Mathematical Inequalities in Fractional Calculus and Applications

Mathematical Inequalities in Fractional Calculus and Applications

Editors

Seth Kermausuor
Eze Nwaeze

MDPI

Basel • Beijing • Wuhan • Barcelona • Belgrade • Novi Sad • Cluj • Manchester

Editors

Seth Kermausuor
Mathematics and
Computer Science
Alabama State University
Montgomery, AL,
USA

Eze Nwaeze
Mathematics and
Computer Science
Alabama State University
Montgomery, AL,
USA

Editorial Office
MDPI AG
Grosspeteranlage 5
4052 Basel, Switzerland

This is a reprint of articles from the Special Issue published online in the open access journal *Fractal and Fractional* (ISSN 2504-3110) (available at: www.mdpi.com/journal/fractalfract/special_issues/MIFCA).

For citation purposes, cite each article independently as indicated on the article page online and as indicated below:

Lastname, A.A.; Lastname, B.B. Article Title. *Journal Name* **Year**, *Volume Number*, Page Range.

ISBN 978-3-7258-2002-3 (Hbk)
ISBN 978-3-7258-2001-6 (PDF)
doi.org/10.3390/books978-3-7258-2001-6

Contents

About the Editors

Seth Kermausuor

Seth Kermausuor is a Ghanaian mathematician who graduated with a Bachelor of Arts in Mathematics and Economics from the University of Ghana, Legon in May 2007. He obtained a Master of Science in Pure and Applied Mathematics from the African University of Science and Technology, Abuja, Nigeria in 2009 and a Master of Applied Mathematics from Auburn University, Auburn, USA in 2010. He earned his PhD in Pure Mathematics with specialization in Harmonic Analysis from Auburn University in 2016. Kermausuor is currently an associate professor of mathematics at Alabama State University, Montgomery, Alabama, USA, a position he has held since January 2017. He has taught various mathematics courses at undergraduate and graduate levels. His research interests are mathematical inequalities, fractional calculus, time scales calculus, mathematical modeling, and harmonic analysis. He has published 2 book chapters and over 35 original research articles in reputable journals. He has also served as an external examiner to many doctoral candidates.

Eze Nwaeze

Eze R. Nwaeze received his Bachelor of Science (BSc) in Mathematics from Ebonyi State University, Abakaliki, Nigeria in 2008, his Master of Science (MSc) in Pure and Applied Mathematics from the African University of Science and Technology, Abuja, Nigeria in 2009, and a Master of Applied Mathematics (MAM) and Doctor of Philosophy (PhD) in Mathematics from Auburn University, Auburn, Alabama, USA in 2010 and 2015, respectively. Currently, he serves as a full graduate faculty and tenured associate professor in the Mathematics and Computer Science Department at the Alabama State University, Montgomery Alabama, USA. Eze Nwaeze's research expertise encompasses areas such as time scale theory, general mathematical inequalities, fractional calculus and its applications in differential equation models, and the growth properties and geometry of zeros of complex polynomials. He has published four book chapters and more than 70 original research articles in reputable journals. He has also served as an external examiner to many doctoral candidates.

fractal and fractional

Editorial

Mathematical Inequalities in Fractional Calculus and Applications

Seth Kermausuor * and Eze R. Nwaeze *

Department of Mathematics and Computer Science, Alabama State University, Montgomery, AL 36101, USA
* Correspondence: skermausour@alasu.edu (S.K.); enwaeze@alasu.edu (E.R.N.)

All types of inequalities play a very important role in various aspects of mathematical analysis, such as approximation theory and differential equation theory. The theory of fractional calculus, which deals with the study and applications of derivatives and integrals of arbitrary orders, has received considerable attention due to its many applications in the applied sciences. Recently, a wide range of applied sciences have relied heavily on fractional differential equations for modeling real systems. Fractional inequalities, also known as the inequalities involving derivatives and integrals of arbitrary orders, have been used to investigate the existence, uniqueness, and stability of solutions to a system of fractional differential equations. Upper and lower bounds of solutions to a system of fractional differential equations are sometimes found by using fractional inequalities. Furthermore, numerical quadrature, probability, and many other related areas also use fractional inequalities. Numerous writers have developed numerous extensions of the different classical inequalities to fractional calculus in the literature over time.

This Special Issue is a compilation of original research on mathematical inequalities involving fractional derivatives and fractional integral operators and their many applications in various mathematical and related fields. The papers in this Special Issue offer deep insight into the interplay between inequalities and fractional calculus, shedding light on new mathematical results, analytical techniques, and computational methods. The Special Issue contains fifteen articles with novel results, and below is an overview of the contributions.

In the first article by Stojiljković et al. [1], a new type of convexity for set-valued function is introduced. Utilizing the definition of this new convexity, the authors prove the Hadamard inequalities involving the Katugampola fractional integrals. These inequalities generalize the non-integer Hadamard inequalities for a convex IVM, (p,h)-convex IVM, p-convex IVM, h-convex, and s-convex in the second sense and many other related well-known classes of functions implicitly. In addition, some numerical examples are provided as supplements to the derived results.

In the second article by Ciurdariu and Grecu [2], several improved quantum Hermite–Hadamard-type integral inequalities for convex functions using a parameter are presented. For this, a new quantum identity is established as the main tool in the proof of the main results. Consequently, in some special cases, several new quantum estimations for q-midpoints and q-trapezoidal-type inequalities are derived with an example.

In [3], Yıldız et al. derived several inequalities for convex functions by using the monotonicity properties of functions and a generalized weighted-type fractional integral operator, which allows the integration of a function with respect to another function in fractional order. The results obtained herein are generalizations of some previously presented findings.

In [4], Vivas-Cortez et al. studied a new class of mean-type inequalities by incorporating Riemann-type fractional integrals. By doing so, a novel set of such inequalities is discovered and analyzed by using different mathematical identities. This class of inequalities is introduced by employing a generalized concept of convexity known as h-convexity. To validate the work, the authors created visual graphs and a table of values using specific

Citation: Kermausuor, S.; Nwaeze, E.R. Mathematical Inequalities in Fractional Calculus and Applications. *Fractal Fract.* **2024**, *8*, 471. https://doi.org/10.3390/fractalfract8080471

Received: 5 August 2024
Accepted: 10 August 2024
Published: 13 August 2024

functions to represent the various parts of the inequalities. This approach presents the opportunity to demonstrate the validity of the findings and further solidify the conclusions. Moreover, some previously published results emerged as special consequences of the main findings. This research serves as a catalyst for future investigations, encouraging researchers to explore more comprehensive outcomes by using generalized fractional operators and expanding the concept of convexity.

Fuzzy-interval-valued functions (FIVFs) are the generalization of interval-valued and real-valued functions, which contribute significantly to resolving the problems arising in the theory of interval analysis. In [5], Vivas-Cortez et al. explored the convexities and pre-invexities of FIVFs and defined some fuzzy fractional integral operators (FFIOs) with a generalized Bessel–Maitland function as their kernel. Using the class of convexities and pre-invexities of FIVFs, some Hermite–Hadamard and trapezoid-type inequalities via the FFIOs are derived. In [6], Yang established certain novel reverse Hölder- and Minkowski-type inequalities for modified unified generalized fractional integral operators (FIOs) with extended unified Mittag–Leffler functions (MLFs). The predominant results of this article generalize and extend the existing fractional Hölder- and Minkowski-type integral inequalities in the literature. As applications, the reverse versions of weighted Radon-, Jensen-, and power-mean-type inequalities for modified unified generalized FIOs with extended unified MLFs are also investigated.

Farid et al. studied and established some bounds of k-integral operators with the Mittag–Leffler kernel in a unified form in [7]. These bounds are obtained by applying the definition of exponentially $(\alpha, h\text{—}p)$-convexity. The presented results provide a large number of new bounds of several integral operators for various kinds of convexities by using appropriate substitutions. In addition, a fractional Hadamard-type inequality that shows the upper and lower bounds of k-integral operators exponentially $(\alpha, h\text{—}p)$-convexity is presented. The results in this paper have some direct links with the results of many published articles.

In the study conducted by Vivas-Cortex et al. [8], the researchers explore some new aspects of Ostrowski-type integral inequalities by implementing the generalized Jensen–Mercer inequality established for generalized s-convexity in fractal space. In this light, the authors construct a new generalized integral equality for first-order local differentiable functions, which serves as an auxiliary result for the main results. The desired results are obtained by employing the new generalized integral equality and some renowned generalized integral inequalities like Hölder's, power mean, and Yang–Hölder's under the conditions of boundedness and generalized s-convexity of the functions. Moreover, in support of the main findings, specific applications to means, numerical integration, and some graphical visualizations are presented.

In the study carried out by Nazir et al. [9], a new filtration class associated with the filtration of infinitesimal generators by using the nonlinear fractional differential operator is studied. The authors establish a connection between the Fekete–Szegö quadratic functional and the class of infinitesimal generators. Certain properties, like sharp Fekete–Szegö inequalities and filtration problems, are also considered.

Kermausuor and Nwaeze [10] propose the definitions of some new fractional integral operators called k-Atangana–Baleanu fractional integral operators. These newly proposed operators are generalizations of the well-known Atangana–Baleanu fractional integral operators. As an application, a generalization of the Hermite–Hadamard inequality is established. Additionally, some new identities involving these new integral operators and new fractional integral inequalities of the midpoint and trapezoidal type for functions whose derivatives are bounded or convex are obtained.

In the article by Ramzan et al. [11], the authors present a novel parameterized fractional integral identity. By using this auxiliary result and the s-convexity property of the function, a series of fractional variants of certain classical inequalities, including Simpson's, midpoint, and trapezoidal-type inequalities, are derived. Additionally, some applications of the main results to special means of real numbers are also explored. Moreover, a new generic numerical scheme for solving nonlinear equations is derived to demonstrate an application of the main results in numerical analysis.

Saeed et al., in [12], propose some new concepts of coordinated up and down convex mappings with fuzzy-number values (coordinated UD-convex FNVMs). Thereafter, Hermite–Hadamard-type inequalities via coordinated up and down convex fuzzy-number-valued mappings are introduced. By taking the products of two coordinated UD-convex FNVMs, Pachpatte-type inequalities are also obtained. Some nontrivial examples are further presented to show the validity of the main results.

The study by Chiheb et al. in [13] deals with the Newton–Cotes-type inequalities involving three points for geometrically arithmetic-convex (GA-convex) functions. The authors first established a new integral identity involving the Hadamard integral operators. Using this new identity, they established some new Maclaurin-type inequalities for functions whose first derivatives in absolute value are GA-convex functions.

Symmetric derivatives and integrals are extensively studied to overcome the limitations of classical derivatives and integral operators. In the study by Vivas-Cortez et al. [14], they explored the quantum symmetric derivatives on finite intervals. They introduce the idea of right quantum symmetric derivatives and integral operators and study various properties of both operators as well. Using these concepts, new variants of Young's inequality, Hölder's inequality, Minkowski's inequality, Hermite–Hadamard's inequality, Ostrowski's inequality, and Gruss–Chebysev inequality are obtained. Furthermore, the Hermite–Hadamard's inequalities, by considering the differentiability of convex mappings, are established. These fundamental results are pivotal to studying the various other problems in the field of inequalities. The authors provide some numerical and visual examples to verify the correctness of the main results.

Finally, in [15], Saeed et al. introduce a new extension of interval-valued convexity, namely, coordinated LR-h-convexity. By using the double Riemann–Liouville fractional integrals, they derive fractional forms of the Hermite–Hadamard inequality for the newly defined class of convex mappings. By taking the product of two LR-$\hbar$-convex functions, some new versions of fractional integral inequalities are also obtained. Moreover, some new and classical exceptional cases are also discussed by taking some restrictions on endpoint functions of interval-valued functions that can be seen as applications of these new outcomes.

In conclusion, this Special Issue serves as a testament to the vibrancy of research in this burgeoning field. We trust that the findings presented here will inspire further exploration and collaboration, leading to new breakthroughs in both theoretical developments and practical applications of fractional calculus. We invite readers to delve into the rich array of articles contained within this Special Issue and to join us in advancing the frontiers of knowledge in fractional calculus and mathematical inequalities.

As editors, we extend our sincere gratitude to all of the authors who have contributed their innovative research to this issue. Their dedication and intellectual rigor have enriched the discourse surrounding mathematical inequalities in fractional calculus. We also thank the reviewers for their constructive feedback and insightful comments, which have been crucial in maintaining the quality and relevance of the articles.

Acknowledgments: Many thanks to all authors who contributed to the success of this special issue.

Conflicts of Interest: The authors declare no conflicts of interest.

References

1. Stojiljković, V.; Ramaswamy, R.; Abdelnaby, O.A.A.; Radenović, S. Some Novel Inequalities for LR-(k,h-m)-p Convex Interval Valued Functions by Means of Pseudo Order Relation. *Fractal Fract.* **2022**, *6*, 726. [CrossRef]
2. Ciurdariu, L.; Grecu, E. Several Quantum Hermite–Hadamard-Type Integral Inequalities for Convex Functions. *Fractal Fract.* **2023**, *7*, 463. [CrossRef]
3. Yıldız, Ç.; Rahman, G.; Cotîrlă, L.-I. On Further Inequalities for Convex Functions via Generalized Weighted-Type Fractional Operators. *Fractal Fract.* **2023**, *7*, 513. [CrossRef]

4. Vivas-Cortez, M.; Samraiz, M.; Ghaffar, M.T.; Naheed, S.; Rahman, G.; Elmasry, Y. Exploration of Hermite–Hadamard-Type Integral Inequalities for Twice Differentiable h-Convex Functions. *Fractal Fract.* **2023**, *7*, 532. [CrossRef]
5. Vivas-Cortez, M.; Ali, R.S.; Saif, H.; Jeelani, M.B.; Rahman, G.; Elmasry, Y. Certain Novel Fractional Integral Inequalities via Fuzzy Interval Valued Functions. *Fractal Fract.* **2023**, *7*, 580. [CrossRef]
6. Yang, W. Certain New Reverse Hölder- and Minkowski-Type Inequalities for Modified Unified Generalized Fractional Integral Operators with Extended Unified Mittag–Leffler Functions. *Fractal Fract.* **2023**, *7*, 613. [CrossRef]
7. Farid, G.; Khan, H.S.; Tawfiq, F.M.O.; Ro, J.-S.; Zainab, S. On Bounds of k-Fractional Integral Operators with Mittag-Leffler Kernels for Several Types of Exponentially Convexities. *Fractal Fract.* **2023**, *7*, 617. [CrossRef]
8. Vivas-Cortez, M.; Awan, M.U.; Asif, U.; Javed, M.Z.; Budak, H. Advances in Ostrowski-Mercer Like Inequalities within Fractal Space. *Fractal Fract.* **2023**, *7*, 689. [CrossRef]
9. Nazir, M.; Bukhari, S.Z.H.; Ro, J.-S.; Tchier, F.; Malik, S.N. On Inequalities and Filtration Associated with the Nonlinear Fractional Operator. *Fractal Fract.* **2023**, *7*, 726. [CrossRef]
10. Kermausuor, S.; Nwaeze, E.R. New Fractional Integral Inequalities via k-Atangana–Baleanu Fractional Integral Operators. *Fractal Fract.* **2023**, *7*, 740. [CrossRef]
11. Ramzan, S.; Awan, M.U.; Dragomir, S.S.; Bin-Mohsin, B.; Noor, M.A. Analysis and Applications of Some New Fractional Integral Inequalities. *Fractal Fract.* **2023**, *7*, 797. [CrossRef]
12. Saeed, T.; Cătaș, A.; Khan, M.B.; Alshehri, A.M. Some New Fractional Inequalities for Coordinated Convexity over Convex Set Pertaining to Fuzzy-Number-Valued Settings Governed by Fractional Integrals. *Fractal Fract.* **2023**, *7*, 856. [CrossRef]
13. Chiheb, T.; Meftah, B.; Moumen, A.; Bouye, M. Maclaurin-Type Integral Inequalities for *GA*-Convex Functions Involving Confluent Hypergeometric Function via Hadamard Fractional Integrals. *Fractal Fract.* **2023**, *7*, 860. [CrossRef]
14. Vivas-Cortez, M.; Javed, M.Z.; Awan, M.U.; Dragomir, S.S.; Zidan, A.M. Properties and Applications of Symmetric Quantum Calculus. *Fractal Fract.* **2024**, *8*, 107. [CrossRef]
15. Saeed, T.; Nwaeze, E.R.; Khan, M.B.; Hakami, K.H. New Version of Fractional Pachpatte-Type Integral Inequalities via Coordinated $\hbar$-Convexity via Left and Right Order Relation. *Fractal Fract.* **2024**, *8*, 125. [CrossRef]

fractal and fractional

Article

New Version of Fractional Pachpatte-Type Integral Inequalities via Coordinated ℏ-Convexity via Left and Right Order Relation

Tareq Saeed [1], Eze R. Nwaeze [2,*], Muhammad Bilal Khan [3,*] and Khalil Hadi Hakami [4]

1 Financial Mathematics and Actuarial Science (FMAS)-Research Group, Department of Mathematics, Faculty of Science, King Abdulaziz University, P.O. Box 80203, Jeddah 21589, Saudi Arabia; tsalmalki@kau.edu.sa
2 Department of Mathematics and Computer Science, Alabama State University, Montgomery, AL 36101, USA
3 Department of Mathematics and Computer Science, Transilvania University of Brasov, 29 Eroilor Boulevard, 500036 Brasov, Romania
4 Department of Mathematics, Faculty of Science, Jazan University, Jazan 45142, Saudi Arabia; khakami@jazanu.edu.sa
* Correspondence: enwaeze@alasu.edu (E.R.N.); muhammad.bilal@unitbv.ro (M.B.K.)

Abstract: In particular, the fractional forms of Hermite–Hadamard inequalities for the newly defined class of convex mappings proposed that are known as coordinated left and right ℏ-convexity (*LR*-ℏ-convexity) over interval-valued codomain. We exploit the use of double Riemann–Liouville fractional integral to derive the major results of the research. We also examine the key results' numerical validations that examples are nontrivial. By taking the product of two left and right coordinated ℏ-convexity, some new versions of fractional integral inequalities are also obtained. Moreover, some new and classical exceptional cases are also discussed by taking some restrictions on endpoint functions of interval-valued functions that can be seen as applications of these new outcomes.

Keywords: interval-valued mappings over coordinates; left and right ℏ-convexity; double Riemann–Liouville fractional integral operator; Pachpatte-type inequalities

Citation: Saeed, T.; Nwaeze, E.R.; Khan, M.B.; Hakami, K.H. New Version of Fractional Pachpatte-Type Integral Inequalities via Coordinated ℏ-Convexity via Left and Right Order Relation. *Fractal Fract.* **2024**, *8*, 125. https://doi.org/10.3390/fractalfract8030125

Academic Editor: Bruce Henry

Received: 14 November 2023
Revised: 5 February 2024
Accepted: 6 February 2024
Published: 20 February 2024

1. Introduction

There are many uses for the concepts of convex sets and convex functions in the realms of applied and pure sciences. Furthermore, because of its many applications and tight relationship to the theory of inequalities, convexity has advanced quickly in recent years. When determining exact values for a mathematical problem proves to be challenging, inequalities can be used to approximate the solution. Since many inequalities can be directly derived from convex functions, there is a close relationship between convexity and the theory of inequalities.

The Hermite–Hadamard inequality is one of the most well-known findings in the category of classical convex functions, according to Dragomir and Pearce [1]. This inequality has several applications and a straightforward intrinsic geometric explanation. The result was mainly credited to Hermite (1822–1901), even though Hadamard (1865–1963) was the one who first identified it [2,3]. The following is how this inequality is stated:

Theorem 1. *Assume that the convex mapping $\mathcal{J}: [\sigma, \mathrm{i}] \to \Re$. Then, the following double inequality holds:*

$$\mathcal{J}\left(\frac{\sigma+\mathrm{i}}{2}\right) \leq \frac{1}{\mathrm{i}-\sigma}\int_{\sigma}^{\mathrm{i}} \mathcal{J}(x)dx \leq \frac{\mathcal{J}(\mathrm{i})+\mathcal{J}(\sigma)}{2}, \tag{1}$$

where $\Re$ is a set of real numbers. One can check the concavity of the mappings by replacing the symbol "≤" with "≥" in double inequality (1).

The midpoint and trapezoidal-type inequalities, which are the two sides of the Hermite–Hadamard inequality, are used to estimate error boundaries for specific quadrature rules. The original derivation of these inequalities was in [4,5].

New extended versions of Simpson-type inequalities were derived by Awan et al. [6] using differentiable, strongly (s, m)-convex maps. Simpson's integral inequality has been further expanded upon, refined, and generalized in [7–10].

In the course of research, various variations of the Hermite–Hadamard inequality have been derived by expanding the definition of convex functions. Conversely, the notion of s}-convexity [11,12] is divided into two halves, as follows, with the fundamental requirement that $1 \geq s > 0$. The following references [13–17] contain more generalizations and expansions of classical convex functions.

Fractional calculus is the study of integrals and derivatives of any real order. Fractional integrals are used to solve a wide range of problems involving mathematical science's special functions, as well as their generalizations and extensions to one or more variables. Furthermore, compared to traditional derivatives, fractional-order derivatives describe the memory and hereditary characteristics of distinct processes far better. Actually, current applications in fluid mechanics, mathematical biology, electrochemistry, physics, differential and integral equations, signal processing, and fluid mechanics have been the driving forces behind the recent developments in fractional calculus. Without a doubt, fractional calculus can be used to solve a wide range of diverse problems in science, engineering, and mathematics [18–20]. The reference [21] provides a thorough history of fractional calculus.

Creating different kinds of integral inequalities is a modern issue. Utilizing a range of integrals, including the Sugeno integral [22,23], the pseudo integral [24], the Choquet integral [25], and others, a significant amount of important work has been accomplished in recent years. As a notion of generalization of functions and a significant mathematical subject, interval-valued functions [26] have grown in importance as a tool for resolving real-world problems, especially in mathematical economics [27]. Certain classical integral inequalities have been expanded to the domain of interval-valued functions through recent studies. New interval variations of Minkowski and Beckenbach's integral inequalities were introduced by Costa et al. [28]. This generalization established Jensen, Ostrowski, and Hermite–Hadamard-type inequalities [29]. Fractional integrals of Riemann–Liouville with interval values were also used to solve Hermite–Hadamard and Hermite–Hadamard-type inequalities [30]. Zhao and colleagues [31–33] employed the gH -differentiable or h-convex notion to study Jensen and Hermite–Hadamard-type inequalities, Opial-type integral inequalities, and Chebyshev-type inequalities for interval-valued functions. Budaka et al. [34] used the definitions of gH-derivatives to develop new fractional inequalities of the Ostrowski type for interval-valued functions. Log-h-convex fuzzy-interval-valued functions are a new class of convex fuzzy-interval-valued functions that were introduced by Khan et al. [35] using a fuzzy order relation. The Jensen and Hermite–Hadamard inequalities were established in this class. To include the Ostrowski-type inequality in the domain of fuzzy-valued functions, the Hukuhara derivative had to be applied, as Anastassiou [36] showed. Anastassiou's research focused heavily on fuzzy-valued functions, commonly referred to as functions with an interval value. An interesting finding is that Anastassiou's fuzzy Ostrowski-type inequalities could also be used for interval-valued functions. Bede and Gal's [37] and Chalco-Cano et al.'s [38] publications should be studied in order to gain a thorough grasp of the limitations placed on interval-valued functions by the idea of the H-derivative. Significantly, Chalco-Cano et al.'s recent work [39] has produced an Ostrowski-type inequality that is tailored to generalized Hukuhara differentiable interval-valued functions. On the other hand, Lupulescu [40] introduced the concept of left-fractional integral in interval-valued calculus. Then, right fractional integrals are proposed by Budak et al. [41], as well as providing the fractional Hermite–Hadamard-type inequalities for interval-valued mappings over coordinates. Zhao et al. [42] generalized the Riemann integral inequalities for coordinated convex interval-valued mappings and produced the inequalities for the product of coordinated convexity. After that, Khan et al. [43]

provide a new direction in interval-valued calculus by introducing new versions of coordinated integral inequalities via double Riemann integrals and left and right relations. Budak and Sarıkaya [44] and Khan et al. [45] defined Pachpatte's inequalities for the product of coordinated and left and right coordinated convex mappings via fractional integrals, respectively. By using this approach, Khan et al. [46] obtained the left- and right-coordinated interval-valued functions and acquired some integral inequalities in interval fractional calculus for left- and right-coordinated interval-valued functions. Zhang et al. [47] first defined the up and down relations and then discussed some of the properties of these relations. Moreover, he defined the new versions of Jensen-type inequalities using up and down relations.

The structure of this research article is as follows. Some classical notions, definitions, and results are recalled and a new definition of convexity over interval-valued mapping is also introduced, which is known as coordinated LR-$\hbar$-convexity in Section 2. We also report several other findings that follow from this definition of convexity. Using coordinated LR-$\hbar$-convexity defined in Section 2, some new and classical exceptional cases are also obtained in Section 2. In Section 3, involving interval fractional integrals for LR-$\hbar$-convexity, some well-known inequalities have been generalized, as well as nontrivial examples have also been provided to validate the main outcomes of this paper. Section 4 concludes this study and discusses future work.

2. Preliminaries

Let $\mathbb{R}$ be the set of real numbers and $\mathbb{R}_I$ containing all bounded and closed intervals within $\mathbb{R}$. $\imath \in \mathbb{R}_I$ should be defined as follows:

$$\imath = [\imath_*, \imath^*] = \{y \in \mathbb{R} | \imath_* \le y \le \imath^*\}, (\imath_*, \imath^* \in \mathbb{R}). \quad (2)$$

It is argued that $\imath$ is degenerate if $\imath_* = \imath^*$. The interval $[\imath_*, \imath^*]$ is referred to as positive if $\imath_* \ge 0$, $\mathbb{R}_I^+$ represents the set of all positive intervals and is defined as $\mathbb{R}_I^+ = \{[\imath_*, \imath^*] : [\imath_*, \imath^*] \in \mathbb{R}_I \text{ and } \imath_* \ge 0\}$.

Let $\varrho \in \mathbb{R}$, $\imath, \jmath \in \mathbb{R}_I$ be defined by, with $\jmath = [\jmath_*, \jmath^*]$ and $\imath = [\imath_*, \imath^*]$, and we may define the interval arithmetic as follows:

- Scaler multiplication:

$$\varrho.\imath = \begin{cases} [\varrho\imath_*, \varrho\imath^*] & \text{if } \varrho > 0, \\ \{0\} & \text{if } \varrho = 0, \\ [\varrho\imath^*, \varrho\imath_*] & \text{if } \varrho < 0. \end{cases} \quad (3)$$

- Addition:

$$[\jmath_*, \jmath^*] + [\imath_*, \imath^*] = [\jmath_* + \imath_*, \jmath^* + \imath^*]. \quad (4)$$

- Multiplication:

$$[\jmath_*, \jmath^*] \times [\imath_*, \imath^*] = [min\{\jmath_*\imath_*, \jmath^*\imath_*, \jmath_*\imath^*, \jmath^*\imath^*\}, max\{\jmath_*\imath_*, \jmath^*\imath_*, \jmath_*\imath^*, \jmath^*\imath^*\}]. \quad (5)$$

The inclusion " $\supseteq$ " means that $\imath \supseteq \jmath$ if and only if, $[\imath_*, \imath^*] \supseteq [\jmath_*, \jmath^*]$, and if and only if $\imath_* \le \jmath_*, \jmath^* \le \imath^*$.

Remark 1 ([47]). *(i) The relation " $\le_p$" is defined on $\mathbb{R}_I$ by*

$$[\jmath_*, \jmath^*] \le_p [\imath_*, \imath^*] \text{ if and only if } \jmath_* \le \imath_*, \ \jmath^* \le \imath^*, \quad (6)$$

for all $[\jmath_*, \jmath^*]$, $[\imath_*, \imath^*] \in \mathbb{R}_I$, and it is a pseudo-order relation. The relation $[\jmath_*, \jmath^*] \le_p [\imath_*, \imath^*]$ coincident to $[\jmath_*, \jmath^*] \le [\imath_*, \imath^*]$ on $\mathbb{R}_I$ when it is " $\le_p$".

(ii) It can be easily seen that " $\leq_p$ " looks like "left and right" on the real line $\mathbb{R}$, so we call " $\leq_p$ " "left and right" (or "LR" order, in short).

The Hausdorff–Pompeiu distance between intervals $[\jmath_*, \jmath^*]$, $[\imath_*, \imath^*] \in \mathbb{R}_I$ is given by

$$d([\jmath_*, \jmath^*], [\imath_*, \imath^*]) = max\{|\jmath_* - \imath_*|, |\jmath^* - \imath^*|\}. \quad (7)$$

It is a familiar fact that $(\mathbb{R}_I, d)$ is a complete metric space.

Definition 1 ([30,40]). *Let $\mathcal{J} : [\sigma, \mathfrak{i}] \to \mathbb{R}_I^+$ be an interval-valued mapping (IVM) and $\mathcal{J} \in \mathcal{IR}_{[\sigma,\mathfrak{i}]}$. Then, interval Riemann–Liouville-type integrals of $\mathcal{J}$ are defined as*

$$\mathcal{I}^{\alpha}_{\sigma^+}\mathcal{J}(y) = \frac{1}{\Gamma(\alpha)}\int_{\sigma}^{y} (y - \mathrm{t})^{\alpha-1}\mathcal{J}(\mathrm{t})d\mathrm{t} \ (y > \sigma), \quad (8)$$

$$\mathcal{I}^{\alpha}_{\mathfrak{i}^-}\mathcal{J}(y) = \frac{1}{\Gamma(\alpha)}\int_{y}^{\mathfrak{i}} (\mathrm{t} - y)^{\alpha-1}\mathcal{J}(\mathrm{t})d\mathrm{t} \ (y < \mathfrak{i}), \quad (9)$$

where $\alpha > 0$ and Γ is the gamma function.

Interval and fuzzy Riemann-type integrals are defined as follows for coordinated VM $\mathcal{J}(x, y)$.

Theorem 2 ([42]). *Let $\mathcal{J} : [\sigma, \mathfrak{i}] \subset \mathbb{R} \to \mathbb{R}_I$ be an IVM, given by $\mathcal{J}(x) = [\mathcal{J}_*(x), \mathcal{J}^*(x)]$ for all $x \in [\sigma, \mathfrak{i}]$. Then, $\mathcal{J}$ is Riemann integrable (IR-integrable) over $[\sigma, \mathfrak{i}]$ if and only if $\mathcal{J}_*(x)$ and $\mathcal{J}^*(x)$ both are Riemann integrable (R-integrable) over $[\sigma, \mathfrak{i}]$. Moreover, if $\mathcal{J}$ is IR-integrable over $[\sigma, \mathfrak{i}]$, then*

$$(IR)\int_{\sigma}^{\mathfrak{i}} \mathcal{J}(x)dx = \left[(R)\int_{\sigma}^{\mathfrak{i}} \mathcal{J}_*(x)dx,\ (R)\int_{\sigma}^{\mathfrak{i}} \mathcal{J}^*(x)dx\right]. \quad (10)$$

The family of all IR-integrable of IVMs over coordinates and R-integrable functions over $[\sigma, \mathfrak{i}]$ are denoted by $IR_{[\sigma,\mathfrak{i}]}$ and $R_{[\sigma,\mathfrak{i}]}$, respectively.

Theorem 3 ([31]). *Let $\mathcal{J} : \Omega = [\sigma, \mathfrak{i}] \times [\varepsilon, \mathfrak{v}] \subset \mathbb{R}^2 \to \mathbb{R}_I$ be an IVM on coordinates, given by $\mathcal{J}(x, y) = [\mathcal{J}_*(x, y), \mathcal{J}^*(x, y)]$ for all $(x, y) \in \Omega = [\sigma, \mathfrak{i}] \times [\varepsilon, \mathfrak{v}]$. Then, $\mathcal{J}$ is double integrable (ID-integrable) over Ω if and only if $\mathcal{J}_*(x, y)$ and $\mathcal{J}^*(x, y)$ both are D-integrable over Ω. Moreover, if $\mathcal{J}$ is FD-integrable over Ω, then*

$$(ID)\int_{\sigma}^{\mathfrak{i}}\int_{\varepsilon}^{\mathfrak{v}} \mathcal{J}(x, y)dydx = (IR)\int_{\sigma}^{\mathfrak{i}}(IR)\int_{\varepsilon}^{\mathfrak{v}} \mathcal{J}(x, y)dydx. \quad (11)$$

The family of all ID-integrable of IVMs over coordinates over coordinates is denoted by $\mathfrak{ID}_{\Omega}$.

Here is the main definition of fuzzy Riemann–Liouville fractional integral on the coordinates of the function $\mathcal{J}(x, y)$ by:

Definition 2 ([41]). *Let $\mathcal{J} : \Omega \to \mathbb{R}_I$ and $\mathcal{J} \in \mathfrak{ID}_{\Omega}$. The double fuzzy interval Rieman—Liouville-type integrals $\mathcal{I}^{\alpha,\,\beta}_{\sigma^+,\varepsilon^+}$, $\mathcal{I}^{\alpha,\,\beta}_{\sigma^+,\mathfrak{v}^-}$, $\mathcal{I}^{\alpha,\,\beta}_{\mathfrak{i}^-,\varepsilon^+}$, $\mathcal{I}^{\alpha,\,\beta}_{\mathfrak{i}^-,\mathfrak{v}^-}$ of $\mathcal{J}$ order α, $\beta > 0$ are defined by:*

$$\mathcal{I}^{\alpha,\,\beta}_{\sigma^+,\varepsilon^+}\mathcal{J}(x, y) = \frac{1}{\Gamma(\alpha)\Gamma(\beta)}\int_{\sigma}^{x}\int_{\varepsilon}^{y} (x - \mathrm{t})^{\alpha-1}(y - \mathrm{s})^{\beta-1}\mathcal{J}(\mathrm{t}, \mathrm{s})d\mathrm{s}d\mathrm{t}, \ (x > \sigma, y > \varepsilon), \quad (12)$$

$$\mathcal{I}^{\alpha,\,\beta}_{\sigma^+,\mathfrak{v}^-}\mathcal{J}(x, y) = \frac{1}{\Gamma(\alpha)\Gamma(\beta)}\int_{\sigma}^{x}\int_{y}^{\mathfrak{v}} (x - \mathrm{t})^{\alpha-1}(\mathrm{s} - y)^{\beta-1}\mathcal{J}(\mathrm{t}, \mathrm{s})d\mathrm{s}d\mathrm{t}, \ (x > \sigma, y < \mathfrak{v}), \quad (13)$$

$$\mathcal{J}^{\alpha,\beta}_{\mathrm{i}^-,\varepsilon^+}\mathcal{J}(x,y)=\frac{1}{\Gamma(\alpha)\Gamma(\beta)}\int_x^{\mathrm{i}}\int_{\varepsilon}^{y}(\mathrm{t}-x)^{\alpha-1}(y-\mathrm{s})^{\beta-1}\mathcal{J}(\mathrm{t},\mathrm{s})d\mathrm{s}d\mathrm{t},\ (x<\mathrm{i},y>\varepsilon),\quad(14)$$

$$\mathcal{J}^{\alpha,\beta}_{\mathrm{i}^-,\mathfrak{v}^-}\mathcal{J}(x,y)=\frac{1}{\Gamma(\alpha)\Gamma(\beta)}\int_x^{\mathrm{i}}\int_{y}^{\mathfrak{v}}(\mathrm{t}-x)^{\alpha-1}(\mathrm{s}-y)^{\beta-1}\mathcal{J}(\mathrm{t},\mathrm{s})d\mathrm{s}d\mathrm{t},\ (x<\mathrm{i},y<\mathfrak{v}).\quad(15)$$

Here is the classical and newly defined concept of coordinated LR-$\hbar$-convexity over fuzzy number space in the codomain via fuzzy relation given by:

Definition 3 ([45])**.** *The IVM $\mathcal{J}:[\varepsilon,\mathfrak{v}]\to\mathbb{R}_I^+$ is referred to be LR-$\hbar$-convex IVM on $[\varepsilon,\mathfrak{v}]$ if*

$$\mathcal{J}(\kappa\varepsilon+(1-\kappa)\mathfrak{v})\leq_p\hbar(\kappa)\mathcal{J}(\varepsilon)+\hbar(1-\kappa)\mathcal{J}(\mathfrak{v}),\quad(16)$$

where $\hbar:[0,1]\to\mathbb{R}^+$. If inequality (16) is reversed, then $\mathcal{J}$ is referred to be $\hbar$-concave IVM on $[\varepsilon,\mathfrak{v}]$.

Theorem 4 ([45])**.** *Let $\hbar:[0,1]\to\mathbb{R}^+$ and $\mathcal{J}:[\varepsilon,\mathfrak{v}]\to\mathbb{R}_I^+$ be a LR-$\hbar$-convex IVM on $[\varepsilon,\mathfrak{v}]$, given by $\mathcal{J}(y)=[\mathcal{J}_*(y),\mathcal{J}^*(y)]$ for all $y\in[\varepsilon,\mathfrak{v}]$. If $\mathcal{J}\in L([\varepsilon,\mathfrak{v}],\mathbb{R}_I^+)$, then*

$$\frac{1}{\alpha\hbar\left(\frac{1}{2}\right)}\mathcal{J}\left(\frac{\varepsilon+\mathfrak{v}}{2}\right)\leq_p\frac{\Gamma(\alpha)}{(\mathfrak{v}-\varepsilon)^{\alpha}}\left[\mathcal{J}^{\alpha}_{\varepsilon^+}\mathcal{J}(\mathfrak{v})+\mathcal{J}^{\alpha}_{\mathfrak{v}^-}\mathcal{J}(\varepsilon)\right]\leq_p[\mathcal{J}(\varepsilon)+\mathcal{J}(\mathfrak{v})]\int_0^1 \upsilon^{\alpha-1}[\hbar(\upsilon)+\hbar(1-\upsilon)]d\upsilon.\quad(17)$$

Definition 4. *The IVM $\mathcal{J}:\Omega\to\mathbb{R}_I^+$ is referred to be coordinated LR-$\hbar$-convex IVM on Ω if*

$$\begin{aligned}&\mathcal{J}(\upsilon\sigma+(1-\upsilon)\mathrm{i},\kappa\varepsilon+(1-\kappa)\mathfrak{v})\\&\leq_p\hbar(\upsilon)\hbar(\kappa)\mathcal{J}(\sigma,\varepsilon)+\hbar(\upsilon)\hbar(1-\kappa)\mathcal{J}(\sigma,\mathfrak{v})+\hbar(1-\upsilon)\hbar(\kappa)\mathcal{J}(\mathrm{i},\varepsilon)+\hbar(1-\upsilon)\hbar(1-\kappa)\mathcal{J}(\mathrm{i},\mathfrak{v})\end{aligned}\quad(18)$$

for all (σ,i), $(\varepsilon,\mathfrak{v})\in\Omega$, and $\upsilon,\kappa\in[0,1]$, where $\mathcal{J}(x)\geq_p 0$. If inequality (18) is reversed, then $\mathcal{J}$ is referred to be coordinate $\hbar$-concave IVM on Ω. If $\hbar$ is the identity function, we recover the LR-convex IVM on Ω given in [46].

Lemma 1. *Let $\mathcal{J}:\Omega\to\mathbb{R}_I^+$ be a coordinated IVM on Ω. Then, $\mathcal{J}$ is coordinated LR-$\hbar$-convex IVM on Ω if and only if there exist two coordinated LR-$\hbar$-convex $IVMs$ $\mathcal{J}_x:[\varepsilon,\mathfrak{v}]\to\mathbb{R}_I^+$, $\mathcal{J}_x(w)=\mathcal{J}(x,w)$ and $\mathcal{J}_y:[\sigma,\mathrm{i}]\to\mathbb{R}_I^+$, $\mathcal{J}_y(z)=\mathcal{J}(z,y)$.*

Theorem 5. *Let $\mathcal{J}:\Omega\to\mathbb{R}_I^+$ be a IVM on Ω, given by*

$$\mathcal{J}(x,y)=[\mathcal{J}_*(x,y),\mathcal{J}^*(x,y)],\quad(19)$$

for all $(x,y)\in\Omega$. Then, $\mathcal{J}$ is coordinated LR-$\hbar$-convex IVM on Ω, if and only if both $\mathcal{J}_*(x,y)$ and $\mathcal{J}^*(x,y)$ are coordinated LR-$\hbar$-convex.

Proof. Assume that $\mathcal{J}_*(x)$ and $\mathcal{J}^*(x)$ are coordinated LR-$\hbar$-convex and $\hbar$-concave on Ω, respectively. Then, from Equation (19), for all (σ,i), $(\varepsilon,\mathfrak{v})\in\Omega$, υ and $\kappa\in[0,1]$, we have

$$\begin{aligned}&\mathcal{J}_*(\upsilon\sigma+(1-\upsilon)\mathrm{i},\kappa\varepsilon+(1-\kappa)\mathfrak{v})\\&\leq\hbar(\upsilon)\hbar(\kappa)\mathcal{J}_*(\sigma,\varepsilon)+\hbar(\upsilon)\hbar(1-\kappa)\mathcal{J}_*(\sigma,\mathfrak{v})+\hbar(\kappa)\hbar(1-\upsilon)\mathcal{J}_*(\mathrm{i},\varepsilon)+\hbar(1-\upsilon)\hbar(1-\kappa)\mathcal{J}_*(\mathrm{i},\mathfrak{v})\end{aligned}\quad(20)$$

and

$$\begin{aligned}&\mathcal{J}^*(\upsilon\sigma+(1-\upsilon)\mathrm{i},\kappa\varepsilon+(1-\kappa)\mathfrak{v})\\&\leq\hbar(\upsilon)\hbar(\kappa)\mathcal{J}^*(\sigma,\varepsilon)+\hbar(\upsilon)\hbar(1-\kappa)\mathcal{J}^*(\sigma,\mathfrak{v})+\hbar(\kappa)\hbar(1-\upsilon)\mathcal{J}^*(\mathrm{i},\varepsilon)+\hbar(1-\upsilon)\hbar(1-\kappa)\mathcal{J}^*(\mathrm{i},\mathfrak{v}).\end{aligned}\quad(21)$$

Then, by Equations (19), (3) and (4), we obtain

$$\begin{aligned}\mathcal{J}(\upsilon\sigma &+ (1-\upsilon)\mathfrak{i}, \kappa\varepsilon + (1-\kappa)\mathfrak{v}) \\ &= \left[\mathcal{J}_*(\upsilon\sigma + (1-\upsilon)\mathfrak{i}, \kappa\varepsilon + (1-\kappa)\mathfrak{v}),\ \mathcal{J}^*(\upsilon\sigma + (1-\upsilon)\mathfrak{i}, \kappa\varepsilon + (1-\kappa)\mathfrak{v})\right] \\ &\leq_p \hbar(\upsilon)\hbar(\kappa)\left[\mathcal{J}_*(\sigma,\varepsilon),\ \mathcal{J}^*(\sigma,\varepsilon)\right] + \hbar(\upsilon)\hbar(1-\kappa)\left[\mathcal{J}_*(\sigma,\mathfrak{v}),\ \mathcal{J}^*(\sigma,\mathfrak{v})\right] \\ &+ \hbar(\kappa)\hbar(1-\upsilon)\left[\mathcal{J}_*(\mathfrak{i},\varepsilon),\ \mathcal{J}^*(\mathfrak{i},\varepsilon)\right] + \hbar(1-\upsilon)\hbar(1-\kappa)\left[\mathcal{J}_*(\mathfrak{i},\mathfrak{v}),\ \mathcal{J}^*(\mathfrak{i},\mathfrak{v})\right]\end{aligned}$$

From (20) and (21), we have

$$\begin{aligned}\mathcal{J}(\upsilon\sigma &+ (1-\upsilon)\mathfrak{i}, \kappa\varepsilon + (1-\kappa)\mathfrak{v}) \\ &\leq_p \hbar(\upsilon)\hbar(\kappa)\mathcal{J}(\sigma,\varepsilon) + \hbar(\upsilon)\hbar(1-\kappa)\mathcal{J}(\sigma,\mathfrak{v}) + \hbar(1-\upsilon)\hbar(1-\kappa)\mathcal{J}(\mathfrak{i},\varepsilon) + \hbar(1-\upsilon)\hbar(1-\kappa)\mathcal{J}(\mathfrak{i},\mathfrak{v}),\end{aligned}$$

hence, $\mathcal{J}$ is coordinated LR-$\hbar$-convex IVM on Ω.

Conversely, let $\mathcal{J}$ be coordinated LR-$\hbar$-convex IVM on Ω. Then, for all $(\sigma,\mathfrak{i})$, $(\varepsilon,\mathfrak{v}) \in \Omega$, υ and $\kappa \in [0,\ 1]$, we have

$$\begin{aligned}&\mathcal{J}(\upsilon\sigma + (1-\upsilon)\mathfrak{i}, \kappa\varepsilon + (1-\kappa)\mathfrak{v}) \\ &\leq_p \hbar(\upsilon)\hbar(\kappa)\mathcal{J}(\sigma,\varepsilon) + \hbar(\upsilon)\hbar(1-\kappa)\mathcal{J}(\sigma,\mathfrak{v}) + \hbar(1-\upsilon)\hbar(\kappa)\mathcal{J}(\mathfrak{i},\varepsilon) + \hbar(1-\upsilon)\hbar(1-\kappa)\mathcal{J}(\mathfrak{i},\mathfrak{v}).\end{aligned}$$

Therefore, again from Equation (20), we have

$$\begin{aligned}&\mathcal{J}((\upsilon\sigma + (1-\upsilon)\mathfrak{i}, \kappa\varepsilon + (1-\kappa)\mathfrak{v})) \\ &= \left[\mathcal{J}_*(\upsilon\sigma + (1-\upsilon)\mathfrak{i}, \kappa\varepsilon + (1-\kappa)\mathfrak{v}),\ \mathcal{J}^*(\upsilon\sigma + (1-\upsilon)\mathfrak{i}, \kappa\varepsilon + (1-\kappa)\mathfrak{v})\right].\end{aligned} \tag{22}$$

Again, Equations (3) and (4), we obtain

$$\begin{aligned}&\hbar(\upsilon)\hbar(\kappa)\mathcal{J}(\sigma,\varepsilon) + \hbar(\upsilon)\hbar(1-\kappa)\mathcal{J}(\sigma,\mathfrak{v}) + \hbar(1-\upsilon)\hbar(\kappa)\mathcal{J}(\mathfrak{i},\varepsilon) + \hbar(1-\upsilon)\hbar(1-\kappa)\mathcal{J}(\mathfrak{i},\mathfrak{v}) \\ &= \hbar(\upsilon)\hbar(\kappa)\left[\mathcal{J}_*(\sigma,\varepsilon),\ \mathcal{J}^*(\sigma,\varepsilon)\right] + \hbar(\upsilon)\hbar(1-\kappa)\left[\mathcal{J}_*(\sigma,\mathfrak{v}),\ \mathcal{J}^*(\sigma,\mathfrak{v})\right] \\ &+ \hbar(\kappa)\hbar(1-\upsilon)\left[\mathcal{J}_*(\sigma,\varepsilon),\ \mathcal{J}^*(\sigma,\varepsilon)\right] + \hbar(1-\upsilon)\hbar(1-\kappa)\left[\mathcal{J}_*(\sigma,\mathfrak{v}),\ \mathcal{J}^*(\sigma,\mathfrak{v})\right],\end{aligned} \tag{23}$$

for all $x,\omega \in \Omega$ and $\upsilon \in [0,\ 1]$. Then, from (22) and (23), we have for all $x,\omega \in \Omega$ and $\upsilon \in [0,\ 1]$, such that

$$\begin{aligned}&\mathcal{J}_*(\upsilon\sigma + (1-\upsilon)\mathfrak{i}, \kappa\varepsilon + (1-\kappa)\mathfrak{v}) \\ &\leq \hbar(\upsilon)\hbar(\kappa)\mathcal{J}_*(\sigma,\varepsilon) + \hbar(\upsilon)\hbar(1-\kappa)\mathcal{J}_*(\sigma,\mathfrak{v}) + \hbar(1-\upsilon)\hbar(\kappa)\mathcal{J}_*(\mathfrak{i},\varepsilon) + \hbar(1-\upsilon)\hbar(1- \\ &\kappa)\mathcal{J}_*(\mathfrak{i},\mathfrak{v}),\end{aligned}$$

and

$$\begin{aligned}&\mathcal{J}^*(\upsilon\sigma + (1-\upsilon)\mathfrak{i}, \kappa\varepsilon + (1-\kappa)\mathfrak{v}) \\ &\leq \hbar(\upsilon)\hbar(\kappa)\mathcal{J}^*(\sigma,\varepsilon) + \hbar(\upsilon)\hbar(1-\kappa)\mathcal{J}^*(\sigma,\mathfrak{v}) + \hbar(1-\upsilon)\hbar(\kappa)\mathcal{J}^*(\mathfrak{i},\varepsilon) + \\ &\hbar(1-\upsilon)\hbar(1-\kappa)\mathcal{J}^*(\mathfrak{i},\mathfrak{v}),\end{aligned}$$

hence, the result follows. □

Example 1. *We consider the IVM* $\mathcal{J} : [0,\ 1] \times [0,\ 1] \to \mathbb{R}_I^+$ *defined by,*

$$\mathcal{J}(x) = [xy, (6 + e^x)(6 + e^y)].$$

Endpoint functions $\mathcal{J}_*(x,y)$, $\mathcal{J}^*(x,y)$ *are coordinate* $\hbar$*-concave functions. Hence,* $\mathcal{J}(x,y)$ *is coordinated LR-*$\hbar$*-convex IVM.*

From Lemma 1 and Example 1, we can easily note that each LR-$\hbar$-convex IVM is coordinated LR-$\hbar$-convex IVM. But the inverse is not true.

Remark 2. *If one assumes that* $\mathcal{J}_*(x,y) = \mathcal{J}^*(x,y)$*, then* $\mathcal{J}$ *is referred to as a classical coordinated LR-*$\hbar$*-convex function if* $\mathcal{J}$ *meets the stated inequality here:*

$$\begin{aligned}&\mathcal{J}(\upsilon\sigma + (1-\upsilon)\mathfrak{i}, \kappa\varepsilon + (1-\kappa)\mathfrak{v}) \\ &\leq \hbar(\upsilon)\hbar(\kappa)\mathcal{J}(\sigma,\varepsilon) + \hbar(\upsilon)\hbar(1-\kappa)\mathcal{J}(\sigma,\mathfrak{v}) + \hbar(\kappa)\hbar(1-\upsilon)\mathcal{J}(\sigma,\varepsilon) + \hbar(1-\upsilon)\hbar(1-\kappa)\mathcal{J}(\sigma,\mathfrak{v}).\end{aligned} \tag{24}$$

If one assumes that $\hbar(\upsilon) = \upsilon$, $\hbar(\kappa) = \kappa$ *and* $\mathfrak{J}_*(x,y) = \mathfrak{J}^*(x,y)$, *then* $\mathfrak{J}$ *is referred to as a classical coordinated convex function if* $\mathfrak{J}$ *meets the stated inequality here:*

$$\begin{aligned}&\mathfrak{J}(\upsilon\sigma + (1-\upsilon)\mathrm{i}, \kappa\varepsilon + (1-\kappa)\mathfrak{v})\\&\leq \upsilon\kappa\mathfrak{J}(\sigma,\varepsilon) + \upsilon(1-\kappa)\mathfrak{J}(\sigma,\mathfrak{v}) + (1-\upsilon)\kappa\mathfrak{J}(\mathrm{i},\varepsilon) + (1-\upsilon)(1-\kappa)\mathfrak{J}(\mathrm{i},\mathfrak{v}).\end{aligned} \tag{25}$$

Let one assume that $\hbar(\upsilon) = \upsilon$, $\hbar(\kappa) = \kappa$ *and* $\mathfrak{J}_*(x,y) \neq \mathfrak{J}^*(x,y)$, *and* $\mathfrak{J}_*(x,y)$ *is an affine function and* $\mathfrak{J}^*(x,y)$ *is a concave function for the stated inequality here (see [42])*

$$\begin{aligned}&\mathfrak{J}(\upsilon\sigma + (1-\upsilon)\mathrm{i}, \kappa\varepsilon + (1-\kappa)\mathfrak{v})\\&\supseteq \upsilon\kappa\mathfrak{J}(\sigma,\varepsilon) + \upsilon(1-\kappa)\mathfrak{J}(\sigma,\mathfrak{v}) + (1-\upsilon)\kappa\mathfrak{J}(\mathrm{i},\varepsilon) + (1-\upsilon)(1-\kappa)\mathfrak{J}(\mathrm{i},\mathfrak{v}),\end{aligned} \tag{26}$$

is true.

Definition 5. *Let* $\mathfrak{J} : \Omega \to \mathbb{R}_I^+$ *be a* IVM *on* Ω. *Then, we have*

$$\mathfrak{J}(x,y) = \left[\mathfrak{J}_*(x,y),\ \mathfrak{J}^*(x,y)\right],$$

for all $(x,y) \in \Omega$. *Then,* $\mathfrak{J}$ *is coordinated left-LR-*$\hbar$*-convex (concave)* IVM *on* Ω, *if and only if,* $\mathfrak{J}_*(x,y)$ *and* $\mathfrak{J}^*(x,y)$ *are coordinated LR-*$\hbar$*-convex (concave) and affine functions on* Ω, *respectively.*

Definition 6. *Let* $\mathfrak{J} : \Omega \to \mathbb{R}_I^+$ *be a* IVM *on* Ω. *Then, we have*

$$\mathfrak{J}(x,y) = \left[\mathfrak{J}_*(x,y),\ \mathfrak{J}^*(x,y)\right],$$

for all $(x,y) \in \Omega$. *Then,* $\mathfrak{J}$ *is coordinated right-LR-*$\hbar$*-convex (concave)* IVM *on* Ω, *if and only if* $\mathfrak{J}_*(x,y)$ *and* $\mathfrak{J}^*(x,y)$ *are coordinated* $\hbar$*-affine and* $\hbar$*-(concave) functions on* Ω, *respectively.*

Theorem 6. *Let* Ω *be a coordinated convex set, and let* $\mathfrak{J} : \Omega \to \mathbb{R}_I^+$ *be a* IVM, *defined by*

$$\mathfrak{J}(x,y) = \left[\mathfrak{J}_*(x,y),\ \mathfrak{J}^*(x,y)\right],$$

for all $(x,y) \in \Omega$. *Then,* $\mathfrak{J}$ *is coordinated* $\hbar$*-concave* IVM *on* Ω, *if and only if* $\mathfrak{J}_*(x,y)$ *and* $\mathfrak{J}^*(x,y)$ *are coordinated* $\hbar$*-concave and LR-*$\hbar$*-convex functions, respectively.*

Proof. The demonstration of proof of Theorem 6 is similar to the demonstration proof of Theorem 5. □

Example 2. *We consider the* $IVMs$ $\mathfrak{J} : [0,\ 1] \times [0,\ 1] \to \mathbb{R}_I^+$ *defined by,*

$$\mathfrak{J}(x,y) = [(6 - e^x)(6 - e^y), 40xy].$$

Then, we have endpoint functions $\mathfrak{J}_*(x,y)$, $\mathfrak{J}^*(x,y)$, *which are both coordinated* $\hbar$*-concave functions. Hence,* $\mathfrak{J}(x,y)$ *is coordinated LR-*$\hbar$*-concave* IVM.

In the next results, to avoid confusion, we will not include the symbols (R), (IR), and (ID) before the integral sign.

3. Main Results

In this section, Hermite–Hadamard and Pachpatte-type inequalities for interval-value functions are given. We first present an inequality of Hermite–Hadamard via coordinated LR-$\hbar$-concave $IVMs$.

Theorem 7. *Let* $\mathfrak{J} : \Omega \to \mathbb{R}_I^+$ *be a coordinate LR-*$\hbar$*-convex* IVM *on* Ω, *where* $\mathfrak{J}(x,y) = \left[\mathfrak{J}_*(x,y),\ \mathfrak{J}^*(x,y)\right]$ *for all* $(x,y) \in \Omega$ *and let* $\hbar : [0,\ 1] \to \mathbb{R}^+$. *If* $\mathfrak{J} \in \mathfrak{TD}_\Omega$, *then the following inequalities hold:*

$$\begin{aligned}
&\frac{1}{\hbar^2\left(\frac{1}{2}\right)}\mathcal{J}\left(\frac{\sigma+\mathrm{i}}{2},\ \frac{\varepsilon+\mathfrak{v}}{2}\right)\\
&\leq_p \frac{\Gamma(\alpha+1)}{2\hbar\left(\frac{1}{2}\right)(\mathrm{i}-\sigma)^{\alpha}}\left[\mathcal{J}^{\alpha}_{\sigma^+}\mathcal{J}\left(\mathrm{i},\frac{\varepsilon+\mathfrak{v}}{2}\right)+\mathcal{J}^{\alpha}_{\mathrm{i}^-}\mathcal{J}\left(\sigma,\frac{\varepsilon+\mathfrak{v}}{2}\right)\right]+\frac{\Gamma(\beta+1)}{2\hbar\left(\frac{1}{2}\right)(\mathfrak{v}-\varepsilon)^{\beta}}\left[\mathcal{J}^{\beta}_{\varepsilon^+}\mathcal{J}\left(\frac{\sigma+\mathrm{i}}{2},\mathfrak{v}\right)+\mathcal{J}^{\beta}_{\mathfrak{v}^-}\mathcal{J}\left(\frac{\sigma+\mathrm{i}}{2},\varepsilon\right)\right]\\
&\leq_p \frac{\Gamma(\alpha+1)\Gamma(\beta+1)}{(\mathrm{i}-\sigma)^{\alpha}(\mathfrak{v}-\varepsilon)^{\beta}}\left[\mathcal{J}^{\alpha,\,\beta}_{\sigma^+,\varepsilon^+}\mathcal{J}(\mathrm{i},\mathfrak{v})+\mathcal{J}^{\alpha,\,\beta}_{\sigma^+,\mathfrak{v}^-}\mathcal{J}(\mathrm{i},\varepsilon)+\mathcal{J}^{\alpha,\,\beta}_{\mathrm{i}^-,\varepsilon^+}\mathcal{J}(\sigma,\mathfrak{v})+\mathcal{J}^{\alpha,\,\beta}_{\mathrm{i}^-,\mathfrak{v}^-}\mathcal{J}(\sigma,\varepsilon)\right]\\
&\leq_p \frac{\beta\Gamma(\alpha+1)}{(\mathrm{i}-\sigma)^{\alpha}}\left[\mathcal{J}^{\alpha}_{\sigma^+}\mathcal{J}(\mathrm{i},\varepsilon)+\mathcal{J}^{\alpha}_{\sigma^+}\mathcal{J}(\mathrm{i},\mathfrak{v})+\mathcal{J}^{\alpha}_{\mathrm{i}^-}\mathcal{J}(\sigma,\varepsilon)+\mathcal{J}^{\alpha}_{\mathrm{i}^-}\mathcal{J}(\sigma,\mathfrak{v})\right]\times\int_0^1\kappa^{\beta-1}[\hbar(\kappa)+\hbar(1-\kappa)]d\kappa\\
&+\frac{\alpha\Gamma(\beta+1)}{(\mathfrak{v}-\varepsilon)^{\beta}}\left[\mathcal{J}^{\beta}_{\varepsilon^+}\mathcal{J}(\sigma,\mathfrak{v})+\mathcal{J}^{\beta}_{\mathfrak{v}^-}\mathcal{J}(\mathrm{i},\varepsilon)+\mathcal{J}^{\beta}_{\varepsilon^+}\mathcal{J}(\mathrm{i},\mathfrak{v})+\mathcal{J}^{\beta}_{\mathfrak{v}^-}\mathcal{J}(\mathrm{i},\varepsilon)\right]\times\int_0^1 \upsilon^{\alpha-1}\hbar(\upsilon)+\hbar(1-\upsilon)d\upsilon\\
&\leq_p \alpha\beta[\mathcal{J}(\sigma,\varepsilon)+\mathcal{J}(\mathrm{i},\varepsilon)+\mathcal{J}(\sigma,\mathfrak{v})+\mathcal{J}(\mathrm{i},\mathfrak{v})]\times\int_0^1\kappa^{\beta-1}[\hbar(\kappa)+\hbar(1-\kappa)]d\kappa\int_0^1\upsilon^{\alpha-1}[\hbar(\upsilon)+\hbar(1-\upsilon)]d\upsilon.
\end{aligned}\tag{27}$$

If $\mathcal{J}(x,y)$ coordinated $\hbar$-concave IVM, then,

$$\begin{aligned}
&\frac{1}{\hbar^2\left(\frac{1}{2}\right)}\mathcal{J}\left(\frac{\sigma+\mathrm{i}}{2},\ \frac{\varepsilon+\mathfrak{v}}{2}\right)\\
&\geq_p \frac{\Gamma(\alpha+1)}{2\hbar\left(\frac{1}{2}\right)(\mathrm{i}-\sigma)^{\alpha}}\left[\mathcal{J}^{\alpha}_{\sigma^+}\mathcal{J}\left(\mathrm{i},\frac{\varepsilon+\mathfrak{v}}{2}\right)+\mathcal{J}^{\alpha}_{\mathrm{i}^-}\mathcal{J}\left(\sigma,\frac{\varepsilon+\mathfrak{v}}{2}\right)\right]+\frac{\Gamma(\beta+1)}{2\hbar\left(\frac{1}{2}\right)(\mathfrak{v}-\varepsilon)^{\beta}}\left[\mathcal{J}^{\beta}_{\varepsilon^+}\mathcal{J}\left(\frac{\sigma+\mathrm{i}}{2},\mathfrak{v}\right)+\mathcal{J}^{\beta}_{\mathfrak{v}^-}\mathcal{J}\left(\frac{\sigma+\mathrm{i}}{2},\varepsilon\right)\right]\\
&\geq_p \frac{\Gamma(\alpha+1)\Gamma(\beta+1)}{(\mathrm{i}-\sigma)^{\alpha}(\mathfrak{v}-\varepsilon)^{\beta}}\left[\mathcal{J}^{\alpha,\,\beta}_{\sigma^+,\varepsilon^+}\mathcal{J}(\mathrm{i},\mathfrak{v})+\mathcal{J}^{\alpha,\,\beta}_{\sigma^+,\mathfrak{v}^-}\mathcal{J}(\mathrm{i},\varepsilon)+\mathcal{J}^{\alpha,\,\beta}_{\mathrm{i}^-,\varepsilon^+}\mathcal{J}(\sigma,\mathfrak{v})+\mathcal{J}^{\alpha,\,\beta}_{\mathrm{i}^-,\mathfrak{v}^-}\mathcal{J}(\sigma,\varepsilon)\right]\\
&\geq_p \frac{\beta\Gamma(\alpha+1)}{(\mathrm{i}-\sigma)^{\alpha}}\left[\mathcal{J}^{\alpha}_{\sigma^+}\mathcal{J}(\mathrm{i},\varepsilon)+\mathcal{J}^{\alpha}_{\sigma^+}\mathcal{J}(\mathrm{i},\mathfrak{v})+\mathcal{J}^{\alpha}_{\mathrm{i}^-}\mathcal{J}(\sigma,\varepsilon)+\mathcal{J}^{\alpha}_{\mathrm{i}^-}\mathcal{J}(\sigma,\mathfrak{v})\right]\times\int_0^1\kappa^{\beta-1}[\hbar(\kappa)+\hbar(1-\kappa)]d\kappa\\
&+\frac{\alpha\Gamma(\beta+1)}{(\mathfrak{v}-\varepsilon)^{\beta}}\left[\mathcal{J}^{\beta}_{\varepsilon^+}\mathcal{J}(\sigma,\mathfrak{v})+\mathcal{J}^{\beta}_{\mathfrak{v}^-}\mathcal{J}(\mathrm{i},\varepsilon)+\mathcal{J}^{\beta}_{\varepsilon^+}\mathcal{J}(\mathrm{i},\mathfrak{v})+\mathcal{J}^{\beta}_{\mathfrak{v}^-}\mathcal{J}(\mathrm{i},\varepsilon)\right]\times\int_0^1 \upsilon^{\alpha-1}[\hbar(\upsilon)+\hbar(1-\upsilon)]d\upsilon\\
&\geq_p \alpha\beta[\mathcal{J}(\sigma,\varepsilon)+\mathcal{J}(\mathrm{i},\varepsilon)+\mathcal{J}(\sigma,\mathfrak{v})+\mathcal{J}(\mathrm{i},\mathfrak{v})]\times\int_0^1\kappa^{\beta-1}[\hbar(\kappa)+\hbar(1-\kappa)]d\kappa\int_0^1\upsilon^{\alpha-1}[\hbar(\upsilon)+\hbar(1-\upsilon)]d\upsilon.
\end{aligned}\tag{28}$$

Proof. Let $\mathcal{J}:[\sigma,\mathrm{i}]\to\mathbb{R}^+_I$ be a coordinated LR-$\hbar$-convex IVM. Then, by hypothesis, we have

$$\frac{1}{\hbar^2\left(\frac{1}{2}\right)}\mathcal{J}\left(\frac{\sigma+\mathrm{i}}{2},\frac{\varepsilon+\mathfrak{v}}{2}\right)\leq_p \mathcal{J}(\upsilon\sigma+(1-\upsilon)\mathrm{i},\upsilon\varepsilon+(1-\upsilon)\mathfrak{v})+\mathcal{J}((1-\upsilon)\sigma+\upsilon\mathrm{i},(1-\upsilon)\varepsilon+\upsilon\mathfrak{v})$$

By using Theorem 5, we have

$$\begin{aligned}
&\frac{1}{\hbar^2\left(\frac{1}{2}\right)}\mathcal{J}_*\left(\frac{\sigma+\mathrm{i}}{2},\frac{\varepsilon+\mathfrak{v}}{2}\right)\\
&\leq \mathcal{J}_*(\upsilon\sigma+(1-\upsilon)\mathrm{i},\upsilon\varepsilon+(1-\upsilon)\mathfrak{v})+\mathcal{J}_*((1-\upsilon)\sigma+\upsilon\mathrm{i},(1-\upsilon)\varepsilon+\upsilon\mathfrak{v}),\\
&\frac{1}{\hbar^2\left(\frac{1}{2}\right)}\mathcal{J}^*\left(\frac{\sigma+\mathrm{i}}{2},\frac{\varepsilon+\mathfrak{v}}{2}\right)\\
&\leq \mathcal{J}^*(\upsilon\sigma+(1-\upsilon)\mathrm{i},\upsilon\varepsilon+(1-\upsilon)\mathfrak{v})+\mathcal{J}^*((1-\upsilon)\sigma+\upsilon\mathrm{i},(1-\upsilon)\varepsilon+\upsilon\mathfrak{v}).
\end{aligned}$$

By using Lemma 1, we have

$$\begin{aligned}
\frac{1}{\hbar\left(\frac{1}{2}\right)}\mathcal{J}_*\left(x,\frac{\varepsilon+\mathfrak{v}}{2}\right)&\leq \mathcal{J}_*(x,\ \upsilon\varepsilon+(1-\upsilon)\mathfrak{v})+\mathcal{J}_*(x,\ (1-\upsilon)\varepsilon+\upsilon\mathfrak{v}),\\
\frac{1}{\hbar\left(\frac{1}{2}\right)}\mathcal{J}^*\left(x,\frac{\varepsilon+\mathfrak{v}}{2}\right)&\leq \mathcal{J}^*(x,\ \upsilon\varepsilon+(1-\upsilon)\mathfrak{v})+\mathcal{J}^*(x,\ (1-\upsilon)\varepsilon+\upsilon\mathfrak{v}),
\end{aligned}\tag{29}$$

and

$$\begin{aligned}
\frac{1}{\hbar\left(\frac{1}{2}\right)}\mathcal{J}_*\left(\frac{\sigma+\mathrm{i}}{2},y\right)&\leq \mathcal{J}_*(\upsilon\sigma+(1-\upsilon)\mathrm{i},y)+\mathcal{J}_*((1-\upsilon)\sigma+\upsilon\mathrm{i},y),\\
\frac{1}{\hbar\left(\frac{1}{2}\right)}\mathcal{J}^*\left(\frac{\sigma+\mathrm{i}}{2},y\right)&\leq \mathcal{J}^*(\upsilon\sigma+(1-\upsilon)\mathrm{i},y)+\mathcal{J}^*((1-\upsilon)\sigma+\upsilon\mathrm{i},y).
\end{aligned}\tag{30}$$

From (29) and (30), we have

$$\begin{aligned}
&\frac{1}{\hbar\left(\frac{1}{2}\right)}\left[\mathcal{J}_*\left(x,\frac{\varepsilon+\mathfrak{v}}{2}\right),\mathcal{J}^*\left(x,\frac{\varepsilon+\mathfrak{v}}{2}\right)\right]\\
&\leq_p \left[\mathcal{J}_*(x,\ \upsilon\varepsilon+(1-\upsilon)\mathfrak{v}),\mathcal{J}^*(x,\ \upsilon\varepsilon+(1-\upsilon)\mathfrak{v})\right]\\
&+\left[\mathcal{J}_*(x,\ (1-\upsilon)\varepsilon+\upsilon\mathfrak{v}),\mathcal{J}^*(x,\ (1-\upsilon)\varepsilon+\upsilon\mathfrak{v})\right],
\end{aligned}$$

and

$$\begin{aligned}&\frac{1}{\hbar\left(\frac{1}{2}\right)}\left[\mathcal{J}_*\left(\frac{\sigma+\mathrm{i}}{2},y\right),\mathcal{J}^*\left(\frac{\sigma+\mathrm{i}}{2},y\right)\right]\\&\leq_p\left[\mathcal{J}_*(v\sigma+(1-v)\mathrm{i},y),\mathcal{J}^*(v\sigma+(1-v)\mathrm{i},y)\right]\\&\quad+\left[\mathcal{J}_*(v\sigma+(1-v)\mathrm{i},y),\mathcal{J}^*(v\sigma+(1-v)\mathrm{i},y)\right],\end{aligned}$$

It follows that

$$\frac{1}{\hbar\left(\frac{1}{2}\right)}\mathcal{J}\left(x,\frac{\varepsilon+\mathfrak{v}}{2}\right)\leq_p\mathcal{J}(x,\ v\varepsilon+(1-v)\mathfrak{v})+\mathcal{J}(x,\ (1-v)\varepsilon+v\mathfrak{v}),\tag{31}$$

and

$$\frac{1}{\hbar\left(\frac{1}{2}\right)}\mathcal{J}\left(\frac{\sigma+\mathrm{i}}{2},y\right)\leq_p\mathcal{J}(v\sigma+(1-v)\mathrm{i},y)+\mathcal{J}(v\sigma+(1-v)\mathrm{i},y).\tag{32}$$

Since $\mathcal{J}(x,.)$ and $\mathcal{J}(.,y)$ are both coordinated LR-$\hbar$-convex-IVMs; then, from (17), (31), and (32), we have

$$\frac{1}{\beta\hbar\left(\frac{1}{2}\right)}\mathcal{J}_x\left(\frac{\varepsilon+\mathfrak{v}}{2}\right)\leq_p\frac{\Gamma(\beta)}{(\mathfrak{v}-\varepsilon)^{\beta}}\left[\mathcal{I}^{\beta}_{\varepsilon^+}\mathcal{J}_x(\mathfrak{v})+\mathcal{I}^{\beta}_{\mathfrak{v}^-}\mathcal{J}_x(\varepsilon)\right]\leq_p\left[\mathcal{J}_x(\varepsilon)+\mathcal{J}_x(\mathfrak{v})\right]\int_0^1\kappa^{\beta-1}[\hbar(\kappa)+\hbar(1-\kappa)]d\kappa\tag{33}$$

and

$$\frac{1}{\alpha\hbar\left(\frac{1}{2}\right)}\mathcal{J}_y\left(\frac{\sigma+\mathrm{i}}{2}\right)\leq_p\frac{\Gamma(\alpha)}{(\mathrm{i}-\sigma)^{\alpha}}\left[\mathcal{I}^{\alpha}_{\sigma^+}\mathcal{J}_y(\mathrm{i})+\mathcal{I}^{\alpha}_{\mathrm{i}^-}\mathcal{J}_y(\sigma)\right]\leq_p\left[\mathcal{J}_y(\sigma)+\mathcal{J}_y(\mathrm{i})\right]\int_0^1 v^{\alpha-1}\hbar(v)+\hbar(1-v)dv\tag{34}$$

Since $\mathcal{J}_x(w)=\mathcal{J}(x,w)$, then (34) can be written as

$$\frac{1}{\beta\hbar\left(\frac{1}{2}\right)}\mathcal{J}\left(x,\frac{\varepsilon+\mathfrak{v}}{2}\right)\leq_p\frac{\Gamma(\beta)}{(\mathfrak{v}-\varepsilon)^{\beta}}\left[\mathcal{I}^{\alpha}_{\varepsilon^+}\mathcal{J}(x,\mathfrak{v})+\mathcal{I}^{\alpha}_{\mathfrak{v}^-}\mathcal{J}(x,\varepsilon)\right]\leq_p[\mathcal{J}(x,\varepsilon)+\mathcal{J}(x,\mathfrak{v})]\int_0^1\kappa^{\beta-1}[\hbar(\kappa)+\hbar(1-\kappa)]d\kappa.\tag{35}$$

That is,

$$\begin{aligned}&\frac{1}{\beta\hbar\left(\frac{1}{2}\right)}\mathcal{J}\left(x,\tfrac{\varepsilon+\mathfrak{v}}{2}\right)\leq_p\frac{1}{(\mathfrak{v}-\varepsilon)^{\beta}}\left[\int_{\varepsilon}^{\mathfrak{v}}(\mathfrak{v}-\kappa)^{\beta-1}\mathcal{J}(x,\kappa)d\kappa+\int_{\varepsilon}^{\mathfrak{v}}(\kappa-\varepsilon)^{\beta-1}\mathcal{J}(x,\kappa)d\kappa\right]\\&\leq_p[\mathcal{J}(x,\varepsilon)+\mathcal{J}(x,\mathfrak{v})]\int_0^1\kappa^{\beta-1}[\hbar(\kappa)+\hbar(1-\kappa)]d\kappa.\end{aligned}\tag{36}$$

Multiplying double inequality (36) by $\frac{(\mathrm{i}-x)^{\alpha-1}}{(\mathrm{i}-\sigma)^{\alpha}}$ and integrating with respect to x over $[\sigma,\mathrm{i}]$, we have

$$\begin{aligned}&\frac{1}{\beta(\mathrm{i}-\sigma)^{\alpha}\hbar\left(\frac{1}{2}\right)}\int_{\sigma}^{\mathrm{i}}\mathcal{J}\left(x,\tfrac{\varepsilon+\mathfrak{v}}{2}\right)(\mathrm{i}-x)^{\alpha-1}dx\\&\leq_p\frac{1}{(\mathrm{i}-\sigma)^{\alpha}(\mathfrak{v}-\varepsilon)^{\beta}}\int_{\sigma}^{\mathrm{i}}\int_{\varepsilon}^{\mathfrak{v}}(\mathrm{i}-x)^{\alpha-1}(\mathfrak{v}-\kappa)^{\beta-1}\mathcal{J}(x,\kappa)d\kappa dx+\int_{\sigma}^{\mathrm{i}}\int_{\varepsilon}^{\mathfrak{v}}(\mathrm{i}-x)^{\alpha-1}(\kappa-\varepsilon)^{\beta-1}\mathcal{J}(x,\kappa)d\kappa dx\\&\leq_p\frac{1}{(\mathrm{i}-\sigma)^{\alpha}}\left[\int_{\sigma}^{\mathrm{i}}(\mathrm{i}-x)^{\alpha-1}\mathcal{J}(x,\varepsilon)dx+\int_{\sigma}^{\mathrm{i}}(\mathrm{i}-x)^{\alpha-1}\mathcal{J}(x,\mathfrak{v})dx\right]\int_0^1\kappa^{\beta-1}[\hbar(\kappa)+\hbar(1-\kappa)]d\kappa.\end{aligned}\tag{37}$$

Again, multiplying double inequality (36) by $\frac{(x-\sigma)^{\alpha-1}}{(\mathrm{i}-\sigma)^{\alpha}}$ and integrating with respect to x over $[\sigma,\mathrm{i}]$, we have

$$\begin{aligned}&\frac{1}{\beta(\mathrm{i}-\sigma)^{\alpha}\hbar\left(\frac{1}{2}\right)}\int_{\sigma}^{\mathrm{i}}\mathcal{J}\left(x,\tfrac{\varepsilon+\mathfrak{v}}{2}\right)(x-\sigma)^{\alpha-1}dx\\&\leq_p\frac{1}{(\mathrm{i}-\sigma)^{\alpha}(\mathfrak{v}-\varepsilon)^{\beta}}\int_{\sigma}^{\mathrm{i}}\int_{\varepsilon}^{\mathfrak{v}}(x-\sigma)^{\alpha-1}(\mathfrak{v}-\kappa)^{\beta-1}\mathcal{J}(x,\kappa)d\kappa dx\\&+\frac{1}{(\mathrm{i}-\sigma)^{\alpha}(\mathfrak{v}-\varepsilon)^{\beta}}\int_{\sigma}^{\mathrm{i}}\int_{\varepsilon}^{\mathfrak{v}}(x-\sigma)^{\alpha-1}(\kappa-\varepsilon)^{\beta-1}\mathcal{J}(x,\kappa)d\kappa dx\\&\leq_p\frac{1}{(\mathrm{i}-\sigma)^{\alpha}}\left[\int_{\sigma}^{\mathrm{i}}(x-\sigma)^{\alpha-1}\mathcal{J}(x,\varepsilon)dx+\int_{\sigma}^{\mathrm{i}}(x-\sigma)^{\alpha-1}\mathcal{J}(x,\mathfrak{v})dx\right]\int_0^1\kappa^{\beta-1}[\hbar(\kappa)+\hbar(1-\kappa)]d\kappa.\end{aligned}\tag{38}$$

From (37), we have

$$\begin{aligned}&\frac{\Gamma(\alpha+1)}{2\hbar\left(\frac{1}{2}\right)(\mathrm{i}-\sigma)^{\alpha}}\left[\mathcal{J}^{\alpha}_{\sigma^{+}}\mathcal{J}\left(\mathrm{i},\tfrac{\varepsilon+\upsilon}{2}\right)\right]\\&\leq_{p}\frac{\Gamma(\alpha+1)\Gamma(\beta+1)}{(\mathrm{i}-\sigma)^{\alpha}(\upsilon-\varepsilon)^{\beta}}\left[\mathcal{J}^{\alpha,\,\beta}_{\sigma^{+},\varepsilon^{+}}\mathcal{J}(\mathrm{i},\upsilon)+\mathcal{J}^{\alpha,\,\beta}_{\mathrm{i}^{-},\varepsilon^{+}}\mathcal{J}(\mathrm{i},\varepsilon)\right]\\&\leq_{p}\frac{\beta\Gamma(\alpha+1)}{(\mathrm{i}-\sigma)^{\alpha}}\left[\mathcal{J}^{\alpha}_{\sigma^{+}}\mathcal{J}(\mathrm{i},\varepsilon)+\mathcal{J}^{\alpha}_{\sigma^{+}}\mathcal{J}(\mathrm{i},\upsilon)\right]\int_0^1\kappa^{\beta-1}[\hbar(\kappa)+\hbar(1-\kappa)]d\kappa.\end{aligned}\tag{39}$$

From (38), we have

$$\begin{aligned}&\frac{\Gamma(\alpha+1)}{2\hbar\left(\frac{1}{2}\right)(\mathrm{i}-\sigma)^{\alpha}}\left[\mathcal{J}^{\alpha}_{\mathrm{i}^{-}}\mathcal{J}\left(\sigma,\tfrac{\varepsilon+\upsilon}{2}\right)\right]\\&\leq_{p}\frac{\Gamma(\alpha+1)\Gamma(\beta+1)}{(\mathrm{i}-\sigma)^{\alpha}(\upsilon-\varepsilon)^{\beta}}\left[\mathcal{J}^{\alpha,\,\beta}_{\mathrm{i}^{-},\varepsilon^{+}}\mathcal{J}(\sigma,\upsilon)+\mathcal{J}^{\alpha,\,\beta}_{\mathrm{i}^{-},\upsilon^{-}}\mathcal{J}(\sigma,\varepsilon)\right]\\&\leq_{p}\frac{\beta\Gamma(\alpha+1)}{(\mathrm{i}-\sigma)^{\alpha}}\left[\mathcal{J}^{\alpha}_{\mathrm{i}^{-}}\mathcal{J}(\sigma,\varepsilon)+\mathcal{J}^{\alpha}_{\mathrm{i}^{-}}\mathcal{J}(\sigma,\upsilon)\right]\int_0^1\kappa^{\beta-1}[\hbar(\kappa)+\hbar(1-\kappa)]d\kappa.\end{aligned}\tag{40}$$

Similarly, since $\mathcal{J}_y(z)=\mathcal{J}(z,y)$, then, from (35), (41), and (42), we have

$$\begin{aligned}&\frac{\Gamma(\beta+1)}{2\hbar\left(\frac{1}{2}\right)(\upsilon-\varepsilon)^{\beta}}\left[\mathcal{J}^{\beta}_{\varepsilon^{+}}\mathcal{J}\left(\frac{\sigma+\mathrm{i}}{2},\upsilon\right)\right]\\&\leq_{p}\frac{\Gamma(\alpha+1)\Gamma(\beta+1)}{(\mathrm{i}-\sigma)^{\alpha}(\upsilon-\varepsilon)^{\beta}}\left[\mathcal{J}^{\alpha,\,\beta}_{\sigma^{+},\varepsilon^{+}}\mathcal{J}(\mathrm{i},\upsilon)+\mathcal{J}^{\alpha,\,\beta}_{\mathrm{i}^{-},\varepsilon^{+}}\mathcal{J}(\sigma,\upsilon)\right]\\&\leq_{p}\frac{\alpha\Gamma(\beta+1)}{(\upsilon-\varepsilon)^{\beta}}\left[\mathcal{J}^{\beta}_{\varepsilon^{+}}\mathcal{J}(\sigma,\upsilon)+\mathcal{J}^{\beta}_{\varepsilon^{+}}\mathcal{J}(\mathrm{i},\upsilon)\right].\end{aligned}\tag{41}$$

and

$$\begin{aligned}&\frac{\Gamma(\beta+1)}{2\hbar\left(\frac{1}{2}\right)(\upsilon-\varepsilon)^{\alpha}}\left[\mathcal{J}^{\beta}_{\upsilon^{-}}\mathcal{J}\left(\frac{\sigma+\mathrm{i}}{2},\varepsilon\right)\right]\\&\leq_{p}\frac{\Gamma(\alpha+1)\Gamma(\beta+1)}{(\mathrm{i}-\sigma)^{\alpha}(\upsilon-\varepsilon)^{\beta}}\left[\mathcal{J}^{\alpha,\,\beta}_{\sigma^{+},\upsilon^{-}}\mathcal{J}(\mathrm{i},\varepsilon)+\mathcal{J}^{\alpha,\,\beta}_{\mathrm{i}^{-},\upsilon^{-}}\mathcal{J}(\sigma,\varepsilon)\right]\\&\leq_{p}\frac{\alpha\Gamma(\beta+1)}{(\upsilon-\varepsilon)^{\beta}}\left[\mathcal{J}^{\beta}_{\upsilon^{-}}\mathcal{J}(\sigma,\varepsilon)+\mathcal{J}^{\beta}_{\upsilon^{-}}\mathcal{J}(\mathrm{i},\varepsilon)\right].\end{aligned}\tag{42}$$

The second, third, and fourth inequalities of (27) will be the consequence of adding the inequalities (41) and (42).

Now, we have inequality (17)'s left portion.

$$\frac{1}{\hbar^2\left(\frac{1}{2}\right)}\mathcal{J}\left(\frac{\sigma+\mathrm{i}}{2},\frac{\varepsilon+\upsilon}{2}\right)\leq_{p}\frac{\Gamma(\beta+1)}{\hbar\left(\frac{1}{2}\right)(\upsilon-\varepsilon)^{\beta}}\left[\mathcal{J}^{\beta}_{\varepsilon^{+}}\mathcal{J}\left(\frac{\sigma+\mathrm{i}}{2},\upsilon\right)+\mathcal{J}^{\beta}_{\upsilon^{-}}\mathcal{J}\left(\frac{\sigma+\mathrm{i}}{2},\varepsilon\right)\right]\tag{43}$$

and

$$\frac{1}{\hbar^2\left(\frac{1}{2}\right)}\mathcal{J}\left(\frac{\sigma+\mathrm{i}}{2},\frac{\varepsilon+\upsilon}{2}\right)\leq_{p}\frac{\Gamma(\alpha+1)}{\hbar\left(\frac{1}{2}\right)(\mathrm{i}-\sigma)^{\alpha}}\left[\mathcal{J}^{\alpha}_{\sigma^{+}}\mathcal{J}\left(\mathrm{i},\frac{\varepsilon+\upsilon}{2}\right)+\mathcal{J}^{\alpha}_{\mathrm{i}^{-}}\mathcal{J}\left(\sigma,\frac{\varepsilon+\upsilon}{2}\right)\right]\tag{44}$$

The following inequality is created by adding the two inequalities (43) and (44):

$$\begin{aligned}\frac{1}{\hbar^2\left(\frac{1}{2}\right)}\mathcal{J}\left(\frac{\sigma+\mathrm{i}}{2},\frac{\varepsilon+\upsilon}{2}\right)&\leq_{p}\frac{\Gamma(\alpha+1)}{\hbar\left(\frac{1}{2}\right)(\mathrm{i}-\sigma)^{\alpha}}\left[\mathcal{J}^{\alpha}_{\sigma^{+}}\mathcal{J}\left(\mathrm{i},\tfrac{\varepsilon+\upsilon}{2}\right)+\mathcal{J}^{\alpha}_{\mathrm{i}^{-}}\mathcal{J}\left(\sigma,\tfrac{\varepsilon+\upsilon}{2}\right)\right]\\&+\frac{\Gamma(\beta+1)}{\hbar\left(\frac{1}{2}\right)(\upsilon-\varepsilon)^{\beta}}\left[\mathcal{J}^{\beta}_{\varepsilon^{+}}\mathcal{J}\left(\frac{\sigma+\mathrm{i}}{2},\upsilon\right)+\mathcal{J}^{\beta}_{\upsilon^{-}}\mathcal{J}\left(\frac{\sigma+\mathrm{i}}{2},\varepsilon\right)\right].\end{aligned}$$

Similarly, since we obtain the set of $IVMs$ $\mathcal{J}:\Omega\to\mathbb{R}^{+}_{I}$, the inequality can be expressed as follows:

$$\begin{aligned}&\frac{1}{\hbar^2\left(\frac{1}{2}\right)}\mathfrak{J}\left(\frac{\sigma+\mathrm{i}}{2},\frac{\varepsilon+\mathfrak{v}}{2}\right)\\&\leq_p\frac{\Gamma(\alpha+1)}{\hbar\left(\frac{1}{2}\right)(\mathrm{i}-\sigma)^\alpha}\left[\mathcal{J}^\alpha_{\sigma^+}\mathfrak{J}\left(\mathrm{i},\frac{\varepsilon+\mathfrak{v}}{2}\right)+\mathcal{J}^\alpha_{\mathrm{i}^-}\mathfrak{J}\left(\sigma,\frac{\varepsilon+\mathfrak{v}}{2}\right)\right]+\frac{\Gamma(\beta+1)}{\hbar\left(\frac{1}{2}\right)(\mathfrak{v}-\varepsilon)^\beta}\left[\mathcal{J}^\beta_{\varepsilon^+}\mathfrak{J}\left(\frac{\sigma+\mathrm{i}}{2},\mathfrak{v}\right)+\mathcal{J}^\beta_{\mathfrak{v}^-}\mathfrak{J}\left(\frac{\sigma+\mathrm{i}}{2},\varepsilon\right)\right].\end{aligned}\tag{45}$$

The first inequality of (27) is this one.

Now, we have inequality (17)'s right portion:

$$\frac{\Gamma(\beta)}{(\mathfrak{v}-\varepsilon)^\beta}\left[\mathcal{J}^\beta_{\varepsilon^+}\mathfrak{J}(\sigma,\mathfrak{v})+\mathcal{J}^\beta_{\mathfrak{v}^-}\mathfrak{J}(\sigma,\varepsilon)\right]\leq_p[\mathfrak{J}(\sigma,\varepsilon)+\mathfrak{J}(\sigma,\mathfrak{v})]\times\int_0^1\kappa^{\beta-1}[\hbar(\kappa)+\hbar(1-\kappa)]d\kappa\tag{46}$$

$$\frac{\Gamma(\beta)}{(\mathfrak{v}-\varepsilon)^\beta}\left[\mathcal{J}^\beta_{\varepsilon^+}\mathfrak{J}(\mathrm{i},\mathfrak{v})+\mathcal{J}^\beta_{\mathfrak{v}^-}\mathfrak{J}(\mathrm{i},\varepsilon)\right]\leq_p[\mathfrak{J}(\mathrm{i},\varepsilon)+\mathfrak{J}(\mathrm{i},\mathfrak{v})]\times\int_0^1\kappa^{\beta-1}[\hbar(\kappa)+\hbar(1-\kappa)]d\kappa\tag{47}$$

$$\frac{\Gamma(\alpha)}{(\mathrm{i}-\sigma)^\alpha}\left[\mathcal{J}^\alpha_{\sigma^+}\mathfrak{J}(\mathrm{i},\varepsilon)+\mathcal{J}^\alpha_{\mathrm{i}^-}\mathfrak{J}(\sigma,\varepsilon)\right]\leq_p[\mathfrak{J}(\sigma,\varepsilon)+\mathfrak{J}(\mathrm{i},\varepsilon)]\times\int_0^1 v^{\alpha-1}\hbar(v)+\hbar(1-v)dv\tag{48}$$

$$\frac{\Gamma(\alpha)}{(\mathrm{i}-\sigma)^\alpha}\left[\mathcal{J}^\alpha_{\sigma^+}\mathfrak{J}(\mathrm{i},\mathfrak{v})+\mathcal{J}^\alpha_{\mathrm{i}^-}\mathfrak{J}(\sigma,\mathfrak{v})\right]\leq_p[\mathfrak{J}(\sigma,\mathfrak{v})+\mathfrak{J}(\mathrm{i},\mathfrak{v})]\times\int_0^1 v^{\alpha-1}\hbar(v)+\hbar(1-v)dv\tag{49}$$

Summing inequalities (46), (47), (48), and (49), and then taking the multiplication of the resultant with $\alpha\beta$, we have

$$\begin{aligned}&\frac{\beta\Gamma(\alpha+1)}{(\mathrm{i}-\sigma)^\alpha}\left[\mathcal{J}^\alpha_{\sigma^+}\mathfrak{J}(\mathrm{i},\varepsilon)+\mathcal{J}^\alpha_{\mathrm{i}^-}\mathfrak{J}(\sigma,\varepsilon)+\mathcal{J}^\alpha_{\sigma^+}\mathfrak{J}(\mathrm{i},\mathfrak{v})+\mathcal{J}^\alpha_{\mathrm{i}^-}\mathfrak{J}(\sigma,\mathfrak{v})\right]\\&+\frac{\alpha\Gamma(\beta+1)}{(\mathfrak{v}-\varepsilon)^\beta}\left[\mathcal{J}^\beta_{\varepsilon^+}\mathfrak{J}(\sigma,\mathfrak{v})+\mathcal{J}^\beta_{\mathfrak{v}^-}\mathfrak{J}(\sigma,\varepsilon)+\mathcal{J}^\beta_{\varepsilon^+}\mathfrak{J}(\mathrm{i},\mathfrak{v})+\mathcal{J}^\beta_{\mathfrak{v}^-}\mathfrak{J}(\mathrm{i},\varepsilon)\right]\\&\leq_p[\mathfrak{J}(\sigma,\varepsilon)+\mathfrak{J}(\sigma,\mathfrak{v})+\mathfrak{J}(\mathrm{i},\varepsilon)+\mathfrak{J}(\mathrm{i},\mathfrak{v})]\times\int_0^1\kappa^{\beta-1}[\hbar(\kappa)+\hbar(1-\kappa)]d\kappa\int_0^1 v^{\alpha-1}\hbar(v)+\hbar(1-v)dv.\end{aligned}\tag{50}$$

This is the final inequality of (27) and the conclusion has been established. □

Example 3. *We assume the IVMs $\mathfrak{J}:[0,2]\times[0,2]\to\mathbb{R}^+_I$ defined by*

$$\mathfrak{J}(x,y)=\left[(2-\sqrt{x})(2-\sqrt{y}),2(2-\sqrt{x})(2-\sqrt{y})\right],\tag{51}$$

then, for each $\gamma\in[0,1]$, we have. Endpoint functions $\mathfrak{J}_*(x,y)$, $\mathfrak{J}^*(x,y)$ are coordinate LR-$\hbar$-convex and $\hbar$-concave functions. Hence, $\widetilde{\mathfrak{J}}(x,y)$ is $\hbar$-coordinated LR-$\hbar$-convex IVM.

$$\begin{aligned}&\mathfrak{J}\left(\frac{\sigma+\mathrm{i}}{2},\frac{\varepsilon+\mathfrak{v}}{2}\right)=[1,2],\\&\frac{\Gamma(\alpha+1)}{4(\mathrm{i}-\sigma)^\alpha}\left[\mathcal{J}^\alpha_{\sigma^+}\mathfrak{J}\left(\mathrm{i},\frac{\varepsilon+\mathfrak{v}}{2}\right)+\mathcal{J}^\alpha_{\mathrm{i}^-}\mathfrak{J}\left(\sigma,\frac{\varepsilon+\mathfrak{v}}{2}\right)\right]+\frac{\Gamma(\beta+1)}{4(\mathfrak{v}-\varepsilon)^\beta}\left[\mathcal{J}^\beta_{\varepsilon^+}\mathfrak{J}\left(\frac{\sigma+\mathrm{i}}{2},\mathfrak{v}\right)+\mathcal{J}^\beta_{\mathfrak{v}^-}\mathfrak{J}\left(\frac{\sigma+\mathrm{i}}{2},\varepsilon\right)\right]\\&=2-\frac{\sqrt{2}}{4}-\frac{\sqrt{2}}{8}\pi\cdot[1,2]\\&\frac{\Gamma(\alpha+1)\Gamma(\beta+1)}{4(\mathrm{i}-\sigma)^\alpha(\mathfrak{v}-\varepsilon)^\beta}\left[\mathcal{J}^{\alpha,\beta}_{\sigma^+,\varepsilon^+}\mathfrak{J}(\mathrm{i},\mathfrak{v})+\mathcal{J}^{\alpha,\beta}_{\sigma^+,\mathfrak{v}^-}\mathfrak{J}(\mathrm{i},\varepsilon)+\mathcal{J}^{\alpha,\beta}_{\mathrm{i}^-,\varepsilon^+}\mathfrak{J}(\sigma,\mathfrak{v})+\mathcal{J}^{\alpha,\beta}_{\mathrm{i}^-,\mathfrak{v}^-}\mathfrak{J}(\sigma,\varepsilon)\right]\\&=\frac{33}{8}-\sqrt{2}-\frac{\sqrt{2}}{2}\pi+\frac{\pi}{8}+\frac{\pi^2}{32}\cdot[1,2]\\&\frac{\Gamma(\alpha+1)}{8(\mathrm{i}-\sigma)^\alpha}\left[\mathcal{J}^\alpha_{\sigma^+}\mathfrak{J}(\mathrm{i},\varepsilon)+\mathcal{J}^\alpha_{\sigma^+}\mathfrak{J}(\mathrm{i},\mathfrak{v})+\mathcal{J}^\alpha_{\mathrm{i}^-}\mathfrak{J}(\sigma,\varepsilon)+\mathcal{J}^\alpha_{\mathrm{i}^-}\mathfrak{J}(\sigma,\mathfrak{v})\right]\\&+\frac{\Gamma(\beta+1)}{8(\mathfrak{v}-\varepsilon)^\beta}\left[\mathcal{J}^\beta_{\varepsilon^+}\mathfrak{J}(\sigma,\mathfrak{v})+\mathcal{J}^\beta_{\varepsilon^+}\mathfrak{J}(\mathrm{i},\mathfrak{v})+\mathcal{J}^\beta_{\mathfrak{v}^-}\mathfrak{J}(\sigma,\varepsilon)+\mathcal{J}^\beta_{\mathfrak{v}^-}\mathfrak{J}(\mathrm{i},\varepsilon)\right]\\&=\frac{34\sqrt{2}+\left(\sqrt{2}-4\right)\pi-24}{8\sqrt{2}}\cdot[1,2]\\&\frac{\mathfrak{J}(\varepsilon,\mathrm{i})+\mathfrak{J}(\sigma,\mathrm{i})+\mathfrak{J}(\varepsilon,\mathfrak{v})+\mathfrak{J}(\sigma,\mathfrak{v})}{4}=\left(\frac{9}{2}-2\sqrt{2}\right)\cdot[1,2].\end{aligned}$$

That is

$$\begin{aligned}&[1,2]\leq_p 2-\frac{\sqrt{2}}{4}-\frac{\sqrt{2}}{8}\pi\cdot[1,2]\leq_p\frac{33}{8}-\sqrt{2}-\frac{\sqrt{2}}{2}\pi+\frac{\pi}{8}+\frac{\pi^2}{32}\cdot[1,2]\leq_p\frac{34\sqrt{2}+\left(\sqrt{2}-4\right)\pi-24}{8\sqrt{2}}\cdot[1,2]\leq_p\left(\frac{9}{2}-2\sqrt{2}\right)\\&\cdot[1,2]\end{aligned}$$

Hence, Theorem 6 has been verified.

Remark 3. *If one assumes that $\alpha = 1$ and $\beta = 1$, and $\hbar(\upsilon) = \upsilon$, $\hbar(\kappa) = \kappa$, then from (27), as a result, there will be inequality (see [43]):*

$$\begin{aligned}
&\mathfrak{J}\left(\frac{\sigma+\mathrm{i}}{2}, \frac{\varepsilon+\mathfrak{v}}{2}\right)\\
&\leq_p \frac{1}{2}\left[\frac{1}{\mathrm{i}-\sigma}\int_\sigma^{\mathrm{i}} \mathfrak{J}\left(x, \frac{\varepsilon+\mathfrak{v}}{2}\right)dx + \frac{1}{\mathfrak{v}-\varepsilon}\int_\varepsilon^{\mathfrak{v}} \mathfrak{J}\left(\frac{\sigma+\mathrm{i}}{2}, y\right)dy\right] \leq_p \frac{1}{(\mathrm{i}-\sigma)(\mathfrak{v}-\varepsilon)}\int_\sigma^{\mathrm{i}}\int_\varepsilon^{\mathfrak{v}} \mathfrak{J}(x,y)dydx\\
&\leq_p \frac{1}{4(\mathrm{i}-\sigma)}\left[\int_\sigma^{\mathrm{i}} \mathfrak{J}(x,\varepsilon)dx + \int_\sigma^{\mathrm{i}} \mathfrak{J}(x,\mathfrak{v})dx\right] + \frac{1}{4(\mathfrak{v}-\varepsilon)}\left[\int_\varepsilon^{\mathfrak{v}} \mathfrak{J}(\sigma,y)dy + \int_\varepsilon^{\mathfrak{v}} \mathfrak{J}(\mathrm{i},y)dy\right]\\
&\leq_p \frac{\mathfrak{J}(\sigma,\varepsilon)+\mathfrak{J}(\mathrm{i},\varepsilon)+\mathfrak{J}(\sigma,\mathfrak{v})+\mathfrak{J}(\mathrm{i},\mathfrak{v})}{4}.
\end{aligned} \tag{52}$$

If one assumes that $\alpha = 1$ and $\beta = 1$, $\hbar(\upsilon) = \upsilon$, $\hbar(\kappa) = \kappa$ and $\mathfrak{J}$ is coordinated left-LR-$\hbar$-convex, then from (27), as a result, there will be inequality (see [42]):

$$\begin{aligned}
&\mathfrak{J}\left(\frac{\sigma+\mathrm{i}}{2}, \frac{\varepsilon+\mathfrak{v}}{2}\right)\\
&\supseteq \frac{1}{2}\left[\frac{1}{\mathrm{i}-\sigma}\int_\sigma^{\mathrm{i}} \mathfrak{J}\left(x, \frac{\varepsilon+\mathfrak{v}}{2}\right)dx + \frac{1}{\mathfrak{v}-\varepsilon}\int_\varepsilon^{\mathfrak{v}} \mathfrak{J}\left(\frac{\sigma+\mathrm{i}}{2}, y\right)dy\right] \supseteq \frac{1}{(\mathrm{i}-\sigma)(\mathfrak{v}-\varepsilon)}\int_\sigma^{\mathrm{i}}\int_\varepsilon^{\mathfrak{v}} \mathfrak{J}(x,y)dydx\\
&\supseteq \frac{1}{4(\mathrm{i}-\sigma)}\left[\int_\sigma^{\mathrm{i}} \mathfrak{J}(x,\varepsilon)dx + \int_\sigma^{\mathrm{i}} \mathfrak{J}(x,\mathfrak{v})dx\right] + \frac{1}{4(\mathfrak{v}-\varepsilon)}\left[\int_\varepsilon^{\mathfrak{v}} \mathfrak{J}(\sigma,y)dy + \int_\varepsilon^{\mathfrak{v}} \mathfrak{J}(\mathrm{i},y)dy\right]\\
&\supseteq \frac{\mathfrak{J}(\sigma,\varepsilon)+\mathfrak{J}(\mathrm{i},\varepsilon)+\mathfrak{J}(\sigma,\mathfrak{v})+\mathfrak{J}(\mathrm{i},\mathfrak{v})}{4}.
\end{aligned} \tag{53}$$

If $\hbar(\upsilon) = \upsilon$, $\hbar(\kappa) = \kappa$ and $\mathfrak{J}_*(x,y) \neq \mathfrak{J}^*(x,y)$, then from (27), we succeed in bringing about the upcoming inequality (see [46]):

$$\begin{aligned}
&\mathfrak{J}\left(\frac{\sigma+\mathrm{i}}{2}, \frac{\varepsilon+\mathfrak{v}}{2}\right)\\
&\leq_p \frac{\Gamma(\alpha+1)}{4(\mathrm{i}-\sigma)^\alpha}\left[\mathcal{J}^\alpha_{\sigma^+}\mathfrak{J}\left(\mathrm{i}, \frac{\varepsilon+\mathfrak{v}}{2}\right) + \mathcal{J}^\alpha_{\mathrm{i}^-}\mathfrak{J}\left(\sigma, \frac{\varepsilon+\mathfrak{v}}{2}\right)\right] + \frac{\Gamma(\beta+1)}{4(\mathfrak{v}-\varepsilon)^\beta}\left[\mathcal{J}^\beta_{\varepsilon^+}\mathfrak{J}\left(\frac{\sigma+\mathrm{i}}{2}, \mathfrak{v}\right) + \mathcal{J}^\beta_{\mathfrak{v}^-}\mathfrak{J}\left(\frac{\sigma+\mathrm{i}}{2}, \varepsilon\right)\right]\\
&\leq_p \frac{\Gamma(\alpha+1)\Gamma(\beta+1)}{4(\mathrm{i}-\sigma)^\alpha(\mathfrak{v}-\varepsilon)^\beta}\left[\mathcal{J}^{\alpha,\beta}_{\sigma^+,\varepsilon^+}\mathfrak{J}(\mathrm{i},\mathfrak{v}) + \mathcal{J}^{\alpha,\beta}_{\sigma^+,\mathfrak{v}^-}\mathfrak{J}(\mathrm{i},\varepsilon) + \mathcal{J}^{\alpha,\beta}_{\mathrm{i}^-,\varepsilon^+}\mathfrak{J}(\sigma,\mathfrak{v}) + \mathcal{J}^{\alpha,\beta}_{\mathrm{i}^-,\mathfrak{v}^-}\mathfrak{J}(\sigma,\varepsilon)\right]\\
&\leq_p \frac{\Gamma(\alpha+1)}{8(\mathrm{i}-\sigma)^\alpha}\left[\mathcal{J}^\alpha_{\sigma^+}\mathfrak{J}(\mathrm{i},\varepsilon) + \mathcal{J}^\alpha_{\sigma^+}\mathfrak{J}(\mathrm{i},\mathfrak{v}) + \mathcal{J}^\alpha_{\mathrm{i}^-}\mathfrak{J}(\sigma,\varepsilon) + \mathcal{J}^\alpha_{\mathrm{i}^-}\mathfrak{J}(\sigma,\mathfrak{v})\right].\\
&+\frac{\Gamma(\beta+1)}{8(\mathfrak{v}-\varepsilon)^\beta}\left[\mathcal{J}^\beta_{\varepsilon^+}\mathfrak{J}(\sigma,\mathfrak{v}) + \mathcal{J}^\beta_{\mathfrak{v}^-}\mathfrak{J}(\sigma,\varepsilon) + \mathcal{J}^\beta_{\varepsilon^+}\mathfrak{J}(\mathrm{i},\mathfrak{v}) + \mathcal{J}^\beta_{\mathfrak{v}^-}\mathfrak{J}(\mathrm{i},\varepsilon)\right]\\
&\leq_p \frac{\mathfrak{J}(\sigma,\varepsilon)+\mathfrak{J}(\mathrm{i},\varepsilon)+\mathfrak{J}(\sigma,\mathfrak{v})+\mathfrak{J}(\mathrm{i},\mathfrak{v})}{4}.
\end{aligned} \tag{54}$$

If $\hbar(\upsilon) = \upsilon$, $\hbar(\kappa) = \kappa$ and $\mathfrak{J}_*(x,y) \neq \mathfrak{J}^*(x,y)$, then by (27), we succeed in bringing about the upcoming inequality (see [43]):

$$\begin{aligned}
&\mathfrak{J}\left(\frac{\sigma+\mathrm{i}}{2}, \frac{\varepsilon+\mathfrak{v}}{2}\right)\\
&\leq_p \frac{1}{2}\left[\frac{1}{\mathrm{i}-\sigma}\int_\sigma^{\mathrm{i}} \mathfrak{J}\left(x, \frac{\varepsilon+\mathfrak{v}}{2}\right)dx + \frac{1}{\mathfrak{v}-\varepsilon}\int_\varepsilon^{\mathfrak{v}} \mathfrak{J}\left(\frac{\sigma+\mathrm{i}}{2}, y\right)dy\right] \leq_p \frac{1}{(\mathrm{i}-\sigma)(\mathfrak{v}-\varepsilon)}\int_\sigma^{\mathrm{i}}\int_\varepsilon^{\mathfrak{v}} \mathfrak{J}(x,y)dydx\\
&\leq_p \frac{1}{4(\mathrm{i}-\sigma)}\left[\int_\sigma^{\mathrm{i}} \mathfrak{J}(x,\varepsilon)dx + \int_\sigma^{\mathrm{i}} \mathfrak{J}(x,\mathfrak{v})dx\right] + \frac{1}{4(\mathfrak{v}-\varepsilon)}\left[\int_\varepsilon^{\mathfrak{v}} \mathfrak{J}(\sigma,y)dy + \int_\varepsilon^{\mathfrak{v}} \mathfrak{J}(\mathrm{i},y)dy\right]\\
&\leq_p \frac{\mathfrak{J}(\sigma,\varepsilon)+\mathfrak{J}(\mathrm{i},\varepsilon)+\mathfrak{J}(\sigma,\mathfrak{v})+\mathfrak{J}(\mathrm{i},\mathfrak{v})}{4}.
\end{aligned} \tag{55}$$

If $\mathfrak{J}$ is coordinated LR-$\hbar$-convex with $\hbar(\upsilon) = \upsilon$, $\hbar(\kappa) = \kappa$ and $\mathfrak{J}_*(x,y) = \mathfrak{J}^*(x,y)$, then from (28), we succeed in bringing about the upcoming classical inequality:

$$
\begin{aligned}
&\mathcal{J}\left(\tfrac{\sigma+i}{2}, \tfrac{\varepsilon+\upsilon}{2}\right)\\
&\leq \frac{\Gamma(\alpha+1)}{4(i-\sigma)^{\alpha}}\left[\mathcal{I}^{\alpha}_{\sigma^+}\mathcal{J}\left(i,\tfrac{\varepsilon+\upsilon}{2}\right)+\mathcal{I}^{\alpha}_{i^-}\mathcal{J}\left(\sigma,\tfrac{\varepsilon+\upsilon}{2}\right)\right]+\frac{\Gamma(\beta+1)}{4(\upsilon-\varepsilon)^{\beta}}\left[\mathcal{I}^{\beta}_{\varepsilon^+}\mathcal{J}\left(\tfrac{\sigma+i}{2},\upsilon\right)+\mathcal{I}^{\beta}_{\upsilon^-}\mathcal{J}\left(\tfrac{\sigma+i}{2},\varepsilon\right)\right]\\
&\leq \frac{\Gamma(\alpha+1)\Gamma(\beta+1)}{4(i-\sigma)^{\alpha}(\upsilon-\varepsilon)^{\beta}}\left[\mathcal{I}^{\alpha,\beta}_{\sigma^+,\varepsilon^+}\mathcal{J}(i,\upsilon)+\mathcal{I}^{\alpha,\beta}_{\sigma^+,\upsilon^-}\mathcal{J}(i,\varepsilon)+\mathcal{I}^{\alpha,\beta}_{i^-,\varepsilon^+}\mathcal{J}(\sigma,\upsilon)+\mathcal{I}^{\alpha,\beta}_{i^-,\upsilon^-}\mathcal{J}(\sigma,\varepsilon)\right]\\
&\leq \frac{\Gamma(\alpha+1)}{8(i-\sigma)^{\alpha}}\left[\mathcal{I}^{\alpha}_{\sigma^+}\mathcal{J}(i,\varepsilon)\mathcal{J}\mathcal{I}^{\alpha}_{\sigma^+}\mathcal{J}(i,\upsilon)+\mathcal{I}^{\alpha}_{i^-}\mathcal{J}(\sigma,\varepsilon)+\mathcal{I}^{\alpha}_{i^-}\mathcal{J}(\sigma,\upsilon)\right].\\
&\quad+\frac{\Gamma(\beta+1)}{8(\upsilon-\varepsilon)^{\beta}}\left[\mathcal{I}^{\beta}_{\varepsilon^+}\mathcal{J}(\sigma,\upsilon)\tilde{+}\mathcal{I}^{\beta}_{\upsilon^-}\mathcal{J}(\sigma,\varepsilon)+\mathcal{I}^{\beta}_{\varepsilon^+}\mathcal{J}(i,\upsilon)+\mathcal{I}^{\beta}_{\upsilon^-}\mathcal{J}(i,\varepsilon)\right]\\
&\leq \frac{\mathcal{J}(\sigma,\varepsilon)+\mathcal{J}(i,\varepsilon)+\mathcal{J}(\sigma,\upsilon)+\mathcal{J}(i,\upsilon)}{4}.
\end{aligned} \tag{56}
$$

In the next outcomes, we are going to find very interesting outcomes that will be obtained over the product of two coordinated LR-ħ-convex IVMs. These inequalities are known as Pachpatte's inequalities.

Theorem 7. *Let $\mathcal{J}$, $\mathcal{g}:\Omega\to\mathbb{R}^+_I$ be two coordinated LR-ħ-convex IVMs on Ω, given by $\mathcal{J}(x,y)=[\mathcal{J}_*(x,y),\mathcal{J}^*(x,y)]$ and $\mathcal{g}(x,y)=[\mathcal{g}_*(x,y),\mathcal{g}^*(x,y)]$ for all $(x,y)\in\Omega$ and let $\hbar_1,\hbar_2:[0,1]\to\mathbb{R}^+$. If $\mathcal{J}\times\mathcal{g}\in\mathfrak{TD}_{\Omega}$, then the following inequalities hold:*

$$
\begin{aligned}
&\frac{\Gamma(\alpha)\Gamma(\beta)}{(i-\sigma)^{\alpha}(\upsilon-\varepsilon)^{\beta}}\left[\mathcal{I}^{\alpha,\beta}_{\sigma^+,\varepsilon^+}\mathcal{J}(i,\upsilon)\times\mathcal{g}(i,\upsilon)+\mathcal{I}^{\alpha,\beta}_{\sigma^+,\upsilon^-}\mathcal{J}(i,\varepsilon)\times\mathcal{g}(i,\varepsilon)\right]\\
&\quad+\frac{\Gamma(\alpha)\Gamma(\beta)}{(i-\sigma)^{\alpha}(\upsilon-\varepsilon)^{\beta}}\left[\mathcal{I}^{\alpha,\beta}_{i^-,\varepsilon^+}\mathcal{J}(\sigma,\upsilon)\times\mathcal{g}(\sigma,\upsilon)+\mathcal{I}^{\alpha,\beta}_{i^-,\upsilon^-}\mathcal{J}(\sigma,\varepsilon)\times\mathcal{g}(\sigma,\varepsilon)\right]\\
&\leq_p \mathcal{M}(\sigma,i,\varepsilon,\upsilon)\int_0^1 v^{\alpha-1}\kappa^{\beta-1}[\hbar_1(1-v)\hbar_2(1-v)\hbar_1(1-\kappa)\hbar_2(1-\kappa)\\
&\quad+\hbar_1(1-v)\hbar_2(1-v)\hbar_1(\kappa)\hbar_2(\kappa)+\hbar_1(v)\hbar_2(v)\hbar_1(1-\kappa)\hbar_2(1-\kappa)\\
&\quad+\hbar_1(v)\hbar_2(v)\hbar_1(\kappa)\hbar_2(\kappa)]dvd\kappa\\
&\quad+P(\sigma,i,\varepsilon,\upsilon)\int_0^1 v^{\alpha-1}\kappa^{\beta-1}[\hbar_1(v)\hbar_2(1-v)\hbar_1(1-\kappa)\hbar_2(1-\kappa)+\hbar_1(1-\\
&\quad v)\hbar_2(v)\hbar_1(1-\kappa)\hbar_2(1-\kappa)+\hbar_1(v)\hbar_2(1-v)\hbar_1(\kappa)\hbar_2(\kappa)+\hbar_1(1-\\
&\quad v)\hbar_2(v)\hbar_1(\kappa)\hbar_2(\kappa)]dvd\kappa\\
&\quad+\mathcal{N}(\sigma,i,\varepsilon,\upsilon)\int_0^1 v^{\alpha-1}\kappa^{\beta-1}[\hbar_1(1-v)\hbar_2(1-v)\hbar_1(\kappa)\hbar_2(1-\kappa)\\
&\quad+\hbar_1(1-v)\hbar_2(1-v)\hbar_1(1-\kappa)\hbar_2(\kappa)+\hbar_1(v)\hbar_2(v)\hbar_1(1-\kappa)\hbar_2(\kappa)\\
&\quad+\hbar_1(v)\hbar_2(v)\hbar_1(\kappa)\hbar_2(1-\kappa)]dvd\kappa\\
&+Q(\sigma,i,\varepsilon,\upsilon)\int_0^1 v^{\alpha-1}\kappa^{\beta-1}[\hbar_1(v)\hbar_2(1-v)\hbar_1(\kappa)\hbar_2(1-\kappa)+\hbar_1(v)\hbar_2(1-v)\hbar_1(1-\kappa)\hbar_2(\kappa)+\\
&\quad\hbar_1(1-v)\hbar_2(v)\hbar_1(\kappa)\hbar_2(1-\kappa)+\hbar_1(v)\hbar_2(1-v)\hbar_1(\kappa)\hbar_2(1-\kappa)]dvd\kappa.
\end{aligned} \tag{57}
$$

If $\mathcal{J}$ and $\mathcal{g}$ are both coordinated ħ-concave IVMs on Ω, then the inequality above can be expressed as follows:

$$
\begin{aligned}
&\frac{\Gamma(\alpha)\Gamma(\beta)}{(i-\sigma)^{\alpha}(\upsilon-\varepsilon)^{\beta}}\left[\mathcal{I}^{\alpha,\beta}_{\sigma^+,\varepsilon^+}\mathcal{J}(i,\upsilon)\times\mathcal{g}(i,\upsilon)+\mathcal{I}^{\alpha,\beta}_{\sigma^+,\upsilon^-}\mathcal{J}(i,\varepsilon)\times\mathcal{g}(i,\varepsilon)\right]\\
&\quad+\frac{\Gamma(\alpha)\Gamma(\beta)}{(i-\sigma)^{\alpha}(\upsilon-\varepsilon)^{\beta}}\left[\mathcal{I}^{\alpha,\beta}_{i^-,\varepsilon^+}\mathcal{J}(\sigma,\upsilon)\times\mathcal{g}(\sigma,\upsilon)+\mathcal{I}^{\alpha,\beta}_{i^-,\upsilon^-}\mathcal{J}(\sigma,\varepsilon)\times\mathcal{g}(\sigma,\varepsilon)\right]\\
&\geq_p \mathcal{M}(\sigma,i,\varepsilon,\upsilon)\int_0^1 v^{\alpha-1}\kappa^{\beta-1}[\hbar_1(1-v)\hbar_2(1-v)\hbar_1(1-\kappa)\hbar_2(1-\kappa)\\
&\quad+\hbar_1(1-v)\hbar_2(1-v)\hbar_1(\kappa)\hbar_2(\kappa)+\hbar_1(v)\hbar_2(v)\hbar_1(1-\kappa)\hbar_2(1-\kappa)\\
&\quad+\hbar_1(v)\hbar_2(v)\hbar_1(\kappa)\hbar_2(\kappa)]dvd\kappa\\
&\quad+P(\sigma,i,\varepsilon,\upsilon)\int_0^1 v^{\alpha-1}\kappa^{\beta-1}[\hbar_1(v)\hbar_2(1-v)\hbar_1(1-\kappa)\hbar_2(1-\kappa)+\hbar_1(1-\\
&\quad v)\hbar_2(v)\hbar_1(1-\kappa)\hbar_2(1-\kappa)+\hbar_1(v)\hbar_2(1-v)\hbar_1(\kappa)\hbar_2(\kappa)+\hbar_1(1-\\
&\quad v)\hbar_2(v)\hbar_1(\kappa)\hbar_2(\kappa)]dvd\kappa\\
&\quad+\mathcal{N}(\sigma,i,\varepsilon,\upsilon)\int_0^1 v^{\alpha-1}\kappa^{\beta-1}[\hbar_1(1-v)\hbar_2(1-v)\hbar_1(\kappa)\hbar_2(1-\kappa)\\
&\quad+\hbar_1(1-v)\hbar_2(1-v)\hbar_1(1-\kappa)\hbar_2(\kappa)+\hbar_1(v)\hbar_2(v)\hbar_1(1-\kappa)\hbar_2(\kappa)\\
&\quad+\hbar_1(v)\hbar_2(v)\hbar_1(\kappa)\hbar_2(1-\kappa)]dvd\kappa\\
&+Q(\sigma,i,\varepsilon,\upsilon)\int_0^1 v^{\alpha-1}\kappa^{\beta-1}[\hbar_1(v)\hbar_2(1-v)\hbar_1(\kappa)\hbar_2(1-\kappa)+\hbar_1(v)\hbar_2(1-v)\hbar_1(1-\kappa)\hbar_2(\kappa)+\\
&\quad\hbar_1(1-v)\hbar_2(v)\hbar_1(\kappa)\hbar_2(1-\kappa)+\hbar_1(v)\hbar_2(1-v)\hbar_1(\kappa)\hbar_2(1-\kappa)]dvd\kappa
\end{aligned} \tag{58}
$$

where

$$\begin{aligned}
\mathcal{M}(\sigma, i, \varepsilon, \mathfrak{v}) &= \mathfrak{J}(\sigma, \varepsilon) \times \mathfrak{g}(\sigma, \varepsilon) + \mathfrak{J}(i, \varepsilon) \times \mathfrak{g}(i, \varepsilon) + \mathfrak{J}(\sigma, \mathfrak{v}) \times \mathfrak{g}(\sigma, \mathfrak{v}) + \mathfrak{J}(i, \mathfrak{v}) \times \mathfrak{g}(i, \mathfrak{v}),\\
P(\sigma, i, \varepsilon, \mathfrak{v}) &= \mathfrak{J}(\sigma, \varepsilon) \times \mathfrak{g}(i, \varepsilon) + \mathfrak{J}(i, \varepsilon) \times \mathfrak{g}(\sigma, \varepsilon) + \mathfrak{J}(\sigma, \mathfrak{v}) \times \mathfrak{g}(i, \mathfrak{v}) + \mathfrak{J}(i, \mathfrak{v}) \times \mathfrak{g}(\sigma, \mathfrak{v}),\\
\mathcal{N}(\sigma, i, \varepsilon, \mathfrak{v}) &= \mathfrak{J}(\sigma, \varepsilon) \times \mathfrak{g}(\sigma, \mathfrak{v}) + \mathfrak{J}(i, \varepsilon) \times \mathfrak{g}(i, \mathfrak{v}) + \mathfrak{J}(\sigma, \mathfrak{v}) \times \mathfrak{g}(\sigma, \varepsilon) + \mathfrak{J}(i, \mathfrak{v}) \times \mathfrak{g}(i, \varepsilon),\\
Q(\sigma, i, \varepsilon, \mathfrak{v}) &= \mathfrak{J}(\sigma, \varepsilon) \times \mathfrak{g}(i, \mathfrak{v}) + \mathfrak{J}(i, \varepsilon) \times \mathfrak{g}(\sigma, \mathfrak{v}) + \mathfrak{J}(\sigma, \mathfrak{v}) \times \mathfrak{g}(i, \varepsilon) + \mathfrak{J}(i, \mathfrak{v}) \times \mathfrak{g}(\sigma, \varepsilon)\,,
\end{aligned}$$

and $\mathcal{M}(\sigma, i, \varepsilon, \mathfrak{v})$, $P(\sigma, i, \varepsilon, \mathfrak{v})$, $\mathcal{N}(\sigma, i, \varepsilon, \mathfrak{v})$ *and* $Q(\sigma, i, \varepsilon, \mathfrak{v})$ *are defined as follows:*

$$\mathcal{M}(\sigma, i, \varepsilon, \mathfrak{v}) = [\mathcal{M}_*(\sigma, i, \varepsilon, \mathfrak{v}),\ \mathcal{M}^*(\sigma, i, \varepsilon, \mathfrak{v})],$$

$$P(\sigma, i, \varepsilon, \mathfrak{v}) = [P_*(\sigma, i, \varepsilon, \mathfrak{v}),\ P^*(\sigma, i, \varepsilon, \mathfrak{v})],$$

$$\mathcal{N}(\sigma, i, \varepsilon, \mathfrak{v}) = [\mathcal{N}_*(\sigma, i, \varepsilon, \mathfrak{v}),\ \mathcal{N}^*(\sigma, i, \varepsilon, \mathfrak{v})],$$

$$Q(\sigma, i, \varepsilon, \mathfrak{v}) = [Q_*(\sigma, i, \varepsilon, \mathfrak{v}),\ Q^*(\sigma, i, \varepsilon, \mathfrak{v})].$$

Proof. Let $\mathfrak{J}$ and $\mathfrak{g}$ be two coordinated LR-$\hbar_1$ and LR-$\hbar_2$-convex IVMs on $[\sigma, i] \times [\varepsilon,\ \mathfrak{v}]$, respectively. Then,

$$\begin{gathered}
\mathfrak{J}(v\sigma + (1-v)i, \kappa\varepsilon + (1-\kappa)\mathfrak{v})\\
\leq_p \hbar_1(v)\hbar_1(\kappa)\mathfrak{J}(\sigma, \varepsilon) + \hbar_1(v)\hbar_1(1-\kappa)\mathfrak{J}(\sigma, \mathfrak{v}) + \hbar_1(1-v)\hbar_1(\kappa)\mathfrak{J}(i, \varepsilon)\\
+\hbar_1(1-v)\hbar_1(1-\kappa)\mathfrak{J}(i, \mathfrak{v}),\\
\mathfrak{J}(v\sigma + (1-v)i, (1-\kappa)\varepsilon + \kappa\mathfrak{v})\\
\leq_p \hbar_1(v)\hbar_1(1-\kappa)\mathfrak{J}(\sigma, \varepsilon) + \hbar_1(v)\hbar_1(\kappa)\mathfrak{J}(\sigma, \mathfrak{v}) + \hbar_1(1-v)\hbar_1(1-\kappa)\mathfrak{J}(i, \varepsilon) + \hbar_1(1-v)\hbar_1(\kappa)\mathfrak{J}(i, \mathfrak{v}),
\end{gathered}$$

$$\begin{gathered}
\mathfrak{J}((1-v)\sigma + vi, \kappa\varepsilon + (1-\kappa)\mathfrak{v})\\
\leq_p \hbar_1(1-v)\hbar_1(\kappa)\mathfrak{J}(\sigma, \varepsilon) + \hbar_1(1-v)\hbar_1(1-\kappa)\mathfrak{J}(\sigma, \mathfrak{v}) + \hbar_1(v)\hbar_1(\kappa)\mathfrak{J}(i, \varepsilon)\\
+\hbar_1(v)\hbar_1(1-\kappa)\mathfrak{J}(i, \mathfrak{v}),\\
\mathfrak{J}((1-v)\sigma + vi, (1-\kappa)\varepsilon + \kappa\mathfrak{v})\\
\leq_p \hbar_1(1-v)\hbar_1(1-\kappa)\mathfrak{J}(\sigma, \varepsilon) + \hbar_1(1-v)\hbar_1(\kappa)\mathfrak{J}(\sigma, \mathfrak{v}) + \hbar_1(v)\hbar_1(1-\kappa)\mathfrak{J}(i, \varepsilon)\\
+\hbar_1(v)\hbar_1(\kappa)\mathfrak{J}(i, \mathfrak{v}),
\end{gathered}$$

and

$$\begin{gathered}
\mathfrak{g}(v\sigma + (1-v)i, \kappa\varepsilon + (1-\kappa)\mathfrak{v})\\
\leq_p \hbar_2(v)\hbar_2(\kappa)\mathfrak{g}(\sigma, \varepsilon) + \hbar_2(v)\hbar_2(1-\kappa)\mathfrak{g}(\sigma, \mathfrak{v}) + \hbar_2(1-v)\hbar_2(\kappa)\mathfrak{g}(i, \varepsilon)\\
+\hbar_2(1-v)\hbar_2(1-\kappa)\mathfrak{g}(i, \mathfrak{v}),\\
\mathfrak{g}(v\sigma + (1-v)i, (1-\kappa)\varepsilon + \kappa\mathfrak{v})\\
\leq_p \hbar_2(v)\hbar_2(1-\kappa)\mathfrak{g}(\sigma, \varepsilon) + \hbar_2(v)\hbar_2(\kappa)\mathfrak{g}(\sigma, \mathfrak{v}) + \hbar_2(1-v)\hbar_2(1-\kappa)\mathfrak{g}(i, \varepsilon) + \hbar_2(1-v)\hbar_2(\kappa)\mathfrak{g}(i, \mathfrak{v}),
\end{gathered}$$

$$\begin{gathered}
((1-v)\sigma + vi, \kappa\varepsilon + (1-\kappa)\mathfrak{v})\\
\leq_p \hbar_2(1-v)\hbar_2(\kappa)\mathfrak{g}(\sigma, \varepsilon) + \hbar_2(1-v)\hbar_2(1-\kappa)\mathfrak{g}(\sigma, \mathfrak{v}) + \hbar_2(v)\hbar_2(\kappa)\mathfrak{g}(i, \varepsilon)\\
+\hbar_2(v)\hbar_2(1-\kappa)\mathfrak{g}(i, \mathfrak{v}),\\
\mathfrak{g}((1-v)\sigma + vi, (1-\kappa)\varepsilon + \kappa\mathfrak{v})\\
\leq_p \hbar_2(1-v)\hbar_2(1-\kappa)\mathfrak{g}(\sigma, \varepsilon) + \hbar_2(1-v)\hbar_2(\kappa)\mathfrak{g}(\sigma, \mathfrak{v}) + \hbar_2(v)\hbar_2(1-\kappa)\mathfrak{g}(i, \varepsilon)\\
+\hbar_2(v)\hbar_2(\kappa)\mathfrak{g}(i, \mathfrak{v}),
\end{gathered}$$

Since $\mathcal{J}$ and $\jmath$ both are coordinated LR-$\hbar_1$ and LR-$\hbar_2$-convex IVMs on $[\sigma, \mathrm{i}] \times [\varepsilon, \mathfrak{v}]$, respectively, we have

$$\begin{aligned}
&\mathcal{J}(v\sigma + (1-v)\mathrm{i}, \kappa\varepsilon + (1-\kappa)\mathfrak{v}) \times \jmath(v\sigma + (1-v)\mathrm{i}, \kappa\varepsilon + (1-\kappa)\mathfrak{v}) \\
&\quad + \mathcal{J}(v\sigma + (1-v)\mathrm{i}, (1-\kappa)\varepsilon + \kappa\mathfrak{v}) \times \jmath(v\sigma + (1-v)\mathrm{i}, (1-\kappa)\varepsilon + \kappa\mathfrak{v}) \\
&\quad + \mathcal{J}((1-v)\sigma + v\mathrm{i}, \kappa\varepsilon + (1-\kappa)\mathfrak{v}) \times \jmath((1-v)\sigma + v\mathrm{i}, \kappa\varepsilon + (1-\kappa)\mathfrak{v}) \\
&+ \mathcal{J}((1-v)\sigma + v\mathrm{i}, (1-\kappa)\varepsilon + \kappa\mathfrak{v}) \times \jmath((1-v)\sigma + v\mathrm{i}, (1-\kappa)\varepsilon + \kappa\mathfrak{v}) \\
&\leq_p \mathcal{M}(\sigma, \mathrm{i}, \varepsilon, \mathfrak{v})[\hbar_1(1-v)\hbar_2(1-v)\hbar_1(1-\kappa)\hbar_2(1-\kappa) \\
&\quad + \hbar_1(1-v)\hbar_2(1-v)\hbar_1(\kappa)\hbar_2(\kappa) + \hbar_1(v)\hbar_2(v)\hbar_1(1-\kappa)\hbar_2(1-\kappa) \\
&\quad + \hbar_1(v)\hbar_2(v)\hbar_1(\kappa)\hbar_2(\kappa)] \\
&+ P(\sigma, \mathrm{i}, \varepsilon, \mathfrak{v})[\hbar_1(v)\hbar_2(1-v)\hbar_1(1-\kappa)\hbar_2(1-\kappa) \\
&\quad + \hbar_1(1-v)\hbar_2(v)\hbar_1(1-\kappa)\hbar_2(1-\kappa) + \hbar_1(v)\hbar_2(1-v)\hbar_1(\kappa)\hbar_2(\kappa) \\
&\quad + \hbar_1(1-v)\hbar_2(v)\hbar_1(\kappa)\hbar_2(\kappa)] \\
&+ \mathcal{N}(\sigma, \mathrm{i}, \varepsilon, \mathfrak{v})[\hbar_1(1-v)\hbar_2(1-v)\hbar_1(\kappa)\hbar_2(1-\kappa) \\
&\quad + \hbar_1(1-v)\hbar_2(1-v)\hbar_1(1-\kappa)\hbar_2(\kappa) + \hbar_1(v)\hbar_2(v)\hbar_1(1-\kappa)\hbar_2(\kappa) \\
&\quad + \hbar_1(v)\hbar_2(v)\hbar_1(\kappa)\hbar_2(1-\kappa)] \\
&+ Q(\sigma, \mathrm{i}, \varepsilon, \mathfrak{v})[\hbar_1(v)\hbar_2(1-v)\hbar_1(\kappa)\hbar_2(1-\kappa) + \hbar_1(v)\hbar_2(1-v)\hbar_1(1-\kappa)\hbar_2(\kappa) \\
&\quad + \hbar_1(1-v)\hbar_2(v)\hbar_1(\kappa)\hbar_2(1-\kappa) + \hbar_1(v)\hbar_2(1-v)\hbar_1(\kappa)\hbar_2(1-\kappa)].
\end{aligned}$$

Taking the multiplication of the above fuzzy inclusion with $v^{\alpha-1}\kappa^{\beta-1}$ and then taking the double integration of the resultant over $[0, 1] \times [0, 1]$ with respect to (v, κ), such that

$$\begin{aligned}
&\int_0^1 \int_0^1 v^{\alpha-1}\kappa^{\beta-1} \mathcal{J}(v\sigma + (1-v)\mathrm{i}, \kappa\varepsilon + (1-\kappa)\mathfrak{v}) \times \jmath(v\sigma + (1-v)\mathrm{i}, \kappa\varepsilon + (1-\kappa)\mathfrak{v}) dv d\kappa \\
&\quad + \int_0^1 \int_0^1 v^{\alpha-1}\kappa^{\beta-1} \mathcal{J}(v\sigma + (1-v)\mathrm{i}, (1-\kappa)\varepsilon + \kappa\mathfrak{v}) \times \jmath(v\sigma + (1-v)\mathrm{i}, (1-\kappa)\varepsilon + \\
&\quad \kappa\mathfrak{v}) dv d\kappa \\
&\quad + \int_0^1 \int_0^1 v^{\alpha-1}\kappa^{\beta-1} \mathcal{J}((1-v)\sigma + v\mathrm{i}, \kappa\varepsilon + (1-\kappa)\mathfrak{v}) \times \jmath((|1-v)\sigma + v\mathrm{i}, \kappa\varepsilon + (1- \\
&\quad \kappa)\mathfrak{v}) dv d\kappa \\
&+ \int_0^1 \int_0^1 v^{\alpha-1}\kappa^{\beta-1} \mathcal{J}((1-v)\sigma + v\mathrm{i}, (1-\kappa)\varepsilon + \kappa\mathfrak{v}) \times \jmath((1-v)\sigma + v\mathrm{i}, (1-\kappa)\varepsilon + \kappa\mathfrak{v}) dv d\kappa \\
&\leq_p \mathcal{M}(\sigma, \mathrm{i}, \varepsilon, \mathfrak{v}) \int_0^1 \int_0^1 v^{\alpha-1}\kappa^{\beta-1} [\hbar_1(1-v)\hbar_2(1-v)\hbar_1(1-\kappa)\hbar_2(1-\kappa) \\
&\quad + \hbar_1(1-v)\hbar_2(1-v)\hbar_1(\kappa)\hbar_2(\kappa) + \hbar_1(v)\hbar_2(v)\hbar_1(1-\kappa)\hbar_2(1-\kappa) \\
&\quad + \hbar_1(v)\hbar_2(v)\hbar_1(\kappa)\hbar_2(\kappa)] dv d\kappa \\
&+ P(\sigma, \mathrm{i}, \varepsilon, \mathfrak{v}) \int_0^1 \int_0^1 v^{\alpha-1}\kappa^{\beta-1} [\hbar_1(v)\hbar_2(1-v)\hbar_1(1-\kappa)\hbar_2(1-\kappa) \\
&\quad + \hbar_1(1-v)\hbar_2(v)\hbar_1(1-\kappa)\hbar_2(1-\kappa) + \hbar_1(v)\hbar_2(1-v)\hbar_1(\kappa)\hbar_2(\kappa) \\
&\quad + \hbar_1(1-v)\hbar_2(v)\hbar_1(\kappa)\hbar_2(\kappa)] dv d\kappa \\
&+ \mathcal{N}(\sigma, \mathrm{i}, \varepsilon, \mathfrak{v}) \int_0^1 \int_0^1 v^{\alpha-1}\kappa^{\beta-1} [\hbar_1(1-v)\hbar_2(1-v)\hbar_1(\kappa)\hbar_2(1-\kappa) \\
&\quad + \hbar_1(1-v)\hbar_2(1-v)\hbar_1(1-\kappa)\hbar_2(\kappa) + \hbar_1(v)\hbar_2(v)\hbar_1(1-\kappa)\hbar_2(\kappa) \\
&\quad + \hbar_1(v)\hbar_2(v)\hbar_1(\kappa)\hbar_2(1-\kappa)] dv d\kappa \\
&+ Q(\sigma, \mathrm{i}, \varepsilon, \mathfrak{v}) \int_0^1 \int_0^1 v^{\alpha-1}\kappa^{\beta-1} [\hbar_1(v)\hbar_2(1-v)\hbar_1(\kappa)\hbar_2(1-\kappa) + \hbar_1(v)\hbar_2(1-v)\hbar_1(1-\kappa)\hbar_2(\kappa) \\
&\quad + \hbar_1(1-v)\hbar_2(v)\hbar_1(\kappa)\hbar_2(1-\kappa) + \hbar_1(v)\hbar_2(1-v)\hbar_1(\kappa)\hbar_2(1-\kappa)] dv d\kappa
\end{aligned} \tag{59}$$

From the right-hand side of (59), we have

$$\begin{aligned}
&\int_0^1 \int_0^1 v^{\alpha-1}\kappa^{\beta-1} \mathcal{J}(v\sigma + (1-v)\mathrm{i}, \kappa\varepsilon + (1-\kappa)\mathfrak{v}) \times \jmath(v\sigma + (1-v)\mathrm{i}, \kappa\varepsilon + (1-\kappa)\mathfrak{v}) dv d\kappa \\
&\quad + \int_0^1 \int_0^1 v^{\alpha-1}\kappa^{\beta-1} \mathcal{J}(v\sigma + (1-v)\mathrm{i}, (1-\kappa)\varepsilon + \kappa\mathfrak{v}) \times \jmath(v\sigma + (1-v)\mathrm{i}, (1-\kappa)\varepsilon + \\
&\quad \kappa\mathfrak{v}) dv d\kappa \\
&\quad + \int_0^1 \int_0^1 v^{\alpha-1}\kappa^{\beta-1} \mathcal{J}((1-v)\sigma + v\mathrm{i}, \kappa\varepsilon + (1-\kappa)\mathfrak{v}) \times \jmath((1-v)\sigma + v\mathrm{i}, \kappa\varepsilon + (1- \\
&\quad \kappa)\mathfrak{v}) dv d\kappa \\
&+ \int_0^1 \int_0^1 v^{\alpha-1}\kappa^{\beta-1} \mathcal{J}((1-v)\sigma + v\mathrm{i}, (1-\kappa)\varepsilon + \kappa\mathfrak{v}) \times \jmath((1-v)\sigma + v\mathrm{i}, (1-\kappa)\varepsilon + \kappa\mathfrak{v}) dv d\kappa \\
&= \frac{\Gamma(\alpha)\Gamma(\beta)}{(\mathrm{i}-\sigma)^{\alpha}(\mathfrak{v}-\varepsilon)^{\beta}} \left[\jmath^{\alpha,\beta}_{\sigma^+,\varepsilon^+} \mathcal{J}(\mathrm{i}, \mathfrak{v}) \times \jmath(\mathrm{i}, \mathfrak{v}) + \jmath^{\alpha,\beta}_{\sigma^+,\mathfrak{v}^-} \mathcal{J}(\mathrm{i}, \varepsilon) \times \jmath(\mathrm{i}, \varepsilon) \right]
\end{aligned} \tag{60}$$

Combining (59) and (60), we have

$$\begin{aligned}
&\frac{\Gamma(\alpha)\Gamma(\beta)}{(\mathfrak{i}-\sigma)^{\alpha}(\mathfrak{v}-\varepsilon)^{\beta}}\left[\mathcal{J}^{\alpha,\,\beta}_{\sigma^+,\varepsilon^+}\mathfrak{J}(\mathfrak{i},\mathfrak{v})\times\jmath(\mathfrak{i},\mathfrak{v})+\mathcal{J}^{\alpha,\,\beta}_{\sigma^+,\mathfrak{v}^-}\mathfrak{J}(\mathfrak{i},\varepsilon)\times\jmath(\mathfrak{i},\varepsilon)\right]\\
&\leq_p \mathcal{M}(\sigma,\mathfrak{i},\varepsilon,\mathfrak{v})\int_0^1\int_0^1 v^{\alpha-1}\kappa^{\beta-1}[\hbar_1(1-v)\hbar_2(1-v)\hbar_1(1-\kappa)\hbar_2(1-\kappa)\\
&+\hbar_1(1-v)\hbar_2(1-v)\hbar_1(\kappa)\hbar_2(\kappa)+\hbar_1(v)\hbar_2(v)\hbar_1(1-\kappa)\hbar_2(1-\kappa)\\
&+\hbar_1(v)\hbar_2(v)\hbar_1(\kappa)\hbar_2(\kappa)]dvd\kappa\\
&+P(\sigma,\mathfrak{i},\varepsilon,\mathfrak{v})\int_0^1\int_0^1 v^{\alpha-1}\kappa^{\beta-1}[\hbar_1(v)\hbar_2(1-v)\hbar_1(1-\kappa)\hbar_2(1-\kappa)\\
&+\hbar_1(1-v)\hbar_2(v)\hbar_1(1-\kappa)\hbar_2(1-\kappa)+\hbar_1(v)\hbar_2(1-v)\hbar_1(\kappa)\hbar_2(\kappa)\\
&+\hbar_1(1-v)\hbar_2(v)\hbar_1(\kappa)\hbar_2(\kappa)]dvd\kappa\\
&+\mathcal{N}(\sigma,\mathfrak{i},\varepsilon,\mathfrak{v})\int_0^1\int_0^1 v^{\alpha-1}\kappa^{\beta-1}[\hbar_1(1-v)\hbar_2(1-v)\hbar_1(\kappa)\hbar_2(1-\kappa)\\
&+\hbar_1(1-v)\hbar_2(1-v)\hbar_1(1-\kappa)\hbar_2(\kappa)+\hbar_1(v)\hbar_2(v)\hbar_1(1-\kappa)\hbar_2(\kappa)\\
&+\hbar_1(v)\hbar_2(v)\hbar_1(\kappa)\hbar_2(1-\kappa)]dvd\kappa\\
&+Q(\sigma,\mathfrak{i},\varepsilon,\mathfrak{v})\int_0^1\int_0^1 v^{\alpha-1}\kappa^{\beta-1}[\hbar_1(v)\hbar_2(1-v)\hbar_1(\kappa)\hbar_2(1-\kappa)\\
&+\hbar_1(v)\hbar_2(1-v)\hbar_1(1-\kappa)\hbar_2(\kappa)+\hbar_1(1-v)\hbar_2(v)\hbar_1(\kappa)\hbar_2(1-\kappa)\\
&+\hbar_1(v)\hbar_2(1-v)\hbar_1(\kappa)\hbar_2(1-\kappa)]dvd\kappa.
\end{aligned}$$

Hence, the required result. □

Remark 4. *If one assumes that $\mathfrak{J}$ is coordinated left-LR-$\hbar$-convex with $\hbar(v)=v$, $\hbar(\kappa)=\kappa$ and $\alpha=1$ and $\beta=1$, then from (59), as a result, there will be inequality (see [42]):*

$$\begin{aligned}
&\frac{1}{(\mathfrak{i}-\sigma)(\mathfrak{v}-\varepsilon)}\int_{\sigma}^{\mathfrak{i}}\int_{\varepsilon}^{\mathfrak{v}}\mathfrak{J}(x,y)\times\jmath(x,y)dydx\\
&\supseteq \tfrac{1}{9}\mathcal{M}(\sigma,\mathfrak{i},\varepsilon,\mathfrak{v})+\tfrac{1}{18}[P(\sigma,\mathfrak{i},\varepsilon,\mathfrak{v})+\mathcal{N}(\sigma,\mathfrak{i},\varepsilon,\mathfrak{v})]+\tfrac{1}{36}Q(\sigma,\mathfrak{i},\varepsilon,\mathfrak{v}).
\end{aligned}\tag{61}$$

If $\mathfrak{J}$ is coordinated LR-$\hbar$-convex with $\hbar(v)=v$, $\hbar(\kappa)=\kappa$ and one assumes that $\alpha=1$ and $\beta=1$, then from (59), as a result, there will be inequality (see [43]):

$$\begin{aligned}
&\frac{1}{(\mathfrak{i}-\sigma)(\mathfrak{v}-\varepsilon)}\int_{\sigma}^{\mathfrak{i}}\int_{\varepsilon}^{\mathfrak{v}}\mathfrak{J}(x,y)\times\jmath(x,y)dydx\\
&\leq_p \tfrac{1}{9}\mathcal{M}(\sigma,\mathfrak{i},\varepsilon,\mathfrak{v})+\tfrac{1}{18}[P(\sigma,\mathfrak{i},\varepsilon,\mathfrak{v})+\mathcal{N}(\sigma,\mathfrak{i},\varepsilon,\mathfrak{v})]+\tfrac{1}{36}Q(\sigma,\mathfrak{i},\varepsilon,\mathfrak{v}).
\end{aligned}\tag{62}$$

If $\mathfrak{J}_*(x,y)\neq\mathfrak{J}^*(x,y)$ and $\hbar(v)=v$, $\hbar(\kappa)=\kappa$ then, by (57), we succeed in bringing about the upcoming inequality (see [46]):

$$\begin{aligned}
&\frac{\Gamma(\alpha+1)\Gamma(\beta+1)}{4(\mathfrak{i}-\sigma)^{\alpha}(\mathfrak{v}-\varepsilon)^{\beta}}\left[\mathcal{J}^{\alpha,\,\beta}_{\sigma^+,\varepsilon^+}\mathfrak{J}(\mathfrak{i},\mathfrak{v})\times J(\mathfrak{i},\mathfrak{v})+\mathcal{J}^{\alpha,\,\beta}_{\sigma^+,\mathfrak{v}^-}\mathfrak{J}(\mathfrak{i},\varepsilon)\times J(\mathfrak{i},\varepsilon)\right]\\
&+\frac{\Gamma(\alpha+1)\Gamma(\beta+1)}{4(\mathfrak{i}-\sigma)^{\alpha}(\mathfrak{v}-\varepsilon)^{\beta}}\left[\mathcal{J}^{\alpha,\,\beta}_{\mathfrak{i}^-,\varepsilon^+}\mathfrak{J}(\sigma,\mathfrak{v})\times J(\sigma,\mathfrak{v})+\mathcal{J}^{\alpha,\,\beta}_{\mathfrak{i}^-,\mathfrak{v}^-}\mathfrak{J}(\sigma,\varepsilon)\times J(\sigma,\varepsilon)\right]\\
&\leq_p\left(\frac{1}{2}-\frac{\alpha}{(\alpha+1)(\alpha+2)}\right)\left(\frac{1}{2}-\frac{\beta}{(\beta+1)(\beta+2)}\right)\mathcal{M}(\sigma,\mathfrak{i},\varepsilon,\mathfrak{v})\\
&+\frac{\alpha}{(\alpha+1)(\alpha+2)}\left(\frac{1}{2}-\frac{\beta}{(\beta+1)(\beta+2)}\right)P(\sigma,\mathfrak{i},\varepsilon,\mathfrak{v})\\
&+\left(\frac{1}{2}-\frac{\alpha}{(\alpha+1)(\alpha+2)}\right)\frac{\beta}{(\beta+1)(\beta+2)}\mathcal{N}(\sigma,\mathfrak{i},\varepsilon,\mathfrak{v})+\frac{\beta}{(\beta+1)(\beta+2)}\frac{\alpha}{(\alpha+1)(\alpha+2)}Q(\sigma,\mathfrak{i},\varepsilon,\mathfrak{v}).
\end{aligned}\tag{63}$$

If $\hbar(v)=v$, $\hbar(\kappa)=\kappa$ and $\mathfrak{J}_*(x,y)\neq\mathfrak{J}^*(x,y)$, then by (57), we succeed in bringing about the upcoming inequality (see [43]):

$$\begin{aligned}
&\frac{1}{(\mathfrak{i}-\sigma)(\mathfrak{v}-\varepsilon)}\int_{\sigma}^{\mathfrak{i}}\int_{\varepsilon}^{\mathfrak{v}}\mathfrak{J}(x,y)\times\jmath(x,y)dydx\\
&\leq_p \tfrac{1}{9}\mathcal{M}(\sigma,\mathfrak{i},\varepsilon,\mathfrak{v})+\tfrac{1}{18}[P(\sigma,\mathfrak{i},\varepsilon,\mathfrak{v})+\mathcal{N}(\sigma,\mathfrak{i},\varepsilon,\mathfrak{v})]+\tfrac{1}{36}Q(\sigma,\mathfrak{i},\varepsilon,\mathfrak{v}).
\end{aligned}\tag{64}$$

If $\mathfrak{J}_*(x,y) = \mathfrak{J}^*(x,y)$ and $\jmath_*(x,y) = \jmath^*(x,y)$ and $\hbar(\upsilon) = \upsilon$, $\hbar(\kappa) = \kappa$, then from (57), we succeed in bringing about the upcoming classical inequality:

$$\begin{aligned}
&\frac{\Gamma(\alpha+1)\Gamma(\beta+1)}{4(\mathrm{i}-\sigma)^{\alpha}(\mathfrak{v}-\varepsilon)^{\beta}}\left[\mathcal{J}^{\alpha,\,\beta}_{\sigma^+,\varepsilon^+}\mathfrak{J}(\mathrm{i},\mathfrak{v}) \times \jmath(\mathrm{i},\mathfrak{v}) + \mathcal{J}^{\alpha,\,\beta}_{\sigma^+,\mathfrak{v}^-}\mathfrak{J}(\mathrm{i},\varepsilon) \times \jmath(\mathrm{i},\varepsilon)\right] \\
&+\frac{\Gamma(\alpha+1)\Gamma(\beta+1)}{4(\mathrm{i}-\sigma)^{\alpha}(\mathfrak{v}-\varepsilon)^{\beta}}\left[+\mathcal{J}^{\alpha,\,\beta}_{\mathrm{i}^-,\varepsilon^+}\mathfrak{J}(\sigma,\mathfrak{v}) \times \jmath(\sigma,\mathfrak{v}) + \mathcal{J}^{\alpha,\,\beta}_{\mathrm{i}^-,\mathfrak{v}^-}\mathfrak{J}(\sigma,\varepsilon) \times \jmath(\sigma,\varepsilon)\right] \\
&\leq \left(\frac{1}{2} - \frac{\alpha}{(\alpha+1)(\alpha+2)}\right)\left(\frac{1}{2} - \frac{\beta}{(\beta+1)(\beta+2)}\right)\mathcal{M}(\sigma,\mathrm{i},\varepsilon,\mathfrak{v}) + \frac{\alpha}{(\alpha+1)(\alpha+2)}\left(\frac{1}{2} - \right. \\
&\left.\frac{\beta}{(\beta+1)(\beta+2)}\right)P(\sigma,\mathrm{i},\varepsilon,\mathfrak{v}) \\
&+\left(\frac{1}{2} - \frac{\alpha}{(\alpha+1)(\alpha+2)}\right)\frac{\beta}{(\beta+1)(\beta+2)}\mathcal{N}(\sigma,\mathrm{i},\varepsilon,\mathfrak{v}) + \frac{\beta}{(\beta+1)(\beta+2)}\frac{\alpha}{(\alpha+1)(\alpha+2)}Q(\sigma,\mathrm{i},\varepsilon,\mathfrak{v}).
\end{aligned} \tag{65}$$

Theorem 8. *Let $\mathfrak{J}$, $\jmath : \Omega \to \mathbb{R}^+_I$ be two coordinated LR-$\hbar$-convex IVMs on Ω, given by $\mathfrak{J}(x,y) = [\mathfrak{J}_*(x,y), \mathfrak{J}^*(x,y)]$ and $\jmath(x,y) = [\jmath_*(x,y), \jmath^*(x,y)]$ for all $(x,y) \in \Omega$ and let $\hbar : [0, 1] \to \mathbb{R}^+$. If $\mathfrak{J} \times \jmath \in \mathfrak{TD}_{\Omega}$, then the following inequalities hold:*

$$\begin{aligned}
&\frac{1}{2\alpha\beta\hbar_1{}^2\left(\frac{1}{2}\right)\hbar_2{}^2\left(\frac{1}{2}\right)}\mathfrak{J}\left(\frac{\sigma+\mathrm{i}}{2}, \frac{\varepsilon+\mathfrak{v}}{2}\right) \times \jmath\left(\frac{\sigma+\mathrm{i}}{2}, \frac{\varepsilon+\mathfrak{v}}{2}\right) \\
&\leq_p \frac{\Gamma(\alpha)\Gamma(\beta)}{2(\mathrm{i}-\sigma)^{\alpha}(\mathfrak{v}-\varepsilon)^{\beta}}\left[\mathcal{J}^{\alpha,\,\beta}_{\sigma^+,\varepsilon^+}\mathfrak{J}(\mathrm{i},\mathfrak{v}) \times \jmath(\mathrm{i},\mathfrak{v}) + \mathcal{J}^{\alpha,\,\beta}_{\sigma^+,\mathfrak{v}^-}\mathfrak{J}(\mathrm{i},\varepsilon) \times \jmath(\mathrm{i},\varepsilon)\right] \\
&+\frac{\Gamma(\alpha)\Gamma(\beta)}{2(\mathrm{i}-\sigma)^{\alpha}(\mathfrak{v}-\varepsilon)^{\beta}}\left[\mathcal{J}^{\alpha,\,\beta}_{\mathrm{i}^-,\varepsilon^+}\mathfrak{J}(\sigma,\mathfrak{v}) \times \jmath(\sigma,\mathfrak{v}) + \mathcal{J}^{\alpha,\,\beta}_{\mathrm{i}^-,\mathfrak{v}^-}\mathfrak{J}(\sigma,\varepsilon) \times \jmath(\sigma,\varepsilon)\right] \\
&+\mathcal{M}(\sigma,\mathrm{i},\varepsilon,\mathfrak{v})\int_0^1 \upsilon^{\alpha-1}\kappa^{\beta-1}[\hbar_1(\upsilon)\hbar_1(\kappa)[\hbar_2(\upsilon)\hbar_2(1-\kappa) + \hbar_2(1-\upsilon)\hbar_2(\kappa) \\
&\quad+\hbar_2(1-\upsilon)\hbar_2(1-\kappa)] \\
&\quad+\hbar_1(\upsilon)\hbar_1(1-\kappa)[\hbar_2(\upsilon)\hbar_2(\kappa) + \hbar_2(1-\upsilon)\hbar_2(1-\kappa) \\
&\quad+\hbar_2(1-\upsilon)\hbar_2(\kappa)]]d\upsilon d\kappa \\
&+P(\sigma,\mathrm{i},\varepsilon,\mathfrak{v})\int_0^1 \upsilon^{\alpha-1}\kappa^{\beta-1}[\hbar_1(\upsilon)\hbar_1(\kappa)[\hbar_2(1-\upsilon)\hbar_2(1-\kappa) + \hbar_2(\upsilon)\hbar_2(\kappa) + \\
&\hbar_2(\upsilon)\hbar_2(1-\kappa)] + \hbar_1(\upsilon)\hbar_1(1-\kappa)[\hbar_2(1-\upsilon)\hbar_2(\kappa) + \hbar_2(\upsilon)\hbar_2(1-\kappa) + \\
&\hbar_2(\upsilon)\hbar_2(\kappa)]]d\upsilon d\kappa \\
&+\mathcal{N}(\sigma,\mathrm{i},\varepsilon,\mathfrak{v})\int_0^1 \upsilon^{\alpha-1}\kappa^{\beta-1}[\hbar_1(\upsilon)\hbar_1(\kappa)[\hbar_2(\upsilon)\hbar_2(\kappa) + \hbar_2(1-\upsilon)\hbar_2(1-\kappa) \\
&\quad+\hbar_2(1-\upsilon)\hbar_2(\kappa)] \\
&\quad+\hbar_1(\upsilon)\hbar_1(1-\kappa)[\hbar_2(\upsilon)\hbar_2(1-\kappa) + \hbar_2(1-\upsilon)\hbar_2(\kappa) \\
&\quad+\hbar_2(1-\upsilon)\hbar_2(1-\kappa)]]d\upsilon d\kappa \\
&+Q(\sigma,\mathrm{i},\varepsilon,\mathfrak{v})\int_0^1 \upsilon^{\alpha-1}\kappa^{\beta-1}[\hbar_1(\upsilon)\hbar_1(\kappa)[\hbar_2(1-\upsilon)\hbar_2(\kappa) + \hbar_2(\upsilon)\hbar_2(1-\kappa) + \hbar_2(\upsilon)\hbar_2(\kappa)] + \\
&\hbar_1(\upsilon)\hbar_1(1-\kappa)[\hbar_2(1-\upsilon)\hbar_2(1-\kappa) + \hbar_2(\upsilon)\hbar_2(\kappa) + \hbar_2(\upsilon)\hbar_2(1-\kappa)]]d\upsilon d\kappa.
\end{aligned} \tag{66}$$

If $\mathfrak{J}$ and $\jmath$ both are coordinate $\hbar$-concave IVMs on Ω, then the inequality above can be expressed as follows:

$$
\begin{aligned}
&\frac{1}{2\alpha\beta\hbar_1{}^2\left(\frac{1}{2}\right)\hbar_2{}^2\left(\frac{1}{2}\right)}\mathcal{J}\left(\frac{\sigma+\mathrm{i}}{2},\ \frac{\varepsilon+\mathfrak{v}}{2}\right)\times \jmath\left(\frac{\sigma+\mathrm{i}}{2},\ \frac{\varepsilon+\mathfrak{v}}{2}\right)\\
&\geq_p \frac{\Gamma(\alpha)\Gamma(\beta)}{2(\mathrm{i}-\sigma)^{\alpha}(\mathfrak{v}-\varepsilon)^{\beta}}\left[\mathcal{I}^{\alpha,\,\beta}_{\sigma^+,\varepsilon^+}\mathcal{J}(\mathrm{i},\mathfrak{v})\times \jmath(\mathrm{i},\mathfrak{v})+\mathcal{I}^{\alpha,\,\beta}_{\sigma^+,\mathfrak{v}^-}\mathcal{J}(\mathrm{i},\varepsilon)\times \jmath(\mathrm{i},\varepsilon)\right]\\
&+\frac{\Gamma(\alpha)\Gamma(\beta)}{2(\mathrm{i}-\sigma)^{\alpha}(\mathfrak{v}-\varepsilon)^{\beta}}\left[\mathcal{I}^{\alpha,\,\beta}_{\mathrm{i}^-,\varepsilon^+}\mathcal{J}(\sigma,\mathfrak{v})\times \jmath(\sigma,\mathfrak{v})+\mathcal{I}^{\alpha,\,\beta}_{\mathrm{i}^-,\mathfrak{v}^-}\mathcal{J}(\sigma,\varepsilon)\times \jmath(\sigma,\varepsilon)\right]\\
&+\mathcal{M}(\sigma,\mathrm{i},\varepsilon,\mathfrak{v})\int_0^1 \upsilon^{\alpha-1}\kappa^{\beta-1}[\hbar_1(\upsilon)\hbar_1(\kappa)[\hbar_2(\upsilon)\hbar_2(1-\kappa)+\hbar_2(1-\upsilon)\hbar_2(\kappa)\\
&\quad+\hbar_2(1-\upsilon)\hbar_2(1-\kappa)]\\
&\quad+\hbar_1(\upsilon)\hbar_1(1-\kappa)[\hbar_2(\upsilon)\hbar_2(\kappa)+\hbar_2(1-\upsilon)\hbar_2(1-\kappa)\\
&\quad+\hbar_2(1-\upsilon)\hbar_2(\kappa)]]d\upsilon d\kappa\\
&+P(\sigma,\mathrm{i},\varepsilon,\mathfrak{v})\int_0^1 \upsilon^{\alpha-1}\kappa^{\beta-1}[\hbar_1(\upsilon)\hbar_1(\kappa)[\hbar_2(1-\upsilon)\hbar_2(1-\kappa)+\hbar_2(\upsilon)\hbar_2(\kappa)+\\
&\hbar_2(\upsilon)\hbar_2(1-\kappa)]+\hbar_1(\upsilon)\hbar_1(1-\kappa)[\hbar_2(1-\upsilon)\hbar_2(\kappa)+\hbar_2(\upsilon)\hbar_2(1-\kappa)+\\
&\hbar_2(\upsilon)\hbar_2(\kappa)]]d\upsilon d\kappa\\
&+\mathcal{N}(\sigma,\mathrm{i},\varepsilon,\mathfrak{v})\int_0^1 \upsilon^{\alpha-1}\kappa^{\beta-1}[\hbar_1(\upsilon)\hbar_1(\kappa)[\hbar_2(\upsilon)\hbar_2(\kappa)+\hbar_2(1-\upsilon)\hbar_2(1-\kappa)\\
&\quad+\hbar_2(1-\upsilon)\hbar_2(\kappa)]\\
&\quad+\hbar_1(\upsilon)\hbar_1(1-\kappa)[\hbar_2(\upsilon)\hbar_2(1-\kappa)+\hbar_2(1-\upsilon)\hbar_2(\kappa)\\
&\quad+\hbar_2(1-\upsilon)\hbar_2(1-\kappa)]]d\upsilon d\kappa\\
&+Q(\sigma,\mathrm{i},\varepsilon,\mathfrak{v})\int_0^1 \upsilon^{\alpha-1}\kappa^{\beta-1}[\hbar_1(\upsilon)\hbar_1(\kappa)[\hbar_2(1-\upsilon)\hbar_2(\kappa)+\hbar_2(\upsilon)\hbar_2(1-\kappa)+\hbar_2(\upsilon)\hbar_2(\kappa)]+\\
&\hbar_1(\upsilon)\hbar_1(1-\kappa)[\hbar_2(1-\upsilon)\hbar_2(1-\kappa)+\hbar_2(\upsilon)\hbar_2(\kappa)+\hbar_2(\upsilon)\hbar_2(1-\kappa)]]d\upsilon d\kappa.
\end{aligned}
\tag{67}
$$

where $\mathcal{M}(\sigma,\mathrm{i},\varepsilon,\mathfrak{v})$, $P(\sigma,\mathrm{i},\varepsilon,\mathfrak{v})$, $\mathcal{N}(\sigma,\mathrm{i},\varepsilon,\mathfrak{v})$, *and* $Q(\sigma,\mathrm{i},\varepsilon,\mathfrak{v})$ *are given in Theorem 7.*

Proof. Since $\mathcal{J}, \jmath : \Omega \to \mathbb{R}_I^+$ is two LR-$\hbar$-convex IVMs, then from inequality (17), we have

$$
\mathcal{J}\left(\frac{\sigma+\mathrm{i}}{2},\frac{\varepsilon+\mathfrak{v}}{2}\right)\times \jmath\left(\frac{\sigma+\mathrm{i}}{2},\frac{\varepsilon+\mathfrak{v}}{2}\right)
$$

$$= \mathcal{J}\left(\frac{\upsilon\sigma+(1-\upsilon)\mathrm{i}}{2}+\frac{(1-\upsilon)\sigma+\upsilon\mathrm{i}}{2},\frac{\kappa\varepsilon+(1-\kappa)\mathfrak{v}}{2}+\frac{\varepsilon+\mathfrak{v}}{2}\right)$$
$$\times\jmath\left(\frac{\upsilon\sigma+(1-\upsilon)\mathrm{i}}{2}+\frac{(1-\upsilon)\sigma+\upsilon\mathrm{i}}{2},\frac{\kappa\varepsilon+(1-\kappa)\mathfrak{v}}{2}+\frac{(1-\kappa)\varepsilon+\kappa\mathfrak{v}}{2}\right)$$
$$\leq_p \hbar_1{}^2\left(\tfrac{1}{2}\right)\hbar_2{}^2\left(\tfrac{1}{2}\right)\times\begin{bmatrix}\mathcal{J}(\upsilon\sigma+(1-\upsilon)\mathrm{i},\kappa\varepsilon+(1-\kappa)\mathfrak{v})+\mathcal{J}((1-\upsilon)\sigma+\upsilon\mathrm{i},\kappa\varepsilon+(1-\kappa)\mathfrak{v})\\+\mathcal{J}(\upsilon\sigma+(1-\upsilon)\mathrm{i},(1-\kappa)\varepsilon+\kappa\mathfrak{v})+\mathcal{J}((1-\upsilon)\sigma+\upsilon\mathrm{i},(1-\kappa)\varepsilon+\kappa\mathfrak{v})\end{bmatrix}$$
$$\times\begin{bmatrix}\jmath(\upsilon\sigma+(1-\upsilon)\mathrm{i},\kappa\varepsilon+(1-\kappa)\mathfrak{v})+\jmath((1-\upsilon)\sigma+\upsilon\mathrm{i},\kappa\varepsilon+(1-\kappa)\mathfrak{v})\\+\jmath(\upsilon\sigma+(1-\upsilon)\mathrm{i},(1-\kappa)\varepsilon+\kappa\mathfrak{v})+\jmath((1-\upsilon)\sigma+\upsilon\mathrm{i},(1-\kappa)\varepsilon+\kappa\mathfrak{v})\end{bmatrix}$$
$$\leq_p \hbar_1{}^2\left(\tfrac{1}{2}\right)\hbar_2{}^2\left(\tfrac{1}{2}\right)\times\begin{bmatrix}\mathcal{J}(\upsilon\sigma+(1-\upsilon)\mathrm{i},\kappa\varepsilon+(1-\kappa)\mathfrak{v})\times\jmath(\upsilon\sigma+(1-\upsilon)\mathrm{i},\kappa\varepsilon+(1-\kappa)\mathfrak{v})\\+\mathcal{J}((1-\upsilon)\sigma+\upsilon\mathrm{i},\kappa\varepsilon+(1-\kappa)\mathfrak{v})\times\jmath((1-\upsilon)\sigma+\upsilon\mathrm{i},\kappa\varepsilon+(1-\kappa)\mathfrak{v})\\+\mathcal{J}(\upsilon\sigma+(1-\upsilon)\mathrm{i},(1-\kappa)\varepsilon+\kappa\mathfrak{v})\times\jmath(\upsilon\sigma+(1-\upsilon)\mathrm{i},(1-\kappa)\varepsilon+\kappa\mathfrak{v})\\+\mathcal{J}((1-\upsilon)\sigma+\upsilon\mathrm{i},(1-\kappa)\varepsilon+\kappa\mathfrak{v})\times\jmath((1-\upsilon)\sigma+\upsilon\mathrm{i},(1-\kappa)\varepsilon+\kappa\mathfrak{v})\end{bmatrix}$$
$$+\hbar_1{}^2\left(\tfrac{1}{2}\right)\hbar_2{}^2\left(\tfrac{1}{2}\right)$$
$$\times\begin{bmatrix}\hbar_1(\upsilon)\hbar_1(\kappa)[\hbar_2(\upsilon)\hbar_2(1-\kappa)+\hbar_2(1-\upsilon)\hbar_2(\kappa)+\hbar_2(1-\upsilon)\hbar_2(1-\kappa)]\\+\hbar_1(\upsilon)\hbar_1(1-\kappa)[\hbar_2(\upsilon)\hbar_2(\kappa)+\hbar_2(1-\upsilon)\hbar_2(1-\kappa)+\hbar_2(1-\upsilon)\hbar_2(\kappa)]\\+\hbar_1(1-\upsilon)\hbar_1(\kappa)[\hbar_2(1-\upsilon)\hbar_2(1-\kappa)+\hbar_2(\upsilon)\hbar_2(\kappa)+\hbar_2(\upsilon)\hbar_2(1-\kappa)]\\+\hbar_1(1-\upsilon)\hbar_1(1-\kappa)[\hbar_2(\upsilon)\hbar_2(\kappa)+\hbar_2(1-\upsilon)\hbar_2(\kappa)+\hbar_2(\upsilon)\hbar_2(1-\kappa)]\end{bmatrix}\mathcal{M}(\sigma,\mathrm{i},\varepsilon,\mathfrak{v})$$
$$+\hbar_1{}^2\left(\tfrac{1}{2}\right)\hbar_2{}^2\left(\tfrac{1}{2}\right)$$
$$\times\begin{bmatrix}\hbar_1(\upsilon)\hbar_1(\kappa)[\hbar_2(1-\upsilon)\hbar_2(1-\kappa)+\hbar_2(\upsilon)\hbar_2(\kappa)+\hbar_2(\upsilon)\hbar_2(1-\kappa)]\\+\hbar_1(\upsilon)\hbar_1(1-\kappa)[\hbar_2(1-\upsilon)\hbar_2(\kappa)+\hbar_2(\upsilon)\hbar_2(1-\kappa)+\hbar_2(\upsilon)\hbar_2(\kappa)]\\+\hbar_1(1-\upsilon)\hbar_1(\kappa)[\hbar_2(\upsilon)\hbar_2(1-\kappa)+\hbar_2(1-\upsilon)\hbar_2(\kappa)+\hbar_2(1-\upsilon)\hbar_2(1-\kappa)]\\+\hbar_1(1-\upsilon)\hbar_1(1-\kappa)[\hbar_2(\upsilon)\hbar_2(\kappa)+\hbar_2(1-\upsilon)\hbar_2(1-\kappa)+\hbar_2(1-\upsilon)\hbar_2(\kappa)]\end{bmatrix}P(\sigma,\mathrm{i},\varepsilon,\mathfrak{v})$$
$$+\hbar_1{}^2\left(\tfrac{1}{2}\right)\hbar_2{}^2\left(\tfrac{1}{2}\right)$$
$$\times\begin{bmatrix}\hbar_1(\upsilon)\hbar_1(\kappa)[\hbar_2(\upsilon)\hbar_2(\kappa)+\hbar_2(1-\upsilon)\hbar_2(1-\kappa)+\hbar_2(1-\upsilon)\hbar_2(\kappa)]\\+\hbar_1(\upsilon)\hbar_1(1-\kappa)[\hbar_2(\upsilon)\hbar_2(1-\kappa)+\hbar_2(1-\upsilon)\hbar_2(\kappa)+\hbar_2(1-\upsilon)\hbar_2(1-\kappa)]\\+\hbar_1(1-\upsilon)\hbar_1(\kappa)[\hbar_2(1-\upsilon)\hbar_2(\kappa)+\hbar_2(\upsilon)\hbar_2(1-\kappa)+\hbar_2(\upsilon)\hbar_2(\kappa)]\\+\hbar_1(1-\upsilon)\hbar_1(1-\kappa)[\hbar_2(1-\upsilon)\hbar_2(1-\kappa)+\hbar_2(\upsilon)\hbar_2(\kappa)+\hbar_2(\upsilon)\hbar_2(1-\kappa)]\end{bmatrix}\mathcal{N}(\sigma,\mathrm{i},\varepsilon,\mathfrak{v})$$
$$+\hbar_1{}^2\left(\tfrac{1}{2}\right)\hbar_2{}^2\left(\tfrac{1}{2}\right)$$
$$\times\begin{bmatrix}\hbar_1(\upsilon)\hbar_1(\kappa)[\hbar_2(1-\upsilon)\hbar_2(\kappa)+\hbar_2(\upsilon)\hbar_2(1-\kappa)+\hbar_2(\upsilon)\hbar_2(\kappa)]\\+\hbar_1(\upsilon)\hbar_1(1-\kappa)[\hbar_2(1-\upsilon)\hbar_2(1-\kappa)+\hbar_2(\upsilon)\hbar_2(\kappa)+\hbar_2(\upsilon)\hbar_2(1-\kappa)]\\+\hbar_1(1-\upsilon)\hbar_1(\kappa)[\hbar_2(\upsilon)\hbar_2(\kappa)+\hbar_2(1-\upsilon)\hbar_2(1-\kappa)+\hbar_2(1-\upsilon)\hbar_2(\kappa)]\\+\hbar_1(\upsilon)\hbar_1(1-\kappa)[\hbar_2(\upsilon)\hbar_2(1-\kappa)+\hbar_2(1-\upsilon)\hbar_2(1-\kappa)+\hbar_2(1-\upsilon)\hbar_2(\kappa)]\end{bmatrix}Q(\sigma,\mathrm{i},\varepsilon,\mathfrak{v}).$$

Taking the multiplication of the above fuzzy inclusion with $\upsilon^{\alpha-1}\kappa^{\beta-1}$ and then taking the double integration of the resultant over $[0,\ 1]\times[0,\ 1]$ with respect to $(\upsilon,\ \kappa)$, we have

$$\int_0^1\int_0^1 \upsilon^{\alpha-1}\kappa^{\beta-1}\mathcal{J}\left(\frac{\sigma+\mathrm{i}}{2},\frac{\varepsilon+\mathfrak{v}}{2}\right)\times\jmath\left(\frac{\sigma+\mathrm{i}}{2},\frac{\varepsilon+\mathfrak{v}}{2}\right)d\upsilon d\kappa$$

$$\leq_p \hbar_1{}^2\left(\tfrac{1}{2}\right)\hbar_2{}^2\left(\tfrac{1}{2}\right)$$
$$\times \int_0^1\int_0^1 v^{\alpha-1}\kappa^{\beta-1}\begin{bmatrix} \mathcal{J}(v\sigma+(1-v)\mathrm{i},\kappa\varepsilon+(1-\kappa)\mathfrak{v})\times \mathcal{g}(v\sigma+(1-v)\mathrm{i},\kappa\varepsilon+(1-\kappa)\mathfrak{v}) \\ +\mathcal{J}((1-v)\sigma+v\mathrm{i},\kappa\varepsilon+(1-\kappa)\mathfrak{v})\times \mathcal{g}((1-v)\sigma+v\mathrm{i},\kappa\varepsilon+(1-\kappa)\mathfrak{v}) \\ +\mathcal{J}(v\sigma+(1-v)\mathrm{i},(1-\kappa)\varepsilon+\kappa\mathfrak{v})\times \mathcal{g}(v\sigma+(1-v)\mathrm{i},(1-\kappa)\varepsilon+\kappa\mathfrak{v}) \\ +\mathcal{J}((1-v)\sigma+v\mathrm{i},(1-\kappa)\varepsilon+\kappa\mathfrak{v})\times \mathcal{g}((1-v)\sigma+v\mathrm{i},(1-\kappa)\varepsilon+\kappa\mathfrak{v}) \end{bmatrix} dv d\kappa$$
$$+\hbar_1{}^2\left(\tfrac{1}{2}\right)\hbar_2{}^2\left(\tfrac{1}{2}\right)\mathcal{M}(\sigma,\mathrm{i},\varepsilon,\mathfrak{v})$$
$$\times \int_0^1\int_0^1 v^{\alpha-1}\kappa^{\beta-1}\begin{bmatrix} \hbar_1(v)\hbar_1(\kappa)[\hbar_2(v)\hbar_2(1-\kappa)+\hbar_2(1-v)\hbar_2(\kappa)+\hbar_2(1-v)\hbar_2(1-\kappa)] \\ +\hbar_1(v)\hbar_1(1-\kappa)[\hbar_2(v)\hbar_2(\kappa)+\hbar_2(1-v)\hbar_2(1-\kappa)+\hbar_2(1-v)\hbar_2(\kappa)] \\ +\hbar_1(1-v)\hbar_1(\kappa)[\hbar_2(1-v)\hbar_2(1-\kappa)+\hbar_2(v)\hbar_2(\kappa)+\hbar_2(v)\hbar_2(1-\kappa)] \\ +\hbar_1(1-v)\hbar_1(1-\kappa)[\hbar_2(v)\hbar_2(\kappa)+\hbar_2(1-v)\hbar_2(\kappa)+\hbar_2(v)\hbar_2(1-\kappa)] \end{bmatrix} dv d\kappa$$
$$+\hbar_1{}^2\left(\tfrac{1}{2}\right)\hbar_2{}^2\left(\tfrac{1}{2}\right)P(\sigma,\mathrm{i},\varepsilon,\mathfrak{v})$$
$$\times \int_0^1\int_0^1 v^{\alpha-1}\kappa^{\beta-1}\begin{bmatrix} \hbar_1(v)\hbar_1(\kappa)[\hbar_2(1-v)\hbar_2(1-\kappa)+\hbar_2(v)\hbar_2(\kappa)+\hbar_2(v)\hbar_2(1-\kappa)] \\ +\hbar_1(v)\hbar_1(1-\kappa)[\hbar_2(1-v)\hbar_2(\kappa)+\hbar_2(v)\hbar_2(1-\kappa)+\hbar_2(v)\hbar_2(\kappa)] \\ +\hbar_1(1-v)\hbar_1(\kappa)[\hbar_2(v)\hbar_2(1-\kappa)+\hbar_2(1-v)\hbar_2(\kappa)+\hbar_2(1-v)\hbar_2(1-\kappa)] \\ +\hbar_1(1-v)\hbar_1(1-\kappa)[\hbar_2(v)\hbar_2(\kappa)+\hbar_2(1-v)\hbar_2(1-\kappa)+\hbar_2(1-v)\hbar_2(\kappa)] \end{bmatrix} dv d\kappa$$
$$+\hbar_1{}^2\left(\tfrac{1}{2}\right)\hbar_2{}^2\left(\tfrac{1}{2}\right)\mathcal{N}(\sigma,\mathrm{i},\varepsilon,\mathfrak{v})$$
$$\times \int_0^1\int_0^1 v^{\alpha-1}\kappa^{\beta-1}\begin{bmatrix} \hbar_1(v)\hbar_1(\kappa)[\hbar_2(v)\hbar_2(\kappa)+\hbar_2(1-v)\hbar_2(1-\kappa)+\hbar_2(1-v)\hbar_2(\kappa)] \\ +\hbar_1(v)\hbar_1(1-\kappa)[\hbar_2(v)\hbar_2(1-\kappa)+\hbar_2(1-v)\hbar_2(\kappa)+\hbar_2(1-v)\hbar_2(1-\kappa)] \\ +\hbar_1(1-v)\hbar_1(\kappa)[\hbar_2(1-v)\hbar_2(\kappa)+\hbar_2(v)\hbar_2(1-\kappa)+\hbar_2(v)\hbar_2(\kappa)] \\ +\hbar_1(1-v)\hbar_1(1-\kappa)[\hbar_2(1-v)\hbar_2(1-\kappa)+\hbar_2(v)\hbar_2(\kappa)+\hbar_2(v)\hbar_2(1-\kappa)] \end{bmatrix} dv d\kappa$$
$$+\hbar_1{}^2\left(\tfrac{1}{2}\right)\hbar_2{}^2\left(\tfrac{1}{2}\right)Q(\sigma,\mathrm{i},\varepsilon,\mathfrak{v})$$
$$\times \int_0^1\int_0^1 v^{\alpha-1}\kappa^{\beta-1}\begin{bmatrix} \hbar_1(v)\hbar_1(\kappa)[\hbar_2(1-v)\hbar_2(\kappa)+\hbar_2(v)\hbar_2(1-\kappa)+\hbar_2(v)\hbar_2(\kappa)] \\ +\hbar_1(v)\hbar_1(1-\kappa)[\hbar_2(1-v)\hbar_2(1-\kappa)+\hbar_2(v)\hbar_2(\kappa)+\hbar_2(v)\hbar_2(1-\kappa)] \\ +\hbar_1(1-v)\hbar_1(\kappa)[\hbar_2(v)\hbar_2(\kappa)+\hbar_2(1-v)\hbar_2(1-\kappa)+\hbar_2(1-v)\hbar_2(\kappa)] \\ +\hbar_1(v)\hbar_1(1-\kappa)[\hbar_2(v)\hbar_2(1-\kappa)+\hbar_2(1-v)\hbar_2(1-\kappa)+\hbar_2(1-v)\hbar_2(\kappa)] \end{bmatrix} dv d\kappa,$$

which implies that

$$\frac{1}{\alpha\beta}\mathcal{J}\left(\frac{\sigma+\mathrm{i}}{2},\frac{\varepsilon+\mathfrak{v}}{2}\right)\times \mathcal{g}\left(\frac{\sigma+\mathrm{i}}{2},\frac{\varepsilon+\mathfrak{v}}{2}\right)$$
$$\leq_p \frac{\Gamma(\alpha)\Gamma(\beta)\hbar_1{}^2\left(\frac{1}{2}\right)\hbar_2{}^2\left(\frac{1}{2}\right)}{(\mathrm{i}-\sigma)^{\alpha}(\mathfrak{v}-\varepsilon)^{\beta}}\left[\mathcal{I}^{\alpha,\,\beta}_{\sigma^+,\varepsilon^+}\mathcal{J}(\mathrm{i},\mathfrak{v})\times \mathcal{g}(\mathrm{i},\mathfrak{v})+\mathcal{I}^{\alpha,\,\beta}_{\sigma^+,\mathfrak{v}^-}\mathcal{J}(\mathrm{i},\varepsilon)\times \mathcal{g}(\mathrm{i},\varepsilon)\right]$$
$$+\frac{\Gamma(\alpha)\Gamma(\beta)\hbar_1{}^2\left(\frac{1}{2}\right)\hbar_2{}^2\left(\frac{1}{2}\right)}{(\mathrm{i}-\sigma)^{\alpha}(\mathfrak{v}-\varepsilon)^{\beta}}\left[\mathcal{I}^{\alpha,\,\beta}_{\mathrm{i}^-,\varepsilon^+}\mathcal{J}(\sigma,\mathfrak{v})\times \mathcal{g}(\sigma,\mathfrak{v})+\mathcal{I}^{\alpha,\,\beta}_{\mathrm{i}^-,\mathfrak{v}^-}\mathcal{J}(\sigma,\varepsilon)\times \mathcal{g}(\sigma,\varepsilon)\right]$$
$$+2\hbar_1{}^2\left(\tfrac{1}{2}\right)\hbar_2{}^2\left(\tfrac{1}{2}\right)\mathcal{M}(\sigma,\mathrm{i},\varepsilon,\mathfrak{v})\int_0^1 v^{\alpha-1}\kappa^{\beta-1}[\hbar_1(v)\hbar_1(\kappa)[\hbar_2(v)\hbar_2(1-\kappa)$$
$$+\hbar_2(1-v)\hbar_2(\kappa)+\hbar_2(1-v)\hbar_2(1-\kappa)]$$
$$+\hbar_1(v)\hbar_1(1-\kappa)[\hbar_2(v)\hbar_2(\kappa)+\hbar_2(1-v)\hbar_2(1-\kappa)$$
$$+\hbar_2(1-v)\hbar_2(\kappa)]]dv d\kappa$$
$$+2\hbar_1{}^2\left(\tfrac{1}{2}\right)\hbar_2{}^2\left(\tfrac{1}{2}\right)P(\sigma,\mathrm{i},\varepsilon,\mathfrak{v})\int_0^1 v^{\alpha-1}\kappa^{\beta-1}[\hbar_1(v)\hbar_1(\kappa)[\hbar_2(1-v)\hbar_2(1-\kappa)$$
$$+\hbar_2(v)\hbar_2(\kappa)+\hbar_2(v)\hbar_2(1-\kappa)]$$
$$+\hbar_1(v)\hbar_1(1-\kappa)[\hbar_2(1-v)\hbar_2(\kappa)+\hbar_2(v)\hbar_2(1-\kappa)$$
$$+\hbar_2(v)\hbar_2(\kappa)]]dv d\kappa$$
$$+2\hbar_1{}^2\left(\tfrac{1}{2}\right)\hbar_2{}^2\left(\tfrac{1}{2}\right)\mathcal{N}(\sigma,\mathrm{i},\varepsilon,\mathfrak{v})\int_0^1 v^{\alpha-1}\kappa^{\beta-1}[\hbar_1(v)\hbar_1(\kappa)[\hbar_2(v)\hbar_2(\kappa)$$
$$+\hbar_2(1-v)\hbar_2(1-\kappa)+\hbar_2(1-v)\hbar_2(\kappa)]$$
$$+\hbar_1(v)\hbar_1(1-\kappa)[\hbar_2(v)\hbar_2(1-\kappa)+\hbar_2(1-v)\hbar_2(\kappa)$$
$$+\hbar_2(1-v)\hbar_2(1-\kappa)]]dv d\kappa$$
$$+2\hbar_1{}^2\left(\tfrac{1}{2}\right)\hbar_2{}^2\left(\tfrac{1}{2}\right)Q(\sigma,\mathrm{i},\varepsilon,\mathfrak{v})\int_0^1 v^{\alpha-1}\kappa^{\beta-1}[\hbar_1(v)\hbar_1(\kappa)[\hbar_2(1-v)\hbar_2(\kappa)+\hbar_2(v)\hbar_2(1-\kappa)+\hbar_2(v)\hbar_2(\kappa)]+\hbar_1(v)\hbar_1(1-\kappa)[\hbar_2(1-v)\hbar_2(1-\kappa)+\hbar_2(v)\hbar_2(\kappa)+\hbar_2(v)\hbar_2(1-\kappa)]]dv d\kappa,$$

hence, the required result. □

Remark 5. *If one assumes that* $\mathcal{J}$ *is coordinated left-LR-*$\hbar$*-convex with* $\hbar(v) = v$, $\hbar(\kappa) = \kappa$ *and* $\alpha = 1$ *and* $\beta = 1$*, then from (66), as a result, there will be inequality (see [42]):*

$$\begin{aligned} &4\mathcal{J}\left(\frac{\sigma+\mathrm{i}}{2}, \frac{\varepsilon+\mathfrak{v}}{2}\right) \times \jmath\left(\frac{\sigma+\mathrm{i}}{2}, \frac{\varepsilon+\mathfrak{v}}{2}\right) \\ &\supseteq \frac{1}{(\mathrm{i}-\sigma)(\mathfrak{v}-\varepsilon)} \int_{\sigma}^{\mathrm{i}} \int_{\varepsilon}^{\mathfrak{v}} \mathcal{J}(x,y) \times \jmath(x,y)dydx + \frac{5}{36}\mathcal{M}(\sigma,\mathrm{i},\varepsilon,\mathfrak{v}) \\ &+\frac{7}{36}[P(\sigma,\mathrm{i},\varepsilon,\mathfrak{v}) + \mathcal{N}(\sigma,\mathrm{i},\varepsilon,\mathfrak{v})] + \frac{2}{9}Q(\sigma,\mathrm{i},\varepsilon,\mathfrak{v}). \end{aligned} \tag{68}$$

If $\mathcal{J}$ *is coordinated LR-*$\hbar$*-convex with* $\hbar(v) = v$, $\hbar(\kappa) = \kappa$ *and one assumes that* $\alpha = 1$ *and* $\beta = 1$*, then from (66), as a result, there will be inequality (see [43]):*

$$\begin{aligned} &4\mathcal{J}\left(\frac{\sigma+\mathrm{i}}{2}, \frac{\varepsilon+\mathfrak{v}}{2}\right) \times \jmath\left(\frac{\sigma+\mathrm{i}}{2}, \frac{\varepsilon+\mathfrak{v}}{2}\right) \\ &\leq_p \frac{1}{(\mathrm{i}-\sigma)(\mathfrak{v}-\varepsilon)} \int_{\sigma}^{\mathrm{i}} \int_{\varepsilon}^{\mathfrak{v}} \mathcal{J}(x,y) \times \jmath(x,y)dydx + \frac{5}{36}\mathcal{M}(\sigma,\mathrm{i},\varepsilon,\mathfrak{v}) \\ &+\frac{7}{36}[P(\sigma,\mathrm{i},\varepsilon,\mathfrak{v}) + \mathcal{N}(\sigma,\mathrm{i},\varepsilon,\mathfrak{v})] + \frac{2}{9}Q(\sigma,\mathrm{i},\varepsilon,\mathfrak{v}). \end{aligned} \tag{69}$$

If $\mathcal{J}$ *is coordinated left-LR-*$\hbar$*-convex and* $\mathcal{J}_*(x,y) \neq \mathcal{J}^*(x,y)$ *with* $\hbar(v) = v$, $\hbar(\kappa) = \kappa$*, then from (66), we succeed in bringing about the upcoming inequality (see [41]):*

$$\begin{aligned} &4\mathcal{J}\left(\frac{\sigma+\mathrm{i}}{2}, \frac{\varepsilon+\mathfrak{v}}{2}\right) \times \jmath\left(\frac{\sigma+\mathrm{i}}{2}, \frac{\varepsilon+\mathfrak{v}}{2}\right) \\ &\supseteq \frac{\Gamma(\alpha+1)\Gamma(\beta+1)}{4(\mathrm{i}-\sigma)^{\alpha}(\mathfrak{v}-\varepsilon)^{\beta}} \left[\begin{array}{c} \mathcal{J}_{\sigma^+,\varepsilon^+}^{\alpha,\,\beta} \mathcal{J}(\mathrm{i},\mathfrak{v}) \times \jmath(\mathrm{i},\mathfrak{v}) + \mathcal{J}_{\sigma^+,\mathfrak{v}^-}^{\alpha,\,\beta} \mathcal{J}(\mathrm{i},\varepsilon) \times \jmath(\mathrm{i},\varepsilon) \\ +\mathcal{J}_{\mathrm{i}^-,\varepsilon^+}^{\alpha,\,\beta} \mathcal{J}(\sigma,\mathfrak{v}) \times \jmath(\sigma,\mathfrak{v}) + \mathcal{J}_{\mathrm{i}^-,\mathfrak{v}^-}^{\alpha,\,\beta} \mathcal{J}(\sigma,\varepsilon) \times \jmath(\sigma,\varepsilon) \end{array}\right] \\ &+\left[\frac{\alpha}{2(\alpha+1)(\alpha+2)} + \frac{\beta}{(\beta+1)(\beta+2)}\left(\frac{1}{2} - \frac{\alpha}{(\alpha+1)(\alpha+2)}\right)\right]\mathcal{M}(\sigma,\mathrm{i},\varepsilon,\mathfrak{v}) \\ &+\left[\frac{1}{2}\left(\frac{1}{2} - \frac{\alpha}{(\alpha+1)(\alpha+2)}\right) + \frac{\alpha}{(\alpha+1)(\alpha+2)}\frac{\beta}{(\beta+1)(\beta+2)}\right]P(\sigma,\mathrm{i},\varepsilon,\mathfrak{v}) \\ &+\left[\frac{1}{2}\left(\frac{1}{2} - \frac{\beta}{(\beta+1)(\beta+2)}\right) + \frac{\alpha}{(\alpha+1)(\alpha+2)}\frac{\beta}{(\beta+1)(\beta+2)}\right]\mathcal{N}(\sigma,\mathrm{i},\varepsilon,\mathfrak{v}) \\ &+\left[\frac{1}{4} - \frac{\alpha}{(\alpha+1)(\alpha+2)}\frac{\beta}{(\beta+1)(\beta+2)}\right]Q(\sigma,\mathrm{i},\varepsilon,\mathfrak{v}). \end{aligned} \tag{70}$$

If $\mathcal{J}_*(x,y) \neq \mathcal{J}^*(x,y)$ *and* $\hbar(v) = v$, $\hbar(\kappa) = \kappa$*, then from (66), we succeed in bringing about the upcoming inequality (see [46]):*

$$\begin{aligned} &4\mathcal{J}\left(\frac{\sigma+\mathrm{i}}{2}, \frac{\varepsilon+\mathfrak{v}}{2}\right) \times \jmath\left(\frac{\sigma+\mathrm{i}}{2}, \frac{\varepsilon+\mathfrak{v}}{2}\right) \\ &\leq_p \frac{\Gamma(\alpha+1)\Gamma(\beta+1)}{4(\mathrm{i}-\sigma)^{\alpha}(\mathfrak{v}-\varepsilon)^{\beta}} \left[\begin{array}{c} \mathcal{J}_{\sigma^+,\varepsilon^+}^{\alpha,\,\beta} \mathcal{J}(\mathrm{i},\mathfrak{v}) \times \jmath(\mathrm{i},\mathfrak{v}) + \mathcal{J}_{\sigma^+,\mathfrak{v}^-}^{\alpha,\,\beta} \mathcal{J}(\mathrm{i},\varepsilon) \times \jmath(\mathrm{i},\varepsilon) \\ +\mathcal{J}_{\mathrm{i}^-,\varepsilon^+}^{\alpha,\,\beta} \mathcal{J}(\sigma,\mathfrak{v}) \times \jmath(\sigma,\mathfrak{v}) + \mathcal{J}_{\mathrm{i}^-,\mathfrak{v}^-}^{\alpha,\,\beta} \mathcal{J}(\sigma,\varepsilon) \times \jmath(\sigma,\varepsilon) \end{array}\right] \\ &+\left[\frac{\alpha}{2(\alpha+1)(\alpha+2)} + \frac{\beta}{(\beta+1)(\beta+2)}\left(\frac{1}{2} - \frac{\alpha}{(\alpha+1)(\alpha+2)}\right)\right]\mathcal{M}(\sigma,\mathrm{i},\varepsilon,\mathfrak{v}) \\ &+\left[\frac{1}{2}\left(\frac{1}{2} - \frac{\alpha}{(\alpha+1)(\alpha+2)}\right) + \frac{\alpha}{(\alpha+1)(\alpha+2)}\frac{\beta}{(\beta+1)(\beta+2)}\right]P(\sigma,\mathrm{i},\varepsilon,\mathfrak{v}) \\ &+\left[\frac{1}{2}\left(\frac{1}{2} - \frac{\beta}{(\beta+1)(\beta+2)}\right) + \frac{\alpha}{(\alpha+1)(\alpha+2)}\frac{\beta}{(\beta+1)(\beta+2)}\right]\mathcal{N}(\sigma,\mathrm{i},\varepsilon,\mathfrak{v}) \\ &+\left[\frac{1}{4} - \frac{\alpha}{(\alpha+1)(\alpha+2)}\frac{\beta}{(\beta+1)(\beta+2)}\right]Q(\sigma,\mathrm{i},\varepsilon,\mathfrak{v}). \end{aligned} \tag{71}$$

If $\mathfrak{J}_*(x,y) = \mathfrak{J}^*(x,y)$ *and* $\jmath_*(x,y) = \jmath^*(x,y)$ *and* $\hbar(\upsilon) = \upsilon$, $\hbar(\kappa) = \kappa$, *then from (66), we succeed in bringing about the upcoming classical inequality.*

$$\begin{aligned}
&4\mathfrak{J}\left(\frac{\sigma+\mathrm{i}}{2}, \frac{\varepsilon+\mathfrak{v}}{2}\right) \times \jmath\left(\frac{\sigma+\mathrm{i}}{2}, \frac{\varepsilon+\mathfrak{v}}{2}\right) \\
&\leq \frac{\Gamma(\alpha+1)\Gamma(\beta+1)}{4(\mathrm{i}-\sigma)^{\alpha}(\mathfrak{v}-\varepsilon)^{\beta}} \begin{bmatrix} \mathcal{J}^{\alpha,\,\beta}_{\sigma^+,\varepsilon^+}\mathfrak{J}(\mathrm{i},\mathfrak{v}) \times \jmath(\mathrm{i},\mathfrak{v}) + \mathcal{J}^{\alpha,\,\beta}_{\sigma^+,\mathfrak{v}^-}\mathfrak{J}(\mathrm{i},\varepsilon) \times \jmath(\mathrm{i},\varepsilon) \\ +\mathcal{J}^{\alpha,\,\beta}_{\mathrm{i}^-,\varepsilon^+}\mathfrak{J}(\sigma,\mathfrak{v}) \times \jmath(\sigma,\mathfrak{v}) + \mathcal{J}^{\alpha,\,\beta}_{\mathrm{i}^-,\mathfrak{v}^-}\mathfrak{J}(\sigma,\varepsilon) \times \jmath(\sigma,\varepsilon) \end{bmatrix} \\
&\quad + \left[\frac{\alpha}{2(\alpha+1)(\alpha+2)} + \frac{\beta}{(\beta+1)(\beta+2)}\left(\frac{1}{2} - \frac{\alpha}{(\alpha+1)(\alpha+2)}\right)\right]\mathcal{M}(\sigma,\mathrm{i},\varepsilon,\mathfrak{v}) \\
&\quad + \left[\frac{1}{2}\left(\frac{1}{2} - \frac{\alpha}{(\alpha+1)(\alpha+2)}\right) + \frac{\alpha}{(\alpha+1)(\alpha+2)}\frac{\beta}{(\beta+1)(\beta+2)}\right]P(\sigma,\mathrm{i},\varepsilon,\mathfrak{v}) \\
&\quad + \left[\frac{1}{2}\left(\frac{1}{2} - \frac{\beta}{(\beta+1)(\beta+2)}\right) + \frac{\alpha}{(\alpha+1)(\alpha+2)}\frac{\beta}{(\beta+1)(\beta+2)}\right]\mathcal{N}(\sigma,\mathrm{i},\varepsilon,\mathfrak{v}) \\
&\quad + \left[\frac{1}{4} - \frac{\alpha}{(\alpha+1)(\alpha+2)}\frac{\beta}{(\beta+1)(\beta+2)}\right]Q(\sigma,\mathrm{i},\varepsilon,\mathfrak{v}).
\end{aligned} \tag{72}$$

4. Conclusions and Future Plans

To sum up, this study offers a new extension of interval-valued convexity. Through the use of fractional integral operators, various inequalities for *LR*-$\hbar$-convexity are produced by applying interval-valued mapping. Many exceptional cases are discussed and new and classical versions of integral inequalities are also acquired that can be considered as applications of this article's outcomes. Some very interesting examples are also given to discuss the validation of the main results. The results of this research paper could potentially have applications in various areas of mathematics, physics, and engineering. The extension of the proposed iterative method to systems of equations could be an interesting future research problem. In the future, we will try to explore these concepts in quantum calculus.

Author Contributions: Conceptualization, M.B.K.; validation, E.R.N.; formal analysis, E.R.N.; investigation, M.B.K. and T.S.; resources, M.B.K. and T.S.; writing—original draft, M.B.K. and T.S.; writing—review and editing, M.B.K. and K.H.H.; visualization, T.S. and K.H.H.; supervision, T.S. and K.H.H.; project administration, T.S. and E.R.N. All authors have read and agreed to the published version of the manuscript.

Funding: This research received no external funding.

Data Availability Statement: No new data were created or analyzed in this study. Data sharing is not applicable to this article.

Acknowledgments: The Transilvania University of Brasov, 29 Eroilor Boulevard, 500036 Brasov, Romania, is acknowledged by the authors for offering top-notch research and academic environments.

Conflicts of Interest: The authors claim to have no conflicts of interest.

References

1. Dragomir, S.S.; Pearce, C. *Selected Topics on Hermite-Hadamard Inequality and Applications*; Victoria University: Melbourne, Australia, 2000.
2. Hadamard, J. Étude sur les propriétés des fonctions entiéres et en particulier d'une fonction considérée par Riemann. *J. Math. Pures Appl.* **1893**, *9*, 171–216.
3. Hermite, C. Sur deux limites d'une intégrale définie. *Mathesis* **1883**, *3*, 1–82.
4. Dragomir, S.S.; Agarwal, R. Two inequalities for differentiable mappings and applications to special means of real numbers and to trapezoidal formula. *Appl. Math. Lett.* **1998**, *11*, 91–95. [CrossRef]
5. Kirmaci, U.S. Inequalities for differentiable mappings and applications to special means of real numbers and to midpoint formula. *Appl. Math. Comput.* **2004**, *147*, 137–146. [CrossRef]
6. Awan, M.U.; Javed, M.Z.; Rassias, M.T.; Noor, M.A.; Noor, K.I. Simpson type inequalities and applications. *J. Anal.* **2021**, *29*, 1403–1419. [CrossRef]
7. Alomari, M.; Darus, M. On some inequalities of Simpson-type via quasi-convex functions and applications. *Transylv. J. Math.* **2010**, *2*, 15–24.
8. İşcan, İ. Hermite-Hadamard and Simpson-like type inequalities for differentiable harmonically convex functions. *J. Math.* **2014**, *2014*, 346305. [CrossRef]

9. Sarikaya, M.Z.; Set, E.; Özdemir, M.E. On new inequalities of Simpson's type for convex functions. *Res. Group Math. Inequalities Appl.* **2010**, *60*, 2191–2199. [CrossRef]
10. Set, E.; Akdemir, A.O.; Özdemir, E.M. Simpson type integral inequalities for convex functions via Riemann-Liouville integrals. *Filomat* **2017**, *31*, 4415–4420. [CrossRef]
11. Breckner, W.W. Stetigkeitsaussagen für eine Klasse verallgemeinerter konvexer Funktionen in topologischen linearen Räumen. *Publ. Inst. Math.* **1978**, *23*, 13–20.
12. Hudzik, H.; Maligranda, L. Some remarks on *s*-convex functions. *Aequationes Math.* **1994**, *48*, 100–111. [CrossRef]
13. Godunova, E.K.; Levin, V.I. Inequalities for functions of a broad class that contains convex, monotone and some other forms of functions. *Numer. Math. Math. Phys.* **1985**, *138*, 166.
14. Noor, M.A.; Noor, K.I.; Awan, M.U.; Li, J. On Hermite-Hadamard Inequalities for *h*-Preinvex Functions. *Filomat* **2014**, *28*, 1463–1474. [CrossRef]
15. Awan, M.U.; Talib, S.; Noor, M.A.; Noor, K.I. On γ-preinvex functions. *Filomat* **2020**, *34*, 4137–4159. [CrossRef]
16. Tunç, M.; Göv, E.; Sanal, Ü. On *tgs*-convex function and their inequalities. *Facta Univ. Ser. Math. Inform.* **2015**, *30*, 679–691.
17. Varošanec, S. On *h*-convexity. *J. Math. Anal. Appl.* **2007**, *326*, 303–311. [CrossRef]
18. Rentería-Baltiérrez, F.Y.; Reyes-Melo, M.E.; Puente-Córdova, J.G.; López-Walle, B. Application of fractional calculus in the mechanical and dielectric correlation model of hybrid polymer films with different average molecular weight matrices. *Polym. Bull.* **2023**, *80*, 6327–6347. [CrossRef]
19. Sun, H.; Zhang, Y.; Baleanu, D.; Chen, W.; Chen, Y. A new collection of real world applications of fractional calculus in science and engineering. *Commun. Nonlinear Sci. Numer. Simul.* **2018**, *64*, 213–231. [CrossRef]
20. Viera-Martin, E.; Gómez-Aguilar, J.F.; Solís-Pérez, J.E.; Hernández-Pérez, J.A.; Escobar-Jiménez, R.F. Artificial neural networks: A practical review of applications involving fractional calculus. *Eur. Phys. J. Spec. Top.* **2022**, *231*, 2059–2095. [CrossRef]
21. Kilbas, A.A.; Srivastava, H.M.; Trujillo, J.J. *Theory and Applications of Fractional Differential Equations*; Elsevier: Amsterdam, The Netherlands, 2006.
22. Abbaszadeh, S.; Gordji, M.E.; Pap, E.; Szakál, A. Jensen-type inequalities for Sugeno integral. *Inf. Sci.* **2017**, *376*, 148–157. [CrossRef]
23. Agahi, H.; Mesiar, R.; Ouyang, Y. General Minkowski type inequalities for Sugeno integrals. *Fuzzy Sets Syst.* **2010**, *161*, 708–715. [CrossRef]
24. Pap, E.; Štrboja, M. Generalization of the Jensen inequality for pseudo-integral. *Inf. Sci.* **2010**, *180*, 543–548. [CrossRef]
25. Wang, R.S. Some inequalities and convergence theorems for Choquet integral. *J. Appl. Math. Comput.* **2011**, *35*, 305–321. [CrossRef]
26. Aumann, R.J. Integrals of set-valued functions. *J. Math. Anal. Appl.* **1965**, *12*, 1–12. [CrossRef]
27. Klein, E.; Thompson, A.C. *Theory of Correspondences*; A Wiley-Interscience Publication: New York, NY, USA, 1984.
28. Costa, T.M.; Román-Flores, H. Some integral inequalities for fuzzy-interval-valued functions. *Inf. Sci.* **2017**, *420*, 110–125. [CrossRef]
29. Khan, M.B.; Zaini, H.G.; Treanţă, S.; Soliman, M.S.; Nonlaopon, K. Riemann–liouville fractional integral inequalities for generalized pre-invex functions of interval-valued settings based upon pseudo order relation. *Mathematics* **2022**, *10*, 204. [CrossRef]
30. Budak, H.; Tun, T.; Sarikaya, M.Z. Fractional hermite-hadamard-type inequalities for interval-valued functions. *Proc. Am. Math. Soc.* **2019**, *148*, 705–718. [CrossRef]
31. Zhao, D.; An, T.; Ye, G.; Liu, W. Chebyshev type inequalities for interval-valued functions. *Fuzzy Sets Syst.* **2020**, *396*, 82–101. [CrossRef]
32. Zhao, D.; An, T.; Ye, G.; Liu, W. Some generalizations of opial type inequalities for interval-valued functions. *Fuzzy Sets Syst.* **2021**, *436*, 128–151. [CrossRef]
33. Zhao, D.; Zhao, G.; Ye, G.; Liu, W.; Dragomir, S.S. On hermite–hadamard-type inequalities for coordinated h-convex interval-valued functions. *Mathematics* **2021**, *9*, 2352. [CrossRef]
34. Budak, H.; Kashuri, A.; Butt, S. Fractional Ostrowski type inequalities for interval valued functions. *Mathematics* **2022**, *36*, 2531–2540. [CrossRef]
35. Khan, M.B.; Abdullah, L.; Noor, M.A.; Noor, K.I. New hermite–hadamard and jensen inequalities for log-h-convex fuzzy interval valued functions. *Int. J. Comput. Intell. Syst.* **2021**, *14*, 155. [CrossRef]
36. Anastassiou, G.A. Fuzzy ostrowski type inequalities. *Comput. Appl. Math.* **2003**, *22*, 279–292. [CrossRef]
37. Bede, B.; Gal, S.G. Generalizations of the differentiability of fuzzy-number-valued functions with applications to fuzzy differential equations. *Fuzzy Sets Syst.* **2005**, *151*, 581–599. [CrossRef]
38. Chalco-Cano, Y.; Román-Flores, H.; Jiménez-Gamero, M.D. Generalized derivative and π-derivative for set-valued functions. *Inf. Sci.* **2011**, *181*, 2177–2188. [CrossRef]
39. Chalco-Cano, Y.; Román-Flores, H.; Jiménez-Gamero, M.D. Ostrowski type inequalities for interval-valued functions using generalized Hukuhara derivative. *Comput. Appl. Math.* **2011**, *181*, 2177–2188.
40. Lupulescu, V. Fractional calculus for interval-valued functions. *Fuzzy Set. Syst.* **2015**, *265*, 63–85. [CrossRef]
41. Budak, H.; Kara, H.; Ali, M.A.; Khan, S.; Chu, Y. Fractional Hermite-Hadamard-type inequalities for interval-valued co-ordinated convex functions. *Open Math.* **2021**, *19*, 1081–1097. [CrossRef]
42. Zhao, D.F.; Ali, M.A.; Murtaza, G. On the Hermite-Hadamard inequalities for interval-valued coordinated convex functions. *Adv. Differ. Equ.* **2020**, *2020*, 570. [CrossRef]

43. Khan, M.B.; Srivastava, H.M.; Mohammed, P.O.; Nonlaopon, K.; Hamed, Y.S. Some new estimates on coordinates of left and right convex interval-valued functions based on pseudo order relation. *Symmetry* **2022**, *14*, 473. [CrossRef]
44. Budak, H.; Sarıkaya, M.Z. Hermite-Hadamard type inequalities for products of two coordinated convex mappings via fractional integrals. *Int. J. Appl. Math. Stat.* **2019**, *58*, 11–30.
45. Khan, M.B.; Treanță, T.; Alrweili, H.; Saeed, T.; Soliman, M.S. Some new Riemann-Liouville fractional integral inequalities for interval-valued mappings. *AIMS Math.* **2022**, *7*, 15659–15679. [CrossRef]
46. Khan, M.B.; Zaini, H.G.; Macías-Díaz, J.E.; Treanţă, S.; Soliman, M.S. Some integral inequalities in interval fractional calculus for left and right coordinated interval-valued functions. *AIMS Math.* **2022**, *7*, 10454–10482. [CrossRef]
47. Zhang, D.; Guo, C.; Chen, D.; Wang, G. Jensen's inequalities for set-valued and fuzzy set-valued functions. *Fuzzy Sets Syst.* **2020**, *404*, 178–204. [CrossRef]

fractal and fractional

Article

Properties and Applications of Symmetric Quantum Calculus

Miguel Vivas-Cortez [1], Muhammad Zakria Javed [2], Muhammad Uzair Awan [2,*], Silvestru Sever Dragomir [3] and Ahmed M. Zidan [4]

1 Escuela de Ciencias Físicas y Matemáticas, Facultad de Ciencias Exactas y Naturales, Pontificia Universidad Católica del Ecuador, Av. 12 de Octubre 1076, Apartado, Quito 17-01-2184, Ecuador; mjvivas@puce.edu.ec
2 Department of Mathematics, Government College University, Faisalabad 38000, Pakistan; zakria.201603943@gcuf.edu.pk or zakriajaved071@gmail.com
3 Mathematics, College of Engineering & Science, Victoria University, P.O. Box 14428, Melbourne City, VIC 8001, Australia; sever.dragomir@vu.edu.au
4 Department of Mathematics, College of Science, King Khalid University, Abha 61413, Saudi Arabia; ahmoahmed@kku.edu.sa
* Correspondence: muawan@gcuf.edu.pk or awan.uzair@gmail.com

Abstract: Symmetric derivatives and integrals are extensively studied to overcome the limitations of classical derivatives and integral operators. In the current investigation, we explore the quantum symmetric derivatives on finite intervals. We introduced the idea of right quantum symmetric derivatives and integral operators and studied various properties of both operators as well. Using these concepts, we deliver new variants of Young's inequality, Hölder's inequality, Minkowski's inequality, Hermite–Hadamard's inequality, Ostrowski's inequality, and Gruss–Chebysev inequality. We report the Hermite–Hadamard's inequalities by taking into account the differentiability of convex mappings. These fundamental results are pivotal to studying the various other problems in the field of inequalities. The validation of results is also supported with some visuals.

Keywords: convex; function; Hermite–Hadamard; Holder's; symmetric; quantum; Ostrowski

Citation: Vivas-Cortez, M.; Javed, M.Z.; Awan, M.U.; Dragomir, S.S.; Zidan, A.M. Properties and Applications of Symmetric Quantum Calculus. *Fractal Fract.* **2024**, *8*, 107. https://doi.org/10.3390/fractalfract8020107

Academic Editor: Ivanka Stamova

Received: 21 November 2023
Revised: 30 January 2024
Accepted: 31 January 2024
Published: 12 February 2024

1. Introduction

The theory of convex functions has diverse applications in several fields of science but its impact on the growth of inequalities is very significant. Most of the fundamental results related to inequalities are derived through convex mappings.

Several innovative and novel techniques are utilized to derive new counterparts of fundamental results of inequalities. One of them is $\hat{q}_1$-calculus because it has advantages over classical concepts. In the perspective of $\hat{q}_1$-calculus one can obtain the quantum derivatives of piecewise discontinuous mappings. Meanwhile symmetric calculus is applied to study the non-differentiable mappings for example absolute functions. Quantum symmetric calculus is also a very interesting and intriguing aspect of mathematical analysis. It generalizes the classical symmetric concepts by $\hat{q}_1 \to 1$.

In Ref. [1] Sudsutad et al. explored the various famous inequalities over finite intervals. In 2018, Alp et al. [2] explored the correct version of Hermite–Hadamard inequality by utilizing the differentiability of convex functions and several other important inequalities. Bin-Mohsin et al. [3] explored the error boundaries for an open method known as the Milne rule implementing the Mercer inequality and quantum calculus. In Ref. [4], Kunt and his fellows gave the idea of right-sided quantum derivatives and integral operators and provided a detailed discussion about these operators. In Ref. [5], Nwaeze and Tameru examined the unified integral inequalities through η-convex functions. Different values of η and other parameters involved in identity produced innovative results. Asawasamrit et al. [6] reported some new integral inequality results concerning Hahn quantum operators. The results produced in the paper can be reduced to integral inequalities established via well-known quantum operators defined on finite intervals. Kunt et al. [7] provided the quantum Montgomery equality and concluded some of Ostrowski's type bounds. In the sequel, Kalsoom et al. [8] devoted their efforts to come up with Ostrowski estimates by invoking the notion of higher order n-polynomial preinvex functions. In Ref. [9], Ali and his colleagues purported new variants of both midpoint and trapezoidal rule via quantum concepts. In Ref. [10], the authors presented the trapezium-type inequalities in a more general form and deduced some inequalities for comparative study with existing outcomes. In Ref. [11], the authors focused on establishing the post-quantum analogues of trapezium inequality via generalized m-convex mappings. Duo et al. [12] analyzed some quantum estimates through a unified approach to obtain several type inequalities by specifying the values for parameters. In Ref. [13], Khan and his co-authors developed the trapezium type inequalities by taking into account the green functions via quantum calculus and have investigated the post-quantum analogues of Hermite–Hadamard type involving generalized m-convexity. Saleh et al. [14] derived quantum dual Simpson-type error estimates involving convex functions and presented some implications as well. In Ref. [15], the authors utilized the majorization approach and quantum calculus to develop new counterparts of Hermite–Hadamard–Mercer type inequalities. In Ref. [16], Alomari derived the quantum variant of Bernoulli's inequality and its consequences. In Ref. [17], Alp and Sarikaya established the quantum integral inequalities based on newly developed quantum operators known as second sense quantum integral operators. Nosheen et al. [18] studied Ostrowski's type variants through s-convex mappings and quantum symmetric calculus. For further details, see Refs. [19–21].

The principal inspiration of the current study is to investigate the right symmetric derivative and integral operator. To accomplish this study, we divide our complete study into three parts. In the first part of the study, we provide some essential facts and a literature review related to the problem. In successive segments, we introduce the notions of right quantum symmetric operators and explore their essential properties as well. In the third part, we discuss the applications of newly studied concepts in previous sections to integral inequalities. Later on, concluding remarks and future insights are provided. We hope this will create new venues for the investigation.

2. Preliminaries

Let us report the notion of convex mappings:

Definition 1 ([22])**.** *Any mapping* $\mathcal{Z} : [\mathcal{C}_1, \mathcal{C}_2] \to \mathbb{R}$ *is referred to be a convex mapping if,*

$$\mathcal{Z}((1-\tau)x + \tau y) \leq (1-\tau)\mathcal{Z}(x) + \tau\mathcal{Z}(y), \quad \forall x, y \in [\mathcal{C}_1, \mathcal{C}_2] \tag{1}$$

where $\tau \in [0,1]$.

The geometrical interpretation of convex mapping is described as if the chord line joining the point $(\mathcal{C}_1, \mathcal{Z}(\mathcal{C}_1))$ and $(\mathcal{C}_2, \mathcal{Z}(\mathcal{C}_2))$ always lies on or above the graph of a mapping. In addition, any mapping is convex if and only if its epigraph is a convex set.

Now we recall a famous consequence of convex mappings, which is known as trapezium inequality proved by Hermite and Hadamard separately and is demonstrated as:

Let $\mathcal{Z} : [\mathcal{C}_1, \mathcal{C}_2] \to \mathbb{R}$ be a convex mapping, then

$$\mathcal{Z}\left(\frac{\mathcal{C}_1+\mathcal{C}_2}{2}\right) \leq \frac{1}{\mathcal{C}_2-\mathcal{C}_1}\int_{\mathcal{C}_1}^{\mathcal{C}_2} \mathcal{Z}(x)\mathrm{d}x \leq \frac{\mathcal{Z}(\mathcal{C}_1)+\mathcal{Z}(\mathcal{C}_2)}{2}.$$

This inequality serves as criteria for convex mappings and it is widely utilized to determine the error bounds of both mid-point and trapezoidal rules. Moreover, it determines the bounds of the average mean integral. Several studies have been carried out regarding this inequality. For further detail, one may consult the following Refs. [23–25].

Now we will recollect some facts regarding symmetric quantum calculus.

Let $\hat{q}_1 \in (0,1)$ and let I be arbitrary interval of $\mathbb{R}$ containing 0,

$$I_{\hat{q}_1} = \{\hat{q}_1 x | x \in I\}.$$

Clearly $I_{\hat{q}_1} \subset I$.

Definition 2. ([26]). *Let $\mathcal{Z} : I \to \mathbb{R}$. Then the symmetric quantum derivative operator is described as:*

$$D^s_{\hat{q}_1} \mathcal{Z}(\tau) = \frac{\mathcal{Z}(\hat{q}_1^{-1}\tau) - \mathcal{Z}(\hat{q}_1\tau)}{(\hat{q}_1^{-1} - \hat{q}_1)\tau}, \tau \neq 0.$$

Additionally, $D^s_{\hat{q}_1} \mathcal{Z}(0) = \mathcal{Z}'(0), \tau = 0$ provided that $\mathcal{Z}$ is differentiable at $\tau = 0$. If $\mathcal{Z}$ is differentiable mapping at $\tau \in I_{\hat{q}_1}$ then $\lim_{\hat{q}_1 \to 1} D^s_{\hat{q}_1} \mathcal{Z}(\tau) = \mathcal{Z}'(\tau)$.

Theorem 1. *Suppose that $\mathcal{Z}$ and g are two $\hat{q}_1$-symmetric differentiable on I°, then for any $c, m_1, n_1 \in \mathbb{R}$ and $\tau \in I_{\hat{q}_1}$*

1. $D^s_{\hat{q}_1} \mathcal{Z}(\tau) = 0 \Leftrightarrow \mathcal{Z} = c.$
2. $D^s_{\hat{q}_1} [m_1 \mathcal{Z}(\tau) + n_1 \mathcal{G}(\tau)] = m_1 D^s_{\hat{q}_1} \mathcal{Z}(\tau) + n_1 D^s_{\hat{q}_1} \mathcal{Z}(\tau).$
3. $D^s_{\hat{q}_1} \mathcal{Z}(\tau)\mathcal{G}(\tau) = \mathcal{G}(\hat{q}_1\tau) D^s_{\hat{q}_1} \mathcal{Z}(\tau) + \mathcal{Z}(\hat{q}_1^{-1}\tau) D^s_{\hat{q}_1} \mathcal{G}(\tau).$

Moreover, In 2023, Khan et al. [27] explored the concept of left quantum symmetric derivatives and integrals over finite intervals. Assume that $J = [\mathcal{C}_1, \mathcal{C}_2] \subset \mathbb{R}$, $0 \in J$ and $0 < \hat{q}_1 < 1$, then the left quantum symmetric derivative is described as:

Definition 3 ([27]). *Let $\mathcal{Z} : J \to \mathbb{R}$ be a continuous mapping, then*

$${}_{\mathcal{C}_1}D^s_{\hat{q}_1} \mathcal{Z}(\tau) = \frac{\mathcal{Z}(\hat{q}_1^{-1}\tau + (1 - \hat{q}_1^{-1})\mathcal{C}_1) - \mathcal{Z}(\hat{q}_1\tau + (1 - \hat{q}_1)\mathcal{C}_1)}{(\hat{q}_1^{-1} - \hat{q}_1)(\tau - \mathcal{C}_1)}, \tau \neq \mathcal{C}_1.$$

And ${}_{\mathcal{C}_1}D^s_{\hat{q}_1} \mathcal{Z}(\mathcal{C}_1) = \lim_{\hat{q}_1 \to 1} {}_{\mathcal{C}_1}D^s_{\hat{q}_1} \mathcal{Z}(\tau)$, if limit exist. If $\mathcal{C}_1 = 0$ then ${}_{\mathcal{C}_1}D^s_{\hat{q}_1} \mathcal{Z} = D^s_{\hat{q}_1} \mathcal{Z}$.

Theorem 2. *Suppose that $\mathcal{Z}, \mathcal{G} : J \to \mathbb{R}$ is quantum symmetric differentiable mapping, then*

1. ${}_{\mathcal{C}_1}D^s_{\hat{q}_1} [m_1 \mathcal{Z}(\tau) + n_1 \mathcal{G}(\tau)] = m_1 {}_{\mathcal{C}_1}D^s_{\hat{q}_1} \mathcal{Z}(\tau) + n_1 {}_{\mathcal{C}_1}D^s_{\hat{q}_1} \mathcal{Z}(\tau).$
2. ${}_{\mathcal{C}_1}D^s_{\hat{q}_1} \mathcal{Z}(\tau)\mathcal{G}(\tau) = \mathcal{G}(\hat{q}_1\tau + (1 - \hat{q}_1)\mathcal{C}_1) {}_{\mathcal{C}_1}D^s_{\hat{q}_1} \mathcal{Z}(\tau) + \mathcal{Z}(\hat{q}_1^{-1}\tau + (1 - \hat{q}_1^{-1})\mathcal{C}_1) {}_{\mathcal{C}_1}D^s_{\hat{q}_1} \mathcal{G}(\tau).$

Similarly, they investigated the corresponding symmetric quantum integral, which is stated as:

Definition 4. *Suppose $\mathcal{Z} : J \to \mathbb{R}$ is a continuous mapping, then*

$$\begin{aligned}
\int_{\mathcal{C}_1}^{\mathcal{C}_2} \mathcal{Z}(\tau) {}_{\mathcal{C}_1}d^s_{\hat{q}_1}\tau &= (\mathcal{C}_2 - \mathcal{C}_1)(\hat{q}_1^{-1} - \hat{q}_1) \sum_{n=0}^{\infty} \hat{q}_1^{2n+1} \mathcal{Z}(\hat{q}_1^{2n+1}\mathcal{C}_2 + (1 - \hat{q}_1^{2n+1})\mathcal{C}_1) \\
&= (\mathcal{C}_2 - \mathcal{C}_1)(1 - \hat{q}_1^2) \sum_{n=0}^{\infty} \hat{q}_1^{2n} \mathcal{Z}(\hat{q}_1^{2n+1}\mathcal{C}_2 + (1 - \hat{q}_1^{2n+1})\mathcal{C}_1).
\end{aligned}$$

If $\mathcal{C}_1 = 0$, then it reduces to classical symmetric quantum integrals in Ref. [26]. To get more information about quantum symmetric differences, one may consult Ref. [28].

3. Main Findings

In the following perspective, we introduce the idea of right quantum symmetric derivative and integral operators, which is stated as:

Definition 5. *Let $\mathcal{Z} : J \to \mathbb{R}$ be a continuous mapping, then*

$${}^{\mathcal{C}_2}D^s_{\hat{q}_1} \mathcal{Z}(\tau) = \frac{\mathcal{Z}(\hat{q}_1\tau + (1 - \hat{q}_1)\mathcal{C}_2) - \mathcal{Z}(\hat{q}_1^{-1}\tau + (1 - \hat{q}_1^{-1})\mathcal{C}_2)}{(\hat{q}_1^{-1} - \hat{q}_1)(\mathcal{C}_2 - \tau)}, \tau \neq \mathcal{C}_2.$$

And ${}^{\mathcal{C}_2}D^{s}_{\hat{q}_1}\mathcal{Z}(\mathcal{C}_2) = \lim_{\hat{q}_1\to 1}{}^{\mathcal{C}_2}D^{s}_{\hat{q}_1}\mathcal{Z}(\tau)$, *if limit exist. If* $\mathcal{C}_2 = 0$ *then* ${}^{\mathcal{C}_2}D^{s}_{\hat{q}_1}\mathcal{Z} = D^{s}_{\hat{q}_1}\mathcal{Z}$.

Example 1. *If* $\mathcal{Z}(\tau) = (\mathcal{C}_2 - \tau)^{\alpha}$, *then*

$$\begin{aligned}{}^{\mathcal{C}_2}D^{s}_{\hat{q}_1}\mathcal{Z}(\tau) &= \frac{(\mathcal{C}_2 - \hat{q}_1\tau - (1-\hat{q}_1)\mathcal{C}_2)^{\alpha} - (\mathcal{C}_2 - \hat{q}_1^{-1}\tau - (1-\hat{q}_1^{-1})\mathcal{C}_2)^{\alpha}}{(\hat{q}_1^{-1} - \hat{q}_1)(\mathcal{C}_2 - \tau)} \\ &= \frac{\hat{q}_1^{\alpha}(\mathcal{C}_2-\tau)^{\alpha} - \hat{q}_1^{-\alpha}(\mathcal{C}_2-\tau)^{\alpha}}{(\hat{q}_1^{-1} - \hat{q}_1)(\mathcal{C}_2 - \tau)} \\ &= \frac{(\hat{q}_1^{\alpha} - \hat{q}_1^{-\alpha})}{\hat{q}_1^{-1} - \hat{q}_1}(\mathcal{C}_2-\tau)^{\alpha-1}.\end{aligned}$$

Now, we discuss the algebraic properties of ${}^{\mathcal{C}_2}D^{s}_{\hat{q}_1}$.

Theorem 3. *Suppose that* $\mathcal{Z}, \mathcal{G} : J \to \mathbb{R}$ *is a right quantum symmetric differentiable mapping, then*

1. ${}^{\mathcal{C}_2}D^{s}_{\hat{q}_1}[m\mathcal{Z}(\tau) + n\mathcal{G}(\tau)] = m\,{}^{\mathcal{C}_2}D^{s}_{\hat{q}_1}\mathcal{Z}(\tau) + n\,{}^{\mathcal{C}_2}D^{s}_{\hat{q}_1}\mathcal{G}(\tau)$.
2. ${}^{\mathcal{C}_2}D^{s}_{\hat{q}_1}[\mathcal{Z}(\tau)\mathcal{G}(\tau)] = \mathcal{G}(\hat{q}_1\tau + (1-\hat{q}_1)\mathcal{C}_2)\,{}^{\mathcal{C}_2}D^{s}_{\hat{q}_1}\mathcal{Z}(\tau) + \mathcal{Z}(\hat{q}_1^{-1}\tau + (1-\hat{q}_1^{-1})\mathcal{C}_2)\,{}^{\mathcal{C}_2}D^{s}_{\hat{q}_1}\mathcal{G}(\tau)$.
   or,
   ${}^{\mathcal{C}_2}D^{s}_{\hat{q}_1}[\mathcal{Z}(\tau)\mathcal{G}(\tau)] = \mathcal{Z}(\hat{q}_1\tau + (1-\hat{q}_1)\mathcal{C}_2)\,{}^{\mathcal{C}_2}D^{s}_{\hat{q}_1}\mathcal{G}(\tau) + \mathcal{G}(\hat{q}_1^{-1}\tau + (1-\hat{q}_1^{-1})\mathcal{C}_2)\,{}^{\mathcal{C}_2}D^{s}_{\hat{q}_1}\mathcal{Z}(\tau)$.
3. ${}^{\mathcal{C}_2}D^{s}_{\hat{q}_1}\left[\frac{\mathcal{Z}(\tau)}{\mathcal{G}(\tau)}\right] = \frac{\mathcal{G}(\hat{q}_1\tau+(1-\hat{q}_1)\mathcal{C}_2)\,{}^{\mathcal{C}_2}D^{s}_{\hat{q}_1}\mathcal{Z}(\tau) - \mathcal{Z}(\hat{q}_1\tau+(1-\hat{q}_1)\mathcal{C}_2)\,{}^{\mathcal{C}_2}D^{s}_{\hat{q}_1}\mathcal{G}(\tau)}{\mathcal{G}(\hat{q}_1^{-1}\tau+(1-\hat{q}_1^{-1})\mathcal{C}_2)\mathcal{G}(\hat{q}_1\tau+(1-\hat{q}_1)\mathcal{C}_2)}$,
   where $\mathcal{G}(\hat{q}_1^{-1}\tau + (1-\hat{q}_1^{-1})\mathcal{C}_2)\mathcal{G}(\hat{q}_1\tau + (1-\hat{q}_1)\mathcal{C}_2) \neq 0$.

Proof. We omit the proof for interested readers. □

Based on the right symmetric quantum derivative, we construct the quantum symmetric definite integral. For this purpose, we define a new shifting operator

$$E_{\hat{q}_1,s}\mathcal{Z}(\tau) = \mathcal{Z}(\hat{q}_1\tau + (1-\hat{q}_1)\mathcal{C}_2)$$

Additionally,

$$E^{s}_{\hat{q}_1^{-1},s}\mathcal{Z}(\tau) = \mathcal{Z}(\hat{q}_1^{-1}\tau + (1-\hat{q}_1^{-1})\mathcal{C}_2)$$

Similarly,

$$\begin{aligned}E^{2}_{\hat{q}_1,s} &= E_{\hat{q}_1,s}(E_{\hat{q}_1,s}\mathcal{Z}(\tau)) \\ &= E_{\hat{q}_1,s}(\mathcal{Z}(\hat{q}_1\tau + (1-\hat{q}_1)\mathcal{C}_2)) \\ &= \mathcal{Z}(\hat{q}_1(\hat{q}_1\tau + (1-\hat{q}_1)\mathcal{C}_2) + (1-\hat{q}_1)\mathcal{C}_2) \\ &= \mathcal{Z}(\hat{q}_1^{2}\tau + (1-\hat{q}_1^{2})\mathcal{C}_2).\end{aligned}$$

Applying mathematical induction, we gain

$$E^{n}_{\hat{q}_1,s}\mathcal{Z}(\tau) = \mathcal{Z}(\hat{q}_1^{n}\tau + (1-\hat{q}_1^{n})\mathcal{C}_2).$$

Moreover, we note that

$$\begin{aligned}&E_{\hat{q}_1,s}E_{\hat{q}_1^{-1},s}\mathcal{Z}(\tau) = \mathcal{Z}(\hat{q}_1^{-1}\tau + (1-\hat{q}_1^{-1})\mathcal{C}_2) \\ &= \mathcal{Z}(\hat{q}_1(\hat{q}_1^{-1}\tau + (1-\hat{q}_1^{-1})\mathcal{C}_2) + (1-\hat{q}_1)\mathcal{C}_2) \\ &= \mathcal{Z}(\tau)\end{aligned} \tag{2}$$

From (2), we have

$$E_{\hat{q}_1^{-1},s} = \frac{1}{E_{\hat{q}_1,s}}.$$

Utilizing this fact, the notion of the right quantum symmetric derivative can be transformed as:

$$\mathcal{G}(\tau) = \frac{(E_{\hat{q}_1^{-1},s} - E_{\hat{q}_1,s})\mathcal{Z}(\tau)}{(\hat{q}_1^{-1} - \hat{q}_1)(\tau - \mathcal{C}_2)}$$

Then right quantum symmetric can be defined as:

$$\begin{aligned}
\mathcal{Z}(\tau) &= \frac{\mathcal{G}(\tau)(\hat{q}_1^{-1} - \hat{q}_1)(\tau - \mathcal{C}_2)}{E_{\hat{q}_1^{-1},s} - E_{\hat{q}_1,s}} \\
&= \frac{\mathcal{G}(\tau)(\hat{q}_1^{-1} - \hat{q}_1)(\tau - \mathcal{C}_2)E_{\hat{q}_1,s}}{1 - E^2_{\hat{q}_1,s}} \\
&= (\hat{q}_1^{-1} - \hat{q}_1)E_{\hat{q}_1,s}(1 - E^2_{\hat{q}_1,s})^{-1}(\tau - \mathcal{C}_2)\mathcal{G}(\tau) \\
&= (\hat{q}_1^{-1} - \hat{q}_1)(E_{\hat{q}_1,s} + E^3_{\hat{q}_1,s} + E^5_{\hat{q}_1,s} + \ldots)(\tau - \mathcal{C}_2)\mathcal{G}(\tau) \\
&= (\hat{q}_1^{-1} - \hat{q}_1)\sum_{n=0}^{\infty} E^{2n+1}_{\hat{q}_1,s}(\tau - \mathcal{C}_2)\mathcal{G}(\tau) \\
&= (\hat{q}_1^{-1} - \hat{q}_1)\sum_{n=0}^{\infty} (\hat{q}_1^{2n+1}\tau + (1 - \hat{q}_1^{2n+1})\mathcal{C}_2 - \mathcal{C}_2)\mathcal{G}(\hat{q}_1^{2n+1}\tau + (1 - \hat{q}_1^{2n+1})\mathcal{C}_2) \\
&= (\hat{q}_1^{-1} - \hat{q}_1)(\tau - \mathcal{C}_2)\sum_{n=0}^{\infty} \hat{q}_1^{2n+1}\mathcal{G}(\hat{q}_1^{2n+1}\tau + (1 - \hat{q}_1^{2n+1})\mathcal{C}_2) \\
&= (1 - \hat{q}_1^2)(\tau - \mathcal{C}_2)\sum_{n=0}^{\infty} \hat{q}_1^{2n}\mathcal{G}(\hat{q}_1^{2n+1}\tau + (1 - \hat{q}_1^{2n+1})\mathcal{C}_2).
\end{aligned}$$

Our next definition is the definite right quantum symmetric integral operator.

Definition 6. *Assume that* $\mathcal{Z} : J \to \mathbb{R}$ *is a continuous mapping, then*

$$\begin{aligned}
\int_{\mathcal{C}_1}^{\mathcal{C}_2} \mathcal{Z}(\tau)^{\mathcal{C}_2} d^s_{\hat{q}_1}\tau &= (\mathcal{C}_2 - \mathcal{C}_1)(\hat{q}_1^{-1} - \hat{q}_1)\sum_{n=0}^{\infty} \hat{q}_1^{2n+1}\mathcal{Z}(\hat{q}_1^{2n+1}\mathcal{C}_1 + (1 - \hat{q}_1^{2n+1})\mathcal{C}_2) \\
&= (\mathcal{C}_2 - \mathcal{C}_1)(1 - \hat{q}_1^2)\sum_{n=0}^{\infty} \hat{q}_1^{2n}\mathcal{Z}(\hat{q}_1^{2n+1}\mathcal{C}_1 + (1 - \hat{q}_1^{2n+1})\mathcal{C}_2).
\end{aligned}$$

Clearly, a mapping is said to be right quantum symmetric integrable if $\sum_{n=0}^{\infty} \hat{q}_1^{2n+1}\mathcal{Z}(\hat{q}_1^{2n+1}\mathcal{C}_1 + (1 - \hat{q}_1^{2n+1})\mathcal{C}_2)$ converges.

Further, we explore some fundamental properties of both right and left quantum symmetric integrals.

Theorem 4. *Assume that* $\mathcal{Z} : J \to \mathbb{R}$ *is a continuous mapping and* $m_1, n_1 \in \mathbb{R}$, *then*

1. $\int_{\mathcal{C}_1}^{\mathcal{C}_2} [m_1\mathcal{Z}(\tau) + n_1\mathcal{G}(\tau)]_{\mathcal{C}_1} d^s_{\hat{q}_1}\tau = m_1\int_{\mathcal{C}_1}^{\mathcal{C}_2} \mathcal{Z}(\tau)_{\mathcal{C}_1} d^s_{\hat{q}_1}\tau + n_1\int_{\mathcal{C}_1}^{\mathcal{C}_2} \mathcal{G}(\tau)_{\mathcal{C}_1} d^s_{\hat{q}_1}\tau.$
2. $\int_0^1 \mathcal{Z}(\tau\mathcal{C}_2 + (1 - \tau)\mathcal{C}_1) d^s_{\hat{q}_1}\tau = \frac{1}{\mathcal{C}_2 - \mathcal{C}_1}\int_{\mathcal{C}_1}^{\mathcal{C}_2} \mathcal{Z}(u)_{\mathcal{C}_1} d^s_{\hat{q}_1}u.$
3. $\int_{\mathcal{C}_1}^{t} {}_{\mathcal{C}_1}D^s_{\hat{q}_1}\mathcal{Z}(u)_{\mathcal{C}_1} d^s_{\hat{q}_1}u = \mathcal{Z}(t)$
4. ${}_{\mathcal{C}_1}D^s_{\hat{q}_1}\int_{\mathcal{C}_1}^{t} \mathcal{Z}(u)_{\mathcal{C}_1} d^s_{\hat{q}_1}u = \mathcal{Z}(t)$
5. $\int_e^{\mathcal{C}_2} {}_{\mathcal{C}_1}D^s_{\hat{q}_1}\mathcal{Z}(\tau)_{\mathcal{C}_1} d^s_{\hat{q}_1}\tau = \mathcal{Z}(\mathcal{C}_2) - \mathcal{Z}(e), e \in (\mathcal{C}_1, \mathcal{C}_2).$

Proof. From the definition of the right quantum symmetric integral, we have

$$\int_{C_1}^{C_2}[m_1\mathcal{Z}(\tau)+n_1\mathcal{G}(\tau)]_{C_1}d^s_{\hat{q}_1}\tau$$
$$=(C_2-C_1)(1-\hat{q}_1^2)\sum_{n=0}^{\infty}\hat{q}_1^{2n}[m_1\mathcal{Z}((\hat{q}_1^{2n+1}\tau+(1-\hat{q}_1^{2n+1})C_1))+n_1\mathcal{G}((\hat{q}_1^{2n+1}\tau+(1-\hat{q}_1^{2n+1})C_1))]$$
$$=m_1(C_2-C_1)(1-\hat{q}_1^2)\sum_{n=0}^{\infty}\hat{q}_1^{2n}\mathcal{Z}((\hat{q}_1^{2n+1}\tau+(1-\hat{q}_1^{2n+1})C_1))$$
$$+n_1(C_2-C_1)(1-\hat{q}_1^2)\sum_{n=0}^{\infty}\hat{q}_1^{2n}\mathcal{G}((\hat{q}_1^{2n+1}\tau+(1-\hat{q}_1^{2n+1})C_1))$$
$$=m_1\int_{C_1}^{C_2}\mathcal{Z}(\tau)_{C_1}d^s_{\hat{q}_1}\tau+n_1\int_{C_1}^{C_2}\mathcal{G}(\tau)_{C_1}d^s_{\hat{q}_1}\tau.$$

For the second property, we again consider the definition of the right symmetric quantum integral,

$$\int_0^1\mathcal{Z}(\tau C_2+(1-\tau)C_1)d^s_{\hat{q}_1}\tau$$
$$=(1-\hat{q}_1^2)\sum_{n=0}^{\infty}\hat{q}_1^{2n}\mathcal{Z}(\hat{q}_1^{2n+1}C_2+(1-\hat{q}_1^{2n+1})C_1)$$
$$=\frac{1}{C_2-C_1}\int_{C_1}^{C_2}\mathcal{Z}(u)_{C_1}d^s_{\hat{q}_1}u.$$

For the third property, we consider Definitions 3 and 4, then

$$\int_{C_1}^{t}{}_{C_1}D^s_{\hat{q}_1}\mathcal{Z}(u)_{C_1}d^s_{\hat{q}_1}u$$
$$=\int_{C_1}^{t}\left[\frac{\mathcal{Z}(\hat{q}_1^{-1}u+(1-\hat{q}_1^{-1})C_1)-\mathcal{Z}(\hat{q}_1u+(1-\hat{q}_1)C_1)}{(\hat{q}_1^{-1}-\hat{q}_1)(u-C_1)}\right]_{C_1}d^s_{\hat{q}_1}u$$
$$=\sum_{n=0}^{\infty}\frac{(t-C_1)\hat{q}_1^{2n+1}}{(\hat{q}_1^{2n+1}t+(1-\hat{q}_1^{2n+1})C_1)-C_1}\Big[\mathcal{Z}\Big(\hat{q}_1^{-1}(\hat{q}_1^{2n+1}t+(1-\hat{q}_1^{2n+1})C_1)+(1-\hat{q}_1^{-1})C_1\Big)$$
$$-\mathcal{Z}\Big(\hat{q}_1(\hat{q}_1^{2n+1}t+(1-\hat{q}_1^{2n+1})C_1)+(1-\hat{q}_1)C_1\Big)\Big]$$
$$=\sum_{n=0}^{\infty}\mathcal{Z}\Big(\hat{q}_1^{2n}t+(1-\hat{q}_1^{2n})C_1\Big)-\sum_{n=0}^{\infty}\mathcal{Z}\Big(\hat{q}_1^{2n+2}t+(1-\hat{q}_1^{2n+2})C_1\Big)$$
$$=\sum_{n=0}^{\infty}\mathcal{Z}\Big(\hat{q}_1^{2n}t+(1-\hat{q}_1^{2n})C_1\Big)-\sum_{n=1}^{\infty}\mathcal{Z}\Big(\hat{q}_1^{2n}t+(1-\hat{q}_1^{2n})C_1\Big)$$
$$=\mathcal{Z}(t).$$

Again, we consider the Definitions 3 and 4, then

$${}_{C_1}D^s_{\hat{q}_1}\int_{C_1}^{t}\mathcal{Z}(u)^{C_2}d^s_{\hat{q}_1}u$$
$$={}_{C_1}D^s_{\hat{q}_1}\left[(\hat{q}_1^{-1}-\hat{q}_1)(t-C_1)\sum_{n=0}^{\infty}\hat{q}_1^{2n+1}\mathcal{Z}(\hat{q}_1^{2n+1}t+(1-\hat{q}_1^{2n+1})C_1)\right]$$
$$=\frac{(\hat{q}_1^{-1}t+(1-\hat{q}_1^{-1})C_1-C_1)\sum_{n=0}^{\infty}\hat{q}_1^{2n+1}\mathcal{Z}(\hat{q}_1^{2n+1}(\hat{q}_1^{-1}t+(1-\hat{q}_1^{-1})C_1)+(1-\hat{q}_1^{2n+1})C_1)}{(t-C_1)}$$
$$-\frac{(\hat{q}_1t+(1-\hat{q}_1)C_1-C_1)\sum_{n=0}^{\infty}\hat{q}_1^{2n+1}\mathcal{Z}(\hat{q}_1^{2n+1}(\hat{q}_1t+(1-\hat{q}_1)C_1)+(1-\hat{q}_1^{2n+1})C_1)}{(t-C_1)}$$
$$=\sum_{n=0}^{\infty}\hat{q}_1^{2n}\mathcal{Z}(\hat{q}_1^{2n}t+(1-\hat{q}_1^{2n})C_1)-\sum_{n=0}^{\infty}\hat{q}_1^{2n+2}\mathcal{Z}(\hat{q}_1^{2n+2}t+(1-\hat{q}_1^{2n+2})C_1)$$
$$=\sum_{n=0}^{\infty}\hat{q}_1^{2n}\mathcal{Z}(\hat{q}_1^{2n}t+(1-\hat{q}_1^{2n})C_1)-\sum_{n=1}^{\infty}\hat{q}_1^{2n}\mathcal{Z}(\hat{q}_1^{2n}t+(1-\hat{q}_1^{2n})C_1)$$
$$=\mathcal{Z}(t).$$

Now we prove our last property by using simple facts,

$$\int_{e}^{\mathcal{C}_2} {}_{\mathcal{C}_1}D^{s}_{\hat{q}_1}\mathcal{Z}(\tau)_{\mathcal{C}_1}\mathrm{d}^{s}_{\hat{q}_1}\tau = \int_{0}^{\mathcal{C}_2} {}_{\mathcal{C}_1}D^{s}_{\hat{q}_1}\mathcal{Z}(\tau)_0\mathrm{d}^{s}_{\hat{q}_1}\tau - \int_{0}^{e} {}_{\mathcal{C}_1}D^{s}_{\hat{q}_1}\mathcal{Z}(\tau)_0\mathrm{d}^{s}_{\hat{q}_1}\tau$$
$$= \mathcal{Z}(\mathcal{C}_2) - \mathcal{Z}(e).$$

Hence the result is achieved. □

Theorem 5. *Assume that $\mathcal{Z},\mathcal{G} : J \to \mathbb{R}$ be a continuous mapping and $m,n \in \mathbb{R}$, then*

1. $\int_{\mathcal{C}_1}^{\mathcal{C}_2} [m\mathcal{Z}(\tau) + n\mathcal{G}(\tau)]^{\mathcal{C}_2}d^{s}_{\hat{q}_1}\tau = m\int_{\mathcal{C}_1}^{\mathcal{C}_2} \mathcal{Z}(\tau)^{\mathcal{C}_2}d^{s}_{\hat{q}_1}\tau + n\int_{\mathcal{C}_1}^{\mathcal{C}_2} \mathcal{G}(\tau)^{\mathcal{C}_2}d^{s}_{\hat{q}_1}\tau.$
2. $\int_{0}^{1} \mathcal{Z}(\tau\mathcal{C}_2 + (1-\tau)\mathcal{C}_1)^{1}d^{s}_{\hat{q}_1}\tau = \frac{1}{\mathcal{C}_2-\mathcal{C}_1}\int_{\mathcal{C}_1}^{\mathcal{C}_2} \mathcal{Z}(u)^{\mathcal{C}_2}d^{s}_{\hat{q}_1}u.$
3. ${}^{\mathcal{C}_2}D^{s}_{\hat{q}_1}\int_{t}^{\mathcal{C}_2} \mathcal{Z}(u)^{\mathcal{C}_2}\mathrm{d}^{s}_{\hat{q}_1}u = -\mathcal{Z}(t)$
4. $\int_{t}^{\mathcal{C}_2} {}^{\mathcal{C}_2}D^{s}_{\hat{q}_1}\mathcal{Z}(u)_{\mathcal{C}_1}\mathrm{d}^{s}_{\hat{q}_1}u = -\mathcal{Z}(t)$
5. $\int_{e}^{\mathcal{C}_2} {}^{\mathcal{C}_2}D^{s}_{\hat{q}_1}\mathcal{Z}(\tau)_{\mathcal{C}_1}d^{s}_{\hat{q}_1}\tau = \mathcal{Z}(\mathcal{C}_2) - \mathcal{Z}(e).$
6. $\int_{\mathcal{C}_1}^{c} f(\hat{q}_1^{-1}\tau + (1-\hat{q}_1^{-1})\mathcal{C}_2)^{\mathcal{C}_2}D^{s}_{\hat{q}_1}\mathcal{G}(\tau)\,{}^{\mathcal{C}_2}d^{s}_{\hat{q}_1}\tau$
   $= \mathcal{Z}(c)\mathcal{G}(c) - \mathcal{Z}(\mathcal{C}_1)\mathcal{G}(\mathcal{C}_1) - \int_{\mathcal{C}_1}^{c} g(\hat{q}_1\tau + (1-\hat{q}_1\tau)\mathcal{C}_2)^{\mathcal{C}_2}D^{s}_{\hat{q}_1}\mathcal{Z}(\tau)\,{}^{\mathcal{C}_2}d^{s}_{\hat{q}_1}\tau.$

Proof. The proofs of Properties 1 and 2 are straightforward from Definition 6.
Now we prove the third property,

$$\int_{0}^{1} \mathcal{Z}(\tau\mathcal{C}_2 + (1-\tau)\mathcal{C}_1)^{1}\mathrm{d}^{s}_{\hat{q}_1}\tau$$
$$= (\hat{q}_1^{-1} - \hat{q}_1)\sum_{n=0}^{\infty}\hat{q}_1^{2n+1}\mathcal{Z}((1-\hat{q}_1^{2n+1})\mathcal{C}_2 + \hat{q}_1^{2n+1}\mathcal{C}_1)$$
$$= \frac{1}{\mathcal{C}_2 - \mathcal{C}_1}\int_{\mathcal{C}_1}^{\mathcal{C}_2} \mathcal{Z}(u)^{\mathcal{C}_2}\mathrm{d}^{s}_{\hat{q}_1}u.$$

For the fourth property, we consider Definitions 5 and 6, then

$$\int_{t}^{\mathcal{C}_2} {}^{\mathcal{C}_2}D^{s}_{\hat{q}_1}\mathcal{Z}(u)^{\mathcal{C}_2}\mathrm{d}^{s}_{\hat{q}_1}u$$
$$= \int_{t}^{\mathcal{C}_2}\left[\frac{\mathcal{Z}(\hat{q}_1^{-1}u + (1-\hat{q}_1^{-1})\mathcal{C}_2) - \mathcal{Z}(\hat{q}_1u + (1-\hat{q}_1)\mathcal{C}_2)}{(\hat{q}_1^{-1} - \hat{q}_1)(u - \mathcal{C}_2)}\right]{}^{\mathcal{C}_2}\mathrm{d}^{s}_{\hat{q}_1}u$$
$$= \sum_{n=0}^{\infty}\frac{(\mathcal{C}_2 - t)\hat{q}_1^{2n+1}}{(\hat{q}_1^{2n+1}t + (1-\hat{q}_1^{2n+1})\mathcal{C}_2) - \mathcal{C}_2}\Big[\mathcal{Z}\Big(\hat{q}_1^{-1}(\hat{q}_1^{2n+1}t + (1-\hat{q}_1^{2n+1})\mathcal{C}_2) + (1-\hat{q}_1^{-1})\mathcal{C}_2\Big)$$
$$-\mathcal{Z}\Big(\hat{q}_1(\hat{q}_1^{2n+1}t + (1-\hat{q}_1^{2n+1})\mathcal{C}_2) + (1-\hat{q}_1)\mathcal{C}_2\Big)\Big]$$
$$= \sum_{n=0}^{\infty}\mathcal{Z}\Big(\hat{q}_1^{2n+2}t + (1-\hat{q}_1^{2n+2})\mathcal{C}_2\Big) - \sum_{n=0}^{\infty}\mathcal{Z}\Big(\hat{q}_1^{2n}t + (1-\hat{q}_1^{2n})\mathcal{C}_2\Big)$$
$$= \sum_{n=1}^{\infty}\mathcal{Z}\Big(\hat{q}_1^{2n}t + (1-\hat{q}_1^{2n})\mathcal{C}_2\Big) - \sum_{n=0}^{\infty}\mathcal{Z}\Big(\hat{q}_1^{2n}t + (1-\hat{q}_1^{2n})\mathcal{C}_2\Big)$$
$$= -\mathcal{Z}(t).$$

Again, we consider Definitions 5 and 6, then

$$
\begin{aligned}
&{}^{\mathcal{C}_2}D^{s}_{\hat{q}_1}\int_t^{\mathcal{C}_2}\mathcal{Z}(u)^{\mathcal{C}_2}d^{s}_{\hat{q}_1}u\\
&={}^{\mathcal{C}_2}D^{s}_{\hat{q}_1}\left[(\hat{q}_1^{-1}-\hat{q}_1)(\mathcal{C}_2-t)\sum_{n=0}^{\infty}\hat{q}_1^{2n+1}\mathcal{Z}(\hat{q}_1^{2n+1}t+(1-\hat{q}_1^{2n+1})\mathcal{C}_2)\right]\\
&=\frac{(\mathcal{C}_2-\hat{q}_1^{-1}t-(1-\hat{q}_1^{-1})\mathcal{C}_2)\sum_{n=0}^{\infty}\hat{q}_1^{2n+1}\mathcal{Z}(\hat{q}_1^{2n+1}(\hat{q}_1^{-1}t+(1-\hat{q}_1^{-1})\mathcal{C}_2)+(1-\hat{q}_1^{2n+1})\mathcal{C}_2)}{(t-\mathcal{C}_2)}\\
&-\frac{(\mathcal{C}_2-\hat{q}_1t-(1-\hat{q}_1)\mathcal{C}_1)\sum_{n=0}^{\infty}\hat{q}_1^{2n+1}\mathcal{Z}(\hat{q}_1^{2n+1}(\hat{q}_1t+(1-\hat{q}_1)\mathcal{C}_2)+(1-\hat{q}_1^{2n+1})\mathcal{C}_2)}{(t-\mathcal{C}_2)}\\
&=\sum_{n=0}^{\infty}\hat{q}_1^{2n+2}\mathcal{Z}(\hat{q}_1^{2n+2}t+(1-\hat{q}_1^{2n+2})\mathcal{C}_2)-\sum_{n=0}^{\infty}\hat{q}_1^{2n}\mathcal{Z}(\hat{q}_1^{2n}t+(1-\hat{q}_1^{2n})\mathcal{C}_2)\\
&=\sum_{n=1}^{\infty}\hat{q}_1^{2n}\mathcal{Z}(\hat{q}_1^{2n}t+(1-\hat{q}_1^{2n})\mathcal{C}_2)-\sum_{n=0}^{\infty}\hat{q}_1^{2n}\mathcal{Z}(\hat{q}_1^{2n}t+(1-\hat{q}_1^{2n})\mathcal{C}_2)\\
&=-\mathcal{Z}(t).
\end{aligned}
$$

Now lastly, we prove the integration by parts formula. For this purpose, we consider the product rule property, which is proved in Theorem 4.

$$
{}^{\mathcal{C}_2}D^{s}_{\hat{q}_1}[\mathcal{Z}(\tau)\mathcal{G}(\tau)]=\mathcal{G}(\hat{q}_1\tau+(1-\hat{q}_1)\mathcal{C}_2)^{\mathcal{C}_2}D^{s}_{\hat{q}_1}\mathcal{Z}(\tau)+\mathcal{Z}(\hat{q}_1^{-1}\tau+(1-\hat{q}_1^{-1})\mathcal{C}_2)^{\mathcal{C}_2}D^{s}_{\hat{q}_1}\mathcal{G}(\tau)
$$

Applying the right quantum symmetric integral operator on the above expression with respect to τ over $[\mathcal{C}_1,c]\subset[\mathcal{C}_1,\mathcal{C}_2]$, then

$$
\begin{aligned}
&\int_{\mathcal{C}_1}^{\mathcal{C}_2}D^{s}_{\hat{q}_1}[\mathcal{Z}(\tau)\mathcal{G}(\tau)]\,{}^{\mathcal{C}_2}d^{s}_{\hat{q}_1}\tau\\
&=\int_{\mathcal{C}_1}^{c}g(\hat{q}_1\tau+(1-\hat{q}_1)\mathcal{C}_2)^{\mathcal{C}_2}D^{s}_{\hat{q}_1}\mathcal{Z}(\tau)\,{}^{\mathcal{C}_2}d^{s}_{\hat{q}_1}\tau+\int_{\mathcal{C}_1}^{c}f(\hat{q}_1^{-1}\tau+(1-\hat{q}_1^{-1})\mathcal{C}_2)^{\mathcal{C}_2}D^{s}_{\hat{q}_1}\mathcal{G}(\tau)\,{}^{\mathcal{C}_2}d^{s}_{\hat{q}_1}\tau.
\end{aligned}
$$

This implies that

$$
\begin{aligned}
&\int_{\mathcal{C}_1}^{c}f(\hat{q}_1^{-1}\tau+(1-\hat{q}_1^{-1})\mathcal{C}_2)^{\mathcal{C}_2}D^{s}_{\hat{q}_1}\mathcal{G}(\tau)\,{}^{\mathcal{C}_2}d^{s}_{\hat{q}_1}\tau\\
&=\mathcal{Z}(c)\mathcal{G}(c)-\mathcal{Z}(\mathcal{C}_1)\mathcal{G}(\mathcal{C}_1)-\int_{\mathcal{C}_1}^{c}g(\hat{q}_1\tau+(1-\hat{q}_1)\mathcal{C}_2)^{\mathcal{C}_2}D^{s}_{\hat{q}_1}\mathcal{Z}(\tau)\,{}^{\mathcal{C}_2}d^{s}_{\hat{q}_1}\tau.
\end{aligned}
$$

Hence, the result is acquired. □

Lemma 1. *For $\alpha\in\mathbb{R}-\{-1\}$, then*

$$
\int_{\mathcal{C}_1}^{\tau}(u-\mathcal{C}_1)^{\alpha}\,{}_{\mathcal{C}_1}d^{s}_{\hat{q}_1}u=\left(\frac{\hat{q}_1^{-1}-\hat{q}_1}{\hat{q}_1^{-\alpha}-\hat{q}_1^{\alpha}}\right)(\tau-\mathcal{C}_1)^{\alpha+1}.
$$

Proof. Let $\mathcal{Z}(u)=(u-\mathcal{C}_1)^{\alpha+1}$, then

$$
{}_{\mathcal{C}_1}D^{s}_{\hat{q}_1}\mathcal{Z}(u)=\left(\frac{\hat{q}_1^{-(\alpha+1)}-\hat{q}_1^{\alpha+1}}{\hat{q}_1^{-1}-\hat{q}_1}\right)(\tau-\mathcal{C}_1)^{\alpha}
$$

Now applying the left symmetric integral operator with respect to u over $[\mathcal{C}_1,\tau]$, then we acquired our desired outcome. □

Lemma 2. *For* $\alpha \in \mathbb{R} - \{-1\}$, *then*

$$\int_{\tau}^{C_2} (C_2 - u)^{\alpha}\, {}^{C_2}d^s_{\hat{q}_1} u = \left(\frac{\hat{q}_1 - \hat{q}_1^{-1}}{\hat{q}_1^{-\alpha} - \hat{q}_1^{\alpha}}\right)(C_2 - \tau)^{\alpha+1}.$$

Proof. Let $\mathcal{Z}(u) = (C_2 - u)^{\alpha+1}$, then

$${}^{C_2}D^s_{\hat{q}_1} \mathcal{Z}(u) = \left(\frac{\hat{q}_1^{-(\alpha+1)} - \hat{q}_1^{\alpha+1}}{\hat{q}_1^{-1} - \hat{q}_1}\right)(C_2 - u)^{\alpha}$$

Now, by applying the right quantum symmetric integral operator with respect to u over $[\tau, C_2]$, we have acquired our desired outcome. □

Now we give the quantum symmetric analogue of Young's inequality.

Theorem 6. *For* $C_1, C_2 > 0$ *and* $\frac{1}{p} + \frac{1}{r} = 1$ *with* $p, \hat{q}_1 > 1$, *then*

$$C_1 C_2 \leq \frac{C_1{}^p}{[p]_{\hat{q}_1,s}} + \frac{C_2{}^r}{[r]_{\hat{q}_1,s}}.$$

Proof. Consider $y = x^{p-1}$ and $x = y^{\frac{1}{p-1}}$ for $p > 1$ and $\frac{1}{p} + \frac{1}{r} = 1$, let us draw the graph of $y = x^{p-1}$ as shown in Figure 1,

$$s_1 = \int_0^{C_1} x^{p-1}\, {}_0d^s_{\hat{q}_1} x = \frac{C_1{}^p}{[p]_{\hat{q}_1,s}}.$$

And

$$s_2 = \int_0^{C_2} y^{\frac{1}{p-1}}\, {}_0d^s_{\hat{q}_1} y = \frac{C_2{}^r}{[r]_{\hat{q}_1,s}}.$$

According to the graph, we have

$$C_1 C_2 \leq s_1 + s_2 = \frac{C_1{}^p}{[p]_{\hat{q}_1,s}} + \frac{C_2{}^r}{[r]_{\hat{q}_1,s}}.$$

Hence, the proof is completed.

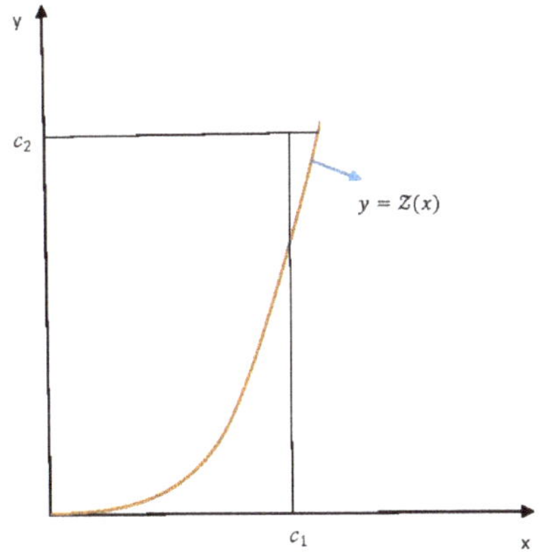

Figure 1. This figure shows the graph of $\mathcal{Z}(x) = x^{p-1}$.

□

Theorem 7. *Let $x \in [\mathcal{C}_1, \mathcal{C}_2]$, $0 < \hat{q}_1 < 1$ and $p, r > 1$ such that $\frac{1}{p} + \frac{1}{r} = 1$, then*

$$\int_x^{\mathcal{C}_2} |\mathcal{Z}(\tau)\mathcal{G}(\tau)|^{\mathcal{C}_2} d_{\hat{q}_1}^s \tau \leq \left(\int_x^{\mathcal{C}_2} |\mathcal{Z}(\tau)|^{p\,\mathcal{C}_2} d_{\hat{q}_1}^s \tau\right)^{\frac{1}{p}} \left(\int_x^{\mathcal{C}_2} |\mathcal{G}(\tau)|^{r\,\mathcal{C}_2} d_{\hat{q}_1}^s \tau\right)^{\frac{1}{r}}.$$

Proof. Considering the Definition of the right quantum symmetric integral operator, we have

$$\begin{aligned}
&\int_x^{\mathcal{C}_2} |\mathcal{Z}(\tau)\mathcal{G}(\tau)|^{\mathcal{C}_2} d_{\hat{q}_1}^s \tau \\
&= (1-\hat{q}_1^2)(\mathcal{C}_2 - x)\sum_{n=0}^{\infty} \hat{q}_1^{2n} |\mathcal{Z}(\hat{q}_1^{2n+1}x + (1-\hat{q}_1^{2n+1})\mathcal{C}_2)\mathcal{G}(\hat{q}_1^{2n+1}x + (1-\hat{q}_1^{2n+1})\mathcal{C}_2)| \\
&\leq (1-\hat{q}_1^2)^{\frac{1}{p}+\frac{1}{r}}(\mathcal{C}_2 - x)^{\frac{1}{p}+\frac{1}{r}}\sum_{n=0}^{\infty} (\hat{q}_1^{2n})^{\frac{1}{p}+\frac{1}{r}} |\mathcal{Z}(\hat{q}_1^{2n+1}x + (1-\hat{q}_1^{2n+1})\mathcal{C}_2)| \\
&|\mathcal{G}(\hat{q}_1^{2n+1}x + (1-\hat{q}_1^{2n+1})\mathcal{C}_2)| \\
&\leq \left((1-\hat{q}_1^2)(\mathcal{C}_2 - x)\sum_{n=0}^{\infty} (\hat{q}_1^{2n}) |\mathcal{Z}(\hat{q}_1^{2n+1}x + (1-\hat{q}_1^{2n+1})\mathcal{C}_2)|^p\right)^{\frac{1}{p}} \\
&\times\left((1-\hat{q}_1^2)(\mathcal{C}_2 - x)\sum_{n=0}^{\infty} (\hat{q}_1^{2n}) |\mathcal{G}(\hat{q}_1^{2n+1}x + (1-\hat{q}_1^{2n+1})\mathcal{C}_2)|^r\right)^{\frac{1}{r}} \\
&= \left(\int_x^{\mathcal{C}_2} |\mathcal{Z}(\tau)|^{p\,\mathcal{C}_2} d_{\hat{q}_1}^s \tau\right)^{\frac{1}{p}} \left(\int_x^{\mathcal{C}_2} |\mathcal{G}(\tau)|^{r\,\mathcal{C}_2} d_{\hat{q}_1}^s \tau\right)^{\frac{1}{r}}.
\end{aligned}$$

This completes the proof. □

Theorem 8. *Assume that $\mathcal{Z}, \mathcal{G} : J \to \mathbb{R}$ are continuous mappings, then*

$$\left(\int_{\mathcal{C}_1}^{\mathcal{C}_2} |\mathcal{Z}(\tau) + \mathcal{G}(\tau)|^{p\,\mathcal{C}_2} d_{\hat{q}_1}^s \tau\right)^{\frac{1}{p}} \leq \left(\int_{\mathcal{C}_1}^{\mathcal{C}_2} |\mathcal{Z}(\tau)|^{p\,\mathcal{C}_2} d_{\hat{q}_1}^s \tau\right)^{\frac{1}{p}} \left(\int_{\mathcal{C}_1}^{\mathcal{C}_2} |\mathcal{G}(\tau)|^{p\,\mathcal{C}_2} d_{\hat{q}_1}^s \tau\right)^{\frac{1}{p}},$$

where $\frac{1}{p} + \frac{1}{r} = 1$.

Proof. From the following expression, we have

$$\begin{aligned}
&\int_{\mathcal{C}_1}^{\mathcal{C}_2} |\mathcal{Z}(\tau) + \mathcal{G}(\tau)|^{p\,\mathcal{C}_2} d_{\hat{q}_1}^s \tau \\
&= \int_{\mathcal{C}_1}^{\mathcal{C}_2} |\mathcal{Z}(\tau) + \mathcal{G}(\tau)|^{p-1} |\mathcal{Z}(\tau) + \mathcal{G}(\tau)|^{\mathcal{C}_2} d_{\hat{q}_1}^s \tau \\
&\leq \int_{\mathcal{C}_1}^{\mathcal{C}_2} |\mathcal{Z}(\tau) + \mathcal{G}(\tau)|^{p-1} |\mathcal{Z}(\tau)|^{\mathcal{C}_2} d_{\hat{q}_1}^s \tau + \int_{\mathcal{C}_1}^{\mathcal{C}_2} |\mathcal{Z}(\tau) + \mathcal{G}(\tau)|^{p-1} |\mathcal{G}(\tau)|^{\mathcal{C}_2} d_{\hat{q}_1}^s \tau.
\end{aligned}$$

Implementing the classical Hölder's inequality on the above relation

$$\begin{aligned}
&\int_{\mathcal{C}_1}^{\mathcal{C}_2} |\mathcal{Z}(\tau) + \mathcal{G}(\tau)|^{p-1} |\mathcal{Z}(\tau)|^{\mathcal{C}_2} d_{\hat{q}_1}^s \tau + \int_{\mathcal{C}_1}^{\mathcal{C}_2} |\mathcal{Z}(\tau) + \mathcal{G}(\tau)|^{p-1} |\mathcal{G}(\tau)|^{\mathcal{C}_2} d_{\hat{q}_1}^s \tau \\
&\leq \left(\int_{\mathcal{C}_1}^{\mathcal{C}_2} |\mathcal{Z}(\tau) + \mathcal{G}(\tau)|^{r(p-1)\,\mathcal{C}_2} d_{\hat{q}_1}^s \tau\right)^{\frac{1}{r}} \left(\int_{\mathcal{C}_1}^{\mathcal{C}_2} |\mathcal{Z}(\tau)|^{p\,\mathcal{C}_2} d_{\hat{q}_1}^s \tau\right)^{\frac{1}{p}} \\
&+\left(\int_{\mathcal{C}_1}^{\mathcal{C}_2} |\mathcal{Z}(\tau) + \mathcal{G}(\tau)|^{r(p-1)\,\mathcal{C}_2} d_{\hat{q}_1}^s \tau\right)^{\frac{1}{r}} \left(\int_{\mathcal{C}_1}^{\mathcal{C}_2} |\mathcal{G}(\tau)|^{p\,\mathcal{C}_2} d_{\hat{q}_1}^s \tau\right)^{\frac{1}{p}} \\
&= \left(\int_{\mathcal{C}_1}^{\mathcal{C}_2} |\mathcal{Z}(\tau) + \mathcal{G}(\tau)|^{r(p-1)\,\mathcal{C}_2} d_{\hat{q}_1}^s \tau\right)^{\frac{1}{r}} \left[\left(\int_{\mathcal{C}_1}^{\mathcal{C}_2} |\mathcal{Z}(\tau)|^{p\,\mathcal{C}_2} d_{\hat{q}_1}^s \tau\right)^{\frac{1}{p}} + \left(\int_{\mathcal{C}_1}^{\mathcal{C}_2} |\mathcal{G}(\tau)|^{p\,\mathcal{C}_2} d_{\hat{q}_1}^s \tau\right)^{\frac{1}{p}}\right].
\end{aligned}$$

After simple computations, we obtain our required result. □

Now, we give the Hermite–Hadamard's inequalities involving new quantum symmetric calculus. To prove the Hermite–Hadamard's inequalities, we draw the following Figure 2.

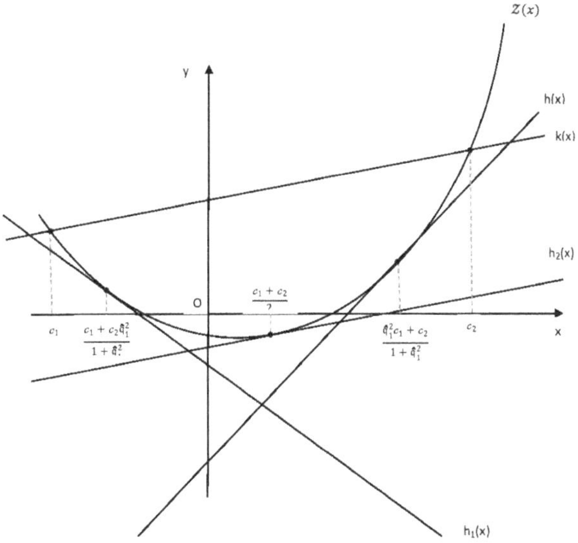

Figure 2. This figure presents the secant and tangent lines of convex mapping.

Theorem 9. *Assume that $\mathcal{Z}: J \to \mathbb{R}$ is a differentiable convex mapping on $(\mathcal{C}_1, \mathcal{C}_2)$ and $\hat{q}_1 \in (0,1)$, then*

$$\mathcal{Z}\left(\frac{\mathcal{C}_1\hat{q}_1^2+\mathcal{C}_2}{1+\hat{q}_1^2}\right) - \frac{\hat{q}_1(\mathcal{C}_2-\mathcal{C}_1)}{1+\hat{q}_1}\mathcal{Z}'\left(\frac{\mathcal{C}_1\hat{q}_1^2+\mathcal{C}_2}{1+\hat{q}_1^2}\right) \leq \frac{1}{\mathcal{C}_2-\mathcal{C}_1}\int_{\mathcal{C}_1}^{\mathcal{C}_2}\mathcal{Z}(x)^{\mathcal{C}_2}d^s_{\hat{q}_1}x$$
$$\leq \frac{\hat{q}_1\mathcal{Z}(\mathcal{C}_1)+(1+\hat{q}_1^2-\hat{q}_1)\mathcal{Z}(\mathcal{C}_2)}{1+\hat{q}_1^2}.$$

Proof. From the given assumption, $\mathcal{Z}$ is a differentiable convex mapping on $(\mathcal{C}_1, \mathcal{C}_2)$, so there exists a tangent line for point $\frac{\mathcal{C}_1\hat{q}_1^2+\mathcal{C}_2}{1+\hat{q}_1^2} \in (\mathcal{C}_1, \mathcal{C}_2)$ and the equation of the tangent line is given as:

$$h(u) = \mathcal{Z}\left(\frac{\mathcal{C}_1\hat{q}_1^2+\mathcal{C}_2}{1+\hat{q}_1^2}\right) + \mathcal{Z}'\left(\frac{\mathcal{C}_1\hat{q}_1^2+\mathcal{C}_2}{1+\hat{q}_1^2}\right)\left(u - \frac{\mathcal{C}_1\hat{q}_1^2+\mathcal{C}_2}{1+\hat{q}_1^2}\right).$$

As $\mathcal{Z}$ is convex mapping, then $h(u) \leq \mathcal{Z}(u)$. Now taking the right quantum symmetric integral on both sides of the preceding inequality, we have

$$\begin{aligned}
&\int_{\mathcal{C}_1}^{\mathcal{C}_2} h(u)\,^{\mathcal{C}_2}\mathrm{d}^s_{\hat{q}_1} u \\
&= \int_{\mathcal{C}_1}^{\mathcal{C}_2}\left[\mathcal{Z}\left(\frac{\mathcal{C}_1\hat{q}_1^2+\mathcal{C}_2}{1+\hat{q}_1^2}\right)+\mathcal{Z}'\left(\frac{\mathcal{C}_1\hat{q}_1^2+\mathcal{C}_2}{1+\hat{q}_1^2}\right)\left(u-\frac{\mathcal{C}_1\hat{q}_1^2+\mathcal{C}_2}{1+\hat{q}_1^2}\right)\right]^{\mathcal{C}_2}\mathrm{d}^s_{\hat{q}_1} u \\
&= (\mathcal{C}_2-\mathcal{C}_1)\mathcal{Z}\left(\frac{\mathcal{C}_1\hat{q}_1^2+\mathcal{C}_2}{1+\hat{q}_1^2}\right)+\mathcal{Z}'\left(\frac{\mathcal{C}_1\hat{q}_1^2+\mathcal{C}_2}{1+\hat{q}_1^2}\right)\int_{\mathcal{C}_1}^{\mathcal{C}_2}\left(u-\frac{\mathcal{C}_1\hat{q}_1^2+\mathcal{C}_2}{1+\hat{q}_1^2}\right)^{\mathcal{C}_2}\mathrm{d}^s_{\hat{q}_1} u \\
&= (\mathcal{C}_2-\mathcal{C}_1)\mathcal{Z}\left(\frac{\mathcal{C}_1\hat{q}_1^2+\mathcal{C}_2}{1+\hat{q}_1^2}\right)+\mathcal{Z}'\left(\frac{\mathcal{C}_1\hat{q}_1^2+\mathcal{C}_2}{1+\hat{q}_1^2}\right)\left(\int_{\mathcal{C}_1}^{b} u\,^{\mathcal{C}_2}\mathrm{d}^s_{\hat{q}_1} u-(\mathcal{C}_2-\mathcal{C}_1)\frac{\mathcal{C}_1\hat{q}_1^2+\mathcal{C}_2}{1+\hat{q}_1^2}\right) \\
&= (\mathcal{C}_2-\mathcal{C}_1)\mathcal{Z}\left(\frac{\mathcal{C}_1\hat{q}_1^2+\mathcal{C}_2}{1+\hat{q}_1^2}\right)+(\mathcal{C}_2-\mathcal{C}_1)\mathcal{Z}'\left(\frac{\mathcal{C}_1\hat{q}_1^2+\mathcal{C}_2}{1+\hat{q}_1^2}\right)\left(\frac{(1+\hat{q}_1^2)\mathcal{C}_2-\hat{q}_1(\mathcal{C}_2-\mathcal{C}_1)}{1+\hat{q}_1^2}-\frac{\mathcal{C}_1\hat{q}_1^2+\mathcal{C}_2}{1+\hat{q}_1^2}\right) \\
&= (\mathcal{C}_2-\mathcal{C}_1)\left[\mathcal{Z}\left(\frac{\mathcal{C}_1\hat{q}_1^2+\mathcal{C}_2}{1+\hat{q}_1^2}\right)-\mathcal{Z}'\left(\frac{\mathcal{C}_1\hat{q}_1^2+\mathcal{C}_2}{1+\hat{q}_1^2}\right)\frac{\hat{q}_1(\mathcal{C}_2-\mathcal{C}_1)}{1+\hat{q}_1^2}\right] \\
&\le \int_{\mathcal{C}_1}^{\mathcal{C}_2}\mathcal{Z}(u)\,^{\mathcal{C}_2}\mathrm{d}^s_{\hat{q}_1} u.
\end{aligned}$$

In addition, due to convexity of $\mathcal{Z}$ then secant lines $k(u)$ joining the points $(\mathcal{C}_1, \mathcal{Z}(\mathcal{C}_1))$ and $(\mathcal{C}_2, \mathcal{Z}(\mathcal{C}_2))$ always lies on or above the graph of $\mathcal{Z}$, so $\mathcal{Z}(u) \le k(u)$, where $k(u)$ is given as:

$$k(u) = \mathcal{Z}(\mathcal{C}_1) + \tfrac{\mathcal{Z}(\mathcal{C}_2)-\mathcal{Z}(\mathcal{C}_1)}{\mathcal{C}_2-\mathcal{C}_1}(u-\mathcal{C}_1), \forall u \in [\mathcal{C}_1, \mathcal{C}_2].$$

Now, implementing the right quantum symmetric integral operator, we have

$$\begin{aligned}
&\int_{\mathcal{C}_1}^{\mathcal{C}_2}\mathcal{Z}(u)\,^{\mathcal{C}_2}\mathrm{d}^s_{\hat{q}_1} u \\
&\le \int_{\mathcal{C}_1}^{b} k(u)\,^{\mathcal{C}_2}\mathrm{d}^s_{\hat{q}_1} u \\
&= \int_{\mathcal{C}_1}^{\mathcal{C}_2}\left[\mathcal{Z}(\mathcal{C}_1)+\frac{\mathcal{Z}(\mathcal{C}_2)-\mathcal{Z}(\mathcal{C}_1)}{\mathcal{C}_2-\mathcal{C}_1}(u-\mathcal{C}_1)\right]^{\mathcal{C}_2}\mathrm{d}^s_{\hat{q}_1} u \\
&= (\mathcal{C}_2-\mathcal{C}_1)\mathcal{Z}(\mathcal{C}_1)+(\mathcal{Z}(\mathcal{C}_2)-\mathcal{Z}(\mathcal{C}_1))\left(\frac{(1+\hat{q}_1^2)\mathcal{C}_2-\hat{q}_1(\mathcal{C}_2-\mathcal{C}_1)}{1+\hat{q}_1^2}-\mathcal{C}_1\right) \\
&= (\mathcal{C}_2-\mathcal{C}_1)\left[\frac{\hat{q}_1\mathcal{Z}(\mathcal{C}_1)+(1+\hat{q}_1^2-\hat{q}_1)\mathcal{Z}(\mathcal{C}_2)}{1+\hat{q}_1^2}\right].
\end{aligned} \tag{3}$$

In the following manner, we reach our desired result. □

Example 2. *We consider* $\mathcal{Z} : [0,2] \to \mathbb{R}$ *such that* $\mathcal{Z}(x) = x^2$ *is a differentiable convex functions, then applying Theorem 9 for* $\hat{q}_1 \in (0,1)$*, we have*

$$\tfrac{4}{(1+\hat{q}_1^2)^2} - \tfrac{8}{(1+\hat{q}_1)(1+\hat{q}_1^2)} \le 4 + \tfrac{4\hat{q}_1^2}{1+\hat{q}_1^2+\hat{q}_1^4} - \tfrac{8\hat{q}_1}{1+\hat{q}_1^2} \le \tfrac{4(1+\hat{q}_1^2-\hat{q}_1)}{1+\hat{q}_1^2}.$$

For $\hat{q}_1 = 0.6$*, we obtain*

$$-1.70667 < 1.5619 < 2.4.$$

For graphic visualization, we use $\hat{q}_1 \in (0,1)$ as the variable. Figure 3 gives a validation of Theorem 9.

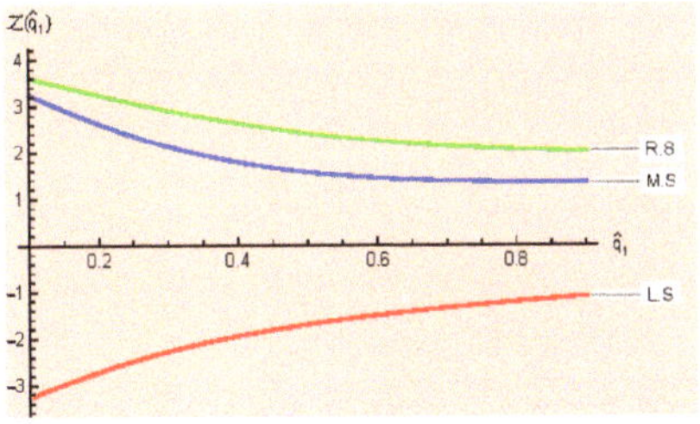

Figure 3. This figure validates the accuracy of Theorem 9.

Theorem 10. *Assume that $\mathcal{Z} : J \to \mathbb{R}$ is a differentiable convex mapping on $(\mathcal{C}_1, \mathcal{C}_2)$ and $\hat{q}_1 \in (0,1)$, then*

$$\mathcal{Z}\left(\frac{\mathcal{C}_1 + bq^2}{1+\hat{q}_1^2}\right) + \frac{(1-\hat{q}_1)(\mathcal{C}_2 - \mathcal{C}_1)}{1+\hat{q}_1^2}\mathcal{Z}'\left(\frac{\mathcal{C}_1 + bq^2}{1+\hat{q}_1^2}\right) \le \frac{1}{\mathcal{C}_2 - \mathcal{C}_1}\int_{\mathcal{C}_1}^{\mathcal{C}_2} \mathcal{Z}(x)^{\mathcal{C}_2} d^s_{\hat{q}_1} x \le \frac{\hat{q}_1 \mathcal{Z}(\mathcal{C}_1) + (1+\hat{q}_1^2 - \hat{q}_1)\mathcal{Z}(\mathcal{C}_2)}{1+\hat{q}_1^2}.$$

Proof. From the given assumption, $\mathcal{Z}$ is a differentiable convex mapping on $(\mathcal{C}_1, \mathcal{C}_2)$, so there exists a tangent line for point $\frac{\mathcal{C}_1+bq^2}{1+\hat{q}_1^2} \in (\mathcal{C}_1, \mathcal{C}_2)$ and the equation of the tangent line is given as:

$$h_1(u) = \mathcal{Z}\left(\frac{\mathcal{C}_1+bq^2}{1+\hat{q}_1^2}\right) + \mathcal{Z}'\left(\frac{\mathcal{C}_1+bq^2}{1+\hat{q}_1^2}\right)\left(u - \frac{\mathcal{C}_1+bq^2}{1+\hat{q}_1^2}\right).$$

As $\mathcal{Z}$ is convex mapping, then $h_1(u) \le \mathcal{Z}(u)$, Now, taking the right quantum symmetric integral on both sides of the preceding inequality, we have

$$\begin{aligned}
&\int_{\mathcal{C}_1}^{\mathcal{C}_2} h_1(u)^{\mathcal{C}_2} d^s_{\hat{q}_1} u \\
&= \int_{\mathcal{C}_1}^{\mathcal{C}_2}\left[\mathcal{Z}\left(\frac{\mathcal{C}_1+bq^2}{1+\hat{q}_1^2}\right) + \mathcal{Z}'\left(\frac{\mathcal{C}_1+bq^2}{1+\hat{q}_1^2}\right)\left(u - \frac{\mathcal{C}_1+bq^2}{1+\hat{q}_1^2}\right)\right]^{\mathcal{C}_2} d^s_{\hat{q}_1} u \\
&= (\mathcal{C}_2 - \mathcal{C}_1)\mathcal{Z}\left(\frac{\mathcal{C}_1+bq^2}{1+\hat{q}_1^2}\right) + \mathcal{Z}'\left(\frac{\mathcal{C}_1+bq^2}{1+\hat{q}_1^2}\right)\int_{\mathcal{C}_1}^{\mathcal{C}_2}\left(u - \frac{\mathcal{C}_1+bq^2}{1+\hat{q}_1^2}\right)^{\mathcal{C}_2} d^s_{\hat{q}_1} u \\
&= (\mathcal{C}_2 - \mathcal{C}_1)\mathcal{Z}\left(\frac{\mathcal{C}_1+bq^2}{1+\hat{q}_1^2}\right) + \mathcal{Z}'\left(\frac{\mathcal{C}_1+bq^2}{1+\hat{q}_1^2}\right)\left(\int_{\mathcal{C}_1}^{b} u^{\mathcal{C}_2} d^s_{\hat{q}_1} u - (\mathcal{C}_2 - \mathcal{C}_1)\frac{\mathcal{C}_1+bq^2}{1+\hat{q}_1^2}\right) \qquad (4)\\
&= (\mathcal{C}_2 - \mathcal{C}_1)\mathcal{Z}\left(\frac{\mathcal{C}_1+bq^2}{1+\hat{q}_1^2}\right) + (\mathcal{C}_2 - \mathcal{C}_1)\mathcal{Z}'\left(\frac{\mathcal{C}_1+bq^2}{1+\hat{q}_1^2}\right)\left(\frac{(1+\hat{q}_1^2)\mathcal{C}_2 - \hat{q}_1(\mathcal{C}_2 - \mathcal{C}_1)}{1+\hat{q}_1^2} - \frac{\mathcal{C}_1+bq^2}{1+\hat{q}_1^2}\right) \\
&= (\mathcal{C}_2 - \mathcal{C}_1)\left[\mathcal{Z}\left(\frac{\mathcal{C}_1+bq^2}{1+\hat{q}_1^2}\right) + \mathcal{Z}'\left(\frac{\mathcal{C}_1+bq^2}{1+\hat{q}_1^2}\right)\frac{(1-\hat{q}_1)(\mathcal{C}_2 - \mathcal{C}_1)}{1+\hat{q}_1^2}\right] \\
&\le \int_{\mathcal{C}_1}^{\mathcal{C}_2} \mathcal{Z}(u)^{\mathcal{C}_2} d^s_{\hat{q}_1} u.
\end{aligned}$$

Now, comparing (3) and (4), we achieve our desired result. □

Example 3. *We consider $\mathcal{Z} : [0,2] \to \mathbb{R}$ such that $\mathcal{Z}(x) = x^2$ is a differentiable convex functions, then applying on Theorem 10 for $\hat{q}_1 \in (0,1)$, we have*

$$\frac{4\hat{q}_1^4}{(1+\hat{q}_1^2)^2} + \frac{8\hat{q}_1^2(1-\hat{q}_1)}{(1+\hat{q}_1^2)^2} \le 4 + \frac{4\hat{q}_1^2}{1+\hat{q}_1^2+\hat{q}_1^4} - \frac{8\hat{q}_1}{1+\hat{q}_1^2} \le \frac{4(1+\hat{q}_1^2-\hat{q}_1)}{1+\hat{q}_1^2}.$$

For $\hat{q}_1 = 0.6$, we obtain

$$0.903114 < 1.43729 < 2.23529.$$

For graphic visualization, we take $\hat{q}_1 \in (0,1)$ as the variable. Figure 4 gives a validation of Theorem 10.

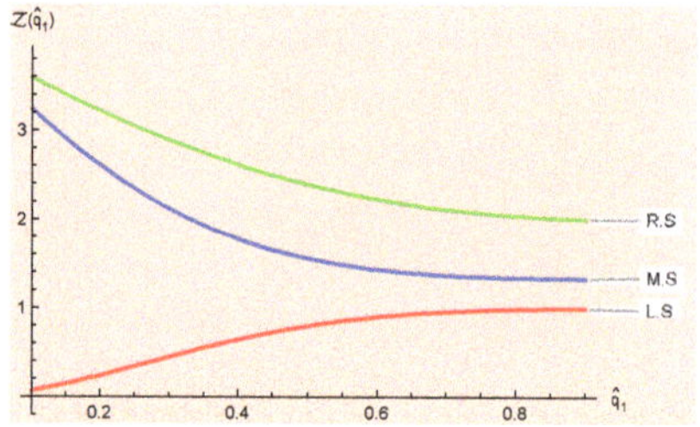

Figure 4. This figure validates the accuracy of Theorem 10.

Theorem 11. *Assume that $\mathcal{Z} : J \to \mathbb{R}$ is a differentiable convex mapping on $(\mathcal{C}_1, \mathcal{C}_2)$ and $\hat{q}_1 \in (0,1)$, then*

$$\mathcal{Z}\left(\frac{\mathcal{C}_1+\mathcal{C}_2}{2}\right) + \frac{(1+\hat{q}_1^2-2\hat{q}_1)(\mathcal{C}_2-\mathcal{C}_1)}{2(1+\hat{q}_1^2)}\mathcal{Z}'\left(\frac{\mathcal{C}_1+\mathcal{C}_2}{2}\right) \le \int_{\mathcal{C}_1}^{\mathcal{C}_2} \mathcal{Z}(x)^{\mathcal{C}_2}\mathrm{d}^s_{\hat{q}_1}x$$
$$\le \frac{\hat{q}_1\mathcal{Z}(\mathcal{C}_1) + (1+\hat{q}_1^2-\hat{q}_1)\mathcal{Z}(\mathcal{C}_2)}{1+\hat{q}_1^2}.$$

Proof. From the given assumption, $\mathcal{Z}$ is a differentiable convex mapping on $(\mathcal{C}_1, \mathcal{C}_2)$, so there exists a tangent line for point $\frac{\mathcal{C}_1+\mathcal{C}_2}{2} \in (\mathcal{C}_1, \mathcal{C}_2)$ and the equation of tangent line is given as:

$$h_2(u) = \mathcal{Z}\left(\tfrac{\mathcal{C}_1+\mathcal{C}_2}{2}\right) + \mathcal{Z}'\left(\tfrac{\mathcal{C}_1+\mathcal{C}_2}{2}\right)\left(u - \tfrac{\mathcal{C}_1+\mathcal{C}_2}{2}\right).$$

As $\mathcal{Z}$ is convex mapping, then $\mathcal{T}_1(u) \le \mathcal{Z}(u)$. Now, taking the right quantum symmetric integral on both sides of the preceding inequality, we have

$$\begin{aligned}
&\int_{\mathcal{C}_1}^{\mathcal{C}_2} h_2(u)^{\mathcal{C}_2}\mathrm{d}^s_{\hat{q}_1}u \\
&= \int_{\mathcal{C}_1}^{\mathcal{C}_2}\left[\mathcal{Z}\left(\frac{\mathcal{C}_1+\mathcal{C}_2}{2}\right) + \mathcal{Z}'\left(\frac{\mathcal{C}_1+\mathcal{C}_2}{2}\right)\left(u - \frac{\mathcal{C}_1+\mathcal{C}_2}{2}\right)\right]^{\mathcal{C}_2}\mathrm{d}^s_{\hat{q}_1}u \\
&= (\mathcal{C}_2-\mathcal{C}_1)\mathcal{Z}\left(\frac{\mathcal{C}_1+\mathcal{C}_2}{2}\right) + \mathcal{Z}'\left(\frac{\mathcal{C}_1+\mathcal{C}_2}{2}\right)\int_{\mathcal{C}_1}^{\mathcal{C}_2}\left(u - \frac{\mathcal{C}_1+\mathcal{C}_2}{2}\right)^{\mathcal{C}_2}\mathrm{d}^s_{\hat{q}_1}u \\
&= (\mathcal{C}_2-\mathcal{C}_1)\mathcal{Z}\left(\frac{\mathcal{C}_1+\mathcal{C}_2}{2}\right) + \mathcal{Z}'\left(\frac{\mathcal{C}_1+\mathcal{C}_2}{2}\right)\left(\int_{\mathcal{C}_1}^{b} u^{\mathcal{C}_2}\mathrm{d}^s_{\hat{q}_1}u - (\mathcal{C}_2-\mathcal{C}_1)\frac{\mathcal{C}_1+\mathcal{C}_2}{2}\right) \qquad (5)\\
&= (\mathcal{C}_2-\mathcal{C}_1)\mathcal{Z}\left(\frac{\mathcal{C}_1+\mathcal{C}_2}{2}\right) + (\mathcal{C}_2-\mathcal{C}_1)\mathcal{Z}'\left(\frac{\mathcal{C}_1+\mathcal{C}_2}{2}\right)\left(\frac{(1+\hat{q}_1^2)\mathcal{C}_2 - \hat{q}_1(\mathcal{C}_2-\mathcal{C}_1)}{1+\hat{q}_1^2} - \frac{\mathcal{C}_1+\mathcal{C}_2}{2}\right) \\
&= (\mathcal{C}_2-\mathcal{C}_1)\left[\mathcal{Z}\left(\frac{\mathcal{C}_1+\mathcal{C}_2}{2}\right) + \mathcal{Z}'\left(\frac{\mathcal{C}_1+\mathcal{C}_2}{2}\right)\frac{(1+\hat{q}_1^2-2\hat{q}_1)(\mathcal{C}_2-\mathcal{C}_1)}{(1+\hat{q}_1^2)2}\right] \\
&\le \int_{\mathcal{C}_1}^{\mathcal{C}_2} \mathcal{Z}(u)^{\mathcal{C}_2}\mathrm{d}^s_{\hat{q}_1}u.
\end{aligned}$$

Now, comparing (3) and (5), we achieve our desired result. □

Example 4. *We consider $\mathcal{Z} : [0,2] \to \mathbb{R}$ such that $\mathcal{Z}(x) = x^2$ is a differentiable convex function, then applying Theorem 11 for $\hat{q}_1 \in (0,1)$, we have*

$$1 + \frac{2(1+\hat{q}_1^2-2\hat{q}_1)}{(1+\hat{q}_1^2)} \le 4 + \frac{4\hat{q}_1^2}{1+\hat{q}_1^2+\hat{q}_1^4} - \frac{8\hat{q}_1}{1+\hat{q}_1^2} \le \frac{4(1+\hat{q}_1^2-\hat{q}_1)}{1+\hat{q}_1^2}.$$

For $\hat{q}_1 = 0.6$, *we obtain*

$$1.23529 < 1.43729 < 2.23529.$$

For graphical visualization, we take $\hat{q}_1 \in (0,1)$ as the variable. Figure 5 gives a validation of Theorem 11.

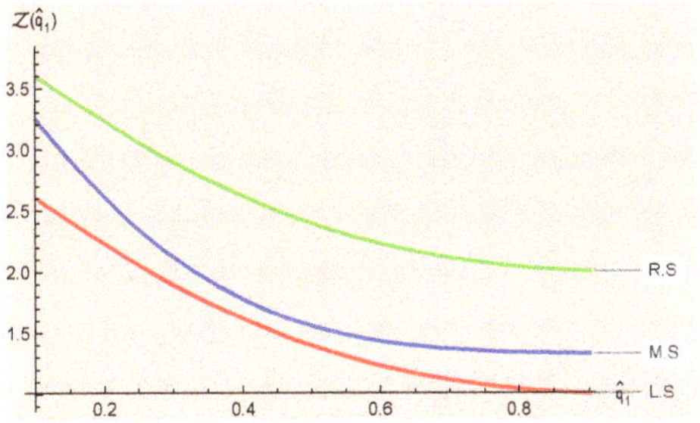

Figure 5. This figure validates the accuracy of Theorem 11.

Now we give an analytical proof of Hermite–Hadamard's inequality.

Theorem 12. *Suppose that* $\mathcal{Z} : J \to \mathbb{R}$ *is a convex mapping, then*

$$\mathcal{Z}\left(\frac{\mathcal{C}_1+\mathcal{C}_2}{2}\right) \leq \frac{1}{2(\mathcal{C}_2-\mathcal{C}_1)}\left[\int_{\mathcal{C}_1}^{\mathcal{C}_2} \mathcal{Z}(x)_{\mathcal{C}_1} d^s_{\hat{q}_1} x + \int_{\mathcal{C}_1}^{\mathcal{C}_2} \mathcal{Z}(x)^{\mathcal{C}_2} d^s_{\hat{q}_1} x\right] \leq \frac{\mathcal{Z}(\mathcal{C}_1)+\mathcal{Z}(\mathcal{C}_2)}{2}.$$

Proof. Since $\mathcal{Z}$ is a convex mapping and for $x, y \in J$ such that $x = \tau\mathcal{C}_1 + (1-\tau)\mathcal{C}_2$ and $y = (1-\tau)\mathcal{C}_1 + \tau\mathcal{C}_2$, we have

$$\mathcal{Z}\left(\frac{\mathcal{C}_1+\mathcal{C}_2}{2}\right) \leq \frac{1}{2}[\mathcal{Z}((1-\tau)\mathcal{C}_1 + \tau\mathcal{C}_2) + \mathcal{Z}(\tau\mathcal{C}_1 + (1-\tau)\mathcal{C}_2)].$$

Now, by applying the quantum symmetric integration with respect to τ over $[0,1]$, then

$$\int_0^1 \mathcal{Z}\left(\frac{\mathcal{C}_1+\mathcal{C}_2}{2}\right)_0 d^s_{\hat{q}_1} x \leq \frac{1}{2}\int_0^1 [\mathcal{Z}((1-\tau)\mathcal{C}_1 + \tau\mathcal{C}_2) + \mathcal{Z}(\tau\mathcal{C}_1 + (1-\tau)\mathcal{C}_2)]_0 d^s_{\hat{q}_1} x. \quad (6)$$

In addition, note that

$$\begin{aligned}
&\int_0^1 \mathcal{Z}((1-\tau)\mathcal{C}_1 + \tau\mathcal{C}_2)_0 d^s_{\hat{q}_1} \tau \\
&= (1-\hat{q}_1^2)\sum_{n=0}^{\infty} \hat{q}_1^{2n} \mathcal{Z}\left((1-\hat{q}_1^{2n+1})\mathcal{C}_1 + \hat{q}_1^{2n+1}\mathcal{C}_2\right) \\
&= \frac{1}{\mathcal{C}_2-\mathcal{C}_1}\int_{\mathcal{C}_1}^{\mathcal{C}_2} \mathcal{Z}(x)_{\mathcal{C}_1} d^s_{\hat{q}_1} x.
\end{aligned} \quad (7)$$

Additionally,

$$\int_0^1 \mathcal{Z}(\tau\mathcal{C}_1 + (1-\tau)\mathcal{C}_2)_0 d^s_{\hat{q}_1} = \frac{1}{\mathcal{C}_2-\mathcal{C}_1}\int_{\mathcal{C}_1}^{\mathcal{C}_2} \mathcal{Z}(x)^{\mathcal{C}_2} d^s_{\hat{q}_1} x. \quad (8)$$

Inserting the values of (7) and (8) in (4), we obtain the left inequality.

To prove the right inequality, we utilize the convexity of $\mathcal{Z}$

$$\frac{\mathcal{Z}((1-\tau)\mathcal{C}_1+\tau\mathcal{C}_2)+\mathcal{Z}(\tau\mathcal{C}_1+(1-\tau)\mathcal{C}_2)}{2} \leq \frac{\mathcal{Z}(\mathcal{C}_1)+\mathcal{Z}(\mathcal{C}_2)}{2}.$$

By implementing the quantum symmetric integration with respect to τ over $[0,1]$, we get the right side inequality. □

Example 5. *We consider* $\mathcal{Z} : [0,2] \to \mathbb{R}$ *such that* $\mathcal{Z}(x) = x^2$ *is a differentiable convex functions, then applying on Theorem 12 for* $\hat{q}_1 \in (0,1)$*, we have*

$$1 \le 2 + \frac{4\hat{q}_1^2}{1+\hat{q}_1^2+\hat{q}_1^4} - \frac{4\hat{q}_1}{1+\hat{q}_1^2} \le 2.$$

For $\hat{q}_1 = 0.6$*, we obtain*

$$1 < 1.202 < 2.$$

For graphical visualization, we take $\hat{q}_1 \in (0,1)$ as the variable. Figure 6 gives a validation of Theorem 12.

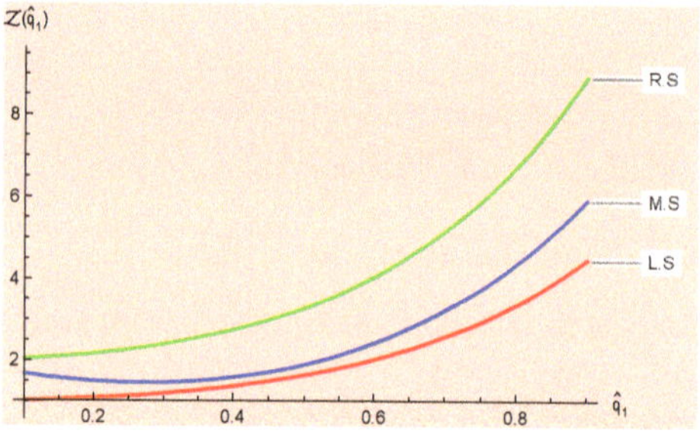

Figure 6. This figure validates the accuracy of Theorem 12.

Next, we compute another quantum symmetric analogue of Ostrowski's inequality.

Theorem 13. *Assume that* $\mathcal{Z} : J \to \mathbb{R}$ *is a continuous and symmetric quantum differentiable mappings, then*

$$\left|\mathcal{Z}(x) - \frac{1}{\mathcal{C}_2 - \mathcal{C}_1}\int_{\mathcal{C}_1}^{\mathcal{C}_2} \mathcal{Z}(\tau)^{\mathcal{C}_2}d^s_{\hat{q}_1}\tau\right| \le \frac{||^{\mathcal{C}_2}D^s_{\hat{q}_1}||}{(\mathcal{C}_2 - \mathcal{C}_1)}\left[\frac{\hat{q}_1^2(x-\mathcal{C}_1)^2 + (1+\hat{q}_1^2-\hat{q}_1)(\mathcal{C}_2 - x)^2}{1+\hat{q}_1^2}\right].$$

Proof. We start with the following expression and make use of the Lagrange mean value theorem,

$$\begin{aligned}
&\left|\mathcal{Z}(x) - \int_{\mathcal{C}_1}^{\mathcal{C}_2} \mathcal{Z}(\tau)\mathcal{Z}(\tau)^{\mathcal{C}_2}d^s_{\hat{q}_1}\tau\right| = \frac{1}{\mathcal{C}_2 - \mathcal{C}_1}\left|\int_{\mathcal{C}_1}^{\mathcal{C}_2} (\mathcal{Z}(\tau) - \mathcal{Z}(x))^{\mathcal{C}_2}d^s_{\hat{q}_1}\tau\right| \\
&\le \frac{1}{\mathcal{C}_2 - \mathcal{C}_1}\int_{\mathcal{C}_1}^{\mathcal{C}_2} |\mathcal{Z}(x) - \mathcal{Z}(\tau)|^{\mathcal{C}_2}d^s_{\hat{q}_1}\tau \\
&\le \frac{||^{\mathcal{C}_2}D^s_{\hat{q}_1}||}{(\mathcal{C}_2 - \mathcal{C}_1)}\int_{\mathcal{C}_1}^{\mathcal{C}_2} |x-\tau|^{\mathcal{C}_2}d^s_{\hat{q}_1}\tau \\
&\le \frac{||^{\mathcal{C}_2}D^s_{\hat{q}_1}||}{(\mathcal{C}_2 - \mathcal{C}_1)}\left[\int_{\mathcal{C}_1}^{x} (x-\tau)^{\mathcal{C}_2}d^s_{\hat{q}_1}\tau + \int_{x}^{\mathcal{C}_2} (\mathcal{C}_2 - x)^{\mathcal{C}_2}d^s_{\hat{q}_1}\tau\right] \\
&\le \frac{||^{\mathcal{C}_2}D^s_{\hat{q}_1}||}{(\mathcal{C}_2 - \mathcal{C}_1)}\left[\frac{\hat{q}_1(x-\mathcal{C}_1)^2}{1+\hat{q}_1^2} + \frac{(1+\hat{q}_1^2-\hat{q}_1)(\mathcal{C}_2 - x)^2}{1+\hat{q}_1^2}\right].
\end{aligned}$$

Hence, we have achieved our desired result. □

Here, we present Korkine's identity, which is beneficial in determining the Guss–Chebysev inequality.

Lemma 3. *Assume that* $\mathcal{Z}, \mathcal{G} : J \to \mathbb{R}$ *is a continuous mapping on J, then*

$$\frac{1}{2}\int_{\mathcal{C}_1}^{\mathcal{C}_2}\int_{\mathcal{C}_1}^{\mathcal{C}_2}(\mathcal{Z}(x)-\mathcal{Z}(y))(\mathcal{G}(x)-\mathcal{G}(y))\,{}^{\mathcal{C}_2}\mathrm{d}^{s}_{\hat{\mathrm{q}}_1}x\,{}^{\mathcal{C}_2}\mathrm{d}^{s}_{\hat{\mathrm{q}}_1}y$$
$$=(\mathcal{C}_2-\mathcal{C}_1)\int_{\mathcal{C}_1}^{\mathcal{C}_2}\mathcal{Z}(x)\mathcal{G}(x)\,{}^{\mathcal{C}_2}\mathrm{d}^{s}_{\hat{\mathrm{q}}_1}x-\left(\int_{\mathcal{C}_1}^{\mathcal{C}_2}\mathcal{Z}(x)\,{}^{\mathcal{C}_2}\mathrm{d}^{s}_{\hat{\mathrm{q}}_1}x\right)\left(\int_{\mathcal{C}_1}^{\mathcal{C}_2}\mathcal{G}(x)\,{}^{\mathcal{C}_2}\mathrm{d}^{s}_{\hat{\mathrm{q}}_1}x\right).$$

Proof. Utilizing the notion of the right quantum symmetric integral operator,

$$\int_{\mathcal{C}_1}^{\mathcal{C}_2}\int_{\mathcal{C}_1}^{\mathcal{C}_2}(\mathcal{Z}(x)-\mathcal{Z}(y))(\mathcal{G}(x)-\mathcal{G}(y))\,{}^{\mathcal{C}_2}\mathrm{d}^{s}_{\hat{\mathrm{q}}_1}x\,{}^{\mathcal{C}_2}\mathrm{d}^{s}_{\hat{\mathrm{q}}_1}y$$
$$=\int_{\mathcal{C}_1}^{\mathcal{C}_2}\int_{\mathcal{C}_1}^{\mathcal{C}_2}(\mathcal{Z}(x)\mathcal{G}(x)-\mathcal{Z}(x)\mathcal{G}(y)-\mathcal{Z}(y)\mathcal{G}(x)+\mathcal{Z}(y)\mathcal{G}(y))\,{}^{\mathcal{C}_2}\mathrm{d}^{s}_{\hat{\mathrm{q}}_1}x\,{}^{\mathcal{C}_2}\mathrm{d}^{s}_{\hat{\mathrm{q}}_1}y$$
$$=(\mathcal{C}_2-\mathcal{C}_1)^2(1-\hat{\mathrm{q}}_1^2)\sum_{n=0}^{\infty}\hat{\mathrm{q}}_1^{2n}\mathcal{Z}(\hat{\mathrm{q}}_1^{2n+1}\mathcal{C}_1+(1-\hat{\mathrm{q}}_1^{2n+1})\mathcal{C}_2)\mathcal{G}(\hat{\mathrm{q}}_1^{2n+1}\mathcal{C}_1+(1-\hat{\mathrm{q}}_1^{2n+1})\mathcal{C}_2)$$
$$+(\mathcal{C}_2-\mathcal{C}_1)^2(1-\hat{\mathrm{q}}_1^2)^2\sum_{n=0}^{\infty}\hat{\mathrm{q}}_1^{2n}\mathcal{Z}(\hat{\mathrm{q}}_1^{2n+1}\mathcal{C}_1+(1-\hat{\mathrm{q}}_1^{2n+1})\mathcal{C}_2)\sum_{n=0}^{\infty}\hat{\mathrm{q}}_1^{2n}\mathcal{G}(\hat{\mathrm{q}}_1^{2n+1}\mathcal{C}_1+(1-\hat{\mathrm{q}}_1^{2n+1})\mathcal{C}_2)$$
$$+(\mathcal{C}_2-\mathcal{C}_1)^2(1-\hat{\mathrm{q}}_1^2)^2\sum_{n=0}^{\infty}\hat{\mathrm{q}}_1^{2n}\mathcal{Z}(\hat{\mathrm{q}}_1^{2n+1}\mathcal{C}_1+(1-\hat{\mathrm{q}}_1^{2n+1})\mathcal{C}_2)\sum_{n=0}^{\infty}\hat{\mathrm{q}}_1^{2n}\mathcal{G}(\hat{\mathrm{q}}_1^{2n+1}\mathcal{C}_1+(1-\hat{\mathrm{q}}_1^{2n+1})\mathcal{C}_2)$$
$$+(\mathcal{C}_2-\mathcal{C}_1)^2(1-\hat{\mathrm{q}}_1^2)\sum_{n=0}^{\infty}\hat{\mathrm{q}}_1^{2n}\mathcal{Z}(\hat{\mathrm{q}}_1^{2n+1}\mathcal{C}_1+(1-\hat{\mathrm{q}}_1^{2n+1})\mathcal{C}_2)\mathcal{G}(\hat{\mathrm{q}}_1^{2n+1}\mathcal{C}_1+(1-\hat{\mathrm{q}}_1^{2n+1})\mathcal{C}_2).$$

We obtain

$$\int_{\mathcal{C}_1}^{\mathcal{C}_2}\int_{\mathcal{C}_1}^{\mathcal{C}_2}(\mathcal{Z}(x)-\mathcal{Z}(y))(\mathcal{G}(x)-\mathcal{G}(y))\,{}^{\mathcal{C}_2}\mathrm{d}^{s}_{\hat{\mathrm{q}}_1}x\,{}^{\mathcal{C}_2}\mathrm{d}^{s}_{\hat{\mathrm{q}}_1}y$$
$$=2(\mathcal{C}_2-\mathcal{C}_1)\int_{\mathcal{C}_1}^{\mathcal{C}_2}\mathcal{Z}(x)\mathcal{G}(x)\,{}^{\mathcal{C}_2}\mathrm{d}^{s}_{\hat{\mathrm{q}}_1}x-2\left(\int_{\mathcal{C}_1}^{\mathcal{C}_2}\mathcal{Z}(x)\,{}^{\mathcal{C}_2}\mathrm{d}^{s}_{\hat{\mathrm{q}}_1}x\right)\left(\int_{\mathcal{C}_1}^{\mathcal{C}_2}\mathcal{G}(x)\,{}^{\mathcal{C}_2}\mathrm{d}^{s}_{\hat{\mathrm{q}}_1}x\right).$$

Hence, the proof is achieved. □

Here, we prove the Cauchy–Bunyakovsky–Schwarz integral inequality for double integrals.

Theorem 14. *Assume that* $\mathcal{Z}, \mathcal{G} : J \to \mathbb{R}$ *is continuous mapping on J, then*

$$\left|\int_{\mathcal{C}_1}^{\mathcal{C}_2}\int_{\mathcal{C}_1}^{\mathcal{C}_2}(\mathcal{Z}(x,y)\mathcal{G}(x,y))\,{}^{\mathcal{C}_2}\mathrm{d}^{s}_{\hat{\mathrm{q}}_1}x\,{}^{\mathcal{C}_2}\mathrm{d}^{s}_{\hat{\mathrm{q}}_1}y\right|$$
$$\leq\left[\int_{\mathcal{C}_1}^{\mathcal{C}_2}\int_{\mathcal{C}_1}^{\mathcal{C}_2}\mathcal{Z}^2(x,y),\,{}^{\mathcal{C}_2}\mathrm{d}^{s}_{\hat{\mathrm{q}}_1}x\,{}^{\mathcal{C}_2}\mathrm{d}^{s}_{\hat{\mathrm{q}}_1}y\right]^{\frac{1}{2}}\left[\int_{\mathcal{C}_1}^{\mathcal{C}_2}\int_{\mathcal{C}_1}^{\mathcal{C}_2}\mathcal{G}^2(x,y)\,{}^{\mathcal{C}_2}\mathrm{d}^{s}_{\hat{\mathrm{q}}_1}x\,{}^{\mathcal{C}_2}\mathrm{d}^{s}_{\hat{\mathrm{q}}_1}y\right]^{\frac{1}{2}}.$$

Proof. To prove our result, we consider the following double symmetric quantum integral,

$$\left[\int_{\mathcal{C}_1}^{\mathcal{C}_2}\int_{\mathcal{C}_1}^{\mathcal{C}_2}(\mathcal{Z}(x,y)\mathcal{G}(x,y))\,{}^{\mathcal{C}_2}\mathrm{d}^{s}_{\hat{\mathrm{q}}_1}x\,{}^{\mathcal{C}_2}\mathrm{d}^{s}_{\hat{\mathrm{q}}_1}y\right]^2$$
$$=\Bigg[(1-\hat{\mathrm{q}}_1)^2(\mathcal{C}_2-\mathcal{C}_1)^2\sum_{n=0}^{\infty}\sum_{m=0}^{\infty}\hat{\mathrm{q}}_1^{2n+2m}\mathcal{Z}\Big((\hat{\mathrm{q}}_1^{2n+1}\mathcal{C}_1+(1-\hat{\mathrm{q}}_1^{2n+1})\mathcal{C}_2),$$
$$\mathcal{Z}(\hat{\mathrm{q}}_1^{2m+1}\mathcal{C}_1+(1-\hat{\mathrm{q}}_1^{2m+1})\mathcal{C}_2)\Big)$$
$$\times\mathcal{G}((\hat{\mathrm{q}}_1^{2n+1}\mathcal{C}_1+(1-\hat{\mathrm{q}}_1^{2n+1})\mathcal{C}_2),\,\mathcal{Z}(\hat{\mathrm{q}}_1^{2m+1}\mathcal{C}_1+(1-\hat{\mathrm{q}}_1^{2m+1})\mathcal{C}_2))\Bigg]^2.$$

Now, employing the discrete Cauchy–Schwarz inequality, we have

$$\Bigg[(1-\hat{q}_1)^2(\mathcal{C}_2-\mathcal{C}_1)^2\sum_{n=0}^{\infty}\sum_{m=0}^{\infty}\hat{q}_1^{2n+2m}\mathcal{Z}((\hat{q}_1^{2n+1}\mathcal{C}_1+(1-\hat{q}_1^{2n+1})\mathcal{C}_2),\ \mathcal{Z}(\hat{q}_1^{2m+1}\mathcal{C}_1+(1-\hat{q}_1^{2m+1})\mathcal{C}_2))$$
$$\times\mathcal{G}((\hat{q}_1^{2n+1}\mathcal{C}_1+(1-\hat{q}_1^{2n+1})\mathcal{C}_2),\ \mathcal{Z}(\hat{q}_1^{2m+1}\mathcal{C}_1+(1-\hat{q}_1^{2m+1})\mathcal{C}_2))\Bigg]^2$$
$$\leq\Bigg[(1-\hat{q}_1)^2(\mathcal{C}_2-\mathcal{C}_1)^2\sum_{n=0}^{\infty}\sum_{m=0}^{\infty}\hat{q}_1^{2n+2m}\mathcal{Z}^2\Big((\hat{q}_1^{2n+1}\mathcal{C}_1+(1-\hat{q}_1^{2n+1})\mathcal{C}_2),$$
$$\mathcal{Z}(\hat{q}_1^{2m+1}\mathcal{C}_1+(1-\hat{q}_1^{2m+1})\mathcal{C}_2)\Big)$$
$$\times(1-\hat{q}_1)^2(\mathcal{C}_2-\mathcal{C}_1)^2\sum_{n=0}^{\infty}\sum_{m=0}^{\infty}\hat{q}_1^{2n+2m}\mathcal{G}^2\Big((\hat{q}_1^{2n+1}\mathcal{C}_1+(1-\hat{q}_1^{2n+1})\mathcal{C}_2),$$
$$\mathcal{Z}(\hat{q}_1^{2m+1}\mathcal{C}_1+(1-\hat{q}_1^{2m+1})\mathcal{C}_2)\Big)\Bigg]^2$$
$$=\left[\int_{\mathcal{C}_1}^{\mathcal{C}_2}\int_{\mathcal{C}_1}^{\mathcal{C}_2}\mathcal{Z}^2(x,y)\,{}^{\mathcal{C}_2}d^s_{\hat{q}_1}x\,{}^{\mathcal{C}_2}d^s_{\hat{q}_1}y\right]^{\frac{1}{2}}\left[\int_{\mathcal{C}_1}^{\mathcal{C}_2}\int_{\mathcal{C}_1}^{\mathcal{C}_2}\mathcal{G}^2(x,y)\,{}^{\mathcal{C}_2}d^s_{\hat{q}_1}x\,{}^{\mathcal{C}_2}d^s_{\hat{q}_1}y\right]^{\frac{1}{2}}.$$

Hence, the proof is obtained. □

Theorem 15. *Assume that $\mathcal{Z},\mathcal{G}:J\to\mathbb{R}$ is two Lipschitzian continuous mappings on J, then*

$$\left|\frac{1}{\mathcal{C}_2-\mathcal{C}_1}\int_{\mathcal{C}_1}^{\mathcal{C}_2}\mathcal{Z}(x)\mathcal{G}(x)^{\mathcal{C}_2}d^s_{\hat{q}_1}x-\left(\frac{1}{\mathcal{C}_2-\mathcal{C}_1}\int_{\mathcal{C}_1}^{\mathcal{C}_2}\mathcal{Z}(x)^{\mathcal{C}_2}d^s_{\hat{q}_1}x\right)\left(\frac{1}{\mathcal{C}_2-\mathcal{C}_1}\int_{\mathcal{C}_1}^{\mathcal{C}_2}\mathcal{G}(x)^{\mathcal{C}_2}d^s_{\hat{q}_1}x\right)\right|$$
$$\leq\frac{L_1L_2\hat{q}_1^4(\mathcal{C}_2-\mathcal{C}_1)^2}{(1+\hat{q}_1^2+\hat{q}_1^4)(1+\hat{q}_1^2)^2}.$$

Proof. Since both $\mathcal{Z},\mathcal{G}$ are Lipschitzian continuous mappings, then for any $L_1,L_2\in\mathbb{R}$, we have

$$|\mathcal{Z}(x)-\mathcal{Z}(y)|\leq L_1|x-y|$$
$$|\mathcal{G}(x)-\mathcal{G}(y)|\leq L_2|x-y|.$$

Then

$$|(\mathcal{Z}(x)-\mathcal{Z}(y))(\mathcal{Z}(x)-\mathcal{Z}(y))|\leq L_1L_2(x-y)^2 \tag{9}$$

Now, applying the double right quantum symmetric integral operator on both sides of (9), then

$$\begin{aligned}&\int_{\mathcal{C}_1}^{\mathcal{C}_2}\int_{\mathcal{C}_1}^{\mathcal{C}_2}|(\mathcal{Z}(x)-\mathcal{Z}(y))(\mathcal{Z}(x)-\mathcal{Z}(y))|\,{}^{\mathcal{C}_2}d^s_{\hat{q}_1}x^{\mathcal{C}_2}d^s_{\hat{q}_1}y\\&\leq L_1L_2\int_{\mathcal{C}_1}^{\mathcal{C}_2}\int_{\mathcal{C}_1}^{\mathcal{C}_2}(x-y)^2\,{}^{\mathcal{C}_2}d^s_{\hat{q}_1}x^{\mathcal{C}_2}d^s_{\hat{q}_1}y\\&=L_1L_2\int_{\mathcal{C}_1}^{\mathcal{C}_2}\int_{\mathcal{C}_1}^{\mathcal{C}_2}(x^2-2xy+y^2)\,{}^{\mathcal{C}_2}d^s_{\hat{q}_1}x^{\mathcal{C}_2}d^s_{\hat{q}_1}y\\&=L_1L_22\left[\int_{\mathcal{C}_1}^{\mathcal{C}_2}x^2\,{}^{\mathcal{C}_2}d^s_{\hat{q}_1}x-\left(\int_{\mathcal{C}_1}^{\mathcal{C}_2}x^{\mathcal{C}_2}d^s_{\hat{q}_1}x\right)^2\right].\end{aligned} \tag{10}$$

Moreover, by taking into account the definition of the right quantum symmetric integral operator, we have

$$\begin{aligned}
&\int_{\mathcal{C}_1}^{\mathcal{C}_2} x^2 \, {}^{\mathcal{C}_2}\mathrm{d}^s_{\hat{q}_1} x \\
&= (\mathcal{C}_2 - \mathcal{C}_1)(1 - \hat{q}_1^2) \sum_{n=0}^{\infty} \hat{q}_1^{2n} \left(\mathcal{C}_2 - \hat{q}_1^{2n+1}(\mathcal{C}_2 - \mathcal{C}_1)\right)^2 \\
&= (\mathcal{C}_2 - \mathcal{C}_1)(1 - \hat{q}_1^2) \sum_{n=0}^{\infty} \hat{q}_1^{2n} \left({\mathcal{C}_2}^2 + \hat{q}_1^{4n+2}(\mathcal{C}_2 - \mathcal{C}_1)^2 - \hat{q}_1^{2n+1}\hat{q}_1\mathcal{C}_2(\mathcal{C}_2 - \mathcal{C}_1)\right) \\
&= (\mathcal{C}_2 - \mathcal{C}_1)(1 - \hat{q}_1^2) \left[\frac{{\mathcal{C}_2}^2}{1 - \hat{q}_1^2} + \frac{\hat{q}_1^2(\mathcal{C}_2 - \mathcal{C}_1)^2}{1 - \hat{q}_1^6} - \frac{2\hat{q}_1\mathcal{C}_2(\mathcal{C}_2 - \mathcal{C}_1)}{1 - \hat{q}_1^4}\right] \\
&= {\mathcal{C}_2}^2(\mathcal{C}_2 - \mathcal{C}_1) + \frac{\hat{q}_1^2(\mathcal{C}_2 - \mathcal{C}_1)^3}{1 + \hat{q}_1^2 + \hat{q}_1^4} - \frac{2\hat{q}_1\mathcal{C}_2(\mathcal{C}_2 - \mathcal{C}_1)^2}{1 + \hat{q}_1^2}.
\end{aligned} \tag{11}$$

Additionally,

$$\begin{aligned}
&\int_{\mathcal{C}_1}^{\mathcal{C}_2} x \, {}^{\mathcal{C}_2}\mathrm{d}^s_{\hat{q}_1} x \\
&= (\mathcal{C}_2 - \mathcal{C}_1)(1 - \hat{q}_1^2) \sum_{n=0}^{\infty} \hat{q}_1^{2n} \left(\mathcal{C}_2 - \hat{q}_1^{2n+1}(\mathcal{C}_2 - \mathcal{C}_1)\right) \\
&= \mathcal{C}_2(\mathcal{C}_2 - \mathcal{C}_1) - \frac{\hat{q}_1(\mathcal{C}_2 - \mathcal{C}_1)^2}{1 + \hat{q}_1^2}.
\end{aligned} \tag{12}$$

Introducing the values of (11) and (12) in (10) results the following inequality,

$$\begin{aligned}
&\int_{\mathcal{C}_1}^{\mathcal{C}_2} \int_{\mathcal{C}_1}^{\mathcal{C}_2} |(\mathcal{Z}(x) - \mathcal{Z}(y))(\mathcal{Z}(x) - \mathcal{Z}(y))| \, {}^{\mathcal{C}_2}\mathrm{d}^s_{\hat{q}_1} x \, {}^{\mathcal{C}_2}\mathrm{d}^s_{\hat{q}_1} y \\
&\leq \frac{2L_1L_2\hat{q}_1^4(\mathcal{C}_2 - \mathcal{C}_1)^4}{(1 + \hat{q}_1^2 + \hat{q}_1^4)(1 + \hat{q}_1^2)^2}.
\end{aligned} \tag{13}$$

Now from Korkine equality and inequality (13), we have

$$\begin{aligned}
&\left|(\mathcal{C}_2 - \mathcal{C}_1)\int_{\mathcal{C}_1}^{\mathcal{C}_2} \mathcal{Z}(x)\mathcal{G}(x) \, {}^{\mathcal{C}_2}\mathrm{d}^s_{\hat{q}_1} x - \left(\int_{\mathcal{C}_1}^{\mathcal{C}_2} \mathcal{Z}(x) \, {}^{\mathcal{C}_2}\mathrm{d}^s_{\hat{q}_1} x\right)\left(\int_{\mathcal{C}_1}^{\mathcal{C}_2} \mathcal{G}(x) \, {}^{\mathcal{C}_2}\mathrm{d}^s_{\hat{q}_1} x\right)\right| \\
&= \left|\frac{1}{2}\int_{\mathcal{C}_1}^{\mathcal{C}_2} \int_{\mathcal{C}_1}^{\mathcal{C}_2} (\mathcal{Z}(x) - \mathcal{Z}(y))(\mathcal{G}(x) \quad \mathcal{G}(y)) \, {}^{\mathcal{C}_2}\mathrm{d}^s_{\hat{q}_1} x \, {}^{\mathcal{C}_2}\mathrm{d}^s_{\hat{q}_1} y\right| \\
&\leq \frac{1}{2}\int_{\mathcal{C}_1}^{\mathcal{C}_2} \int_{\mathcal{C}_1}^{\mathcal{C}_2} |(\mathcal{Z}(x) - \mathcal{Z}(y))(\mathcal{G}(x) - \mathcal{G}(y))| \, {}^{\mathcal{C}_2}\mathrm{d}^s_{\hat{q}_1} x \, {}^{\mathcal{C}_2}\mathrm{d}^s_{\hat{q}_1} y \\
&= \frac{2L_1L_2\hat{q}_1^4(\mathcal{C}_2 - \mathcal{C}_1)^4}{(1 + \hat{q}_1^2 + \hat{q}_1^4)(1 + \hat{q}_1^2)^2}.
\end{aligned} \tag{14}$$

By dividing both sides of (14) by $(\mathcal{C}_2 - \mathcal{C}_1)^2$, we attain our desired result. □

Example 6. *We consider $\mathcal{Z}, \mathcal{G} : [0,2] \to \mathbb{R}$ such that $\mathcal{Z}(x) = \frac{x^2}{2}$ and $\mathcal{G}(x) = \frac{x}{3}$ are two continuous Lipschitzian mappings, then applying on Theorem 15 for $\hat{q}_1 \in (0,1)$, we have*

$$\begin{aligned}
&\left|\frac{4}{3}\left[\frac{1 + \hat{q}_1^2 - 3\hat{q}_1}{1 + \hat{q}_1^2} + \frac{3\hat{q}_1^2}{1 + \hat{q}_1^2 + \hat{q}_1^4} - \frac{\hat{q}_1^3}{(1 + \hat{q}_1^4)(1 + \hat{q}_1^2)}\right] - \frac{(2 + 2\hat{q}_1^2 - 2\hat{q}_1)}{(3(1 + \hat{q}_1^2))}\left(\frac{2 + 4\hat{q}_1^2 + 2\hat{q}_1^4}{1 + \hat{q}_1^2 + \hat{q}_1^4} - \frac{4\hat{q}_1}{1 + \hat{q}_1^2}\right)\right| \\
&\leq \frac{8\hat{q}_1^4}{3(1 + \hat{q}_1^2 + \hat{q}_1^4)(1 + \hat{q}_1^2)^2}.
\end{aligned}$$

For $\hat{q}_1 = 0.6$, we obtain

$$0.0801305 < 0.125437.$$

For graphical visualization, we take $\hat{q}_1 \in (0,1)$ as the variable. Figure 7 gives a validation of Theorem 15.

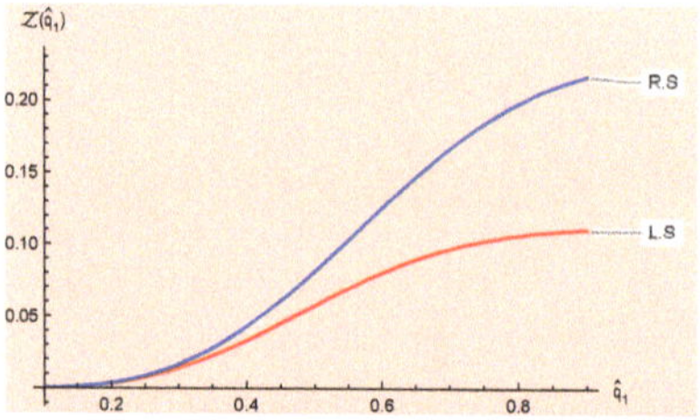

Figure 7. This figure validates the accuracy of Theorem 15.

4. Conclusions

In this study, we introduced the novel concepts of right analogues of symmetric operators and examined some key properties. Additionally, we presented the quantum symmetric analogues of several well-known inequalities, such as Hermite–Hadamard's, Young's, Ostrowski's, and Hölder's inequalities. Moreover, we have proposed the geometrical and analytical proof of Hermite–Hadamard's inequality. Furthermore, the correctness of the results is verified through numerical examples and visuals. These operators will play a significant role in the study of non-differentiable mappings. In the future, we will try to develop new symmetric analogues of Hermite–Hadamard–Mercer inequality, Simpson's inequality, and Newton's inequality associated with various generalizations of convex functions. In addition, based on these derivative operators, new integral operators can be established. Furthermore, we will extend these results for set-valued mappings and will also establish necessary and sufficient conditions for the differentiability of interval-valued mapping. We hope that these results will play a significant contribution to the development of inequalities and optimization theory.

Author Contributions: Conceptualization, M.Z.J. and M.U.A.; software, M.Z.J.; validation, M.V.-C., M.Z.J., M.U.A., M.U.A., S.S.D. and A.M.Z.; formal analysis, M.V.-C., M.Z.J., M.U.A., S.S.D. and A.M.Z.; investigation, M.V.-C., M.Z.J., M.U.A., S.S.D. and A.M.Z.; writing—original draft preparation, M.V.-C., M.Z.J. and A.M.Z.; writing—review and editing, M.U.A. and S.S.D.; visualization, M.V.-C., M.Z.J., M.U.A., S.S.D. and A.M.Z.; supervision, M.U.A. All authors have read and agreed to the published version of the manuscript.

Funding: This Study was supported via funding from Pontificia Universidad Católica del Ecuador project: RESULTADOS CUALITATIVOS DE ECUACIONES DIFERENCIALES FRACCIONARIAS LOCALES Y DESIGUALDADES INTEGRALES Cod: 070-UIO-2022.

Data Availability Statement: No new data were created or analyzed in this study. Data sharing is not applicable to this article.

Acknowledgments: Ahmed M. Zidan extend his appreciation to the Deanship of Scientific Research at King Khalid University for funding this work through large group Research Project under grant number RGP.2/13/44.

Conflicts of Interest: The authors declare no conflict of interest.

References

1. Sudsutad, W.; Ntouyas, S.K.; Tariboon, J. Quantum integral inequalities for convex functions. *J. Math. Inequal.* **2015**, *9*, 781–793. [CrossRef]
2. Alp, N.; Sarıkaya, M.Z.; Kunt, M.; İşcan, İ. *q*-Hermite Hadamard inequalities and quantum estimates for midpoint type inequalities via convex and quasi-convex functions. *J. King Saud Univ. Sci.* **2018**, *30*, 193–203. [CrossRef]
3. Bin-Mohsin, B.; Javed, M.Z.; Awan, M.U.; Khan, A.G.; Cesarano, C.; Noor, M.A. Exploration of Quantum Milne-Mercer-Type Inequalities with Applications. *Symmetry* **2023**, *15*, 1096. [CrossRef]
4. Kunt, M.; Baidar, A.W.; Sanli, Z. Some Quantum Integral Inequalities Based on Left-Right Quantum Integrals. *Turk. J. Sci. Technol.* **2022**, *17*, 343–356. [CrossRef]

5. Nwaeze, E.R.; Tameru, A.M. New parameterized quantum integral inequalities via η-quasiconvexity. *Adv. Differ. Equ.* **2019**, *2019*, 425. [CrossRef]
6. Asawasamrit, S.; Sudprasert, C.; Ntouyas, S.K.; Tariboon, J. Some results on quantum Hahn integral inequalities. *J. Inequalities Appl.* **2019**, *2019*, 154. [CrossRef]
7. Kunt, M.; Kashuri, A.; Du, T.; Baidar, A.W. Quantum Montgomery identity and quantum estimates of Ostrowski type inequalities. *AIMS Math* **2020**, *5*, 5439–5457. [CrossRef]
8. Kalsoom, H.; Vivas-Cortez, M. (q_1, q_2)-Ostrowski-Type Integral Inequalities Involving Property of Generalized Higher-Order Strongly n-Polynomial Preinvexity. *Symmetry* **2022**, *14*, 717. [CrossRef]
9. Ali, M.A.; Budak, H.; Feckan, M.; Khan, S. A new version of q-Hermite-Hadamard's midpoint and trapezoid type inequalities for convex functions. *J. Math. Slovaca* **2023**, *73*, 369–386. [CrossRef]
10. Jhanthanam, S.; Tariboon, J.; Ntouyas, S.K.; Nonlaopon, K. On q-Hermite-Hadamard inequalities for differentiable convex functions. *Mathematics* **2019**, *7*, 632. [CrossRef]
11. Awan, M.U.; Javed, M.Z.; Slimane, I.; Kashuri, A.; Cesarano, C.; Nonlaopon, K. (q_1, q_2)-Trapezium-Like Inequalities Involving Twice Differentiable Generalized m-Convex Functions and Applications. *Fractal Fract.* **2022**, *6*, 435. [CrossRef]
12. Du, T.S.; Luo, C.Y.; Yu, B. Certain quantum estimates on the parameterized integral inequalities and their applications. *J. Math. Inequal* **2021**, *15*, 201–228. [CrossRef]
13. Khan, M.A.; Mohammad, N.; Nwaeze, E.R.; Chu, Y.M. Quantum Hermite-Hadamard inequality by means of A Green function. *Adv. Differ. Equ.* **2020**, *2020*, 99. [CrossRef]
14. Saleh, W.; Meftah, B.; Lakhdari, A. Quantum dual Simpson type inequalities for q-differentiable convex functions. *Int. J. Nonlinear Anal. Appl.* **2023**, *14*, 63–76.
15. Bin-Mohsin, B.; Javed, M.Z.; Awan, M.U.; Budak, H.; Kara, H.; Noor, M.A. Quantum Integral Inequalities in the Setting of Majorization Theory and Applications. *Symmetry* **2022**, *14*, 1925. [CrossRef]
16. Alomari, M. q-Bernoulli inequality. *Turk. J. Sci.* **2018**, *3*, 32–39.
17. Alp, N.; Sarikaya, M.Z. q-Inequalities on quantum integral. *Malaya J. Mat.* **2020**, *8*, 2035–2044. [CrossRef] [PubMed]
18. Nosheen, A.; Ijaz, S.; Khan, K.A.; Awan, K.M.; Albahar, M.A.; Thanoon, M. Some q-Symmetric Integral Inequalities Involving s-Convex Functions. *Symmetry* **2023**, *15*, 1169. [CrossRef]
19. Mehmet, K.U.N.T.; Aljasem, M. Fractional quantum Hermite-Hadamard type inequalities. *Konuralp J. Math.* **2020**, *8*, 122–136.
20. Budak, H.; Ali, M.A.; Tarhanaci, M. Some new quantum Hermite–Hadamard-like inequalities for coordinated convex functions. *J. Optim. Theory Appl.* **2020**, *186*, 899–910. [CrossRef]
21. Ali, M.A.; Budak, H.; Abbas, M.; Chu, Y.M. Quantum Hermite–Hadamard-type inequalities for functions with convex absolute values of second q^{t_2}-derivatives. *Adv. Differ. Equ.* **2021**, *2021*, 7. [CrossRef]
22. Niculescu, C.; Persson, L.E. *Convex Functions and Their Applications*; Springer: New York, NY, USA, 2006; Volume 23.
23. Dragomir, S.S.; Pearce, C.E.M. *Selected Topics on Hermite–Hadamard Inequalities and Applications*; RGMIA; Victoria University: Melbourne, Australia, 2000.
24. Peajcariaac, J.E.; Tong, Y.L. *Convex Functions, Partial Orderings, and Statistical Applications*; Academic Press: Cambridge, MA, USA, 1992.
25. Akdemir, A.O.; Butt, S.I.; Nadeem, M.; Ragusa, M.A. New general variants of Chebyshev type inequalities via generalized fractional integral operators. *Mathematics* **2021**, *9*, 122. [CrossRef]
26. Kac, V.G.; Cheung, P. *Quantum Calculus*; Springer: New York, NY, USA, 2002; Volume 113.
27. BilalL, M.; Iqbal, A.; Rastogi, S. Quantum symmetric analogues of various integral inequalities over finite intervals. *J. Math. Inequalities* **2023**, *17*, 615–627. [CrossRef]
28. Zhao, W.; Rexma Sherine, V.; Gerly, T.G.; Britto Antony Xavier, G.; Julietraja, K.; Chellamani, P. Symmetric Difference Operator in Quantum Calculus. *Symmetry* **2022**, *14*, 1317. [CrossRef]

fractal and fractional

MDPI

Article

Maclaurin-Type Integral Inequalities for GA-Convex Functions Involving Confluent Hypergeometric Function via Hadamard Fractional Integrals

Tarek Chiheb [1], Badreddine Meftah [1], Abdelkader Moumen [2,*] and Mohamed Bouye [3]

1 Laboratory of Analysis and Control of Differential Equations "ACED", Facuty MISM, Department of Mathematics, University of 8 May 1945 Guelma, P.O. Box 401, Guelma 24000, Algeria; tchiheb@yahoo.fr (T.C.); badrimeftah@yahoo.fr (B.M.)
2 Department of Mathematics, Faculty of Sciences, University of Ha'il, Ha'il 55473, Saudi Arabia
3 Department of Mathematics, College of Science, King Khalid University, P.O. Box 9004, Abha 61413, Saudi Arabia; mbmahmad@kku.edu.sa
* Correspondence: mo.abdelkader@uoh.edu.sa

Abstract: In this manuscript, by using a new identity, we establish some new Maclaurin-type inequalities for functions whose modulus of the first derivatives are GA-convex functions via Hadamard fractional integrals.

Keywords: Hadamard fractional integrals; confluent hypergeometric function; incomplete confluent hypergeometric function; Maclaurin-type integral inequalities; geometrically arithmetically convex functions

Citation: Chiheb, T.; Meftah, B.; Moumen, A.; Bouye, M. Maclaurin-Type Integral Inequalities for GA-Convex Functions Involving Confluent Hypergeometric Function via Hadamard Fractional Integrals. *Fractal Fract.* **2023**, *7*, 860. https://doi.org/10.3390/fractalfract7120860

Academic Editors: Seth Kermausuor and Eze Nwaeze

Received: 26 October 2023
Revised: 24 November 2023
Accepted: 30 November 2023
Published: 2 December 2023

1. Introduction

It is well known that convexity plays an important and central role in many fields, such as economics, finance, optimization, and game theory. Due to its various applications, this concept has been extended and generalized in several directions.

This concept is closely related to integral inequalities. The literature in this context is rich. One can easily find papers that deal with different types of inequalities via different kinds of convexity.

Over the past few years, numerous scholars have investigated the error estimates associated with specific quadrature formulas. Their aim has been to develop new refinements, generalizations, and variants. For additional details, readers are encouraged to consult references [1–10] for classical inequalities, and [11–14] for fractional inequalities.

In [15], İşcan gave the analogue fractional of Hermite–Hadamard inequality for GA-convex functions as follows:

$$f\left(\sqrt{ab}\right) \leq \frac{\Gamma(\alpha+1)}{2(\ln b-\ln a)^{\alpha}}\left\{{}_H J_{a^+}^{\alpha} f(b) +{}_H J_{b^-}^{\alpha} f(a)\right\} \leq \frac{f(a)+f(b)}{2},$$

where $\alpha > 0$ and $0 < a < b$ and f is an integrable and GA-convex function on $[a,b]$.

Qi and Xi [16] have derived specific Simpson-type inequalities for GA-ε-convex functions. Within the outcomes obtained for differentiable function $f\colon [a,b] \to \mathbb{R}$, with $0 < a < b$ and $f' \in L[a,b]$ and $|f'|^q$ is GA-ε-convex, we have

$$\left|\frac{f(a)+4f\left(\sqrt{ab}\right)+f(b)}{6} - \frac{1}{\ln b-\ln a}\int_a^b f(u)\frac{du}{u}\right|$$
$$\leq \frac{\ln b-\ln a}{4}\left\{M_1^{1-\frac{1}{q}}(a,b)\Big((M_1(a,b)-M_2(a,b))|f'(a)|^q\right.$$
$$+ M_2(a,b)|f'(b)|^q + \varepsilon M_1(a,b)\Big)^{\frac{1}{q}}$$
$$+ M_1^{1-\frac{1}{q}}(b,a)\Big(M_2(b,a)|f'(a)|^q$$
$$\left.+ (M_1(b,a)-M_2(b,a))|f'(b)|^q + \varepsilon M_1(b,a)\Big)^{\frac{1}{q}}\right\},$$

where $q \geq 1$,

$$M_1(x,y) = \frac{2\left(x^{\frac{5}{6}}L\left(x^{\frac{1}{6}},y^{\frac{1}{6}}\right)+x^{\frac{1}{2}}\left(2y^{\frac{1}{2}}-x^{\frac{1}{2}}\right)-2x^{\frac{1}{2}}y^{\frac{1}{6}}L\left(x^{\frac{1}{3}},y^{\frac{1}{3}}\right)\right)}{3(\ln y-\ln x)}$$

and

$$M_1(x,y) = \frac{2x^{\frac{1}{2}}\left(4y^{\frac{1}{6}}L\left(x^{\frac{1}{3}},y^{\frac{1}{3}}\right)+y^{\frac{1}{2}}(\ln y-\ln x)-2x^{\frac{1}{3}}L\left(x^{\frac{1}{6}},y^{\frac{1}{6}}\right)-5y^{\frac{1}{2}}+2x^{\frac{1}{3}}y^{\frac{1}{6}}+x^{\frac{1}{2}}\right)}{3(\ln y-\ln x)^2},$$

with

$$L(x,y) = \begin{cases} \frac{x-y}{\ln x-\ln y} & \text{if } x \neq y \\ x & \text{if } x = y. \end{cases}$$

Motivated by the above results, we propose in this work to study one of the open three-point Newton–Cotes formulas called Maclaurin inequality, which can be declared as follows:

$$\left|\frac{1}{8}\left(3f\left(\frac{5a+b}{6}\right)+2f\left(\frac{a+b}{2}\right)+3f\left(\frac{a+5b}{6}\right)\right)-\frac{1}{b-a}\int_a^b f(u)du\right| \leq \frac{7(\tau-\upsilon)^4}{51840}\left\|f^{(4)}\right\|_\infty (b-a)^4,$$

where f is four times continuously differentiable function on (a,b), and $\left\|f^{(4)}\right\|_\infty = \sup_{x\in(a,b)}\left|f^{(4)}(x)\right|$, (see [17]).

For this, we first prove a new identity involving Hadamard fractional integrals. On the basis of this identity, we establish some new Maclaurin-type inequalities for functions whose modulus of the first derivatives are GA-convex.

2. Preliminaries

This section recalls some known definitions. We denote by $\mathbb{R}$ the set of real numbers, and by $\mathbb{R}^+$ the set of non-negative real numbers.

Definition 1 ([18]). *Let I be a subintervals of $(0,+\infty)$. A function f: $I \to \mathbb{R}^+$ is said to be GA-convex on I, if*

$$f\left(x^t y^{1-t}\right) \leq tf(x) + (1-t)f(y)$$

holds for all $x, y \in I$ and $t \in [0,1]$.

Definition 2 ([19]). *The integral representation of the confluent hypergeometric function is given by*

$$ {}_1F_1(a;b;z) = \frac{1}{B(a,b-a)} \int_0^1 t^{a-1}(1-t)^{b-a-1} e^{zt} dt, $$

where $\Re b > \Re a > 0$ *and B is the beta function.*

Definition 3 ([20]). *The integral representation of the incomplete confluent hypergeometric function is given by*

$$ \begin{aligned} {}_1F_1([a,b;y],z) &= \frac{1}{B(a,b-a)} \int_0^y u^{a-1}(1-u)^{b-a-1} e^{zu} du \\ &= \frac{y^a}{B(a,b-a)} \int_0^1 u^{a-1}(1-uy)^{b-a-1} e^{zuy} du, \end{aligned} $$

where $\Re b > \Re a > 0$ *and B is the Beta function.*

Definition 4 ([21]). *The left-sided and right-sided Hadamard fractional integrals of order* $\alpha \in \mathbb{R}^+$ *of function* $f(x)$ *are defined by*

$$ {}_H J_{a^+}^{\alpha} f(x) = \frac{1}{\Gamma(\alpha)} \int_a^x (\ln x - \ln u)^{\alpha-1} f(u) \frac{du}{u}, (0 < a < x \leq b), $$

and

$$ {}_H J_{b^-}^{\alpha} f(x) = \frac{1}{\Gamma(\alpha)} \int_x^b (\ln u - \ln x)^{\alpha-1} f(u) \frac{du}{u}, (0 < a \leq x < b). $$

Lemma 1 ([22]). *For any* $0 \leq a < b$ *in* $\mathbb{R}$*, and a fixed* $p \geq 1$*, we have*

$$ (b-a)^p \leq b^p - a^p. $$

3. Auxiliary Results

We provide certain lemmas in this section that help with the computations and are utilized in the following section. The following lemma is crucial to establish our main results

Lemma 2. *Let* f*:* $[a,b] \to \mathbb{R}$ *be a differentiable mapping on* $[a,b]$ *with* $0 < a < b$*. Assume that* $f' \in L[a,b]$*. Then, the following equality for fractional integrals holds:*

$$ \begin{aligned} &\frac{1}{8}\left(3f\left(a^{\frac{5}{6}}b^{\frac{1}{6}}\right) + 2f\left(a^{\frac{1}{2}}b^{\frac{1}{2}}\right) + 3f\left(a^{\frac{1}{6}}b^{\frac{5}{6}}\right)\right) - \frac{6^{\alpha-1}\Gamma(\alpha+1)}{(\ln b - \ln a)^{\alpha}} \Upsilon \\ &= \frac{\ln b - \ln a}{9} \left(\int_0^1 \frac{1}{4} \varkappa^{\alpha} a^{\frac{6-\varkappa}{6}} b^{\frac{\varkappa}{6}} f'\left(a^{\frac{6-\varkappa}{6}} b^{\frac{\varkappa}{6}}\right) d\varkappa \right. \\ &\quad - \int_0^1 \left((1-\varkappa)^{\alpha} - \frac{3}{8}\right) a^{\frac{5-2\varkappa}{6}} b^{\frac{1+2\varkappa}{6}} f'\left(a^{\frac{5-2\varkappa}{6}} b^{\frac{1+2\varkappa}{6}}\right) d\varkappa \\ &\quad + \int_0^1 \left(\varkappa^{\alpha} - \frac{3}{8}\right) a^{\frac{3-2\varkappa}{6}} b^{\frac{3+2\varkappa}{6}} f'\left(a^{\frac{3-2\varkappa}{6}} b^{\frac{3+2\varkappa}{6}}\right) d\varkappa \\ &\quad \left. - \int_0^1 \frac{1}{4} (1-\varkappa)^{\alpha} a^{\frac{1-\varkappa}{6}} b^{\frac{5+\varkappa}{6}} f'\left(a^{\frac{1-\varkappa}{6}} b^{\frac{5+\varkappa}{6}}\right) d\varkappa \right) \end{aligned} $$

where $\alpha > 0$ *and*

$$\begin{aligned} \Upsilon = &{}_H J^{\alpha}_{\left(a^{\frac{5}{6}}b^{\frac{1}{6}}\right)^-} f(a) +_H J^{\alpha}_{\left(a^{\frac{1}{6}}b^{\frac{5}{6}}\right)^+} f(b) \\ &+ \frac{1}{2^{\alpha-1}}\left({}_H J^{\alpha}_{\left(a^{\frac{5}{6}}b^{\frac{1}{6}}\right)^+} f\left(a^{\frac{1}{2}}b^{\frac{1}{2}}\right) +_H J^{\alpha}_{\left(a^{\frac{1}{6}}b^{\frac{5}{6}}\right)^-} f\left(a^{\frac{1}{2}}b^{\frac{1}{2}}\right)\right). \end{aligned} \tag{1}$$

Proof. Let

$$I = I_1 - I_2 + I_3 - I_4, \tag{2}$$

where

$$\begin{aligned} I_1 &= \int_0^1 \tfrac{1}{4}\varkappa^{\alpha} a^{\frac{6-\varkappa}{6}} b^{\frac{\varkappa}{6}} f'\left(a^{\frac{6-\varkappa}{6}} b^{\frac{\varkappa}{6}}\right) d\varkappa, \\ I_2 &= \int_0^1 \left((1-\varkappa)^{\alpha} - \tfrac{3}{8}\right) a^{\frac{5-2\varkappa}{6}} b^{\frac{1+2\varkappa}{6}} f'\left(a^{\frac{5-2\varkappa}{6}} b^{\frac{1+2\varkappa}{6}}\right) d\varkappa, \\ I_3 &= \int_0^1 \left(\varkappa^{\alpha} - \tfrac{3}{8}\right) a^{\frac{3-2\varkappa}{6}} b^{\frac{3+2\varkappa}{6}} f'\left(a^{\frac{3-2\varkappa}{6}} b^{\frac{3+2\varkappa}{6}}\right) d\varkappa \end{aligned}$$

and

$$I_4 = \int_0^1 \tfrac{1}{4}(1-\varkappa)^{\alpha} a^{\frac{1-\varkappa}{6}} b^{\frac{5+\varkappa}{6}} f'\left(a^{\frac{1-\varkappa}{6}} b^{\frac{5+\varkappa}{6}}\right) d\varkappa,$$

Integrating by parts I_1, we have

$$\begin{aligned} I_1 &= \int_0^1 \tfrac{1}{4}\varkappa^{\alpha} a^{\frac{6-\varkappa}{6}} b^{\frac{\varkappa}{6}} f'\left(a^{\frac{6-\varkappa}{6}} b^{\frac{\varkappa}{6}}\right) d\varkappa \\ &= \frac{6\varkappa^{\alpha}}{4(\ln b - \ln a)} f\left(a^{\frac{6-\varkappa}{6}} b^{\frac{\varkappa}{6}}\right)\Big|_{t=0}^{t=1} - \frac{6\alpha}{4(\ln b - \ln a)} \int_0^1 \varkappa^{\alpha-1} f\left(a^{\frac{6-\varkappa}{6}} b^{\frac{\varkappa}{6}}\right) d\varkappa \\ &= \frac{3}{2(\ln b - \ln a)} f\left(a^{\frac{5}{6}} b^{\frac{1}{6}}\right) - \frac{6^{\alpha+1}\alpha}{4(\ln b - \ln a)^{\alpha+1}} \int_a^{a^{\frac{5}{6}}b^{\frac{1}{6}}} (\ln u - \ln a)^{\alpha-1} f(u) \frac{du}{u} \\ &= \frac{3}{2(\ln b - \ln a)} f\left(a^{\frac{5}{6}} b^{\frac{1}{6}}\right) - \frac{6^{\alpha+1}\Gamma(\alpha+1)}{4(\ln b - \ln a)^{\alpha+1}} {}_H J^{\alpha}_{\left(a^{\frac{5}{6}}b^{\frac{1}{6}}\right)^-} f(a). \end{aligned} \tag{3}$$

Similarly, we have

$$\begin{aligned} I_2 &= \int_0^1 \left((1-\varkappa)^{\alpha} - \tfrac{3}{8}\right) a^{\frac{5-2\varkappa}{6}} b^{\frac{1+2\varkappa}{6}} f'\left(a^{\frac{5-2\varkappa}{6}} b^{\frac{1+2\varkappa}{6}}\right) d\varkappa \\ &= \frac{3}{\ln b - \ln a}\left((1-\varkappa)^{\alpha} + \tfrac{3}{8}\right) f\left(a^{\frac{5-2\varkappa}{6}} b^{\frac{1+2\varkappa}{6}}\right)\Big|_{t=0}^{t=1} \\ &\quad + \frac{3\alpha}{\ln b - \ln a} \int_0^1 (1-\varkappa)^{\alpha-1} f\left(a^{\frac{5-2\varkappa}{6}} b^{\frac{1+2\varkappa}{6}}\right) d\varkappa \\ &= -\frac{9}{8(\ln b - \ln a)} f\left(a^{\frac{1}{2}} b^{\frac{1}{2}}\right) - \frac{15}{8(\ln b - \ln a)} f\left(a^{\frac{5}{6}} b^{\frac{1}{6}}\right) \end{aligned} \tag{4}$$

$$+\frac{3^{\alpha+1}\alpha}{(\ln b-\ln a)^{\alpha+1}}\int_{a^{\frac{5}{6}}b^{\frac{1}{6}}}^{a^{\frac{1}{2}}b^{\frac{1}{2}}}\left(\ln a^{\frac{1}{2}}b^{\frac{1}{2}}-\ln u\right)^{\alpha-1}f(u)\frac{du}{u}$$

$$=-\frac{9}{8(\ln b-\ln a)}f\left(a^{\frac{1}{2}}b^{\frac{1}{2}}\right)-\frac{15}{8(\ln b-\ln a)}f\left(a^{\frac{5}{6}}b^{\frac{1}{6}}\right)$$

$$+\frac{3^{\alpha+1}\Gamma(\alpha+1)}{(\ln b-\ln a)^{\alpha+1}}\,{}_{H}J^{\alpha}_{\left(a^{\frac{5}{6}}b^{\frac{1}{6}}\right)^{+}}f\left(a^{\frac{1}{2}}b^{\frac{1}{2}}\right),$$

$$I_3=\int_0^1\left(\varkappa^{\alpha}-\tfrac{3}{8}\right)a^{\frac{3-2\varkappa}{6}}b^{\frac{3+2\varkappa}{6}}f'\left(a^{\frac{3-2\varkappa}{6}}b^{\frac{3+2\varkappa}{6}}\right)d\varkappa \tag{5}$$

$$=\frac{3}{\ln b-\ln a}\left(\varkappa^{\alpha}-\tfrac{3}{8}\right)f\left(a^{\frac{3-2\varkappa}{6}}b^{\frac{3+2\varkappa}{6}}\right)\Big|_{t=0}^{t=1}$$

$$-\frac{3\alpha}{\ln b-\ln a}\int_0^1\varkappa^{\alpha-1}f\left(a^{\frac{5-2\varkappa}{6}}b^{\frac{1+2\varkappa}{6}}\right)d\varkappa$$

$$=\frac{15}{8(\ln b-\ln a)}f\left(a^{\frac{1}{6}}b^{\frac{5}{6}}\right)+\frac{9}{8(\ln b-\ln a)}f\left(a^{\frac{1}{2}}b^{\frac{1}{2}}\right)$$

$$-\frac{3^{\alpha+1}\alpha}{(\ln b-\ln a)^{\alpha+1}}\int_{a^{\frac{1}{2}}b^{\frac{1}{2}}}^{a^{\frac{1}{6}}b^{\frac{5}{2}}}\left(\ln u-\ln a^{\frac{5}{6}}b^{\frac{1}{6}}\right)^{\alpha-1}f(u)\frac{du}{u}$$

$$=\frac{15}{8(\ln b-\ln a)}f\left(a^{\frac{1}{6}}b^{\frac{5}{6}}\right)+\frac{9}{8(\ln b-\ln a)}f\left(a^{\frac{1}{2}}b^{\frac{1}{2}}\right)$$

$$-\frac{3^{\alpha+1}\Gamma(\alpha+1)}{(\ln b-\ln a)^{\alpha+1}}\,{}_{H}J^{\alpha}_{\left(a^{\frac{1}{6}}b^{\frac{5}{6}}\right)^{-}}f\left(a^{\frac{1}{2}}b^{\frac{1}{2}}\right)$$

$$I_4=\int_0^1\tfrac{1}{4}(1-\varkappa)^{\alpha}a^{\frac{1-\varkappa}{6}}b^{\frac{5+\varkappa}{6}}f'\left(a^{\frac{1-\varkappa}{6}}b^{\frac{5+\varkappa}{6}}\right)d\varkappa \tag{6}$$

$$=\frac{3}{2(\ln b-\ln a)}(1-\varkappa)^{\alpha}f\left(a^{\frac{1-\varkappa}{6}}b^{\frac{5+\varkappa}{6}}\right)\Big|_{t=0}^{t=1}$$

$$+\frac{3\alpha}{2(\ln b-\ln a)}\int_0^1(1-\varkappa)^{\alpha-1}f\left(a^{\frac{1-\varkappa}{6}}b^{\frac{5+\varkappa}{6}}\right)d\varkappa$$

$$=-\frac{6}{4(\ln b-\ln a)}f\left(a^{\frac{1}{6}}b^{\frac{5}{6}}\right)+\frac{6^{\alpha+1}\alpha}{4(\ln b-\ln a)^{\alpha+1}}\int_{a^{\frac{1}{6}}b^{\frac{5}{6}}}^{b}(\ln b-\ln u)^{\alpha-1}f(u)\frac{du}{u}$$

$$=-\frac{6}{4(\ln b-\ln a)}f\left(a^{\frac{1}{6}}b^{\frac{5}{6}}\right)+\frac{6^{\alpha+1}\Gamma(\alpha+1)}{4(\ln b-\ln a)^{\alpha+1}}\,{}_{H}J^{\alpha}_{\left(a^{\frac{1}{6}}b^{\frac{5}{6}}\right)^{+}}f(b).$$

Using (3)–(6) in (2), and then multiplying the resulting equality by $\frac{\ln b-\ln a}{9}$, we obtain the desired result. □

In order for the paper to be well organized, we calculated the resulting integrals separately, so that there is no confusion.

Lemma 3. *Let λ and η be two positive numbers. Then, the following equality holds:*

$$I_1(\lambda,\eta)=\int_0^{\lambda}e^{\eta\varkappa}d\varkappa=\frac{1}{\eta}\left(e^{\eta\lambda}-1\right) \tag{7}$$

and

$$I_2(\lambda,\eta) = \int_0^{\lambda} \varkappa e^{\eta\varkappa} d\varkappa = \tfrac{1}{\eta}\lambda e^{\eta\lambda} - \tfrac{1}{\eta^2}\left(e^{\eta\lambda} - 1\right). \tag{8}$$

Proof. By computing directly, we have

$$\int_0^{\lambda} e^{\eta\varkappa} d\varkappa = \tfrac{1}{\eta} e^{\eta\varkappa}\Big|_{\varkappa=0}^{\varkappa=\lambda} = \tfrac{1}{\eta}\left(e^{\eta\lambda} - 1\right).$$

By using the integration by parts, we have

$$\begin{aligned}\int_0^{\lambda} \varkappa e^{\eta\varkappa} d\varkappa &= \tfrac{1}{\eta}\varkappa e^{\eta\varkappa}\Big|_{\varkappa=0}^{\varkappa=\lambda} - \int_0^{\lambda} \tfrac{1}{\eta} e^{\eta\varkappa} d\varkappa \\ &= \tfrac{1}{\eta}\lambda e^{\eta\lambda} - \tfrac{1}{\eta^2} e^{\eta\varkappa}\Big|_{\varkappa=0}^{\varkappa=\lambda} = \tfrac{1}{\eta}\lambda e^{\eta\lambda} - \tfrac{1}{\eta^2}\left(e^{\eta\lambda} - 1\right).\end{aligned}$$

The proof is completed. □

Lemma 4. *Let α and θ be two positive numbers. Then, the following equality holds:*

$$\vartheta_1(\alpha,\theta) = \int_0^1 \varkappa^{\alpha}\left(1 - \tfrac{1}{6}\varkappa\right)\theta^{\frac{\varkappa}{6}} d\varkappa = \frac{6^{\alpha+1} \cdot {}_1F_1\left(\left[\alpha+1, \alpha+3; \tfrac{1}{6}\right], \ln\theta\right)}{(\alpha+1)(\alpha+2)}. \tag{9}$$

Proof. By computing directly, we have

$$\begin{aligned}\int_0^1 \varkappa^{\alpha}\left(1 - \tfrac{1}{6}\varkappa\right)\theta^{\frac{\varkappa}{6}} d\varkappa &= \int_0^1 \varkappa^{\alpha}\left(1 - \tfrac{1}{6}\varkappa\right) e^{\frac{1}{6}\varkappa\ln\theta} d\varkappa \\ &= \frac{6^{\alpha+1} \cdot {}_1F_1\left(\left[\alpha+1, \alpha+3; \tfrac{1}{6}\right], \ln\theta\right)}{(\alpha+1)(\alpha+2)}.\end{aligned}$$

The proof is completed. □

Lemma 5. *Let α and θ be two positive numbers. Then, the following equality holds:*

$$\int_0^1 \left|\varkappa^{\alpha} - \tfrac{3}{8}\right|(3+2\varkappa)\theta^{\frac{\varkappa}{3}} d\varkappa = \mu_1(\alpha,\theta) + \mu_2(\alpha,\theta). \tag{10}$$

Proof. Clearly, we have

$$\begin{aligned}&\int_0^1 \left|\varkappa^{\alpha} - \tfrac{3}{8}\right|(3+2\varkappa)\theta^{\frac{\varkappa}{3}} d\varkappa \\ &= \int_0^{\left(\frac{3}{8}\right)^{\frac{1}{\alpha}}} \left(\tfrac{3}{8} - \varkappa^{\alpha}\right)(3+2\varkappa)\theta^{\frac{\varkappa}{3}} d\varkappa + \int_{\left(\frac{3}{8}\right)^{\frac{1}{\alpha}}}^1 \left(\varkappa^{\alpha} - \tfrac{3}{8}\right)(3+2\varkappa)\theta^{\frac{\varkappa}{3}} d\varkappa. \end{aligned} \tag{11}$$

By computing directly, we obtain

$$\mu_1(\alpha,\theta) = \int_0^{\left(\frac{3}{8}\right)^{\frac{1}{\alpha}}} \left(\tfrac{3}{8} - \varkappa^{\alpha}\right)(3+2\varkappa)\theta^{\frac{\varkappa}{3}}d\varkappa \tag{12}$$

$$=\tfrac{1}{8}\int_0^{\left(\frac{3}{8}\right)^{\frac{1}{\alpha}}} \left(9+6\varkappa-24\varkappa^{\alpha}-16\varkappa^{\alpha+1}\right)e^{\frac{\varkappa}{3}\ln\theta}d\varkappa$$

$$=\tfrac{9}{8}\int_0^{\left(\frac{3}{8}\right)^{\frac{1}{\alpha}}} e^{\frac{\varkappa}{3}\ln\theta}d\varkappa + \tfrac{6}{8}\int_0^{\left(\frac{3}{8}\right)^{\frac{1}{\alpha}}} \varkappa e^{\frac{\varkappa}{3}\ln\theta}d\varkappa$$

$$-3\int_0^{\left(\frac{3}{8}\right)^{\frac{1}{\alpha}}} \varkappa^{\alpha}e^{\frac{\varkappa}{3}\ln\theta}d\varkappa - 2\int_0^{\left(\frac{3}{8}\right)^{\frac{1}{\alpha}}} \varkappa^{\alpha+1}e^{\frac{\varkappa}{3}\ln\theta}d\varkappa$$

$$=\tfrac{9}{8}I_1\left(\left(\tfrac{3}{8}\right)^{\frac{1}{\alpha}},\tfrac{1}{3}\ln\theta\right)+\tfrac{6}{8}I_2\left(\left(\tfrac{3}{8}\right)^{\frac{1}{\alpha}},\tfrac{1}{3}\ln\theta\right)$$

$$-\frac{3._1F_1\left(\left[\alpha+1,\alpha+2;\left(\frac{3}{8}\right)^{\frac{1}{\alpha}}\right],\frac{1}{3}\ln\theta\right)}{\alpha+1}-\frac{2._1F_1\left(\left[\alpha+2,\alpha+3;\left(\frac{3}{8}\right)^{\frac{1}{\alpha}}\right],\frac{1}{3}\ln\theta\right)}{\alpha+2}.$$

On the other hand, we have

$$\mu_2(\alpha,\theta) = \int_{\left(\frac{3}{8}\right)^{\frac{1}{\alpha}}}^{1} \left(\varkappa^{\alpha}-\tfrac{3}{8}\right)(3+2\varkappa)\theta^{\frac{\varkappa}{3}}d\varkappa \tag{13}$$

$$=\frac{\theta^{\frac{1}{3}}}{8}\int_0^{1-\left(\frac{3}{8}\right)^{\frac{1}{\alpha}}} \left(40(1-\varkappa)^{\alpha}-16\varkappa(1-\varkappa)^{\alpha}-15+6\varkappa\right)e^{-\frac{\varkappa}{3}\ln\theta}d\varkappa$$

$$=5\theta^{\frac{1}{3}}\int_0^{1-\left(\frac{3}{8}\right)^{\frac{1}{\alpha}}} (1-\varkappa)^{\alpha}e^{-\frac{\varkappa}{3}\ln\theta}d\varkappa - 2\theta^{\frac{1}{3}}\int_0^{1-\left(\frac{3}{8}\right)^{\frac{1}{\alpha}}} \varkappa(1-\varkappa)^{\alpha}e^{-\frac{\varkappa}{3}\ln\theta}d\varkappa$$

$$-\frac{15\theta^{\frac{1}{3}}}{8}\int_0^{1-\left(\frac{3}{8}\right)^{\frac{1}{\alpha}}} e^{-\frac{\varkappa}{3}\ln\theta}d\varkappa + \frac{3\theta^{\frac{1}{3}}}{4}\int_0^{1-\left(\frac{3}{8}\right)^{\frac{1}{\alpha}}} \varkappa e^{-\frac{\varkappa}{3}\ln\theta}d\varkappa$$

$$=5\theta^{\frac{1}{3}}\frac{{}_1F_1\left(\left[1,\alpha+2;1-\left(\frac{3}{8}\right)^{\frac{1}{\alpha}}\right],-\frac{1}{3}\ln\theta\right)}{\alpha+1}-2\theta^{\frac{1}{3}}\frac{{}_1F_1\left(\left[2,\alpha+3;1-\left(\frac{3}{8}\right)^{\frac{1}{\alpha}}\right],-\frac{1}{3}\ln\theta\right)}{(\alpha+1)(\alpha+2)}$$

$$-\frac{15\theta^{\frac{1}{3}}}{8}I_1\left(1-\left(\tfrac{3}{8}\right)^{\frac{1}{\alpha}},-\tfrac{1}{3}\ln\theta\right)+\frac{3\theta^{\frac{1}{3}}}{4}I_2\left(1-\left(\tfrac{3}{8}\right)^{\frac{1}{\alpha}},-\tfrac{1}{3}\ln\theta\right).$$

Using (12) and (13) in (11), we obtain the desired result. The proof is completed. □

Lemma 6. *Let α and θ be two positive numbers. Then, the following equality holds:*

$$\int_0^1 \left|\varkappa^{\alpha}-\tfrac{3}{8}\right|(3-2\varkappa)\theta^{\frac{\varkappa}{3}}d\varkappa = \mu_3(\alpha,\theta)+\mu_4(\alpha,\theta). \tag{14}$$

Proof. Clearly, we have

$$\int_0^1 \left|\varkappa^\alpha - \tfrac{3}{8}\right|(3-2\varkappa)\theta^{\frac{\varkappa}{3}}d\varkappa$$

$$= \int_0^{\left(\frac{3}{8}\right)^{\frac{1}{\alpha}}} \left(\tfrac{3}{8} - \varkappa^\alpha\right)(3-2\varkappa)\theta^{\frac{\varkappa}{3}}d\varkappa + \int_{\left(\frac{3}{8}\right)^{\frac{1}{\alpha}}}^1 \left(\varkappa^\alpha - \tfrac{3}{8}\right)(3-2\varkappa)\theta^{\frac{\varkappa}{3}}d\varkappa. \tag{15}$$

By computing directly, we obtain

$$\begin{aligned}
\mu_3(\alpha,\theta) &= \int_0^{\left(\frac{3}{8}\right)^{\frac{1}{\alpha}}} \left(\tfrac{3}{8} - \varkappa^\alpha\right)(3-2\varkappa)\theta^{\frac{\varkappa}{3}}d\varkappa \qquad (16)\\
&= \tfrac{1}{8}\int_0^{\left(\frac{3}{8}\right)^{\frac{1}{\alpha}}} \left(9 - 6\varkappa - 24\varkappa^\alpha + 16\varkappa^{\alpha+1}\right)e^{\frac{\varkappa}{3}\ln\theta}d\varkappa\\
&= \tfrac{9}{8}\int_0^{\left(\frac{3}{8}\right)^{\frac{1}{\alpha}}} e^{\frac{\varkappa}{3}\ln\theta}d\varkappa - \frac{3}{4}\int_0^{\left(\frac{3}{8}\right)^{\frac{1}{\alpha}}} \varkappa e^{\frac{\varkappa}{3}\ln\theta}d\varkappa\\
&\quad - 3\int_0^{\left(\frac{3}{8}\right)^{\frac{1}{\alpha}}} \varkappa^\alpha e^{\frac{\varkappa}{3}\ln\theta}d\varkappa + 2\int_0^{\left(\frac{3}{8}\right)^{\frac{1}{\alpha}}} \varkappa^{\alpha+1} e^{\frac{\varkappa}{3}\ln\theta}d\varkappa\\
&= \tfrac{9}{8}I_1\left(\left(\tfrac{3}{8}\right)^{\frac{1}{\alpha}}, \tfrac{1}{3}\ln\theta\right) - \tfrac{3}{4}I_2\left(\left(\tfrac{3}{8}\right)^{\frac{1}{\alpha}}, \tfrac{1}{3}\ln\theta\right)\\
&\quad - 3\frac{{}_1F_1\left(\left[\alpha+1,\alpha+2;\left(\frac{3}{8}\right)^{\frac{1}{\alpha}}\right], \frac{1}{3}\ln\theta\right)}{\alpha+1} + 2\frac{{}_1F_1\left(\left[\alpha+2,\alpha+3;\left(\frac{3}{8}\right)^{\frac{1}{\alpha}}\right], \frac{1}{3}\ln\theta\right)}{\alpha+2}.
\end{aligned}$$

And on the other hand, we have

$$\begin{aligned}
\mu_4(\alpha,\theta) &= \int_{\left(\frac{3}{8}\right)^{\frac{1}{\alpha}}}^1 \left(\varkappa^\alpha - \tfrac{3}{8}\right)(3-2\varkappa)\theta^{\frac{\varkappa}{3}}d\varkappa \qquad (17)\\
&= \tfrac{\theta^{\frac{1}{3}}}{8}\int_0^{1-\left(\frac{3}{8}\right)^{\frac{1}{\alpha}}} \left(8(1-\varkappa)^\alpha + 16\varkappa(1-\varkappa)^\alpha - 3 - 6\varkappa\right)e^{-\frac{\varkappa}{3}\ln\theta}d\varkappa\\
&= \theta^{\frac{1}{3}}\int_0^{1-\left(\frac{3}{8}\right)^{\frac{1}{\alpha}}} (1-\varkappa)^\alpha e^{-\frac{\varkappa}{3}\ln\theta}d\varkappa + 2\theta^{\frac{1}{3}}\int_0^{1-\left(\frac{3}{8}\right)^{\frac{1}{\alpha}}} \varkappa(1-\varkappa)^\alpha e^{-\frac{\varkappa}{3}\ln\theta}d\varkappa\\
&\quad - \tfrac{3\theta^{\frac{1}{3}}}{8}\int_0^{1-\left(\frac{3}{8}\right)^{\frac{1}{\alpha}}} e^{-\frac{\varkappa}{3}\ln\theta}d\varkappa - \tfrac{3\theta^{\frac{1}{3}}}{4}\int_0^{1-\left(\frac{3}{8}\right)^{\frac{1}{\alpha}}} \varkappa e^{-\frac{\varkappa}{3}\ln\theta}d\varkappa\\
&= \theta^{\frac{1}{3}}\frac{{}_1F_1\left(\left[1,\alpha+2;1-\left(\frac{3}{8}\right)^{\frac{1}{\alpha}}\right], -\frac{1}{3}\ln\theta\right)}{\alpha+1} + 2\theta^{\frac{1}{3}}\frac{{}_1F_1\left(\left[2,\alpha+3;1-\left(\frac{3}{8}\right)^{\frac{1}{\alpha}}\right], -\frac{1}{3}\ln\theta\right)}{(\alpha+1)(\alpha+2)}\\
&\quad - \tfrac{3\theta^{\frac{1}{3}}}{8}I_1\left(1-\left(\tfrac{3}{8}\right)^{\frac{1}{\alpha}}, -\tfrac{1}{3}\ln\theta\right) - \tfrac{3\theta^{\frac{1}{3}}}{4}I_2\left(1-\left(\tfrac{3}{8}\right)^{\frac{1}{\alpha}}, -\tfrac{1}{3}\ln\theta\right).
\end{aligned}$$

Using (15) and (16) in (14), we obtain the desired result. The proof is completed. □

Lemma 7. *Let α and θ be two positive numbers. Then, the following equality holds:*

$$\vartheta_2(\alpha,\theta) = \int_0^1 \varkappa^{\alpha+1}\theta^{\frac{\varkappa}{6}}d\varkappa = \frac{{}_1F_1\left(\alpha+2,\alpha+3,\frac{1}{6}\ln\theta\right)}{\alpha+2}. \tag{18}$$

Proof. By computing directly, we obtain

$$\int_0^1 \varkappa^{\alpha+1}\theta^{\frac{\varkappa}{6}}d\varkappa = \int_0^1 \varkappa^{\alpha+1}e^{\frac{\varkappa}{6}\ln\theta}d\varkappa = \frac{{}_1F_1\left(\alpha+2,\alpha+3,\frac{1}{6}\ln\theta\right)}{\alpha+2}.$$

The proof is completed. □

Lemma 8. *Let λ, β and η be a positive numbers. Then, the following equality holds*

$$J_1(\lambda,\eta) = \int_0^\lambda \varkappa^{\beta}\theta^{\eta\varkappa}d\varkappa = \frac{{}_1F_1([\beta+1,\beta+2;\lambda],\eta\ln\theta)}{\beta+1} \tag{19}$$

and

$$J_2(\lambda,\eta) = \int_0^\lambda (1-\varkappa)^{\beta}\theta^{\eta\varkappa}d\varkappa = \frac{{}_1F_1([1,\beta+2;\lambda],\eta\ln\theta)}{\beta+1}. \tag{20}$$

Proof. By computing directly, we have

$$\begin{aligned} J_1(\lambda,\eta) &= \int_0^\lambda \varkappa^{\beta}\theta^{\eta\varkappa}d\varkappa = J_1(\lambda,\eta) = \int_0^\lambda \varkappa^{\beta}e^{\eta\varkappa\ln\theta}d\varkappa \\ &= \frac{{}_1F_1([\beta+1,\beta+2;\lambda],\eta\ln\theta)}{\beta+1}. \end{aligned}$$

For $J_2(\lambda,\eta)$, we have

$$\begin{aligned} J_2(\lambda,\eta) &= \int_0^\lambda (1-\varkappa)^{\beta}\theta^{\eta\varkappa}d\varkappa = \int_0^\lambda (1-\varkappa)^{\beta}e^{\eta\varkappa\ln\theta}d\varkappa \\ &= \frac{{}_1F_1([1,\beta+2;\lambda],\eta\ln\theta)}{\beta+1}. \end{aligned}$$

The proof is completed. □

Lemma 9. *Let α and θ be two positive numbers. Then, the following equality holds:*

$$\begin{aligned} \Phi(\alpha,\theta) &= \int_0^1 \left|\varkappa^{\alpha} - \tfrac{3}{8}\right|\theta^{\frac{\varkappa}{3}}d\varkappa \\ &= \frac{9}{8\ln\theta}\left(e^{\frac{1}{3}\left(\frac{3}{8}\right)^{\frac{1}{\alpha}}\ln\theta} + \theta^{\frac{1}{3}}e^{\frac{1}{3}\left(1-\left(\frac{3}{8}\right)^{\frac{1}{\alpha}}\right)\ln\theta^{-1}} - \theta^{\frac{1}{3}} - 1\right) \\ &\quad + \frac{\theta^{\frac{1}{3}}\cdot{}_1F_1\left(\left[1,\alpha+2;1-\left(\frac{3}{8}\right)^{\frac{1}{\alpha}}\right],\frac{1}{3}\ln\theta^{-1}\right) - {}_1F_1\left(\left[\alpha+1,\alpha+2;\left(\frac{3}{8}\right)^{\frac{1}{\alpha}}\right],\frac{1}{3}\ln\theta\right)}{\alpha+1}. \end{aligned} \tag{21}$$

Proof. By computing directly, we have

$$\int_0^1 \left|\varkappa^\alpha - \tfrac{3}{8}\right| \theta^{\frac{\varkappa}{3}} d\varkappa = \int_0^{\left(\frac{3}{8}\right)^{\frac{1}{\alpha}}} \left(\tfrac{3}{8} - \varkappa^\alpha\right)\theta^{\frac{\varkappa}{3}} d\varkappa + \int_{\left(\frac{3}{8}\right)^{\frac{1}{\alpha}}}^1 \left(\varkappa^\alpha - \tfrac{3}{8}\right)\theta^{\frac{\varkappa}{3}} d\varkappa$$

$$= \int_0^{\left(\frac{3}{8}\right)^{\frac{1}{\alpha}}} \left(\tfrac{3}{8} - \varkappa^\alpha\right)\theta^{\frac{\varkappa}{3}} d\varkappa + \theta^{\frac{1}{3}} \int_0^{1-\left(\frac{3}{8}\right)^{\frac{1}{\alpha}}} \left((1-\varkappa)^\alpha - \tfrac{3}{8}\right)\theta^{-\frac{\varkappa}{3}} d\varkappa$$

$$= \tfrac{3}{8}\int_0^{\left(\frac{3}{8}\right)^{\frac{1}{\alpha}}} e^{\frac{\varkappa}{3}\ln\theta} d\varkappa - \int_0^{\left(\frac{3}{8}\right)^{\frac{1}{\alpha}}} \varkappa^\alpha \theta^{\frac{\varkappa}{3}} d\varkappa + \theta^{\frac{1}{3}} \int_0^{1-\left(\frac{3}{8}\right)^{\frac{1}{\alpha}}} (1-\varkappa)^\alpha \theta^{-\frac{\varkappa}{3}} d\varkappa$$

$$- \tfrac{3\theta^{\frac{1}{3}}}{8} \int_0^{1-\left(\frac{3}{8}\right)^{\frac{1}{\alpha}}} e^{-\frac{\varkappa}{3}\ln\theta} d\varkappa$$

$$= \tfrac{9}{8\ln\theta}\left(e^{\frac{1}{3}\left(\frac{3}{8}\right)^{\frac{1}{\alpha}}\ln\theta} - 1\right) + \tfrac{9\theta^{\frac{1}{3}}}{8\ln\theta}\left(e^{\frac{1}{3}\left(1-\left(\frac{3}{8}\right)^{\frac{1}{\alpha}}\right)\ln\theta^{-1}} - 1\right)$$

$$+ \frac{\theta^{\frac{1}{3}} \cdot {}_1F_1\left(\left[1,\alpha+2;1-\left(\frac{3}{8}\right)^{\frac{1}{\alpha}}\right], \frac{1}{3}\ln\theta^{-1}\right) - {}_1F_1\left(\left[\alpha+1,\alpha+2;\left(\frac{3}{8}\right)^{\frac{1}{\alpha}}\right], \frac{1}{3}\ln\theta\right)}{\alpha+1}. \tag{22}$$

The proof is completed. □

4. Main Results

Our first result concerns functions whose absolute values of the first derivatives are GA-convex functions.

Theorem 1. *Let $f\colon [a,b] \to \mathbb{R}$ be a differentiable mapping on $[a,b]$ with $0 < a < b$, and $f' \in L^1[a,b]$. If $|f'|$ is GA-convex function, then the following inequality for fractional integrals holds:*

$$\left|\tfrac{1}{8}\left(3f\left(a^{\frac{5}{6}}b^{\frac{1}{6}}\right) + 2f\left(a^{\frac{1}{2}}b^{\frac{1}{2}}\right) + 3f\left(a^{\frac{1}{6}}b^{\frac{5}{6}}\right)\right) - \tfrac{6^{\alpha-1}\Gamma(\alpha+1)}{(\ln b - \ln a)^\alpha}\Upsilon\right|$$

$$\leq \tfrac{\ln b - \ln a}{9}\left(|f'(a)|\left(\tfrac{a\times 6^{\alpha+1}\cdot{}_1F_1\left(\left[\alpha+1,\alpha+3;\frac{1}{6}\right],\ln\frac{b}{a}\right)}{4(\alpha+1)(\alpha+2)} + \tfrac{b\times{}_1F_1\left(\alpha+2,\alpha+3,\frac{1}{6}\ln\frac{a}{b}\right)}{24(\alpha+2)}\right.\right.$$

$$\left.+ \tfrac{a^{\frac{1}{2}}b^{\frac{1}{2}}}{6}\left(\mu_1\left(\alpha,\tfrac{a}{b}\right) + \mu_2\left(\alpha,\tfrac{a}{b}\right) + \mu_3\left(\alpha,\tfrac{b}{a}\right) + \mu_4\left(\alpha,\tfrac{b}{a}\right)\right)\right)$$

$$+ |f'(b)|\left(\tfrac{a\times{}_1F_1\left(\alpha+2,\alpha+3,\frac{1}{6}\ln\frac{b}{a}\right)}{24(\alpha+2)} + \tfrac{b\times 6^{\alpha+1}\cdot{}_1F_1\left(\left[\alpha+1,\alpha+3;\frac{1}{6}\right],\ln\frac{a}{b}\right)}{4(\alpha+1)(\alpha+2)}\right.$$

$$\left.\left.+ \tfrac{a^{\frac{1}{2}}b^{\frac{1}{2}}}{6}\left(\mu_1\left(\alpha,\tfrac{b}{a}\right) + \mu_2\left(\alpha,\tfrac{b}{a}\right) + \mu_3\left(\alpha,\tfrac{a}{b}\right) + \mu_4\left(\alpha,\tfrac{a}{b}\right)\right)\right)\right),$$

where $\alpha > 0$, $\Upsilon, \mu_1, \mu_2, \mu_3, \mu_4$ are defined by (1), (12), (13), (16), and (17), respectively, where ${}_1F_1(.;.;.)$ and ${}_1F_1([.,.;.],.)$ are the confluent and the incomplete confluent hypergeometric functions, respectively.

Proof. From Lemma 2, and the properties of modulus and GA-convexity of $|f'|$, we obtain

$$\left|\tfrac{1}{8}\left(3f\left(a^{\frac{5}{6}}b^{\frac{1}{6}}\right) + 2f\left(a^{\frac{1}{2}}b^{\frac{1}{2}}\right) + 3f\left(a^{\frac{1}{6}}b^{\frac{5}{6}}\right)\right) - \tfrac{6^{\alpha-1}\Gamma(\alpha+1)}{(\ln b - \ln a)^\alpha}\Upsilon\right|$$

$$\leq \tfrac{\ln b - \ln a}{9}\left(\int_0^1 \tfrac{1}{4}\varkappa^\alpha a^{\frac{6-\varkappa}{6}} b^{\frac{\varkappa}{6}} \left|f'\left(a^{\frac{6-\varkappa}{6}} b^{\frac{\varkappa}{6}}\right)\right| d\varkappa\right.$$

$$
\begin{aligned}
&+\int_0^1 \left|(1-\varkappa)^{\alpha}-\tfrac{3}{8}\right| a^{\frac{5-2\varkappa}{6}} b^{\frac{1+2\varkappa}{6}} \left|f'\left(a^{\frac{5-2\varkappa}{6}} b^{\frac{1+2\varkappa}{6}}\right)\right| d\varkappa \\
&+\int_0^1 \left(\left|\varkappa^{\alpha}-\tfrac{3}{8}\right|\right) a^{\frac{3-2\varkappa}{6}} b^{\frac{3+2\varkappa}{6}} \left|f'\left(a^{\frac{3-2\varkappa}{6}} b^{\frac{3+2\varkappa}{6}}\right)\right| d\varkappa \\
&+\left.\int_0^1 \tfrac{1}{4}(1-\varkappa)^{\alpha} a^{\frac{1-\varkappa}{6}} b^{\frac{5+\varkappa}{6}} \left|f'\left(a^{\frac{1-\varkappa}{6}} b^{\frac{5+\varkappa}{6}}\right)\right| d\varkappa \right) \\
\leq & \tfrac{\ln b-\ln a}{9}\left(\int_0^1 \tfrac{1}{4}\varkappa^{\alpha} a^{\frac{6-\varkappa}{6}} b^{\frac{\varkappa}{6}} \left(\tfrac{6-\varkappa}{6}|f'(a)|+\tfrac{\varkappa}{6}|f'(b)|\right) d\varkappa\right. \\
&+\int_0^1 \left|(1-\varkappa)^{\alpha}-\tfrac{3}{8}\right| a^{\frac{5-2\varkappa}{6}} b^{\frac{1+2\varkappa}{6}} \left(\tfrac{5-2\varkappa}{6}|f'(a)|+\tfrac{1+2\varkappa}{6}|f'(b)|\right) d\varkappa \\
&+\int_0^1 \left|\varkappa^{\alpha}-\tfrac{3}{8}\right| a^{\frac{3-2\varkappa}{6}} b^{\frac{3+2\varkappa}{6}} \left(\tfrac{3-2\varkappa}{6}|f'(a)|+\tfrac{3+2\varkappa}{6}|f'(b)|\right) d\varkappa \\
&+\left.\int_0^1 \tfrac{1}{4}(1-\varkappa)^{\alpha} a^{\frac{1-\varkappa}{6}} b^{\frac{5+\varkappa}{6}} \left(\tfrac{1-\varkappa}{6}|f'(a)|+\tfrac{5+\varkappa}{6}|f'(b)|\right) d\varkappa\right) \\
= & \tfrac{\ln b-\ln a}{9}\left(|f'(a)|\int_0^1 \tfrac{1}{4}\varkappa^{\alpha}\left(1-\tfrac{1}{6}\varkappa\right) a^{\frac{6-\varkappa}{6}} b^{\frac{\varkappa}{6}} d\varkappa+|f'(b)|\int_0^1 \tfrac{1}{24}\varkappa^{\alpha+1} a^{\frac{6-\varkappa}{6}} b^{\frac{\varkappa}{6}} d\varkappa\right. \\
&+|f'(a)|\int_0^1 \left|(1-\varkappa)^{\alpha}-\tfrac{3}{8}\right| a^{\frac{5-2\varkappa}{6}} b^{\frac{1+2\varkappa}{6}} \left(\tfrac{5-2\varkappa}{6}\right) d\varkappa \\
&+|f'(b)|\int_0^1 \left|(1-\varkappa)^{\alpha}-\tfrac{3}{8}\right| a^{\frac{5-2\varkappa}{6}} b^{\frac{1+2\varkappa}{6}} \left(\tfrac{1+2\varkappa}{6}\right) d\varkappa \\
&+|f'(a)|\int_0^1 \left|\varkappa^{\alpha}-\tfrac{3}{8}\right| a^{\frac{3-2\varkappa}{6}} b^{\frac{3+2\varkappa}{6}} \left(\tfrac{3-2\varkappa}{6}\right) d\varkappa \\
&+|f'(b)|\int_0^1 \left|\varkappa^{\alpha}-\tfrac{3}{8}\right| a^{\frac{3-2\varkappa}{6}} b^{\frac{3+2\varkappa}{6}} \left(\tfrac{3+2\varkappa}{6}\right) d\varkappa \\
&+|f'(a)|\int_0^1 \tfrac{1}{4}(1-\varkappa)^{\alpha} a^{\frac{1-\varkappa}{6}} b^{\frac{5+\varkappa}{6}} \left(\tfrac{1-\varkappa}{6}\right) d\varkappa \\
&+\left.|f'(b)|\int_0^1 \tfrac{1}{4}(1-\varkappa)^{\alpha} a^{\frac{1-\varkappa}{6}} b^{\frac{5+\varkappa}{6}} \left(\tfrac{5+\varkappa}{6}\right) d\varkappa\right) \\
= & \tfrac{\ln b-\ln a}{9}\left(|f'(a)|\left(\tfrac{a}{4}\int_0^1 \varkappa^{\alpha}\left(1-\tfrac{1}{6}\varkappa\right)\left(\tfrac{b}{a}\right)^{\frac{\varkappa}{6}} d\varkappa\right.\right. \\
&+\tfrac{a^{\frac{1}{2}}b^{\frac{1}{2}}}{6}\int_0^1 \left|\varkappa^{\alpha}-\tfrac{3}{8}\right|(3+2\varkappa)\left(\tfrac{a}{b}\right)^{\frac{\varkappa}{3}} d\varkappa \\
&+\left.\tfrac{a^{\frac{1}{2}}b^{\frac{1}{2}}}{6}\int_0^1 \left|\varkappa^{\alpha}-\tfrac{3}{8}\right|(3-2\varkappa)\left(\tfrac{b}{a}\right)^{\frac{\varkappa}{3}} d\varkappa+\tfrac{b}{24}\int_0^1 \varkappa^{\alpha+1}\left(\tfrac{a}{b}\right)^{\frac{\varkappa}{6}} d\varkappa\right)
\end{aligned}
$$

$$
\begin{aligned}
&+\left|f'(b)\right|\left(\frac{a}{24}\int_0^1 \varkappa^{\alpha+1}\left(\frac{b}{a}\right)^{\frac{\varkappa}{6}}d\varkappa+\frac{a^{\frac{1}{2}}b^{\frac{1}{2}}}{6}\int_0^1\left|\varkappa^{\alpha}-\frac{3}{8}\right|(3-2\varkappa)\left(\frac{a}{b}\right)^{\frac{\varkappa}{3}}d\varkappa\right.\\
&\left.\left.+\frac{a^{\frac{1}{2}}b^{\frac{1}{2}}}{6}\int_0^1\left|\varkappa^{\alpha}-\frac{3}{8}\right|(3+2\varkappa)\left(\frac{b}{a}\right)^{\frac{\varkappa}{3}}d\varkappa+\frac{b}{4}\int_0^1\varkappa^{\alpha}\left(1-\frac{1}{6}\varkappa\right)\left(\frac{a}{b}\right)^{\frac{\varkappa}{6}}d\varkappa\right)\right)\\
&=\frac{\ln b-\ln a}{9}\left(\left|f'(a)\right|\left(\frac{a\times 6^{\alpha+1}\cdot{}_1F_1\left(\left[\alpha+1,\alpha+3;\frac{1}{6}\right],\ln\frac{b}{a}\right)}{4(\alpha+1)(\alpha+2)}+\frac{b\times{}_1F_1\left(\alpha+2,\alpha+3,\frac{1}{6}\ln\frac{a}{b}\right)}{24(\alpha+2)}\right.\right.\\
&\left.+\frac{a^{\frac{1}{2}}b^{\frac{1}{2}}}{6}\left(\mu_1\left(\alpha,\frac{a}{b}\right)+\mu_2\left(\alpha,\frac{a}{b}\right)+\mu_3\left(\alpha,\frac{b}{a}\right)+\mu_4\left(\alpha,\frac{b}{a}\right)\right)\right)\\
&+\left|f'(b)\right|\left(\frac{a\times{}_1F_1\left(\alpha+2,\alpha+3,\frac{1}{6}\ln\frac{b}{a}\right)}{24(\alpha+2)}+\frac{b\times 6^{\alpha+1}\cdot{}_1F_1\left(\left[\alpha+1,\alpha+3;\frac{1}{6}\right],\ln\frac{a}{b}\right)}{4(\alpha+1)(\alpha+2)}\right.\\
&\left.\left.+\frac{a^{\frac{1}{2}}b^{\frac{1}{2}}}{6}\left(\mu_1\left(\alpha,\frac{b}{a}\right)+\mu_2\left(\alpha,\frac{b}{a}\right)+\mu_3\left(\alpha,\frac{a}{b}\right)+\mu_4\left(\alpha,\frac{a}{b}\right)\right)\right)\right),
\end{aligned}
$$

which we have used. The proof is completed. □

The following result deals with the case where the absolute values of the first derivatives at a certain power q are GA-convex functions.

Theorem 2. *Let $f\colon [a,b]\to\mathbb{R}$ be a differentiable mapping on $[a,b]$ with $0<a<b$, and $f'\in L^1[a,b]$. If $|f'|^q$ is GA-convex function and $q>1$ with $\frac{1}{p}+\frac{1}{q}=1$, then the following inequality for fractional integrals holds:*

$$
\begin{aligned}
&\left|\frac{1}{8}\left(3f\left(a^{\frac{5}{6}}b^{\frac{1}{6}}\right)+2f\left(a^{\frac{1}{2}}b^{\frac{1}{2}}\right)+3f\left(a^{\frac{1}{6}}b^{\frac{5}{6}}\right)\right)-\frac{6^{\alpha-1}\Gamma(\alpha+1)}{(\ln b-\ln a)^{\alpha}}\Upsilon\right|\\
&\leq\frac{\ln b-\ln a}{9}\left(\frac{a}{4}\left(\frac{{}_1F_1\left(p\alpha+1,p\alpha+2,\frac{p}{6}\ln\left(\frac{b}{a}\right)\right)}{p\alpha+1}\right)^{\frac{1}{p}}\left(\frac{11|f'(a)|^q+|f'(b)|^q}{12}\right)^{\frac{1}{q}}\right.\\
&+a^{\frac{1}{2}}b^{\frac{1}{2}}\left(\frac{2|f'(a)|^q+|f'(b)|^q}{3}\right)^{\frac{1}{q}}\left(\frac{3^{p+1}\left(e^{\frac{p}{3}\left(\frac{3}{8}\right)^{\frac{1}{\alpha}}\ln\left(\frac{a}{b}\right)}-1\right)}{8^p p\ln\left(\frac{a}{b}\right)}-\frac{{}_1F_1\left(\left[p\alpha+1,p\alpha+2;\left(\frac{3}{8}\right)^{\frac{1}{\alpha}}\right],\frac{p}{3}\ln\frac{a}{b}\right)}{p\alpha+1}\right.\\
&\left.+\left(\frac{a}{b}\right)^{\frac{p}{3}}\left(\frac{{}_1F_1\left(\left[1,p\alpha+2;1-\left(\frac{3}{8}\right)^{\frac{1}{\alpha}}\right],\frac{p}{3}\ln\frac{b}{a}\right)}{p\alpha+1}-\frac{3^{p+1}}{8^p p\ln\left(\frac{a}{b}\right)}\left(e^{\frac{p}{3}\left(1-\left(\frac{3}{8}\right)^{\frac{1}{\alpha}}\right)\ln\left(\frac{a}{b}\right)}-1\right)\right)\right)^{\frac{1}{p}}\\
&+a^{\frac{1}{2}}b^{\frac{1}{2}}\left(\frac{|f'(a)|^q+2|f'(b)|^q}{3}\right)^{\frac{1}{q}}\left(\frac{3^{p+1}\left(e^{\frac{p}{3}\left(\frac{3}{8}\right)^{\frac{1}{\alpha}}\ln\left(\frac{b}{a}\right)}-1\right)}{8^p p\ln\left(\frac{a}{b}\right)}-\frac{{}_1F_1\left(\left[p\alpha+1,p\alpha+2;\left(\frac{3}{8}\right)^{\frac{1}{\alpha}}\right],\frac{p}{3}\ln\frac{b}{a}\right)}{p\alpha+1}\right.\\
&\left.+\left(\frac{b}{a}\right)^{\frac{p}{3}}\left(\frac{{}_1F_1\left(\left[1,p\alpha+2;1-\left(\frac{3}{8}\right)^{\frac{1}{\alpha}}\right],\frac{p}{3}\ln\frac{a}{b}\right)}{p\alpha+1}-\left(\frac{3}{8}\right)^{p}\frac{{}_1F_1\left(\left[p\alpha+1,p\alpha+2;1-\left(\frac{3}{8}\right)^{\frac{1}{\alpha}}\right],\frac{p}{3}\ln\frac{a}{b}\right)}{p\alpha+1}\right)\right)^{\frac{1}{p}}\\
&\left.+\frac{b}{4}\left(\frac{{}_1F_1\left(p\alpha+1,p\alpha+2,\frac{p}{6}\ln\frac{a}{b}\right)}{p\alpha+1}\right)^{\frac{1}{p}}\left(\frac{|f'(a)|^q+11|f'(b)|^q}{12}\right)^{\frac{1}{q}}\right),
\end{aligned}
$$

where $\alpha>0$, Υ is given by (1), and ${}_1F_1(.;.;.)$ and ${}_1F_1([.,.;.],.)$ are the confluent and the incomplete confluent hypergeometric functions, respectively.

Proof. From Lemma 2, the modulus, Hölder's inequality, *GA*-convexity of $|f'|^q$, and Lemma 1, we have

$$
\begin{aligned}
&\left|\tfrac{1}{8}\left(3f\left(a^{\frac{5}{6}}b^{\frac{1}{6}}\right)+2f\left(a^{\frac{1}{2}}b^{\frac{1}{2}}\right)+3f\left(a^{\frac{1}{6}}b^{\frac{5}{6}}\right)\right)-\tfrac{6^{\alpha-1}\Gamma(\alpha+1)}{(\ln b-\ln a)^{\alpha}}\Upsilon\right| \\
&\le \tfrac{\ln b-\ln a}{9}\left(\left(\int_0^1\left(\tfrac{1}{4}\varkappa^{\alpha}a^{\frac{6-\varkappa}{6}}b^{\frac{\varkappa}{6}}\right)^{p}d\varkappa\right)^{\frac{1}{p}}\left(\int_0^1\left|f'\left(a^{\frac{6-\varkappa}{6}}b^{\frac{\varkappa}{6}}\right)\right|^{q}d\varkappa\right)^{\frac{1}{q}}\right.\\
&\quad+\left(\int_0^1\left(\left|(1-\varkappa)^{\alpha}-\tfrac{3}{8}\right|a^{\frac{5-2\varkappa}{6}}b^{\frac{1+2\varkappa}{6}}\right)^{p}d\varkappa\right)^{\frac{1}{p}}\left(\int_0^1\left|f'\left(a^{\frac{5-2\varkappa}{6}}b^{\frac{1+2\varkappa}{6}}\right)\right|^{q}d\varkappa\right)^{\frac{1}{q}}\\
&\quad+\left(\int_0^1\left(\left|\varkappa^{\alpha}-\tfrac{3}{8}\right|a^{\frac{3-2\varkappa}{6}}b^{\frac{3+2\varkappa}{6}}\right)^{p}d\varkappa\right)^{\frac{1}{p}}\left(\int_0^1\left|f'\left(a^{\frac{3-2\varkappa}{6}}b^{\frac{3+2\varkappa}{6}}\right)\right|^{q}d\varkappa\right)^{\frac{1}{q}}\\
&\quad\left.+\left(\int_0^1\left(\tfrac{1}{4}(1-\varkappa)^{\alpha}a^{\frac{1-\varkappa}{6}}b^{\frac{5+\varkappa}{6}}\right)^{p}d\varkappa\right)^{\frac{1}{p}}\left(\int_0^1\left|f'\left(a^{\frac{1-\varkappa}{6}}b^{\frac{5+\varkappa}{6}}\right)\right|^{q}d\varkappa\right)^{\frac{1}{q}}\right)\\
&\le \tfrac{\ln b-\ln a}{9}\left(\tfrac{a}{4}\left(\int_0^1\varkappa^{p\alpha}\left(\tfrac{b}{a}\right)^{\frac{p}{6}\varkappa}d\varkappa\right)^{\frac{1}{p}}\left(\int_0^1\left(\tfrac{6-\varkappa}{6}|f'(a)|^{q}+\tfrac{\varkappa}{6}|f'(b)|^{q}\right)d\varkappa\right)^{\frac{1}{q}}\right.\\
&\quad+a^{\frac{1}{2}}b^{\frac{1}{2}}\left(\int_0^{\left(\frac{3}{8}\right)^{\frac{1}{\alpha}}}\left(\tfrac{3}{8}-\varkappa^{\alpha}\right)^{p}\left(\tfrac{a}{b}\right)^{\frac{p}{3}\varkappa}d\varkappa+\int_{\left(\frac{3}{8}\right)^{\frac{1}{\alpha}}}^{1}\left(\varkappa^{\alpha}-\tfrac{3}{8}\right)^{p}\left(\tfrac{a}{b}\right)^{\frac{p}{3}\varkappa}d\varkappa\right)^{\frac{1}{p}}\\
&\quad\times\left(\int_0^1\left(\tfrac{5-2\varkappa}{6}|f'(a)|^{q}+\tfrac{1+2\varkappa}{6}|f'(b)|^{q}\right)d\varkappa\right)^{\frac{1}{q}}\\
&\quad+a^{\frac{1}{2}}b^{\frac{1}{2}}\left(\int_0^{\left(\frac{3}{8}\right)^{\frac{1}{\alpha}}}\left(\tfrac{3}{8}-\varkappa^{\alpha}\right)^{p}\left(\tfrac{b}{a}\right)^{\frac{p}{3}\varkappa}d\varkappa+\int_{\left(\frac{3}{8}\right)^{\frac{1}{\alpha}}}^{1}\left(\varkappa^{\alpha}-\tfrac{3}{8}\right)^{p}\left(\tfrac{b}{a}\right)^{\frac{p}{3}\varkappa}d\varkappa\right)^{\frac{1}{p}}\\
&\quad\times\left(\int_0^1\left(\tfrac{3-2\varkappa}{6}|f'(a)|^{q}+\tfrac{3+2\varkappa}{6}|f'(b)|^{q}\right)d\varkappa\right)^{\frac{1}{q}}\\
&\quad\left.+\tfrac{b}{4}\left(\int_0^1\varkappa^{p\alpha}\left(\tfrac{a}{b}\right)^{\frac{p}{6}\varkappa}d\varkappa\right)^{\frac{1}{p}}\left(\int_0^1\left(\tfrac{1-\varkappa}{6}|f'(a)|^{q}+\tfrac{5+\varkappa}{6}|f'(b)|^{q}\right)d\varkappa\right)^{\frac{1}{q}}\right)\\
&\le \tfrac{\ln b-\ln a}{9}\left(\tfrac{a}{4}\left(\int_0^1\varkappa^{(p\alpha-1)+1}\left(\left(\tfrac{b}{a}\right)^{p}\right)^{\frac{1}{6}\varkappa}d\varkappa\right)^{\frac{1}{p}}\left(|f'(a)|^{q}\int_0^1\tfrac{6-\varkappa}{6}d\varkappa+|f'(b)|^{q}\int_0^1\tfrac{\varkappa}{6}d\varkappa\right)^{\frac{1}{q}}\right.\\
&\quad+a^{\frac{1}{2}}b^{\frac{1}{2}}\left(\int_0^{\left(\frac{3}{8}\right)^{\frac{1}{\alpha}}}\left(\left(\tfrac{3}{8}\right)^{p}e^{\frac{p}{3}\varkappa\ln\left(\frac{a}{b}\right)}-\varkappa^{p\alpha}\left(\tfrac{a}{b}\right)^{\frac{p}{3}\varkappa}\right)d\varkappa\right.
\end{aligned}
$$

$$
\begin{aligned}
&+\left(\tfrac{a}{b}\right)^{\frac{p}{3}}\int_0^{1-\left(\frac{3}{8}\right)^{\frac{1}{\alpha}}}\left((1-\varkappa)^{p\alpha}\left(\tfrac{b}{a}\right)^{\frac{p}{3}\varkappa}-\left(\tfrac{3}{8}\right)^{p}e^{\frac{p}{3}\varkappa\ln\left(\frac{b}{a}\right)}\right)d\varkappa\Bigg)^{\frac{1}{p}}\\
&\times\left(|f'(a)|^q\int_0^1\tfrac{5-2\varkappa}{6}d\varkappa+|f'(b)|^q\int_0^1\tfrac{1+2\varkappa}{6}d\varkappa\right)^{\frac{1}{q}}\\
&+a^{\frac{1}{2}}b^{\frac{1}{2}}\Bigg(\int_0^{\left(\frac{3}{8}\right)^{\frac{1}{\alpha}}}\left(\left(\tfrac{3}{8}\right)^{p}e^{\frac{p}{3}\varkappa\ln\left(\frac{b}{a}\right)}-\varkappa^{p\alpha}\left(\tfrac{b}{a}\right)^{\frac{p}{3}\varkappa}\right)d\varkappa\\
&+\left(\tfrac{b}{a}\right)^{\frac{p}{3}}\int_0^{1-\left(\frac{3}{8}\right)^{\frac{1}{\alpha}}}\left((1-\varkappa)^{p\alpha}\left(\tfrac{a}{b}\right)^{\frac{p}{3}\varkappa}-\left(\tfrac{3}{8}\right)^{p}\varkappa^{p\alpha}\left(\tfrac{a}{b}\right)^{\frac{p}{3}\varkappa}\right)d\varkappa\Bigg)^{\frac{1}{p}}\\
&\times\left(|f'(a)|^q\int_0^1\tfrac{3-2\varkappa}{6}d\varkappa+|f'(b)|^q\int_0^1\tfrac{3+2\varkappa}{6}d\varkappa\right)^{\frac{1}{q}}\\
&+\tfrac{b}{4}\left(\int_0^1\varkappa^{(p\alpha-1)+1}\left(\left(\tfrac{a}{b}\right)^{p}\right)^{\frac{1}{6}\varkappa}d\varkappa\right)^{\frac{1}{p}}\left(|f'(a)|^q\int_0^1\tfrac{1-\varkappa}{6}d\varkappa+|f'(b)|^q\int_0^1\tfrac{5+\varkappa}{6}d\varkappa\right)^{\frac{1}{q}}\Bigg)\\
=&\frac{\ln b-\ln a}{9}\Bigg(\frac{a}{4}\left(\frac{{}_1F_1\left(p\alpha+1,p\alpha+2,\frac{p}{6}\ln\left(\frac{b}{a}\right)\right)}{p\alpha+1}\right)^{\frac{1}{p}}\left(\frac{11|f'(a)|^q+|f'(b)|^q}{12}\right)^{\frac{1}{q}}\\
&+a^{\frac{1}{2}}b^{\frac{1}{2}}\left(\frac{2|f'(a)|^q+|f'(b)|^q}{3}\right)^{\frac{1}{q}}\Bigg(\frac{3^{p+1}\left(e^{\frac{p}{3}\left(\frac{3}{8}\right)^{\frac{1}{\alpha}}\ln\left(\frac{a}{b}\right)}-1\right)}{8^p p\ln\left(\frac{a}{b}\right)}-\frac{{}_1F_1\left(\left[p\alpha+1,p\alpha+2;\left(\frac{3}{8}\right)^{\frac{1}{\alpha}}\right],\frac{p}{3}\ln\frac{a}{b}\right)}{p\alpha+1}\\
&+\left(\tfrac{a}{b}\right)^{\frac{p}{3}}\left(\frac{{}_1F_1\left(\left[1,p\alpha+2;1-\left(\frac{3}{8}\right)^{\frac{1}{\alpha}}\right],\frac{p}{3}\ln\frac{b}{a}\right)}{p\alpha+1}-\frac{3^{p+1}}{8^p p\ln\left(\frac{a}{b}\right)}\left(e^{\frac{p}{3}\left(1-\left(\frac{3}{8}\right)^{\frac{1}{\alpha}}\right)\ln\left(\frac{a}{b}\right)}-1\right)\right)\Bigg)^{\frac{1}{p}}\\
&+a^{\frac{1}{2}}b^{\frac{1}{2}}\left(\frac{|f'(a)|^q+2|f'(b)|^q}{3}\right)^{\frac{1}{q}}\Bigg(\frac{3^{p+1}\left(e^{\frac{p}{3}\left(\frac{3}{8}\right)^{\frac{1}{\alpha}}\ln\left(\frac{b}{a}\right)}-1\right)}{8^p p\ln\left(\frac{a}{b}\right)}-\frac{{}_1F_1\left(\left[p\alpha+1,p\alpha+2;\left(\frac{3}{8}\right)^{\frac{1}{\alpha}}\right],\frac{p}{3}\ln\frac{b}{a}\right)}{p\alpha+1}\\
&+\left(\tfrac{b}{a}\right)^{\frac{p}{3}}\left(\frac{{}_1F_1\left(\left[1,p\alpha+2;1-\left(\frac{3}{8}\right)^{\frac{1}{\alpha}}\right],\frac{p}{3}\ln\frac{a}{b}\right)}{p\alpha+1}-\left(\frac{3}{8}\right)^{p}\frac{{}_1F_1\left(\left[p\alpha+1,p\alpha+2;1-\left(\frac{3}{8}\right)^{\frac{1}{\alpha}}\right],\frac{p}{3}\ln\frac{a}{b}\right)}{p\alpha+1}\right)\Bigg)^{\frac{1}{p}}\\
&+\frac{b}{4}\left(\frac{{}_1F_1\left(p\alpha+1,p\alpha+2,\frac{p}{6}\ln\frac{a}{b}\right)}{p\alpha+1}\right)^{\frac{1}{p}}\left(\frac{|f'(a)|^q+11|f'(b)|^q}{12}\right)^{\frac{1}{q}}\Bigg),
\end{aligned}
$$

The proof is completed. □

The following theorem represents a variation of Theorem 2.

Theorem 3. *Let $f\colon [a,b] \to \mathbb{R}$ be a differentiable mapping on $[a,b]$ with $0<a<b$, and $f' \in L^1[a,b]$. If $|f'|^q$ is GA-convex function and $q \geq 1$, then the following inequality for fractional integrals holds:*

$$\left|\frac{1}{8}\left(3f\left(a^{\frac{5}{6}}b^{\frac{1}{6}}\right)+2f\left(a^{\frac{1}{2}}b^{\frac{1}{2}}\right)+3f\left(a^{\frac{1}{6}}b^{\frac{5}{6}}\right)\right)-\frac{6^{\alpha-1}\Gamma(\alpha+1)}{(\ln b-\ln a)^{\alpha}}\Upsilon\right|$$
$$\leq\frac{\ln b-\ln a}{9}\left(\frac{a}{4}\left(\frac{{}_1F_1\left(\alpha+1,\alpha+2,\frac{1}{6}\ln\frac{b}{a}\right)}{\alpha+1}\right)^{1-\frac{1}{q}}\right.$$
$$\times\left(\frac{6^{\alpha+2}\cdot{}_1F_1\left(\left[\alpha+1,\alpha+3;\frac{1}{6}\right],\ln\frac{b}{a}\right)|f'(a)|^q+(\alpha+1){}_1F_1\left(\alpha+2,\alpha+3,\frac{1}{6}\ln\frac{b}{a}\right)|f'(b)|^q}{6(\alpha+1)(\alpha+2)}\right)^{\frac{1}{q}}$$
$$+a^{\frac{1}{2}}b^{\frac{1}{2}}\left(\Phi\left(\alpha,\frac{a}{b}\right)\right)^{1-\frac{1}{q}}\left(\frac{\left(\mu_1\left(\alpha,\frac{a}{b}\right)+\mu_2\left(\alpha,\frac{a}{b}\right)\right)|f'(a)|^q+\left(\mu_3\left(\alpha,\frac{a}{b}\right)+\mu_4\left(\alpha,\frac{a}{b}\right)\right)|f'(b)|^q}{6}\right)^{\frac{1}{q}}$$
$$+a^{\frac{1}{2}}b^{\frac{1}{2}}\left(\Phi\left(\alpha,\frac{b}{a}\right)\right)^{1-\frac{1}{q}}\left(\frac{\left(\mu_3\left(\alpha,\frac{b}{a}\right)+\mu_4\left(\alpha,\frac{b}{a}\right)\right)|f'(a)|^q+\left(\mu_1\left(\alpha,\frac{b}{a}\right)+\mu_2\left(\alpha,\frac{b}{a}\right)\right)|f'(b)|^q}{6}\right)^{\frac{1}{q}}$$
$$+\frac{b}{4}\left(\frac{{}_1F_1\left(\alpha+1,\alpha+2,\frac{1}{6}\ln\frac{a}{b}\right)}{\alpha+1}\right)^{1-\frac{1}{q}}$$
$$\left.\times\left(\frac{(\alpha+1){}_1F_1\left(\alpha+2,\alpha+3,\frac{1}{6}\ln\frac{a}{b}\right)|f'(a)|^q+6^{\alpha+2}\cdot{}_1F_1\left(\left[\alpha+1,\alpha+3;\frac{1}{6}\right],\ln\frac{a}{b}\right)|f'(b)|^q}{6(\alpha+1)(\alpha+2)}\right)^{\frac{1}{q}}\right),$$

where $\alpha>0, \Upsilon, \mu_1, \mu_2, \mu_3, \mu_4, \Phi$ are defined by (1), (12), (13), (16), (17) *and* (20), *respectively, where ${}_1F_1(.;.;.)$ and ${}_1F_1([.,.;.],.)$ are the confluent and the incomplete confluent hypergeometric functions, respectively.*

Proof. From Lemma 2, the modulus, the power mean inequality, and the GA-convexity of $|f'|^q$, we have

$$\left|\frac{1}{8}\left(3f\left(a^{\frac{5}{6}}b^{\frac{1}{6}}\right)+2f\left(a^{\frac{1}{2}}b^{\frac{1}{2}}\right)+3f\left(a^{\frac{1}{6}}b^{\frac{5}{6}}\right)\right)-\frac{6^{\alpha-1}\Gamma(\alpha+1)}{(\ln b-\ln a)^{\alpha}}\Upsilon\right|$$
$$\leq\frac{\ln b-\ln a}{9}\left(\left(\int_0^1\frac{1}{4}\varkappa^{\alpha}a^{\frac{6-\varkappa}{6}}b^{\frac{\varkappa}{6}}d\varkappa\right)^{1-\frac{1}{q}}\left(\int_0^1\frac{1}{4}\varkappa^{\alpha}a^{\frac{6-\varkappa}{6}}b^{\frac{\varkappa}{6}}\left|f'\left(a^{\frac{6-\varkappa}{6}}b^{\frac{\varkappa}{6}}\right)\right|^q d\varkappa\right)^{\frac{1}{q}}\right.$$
$$+\left(\int_0^1\left|(1-\varkappa)^{\alpha}-\frac{3}{8}\right|a^{\frac{5-2\varkappa}{6}}b^{\frac{1+2\varkappa}{6}}d\varkappa\right)^{1-\frac{1}{q}}$$
$$\times\left(\int_0^1\left|(1-\varkappa)^{\alpha}-\frac{3}{8}\right|a^{\frac{5-2\varkappa}{6}}b^{\frac{1+2\varkappa}{6}}\left|f'\left(a^{\frac{5-2\varkappa}{6}}b^{\frac{1+2\varkappa}{6}}\right)\right|^q d\varkappa\right)^{\frac{1}{q}}$$
$$+\left(\int_0^1\left|\varkappa^{\alpha}-\frac{3}{8}\right|a^{\frac{3-2\varkappa}{6}}b^{\frac{3+2\varkappa}{6}}d\varkappa\right)^{1-\frac{1}{q}}$$
$$\times\left(\int_0^1\left|\varkappa^{\alpha}-\frac{3}{8}\right|a^{\frac{3-2\varkappa}{6}}b^{\frac{3+2\varkappa}{6}}\left|f'\left(a^{\frac{3-2\varkappa}{6}}b^{\frac{3+2\varkappa}{6}}\right)\right|^q d\varkappa\right)^{\frac{1}{q}}$$
$$+\left(\int_0^1\frac{1}{4}(1-\varkappa)^{\alpha}a^{\frac{1-\varkappa}{6}}b^{\frac{5+\varkappa}{6}}d\varkappa\right)^{1-\frac{1}{q}}$$

$$
\begin{aligned}
&\times \left(\int_0^1 \tfrac{1}{4}(1-\varkappa)^{\alpha} a^{\frac{1-\varkappa}{6}} b^{\frac{5+\varkappa}{6}} \left| f'\left(a^{\frac{1-\varkappa}{6}} b^{\frac{5+\varkappa}{6}}\right)\right|^q d\varkappa \right)^{\frac{1}{q}} \Bigg) \\
&\leq \frac{\ln b - \ln a}{9} \left(\frac{a}{4} \left(\int_0^1 \varkappa^{\alpha} \left(\tfrac{b}{a}\right)^{\frac{\varkappa}{6}} d\varkappa \right)^{1-\frac{1}{q}} \right. \\
&\times \left(|f'(a)|^q \int_0^1 \varkappa^{\alpha} \left(1-\tfrac{\varkappa}{6}\right)\left(\tfrac{b}{a}\right)^{\frac{\varkappa}{6}} d\varkappa + \tfrac{1}{6}|f'(b)|^q \int_0^1 \varkappa^{\alpha+1} \left(\tfrac{b}{a}\right)^{\frac{\varkappa}{6}} d\varkappa \right)^{\frac{1}{q}} \\
&+ \frac{a^{\frac{1}{2}} b^{\frac{1}{2}}}{6} \left(6 \int_0^1 \left|\varkappa^{\alpha} - \tfrac{3}{8}\right| \left(\tfrac{a}{b}\right)^{\frac{\varkappa}{3}} d\varkappa \right)^{1-\frac{1}{q}} \\
&\times \left(|f'(a)|^q \int_0^1 \left|\varkappa^{\alpha} - \tfrac{3}{8}\right| (3+2\varkappa) \left(\tfrac{a}{b}\right)^{\frac{\varkappa}{3}} d\varkappa + |f'(b)|^q \int_0^1 \left|\varkappa^{\alpha} - \tfrac{3}{8}\right| (3-2\varkappa) \left(\tfrac{a}{b}\right)^{\frac{\varkappa}{3}} d\varkappa \right)^{\frac{1}{q}} \\
&+ \frac{a^{\frac{1}{2}} b^{\frac{1}{2}}}{6} \left(6 \int_0^1 \left|\varkappa^{\alpha} - \tfrac{3}{8}\right| \left(\tfrac{b}{a}\right)^{\frac{\varkappa}{3}} d\varkappa \right)^{1-\frac{1}{q}} \\
&\times \left(|f'(a)|^q \int_0^1 \left|\varkappa^{\alpha} - \tfrac{3}{8}\right| (3-2\varkappa) \left(\tfrac{b}{a}\right)^{\frac{\varkappa}{3}} d\varkappa + |f'(b)|^q \int_0^1 \left|\varkappa^{\alpha} - \tfrac{3}{8}\right| (3+2\varkappa) \left(\tfrac{b}{a}\right)^{\frac{\varkappa}{3}} d\varkappa \right)^{\frac{1}{q}} \\
&+ \frac{b}{4} \left(\int_0^1 \varkappa^{\alpha} \left(\tfrac{a}{b}\right)^{\frac{\varkappa}{6}} d\varkappa \right)^{1-\frac{1}{q}} \\
&\times \left. \left(\tfrac{1}{6}|f'(a)|^q \int_0^1 \varkappa^{\alpha+1} \left(\tfrac{a}{b}\right)^{\frac{\varkappa}{6}} d\varkappa + |f'(b)|^q \int_0^1 \varkappa^{\alpha} \left(1 - \tfrac{1}{6}\varkappa\right) \left(\tfrac{a}{b}\right)^{\frac{\varkappa}{6}} d\varkappa \right)^{\frac{1}{q}} \right) \\
&= \frac{\ln b - \ln a}{9} \left(\frac{a}{4} \left(\frac{{}_1F_1\left(\alpha+1, \alpha+2, \frac{1}{6}\ln\frac{b}{a}\right)}{\alpha+1} \right)^{1-\frac{1}{q}} \right. \\
&\times \left(\frac{6^{\alpha+2} \cdot {}_1F_1\left(\left[\alpha+1, \alpha+3; \frac{1}{6}\right], \ln\frac{b}{a}\right)|f'(a)|^q + (\alpha+1)\,{}_1F_1\left(\alpha+2, \alpha+3, \frac{1}{6}\ln\frac{b}{a}\right)|f'(b)|^q}{6(\alpha+1)(\alpha+2)} \right)^{\frac{1}{q}} \\
&+ a^{\frac{1}{2}} b^{\frac{1}{2}} \left(\Phi\left(\alpha, \tfrac{a}{b}\right)\right)^{1-\frac{1}{q}} \left(\frac{\left(\mu_1\left(\alpha, \frac{a}{b}\right) + \mu_2\left(\alpha, \frac{a}{b}\right)\right)|f'(a)|^q + \left(\mu_3\left(\alpha, \frac{a}{b}\right) + \mu_4\left(\alpha, \frac{a}{b}\right)\right)|f'(b)|^q}{6} \right)^{\frac{1}{q}} \\
&+ a^{\frac{1}{2}} b^{\frac{1}{2}} \left(\Phi\left(\alpha, \tfrac{b}{a}\right)\right)^{1-\frac{1}{q}} \left(\frac{\left(\mu_3\left(\alpha, \frac{b}{a}\right) + \mu_4\left(\alpha, \frac{b}{a}\right)\right)|f'(a)|^q + \left(\mu_1\left(\alpha, \frac{b}{a}\right) + \mu_2\left(\alpha, \frac{b}{a}\right)\right)|f'(b)|^q}{6} \right)^{\frac{1}{q}} \\
&+ \frac{b}{4} \left(\frac{{}_1F_1\left(\alpha+1, \alpha+2, \frac{1}{6}\ln\frac{a}{b}\right)}{\alpha+1} \right)^{1-\frac{1}{q}} \\
&\times \left. \left(\frac{(\alpha+1)\,{}_1F_1\left(\alpha+2, \alpha+3, \frac{1}{6}\ln\frac{a}{b}\right)|f'(a)|^q + 6^{\alpha+2} \cdot {}_1F_1\left(\left[\alpha+1, \alpha+3; \frac{1}{6}\right], \ln\frac{a}{b}\right)|f'(b)|^q}{6(\alpha+1)(\alpha+2)} \right)^{\frac{1}{q}} \right),
\end{aligned}
$$

The proof is completed. □

5. Conclusions

This study deals with the fractional Newton–Cotes-type inequalities involving three points by applying one of a novel generalizations of convexity, called geometrically arithmetically convexity. To study this, we have firstly proved a new integral identity. Based on this identity, we have establish some new Maclaurin-type inequalities for functions whose modulus of the first derivatives are geometrically arithmetically convex via Hadamard fractional integral operators, which are very useful and important fractional integral operators in fractional calculus. We hope that the obtained results could be motivation researchers working in the of fractional calculus, and serve as inspiration for academics to prove novel results using more generalized forms of convexity together with other fractional integral operators.

Author Contributions: Conceptualization, T.C., B.M. and A.M.; Methodology, T.C., B.M. and A.M.; Formal analysis, T.C., B.M. and A.M.; Writing—original draft, T.C., B.M., A.M. and M.B.; Writing—review and editing, T.C., B.M., A.M. and M.B.; Project administration, A.M.; Funding acquisition, M.B. All authors have read and agreed to the published version of the manuscript.

Funding: This research was funded by King Khalid University through large research project under grant number R.G.P.2/252/44.

Data Availability Statement: No new data were created or analyzed in this study. Data sharing is not applicable to this article.

Conflicts of Interest: The authors declare no conflict of interest.

References

1. Awan, M.U.; Noor, M.A.; Mihai, M.V.; Noor, K.I.; Khan, A.G. Some new bounds for Simpson's rule involving special functions via harmonic h-convexity. *J. Nonlinear Sci. Appl.* **2017**, *10*, 1755–1766. [CrossRef]
2. Chiheb, T.; Boumaza, N.; Meftah, B. Some new Simpson-like type inequalities via preqausiinvexity. *Transylv. J. Math. Mech.* **2020**, *12*, 1–10.
3. Delavar, M.R.; De La Sen, M. Some generalizations of Hermite–Hadamard type inequalities. *Springer Plus* **2016**, *5*, 1661. [CrossRef] [PubMed]
4. Dragomir, S.S.; Agarwal, R.P.; Cerone, P. On Simpson's inequality and applications. *J. Inequal. Appl.* **2000**, *5*, 533–579. [CrossRef]
5. İmdat, İ.; Bekar, K.; Numan, S. Hermite-Hadamard and Simpson type inequalities for differentiable quasi-geometrically convex functions. *Turk. J. Anal. Number Theory* **2014**, *2*, 42–46.
6. İmdat, İ. Hermite-Hadamard and Simpson type inequalities for differentiable P-GA-functions. *Int. J. Anal.* **2014**, *2014*, 125439.
7. Kashuri, A.; Mohammed, P.O.; Abdeljawad, T.; Hamasalh, F.; Chu, Y. New Simpson Type Integral Inequalities for s-Convex Functions and Their Applications. *Math. Probl. Eng.* **2020**, *31*, 4415–4420. [CrossRef]
8. Kashuri, A.; Meftah, B.; Mohammed, P.O. Some weighted Simpson type inequalities for differentiable s-convex functions and their applications. *J. Frac. Calc. Nonlinear Sys.* **2021**, *1*, 75–94. [CrossRef]
9. Noor, M.A.; Noor, K.I.; Awan, M.U. Simpson-type inequalities for geometrically relative convex functions. *Ukr. Math. J.* **2018**, *70*, 1145–1154. [CrossRef]
10. Sarikaya, M.Z. New generalizations of Hermite-Hadamard type inequalities. *Turk. J. Ineq.* **2023**, *7*, 29–39.
11. Deng, J.; Wang, J. Fractional Hermite-Hadamard inequalities for (α, m)-logarithmically convex functions. *J. Inequal. Appl.* **2013**, *2013*, 364. [CrossRef]
12. İmdat, İ. New general integral inequalities for quasi-geometrically convex functions via fractional integrals. *J. Inequal. Appl.* **2013**, *2013*, 491.
13. Kashuri, A.; Meftah, B.; Mohammed, P.O.; Lupaş, A.A.; Abdalla, B.; Hamed, Y.S.; Abdeljawad, T. Fractional weighted Ostrowski-type inequalities and their applications. *Symmetry* **2021**, *13*, 968. [CrossRef]
14. Meftah, B.; Azaizia, A. Fractional Ostrowski type inequalities for functions whose first derivatives are MT-preinvex. *Rev. DeMatemáticas Univ. Del Atlántico Páginas* **2019**, *6*, 33–43.
15. İmdat, İ.; Aydin, M. Some new generalized integral inequalities for GA-s-convex functions via Hadamard fractional integrals. *Chin. J. Math.* **2016**, *2016*, 4361806.
16. Qi, F.; Xi, B.-Y. Some integral inequalities of Simpson type for GA-ε-convex functions. *Georgian Math. J.* **2013**, *20*, 775–788. [CrossRef]
17. Alomari, M.W.; Dragomir, S.S. Various error estimations for several Newton-Cotes quadrature formulae in terms of at most first derivative and applications in numerical integration. *Jordan J. Math. Stat.* **2014**, *7*, 89–108.
18. Niculescu, C.P. Convexity according to the geometric mean. *Math. Inequal. Appl.* **2000**, *3*, 155–167. [CrossRef]
19. Rainville, E.D. *Special Functions*; Macmillan Company: New York, NY, USA, 1960; Reprinted by Chelsea Publishing Company: Bronx, NY, USA, 1971.
20. Özarslan, M.A.; Ustaoğlu, C. Some incomplete hypergeometric functions and incomplete Riemann-Liouville fractional integral operators. *Mathematics* **2019**, *7*, 483. [CrossRef]

21. Kilbas, A.A.; Srivastava, H.M.; Trujillo, J.J. Theory and applications of fractional differential equations. In *North-Holland Mathematics Studies*; Elsevier Science B.V.: Amsterdam, The Netherlands, 2006; Volume 204.
22. Park, J. Some Hermite-Hadamard-like type inequalities for logarithmically convex functions. *Int. J. Math. Anal.* **2013**, *7*, 2217–2233. [CrossRef]

fractal and fractional

MDPI

Article

Some New Fractional Inequalities for Coordinated Convexity over Convex Set Pertaining to Fuzzy-Number-Valued Settings Governed by Fractional Integrals

Tareq Saeed [1], Adriana Cătaş [2,*], Muhammad Bilal Khan [3,*] and Ahmed Mohammed Alshehri [1]

1 Financial Mathematics and Actuarial Science (FMAS)—Research Group, Department of Mathematics, Faculty of Science, King Abdulaziz University, Jeddah 21589, Saudi Arabia; tsalmalki@kau.edu.sa (T.S.); amalshehre@kau.edu.sa (A.M.A.)

2 Department of Mathematics and Computer Science, University of Oradea, 1 University Street, 410087 Oradea, Romania

3 Department of Mathematics and Computer Science, Transilvania University of Brasov, 29 Eroilor Boulevard, 500036 Brasov, Romania

* Correspondence: acatas@uoradea.ro (A.C.); muhammad.bilal@unitbv.ro (M.B.K.)

Abstract: In this study, we first propose some new concepts of coordinated up and down convex mappings with fuzzy-number values. Then, Hermite–Hadamard-type inequalities via coordinated up and down convex fuzzy-number-valued mapping (coordinated UD-convex $FNVMs$) are introduced. By taking the products of two coordinated UD-convex $FNVMs$, Pachpatte-type inequalities are also obtained. Some new conclusions are also derived by making particular decisions with the newly defined inequalities, and it is demonstrated that the recently discovered inequalities are expansions of comparable findings in the literature. It is important to note that the main outcomes are validated using nontrivial examples.

Keywords: fuzzy-number-valued mappings; generalized fractional integral; coordinated convex mappings; coordinated UD-convexity; Hermite–Hadamard's inequalities

Citation: Saeed, T.; Cătaş, A.; Khan, M.B.; Alshehri, A.M. Some New Fractional Inequalities for Coordinated Convexity over Convex Set Pertaining to Fuzzy-Number-Valued Settings Governed by Fractional Integrals. *Fractal Fract.* **2023**, *7*, 856. https://doi.org/10.3390/fractalfract7120856

Academic Editor: Ivanka Stamova

Received: 13 October 2023
Revised: 23 November 2023
Accepted: 28 November 2023
Published: 30 November 2023

1. Introduction

One of the most well-known concepts in the field of function theory is the Hermite–Hadamard inequality, which was found by C. Hermite and J. Hadamard (and described in sources such as [1] and [2] (p. 137)). This inequality has several real-world applications in addition to its geometric interpretation.

The Hermite–Hadamard inequalities have been established by numerous mathematicians. It is important to note that the Hermite–Hadamard inequality, which naturally follows on from Jensen's inequality, can be seen as a development of the idea of convexity. Recently, there has been renewed interest in the Hermite–Hadamard inequality for convex functions, leading to a wide range of improvements and expansions that have been thoroughly investigated (see, for example, publications like [3–12]).

Interval analysis is a crucial topic since it is used in math and computer models as one method of addressing interval uncertainty. Even though this theory has a long history, going back to Archimedes' calculation of a circle's circumference, significant research on the subject was not published until the 1950s. The first book [13] on interval analysis was published in 1966 by Ramon E. Moore, who is credited with developing interval calculus. After that, other academics studied the theory and uses of interval analysis.

Furthermore, well-known inequality types, such as Ostrowski, Minkowski, and Beckenbach, as well as some of their applications were supplied by taking into account the interval-valued functions (see [14–18]). Additionally, Budak et al. [19] developed a few inequalities utilizing the interval-valued Riemann–Liouville fractional integrals. The definition of interval-valued harmonically convex functions was provided by Liu et al. [20], and, as a result, they were able to derive several Hermite–Hadamard-type inequalities, including interval fractional integrals. The authors provided a fuzzy integral-based variation of Jensen's inequality for interval-valued functions [21,22] and demonstrated several integral inequalities [23–26]. In their proofs of Hermite–Hadamard-type inequalities for set-valued functions [27–29], Mitroi et al. made use of the general forms of interval-valued convex functions. Rom'an Flores et al. found a few Gronwal-type inequalities for interval-valued functions [30]. Zhao et al. showed many kinds of integral inequalities for interval-valued functions [31–42].

In [43], Jleli and Samet discovered a brand-new Hermite–Hadamard-type inequality involving fractional integrals with regard to a different function. The fractional integrals of a function with respect to another function were first introduced by Tunc in [44]. The Riemann–Liouville and Hadamard fractional integrals were generalized into a single form by Katugompala's novel fractional integration. Budak and Agarwal used generalized fractional integrals, which generalize some significant fractional integrals like the Riemann–Liouville fractional integrals, the Hadamard fractional integrals, and the Katugampola fractional integrals in [45] to establish the Hermite–Hadamard-type inequalities for coordinated convex functions. The interval-valued left- and right-sided generalized fractional double integrals were defined by Kara et al. [46]. Numerous authors have concentrated on interval-valued functions in recent years. The authors of [47] introduced the idea of interval-valued general convex functions and used it to demonstrate a number of novel Hermite–Hadamard-type inequalities. A fractional version of Hermite–Hadamard-type inequalities for interval-valued harmonically convex functions was also provided by the authors in [48]. Researchers recently expanded the idea of interval-valued convexity and described various types of UD-convexity for interval-valued functions in [49,50]. For UD-fuzzy-number-valued convex functions, they also discovered a large number of Hermite–Hadmard type inequalities.

To express the collection of all the positive fuzzy numbers over real numbers, we introduce the notation $\mathbb{F}_0$ in the context of this article. The terms $\mathcal{A}_{[\upsilon,\ d]}$, $\mathcal{IA}_{[\upsilon,\ d]}$, and $\mathcal{FA}_{([\upsilon,\ d])}$ refer to the set of all $FNVMFNVMs$ that are Riemann integrable real-valued functions, Aumann's integrable *IV-Fs*, and fuzzy Aumann's integrable on the interval $[\upsilon,\ d]$. The following theorem draws a link between the functions that are integrable in terms of Riemann ($\mathcal{A}$-integrable) and functions that are integrable in terms of $\mathcal{FA}$. Additionally, the sign "$\supseteq_{\mathbb{F}}$" is used to denote the up and down (UD) fuzzy inclusion relationship for $\widetilde{Đ}$ and $\widetilde{ɱ}$ belonging to $\mathbb{F}_0$, where $\widetilde{ɱ}$ is thought of as a fuzzy subset of $\widetilde{Đ}$. If and only if for $\mathfrak{z}$-levels, the condition $[\widetilde{Đ}]^{\mathfrak{z}} \supseteq_I [\widetilde{ɱ}]^{\mathfrak{z}}$ is met, this UD-inclusion is true. Integral fuzzy inequalities generated from $FNVMs$ have recently attracted the attention of several academics.

Theorem 1 ([51]). *Assume that the UD-convex FNVM* $\widetilde{\gamma} : [\upsilon,\ d] \to \mathbb{F}_0$ *is an IVM with* $\gamma_{\mathfrak{z}}(\theta) = [\gamma_*(\theta, \mathfrak{z}),\ \gamma^*(\theta, \mathfrak{z})]$ *for all* $\theta \in [\upsilon,\ d]$ *and for all* $\mathfrak{z} \in [0,\ 1]$. *Then, there are disparities:*

$$\widetilde{\gamma}\left(\frac{\upsilon + d}{2}\right) \supseteq_{\mathbb{F}} \frac{1}{d - \upsilon} \odot (FA)\int_{\upsilon}^{d} \widetilde{\gamma}(\theta)d\theta \supseteq_{\mathbb{F}} \frac{\widetilde{\gamma}(d) \oplus \widetilde{\gamma}(\upsilon)}{2}. \tag{1}$$

We provide the ideas of generalized fractional integrals for two-variable $FNVMs$ in order to demonstrate Hermite–Hadmard-type inequalities for the convex and coordinated convex functions, which are inspired by ongoing investigations. The main benefit of the newly established inequalities is that they can be converted into classical Hermite–Hadamard integral inequalities for coordinated UD-convex $FNVMs$ and fuzzy Riemann–Liouville fractional Hermite–Hadamard, Hadamard, and Katugampola fractional Hermite–Hadamard inequalities without having to prove each one separately; for more information, see [52–64] and the references therein.

The format of this paper is as follows: A brief summary of the foundations of fuzzy-number-valued calculus and other relevant works in this area are presented in Section 2. In Section 3, we provide some generalized fractional integrals for *UD*-convex *FNVMFNVMs* with two variables. For *UD*-convex *FNVMFNVMs*, we create a novel Hermite–Hadamard-type inequality. Several Hermite–Hadamard-type inequalities for coordinated *UD*-convex *FNVMFNVMs* are presented in Section 3. It is also taken into consideration how these findings compare with the findings of a similar nature in the literature. Finally, Section 4 makes some suggestions for additional studies.

2. Preliminaries

We will go through the fundamental terminologies and findings in this section, which helps to comprehend the ideas behind our fresh findings.

Definition 1 ([58,59]). *Given $\widetilde{Đ} \in \mathbb{F}_0$, the level or cut sets are given by $[\widetilde{Đ}]^{\mathfrak{z}} = \{\theta \in \mathfrak{R} | \widetilde{Đ}(\theta) > \mathfrak{z}\}$ $\forall\, \mathfrak{z} \in [0,\ 1]$ and by*

$$[\widetilde{Đ}]^0 = \{\theta \in \mathfrak{R} | \widetilde{Đ}(\theta) > 0\}. \tag{2}$$

These sets are known as the $\mathfrak{z}$-level or $\mathfrak{z}$-cut sets of $\widetilde{Đ}$.

Proposition 1 ([22]). *Let $\widetilde{Đ}, \widetilde{₼} \in \mathbb{F}_0$. Then, the relation "$\leq_{\mathbb{F}}$" is given on $\mathbb{F}_0$ by $\widetilde{Đ} \leq_{\mathbb{F}} \widetilde{₼}$ when and only when $[\widetilde{Đ}]^{\mathfrak{z}} \leq_I [\widetilde{₼}]^{\mathfrak{z}}$, for every $\mathfrak{z} \in [0,\ 1]$, which are left- and right-order relations.*

Proposition 2 ([57]). *Let $\widetilde{Đ}, \widetilde{₼} \in \mathbb{F}_0$. Then, the relation " $\supseteq_{\mathbb{F}}$ " is given on $\mathbb{F}_0$ by $\widetilde{Đ} \supseteq_{\mathbb{F}} \widetilde{₼}$ when and only when $[\widetilde{Đ}]^{\mathfrak{z}} \supseteq_I [\widetilde{₼}]^{\mathfrak{z}}$ for every $\mathfrak{z} \in [0,\ 1]$, which is the UD-order relation on $\mathbb{F}_0$.*

Remember the approaching notions, which are offered in the literature. If $\widetilde{Đ}, \widetilde{₼} \in \mathbb{F}_0$ and $t \in \mathfrak{R}$, then, for every $\mathfrak{z} \in [0,\ 1]$, the arithmetic operation addition " $\oplus$", multiplication "$\otimes$", and scalar multiplication "$\odot$" are defined by

$$[\widetilde{Đ} \oplus \widetilde{₼}]^{\mathfrak{z}} = [\widetilde{Đ}]^{\mathfrak{z}} + [\widetilde{₼}]^{\mathfrak{z}}, \tag{3}$$

$$[\widetilde{Đ} \otimes \widetilde{₼}]^{\mathfrak{z}} = [\widetilde{Đ}]^{\mathfrak{z}} \times [\widetilde{₼}]^{\mathfrak{z}}, \tag{4}$$

$$[t \odot \widetilde{Đ}]^{\mathfrak{z}} = t\,[\widetilde{Đ}]^{\mathfrak{z}}. \tag{5}$$

Equations (4) to (6) have immediate consequences for these outcomes.

Theorem 2 ([22]). *The space $\mathbb{F}_0$ dealing with a supremum metric, i.e., for $\widetilde{Đ},\ \widetilde{₼} \in \mathbb{F}_0$*

$$d_\infty(\widetilde{Đ},\ \widetilde{₼}) = \sup_{0 \leq \mathfrak{z} \leq 1} d_H([\widetilde{Đ}]^{\mathfrak{z}},\ [\widetilde{₼}]^{\mathfrak{z}}), \tag{6}$$

is a complete metric space, where H indicates the well-known Hausdorff metric on the space of the intervals.

Theorem 3. *Let $\widetilde{\mathrm{Y}} : [\upsilon,\ d] \subset \mathfrak{R} \to \mathbb{F}_0$ be an FNVM, and the IVMs classified according to their $\mathfrak{z}$-levels $\mathrm{Y}_{\mathfrak{z}} : [\upsilon,\ d] \subset \mathfrak{R} \to \mathbb{R}_I$ are given by $\mathrm{Y}_{\mathfrak{z}}(\theta) = [\mathrm{Y}_*(\theta, \mathfrak{z}),\ \mathrm{Y}^*(\theta, \mathfrak{z})]$ $\forall\ \theta \in [\upsilon,\ d]$ and $\forall$ $\mathfrak{z} \in (0,\ 1]$. Then, $\widetilde{\mathrm{Y}}$ is FA-integrable over $[\upsilon,\ d]$ if and only if, $\mathrm{Y}_*(\theta, \mathfrak{z})$ and $\mathrm{Y}^*(\theta, \mathfrak{z})$ are both A-integrable over $[\upsilon,\ d]$. Moreover, if $\widetilde{\mathrm{Y}}$ is FA-integrable over $[\upsilon,\ d]$, then*

$$\begin{aligned}\left[(FA)\int_{\upsilon}^{d} \widetilde{\mathrm{Y}}(\theta)d\theta\right]^{\mathfrak{z}} &= \left[(A)\int_{\upsilon}^{d} \mathrm{Y}_*(\theta, \mathfrak{z})d\theta,\ (A)\int_{\upsilon}^{d} \mathrm{Y}^*(\theta, \mathfrak{z})d\theta\right] \\ &= (IA)\int_{\upsilon}^{d} \mathrm{Y}_{\mathfrak{z}}(\theta)d\theta,\end{aligned} \tag{7}$$

$\forall\, \mathfrak{z} \in (0,\, 1]$, *where* $\mathcal{FA}_{([\upsilon,\, \mathrm{d}],\, \mathfrak{z})}$ *denotes the collection of all FA-integrable FNVMs over* $[\upsilon,\, \mathrm{d}]$.

Fuzzy Aumann's and Fractional Calculus on Coordinates

Definition 2. ([19,38]). *Let* $\mathrm{Y} : [\eth,\, \mathrm{n}] \to \mathbb{R}_I^+$ *be an IVM and* $\mathrm{Y} \in \mathcal{IR}_{[\eth,\, \mathrm{n}]}$. *Then, the interval Riemann–Liouville type integrals of* Y *are defined as*

$$\mathcal{I}_{\eth^+}^{\Upsilon}\, \mathrm{Y}(\psi) = \frac{1}{\Gamma(\Upsilon)} \int_{\eth}^{\psi} (\psi - \mathrm{t})^{\Upsilon - 1} \mathrm{Y}(\mathrm{t}) d\mathrm{t} \quad (\psi > \eth), \tag{8}$$

$$\mathcal{I}_{\mathrm{n}^-}^{\Upsilon}\, \mathrm{Y}(\psi) = \frac{1}{\Gamma(\Upsilon)} \int_{\psi}^{\mathrm{n}} (\mathrm{t} - \psi)^{\Upsilon - 1} \mathrm{Y}(\mathrm{t}) d\mathrm{t} \quad (\psi < \mathrm{n}), \tag{9}$$

where $\Upsilon > 0$ *and* Γ *is the gamma function.*

Recently, Allahviranloo et al. [39] introduced the fuzzy version of the defined fractional integral integrals such that:

Definition 3. *Let* $\Upsilon > 0$ *and* $L([\eth,\, \mathrm{n}], \mathbb{F}_0)$ *be the collection of all the Lebesgue measurable FNVMs on* $[\eth, \mathrm{n}]$. *Then, the fuzzy left and right Riemann–Liouville fractional integrals of* $\widetilde{\mathrm{Y}} \in L([\eth,\, \mathrm{n}], \mathbb{F}_0)$ *with the order* $\Upsilon > 0$ *are defined by*

$$\mathcal{I}_{\eth^+}^{\Upsilon}\, \widetilde{\mathrm{Y}}(\psi) = \frac{1}{\Gamma(\Upsilon)} \int_{\eth}^{\psi} (\psi - \mathrm{t})^{\Upsilon - 1} \widetilde{\mathrm{Y}}(\mathrm{t}) d\mathrm{t}, \quad (\psi > \eth), \tag{10}$$

and

$$\mathcal{I}_{\mathrm{n}^-}^{\Upsilon}\, \widetilde{\mathrm{Y}}(\psi) = \frac{1}{\Gamma(\Upsilon)} \int_{\psi}^{\mathrm{n}} (\mathrm{t} - \psi)^{\Upsilon - 1} \widetilde{\mathrm{Y}}(\mathrm{t}) d\mathrm{t}, \quad (\psi < \mathrm{n}), \tag{11}$$

respectively, where $\Gamma(\psi) = \int_0^\infty \mathrm{t}^{\psi - 1} e^{-\mathrm{t}} d\mathrm{t}$ *is the Euler gamma function. The fuzzy left and right Riemann–Liouville fractional integral* ψ *based on the left and right end point functions can be defined, that is*

$$\begin{aligned} [\mathcal{I}_{\eth^+}^{\Upsilon}\, \widetilde{\mathrm{Y}}(\psi)]^{\mathfrak{z}} &= \tfrac{1}{\Gamma(\Upsilon)} \int_{\eth}^{\psi} (\psi - \mathrm{t})^{\Upsilon - 1} \mathrm{Y}_{\mathfrak{z}}(\mathrm{t}) d\mathrm{t} \\ &= \tfrac{1}{\Gamma(\Upsilon)} \int_{\eth}^{\psi} (\psi - \mathrm{t})^{\Upsilon - 1} [\mathrm{Y}_*(\mathrm{t}, \mathfrak{z}), \mathrm{Y}^*(\mathrm{t}, \mathfrak{z})] d\mathrm{t}, (\psi > \eth), \end{aligned} \tag{12}$$

where

$$\mathcal{I}_{\eth^+}^{\Upsilon}\, \mathrm{Y}_*(\psi,\, \mathfrak{z}) = \frac{1}{\Gamma(\Upsilon)} \int_{\eth}^{\psi} (\psi - \mathrm{t})^{\Upsilon - 1} \mathrm{Y}_*(\mathrm{t}, \mathfrak{z}) d\mathrm{t}, \quad (\psi > \eth), \tag{13}$$

and

$$\mathcal{I}_{\eth^+}^{\Upsilon}\, \mathrm{Y}^*(\psi,\, \mathfrak{z}) = \frac{1}{\Gamma(\Upsilon)} \int_{\eth}^{\psi} (\psi - \mathrm{t})^{\Upsilon - 1} \mathrm{Y}^*(\mathrm{t}, \mathfrak{z}) d\mathrm{t}, \quad (\psi > \eth). \tag{14}$$

The right Riemann–Liouville fractional integral, denoted by $[\mathcal{I}_{\mathrm{n}^-}^{\Upsilon}\, \widetilde{\mathrm{Y}}(\psi)]^{\mathfrak{z}}$, *can also be defined using the left and right end point functions.*

Theorem 4 ([57]). *Let* $\widetilde{\mathrm{Y}} : [\upsilon,\, \mathrm{d}] \to \mathbb{F}_0$ *be a UD-convex FNVM on* $[\upsilon,\, \mathrm{d}]$, *whose* $\mathfrak{z}$*-cuts set up the sequence of IVMs* $\mathrm{Y}_{\mathfrak{z}} : [\upsilon,\, \mathrm{d}] \subset \mathbb{R} \to \mathbb{R}_C{}^+$ *are given by* $\mathrm{Y}_{\mathfrak{z}}(\psi) = [\mathrm{Y}_*(\psi, \mathfrak{z}),\, \mathrm{Y}^*(\psi, \mathfrak{z})]$ *for all* $\psi \in [\upsilon,\, \mathrm{d}]$ *and for all* $\mathfrak{z} \in [0,\, 1]$. *If* $\widetilde{\mathrm{Y}} \in L([\upsilon,\, \mathrm{d}], \mathbb{F}_0)$, *then*

$$\widetilde{\mathrm{Y}}\left(\frac{\upsilon + \mathrm{d}}{2}\right) \supseteq_{\mathbb{F}} \frac{\Gamma(\Upsilon + 1)}{2(\mathrm{d} - \upsilon)^{\Upsilon}} \left[\mathcal{I}_{\upsilon^+}^{\Upsilon}\, \widetilde{\mathrm{Y}}(\mathrm{d}) \oplus \mathcal{I}_{\mathrm{d}^-}^{\Upsilon}\, \widetilde{\mathrm{Y}}(\upsilon)\right] \supseteq_{\mathbb{F}} \frac{\widetilde{\mathrm{Y}}(\upsilon) \oplus \widetilde{\mathrm{Y}}(\mathrm{d})}{2}. \tag{15}$$

Theorem 5 ([57]). *Let* $\widetilde{\mathrm{Y}}, \widetilde{\mathcal{J}} : [\upsilon,\, \mathrm{d}] \to \mathbb{F}_0$ *be two UD-convex FNVMs. Then, from the* $\mathfrak{z}$*-cuts, we set up the sequence of IVMs* $\mathrm{Y}_{\mathfrak{z}},\, \mathcal{J}_{\mathfrak{z}} : [\upsilon,\, \mathrm{d}] \subset \mathbb{R} \to \mathbb{R}_I^+$ *are given by* $\mathrm{Y}_{\mathfrak{z}}(\theta) = [\mathrm{Y}_*(\theta, \mathfrak{z}),\, \mathrm{Y}^*(\theta, \mathfrak{z})]$

and $\mathcal{J}_\mathfrak{z}(\theta) = [\mathcal{J}_*(\theta, \mathfrak{z}), \mathcal{J}^*(\theta, \mathfrak{z})]$ for all $\theta \in [\upsilon, d]$ and for all $\mathfrak{z} \in [0, 1]$. If $\widetilde{\Upsilon} \otimes \widetilde{\mathcal{J}} \in L([\upsilon, d], \mathbb{F}_0)$ is the fuzzy Riemann integrable, then

$$\frac{\Gamma(\Upsilon+1)}{2(d-\upsilon)^\Upsilon} [\mathcal{I}^\Upsilon_{\upsilon^+} \widetilde{\Upsilon}(d) \otimes \widetilde{\mathcal{J}}(d) \oplus \mathcal{I}^\Upsilon_{d^-} \widetilde{\Upsilon}(\upsilon) \otimes \widetilde{\mathcal{J}}(\upsilon)]$$
$$\supseteq_\mathbb{F} \left(\frac{1}{2} - \frac{\Upsilon}{(\Upsilon+1)(\Upsilon+2)}\right) \widetilde{\mathcal{M}}(\upsilon, d) \oplus \left(\frac{\Upsilon}{(\Upsilon+1)(\Upsilon+2)}\right) \widetilde{\mathcal{N}}(\upsilon, d), \quad (16)$$

and

$$\widetilde{\Upsilon}\left(\frac{\upsilon+d}{2}\right) \otimes \widetilde{\mathcal{J}}\left(\frac{\upsilon+d}{2}\right)$$
$$\supseteq_\mathbb{F} \frac{\Gamma(\Upsilon+1)}{4(d-\upsilon)^\Upsilon} \left[\mathcal{I}^\Upsilon_{\upsilon^+} \widetilde{\Upsilon}(d) \otimes \widetilde{\mathcal{J}}(d) \oplus \mathcal{I}^\Upsilon_{d^-} \widetilde{\Upsilon}(\upsilon) \otimes \widetilde{\mathcal{J}}(\upsilon)\right] \quad (17)$$
$$+\frac{1}{2}\left(\frac{1}{2} - \frac{\Upsilon}{(\Upsilon+1)(\Upsilon+2)}\right) \widetilde{\mathcal{M}}(\upsilon, d) \oplus \frac{1}{2}\left(\frac{\Upsilon}{(\Upsilon+1)(\Upsilon+2)}\right) \widetilde{\mathcal{N}}(\upsilon, d),$$

where $\widetilde{\mathcal{M}}(\upsilon, d) = \widetilde{\Upsilon}(\upsilon) \otimes \widetilde{\mathcal{J}}(\upsilon) \oplus \widetilde{\Upsilon}(d) \otimes \widetilde{\mathcal{J}}(d)$, $\widetilde{\mathcal{N}}(\upsilon, d) = \widetilde{\Upsilon}(\upsilon) \otimes \widetilde{\mathcal{J}}(d) \oplus \widetilde{\Upsilon}(d) \otimes \widetilde{\mathcal{J}}(\upsilon)$, $\mathcal{M}_\mathfrak{z}(\upsilon, d) = [\mathcal{M}_*((\upsilon, d), \mathfrak{z}), \mathcal{M}^*((\upsilon, d), \mathfrak{z})]$, and $\mathcal{N}_\mathfrak{z}(\upsilon, d) = [\mathcal{N}_*((\upsilon, d), \mathfrak{z}), \mathcal{N}^*((\upsilon, d), \mathfrak{z})]$.

The interval and fuzzy Aumann's type integrals are defined as follows for the coordinated IVM $\Upsilon(\theta, \psi)$ and coordinated $FNVM$ $\widetilde{\Upsilon}(\theta, \psi)$:

Theorem 6 ([57]). *Let $\widetilde{\Upsilon}: \Delta[\delta, n] \times [\upsilon, d] \subset \mathbb{R}^2 \to \mathbb{F}_0$ be an FNVM on the coordinates, whose $\mathfrak{z}$-cuts set up the sequence of IVMs $\Upsilon_\mathfrak{z}: \Delta \subset \mathbb{R}^2 \to \mathbb{R}_I$ are given by $\Upsilon_\mathfrak{z}(\theta, \psi) = [\Upsilon_*((\theta, \psi), \mathfrak{z}), \Upsilon^*((\theta, \psi), \mathfrak{z})]$ for all $(\theta, \psi) \in \Delta = [\delta, n] \times [\upsilon, d]$ and for all $\mathfrak{z} \in [0, 1]$. Then, $\widetilde{\Upsilon}$ is fuzzy double integrable (FD-integrable) over Δ if and only if $\Upsilon_*(\theta, \mathfrak{z})$ and $\Upsilon^*(\theta, \mathfrak{z})$ are both D-integrable over Δ. Moreover, if $\widetilde{\Upsilon}$ is FD-integrable over Δ, then*

$$\left[(FD)\int_\delta^n \int_\upsilon^d \widetilde{\Upsilon}(\theta, \psi) d\psi d\theta\right]^\mathfrak{z} = \left[(D)\int_\delta^n \int_\upsilon^d \Upsilon_*((\theta, \psi), \mathfrak{z}) d\psi d\theta, (D)\int_\delta^n \int_\upsilon^d \Upsilon^*((\theta, \psi), \mathfrak{z}) d\psi d\theta\right] \quad (18)$$
$$= (ID)\int_\delta^n \int_\upsilon^d \Upsilon_\mathfrak{z}(\theta, \psi) d\psi d\theta,$$

for all $\mathfrak{z} \in [0, 1]$.

The family of all FD-integrable functions of $FNVMs$ over coordinates and D-integrable functions over coordinates are denoted by $\mathcal{FD}_\Delta$ and $\mathfrak{D}_{(\Delta, \mathfrak{z})}$ for all $\mathfrak{z} \in [0, 1]$.

The following is the main definition of the fuzzy Riemann–Liouville fractional integral on the coordinates of the function $\widetilde{\Upsilon}(\theta, \psi)$:

Definition 4. *([42]). Let $\widetilde{\Upsilon}: \Delta \to \mathbb{F}_0$ and $\widetilde{\Upsilon} \in \mathcal{FD}_\Delta$. The double fuzzy interval Riemann–Liouville-type integrals $\mathcal{I}^{\Upsilon, \beta}_{\delta^+, \upsilon^+}$, $\mathcal{I}^{\Upsilon, \beta}_{\delta^+, d^-}$, $\mathcal{I}^{\Upsilon, \beta}_{n^-, \upsilon^+}$, $\mathcal{I}^{\Upsilon, \beta}_{n^-, d^-}$ of Υ order $\Upsilon, \beta > 0$ are defined by the following:*

$$\mathcal{I}^{\Upsilon, \beta}_{\delta^+, \upsilon^+} \widetilde{\Upsilon}(\theta, \psi) = \frac{1}{\Gamma(\Upsilon)\Gamma(\beta)} \int_\delta^\theta \int_\upsilon^\psi (\theta - t)^{\Upsilon-1}(\psi - s)^{\beta-1} \widetilde{\Upsilon}(t, s) ds dt, \quad (\theta > \delta, \psi > \upsilon), \quad (19)$$

$$\mathcal{I}^{\Upsilon, \beta}_{\delta^+, d^-} \widetilde{\Upsilon}(\theta, \psi) = \frac{1}{\Gamma(\Upsilon)\Gamma(\beta)} \int_\delta^\theta \int_\psi^d (\theta - t)^{\Upsilon-1}(s - \psi)^{\beta-1} \widetilde{\Upsilon}(t, s) ds dt, \quad (\theta > \delta, \psi < d), \quad (20)$$

$$\mathcal{I}^{\Upsilon, \beta}_{n^-, \upsilon^+} \widetilde{\Upsilon}(\theta, \psi) = \frac{1}{\Gamma(\Upsilon)\Gamma(\beta)} \int_\theta^n \int_\upsilon^\psi (t - \theta)^{\Upsilon-1}(\psi - s)^{\beta-1} \widetilde{\Upsilon}(t, s) ds dt, \quad (\theta < n, \psi > \upsilon), \quad (21)$$

$$\mathcal{I}^{\Upsilon, \beta}_{n^-, d^-} \widetilde{\Upsilon}(\theta, \psi) = \frac{1}{\Gamma(\Upsilon)\Gamma(\beta)} \int_\theta^n \int_\psi^d (t - \theta)^{\Upsilon-1}(s - \psi)^{\beta-1} \widetilde{\Upsilon}(t, s) ds dt, \quad (\theta < n, \psi < d). \quad (22)$$

The following is the newly defined concept of coordinated convexity over fuzzy-number space in the codomain via the UD-relation:

Definition 5 ([42]). *The FNVM* $\widetilde{\mathrm{y}} : \Delta \to \mathbb{F}_0$ *is referred to as a coordinated UD-convex FNVM on* Δ *if*

$$\begin{aligned}&\widetilde{\mathrm{y}}(\varepsilon\eth + (1-\varepsilon)\mathrm{n},\ s\upsilon + (1-s)\mathrm{d})\\ &\supseteq_{\mathbb{F}} \varepsilon s\widetilde{\mathrm{y}}(\eth,\upsilon) \oplus \varepsilon(1-s)\widetilde{\mathrm{y}}(\eth,\mathrm{d}) \oplus (1-\varepsilon)s\widetilde{\mathrm{y}}(\mathrm{n},\upsilon) \oplus (1-\varepsilon)(1-s)\widetilde{\mathrm{y}}(\mathrm{n},\mathrm{d}),\end{aligned} \tag{23}$$

for all $(\eth,\ \mathrm{n}),\ (\upsilon,\mathrm{d}) \in \Delta$, *and* $\varepsilon, s \in [0,\ 1]$, *where* $\widetilde{\mathrm{y}}(\theta) \geq_{\mathbb{F}} \widetilde{0}$. *If inequality (23) is reversed, then* $\widetilde{\mathrm{y}}$ *is referred to as a coordinate concave FNVM on* Δ.

Lemma 1 ([42]). *Let* $\widetilde{\mathrm{y}} : \Delta \to \mathbb{F}_0$ *be a coordinated FNVM on* Δ. *Then,* $\widetilde{\mathrm{y}}$ *is a coordinated UD-convex FNVM on* Δ *if and only if there are two coordinated UD-convex FNVMs* $\widetilde{\mathrm{y}}_\theta : [\upsilon,\mathrm{d}] \to \mathbb{F}_0$, $\widetilde{\mathrm{y}}_\theta(w) = \widetilde{\mathrm{y}}(\theta, w)$ *and* $\widetilde{\mathrm{y}}_\psi : [\eth,\mathrm{n}] \to \mathbb{F}_0$, $\widetilde{\mathrm{y}}_\psi(z) = \widetilde{\mathrm{y}}(z,\psi)$.

Theorem 7 ([42]). *Let* $\widetilde{\mathrm{y}} : \Delta \to \mathbb{F}_0$ *be an FNVM on* Δ. *Then, from the* $\mathfrak{z}$*-levels, we obtain the collection of IVMs* $\mathrm{y}_\mathfrak{z} : \Delta \to \mathbb{R}_I^+ \subset \mathbb{R}_I$ *are given by*

$$\mathrm{y}_\mathfrak{z}(\theta,\psi) = [\mathrm{y}_*((\theta,\psi),\mathfrak{z}),\ \mathrm{y}^*((\theta,\psi),\mathfrak{z})] \tag{24}$$

for all $(\theta,\psi) \in \Delta$ *and for all* $\mathfrak{z} \in [0,\ 1]$. *Then,* $\widetilde{\mathrm{y}}$ *is a coordinated UD-convex FNVM on* Δ, *if and only if, for all* $\mathfrak{z} \in [0,\ 1]$, $\mathrm{y}_*((\theta,\psi),\ \mathfrak{z})$ *and* $\mathrm{y}^*((\theta,\psi),\ \mathfrak{z})$ *are coordinated convex and concave functions, respectively.*

Example 1. *We consider the FNVM* $\widetilde{\mathrm{y}} : [0,\ 1] \times [0,\ 1] \to \mathbb{F}_0$ *defined by*

$$\mathrm{y}(\theta)(\sigma) = \begin{cases} \frac{\sigma-\theta\psi}{5-\theta\psi}, & \sigma \in [\theta\psi,\ 5] \\ \frac{(6+e^\theta)(6+e^\psi)-\sigma}{(6+e^\theta)(6+e^\psi)-5}, & \sigma \in (5,\ (6+e^\theta)(6+e^\psi)] \\ 0\quad, & \text{otherwise.} \end{cases} \tag{25}$$

Then, for each $\mathfrak{z} \in [0,\ 1]$, *we have* $\mathrm{y}_\mathfrak{z}(\theta) = [(1-\mathfrak{z})\theta\psi + 5\mathfrak{z}, (1-\mathfrak{z})\left(6+e^\theta\right)(6+e^\psi) + 5\mathfrak{z}]$. *Since the endpoint functions* $\mathrm{y}_*((\theta,\psi),\mathfrak{z}), \mathrm{y}^*((\theta,\psi),\mathfrak{z})$ *are coordinate concave functions for each* $\mathfrak{z} \in [0,\ 1]$, *hence* $\widetilde{\mathrm{y}}(\theta,\psi)$ *is a coordinate UD-convex FNVM.*

From Lemma 1 and Example 1, we can easily note that each UD-convex $FNVM$ is a coordinated UD-convex $FNVM$. But the converse is not true.

Remark 1. *If one assumes that* $\mathrm{y}_*((\theta,\psi),\mathfrak{z}) = \mathrm{y}^*((\theta,\psi),\mathfrak{z})$ *with* $\mathfrak{z} = 1$, *then* y *is referred to as a classical coordinated convex function if* y *meets the stated inequality here:*

$$\begin{aligned}&\mathrm{y}(\varepsilon\eth + (1-\varepsilon)\mathrm{n},\ s\upsilon + (1-s)\mathrm{d})\\ &\quad\leq \varepsilon s\mathrm{y}(\eth,\upsilon) + \varepsilon(1-s)\mathrm{y}(\eth,\mathrm{d}) + (1-\varepsilon)s\mathrm{y}(\mathrm{n},\upsilon) + (1-\varepsilon)(1-s)\mathrm{y}(\mathrm{n},\mathrm{d}).\end{aligned}$$

Let one assume that $\mathrm{y}_*((\theta,\psi),\mathfrak{z}) \neq \mathrm{y}^*((\theta,\psi),\mathfrak{z})$ *with* $\mathfrak{z} = 1$ *and* $\mathrm{y}_*((\theta,\psi),\mathfrak{z})$ *is an affine function and* $\mathrm{y}^*((\theta,\psi),\mathfrak{z})$ *is a concave function. If the stated inequality is present (see [25]), then*

$$\begin{aligned}&\mathrm{y}(\varepsilon\eth + (1-\varepsilon)\mathrm{n},\ s\upsilon + (1-s)\mathrm{d})\\ &\quad\supseteq \varepsilon s\mathrm{y}(\eth,\upsilon) + \varepsilon(1-s)\mathrm{y}(\eth,\mathrm{d}) + (1-\varepsilon)s\mathrm{y}(\mathrm{n},\upsilon) + (1-\varepsilon)(1-s)\mathrm{y}(\mathrm{n},\mathrm{d}),\end{aligned}$$

is true.

Definition 6. *Let* $\curlyvee_{\mathfrak{z}} : \Delta \to \mathbb{R}_I^+ \subset \mathbb{R}_I$ *be the collection of IVMs such that for each* $\mathfrak{z} \in [0,\ 1]$, $\curlyvee_{\mathfrak{z}}(\theta, \psi) = [\curlyvee_*((\theta, \psi), \mathfrak{z}),\ \curlyvee^*((\theta, \psi), \mathfrak{z})]$ *with* $\curlyvee_*((\theta, \psi),\ \mathfrak{z})$ *and* $\curlyvee^*((\theta, \psi),\ \mathfrak{z})$ *are coordinated convex (concave) and affine functions on* Δ*, respectively. Then,* $\widetilde{\curlyvee} : \Delta \to \mathbb{F}_0$ *is called a coordinated left-UD-convex (concave) FNVM on* Δ.

Definition 7. *Let* $\curlyvee_{\mathfrak{z}} : \Delta \to \mathbb{R}_I^+ \subset \mathbb{R}_I$ *be the collection of IVMs such that for each* $\mathfrak{z} \in [0,\ 1]$, $\curlyvee_{\mathfrak{z}}(\theta, \psi) = [\curlyvee_*((\theta, \psi), \mathfrak{z}),\ \curlyvee^*((\theta, \psi), \mathfrak{z})]$ *with* $\curlyvee_*((\theta, \psi),\ \mathfrak{z})$ *and* $\curlyvee^*((\theta, \psi),\ \mathfrak{z})$ *are coordinated affine and convex (concave) functions on* Δ*, respectively. Then,* $\widetilde{\curlyvee} : \Delta \to \mathbb{F}_0$ *is called a coordinated right-UD-convex (concave) FNVM on* Δ.

Theorem 8. *Let* Δ *be a coordinated convex set, and let* $\widetilde{\curlyvee} : \Delta \to \mathbb{F}_0$ *be an FNVM. Then, from the* $\mathfrak{z}$*-levels, we obtain the collection of IVMs* $\curlyvee_{\mathfrak{z}} : \Delta \to \mathbb{R}_I^+ \subset \mathbb{R}_I$*, which are given by*

$$\curlyvee_{\mathfrak{z}}(\theta, \psi) = [\curlyvee_*((\theta, \psi), \mathfrak{z}),\ \curlyvee^*((\theta, \psi), \mathfrak{z})], \tag{26}$$

for all $(\theta, \psi) \in \Delta$ *and for all* $\mathfrak{z} \in [0,\ 1]$*. Then,* $\widetilde{\curlyvee}$ *is a coordinated UD-concave FNVM on* Δ*, if and only if, for all* $\mathfrak{z} \in [0,\ 1]$, $\curlyvee_*((\theta, \psi),\ \mathfrak{z})$ *and* $\curlyvee^*((\theta, \psi),\ \mathfrak{z})$ *are coordinated concave and convex functions, respectively.*

Proof. The demonstration of proof of Theorem 8 is similar to the demonstration of proof of Theorem 7. □

Example 2. *We consider the FNVMs* $\widetilde{\curlyvee} : [0,\ 1] \times [0,\ 1] \to \mathbb{F}_0$ *defined by*

$$\widetilde{\curlyvee}(\theta)(\sigma) = \begin{cases} \frac{\sigma - \left(6-e^{\theta}\right)\left(6-e^{\psi}\right)}{\left(6-e^{\theta}\right)\left(6-e^{\psi}\right)-25}, & \sigma \in \left[\left(6-e^{\theta}\right)\left(6-e^{\psi}\right),\ 25\right] \\ \frac{35\theta\psi - \sigma}{35\theta\psi - 25}, & \sigma \in (25,\ 35\theta\psi] \\ 0, & \text{otherwise.} \end{cases} \tag{27}$$

Then, for each $\mathfrak{z} \in [0,\ 1]$*, we have* $\curlyvee_{\mathfrak{z}}(\theta, \psi) = \left[(1-\mathfrak{z})\left(6-e^{\theta}\right)\left(6-e^{\psi}\right) + 25\mathfrak{z}, 35(1-\mathfrak{z})\theta\psi + 25\mathfrak{z}\right]$*. Since the endpoint functions* $\curlyvee_*((\theta, \psi), \mathfrak{z})$, $\curlyvee^*((\theta, \psi), \mathfrak{z})$ *are coordinate concave and convex functions for each* $\mathfrak{z} \in [0,\ 1]$*, hence* $\widetilde{\curlyvee}(\theta, \psi)$ *is a coordinated UD-concave FNVM.*

In the next results, to avoid confusion, we will not include the symbols (R), (IR), (FR), (ID), and (FD) before the integral sign.

The main goal of this article is to develop a number of original fractional coordinated integral inequalities for the Hermite–Hadamard types using a coordinated UD-concave $FNVM$. We acquired the most recent estimates for mappings whose products are coordinated UD-concave $FNVMs$ using the fuzzy fractional operators.

3. Main Results

The following is the first result of coordinated integral inequalities for the Hermite–Hadamard type using the fuzzy fractional operators via coordinated UD-concave $FNVMs$.

Theorem 9. *Let* $\widetilde{\curlyvee} : \Delta \to \mathbb{F}_0$ *be a coordinate UD-convex FNVM on* Δ*. Then, from the* $\mathfrak{z}$*-cuts, we set up the sequence of IVMs* $\curlyvee_{\mathfrak{z}} : \Delta \to \mathbb{R}_I^+$ *are given by* $\curlyvee_{\mathfrak{z}}(\theta, \psi) = [\curlyvee_*((\theta, \psi), \mathfrak{z}),\ \curlyvee^*((\theta, \psi), \mathfrak{z})]$ *for all* $(\theta, \psi) \in \Delta$ *and for all* $\mathfrak{z} \in [0,\ 1]$*. If* $\widetilde{\curlyvee} \in \mathcal{FD}_{\Delta}$*, then the following inequalities hold:*

$$\begin{aligned}
&\widetilde{\mathrm{Y}}\left(\frac{\eth+\mathrm{n}}{2}, \frac{\upsilon+\mathrm{d}}{2}\right) \\
&\supseteq_{\mathbb{F}} \frac{\Gamma(\gamma+1)}{4(\mathrm{n}-\eth)^{\gamma}}\left[\mathcal{I}_{\eth^+}^{\gamma}\widetilde{\mathrm{Y}}\left(\mathrm{n}, \frac{\upsilon+\mathrm{d}}{2}\right) \oplus \mathcal{I}_{\mathrm{n}^-}^{\gamma}\widetilde{\mathrm{Y}}\left(\eth, \frac{\upsilon+\mathrm{d}}{2}\right)\right] \oplus \frac{\Gamma(\beta+1)}{4(\mathrm{d}-\upsilon)^{\beta}}\left[\mathcal{I}_{\upsilon^+}^{\beta}\widetilde{\mathrm{Y}}\left(\frac{\eth+\mathrm{n}}{2}, \mathrm{d}\right) \oplus \mathcal{I}_{\mathrm{d}^-}^{\beta}\widetilde{\mathrm{Y}}\left(\frac{\eth+\mathrm{n}}{2}, \upsilon\right)\right] \\
&\supseteq_{\mathbb{F}} \frac{\Gamma(\gamma+1)\Gamma(\beta+1)}{4(\mathrm{n}-\eth)^{\gamma}(\mathrm{d}-\upsilon)^{\beta}}\left[\mathcal{I}_{\eth^+,\upsilon^+}^{\gamma,\beta}\widetilde{\mathrm{Y}}(\mathrm{n},\mathrm{d}) \oplus \mathcal{I}_{\eth^+,\mathrm{d}^-}^{\gamma,\beta}\widetilde{\mathrm{Y}}(\mathrm{n},\upsilon) \oplus \mathcal{I}_{\mathrm{n}^-,\upsilon^+}^{\gamma,\beta}\widetilde{\mathrm{Y}}(\eth,\mathrm{d}) \oplus \mathcal{I}_{\mathrm{n}^-,\mathrm{d}^-}^{\gamma,\beta}\widetilde{\mathrm{Y}}(\eth,\upsilon)\right] \\
&\supseteq_{\mathbb{F}} \frac{\Gamma(\gamma+1)}{8(\mathrm{n}-\eth)^{\gamma}}\left[\mathcal{I}_{\eth^+}^{\gamma}\widetilde{\mathrm{Y}}(\mathrm{n},\upsilon) \oplus \mathcal{I}_{\eth^+}^{\gamma}\widetilde{\mathrm{Y}}(\mathrm{n},\mathrm{d}) \oplus \mathcal{I}_{\mathrm{n}^-}^{\gamma}\widetilde{\mathrm{Y}}(\eth,\upsilon) \oplus \mathcal{I}_{\mathrm{n}^-}^{\gamma}\widetilde{\mathrm{Y}}(\eth,\mathrm{d})\right] \\
&\oplus \frac{\Gamma(\beta+1)}{8(\mathrm{d}-\upsilon)^{\beta}}\left[\mathcal{I}_{\upsilon^+}^{\beta}\widetilde{\mathrm{Y}}(\eth,\mathrm{d}) \oplus \mathcal{I}_{\mathrm{d}^-}^{\beta}\widetilde{\mathrm{Y}}(\mathrm{n},\upsilon) \oplus \mathcal{I}_{\upsilon^+}^{\beta}\widetilde{\mathrm{Y}}(\mathrm{n},\mathrm{d}) \oplus \mathcal{I}_{\mathrm{d}^-}^{\beta}\widetilde{\mathrm{Y}}(\mathrm{n},\upsilon)\right] \\
&\supseteq_{\mathbb{F}} \frac{\widetilde{\mathrm{Y}}(\eth,\upsilon)\oplus\widetilde{\mathrm{Y}}(\mathrm{n},\upsilon)\oplus\widetilde{\mathrm{Y}}(\eth,\mathrm{d})\oplus\widetilde{\mathrm{Y}}(\mathrm{n},\mathrm{d})}{4}.
\end{aligned} \tag{28}$$

If $\mathrm{Y}(\theta)$ *is a coordinated concave FNVM then,*

$$\begin{aligned}
&\widetilde{\mathrm{Y}}\left(\frac{\eth+\mathrm{n}}{2}, \frac{\upsilon+\mathrm{d}}{2}\right) \\
&\subseteq_{\mathbb{F}} \frac{\Gamma(\gamma+1)}{4(\mathrm{n}-\eth)^{\gamma}}\left[\mathcal{I}_{\eth^+}^{\gamma}\widetilde{\mathrm{Y}}\left(\mathrm{n}, \frac{\upsilon+\mathrm{d}}{2}\right) \oplus \mathcal{I}_{\mathrm{n}^-}^{\gamma}\widetilde{\mathrm{Y}}\left(\eth, \frac{\upsilon+\mathrm{d}}{2}\right)\right] \oplus \frac{\Gamma(\beta+1)}{4(\mathrm{d}-\upsilon)^{\beta}}\left[\mathcal{I}_{\upsilon^+}^{\beta}\widetilde{\mathrm{Y}}\left(\frac{\eth+\mathrm{n}}{2}, \mathrm{d}\right) \oplus \mathcal{I}_{\mathrm{d}^-}^{\beta}\widetilde{\mathrm{Y}}\left(\frac{\eth+\mathrm{n}}{2}, \upsilon\right)\right] \\
&\subseteq_{\mathbb{F}} \frac{\Gamma(\gamma+1)\Gamma(\beta+1)}{4(\mathrm{n}-\eth)^{\gamma}(\mathrm{d}-\upsilon)^{\beta}}\left[\mathcal{I}_{\eth^+,\upsilon^+}^{\gamma,\beta}\widetilde{\mathrm{Y}}(\mathrm{n},\mathrm{d}) \oplus \mathcal{I}_{\eth^+,\mathrm{d}^-}^{\gamma,\beta}\widetilde{\mathrm{Y}}(\mathrm{n},\upsilon) \oplus \mathcal{I}_{\mathrm{n}^-,\upsilon^+}^{\gamma,\beta}\widetilde{\mathrm{Y}}(\eth,\mathrm{d}) \oplus \mathcal{I}_{\mathrm{n}^-,\mathrm{d}^-}^{\gamma,\beta}\widetilde{\mathrm{Y}}(\eth,\upsilon)\right] \\
&\subseteq_{\mathbb{F}} \frac{\Gamma(\gamma+1)}{8(\mathrm{n}-\eth)^{\gamma}}\left[\mathcal{I}_{\eth^+}^{\gamma}\widetilde{\mathrm{Y}}(\mathrm{n},\upsilon) \oplus \mathcal{I}_{\eth^+}^{\gamma}\widetilde{\mathrm{Y}}(\mathrm{n},\mathrm{d}) \oplus \mathcal{I}_{\mathrm{n}^-}^{\gamma}\widetilde{\mathrm{Y}}(\eth,\upsilon) \oplus \mathcal{I}_{\mathrm{n}^-}^{\gamma}\widetilde{\mathrm{Y}}(\eth,\mathrm{d})\right] \\
&\oplus \frac{\Gamma(\beta+1)}{8(\mathrm{d}-\upsilon)^{\beta}}\left[\mathcal{I}_{\upsilon^+}^{\beta}\widetilde{\mathrm{Y}}(\eth,\mathrm{d}) \oplus \mathcal{I}_{\mathrm{d}^-}^{\beta}\widetilde{\mathrm{Y}}(\mathrm{n},\upsilon) \oplus \mathcal{I}_{\upsilon^+}^{\beta}\widetilde{\mathrm{Y}}(\mathrm{n},\mathrm{d}) \oplus \mathcal{I}_{\mathrm{d}^-}^{\beta}\widetilde{\mathrm{Y}}(\eth,\upsilon)\right] \\
&\subseteq_{\mathbb{F}} \frac{\widetilde{\mathrm{Y}}(\eth,\upsilon)\oplus\widetilde{\mathrm{Y}}(\mathrm{n},\upsilon)\oplus\widetilde{\mathrm{Y}}(\eth,\mathrm{d})\oplus\widetilde{\mathrm{Y}}(\mathrm{n},\mathrm{d})}{4}.
\end{aligned} \tag{29}$$

Proof. Let $\widetilde{\mathrm{Y}} : [\eth, \mathrm{n}] \to \mathbb{F}_0$ be a coordinated *UD*-convex *FNVM*. Then, by hypothesis, we have

$$4\widetilde{\mathrm{Y}}\left(\frac{\eth+\mathrm{n}}{2}, \frac{\upsilon+\mathrm{d}}{2}\right) \supseteq_{\mathbb{F}} \widetilde{\mathrm{Y}}(\varepsilon\eth+(1-\varepsilon)\mathrm{n},\ \varepsilon\upsilon+(1-\varepsilon)\mathrm{d}) \oplus \widetilde{\mathrm{Y}}((1-\varepsilon)\eth+\varepsilon\mathrm{n},\ (1-\varepsilon)\upsilon+\varepsilon\mathrm{d}).$$

Using Theorem 7, for every $\mathfrak{z} \in [0, 1]$, we have

$$\begin{aligned}
&4\mathrm{Y}_*\left(\left(\frac{\eth+\mathrm{n}}{2}, \frac{\upsilon+\mathrm{d}}{2}\right), \mathfrak{z}\right) \\
&\leq \mathrm{Y}_*((\varepsilon\eth+(1-\varepsilon)\mathrm{n},\ \varepsilon\upsilon+(1-\varepsilon)\mathrm{d}),\ \mathfrak{z}) + \mathrm{Y}_*(((1-\varepsilon)\eth+\varepsilon\mathrm{n},\ (1-\varepsilon)\upsilon+\varepsilon\mathrm{d}),\ \mathfrak{z}), \\
&4\mathrm{Y}^*\left(\left(\frac{\eth+\mathrm{n}}{2}, \frac{\upsilon+\mathrm{d}}{2}\right), \mathfrak{z}\right) \\
&\geq \mathrm{Y}^*((\varepsilon\eth+(1-\varepsilon)\mathrm{n},\ \varepsilon\upsilon+(1-\varepsilon)\mathrm{d}),\ \mathfrak{z}) + \mathrm{Y}^*(((1-\varepsilon)\eth+\varepsilon\mathrm{n},\ (1-\varepsilon)\upsilon+\varepsilon\mathrm{d}),\mathfrak{z}).
\end{aligned}$$

Using Lemma 1, we have

$$\begin{aligned}
2\mathrm{Y}_*\left(\left(\theta, \frac{\upsilon+\mathrm{d}}{2}\right), \mathfrak{z}\right) &\leq \mathrm{Y}_*((\theta,\ \varepsilon\upsilon+(1-\varepsilon)\mathrm{d}),\ \mathfrak{z}) + \mathrm{Y}_*((\theta,\ (1-\varepsilon)\upsilon+\varepsilon\mathrm{d}),\ \mathfrak{z}), \\
2\mathrm{Y}^*\left(\left(\theta, \frac{\upsilon+\mathrm{d}}{2}\right), \mathfrak{z}\right) &\geq \mathrm{Y}^*((\theta,\ \varepsilon\upsilon+(1-\varepsilon)\mathrm{d}),\ \mathfrak{z}) + \mathrm{Y}^*((\theta,\ (1-\varepsilon)\upsilon+\varepsilon\mathrm{d}),\mathfrak{z}),
\end{aligned} \tag{30}$$

and

$$\begin{aligned}
2\mathrm{Y}_*\left(\left(\frac{\eth+\mathrm{n}}{2}, \psi\right), \mathfrak{z}\right) &\leq \mathrm{Y}_*((\varepsilon\eth+(1-\varepsilon)\mathrm{n},\ \psi),\ \mathfrak{z}) + \mathrm{Y}_*(((1-\varepsilon)\eth+t\mathrm{n},\ \psi),\ \mathfrak{z}), \\
2\mathrm{Y}^*\left(\left(\frac{\eth+\mathrm{n}}{2}, \psi\right), \mathfrak{z}\right) &\geq \mathrm{Y}^*((\varepsilon\eth+(1-\varepsilon)\mathrm{n},\ \psi),\ \mathfrak{z}) + \mathrm{Y}^*(((1-\varepsilon)\eth+t\mathrm{n},\ \psi),\mathfrak{z}).
\end{aligned} \tag{31}$$

From (30) and (31), we have

$$2\left[\Upsilon_*\left(\left(\theta, \frac{\upsilon+d}{2}\right), \mathfrak{z}\right), \Upsilon^*\left(\left(\theta, \frac{\upsilon+d}{2}\right), \mathfrak{z}\right)\right]$$
$$\supseteq_I [\Upsilon_*((\theta, \varepsilon\upsilon + (1-\varepsilon)d), \mathfrak{z}), \Upsilon^*((\theta, \varepsilon\upsilon + (1-\varepsilon)d), \mathfrak{z})]$$
$$+ [\Upsilon_*((\theta, (1-\varepsilon)\upsilon + \varepsilon d), \mathfrak{z}), \Upsilon^*((\theta, (1-\varepsilon)\upsilon + \varepsilon d), \mathfrak{z})],$$

and

$$2\left[\Upsilon_*\left(\left(\frac{\delta+n}{2}, \psi\right), \mathfrak{z}\right), \Upsilon^*\left(\left(\frac{\delta+n}{2}, \psi\right), \mathfrak{z}\right)\right]$$
$$\supseteq_I [\Upsilon_*((\varepsilon\delta + (1-\varepsilon)n, \psi), \mathfrak{z}), \Upsilon^*((\varepsilon\delta + (1-\varepsilon)n, \psi), \mathfrak{z})]$$
$$+ [\Upsilon_*((\varepsilon\delta + (1-\varepsilon)n, \psi), \mathfrak{z}), \Upsilon^*((\varepsilon\delta + (1-\varepsilon)n, \psi), \mathfrak{z})].$$

It follows that

$$\Upsilon_{\mathfrak{z}}\left(\theta, \frac{\upsilon+d}{2}\right) \supseteq_I \Upsilon_{\mathfrak{z}}(\theta, \varepsilon\upsilon + (1-\varepsilon)d) + \Upsilon_{\mathfrak{z}}(\theta, (1-\varepsilon)\upsilon + \varepsilon d), \quad (32)$$

and

$$\Upsilon_{\mathfrak{z}}\left(\frac{\delta+n}{2}, \psi\right) \supseteq_I \Upsilon_{\mathfrak{z}}(\varepsilon\delta + (1-\varepsilon)n, \psi) + \Upsilon_{\mathfrak{z}}(\varepsilon\delta + (1-\varepsilon)n, \psi). \quad (33)$$

Since $\Upsilon_{\mathfrak{z}}(\theta, .)$ and $\Upsilon_{\mathfrak{z}}(., \psi)$, are both coordinated UD-convex-IVMs, then from inequality (15), for every $\mathfrak{z} \in [0, 1]$, inequalities (32) and (43), we have

$$\Upsilon_{\mathfrak{z}\theta}\left(\frac{\upsilon+d}{2}\right) \supseteq_I \frac{\Gamma(\beta+1)}{2(d-\upsilon)^\beta}\left[\mathcal{I}^\beta_{\upsilon^+}\Upsilon_{\mathfrak{z}\theta}(d) + \mathcal{I}^\beta_{d^-}\Upsilon_{\mathfrak{z}\theta}(\upsilon)\right] \supseteq_I \frac{\Upsilon_{\mathfrak{z}\theta}(\upsilon) + \Upsilon_{\mathfrak{z}\theta}(d)}{2}, \quad (34)$$

and

$$\Upsilon_{\mathfrak{z}\psi}\left(\frac{\delta+n}{2}\right) \supseteq_I \frac{\Gamma(\gamma+1)}{2(n-\delta)^\gamma}\left[\mathcal{I}^\gamma_{\delta^+}\Upsilon_{\mathfrak{z}\psi}(n) + \mathcal{I}^\gamma_{n^-}\Upsilon_{\mathfrak{z}\psi}(\delta)\right] \supseteq_I \frac{\Upsilon_{\mathfrak{z}\psi}(\delta) + \Upsilon_{\mathfrak{z}\psi}(n)}{2}. \quad (35)$$

Since $\Upsilon_{\mathfrak{z}\theta}(w) = \Upsilon_{\mathfrak{z}}(\theta, w)$, then (34) can be written as

$$\Upsilon_{\mathfrak{z}}\left(\theta, \frac{\upsilon+d}{2}\right) \supseteq_I \frac{\Gamma(\beta+1)}{2(d-\upsilon)^\beta}\left[\mathcal{I}^\gamma_{\upsilon^+}\Upsilon_{\mathfrak{z}}(\theta, d) + \mathcal{I}^\gamma_{d^-}\Upsilon_{\mathfrak{z}}(\theta, \upsilon)\right] \supseteq_I \frac{\Upsilon_{\mathfrak{z}}(\theta, \upsilon) + \Upsilon_{\mathfrak{z}}(\theta, d)}{2}. \quad (36)$$

That is

$$\Upsilon_{\mathfrak{z}}\left(\theta, \frac{\upsilon+d}{2}\right) \supseteq_I \frac{\beta}{2(d-\upsilon)^\beta}\left[\int_\upsilon^d (d-s)^{\beta-1}\Upsilon_{\mathfrak{z}}(\theta, s)ds + \int_\upsilon^d (s-\upsilon)^{\beta-1}\Upsilon_{\mathfrak{z}}(\theta, s)ds\right] \supseteq_I \frac{\Upsilon_{\mathfrak{z}}(\theta, \upsilon) + \Upsilon_{\mathfrak{z}}(\theta, d)}{2}.$$

Multiplying double inequality (36) by $\frac{\gamma(n-\theta)^{\gamma-1}}{2(n-\delta)^\gamma}$ and integrating it with respect to θ over $[\delta, n]$, we have

$$\frac{\gamma}{2(n-\delta)^\gamma} \int_\delta^n \Upsilon_{\mathfrak{z}}\left(\theta, \frac{\upsilon+d}{2}\right)(n-\theta)^{\gamma-1}d\theta$$
$$\supseteq_I \int_\delta^n \int_\upsilon^d (n-\theta)^{\gamma-1}(d-s)^{\beta-1}\Upsilon_{\mathfrak{z}}(\theta, s)dsd\theta + \int_\delta^n \int_\upsilon^d (n-\theta)^{\gamma-1}(s-\upsilon)^{\beta-1}\Upsilon_{\mathfrak{z}}(\theta, s)dsd\theta \quad (37)$$
$$\supseteq_I \frac{\gamma}{4(n-\delta)^\gamma}\left[\int_\delta^n (n-\theta)^{\gamma-1}\Upsilon_{\mathfrak{z}}(\theta, \upsilon)d\theta + \int_\delta^n (n-\theta)^{\gamma-1}\Upsilon_{\mathfrak{z}}(\theta, d)d\theta\right].$$

Again, multiplying double inequality (36) by $\frac{\gamma(\theta-\delta)^{\gamma-1}}{2(n-\delta)^{\gamma}}$ and integrating it with respect to θ over $[\delta, n]$, we have

$$
\begin{aligned}
&\frac{\gamma}{2(n-\delta)^{\gamma}}\int_{\delta}^{n} \gamma_{\mathfrak{z}}\left(\theta, \frac{\upsilon+d}{2}\right)(n-\theta)^{\gamma-1}d\theta \\
&\supseteq_{I} \frac{\gamma\beta}{4(n-\delta)^{\gamma}(d-\upsilon)^{\beta}}\int_{\delta}^{n}\int_{\upsilon}^{d}(\theta-\delta)^{\gamma-1}(d-s)^{\beta-1}\gamma_{\mathfrak{z}}(\theta,s)dsd\theta \\
&+\frac{\gamma\beta}{4(n-\delta)^{\gamma}(d-\upsilon)^{\beta}}\int_{\delta}^{n}\int_{\upsilon}^{d}(\theta-\delta)^{\gamma-1}(s-\upsilon)^{\beta-1}\gamma_{\mathfrak{z}}(\theta,s)dsd\theta \\
&\supseteq_{I} \frac{\gamma}{4(n-\delta)^{\gamma}}\left[\int_{\delta}^{n}(\theta-\delta)^{\gamma-1}\gamma_{\mathfrak{z}}(\theta,\upsilon)d\theta+\int_{\delta}^{n}(\theta-\delta)^{\gamma-1}\gamma_{\mathfrak{z}}(\theta,d)d\theta\right].
\end{aligned} \tag{38}
$$

From (37), we have

$$
\begin{aligned}
&\frac{\Gamma(\gamma+1)}{2(n-\delta)^{\gamma}}\left[\mathcal{I}_{\delta^{+}}^{\gamma}\gamma_{\mathfrak{z}}\left(n, \frac{\upsilon+d}{2}\right)\right] \\
&\supseteq_{I} \frac{\Gamma(\gamma+1)\Gamma(\beta+1)}{4(n-\delta)^{\gamma}(d-\upsilon)^{\beta}}\left[\mathcal{I}_{\delta^{+},\upsilon^{+}}^{\gamma,\beta}\gamma_{\mathfrak{z}}(n,d)+\mathcal{I}_{n^{-},\upsilon^{+}}^{\gamma,\beta}\gamma_{\mathfrak{z}}(n,\upsilon)\right] \\
&\supseteq_{I} \frac{\Gamma(\gamma+1)}{4(n-\delta)^{\gamma}}\left[\mathcal{I}_{\delta^{+}}^{\gamma}\gamma_{\mathfrak{z}}(n,\upsilon)+\mathcal{I}_{\delta^{+}}^{\gamma}\gamma_{\mathfrak{z}}(n,d)\right].
\end{aligned} \tag{39}
$$

From (38), we have

$$
\begin{aligned}
&\frac{\Gamma(\gamma+1)}{2(n-\delta)^{\gamma}}\left[\mathcal{I}_{n^{-}}^{\gamma}\gamma_{\mathfrak{z}}\left(\delta, \frac{\upsilon+d}{2}\right)\right] \\
&\supseteq_{I} \frac{\Gamma(\gamma+1)\Gamma(\beta+1)}{4(n-\delta)^{\gamma}(d-\upsilon)^{\beta}}\left[\mathcal{I}_{n^{-},\upsilon^{+}}^{\gamma,\beta}\gamma_{\mathfrak{z}}(\delta,d)+\mathcal{I}_{n^{-},d^{-}}^{\gamma,\beta}\gamma_{\mathfrak{z}}(\delta,\upsilon)\right] \\
&\supseteq_{I} \frac{\Gamma(\gamma+1)}{4(n-\delta)^{\gamma}}\left[\mathcal{I}_{n^{-}}^{\gamma}\gamma_{\mathfrak{z}}(\delta,\upsilon)+\mathcal{I}_{n^{-}}^{\gamma}\gamma_{\mathfrak{z}}(\delta,d)\right].
\end{aligned} \tag{40}
$$

Since from the $\mathfrak{z}$-cuts, we obtain the collection of $IVMs$ $\gamma_{\mathfrak{z}} : \Delta \rightarrow \mathbb{R}_{I}^{+}$, hence we have

$$
\begin{aligned}
&\frac{\Gamma(\gamma+1)}{2(n-\delta)^{\gamma}}\left[\mathcal{I}_{\delta^{+}}^{\gamma}\widetilde{\gamma}\left(n, \frac{\upsilon+d}{2}\right)\right] \\
&\supseteq_{\mathbb{F}} \frac{\Gamma(\gamma+1)\Gamma(\beta+1)}{4(n-\delta)^{\gamma}(d-\upsilon)^{\beta}}\left[\mathcal{I}_{\delta^{+},\upsilon^{+}}^{\gamma,\beta}\widetilde{\gamma}(n,d)\oplus\mathcal{I}_{n^{-},\upsilon^{+}}^{\gamma,\beta}\widetilde{\gamma}(n,\upsilon)\right] \\
&\supseteq_{\mathbb{F}} \frac{\Gamma(\gamma+1)}{4(n-\delta)^{\gamma}}\left[\mathcal{I}_{\delta^{+}}^{\gamma}\widetilde{\gamma}(n,\upsilon)\oplus\mathcal{I}_{\delta^{+}}^{\gamma}\widetilde{\gamma}(n,d)\right],
\end{aligned} \tag{41}
$$

and

$$
\begin{aligned}
&\frac{\Gamma(\gamma+1)}{2(n-\delta)^{\gamma}}\left[\mathcal{I}_{n^{-}}^{\gamma}\widetilde{\gamma}\left(\delta, \frac{\upsilon+d}{2}\right)\right] \\
&\supseteq_{\mathbb{F}} \frac{\Gamma(\gamma+1)\Gamma(\beta+1)}{4(n-\delta)^{\gamma}(d-\upsilon)^{\beta}}\left[\mathcal{I}_{n^{-},\upsilon^{+}}^{\gamma,\beta}\widetilde{\gamma}(\delta,d)\oplus\mathcal{I}_{n^{-},d^{-}}^{\gamma,\beta}\widetilde{\gamma}(\delta,\upsilon)\right] \\
&\supseteq_{\mathbb{F}} \frac{\Gamma(\gamma+1)}{4(n-\delta)^{\gamma}}\left[\mathcal{I}_{n^{-}}^{\gamma}\widetilde{\gamma}(\delta,\upsilon)\oplus\mathcal{I}_{n^{-}}^{\gamma}\widetilde{\gamma}(\delta,d)\right].
\end{aligned} \tag{42}
$$

Similarly, since $\widetilde{\gamma}_{\psi}(z) = \widetilde{\gamma}(z, \psi)$ then, from (35), (41), and (42), we have

$$
\begin{aligned}
&\frac{\Gamma(\beta+1)}{2(d-\upsilon)^{\beta}}\left[\mathcal{I}_{\upsilon^{+}}^{\beta}\widetilde{\gamma}\left(\frac{\delta+n}{2}, d\right)\right] \\
&\supseteq_{\mathbb{F}} \frac{\Gamma(\gamma+1)\Gamma(\beta+1)}{4(n-\delta)^{\gamma}(d-\upsilon)^{\beta}}\left[\mathcal{I}_{\delta^{+},\upsilon^{+}}^{\gamma,\beta}\widetilde{\gamma}(n,d)\oplus\mathcal{I}_{n^{-},\upsilon^{+}}^{\gamma,\beta}\widetilde{\gamma}(\delta,d)\right] \\
&\supseteq_{\mathbb{F}} \frac{\Gamma(\beta+1)}{4(d-\upsilon)^{\beta}}\left[\mathcal{I}_{\upsilon^{+}}^{\beta}\widetilde{\gamma}(\delta,d)\oplus\mathcal{I}_{\upsilon^{+}}^{\beta}\widetilde{\gamma}(n,d)\right],
\end{aligned} \tag{43}
$$

and

$$\begin{aligned}&\frac{\Gamma(\beta+1)}{2(\mathrm{d}-\upsilon)^{\gamma}}\left[\mathcal{I}^{\beta}_{\mathrm{d}^-}\widetilde{\Upsilon}\left(\frac{\eth+\mathrm{n}}{2},\upsilon\right)\right]\\ &\qquad\supseteq_{\mathbb{F}}\frac{\Gamma(\gamma+1)\Gamma(\beta+1)}{4(\mathrm{n}-\eth)^{\gamma}(\mathrm{d}-\upsilon)^{\beta}}\left[\mathcal{I}^{\gamma,\beta}_{\eth^+,\mathrm{d}^-}\widetilde{\Upsilon}(\mathrm{n},\upsilon)\oplus\mathcal{I}^{\gamma,\beta}_{\mathrm{n}^-,\mathrm{d}^-}\widetilde{\Upsilon}(\eth,\upsilon)\right]\\ &\qquad\supseteq_{\mathbb{F}}\frac{\Gamma(\beta+1)}{4(\mathrm{d}-\upsilon)^{\beta}}\left[\mathcal{I}^{\beta}_{\mathrm{d}^-}\widetilde{\Upsilon}(\eth,\upsilon)\oplus\mathcal{I}^{\beta}_{\mathrm{d}^-}\widetilde{\Upsilon}(\mathrm{n},\upsilon)\right].\end{aligned} \tag{44}$$

The second, third, and fourth inequalities of (28) will be the consequence of adding the inequalities (41)–(44).

Now, for any $\mathfrak{z}\in[0,\ 1]$, we have inequality (15)'s left portion:

$$\Upsilon_{\mathfrak{z}}\left(\frac{\eth+\mathrm{n}}{2},\frac{\upsilon+\mathrm{d}}{2}\right)\supseteq_I\frac{\Gamma(\beta+1)}{2(\mathrm{d}-\upsilon)^{\beta}}\left[\mathcal{I}^{\beta}_{\upsilon^+}\Upsilon_{\mathfrak{z}}\left(\frac{\eth+\mathrm{n}}{2},\mathrm{d}\right)+\mathcal{I}^{\beta}_{\mathrm{d}^-}\Upsilon_{\mathfrak{z}}\left(\frac{\eth+\mathrm{n}}{2},\upsilon\right)\right], \tag{45}$$

and

$$\Upsilon_{\mathfrak{z}}\left(\frac{\eth+\mathrm{n}}{2},\frac{\upsilon+\mathrm{d}}{2}\right)\supseteq_I\frac{\Gamma(\gamma+1)}{2(\mathrm{n}-\eth)^{\gamma}}\left[\mathcal{I}^{\gamma}_{\eth^+}\Upsilon_{\mathfrak{z}}\left(\mathrm{n},\frac{\upsilon+\mathrm{d}}{2}\right)+\mathcal{I}^{\gamma}_{\mathrm{n}^-}\Upsilon_{\mathfrak{z}}\left(\eth,\frac{\upsilon+\mathrm{d}}{2}\right)\right]. \tag{46}$$

The following inequality is created by adding two inequalities (45) and (46):

$$\begin{aligned}\Upsilon_{\mathfrak{z}}\left(\frac{\eth+\mathrm{n}}{2},\frac{\upsilon+\mathrm{d}}{2}\right)\supseteq_I&\frac{\Gamma(\gamma+1)}{4(\mathrm{n}-\eth)^{\gamma}}\left[\mathcal{I}^{\gamma}_{\eth^+}\Upsilon_{\mathfrak{z}}\left(\mathrm{n},\frac{\upsilon+\mathrm{d}}{2}\right)+\mathcal{I}^{\gamma}_{\mathrm{n}^-}\Upsilon_{\mathfrak{z}}\left(\eth,\frac{\upsilon+\mathrm{d}}{2}\right)\right]\\ &+\frac{\Gamma(\beta+1)}{4(\mathrm{d}-\upsilon)^{\beta}}\left[\mathcal{I}^{\beta}_{\upsilon^+}\Upsilon_{\mathfrak{z}}\left(\frac{\eth+\mathrm{n}}{2},\mathrm{d}\right)+\mathcal{I}^{\beta}_{\mathrm{d}^-}\Upsilon_{\mathfrak{z}}\left(\frac{\eth+\mathrm{n}}{2},\upsilon\right)\right].\end{aligned}$$

Similarly, since we obtain the set of $IVMs$ $\Upsilon_{\mathfrak{z}}:\Delta\to\mathbb{R}^+_I$ for for $\mathfrak{z}\in[0,\ 1]$, the inequality can be expressed as follows:

$$\begin{aligned}&\widetilde{\Upsilon}\left(\frac{\eth+\mathrm{n}}{2},\frac{\upsilon+\mathrm{d}}{2}\right)\\ &\supseteq_{\mathbb{F}}\frac{\Gamma(\gamma+1)}{4(\mathrm{n}-\eth)^{\gamma}}\left[\mathcal{I}^{\gamma}_{\eth^+}\widetilde{\Upsilon}\left(\mathrm{n},\frac{\upsilon+\mathrm{d}}{2}\right)\oplus\mathcal{I}^{\gamma}_{\mathrm{n}^-}\widetilde{\Upsilon}\left(\eth,\frac{\upsilon+\mathrm{d}}{2}\right)\right]\oplus\frac{\Gamma(\beta+1)}{4(\mathrm{d}-\upsilon)^{\beta}}\left[\mathcal{I}^{\beta}_{\upsilon^+}\widetilde{\Upsilon}\left(\frac{\eth+\mathrm{n}}{2},\mathrm{d}\right)\oplus\mathcal{I}^{\beta}_{\mathrm{d}^-}\widetilde{\Upsilon}\left(\frac{\eth+\mathrm{n}}{2},\upsilon\right)\right].\end{aligned} \tag{47}$$

The first inequality of (28) is this one.

Now, for any $\mathfrak{z}\in[0,\ 1]$, we have inequality (15)'s right portion:

$$\frac{\Gamma(\beta+1)}{2(\mathrm{d}-\upsilon)^{\beta}}\left[\mathcal{I}^{\beta}_{\upsilon^+}\Upsilon_{\mathfrak{z}}(\eth,\mathrm{d})+\mathcal{I}^{\beta}_{\mathrm{d}^-}\Upsilon_{\mathfrak{z}}(\eth,\upsilon)\right]\supseteq_I\frac{\Upsilon_{\mathfrak{z}}(\eth,\upsilon)+\Upsilon_{\mathfrak{z}}(\eth,\mathrm{d})}{2}. \tag{48}$$

$$\frac{\Gamma(\beta+1)}{2(\mathrm{d}-\upsilon)^{\beta}}\left[\mathcal{I}^{\beta}_{\upsilon^+}\Upsilon_{\mathfrak{z}}(\mathrm{n},\mathrm{d})+\mathcal{I}^{\beta}_{\mathrm{d}^-}\Upsilon_{\mathfrak{z}}(\mathrm{n},\upsilon)\right]\supseteq_I\frac{\Upsilon_{\mathfrak{z}}(\mathrm{n},\upsilon)+\Upsilon_{\mathfrak{z}}(\mathrm{n},\mathrm{d})}{2}. \tag{49}$$

$$\frac{\Gamma(\gamma+1)}{2(\mathrm{n}-\eth)^{\gamma}}\left[\mathcal{I}^{\gamma}_{\eth^+}\Upsilon_{\mathfrak{z}}(\mathrm{n},\upsilon)+\mathcal{I}^{\gamma}_{\mathrm{n}^-}\Upsilon_{\mathfrak{z}}(\eth,\upsilon)\right]\supseteq_I\frac{\Upsilon_{\mathfrak{z}}(\eth,\upsilon)+\Upsilon_{\mathfrak{z}}(\mathrm{n},\upsilon)}{2} \tag{50}$$

$$\frac{\Gamma(\gamma+1)}{2(\mathrm{n}-\eth)^{\gamma}}\left[\mathcal{I}^{\gamma}_{\eth^+}\Upsilon_{\mathfrak{z}}(\mathrm{n},\mathrm{d})+\mathcal{I}^{\gamma}_{\mathrm{n}^-}\Upsilon_{\mathfrak{z}}(\eth,\mathrm{d})\right]\supseteq_I\frac{\Upsilon_{\mathfrak{z}}(\eth,\mathrm{d})+\Upsilon_{\mathfrak{z}}(\mathrm{n},\mathrm{d})}{2} \tag{51}$$

Summing inequalities (48)–(51), and then multiplying the resultant with $\frac{1}{4}$, we have

$$\begin{aligned}\frac{\Gamma(\gamma+1)}{8(\mathrm{n}-\eth)^{\gamma}}\left[\mathcal{I}^{\gamma}_{\eth^+}\Upsilon_{\mathfrak{z}}(\mathrm{n},\upsilon)\right.&\left.+\mathcal{I}^{\gamma}_{\mathrm{n}^-}\Upsilon_{\mathfrak{z}}(\eth,\upsilon)+\mathcal{I}^{\gamma}_{\eth^+}\Upsilon_{\mathfrak{z}}(\mathrm{n},\mathrm{d})+\mathcal{I}^{\gamma}_{\mathrm{n}^-}\Upsilon_{\mathfrak{z}}(\eth,\mathrm{d})\right]\\ &+\frac{\Gamma(\beta+1)}{8(\mathrm{d}-\upsilon)^{\beta}}\left[\mathcal{I}^{\beta}_{\upsilon^+}\Upsilon_{\mathfrak{z}}(\eth,\mathrm{d})+\mathcal{I}^{\beta}_{\mathrm{d}^-}\Upsilon_{\mathfrak{z}}(\eth,\upsilon)+\mathcal{I}^{\beta}_{\upsilon^+}\Upsilon_{\mathfrak{z}}(\mathrm{n},\mathrm{d})+\mathcal{I}^{\beta}_{\mathrm{d}^-}\Upsilon_{\mathfrak{z}}(\mathrm{n},\upsilon)\right]\\ &\supseteq_I\frac{\Upsilon_{\mathfrak{z}}(\eth,\upsilon)+\Upsilon_{\mathfrak{z}}(\eth,\mathrm{d})+\Upsilon_{\mathfrak{z}}(\mathrm{n},\upsilon)+\Upsilon_{\mathfrak{z}}(\mathrm{n},\mathrm{d})}{4}.\end{aligned}$$

Since we receive the collection of $IVMs$ $\mathfrak{Y}_{\mathfrak{z}} : \Delta \to \mathbb{R}_I^+$ from the $\mathfrak{z}$-cuts, we have

$$\begin{aligned}&\frac{\Gamma(\Upsilon+1)}{8(\mathfrak{n}-\mathfrak{d})^{\Upsilon}}\left[\mathcal{I}_{\mathfrak{d}^+}^{\Upsilon}\widetilde{\mathfrak{Y}}(\mathfrak{n},\upsilon) \oplus \mathcal{I}_{\mathfrak{n}^-}^{\Upsilon}\widetilde{\mathfrak{Y}}(\mathfrak{d},\upsilon) \oplus \mathcal{I}_{\mathfrak{d}^+}^{\Upsilon}\widetilde{\mathfrak{Y}}(\mathfrak{n},\mathfrak{d}) \oplus \mathcal{I}_{\mathfrak{n}^-}^{\Upsilon}\widetilde{\mathfrak{Y}}(\mathfrak{d},\mathfrak{d})\right]\\ &\oplus\frac{\Gamma(\beta+1)}{8(\mathfrak{d}-\upsilon)^{\beta}}\left[\mathcal{I}_{\upsilon^+}^{\beta}\widetilde{\mathfrak{Y}}(\mathfrak{d},\mathfrak{d}) \oplus \mathcal{I}_{\mathfrak{d}^-}^{\beta}\widetilde{\mathfrak{Y}}(\mathfrak{d},\upsilon) \oplus \mathcal{I}_{\upsilon^+}^{\beta}\widetilde{\mathfrak{Y}}(\mathfrak{n},\mathfrak{d}) \oplus \mathcal{I}_{\mathfrak{d}^-}^{\beta}\widetilde{\mathfrak{Y}}(\mathfrak{n},\upsilon)\right]\\ &\supseteq_{\mathbb{F}} \frac{\widetilde{\mathfrak{Y}}(\mathfrak{d},\upsilon)\oplus\widetilde{\mathfrak{Y}}(\mathfrak{d},\mathfrak{d})\oplus\widetilde{\mathfrak{Y}}(\mathfrak{n},\upsilon)\oplus\widetilde{\mathfrak{Y}}(\mathfrak{n},\mathfrak{d})}{4}.\end{aligned}$$

This is the final inequality of (28), and the conclusion has been established. □

Example 3. *We assume the $FNVMs$ $\widetilde{\mathfrak{Y}} : [0,\ 2] \times [0,\ 2] \to \mathbb{F}_0$ defined by*

$$\mathfrak{Y}(\theta,\psi)(\sigma) = \begin{cases} \dfrac{\sigma-\left(2-\sqrt{\theta}\right)(2-\sqrt{\psi})}{4-\left(2-\sqrt{\theta}\right)(2-\sqrt{\psi})}, & \sigma \in \left[\left(2-\sqrt{\theta}\right)(2-\sqrt{\psi}),\ 4\right] \\ \dfrac{\left(2+\sqrt{\theta}\right)(2+\sqrt{\psi})-\sigma}{\left(2+\sqrt{\theta}\right)(2+\sqrt{\psi})-4}, & \sigma \in \left(4,\ \left(2+\sqrt{\theta}\right)(2+\sqrt{\psi})\right] \\ 0, & \text{otherwise,} \end{cases}$$

Then, for each $\mathfrak{z} \in [0,\ 1]$, we have $\mathfrak{Y}_{\mathfrak{z}}(\theta,\psi) = \left[(1-\mathfrak{z})\left(2-\sqrt{\theta}\right)(2-\sqrt{\psi})+4\mathfrak{z}, (1-\mathfrak{z})(2+\sqrt{\theta})\right.$ $\left.(2+\sqrt{\psi})+4\mathfrak{z}\right]$. Since the end point functions $\mathfrak{Y}_*((\theta,\psi),\mathfrak{z})$, $\mathfrak{Y}^*((\theta,\psi),\mathfrak{z})$ are coordinate concave functions for each $\mathfrak{z} \in [0,\ 1]$, hence $\widetilde{\mathfrak{Y}}(\theta,\psi)$ is a coordinate concave $FNVM$.

$$\begin{aligned}&\mathfrak{Y}_{\mathfrak{z}}\left(\tfrac{\mathfrak{d}+\mathfrak{n}}{2},\ \tfrac{\upsilon+\mathfrak{d}}{2}\right) = [(1-\mathfrak{z})+4\mathfrak{z}, 9(1-\mathfrak{z})+4\mathfrak{z}],\\ &\frac{\Gamma(\Upsilon+1)}{4(\mathfrak{n}-\mathfrak{d})^{\Upsilon}}\left[\mathcal{I}_{\mathfrak{d}^+}^{\Upsilon}\widetilde{\mathfrak{Y}}\left(\mathfrak{n},\tfrac{\upsilon+\mathfrak{d}}{2}\right) \oplus \mathcal{I}_{\mathfrak{n}^-}^{\Upsilon}\widetilde{\mathfrak{Y}}\left(\mathfrak{d},\tfrac{\upsilon+\mathfrak{d}}{2}\right)\right] \oplus \frac{\Gamma(\beta+1)}{4(\mathfrak{d}-\upsilon)^{\beta}}\left[\mathcal{I}_{\upsilon^+}^{\beta}\widetilde{\mathfrak{Y}}\left(\tfrac{\mathfrak{d}+\mathfrak{n}}{2},\mathfrak{d}\right) \oplus \mathcal{I}_{\mathfrak{d}^-}^{\beta}\widetilde{\mathfrak{Y}}\left(\tfrac{\mathfrak{d}+\mathfrak{n}}{2},\upsilon\right)\right]\\ &= \left[(1-\mathfrak{z})\left(2-\tfrac{\sqrt{2}}{4}-\tfrac{\sqrt{2}}{8}\pi\right)+4\mathfrak{z}, (1-\mathfrak{z})\left(2+\tfrac{\sqrt{2}}{4}+\tfrac{\sqrt{2}}{8}\pi\right)+4\mathfrak{z}\right]\\ &\frac{\Gamma(\Upsilon+1)\Gamma(\beta+1)}{4(\mathfrak{n}-\mathfrak{d})^{\Upsilon}(\mathfrak{d}-\upsilon)^{\beta}}\left[\mathcal{I}_{\mathfrak{d}^+,\upsilon^+}^{\Upsilon,\beta}\mathfrak{Y}_{\mathfrak{z}}(\mathfrak{n},\mathfrak{d}) \oplus \mathcal{I}_{\mathfrak{d}^+,\mathfrak{d}^-}^{\Upsilon,\beta}\mathfrak{Y}_{\mathfrak{z}}(\mathfrak{n},\upsilon) \oplus \mathcal{I}_{\mathfrak{n}^-,\upsilon^+}^{\Upsilon,\beta}\mathfrak{Y}_{\mathfrak{z}}(\mathfrak{d},\mathfrak{d}) \oplus \mathcal{I}_{\mathfrak{n}^-,\mathfrak{d}^-}^{\Upsilon,\beta}\mathfrak{Y}_{\mathfrak{z}}(\mathfrak{d},\upsilon)\right]\\ &= \left[(1-\mathfrak{z})\left(\tfrac{33}{8}-\sqrt{2}-\tfrac{\sqrt{2}}{2}\pi+\tfrac{\pi}{8}+\tfrac{\pi^2}{32}\right)+4\mathfrak{z}, (1-\mathfrak{z})\left(\tfrac{33}{8}+\sqrt{2}+\tfrac{\sqrt{2}}{2}\pi+\tfrac{\pi}{8}+\tfrac{\pi^2}{32}\right)+4\mathfrak{z}\right]\\ &\frac{\Gamma(\Upsilon+1)}{8(\mathfrak{n}-\mathfrak{d})^{\Upsilon}}\left[\mathcal{I}_{\mathfrak{d}^+}^{\Upsilon}\widetilde{\mathfrak{Y}}(\mathfrak{n},\upsilon) \oplus \mathcal{I}_{\mathfrak{d}^+}^{\Upsilon}\widetilde{\mathfrak{Y}}(\mathfrak{n},\mathfrak{d}) \oplus \mathcal{I}_{\mathfrak{n}^-}^{\Upsilon}\widetilde{\mathfrak{Y}}(\mathfrak{d},\upsilon) \oplus \mathcal{I}_{\mathfrak{n}^-}^{\Upsilon}\widetilde{\mathfrak{Y}}(\mathfrak{d},\mathfrak{d})\right]\\ &\oplus\frac{\Gamma(\beta+1)}{8(\mathfrak{d}-\upsilon)^{\beta}}\left[\mathcal{I}_{\upsilon^+}^{\beta}\widetilde{\mathfrak{Y}}(\mathfrak{d},\mathfrak{d}) \oplus \mathcal{I}_{\upsilon^+}^{\beta}\widetilde{\mathfrak{Y}}(\mathfrak{n},\mathfrak{d}) \oplus \mathcal{I}_{\mathfrak{d}^-}^{\beta}\widetilde{\mathfrak{Y}}(\mathfrak{d},\upsilon) \oplus \mathcal{I}_{\mathfrak{d}^-}^{\beta}\widetilde{\mathfrak{Y}}(\mathfrak{n},\upsilon)\right]\\ &= \left[\frac{34\sqrt{2}+\left(\sqrt{2}-4\right)\pi-24}{8\sqrt{2}}(1-\mathfrak{z})+4\mathfrak{z}, \frac{34\sqrt{2}+\left(\sqrt{2}+4\right)\pi+24}{8\sqrt{2}}(1-\mathfrak{z})+4\mathfrak{z}\right]\\ &\frac{\mathfrak{Y}_{\mathfrak{z}}(\upsilon,n)+\mathfrak{Y}_{\mathfrak{z}}(\sigma,n)+\mathfrak{Y}_{\mathfrak{z}}(\upsilon,\mathfrak{d})+\mathfrak{Y}_{\mathfrak{z}}(\sigma,\mathfrak{d})}{4} = \left[(1-\mathfrak{z})\left(\tfrac{9}{2}-2\sqrt{2}\right)+4\mathfrak{z}, (1-\mathfrak{z})\left(\tfrac{9}{2}+2\sqrt{2}\right)+4\mathfrak{z}\right].\end{aligned}$$

That is

$$\begin{aligned}[(1-\mathfrak{z})+\ &4\mathfrak{z}, 9(1-\mathfrak{z})+4\mathfrak{z}] \supseteq_I \left[(1-\mathfrak{z})\left(2-\tfrac{\sqrt{2}}{4}-\tfrac{\sqrt{2}}{8}\pi\right)+4\mathfrak{z}, (1-\mathfrak{z})\left(2+\tfrac{\sqrt{2}}{4}+\tfrac{\sqrt{2}}{8}\pi\right)+4\mathfrak{z}\right]\\ &\supseteq_I \left[(1-\mathfrak{z})\left(\tfrac{33}{8}-\sqrt{2}-\tfrac{\sqrt{2}}{2}\pi+\tfrac{\pi}{8}+\tfrac{\pi^2}{32}\right)+4\mathfrak{z}, (1-\mathfrak{z})\left(\tfrac{33}{8}+\sqrt{2}+\tfrac{\sqrt{2}}{2}\pi+\tfrac{\pi}{8}+\tfrac{\pi^2}{32}\right)+4\mathfrak{z}\right]\\ &\supseteq_I \left[\frac{34\sqrt{2}+\left(\sqrt{2}-4\right)\pi-24}{8\sqrt{2}}(1-\mathfrak{z})+4\mathfrak{z}, \frac{34\sqrt{2}+\left(\sqrt{2}+4\right)\pi+24}{8\sqrt{2}}(1-\mathfrak{z})+4\mathfrak{z}\right]\\ &\supseteq_I \frac{34\sqrt{2}+\left(\sqrt{2}-4\right)\pi-24}{8\sqrt{2}}(1-\mathfrak{z})+4\mathfrak{z}.\end{aligned}$$

Hence, Theorem 9 has been verified. □

Remark 2. *If one assumes that* $\gamma = 1 = \beta$, *then from (28), as a result, there will be inequity (see [42]):*

$$\begin{aligned}
&\widetilde{\mathtt{Y}}\left(\frac{\eth+n}{2}, \frac{\upsilon+d}{2}\right)\\
&\supseteq_{\mathbb{F}} \frac{1}{2}\left[\frac{1}{n-\eth}\int_{\eth}^{n}\widetilde{\mathtt{Y}}\left(\theta, \frac{\upsilon+d}{2}\right)d\theta \oplus \frac{1}{d-\upsilon}\int_{\upsilon}^{d}\widetilde{\mathtt{Y}}\left(\frac{\eth+n}{2}, \psi\right)d\psi\right] \supseteq_{\mathbb{F}} \frac{1}{(n-\eth)(d-\upsilon)}\int_{\eth}^{n}\int_{\upsilon}^{d}\widetilde{\mathtt{Y}}(\theta,\psi)d\psi d\theta\\
&\supseteq_{\mathbb{F}} \frac{1}{4(n-\eth)}\left[\int_{\eth}^{n}\widetilde{\mathtt{Y}}(\theta,\upsilon)d\theta \oplus \int_{\eth}^{n}\widetilde{\mathtt{Y}}(\theta,d)d\theta\right] \oplus \frac{1}{4(d-\upsilon)}\left[\int_{\upsilon}^{d}\widetilde{\mathtt{Y}}(\eth,\psi)d\psi \oplus \int_{\upsilon}^{d}\widetilde{\mathtt{Y}}(n,\psi)d\psi\right]\\
&\qquad\supseteq_{\mathbb{F}} \frac{\widetilde{\mathtt{Y}}(\eth,\upsilon)\oplus\widetilde{\mathtt{Y}}(n,\upsilon)\oplus\widetilde{\mathtt{Y}}(\eth,d)\oplus\widetilde{\mathtt{Y}}(n,d)}{4}.
\end{aligned}$$

If one assumes that $\gamma = 1 = \beta$ *and* $\widetilde{\mathtt{Y}}$ *is a coordinated left-UD-convex, then from (28), as a result, there will be inequity (see [27]):*

$$\begin{aligned}
&\widetilde{\mathtt{Y}}\left(\frac{\eth+n}{2}, \frac{\upsilon+d}{2}\right)\\
&\leq_{\mathbb{F}} \frac{1}{2}\left[\frac{1}{n-\eth}\int_{\eth}^{n}\widetilde{\mathtt{Y}}\left(\theta, \frac{\upsilon+d}{2}\right)d\theta \oplus \frac{1}{d-\upsilon}\int_{\upsilon}^{d}\widetilde{\mathtt{Y}}\left(\frac{\eth+n}{2}, \psi\right)d\psi\right] \leq_{\mathbb{F}} \frac{1}{(n-\eth)(d-\upsilon)}\int_{\eth}^{n}\int_{\upsilon}^{d}\widetilde{\mathtt{Y}}(\theta,\psi)d\psi d\theta\\
&\leq_{\mathbb{F}} \frac{1}{4(n-\eth)}\left[\int_{\eth}^{n}\widetilde{\mathtt{Y}}(\theta,\upsilon)d\theta \oplus \int_{\eth}^{n}\widetilde{\mathtt{Y}}(\theta,d)d\theta\right] \oplus \frac{1}{4(d-\upsilon)}\left[\int_{\upsilon}^{d}\widetilde{\mathtt{Y}}(\eth,\psi)d\psi \oplus \int_{\upsilon}^{d}\widetilde{\mathtt{Y}}(n,\psi)d\psi\right]\\
&\leq_{\mathbb{F}} \frac{\widetilde{\mathtt{Y}}(\eth,\upsilon)\oplus\widetilde{\mathtt{Y}}(n,\upsilon)\oplus\widetilde{\mathtt{Y}}(\eth,d)\oplus\widetilde{\mathtt{Y}}(n,d)}{4}.
\end{aligned}$$

If $\mathtt{Y}_*((\theta,\psi), z) \neq \mathtt{Y}^*((\theta,\psi), z)$ *with* $z = 1$, *then from (28), we succeed in bringing about the upcoming inequity (see [26]):*

$$\begin{aligned}
&\mathtt{Y}\left(\frac{\eth+n}{2}, \frac{\upsilon+d}{2}\right)\\
&\supseteq \frac{\Gamma(\gamma+1)}{4(n-\eth)^{\gamma}}\left[\mathcal{I}_{\eth^+}^{\gamma}\mathtt{Y}\left(n, \frac{\upsilon+d}{2}\right) + \mathcal{I}_{n^-}^{\gamma}\mathtt{Y}\left(\eth, \frac{\upsilon+d}{2}\right)\right] + \frac{\Gamma(\beta+1)}{4(d-\upsilon)^{\beta}}\left[\mathcal{I}_{\upsilon^+}^{\beta}\mathtt{Y}\left(\frac{\eth+n}{2}, d\right) + \mathcal{I}_{d^-}^{\beta}\mathtt{Y}\left(\frac{\eth+n}{2}, \upsilon\right)\right]\\
&\supseteq \frac{\Gamma(\gamma+1)\Gamma(\beta+1)}{4(n-\eth)^{\gamma}(d-\upsilon)^{\beta}}\left[\mathcal{I}_{\eth^+,\upsilon^+}^{\gamma,\beta}\mathtt{Y}(n,d) + \mathcal{I}_{\eth^+,d^-}^{\gamma,\beta}\mathtt{Y}(n,\upsilon) + \mathcal{I}_{n^-,\upsilon^+}^{\gamma,\beta}\mathtt{Y}(\eth,d) + \mathcal{I}_{n^-,d^-}^{\gamma,\beta}\mathtt{Y}(\eth,\upsilon)\right]\\
&\supseteq \frac{\Gamma(\gamma+1)}{8(n-\eth)^{\gamma}}\left[\mathcal{I}_{\eth^+}^{\gamma}\mathtt{Y}(n,\upsilon) + \mathcal{I}_{\eth^+}^{\gamma}\mathtt{Y}(n,d) + \mathcal{I}_{n^-}^{\gamma}\mathtt{Y}(\eth,\upsilon) + \mathcal{I}_{n^-}^{\gamma}\mathtt{Y}(\eth,d)\right]\\
&+\frac{\Gamma(\beta+1)}{8(d-\upsilon)^{\beta}}\left[\mathcal{I}_{\upsilon^+}^{\beta}\mathtt{Y}(\eth,d) + \mathcal{I}_{d^-}^{\beta}\mathtt{Y}(\eth,\upsilon) + \mathcal{I}_{\upsilon^+}^{\beta}\mathtt{Y}(n,d) + \mathcal{I}_{d^-}^{\beta}\mathtt{Y}(n,\upsilon)\right]\\
&\supseteq \frac{\mathtt{Y}(\eth,\upsilon)+\mathtt{Y}(n,\upsilon)+\mathtt{Y}(\eth,d)+\mathtt{Y}(n,d)}{4}.
\end{aligned}$$

If $\mathtt{Y}_*((\theta,\psi), z) \neq \mathtt{Y}^*((\theta,\psi), z)$ *with* $z = 1$, *then from (28), we succeed in bringing about the upcoming inequity (see [25]):*

$$\begin{aligned}
&\mathtt{Y}\left(\frac{\eth+n}{2}, \frac{\upsilon+d}{2}\right)\\
&\supseteq \frac{1}{2}\left[\frac{1}{n-\eth}\int_{\eth}^{n}\mathtt{Y}\left(\theta, \frac{\upsilon+d}{2}\right)d\theta + \frac{1}{d-\upsilon}\int_{\upsilon}^{d}\mathtt{Y}\left(\frac{\eth+n}{2}, \psi\right)d\psi\right] \subseteq \frac{1}{(n-\eth)(d-\upsilon)}\int_{\eth}^{n}\int_{\upsilon}^{d}\mathtt{Y}(\theta,\psi)d\psi d\theta\\
&\supseteq \frac{1}{4(n-\eth)}\left[\int_{\eth}^{n}\mathtt{Y}(\theta,\upsilon)d\theta + \int_{\eth}^{n}\mathtt{Y}(\theta,d)d\theta\right] + \frac{1}{4(d-\upsilon)}\left[\int_{\upsilon}^{d}\mathtt{Y}(\eth,\psi)d\psi + \int_{\upsilon}^{d}\mathtt{Y}(n,\psi)d\psi\right]\\
&\supseteq \frac{\mathtt{Y}(\eth,\upsilon)+\mathtt{Y}(n,\upsilon)+\mathtt{Y}(\eth,d)+\mathtt{Y}(n,d)}{4}.
\end{aligned}$$

If $\widetilde{\mathtt{Y}}$ *is coordinated right-UD-convex and* $\mathtt{Y}_*((\theta,\psi), z) = \mathtt{Y}^*((\theta,\psi), z)$ *with* $z = 1$, *then from (28), we succeed in bringing about the upcoming inequity (see [37]):*

$$\begin{aligned}
&\mathrm{Y}\left(\frac{\eth+n}{2},\frac{\upsilon+\mathrm{d}}{2}\right)\\
&\leq \frac{\Gamma(\mathrm{Y}+1)}{4(n-\eth)^{\mathrm{Y}}}\left[\mathcal{I}^{\mathrm{Y}}_{\eth^+}\,\mathrm{Y}\left(n,\frac{\upsilon+\mathrm{d}}{2}\right)+\mathcal{I}^{\mathrm{Y}}_{n^-}\mathrm{Y}\left(\eth,\frac{\upsilon+\mathrm{d}}{2}\right)\right]+\frac{\Gamma(\beta+1)}{4(\mathrm{d}-\upsilon)^{\beta}}\left[\mathcal{I}^{\beta}_{\upsilon^+}\,\mathrm{Y}\left(\frac{\eth+n}{2},\mathrm{d}\right)+\mathcal{I}^{\beta}_{\mathrm{d}^-}\,\mathrm{Y}\left(\frac{\eth+n}{2},\upsilon\right)\right]\\
&\leq \frac{\Gamma(\mathrm{Y}+1)\Gamma(\beta+1)}{4(n-\eth)^{\mathrm{Y}}(\mathrm{d}-\upsilon)^{\beta}}\left[\mathcal{I}^{\mathrm{Y},\,\beta}_{\eth^+,\upsilon^+}\,\mathrm{Y}(n,\mathrm{d})+\mathcal{I}^{\mathrm{Y},\,\beta}_{\eth^+,\mathrm{d}^-}\,\mathrm{Y}(n,\upsilon)+\mathcal{I}^{\mathrm{Y},\,\beta}_{n^-,\upsilon^+}\,\mathrm{Y}(\eth,\mathrm{d})+\mathcal{I}^{\mathrm{Y},\,\beta}_{n^-,\mathrm{d}^-}\,\mathrm{Y}(\eth,\upsilon)\right]\\
&\leq \frac{\Gamma(\mathrm{Y}+1)}{8(n-\eth)^{\mathrm{Y}}}\left[\mathcal{I}^{\mathrm{Y}}_{\eth^+}\,\mathrm{Y}(n,\upsilon)\mathrm{Y}\mathcal{I}^{\mathrm{Y}}_{\eth^+}\,\mathrm{Y}(n,\mathrm{d})+\mathcal{I}^{\mathrm{Y}}_{n^-}\,\mathrm{Y}(\eth,\upsilon)+\mathcal{I}^{\mathrm{Y}}_{n^-}\,\mathrm{Y}(\eth,\mathrm{d})\right].\\
&+\frac{\Gamma(\beta+1)}{8(\mathrm{d}-\upsilon)^{\beta}}\left[\mathcal{I}^{\beta}_{\upsilon^+}\,\mathrm{Y}(\eth,\mathrm{d})\tilde{+}\mathcal{I}^{\beta}_{\mathrm{d}^-}\,\mathrm{Y}(\eth,\upsilon)+\mathcal{I}^{\beta}_{\upsilon^+}\,\mathrm{Y}(n,\mathrm{d})+\mathcal{I}^{\beta}_{\mathrm{d}^-}\,\mathrm{Y}(n,\upsilon)\right]\\
&\leq \frac{\mathrm{Y}(\eth,\upsilon)+\mathrm{Y}(n,\upsilon)+\mathrm{Y}(\eth,\mathrm{d})+\mathrm{Y}(n,\mathrm{d})}{4}.
\end{aligned}$$

Theorem 10. *Let* $\widetilde{\mathrm{Y}},\ \widetilde{\mathcal{J}}:\Delta\to\mathbb{F}_0$ *be a coordinated UD-convex FNVMFNVM on* Δ. *Then, from the* $\mathfrak{z}$*-cuts, we set up the sequence of IVMs* $\mathrm{Y}_{\mathfrak{z}},\mathcal{J}_{\mathfrak{z}}:\Delta\to\mathbb{R}^+_I$ *are given by* $\mathrm{Y}_{\mathfrak{z}}(\theta,\psi)=[\mathrm{Y}_*((\theta,\psi),\mathfrak{z}),\ \mathrm{Y}^*((\theta,\psi),\mathfrak{z})]$ *and* $\mathcal{J}_{\mathfrak{z}}(\theta,\psi)=[\mathcal{J}_*((\theta,\psi),\mathfrak{z}),\ \mathcal{J}^*((\theta,\psi),\mathfrak{z})]$ *for all* $(\theta,\psi)\in\Delta$ *and for all* $\mathfrak{z}\in[0,\ 1]$. *If* $\widetilde{\mathrm{Y}}\otimes\widetilde{\mathcal{J}}\in\mathcal{FD}_\Delta$, *then the following inequalities hold:*

$$\begin{aligned}
&\frac{\Gamma(\mathrm{Y}+1)\Gamma(\beta+1)}{4(n-\eth)^{\mathrm{Y}}(\mathrm{d}-\upsilon)^{\beta}}\left[\mathcal{I}^{\mathrm{Y},\,\beta}_{\eth^+,\upsilon^+}\,\widetilde{\mathrm{Y}}(n,\mathrm{d})\otimes\widetilde{\mathcal{J}}(n,\mathrm{d})\oplus\mathcal{I}^{\mathrm{Y},\,\beta}_{\eth^+,\mathrm{d}^-}\,\widetilde{\mathrm{Y}}(n,\upsilon)\otimes\widetilde{\mathcal{J}}(n,\upsilon)\right]\\
&\oplus\frac{\Gamma(\mathrm{Y}+1)\Gamma(\beta+1)}{4(n-\eth)^{\mathrm{Y}}(\mathrm{d}-\upsilon)^{\beta}}\left[\mathcal{I}^{\mathrm{Y},\,\beta}_{n^-,\upsilon^+}\,\widetilde{\mathrm{Y}}(\eth,\mathrm{d})\otimes\widetilde{\mathcal{J}}(\eth,\mathrm{d})\oplus\mathcal{I}^{\mathrm{Y},\,\beta}_{n^-,\mathrm{d}^-}\,\widetilde{\mathrm{Y}}(\eth,\upsilon)\otimes\widetilde{\mathcal{J}}(\eth,\upsilon)\right]\\
&\supseteq_{\mathbb{F}}\left(\frac{1}{2}-\frac{\mathrm{Y}}{(\mathrm{Y}+1)(\mathrm{Y}+2)}\right)\left(\frac{1}{2}-\frac{\beta}{(\beta+1)(\beta+2)}\right)\widetilde{K}(\eth,n,\upsilon,\mathrm{d})\oplus\frac{\mathrm{Y}}{(\mathrm{Y}+1)(\mathrm{Y}+2)}\left(\frac{1}{2}-\frac{\beta}{(\beta+1)(\beta+2)}\right)\widetilde{L}(\eth,n,\upsilon,\mathrm{d})\\
&\oplus\left(\frac{1}{2}-\frac{\mathrm{Y}}{(\mathrm{Y}+1)(\mathrm{Y}+2)}\right)\frac{\beta}{(\beta+1)(\beta+2)}\widetilde{\mathcal{M}}(\eth,n,\upsilon,\mathrm{d})\oplus\frac{\beta}{(\beta+1)(\beta+2)}\frac{\mathrm{Y}}{(\mathrm{Y}+1)(\mathrm{Y}+2)}\widetilde{\mathcal{N}}(\eth,n,\upsilon,\mathrm{d}).
\end{aligned}\tag{52}$$

If $\widetilde{\mathrm{Y}}$ *and* $\widetilde{\mathcal{J}}$ *are both coordinated concave FNVMs on* Δ, *then the above inequality can be expressed as follows:*

$$\begin{aligned}
&\frac{\Gamma(\mathrm{Y}+1)\Gamma(\beta+1)}{4(n-\eth)^{\mathrm{Y}}(\mathrm{d}-\upsilon)^{\beta}}\left[\mathcal{I}^{\mathrm{Y},\,\beta}_{\eth^+,\upsilon^+}\,\widetilde{\mathrm{Y}}(n,\mathrm{d})\otimes\widetilde{\mathcal{J}}(n,\mathrm{d})\oplus\mathcal{I}^{\mathrm{Y},\,\beta}_{\eth^+,\mathrm{d}^-}\,\widetilde{\mathrm{Y}}(n,\upsilon)\otimes\widetilde{\mathcal{J}}(n,\upsilon)\right]\\
&\oplus\frac{\Gamma(\mathrm{Y}+1)\Gamma(\beta+1)}{4(n-\eth)^{\mathrm{Y}}(\mathrm{d}-\upsilon)^{\beta}}\left[\mathcal{I}^{\mathrm{Y},\,\beta}_{n^-,\upsilon^+}\,\widetilde{\mathrm{Y}}(\eth,\mathrm{d})\otimes\widetilde{\mathcal{J}}(\eth,\mathrm{d})\oplus\mathcal{I}^{\mathrm{Y},\,\beta}_{n^-,\mathrm{d}^-}\,\widetilde{\mathrm{Y}}(\eth,\upsilon)\otimes\widetilde{\mathcal{J}}(\eth,\upsilon)\right]\\
&\subseteq_{\mathbb{F}}\left(\frac{1}{2}-\frac{\mathrm{Y}}{(\mathrm{Y}+1)(\mathrm{Y}+2)}\right)\left(\frac{1}{2}-\frac{\beta}{(\beta+1)(\beta+2)}\right)\widetilde{K}(\eth,n,\upsilon,\mathrm{d})\oplus\frac{\mathrm{Y}}{(\mathrm{Y}+1)(\mathrm{Y}+2)}\left(\frac{1}{2}-\frac{\beta}{(\beta+1)(\beta+2)}\right)\widetilde{L}(\eth,n,\upsilon,\mathrm{d})\\
&\oplus\left(\frac{1}{2}-\frac{\mathrm{Y}}{(\mathrm{Y}+1)(\mathrm{Y}+2)}\right)\frac{\beta}{(\beta+1)(\beta+2)}\widetilde{\mathcal{M}}(\eth,n,\upsilon,\mathrm{d})\oplus\frac{\beta}{(\beta+1)(\beta+2)}\frac{\mathrm{Y}}{(\mathrm{Y}+1)(\mathrm{Y}+2)}\widetilde{\mathcal{N}}(\eth,n,\upsilon,\mathrm{d}),
\end{aligned}$$

where

$$\begin{aligned}
\widetilde{K}(\eth,n,\upsilon,\mathrm{d})&=\widetilde{\mathrm{Y}}(\eth,\upsilon)\otimes\widetilde{\mathcal{J}}(\eth,\upsilon)\oplus\widetilde{\mathrm{Y}}(n,\upsilon)\otimes\widetilde{\mathcal{J}}(n,\upsilon)\\
&\oplus\widetilde{\mathrm{Y}}(\eth,\mathrm{d})\otimes\widetilde{\mathcal{J}}(\eth,\mathrm{d})\oplus\widetilde{\mathrm{Y}}(n,\mathrm{d})\otimes\widetilde{\mathcal{J}}(n,\mathrm{d}),\\
\widetilde{L}(\eth,n,\upsilon,\mathrm{d})&=\widetilde{\mathrm{Y}}(\eth,\upsilon)\otimes\widetilde{\mathcal{J}}(n,\upsilon)\oplus\widetilde{\mathrm{Y}}(n,\mathrm{d})\\
&\otimes\widetilde{\mathcal{J}}(\eth,\mathrm{d})\oplus\widetilde{\mathrm{Y}}(n,\upsilon)\otimes\widetilde{\mathcal{J}}(\eth,\upsilon)\oplus\widetilde{\mathrm{Y}}(\eth,\mathrm{d})\otimes\widetilde{\mathcal{J}}(n,\mathrm{d}),\\
\widetilde{\mathcal{M}}(\eth,n,\upsilon,\mathrm{d})&=\widetilde{\mathrm{Y}}(\eth,\upsilon)\otimes\widetilde{\mathcal{J}}(\eth,\mathrm{d})\oplus\widetilde{\mathrm{Y}}(n,\upsilon)\otimes\widetilde{\mathcal{J}}(n,\mathrm{d})\\
&\oplus\widetilde{\mathrm{Y}}(\eth,\mathrm{d})\otimes\widetilde{\mathcal{J}}(\eth,\upsilon)\oplus\widetilde{\mathrm{Y}}(n,\mathrm{d})\otimes\widetilde{\mathcal{J}}(n,\upsilon),\\
\widetilde{\mathcal{N}}(\eth,n,\upsilon,\mathrm{d})&=\widetilde{\mathrm{Y}}(\eth,\upsilon)\otimes\widetilde{\mathcal{J}}(n,\mathrm{d})\oplus\widetilde{\mathrm{Y}}(n,\upsilon)\otimes\widetilde{\mathcal{J}}(\eth,\mathrm{d})\\
&\oplus\widetilde{\mathrm{Y}}(\eth,\mathrm{d})\otimes\widetilde{\mathcal{J}}(n,\upsilon)\oplus\widetilde{\mathrm{Y}}(n,\mathrm{d})\otimes\widetilde{\mathcal{J}}(\eth,\upsilon),
\end{aligned}$$

and for each $\mathfrak{z} \in [0,\ 1]$, $\widetilde{K}(\eth, \mathrm{n}, \upsilon, \mathrm{d})$, $\widetilde{L}(\eth, \mathrm{n}, \upsilon, \mathrm{d})$, $\widetilde{\mathcal{M}}(\eth, \mathrm{n}, \upsilon, \mathrm{d})$, *and* $\widetilde{\mathcal{N}}(\eth, \mathrm{n}, \upsilon, \mathrm{d})$ *are defined as follows:*

$$\begin{aligned} K_{\mathfrak{z}}(\eth, \mathrm{n}, \upsilon, \mathrm{d}) &= [K_*((\eth, \mathrm{n}, \upsilon, \mathrm{d}),\ \mathfrak{z}),\ K^*((\eth, \mathrm{n}, \upsilon, \mathrm{d}),\ \mathfrak{z})], \\ L_{\mathfrak{z}}(\eth, \mathrm{n}, \upsilon, \mathrm{d}) &= [L_*((\eth, \mathrm{n}, \upsilon, \mathrm{d}),\ \mathfrak{z}),\ L^*((\eth, \mathrm{n}, \upsilon, \mathrm{d}),\ \mathfrak{z})], \\ \mathcal{M}_{\mathfrak{z}}(\eth, \mathrm{n}, \upsilon, \mathrm{d}) &= [\mathcal{M}_*((\eth, \mathrm{n}, \upsilon, \mathrm{d}),\ \mathfrak{z}),\ \mathcal{M}^*((\eth, \mathrm{n}, \upsilon, \mathrm{d}),\ \mathfrak{z})], \\ \mathcal{N}_{\mathfrak{z}}(\eth, \mathrm{n}, \upsilon, \mathrm{d}) &= [\mathcal{N}_*((\eth, \mathrm{n}, \upsilon, \mathrm{d}),\ \mathfrak{z}),\ \mathcal{N}^*((\eth, \mathrm{n}, \upsilon, \mathrm{d}),\ \mathfrak{z})] \end{aligned}$$

Proof. Let $\widetilde{\gamma}$ and $\widetilde{\mathcal{J}}$ be two coordinated UD-convex $FNVM$s on $[\eth,\ \mathrm{n}] \times [\upsilon,\ \mathrm{d}]$. Then

$$\begin{aligned} &\widetilde{\gamma}(\varepsilon\eth + (1-\varepsilon)\mathrm{n},\ s\upsilon + (1-s)\mathrm{d}) \\ &\quad \supseteq_{\mathbb{F}} \varepsilon s\widetilde{\gamma}(\eth, \upsilon) \oplus \varepsilon(1-s)\widetilde{\gamma}(\eth, \mathrm{d}) \oplus (1-\varepsilon)s\widetilde{\gamma}(\mathrm{n}, \upsilon) \oplus (1-\varepsilon)(1-s)\widetilde{\gamma}(\mathrm{n}, \mathrm{d}), \end{aligned}$$

And

$$\begin{aligned} &\widetilde{\mathcal{J}}(\varepsilon\eth + (1-\varepsilon)\mathrm{n},\ s\upsilon + (1-s)\mathrm{d}) \\ &\quad \supseteq_{\mathbb{F}} \varepsilon s\widetilde{\mathcal{J}}(\eth, \upsilon) \oplus \varepsilon(1-s)\widetilde{\mathcal{J}}(\eth, \mathrm{d}) \oplus (1-\varepsilon)s\widetilde{\mathcal{J}}(\mathrm{n}, \upsilon) \oplus (1-\varepsilon)(1-s)\widetilde{\mathcal{J}}(\mathrm{n}, \mathrm{d}). \end{aligned}$$

Since $\widetilde{\gamma}$ and $\widetilde{\mathcal{J}}$ are both coordinated UD-convex $FNVM$s, Lemma 1 states that

$$\widetilde{\gamma}_{\theta} : [\upsilon, \mathrm{d}] \to \mathbb{F}_0,\ \widetilde{\gamma}_{\theta}(\psi) = \widetilde{\gamma}(\theta, \psi),\ \widetilde{\mathcal{J}}_{\theta} : [\upsilon, \mathrm{d}] \to \mathbb{F}_0,\ \widetilde{\mathcal{J}}_{\theta}(\psi) = \widetilde{\mathcal{J}}(\theta, \psi).$$

Since $\widetilde{\gamma}_{\theta}$ and $\widetilde{\mathcal{J}}_{\theta}$ are $FNVM$s, then by inequality (16), we have

$$\begin{aligned} &\frac{\Gamma(\beta+1)}{2(\mathrm{d}-\upsilon)^{\beta}} \left[\mathcal{I}^{\beta}_{\upsilon^+}\widetilde{\gamma}_{\theta}(\mathrm{d}) \otimes \widetilde{\mathcal{J}}_{\theta}(\mathrm{d}) \oplus \mathcal{I}^{\beta}_{\mathrm{d}^-}\widetilde{\gamma}_{\theta}(\upsilon) \otimes \widetilde{\mathcal{J}}_{\theta}(\upsilon)\right] \\ &\quad \supseteq_{\mathbb{F}} \left(\tfrac{1}{2} - \tfrac{\beta}{(\beta+1)(\beta+2)}\right)\left(\widetilde{\gamma}_{\theta}(\upsilon) \otimes \widetilde{\mathcal{J}}_{\theta}(\upsilon) \oplus \widetilde{\gamma}_{\theta}(\mathrm{d}) \otimes \widetilde{\mathcal{J}}_{\theta}(\mathrm{d})\right) \\ &\quad \oplus\left(\tfrac{\beta}{(\beta+1)(\beta+2)}\right)\left(\widetilde{\gamma}_{\theta}(\upsilon) \otimes \widetilde{\mathcal{J}}_{\theta}(\mathrm{d}) \oplus \widetilde{\gamma}_{\theta}(\mathrm{d}) \otimes \widetilde{\mathcal{J}}_{\theta}(\upsilon)\right). \end{aligned}$$

Now, for all $\mathfrak{z} \in [0,\ 1]$, we have

$$\begin{aligned} &\frac{\Gamma(\beta+1)}{2(\mathrm{d}-\upsilon)^{\beta}} \left[\mathcal{I}^{\beta}_{\upsilon^+}\gamma_{\mathfrak{z}\theta}(\mathrm{d}) \times \mathcal{J}_{\mathfrak{z}\theta}(\mathrm{d}) + \mathcal{I}^{\beta}_{\mathrm{d}^-}\gamma_{\mathfrak{z}\theta}(\upsilon) \times \mathcal{J}_{\mathfrak{z}\theta}(\upsilon)\right] \\ &\quad \supseteq_I \left(\tfrac{1}{2} - \tfrac{\beta}{(\beta+1)(\beta+2)}\right)\left(\gamma_{\mathfrak{z}\theta}(\upsilon) \times \mathcal{J}_{\mathfrak{z}\theta}(\upsilon) + \gamma_{\mathfrak{z}\theta}(\mathrm{d}) \times \mathcal{J}_{\mathfrak{z}\theta}(\mathrm{d})\right) \\ &\quad +\left(\tfrac{\beta}{(\beta+1)(\beta+2)}\right)\left(\gamma_{\mathfrak{z}\theta}(\upsilon) \times \mathcal{J}_{\mathfrak{z}\theta}(\mathrm{d}) + \gamma_{\mathfrak{z}\theta}(\mathrm{d}) \times \mathcal{J}_{\mathfrak{z}\theta}(\upsilon)\right). \end{aligned}$$

That is

$$\begin{aligned} &\frac{\beta}{2(\mathrm{d}-\upsilon)^{\beta}} \left[\int_{\upsilon}^{\mathrm{d}} (\mathrm{d}-\psi)^{\beta-1}\gamma_{\mathfrak{z}}(\theta, \psi) \times \mathcal{J}_{\mathfrak{z}}(\theta, \psi)d\psi + \int_{\upsilon}^{\mathrm{d}} (\psi-\upsilon)^{\beta-1}\gamma_{\mathfrak{z}}(\theta, \psi) \times \mathcal{J}_{\mathfrak{z}}(\theta, \psi)d\psi\right] \\ &\quad \supseteq_I \left(\tfrac{1}{2} - \tfrac{\beta}{(\beta+1)(\beta+2)}\right)\left(\gamma_{\mathfrak{z}}(\theta, \upsilon) \times \mathcal{J}_{\mathfrak{z}}(\theta, \upsilon) + \gamma_{\mathfrak{z}}(\theta, \mathrm{d}) \times \mathcal{J}_{\mathfrak{z}}(\theta, \mathrm{d})\right) \\ &\quad +\left(\tfrac{\beta}{(\beta+1)(\beta+2)}\right)\left(\gamma_{\mathfrak{z}}(\theta, \upsilon) \times \mathcal{J}_{\mathfrak{z}}(\theta, \mathrm{d}) + \gamma_{\mathfrak{z}}(\theta, \mathrm{d}) \times \mathcal{J}_{\mathfrak{z}}(\theta, \upsilon)\right). \end{aligned} \quad (53)$$

Multiplying double inequality (53) by $\frac{\gamma(\mathrm{n}-\theta)^{\gamma-1}}{2(\mathrm{n}-\eth)^{\gamma}}$ and integrating it with respect to θ over $[\eth,\ \mathrm{n}]$, we obtain

$$\begin{aligned} &\frac{\Gamma(\gamma+1)\Gamma(\beta+1)}{4(\mathrm{n}-\eth)^{\gamma}(\mathrm{d}-\upsilon)^{\beta}} \left[\mathcal{I}^{\gamma,\beta}_{\eth^+,\upsilon^+}\gamma_{\mathfrak{z}}(\mathrm{n}, \mathrm{d}) \times \mathcal{J}_{\mathfrak{z}}(\mathrm{n}, \mathrm{d}) + \mathcal{I}^{\gamma,\beta}_{\eth^+,\mathrm{d}^-}\gamma_{\mathfrak{z}}(\mathrm{n}, \upsilon) \times \mathcal{J}_{\mathfrak{z}}(\mathrm{n}, \upsilon)\right] \\ &\quad \supseteq_I \frac{\Gamma(\gamma+1)}{2(\mathrm{n}-\eth)^{\gamma}}\left(\tfrac{1}{2} - \tfrac{\beta}{(\beta+1)(\beta+2)}\right)\left(\mathcal{I}^{\gamma}_{\eth^+}\gamma_{\mathfrak{z}}(\mathrm{n}, \upsilon) \times \mathcal{J}_{\mathfrak{z}}(\mathrm{n}, \upsilon) + \mathcal{I}^{\gamma}_{\eth^+}\gamma_{\mathfrak{z}}(\mathrm{n}, \mathrm{d}) \times \mathcal{J}_{\mathfrak{z}}(\mathrm{n}, \mathrm{d})\right) \\ &\quad +\frac{\Gamma(\gamma+1)}{2(\mathrm{n}-\eth)^{\gamma}}\frac{\beta}{(\beta+1)(\beta+2)}\left(\mathcal{I}^{\gamma}_{\eth^+}\gamma_{\mathfrak{z}}(\mathrm{n}, \upsilon) \times \mathcal{J}_{\mathfrak{z}}(\mathrm{n}, \mathrm{d}) + \mathcal{I}^{\gamma}_{\eth^+}\gamma_{\mathfrak{z}}(\mathrm{n}, \mathrm{d}) \times \mathcal{J}_{\mathfrak{z}}(\mathrm{n}, \upsilon)\right). \end{aligned} \quad (54)$$

Again, multiplying inequality (54) by $\frac{\gamma(\theta-\delta)^{\gamma-1}}{2(n-\delta)^{\gamma}}$ and integrating it with respect to θ over $[\delta,\ n]$, we obtain

$$\begin{aligned}&\frac{\Gamma(\gamma+1)\Gamma(\beta+1)}{4(n-\delta)^{\gamma}(d-\upsilon)^{\beta}}\left[\mathcal{I}^{\gamma,\beta}_{n^-,\upsilon^+}\Upsilon_{\mathfrak{z}}(\delta,d)\times\mathcal{J}_{\mathfrak{z}}(\delta,d)+\mathcal{I}^{\gamma,\beta}_{n^-,d^-}\Upsilon_{\mathfrak{z}}(\delta,\upsilon)\times\mathcal{J}_{\mathfrak{z}}(\delta,\upsilon)\right]\\&\supseteq_I\frac{\Gamma(\gamma+1)}{2(n-\delta)^{\gamma}}\left(\frac{1}{2}-\frac{\beta}{(\beta+1)(\beta+2)}\right)\left(\mathcal{I}^{\gamma}_{n^-}\Upsilon_{\mathfrak{z}}(\delta,\upsilon)\times\mathcal{J}_{\mathfrak{z}}(\delta,\upsilon)+\mathcal{I}^{\gamma}_{n^-}\Upsilon_{\mathfrak{z}}(\delta,d)\times\mathcal{J}_{\mathfrak{z}}(\delta,d)\right)\\&+\frac{\Gamma(\gamma+1)}{2(n-\delta)^{\gamma}}\frac{\beta}{(\beta+1)(\beta+2)}\left(\mathcal{I}^{\gamma}_{n^-}\Upsilon_{\mathfrak{z}}(\delta,\upsilon)\times\mathcal{J}_{\mathfrak{z}}(\delta,d)+\mathcal{I}^{\gamma}_{n^-}\Upsilon_{\mathfrak{z}}(\delta,d)\times\mathcal{J}_{\mathfrak{z}}(\delta,\upsilon)\right).\end{aligned}\tag{55}$$

Summing (54) and (55), we have

$$\begin{aligned}&\frac{\Gamma(\gamma+1)\Gamma(\beta+1)}{4(n-\delta)^{\gamma}(d-\upsilon)^{\beta}}\left[\begin{array}{c}\mathcal{I}^{\gamma,\beta}_{\delta^+,\upsilon^+}\Upsilon_{\mathfrak{z}}(n,d)\times\mathcal{J}_{\mathfrak{z}}(n,d)+\mathcal{I}^{\gamma,\beta}_{\delta^+,d^-}\Upsilon_{\mathfrak{z}}(n,\upsilon)\times\mathcal{J}_{\mathfrak{z}}(n,\upsilon)\\+\mathcal{I}^{\gamma,\beta}_{n^-,\upsilon^+}\Upsilon_{\mathfrak{z}}(\delta,d)\times\mathcal{J}_{\mathfrak{z}}(\delta,d)+\mathcal{I}^{\gamma,\beta}_{n^-,d^-}\Upsilon_{\mathfrak{z}}(\delta,\upsilon)\times\mathcal{J}_{\mathfrak{z}}(\delta,\upsilon)\end{array}\right]\\&\supseteq_I\frac{\Gamma(\gamma+1)}{2(n-\delta)^{\gamma}}\left(\frac{1}{2}-\frac{\beta}{(\beta+1)(\beta+2)}\right)\left(\mathcal{I}^{\gamma}_{\delta^+}\Upsilon_{\mathfrak{z}}(n,\upsilon)\times\mathcal{J}_{\mathfrak{z}}(n,\upsilon)+\mathcal{I}^{\gamma}_{n^-}\Upsilon_{\mathfrak{z}}(\delta,\upsilon)\times\mathcal{J}_{\mathfrak{z}}(\delta,\upsilon)\right)\\&+\frac{\Gamma(\gamma+1)}{2(n-\delta)^{\gamma}}\left(\frac{1}{2}-\frac{\beta}{(\beta+1)(\beta+2)}\right)\left(\mathcal{I}^{\gamma}_{\delta^+}\Upsilon_{\mathfrak{z}}(n,d)\times\mathcal{J}_{\mathfrak{z}}(n,d)+\mathcal{I}^{\gamma}_{n^-}\Upsilon_{\mathfrak{z}}(\delta,d)\times\mathcal{J}_{\mathfrak{z}}(\delta,d)\right)\\&+\frac{\Gamma(\gamma+1)}{2(n-\delta)^{\gamma}}\frac{\beta}{(\beta+1)(\beta+2)}\left(\mathcal{I}^{\gamma}_{\delta^+}\Upsilon_{\mathfrak{z}}(n,\upsilon)\times\mathcal{J}_{\mathfrak{z}}(n,d)+\mathcal{I}^{\gamma}_{n^-}\Upsilon_{\mathfrak{z}}(\delta,\upsilon)\times\mathcal{J}_{\mathfrak{z}}(\delta,d)\right)\\&+\frac{\Gamma(\gamma+1)}{2(n-\delta)^{\gamma}}\frac{\beta}{(\beta+1)(\beta+2)}\left(\mathcal{I}^{\gamma}_{\delta^+}\Upsilon_{\mathfrak{z}}(n,d)\times\mathcal{J}_{\mathfrak{z}}(n,\upsilon)+\mathcal{I}^{\gamma}_{n^-}\Upsilon_{\mathfrak{z}}(\delta,d)\times\mathcal{J}_{\mathfrak{z}}(\delta,\upsilon)\right).\end{aligned}\tag{56}$$

Now, once more with the aid of integral inequality (16), we obtain the following relationship for the first two integrals on the right-hand side of (56):

$$\begin{aligned}&\frac{\Gamma(\gamma+1)}{2(n-\delta)^{\gamma}}\left(\mathcal{I}^{\gamma}_{\delta^+}\Upsilon_{\mathfrak{z}}(n,\upsilon)\times\mathcal{J}_{\mathfrak{z}}(n,\upsilon)+\mathcal{I}^{\gamma}_{n^-}\Upsilon_{\mathfrak{z}}(\delta,\upsilon)\times\mathcal{J}_{\mathfrak{z}}(\delta,\upsilon)\right)\\&\supseteq_I\left(\frac{1}{2}-\frac{\gamma}{(\gamma+1)(\gamma+2)}\right)\left(\Upsilon_{\mathfrak{z}}(\delta,\upsilon)\times\mathcal{J}_{\mathfrak{z}}(\delta,\upsilon)+\Upsilon_{\mathfrak{z}}(n,\upsilon)\times\mathcal{J}_{\mathfrak{z}}(n,\upsilon)\right)\\&+\left(\frac{\gamma}{(\gamma+1)(\gamma+2)}\right)\left(\Upsilon_{\mathfrak{z}}(\delta,\upsilon)\times\mathcal{J}_{\mathfrak{z}}(n,\upsilon)+\Upsilon_{\mathfrak{z}}(n,\upsilon)\times\mathcal{J}_{\mathfrak{z}}(\delta,\upsilon)\right).\end{aligned}\tag{57}$$

$$\begin{aligned}&\frac{\Gamma(\gamma+1)}{2(n-\delta)^{\gamma}}\left(\mathcal{I}^{\gamma}_{\delta^+}\Upsilon_{\mathfrak{z}}(n,d)\times\mathcal{J}_{\mathfrak{z}}(n,d)+\mathcal{I}^{\gamma}_{n^-}\Upsilon_{\mathfrak{z}}(\delta,d)\times\mathcal{J}_{\mathfrak{z}}(\delta,d)\right)\\&\supseteq_I\left(\frac{1}{2}-\frac{\gamma}{(\gamma+1)(\gamma+2)}\right)\left(\Upsilon_{\mathfrak{z}}(\delta,d)\times\mathcal{J}_{\mathfrak{z}}(\delta,d)+\Upsilon_{\mathfrak{z}}(n,d)\times\mathcal{J}_{\mathfrak{z}}(n,d)\right)\\&+\left(\frac{\gamma}{(\gamma+1)(\gamma+2)}\right)\left(\Upsilon_{\mathfrak{z}}(\delta,d)\times\mathcal{J}_{\mathfrak{z}}(n,d)+\Upsilon_{\mathfrak{z}}(n,d)\times\mathcal{J}_{\mathfrak{z}}(\delta,d)\right).\end{aligned}\tag{58}$$

$$\begin{aligned}&\frac{\Gamma(\gamma+1)}{2(n-\delta)^{\gamma}}\left(\mathcal{I}^{\gamma}_{\delta^+}\Upsilon_{\mathfrak{z}}(n,\upsilon)\times\mathcal{J}_{\mathfrak{z}}(n,d)+\mathcal{I}^{\gamma}_{n^-}\Upsilon_{\mathfrak{z}}(\delta,\upsilon)\times\mathcal{J}_{\mathfrak{z}}(\delta,d)\right)\\&\supseteq_I\left(\frac{1}{2}-\frac{\gamma}{(\gamma+1)(\gamma+2)}\right)\left(\Upsilon_{\mathfrak{z}}(\delta,\upsilon)\times\mathcal{J}_{\mathfrak{z}}(\delta,d)+\Upsilon_{\mathfrak{z}}(n,\upsilon)\times\mathcal{J}_{\mathfrak{z}}(n,d)\right)\\&+\left(\frac{\gamma}{(\gamma+1)(\gamma+2)}\right)\left(\Upsilon_{\mathfrak{z}}(\delta,\upsilon)\times\mathcal{J}_{\mathfrak{z}}(n,d)+\Upsilon_{\mathfrak{z}}(n,\upsilon)\times\mathcal{J}_{\mathfrak{z}}(\delta,d)\right).\end{aligned}\tag{59}$$

And

$$\begin{aligned}&\frac{\Gamma(\gamma+1)}{2(n-\delta)^{\gamma}}\left(\mathcal{I}^{\gamma}_{\delta^+}\Upsilon_{\mathfrak{z}}(n,d)\times\mathcal{J}_{\mathfrak{z}}(n,\upsilon)+\mathcal{I}^{\gamma}_{n^-}\Upsilon_{\mathfrak{z}}(\delta,d)\times\mathcal{J}_{\mathfrak{z}}(\delta,\upsilon)\right)\\&\supseteq_I\left(\frac{1}{2}-\frac{\gamma}{(\gamma+1)(\gamma+2)}\right)\left(\Upsilon_{\mathfrak{z}}(\delta,d)\times\mathcal{J}_{\mathfrak{z}}(\delta,\upsilon)+\Upsilon_{\mathfrak{z}}(n,d)\times\mathcal{J}_{\mathfrak{z}}(n,\upsilon)\right)\\&+\left(\frac{\gamma}{(\gamma+1)(\gamma+2)}\right)\left(\Upsilon_{\mathfrak{z}}(\delta,d)\times\mathcal{J}_{\mathfrak{z}}(n,\upsilon)+\Upsilon_{\mathfrak{z}}(n,d)\times\mathcal{J}_{\mathfrak{z}}(\delta,\upsilon)\right).\end{aligned}\tag{60}$$

From (57)–(60), inequality (54) we have

$$\frac{\Gamma(\gamma+1)\Gamma(\beta+1)}{4(n-\delta)^{\gamma}(d-\upsilon)^{\beta}}\begin{bmatrix}\mathcal{I}^{\gamma,\beta}_{\delta^+,\upsilon^+}\,\gamma_{\mathfrak{z}}(n,d)\times\mathcal{J}_{\mathfrak{z}}(n,d)+\mathcal{I}^{\gamma,\beta}_{\delta^+,d^-}\gamma_{\mathfrak{z}}(n,\upsilon)\times\mathcal{J}_{\mathfrak{z}}(n,\upsilon)\\+\mathcal{I}^{\gamma,\beta}_{n^-,\upsilon^+}\,\gamma_{\mathfrak{z}}(\delta,d)\times\mathcal{J}_{\mathfrak{z}}(\delta,d)+\mathcal{I}^{\gamma,\beta}_{n^-,d^-}\gamma_{\mathfrak{z}}(\delta,\upsilon)\times\mathcal{J}_{\mathfrak{z}}(\delta,\upsilon)\end{bmatrix}$$
$$\supseteq_I\left(\tfrac{1}{2}-\tfrac{\gamma}{(\gamma+1)(\gamma+2)}\right)\left(\tfrac{1}{2}-\tfrac{\beta}{(\beta+1)(\beta+2)}\right)K_{\mathfrak{z}}(\delta,n,\upsilon,d)+\tfrac{\gamma}{(\gamma+1)(\gamma+2)}\left(\tfrac{1}{2}-\tfrac{\beta}{(\beta+1)(\beta+2)}\right)L_{\mathfrak{z}}(\delta,n,\upsilon,d)$$
$$+\left(\tfrac{1}{2}-\tfrac{\gamma}{(\gamma+1)(\gamma+2)}\right)\tfrac{\beta}{(\beta+1)(\beta+2)}\mathcal{M}_{\mathfrak{z}}(\delta,n,\upsilon,d)+\tfrac{\beta}{(\beta+1)(\beta+2)}\tfrac{\gamma}{(\gamma+1)(\gamma+2)}\mathcal{N}_{\mathfrak{z}}(\delta,n,\upsilon,d).$$

Since we obtain the collection of $IVMs$ $\gamma_{\mathfrak{z}}$, $\mathcal{J}_{\mathfrak{z}}:\Delta\to\mathbb{R}_I^+$ from the $\mathfrak{z}$-cuts, the aforementioned inequality can be expressed as an inequality (52). A conclusion has, therefore, been established. □

Remark 3. *If one assumes that* $\gamma=1=\beta$*, then from (52), as a result, there will be inequity (see [42]):*

$$\frac{1}{(n-\delta)(d-\upsilon)}\int_{\delta}^{n}\int_{\upsilon}^{d}\widetilde{\gamma}(\theta,\psi)\otimes\widetilde{\mathcal{J}}(\theta,\psi)d\psi d\theta$$
$$\supseteq_{\mathbb{F}}\tfrac{1}{9}\widetilde{K}(\delta,n,\upsilon,d)\oplus\tfrac{1}{18}\left[\widetilde{L}(\delta,n,\upsilon,d)\oplus\widetilde{\mathcal{M}}(\delta,n,\upsilon,d)\right]\oplus\tfrac{1}{36}\widetilde{\mathcal{N}}(\delta,n,\upsilon,d).$$

If $\widetilde{\gamma}$ *is coordinated left-UD-convex and one assumes that* $\gamma=1=\beta$*, then from (52), as a result, there will be inequity (see [27]):*

$$\frac{1}{(n-\delta)(d-\upsilon)}\int_{\delta}^{n}\int_{\upsilon}^{d}\widetilde{\gamma}(\theta,\psi)\otimes\widetilde{\mathcal{J}}(\theta,\psi)d\psi d\theta$$
$$\leq_{\mathbb{F}}\tfrac{1}{9}\widetilde{K}(\delta,n,\upsilon,d)\oplus\tfrac{1}{18}\left[\widetilde{L}(\delta,n,\upsilon,d)\oplus\widetilde{\mathcal{M}}(\delta,n,\upsilon,d)\right]\oplus\tfrac{1}{36}\widetilde{\mathcal{N}}(\delta,n,\upsilon,d).$$

If $\gamma_*((\theta,\psi),\mathfrak{z})\neq\gamma^*((\theta,\psi),\mathfrak{z})$ *with* $\mathfrak{z}=1$*, then from (52), we succeed in bringing about the upcoming inequity (see [26]):*

$$\frac{\Gamma(\gamma+1)\Gamma(\beta+1)}{4(n-\delta)^{\gamma}(d-\upsilon)^{\beta}}\left[\mathcal{I}^{\gamma,\beta}_{\delta^+,\upsilon^+}\gamma(n,d)\times J(n,d)+\mathcal{I}^{\gamma,\beta}_{\delta^+,d^-}\gamma(n,\upsilon)\times J(n,\upsilon)\right]$$
$$+\frac{\Gamma(\gamma+1)\Gamma(\beta+1)}{4(n-\delta)^{\gamma}(d-\upsilon)^{\beta}}\left[\mathcal{I}^{\gamma,\beta}_{n^-,\upsilon^+}\gamma(\delta,d)\times J(\delta,d)+\mathcal{I}^{\gamma,\beta}_{n^-,d^-}\gamma(\delta,\upsilon)\times J(\delta,\upsilon)\right]$$
$$\supseteq\left(\tfrac{1}{2}-\tfrac{\gamma}{(\gamma+1)(\gamma+2)}\right)\left(\tfrac{1}{2}-\tfrac{\beta}{(\beta+1)(\beta+2)}\right)K(\delta,n,\upsilon,d)+\tfrac{\gamma}{(\gamma+1)(\gamma+2)}\left(\tfrac{1}{2}-\tfrac{\beta}{(\beta+1)(\beta+2)}\right)L(\delta,n,\upsilon,d)$$
$$+\left(\tfrac{1}{2}-\tfrac{\gamma}{(\gamma+1)(\gamma+2)}\right)\tfrac{\beta}{(\beta+1)(\beta+2)}\mathcal{M}(\delta,n,\upsilon,d)+\tfrac{\beta}{(\beta+1)(\beta+2)}\tfrac{\gamma}{(\gamma+1)(\gamma+2)}\mathcal{N}(\delta,n,\upsilon,d).$$

If $\gamma_*((\theta,\psi),\mathfrak{z})\neq\gamma^*((\theta,\psi),\mathfrak{z})$ *with* $\mathfrak{z}=1$*, then from (52), we succeed in bringing about the upcoming inequity (see [25]):*

$$\frac{1}{(n-\delta)(d-\upsilon)}\int_{\delta}^{n}\int_{\upsilon}^{d}\gamma(\theta,\psi)\times\mathcal{J}(\theta,\psi)d\psi d\theta$$
$$\supseteq\tfrac{1}{9}K(\delta,n,\upsilon,d)+\tfrac{1}{18}[L(\delta,n,\upsilon,d)+\mathcal{M}(\delta,n,\upsilon,d)]+\tfrac{1}{36}\mathcal{N}(\delta,n,\upsilon,d).$$

If $\gamma_*((\theta,\psi),\mathfrak{z})=\gamma^*((\theta,\psi),\mathfrak{z})$ *and* $\mathcal{J}_*((\theta,\psi),\mathfrak{z})=\mathcal{J}^*((\theta,\psi),\mathfrak{z})$ *with* $\mathfrak{z}=1$*, then from (52), we succeed in bringing about the upcoming inequity (see [41]):*

$$\frac{\Gamma(\gamma+1)\Gamma(\beta+1)}{4(n-\delta)^{\gamma}(d-\upsilon)^{\beta}}\left[\mathcal{I}^{\gamma,\beta}_{\delta^+,\upsilon^+}\gamma(n,d)\times J(n,d)+\mathcal{I}^{\gamma,\beta}_{\delta^+,d^-}\gamma(n,\upsilon)\times J(n,\upsilon)\right]$$
$$+\frac{\Gamma(\gamma+1)\Gamma(\beta+1)}{4(n-\delta)^{\gamma}(d-\upsilon)^{\beta}}\left[+\mathcal{I}^{\gamma,\beta}_{n^-,\upsilon^+}\gamma(\delta,d)\times J(\delta,d)+\mathcal{I}^{\gamma,\beta}_{n^-,d^-}\gamma(\delta,\upsilon)\times J(\delta,\upsilon)\right]$$
$$\leq\left(\tfrac{1}{2}-\tfrac{\gamma}{(\gamma+1)(\gamma+2)}\right)\left(\tfrac{1}{2}-\tfrac{\beta}{(\beta+1)(\beta+2)}\right)K(\delta,n,\upsilon,d)+\tfrac{\gamma}{(\gamma+1)(\gamma+2)}\left(\tfrac{1}{2}-\tfrac{\beta}{(\beta+1)(\beta+2)}\right)L(\delta,n,\upsilon,d)$$
$$+\left(\tfrac{1}{2}-\tfrac{\gamma}{(\gamma+1)(\gamma+2)}\right)\tfrac{\beta}{(\beta+1)(\beta+2)}\mathcal{M}(\delta,n,\upsilon,d)+\tfrac{\beta}{(\beta+1)(\beta+2)}\tfrac{\gamma}{(\gamma+1)(\gamma+2)}\mathcal{N}(\delta,n,\upsilon,d).$$

Theorem 11. *Let $\widetilde{\gamma}$, $\widetilde{\mathcal{J}} : \Delta \to \mathbb{F}_0$ be a coordinated UD-convex FNVMFNVM on Δ. Then, from the $\mathfrak{z}$-cuts, we set up the sequence of IVMs $\gamma_{\mathfrak{z}}, \mathcal{J}_{\mathfrak{z}} : \Delta \to \mathbb{R}_I^+$ that are given by $\gamma_{\mathfrak{z}}(\theta,\psi) = [\gamma_*((\theta,\psi),\mathfrak{z}),\ \gamma^*((\theta,\psi),\mathfrak{z})]$ and $\mathcal{J}_{\mathfrak{z}}(\theta,\psi) = [\mathcal{J}_*((\theta,\psi),\mathfrak{z}),\ \mathcal{J}^*((\theta,\psi),\mathfrak{z})]$ for all $(\theta,\psi) \in \Delta$ and for all $\mathfrak{z} \in [0,\ 1]$. If $\widetilde{\gamma} \otimes \widetilde{\mathcal{J}} \in \mathcal{FD}_\Delta$, then the following inequalities hold:*

$$\begin{aligned} 4\widetilde{\gamma}\left(\tfrac{\delta+n}{2}, \tfrac{\upsilon+d}{2}\right) &\otimes \widetilde{\mathcal{J}}\left(\tfrac{\delta+n}{2}, \tfrac{\upsilon+d}{2}\right) \\ &\supseteq_{\mathbb{F}} \frac{\Gamma(\gamma+1)\Gamma(\beta+1)}{4(n-\delta)^{\gamma}(d-\upsilon)^{\beta}}\left[\mathcal{I}^{\gamma,\beta}_{\delta^+,\upsilon^+}\widetilde{\gamma}(n,d)\otimes\widetilde{\mathcal{J}}(n,d)\oplus\mathcal{I}^{\gamma,\beta}_{\delta^+,d^-}\widetilde{\gamma}(n,\upsilon)\otimes\widetilde{\mathcal{J}}(n,\upsilon)\right] \\ &\oplus \frac{\Gamma(\gamma+1)\Gamma(\beta+1)}{4(n-\delta)^{\gamma}(d-\upsilon)^{\beta}}\left[\mathcal{I}^{\gamma,\beta}_{n^-,\upsilon^+}\widetilde{\gamma}(\delta,d)\otimes\widetilde{\mathcal{J}}(\delta,d)\oplus\mathcal{I}^{\gamma,\beta}_{n^-,d^-}\widetilde{\gamma}(\delta,\upsilon)\otimes\widetilde{\mathcal{J}}(\delta,\upsilon)\right] \\ &\oplus \left[\frac{\gamma}{2(\gamma+1)(\gamma+2)} + \frac{\beta}{(\beta+1)(\beta+2)}\left(\frac{1}{2} - \frac{\gamma}{(\gamma+1)(\gamma+2)}\right)\right]\widetilde{K}(\delta,n,\upsilon,d) \\ &\oplus \left[\frac{1}{2}\left(\frac{1}{2} - \frac{\gamma}{(\gamma+1)(\gamma+2)}\right) + \frac{\gamma}{(\gamma+1)(\gamma+2)}\frac{\beta}{(\beta+1)(\beta+2)}\right]\widetilde{L}(\delta,n,\upsilon,d) \\ &\oplus \left[\frac{1}{2}\left(\frac{1}{2} - \frac{\beta}{(\beta+1)(\beta+2)}\right) + \frac{\gamma}{(\gamma+1)(\gamma+2)}\frac{\beta}{(\beta+1)(\beta+2)}\right]\widetilde{\mathcal{M}}(\delta,n,\upsilon,d) \\ &\oplus \left[\frac{1}{4} - \frac{\gamma}{(\gamma+1)(\gamma+2)}\frac{\beta}{(\beta+1)(\beta+2)}\right]\widetilde{\mathcal{N}}(\delta,n,\upsilon,d). \end{aligned} \tag{61}$$

If $\widetilde{\gamma}$ and $\widetilde{\mathcal{J}}$ are both coordinated concave FNVMs on Δ, then the above inequality can be expressed as follows:

$$\begin{aligned} 4\widetilde{\gamma}\left(\tfrac{\delta+n}{2}, \tfrac{\upsilon+d}{2}\right) &\otimes \widetilde{\mathcal{J}}\left(\tfrac{\delta+n}{2}, \tfrac{\upsilon+d}{2}\right) \\ &\subseteq_{\mathbb{F}} \frac{\Gamma(\gamma+1)\Gamma(\beta+1)}{4(n-\delta)^{\gamma}(d-\upsilon)^{\beta}}\left[\mathcal{I}^{\gamma,\beta}_{\delta^+,\upsilon^+}\widetilde{\gamma}(n,d)\otimes\widetilde{\mathcal{J}}(n,d)\oplus\mathcal{I}^{\gamma,\beta}_{\delta^+,d^-}\widetilde{\gamma}(n,\upsilon)\otimes\widetilde{\mathcal{J}}(n,\upsilon)\right] \\ &\oplus \frac{\Gamma(\gamma+1)\Gamma(\beta+1)}{4(n-\delta)^{\gamma}(d-\upsilon)^{\beta}}\left[\mathcal{I}^{\gamma,\beta}_{n^-,\upsilon^+}\widetilde{\gamma}(\delta,d)\otimes\widetilde{\mathcal{J}}(\delta,d)\oplus\mathcal{I}^{\gamma,\beta}_{n^-,d^-}\widetilde{\gamma}(\delta,\upsilon)\otimes\widetilde{\mathcal{J}}(\delta,\upsilon)\right] \\ &\oplus \left[\frac{\gamma}{2(\gamma+1)(\gamma+2)} + \frac{\beta}{(\beta+1)(\beta+2)}\left(\frac{1}{2} - \frac{\gamma}{(\gamma+1)(\gamma+2)}\right)\right]\widetilde{K}(\delta,n,\upsilon,d) \\ &\oplus \left[\frac{1}{2}\left(\frac{1}{2} - \frac{\gamma}{(\gamma+1)(\gamma+2)}\right) + \frac{\gamma}{(\gamma+1)(\gamma+2)}\frac{\beta}{(\beta+1)(\beta+2)}\right]\widetilde{L}(\delta,n,\upsilon,d) \\ &\oplus \left[\frac{1}{2}\left(\frac{1}{2} - \frac{\beta}{(\beta+1)(\beta+2)}\right) + \frac{\gamma}{(\gamma+1)(\gamma+2)}\frac{\beta}{(\beta+1)(\beta+2)}\right]\widetilde{\mathcal{M}}(\delta,n,\upsilon,d) \\ &\oplus \left[\frac{1}{4} - \frac{\gamma}{(\gamma+1)(\gamma+2)}\frac{\beta}{(\beta+1)(\beta+2)}\right]\widetilde{\mathcal{N}}(\delta,n,\upsilon,d), \end{aligned} \tag{62}$$

where $\widetilde{K}(\delta,n,\upsilon,d)$, $\widetilde{L}(\delta,n,\upsilon,d)$, $\widetilde{\mathcal{M}}(\delta,n,\upsilon,d)$, and $\widetilde{\mathcal{N}}(\delta,n,\upsilon,d)$ are given in Theorem 10.

Proof. Since $\widetilde{\gamma}, \widetilde{\mathcal{J}} : \Delta \to \mathbb{F}_0$ are two *UD*-convex *FNVMs*, then from inequality (17) and for each $\mathfrak{z} \in [0,\ 1]$, we have

$$\begin{aligned} 2\gamma_{\mathfrak{z}}\left(\tfrac{\delta+n}{2}, \tfrac{\upsilon+d}{2}\right) &\times \mathcal{J}_{\mathfrak{z}}\left(\tfrac{\delta+n}{2}, \tfrac{\upsilon+d}{2}\right) \\ &\supseteq_I \frac{\gamma}{2(n-\delta)^{\gamma}}\left[\begin{array}{c} \int_\delta^n (n-\theta)^{\gamma-1}\gamma_{\mathfrak{z}}\left(\theta,\tfrac{\upsilon+d}{2}\right)\times\mathcal{J}_{\mathfrak{z}}\left(\theta,\tfrac{\upsilon+d}{2}\right)d\theta \\ +\int_\delta^n (\theta-\delta)^{\gamma-1}\gamma_{\mathfrak{z}}\left(\theta,\tfrac{\upsilon+d}{2}\right)\times\mathcal{J}_{\mathfrak{z}}\left(\theta,\tfrac{\upsilon+d}{2}\right)d\theta \end{array}\right] \\ &+\left(\frac{\gamma}{(\gamma+1)(\gamma+2)}\right)\left(\gamma_{\mathfrak{z}}\left(\delta,\tfrac{\upsilon+d}{2}\right)\times\mathcal{J}_{\mathfrak{z}}\left(\delta,\tfrac{\upsilon+d}{2}\right)+\gamma_{\mathfrak{z}}\left(n,\tfrac{\upsilon+d}{2}\right)\times\mathcal{J}_{\mathfrak{z}}\left(n,\tfrac{\upsilon+d}{2}\right)\right) \\ &+\left(\frac{1}{2}-\frac{\gamma}{(\gamma+1)(\gamma+2)}\right)\left(\gamma_{\mathfrak{z}}\left(\delta,\tfrac{\upsilon+d}{2}\right)\times\mathcal{J}_{\mathfrak{z}}\left(n,\tfrac{\upsilon+d}{2}\right)+\gamma_{\mathfrak{z}}\left(n,\tfrac{\upsilon+d}{2}\right)\times\mathcal{J}_{\mathfrak{z}}\left(\delta,\tfrac{\upsilon+d}{2}\right)\right), \end{aligned} \tag{63}$$

and

$$
\begin{aligned}
2\mathrm{Y}_{\mathfrak{z}}\left(\tfrac{\eth+n}{2},\tfrac{\upsilon+d}{2}\right) & \times \mathcal{J}_{\mathfrak{z}}\left(\tfrac{\eth+n}{2},\tfrac{\upsilon+d}{2}\right) \\
& \supseteq_I \frac{\beta}{2(d-\upsilon)^{\beta}}\begin{bmatrix} \int_{\upsilon}^{d}(d-\psi)^{\beta-1}\mathrm{Y}_{\mathfrak{z}}\left(\tfrac{\eth+n}{2},\psi\right)\times\mathcal{J}_{\mathfrak{z}}\left(\tfrac{\eth+n}{2},\psi\right)d\psi \\ +\int_{\upsilon}^{d}(\psi-\upsilon)^{\beta-1}\mathrm{Y}_{\mathfrak{z}}\left(\tfrac{\eth+n}{2},\psi\right)\times\mathcal{J}_{\mathfrak{z}}\left(\tfrac{\eth+n}{2},\psi\right)d\psi \end{bmatrix} \\
& +\left(\tfrac{\beta}{(\beta+1)(\beta+2)}\right)\left(\mathrm{Y}_{\mathfrak{z}}\left(\tfrac{\eth+n}{2},\upsilon\right)\times\mathcal{J}_{\mathfrak{z}}\left(\tfrac{\eth+n}{2},\upsilon\right)+\mathrm{Y}_{\mathfrak{z}}\left(\tfrac{\eth+n}{2},d\right)\times\mathcal{J}_{\mathfrak{z}}\left(\tfrac{\eth+n}{2},d\right)\right) \\
& +\left(\tfrac{1}{2}-\tfrac{\beta}{(\beta+1)(\beta+2)}\right)\left(\mathrm{Y}_{\mathfrak{z}}\left(\tfrac{\eth+n}{2},\upsilon\right)\times\mathcal{J}_{\mathfrak{z}}\left(\tfrac{\eth+n}{2},d\right)+\mathrm{Y}_{\mathfrak{z}}\left(\tfrac{\eth+n}{2},d\right)\times\mathcal{J}_{\mathfrak{z}}\left(\tfrac{\eth+n}{2},\upsilon\right)\right)
\end{aligned} \tag{64}
$$

By adding (63) and (64) and multiplying the result by 2, we obtain:

$$
\begin{aligned}
8\mathrm{Y}_{\mathfrak{z}}\left(\tfrac{\eth+n}{2},\tfrac{\upsilon+d}{2}\right) & \times \mathcal{J}_{\mathfrak{z}}\left(\tfrac{\eth+n}{2},\tfrac{\upsilon+d}{2}\right) \\
& \supseteq_I \frac{\Upsilon}{2(n-\eth)^{\Upsilon}}\begin{bmatrix} \int_{\eth}^{n}2(n-\theta)^{\Upsilon-1}\mathrm{Y}_{\mathfrak{z}}\left(\theta,\tfrac{\upsilon+d}{2}\right)\times\mathcal{J}_{\mathfrak{z}}\left(\theta,\tfrac{\upsilon+d}{2}\right)d\theta \\ +\int_{\eth}^{n}2(\theta-\eth)^{\Upsilon-1}\mathrm{Y}_{\mathfrak{z}}\left(\theta,\tfrac{\upsilon+d}{2}\right)\times\mathcal{J}_{\mathfrak{z}}\left(\theta,\tfrac{\upsilon+d}{2}\right)d\theta \end{bmatrix} \\
& +\frac{\beta}{2(d-\upsilon)^{\beta}}\begin{bmatrix} \int_{\upsilon}^{d}2(d-\psi)^{\beta-1}\mathrm{Y}_{\mathfrak{z}}\left(\tfrac{\eth+n}{2},\psi\right)\times\mathcal{J}_{\mathfrak{z}}\left(\tfrac{\eth+n}{2},\psi\right)d\psi \\ +\int_{\upsilon}^{d}2(\psi-\upsilon)^{\beta-1}\mathrm{Y}_{\mathfrak{z}}\left(\tfrac{\eth+n}{2},\psi\right)\times\mathcal{J}_{\mathfrak{z}}\left(\tfrac{\eth+n}{2},\psi\right)d\psi \end{bmatrix} \\
& +\left(\tfrac{\Upsilon}{(\Upsilon+1)(\Upsilon+2)}\right)\left(2\mathrm{Y}_{\mathfrak{z}}\left(\eth,\tfrac{\upsilon+d}{2}\right)\times\mathcal{J}_{\mathfrak{z}}\left(\eth,\tfrac{\upsilon+d}{2}\right)+2\mathrm{Y}_{\mathfrak{z}}\left(n,\tfrac{\upsilon+d}{2}\right)\times\mathcal{J}_{\mathfrak{z}}\left(n,\tfrac{\upsilon+d}{2}\right)\right) \\
& +\left(\tfrac{1}{2}-\tfrac{\Upsilon}{(\Upsilon+1)(\Upsilon+2)}\right)\left(2\mathrm{Y}_{\mathfrak{z}}\left(\eth,\tfrac{\upsilon+d}{2}\right)\times\mathcal{J}_{\mathfrak{z}}\left(n,\tfrac{\upsilon+d}{2}\right)+2\mathrm{Y}_{\mathfrak{z}}\left(n,\tfrac{\upsilon+d}{2}\right)\times\mathcal{J}_{\mathfrak{z}}\left(\eth,\tfrac{\upsilon+d}{2}\right)\right) \\
& +\left(\tfrac{\beta}{(\beta+1)(\beta+2)}\right)\left(2\mathrm{Y}_{\mathfrak{z}}\left(\tfrac{\eth+n}{2},\upsilon\right)\times\mathcal{J}_{\mathfrak{z}}\left(\tfrac{\eth+n}{2},\upsilon\right)+2\mathrm{Y}_{\mathfrak{z}}\left(\tfrac{\eth+n}{2},d\right)\times\mathcal{J}_{\mathfrak{z}}\left(\tfrac{\eth+n}{2},d\right)\right) \\
& +\left(\tfrac{1}{2}-\tfrac{\beta}{(\beta+1)(\beta+2)}\right)\left(2\mathrm{Y}_{\mathfrak{z}}\left(\tfrac{\eth+n}{2},\upsilon\right)\times\mathcal{J}_{\mathfrak{z}}\left(\tfrac{\eth+n}{2},d\right)+2\mathrm{Y}_{\mathfrak{z}}\left(\tfrac{\eth+n}{2},d\right)\times\mathcal{J}_{\mathfrak{z}}\left(\tfrac{\eth+n}{2},\upsilon\right)\right).
\end{aligned} \tag{65}
$$

Using Lemma 1 for each integral on the right-hand side of (65) and the integral inequality (17) once more leads us to obtain the following:

$$
\begin{aligned}
\frac{\Upsilon}{2(n-\eth)^{\Upsilon}} & \int_{\eth}^{n}2(n-\theta)^{\Upsilon-1}\mathrm{Y}_{\mathfrak{z}}\left(\theta,\tfrac{\upsilon+d}{2}\right)\times\mathcal{J}_{\mathfrak{z}}\left(\theta,\tfrac{\upsilon+d}{2}\right)d\theta \\
& \supseteq_I \frac{\Upsilon\beta}{4(n-\eth)^{\Upsilon}(d-\upsilon)^{\beta}}\left[\int_{\eth}^{n}\int_{\upsilon}^{d}(n-\theta)^{\Upsilon-1}(d-\psi)^{\beta-1}\mathrm{Y}_{\mathfrak{z}}(\theta,\psi)d\psi d\theta\right] \\
& +\frac{\Upsilon\beta}{4(n-\eth)^{\Upsilon}(d-\upsilon)^{\beta}}\left[\int_{\eth}^{n}\int_{\upsilon}^{d}(n-\theta)^{\Upsilon-1}(\psi-\upsilon)^{\beta-1}\mathrm{Y}_{\mathfrak{z}}(\theta,\psi)d\psi d\theta\right] \\
& +\frac{\beta}{(\beta+1)(\beta+2)}\frac{\Upsilon}{2(n-\eth)^{\Upsilon}}\int_{\eth}^{n}(n-\theta)^{\Upsilon-1}\left(\mathrm{Y}_{\mathfrak{z}}(\theta,\upsilon)\times\mathcal{J}_{\mathfrak{z}}(\theta,\upsilon)+\mathrm{Y}_{\mathfrak{z}}(\theta,d)\times\mathcal{J}_{\mathfrak{z}}(\theta,d)\right)d\theta \\
& +\left(\tfrac{1}{2}-\tfrac{\beta}{(\beta+1)(\beta+2)}\right)\frac{\Upsilon}{2(n-\eth)^{\Upsilon}}\int_{\eth}^{n}(n-\theta)^{\Upsilon-1}\left(\mathrm{Y}_{\mathfrak{z}}(\theta,\upsilon)\times\mathcal{J}_{\mathfrak{z}}(\theta,d)+\mathrm{Y}_{\mathfrak{z}}(\theta,d)\times\mathcal{J}_{\mathfrak{z}}(\theta,\upsilon)\right)d\theta, \\
& =\frac{\Gamma(\Upsilon+1)\Gamma(\beta+1)}{4(n-\eth)^{\Upsilon}(d-\upsilon)^{\beta}}\left[\mathcal{I}_{\eth^+,\upsilon^+}^{\Upsilon,\beta}\,\mathrm{Y}_{\mathfrak{z}}(n,d)\times\mathcal{J}_{\mathfrak{z}}(n,d)+\mathcal{I}_{\eth^+,d^-}^{\Upsilon,\beta}\,\mathrm{Y}_{\mathfrak{z}}(n,\upsilon)\times\mathcal{J}_{\mathfrak{z}}(n,\upsilon)\right] \\
& +\frac{\Gamma(\Upsilon+1)}{2(n-\eth)^{\Upsilon}}\left(\frac{\beta}{(\beta+1)(\beta+2)}\right)\left(\mathcal{I}_{\eth^+}^{\Upsilon}\,\mathrm{Y}_{\mathfrak{z}}(n,\upsilon)\times\mathcal{J}_{\mathfrak{z}}(n,\upsilon)+\mathcal{I}_{\eth^+}^{\Upsilon}\,\mathrm{Y}_{\mathfrak{z}}(n,d)\times\mathcal{J}_{\mathfrak{z}}(n,d)\right) \\
& +\frac{\Gamma(\Upsilon+1)}{2(n-\eth)^{\Upsilon}}\left(\tfrac{1}{2}-\frac{\beta}{(\beta+1)(\beta+2)}\right)\left(\mathcal{I}_{\eth^+}^{\Upsilon}\,\mathrm{Y}_{\mathfrak{z}}(n,\upsilon)\times\mathcal{J}_{\mathfrak{z}}(n,d)+\mathcal{I}_{\eth^+}^{\Upsilon}\,\mathrm{Y}_{\mathfrak{z}}(n,d)\times\mathcal{J}_{\mathfrak{z}}(n,\upsilon)\right).
\end{aligned} \tag{66}
$$

$$\begin{aligned}\frac{\gamma}{2(\mathrm{n}-\eth)^{\gamma}} & \int_{\eth}^{\mathrm{n}} 2(\theta-\eth)^{\gamma-1}\Upsilon_{\mathfrak{z}}\left(\theta,\frac{\upsilon+\mathrm{d}}{2}\right)\times\mathcal{J}_{\mathfrak{z}}\left(\theta,\frac{\upsilon+\mathrm{d}}{2}\right)d\theta \\ & \supseteq_{I} \frac{\gamma\beta}{4(\mathrm{n}-\eth)^{\gamma}(\mathrm{d}-\upsilon)^{\beta}}\left[\int_{\eth}^{\mathrm{n}}\int_{\upsilon}^{\mathrm{d}}(\theta-\eth)^{\gamma-1}(\mathrm{d}-\psi)^{\beta-1}\Upsilon_{\mathfrak{z}}(\theta,\psi)d\psi d\theta\right] \\ & +\frac{\gamma\beta}{4(\mathrm{n}-\eth)^{\gamma}(\mathrm{d}-\upsilon)^{\beta}}\left[\int_{\eth}^{\mathrm{n}}\int_{\upsilon}^{\mathrm{d}}(\theta-\eth)^{\gamma-1}(\psi-\upsilon)^{\beta-1}\Upsilon_{\mathfrak{z}}(\theta,\psi)d\psi d\theta\right] \\ & +\frac{\beta}{(\beta+1)(\beta+2)}\frac{\gamma}{2(\mathrm{n}-\eth)^{\gamma}}\int_{\eth}^{\mathrm{n}}(\theta-\eth)^{\gamma-1}\Big(\Upsilon_{\mathfrak{z}}(\theta,\upsilon)\times\mathcal{J}_{\mathfrak{z}}(\theta,\upsilon)+\Upsilon_{\mathfrak{z}}(\theta,\mathrm{d})\times\mathcal{J}_{\mathfrak{z}}(\theta,\mathrm{d})\Big)d\theta \\ & +\left(\frac{1}{2}-\frac{\beta}{(\beta+1)(\beta+2)}\right)\frac{\gamma}{2(\mathrm{n}-\eth)^{\gamma}}\int_{\eth}^{\mathrm{n}}(\theta-\eth)^{\gamma-1}\Big(\Upsilon_{\mathfrak{z}}(\theta,\upsilon)\times\mathcal{J}_{\mathfrak{z}}(\theta,\mathrm{d})+\Upsilon_{\mathfrak{z}}(\theta,\mathrm{d})\times\mathcal{J}_{\mathfrak{z}}(\theta,\upsilon)\Big)d\theta, \\ & = \frac{\Gamma(\gamma+1)\Gamma(\beta+1)}{4(\mathrm{n}-\eth)^{\gamma}(\mathrm{d}-\upsilon)^{\beta}}\left[\mathcal{I}_{\mathrm{n}^-,\upsilon^+}^{\gamma,\,\beta}\Upsilon_{\mathfrak{z}}(\eth,\mathrm{d})\times\mathcal{J}_{\mathfrak{z}}(\eth,\mathrm{d})+\mathcal{I}_{\mathrm{n}^-,\mathrm{d}^-}^{\gamma,\,\beta}\Upsilon_{\mathfrak{z}}(\eth,\upsilon)\times\mathcal{J}_{\mathfrak{z}}(\eth,\upsilon)\right] \\ & +\frac{\Gamma(\gamma+1)}{2(\mathrm{n}-\eth)^{\gamma}}\left(\frac{\beta}{(\beta+1)(\beta+2)}\right)\Big(\mathcal{I}_{\mathrm{n}^-}^{\gamma}\Upsilon_{\mathfrak{z}}(\eth,\upsilon)\times\mathcal{J}_{\mathfrak{z}}(\eth,\upsilon)+\mathcal{I}_{\mathrm{n}^-}^{\gamma}\Upsilon_{\mathfrak{z}}(\eth,\mathrm{d})\times\mathcal{J}_{\mathfrak{z}}(\eth,\mathrm{d})\Big) \\ & +\frac{\Gamma(\gamma+1)}{2(\mathrm{n}-\eth)^{\gamma}}\left(\frac{1}{2}-\frac{\beta}{(\beta+1)(\beta+2)}\right)\Big(\mathcal{I}_{\mathrm{n}^-}^{\gamma}\Upsilon_{\mathfrak{z}}(\eth,\upsilon)\times\mathcal{J}_{\mathfrak{z}}(\eth,\mathrm{d})+\mathcal{I}_{\mathrm{n}^-}^{\gamma}\Upsilon_{\mathfrak{z}}(\eth,\mathrm{d})\times\mathcal{J}_{\mathfrak{z}}(\eth,\upsilon)\Big).\end{aligned} \tag{67}$$

$$\begin{aligned}\frac{\beta}{2(\mathrm{d}-\upsilon)^{\beta}} & \left[\int_{\upsilon}^{\mathrm{d}} 2(\mathrm{d}-\psi)^{\beta-1}\Upsilon_{\mathfrak{z}}\left(\frac{\eth+\mathrm{n}}{2},\psi\right)\times\mathcal{J}_{\mathfrak{z}}\left(\frac{\eth+\mathrm{n}}{2},\psi\right)d\psi\right] \\ & \supseteq_{I} \frac{\Gamma(\gamma+1)\Gamma(\beta+1)}{4(\mathrm{n}-\eth)^{\gamma}(\mathrm{d}-\upsilon)^{\beta}}\left[\mathcal{I}_{\eth^+,\upsilon^+}^{\gamma,\,\beta}\Upsilon_{\mathfrak{z}}(\mathrm{n},\mathrm{d})\times\mathcal{J}_{\mathfrak{z}}(\mathrm{n},\mathrm{d})+\mathcal{I}_{\mathrm{n}^-,\upsilon^+}^{\gamma,\,\beta}\Upsilon_{\mathfrak{z}}(\eth,\mathrm{d})\times\mathcal{J}_{\mathfrak{z}}(\eth,\mathrm{d})\right] \\ & +\frac{\Gamma(\beta+1)}{2(\mathrm{d}-\upsilon)^{\beta}}\left(\frac{\gamma}{(\gamma+1)(\gamma+2)}\right)\Big(\mathcal{I}_{\upsilon^+}^{\beta}\Upsilon_{\mathfrak{z}}(\eth,\mathrm{d})\times\mathcal{J}_{\mathfrak{z}}(\eth,\mathrm{d})+\mathcal{I}_{\upsilon^+}^{\beta}\Upsilon_{\mathfrak{z}}(\mathrm{n},\mathrm{d})\times\mathcal{J}_{\mathfrak{z}}(\mathrm{n},\mathrm{d})\Big) \\ & +\frac{\Gamma(\beta+1)}{2(\mathrm{d}-\upsilon)^{\beta}}\left(\frac{1}{2}-\frac{\gamma}{(\gamma+1)(\gamma+2)}\right)\Big(\mathcal{I}_{\upsilon^+}^{\beta}\Upsilon_{\mathfrak{z}}(\eth,\mathrm{d})\times\mathcal{J}_{\mathfrak{z}}(\mathrm{n},\mathrm{d})+\mathcal{I}_{\upsilon^+}^{\beta}\Upsilon_{\mathfrak{z}}(\mathrm{n},\mathrm{d})\times\mathcal{J}_{\mathfrak{z}}(\mathrm{n},\mathrm{d})\Big).\end{aligned} \tag{68}$$

$$\begin{aligned}\frac{\beta}{2(\mathrm{d}-\upsilon)^{\beta}} & \left[\int_{\upsilon}^{\mathrm{d}} 2(\psi-\upsilon)^{\beta-1}\Upsilon_{\mathfrak{z}}\left(\frac{\eth+\mathrm{n}}{2},\psi\right)\times\mathcal{J}_{\mathfrak{z}}\left(\frac{\eth+\mathrm{n}}{2},\psi\right)d\psi\right] \\ & \supseteq_{I} \frac{\Gamma(\gamma+1)\Gamma(\beta+1)}{4(\mathrm{n}-\eth)^{\gamma}(\mathrm{d}-\upsilon)^{\beta}}\left[\mathcal{I}_{\eth^+,\mathrm{d}^-}^{\gamma,\,\beta}\Upsilon_{\mathfrak{z}}(\mathrm{n},\upsilon)\times\mathcal{J}_{\mathfrak{z}}(\mathrm{n},\upsilon)+\mathcal{I}_{\mathrm{n}^-,\mathrm{d}^-}^{\gamma,\,\beta}\Upsilon_{\mathfrak{z}}(\mathrm{n},\upsilon)\times\mathcal{J}_{\mathfrak{z}}(\mathrm{n},\upsilon)\right] \\ & +\frac{\Gamma(\beta+1)}{2(\mathrm{d}-\upsilon)^{\beta}}\left(\frac{\gamma}{(\gamma+1)(\gamma+2)}\right)\Big(\mathcal{I}_{\mathrm{d}^-}^{\beta}\Upsilon_{\mathfrak{z}}(\eth,\upsilon)\times\mathcal{J}_{\mathfrak{z}}(\eth,\upsilon)+\mathcal{I}_{\mathrm{d}^-}^{\beta}\Upsilon_{\mathfrak{z}}(\mathrm{n},\upsilon)\times\mathcal{J}_{\mathfrak{z}}(\mathrm{n},\upsilon)\Big) \\ & +\frac{\Gamma(\beta+1)}{2(\mathrm{d}-\upsilon)^{\beta}}\left(\frac{1}{2}-\frac{\gamma}{(\gamma+1)(\gamma+2)}\right)\Big(\mathcal{I}_{\mathrm{d}^-}^{\beta}\Upsilon_{\mathfrak{z}}(\eth,\upsilon)\times\mathcal{J}_{\mathfrak{z}}(\mathrm{n},\upsilon)+\mathcal{I}_{\mathrm{d}^-}^{\beta}\Upsilon_{\mathfrak{z}}(\mathrm{n},\upsilon)\times\mathcal{J}_{\mathfrak{z}}(\mathrm{n},\upsilon)\Big).\end{aligned} \tag{69}$$

And

$$\begin{aligned}2\Upsilon_{\mathfrak{z}}\left(\frac{\eth+\mathrm{n}}{2},\upsilon\right) & \times\mathcal{J}_{\mathfrak{z}}\left(\frac{\eth+\mathrm{n}}{2},\upsilon\right) \\ & \supseteq_{I} \frac{\Gamma(\gamma+1)}{2(\mathrm{n}-\eth)^{\gamma}}\left[\mathcal{I}_{\eth^+}^{\gamma}\Upsilon_{\mathfrak{z}}(\mathrm{n},\upsilon)\times\mathcal{J}_{\mathfrak{z}}(\mathrm{n},\upsilon)+\mathcal{I}_{\mathrm{n}^-}^{\gamma}\Upsilon_{\mathfrak{z}}(\eth,\upsilon)\times\mathcal{J}_{\mathfrak{z}}(\eth,\upsilon)\right] \\ & +\frac{\gamma}{(\gamma+1)(\gamma+2)}\Big(\Upsilon_{\mathfrak{z}}(\eth,\upsilon)\times\mathcal{J}_{\mathfrak{z}}(\eth,\upsilon)+\Upsilon_{\mathfrak{z}}(\mathrm{n},\upsilon)\times\mathcal{J}_{\mathfrak{z}}(\mathrm{n},\upsilon)\Big) \\ & +\left(\frac{1}{2}-\frac{\gamma}{(\gamma+1)(\gamma+2)}\right)\Big(\Upsilon_{\mathfrak{z}}(\eth,\upsilon)\times\mathcal{J}_{\mathfrak{z}}(\mathrm{n},\upsilon)+\Upsilon_{\mathfrak{z}}(\mathrm{n},\upsilon)\times\mathcal{J}_{\mathfrak{z}}(\eth,\upsilon)\Big),\end{aligned} \tag{70}$$

$$\begin{aligned}2\Upsilon_{\mathfrak{z}}\left(\frac{\eth+\mathrm{n}}{2},\mathrm{d}\right) & \times\mathcal{J}_{\mathfrak{z}}\left(\frac{\eth+\mathrm{n}}{2},\mathrm{d}\right) \\ & \supseteq_{I} \frac{\Gamma(\gamma+1)}{2(\mathrm{n}-\eth)^{\gamma}}\left[\mathcal{I}_{\eth^+}^{\gamma}\Upsilon_{\mathfrak{z}}(\mathrm{n},\mathrm{d})\times\mathcal{J}_{\mathfrak{z}}(\mathrm{n},\mathrm{d})+\mathcal{I}_{\mathrm{n}^-}^{\gamma}\Upsilon_{\mathfrak{z}}(\eth,\mathrm{d})\times\mathcal{J}_{\mathfrak{z}}(\eth,\mathrm{d})\right] \\ & +\frac{\gamma}{(\gamma+1)(\gamma+2)}\Big(\Upsilon_{\mathfrak{z}}(\eth,\mathrm{d})\times\mathcal{J}_{\mathfrak{z}}(\eth,\mathrm{d})+\Upsilon_{\mathfrak{z}}(\mathrm{n},\mathrm{d})\times\mathcal{J}_{\mathfrak{z}}(\mathrm{n},\mathrm{d})\Big) \\ & +\left(\frac{1}{2}-\frac{\gamma}{(\gamma+1)(\gamma+2)}\right)\Big(\Upsilon_{\mathfrak{z}}(\eth,\mathrm{d})\times\mathcal{J}_{\mathfrak{z}}(\mathrm{n},\mathrm{d})+\Upsilon_{\mathfrak{z}}(\mathrm{n},\mathrm{d})\times\mathcal{J}_{\mathfrak{z}}(\eth,\mathrm{d})\Big),\end{aligned} \tag{71}$$

$$\begin{aligned}2\gamma_{\mathfrak{z}}\left(\frac{\eth+\mathfrak{n}}{2},\upsilon\right) &\times \mathcal{J}_{\mathfrak{z}}\left(\frac{\eth+\mathfrak{n}}{2},\mathfrak{d}\right)\\ &\supseteq_I \frac{\Gamma(\gamma+1)}{2(\mathfrak{n}-\eth)^{\gamma}}\left[\mathcal{I}_{\eth^+}^{\gamma}\,\gamma_{\mathfrak{z}}(\mathfrak{n},\upsilon)\times\mathcal{J}_{\mathfrak{z}}(\mathfrak{n},\mathfrak{d})+\mathcal{I}_{\mathfrak{n}^-}^{\gamma}\,\gamma_{\mathfrak{z}}(\eth,\upsilon)\times\mathcal{J}_{\mathfrak{z}}(\eth,\mathfrak{d})\right]\\ &+\frac{\gamma}{(\gamma+1)(\gamma+2)}\left(\gamma_{\mathfrak{z}}(\eth,\upsilon)\times\mathcal{J}_{\mathfrak{z}}(\eth,\mathfrak{d})+\gamma_{\mathfrak{z}}(\mathfrak{n},\upsilon)\times\mathcal{J}_{\mathfrak{z}}(\mathfrak{n},\mathfrak{d})\right)\\ &+\left(\frac{1}{2}-\frac{\gamma}{(\gamma+1)(\gamma+2)}\right)\left(\gamma_{\mathfrak{z}}(\eth,\upsilon)\times\mathcal{J}_{\mathfrak{z}}(\mathfrak{n},\mathfrak{d})+\gamma_{\mathfrak{z}}(\mathfrak{n},\upsilon)\times\mathcal{J}_{\mathfrak{z}}(\eth,\mathfrak{d})\right),\end{aligned} \tag{72}$$

$$\begin{aligned}2\gamma_{\mathfrak{z}}\left(\frac{\eth+\mathfrak{n}}{2},\mathfrak{d}\right) &\times \mathcal{J}_{\mathfrak{z}}\left(\frac{\eth+\mathfrak{n}}{2},\upsilon\right)\\ &\supseteq_I \frac{\Gamma(\gamma+1)}{2(\mathfrak{n}-\eth)^{\gamma}}\left[\mathcal{I}_{\eth^+}^{\gamma}\,\gamma_{\mathfrak{z}}(\mathfrak{n},\mathfrak{d})\times\mathcal{J}_{\mathfrak{z}}(\mathfrak{n},\upsilon)+\mathcal{I}_{\mathfrak{n}^-}^{\gamma}\,\gamma_{\mathfrak{z}}(\eth,\mathfrak{d})\times\mathcal{J}_{\mathfrak{z}}(\eth,\upsilon)\right]\\ &+\frac{\gamma}{(\gamma+1)(\gamma+2)}\left(\gamma_{\mathfrak{z}}(\eth,\mathfrak{d})\times\mathcal{J}_{\mathfrak{z}}(\eth,\upsilon)+\gamma_{\mathfrak{z}}(\mathfrak{n},\mathfrak{d})\times\mathcal{J}_{\mathfrak{z}}(\mathfrak{n},\upsilon)\right)\\ &+\left(\frac{1}{2}-\frac{\gamma}{(\gamma+1)(\gamma+2)}\right)\left(\gamma_{\mathfrak{z}}(\eth,\mathfrak{d})\times\mathcal{J}_{\mathfrak{z}}(\mathfrak{n},\upsilon)+\gamma_{\mathfrak{z}}(\mathfrak{n},\mathfrak{d})\times\mathcal{J}_{\mathfrak{z}}(\eth,\upsilon)\right),\end{aligned} \tag{73}$$

$$\begin{aligned}2\gamma_{\mathfrak{z}}\left(\eth,\frac{\upsilon+\mathfrak{d}}{2}\right) &\times \mathcal{J}_{\mathfrak{z}}\left(\eth,\frac{\upsilon+\mathfrak{d}}{2}\right)\\ &\supseteq_I \frac{\Gamma(\beta+1)}{2(\mathfrak{d}-\upsilon)^{\beta}}\left[\mathcal{I}_{\upsilon^+}^{\beta}\,\gamma_{\mathfrak{z}}(\eth,\mathfrak{d})\times\mathcal{J}_{\mathfrak{z}}(\eth,\mathfrak{d})+\mathcal{I}_{\mathfrak{d}^-}^{\beta}\,\gamma_{\mathfrak{z}}(\eth,\mathfrak{d})\times\mathcal{J}_{\mathfrak{z}}(\eth,\upsilon)\right]\\ &+\frac{\beta}{(\beta+1)(\beta+2)}\left(\gamma_{\mathfrak{z}}(\eth,\upsilon)\times\mathcal{J}_{\mathfrak{z}}(\eth,\upsilon)+\gamma_{\mathfrak{z}}(\eth,\mathfrak{d})\times\mathcal{J}_{\mathfrak{z}}(\eth,\mathfrak{d})\right)\\ &+\left(\frac{1}{2}-\frac{\beta}{(\beta+1)(\beta+2)}\right)\left(\gamma_{\mathfrak{z}}(\eth,\upsilon)\times\mathcal{J}_{\mathfrak{z}}(\eth,\mathfrak{d})+\gamma_{\mathfrak{z}}(\eth,\mathfrak{d})\times\mathcal{J}_{\mathfrak{z}}(\eth,\upsilon)\right),\end{aligned} \tag{74}$$

$$\begin{aligned}2\gamma_{\mathfrak{z}}\left(\mathfrak{n},\frac{\upsilon+\mathfrak{d}}{2}\right) &\times \mathcal{J}_{\mathfrak{z}}\left(\mathfrak{n},\frac{\upsilon+\mathfrak{d}}{2}\right)\\ &\supseteq_I \frac{\Gamma(\beta+1)}{2(\mathfrak{d}-\upsilon)^{\beta}}\left[\mathcal{I}_{\upsilon^+}^{\beta}\,\gamma_{\mathfrak{z}}(\mathfrak{n},\mathfrak{d})\times\mathcal{J}_{\mathfrak{z}}(\mathfrak{n},\mathfrak{d})+\mathcal{I}_{\mathfrak{d}^-}^{\beta}\,\gamma_{\mathfrak{z}}(\mathfrak{n},\mathfrak{d})\times\mathcal{J}_{\mathfrak{z}}(\mathfrak{n},\upsilon)\right]\\ &+\frac{\beta}{(\beta+1)(\beta+2)}\left(\gamma_{\mathfrak{z}}(\mathfrak{n},\upsilon)\times\mathcal{J}_{\mathfrak{z}}(\mathfrak{n},\upsilon)+\gamma_{\mathfrak{z}}(\mathfrak{n},\mathfrak{d})\times\mathcal{J}_{\mathfrak{z}}(\mathfrak{n},\mathfrak{d})\right)\\ &+\left(\frac{1}{2}-\frac{\beta}{(\beta+1)(\beta+2)}\right)\left(\gamma_{\mathfrak{z}}(\mathfrak{n},\upsilon)\times\mathcal{J}_{\mathfrak{z}}(\mathfrak{n},\mathfrak{d})+\gamma_{\mathfrak{z}}(\mathfrak{n},\mathfrak{d})\times\mathcal{J}_{\mathfrak{z}}(\mathfrak{n},\upsilon)\right),\end{aligned} \tag{75}$$

$$\begin{aligned}2\gamma_{\mathfrak{z}}\left(\eth,\frac{\upsilon+\mathfrak{d}}{2}\right) &\times \mathcal{J}_{\mathfrak{z}}\left(\mathfrak{n},\frac{\upsilon+\mathfrak{d}}{2}\right)\\ &\supseteq_I \frac{\Gamma(\beta+1)}{2(\mathfrak{d}-\upsilon)^{\beta}}\left[\mathcal{I}_{\upsilon^+}^{\beta}\,\gamma_{\mathfrak{z}}(\eth,\mathfrak{d})\times\mathcal{J}_{\mathfrak{z}}(\mathfrak{n},\mathfrak{d})+\mathcal{I}_{\mathfrak{d}^-}^{\beta}\,\gamma_{\mathfrak{z}}(\eth,\mathfrak{d})\times\mathcal{J}_{\mathfrak{z}}(\mathfrak{n},\upsilon)\right]\\ &+\frac{\beta}{(\beta+1)(\beta+2)}\left(\gamma_{\mathfrak{z}}(\eth,\upsilon)\times\mathcal{J}_{\mathfrak{z}}(\mathfrak{n},\upsilon)+\gamma_{\mathfrak{z}}(\eth,\mathfrak{d})\times\mathcal{J}_{\mathfrak{z}}(\mathfrak{n},\mathfrak{d})\right)\\ &+\left(\frac{1}{2}-\frac{\beta}{(\beta+1)(\beta+2)}\right)\left(\gamma_{\mathfrak{z}}(\eth,\upsilon)\times\mathcal{J}_{\mathfrak{z}}(\mathfrak{n},\mathfrak{d})+\gamma_{\mathfrak{z}}(\eth,\mathfrak{d})\times\mathcal{J}_{\mathfrak{z}}(\mathfrak{n},\upsilon)\right),\end{aligned} \tag{76}$$

and

$$\begin{aligned}2\gamma_{\mathfrak{z}}\left(\mathfrak{n},\frac{\upsilon+\mathfrak{d}}{2}\right) &\times \mathcal{J}_{\mathfrak{z}}\left(\eth,\frac{\upsilon+\mathfrak{d}}{2}\right)\\ &\supseteq_I \frac{\Gamma(\beta+1)}{2(\mathfrak{d}-\upsilon)^{\beta}}\left[\mathcal{I}_{\upsilon^+}^{\beta}\,\gamma_{\mathfrak{z}}(\mathfrak{n},\mathfrak{d})\times\mathcal{J}_{\mathfrak{z}}(\eth,\mathfrak{d})+\mathcal{I}_{\mathfrak{d}^-}^{\beta}\,\gamma_{\mathfrak{z}}(\mathfrak{n},\mathfrak{d})\times\mathcal{J}_{\mathfrak{z}}(\eth,\upsilon)\right]\\ &+\frac{\beta}{(\beta+1)(\beta+2)}\left(\gamma_{\mathfrak{z}}(\mathfrak{n},\upsilon)\times\mathcal{J}_{\mathfrak{z}}(\eth,\upsilon)+\gamma_{\mathfrak{z}}(\mathfrak{n},\mathfrak{d})\times\mathcal{J}_{\mathfrak{z}}(\eth,\mathfrak{d})\right)\\ &+\left(\frac{1}{2}-\frac{\beta}{(\beta+1)(\beta+2)}\right)\left(\gamma_{\mathfrak{z}}(\mathfrak{n},\upsilon)\times\mathcal{J}_{\mathfrak{z}}(\eth,\mathfrak{d})+\gamma_{\mathfrak{z}}(\mathfrak{n},\mathfrak{d})\times\mathcal{J}_{\mathfrak{z}}(\eth,\upsilon)\right).\end{aligned} \tag{77}$$

From inequalities (66)–(77) and inequality (65), we have

$$
\begin{aligned}
8\mathrm{Y}_{\mathfrak{z}}\left(\frac{\eth+\mathrm{n}}{2},\frac{\upsilon+\mathrm{d}}{2}\right) & \times \mathcal{J}_{\mathfrak{z}}\left(\frac{\eth+\mathrm{n}}{2},\frac{\upsilon+\mathrm{d}}{2}\right) \\
& \supseteq_I \frac{\Gamma(\Upsilon+1)\Gamma(\beta+1)}{2(\mathrm{n}-\eth)^{\Upsilon}(\mathrm{d}-\upsilon)^{\beta}}\begin{bmatrix} \mathcal{I}^{\Upsilon,\beta}_{\eth^+,\upsilon^+}\mathrm{Y}_{\mathfrak{z}}(\mathrm{n},\mathrm{d})\times\mathcal{J}_{\mathfrak{z}}(\mathrm{n},\mathrm{d})+\mathcal{I}^{\Upsilon,\beta}_{\eth^+,\mathrm{d}^-}\mathrm{Y}_{\mathfrak{z}}(\mathrm{n},\upsilon)\times\mathcal{J}_{\mathfrak{z}}(\mathrm{n},\upsilon) \\ +\mathcal{I}^{\Upsilon,\beta}_{\mathrm{n}^-,\upsilon^+}\mathrm{Y}_{\mathfrak{z}}(\eth,\mathrm{d})\times\mathcal{J}_{\mathfrak{z}}(\eth,\mathrm{d})+\mathcal{I}^{\Upsilon,\beta}_{\mathrm{n}^-,\mathrm{d}^-}\mathrm{Y}_{\mathfrak{z}}(\eth,\upsilon)\times\mathcal{J}_{\mathfrak{z}}(\eth,\upsilon) \end{bmatrix} \\
& +\left(\frac{2\Upsilon}{(\Upsilon+1)(\Upsilon+2)}\right)\begin{bmatrix} \frac{\Gamma(\beta+1)}{2(\mathrm{d}-\upsilon)^{\beta}}\left(\mathcal{I}^{\beta}_{\upsilon^+}\mathrm{Y}_{\mathfrak{z}}(\eth,\mathrm{d})\times\mathcal{J}_{\mathfrak{z}}(\eth,\mathrm{d})+\mathcal{I}^{\beta}_{\upsilon^+}\mathrm{Y}_{\mathfrak{z}}(\mathrm{n},\mathrm{d})\times\mathcal{J}_{\mathfrak{z}}(\mathrm{n},\mathrm{d})\right) \\ +\frac{\Gamma(\beta+1)}{2(\mathrm{d}-\upsilon)^{\beta}}\left(\mathcal{I}^{\beta}_{\mathrm{d}^-}\mathrm{Y}_{\mathfrak{z}}(\eth,\upsilon)\times\mathcal{J}_{\mathfrak{z}}(\eth,\upsilon)+\mathcal{I}^{\beta}_{\mathrm{d}^-}\mathrm{Y}_{\mathfrak{z}}(\mathrm{n},\upsilon)\times\mathcal{J}_{\mathfrak{z}}(\mathrm{n},\upsilon)\right) \end{bmatrix} \\
& +2\left(\frac{1}{2}-\frac{\Upsilon}{(\Upsilon+1)(\Upsilon+2)}\right)\begin{bmatrix} \frac{\Gamma(\beta+1)}{2(\mathrm{d}-\upsilon)^{\beta}}\left(\mathcal{I}^{\beta}_{\upsilon^+}\mathrm{Y}_{\mathfrak{z}}(\eth,\mathrm{d})\times\mathcal{J}_{\mathfrak{z}}(\mathrm{n},\mathrm{d})+\mathcal{I}^{\beta}_{\upsilon^+}\mathrm{Y}_{\mathfrak{z}}(\mathrm{n},\mathrm{d})\times\mathcal{J}_{\mathfrak{z}}(\mathrm{n},\mathrm{d})\right) \\ +\frac{\Gamma(\beta+1)}{2(\mathrm{d}-\upsilon)^{\beta}}\left(\mathcal{I}^{\beta}_{\mathrm{d}^-}\mathrm{Y}_{\mathfrak{z}}(\eth,\upsilon)\times\mathcal{J}_{\mathfrak{z}}(\mathrm{n},\upsilon)+\mathcal{I}^{\beta}_{\mathrm{d}^-}\mathrm{Y}_{\mathfrak{z}}(\mathrm{n},\upsilon)\times\mathcal{J}_{\mathfrak{z}}(\mathrm{n},\upsilon)\right) \end{bmatrix} \\
& +2\left(\frac{\beta}{(\beta+1)(\beta+2)}\right)\begin{bmatrix} \frac{\Gamma(\Upsilon+1)}{2(\mathrm{n}-\eth)^{\Upsilon}}\left(\mathcal{I}^{\Upsilon}_{\eth^+}\mathrm{Y}_{\mathfrak{z}}(\mathrm{n},\upsilon)\times\mathcal{J}_{\mathfrak{z}}(\mathrm{n},\upsilon)+\mathcal{I}^{\Upsilon}_{\eth^+}\mathrm{Y}_{\mathfrak{z}}(\mathrm{n},\mathrm{d})\times\mathcal{J}_{\mathfrak{z}}(\mathrm{n},\mathrm{d})\right) \\ +\frac{\Gamma(\Upsilon+1)}{2(\mathrm{n}-\eth)^{\Upsilon}}\left(\mathcal{I}^{\Upsilon}_{\mathrm{n}^-}\mathrm{Y}_{\mathfrak{z}}(\eth,\upsilon)\times\mathcal{J}_{\mathfrak{z}}(\eth,\upsilon)+\mathcal{I}^{\Upsilon}_{\mathrm{n}^-}\mathrm{Y}_{\mathfrak{z}}(\eth,\mathrm{d})\times\mathcal{J}_{\mathfrak{z}}(\eth,\mathrm{d})\right) \end{bmatrix} \\
& +2\left(\frac{1}{2}-\frac{\beta}{(\beta+1)(\beta+2)}\right)\begin{bmatrix} \frac{\Gamma(\Upsilon+1)}{2(\mathrm{n}-\eth)^{\Upsilon}}\left(\mathcal{I}^{\Upsilon}_{\eth^+}\mathrm{Y}_{\mathfrak{z}}(\mathrm{n},\upsilon)\times\mathcal{J}_{\mathfrak{z}}(\mathrm{n},\mathrm{d})+\mathcal{I}^{\Upsilon}_{\eth^+}\mathrm{Y}_{\mathfrak{z}}(\mathrm{n},\mathrm{d})\times\mathcal{J}_{\mathfrak{z}}(\mathrm{n},\upsilon)\right) \\ +\frac{\Gamma(\Upsilon+1)}{2(\mathrm{n}-\eth)^{\Upsilon}}\left(\mathcal{I}^{\Upsilon}_{\mathrm{n}^-}\mathrm{Y}_{\mathfrak{z}}(\eth,\upsilon)\times\mathcal{J}_{\mathfrak{z}}(\eth,\mathrm{d})+\mathcal{I}^{\Upsilon}_{\mathrm{n}^-}\mathrm{Y}_{\mathfrak{z}}(\eth,\mathrm{d})\times\mathcal{J}_{\mathfrak{z}}(\eth,\upsilon)\right) \end{bmatrix} \\
& +\frac{2\Upsilon}{(\Upsilon+1)(\Upsilon+2)}\frac{\beta}{(\beta+1)(\beta+2)}K_{\mathfrak{z}}(\eth,\mathrm{n},\upsilon,\mathrm{d})++\left(\frac{1}{2}-\frac{\Upsilon}{(\Upsilon+1)(\Upsilon+2)}\right)\frac{2\beta}{(\beta+1)(\beta+2)}L_{\mathfrak{z}}(\eth,\mathrm{n},\upsilon,\mathrm{d}) \\
& +\frac{2\Upsilon}{(\Upsilon+1)(\Upsilon+2)}\left(\frac{1}{2}-\frac{\beta}{(\beta+1)(\beta+2)}\right)\mathcal{M}_{\mathfrak{z}}(\eth,\mathrm{n},\upsilon,\mathrm{d}) \\
& +2\left(\frac{1}{2}-\frac{\Upsilon}{(\Upsilon+1)(\Upsilon+2)}\right)\left(\frac{1}{2}-\frac{\beta}{(\beta+1)(\beta+2)}\right)\mathcal{N}_{\mathfrak{z}}(\eth,\mathrm{n},\upsilon,\mathrm{d}).
\end{aligned} \tag{78}
$$

Using Lemma 1 for each integral on the right-hand side of (78) and the integral inequality (16) once more leads us to arrive at:

$$
\begin{aligned}
\frac{\Gamma(\beta+1)}{2(\mathrm{d}-\upsilon)^{\beta}} & \left(\mathcal{I}^{\beta}_{\upsilon^+}\mathrm{Y}_{\mathfrak{z}}(\eth,\mathrm{d})\times\mathcal{J}_{\mathfrak{z}}(\eth,\mathrm{d})+\mathcal{I}^{\beta}_{\upsilon^+}\mathrm{Y}_{\mathfrak{z}}(\mathrm{n},\mathrm{d})\times\mathcal{J}_{\mathfrak{z}}(\mathrm{n},\mathrm{d})\right) \\
& +\frac{\Gamma(\beta+1)}{2(\mathrm{d}-\upsilon)^{\beta}}\left(\mathcal{I}^{\beta}_{\mathrm{d}^-}\mathrm{Y}_{\mathfrak{z}}(\eth,\upsilon)\times\mathcal{J}_{\mathfrak{z}}(\eth,\upsilon)+\mathcal{I}^{\beta}_{\mathrm{d}^-}\mathrm{Y}_{\mathfrak{z}}(\mathrm{n},\upsilon)\times\mathcal{J}_{\mathfrak{z}}(\mathrm{n},\upsilon)\right) \\
& \supseteq_I \left(\frac{1}{2}-\frac{\beta}{(\beta+1)(\beta+2)}\right)K_{\mathfrak{z}}(\eth,\mathrm{n},\upsilon,\mathrm{d})+\frac{\beta}{(\beta+1)(\beta+2)}\mathcal{M}_{\mathfrak{z}}(\eth,\mathrm{n},\upsilon,\mathrm{d}).
\end{aligned} \tag{79}
$$

$$
\begin{aligned}
\frac{\Gamma(\beta+1)}{2(\mathrm{d}-\upsilon)^{\beta}} & \left(\mathcal{I}^{\beta}_{\upsilon^+}\mathrm{Y}_{\mathfrak{z}}(\eth,\mathrm{d})\times\mathcal{J}_{\mathfrak{z}}(\mathrm{n},\mathrm{d})+\mathcal{I}^{\beta}_{\upsilon^+}\mathrm{Y}_{\mathfrak{z}}(\mathrm{n},\mathrm{d})\times\mathcal{J}_{\mathfrak{z}}(\mathrm{n},\mathrm{d})\right) \\
& +\frac{\Gamma(\beta+1)}{2(\mathrm{d}-\upsilon)^{\beta}}\left(\mathcal{I}^{\beta}_{\mathrm{d}^-}\mathrm{Y}_{\mathfrak{z}}(\eth,\upsilon)\times\mathcal{J}_{\mathfrak{z}}(\mathrm{n},\upsilon)+\mathcal{I}^{\beta}_{\mathrm{d}^-}\mathrm{Y}_{\mathfrak{z}}(\mathrm{n},\upsilon)\times\mathcal{J}_{\mathfrak{z}}(\mathrm{n},\upsilon)\right) \\
& \supseteq_I \left(\frac{1}{2}-\frac{\beta}{(\beta+1)(\beta+2)}\right)L_{\mathfrak{z}}(\eth,\mathrm{n},\upsilon,\mathrm{d})+\frac{\beta}{(\beta+1)(\beta+2)}\mathcal{N}_{\mathfrak{z}}(\eth,\mathrm{n},\upsilon,\mathrm{d}).
\end{aligned} \tag{80}
$$

$$
\begin{aligned}
\frac{\Gamma(\Upsilon+1)}{2(\mathrm{n}-\eth)^{\Upsilon}} & \left(\mathcal{I}^{\Upsilon}_{\eth^+}\mathrm{Y}_{\mathfrak{z}}(\mathrm{n},\upsilon)\times\mathcal{J}_{\mathfrak{z}}(\mathrm{n},\upsilon)+\mathcal{I}^{\Upsilon}_{\eth^+}\mathrm{Y}_{\mathfrak{z}}(\mathrm{n},\mathrm{d})\times\mathcal{J}_{\mathfrak{z}}(\mathrm{n},\mathrm{d})\right) \\
& +\frac{\Gamma(\Upsilon+1)}{2(\mathrm{n}-\eth)^{\Upsilon}}\left(\mathcal{I}^{\Upsilon}_{\mathrm{n}^-}\mathrm{Y}_{\mathfrak{z}}(\eth,\upsilon)\times\mathcal{J}_{\mathfrak{z}}(\eth,\upsilon)+\mathcal{I}^{\Upsilon}_{\mathrm{n}^-}\mathrm{Y}_{\mathfrak{z}}(\eth,\mathrm{d})\times\mathcal{J}_{\mathfrak{z}}(\eth,\mathrm{d})\right) \\
& \supseteq_I \left(\frac{1}{2}-\frac{\Upsilon}{(\Upsilon+1)(\Upsilon+2)}\right)K_{\mathfrak{z}}(\eth,\mathrm{n},\upsilon,\mathrm{d})+\frac{\Upsilon}{(\Upsilon+1)(\Upsilon+2)}L_{\mathfrak{z}}(\eth,\mathrm{n},\upsilon,\mathrm{d}).
\end{aligned} \tag{81}
$$

$$
\begin{aligned}
\frac{\Gamma(\Upsilon+1)}{2(\mathrm{n}-\eth)^{\Upsilon}} & \left(\mathcal{I}^{\Upsilon}_{\mathrm{n}^-}\mathrm{Y}_{\mathfrak{z}}(\eth,\upsilon)\times\mathcal{J}_{\mathfrak{z}}(\eth,\mathrm{d})+\mathcal{I}^{\Upsilon}_{\mathrm{n}^-}\mathrm{Y}_{\mathfrak{z}}(\eth,\mathrm{d})\times\mathcal{J}_{\mathfrak{z}}(\eth,\upsilon)\right) \\
& +\frac{\Gamma(\Upsilon+1)}{2(\mathrm{n}-\eth)^{\Upsilon}}\left(\mathcal{I}^{\Upsilon}_{\mathrm{n}^-}\mathrm{Y}_{\mathfrak{z}}(\eth,\upsilon)\times\mathcal{J}_{\mathfrak{z}}(\eth,\mathrm{d})+\mathcal{I}^{\Upsilon}_{\mathrm{n}^-}\mathrm{Y}_{\mathfrak{z}}(\eth,\mathrm{d})\times\mathcal{J}_{\mathfrak{z}}(\eth,\upsilon)\right) \\
& \supseteq_I \left(\frac{1}{2}-\frac{\Upsilon}{(\Upsilon+1)(\Upsilon+2)}\right)\mathcal{M}_{\mathfrak{z}}(\eth,\mathrm{n},\upsilon,\mathrm{d})+\frac{\Upsilon}{(\Upsilon+1)(\Upsilon+2)}\mathcal{N}_{\mathfrak{z}}(\eth,\mathrm{n},\upsilon,\mathrm{d}).
\end{aligned} \tag{82}
$$

From (79)–(82) we have

$$
\begin{aligned}
4\mathrm{Y}_{\mathfrak{z}}\left(\tfrac{\eth+\mathrm{n}}{2},\tfrac{\upsilon+\mathrm{d}}{2}\right) &\times \mathcal{J}_{\mathfrak{z}}\left(\tfrac{\eth+\mathrm{n}}{2},\tfrac{\upsilon+\mathrm{d}}{2}\right)\\
&\supseteq_I \frac{\Gamma(\Upsilon+1)\Gamma(\beta+1)}{4(\mathrm{n}-\eth)^{\Upsilon}(\mathrm{d}-\upsilon)^{\beta}}\left[\begin{array}{l}\mathcal{I}^{\Upsilon,\beta}_{\eth^+,\upsilon^+}\mathrm{Y}_{\mathfrak{z}}(\mathrm{n},\mathrm{d})\times\mathcal{J}_{\mathfrak{z}}(\mathrm{n},\mathrm{d})+\mathcal{I}^{\Upsilon,\beta}_{\eth^+,\mathrm{d}^-}\mathrm{Y}_{\mathfrak{z}}(\mathrm{n},\upsilon)\times\mathcal{J}_{\mathfrak{z}}(\mathrm{n},\upsilon)\\ +\mathcal{I}^{\Upsilon,\beta}_{\mathrm{n}^-,\upsilon^+}\mathrm{Y}_{\mathfrak{z}}(\eth,\mathrm{d})\times\mathcal{J}_{\mathfrak{z}}(\eth,\mathrm{d})+\mathcal{I}^{\Upsilon,\beta}_{\mathrm{n}^-,\mathrm{d}^-}\mathrm{Y}_{\mathfrak{z}}(\eth,\upsilon)\times\mathcal{J}_{\mathfrak{z}}(\eth,\upsilon)\end{array}\right]\\
&+\left[\tfrac{\Upsilon}{2(\Upsilon+1)(\Upsilon+2)}+\tfrac{\beta}{(\beta+1)(\beta+2)}\left(\tfrac{1}{2}-\tfrac{\Upsilon}{(\Upsilon+1)(\Upsilon+2)}\right)\right]K_{\mathfrak{z}}(\eth,\mathrm{n},\upsilon,\mathrm{d})\\
&+\left[\tfrac{1}{2}\left(\tfrac{1}{2}-\tfrac{\Upsilon}{(\Upsilon+1)(\Upsilon+2)}\right)+\tfrac{\Upsilon}{(\Upsilon+1)(\Upsilon+2)}\tfrac{\beta}{(\beta+1)(\beta+2)}\right]L_{\mathfrak{z}}(\eth,\mathrm{n},\upsilon,\mathrm{d})\\
&+\left[\tfrac{1}{2}\left(\tfrac{1}{2}-\tfrac{\beta}{(\beta+1)(\beta+2)}\right)+\tfrac{\Upsilon}{(\Upsilon+1)(\Upsilon+2)}\tfrac{\beta}{(\beta+1)(\beta+2)}\right]\mathcal{M}_{\mathfrak{z}}(\eth,\mathrm{n},\upsilon,\mathrm{d})\\
&+\left[\tfrac{1}{4}-\tfrac{\Upsilon}{(\Upsilon+1)(\Upsilon+2)}\tfrac{\beta}{(\beta+1)(\beta+2)}\right]\mathcal{N}_{\mathfrak{z}}(\eth,\mathrm{n},\upsilon,\mathrm{d}).
\end{aligned}
\tag{83}
$$

That is

$$
\begin{aligned}
4\widetilde{\mathrm{Y}}\left(\tfrac{\eth+\mathrm{n}}{2},\tfrac{\upsilon+\mathrm{d}}{2}\right) &\otimes \widetilde{\mathcal{J}}\left(\tfrac{\eth+\mathrm{n}}{2},\tfrac{\upsilon+\mathrm{d}}{2}\right)\\
&\supseteq_{\mathbb{F}} \frac{\Gamma(\Upsilon+1)\Gamma(\beta+1)}{4(\mathrm{n}-\eth)^{\Upsilon}(\mathrm{d}-\upsilon)^{\beta}}\left[\begin{array}{l}\mathcal{I}^{\Upsilon,\beta}_{\eth^+,\upsilon^+}\widetilde{\mathrm{Y}}(\mathrm{n},\mathrm{d})\otimes\widetilde{\mathcal{J}}(\mathrm{n},\mathrm{d})\oplus\mathcal{I}^{\Upsilon,\beta}_{\eth^+,\mathrm{d}^-}\widetilde{\mathrm{Y}}(\mathrm{n},\upsilon)\otimes\widetilde{\mathcal{J}}(\mathrm{n},\upsilon)\\ \oplus\mathcal{I}^{\Upsilon,\beta}_{\mathrm{n}^-,\upsilon^+}\widetilde{\mathrm{Y}}(\eth,\mathrm{d})\otimes\widetilde{\mathcal{J}}(\eth,\mathrm{d})\oplus\mathcal{I}^{\Upsilon,\beta}_{\mathrm{n}^-,\mathrm{d}^-}\widetilde{\mathrm{Y}}(\eth,\upsilon)\otimes\widetilde{\mathcal{J}}(\eth,\upsilon)\end{array}\right]\\
&\oplus\left[\tfrac{\Upsilon}{2(\Upsilon+1)(\Upsilon+2)}+\tfrac{\beta}{(\beta+1)(\beta+2)}\left(\tfrac{1}{2}-\tfrac{\Upsilon}{(\Upsilon+1)(\Upsilon+2)}\right)\right]\widetilde{K}(\eth,\mathrm{n},\upsilon,\mathrm{d})\\
&\oplus\left[\tfrac{1}{2}\left(\tfrac{1}{2}-\tfrac{\Upsilon}{(\Upsilon+1)(\Upsilon+2)}\right)+\tfrac{\Upsilon}{(\Upsilon+1)(\Upsilon+2)}\tfrac{\beta}{(\beta+1)(\beta+2)}\right]\widetilde{L}(\eth,\mathrm{n},\upsilon,\mathrm{d})\\
&\oplus\left[\tfrac{1}{2}\left(\tfrac{1}{2}-\tfrac{\beta}{(\beta+1)(\beta+2)}\right)+\tfrac{\Upsilon}{(\Upsilon+1)(\Upsilon+2)}\tfrac{\beta}{(\beta+1)(\beta+2)}\right]\widetilde{\mathcal{M}}(\eth,\mathrm{n},\upsilon,\mathrm{d})\\
&\oplus\left[\tfrac{1}{4}-\tfrac{\Upsilon}{(\Upsilon+1)(\Upsilon+2)}\tfrac{\beta}{(\beta+1)(\beta+2)}\right]\widetilde{\mathcal{N}}(\eth,\mathrm{n},\upsilon,\mathrm{d}).
\end{aligned}
$$

A conclusion has, therefore, been established. □

Remark 4. *If one assumes that $\Upsilon = 1 = \beta$, then from (61), as a result, there will be inequity (see [42]):*

$$
\begin{aligned}
4\widetilde{\mathrm{Y}}\left(\tfrac{\eth+\mathrm{n}}{2},\tfrac{\upsilon+\mathrm{d}}{2}\right) &\otimes \widetilde{\mathcal{J}}\left(\tfrac{\eth+\mathrm{n}}{2},\tfrac{\upsilon+\mathrm{d}}{2}\right)\\
&\supseteq_{\mathbb{F}} \tfrac{1}{(\mathrm{n}-\eth)(\mathrm{d}-\upsilon)}\int_{\eth}^{\mathrm{n}}\int_{\upsilon}^{\mathrm{d}}\widetilde{\mathrm{Y}}(\theta,\psi)\otimes\widetilde{\mathcal{J}}(\theta,\psi)d\psi d\theta\oplus\tfrac{5}{36}\widetilde{K}(\eth,\mathrm{n},\upsilon,\mathrm{d})\\
&\oplus\tfrac{7}{36}\left[\widetilde{L}(\eth,\mathrm{n},\upsilon,\mathrm{d})\,\widetilde{+}\,\widetilde{\mathcal{M}}(\eth,\mathrm{n},\upsilon,\mathrm{d})\right]\oplus\tfrac{2}{9}\widetilde{\mathcal{N}}(\eth,\mathrm{n},\upsilon,\mathrm{d}).
\end{aligned}
$$

If $\widetilde{\mathrm{Y}}$ is coordinated left-UD-convex and one assumes that $\Upsilon = 1 = \beta$, then from (61), as a result, there will be inequity (see [27]):

$$
\begin{aligned}
4\widetilde{\mathrm{Y}}\left(\tfrac{\eth+\mathrm{n}}{2},\tfrac{\upsilon+\mathrm{d}}{2}\right) &\otimes \widetilde{\mathcal{J}}\left(\tfrac{\eth+\mathrm{n}}{2},\tfrac{\upsilon+\mathrm{d}}{2}\right)\\
&\leq_{\mathbb{F}} \tfrac{1}{(\mathrm{n}-\eth)(\mathrm{d}-\upsilon)}\int_{\eth}^{\mathrm{n}}\int_{\upsilon}^{\mathrm{d}}\widetilde{\mathrm{Y}}(\theta,\psi)\otimes\widetilde{\mathcal{J}}(\theta,\psi)d\psi d\theta\oplus\tfrac{5}{36}\widetilde{K}(\eth,\mathrm{n},\upsilon,\mathrm{d})\\
&\oplus\tfrac{7}{36}\left[\widetilde{L}(\eth,\mathrm{n},\upsilon,\mathrm{d})\,\widetilde{+}\,\widetilde{\mathcal{M}}(\eth,\mathrm{n},\upsilon,\mathrm{d})\right]\oplus\tfrac{2}{9}\widetilde{\mathcal{N}}(\eth,\mathrm{n},\upsilon,\mathrm{d}).
\end{aligned}
$$

If $\mathrm{Y}_*((\theta,\psi),\,\mathfrak{z}) \neq \mathrm{Y}^*((\theta,\psi),\,\mathfrak{z})$ with $\mathfrak{z} = 1$, then from (61), we succeed in bringing about the upcoming inequity (see [25]):

$$
\begin{aligned}
4\,\mathrm{Y}\left(\tfrac{\eth+\mathrm{n}}{2},\tfrac{\upsilon+\mathrm{d}}{2}\right) &\times \mathcal{J}\left(\tfrac{\eth+\mathrm{n}}{2},\tfrac{\upsilon+\mathrm{d}}{2}\right)\\
&\supseteq \tfrac{1}{(\mathrm{n}-\eth)(\mathrm{d}-\upsilon)}\int_{\eth}^{\mathrm{n}}\int_{\upsilon}^{\mathrm{d}}\mathrm{Y}(\theta,\psi)\times\mathcal{J}(\theta,\psi)d\psi d\theta+\tfrac{5}{36}K(\eth,\mathrm{n},\upsilon,\mathrm{d})\\
&+\tfrac{7}{36}[L(\eth,\mathrm{n},\upsilon,\mathrm{d})+\mathcal{M}(\eth,\mathrm{n},\upsilon,\mathrm{d})]+\tfrac{2}{9}\mathcal{N}(\eth,\mathrm{n},\upsilon,\mathrm{d}).
\end{aligned}
$$

If $\gamma_*((\theta,\psi),\mathfrak{z}) \neq \gamma^*((\theta,\psi),\mathfrak{z})$ *with* $\mathfrak{z}=1$*, then from (61), we succeed in bringing about the upcoming inequity (see [26]):*

$$
\begin{aligned}
4\gamma\left(\tfrac{\mathfrak{d}+\mathfrak{n}}{2},\tfrac{\upsilon+\mathfrak{d}}{2}\right) &\times \mathcal{J}\left(\tfrac{\mathfrak{d}+\mathfrak{n}}{2},\tfrac{\upsilon+\mathfrak{d}}{2}\right) \\
&\supseteq \frac{\Gamma(\gamma+1)\Gamma(\beta+1)}{4(\mathfrak{n}-\mathfrak{d})^{\gamma}(\mathfrak{d}-\upsilon)^{\beta}}\left[\begin{array}{l}\mathcal{I}^{\gamma,\beta}_{\mathfrak{d}^+,\upsilon^+}\,\gamma(\mathfrak{n},\mathfrak{d})\times J(\mathfrak{n},\mathfrak{d})+\mathcal{I}^{\gamma,\beta}_{\mathfrak{d}^+,\mathfrak{d}^-}\,\gamma(\mathfrak{n},\upsilon)\times J(\mathfrak{n},\upsilon)\\ +\mathcal{I}^{\gamma,\beta}_{\mathfrak{n}^-,\upsilon^+}\,\gamma(\mathfrak{d},\mathfrak{d})\times J(\mathfrak{d},\mathfrak{d})+\mathcal{I}^{\gamma,\beta}_{\mathfrak{n}^-,\mathfrak{d}^-}\,\gamma(\mathfrak{d},\upsilon)\times J(\mathfrak{d},\upsilon)\end{array}\right] \\
&+\left[\frac{\gamma}{2(\gamma+1)(\gamma+2)}+\frac{\beta}{(\beta+1)(\beta+2)}\left(\frac{1}{2}-\frac{\gamma}{(\gamma+1)(\gamma+2)}\right)\right]K(\mathfrak{d},\mathfrak{n},\upsilon,\mathfrak{d}) \\
&+\left[\frac{1}{2}\left(\frac{1}{2}-\frac{\gamma}{(\gamma+1)(\gamma+2)}\right)+\frac{\gamma}{(\gamma+1)(\gamma+2)}\frac{\beta}{(\beta+1)(\beta+2)}\right]L(\mathfrak{d},\mathfrak{n},\upsilon,\mathfrak{d}) \\
&+\left[\frac{1}{2}\left(\frac{1}{2}-\frac{\beta}{(\beta+1)(\beta+2)}\right)+\frac{\gamma}{(\gamma+1)(\gamma+2)}\frac{\beta}{(\beta+1)(\beta+2)}\right]\mathcal{M}(\mathfrak{d},\mathfrak{n},\upsilon,\mathfrak{d}) \\
&+\left[\frac{1}{4}-\frac{\gamma}{(\gamma+1)(\gamma+2)}\frac{\beta}{(\beta+1)(\beta+2)}\right]\mathcal{N}(\mathfrak{d},\mathfrak{n},\upsilon,\mathfrak{d}).
\end{aligned}
$$

If $\gamma_*((\theta,\psi),\mathfrak{z}) = \gamma^*((\theta,\psi),\mathfrak{z})$ *and* $\mathcal{J}_*((\theta,\psi),\mathfrak{z}) = \mathcal{J}^*((\theta,\psi),\mathfrak{z})$ *with* $\mathfrak{z}=1$*, then from (61) , we succeed in bringing about the upcoming inequity (see [41]):*

$$
\begin{aligned}
4\gamma\left(\tfrac{\mathfrak{d}+\mathfrak{n}}{2},\tfrac{\upsilon+\mathfrak{d}}{2}\right) &\times \mathcal{J}\left(\tfrac{\mathfrak{d}+\mathfrak{n}}{2},\tfrac{\upsilon+\mathfrak{d}}{2}\right) \\
&\leq \frac{\Gamma(\gamma+1)\Gamma(\beta+1)}{4(\mathfrak{n}-\mathfrak{d})^{\gamma}(\mathfrak{d}-\upsilon)^{\beta}}\left[\begin{array}{l}\mathcal{I}^{\gamma,\beta}_{\mathfrak{d}^+,\upsilon^+}\,\gamma(\mathfrak{n},\mathfrak{d})\times J(\mathfrak{n},\mathfrak{d})+\mathcal{I}^{\gamma,\beta}_{\mathfrak{d}^+,\mathfrak{d}^-}\,\gamma(\mathfrak{n},\upsilon)\times J(\mathfrak{n},\upsilon)\\ +\mathcal{I}^{\gamma,\beta}_{\mathfrak{n}^-,\upsilon^+}\,\gamma(\mathfrak{d},\mathfrak{d})\times J(\mathfrak{d},\mathfrak{d})+\mathcal{I}^{\gamma,\beta}_{\mathfrak{n}^-,\mathfrak{d}^-}\,\gamma(\mathfrak{d},\upsilon)\times J(\mathfrak{d},\upsilon)\end{array}\right] \\
&+\left[\frac{\gamma}{2(\gamma+1)(\gamma+2)}+\frac{\beta}{(\beta+1)(\beta+2)}\left(\frac{1}{2}-\frac{\gamma}{(\gamma+1)(\gamma+2)}\right)\right]K(\mathfrak{d},\mathfrak{n},\upsilon,\mathfrak{d}) \\
&+\left[\frac{1}{2}\left(\frac{1}{2}-\frac{\gamma}{(\gamma+1)(\gamma+2)}\right)+\frac{\gamma}{(\gamma+1)(\gamma+2)}\frac{\beta}{(\beta+1)(\beta+2)}\right]L(\mathfrak{d},\mathfrak{n},\upsilon,\mathfrak{d}) \\
&+\left[\frac{1}{2}\left(\frac{1}{2}-\frac{\beta}{(\beta+1)(\beta+2)}\right)+\frac{\gamma}{(\gamma+1)(\gamma+2)}\frac{\beta}{(\beta+1)(\beta+2)}\right]\mathcal{M}(\mathfrak{d},\mathfrak{n},\upsilon,\mathfrak{d}) \\
&+\left[\frac{1}{4}-\frac{\gamma}{(\gamma+1)(\gamma+2)}\frac{\beta}{(\beta+1)(\beta+2)}\right]\mathcal{N}(\mathfrak{d},\mathfrak{n},\upsilon,\mathfrak{d})
\end{aligned}
$$

4. Conclusions and Future Plans

In this study, Hermite–Hadamard-type inequalities for coordinated UD-convex $FNVM$ were established. These inequalities are very important in the field of inequalities because the findings in this research constitute an expansion of a number of earlier findings. A coordinated fuzzy-number-valued convexity is a novel type of class and, by using this class and other fractional integrals, new fractional inequalities can be found that are available to interested authors.

Author Contributions: Conceptualization, M.B.K.; validation, A.C.; formal analysis, A.C.; investigation, M.B.K. and T.S.; resources, M.B.K. and T.S.; writing—original draft, M.B.K. and T.S.; writing—review and editing, M.B.K. and A.M.A.; visualization, T.S. and A.M.A.; supervision, T.S. and A.M.A.; project administration, T.S. and A.C. All authors have read and agreed to the published version of the manuscript.

Funding: The research was funded by the University of Oradea, Romania.

Data Availability Statement: Data are contained within the article.

Acknowledgments: The Rector of the Transilvania University of Brasov, 29 Eroilor Boulevard, 500036 Brasov, Romania, is acknowledged by the author "M.B.K" for offering top-notch research and academic environments.

Conflicts of Interest: The authors declare no conflict of interest.

References

1. Peajcariaac, J.E.; Proschan, F.; Tong, Y.L. *Convex Functions, Partial Orderings and Statistical Applications*; Academic Press: Boston, MA, USA, 1992.
2. Dragomir, S.S.; Pearce, C.E.M. *Selected Topics on Hermite–Hadamard Inequalities and Applications*; RGMIA Monographs; Victoria University: Melbourne, Australia, 2000.
3. Aldawish, I.; Jleli, M.; Samet, B. On Hermite–Hadamard-Type Inequalities for Functions Satisfying Second-Order Differential Inequalities. *Axioms* **2023**, *12*, 443. [CrossRef]
4. Chen, F. A note on Hermite–Hadamard inequalities for products of convex functions. *J. Appl. Math.* **2013**, *2013*, 935020. [CrossRef]
5. Dragomir, S.S.; Pecaric, J.; Persson, L.E. Some inequalities of Hadamard type. *Soochow J. Math.* **1995**, *21*, 335–341.
6. Pavic, Z. Improvements of the Hermite–Hadamard inequality. *J. Inequalities Appl.* **2015**, *2015*, 222. [CrossRef]
7. Zhao, T.H.; Wang, M.K.; Hai, G.J.; Chu, Y.M. Landen inequalities for Gaussian hypergeometric function. *RACSAM Rev. R. Acad. A* **2022**, *116*, 53. [CrossRef]
8. Wang, M.K.; Hong, M.Y.; Xu, Y.F.; Shen, Z.H.; Chu, Y.M. Inequalities for generalized trigonometric and hyperbolic functions with one parameter. *J. Math. Inequal.* **2020**, *14*, 1–21. [CrossRef]
9. Zhao, T.H.; Qian, W.M.; Chu, Y.M. Sharp power mean bounds for the tangent and hyperbolic sine means. *J. Math. Inequal.* **2021**, *15*, 1459–1472. [CrossRef]
10. Chu, Y.M.; Wang, G.D.; Zhang, X.H. The Schur multiplicative and harmonic convexities of the complete symmetric function. *Math. Nachr.* **2011**, *284*, 53–663. [CrossRef]
11. Chu, Y.M.; Xia, W.F.; Zhang, X.H. The Schur concavity, Schur multiplicative and harmonic convexities of the second dual form of the Hamy symmetric function with applications. *J. Multivar. Anal.* **2012**, *105*, 412–442. [CrossRef]
12. Chu, Y.M.; Rauf, A.; Ishtiaq, M.; Siddiqui, M.K.; Muhammad, M.H. Topological properties of polycyclic aromatic nanostars dendrimers. *Polycycl. Aromat. Compd.* **2022**, *42*, 1891–1908. [CrossRef]
13. Moore, R.E. *Interval Analysis*; Prentice-Hall: Englewood Cliffs, NJ, USA, 1966.
14. Chalco-Cano, Y.; Flores-Franulič, A.; Román-Flores, H. Ostrowski type inequalities for interval-valued functions using generalized Hukuhara derivative. *Comput. Appl. Math.* **2012**, *31*, 457–472.
15. Chalco-Cano, Y.; Lodwick, W.A.; Condori-Equice, W. Ostrowski type inequalities and applications in numerical integration for interval-valued functions. *Soft Comput.* **2015**, *19*, 3293–3300. [CrossRef]
16. Flores-Franulič, A.; Chalco-Cano, Y.; Román-Flores, H. An Ostrowski type inequality for interval-valued functions. In Proceedings of the 2013 Joint IFSA World Congress and NAFIPS Annual Meeting (IFSA/NAFIPS) (2013), Edmonton, AB, Canada, 24–28 June 2013; pp. 1459–1462.
17. Román-Flores, H.; Chalco-Cano, Y.; Lodwick, W.A. Some integral inequalities for interval-valued functions. *Comput. Appl. Math.* **2018**, *37*, 1306–1318. [CrossRef]
18. Nwaeze, E.R.; Khan, M.A.; Chu, Y.M. Fractional inclusions of the Hermite-Hadamard type for m-polynomial convex interval valued functions. *Adv. Differ. Equ.* **2020**, *2020*, 507. [CrossRef]
19. Budak, H.; Tunc, T.; Sarikaya, M.Z. Fractional Hermite-Hadamard-type inequalities for interval-valued functions. *Proc. Am. Math. Soc.* **2020**, *148*, 705–718. [CrossRef]
20. Liu, X.; Ye, G.; Zhao, D.; Liu, W. Fractional Hermite-Hadamard type inequalities for interval-valued functions. *J. Inequal. Appl.* **2019**, *2019*, 266. [CrossRef]
21. Costa, T.M. Jensen's inequality type integral for fuzzy-interval-valued functions. *Fuzzy Sets Syst.* **2017**, *327*, 31–47. [CrossRef]
22. Costa, T.M.; Román-Flores, H. Some integral inequalities for fuzzy-interval-valued functions. *Inf. Sci.* **2017**, *420*, 110–125. [CrossRef]
23. Wang, M.-K.; Chu, H.-H.; Li, Y.-M.; Chu, Y.-M. Answers to three conjectures on convexity of three functions involving complete elliptic integrals of the first kind. *Appl. Anal. Discrete Math.* **2020**, *14*, 255–271. [CrossRef]
24. Zhao, D.F.; Ali, M.A.; Murtaza, G. On the Hermite-Hadamard inequalities for interval-valued coordinated convex functions. *Adv. Differ. Equ.* **2020**, *2020*, 570.
25. Budak, H.; Kara, H.; Ali, M.A.; Khan, S.; Chu, Y.M. Fractional Hermite-Hadamard-type inequalities for interval-valued coordinated convex functions. *Open Math.* **2021**, *19*, 1081–1097. [CrossRef]
26. Khan, M.B.; Mohammed, P.O.; Noor, M.A.; Abuahalnaja, K. Fuzzy integral inequalities on coordinates of convex fuzzy interval-valued functions. *Math. Biosci. Eng.* **2021**, *18*, 6552–6580. [CrossRef]
27. Mitroi, F.-C.; Nikodem, K.; Wasowicz, S. Hermite–Hadamard inequalities for convex set-valued functions. *Demonstr. Math.* **2013**, *46*, 655–662.
28. Osuna-Gómez, R.; Jiménez-Gamero, M.D.; Chalco-Cano, Y.; Rojas-Medar, M.A. Hadamard and Jensen inequalities for s-convex fuzzy processes. In *Soft Methodology and Random Information Systems*; Springer: Berlin/Heidelberg, Germany, 2004; pp. 645–652.
29. Nikodem, K.; Sanchez, J.L.; Sanchez, L. Jensen and Hermite-Hadamard inequalities for strongly convex set-valued maps. *Math. Aeterna* **2014**, *4*, 979–987.
30. Román-Flores, H.; Chalco-Cano, Y.; Silva, G.N. A note on gronwall type inequality for interval-valued functions. In Proceedings of the 2013 Joint IFSA World Congress and NAFIPS Annual Meeting (IFSA/NAFIPS) (2013), Edmonton, AB, Canada, 24–28 June 2013; pp. 1455–1458.

31. Zhao, D.; An, T.; Ye, G.; Liu, W. Chebyshev type inequalities for interval-valued functions. *Fuzzy Sets Syst.* **2020**, *396*, 82–101. [CrossRef]
32. Abbas Baloch, I.; Chu, Y.-M. Petrovic-type inequalities for harmonic h-convex functions. *J. Funct. Spaces* **2020**, *2020*, 3075390. [CrossRef]
33. Chu, Y.-M.; Long, B.-Y. Sharp inequalities between means. *Math. Inequal. Appl.* **2011**, *14*, 647–655.
34. Chu, Y.-M.; Qiu, Y.-F.; Wang, M.-K. Hölder mean inequalities for the complete elliptic integrals. *Integral Transform. Spec. Funct.* **2012**, *23*, 521–527. [CrossRef]
35. Chu, Y.-M.; Wang, M.-K. Inequalities between arithmetic geometric, Gini, and Toader means. *Abstr. Appl. Anal.* **2012**, *2012*, 830585. [CrossRef]
36. Sarikaya, M.Z. On the Hermite-Hadamard-type inequalities for co-ordinated convex function via fractional integrals. *Integral Transform. Spec. Funct.* **2013**, *25*, 134–147. [CrossRef]
37. Dragomir, S.S. On the Hadamard's inequality for convex functions on the co-ordinates in a rectangle from the plane. *Taiwan J. Math.* **2001**, *5*, 775–788.
38. Lupulescu, V. Fractional calculus for interval-valued functions. *Fuzzy Sets Sys.* **2015**, *265*, 63–85. [CrossRef]
39. Allahviranloo, T.; Salahshour, S.; Abbasbandy, S. Explicit solutions of fractional differential equations with uncertainty. *Soft Comput.* **2012**, *16*, 297–302. [CrossRef]
40. Budak, H.; Sarikaya, M.Z. Hermite-Hadamard type inequalities for products of two co-ordinated convex mappings via fractional integrals. *Int. J. Appl. Math. Stat.* **2019**, *58*, 11–30.
41. Khan, M.B.; Althobaiti, A.; Lee, C.C.; Soliman, M.S.; Li, C.T. Some New Properties of Convex Fuzzy-Number-Valued Mappings on Coordinates Using Up and Down Fuzzy Relations and Related Inequalities. *Mathematics* **2023**, *11*, 2851. [CrossRef]
42. Khan, M.B.; Santos-García, G.; Zaini, H.G.; Treanţă, S.; Soliman, M.S. Some new concepts related to integral operators and inequalities on coordinates in fuzzy fractional calculus. *Mathematics* **2022**, *10*, 534. [CrossRef]
43. Jleli, M.; Samet, B. On Hermite-Hadamard type inequalities via fractional integrals of a function with respect to another function. *J. Nonlinear Sci. Appl.* **2016**, *9*, 1252–1260. [CrossRef]
44. Tunc, T. Hermite-Hadamard type inequalities for interval-valued fractional integrals with respect to another function. *Math. Slovaca* **2022**, *72*, 1501–1512. [CrossRef]
45. Budak, H.; Agarwal, P. On Hermite-Hadamard-type inequalities for coordinated convex mappings utilizing generalized fractional integrals. In *International Workshop on Advanced Theory and Applications of Fractional Calculus*; Springer: Berlin/Heidelberg, Germany, 2018; pp. 227–249.
46. Kara, H.; Ali, M.A.; Budak, H. Hermite-Hadamard-type inequalities for interval-valued coordinated convex functions involving generalized fractional integrals. *Math. Methods Appl. Sci.* **2021**, *44*, 104–123. [CrossRef]
47. Zhao, D.; Ali, M.A.; Kashuri, A.; Budak, H.; Sarikaya, M.Z. Hermite-Hadamard-type inequalities for the interval-valued approximately h-convex functions via generalized fractional integrals. *J. Inequal. Appl.* **2020**, *2020*, 222. [CrossRef]
48. Budak, H.; Bilisik, C.C.; Kashuri, A.; Ali, M.A. Hermite-Hadamard Type Inequalities for the Interval-Valued Harmonically h-Convex Functions Via Fractional Integrals. *Appl. Math. E-Notes* **2021**, *21*, 12–32.
49. Khan, M.B.; Zaini, H.G.; Macías-Díaz, J.E.; Treanţă, S.; Soliman, M.S. Some Fuzzy Riemann–Liouville Fractional Integral Inequalities for Preinvex Fuzzy Interval-Valued Functions. *Symmetry* **2022**, *14*, 313. [CrossRef]
50. Zhao, D.; Ye, G.; Liu, W.; Torres, D.F.M. Some inequalities for interval-valued functions on time scales. *Soft Comput.* **2019**, *23*, 6005–6015. [CrossRef]
51. Khan, M.B.; Santos-García, G.; Noor, M.A.; Soliman, M.S. Some new concepts related to fuzzy fractional calculus for up and down convex fuzzy-number valued functions and inequalities. *Chaos Solitons Fractals* **2022**, *164*, 112692. [CrossRef]
52. Diamond, P.; Kloeden, P. *Metric Spaces of Fuzzy Sets: Theory and Applications*; World Scientific: Singapore, 1994.
53. Bede, B. *Mathematics of Fuzzy Sets and Fuzzy Logic, Volume 295 of Studies in Fuzziness and Soft Computing*; Springer: Berlin/Heidelberg, Germany, 2013.
54. Zhao, T.H.; Bhayo, B.A.; Chu, Y.M. Inequalities for generalized Grötzsch ring function. *Comput. Methods Funct. Theory* **2022**, *22*, 559–574. [CrossRef]
55. Zhao, T.H.; He, Z.Y.; Chu, Y.M. Sharp bounds for the weighted Hölder mean of the zero-balanced generalized complete elliptic integrals. *Comput. Methods Funct. Theory* **2021**, *21*, 413–426. [CrossRef]
56. Zhao, T.H.; Wang, M.K.; Chu, Y.M. Concavity and bounds involving generalized elliptic integral of the first kind. *J. Math. Inequal.* **2021**, *15*, 701–724. [CrossRef]
57. Zhao, T.H.; Wang, M.K.; Chu, Y.M. Monotonicity and convexity involving generalized elliptic integral of the first kind. *RACSAM Rev. R. Acad. A* **2021**, *115*, 46. [CrossRef]
58. Chu, H.H.; Zhao, T.H.; Chu, Y.M. Sharp bounds for the Toader mean of order 3 in terms of arithmetic, quadratic and contra harmonic means. *Math. Slovaca.* **2020**, *70*, 1097–1112. [CrossRef]
59. Zhao, T.H.; He, Z.Y.; Chu, Y.M. On some refinemens for inequalities involving zero-balanced hyper geometric function. *AIMS Math.* **2020**, *5*, 6479–6495. [CrossRef]
60. Zhao, T.H.; Wang, M.K.; Chu, Y.M. A sharp double inequality involving generalized complete elliptic integral of the first kind. *AIMS Math.* **2020**, *5*, 4512–4528. [CrossRef]

61. Wang, W.; Zhang, H.; Jiang, X.; Yang, X. A high-order and efficient numerical technique for the nonlocal neutron diffusion equation representing neutron transport in a nuclear reactor. *Ann. Nucl. Energy* **2024**, *195*, 110163. [CrossRef]
62. Zhou, Z.; Zhang, H.; Yang, X. H^1-norm error analysis of a robust ADI method on graded mesh for three-dimensional subdiffusion problems. *Numer. Algorithms* **2023**, *2023*, 1–19.
63. Zhang, H.; Liu, Y.; Yang, X. An efficient ADI difference scheme for the nonlocal evolution problem in three-dimensional space. *J. Appl. Math. Comput.* **2023**, *69*, 651–674. [CrossRef]
64. Yang, X.; Zhang, Q.; Yuan, G.; Sheng, Z. On positivity preservation in nonlinear finite volume method for multi-term fractional subdiffusion equation on polygonal meshes. *Nonlinear Dyn.* **2018**, *92*, 595–612. [CrossRef]

fractal and fractional

Article

Analysis and Applications of Some New Fractional Integral Inequalities

Sofia Ramzan [1], Muhammad Uzair Awan [1,*], Silvestru Sever Dragomir [2], Bandar Bin-Mohsin [3,*] and Muhammad Aslam Noor [4]

1 Department of Mathematics, Government College University, Faisalabad 38000, Pakistan
2 Mathematics, College of Engineering & Science, Victoria University, P. O. Box 14428, Melbourne City, MC 8001, Australia
3 Department of Mathematics, College of Science, King Saud University, Riyadh 11451, Saudi Arabia
4 Department of Mathematics, COMSATS University Islamabad, Islamabad 45540, Pakistan; noormaslam@gmail.com
* Correspondence: muawan@gcuf.edu.pk (M.U.A.); balmohsen@ksu.edu.sa (B.B.-M.)

Abstract: This paper presents a novel parameterized fractional integral identity. By using this auxiliary result and the $\mathfrak{s}$-convexity property of the mapping, a series of fractional variants of certain classical inequalities, including Simpson's, midpoint, and trapezoidal-type inequalities, have been derived. Additionally, some applications of our main outcomes to special means of real numbers have been explored. Moreover, we have derived a new generic numerical scheme for solving non-linear equations, demonstrating an application of our main results in numerical analysis.

Keywords: $\mathfrak{s}$-convex mappings; Simpson's $\frac{1}{3}$ formula; midpoint formula; trapezoidal formula; integral inequalities; fractional calculus; basins of attraction

MSC: 26A33; 26A51; 26D07; 26D10; 26D15; 26D20; 58C30; 65H05

Citation: Ramzan, S.; Awan, M.U.; Dragomir, S.S.; Bin-Mohsin, B.; Noor, M.A. Analysis and Applications of Some New Fractional Integral Inequalities. *Fractal Fract.* **2023**, *7*, 797. https://doi.org/10.3390/fractalfract7110797

Academic Editors: Eze Nwaeze and Seth Kermausuor

Received: 17 September 2023
Revised: 17 October 2023
Accepted: 19 October 2023
Published: 31 October 2023

1. Introduction and Preliminaries

The notion of convex sets and convex functions has numerous applications in the fields of both pure and applied sciences. In addition, the theory of convexity has undergone rapid advancements in recent years owing to its numerous applications and its close connection with the theory of inequalities. Solutions to mathematical problems can be approximated using the application of inequalities in cases where there is difficulty in finding the exact values. There is a strong relation between convexity and the theory of inequalities, as convex functions can be directly applied to derive many inequalities.

According to Dragomir and Pearce [1], the Hermite–Hadamard inequality is one of the most renowned results in the class of classical convex functions. This inequality possesses a clear intrinsic geometrical interpretation and finds numerous applications. Although the result was initially identified by Hadamard (1865–1963), it was primarily attributed to Hermite (1822–1901) [2,3]. The statement of this inequality is as follows:

Suppose that $\aleph : \mathcal{I} \subseteq \mathbb{R} \to \mathbb{R}$ is a convex mapping, and let $\tau_1, \tau_2 \in \mathcal{I}$ such that $\tau_1 < \tau_2$. Then,

$$\aleph\left(\frac{\tau_1+\tau_2}{2}\right) \leq \frac{1}{\tau_2-\tau_1}\int_{\tau_1}^{\tau_2} \aleph(\lambda)d\lambda \leq \frac{\aleph(\tau_1)+\aleph(\tau_2)}{2}. \tag{1}$$

The two sides of the Hermite–Hadamard inequality, namely the midpoint and trapezoidal-type inequalities, are utilized for the estimation of error bounds for certain quadrature rules. These inequalities were first derived in [4,5] and are defined as follows:

Suppose that $\aleph : [\tau_1, \tau_2] \to \mathbb{R}$ is a differentiable mapping on (τ_1, τ_2), with $\tau_1 < \tau_2$. If $|\aleph'|$ is convex on $[\tau_1, \tau_2]$, then:

$$\left| \frac{1}{\tau_2 - \tau_1} \int_{\tau_1}^{\tau_2} \aleph(\lambda) d\lambda - \aleph\left(\frac{\tau_1 + \tau_2}{2}\right) \right| \le \frac{\tau_2 - \tau_1}{8} \left[|\aleph'(\tau_1)| + |\aleph'(\tau_2)| \right].$$

Let $\aleph : [\tau_1, \tau_2] \to \mathbb{R}$ be a differentiable mapping on (τ_1, τ_2), with $\tau_1 < \tau_2$. If $|\aleph'|$ is convex on $[\tau_1, \tau_2]$, then:

$$\left| \frac{\aleph(\tau_1) + \aleph(\tau_2)}{2} - \frac{1}{\tau_2 - \tau_1} \int_{\tau_1}^{\tau_2} \aleph(\lambda) d\lambda \right| \le \frac{\tau_2 - \tau_1}{8} \left[|\aleph'(\tau_1)| + |\aleph'(\tau_2)| \right].$$

Another significant inequality in the literature is known as Simpson's integral inequality [6], which yields an error bound for the well-known Simpson's rule and is defined as:

Let $\aleph : [\tau_1, \tau_2] \to \mathbb{R}$ be four times continuously differentiable mapping on (τ_1, τ_2) and $\|\aleph^{(4)}\|_\infty < \infty$, then:

$$\left| \frac{1}{3}\left[\frac{\aleph(\tau_1) + \aleph(\tau_2)}{2} + 2\aleph\left(\frac{\tau_1 + \tau_2}{2}\right) \right] - \frac{1}{\tau_2 - \tau_1} \int_{\tau_1}^{\tau_2} \aleph(\lambda) d\lambda \right| \le \frac{1}{2880} \|\aleph^{(4)}\|_\infty (\tau_2 - \tau_1)^4.$$

Awan et al. [7] obtained some new generalized variants of Simpson-type inequalities based on differentiable, strongly $(\mathfrak{s}, \mathfrak{m})$-convex mappings. Further generalizations, extensions, and refinements of Simpson's integral inequality can be found in [8–11].

Over time, researchers have extended the definition of convex functions to derive different variants of the Hermite–Hadamard inequality. On the other hand, the concept of $\mathfrak{s}$-convexity [12,13] is split into two notions, which are described below, with the basic condition that $0 < \mathfrak{s} \le 1$.

A function $\aleph : [0, \infty) \to \mathbb{R}$ is said to be an $\mathfrak{s}$-convex function in the first sense, denoted by $K_{\mathfrak{s}}^1$, if

$$\aleph(\varkappa_1 \tau_1 + \varkappa_2 \tau_2) \le \varkappa_1{}^{\mathfrak{s}} \aleph(\tau_1) + \varkappa_2{}^{\mathfrak{s}} \aleph(\tau_2), \tag{2}$$

holds for all $\tau_1, \tau_2 \in [0, \infty)$ and all $\varkappa_1, \varkappa_2 \ge 0$ and $\varkappa_1{}^{\mathfrak{s}} + \varkappa_2{}^{\mathfrak{s}} = 1$.

A function $\aleph : [0, \infty) \to \mathbb{R}$ is said to be an $\mathfrak{s}$-convex function in the second sense, or $\mathfrak{s}$-Breckner convex, if the inequality (2) holds for all $\tau_1, \tau_2 \in [0, \infty)$ and all $\varkappa_1, \varkappa_2 \ge 0$ with $\varkappa_1 + \varkappa_2 = 1$. We denote this as $K_{\mathfrak{s}}^2$. Of course, both $\mathfrak{s}$-convexities reduce to standard convexity when $\mathfrak{s} = 1$.

The geometrical meaning of $\mathfrak{s}$-convexity $(0 < \mathfrak{s} < 1)$ is that the graph of the function lies below a curved chord L that is located between any two points.

Example 1. *Let $0 < \mathfrak{s} < 1$ and $a, b, c \in \mathbb{R}$. By defining, for $u \in [0, \infty)$,*

$$\aleph(u) = \begin{cases} a & \text{if } u = 0, \\ bu^{\mathfrak{s}} + c & \text{if } u > 0, \end{cases}$$

we have the following:

1. *If $b \ge 0$ and $c \le a$, then $\aleph \in K_{\mathfrak{s}}^1$.*
2. *If $b \ge 0$ and $c < a$, then $\aleph$ is non-decreasing on $(0, \infty)$ but not on $[0, \infty)$.*
3. *If $b \ge 0$ and $0 \le c \le a$, then $\aleph \in K_{\mathfrak{s}}^2$.*
4. *If $b > 0$ and $c < 0$, then $\aleph \notin K_{\mathfrak{s}}^2$.*

For $\mathfrak{s}$-convexity in the first and second senses, Dragomir and Fitzpatrick [14] described the respective Hermite–Hadamard-type inequalities as follows:

Suppose that $\aleph : [0,\infty) \to [0,\infty)$ is an $\mathfrak{s}$-convex mapping in the first sense, where $\mathfrak{s} \in (0,1]$, and let $\tau_1, \tau_2 \in [0,\infty)$ and $\tau_1 < \tau_2$. Then, the following inequalities hold:

$$\aleph\left(\frac{\tau_1+\tau_2}{2}\right) \leq \frac{1}{\tau_2-\tau_1}\int_{\tau_1}^{\tau_2} \aleph(\lambda)d\lambda \leq \frac{\aleph(\tau_1)+\mathfrak{s}\aleph(\tau_2)}{\mathfrak{s}+1}. \tag{3}$$

Suppose that $\aleph : [0,\infty) \to [0,\infty)$ is an $\mathfrak{s}$-convex mapping in the second sense, where $\mathfrak{s} \in (0,1]$, and let $\tau_1, \tau_2 \in [0,\infty)$ and $\tau_1 < \tau_2$. Then, the following inequalities hold:

$$2^{\mathfrak{s}-1}\aleph\left(\frac{\tau_1+\tau_2}{2}\right) \leq \frac{1}{\tau_2-\tau_1}\int_{\tau_1}^{\tau_2} \aleph(\lambda)d\lambda \leq \frac{\aleph(\tau_1)+\aleph(\tau_2)}{\mathfrak{s}+1}. \tag{4}$$

Further generalizations and extensions of classical convex functions can be found in [15–19].

The study of integrals and derivatives of arbitrary real order is known as fractional calculus. The goal of fractional integrals is to address various problems involving special functions of mathematical science, as well as their extensions and generalizations to one or more variables. Additionally, fractional-order derivatives are much better at describing the memory and hereditary properties of various processes compared to classical derivatives. In fact, the latest advancements in fractional calculus have been driven by current applications in physics, differential and integral equations, signal processing, fluid mechanics, mathematical biology, and electrochemistry. There is no doubt that various diverse problems in mathematics, engineering, and science can be addressed through the application of fractional calculus [20–22]. A detailed history of fractional calculus can be found in [23].

Sarikaya and Ertuğral [24] introduced the idea of generalized fractional integrals and derived Hadamard-type inequalities. The generalized fractional integrals from both the left and right sides of the interval $[\tau_1, \tau_2]$ are defined as:

$${}_{\tau_1^+}I_{\varphi}\aleph(y) = \int_{\tau_1}^{y} \frac{\varphi(y-\lambda)}{y-\lambda}\aleph(\lambda)d\lambda, \quad y > \tau_1, \tag{5}$$

and

$${}_{\tau_2^-}I_{\varphi}\aleph(y) = \int_{y}^{\tau_2} \frac{\varphi(\lambda-y)}{\lambda-y}\aleph(\lambda)d\lambda, \quad y < \tau_2, \tag{6}$$

where $\varphi : [0,\infty) \to [0,\infty)$ is the mapping satisfying the following condition:

$$\int_0^1 \frac{\varphi(\lambda)}{\lambda}d\lambda < \infty.$$

For some suitable choices of the mapping φ in (5) and (6), we can obtain Riemann–Liouville fractional integrals, k-Riemann–Liouville fractional integrals, Katugampola fractional integrals, conformable fractional integrals, and Hadamard fractional integrals as special cases.

From (5) and (6), the following fractional integrals are obtained:

1. For $\varphi(\lambda) = \lambda$, the resulting integrals are Riemann integrals:

$$I_{\tau_1^+}\aleph(y) = \int_{\tau_1}^{y} \aleph(\lambda)d\lambda, \quad y > \tau_1,$$
$$I_{\tau_2^-}\aleph(y) = \int_{y}^{\tau_2} \aleph(\lambda)d\lambda, \quad y < \tau_2.$$

2. By setting $\varphi(\lambda) = \frac{\lambda^\alpha}{\Gamma(\alpha)}$ and $\alpha > 0$, the resulting integrals are Riemann–Liouville integrals:

$$I^\alpha_{\tau_1^+}\aleph(y) = \frac{1}{\Gamma(\alpha)}\int_{\tau_1}^{y}(y-\lambda)^{\alpha-1}\aleph(\lambda)d\lambda, \quad y > \tau_1,$$
$$I^\alpha_{\tau_2^-}\aleph(y) = \frac{1}{\Gamma(\alpha)}\int_{y}^{\tau_2}(\lambda-y)^{\alpha-1}\aleph(\lambda)d\lambda, \quad y < \tau_2,$$

where Γ is the gamma mapping.

3. By taking $\varphi(\lambda) = \frac{1}{k\Gamma_k(\alpha)}\lambda^{\frac{\alpha}{k}}$ and $\alpha, k > 0$, the resulting integrals are k-Riemann–Liouville fractional integrals provided in [25] and defined as:

$$I^\alpha_{\tau_1^+,k}\aleph(y) = \frac{1}{k\Gamma_k(\alpha)}\int_{\tau_1}^{y}(y-\lambda)^{\frac{\alpha}{k}-1}\aleph(\lambda)d\lambda, \quad y > \tau_1,$$
$$I^\alpha_{\tau_2^-,k}\aleph(y) = \frac{1}{k\Gamma_k(\alpha)}\int_{y}^{\tau_2}(\lambda-y)^{\frac{\alpha}{k}-1}\aleph(\lambda)d\lambda, \quad y < \tau_2,$$

where

$$\Gamma_k(\alpha) = \int_0^\infty \lambda^{\alpha-1}e^{\frac{-\lambda^k}{k}}d\lambda, \quad Re(\alpha) > 0,$$

and

$$\Gamma_k(\alpha) = k^{\frac{\alpha}{k}-1}\Gamma\left(\frac{\alpha}{k}\right), \quad \Gamma_k(\alpha+k) = \alpha\Gamma_k(\alpha), \quad Re(\alpha) > 0; \quad k > 0.$$

Now, let us recall some special functions, which we will use in our calculations:
The Euler gamma mapping, or Euler integral of the second kind, is defined as:

$$\Gamma(\alpha) = \int_0^\infty \lambda^{\alpha-1}e^{-\lambda}d\lambda, \quad Re(\alpha) > 0.$$

The beta mapping, or Euler integral of the first kind with two variables, is defined as:

$$B(v_1, v_2) = \int_0^1 \lambda^{v_1-1}(1-\lambda)^{v_2-1}d\lambda, \quad Re(v_1) > 0, \quad Re(v_2) > 0. \tag{7}$$

In terms of gamma mapping, it is defined as:

$$B(v_1, v_2) = \frac{\Gamma(v_1)\Gamma(v_2)}{\Gamma(v_1+v_2)}.$$

The incomplete beta mapping, which is a generalization of the beta mapping, is defined in [26] as:

$$B_x(v_1, v_2) = B(x : v_1, v_2) = \int_0^x \lambda^{v_1-1}(1-\lambda)^{v_2-1}d\lambda, \quad Re(v_1) > 0, \quad Re(v_2) > 0. \tag{8}$$

When $x = 1$ in (8), it coincides with the beta mapping.
The hypergeometric mapping is:

$${}_2F_1(v_1, v_2; \mathfrak{c}; z) = \frac{1}{B(v_2, \mathfrak{c}-v_2)}\int_0^1 \lambda^{v_2-1}(1-\lambda)^{\mathfrak{c}-v_2-1}(1-z\lambda)^{-v_1}d\lambda, \quad Re(\mathfrak{c}) > Re(v_2) > 0, \quad |z| < 1. \tag{9}$$

This research article is organized as follows. In Section 2, we derive a new general parameterized integral identity for differentiable mappings. We also present various additional results that can be deduced from this new identity. In Section 3, we derive some new parameterized inequalities involving generalized fractional integrals for differentiable $\mathfrak{s}$-convex mappings of the second kind, utilizing the identity derived in Section 2. Some detailed graphical visualizations of our main findings are presented in Section 4, which shows the significance and validity of our results. In Section 5, some applications to special means of real numbers and quadrature formulas are presented. As an application, we also derive a new generalized numerical scheme. To the best of our knowledge, this is the first study in the literature pertaining to applications of integral inequalities in numerical analysis. We hope that the ideas and techniques presented in this paper will inspire interested readers working in this field.

2. A Parameterized Integral Identity Involving Generalized Fractional Integrals

In this section, a parameterized identity involving generalized fractional integrals is derived. Further, for some suitable choices of the given parameters, Simpson's, midpoint, and trapezoidal-type identities are also derived.

Lemma 1. *For a differentiable mapping $\aleph : [\tau_1, \tau_2] \to \mathbb{R}$ on (τ_1, τ_2) with continuous and integrable derivative $\aleph'$ on $[\tau_1, \tau_2]$, the following equality holds for $\rho, \sigma \geq 0$ and $n \in \mathbb{N}$:*

$$\begin{aligned}
&(1-\sigma)\aleph(\tau_1) + (1-\rho)\aleph(\tau_2) + \sigma\aleph\left(\frac{n\tau_1+\tau_2}{n+1}\right) + \rho\aleph\left(\frac{\tau_1+n\tau_2}{n+1}\right) \\
&- \frac{1}{\Delta(1)}\left[{}_{\tau_1^+}I_\varphi\aleph\left(\frac{n\tau_1+\tau_2}{n+1}\right) + {}_{\tau_2^-}I_\varphi\aleph\left(\frac{\tau_1+n\tau_2}{n+1}\right)\right] \\
&= \frac{\tau_2-\tau_1}{n+1}\frac{1}{\Delta(1)}\left[\int_0^1 (\Delta(\lambda)-\Delta(1)\rho)\aleph'\left(\frac{1-\lambda}{n+1}\tau_1 + \frac{n+\lambda}{n+1}\tau_2\right)d\lambda\right. \\
&\left.+ \int_0^1 (\Delta(1)\sigma - \Delta(\lambda))\aleph'\left(\frac{n+\lambda}{n+1}\tau_1 + \frac{1-\lambda}{n+1}\tau_2\right)d\lambda\right], \qquad (10)
\end{aligned}$$

where $\Delta : [0,1] \to \mathbb{R}$ is defined as

$$\Delta(\lambda) = \int_0^\lambda \frac{\varphi\left(\left(\frac{\tau_2-\tau_1}{n+1}\right)\mu\right)}{\mu}d\mu.$$

Proof. Let

$$Y_1 = \int_0^1 (\Delta(\lambda)-\Delta(1)\rho)\aleph'\left(\frac{1-\lambda}{n+1}\tau_1 + \frac{n+\lambda}{n+1}\tau_2\right)d\lambda.$$

By applying integration by parts, we obtain

$$
\begin{aligned}
&= \frac{n+1}{\tau_2-\tau_1}(\Delta(\lambda)-\Delta(1)\rho)\aleph\left(\frac{1-\lambda}{n+1}\tau_1+\frac{n+\lambda}{n+1}\tau_2\right)\Big|_0^1 \\
&- \frac{n+1}{\tau_2-\tau_1}\int_0^1 \frac{\varphi\left(\left(\frac{\tau_2-\tau_1}{n+1}\right)\lambda\right)}{\lambda}\aleph\left(\frac{1-\lambda}{n+1}\tau_1+\frac{n+\lambda}{n+1}\tau_2\right)d\lambda \\
&= \frac{n+1}{\tau_2-\tau_1}\left[\Delta(1)\left((1-\rho)\aleph(\tau_2)+\rho\aleph\left(\frac{\tau_1+n\tau_2}{n+1}\right)\right)\right. \\
&\left. - \int_{\frac{\tau_1+n\tau_2}{n+1}}^{\tau_2}\aleph(\mu)\varphi\left(\mu-\frac{\tau_1+n\tau_2}{n+1}\right)\frac{1}{\mu-\frac{\tau_1+n\tau_2}{n+1}}d\mu\right] \\
&= \frac{n+1}{\tau_2-\tau_1}\left[\Delta(1)\left((1-\rho)\aleph(\tau_2)+\rho\aleph\left(\frac{\tau_1+n\tau_2}{n+1}\right)\right)-\left({}_{\tau_2^-}I_\varphi\aleph\left(\frac{\tau_1+n\tau_2}{n+1}\right)\right)\right].
\end{aligned} \tag{11}
$$

and

$$
\begin{aligned}
Y_2 &= \int_0^1 (\Delta(1)\sigma-\Delta(\lambda))\aleph'\left(\frac{n+\lambda}{n+1}\tau_1+\frac{1-\lambda}{n+1}\tau_2\right)d\lambda \\
&= -\frac{n+1}{\tau_2-\tau_1}(\Delta(1)\sigma-\Delta(\lambda))\aleph\left(\frac{n+\lambda}{n+1}\tau_1+\frac{1-\lambda}{n+1}\tau_2\right)\Big|_0^1 \\
&+ \frac{n+1}{\tau_2-\tau_1}\int_0^1 \frac{\varphi\left(\left(\frac{\tau_2-\tau_1}{n+1}\right)\lambda\right)}{\lambda}\aleph\left(\frac{n+\lambda}{n+1}\tau_1+\frac{1-\lambda}{n+1}\tau_2\right)d\lambda \\
&= \frac{n+1}{\tau_2-\tau_1}\left[\Delta(1)\left((1-\sigma)\aleph(\tau_1)+\sigma\aleph\left(\frac{n\tau_1+\tau_2}{n+1}\right)\right)\right. \\
&\left. - \int_{\tau_1}^{\frac{n\tau_1+\tau_2}{n+1}}\aleph(\mu)\varphi\left(\frac{n\tau_1+\tau_2}{n+1}-\mu\right)\frac{1}{\frac{n\tau_1+\tau_2}{n+1}-\mu}d\mu\right] \\
&= \frac{n+1}{\tau_2-\tau_1}\left[\Delta(1)\left((1-\sigma)\aleph(\tau_1)+\sigma\aleph\left(\frac{n\tau_1+\tau_2}{n+1}\right)\right)-\left({}_{\tau_1^+}I_\varphi\aleph\left(\frac{n\tau_1+\tau_2}{n+1}\right)\right)\right].
\end{aligned} \tag{12}
$$

Now, by adding (11) and (12) and multiplying by $\frac{\tau_2-\tau_1}{n+1}\frac{1}{\Delta(1)}$, we obtain

$$
\begin{aligned}
=&(1-\sigma)\aleph(\tau_1)+(1-\rho)\aleph(\tau_2)+\sigma\aleph\left(\frac{n\tau_1+\tau_2}{n+1}\right)+\rho\aleph\left(\frac{\tau_1+n\tau_2}{n+1}\right) \\
&-\frac{1}{\Delta(1)}\left[{}_{\tau_1^+}I_\varphi\aleph\left(\frac{n\tau_1+\tau_2}{n+1}\right)+{}_{\tau_2^-}I_\varphi\aleph\left(\frac{\tau_1+n\tau_2}{n+1}\right)\right].
\end{aligned}
$$

The proof is completed. □

Remark 1. *From Lemma 1:*

1. *By setting $\rho=\sigma=\frac{n+1}{n+2}$, the resulting identity is identical to Lemma 3 in [27] for $n=1$*
2. *By setting $\rho=\sigma=0$, the resulting identity is identical to Corollary 5.2 in [28] for $n=1$.*

Corollary 1. *By setting $\varphi(\lambda) = \lambda$ in Lemma 1, the following equality for Riemann integrals is obtained:*

$$\frac{1}{n+1}\left[(1-\sigma)\aleph(\tau_1) + (1-\rho)\aleph(\tau_2) + \sigma\aleph\left(\frac{n\tau_1+\tau_2}{n+1}\right) + \rho\aleph\left(\frac{\tau_1+n\tau_2}{n+1}\right)\right] - \frac{1}{\tau_2-\tau_1}\int_{\tau_1}^{\tau_2}\aleph(\lambda)d\lambda$$
$$= \frac{\tau_2-\tau_1}{(n+1)^2}\left[\int_0^1 (\lambda-\rho)\aleph'\left(\frac{1-\lambda}{n+1}\tau_1 + \frac{n+\lambda}{n+1}\tau_2\right)d\lambda\right.$$
$$\left.+\int_0^1 (\sigma-\lambda)\aleph'\left(\frac{n+\lambda}{n+1}\tau_1 + \frac{1-\lambda}{n+1}\tau_2\right)d\lambda\right].$$

Remark 2. *From Corollary 1:*

1. *By setting $\rho = \sigma = \frac{n+1}{n+2}$, the resulting identity is identical to Lemma 1 in [10] for $n = 1$.*
2. *By setting $\rho = \sigma = 0$, the resulting identity is identical to Corollary 5.2 in [28] for $n = 1$.*

Corollary 2. *By setting $\varphi(\lambda) = \frac{\lambda^\alpha}{\Gamma(\alpha)}, \alpha > 0$ in Lemma 1, the following equality is obtained for Riemann–Liouville fractional integrals:*

$$(1-\sigma)\aleph(\tau_1) + (1-\rho)\aleph(\tau_2) + \sigma\aleph\left(\frac{n\tau_1+\tau_2}{n+1}\right) + \rho\aleph\left(\frac{\tau_1+n\tau_2}{n+1}\right)$$
$$-\frac{(n+1)^\alpha\Gamma(\alpha+1)}{(\tau_2-\tau_1)^\alpha}\left[I^\alpha_{\tau_1^+}\aleph\left(\frac{n\tau_1+\tau_2}{n+1}\right) + I^\alpha_{\tau_2^-}\aleph\left(\frac{\tau_1+n\tau_2}{n+1}\right)\right]$$
$$= \frac{\tau_2-\tau_1}{n+1}\left[\int_0^1 (\lambda^\alpha-\rho)\aleph'\left(\frac{1-\lambda}{n+1}\tau_1 + \frac{n+\lambda}{n+1}\tau_2\right)d\lambda\right.$$
$$\left.+\int_0^1 (\sigma-\lambda^\alpha)\aleph'\left(\frac{n+\lambda}{n+1}\tau_1 + \frac{1-\lambda}{n+1}\tau_2\right)d\lambda\right].$$

Remark 3. *From Corollary 2:*

1. *By setting $\rho = \sigma = \frac{n+1}{n+2}$, the resulting identity is identical to Lemma 2.1 in [29] for $n = 1$.*
2. *By setting $\rho = \sigma = 0$, the resulting identity is identical to Corollary 5.3 in [28] for $n = 1$.*

Corollary 3. *By setting $\varphi(\lambda) = \frac{\lambda^{\frac{\alpha}{k}}}{k\Gamma_k(\alpha)}$ for $\alpha, k > 0$ in Lemma 1, the following equality is obtained for k-Riemann–Liouville fractional integrals:*

$$(1-\sigma)\aleph(\tau_1) + (1-\rho)\aleph(\tau_2) + \sigma\aleph\left(\frac{n\tau_1+\tau_2}{n+1}\right) + \rho\aleph\left(\frac{\tau_1+n\tau_2}{n+1}\right)$$
$$-\frac{(n+1)^{\frac{\alpha}{k}}\Gamma_k(\alpha+k)}{(\tau_2-\tau_1)^{\frac{\alpha}{k}}}\left[I^\alpha_{\tau_1^+,k}\aleph\left(\frac{n\tau_1+\tau_2}{n+1}\right) + I^\alpha_{\tau_2^-,k}\aleph\left(\frac{\tau_1+n\tau_2}{n+1}\right)\right]$$
$$= \frac{\tau_2-\tau_1}{n+1}\left[\int_0^1 \left(\lambda^{\frac{\alpha}{k}}-\rho\right)\aleph'\left(\frac{1-\lambda}{n+1}\tau_1 + \frac{n+\lambda}{n+1}\tau_2\right)d\lambda\right.$$
$$\left.+\int_0^1 \left(\sigma-\lambda^{\frac{\alpha}{k}}\right)\aleph'\left(\frac{n+\lambda}{n+1}\tau_1 + \frac{1-\lambda}{n+1}\tau_2\right)d\lambda\right].$$

Remark 4. *From Corollary 3:*

1. *By setting $\rho = \sigma = \frac{n+1}{n+2}$, the resulting identity is identical to Corollary 1 in [27] for $n = 1$.*
2. *By setting $\rho = \sigma = 0$, the resulting identity is identical to Corollary 5.4 in [28] for $n = 1$.*

3. Some Parameterized Inequalities Involving Generalized Fractional Integrals

In this section, we establish some parameterized inequalities involving generalized fractional integrals for differentiable $\mathfrak{s}$-convex mappings of the second kind.

Theorem 1. *Let all the conditions of Lemma 1 be satisfied. If $|\aleph'|$ is an $\mathfrak{s}$-convex mapping on $[\tau_1, \tau_2]$ for $\mathfrak{s} \in (0,1]$ and $n \in \mathbb{N}$, then:*

$$\begin{aligned}
&\left|(1-\sigma)\aleph(\tau_1) + (1-\rho)\aleph(\tau_2) + \sigma\aleph\left(\frac{n\tau_1+\tau_2}{n+1}\right) + \rho\aleph\left(\frac{\tau_1+n\tau_2}{n+1}\right)\right. \\
&\left. - \frac{1}{\Delta(1)}\left[{}_{\tau_1^+}I_\varphi\aleph\left(\frac{n\tau_1+\tau_2}{n+1}\right) + {}_{\tau_2^-}I_\varphi\aleph\left(\frac{\tau_1+n\tau_2}{n+1}\right)\right]\right| \\
&\leq \frac{\tau_2-\tau_1}{(n+1)^{\mathfrak{s}+1}}\frac{1}{\Delta(1)}\left[|\aleph'(\tau_1)|\left(\Pi_1^\varphi(\rho,\mathfrak{s}) + \Pi_2^\varphi(\sigma,\mathfrak{s},n)\right) + |\aleph'(\tau_2)|\left(\Pi_2^\varphi(\rho,\mathfrak{s},n) + \Pi_1^\varphi(\sigma,\mathfrak{s})\right)\right], \quad (13)
\end{aligned}$$

where

$$\Pi_1^\varphi(\delta,\mathfrak{s}) = \int_0^1 (1-\lambda)^{\mathfrak{s}}|\Delta(\lambda) - \Delta(1)\delta|d\lambda$$

and

$$\Pi_2^\varphi(\delta,\mathfrak{s},n) = \int_0^1 (n+\lambda)^{\mathfrak{s}}|\Delta(\lambda) - \Delta(1)\delta|d\lambda.$$

Proof. By taking the modulus in Lemma 1 and applying the $\mathfrak{s}$-convexity of $|\aleph'|$, we obtain

$$\begin{aligned}
&\left|(1-\sigma)\aleph(\tau_1) + (1-\rho)\aleph(\tau_2) + \sigma\aleph\left(\frac{n\tau_1+\tau_2}{n+1}\right) + \rho\aleph\left(\frac{\tau_1+n\tau_2}{n+1}\right)\right. \\
&\left. - \frac{1}{\Delta(1)}\left[{}_{\tau_1^+}I_\varphi\aleph\left(\frac{n\tau_1+\tau_2}{n+1}\right) + {}_{\tau_2^-}I_\varphi\aleph\left(\frac{\tau_1+n\tau_2}{n+1}\right)\right]\right| \\
&= \left|\frac{\tau_2-\tau_1}{n+1}\frac{1}{\Delta(1)}\left[\int_0^1 (\Delta(\lambda) - \Delta(1)\rho)\aleph'\left(\frac{1-\lambda}{n+1}\tau_1 + \frac{n+\lambda}{n+1}\tau_2\right)d\lambda\right.\right. \\
&\left.\left. + \int_0^1 (\Delta(1)\sigma - \Delta(\lambda))\aleph'\left(\frac{n+\lambda}{n+1}\tau_1 + \frac{1-\lambda}{n+1}\tau_2\right)d\lambda\right]\right| \\
&\leq \frac{\tau_2-\tau_1}{n+1}\frac{1}{\Delta(1)}\left[\int_0^1 |\Delta(\lambda) - \Delta(1)\rho|\left|\aleph'\left(\frac{1-\lambda}{n+1}\tau_1 + \frac{n+\lambda}{n+1}\tau_2\right)\right|d\lambda\right. \\
&\left. + \int_0^1 |\Delta(1)\sigma - \Delta(\lambda)|\left|\aleph'\left(\frac{n+\lambda}{n+1}\tau_1 + \frac{1-\lambda}{n+1}\tau_2\right)\right|d\lambda\right] \\
&\leq \frac{\tau_2-\tau_1}{n+1}\frac{1}{\Delta(1)}\left[\int_0^1 |\Delta(\lambda) - \Delta(1)\rho|\left[\left(\frac{1-\lambda}{n+1}\right)^{\mathfrak{s}}|\aleph'(\tau_1)| + \left(\frac{n+\lambda}{n+1}\right)^{\mathfrak{s}}|\aleph'(\tau_2)|\right]d\lambda\right. \\
&\left. + \int_0^1 |\Delta(1)\sigma - \Delta(\lambda)|\left[\left(\frac{n+\lambda}{n+1}\right)^{\mathfrak{s}}|\aleph'(\tau_1)| + \left(\frac{1-\lambda}{n+1}\right)^{\mathfrak{s}}|\aleph'(\tau_2)|\right]d\lambda\right] \\
&\leq \frac{\tau_2-\tau_1}{(n+1)^{\mathfrak{s}+1}}\frac{1}{\Delta(1)}\left[|\aleph'(\tau_1)|\left(\int_0^1 |\Delta(\lambda) - \Delta(1)\rho|(1-\lambda)^{\mathfrak{s}}d\lambda + \int_0^1 |\Delta(1)\sigma - \Delta(\lambda)|(n+\lambda)^{\mathfrak{s}}d\lambda\right)\right. \\
&\left. + |\aleph'(\tau_2)|\left(\int_0^1 |\Delta(\lambda) - \Delta(1)\rho|(n+\lambda)^{\mathfrak{s}}d\lambda + \int_0^1 |\Delta(1)\sigma - \Delta(\lambda)|(1-\lambda)^{\mathfrak{s}}d\lambda\right)\right] \\
&\leq \frac{\tau_2-\tau_1}{(n+1)^{\mathfrak{s}+1}}\frac{1}{\Delta(1)}\left[|\aleph'(\tau_1)|\left(\Pi_1^\varphi(\rho,\mathfrak{s}) + \Pi_2^\varphi(\sigma,\mathfrak{s},n)\right) + |\aleph'(\tau_2)|\left(\Pi_2^\varphi(\rho,\mathfrak{s},n) + \Pi_1^\varphi(\sigma,\mathfrak{s})\right)\right].
\end{aligned}$$

The proof is completed. □

Theorem 2. *Let all the conditions of Lemma 1 be satisfied. If* $|\aleph'|^q$ *is an* $\mathfrak{s}$*-convex mapping on* $[\tau_1, \tau_2]$ *for* $\mathfrak{s} \in (0,1]$*,* $n \in \mathbb{N}$ *and* $q > 1$*, then:*

$$\begin{aligned}
&\Bigg|(1-\sigma)\aleph(\tau_1) + (1-\rho)\aleph(\tau_2) + \sigma\aleph\left(\frac{n\tau_1+\tau_2}{n+1}\right) + \rho\aleph\left(\frac{\tau_1+n\tau_2}{n+1}\right) \\
&-\frac{1}{\Delta(1)}\left[{}_{\tau_1^+}I_\varphi\aleph\left(\frac{n\tau_1+\tau_2}{n+1}\right) + {}_{\tau_2^-}I_\varphi\aleph\left(\frac{\tau_1+n\tau_2}{n+1}\right)\right]\Bigg| \\
&\leq \frac{\tau_2-\tau_1}{n+1}\frac{1}{\Delta(1)}\left[\left(\int_0^1 |\Delta(\lambda)-\Delta(1)\rho|^{\frac{q}{q-1}}d\lambda\right)^{\frac{q-1}{q}}\right. \\
&\left(\frac{1}{(\mathfrak{s}+1)(n+1)^{\mathfrak{s}}}|\aleph'(\tau_1)|^q + \frac{(n+1)^{\mathfrak{s}+1}-n^{\mathfrak{s}+1}}{(\mathfrak{s}+1)(n+1)^{\mathfrak{s}}}|\aleph'(\tau_2)|^q\right)^{\frac{1}{q}} \\
&+\left(\int_0^1 |\Delta(1)\sigma-\Delta(\lambda)|^{\frac{q}{q-1}}d\lambda\right)^{\frac{q-1}{q}} \\
&\left.\left(\frac{(n+1)^{\mathfrak{s}+1}-n^{\mathfrak{s}+1}}{(\mathfrak{s}+1)(n+1)^{\mathfrak{s}}}|\aleph'(\tau_1)|^q + \frac{1}{(\mathfrak{s}+1)(n+1)^{\mathfrak{s}}}|\aleph'(\tau_2)|^q\right)^{\frac{1}{q}}\right].
\end{aligned} \tag{14}$$

Proof. By using Lemma 1 and the Hölder integral inequality, we have

$$\begin{aligned}
&\Bigg|(1-\sigma)\aleph(\tau_1) + (1-\rho)\aleph(\tau_2) + \sigma\aleph\left(\frac{n\tau_1+\tau_2}{n+1}\right) + \rho\aleph\left(\frac{\tau_1+n\tau_2}{n+1}\right) \\
&-\frac{1}{\Delta(1)}\left[{}_{\tau_1^+}I_\varphi\aleph\left(\frac{n\tau_1+\tau_2}{n+1}\right) + {}_{\tau_2^-}I_\varphi\aleph\left(\frac{\tau_1+n\tau_2}{n+1}\right)\right]\Bigg| \\
&= \Bigg|\frac{\tau_2-\tau_1}{n+1}\frac{1}{\Delta(1)}\left[\int_0^1 (\Delta(\lambda)-\Delta(1)\rho)\aleph'\left(\frac{1-\lambda}{n+1}\tau_1 + \frac{n+\lambda}{n+1}\tau_2\right)d\lambda\right. \\
&\left.+\int_0^1 (\Delta(1)\sigma-\Delta(\lambda))\aleph'\left(\frac{n+\lambda}{n+1}\tau_1 + \frac{1-\lambda}{n+1}\tau_2\right)d\lambda\right]\Bigg| \\
&\leq \frac{\tau_2-\tau_1}{n+1}\frac{1}{\Delta(1)}\left[\left(\int_0^1 |\Delta(\lambda)-\Delta(1)\rho|^{\frac{q}{q-1}}d\lambda\right)^{\frac{q-1}{q}}\left(\int_0^1 \left|\aleph'\left(\frac{1-\lambda}{n+1}\tau_1 + \frac{n+\lambda}{n+1}\tau_2\right)\right|^q d\lambda\right)^{\frac{1}{q}}\right. \\
&\left.+\left(\int_0^1 |\Delta(1)\sigma-\Delta(\lambda)|^{\frac{q}{q-1}}d\lambda\right)^{\frac{q-1}{q}}\left(\int_0^1 \left|\aleph'\left(\frac{n+\lambda}{n+1}\tau_1 + \frac{1-\lambda}{n+1}\tau_2\right)\right|^q d\lambda\right)^{\frac{1}{q}}\right].
\end{aligned}$$

Since $|\aleph'|^q$ is $\mathfrak{s}$-convex, we obtain

$$\leq \frac{\tau_2-\tau_1}{n+1}\frac{1}{\Delta(1)}\left[\left(\int_0^1 |\Delta(\lambda)-\Delta(1)\rho|^{\frac{q}{q-1}}d\lambda\right)^{\frac{q-1}{q}}\right.$$

$$\left(\int_0^1 \left[\left(\frac{1-\lambda}{n+1}\right)^{\mathfrak{s}}|\aleph'(\tau_1)|^q+\left(\frac{n+\lambda}{n+1}\right)^{\mathfrak{s}}|\aleph'(\tau_2)|^q\right]d\lambda\right)^{\frac{1}{q}}$$

$$+\left(\int_0^1 |\Delta(1)\sigma-\Delta(\lambda)|^{\frac{q}{q-1}}d\lambda\right)^{\frac{q-1}{q}}$$

$$\left.\left(\int_0^1 \left[\left(\frac{n+\lambda}{n+1}\right)^{\mathfrak{s}}|\aleph'(\tau_1)|^q+\left(\frac{1-\lambda}{n+1}\right)^{\mathfrak{s}}|\aleph'(\tau_2)|^q\right]d\lambda\right)^{\frac{1}{q}}\right]$$

$$\leq \frac{\tau_2-\tau_1}{n+1}\frac{1}{\Delta(1)}\left[\left(\int_0^1 |\Delta(\lambda)-\Delta(1)\rho|^{\frac{q}{q-1}}d\lambda\right)^{\frac{q-1}{q}}\right.$$

$$\left(\frac{1}{(\mathfrak{s}+1)(n+1)^{\mathfrak{s}}}|\aleph'(\tau_1)|^q+\frac{(n+1)^{\mathfrak{s}+1}-n^{\mathfrak{s}+1}}{(\mathfrak{s}+1)(n+1)^{\mathfrak{s}}}|\aleph'(\tau_2)|^q\right)^{\frac{1}{q}}$$

$$+\left(\int_0^1 |\Delta(1)\sigma-\Delta(\lambda)|^{\frac{q}{q-1}}d\lambda\right)^{\frac{q-1}{q}}$$

$$\left.\left(\frac{(n+1)^{\mathfrak{s}+1}-n^{\mathfrak{s}+1}}{(\mathfrak{s}+1)(n+1)^{\mathfrak{s}}}|\aleph'(\tau_1)|^q+\frac{1}{(\mathfrak{s}+1)(n+1)^{\mathfrak{s}}}|\aleph'(\tau_2)|^q\right)^{\frac{1}{q}}\right].$$

The proof is completed. □

Theorem 3. *Let all the conditions of Lemma 1 be satisfied. If $|\aleph'|^q$ is an $\mathfrak{s}$-convex mapping on $[\tau_1,\tau_2]$ for $\mathfrak{s}\in(0,1]$, $n\in\mathbb{N}$ and $q>1$, then:*

$$\left|(1-\sigma)\aleph(\tau_1)+(1-\rho)\aleph(\tau_2)+\sigma\aleph\left(\frac{n\tau_1+\tau_2}{n+1}\right)+\rho\aleph\left(\frac{\tau_1+n\tau_2}{n+1}\right)\right.$$
$$\left.-\frac{1}{\Delta(1)}\left[{}_{\tau_1^+}I_{\varphi}\aleph\left(\frac{n\tau_1+\tau_2}{n+1}\right)+{}_{\tau_2^-}I_{\varphi}\aleph\left(\frac{\tau_1+n\tau_2}{n+1}\right)\right]\right|$$
$$\leq \frac{\tau_2-\tau_1}{n+1}\frac{1}{\Delta(1)}\left[\left(\int_0^1|\Delta(\lambda)-\Delta(1)\rho|d\lambda\right)^{1-\frac{1}{q}}\left(\frac{|\aleph'(\tau_1)|^q\Pi_1^{\varphi}(\rho,\mathfrak{s})+|\aleph'(\tau_2)|^q\Pi_2^{\varphi}(\rho,\mathfrak{s},n)}{(n+1)^{\mathfrak{s}}}\right)^{\frac{1}{q}}\right.$$
$$\left.+\left(\int_0^1|\Delta(1)\sigma-\Delta(\lambda)|d\lambda\right)^{1-\frac{1}{q}}\left(\frac{|\aleph'(\tau_1)|^q\Pi_2^{\varphi}(\sigma,\mathfrak{s},n)+|\aleph'(\tau_2)|^q\Pi_1^{\varphi}(\sigma,\mathfrak{s})}{(n+1)^{\mathfrak{s}}}\right)^{\frac{1}{q}}\right], \quad (15)$$

where $\Pi_1^{\varphi}(\delta,\mathfrak{s})$ and $\Pi_2^{\varphi}(\delta,\mathfrak{s},n)$ are defined in Theorem 1.

Proof. By using Lemma 1 and the power mean integral inequality, we deduce that

$$\begin{aligned}
&\Bigg|(1-\sigma)\aleph(\tau_1)+(1-\rho)\aleph(\tau_2)+\sigma\aleph\left(\frac{n\tau_1+\tau_2}{n+1}\right)+\rho\aleph\left(\frac{\tau_1+n\tau_2}{n+1}\right)\\
&-\frac{1}{\Delta(1)}\left[{}_{\tau_1^+}I_\varphi\aleph\left(\frac{n\tau_1+\tau_2}{n+1}\right)+{}_{\tau_2^-}I_\varphi\aleph\left(\frac{\tau_1+n\tau_2}{n+1}\right)\right]\Bigg|\\
&=\Bigg|\frac{\tau_2-\tau_1}{n+1}\frac{1}{\Delta(1)}\left[\int_0^1(\Delta(\lambda)-\Delta(1)\rho)\aleph'\left(\frac{1-\lambda}{n+1}\tau_1+\frac{n+\lambda}{n+1}\tau_2\right)d\lambda\right.\\
&\left.+\int_0^1(\Delta(1)\sigma-\Delta(\lambda))\aleph'\left(\frac{n+\lambda}{n+1}\tau_1+\frac{1-\lambda}{n+1}\tau_2\right)d\lambda\right]\Bigg|\\
&\leq\frac{\tau_2-\tau_1}{n+1}\frac{1}{\Delta(1)}\left[\left(\int_0^1|\Delta(\lambda)-\Delta(1)\rho|d\lambda\right)^{1-\frac{1}{q}}\left(\int_0^1|\Delta(\lambda)-\Delta(1)\rho|\left|\aleph'\left(\frac{1-\lambda}{n+1}\tau_1+\frac{n+\lambda}{n+1}\tau_2\right)\right|^q d\lambda\right)^{\frac{1}{q}}\right.\\
&\left.+\left(\int_0^1|\Delta(1)\sigma-\Delta(\lambda)|d\lambda\right)^{1-\frac{1}{q}}\left(\int_0^1|\Delta(1)\sigma-\Delta(\lambda)|\left|\aleph'\left(\frac{n+\lambda}{n+1}\tau_1+\frac{1-\lambda}{n+1}\tau_2\right)\right|^q d\lambda\right)^{\frac{1}{q}}\right].
\end{aligned}$$

Since $|\aleph'|^q$ is $\mathfrak{s}$-convex, we obtain

$$\begin{aligned}
&\leq\frac{\tau_2-\tau_1}{n+1}\frac{1}{\Delta(1)}\left[\left(\int_0^1|\Delta(\lambda)-\Delta(1)\rho|d\lambda\right)^{1-\frac{1}{q}}\right.\\
&\left(|\aleph'(\tau_1)|^q\int_0^1|\Delta(\lambda)-\Delta(1)\rho|\left(\frac{1-\lambda}{n+1}\right)^{\mathfrak{s}}d\lambda+|\aleph'(\tau_2)|^q\int_0^1|\Delta(\lambda)-\Delta(1)\rho|\left(\frac{n+\lambda}{n+1}\right)^{\mathfrak{s}}d\lambda\right)^{\frac{1}{q}}\\
&+\left(\int_0^1|\Delta(1)\sigma-\Delta(\lambda)|d\lambda\right)^{1-\frac{1}{q}}\\
&\left.\left(|\aleph'(\tau_1)|^q\int_0^1|\Delta(1)\sigma-\Delta(\lambda)|\left(\frac{n+\lambda}{n+1}\right)^{\mathfrak{s}}d\lambda+|\aleph'(\tau_2)|^q\int_0^1|\Delta(1)\sigma-\Delta(\lambda)|\left(\frac{1-\lambda}{n+1}\right)^{\mathfrak{s}}d\lambda\right)^{\frac{1}{q}}\right]\\
&\leq\frac{\tau_2-\tau_1}{n+1}\frac{1}{\Delta(1)}\left[\left(\int_0^1|\Delta(\lambda)-\Delta(1)\rho|d\lambda\right)^{1-\frac{1}{q}}\left(\frac{|\aleph'(\tau_1)|^q\Pi_1^\varphi(\rho,\mathfrak{s})+|\aleph'(\tau_2)|^q\Pi_2^\varphi(\rho,\mathfrak{s},n)}{(n+1)^{\mathfrak{s}}}\right)^{\frac{1}{q}}\right.\\
&\left.+\left(\int_0^1|\Delta(1)\sigma-\Delta(\lambda)|d\lambda\right)^{1-\frac{1}{q}}\left(\frac{|\aleph'(\tau_1)|^q\Pi_2^\varphi(\sigma,\mathfrak{s},n)+|\aleph'(\tau_2)|^q\Pi_1^\varphi(\sigma,\mathfrak{s})}{(n+1)^{\mathfrak{s}}}\right)^{\frac{1}{q}}\right].
\end{aligned}$$

The proof is completed. □

Remark 5. *From Theorems 1, 2, and 3:*

1. *By setting $\varphi(\lambda)=\lambda$, the inequalities for Riemann integrals are obtained.*
2. *By setting $\varphi(\lambda)=\frac{\lambda^\alpha}{\Gamma(\alpha)},\alpha>0$, the inequalities for Riemann–Liouville fractional integrals are obtained.*
3. *By setting $\varphi(\lambda)=\frac{\lambda^{\frac{\alpha}{k}}}{k\Gamma_k(\alpha)},\alpha,k>0$, the inequalities for k-Riemann–Liouville fractional integrals are obtained.*

4. Examples and Graphical Analysis

In this section, we validate the main results of Section 3 through various simulations and numerical examples. It is important to note that by specifying the values for $\varphi(\lambda)$ in Theorems 1–3, we recover several new and novel fractional versions of inequalities, including those involving Riemann integrals, Riemann–Liouville fractional integrals, and k-Riemann–Liouville fractional integrals. Further, by choosing several values for the parameters ρ and σ, we provide graphical visualizations of Simpson's, midpoint, and trapezoidal-type inequalities in Figures 1–3. In addition, from these simulations, one can visualize the comparison between error bounds involving different fractional operators and generalized convexity. The following assumptions are utilized in all the graphs:

$$\aleph(\lambda) = \lambda^{\mathfrak{s}},$$

where $\mathfrak{s} \in (0,1]$, $[\tau_1, \tau_2] = [1,3]$, $n = 1$, $\alpha \in (0,1]$, $k = 2$, and $q = 2$

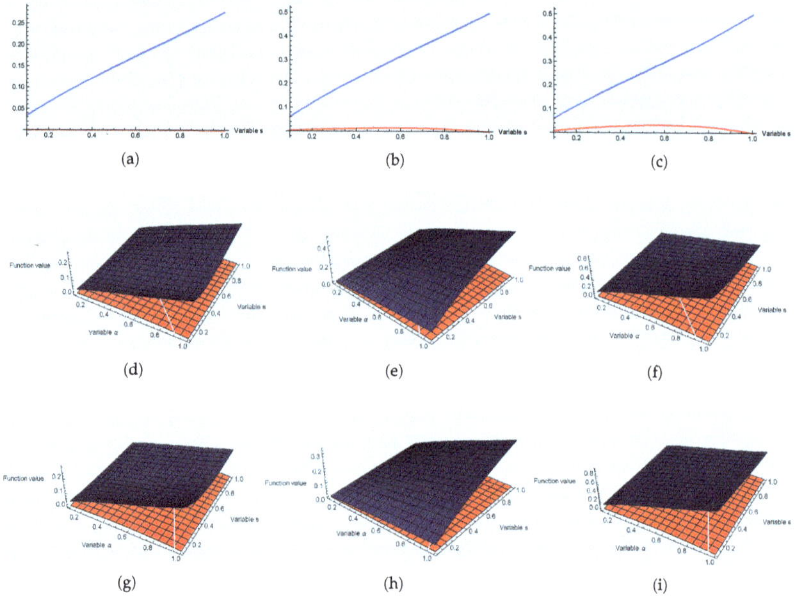

Figure 1. Visual analysis of left (red) and right (blue) sides of (**a**,**d**,**g**) Simpson's inequalities, (**b**,**e**,**h**) midpoint inequalities, (**c**,**f**,**i**) trapezoidal-type inequalities. In figures (**a**,**d**,**g**), the Simpson's inequalities are derived by setting $\varphi(\lambda) = \lambda$, $\varphi(\lambda) = \frac{\lambda^{\alpha}}{\Gamma(\alpha)}, \alpha > 0$ and $\varphi(\lambda) = \frac{\lambda^{\frac{\alpha}{k}}}{k\Gamma_k(\alpha)}, \alpha, k > 0$, respectively, for Remark 5(1) for the choices of the parameters $\sigma = \rho = \frac{2}{3}$. Similar cases hold for the midpoint inequalities in figures (**b**,**e**,**h**) and trapezoidal-type inequalities in figures (**c**,**f**,**i**) for the parametric values $\sigma = \rho = 1$ and $\sigma = \rho = 0$, respectively.

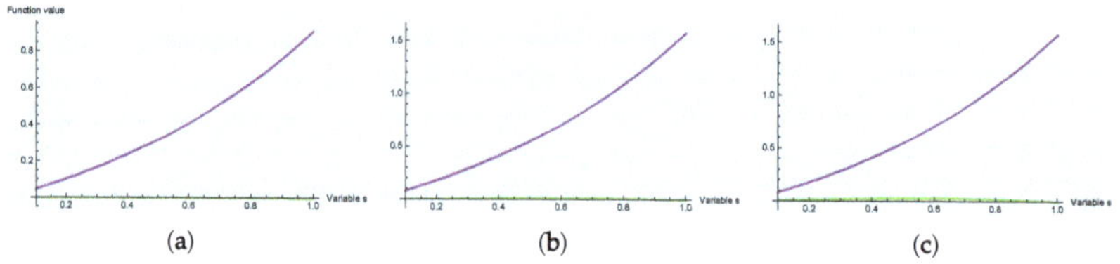

Figure 2. *Cont.*

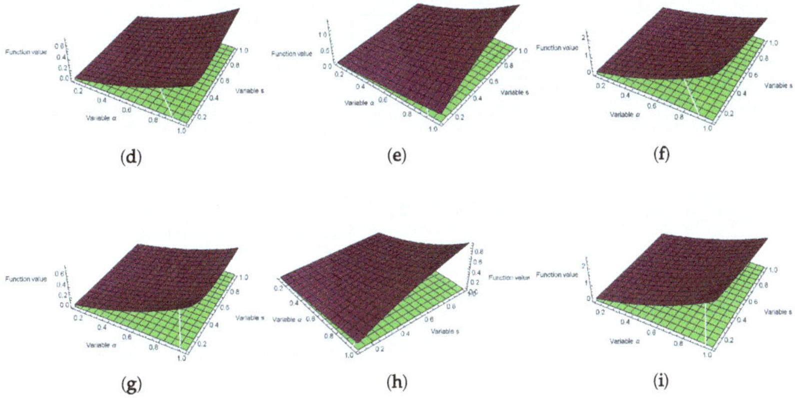

Figure 2. Visual analysis of left (green) and right (purple) sides of (**a**,**d**,**g**) Simpson's inequalities, (**b**,**e**,**h**) midpoint inequalities, (**c**,**f**,**i**) trapezoidal-type inequalities. In figures (**a**,**d**,**g**), the Simpson's inequalities are derived by setting $\varphi(\lambda) = \lambda$, $\varphi(\lambda) = \frac{\lambda^{\alpha}}{\Gamma(\alpha)}, \alpha > 0$ and $\varphi(\lambda) = \frac{\lambda^{\frac{\alpha}{k}}}{k\Gamma_k(\alpha)}, \alpha, k > 0$, respectively, for Remark 5(2) for the choices of the parameters $\sigma = \rho = \frac{2}{3}$. Similar cases hold for the midpoint inequalities in figures (**b**,**e**,**h**) and trapezoidal-type inequalities in figures (**c**,**f**,**i**) for the parametric values $\sigma = \rho = 1$ and $\sigma = \rho = 0$, respectively.

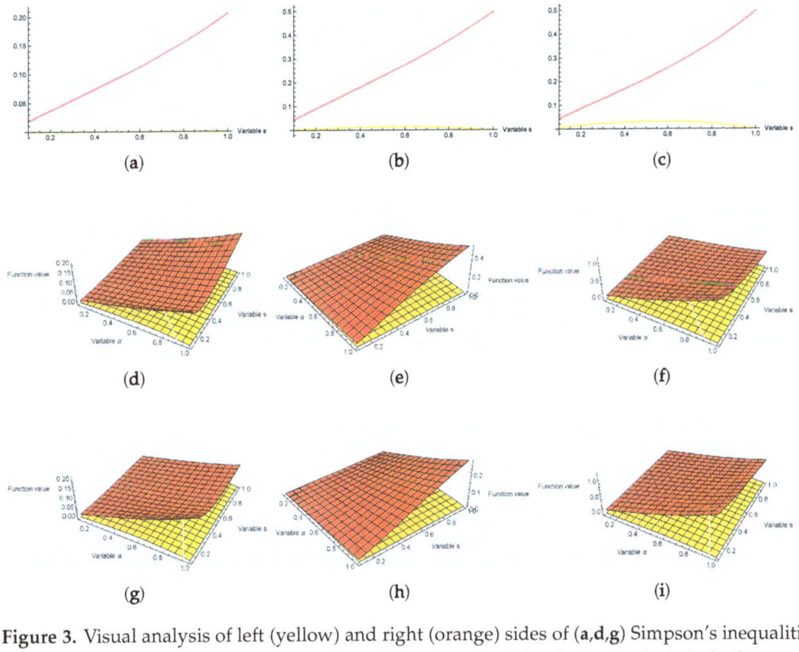

Figure 3. Visual analysis of left (yellow) and right (orange) sides of (**a**,**d**,**g**) Simpson's inequalities, (**b**,**e**,**h**) midpoint inequalities, (**c**,**f**,**i**) trapezoidal-type inequalities. In figures (**a**,**d**,**g**), the Simpson's inequalities are derived by setting $\varphi(\lambda) = \lambda$, $\varphi(\lambda) = \frac{\lambda^{\alpha}}{\Gamma(\alpha)}, \alpha > 0$ and $\varphi(\lambda) = \frac{\lambda^{\frac{\alpha}{k}}}{k\Gamma_k(\alpha)}, \alpha, k > 0$, respectively, for Remark 5(3) for the choices of the parameters $\sigma = \rho = \frac{2}{3}$. Similar cases hold for the midpoint inequalities in figures (**b**,**e**,**h**) and trapezoidal-type inequalities in figures (**c**,**f**,**i**) for the parametric values $\sigma = \rho = 1$ and $\sigma = \rho = 0$, respectively.

5. Applications

In this section, some interesting applications to special means, quadrature formulas, and in numerical analysis for solving non-linear equations are discussed, which highlight the significance and validation of our main findings.

5.1. Special Means

Before we present applications to special means, let us recall some classical concepts. For further details, see [30].

Let $\zeta : \mathcal{I} \to \mathcal{I}_1 \subseteq [0, \infty)$ be a non-negative convex mapping on $\mathcal{I}$. Then, $\zeta^{\mathfrak{s}}$ is $\mathfrak{s}$-convex on $\mathcal{I}, 0 < \mathfrak{s} < 1$.

For positive real numbers $\tau_1, \tau_2, \tau_1 \neq \tau_2$, the following means are well known in the literature:

1. The arithmetic mean

$$A(\tau_1, \tau_2) = \frac{\tau_1 + \tau_2}{2}, \quad \tau_1, \tau_2 \in \mathbb{R}.$$

2. The harmonic mean

$$H(\tau_1, \tau_2) = \frac{2\tau_1\tau_2}{\tau_1 + \tau_2}, \quad \tau_1, \tau_2 \in \mathbb{R} \setminus \{0\}.$$

3. The generalized log mean

$$L_{\mathfrak{m}}(\tau_1, \tau_2) = \left(\frac{{\tau_2}^{\mathfrak{m}+1} - {\tau_1}^{\mathfrak{m}+1}}{(\mathfrak{m}+1)(\tau_2 - \tau_1)}\right)^{\frac{1}{\mathfrak{m}}}, \quad \mathfrak{m} \in \mathbb{R} \setminus \{-1, 0\}, \quad \tau_1, \tau_2 > 0.$$

Now, we will derive some inequalities for special means by utilizing the results from Section 3 for the following assumptions:

Consider $\aleph : [\tau_1, \tau_2] \to \mathbb{R}, \tau_1 < \tau_2$ such that $\aleph(\lambda) = \lambda^{\mathfrak{s}}$ for $\mathfrak{s} \in (0, 1]$, $\varphi(\lambda) = \lambda$ and $n = 1$. Then, from Theorem 1:

1. For $\rho = \sigma = \frac{2}{3}$, we obtain

$$\begin{aligned} &\left|\frac{1}{3}A(\tau_1^{\mathfrak{s}}, \tau_2^{\mathfrak{s}}) + \frac{2}{3}A^{\mathfrak{s}}(\tau_1, \tau_2) - L_{\mathfrak{s}}^{\mathfrak{s}}(\tau_1, \tau_2)\right| \\ &\leq \frac{(\tau_2 - \tau_1)|\mathfrak{s}|}{2^{\mathfrak{s}}} \frac{\left(1 - 2^{2+\mathfrak{s}}3^{1+\mathfrak{s}} - 3^{2+\mathfrak{s}} + 5^{2+\mathfrak{s}} + 2^{\mathfrak{s}}3^{1+\mathfrak{s}}\mathfrak{s}\right)}{3^{2+\mathfrak{s}}(1+\mathfrak{s})(2+\mathfrak{s})} A\left(|\tau_1^{\mathfrak{s}-1}|, |\tau_2^{\mathfrak{s}-1}|\right). \end{aligned} \tag{16}$$

2. For $\rho = \sigma = 1$, we obtain

$$|L_{\mathfrak{s}}^{\mathfrak{s}}(\tau_1, \tau_2) - A^{\mathfrak{s}}(\tau_1, \tau_2)| \leq \frac{(\tau_2 - \tau_1)|\mathfrak{s}|}{2^{\mathfrak{s}+1}} \frac{\left(-1 + 2^{1+\mathfrak{s}}\right)}{(1+\mathfrak{s})(2+\mathfrak{s})} A\left(|\tau_1^{\mathfrak{s}-1}|, |\tau_2^{\mathfrak{s}-1}|\right). \tag{17}$$

3. For $\rho = \sigma = 1$, we obtain

$$|A(\tau_1^{\mathfrak{s}}, \tau_2^{\mathfrak{s}}) - L_{\mathfrak{s}}^{\mathfrak{s}}(\tau_1, \tau_2)| \leq \frac{(\tau_2 - \tau_1)|\mathfrak{s}|}{2^{\mathfrak{s}+1}} \frac{\left(1 + 2^{\mathfrak{s}}\mathfrak{s}\right)}{2 + 3\mathfrak{s} + \mathfrak{s}^2} A\left(|\tau_1^{\mathfrak{s}-1}|, |\tau_2^{\mathfrak{s}-1}|\right). \tag{18}$$

Similarly, from Theorem 2:

1. For $\rho = \sigma = \frac{2}{3}$, we obtain

$$\left|\frac{1}{3}A(\tau_1^{\mathfrak{s}}, \tau_2^{\mathfrak{s}}) + \frac{2}{3}A^{\mathfrak{s}}(\tau_1, \tau_2) - L_{\mathfrak{s}}^{\mathfrak{s}}(\tau_1, \tau_2)\right|$$
$$\leq \frac{(\tau_2 - \tau_1)|\mathfrak{s}|}{2}\left(\frac{4(q-1)(3)^{\frac{1-2q}{q-1}}(2)^{\frac{1}{q-1}}}{2q-1}\right)^{\frac{q-1}{q}}\left(\frac{1}{(\mathfrak{s}+1)2^{\mathfrak{s}}}\right)^{\frac{1}{q}}$$
$$\left[1 + \left(2^{\mathfrak{s}+1} - 1\right)^{\frac{1}{q}}\right]A\left(|\tau_1^{\mathfrak{s}-1}|, |\tau_2^{\mathfrak{s}-1}|\right). \tag{19}$$

2. For $\rho = \sigma = 1$, we obtain

$$|L_{\mathfrak{s}}^{\mathfrak{s}}(\tau_1, \tau_2) - A^{\mathfrak{s}}(\tau_1, \tau_2)|$$
$$\leq \frac{(\tau_2 - \tau_1)|\mathfrak{s}|}{2}\left(\frac{1-q}{1-2q}\right)^{\frac{q-1}{q}}\left(\frac{1}{(\mathfrak{s}+1)2^{\mathfrak{s}}}\right)^{\frac{1}{q}}\left[1 + \left(2^{\mathfrak{s}+1} - 1\right)^{\frac{1}{q}}\right]A\left(|\tau_1^{\mathfrak{s}-1}|, |\tau_2^{\mathfrak{s}-1}|\right). \tag{20}$$

3. For $\rho = \sigma = 0$, we obtain

$$|A(\tau_1^{\mathfrak{s}}, \tau_2^{\mathfrak{s}}) - L_{\mathfrak{s}}^{\mathfrak{s}}(\tau_1, \tau_2)|$$
$$\leq \frac{(\tau_2 - \tau_1)|\mathfrak{s}|}{2}\left(\frac{q-1}{2q-1}\right)^{\frac{q-1}{q}}\left(\frac{1}{(\mathfrak{s}+1)2^{\mathfrak{s}}}\right)^{\frac{1}{q}}\left[1 + \left(2^{\mathfrak{s}+1} - 1\right)^{\frac{1}{q}}\right]A\left(|\tau_1^{\mathfrak{s}-1}|, |\tau_2^{\mathfrak{s}-1}|\right). \tag{21}$$

Similarly, from Theorem 3:

1. For $\rho = \sigma = \frac{2}{3}$, we obtain

$$\left|\frac{1}{3}A(\tau_1^{\mathfrak{s}}, \tau_2^{\mathfrak{s}}) + \frac{2}{3}A^{\mathfrak{s}}(\tau_1, \tau_2) - L_{\mathfrak{s}}^{\mathfrak{s}}(\tau_1, \tau_2)\right|$$
$$\leq \left(\frac{5}{18}\right)^{1-\frac{1}{q}}\frac{(\tau_2 - \tau_1)|\mathfrak{s}|}{2}$$
$$\left[\left(\frac{2 \times 5^{\mathfrak{s}} \times 9^{-1-\mathfrak{s}}\left(50 \times 3^{\mathfrak{s}} - 7 \times 3^{1+2\mathfrak{s}} \times 5^{-\mathfrak{s}} - 2^{3+\mathfrak{s}}3^{1+2\mathfrak{s}}5^{-\mathfrak{s}} - 2 \times 3^{1+2\mathfrak{s}}5^{-\mathfrak{s}}\mathfrak{s} + 2^{1+\mathfrak{s}}3^{1+2\mathfrak{s}}5^{-\mathfrak{s}}\mathfrak{s}\right)}{(1+\mathfrak{s})(2+\mathfrak{s})}\right)^{\frac{1}{q}}\right.$$
$$\left.+\left(\frac{3^{-2-\mathfrak{s}}\left(2 + 3^{1+\mathfrak{s}} + 2 \times 3^{1+\mathfrak{s}}\mathfrak{s}\right)}{2 + 3\mathfrak{s} + \mathfrak{s}^2}\right)^{\frac{1}{q}}\right]A\left(|\tau_1^{\mathfrak{s}-1}|, |\tau_2^{\mathfrak{s}-1}|\right). \tag{22}$$

2. For $\rho = \sigma = 1$, we obtain

$$|L_{\mathfrak{s}}^{\mathfrak{s}}(\tau_1, \tau_2) - A^{\mathfrak{s}}(\tau_1, \tau_2)|$$
$$\leq \frac{(\tau_2 - \tau_1)|\mathfrak{s}|}{2}\left(\frac{1}{1+p}\right)^{1-\frac{1}{q}}\left[\left(\frac{-3 + 2^{2+\mathfrak{s}} - \mathfrak{s}}{2 + 3\mathfrak{s} + \mathfrak{s}^2}\right)^{\frac{1}{q}} + \left(\frac{1}{2+\mathfrak{s}}\right)^{\frac{1}{q}}\right]A\left(|\tau_1^{\mathfrak{s}-1}|, |\tau_2^{\mathfrak{s}-1}|\right). \tag{23}$$

3. For $\rho = \sigma = 0$, we obtain

$$|A(\tau_1^{\mathfrak{s}}, \tau_2^{\mathfrak{s}}) - L_{\mathfrak{s}}^{\mathfrak{s}}(\tau_1, \tau_2)|$$
$$\leq \frac{(\tau_2 - \tau_1)|\mathfrak{s}|}{2}\left(\frac{1}{2}\right)^{1-\frac{1}{q}}\left(\frac{1}{2 + 3\mathfrak{s} + \mathfrak{s}^2}\right)^{\frac{1}{q}}\left[\left(1 + 2^{1+\mathfrak{s}}\mathfrak{s}\right)^{\frac{1}{q}} + 1\right]A\left(|\tau_1^{\mathfrak{s}-1}|, |\tau_2^{\mathfrak{s}-1}|\right). \tag{24}$$

For $\tau_1, \tau_2 \in \mathbb{R} \setminus \{0\}$, $\tau_1 < \tau_2$, ${\tau_1}^{-1} > {\tau_2}^{-1}$ and by substituting $\tau_1 \to (\tau_2)^{-1}$ and $\tau_2 \to (\tau_1)^{-1}$ in (16), we obtain

$$\begin{aligned}&\left|\frac{1}{3}H^{-1}(\tau_2^{\mathfrak{s}}, \tau_1^{\mathfrak{s}}) + \frac{2}{3}H^{-\mathfrak{s}}(\tau_1, \tau_2) - L_{\mathfrak{s}}^{\mathfrak{s}}\left({\tau_2}^{-1}, {\tau_1}^{-1}\right)\right| \\ &\leq \frac{({\tau_1}^{-1} - {\tau_2}^{-1})|\mathfrak{s}|}{2^{\mathfrak{s}}} \frac{\left(1 - 2^{2+\mathfrak{s}}3^{1+\mathfrak{s}} - 3^{2+\mathfrak{s}} + 5^{2+\mathfrak{s}} + 2^{\mathfrak{s}}3^{1+\mathfrak{s}}\mathfrak{s}\right)}{3^{2+\mathfrak{s}}(1+\mathfrak{s})(2+\mathfrak{s})} H^{-1}\left(|\tau_1^{\mathfrak{s}-1}|, |\tau_2^{\mathfrak{s}-1}|\right). \end{aligned} \tag{25}$$

Remark 6. *By setting the same assumptions as those followed in inequality* (25), *we can also obtain the inequalities involving harmonic means for* (17)–(24).

5.2. Quadrature Formulas

In this section, for different choices of the parameters ρ and σ, we provide a range of Simpson's, midpoint, and trapezoidal-type inequalities. These inequalities provide error bounds for several quadrature formulas.

Remark 7. *From Theorem 1, the following inequalities are obtained:*

1. *By setting $\rho = \sigma = \frac{n+1}{n+2}$, we have the Simpson's inequality for generalized fractional integrals:*

$$\begin{aligned}&\left|\frac{1}{(n+1)(n+2)}[\aleph(\tau_1) + \aleph(\tau_2)] + \frac{1}{n+2}\left[\aleph\left(\frac{n\tau_1 + \tau_2}{n+1}\right) + \aleph\left(\frac{\tau_1 + n\tau_2}{n+1}\right)\right]\right. \\ &\left. - \frac{1}{\Delta(1)(n+1)}\left[{}_{\tau_1^+}I_{\varphi}\aleph\left(\frac{n\tau_1 + \tau_2}{n+1}\right) + {}_{\tau_2^-}I_{\varphi}\aleph\left(\frac{\tau_1 + n\tau_2}{n+1}\right)\right]\right| \\ &\leq \frac{\tau_2 - \tau_1}{(n+1)^{\mathfrak{s}+2}}\frac{1}{\Delta(1)}\left[\left(\Pi_1^{\varphi}\left(\frac{n+1}{n+2}, \mathfrak{s}\right) + \Pi_2^{\varphi}\left(\frac{n+1}{n+2}, \mathfrak{s}\right)\right)\left(|\aleph'(\tau_1)| + |\aleph'(\tau_2)|\right)\right], \end{aligned} \tag{26}$$

where

$$\Pi_1^{\varphi}\left(\frac{n+1}{n+2}, \mathfrak{s}\right) = \int_0^1 (1-\lambda)^{\mathfrak{s}}\left|\Delta(\lambda) - \Delta(1)\frac{n+1}{n+2}\right| d\lambda,$$

and

$$\Pi_2^{\varphi}\left(\frac{n+1}{n+2}, \mathfrak{s}\right) = \int_0^1 (n+\lambda)^{\mathfrak{s}}\left|\Delta(\lambda) - \Delta(1)\frac{n+1}{n+2}\right| d\lambda,$$

and the inequality (26) *is identical to Theorem 4 in [27] by taking $n = 1$ and $\mathfrak{s} = 1$.*

2. *By setting $\rho = \sigma = n$, we have the midpoint inequality for generalized fractional integrals:*

$$\begin{aligned}&\left|\frac{n}{n+1}\left[\aleph\left(\frac{n\tau_1 + \tau_2}{n+1}\right) + \aleph\left(\frac{\tau_1 + n\tau_2}{n+1}\right)\right] - \frac{n-1}{n+1}[\aleph(\tau_1) + \aleph(\tau_2)]\right. \\ &\left. - \frac{1}{\Delta(1)(n+1)}\left[{}_{\tau_1^+}I_{\varphi}\aleph\left(\frac{n\tau_1 + \tau_2}{n+1}\right) + {}_{\tau_2^-}I_{\varphi}\aleph\left(\frac{\tau_1 + n\tau_2}{n+1}\right)\right]\right| \\ &\leq \frac{\tau_2 - \tau_1}{(n+1)^{\mathfrak{s}+2}}\frac{1}{\Delta(1)}\left[\left(\Pi_1^{\varphi}(n, \mathfrak{s}) + \Pi_2^{\varphi}(n, \mathfrak{s})\right)\left(|\aleph'(\tau_1)| + |\aleph'(\tau_2)|\right)\right], \end{aligned} \tag{27}$$

where

$$\Pi_1^{\varphi}(n, \mathfrak{s}) = \int_0^1 (1-\lambda)^{\mathfrak{s}}|\Delta(\lambda) - \Delta(1)n| d\lambda,$$

and

$$\Pi_2^{\varphi}(n,\mathfrak{s}) = \int_0^1 (n+\lambda)^{\mathfrak{s}}|\Delta(\lambda) - \Delta(1)n|d\lambda.$$

3. *By setting $\rho = \sigma = 0$, we have the trapezoidal-type inequality for generalized fractional integrals:*

$$\left|\frac{\aleph(\tau_1)+\aleph(\tau_2)}{n+1} - \frac{1}{\Delta(1)(n+1)}\left[{}_{\tau_1^+}I_{\varphi}\aleph\left(\frac{n\tau_1+\tau_2}{n+1}\right) + {}_{\tau_2^-}I_{\varphi}\aleph\left(\frac{\tau_1+n\tau_2}{n+1}\right)\right]\right|$$
$$\leq \frac{\tau_2-\tau_1}{(n+1)^{\mathfrak{s}+2}}\frac{1}{\Delta(1)}\left[\left(\Pi_1^{\varphi}(\mathfrak{s}) + \Pi_2^{\varphi}(n,\mathfrak{s})\right)\left(|\aleph'(\tau_1)| + |\aleph'(\tau_2)|\right)\right], \tag{28}$$

where

$$\Pi_1^{\varphi}(\mathfrak{s}) = \int_0^1 (1-\lambda)^{\mathfrak{s}}|\Delta(\lambda)|d\lambda,$$

and

$$\Pi_2^{\varphi}(n,\mathfrak{s}) = \int_0^1 (n+\lambda)^{\mathfrak{s}}|\Delta(\lambda)|d\lambda,$$

and inequality (28) *is identical to Theorem 5.5 in [28] by taking $n = 1$ and $\mathfrak{s} = 1$.*

Remark 8. *The inequalities that we derived in Remark 7 can also be established for Theorems 2 and 3 and for all the inequalities that can be derived for different choices of the function $\phi(\lambda)$, which are discussed in Remark 5.*

5.3. A Family of Numerical Schemes to Solve Non-Linear Equations

The aim of this section is to present a new iterative scheme as an application of our main results.

Consider a non-linear equation

$$\aleph(\omega) = 0. \tag{29}$$

One of the most significant problems in applied mathematics is finding the solutions to equations of the form (29). There are several methods known in the literature that can be used to find the solutions to equations of the form (29). For further details, see [31–34]. In this section, as an application of our main outcomes, we present a new generalized form of an iterative scheme that can be used to find the solution to (29).

In [35], Weerakoon and Fernando proposed the idea of obtaining quadrature rules through an iterative method. Indeed, they used Newton's method in the integral form given in [36]. The integral representation of Newton's method is

$$\aleph(\omega) = \aleph(\omega_m) + \int_{\omega_m}^{\omega} \aleph'(\lambda)d\lambda. \tag{30}$$

We now present a new generalized iterative scheme by applying the technique of Weerakoon and Fernando in [35] as follows Algorithm 1:

Algorithm 1: Generalized Iterative Scheme

Let $\sigma, \rho \geq 0$ and a non-linear function $\aleph(\omega) = 0$. Then, we have

$$\omega_{\mathrm{m}+1} = \omega_{\mathrm{m}} - \frac{2\aleph(\omega_{\mathrm{m}})}{(1-\sigma)\aleph'(\omega_{\mathrm{m}}) + (1-\rho)\aleph'(v_{\mathrm{m}}) + (\rho+\sigma)\aleph'\left(\frac{\omega_{\mathrm{m}}+v_{\mathrm{m}}}{2}\right)}. \quad (31)$$

Proof. Substituting $\varphi(\lambda) = \lambda$, $n = 1$ and $\mathfrak{s} = 1$ in Theorem 1, using (29) and (30), we deduce

$$\omega = \omega_{\mathrm{m}} - \frac{2\aleph(\omega_{\mathrm{m}})}{(1-\sigma)\aleph'(\omega_{\mathrm{m}}) + (1-\rho)\aleph'(\omega) + (\rho+\sigma)\aleph'\left(\frac{\omega_{\mathrm{m}}+\omega}{2}\right)}. \quad (32)$$

Now, (32) allows us to suggest the following generic iterative scheme for finding the solution to equations of the form (29).

$$\omega_{\mathrm{m}+1} = \omega_{\mathrm{m}} - \frac{2\aleph(\omega_{\mathrm{m}})}{(1-\sigma)\aleph'(\omega_{\mathrm{m}}) + (1-\rho)\aleph'(v_{\mathrm{m}}) + (\rho+\sigma)\aleph'\left(\frac{\omega_{\mathrm{m}}+v_{\mathrm{m}}}{2}\right)}, \quad (33)$$

where v_{m} is some explicit method. This completes the proof. □

Remark 9. *For different values of ρ and σ in* (31), *we derive different classical numerical schemes:*

1. *By setting $\rho = 0$ and $\sigma = 0$, the trapezoidal Newton method is derived and is given in [35].*
2. *By setting $\rho = 1$ and $\sigma = 1$, the midpoint Newton method is derived and is given in [37].*
3. *By setting $\rho = \frac{1}{2}$ and $\sigma = \frac{1}{2}$, the average trapezoidal midpoint Newton method is derived and is given in [38].*
4. *By setting $\rho = \frac{2}{3}$ and $\sigma = \frac{2}{3}$, the Simpson-Newton method is derived and is given in [39].*

We now discuss the convergence analysis of Algorithm 1.

Theorem 4. *Let r be a simple zero of a sufficiently differentiable function $\aleph : \mathcal{I} \subseteq \mathbb{R} \to \mathbb{R}$, where $r \in \mathcal{I}$, provided that ω_0 is in close proximity to r. Then, the generalized iterative scheme given by Algorithm 1 exhibits a quadratic order of convergence, satisfying the following error equation:*

$$e_{\mathrm{m}+1} = -\frac{1}{2}c_2(\sigma-\rho)e_{\mathrm{m}}^2 + \left(\frac{1}{2}c_3 - \frac{9}{8}\sigma c_3 - \rho c_2^2 + c_2^2 + \frac{3}{8}\rho c_3 + \sigma c_2^2 - \frac{1}{4}\sigma^2 c_2^2 + \frac{1}{2}\sigma\rho c_2^2 - \frac{1}{4}\rho^2 c_2^2\right)e_{\mathrm{m}}^3 + O(e_{\mathrm{m}}^4),$$

where $c_k = \frac{1}{k!}\frac{\aleph^k(r)}{\aleph'(r)}$, $k = 1, 2, 3, \ldots$ and $e_{\mathrm{m}} = \omega_{\mathrm{m}} - r$.

Proof. From Algorithm 1, we have

$$\omega_{\mathrm{m}+1} = \omega_{\mathrm{m}} - \frac{2\aleph(\omega_{\mathrm{m}})}{(1-\sigma)\aleph'(\omega_{\mathrm{m}}) + (1-\rho)\aleph'(v_{\mathrm{m}}) + (\rho+\sigma)\aleph'\left(\frac{\omega_{\mathrm{m}}+v_{\mathrm{m}}}{2}\right)}, \quad (34)$$

where v_{m} is some explicit method, so we take the Newton–Raphson method.

$$v_{\mathrm{m}} = \omega_{\mathrm{m}} - \frac{\aleph(\omega_{\mathrm{m}})}{\aleph'(\omega_{\mathrm{m}})}. \quad (35)$$

Since r is a simple zero of $\aleph$, which is sufficiently differentiable, using a Taylor-series expansion of $\aleph(\omega_{\mathrm{m}})$ and $D_q\aleph(\omega_{\mathrm{m}})$ about r, we obtain

$$\aleph(\omega_{\mathrm{m}}) = \aleph'(r)[e_{\mathrm{m}} + c_2 e_{\mathrm{m}}^2 + c_3 e_{\mathrm{m}}^3 + c_4 e_{\mathrm{m}}^4 + O(e_{\mathrm{m}}^5)], \quad (36)$$

$$\aleph'(\omega_m) = \aleph'(r)[1 + 2c_2e_m + 3c_3e_m^2 + 4c_4e_m^3 + O(e_m^4)]. \tag{37}$$

By utilizing (36) and (37), we obtain

$$v_m = c_2e_m^2 + (-2c_2^2 + 2c_3)e_m^3 + O(e_m^4). \tag{38}$$

Now, using (38), we deduce that

$$\aleph(v_m) = c_1 + 2c_1c_2^2e_m^2 - 4c_1(c_2^2 - c_3)c_2e_m^3 + O(e_m^4). \tag{39}$$

Also, we have

$$\aleph\left(\frac{\omega_m + v_m}{2}\right) = c_1 + c_1c_2e_m + \frac{1}{4}c_1(4c_2^2 + 3c_3)e_m^2 - \frac{1}{2}c_1(4c_2^3 - 7c_2c_3 - c_4)e_m^3 + O(e_m^4). \tag{40}$$

Using (36)–(40), we obtain

$$e_{m+1} = -\frac{1}{2}c_2(\sigma - \rho)e_m^2 + \left(\frac{1}{2}c_3 - \frac{9}{8}\sigma c_3 - \rho c_2^2 + c_2^2 + \frac{3}{8}\rho c_3 + \sigma c_2^2 - \frac{1}{4}\sigma^2c_2^2 + \frac{1}{2}\sigma\rho c_2^2 - \frac{1}{4}\rho^2c_2^2\right)e_m^3 + O(e_m^4).$$

This completes the proof. □

Now, we consider the following numerical scheme (Algorithm 2).

Algorithm 2: A new iterative scheme of order 3

For a given x_0, compute the approximate solution x_{n+1} using the following two-step iterative scheme:

$$v_m = x_n - \frac{\aleph(\omega_m)}{\aleph'(\omega_m)},$$
$$\omega_{m+1} = \omega_m - \frac{3\aleph(\omega_m)}{\aleph'(\omega_m) + \aleph'(v_m) + \aleph'\left(\frac{\omega_m + v_m}{2}\right)}. \tag{41}$$

Note that Algorithm 2 can be deduced using our generic iterative Algorithm 1 by taking $\rho = \frac{1}{3} = \sigma$. We would like to mention here that to the best of our knowledge, this iterative scheme is new in the literature.

The convergence analysis of Algorithm 2 can easily be checked from the convergence analysis of Algorithm 1 by taking $\rho = \frac{1}{3} = \sigma$. It can be seen that it satisfies the following error equation:

$$e_{m+1} = \left(c_2^2 + \frac{1}{4}c_3\right)e_m^3 + O(e_m^4).$$

This shows that the iterative scheme provided by (41) exhibits a cubic order of convergence.

5.3.1. Comparison Analysis

In this section, we present some examples that demonstrate the effectiveness of our suggested approach. We compare our proposed method (Algorithm 1) with well-known techniques, including the Newton method (NM) [32], Abbasbandy method (AM) [40], Halley method (HM) [32], and Chun method (CM) [33]. To determine the approximate root, we employed a tolerance of $\epsilon = 10^{-15}$. The following termination conditions were utilized for the computer algorithms:

1. $|\omega_{m+1} - \omega_m| < \epsilon$;
2. $|\aleph(\omega_{m+1})| < \epsilon$.

The numerical tests were conducted on an Intel(R) Core(TM) i5 processor with 1.60 GHz and 16 GB RAM. Maple 2020 was used for coding, while the graphical analysis was carried out using Matlab 2021. For the comparison analysis, we consider the following four types of examples.

1. $\aleph(\omega) = \omega^3 + 4\omega^2 - 15$;
2. $\aleph(\omega) = \omega \exp(\omega^2) - \sin^2 \omega + 3\cos\omega + 5$;
3. $\aleph(\omega) = 10\omega \exp(-\omega^2) - 1$;
4. $\aleph(\omega) = \exp(-\omega) + \cos\omega$.

After carrying out the numerical tests with the software, we prepared tables and visual illustrations of Algorithm 1 for the above-mentioned examples, which are presented below (Tables 1–4).

Table 1. Comparison results for $\aleph(\omega) = \omega^3 + 4\omega^2 - 15$.

Methods	ω_0	IT	ω_m	$\aleph(\omega_m)$	δ
NM	2	6	1.6319808055660635175	0	0
AM	2	4	1.6319808055660635175	0	0
HM	2	4	1.6319808055660635175	0	0
CM	2	4	1.6319808055660635175	0	0
ALG	2	4	1.6319808055660635175	0	0

Table 2. Comparison results for $\aleph(\omega) = \omega \exp(\omega^2) - \sin^2 \omega + 3\cos\omega + 5$.

Methods	ω_0	IT	ω_m	$\aleph(\omega_m)$	δ
NM	−1	6	−1.2076478271309189270	4.0×10^{-19}	7.58×10^{-17}
AM	−1	5	−1.2076478271309189270	4.0×10^{-19}	0
HM	−1	5	−1.2076478271309189270	0	0
CM	−1	6	−1.2076478271309189270	4.0×10^{-19}	0
ALG	−1	5	−1.2076478271309189270	4.0×10^{-19}	0

Table 3. Comparison results for $\aleph(\omega) = 10\omega \exp(-\omega^2) - 1$.

Methods	ω_0	IT	ω_m	$\aleph(\omega_m)$	δ
NM	1.8	5	1.6796306104284499407	-9×10^{-20}	4.7395×10^{-15}
AM	1.8	4	1.6796306104284499407	-9×10^{-20}	1.0×10^{-19}
HM	1.8	4	1.6796306104284499407	-9×10^{-20}	0
CM	1.8	4	1.6796306104284499407	2.0×10^{-19}	0
ALG	1.8	4	1.6796306104284499407	-9×10^{-20}	0

Table 4. Comparison results for $\aleph(\omega) = \exp(-\omega) + \cos\omega$.

Methods	ω_0	IT	ω_m	$\aleph(\omega_m)$	δ
NM	2	5	1.7461395304080124177	6.0×10^{-20}	1.0×10^{-19}
AM	2	4	1.7461395304080124177	-6×10^{-20}	1.0×10^{-19}
HM	2	4	1.7461395304080124177	6.0×10^{-20}	1.0×10^{-19}
CM	2	3	1.7461395304080124177	-6×10^{-20}	4.63×10^{-17}
ALG	2	4	1.7461395304080124177	-6×10^{-20}	1.0×10^{-19}

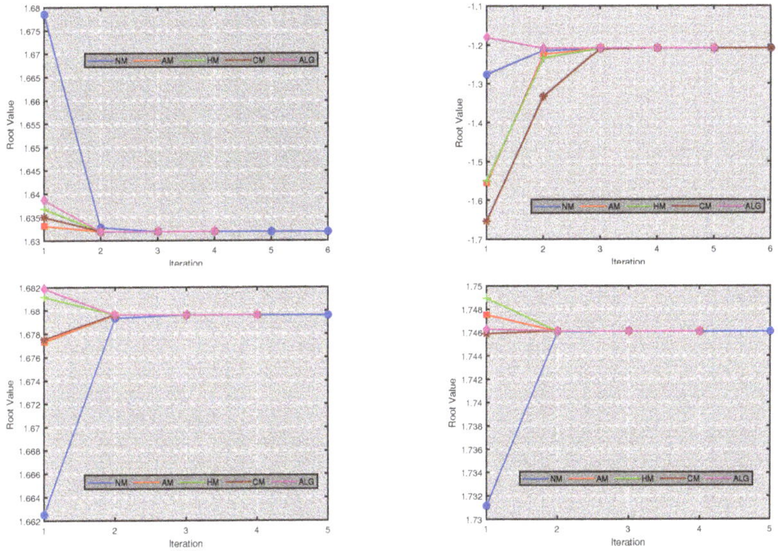

5.3.2. Basins of Attraction

In this section, we discuss the basins of attraction for Algorithm 1. We apply our proposed method to $\mathbb{R} \times \mathbb{R} = [-2, 2] \times [-2, 2]$ with a grid of 500×500 points, employing a tolerance of $|\aleph(\omega_{\mathfrak{m}})| < 1 \times 10^{-10}$ and a maximum of 20 iterations. Additionally, we present graphical representations of the CPU time consumed to generate the basins of attraction per iteration. For this analysis, we consider a famous problem involving finding the roots of $\aleph(\omega) = \omega^{\mathfrak{m}} - 1$. We consider $\mathfrak{m} = 2, 3, 4$. Figures 4–6 gives the visual analysis of basins of attraction for $\aleph(\omega) = \omega^2 - 1$, $\aleph(\omega) = \omega^3 - 1$ and $\aleph(\omega) = \omega^4 - 1$ and also CPU time consumed to generate the basins of attraction per iteration respectively.

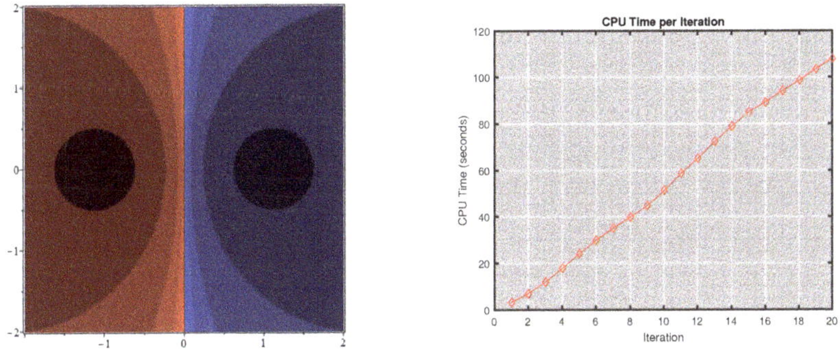

Figure 4. (**Left**) Basins of attraction for $\aleph(\omega) = \omega^2 - 1$. (**Right**) CPU time consumed to generate the basins of attraction per iteration.

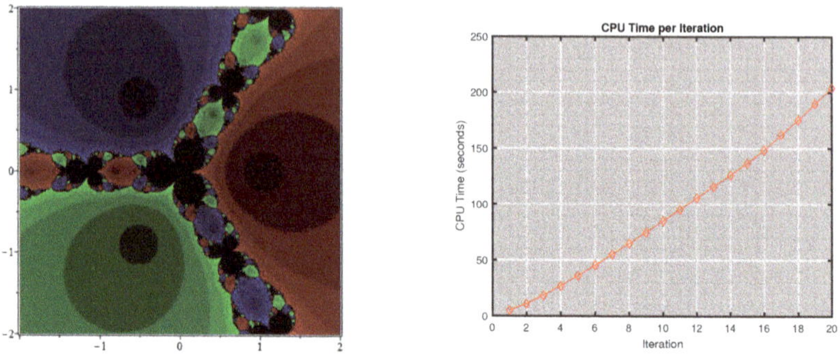

Figure 5. (**Left**) Basins of attraction $\aleph(\omega) = \omega^3 - 1$. (**Right**) CPU time consumed to generate the basins of attraction per iteration.

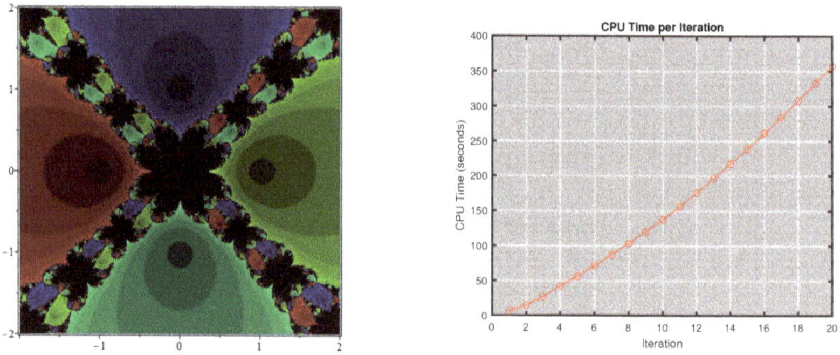

Figure 6. (**Left**) Basins of attraction $\aleph(\omega) = \omega^4 - 1$. (**Right**) CPU time consumed to generate the basins of attraction per iteration.

6. Conclusions

In conclusion, this research paper presents a novel extension of a parameterized identity. By utilizing this identity, some parametric inequalities for differentiable $\mathfrak{s}$-convex mappings through the use of generalized fractional integral operators are obtained. The derived Simpson's, midpoint, and trapezoidal-type inequalities, incorporating different integral operators and parameters, serve as additional contributions to the existing literature on this topic. We also discuss the applicability of the main results to means of real numbers and in numerical analysis for solving non-linear equations. The graphical analysis provided in this paper further supports the importance and practical relevance of our findings. The results of this research paper could potentially have applications in various areas of mathematics, physics, and engineering. The extension of the proposed iterative method to systems of equations could be an interesting future research problem.

Author Contributions: Investigation, S.R., M.U.A., S.S.D., B.B.-M. and M.A.N. All authors have read and agreed to the published version of the manuscript.

Funding: This research is supported by Researchers Supporting Project Number (RSP2023R158), King Saud University, Riyadh, Saudi Arabia.

Data Availability Statement: Not applicable.

Acknowledgments: The authors would like to thank the editor and anonymous reviewers for their valuable comments and suggestions. This research is supported by Researchers Supporting Project Number (RSP2023R158), King Saud University, Riyadh, Saudi Arabia.

Conflicts of Interest: The authors declare no conflict of interest.

References

1. Dragomir, S.S.; Pearce, C. *Selected Topics on Hermite-Hadamard Inequality and Applications*; Victoria University: Melbourne, Australia, 2000.
2. Hadamard, J. Étude sur les propriétés des fonctions entiéres et en particulier d'une fonction considérée par Riemann. *J. Mathématiques Pures Appliquées* **1893**, *9*, 171–216.
3. Hermite, C. Sur deux limites d'une intégrale définie. *Mathesis* **1883**, *3*, 1–82.
4. Dragomir, S.S.; Agarwal, R. Two inequalities for differentiable mappings and applications to special means of real numbers and to trapezoidal formula. *Appl. Math. Lett.* **1998**, *11*, 91–95. [CrossRef]
5. Kirmaci, U.S. Inequalities for differentiable mappings and applications to special means of real numbers and to midpoint formula. *Appl. Math. Comput.* **2004**, *147*, 137–146. [CrossRef]
6. Dragomir, S.S.; Agarwal, R.P.; Cerone, P. On Simpson's inequality and applications. *Res. Group Math. Inequalities Appl.* **1999**, *2*, 1–35. [CrossRef]
7. Awan, M.U.; Javed, M.Z.; Rassias, M.T.; Noor, M.A.; Noor, K.I. Simpson type inequalities and applications. *J. Anal.* **2021**, *29*, 1403–1419. [CrossRef]
8. Alomari, M.; Darus, M. On some inequalities of Simpson-type via quasi-convex functions and applications. *Transylv. J. Math.* **2010**, *2*, 15–24.
9. İşcan, İ. Hermite-Hadamard and Simpson-like type inequalities for differentiable harmonically convex functions. *J. Math.* **2014**, *2014*, 346305. [CrossRef]
10. Sarikaya, M.Z.; Set, E.; Özdemir, M.E. On new inequalities of Simpson's type for convex functions. *Res. Group Math. Inequalities Appl.* **2010**, *60*, 2191–2199. [CrossRef]
11. Set, E.; Akdemir, A.O.; Özdemir, E.M. Simpson type integral inequalities for convex functions via Riemann-Liouville integrals. *Filomat* **2017**, *31*, 4415–4420. [CrossRef]
12. Breckner, W.W. Stetigkeitsaussagen für eine Klasse verallgemeinerter konvexer Funktionen in topologischen linearen Räumen. *Publ. I'Institut Math.* **1978**, *23*, 13–20.
13. Hudzik, H.; Maligranda, L. Some remarks on $\mathfrak{s}$-convex functions. *Aequationes Math.* **1994**, *48*, 100–111. [CrossRef]
14. Dragomir, S.S.; Fitzpatrick, S. The Hadamard inequalities for $\mathfrak{s}$-convex functions in the second sense. *Demonstr. Math.* **1999**, *32*, 687–696. [CrossRef]
15. Godunova, E.K.; Levin, V.I. Inequalities for functions of a broad class that contains convex, monotone and some other forms of functions. *Numer. Math. Math. Phys.* **1985**, *138*, 166.
16. Noor, M.A.; Noor, K.I.; Awan, M.U.; Li, J. On Hermite-Hadamard Inequalities for h-Preinvex Functions. *Filomat* **2014**, *28*, 1463–1474. [CrossRef]
17. Awan, M.U.; Talib, S.; Noor, M.A.; Noor, K.I. On γ-preinvex functions. *Filomat* **2020**, *34*, 4137–4159. [CrossRef]
18. Tunç, M.; Göv, E.; Sanal, Ü. On tgs-convex function and their inequalities. *Facta Univ. Ser. Math. Inform.* **2015**, *30*, 679–691.
19. Varošanec, S. On h-convexity. *J. Math. Anal. Appl.* **2007**, *326*, 303–311. [CrossRef]
20. Rentería-Baltiérrez, F.Y.; Reyes-Melo, M.E.; Puente-Córdova, J.G.; López-Walle, B. Application of fractional calculus in the mechanical and dielectric correlation model of hybrid polymer films with different average molecular weight matrices. *Polym. Bull.* **2023**, *80*, 6327–6347. [CrossRef]
21. Sun, H.; Zhang, Y.; Baleanu, D.; Chen, W.; Chen, Y. A new collection of real world applications of fractional calculus in science and engineering. *Commun. Nonlinear Sci. Numer. Simul.* **2018**, *64*, 213–231. [CrossRef]
22. Viera-Martin, E.; Gómez-Aguilar, J.F.; Solís-Pérez, J.E.; Hernández-Pérez, J.A.; Escobar-Jiménez, R.F. Artificial neural networks: A practical review of applications involving fractional calculus. *Eur. Phys. J. Spec. Top.* **2022**, *231*, 2059–2095. [CrossRef] [PubMed]
23. Kilbas, A.A.; Srivastava, H.M.; Trujillo, J.J. *Theory and Applications of Fractional Differential Equations*; Elsevier: Amsterdam, The Netherlands, 2006.
24. Sarikaya, M.Z.; Ertugral, F. On the generalized Hermite-Hadamard inequalities. *Ann. Univ.-Craiova-Math. Comput. Sci. Ser.* **2020**, *47*, 193–213.
25. Mubeen, S.; Habibullah, G.M. k-Fractional integrals and application. *Int. J. Contemp. Math. Sci.* **2012**, *7*, 89–94.
26. Davis, P. J. *Handbook of Mathematical Functions with Formulas, Graphs, and Mathematical Tables*; US Government Printing Office: New York, NY, USA, 1972.
27. Ertuğral, F.; Sarikaya, M.Z. Simpson type integral inequalities for generalized fractional integral. *Rev. Real Acad. Cienc. Exactas Físicas Nat. Ser. Matemáticas* **2019**, *113*, 3115–3124. [CrossRef]
28. Ertuğral, F.; Sarikaya, M.Z.; Budak, H. On Hermite-Hadamard type inequalities associated with the generalized fractional integrals. *Filomat* **2022**, *36*, 3981–3993. [CrossRef]
29. Chen, J.; Huang, X. Some new inequalities of Simpson's type for $\mathfrak{s}$-convex functions via fractional integrals. *Filomat* **2017**, *31*, 4989–4997. [CrossRef]
30. Alomari, M.; Darus, M.; Dragomir, S.S. New inequalities of Simpson's type for $\mathfrak{s}$-convex functions with applications. *Res. Rep. Collect.* **2009**, *12*, 1–18.

31. Babajee, D.K.R.; Dauhoo, M.Z. An analysis of the properties of the variants of Newton's method with third order convergence. *Appl. Math. Comput.* **2006**, *183*, 659–684.
32. Burden, R.L.; Faires, J.D.; Burden, A.M. *Numerical Analysis*; Richard Stratton: Boston, MA, USA, 2015. [CrossRef]
33. Chun, C. Iterative methods improving Newton's method by the decomposition method. *Comput. Math. Appl.* **2005**, *50*, 1559–1568.
34. Adomian, G. *Nonlinear Stochastis System Theory and Applications to Physics*; Kluwer Academic Publishers: Dordrecht, The Netherlands, 1989. [CrossRef]
35. Weerakoon, S.; Fernando, T. A variant of Newton's method with accelerated third-order convergence. *Appl. Math. Lett.* **2000**, *13*, 87–93.
36. Dennis, J.E.; Schnabel, R.B. *Numerical Methods for Unconstrained Optimization and Nonlinear Equations*; Society for Industrial and Applied Mathematics Philadelphia: Philadelphia, PN, USA, 1996. [CrossRef]
37. Frontini, M.; Sormani, E. Some variant of Newton's method with third-order convergence. *Appl. Math. Comput.* **2003**, *140*, 419–426.
38. Nedzhibov, G. On a few iterative methods for solving nonlinear equations. *Appl. Math. Eng. Econ.* **2002**, *28*, 1–8. [CrossRef]
39. Hasanov, V.I.; Ivanov, I.G.; Nedzhibov, G. A new modification of Newton's method. *Appl. Math. Sci. Eng.* **2002**, *27*, 278–286.
40. Abbasbandy, S. Improving Newton-Raphson method for nonlinear equations by modified Adomian decomposition method. *Appl. Math. Comput.* **2003**, *145*, 887–893.

fractal and fractional

Article

New Fractional Integral Inequalities via k-Atangana–Baleanu Fractional Integral Operators

Seth Kermausuor * and Eze R. Nwaeze

Department of Mathematics and Computer Science, Alabama State University, Montgomery, AL 36101, USA; enwaeze@alasu.edu
* Correspondence: skermausour@alasu.edu

Abstract: We propose the definitions of some fractional integral operators called k-Atangana–Baleanu fractional integral operators. These newly proposed operators are generalizations of the well-known Atangana–Baleanu fractional integral operators. As an application, we establish a generalization of the Hermite–Hadamard inequality. Additionally, we establish some new identities involving these new integral operators and obtained new fractional integral inequalities of the midpoint and trapezoidal type for functions whose derivatives are bounded or convex.

Keywords: Hermite–Hadamard inequality; Atangana–Baleanu fractional integral operators; fractional integral inequalities; convex functions; bounded functions

Citation: Kermausuor, S.; Nwaeze, E. R. New Fractional Integral Inequalities via k-Atangana–Baleanu Fractional Integral Operators. *Fractal Fract.* **2023**, *7*, 740. https://doi.org/10.3390/fractalfract7100740

Academic Editor: Carlo Cattani

Received: 31 August 2023
Revised: 2 October 2023
Accepted: 6 October 2023
Published: 8 October 2023

1. Introduction

Integral inequalities play an indispensable role in mathematical analysis due to their innumerable applications in the analysis of differential equations and approximation theory, amongst others. Several integral inequalities for functions of single variables under various conditions have been established in the literature. Fractional calculus and convex functions have been found to play a fundamental role in the study of integral inequalities in recent years. A great number of researchers have established several integral inequalities under conditions of convexity and its generalizations by utilizing various fractional integral operators. For example, Akdemir et al. established some fractional integral inequalities of the Hermite–Hadamard type for convex and concave functions via the Atagana–Baleanu fractional integral operators in [1], and Ali et al. obtained some parametrized Newton-type inequalities for convex functions using the Riemann–Liouville fractional integrals in [2]. In [3], Butt et al. provided some Hermite–Hadamard-type integral inequalities for convex functions using the ABK-fractional integral operators, and in [4], Chu et al. established some Simpson's type inequalities for n-polynomial convex functions using the Katugampola fractional integrals. Using some generalized fractional integrals by Guzman et al., some Hermite–Hadamard-type inequalities for convex functions were present in [5], and some midpoint-type and trapezoidal-type inequalities for prequasiinvex functions via the Katugampola fractional integrals were provided by Kermausuor and Nwaeze in [6]. Peng et al. established some Simpson's type inequalities for generalized (m, h_1, h_1)-preinvex functions by utilizing the Riemann–Liouville fractional integral operators in [7], and Şanli provided some Simpson's type inequalities for harmonically convex functions via the Katugampola fractional integrals in [8]. In [9], Yu et al. established some Ostrowski-type integral inequalities for p-convex functions by utilizing the Katugampola fractional integral operators, and Zabandan et al. established some integral inequalities of the Hermite–Hadamard type for r-convex functions. For more information about the results mentioned above and other related results, we invite the interested reader to see the papers in [1–22] and the references therein.

The aforementioned results are established via the convexity of the function involved. For this purpose, it is natural to start by first presenting the definition of a convex function.

Definition 1. *A function $\mathcal{J} : I \to \mathbb{R}$ is convex on the interval I if*

$$\mathcal{J}(\lambda\gamma_1 + (1-\lambda)\gamma_2) \leq \lambda\mathcal{J}(\gamma_1) + (1-\lambda)\mathcal{J}(\gamma_2)$$

for all γ_1, $\gamma_2 \in I$ and $\lambda \in [0,1]$.

The double inequality below holds for convex functions and is known in the literature as the Hermite–Hadamard inequality.

Theorem 1 ([23]). *If $\mathcal{J} : I \to \mathbb{R}$ is a convex function, then the double inequality:*

$$\mathcal{J}\left(\frac{\gamma_1+\gamma_2}{2}\right) \leq \frac{1}{\gamma_2-\gamma_1}\int_{\gamma_1}^{\gamma_2} \mathcal{J}(s)ds \leq \frac{\mathcal{J}(\gamma_1)+\mathcal{J}(\gamma_2)}{2} \tag{1}$$

holds for all γ_1, $\gamma_2 \in I$ with $\gamma_1 < \gamma_2$.

The Hermite–Hadamard inequality has been one of the most studied integral inequalities. Several generalizations of this inequality have been introduced in the literature in recent years. For instance, in [21], Sarikaya et al. established the following generalization of the Hermite–Hadamard inequality by utilizing the Riemann–Liouville fractional integrals defined in Definition 2.

Theorem 2. *If $\mathcal{J} : [d_1, d_2] \to \mathbb{R}$ is a positive and convex function on $[d_1, d_2]$ with $d_1 < d_2$ and $\mathcal{J} \in L_1([d_1, d_2])$, then the inequalities:*

$$\mathcal{J}\left(\frac{d_1+d_2}{2}\right) \leq \frac{\Gamma(\alpha+1)}{2(d_2-d_1)^{\alpha}}\left[I^{\alpha}_{d_1^+}\mathcal{J}(d_2) + I^{\alpha}_{d_2^-}\mathcal{J}(d_1)\right] \leq \frac{\mathcal{J}(d_1)+\mathcal{J}(d_2)}{2}$$

hold for all $\alpha > 0$, where Γ denotes the gamma function, and $I^{\alpha}_{d_1^+}\mathcal{J}$ and $I^{\alpha}_{d_2^-}\mathcal{J}$, respectively, denotes the left- and right-sided Riemann–Liouville fractional integrals of $\mathcal{J}$ of order α defined in Definition 2.

Similarly, in [24], Wu et al. obtained a generalization of the Hermite–Hadamard inequality by utilizing the k-Riemann–Liouville fractional integrals defined in Definition 3 as follows.

Theorem 3. *If $\mathcal{J} : [d_1, d_2] \to \mathbb{R}$ is a positive and convex function on $[d_1, d_2]$ with $d_1 < d_2$ and $\mathcal{J} \in L_1([d_1, d_2])$, then the inequalities:*

$$\mathcal{J}\left(\frac{d_1+d_2}{2}\right) \leq \frac{\Gamma_k(\alpha+k)}{2(d_2-d_1)^{\frac{\alpha}{k}}}\left[{}_kI^{\alpha}_{d_1^+}\mathcal{J}(d_2) + {}_kI^{\alpha}_{d_2^-}\mathcal{J}(d_1)\right] \leq \frac{\mathcal{J}(d_1)+\mathcal{J}(d_2)}{2}$$

hold for all $\alpha, k > 0$, where Γ_k denotes the k-gamma function, and ${}_kI^{\alpha}_{d_1^+}\mathcal{J}$ and ${}_kI^{\alpha}_{d_2^-}\mathcal{J}$ denotes the left- and right-sided k-Riemann–Liouville fractional integrals of $\mathcal{J}$ of order α defined in Definition 3.

The Riemann–Liouville and k-Riemann–Liouville fractional integrals are defined as follows.

Definition 2 ([25–27]). *The left- and right-sided Riemann–Liouville fractional integrals of a real-valued function $\mathcal{J}$ of order $\alpha > 0$ are given by*

$$I^{\alpha}_{d_1^+}\mathcal{J}(\lambda) = \frac{1}{\Gamma(\alpha)}\int_{d_1}^{\lambda}(\lambda-u)^{\alpha-1}\mathcal{J}(u)du$$

and

$$I^{\alpha}_{d_2^-}\mathcal{J}(\lambda) = \frac{1}{\Gamma(\alpha)}\int_{\lambda}^{d_2}(u-\lambda)^{\alpha-1}\mathcal{J}(u)du,$$

where Γ *is the gamma function given by*

$$\Gamma(\nu) := \int_0^\infty u^{\nu-1} e^{-u} du, \quad Re(\nu) > 0.$$

Definition 3 ([28]). *The left- and right-sided k-Riemann–Liouville fractional integrals of a real-valued function* $\mathcal{J}$ *of order* $\alpha > 0$ *are given by*

$$_kI^{\alpha}_{d_1^+}\mathcal{J}(\lambda) = \frac{1}{k\Gamma_k(\alpha)}\int_{d_1}^{\lambda}(\lambda - u)^{\frac{\alpha}{k}-1}\mathcal{J}(u)du$$

and

$$_kI^{\alpha}_{d_2^-}\mathcal{J}(\lambda) = \frac{1}{k\Gamma_k(\alpha)}\int_{\lambda}^{d_2}(u - \lambda)^{\frac{\alpha}{k}-1}\mathcal{J}(u)du,$$

where Γ_k *is the k-gamma function presented by Diaz et al. [29] as*

$$\Gamma_k(\nu) := \int_0^\infty u^{\nu-1} e^{-\frac{u^k}{k}} du, \quad Re(\nu) > 0.$$

Recently, Atangana and Baleanu introduced a fractional integral which is known in the literature as the left-sided Atangana–Baleanu fractional integral defined below.

Definition 4 ([30]). *The left-sided Atangana–Baleanu fractional integral of a real-valued function* $\mathcal{J}$ *of order* $\alpha \in (0,1)$ *is given by*

$$^{AB}I^{\alpha}_{d_1^+}\mathcal{J}(\lambda) = \frac{1-\alpha}{B(\alpha)}\mathcal{J}(\lambda) + \frac{\alpha}{B(\alpha)\Gamma(\alpha)}\int_{d_1}^{\lambda}(\lambda - u)^{\alpha-1}\mathcal{J}(u)du,$$

where $B(\alpha) > 0$ *and satisfies the property* $B(0) = B(1) = 1$.

In [31], Abdeljawad and Baleanu introduced the right-sided version of the Atangana–Baleanu fractional integral as follows:

$$^{AB}I^{\alpha}_{d_2^-}\mathcal{J}(\lambda) = \frac{1-\alpha}{B(\alpha)}\mathcal{J}(\lambda) + \frac{\alpha}{B(\alpha)\Gamma(\alpha)}\int_{\lambda}^{d_2}(u - \lambda)^{\alpha-1}\mathcal{J}(u)du.$$

By utilizing the Atangana–Baleanu fractional integral operators, Fernandez and Mohammed [32] established the following generalization of the Hermite–Hadamard inequality.

Theorem 4. *If* $\mathcal{J} : [d_1, d_2] \to \mathbb{R}$ *is convex on* $[d_1, d_2]$ *and* $\mathcal{J} \in L_1([d_1, d_2])$, *then the inequalities*

$$\mathcal{J}\left(\frac{d_1 + d_2}{2}\right) \le \frac{B(\alpha)\Gamma(\alpha)}{2[(d_2 - d_1)^{\alpha} + (1-\alpha)\Gamma(\alpha)]}\left[^{AB}I^{\alpha}_{d_1^+}\mathcal{J}(d_2) + {}^{AB}I^{\alpha}_{d_2^-}\mathcal{J}(d_1)\right] \le \frac{\mathcal{J}(d_1) + \mathcal{J}(d_2)}{2}$$

hold for $\alpha \in (0,1)$.

In [33], Kashuri introduced some fractional integral operators called the ABK-fractional integral operators, which are generalizations of the Atangana–Baleanu fractional operators, and presented the Hermite–Hadamard inequality for these fractional integral operators in the following:

Definition 5. *The left- and right-sided ABK-Atangana–Baleanu fractional integral operators of a real-valued function $\mathcal{J}$ of order $\nu \in (0,1)$ are given by*

$$^{ABK\rho}_{\ d_1^+}I^{\nu}_{\lambda}\mathcal{J}(\lambda) = \frac{1-\nu}{B(\nu)}\mathcal{J}(\lambda) + \frac{\rho^{1-\nu}\nu}{B(\nu)\Gamma(\nu)}\int_{d_1}^{\lambda}\frac{u^{\rho-1}}{(\lambda^{\rho}-u^{\rho})^{1-\nu}}\mathcal{J}(u)du, \quad \lambda > d_1$$

and

$$^{ABK\rho}_{\ d_2^-}I^{\nu}_{\lambda}\mathcal{J}(\lambda) = \frac{1-\nu}{B(\nu)}\mathcal{J}(\lambda) + \frac{\rho^{1-\nu}\nu}{B(\nu)\Gamma(\nu)}\int_{\lambda}^{d_2}\frac{u^{\rho-1}}{(u^{\rho}-t^{\rho})^{1-\nu}}\mathcal{J}(u)du, \quad \lambda < d_2,$$

where $\rho > 0$ and $B(\nu) > 0$ satisfies the property $B(0) = B(1) = 1$.

Theorem 5. *Let $\nu \in (0,1)$ and $\rho > 0$. Let $\mathcal{J} : [d_1^{\rho}, d_2^{\rho}] \to \mathbb{R}$ with $0 \le d_1 < d_2$ be a convex function. Then the following inequalities for the ABK-fractional integrals hold:*

$$\begin{aligned}
&\frac{2(d_2^{\rho}-d_1^{\rho})^{\nu}}{B(\nu)\Gamma(\nu+1)\rho^{2-\rho}}\mathcal{J}\left(\frac{d_1^{\rho}+d_2^{\rho}}{2}\right) + \frac{1-\nu}{B(\nu)}\left[\mathcal{J}(d_1^{\rho}) + \mathcal{J}(d_2^{\rho})\right] \\
&\le {}^{ABK\rho}_{\ d_1^+}I^{\nu}_{d_2^{\rho}}\mathcal{J}(d_2^{\rho}) + {}^{ABK\rho}_{\ d_2^-}I^{\nu}_{d_1^{\rho}}\mathcal{J}(d_1^{\rho}) \\
&\le \left(\frac{(d_2^{\rho}-d_1^{\rho})^{\nu} + \rho(1-\nu)\Gamma(\nu)}{\rho B(\nu)\Gamma(\nu)}\right)\left[\mathcal{J}(d_1^{\rho}) + \mathcal{J}(d_2^{\rho})\right].
\end{aligned}$$

Driven by the ongoing research work on fractional integrals and the crucial role they play in the study of fractional integral inequalities, our aim in this paper is to propose novel definitions of some generalized fractional integral operators called k-Atangana–Baleanu fractional integral operators. As an application, we will establish the Hermite–Hadamard inequality and some new fractional integral inequalities by using these new operators. Our main results are presented in Section 2, followed by a conclusion in Section 3.

2. Main Results

We begin by providing the definition of the new fractional integrals that presents a generalization of the Atangana–Baleanu fractional integrals.

Definition 6. *The left- and right-sided k-Atangana–Baleanu fractional integral operators of a real-valued function $\mathcal{J}$ of order $\alpha > 0$, are defined as*

$$^{AB}{}_{k}I^{\alpha}_{d_1^+}\mathcal{J}(\lambda) = \frac{1-\alpha}{B(\alpha)}\mathcal{J}(\lambda) + \frac{\alpha}{kB(\alpha)\Gamma_k(\alpha)}\int_{d_1}^{\lambda}(\lambda-u)^{\frac{\alpha}{k}-1}\mathcal{J}(u)du, \quad \lambda > d_1$$

and

$$^{AB}{}_{k}I^{\alpha}_{d_2^-}\mathcal{J}(\lambda) = \frac{1-\alpha}{B(\alpha)}\mathcal{J}(\lambda) + \frac{\alpha}{kB(\alpha)\Gamma_k(\alpha)}\int_{\lambda}^{d_2}(u-\lambda)^{\frac{\alpha}{k}-1}\mathcal{J}(u)du, \quad \lambda < d_2,$$

where $k > 0$ and $B(\alpha) > 0$ satisfies the property $B(0) = B(1) = 1$.

Remark 1. *If $k = 1$ in Definition 6, then we have the Atangana–Baleanu fractional integral operators.*

Next, we study the Hermite–Hadamard inequality by utilizing the k-Atangana–Baleanu fractional integral operators.

Theorem 6. *Let $\gamma,\theta \in \mathbb{R}$ with $\gamma < \theta$ and $\mathcal{J} : [\gamma,\theta] \to \mathbb{R}$ be a convex function. Then the inequalities*

$$\mathcal{J}\left(\frac{\theta+\gamma}{2}\right) \leq \frac{B(\alpha)\Gamma_k(\alpha)}{2[(\theta-\gamma)^{\frac{\alpha}{k}} + (1-\alpha)\Gamma_k(\alpha)]}\left[{}^{AB}{}_kI^{\alpha}_{\gamma^+}\mathcal{J}(\theta) + {}^{AB}{}_kI^{\alpha}_{\theta^-}\mathcal{J}(\gamma)\right] \leq \frac{\mathcal{J}(\gamma)+\mathcal{J}(\theta)}{2} \tag{2}$$

hold for all $k > 0$ and $\alpha \in (0,1)$.

Proof. Under the condition of convexity of $\mathcal{J}$ on $[\gamma,\theta]$, it follows that for any $u_1, u_2 \in [\gamma,\theta]$

$$\mathcal{J}\left(\frac{u_1+u_2}{2}\right) \leq \frac{\mathcal{J}(u_1)+\mathcal{J}(u_2)}{2}. \tag{3}$$

If we take $u_1 = \lambda\theta + (1-\lambda)\gamma$ and $u_2 = (1-\lambda)\theta + \lambda\gamma$ for $\lambda \in [0,1]$ in (3), then we obtain

$$2\mathcal{J}\left(\frac{\theta+\gamma}{2}\right) \leq \mathcal{J}(\lambda\theta + (1-\lambda)\gamma) + \mathcal{J}((1-\lambda)\theta + \lambda\gamma). \tag{4}$$

Multiply (4) by $\frac{\alpha}{kB(\alpha)\Gamma_k(\alpha)}\lambda^{\frac{\alpha}{k}-1}$ and integrate both sides of the resulting inequality with respect to λ over $[0,1]$ to obtain

$$\begin{aligned}\frac{2}{B(\alpha)\Gamma_k(\alpha)}\mathcal{J}\left(\frac{\theta+\gamma}{2}\right) &\leq \frac{\alpha}{kB(\alpha)\Gamma_k(\alpha)}\int_0^1 \lambda^{\frac{\alpha}{k}-1}\mathcal{J}(\lambda\theta+(1-\lambda)\gamma)d\lambda \\ &\quad + \frac{\alpha}{kB(\alpha)\Gamma_k(\alpha)}\int_0^1 \lambda^{\frac{\alpha}{k}-1}\mathcal{J}((1-\lambda)\theta+\lambda\gamma)d\lambda \\ &= \frac{\alpha}{kB(\alpha)\Gamma_k(\alpha)(\theta-\gamma)^{\frac{\alpha}{k}}}\int_\gamma^\theta (\theta-u)^{\frac{\alpha}{k}-1}\mathcal{J}(u)du \\ &\quad + \frac{\alpha}{kB(\alpha)\Gamma_k(\alpha)(\theta-\gamma)^{\frac{\alpha}{k}}}\int_\gamma^\theta (v-\gamma)^{\frac{\alpha}{k}-1}\mathcal{J}(v)dv. \end{aligned} \tag{5}$$

Using Definition 6 and (5), we obtain

$$\frac{2(\theta-\gamma)^{\frac{\alpha}{k}}}{B(\alpha)\Gamma_k(\alpha)}\mathcal{J}\left(\frac{\theta+\gamma}{2}\right) + \frac{1-\alpha}{B(\alpha)}[\mathcal{J}(\gamma)+\mathcal{J}(\theta)] \leq {}^{AB}{}_kI^{\alpha}_{\gamma^+}\mathcal{J}(\theta) + {}^{AB}{}_kI^{\alpha}_{\theta^-}\mathcal{J}(\gamma). \tag{6}$$

Now, since $\mathcal{J}$ is convex, we have that $\mathcal{J}\left(\frac{\theta+\gamma}{2}\right) \leq \frac{\mathcal{J}(\theta)+\mathcal{J}(\gamma)}{2}$. Hence, from (6), we have

$$\left[\frac{2(\theta-\gamma)^{\frac{\alpha}{k}}}{B(\alpha)\Gamma_k(\alpha)} + \frac{2(1-\alpha)}{B(\alpha)}\right]\mathcal{J}\left(\frac{\theta+\gamma}{2}\right) \leq {}^{AB}{}_kI^{\alpha}_{\gamma^+}\mathcal{J}(\theta) + {}^{AB}{}_kI^{\alpha}_{\theta^-}\mathcal{J}(\gamma). \tag{7}$$

By rearranging the terms in (7), we obtain the first inequality in (2). To prove the second inequality, we note that if $\mathcal{J}$ is convex, then for $\lambda \in [0,1]$, we have

$$\mathcal{J}(\lambda\theta + (1-\lambda)\gamma) \leq \lambda\mathcal{J}(\theta) + (1-\lambda)\mathcal{J}(\gamma) \tag{8}$$

and

$$\mathcal{J}((1-\lambda)\theta + \lambda\gamma) \leq (1-\lambda)\mathcal{J}(\theta) + \lambda\mathcal{J}(\gamma). \tag{9}$$

Adding (8) and (9), we obtain

$$\mathcal{J}(\lambda\theta + (1-\lambda)\gamma) + \mathcal{J}((1-\lambda)\theta + \lambda\gamma) \leq \mathcal{J}(\gamma) + \mathcal{J}(\theta). \tag{10}$$

Multiply (10) by $\frac{\alpha}{kB(\alpha)\Gamma_k(\alpha)}\lambda^{\frac{\alpha}{k}-1}$ and integrate both sides of the resulting inequality with respect to λ over $[0,1]$ to obtain

$$\frac{\alpha}{kB(\alpha)\Gamma_k(\alpha)}\int_0^1 \lambda^{\frac{\alpha}{k}-1}\mathcal{J}(\lambda\theta + (1-\lambda)\gamma)d\lambda + \frac{\alpha}{kB(\alpha)\Gamma_k(\alpha)}\int_0^1 \lambda^{\frac{\alpha}{k}-1}\mathcal{J}((1-\lambda)\theta + \lambda\gamma)d\lambda \leq \frac{1}{B(\alpha)\Gamma_k(\alpha)}[\mathcal{J}(\gamma) + \mathcal{J}(\theta)]. \tag{11}$$

By using change of variables like in the proof of the first inequality and Definition 6, we deduce from (11) that

$$\begin{aligned} {}^{AB}{}_kI^{\alpha}_{\gamma^+}\mathcal{J}(\theta) + {}^{AB}{}_kI^{\alpha}_{\theta^-}\mathcal{J}(\gamma) &\leq \frac{(\theta-\gamma)^{\frac{\alpha}{k}}}{B(\alpha)\Gamma_k(\alpha)}[\mathcal{J}(\gamma) + \mathcal{J}(\theta)] + \frac{1-\alpha}{B(\alpha)}[\mathcal{J}(\gamma) + \mathcal{J}(\theta)] \\ &= \left[\frac{2(\theta-\gamma)^{\frac{\alpha}{k}}}{B(\alpha)\Gamma_k(\alpha)} + \frac{2(1-\alpha)}{B(\alpha)}\right]\frac{\mathcal{J}(\gamma) + \mathcal{J}(\theta)}{2}. \end{aligned} \tag{12}$$

Thus, the second inequality in (2) is obtained by rearranging the terms in (12). Hence the proof is complete. □

Remark 2. *If $k = 1$ in Theorem 6, then we have the Hermit–Hadamard inequality via the Atangana–Baleanu fractional integrals as stated in Theorem 4.*

In what follows, we present some novel inequalities of the midpoint type and trapezoidal type for functions with bounded derivatives and functions with convex derivatives in absolute value by utilizing the k-Atangana–Baleanu fractional integrals. To do this, we first establish the following crucial identities involving k-Atangana–Baleanu fractional integrals.

Lemma 1. *Let $\gamma, \theta \in \mathbb{R}$ with $\gamma < \theta$ and $\mathcal{J} : [\gamma, \theta] \to \mathbb{R}$ be a function. If $\mathcal{J}$ is differentiable and $\mathcal{J}' \in L_1([\gamma, \theta])$, then the equality*

$$\left(\frac{(\theta-\gamma)^{\frac{\alpha}{k}} + (1-\alpha)\Gamma_k(\alpha)}{\Gamma_k(\alpha)}\right)\frac{\mathcal{J}(\gamma) + \mathcal{J}(\theta)}{B(\alpha)} - \left[{}^{AB}{}_kI^{\alpha}_{\gamma^+}\mathcal{J}(\theta) + {}^{AB}{}_kI^{\alpha}_{\theta^-}\mathcal{J}(\gamma)\right] = \frac{(\theta-\gamma)^{\frac{\alpha}{k}+1}}{B(\alpha)\Gamma_k(\alpha)}\int_0^1 [(1-\lambda)^{\frac{\alpha}{k}} - \lambda^{\frac{\alpha}{k}}]\mathcal{J}'(\lambda\gamma + (1-\lambda)\theta)d\lambda \tag{13}$$

holds for all $\alpha, k > 0$.

Proof. Using integration by parts, we obtain

$$\begin{aligned} &\int_0^1 (1-\lambda)^{\frac{\alpha}{k}}\mathcal{J}'(\lambda\gamma + (1-\lambda)\theta)d\lambda \\ &= \frac{(1-\lambda)^{\frac{\alpha}{k}}}{\gamma-\theta}\mathcal{J}(\lambda\gamma + (1-\lambda)\theta)\Big|_0^1 - \frac{\alpha}{k(\theta-\gamma)}\int_0^1 (1-\lambda)^{\frac{\alpha}{k}-1}\mathcal{J}(\lambda\gamma + (1-\lambda)\theta)d\lambda \\ &= \frac{1}{\theta-\gamma}\mathcal{J}(\theta) - \frac{\alpha}{k(\theta-\gamma)}\int_0^1 (1-\lambda)^{\frac{\alpha}{k}-1}\mathcal{J}(\lambda\gamma + (1-\lambda)\theta)d\lambda \\ &= \frac{1}{\theta-\gamma}\mathcal{J}(\theta) - \frac{\alpha}{k(\theta-\gamma)^{\frac{\alpha}{k}+1}}\int_\gamma^\theta (\theta-u)^{\frac{\alpha}{k}-1}\mathcal{J}(u)du \\ &= \frac{1}{\theta-\gamma}\mathcal{J}(\theta) - \frac{B(\alpha)\Gamma_k(\alpha)}{(\theta-\gamma)^{\frac{\alpha}{k}+1}}\left[{}^{AB}{}_kI^{\alpha}_{\gamma^+}\mathcal{J}(\theta) - \frac{1-\alpha}{B(\alpha)}\mathcal{J}(\theta)\right]. \end{aligned}$$

Thus,

$$\int_0^1 (1-\lambda)^{\frac{\alpha}{k}} \mathcal{J}'(\lambda\gamma+(1-\lambda)\theta)d\lambda$$
$$= \frac{1}{\theta-\gamma}\mathcal{J}(\theta) - \frac{B(\alpha)\Gamma_k(\alpha)}{(\theta-\gamma)^{\frac{\alpha}{k}+1}}\left[{}^{AB}{}_kI^{\alpha}_{\gamma^+}\mathcal{J}(\theta) - \frac{1-\alpha}{B(\alpha)}\mathcal{J}(\theta)\right]. \tag{14}$$

By a similar argument, we deduce that

$$\int_0^1 t^{\frac{\alpha}{k}} \mathcal{J}'(\lambda\gamma+(1-\lambda)\theta)d\lambda$$
$$= -\frac{1}{\theta-\gamma}\mathcal{J}(\gamma) + \frac{B(\alpha)\Gamma_k(\alpha)}{(\theta-\gamma)^{\frac{\alpha}{k}+1}}\left[{}^{AB}{}_kI^{\alpha}_{\theta^-}\mathcal{J}(\gamma) - \frac{1-\alpha}{B(\alpha)}\mathcal{J}(\gamma)\right]. \tag{15}$$

The desired identity in (13) is obtained if we multiply the identities in (14) and (15) by $\frac{(\theta-\gamma)^{\frac{\alpha}{k}+1}}{B(\alpha)\Gamma_k(\alpha)}$, and take the difference between the resulting equations.
□

Lemma 2. *Let $\gamma, \theta \in \mathbb{R}$ with $\gamma < \theta$ and $\mathcal{J} : [\gamma, \theta] \to \mathbb{R}$ be a function. If $\mathcal{J}$ is differentiable and $\mathcal{J}' \in L_1([\gamma, \theta])$, then the equality*

$$\left[{}^{AB}{}_kI^{\alpha}_{(\frac{\gamma+\theta}{2})^+}\mathcal{J}(\theta) + {}^{AB}{}_kI^{\alpha}_{(\frac{\gamma+\theta}{2})^-}\mathcal{J}(\gamma)\right]$$
$$-\left(\frac{(\theta-\gamma)^{\frac{\alpha}{k}}}{2^{\frac{\alpha}{k}-1}B(\alpha)\Gamma_k(\alpha)}\mathcal{J}\left(\frac{\theta+\gamma}{2}\right) + \frac{1-\alpha}{B(\alpha)}\left[\mathcal{J}(\gamma)+\mathcal{J}(\theta)\right]\right)$$
$$= \frac{(\theta-\gamma)^{\frac{\alpha}{k}+1}}{B(\alpha)\Gamma_k(\alpha)}\left[\int_0^{1/2} \lambda^{\frac{\alpha}{k}}\mathcal{J}'(\lambda\gamma+(1-\lambda)\theta)d\lambda - \int_{1/2}^1 (1-\lambda)^{\frac{\alpha}{k}}\mathcal{J}'(\lambda\gamma+(1-\lambda)\theta)d\lambda\right] \tag{16}$$

holds for all $\alpha, k > 0$.

Proof. Using integration by parts, we obtain

$$\int_0^{1/2} \lambda^{\frac{\alpha}{k}}\mathcal{J}'(t\gamma+(1-\lambda)\theta)d\lambda$$
$$= \frac{\lambda^{\frac{\alpha}{k}}}{\gamma-\theta}\mathcal{J}(\lambda\gamma+(1-\lambda)\theta)\bigg|_0^{1/2} - \frac{\alpha}{k(\gamma-\theta)}\int_0^{1/2}\lambda^{\frac{\alpha}{k}-1}\mathcal{J}(\lambda\gamma+(1-\lambda)\theta)d\lambda$$
$$= \frac{1}{2^{\frac{\alpha}{k}}(\gamma-\theta)}\mathcal{J}\left(\frac{\gamma+\theta}{2}\right) - \frac{\alpha}{k(\gamma-\theta)}\int_0^{1/2}\lambda^{\frac{\alpha}{k}-1}\mathcal{J}(\lambda\gamma+(1-\lambda)\theta)d\lambda$$
$$= \frac{1}{2^{\frac{\alpha}{k}}(\gamma-\theta)}\mathcal{J}\left(\frac{\gamma+\theta}{2}\right) + \frac{\alpha}{k(\theta-\gamma)^{\frac{\alpha}{k}+1}}\int_{\frac{\gamma+\theta}{2}}^{\theta}(\theta-u)^{\frac{\alpha}{k}-1}\mathcal{J}(u)du$$
$$= -\frac{1}{2^{\frac{\alpha}{k}}(\theta-\gamma)}\mathcal{J}\left(\frac{\gamma+\theta}{2}\right) + \frac{B(\alpha)\Gamma_k(\alpha)}{(\theta-\gamma)^{\frac{\alpha}{k}+1}}\left[{}^{AB}{}_kI^{\alpha}_{(\frac{\gamma+\theta}{2})^+}\mathcal{J}(\theta) - \frac{1-\alpha}{B(\alpha)}\mathcal{J}(\theta)\right].$$

So,

$$\int_0^{1/2} \lambda^{\frac{\alpha}{k}}\mathcal{J}'(\lambda\gamma+(1-\lambda)\theta)d\lambda$$
$$= -\frac{1}{2^{\frac{\alpha}{k}}(\theta-\gamma)}\mathcal{J}\left(\frac{\gamma+\theta}{2}\right) + \frac{B(\alpha)\Gamma_k(\alpha)}{(\theta-\gamma)^{\frac{\alpha}{k}+1}}\left[{}^{AB}{}_kI^{\alpha}_{(\frac{\gamma+\theta}{2})^+}\mathcal{J}(\theta) - \frac{1-\alpha}{B(\alpha)}\mathcal{J}(\theta)\right]. \tag{17}$$

Similarly,

$$\begin{aligned}
&\int_{1/2}^{1}(1-\lambda)^{\frac{\alpha}{k}}\mathcal{J}'(\lambda\gamma+(1-\lambda)\theta)d\lambda \\
&=\frac{(1-\lambda)^{\frac{\alpha}{k}}}{\gamma-\theta}\mathcal{J}(\lambda\gamma+(1-\lambda)\theta)\Big|_{1/2}^{1}-\frac{\alpha}{k(\theta-\gamma)}\int_{1/2}^{1}(1-\lambda)^{\frac{\alpha}{k}-1}\mathcal{J}(\lambda\gamma+(1-\lambda)\theta)d\lambda \\
&=\frac{1}{2^{\frac{\alpha}{k}}(\theta-\gamma)}\mathcal{J}\left(\frac{\gamma+\theta}{2}\right)-\frac{\alpha}{k(\theta-\gamma)}\int_{1/2}^{1}(1-\lambda)^{\frac{\alpha}{k}-1}\mathcal{J}(\lambda\gamma+(1-\lambda)\theta)d\lambda \\
&=\frac{1}{2^{\frac{\alpha}{k}}(\theta-\gamma)}\mathcal{J}\left(\frac{\gamma+\theta}{2}\right)-\frac{\alpha}{k(\theta-\gamma)^{\frac{\alpha}{k}+1}}\int_{\gamma}^{\frac{\gamma+\theta}{2}}(u-\gamma)^{\frac{\alpha}{k}-1}\mathcal{J}(u)du \\
&=\frac{1}{2^{\frac{\alpha}{k}}(\theta-\gamma)}\mathcal{J}\left(\frac{\gamma+\theta}{2}\right)-\frac{B(\alpha)\Gamma_k(\alpha)}{(\theta-\gamma)^{\frac{\alpha}{k}+1}}\left[{}^{AB}{}_{k}I^{\alpha}_{(\frac{\gamma+\theta}{2})^-}\mathcal{J}(\gamma)-\frac{1-\alpha}{B(\alpha)}\mathcal{J}(\gamma)\right].
\end{aligned}$$

So,

$$\begin{aligned}
&\int_{1/2}^{1}(1-\lambda)^{\frac{\alpha}{k}}\mathcal{J}'(\lambda\gamma+(1-\lambda)\theta)d\lambda \\
&=\frac{1}{2^{\frac{\alpha}{k}}(\theta-\gamma)}\mathcal{J}\left(\frac{\gamma+\theta}{2}\right)-\frac{B(\alpha)\Gamma_k(\alpha)}{(\theta-\gamma)^{\frac{\alpha}{k}+1}}\left[{}^{AB}{}_{k}I^{\alpha}_{(\frac{\gamma+\theta}{2})^-}\mathcal{J}(\gamma)-\frac{1-\alpha}{B(\alpha)}\mathcal{J}(\gamma)\right]. \qquad (18)
\end{aligned}$$

The desired identity in (16) is obtained if we multiply the identities in (17) and (18) by $\frac{(\theta-\gamma)^{\frac{\alpha}{k}+1}}{B(\alpha)\Gamma_k(\alpha)}$, and take the difference between the resulting equations. □

Using Lemma 1, we obtain the following trapezoidal type inequalities.

Theorem 7. *If $\mathcal{J}$ satisfies the conditions of Lemma 1 and $\mathcal{J}'$ is bounded, that is, $\|\mathcal{J}'\|_\infty = \sup_{x\in[\gamma,\theta]}|\mathcal{J}'(x)| < \infty$, then the inequality*

$$\begin{aligned}
&\left|\left(\frac{(\theta-\gamma)^{\frac{\alpha}{k}}+(1-\alpha)\Gamma_k(\alpha)}{\Gamma_k(\alpha)}\right)\frac{\mathcal{J}(\gamma)+\mathcal{J}(\theta)}{B(\alpha)}-\left[{}^{AB}{}_{k}I^{\alpha}_{\gamma^+}\mathcal{J}(\theta)+{}^{AB}{}_{k}I^{\alpha}_{\theta^-}\mathcal{J}(\gamma)\right]\right| \\
&\qquad\le\frac{2k(\theta-\gamma)^{\frac{\alpha}{k}+1}\|\mathcal{J}'\|_\infty}{(\alpha+k)B(\alpha)\Gamma_k(\alpha)}\left(1-\frac{1}{2^{\frac{\alpha}{k}}}\right) \qquad (19)
\end{aligned}$$

holds for all $\alpha, k > 0$.

Proof. By taking the absolute value on both sides of the identity in (13) and using the boundedness of $\mathcal{J}'$, we obtain

$$\begin{aligned}
&\left|\left(\frac{(\theta-\gamma)^{\frac{\alpha}{k}}+(1-\alpha)\Gamma_k(\alpha)}{\Gamma_k(\alpha)}\right)\frac{\mathcal{J}(\gamma)+\mathcal{J}(\theta)}{B(\alpha)}-\left[{}^{AB}{}_{k}I^{\alpha}_{\gamma^+}\mathcal{J}(\theta)+{}^{AB}{}_{k}I^{\alpha}_{\theta^-}\mathcal{J}(\gamma)\right]\right| \\
&\qquad\le\frac{(\theta-\gamma)^{\frac{\alpha}{k}+1}\|\mathcal{J}'\|_\infty}{B(\alpha)\Gamma_k(\alpha)}\int_0^1|(1-\lambda)^{\frac{\alpha}{k}}-\lambda^{\frac{\alpha}{k}}|d\lambda. \qquad (20)
\end{aligned}$$

Now, we observed that for $\lambda\in[0,1]$,

$$(1-\lambda)^{\frac{\alpha}{k}}-\lambda^{\frac{\alpha}{k}}\begin{cases}\ge 0 & \text{for } \lambda\in[0,1/2]\\ <0 & \text{for } \lambda\in(1/2,1]\end{cases}$$

and hence

$$\int_0^1|(1-\lambda)^{\frac{\alpha}{k}}-\lambda^{\frac{\alpha}{k}}|d\lambda=\int_0^{1/2}(1-\lambda)^{\frac{\alpha}{k}}-\lambda^{\frac{\alpha}{k}}d\lambda+\int_{1/2}^{1}\lambda^{\frac{\alpha}{k}}-(1-\lambda)^{\frac{\alpha}{k}}d\lambda$$

$$= \frac{2}{\frac{\alpha}{k}+1}\left(1-\frac{1}{2^{\frac{\alpha}{k}}}\right). \tag{21}$$

The desired inequality in (19) follows by substituting (21) in (20). □

Theorem 8. *If $\mathcal{J}$ satisfies the conditions of Lemma 1 and $\mathcal{J}'$ is convex on $[\gamma,\theta]$, then the inequality*

$$\left|\left(\frac{(\theta-\gamma)^{\frac{\alpha}{k}}+(1-\alpha)\Gamma_k(\alpha)}{\Gamma_k(\alpha)}\right)\frac{\mathcal{J}(\gamma)+\mathcal{J}(\theta)}{B(\alpha)}-\left[{}^{AB}{}_kI^{\alpha}_{\gamma^+}\mathcal{J}(\theta)+{}^{AB}{}_kI^{\alpha}_{\theta^-}\mathcal{J}(\gamma)\right]\right|$$
$$\leq \frac{k(\theta-\gamma)^{\frac{\alpha}{k}+1}}{(\alpha+k)B(\alpha)\Gamma_k(\alpha)}\left(1-\frac{1}{2^{\frac{\alpha}{k}}}\right)\left[|\mathcal{J}'(\gamma)|+|\mathcal{J}'(\theta)|\right] \tag{22}$$

holds for all $\alpha,k>0$

Proof. By taking the absolute value on both sides of the identity in (13) and using the convexity of $|\mathcal{J}'|$, we obtain

$$\left|\left(\frac{(\theta-\gamma)^{\frac{\alpha}{k}}+(1-\alpha)\Gamma_k(\alpha)}{\Gamma_k(\alpha)}\right)\frac{\mathcal{J}(\gamma)+\mathcal{J}(\theta)}{B(\alpha)}-\left[{}^{AB}{}_kI^{\alpha}_{\gamma^+}\mathcal{J}(\theta)+{}^{AB}{}_kI^{\alpha}_{\theta^-}\mathcal{J}(\gamma)\right]\right|$$
$$\leq \frac{(\theta-\gamma)^{\frac{\alpha}{k}+1}}{B(\alpha)\Gamma_k(\alpha)}\int_0^1\left|(1-\lambda)^{\frac{\alpha}{k}}-\lambda^{\frac{\alpha}{k}}\right|(\lambda|f'(\gamma)|+(1-\lambda)|\mathcal{J}'(\theta)|)d\lambda$$
$$=\frac{(\theta-\gamma)^{\frac{\alpha}{k}+1}}{B(\alpha)\Gamma_k(\alpha)}\left[|\mathcal{J}'(\gamma)|\int_0^1\left|(1-\lambda)^{\frac{\alpha}{k}}-\lambda^{\frac{\alpha}{k}}\right|\lambda d\lambda\right.$$
$$\left.+|\mathcal{J}'(\theta)|\int_0^1\left|(1-\lambda)^{\frac{\alpha}{k}}-\lambda^{\frac{\alpha}{k}}\right|(1-\lambda)d\lambda\right]. \tag{23}$$

With an argument similar to the one used in the proof of Theorem 7, we deduce that

$$\int_0^1\left|(1-\lambda)^{\frac{\alpha}{k}}-\lambda^{\frac{\alpha}{k}}\right|\lambda d\lambda=\frac{1}{\frac{\alpha}{k}+1}\left(1-\frac{1}{2^{\frac{\alpha}{k}}}\right) \tag{24}$$

and

$$\int_0^1\left|(1-\lambda)^{\frac{\alpha}{k}}-\lambda^{\frac{\alpha}{k}}\right|(1-\lambda)d\lambda=\frac{1}{\frac{\alpha}{k}+1}\left(1-\frac{1}{2^{\frac{\alpha}{k}}}\right). \tag{25}$$

The desired inequality in (22) follows by substituting (24) and (25) in (23).
□

Using Lemma 2, we obtain the following midpoint type inequalities.

Theorem 9. *If $\mathcal{J}$ satisfies the conditions of Lemma 2 and $\mathcal{J}'$ is bounded, that is, $\|\mathcal{J}'\|_\infty=\sup_{x\in[\gamma,\theta]}|\mathcal{J}'(x)|<\infty$, then the inequality*

$$\left|\left[{}^{AB}{}_kI^{\alpha}_{(\frac{\gamma+\theta}{2})^+}\mathcal{J}(\theta)+{}^{AB}{}_kI^{\alpha}_{(\frac{\gamma+\theta}{2})^-}\mathcal{J}(\gamma)\right]\right.$$
$$\left.-\left(\frac{(\theta-\gamma)^{\frac{\alpha}{k}}}{2^{\frac{\alpha}{k}-1}B(\alpha)\Gamma_k(\alpha)}\mathcal{J}\left(\frac{\theta+\gamma}{2}\right)+\frac{1-\alpha}{B(\alpha)}\left[\mathcal{J}(\gamma)+\mathcal{J}(\theta)\right]\right)\right|$$
$$\leq\frac{k(\theta-\gamma)^{\frac{\alpha}{k}+1}\|\mathcal{J}'\|_\infty}{2^{\frac{\alpha}{k}}(\alpha+k)B(\alpha)\Gamma_k(\alpha)} \tag{26}$$

holds for all $\alpha,k>0$.

Proof. Taking the absolute value on both sides of the identity in (16) and using the boundedness of $\mathcal{J}'$, we obtain

$$\begin{aligned}
&\Bigg|\left[{}^{AB}{}_{k}I^{\alpha}_{(\frac{\gamma+\theta}{2})^{+}}\mathcal{J}(\theta)+{}^{AB}{}_{k}I^{\alpha}_{(\frac{\gamma+\theta}{2})^{-}}\mathcal{J}(\gamma)\right] \\
&\qquad -\left(\frac{(\theta-\gamma)^{\frac{\alpha}{k}}}{2^{\frac{\alpha}{k}-1}B(\alpha)\Gamma_k(\alpha)}\mathcal{J}\left(\frac{\theta+\gamma}{2}\right)+\frac{1-\alpha}{B(\alpha)}[\mathcal{J}(\gamma)+\mathcal{J}(\theta)]\right)\Bigg| \\
&\leq \frac{(\theta-\gamma)^{\frac{\alpha}{k}+1}}{B(\alpha)\Gamma_k(\alpha)}\left[\int_0^{1/2}\lambda^{\frac{\alpha}{k}}|\mathcal{J}'(\lambda\gamma+(1-\lambda)\theta)|d\lambda+\int_{1/2}^{1}(1-\lambda)^{\frac{\alpha}{k}}|\lambda'(\lambda\gamma+(1-\lambda)\theta)|d\lambda\right] \\
&\leq \frac{(\theta-\gamma)^{\frac{\alpha}{k}+1}\|\mathcal{J}'\|_\infty}{B(\alpha)\Gamma_k(\alpha)}\left[\int_0^{1/2}\lambda^{\frac{\alpha}{k}}d\lambda+\int_{1/2}^{1}(1-\lambda)^{\frac{\alpha}{k}}d\lambda\right] \\
&= \frac{k(\theta-\gamma)^{\frac{\alpha}{k}+1}\|\mathcal{J}'\|_\infty}{2^{\frac{\alpha}{k}}(\alpha+k)B(\alpha)\Gamma_k(\alpha)}.
\end{aligned}$$

Hence the proof is complete. □

Theorem 10. *If $\mathcal{J}$ satisfies the conditions of Lemma 1 and $\mathcal{J}'$ is convex on $[\gamma,\theta]$, then the inequality*

$$\begin{aligned}
&\Bigg|\left[{}^{AB}{}_{k}I^{\alpha}_{(\frac{\gamma+\theta}{2})^{+}}\mathcal{J}(\theta)+{}^{AB}{}_{k}I^{\alpha}_{(\frac{\gamma+\theta}{2})^{-}}\mathcal{J}(\gamma)\right] \\
&\qquad -\left(\frac{(\theta-\gamma)^{\frac{\alpha}{k}}}{2^{\frac{\alpha}{k}-1}B(\alpha)\Gamma_k(\alpha)}\mathcal{J}\left(\frac{\theta+\gamma}{2}\right)+\frac{1-\alpha}{B(\alpha)}\Big[\mathcal{J}(\gamma)+\mathcal{J}(\theta)\Big]\right)\Bigg| \\
&\leq \frac{k(\theta-\gamma)^{\frac{\alpha}{k}+1}}{2^{\frac{\alpha}{k}+1}(\alpha+k)B(\alpha)\Gamma_k(\alpha)}\Big[|\mathcal{J}'(\gamma)|+|\mathcal{J}'(\theta)|\Big] \qquad (27)
\end{aligned}$$

holds for all $\alpha, k > 0$.

Proof. Taking the absolute value on both sides of the identity in (16) and using the convexity of $|\mathcal{J}'|$, we obtain

$$\begin{aligned}
&\Bigg|\left[{}^{AB}{}_{k}I^{\alpha}_{(\frac{\gamma+\theta}{2})^{+}}\mathcal{J}(\theta)+{}^{AB}{}_{k}I^{\alpha}_{(\frac{\gamma+\theta}{2})^{-}}\mathcal{J}(\gamma)\right] \\
&\qquad -\left(\frac{(\theta-\gamma)^{\frac{\alpha}{k}}}{2^{\frac{\alpha}{k}-1}B(\alpha)\Gamma_k(\alpha)}\mathcal{J}\left(\frac{\theta+\gamma}{2}\right)+\frac{1-\alpha}{B(\alpha)}[\mathcal{J}(\gamma)+\mathcal{J}(\theta)]\right)\Bigg| \\
&\leq \frac{(\theta-\gamma)^{\frac{\alpha}{k}+1}}{B(\alpha)\Gamma_k(\alpha)}\left[\int_0^{1/2}\lambda^{\frac{\alpha}{k}}|\mathcal{J}'(\lambda\gamma+(1-\lambda)\theta)|d\lambda+\int_{1/2}^{1}(1-\lambda)^{\frac{\alpha}{k}}|\mathcal{J}'(\lambda\gamma+(1-\lambda)\theta)|d\lambda\right] \\
&\leq \frac{(\theta-\gamma)^{\frac{\alpha}{k}+1}}{B(\alpha)\Gamma_k(\alpha)}\left[\int_0^{1/2}\lambda^{\frac{\alpha}{k}}\Big(\lambda|\mathcal{J}'(\gamma)|+(1-\lambda)|\mathcal{J}'(\theta)|\Big)d\lambda\right. \\
&\qquad \left.+\int_{1/2}^{1}(1-\lambda)^{\frac{\alpha}{k}}\Big(\lambda|\mathcal{J}'(\gamma)|+(1-\lambda)|\mathcal{J}'(\theta)|\Big)d\lambda\right] \\
&= \frac{(\theta-\gamma)^{\frac{\alpha}{k}+1}}{B(\alpha)\Gamma_k(\alpha)}\left[|\mathcal{J}'(\gamma)|\left(\int_0^{1/2}\lambda^{\frac{\alpha}{k}+1}d\lambda+\int_{1/2}^{1}(1-\lambda)^{\frac{\alpha}{k}}\lambda d\lambda\right)\right. \\
&\qquad \left.+|\mathcal{J}'(\theta)|\left(\int_0^{1/2}\lambda^{\frac{\alpha}{k}}(1-\lambda)d\lambda+\int_{1/2}^{1}(1-\lambda)^{\frac{\alpha}{k}+1}d\lambda\right)\right] \\
&= \frac{k(\theta-\gamma)^{\frac{\alpha}{k}+1}}{2^{\frac{\alpha}{k}+1}(\alpha+k)B(\alpha)\Gamma_k(\alpha)}\Big[|\mathcal{J}'(\gamma)|+|\mathcal{J}'(\theta)|\Big].
\end{aligned}$$

Hence, the proof is complete. □

Remark 3. *It is worth noting that the inequalities in Theorems 7–10 provide estimates for the absolute of the error between the middle term and left or right terms in the inequality in Theorem 6, with some modifications.*

3. Conclusions

We proposed the definitions of some new generalized fractional integral operators called k-Atangana–Baleanu fractional integrals. The well-known Atangana–Baleanu fractional integrals are special cases of the newly proposed fractional integral operators when $k = 1$; see Remark 1. The Hermite–Hadamard inequality and some fractional integral inequalities involving these new generalized fractional integral operators have been established as an application of these new operators. It has been noted that certain results already provided can be obtained as particular cases from some of our results; see Remark 2. In addition, if we set $k = 1$ in the inequalities of Theorems 7–10, we obtain, respectively, the following inequalities involving the Atangana–Baleanu fractional integrals:

1.
$$\left|\left(\frac{(\theta-\gamma)^{\alpha}+(1-\alpha)\Gamma(\alpha)}{\Gamma(\alpha)}\right)\frac{\mathcal{J}(\gamma)+\mathcal{J}(\theta)}{B(\alpha)}-\left[{}^{AB}I^{\alpha}_{\gamma^+}\mathcal{J}(\theta)+{}^{AB}I^{\alpha}_{\theta^-}\mathcal{J}(\gamma)\right]\right| \leq \frac{2(\theta-\gamma)^{\alpha+1}\|\mathcal{J}'\|_{\infty}}{(\alpha+1)B(\alpha)\Gamma(\alpha)}\left(1-\frac{1}{2^{\alpha}}\right).$$

2.
$$\left|\left(\frac{(\theta-\gamma)^{\alpha}+(1-\alpha)\Gamma(\alpha)}{\Gamma(\alpha)}\right)\frac{\mathcal{J}(\gamma)+\mathcal{J}(\theta)}{B(\alpha)}-\left[{}^{AB}I^{\alpha}_{\gamma^+}\mathcal{J}(\theta)+{}^{AB}I^{\alpha}_{\theta^-}\mathcal{J}(\gamma)\right]\right| \leq \frac{(\theta-\gamma)^{\alpha+1}}{(\alpha+1)B(\alpha)\Gamma(\alpha)}\left(1-\frac{1}{2^{\alpha}}\right)\left[|\mathcal{J}'\gamma|+|\mathcal{J}'(\theta)|\right].$$

3.
$$\left|\left[{}^{AB}I^{\alpha}_{(\frac{\gamma+\theta}{2})^+}\mathcal{J}(\theta)+{}^{AB}I^{\alpha}_{(\frac{\gamma+\theta}{2})^-}\mathcal{J}(\gamma)\right] -\left(\frac{(\theta-\gamma)^{\alpha}}{2^{\alpha-1}B(\alpha)\Gamma(\alpha)}\mathcal{J}\left(\frac{\theta+\gamma}{2}\right)+\frac{1-\alpha}{B(\alpha)}[\mathcal{J}(\gamma)+\mathcal{J}(\theta)]\right)\right| \leq \frac{(\theta-\gamma)^{\alpha+1}\|\mathcal{J}'\|_{\infty}}{2^{\alpha}(\alpha+1)B(\alpha)\Gamma(\alpha)}.$$

4.
$$\left|\left[{}^{AB}I^{\alpha}_{(\frac{\gamma+\theta}{2})^+}\mathcal{J}(\theta)+{}^{AB}I^{\alpha}_{(\frac{\gamma+\theta}{2})^-}\mathcal{J}(\gamma)\right] -\left(\frac{(\theta-\gamma)^{\alpha}}{2^{\alpha-1}B(\alpha)\Gamma(\alpha)}\mathcal{J}\left(\frac{\theta+\gamma}{2}\right)+\frac{1-\alpha}{B(\alpha)}[\mathcal{J}(\gamma)+\mathcal{J}(\theta)]\right)\right| \leq \frac{(\theta-\gamma)^{\alpha+1}}{2^{\alpha+1}(\alpha+1)B(\alpha)\Gamma(\alpha)}\left[|\mathcal{J}'(\gamma)|+|\mathcal{J}'(\theta)|\right].$$

These special cases are new, to the best of our knowledge. We are of the opinion that the results in this paper will stimulate further research on fractional integral operators and their applications.

Author Contributions: Conceptualization, S.K. and E.R.N.; methodology, S.K. and E.R.N.; writing—original draft preparation, S.K. and E.R.N.; writing—review and editing, S.K. and E.R.N. All authors have read and agreed to the published version of the manuscript.

Funding: This research received no external funding.

Data Availability Statement: Not applicable.

Acknowledgments: The authors would like to express their profound gratitude to the anonymous reviewers for their comments and suggestions that have led to improve the final version of the manuscript.

Conflicts of Interest: The authors declare no conflict of interest.

References

1. Akdemir, A.O.; Karaoğlan, A.; Ragusa, M.A.; Set, E. Fractional integral inequalities via Atangana-Baleanu Operators for convex and concave functions. *J. Funct. Spaces* **2021**, *2021*, 1055434. [CrossRef]
2. Ali, M.A.; Goodrich, C.S.; Budak, H. Some new parametrized Newton-type inequalities for differentiable functions via fractional integrals. *J. Inequal. Appl.* **2023**, *2023*, 49. [CrossRef]
3. Butt, S.S.; Yousaf, S.; Akdemir, A.O.; Dokuyucu, M.A. New Hadamard-type integral inequalities via a general form of fractional integral operators. *Chaos Solitons Fractals* **2021**, *148*, 111025.
4. Chu, Y.-M.; Awan, M.U.; Javad, M.Z.; Khan, A.G. Bounds for the remainder in Simpsons inequality via n-convex functions of higher order using Katugampola fractional integrals. *J. Math.* **2020**, *2020*, 4189036. [CrossRef]
5. Guzman, P.M.; Valdes, J.E.N.; Gasimov, Y.S. Integral inequalities within the framework of generalized fractional integrals. *Fract. Differ. Calc.* **2021**, *11*, 69–84. [CrossRef]
6. Kermausuor, S.; Nwaeze, E.R. New midpoint and trapezoidal-type inequalities for prequasiinvex functions via generalized fractional integrals. *Stud. Univ.-Babes-Bolyai Math.* **2022**, *67*, 677–692. [CrossRef]
7. Peng, C.; Zhou, C.; Du, T.S. Riemann–Liouville fractional Simpson's inequalities through generalized $(m, h_1, h_2)-$preinvexity. *Ital. J. Pure Appl. Math.* **2017**, *38*, 345–367.
8. Sanli, Z. Simpson type Katugampola fractional integral inequalities via Harmonic convex functions. *Malaya J. Mat.* **2022**, *10*, 364–373. [CrossRef]
9. Yu, Y.; Lei, H.; Du, T. Estimates of upper bounds for differentiable mappings related to Katugampola fractional integrals and p-convex mappings. *AIMS Math.* **2021**, *64*, 3525–3545. [CrossRef]
10. Ali, M.A.; Kara, H.; Tariboon, J.; Asawasamrit, S.; Budak, H.; Heneci, F. Some new Simpson's-formula-type inequalities for twice differentiable convex functions via generalized fractional operators. *Symmetry* **2021**, *13*, 2249. [CrossRef]
11. Bibi, M.; Muddasar, M. Hermite–Hadamard type fractional integral inequalities for strongly generalized-prequasi-invex function. *Int. J. Nonlinear Anal. Appl.* **2022**, *13*, 515–525.
12. Bohner, M.; Khan, A.; Khan, M.; Mehmood, F.; Shaikh, M.A. Generalized perturbed Ostrowski-type inequalities. *Ann. Univ. Mariae-Curie-Sklodowska Sect. A Math.* **2022**, *75*, 13–29. [CrossRef]
13. Du, T.; Yuan, X. On the parametrized fractional integral inequalities and related applications. *Chaos, Solitons & Fractals* **2023**, *170*, 113375.
14. Farid, G. Some Riemann–Liouville fractional integral inequalities for convex functions. *J. Anal.* **2019**, *27*, 1095–1102. [CrossRef]
15. Farid, G.; Rehman, A.U.; Ain, Q.U. k fractional inequalities of Hadamard type for (h, k)-convex functions. *Computat. Methods Differ. Equ.* **2020**, *8*, 119–140.
16. Hussain, S.; Azhar, F.; Latif, M.A. Generalized fractional Ostrowski type integral inequalities for logarithmically h-convex function. *J. Anal.* **2021**, *29*, 1265–1278. [CrossRef]
17. Mohammed, P.O.; Brevik, I. A new version of the Hermite–Hadamard inequality for Riemann–Liouville fractional integrals. *Symmetry* **2019**, *12*, 610. [CrossRef]
18. Noor, M.A.; Noor, K.I.; Awan, M.U.; Khan, S. Fractional Hermite–Hadamard inequalities for some new classes of Godunova–Levin functions. *Appl. Math. Inf. Sci.* **2014**, *8*, 2865–2872. [CrossRef]
19. Nwaeze, E.R.; Kermausuor, S.; Tameru, A.M. Some new k-Riemann–Liouville fractional integral inequalities associated with the strongly η-quasiconvex functions with modulus $\mu \geq 0$. *J. Inequal. Appl.* **2018**, *2018*, 139. [CrossRef]
20. Sahoo, S.K.; Mohammed, P.O.; Kodamasingh, B.; Tariq, M.; Hamed, Y.S. New fractional integral inequalities for functions pertaining to Caputo-Frabrizio Operator. *Fractal Fract.* **2022**, *6*, 171. [CrossRef]
21. Sarikaya, M.Z.; Set, E.; Yaldiz, H.; Başak, N. Hermite–Hadamard's inequalities for fractional integrals and related fractional inequalities. *Math. Comput. Model.* **2013**, *57*, 2403–2407. [CrossRef]
22. Zabandan, G.; Bodaghi, A.; Kiliçman, A. The Hermite–Hadamard inequality for r-convex functions. *J. Inequal. Appl.* **2012**, *2012*, 215. [CrossRef]
23. Hadamard, J. Etude sur les propriétés des fonctions entiéres et en particulier d'une fonction considérée par Riemann. *J. Math. Pures Appl.* **1893**, *58*, 171–215.

24. Wu, S.; Iqbal, S.; Aamir, M.; Samraiz, M.; Younus, A. On some Hermite–Hadamard inequalities involving *k*-fractional operators. *J. Inequal. Appl.* **2021**, *2021*, 32. [CrossRef]
25. Gorenflo, R.; Mainardi, F. *Fractional Calculus: Integral and Differential Equations of Fractional Order*; Springer: Wien, Austria, 1997; pp. 223–276.
26. Miller, S.; Ross, B. *An Introduction to the Fractional Calculus and Fractional Differential Equations*; John Willey & Sons: Hoboken, NJ, USA, 1993; p. 2.
27. Podlubny, I. *Fractional Differential Equations*; Academic Press: San Diego, CA, USA, 1999.
28. Mubeen, S.; Habibullah, G.M. *k*-fractional integrals and applications. *Int. J. Contem. Math. Sci.* **2012**, *7*, 89–94.
29. Diaz, R.; Pariguan, E. On hypergeometric functions and Pochhammer *k*-symbol. *Divulg. Mat.* **2007**, *15*, 179–192.
30. Atangana, A.; Baleanu, D. New fractional derivatives with non-local and non-singular kernel. *Therm. Sci.* **2016**, *20*, 763–769.
31. Abdeljawad, T.; Baleanu, D. Integration by parts and its applications of a new local fractional derivative with Mittag–Leffler nonsingular kernel. *J. Nonlinear Sci. Appl.* **2017**, *10*, 1098–1107. [CrossRef]
32. Fernandez, A.; Mohammed, P. Hermite–Hadamard inequalities in fractional calculus defined using Mittag–Leffler kernels. *Math. Meth. Appl. Sci.* **2021**, *44*, 8414–8431. [CrossRef]
33. Kashuri, A. Hermite–Hadamard type inequalities for the ABK-fractional integrals. *J. Comput. Anal. Appl.* **2021**, *29*, 309–326.

fractal and fractional

Article

On Inequalities and Filtration Associated with the Nonlinear Fractional Operator

Maryam Nazir [1], Syed Zakir Hussain Bukhari [1], Jong-Suk Ro [2,3,*], Fairouz Tchier [4] and Sarfraz Nawaz Malik [5]

1 Department of Mathematics, Mirpur University of Science and Technology, Mirpur 10250, Pakistan; maryam.maths@must.edu.pk (M.N.); fatmi@must.edu.pk (S.Z.H.B.)
2 School of Electrical and Electronics Engineering, Chung-Ang University, Dongjak-gu, Seoul 06974, Republic of Korea
3 Department of Intelligent Energy and Industry, Chung-Ang University, Dongjak-gu, Seoul 06974, Republic of Korea
4 Mathematics Department, College of Science, King Saud University, P.O. Box 22452, Riyadh 11495, Saudi Arabia; ftchier@ksu.edu.sa
5 Department of Mathematics, COMSATS University Islamabad, Wah Campus, Wah Cantt 47040, Pakistan; snmalik110@ciitwah.edu.pk or snmalik110@yahoo.com
* Correspondence: jsro@cau.ac.kr

Abstract: In this paper, we study a new filtration class $\mathcal{MF}^{\mu}_{\alpha,\beta}$, associated with the filtration of infinitesimal generators, by using the nonlinear fractional differential operator and study certain properties, like sharp Fekete–Szegö inequalities and filtration problems.

Keywords: infinitesimal generator; Fekete–Szegö inequality; semi-group; differential subordination; fractional differential operator

MSC: 30C35; 30C50; 30D05; 37C25; 30C45

Citation: Nazir, M.; Bukhari, S.Z.H.; Ro, J.-S.; Tchier, F.; Malik, S.N. On Inequalities and Filtration Associated with the Nonlinear Fractional Operator. *Fractal Fract.* **2023**, *7*, 726. https://doi.org/10.3390/fractalfract7100726

Academic Editor: Ivanka Stamova

Received: 7 August 2023
Revised: 26 September 2023
Accepted: 28 September 2023
Published: 30 September 2023

1. Introduction and Preliminaries

Assume that $\mathcal{H}$ is a family of analytic functions. For a natural j and $a \in \mathbb{C}$ and let

$$\mathcal{H}^j_a := \left\{ f \in \mathcal{H} : \ f(\xi) = a + \xi + a_{j+1}\xi^{j+1} + a_{j+2}\xi^{j+2} + \ldots, \ \xi \in \mathbb{E} \right\} \tag{1}$$

be the subclass of $\mathcal{H}$. Furthermore, we deduce that

$$\mathcal{H}^j_0 := \left\{ f : f(\xi) = \xi + a_{j+1}\xi^{j+1} + \ldots, \frac{f^{(j+1)}(0)}{(j+1)!} = a_{j+1} \ \xi \in \mathbb{E} \right\}. \tag{2}$$

For $j = 1$, we observe that

$$\mathcal{H}^1_0 = \mathcal{A} := \left\{ f : f(\xi) = \xi + a_2\xi^2 + a_3\xi^3 + \ldots, \ \xi \in \mathbb{E} \right\} \tag{3}$$

and $\Omega = \{s \in \mathcal{A} : s(0) = 0\}$. The family $\mathcal{A}$ is given by (3). For $\lambda \in \mathbb{C}$, let $\phi(f, \lambda) = a_3 - \lambda a_2^2$ be a quadratic functional. The problem related to this function involves the derivation of sharp estimates for the functional absolute values $\phi(., \lambda)$ for certain types of functions over the class $\mathcal{A}$. Keogh and Merks [1] showed that

$$|\phi(f, \lambda)| \leq \begin{cases} \max\left(\frac{1}{3}, |1-\lambda|\right), & f \in \mathcal{C} \\ \max\left(\frac{1}{2}, |1-\lambda|\right), & f \in \mathcal{S}^*_{\frac{1}{2}} \end{cases}, \tag{4}$$

and these inequalities are best possible. In [2], it is shown that for the functions f such that $\Re e\frac{f(\xi)}{\xi} > \frac{1}{2}$, $\xi \in \mathbb{E}$, the following sharp result holds

$$|\phi(f, \lambda)| \le \max(1, |1 - \lambda|).$$

Consider the mapping $f \in \mathcal{A}$, defined by the limit given by

$$\lim_{t \to 0^+} \frac{\xi - u_t(\xi)}{t} = f(\xi), \quad t \ge 0.$$

This mapping is called an infinitesimal generator of one-parameter family of a continuous semi-group, if, for $\xi \in \mathbb{E}$, the Cauchy problem,

$$\begin{cases} \frac{\partial}{\partial t}(u(\xi, t)) + f(u(\xi, t)) = 0, \\ u(\xi, t) = \xi, t = 0 \end{cases} \tag{5}$$

has a unique solution $u = u(\xi, t) \in \mathbb{E}, t \ge 0$. In this case, the solution $u = u(\xi, t) \in \mathbb{E}, t \ge 0$ of (5) forms a semi-group of holomorphic or analytic self-mappings in $\mathbb{E}$ generated by f; for details, see [3–5]. The family of all generators, known as a semi-complete vector field on $\mathbb{E}$, is expressed by $\mathcal{G}$. Another important form of the family $\mathcal{G}$ is studied by Berkson and Porta [6] and can be restated below.

Theorem 1. *For $f \in \mathcal{A}$ with $f(\xi) \neq 0$, f is a generator on $\mathbb{E}$, if and only if $\exists$ a point $\tau \in \overline{\mathbb{E}}$ and a function $h \in \mathcal{A}$ with $\Re e h(\xi) \ge 0$:*

$$f(\xi) = h(\xi)(\tau - \xi)(\xi\overline{\tau} - 1), \ \xi \in \mathbb{E}.$$

In particular, $f \in \mathcal{A}$ is a generator if and only if $\Re e\left(\frac{f(\xi)}{\xi}\right) > 0$. We express the family of such a generator using $\mathcal{G}$. The condition $\Re e\left(\frac{f(\xi)}{\xi}\right) > 0$ seems simple, but often it is hard to verify. The condition $\Re e(f'(\xi)) > 0$, provided by Noshiro and Warschawski [4,7], independently implies that a function $f \in \mathcal{A}$ is univalent. It can be taken as sufficient for $f \in \mathcal{A}$ to consider it a generator. All infinitesimal generators may not be univalent. Then, $\Re e(f'(\xi)) > 0$ cannot ensure that $f \in \mathcal{G}$.

In recent years, many remarkable developments have been made in the study of the generation theory of one parametric semi-group of analytic functions. This study not only answers many diverse questions from different areas of mathematical analysis, but also deals with significantly new developments in the initial and boundary value partial differential equations, approximation theory and the theory of singular integrals. The generation theory of semi-groups has been used in Markov stochastic processes and in the theory of branching processes. This leads to its involvement in one-dimensional complex analysis and is the main motivation of this work.

In this paper, our main task is to establish a connection between the Fekete–Szegö quadratic functional and the class of infinitesimal generators $\mathcal{G}$. For this purpose, we define a class $\mathcal{MF} = \{f_s, s > 0\}$, of all $f \in \mathcal{A}$, such that $\phi(f, \lambda)$ satisfies the sharp estimates $\sup_{f \in \mathcal{MF}}|\phi(f, \lambda)| = \max(s, |1 - \lambda|)$. Moreover, in the case of an invertible function $f \in \mathcal{A}$, we have

$$\sup_{f \in \mathcal{MF}} \left|\phi\left(f^{-1}, \lambda\right)\right| = \sup_{f \in \mathcal{MF}} |\phi(f, \lambda)|.$$

Definition 1. *A filtration of $\mathcal{G}$ is a family $\mathcal{MF} = \{\wp_s : s \in [c, d], \wp_s \subseteq \mathcal{G}\}$, where c, $d \in [-\infty, +\infty]$ and $c < d : \wp_s \subseteq \wp_t$, whenever $c \le s \le t \le d$. Furthermore, a filtration is strict if $\wp_s \subset \wp_t$, $s < t$.*

We are focused on building a relationship between the family $\mathcal{G}$ of infinitesimal generators and the Fekete–Szegö functional $\phi(f, \lambda)$. Here, we establish a more generalized mechanism for $f \in \mathcal{A}$ to be in the family $\mathcal{G}$. Our task is to establish a connection between the family of infinitesimal generators $\mathcal{G}$ and the Fekete–Szegö functional $\phi(f, \lambda)$ by determining a filtration $\{\wp_s, s > 0\}$ such that $\sup_{f \in \mathcal{MF}} |\phi(f, \lambda)| = \max(s, |1 - \lambda|)$. Here, we assume a more generalized condition for $f \in \mathcal{A}$ to be in $\mathcal{G}$ by:

Definition 2. *Assume that $h(\xi) = \frac{f(\xi)}{\xi}$ is strongly starlike of order $\alpha = \frac{1}{\mu}$, such that*

$$\left|\arg\left(\xi^{-1} f(\xi)\right)\right| \leq \frac{\pi}{2\mu}, \quad 0 < \frac{1}{\mu} \leq 1, \; \xi \in \mathbb{E}.$$

A function $f \in \mathcal{A}$ is in $\mathcal{G}$ if and only if $\Re e\left(\frac{f(\xi)}{\xi}\right)^{\mu} > 0$ and $-1 \leq \mu \leq 1$.

By using Definition 2, we now develop some new filtration families by using a nonlinear differential operator

$$\wp^{\mu}_{\alpha,\beta}(f)(\xi) = \alpha\left(\frac{f(\xi)}{\xi}\right)^{\mu} + (\beta\mu + \Lambda) w(\xi) + \Lambda \frac{\xi \mu w'(\xi)}{1 - \mu + \mu w(\xi)}, \tag{6}$$

where $w(\xi) = \frac{\xi f'(\xi)}{f(\xi)}$, $\alpha, \beta \in \mathbb{R}$, $\Lambda = 1 - \alpha - \beta$, $-1 \leq \mu \leq 1$ and $\xi \in \mathbb{E}$, and we establish sharp bounds on the modulus of $\phi(f, \lambda)$ over these filtration classes.

For the sake of completeness, we are required to obtain the following important results from Geometric Function Theory.

2. Preliminaries

Let $\Psi : \mathbb{C}^3 \times \mathbb{E} \to \mathbb{C}$ and let $h \in \mathcal{S}$ in $\mathbb{E}$. If p is analytic in $\mathbb{E}$ and satisfies the nonlinear second order differential subordination

$$\Psi\left(p(\xi), \xi p'(\xi), \xi^2 p''(\xi); \xi\right) \prec h(\xi), \tag{7}$$

then p is called a solution of (7). The function $q \in \mathcal{S}$ is called a dominant of the solutions of (7), or simply a dominant, if $p(\xi) \prec q(\xi)$ for all p satisfying (7). A dominant $q : q(\xi) \prec \tilde{q}(\xi)$ for all dominants q of (7) is said to be the best dominant of (7).

Lemma 1. *Let $\beta, \tau \in \mathbb{C}$ and $\beta \neq 0$. Let $h_1 \in \mathcal{A}$ and $\Re e[\beta h_1(\xi) + \tau] > 0$. Then, the solution h of*

$$h(\xi) + \frac{\xi h'(\xi)}{\beta h(\xi) + \tau} = h_1(\xi)$$

satisfies $\Re e[\beta h(\xi) + \tau] > 0 : h(0) = c$.

For the details of Lemma 1, see [8].

Lemma 2. *Let $\tau \in \mathbb{R}$, $f \in \mathcal{A}$ and $\Omega \subset \mathbb{C}$. Then, $\Re e f(\xi) > \tau$, $\xi \in \mathbb{E}$ if and only if the functional s is defined by*

$$s(\xi) = \frac{f(0) - f(\xi)}{2\tau - f(0) - f(\xi)} \in \mathcal{A}. \tag{8}$$

Lemma 3. *Suppose $h : h(0) = 1, \Omega \subset \mathbb{C}$ and $\Psi : \mathbb{C}^3 \times \mathbb{E} \to \mathbb{C}$ satisfy*

$$\Psi(i\rho, \sigma, u + iv; \xi) \notin \Omega, \qquad (\xi \in \mathbb{E}),$$

for $\rho, \sigma, u, \sigma \in \mathbb{R}$, $\sigma \leq -\frac{1+\rho^2}{2}$ and $\sigma + u \leq 0$. If, for the functional Ψ, we have

$$\Psi\left(h, \xi h', \xi^2 h''\right)(\xi) \in \Omega \qquad (\xi \in \mathbb{E}),$$

then $\Re eh(\xi) > 0, \xi \in \mathbb{E}$.

For the proof of the both Lemmas 2 and 3, we refer to [9].

Lemma 4. *If* $w \in \mathcal{A}$ *and* $w(\xi) = \sum\limits_{j=1}^{\infty} b_j \xi^j$, *then* $|b_2| \leq 1 - |b_1|^2$ *and* $|b_2 - sb_1^2| \leq \max(1, |s|)$ *for* $s \in \mathbb{C}$.

A detailed proof of Lemma 4 can be found in [1].

Lemma 5. *Let* $f \in \mathcal{A} : |f(\xi)| < 1$. *If* $|f(\xi)|$ *attains its highest value at* ξ_0, *then*

$$\frac{\xi_0 f'(\xi_0)}{f(\xi_0)} = m, \; m \geq 1.$$

For detailed information of Lemma 5, see [10].

3. A Function as an Infinitesimal Generator

In the first Theorem, we drive some sufficient conditions on $\wp^{\mu}_{\alpha,\beta}(f)$ which ensure that f is a generator.

Theorem 2. *For* $\alpha, \beta, \mu \in \mathbb{R}$ *and* $-1 \leq \mu \leq 1$, *consider that*

$$\Delta_1 = \left\{ s = x + iy : \mu\beta - \alpha + 1 \geq x; \;\; (x - 1 - \beta\mu)^2 - \alpha^2 \geq y^2; \;\; \alpha \geq 0 \right\},$$

and

$$\Delta_2 = \left\{ s = x + iy : x > \mu\beta - \alpha + 1; \;\; y^2 \leq (x - 1 - \beta\mu)^2 - \alpha^2; \;\; \alpha < 0 \right\}.$$

For the image domain $\Delta \subset \mathbb{C}$ *such that*

$$\Delta = \begin{cases} \mathbb{C} \setminus \Delta_1, & \alpha \geq 0 \\ \mathbb{C} \setminus \Delta_2, & \alpha < 0 \end{cases}, \tag{9}$$

if, for $f \in \mathcal{A}$ *and* $\wp^{\mu}_{\alpha,\beta}(f) \subseteq \Delta$, *then* $f \in \mathcal{G}$.

Proof. For the mapping $f \in \mathcal{A}$ and $h(\xi) = \left(\frac{f(\xi)}{\xi}\right)^{\mu}$, we see that

$$\mu \frac{\xi f'(\xi)}{f(\xi)} = \mu + \frac{\xi h'(\xi)}{h(\xi)}$$

and

$$\frac{\mu\xi\left(\frac{\xi f'(\xi)}{f(\xi)}\right)'}{1 + \mu\left(\frac{\xi f'(\xi)}{f(\xi)} - 1\right)} + \frac{\xi f'(\xi)}{f(\xi)} = \frac{\left(\xi^2 h'(\xi)\right)'}{(\xi h(\xi))'} + 1.$$

Thus, for $\Lambda = 1 - \alpha - \beta$, we find that

$$\begin{aligned} \wp^{\mu}_{\alpha,\beta}(f)(\xi) &= \mu\beta + \Lambda + \alpha h(\xi) + \frac{\beta\xi h'(\xi)}{h(\xi)} + \Lambda \frac{\left(\xi^2 h'(\xi)\right)'}{(\xi h(\xi))'} \\ &= 1 - \alpha + \beta(\mu - 1) + \alpha h(\xi) + \frac{\beta\xi h'(\xi)}{h(\xi)} + \Lambda \frac{\left(\xi^2 h'(\xi)\right)'}{(\xi h(\xi))'}. \end{aligned}$$

By choosing $r = h(\xi)$, $s = \xi h'(\xi)$ and $t = \xi^2 h''(\xi)$, we study the admissibility conditions as:

For $\Lambda = 1 - \beta - \alpha$, consider that

$$\Psi(r,s,t;\xi) = 1 - \alpha + \beta(\mu - 1) + \alpha r + \beta\frac{s}{r} + \Lambda\frac{2s+t}{s+r},$$

and

$$\Psi\left(h, \xi h', \xi^2 h''; \xi\right) = 1 - \alpha + \beta(\mu - 1) + \alpha h(\xi) + \beta\frac{\xi h'(\xi)}{h(\xi)} + \Lambda\frac{\left(\xi^2 h'(\xi)\right)'}{(\xi h(\xi))'}.$$

In view of Lemma 3, we prove that $f \in \mathcal{G}$. To establish this inclusion, it is enough to prove that h maps $\mathbb{E}$ onto the right half plane. For this, we need to show that

$$\Psi(i\rho, \sigma, u + i\sigma; \xi) \notin \Delta, \text{ when } \rho,\ \sigma,\ u,\ \sigma \in \mathbb{R},\ \sigma \leq -\frac{1}{2}\left(1+\rho^2\right),\ \sigma + u \leq 0. \tag{10}$$

For $\Lambda = 1 - \alpha - \beta$, we see that

$$X = \Re e\Psi(i\rho, \sigma, u + i\sigma; \xi) = 1 - \alpha + \beta(\mu - 1) + \frac{\Lambda}{\rho^2 + \sigma^2}[(u + 2\sigma)\sigma + v\rho],$$

and

$$Y = \operatorname{Im}\Psi(i\rho, \sigma, u + i\sigma; \xi) = \Lambda\frac{v\sigma - (u+2\sigma)\rho}{\rho^2 + \sigma^2} - \frac{\beta\sigma}{\rho} + \alpha\rho.$$

This implies that

$$\frac{Y - \alpha\rho + \frac{\beta\sigma}{\rho}}{X - 1 + \alpha - \beta(\mu - 1)} = \frac{v\sigma - (u+2\sigma)\rho}{(u+2\sigma)\sigma + v\rho},$$

or we can write that

$$\frac{Y - \alpha\rho + \frac{\beta\sigma}{\rho}}{(X - 1 + \alpha - \beta\mu) + \beta} = \frac{\sigma}{\rho} - \frac{(u+2\sigma)\left(\rho^2 + \alpha\sigma^2\right)}{\rho(v\rho + (u+2\sigma)\sigma)}. \tag{11}$$

Moreover, if we let $\kappa = X - 1 + \alpha - \beta\mu$ and

$$Y_{\sigma,\rho,u} = \frac{(u+2\sigma)\left(\rho^2 + \sigma^2\right)}{(v\rho + (u+2\sigma)\sigma)},$$

then (11) becomes

$$Y - \alpha\rho + \frac{\beta\sigma}{\rho} = (\kappa + \beta)\frac{\sigma}{\rho} - \frac{\kappa + \beta}{\rho}Y_{\sigma,\rho,u},$$

or

$$Y = \rho\alpha + \kappa\frac{\sigma}{\rho} - \frac{\kappa + \beta}{\rho}Y_{\sigma,\rho,u}.$$

Therefore, we have

$$Y \neq \rho\left[\alpha + \kappa\frac{\sigma}{\rho^2}\right] = Y_{\sigma,\rho,u}(\kappa), \text{ where } \rho \in \mathbb{R} \text{ and } \sigma \leq -\frac{1}{2}\left(1 + \rho^2\right).$$

Condition (10) holds if every point of $\Omega = \{s \in \mathcal{A} : s(0) = 0\}$ is found on the graph of $Y_{\sigma,\rho,u}$, for some σ and ρ. Next, we analyze the range of $Y_{\sigma,\rho,u}(\kappa)$.
Case I: For $\alpha \geq 0$, if we take $\kappa > 0$, then by letting

$$y = \rho\left[\alpha + \kappa\frac{\sigma}{\rho^2}\right], \tag{12}$$

we see that $\alpha\rho^2 - \rho y + \sigma\kappa = 0$ implies that

$$\rho = \frac{y \pm \sqrt{y^2 - 4\alpha\sigma\kappa}}{2\alpha}. \tag{13}$$

Furthermore, by using (12) for $\sigma \leq \frac{-(1+\rho^2)}{2}$, we have

$$y = \alpha\rho - \kappa\frac{(1+\rho^2)}{2\rho}, \text{ implies that } \rho = \frac{-y \pm \sqrt{y^2 - (\kappa - 2\alpha)\kappa}}{2(\kappa - 2\alpha)}.$$

Taking $y^2 - (\kappa - 2\alpha)\kappa \geq 0$, we have $y \geq \sqrt{(\kappa - 2\alpha)\kappa}$, where $(\kappa - 2\alpha)\kappa$ is taken to be positive. Also,

$$\begin{aligned} \left|Y_{\sigma,\rho,u}(\kappa)\right| &= \left|\alpha - \kappa\frac{1}{2\rho^2}\left(1+\rho^2\right)\right||\rho| \geq \left[\alpha - \kappa\frac{(1+\rho^2)}{2\rho^2}\right]|\rho| \\ &\geq \sqrt{(\kappa - 2\alpha)\kappa} = \sqrt{(X - 1 - \beta\mu)^2 - \alpha^2}. \end{aligned}$$

Hence $Y_{\sigma,\rho,u}(X) = \sqrt{(X - 1 - \beta\mu)^2 - \alpha^2}$ holds for all reals. For $y \in \mathbb{R}$, we can select a ρ given by (13), so that (12) holds.
Case II: For $\kappa \leq 0$, we have

$$\left|Y_{\sigma,\rho,u}(\kappa)\right| \geq \sqrt{(\kappa - 2\alpha)\kappa} = \sqrt{(\kappa - \alpha)^2 - \alpha^2} = \sqrt{(X - 1 - \beta\mu)^2 - \alpha^2},$$

where we minimize $\left(\alpha - \kappa\frac{(1+\rho^2)}{2\rho^2}\right)|\rho|$ in respect to ρ. Thus, for $\alpha \geq 0$ and $\kappa \leq 0$, $\left|Y_{\sigma,\rho,u}(X)\right|^2$ assumes all values greater than or equal to $(\kappa - 2\alpha)\kappa = (-1 + X - \beta\mu)^2 - \alpha^2$. Therefore, if $\kappa \leq 0$, then $X \leq 1 - \alpha + \beta\mu$, and in this case the range of $\wp^{\mu}_{\alpha,\beta}$ is

$$\mathbb{C}\backslash\Delta_1 = \left\{s = x + iy : x \leq 1 - \alpha + \beta\mu;\ y^2 \geq (x - 1 - \beta\mu)^2 - \alpha^2;\ \alpha \geq 0\right\}.$$

Case III: Again, for $\kappa \leq 0$, we have

$$\begin{aligned} \left|Y_{\sigma,\rho,u}(\kappa)\right| &= -\left[\alpha - \kappa\frac{1+\rho^2}{2\rho^2}\right]|\rho| \geq |\rho|\left(\kappa\frac{1+\rho^2}{2\rho^2} - \alpha\right) \geq \sqrt{(\kappa - 2\alpha)\kappa} \\ &= (-1 + X - \beta\mu)^2 - \alpha^2. \end{aligned}$$

For $\alpha < 0, \kappa \geq 0$, we observe that $X > 1 - \alpha + \beta\mu$ and $y^2 \geq (x - 1 - \beta\mu)^2 - \alpha^2$, and, in this case, the range for $\wp^{\mu}_{\alpha,\beta}$ is

$$\mathbb{C}\backslash\Delta_2 = \left\{s = x + iy : x > 1 - \alpha + \beta\mu;\ y^2 \geq (x - 1 - \beta\mu)^2 - \alpha^2;\ \alpha < 0\right\}.$$

Thus, for $\alpha < 0$, the union of graphs of $Y_{\sigma,\rho,u}(\kappa)$ lies in the set $\mathbb{C}\backslash\Delta_2$; $\forall\ \rho \in \mathbb{R}$ and $\sigma \leq -\frac{1}{2}(1+\rho^2)$.

Combining the above cases, as well as applying Lemma 3, we complete the proof of the above Theorem. □

Remark 1. *From the geometry of the regions Δ_1 and Δ_2 along with $f \in \mathcal{A}$, $-1 \leq \mu \leq 1$, $\alpha, \beta \in \mathbb{R}$ and $\xi \in \mathbb{E}$, if $\alpha \geq 0$; $\frac{\alpha+\beta}{2} \geq 1 - \alpha + \beta\mu : \beta \geq \frac{2-3\alpha}{1-2\mu}$, then we obtain the results listed below.*

Corollary 1. *Let $\alpha, \beta \in \mathbb{R}$, $f \in \mathcal{A}$, $\alpha, \beta \in \mathbb{R}$, $-1 \leq \mu \leq 1$ and $\xi \in \mathbb{E}$. If either $\alpha \geq 0$; $\beta < \alpha$ and*

$$\Re e\wp^{\mu}_{\alpha,\beta}(f)(\xi) > \beta\mu - \alpha + 1,$$

or $\alpha < 0$; $\beta > \alpha$ *and*

$$\Re e \wp^{\mu}_{\alpha,\beta}(f)(\xi) < \beta\mu - \alpha + 1,$$

then $f \in \mathcal{G}$.

4. Maximization of the Fekete-Szegö Functional

We define a new class $\mathcal{MF}^{\mu}_{\alpha,\beta}$ in connection with the nonlinear operator $\wp^{\mu}_{\alpha,\beta}(f)$.

Definition 3. *For* $f \in \mathcal{A}$, *we have* $f \in \mathcal{MF}^{\mu}_{\alpha,\beta}$, *that is*

$$\Re e \wp^{\mu}_{\alpha,\beta}(f)(\xi) > \frac{\alpha+\beta}{2},$$

where $\beta \geq \frac{2-3\alpha}{1-2\mu}$ *or*

$$\Re e \wp^{\mu}_{\alpha,\beta}(f)(\xi) > \frac{1-\alpha(1+\mu)}{(1-2\mu)}.$$

Thus, we note that
For $\mu = 1$ and $\alpha + \beta \geq 2$, we have $\mathcal{MF}^{\mu}_{\alpha,\beta} = \emptyset$.
For $\alpha = 1$, $\beta = 0$ and $-1 \leq \mu \leq 1$, we have $\mathcal{MF}^{\mu}_{1,0} = \mathcal{G}$.
For $\alpha = 0$ and $-1 \leq \mu \leq 1$, we have $\mathcal{MF}^{\mu}_{\alpha,\beta} = \mathcal{M}_{1-\beta}$ of order $\frac{\beta}{2}$, where $\beta \geq \frac{2}{1-2\mu}$.

Remark 2. *For* $\alpha \geq 0$, $-1 \leq \mu \leq 1$ *and* $\beta \leq \frac{2-3\alpha}{1-2\mu}$, *we have* $\frac{\alpha+\beta}{2} \geq 1 - \alpha + \beta\mu$ *and* $\mathcal{MF}^{\mu}_{\alpha,\beta} \subset \mathcal{G}$.

In the next Theorem, we work out the conditions of α, β and μ, so that for $\phi(.,\lambda)$, we obtain $|\phi(f,\lambda)| \leq \max(s, |1-\lambda|)$.

Theorem 3. *Let* $f \in \mathcal{A}$, $\alpha, \beta \in \mathbb{R}$, $-1 \leq \mu \leq 1$ *and* $\xi \in \mathbb{E}$ *satisfy*

$$\alpha - (2\mu - 3)\beta < 2, \quad (-3\mu - 2)\alpha - (2\mu + 1)\beta < 2(2\mu + 1),$$

and

$$\lambda_0 = (\alpha + 2\beta)\mu + 2(1 - \alpha - \beta)(2\mu + 1),$$

such that $\beta = \frac{2(\mu+1)}{4+3\mu-6\mu^2}$. *If we denote the level set of function*

$$\varphi\binom{\mu}{\alpha,\beta} = \frac{2 + (2\mu - 3)\beta - \alpha}{(\alpha + 2\beta)\mu + 2(1 - \alpha - \beta)(2\mu + 1)} > 0,$$

then $|\phi(f,\lambda)| \leq \max\left(\varphi\binom{\mu}{\alpha,\beta}|1-\lambda|\right)$ *for* $\lambda \in \mathbb{C}$, *over the family* $\mathcal{MF}^{\mu}_{\alpha,\beta}$.

Proof. Let $f \in \mathcal{A}$ be in the family $\mathcal{MF}^{\mu}_{\alpha,\beta}$. Then, $\wp^{\mu}_{\alpha,\beta}(f)(\xi)$ is obtained by using

$$\alpha\left(\frac{f(\xi)}{\xi}\right)^{\mu} = \alpha + \alpha\mu a_2\xi + \alpha\left[\mu a_3 + \frac{\mu(\mu-1)}{2}a_2^2\right]\xi^2 + \ldots,$$

$$\beta\mu\frac{\xi f'(\xi)}{f(\xi)} = \beta\mu + \beta\mu a_2\xi + \beta\mu\left(2a_3 - a_2^2\right)\xi^2 + \ldots,$$

and

$$\frac{\mu\xi\left(\frac{\xi f'(\xi)}{f(\xi)}\right)'}{\mu\frac{\xi f'(\xi)}{f(\xi)} - \mu + 1} + \frac{\xi f'(\xi)}{f(\xi)} = 1 + (1+\mu)a_2\xi + \left[(1+2\mu)2a_3 - (\mu+1)^2a_2^2\right]\xi^2 + \ldots$$

in (6), as seen below

$$\wp^{\mu}_{\alpha,\beta}(f)(\xi) = 1 - (1-\mu)\beta + (\mu+\Lambda)a_2\xi + \left[\lambda_0 a_3 - \lambda_1 a_2^2\right]\xi^2 + ..., \tag{14}$$

where

$$\Lambda = 1-\alpha-\beta, \lambda_0 = (-3\mu-2)\alpha - (2\mu+1)(\beta+2)$$

and

$$\lambda_1 = \left(1 - \frac{3\alpha}{2} - \beta\right)\mu^2 - \left(\frac{3}{2}\alpha + \beta - 2\right)\mu + \Lambda.$$

Now, consider that

$$s(\xi) = \frac{\wp^{\mu}_{\alpha,\beta}(f)(\xi) - \wp^{\mu}_{\alpha,\beta}(f)(0)}{-2\varkappa + \wp^{\mu}_{\alpha,\beta}(f)(0) + \wp^{\mu}_{\alpha,\beta}(f)(\xi)}.$$

By using (14), we see that

$$s(\xi) = \frac{(\Lambda+\mu)a_2\xi}{2+\mu_1\beta-\alpha} + \left[\frac{(\lambda_0+\lambda_1 a_2^2)a_3}{2+\mu_1\beta-\alpha} + \frac{(\Lambda+\mu)^2 a_2^2}{[2+\mu_1\beta-\alpha]^2}\right]\xi^2 + ...,$$

where $\mu_1 = 2\mu - 3$. If we take $s(\xi) = \sum_{j=1}^{\infty} b_j \xi^j$ and $\mu_1 = 2\mu - 3$, then we note that

$$s(\xi) = \frac{(\Lambda+\mu)a_2\xi}{2+\mu_1\beta-\alpha} + \left[\frac{(\lambda_0+\lambda_1 a_2^2)a_3}{2+\mu_1\beta-\alpha} + \frac{(\Lambda+\mu)^2 a_2^2}{[2+\mu_1\beta-\alpha]^2}\right]\xi^2 + \sum_{j=3}^{\infty} b_j \xi^j.$$

On comparison, we have

$$b_1 = \frac{(\Lambda+\mu)}{2+\mu_1\beta-\alpha}a_2 = \tau_0 a_2,$$

$$b_2 = \frac{\lambda_0}{2+\mu_1\beta-\alpha}\left[a_3 - \frac{\lambda_1[\alpha-2-\mu_1\beta] - (\Lambda+\mu)^2}{[2+\mu_1\beta-\alpha]\lambda_0}u_2^2\right] - \tau_1\left[a_3 - \tau_2 a_2^2\right],$$

where $\mu_1 = 2\mu - 3$, $\tau_0 = \frac{(1-\alpha-\beta+\mu)}{2+\mu_1\beta-\alpha}$, $\tau_1 = \frac{\lambda_0}{2+\mu_1\beta-\alpha}$, $\tau_2 = \frac{\lambda_1(\alpha-2-\mu_1\beta)-(1-\alpha-\beta+\mu)^2}{(2+\mu_1\beta-\alpha)\lambda_0}$ and $\tau_3 = \tau_1\tau_2$. Thus, with the help of Lemma 4, we obtain the following relation

$$\left|b_2 - sb_1^2\right| = \left|\tau_1\left[a_3 - \tau_2 a_2^2\right] - s\tau_0^2 a_2^2\right| = \left|\tau_1 a_3 - \left(\tau_3 + s\tau_0^2\right)a_2^2\right|,$$

or we see that

$$\left|b_2 - sb_1^2\right| = |\tau_1|\left|a_3 - \frac{(\tau_3 + s\tau_0^2)}{\tau_1}a_2^2\right|.$$

If we denote $\lambda = \frac{1}{\tau_1}\left(\tau_3 + s\tau_0^2\right)$, then we write

$$\left|a_3 - \lambda a_2^2\right| = \frac{1}{|\tau_1|}\left|b_2 - sb_1^2\right|,$$

or

$$\left|a_3 - \lambda a_2^2\right| = |\tau|\left|b_2 - sb_1^2\right|, \text{ where } |\tau| = \frac{1}{|\tau_1|}$$

and the level set of functions is obtained from

$$\varphi\binom{\mu}{\alpha,\beta} = \left[\frac{\lambda_0}{(2+(2\mu-3)\beta-\alpha)}\right]^{-1} = \frac{(2+(2\mu-3)\beta-\alpha)}{(-3\mu-2)\alpha-(2\mu+1)(\beta+2)}.$$

On setting

$$\alpha = 2 + (2\mu - 3)\beta \text{ and } (-3\mu - 2)\alpha - (2\mu + 1)(\beta + 2) = 0,$$

we obtain

$$\beta = \frac{2(\mu + 1)}{4 + 3\mu - 6\mu^2}.$$

Hence, the level sets are rays starting from the points $\left(2 + \frac{2(\mu+1)(2\mu-3)}{4+3\mu-6\mu^2}, \frac{2(\mu+1)}{4+3\mu-6\mu^2}\right)$ and lying under the lines $\alpha - (2\mu - 3)\beta = 2$ and $(-3\mu - 2)\alpha - (2\mu + 1)\beta = 2(2\mu + 1)$. □

5. Filtration Problems for Some Related Classes

In this section, we take $\alpha = 0$ and consider the class $\mathcal{MF}^{\mu}_{0,\beta}$, consisting of functions $f \in \mathcal{A}$, that satisfy the inequality

$$\Re e\left\{(1 - \beta + \beta\mu)w(\xi) + \frac{(1 - \beta)\mu\xi w'(\xi)}{\mu(w(\xi) - 1) + 1}\right\} > \frac{\beta}{2},$$

or we see that

$$\Re e\left\{\{1 + \beta(\mu - 1)\}w(\xi) + \frac{(1 - \beta)\mu\xi w'(\xi)}{\mu(w(\xi) - 1) + 1}\right\} > \frac{\beta}{2}, \tag{15}$$

where $w(\xi) = \frac{\xi f'(\xi)}{f(\xi)}$. This can also be rewritten as:

$$\mathcal{MF}^{\mu}_{0,\beta} = \left\{f \in \mathcal{A} : 2\Re e\wp^{\mu}_{0,\beta}(f)(\xi) > \beta \text{ for } \beta \geq \frac{2}{1 - 2\mu}\right\}.$$

Theorem 4. *For $\beta \neq 1$, we have*

$$f \in \mathcal{MF}^{\mu}_{0,\beta} \Longleftrightarrow \left[1 - \mu + \mu\frac{\xi f'(\xi)}{f(\xi)}\right]^{1-\beta}[f(\xi)]^{1+\beta\mu-\beta} \in \mathcal{S}^*.$$

Proof. From (15), we note that

$$g(\xi) = [1 - \mu + \mu w(\xi)]^{1-\beta}[f(\xi)]^{1+\beta\mu-\beta},$$

or we see that

$$\frac{\xi g'(\xi)}{g(\xi)} = \{1 - \beta + \beta\mu\}w(\xi) + (1 - \beta)\mu\frac{\xi w'(\xi)}{1 - \mu + \mu w(\xi)}.$$

where $w(\xi) = \frac{\xi f'(\xi)}{f(\xi)}$. Thus, we obtain the desired conclusion. □

We also assume $\alpha = 0$ and $\mu = 1$ to consider the class $\mathcal{MF}^{1}_{0,\beta}$, consisting of functions $f \in \mathcal{A}$, satisfying

$$\mathcal{MF}^{1}_{0,\beta} = \left\{f \in \mathcal{A} : \Re e\left\{(1 - \beta)\frac{(\xi f'(\xi))'}{f'(\xi)} + \beta\frac{\xi f'(\xi)}{f(\xi)}\right\} > \frac{\beta}{2}\right\}.$$

The function in this class is equivalent to the $(1 - \beta)$-convex function of order $\frac{\beta}{2}$, first seen in [11] and then investigated by others. For more details, see [12–15]. Moreover, we obtain the following result, as shown by Elin, see [9].

Corollary 2. *For $\beta < 2$ and $\beta \neq 1$, we have*

$$f \in \mathcal{MF}^1_{0,\beta} \Longleftrightarrow g(\xi) = \xi\left[f'(\xi)\right]^{\frac{2-2\beta}{2-\beta}}\left[\frac{f(\xi)}{\xi}\right]^{\frac{2\beta}{2-\beta}} \in \mathcal{S}^*,$$

where

$$f(\xi) = \left[\frac{1}{1-\beta}\int_0^{\xi} s^{\frac{\beta}{1-\beta}}\left(\frac{g(s)}{s}\right)^{\frac{2-\beta}{2-2\beta}} ds\right]^{1-\beta}.$$

Theorem 5. *Let $0 \leq \beta \leq 1$, $-1 \leq \mu \leq 1$ and $f \in \mathcal{MF}^{\mu}_{0,\beta}$, such that,*

$$\Re e\wp^{\mu}_{0,\beta}(f)(\xi) = \Re e\left\{\{1+\beta(\mu-1)\}w(\xi) + \frac{\mu(1-\beta)\xi w'(\xi)}{\mu(w(\xi)-1)+1}\right\} > \frac{\beta}{2},$$

where $w(\xi) = \frac{\xi f'(\xi)}{f(\xi)}$. Then, $\Re e\frac{\xi f'(\xi)}{f(\xi)} > \frac{1}{2}$, $\xi \in \mathbb{E}$, that is, $f \in \mathcal{S}^*_{\frac{1}{2}}$.

Proof. Here, we use Lemma 2, which implies that $\Re e\frac{\xi f'(\xi)}{f(\xi)} > \frac{1}{2}$, if and only if the function s is defined by (8), such that

$$s(\xi) = 1 - \frac{1}{w(\xi)}, w(\xi) = \frac{\xi f'(\xi)}{f(\xi)},$$

which, on differentiation, leads to the following.

$$\frac{1}{1-s(\xi)} = w(\xi), \text{ and } 1 - w(\xi) + \frac{\xi f''(\xi)}{f'(\xi)} = \frac{\xi s'(\xi)}{1-s(\xi)}. \tag{16}$$

Here, we make use of Jack's Lemma 5 to achieve our task. We assume, on the contrary, that s is not an analytic self-mapping of $\mathbb{E}$. Then, for $\xi_0 \in \mathbb{E} : |s(\xi)| < 1$ for all $|\xi| < |\xi_0|$ and $|s(\xi_0)| = 1$. By Lemma 5, we have

$$\frac{\xi_0 s'(\xi_0)}{s(\xi_0)} = m \geq 1.$$

Using notation $s(\xi_0) = a + ib$, for some $a, b \in \mathbb{R} : a^2 + b^2 = 1$, we have

$$\Re e\left\{\frac{1}{1-s(\xi_0)}\right\} = \frac{1-a}{1-2a+(a^2+b^2)} = \frac{1}{2}.$$

Hence, for $0 \leq \beta \leq 1$ and $-1 \leq \mu \leq 1$, (16) yields

$$\begin{aligned}
&\Re e\wp^{\mu}_{0,\beta}(f)(\xi_0) \\
&= \Re e\left\{\frac{1}{2}\{1+\beta(\mu-1)\} + \frac{m(1-\beta)\mu s(\xi_0)}{\left(1-\frac{1}{2}\mu\right)(1-s(\xi_0))^2} - \frac{\beta}{2}\right\} \\
&= \frac{1+\beta(\mu-1)}{2} - \frac{(1-\beta)\mu}{2-\mu} - \frac{\beta}{2} \leq 0,
\end{aligned}$$

which contradicts our assumption. This completes the desired proof of the Theorem. □

For $\alpha = 0$ and $\mu = 1$, we obtain the following corollary, as seen in [9,13].

Corollary 3. *If* $0 \le \beta \le 1$, $\mu = 1$ *and* $f \in \mathcal{MF}^1_{0,\beta}$, *that is,*

$$\Re e \wp^1_{0,\beta}(\xi_0) = \Re e \left\{ \beta \frac{\xi f'(\xi)}{f(\xi)} + (1-\beta) \frac{(\xi f'(\xi))'}{f'(\xi)} \right\} > \frac{\beta}{2},$$

then we have the assertion $\Re e \frac{\xi f'(\xi)}{f(\xi)} > \frac{1}{2}$, *that is,* $f \in \mathcal{S}^*\left(\frac{1}{2}\right)$.

Theorem 6. *For* $\beta < \beta_1 \le 1$, *we have* $\mathcal{MF}^\mu_{0,\beta} \subseteq \mathcal{MF}^\mu_{0,\beta_1}$.

Proof. Let $f \in \mathcal{MF}^\mu_{0,\beta}$. Then,

$$\Re e \wp^\mu_{0,\beta}(f)(\xi) > \frac{\beta}{2} : \beta \ge \frac{2}{1-2\mu}, \quad -1 \le \mu \le 1$$

implies that there exists $s(\xi) \in \Omega = \{s \in \mathcal{A} : s(0) = 0\}$, such that

$$\begin{aligned} \wp^\mu_{0,\beta}(f)(\xi) &= \frac{(1-\beta)\mu\xi w'(\xi)}{1-\mu+\mu w(\xi)} + (1-\beta+\beta\mu)w(\xi); \qquad \left(w(\xi) = \frac{\xi f'(\xi)}{f(\xi)}\right) \\ &= \frac{1-(1-\mu)\beta}{1-s(\xi)} + \frac{(1-\beta)\mu s(\xi)}{[1-s(\xi)][(1-\mu)(1-s(\xi))+\mu]} \\ &= \frac{1}{1-s(\xi)} \frac{[1-\beta(1-\mu)][(1-\mu)(1-s(\xi))+\mu] + (1-\beta)\mu s(\xi)}{\mu+(1-\mu)(1-s(\xi))}. \end{aligned}$$

Furthermore, by letting, $A = 1+\beta\mu-\beta$, $B = 1-\mu$ and $C = \mu - \beta\mu$, we note that

$$\wp^\mu_{0,\beta}(f)(\xi) - \frac{1}{2}\beta = \frac{1}{1-s(\xi)} \frac{A[B(1-s(\xi))+\mu] + Cs(\xi)}{\mu + B(1-s(\xi))} - \frac{1}{2}\beta$$

or we can write

$$\wp^\mu_{0,\beta}(f)(\xi) = \frac{2A(B+\mu) - \beta(B+\mu) + [\beta(\mu+2B) - 2(AB-C)]s(\xi) - \beta B s^2(\xi)}{2(B+\mu) + 2Bs^2(\xi) - 2(2B+\mu)s(\xi)} + \frac{1}{2}\beta.$$

By using (8), we note that

$$s_\beta(\xi) = -\frac{\wp^\mu_{0,\beta}(f)(0) - \wp^\mu_{0,\beta}(f)(\xi)}{\wp^\mu_{0,\beta}(f)(\xi) - 2\propto + \wp^\mu_{0,\beta}(f)(0)}.$$

That is,

$$s_\beta(\xi) = \frac{1 - \wp^\mu_{0,\beta}(f)(\xi) - (1-\mu)\beta}{-\wp^\mu_{0,\beta}(f)(\xi) - 1 + \beta + (1-\mu)\beta}. \tag{17}$$

Similarly for β_1, we consider that

$$s_{\beta_1}(\xi) = \frac{\wp^\mu_{0,\beta_1}(f)(\xi) + (1-\mu)\beta_1 - 1}{1 - \beta_1 - (1-\mu)\beta_1 + \wp^\mu_{0,\beta_1}(f)(\xi)},$$

which is analytic in the disk or neighbourhood $\mathbb{E}$ and zero at origin. We rewrite (17) as

$$[s_\beta(\xi)]\left[1 - \beta - (1-\mu)\beta + \wp^\mu_{0,\beta_1}(f)(\xi)\right] = \wp^\mu_{0,\beta_1}(f)(\xi) - 1 + \beta(1-\mu). \tag{18}$$

Similarly, we see that

$$[s_{\beta_1}(\xi)]\left[1 - \beta_1 + (\mu-1)\beta_1 + \wp^\mu_{0,\beta_1}(f)(\xi)\right] = \wp^\mu_{0,\beta_1}(f)(\xi) - 1 - (\mu-1)\beta_1. \tag{19}$$

Furthermore, we define the function

$$\wp^{\mu}_{0,\frac{1}{2}}(f)(\xi) = \frac{\frac{1}{2}\mu\xi\left(\frac{\xi f'(\xi)}{f(\xi)}\right)'}{1-\mu+\mu\frac{\xi f'(\xi)}{f(\xi)}} - 1 + \beta(1-\mu),$$

or

$$h(\xi) = \mu\frac{\xi\left(\frac{\xi f'(\xi)}{f(\xi)}\right)'}{1-\mu+\mu\frac{\xi f'(\xi)}{f(\xi)}} + (1+\mu)\frac{\xi f'(\xi)}{f(\xi)},$$

where $h(\xi) = 2\wp^{\mu}_{0,\frac{1}{2}}(f)(\xi)$. Then, (18) implies that

$$\begin{aligned}&(\beta-1)\left[1-s_\beta(\xi)\right]h(\xi)\\&=\{(\mu-1)\beta-1\}+(1-2\beta)\mu\left[1-s_\beta(\xi)\right]\frac{\xi f'(\xi)}{f(\xi)}-\{(\mu-2)\beta+1\}s_\beta(\xi).\end{aligned} \tag{20}$$

We solve (20) to obtain the value of $h(\xi)$ as

$$h(\xi) = \frac{1}{(1-\beta)\left[1-s_\beta(\xi)\right]} + \frac{1-2\beta}{1-\beta}\mu\frac{\xi f'(\xi)}{f(\xi)} + \frac{s_\beta(\xi)}{1-s_\beta(\xi)} + \frac{\beta}{1-\beta}(1-\mu). \tag{21}$$

Furthermore, Equation (19) leads to

$$(1-\beta_1)h(\xi) = (1-2\beta_1)\mu\frac{\xi f'(\xi)}{f(\xi)} + \frac{1}{1-s_{\beta_1}(\xi)} + \frac{(1-\beta_1)s_{\beta_1}(\xi)}{1-s_{\beta_1}(\xi)} + (1-\mu)\beta_1. \tag{22}$$

From (21) and (22), we see that

$$\begin{aligned}&\frac{1}{(1-\beta)\left[1-s_\beta(\xi)\right]} + \left\{\frac{\beta_1}{1-\beta_1} - \frac{\beta}{1-\beta}\right\}\mu\frac{\xi f'(\xi)}{f(\xi)} + \frac{s_\beta(\xi)}{1-s_\beta(\xi)} - \beta\left(\frac{\mu-1}{1-\beta}\right)\\&=\frac{1-\mu}{1-\beta_1}\beta_1 + \frac{s_{\beta_1}(\xi)}{1-s_{\beta_1}(\xi)} + \frac{1}{(1-\beta_1)\left[1-s_{\beta_1}(\xi)\right]}.\end{aligned} \tag{23}$$

On the contrary, we may assume that $s_{\beta_1}(\xi)$ will not be a self mapping of $\mathbb{E}$. Therefore, $\exists$ $\xi_0 \in \mathbb{E} : \left|s_{\beta_1}(\xi)\right| < 1$ for $|\xi| < |\xi_0|$ and $\left|s_{\beta_1}(\xi_0)\right| = 1$. Substitute $\xi = \xi_0$ in (23) to have

$$\frac{s_\beta(\xi)}{1-s_\beta(\xi)} = \frac{-1}{2}, \; \frac{1}{1-s_\beta(\xi)} = \frac{1}{2},$$

and

$$\begin{aligned}&\left\{\frac{\beta_1}{1-\beta_1} - \frac{\beta}{1-\beta}\right\}\mu\Re e\frac{\xi_0 f'(\xi_0)}{f(\xi_0)} + \Re e\frac{1}{(1-\beta)\left[1-s_\beta(\xi_0)\right]} + \Re e\frac{s_\beta(\xi_0)}{1-s_\beta(\xi_0)} - \beta\frac{\mu-1}{1-\beta}\\&= \Re e\frac{1}{(1-\beta_1)\left[1-s_{\beta_1}(\xi_0)\right]} + \Re e\frac{s_{\beta_1}(\xi_0)}{1-s_{\beta_1}(\xi_0)} - \beta_1\left(\frac{\mu-1}{1-\beta_1}\right).\end{aligned}$$

Or, we see that

$$\left\{\frac{\beta_1}{1-\beta_1} - \frac{\beta}{1-\beta}\right\}\mu\Re e\frac{\xi_0 f'(\xi_0)}{f(\xi_0)} + \frac{1}{2-2\beta} - \frac{1}{2} - \beta\frac{\mu-1}{1-\beta} > \frac{1}{2-2\beta_1} - \frac{1}{2} + \frac{1-\mu}{1-\beta_1}\beta_1.$$

By using Theorem 5, we obtain

$$\left\{\frac{\beta_1}{1-\beta_1}-\frac{\beta}{1-\beta}\right\}\mu\Re e\frac{\xi_0 f'(\xi_0)}{f(\xi_0)}+\frac{1}{2-2\beta}-\frac{\mu-1}{1-\beta}\beta$$
$$>\frac{1}{2}\left\{\frac{\beta_1}{1-\beta_1}-\frac{\beta}{1-\beta}\right\}\mu+\frac{1}{2-2\beta}-\frac{\mu-1}{1-\beta}\beta=\frac{1}{2(1-\beta_1)}-\frac{\mu-1}{1-\beta_1}\beta_1.$$

This leads to a contradiction to our assumption. Therefore, it is obvious that the family $\left\{\mathcal{MF}^{\mu}_{0,\beta}, 1\leq\mu\leq 1\right\}$ is a filtration. □

Corollary 4. *If* $\mu=1$, *then for* $\beta<\beta_1\leq 1$, *we have* $\mathcal{MF}^{1}_{0,\beta}\subseteq\mathcal{MF}^{1}_{0,\beta_1}$, *where*

$$\wp^{\mu}_{0,\beta}(f)(\xi)=\frac{1}{2}\beta-\left(\frac{1}{2}\beta-1\right)\frac{1+s(\xi)}{1-s(\xi)}.$$

For the reference of the above inequality, see [9].

6. Interpolation to Fekete-Szegö Functional

In the next Theorem, we work out the interpolation result to estimate the Fekete–Szegö functional $\phi(f,\lambda)$, given by (4).

Theorem 7. *If the family* $\left\{\mathcal{MF}^{\mu}_{0,\beta},\ -1\leq\mu\leq 1\right\}$ *is a filtration of* $\mathcal{G}$ *such that* $\mathcal{MF}^{\mu}_{0,\beta}\subset\mathcal{G}$ *is satisfied, then*

$$\sup_{f\in\mathcal{MF}^{\mu}_{0,\beta}}|\phi(f,\lambda)|\leq\max\left(\mu_{0,\beta},|1-\lambda|\right), \textit{for } \lambda\in\mathbb{C},$$

over the family $\mathcal{MF}^{\mu}_{0,\beta}$, *where* $\mu_{0,\beta}=\frac{2+(2\mu-3)\beta}{2\beta\mu+2(1-\beta)(2\mu+1)}$.

Proof. In Theorem 6, we already proved that the family $\left\{\mathcal{MF}^{\mu}_{0,\beta}, -1\leq\mu\leq 1\right\}$ is a filtration of $\mathcal{G}$. Moreover, applying Theorem 3 for $\alpha=0$ gives the desired result. □

As a special case, if we take $\alpha=0$, $\mu=1$ and $\beta\in\mathbb{R}$, we obtain the following corollary, as seen in [9].

Corollary 5. *The family* $\left\{\mathcal{MF}^{1}_{0,\beta}\right\}$ *is a filtration of* $\mathcal{G}$ *and satisfies* $\mathcal{MF}^{1}_{0,\beta}\subset S^*\left(\frac{1}{2}\right)$. *Also,*

$$\sup_{f\in\mathcal{MF}^{1}_{0,\beta}}|\phi(f,\lambda)|\leq\max\left(\mu_{0,\beta},|1-\lambda|\right),$$

where $\lambda\in\mathbb{C}$ *and* $\mu_{0,\beta}=\frac{2-\beta}{6-4\beta}$. *In view of* (4), *the supremum is obtained; whenever* $\beta=0$ *and* $\beta=1$, *this estimate is sharp for* $\beta\in(0,1)$ *such that there exist two functions,* f_1 *and* $f_2\in\mathcal{MF}^{1}_{0,\beta}$, *so that*

$$\wp^{1}_{0,\beta}(f_1)(\xi)=\left(1-\frac{\beta}{2}\right)\frac{1+\xi}{1-\xi}+\frac{\beta}{2},$$

and

$$\wp^{1}_{0,\beta}(f_2)(\xi)=\left(1-\frac{\beta}{2}\right)\frac{1+\xi^2}{1-\xi^2}+\frac{\beta}{2}$$

are constructed from (6) *and satisfy the Briot–Bouquet differential equation. Hence,* $|\phi(f_1,\lambda)|\leq|1-\lambda|$, $\lambda\in\mathbb{C}$ *and* $|\phi(f_2,\lambda)|\leq\frac{2-\beta}{6-4\beta}$.

7. Some Filtration Classes

Here, we investigate the case where $\beta = -\alpha + 1$ for $\alpha < 2$. The class $\mathcal{MF}^{\mu}_{\alpha,1-\alpha}$ contains functions given by

$$\wp^{\mu}_{\alpha,1-\alpha}(f)(\xi) = \mu(1-\alpha)\frac{\xi f'(\xi)}{f(\xi)} + \alpha\left(\frac{f(\xi)}{\xi}\right)^{\mu},$$

and

$$\mathcal{MF}^{\mu}_{\alpha,1-\alpha} = \left\{ f \in \mathcal{A} : \Re e \wp^{\mu}_{\alpha,1-\alpha}(f)(\xi) > \frac{1}{2} \right\}.$$

For $\mu = 1$, we obtain the known result of Marx-Strohhäcker given by

$$\Re e\left(\frac{\xi f'(\xi)}{f(\xi)}\right) > \frac{1}{2} \iff \Re e\left(\frac{f(\xi)}{\xi}\right) > \frac{1}{2},$$

and, hence, $\mathcal{S}^*\left(\frac{1}{2}\right) \subset \mathcal{MF}^{\mu}_{\alpha,1-\alpha}$ for any $\alpha < 2$.

Theorem 8. *For $f \in \mathcal{S}^*\left(\frac{1}{2}\right)$, $\Re e\left(\frac{f(\xi)}{\xi}\right)^{\mu} > \frac{1}{2}$ and $\mathcal{S}^*\left(\frac{1}{2}\right) \subset \mathcal{MF}^{\mu}_{\alpha,1-\alpha}$, $-1 \le \mu \le 1$. The sharpness occurs for the function $\xi(1-\xi^n)^{-\frac{1}{\mu}}$.*

Proof. Assume that

$$h(\xi) = 2\frac{[f(\xi)]^{\mu}}{\xi^{\mu}} - 1$$

and

$$\frac{1}{\mu}\frac{\xi h'(\xi)}{h(\xi)+1} + 1 = \frac{\xi f'(\xi)}{f(\xi)}.$$

For $s = \xi h'(\xi)$, $r = h(\xi)$, $\Psi(r,s) = \frac{s}{(r+1)\mu} + 1 : \Psi(i\rho,\sigma) = \frac{\sigma}{\mu(\rho^2+1)} + 1$, if $\rho \in \mathbb{R}$ and $\sigma \le -\mu\left(\frac{\rho^2+1}{2}\right)$, then $\Re e[\Psi(i\rho,\sigma)] = \Re e\left(\frac{\sigma}{(\rho^2+1)\mu} + 1\right) \le 0$. Since $f \in \mathcal{S}^*\left(\frac{1}{2}\right)$, we write

$$\Re e\left[\Psi\left(h, \xi h'\right)(\xi)\right] > 0.$$

Therefore, $\Re e h(\xi) > \frac{1}{2}$, and this implies that $\Re e\left(\frac{f(\xi)}{\xi}\right)^{\mu} > \frac{1}{2}$. □

Theorem 9. *Let $\alpha < \alpha_1 \le 1$. Then, we have $\mathcal{MF}^{\mu}_{\alpha,1-\alpha} \subseteq \mathcal{MF}^{\mu}_{\alpha_1,1-\alpha_1}$.*

Proof. Suppose that $f \in \mathcal{MF}^{\mu}_{\alpha,1-\alpha}$ for $-1 \le \mu \le 1$, $\xi \in \mathbb{E}$. Then, $\Re e \wp^{\mu}_{\alpha,1-\alpha}(f)(\xi) > \frac{1}{2}$ proves the existence of a function $s_{\beta}(\xi)$ so that we can write that

$$s_{\beta}(\xi) = \frac{\wp^{\mu}_{\alpha,1-\alpha}(f)(\xi) + 2 - \mu + \alpha\mu - \alpha}{-1 + \mu - \alpha\mu + \alpha + \wp^{\mu}_{\alpha,1-\alpha}(f)(\xi)}.$$

Then, from the above functional equation, we see that

$$\begin{aligned} & s_{\alpha}(\xi)\left[(1-\alpha)\mu\frac{\xi f'(\xi)}{f(\xi)} - 1 + \mu - \alpha\mu + \alpha + \alpha\left(\frac{f(\xi)}{\xi}\right)^{\mu}\right] \\ & = \alpha\left(\frac{f(\xi)}{\xi}\right)^{\mu} - 1 - (1-\mu)(1-\alpha) + (1-\alpha)\mu\frac{\xi f'(\xi)}{f(\xi)}. \end{aligned} \tag{24}$$

Furthermore, we see that

$$-2\wp^{\mu}_{-\frac{1}{2},\frac{1}{2}}(f)(\xi) = -h_1(\xi) = -\mu\frac{\xi f'(\xi)}{f(\xi)} + \left(\frac{f(\xi)}{\xi}\right)^{\mu}. \tag{25}$$

By using (25) in (24), we observe that

$$\{\alpha+\mu(1-\alpha)\}\frac{(f(\xi))^{\mu}}{\xi^{\mu}}-(1-\alpha)\mu\left\{\frac{(f(\xi))^{\mu}}{\xi^{\mu}}-\frac{\xi f'(\xi)}{f(\xi)}\right\}=\frac{1-(1-\alpha)\mu_1[1+s_\alpha(\xi)]}{1-s_\alpha(\xi)},$$

or

$$h_1(\xi)=\frac{1-(1-\alpha)\mu_1[1+s_\alpha(\xi)]}{[1-s_\alpha(\xi)](1-\alpha)}-\frac{\{\mu-\alpha\mu_1\}\left(\frac{f(\xi)}{\xi}\right)^{\mu}}{1-\alpha}, \tag{26}$$

where $\mu_1=1-\mu$. Similarly, in the case of α_1, we have

$$\begin{aligned}&s_{\alpha_1}(\xi)\left[\alpha_1\left(\frac{f(\xi)}{\xi}\right)^{\mu}+(1-\alpha_1)\mu\frac{\xi f'(\xi)}{f(\xi)}-\mu_1(1-\alpha_1)\right]\\&=\alpha_1\left(\frac{f(\xi)}{\xi}\right)^{\mu}+(1-\alpha_1)\mu\frac{\xi f'(\xi)}{f(\xi)}+\mu_1(1-\alpha_1)-1\end{aligned}$$

and

$$h_1(\xi)=\frac{1-(1-\alpha_1)\mu_1[1+s_{\alpha_1}(\xi)]}{(1-\alpha_1)[1-s_{\alpha_1}(\xi)]}-\frac{\{\mu+\alpha_1\mu_1\}\left(\frac{f(\xi)}{\xi}\right)^{\mu}}{1-\alpha}, \tag{27}$$

where $\mu_1=1-\mu$. Equating (26) and (27), we observe that

$$\begin{aligned}&\frac{1-(1-\alpha)\mu_1[1+s_\alpha(\xi)]}{(1-\alpha)[1-s_\alpha(\xi)]}-\frac{\{\mu+\alpha\mu_1\}\left(\frac{f(\xi)}{\xi}\right)^{\mu}}{1-\alpha}\\&=\frac{1-(1-\alpha_1)\mu_1[1+s_{\alpha_1}(\xi)]}{(1-\alpha_1)[1-s_{\alpha_1}(\xi)]}-\frac{\{\mu+\alpha_1\mu_1\}\left(\frac{f(\xi)}{\xi}\right)^{\mu}}{1-\alpha_1}\end{aligned}$$

or we write

$$\begin{aligned}&\left\{\frac{\alpha_1}{1-\alpha_1}-\frac{\alpha}{1-\alpha}\right\}\left(\frac{f(\xi)}{\xi}\right)^{\mu}+\frac{1}{(\alpha-1)[s_\alpha(\xi)-1]}-\mu_1\frac{1+s_\alpha(\xi)}{1-s_\alpha(\xi)}\\&=\left[\frac{1}{[1-s_{\alpha_1}(\xi)](1-\alpha_1)}+\mu_1\frac{1+s_{\alpha_1}(\xi)}{s_{\alpha_1}(\xi)-1}\right]\end{aligned}$$

or, equivalently, we have

$$\begin{aligned}&\left\{\frac{\alpha_1}{1-\alpha_1}-\frac{\alpha}{1-\alpha}\right\}\left(\frac{f(\xi)}{\xi}\right)^{\mu}+\frac{1}{(1-\alpha)[1-s_\alpha(\xi)]}-\frac{\mu_1}{1-s_\alpha(\xi)}-\frac{\mu_1 s_\alpha(\xi)}{1-s_\alpha(\xi)}\\&=-\mu_1\left[\frac{1}{1-s_{\alpha_1}(\xi)}+\frac{s_{\alpha_1}(\xi)}{1-s_{\alpha_1}(\xi)}\right]+\frac{1}{(1-\alpha_1)[1-s_{\alpha_1}(\xi)]},\end{aligned} \tag{28}$$

where $\mu_1=1-\mu$. It is clear that $s_{\alpha_1}(0)=0$ and we assume, on the contrary, that $s_{\alpha_1}(\xi)$ is not a self-mapping of $\mathbb{E}$. Then, there exists $\xi_0\in\mathbb{E}:|s_{\alpha_1}(\xi)|<1\ \forall\ |\xi|<|\xi_0|$ while $|s_{\alpha_1}(\xi_0)|=1$. We substitute $\xi=\xi_0$ in (28) to have

$$\begin{aligned}&\left\{\frac{\alpha_1}{1-\alpha_1}-\frac{\alpha}{1-\alpha}\right\}\Re e\left(\frac{f(\xi)}{\xi}\right)^{\mu}-(1-\mu)\Re e\frac{1+s_\alpha(\xi)}{1-s_\alpha(\xi)}+\Re e\frac{1}{(1-\alpha)[1-s_\alpha(\xi)]}\\&>-\frac{1}{2}\left[\frac{1+\alpha}{1-\alpha}-\frac{\alpha_1}{1-\alpha_1}\right].\end{aligned}$$

Now, applying Theorem 5, we see that

$$-\Re e\frac{1}{(1-\alpha_1)[1-s_{\alpha_1}(\xi)]}-\Re e\left[\frac{(1-\mu)s_{\alpha_1}(\xi)}{1-s_{\alpha_1}(\xi)}+\frac{1-\mu}{1-s_{\alpha_1}(\xi)}\right]>\frac{1}{2(1-\alpha_1)}.$$

Hence, we find that

$$-\frac{1}{2}\left[\frac{1+\alpha}{1-\alpha}-\frac{\alpha_1}{1-\alpha_1}\right]>\frac{1}{2(1-\alpha_1)}$$

or

$$-\left\{\frac{\alpha}{1-\alpha}-\frac{\alpha_1}{1-\alpha_1}\right\}\Re e\left(\frac{f(\xi)}{\xi}\right)^{\mu}+\frac{1}{2(\alpha-1)}>\frac{1}{2(1-\alpha_1)}$$

or

$$-\left\{\frac{\alpha(1-\alpha_1)-\alpha_1(1-\alpha)}{(1-\alpha)(1-\alpha_1)}\right\}\Re e\left(\frac{f(\xi)}{\xi}\right)^{\mu}>\frac{1}{2}\left[\frac{1-\alpha+1-\alpha_1}{(1-\alpha_1)(1-\alpha)}\right].$$

This gives that

$$\Re e\left(\frac{f(\xi)}{\xi}\right)^{\mu}<\frac{1}{2}\left[\frac{\alpha+\alpha_1-2}{\alpha-\alpha_1}\right].$$

This is clearly contradictory to our assumption. Thus, the proof of our Theorem is completed. □

These Theorems show that the class $\mathcal{MF}^{\mu}_{\alpha,1-\alpha}$, with $\frac{1}{2}\leq\alpha<2$, constructs a filtration for generators along with sharp estimates over the bounds of the Fekete–Szegö quadratic functional.

Theorem 10. *Let $f\in\mathcal{MF}^{\mu}_{\alpha,1-\alpha}$ and $\frac{1}{2}\leq\alpha<2$. Then, $\mathcal{MF}^{\mu}_{\alpha,1-\alpha}\subset\mathcal{G}$. Furthermore, for $\frac{1}{2}\leq\alpha\leq1$, each $f\in\mathcal{MF}^{\mu}_{\alpha,1-\alpha}$ leads a semi-group $\{\wp_t,\ t\geq0\}\subset\mathcal{A}$, which satisfies*

$$|\wp_t(\xi)|\leq e^{\frac{1-2\alpha}{2\alpha}t}|\xi|,\ \alpha=1,\frac{1}{2}\ \textit{and}\ \xi\in\mathbb{E}.$$

Furthermore, the family $\left\{\mathcal{MF}^{\mu}_{\alpha,1-\alpha}\right\}$ is a filtration of $\mathcal{G}$ such that

$$\sup_{f\in\mathcal{MF}^{\mu}_{\alpha,1-\alpha}}|\phi(f,\lambda)|\leq\max\{\mu_{\alpha,1-\alpha},|1-\lambda|\}\ \textit{for}\ \lambda\in\mathbb{C}.$$

Proof. Suppose that $f\notin\mathcal{G}:\Re e\left(\frac{f(\xi)}{\xi}\right)^{\mu}>0$ and consider that $s(\xi)$ is as defined by (8) with $\tau=0$, such that

$$s(\xi)=\frac{(w(\xi))^{\mu}-1}{(w(\xi))^{\mu}+1},$$

and

$$\left(\frac{f(\xi)}{\xi}\right)^{\mu}=\frac{1+s(\xi)}{1-s(\xi)},\quad w(\xi)=\frac{f(\xi)}{\xi}.$$

Moreover,

$$\mu\frac{\xi f'(\xi)}{f(\xi)}=\frac{\xi s'(\xi)}{1-s(\xi)}+\frac{\xi s'(\xi)}{1+s(\xi)}+\mu.$$

For some fixed $\xi\in\mathbb{E}$, $s(\xi)\in\mathbb{E}\Longleftrightarrow\Re e\left(\frac{f(\xi)}{\xi}\right)^{\mu}>0$. In view of our supposition, there exists a $\xi_0\in\mathbb{E}$ such that $\Re e\left(\frac{f(\xi)}{\xi}\right)^{\mu}<0:|\xi|<|\xi_0|$ while $\Re e\left(\frac{f(\xi_0)}{\xi_0}\right)^{\mu}<0$ and, hence, $|s(\xi_0)|=1$. Therefore, by Lemma 5, there is $m\geq1$, such that $\xi_0s'(\xi_0)=ms(\xi_0)$. A straightforward calculation leads to

$$\begin{aligned}\wp^{\mu}_{\alpha,1-\alpha}(f)(\xi_0)&=(1-\alpha)\mu\frac{\xi_0f'(\xi_0)}{f(\xi_0)}+\alpha\left(\frac{f(\xi_0)}{\xi_0}\right)^{\mu}\\&=\alpha\frac{1+s(\xi_0)}{1-s(\xi_0)}+\left(\frac{\xi_0s'(\xi_0)}{1+s(\xi_0)}+\frac{\xi_0s'(\xi_0)}{1-s(\xi_0)}+\mu\right)(1-\alpha)\\&=\alpha\frac{1+s(\xi_0)}{1-s(\xi_0)}+\left(\frac{ms(\xi_0)}{1+s(\xi_0)}+\frac{ms(\xi_0)}{1-s(\xi_0)}+\mu\right)(1-\alpha).\end{aligned}\tag{29}$$

Using $s(\xi_0) = a + ib, a, b \in \mathbb{R} : a^2 + b^2 = 1$, we have

$$\Re e\left\{\frac{1}{1 - s(\xi_0)}\right\} = \frac{1 - a}{1 - 2a + a^2 + b^2} = \frac{1}{2},$$

$$\Re e\frac{s(\xi_0)}{1 - s(\xi_0)} = \Re e\frac{(a + ib)((1 - a) + ib)}{1 - 2a + b^2 + a^2} = \frac{a - (a^2 + b^2)}{2(1 - a)} = -\frac{1}{2},$$

$$\Re e\left\{\frac{1}{1 + s(\xi_0)}\right\} = \Re e\left\{\frac{(1 + a) - ib}{1 + 2a + b^2 + a^2}\right\} = \frac{(1 + a)}{2(1 + a)} = \frac{1}{2},$$

and, finally, we see that

$$\Re e\frac{s(\xi_0)}{1 + s(\xi_0)} = \Re e\frac{(a + ib)((1 + a) - ib)}{1 + 2a + b^2 + a^2} = \Re e\frac{a + 1}{2(1 + a)} = \frac{1}{2}.$$

From (29), we note that

$$\begin{aligned}\Re e\wp^{\mu}_{\alpha,1-\alpha}(\xi_0) &= \Re e\left[\alpha\frac{1 + s(\xi_0)}{1 - s(\xi_0)} + \left(\frac{ms(\xi_0)}{1 + s(\xi_0)} + \frac{ms(\xi_0)}{1 - s(\xi_0)} + \mu\right)(1 - \alpha)\right] \\ &= (1 - \alpha)m\mu, \ m \geq 1.\end{aligned}$$

Since $f \in \mathcal{MF}^{\mu}_{\alpha,1-\alpha}$ and $\Re e\wp^{\mu}_{\alpha,1-\alpha}(f)(\xi_0) = (1 - \alpha)\mu$, we conclude that $\alpha < \frac{1}{2}$. Thus, $\mathcal{MF}^{\mu}_{\alpha,1-\alpha} \subset \mathcal{G}$ whenever $\alpha \geq \frac{1}{2}$ (by (9)). For $\alpha = 1$, we observe that

$$\wp^{\mu}_{1,0}(f)(\xi) = \left(\frac{f(\xi)}{\xi}\right)^{\mu}, \ -1 \leq \mu \leq 1$$

and, when $\alpha = \frac{1}{2}$, we observe that

$$\wp^{\mu}_{\frac{1}{2},\frac{1}{2}}(f)(\xi) = \frac{1}{2}\left[\left(\frac{f(\xi)}{\xi}\right)^{\mu} + \mu\frac{\xi f'(\xi)}{f(\xi)}\right].$$

In both of these cases, $f \in \mathcal{MF}^{\mu}_{\alpha,(1-\alpha)}$ leads to a semi-group $\{\wp_t : t \geq 0\} \subset \mathcal{A}$, which satisfies the Cauchy problem given by (5). The mapping $f \in \mathcal{A}$, defined by

$$\left[\lim_{t\to 0^+}\frac{\xi - \wp_t(\xi)}{t}\right]^{\mu} = f_1(\xi) = (f(\xi))^{\mu}, \ \ t \geq 0$$

with $\wp_t(\xi) = \exp(-at)\xi$, $a = \frac{1-2\alpha}{2\alpha} \in \mathbb{C}$, such that

$$\left[\lim_{t\to 0^+}\frac{\xi - \exp(-at)\xi}{t}\right]^{\mu} = \xi^{\mu}\left[\lim_{t\to 0^+}\frac{1 - \exp(-at)}{t}\right]^{\mu} = a^{\mu}\xi^{\mu} = (f(\xi))^{\mu}, \ \ t \geq 0,$$

is obviously an infinitesimal generator for some one-parameter family of semi-group, and for every $\xi \in \mathbb{E}$, the problem from (5) clearly possess a unique solution $u = u_t(\xi) \in \mathbb{E}$, $t \geq 0$ such that $|\wp_t(\xi)| \leq e^{\frac{1-2\alpha}{2\alpha}t}|\xi|$, $\alpha = 1, \frac{1}{2}$ and $\xi \in \mathbb{E}$. Therefore, we take $\alpha \in \left(\frac{1}{2}, 1\right)$. Suppose that

$$w(\xi) = \left(\frac{f(\xi)}{\xi}\right)^{\mu} - \left(\frac{1 - 2\alpha}{2\alpha}\right)^{\mu}.$$

Then,

$$\frac{\xi w'(\xi)}{w(\xi) + \left(\frac{1-2\alpha}{2\alpha}\right)^{\mu}} + \mu = \mu\frac{\xi f'(\xi)}{f(\xi)}.$$

$$\begin{aligned}\wp^{\mu}_{\alpha,\delta}(f)(\xi) &= \alpha\left(\frac{f(\xi)}{\xi}\right)^{\mu} + \delta\mu\frac{\xi f'(\xi)}{f(\xi)}; \qquad (\delta = 1-\alpha)\\ &= \alpha w(\xi) + \alpha\left(\frac{\delta-\alpha}{2\alpha}\right)^{\mu} + \frac{\xi w'(\xi)}{\frac{w(\xi)}{\delta\mu} + \frac{1}{\delta\mu}\left(\frac{\delta-\alpha}{2\alpha}\right)^{\mu}} + \delta\mu^2\\ &= \alpha w(\xi) + \frac{w'(\xi)}{\frac{h(\xi)}{\delta\mu} + \frac{1}{\delta\mu}\left(\frac{\delta-\alpha}{2\alpha}\right)^{\mu}} + \delta\mu^2 + \alpha\left(\frac{\delta-\alpha}{2\alpha}\right)^{\mu}\\ &= \alpha w(\xi) + \frac{\xi w'(\xi)}{\frac{1}{\delta\mu}w(\xi) + \frac{1}{\delta\mu}\left(\frac{\delta-\alpha}{2\alpha}\right)^{\mu}} + \delta\mu^2 + \left(\frac{\delta-\alpha}{2\alpha}\right)^{\mu}.\end{aligned}$$

From the above calculations and for $\delta = 1-\alpha$, we see that

$$\wp^{\mu}_{\alpha,\delta}(f)(\xi) - \delta\mu^2 - \left(\frac{\delta-\alpha}{2\alpha}\right)^{\mu} = \alpha w(\xi) + \frac{\xi w'(\xi)}{\frac{1}{\delta\mu}w(\xi) + \frac{1}{\delta\mu}\left(\frac{\delta-\alpha}{2\alpha}\right)^{\mu}}.$$

Hence, from Lemma 1, we see that the solution $w(\xi) = h(\xi)$ of the above equation is analytic in $\mathbb{E}$ and $\Re e h(\xi) = \Re e\left(\frac{f(\xi)}{\xi}\right)^{\mu} > \frac{1}{2} > 0, \xi \in \mathbb{E}$. Therefore, in this case $\wp^{\mu}_{\alpha,1-\alpha}(f)(\xi)$ also generates a semi-group and the family $\left\{\mathcal{MF}^{\mu}_{\alpha,1-\alpha}\right\}$ is a filtration of $\mathcal{G}$. Moreover, we let $\alpha \in \mathbb{R}$, $f \in \mathcal{A}$, $-1 \le \mu \le 1$ and $\xi \in \mathbb{E}$ such that

$$\mu_{\alpha,1-\alpha} = \frac{2 + (2\mu-3)(1-\alpha) - \alpha}{(2-\alpha)\mu} > 0.$$

Then, $\sup_{f\in\mathcal{MF}^{\mu}_{\alpha,1-\alpha}}|\phi(f,\lambda)| \le \max(\mu_{\alpha,1-\alpha}, |1-\lambda|)$ for $\lambda \in \mathbb{C}$, over the family $\mathcal{MF}^{\mu}_{\alpha,1-\alpha}$. □

8. Open Problems

Recall that, by Theorem 3, $|\phi(f,\lambda)| \le \max\left(\varphi\binom{\mu}{\alpha,\beta}|1-\lambda|\right)$ for $\lambda \in \mathbb{C}$, over the family $\mathcal{MF}^{\mu}_{\alpha,\beta}$, where the level set of function denoted by

$$\varphi\binom{\mu}{\alpha,\beta} = \frac{2 + (2\mu-3)\beta - \alpha}{(\alpha+2\beta)\mu + 2(1-\alpha-\beta)(2\mu+1)} > 0,$$

where $\alpha, \beta \in \mathbb{R}$, $-1 \le \mu \le 1$ and $\xi \in \mathbb{E}$, satisfies

$$\alpha - (2\mu-3)\beta < 2, \quad (-3\mu-2)\alpha - (2\mu+1)\beta < 2(2\mu+1)$$

and

$$\lambda_0 = (\alpha+2\beta)\mu + 2(1-\alpha-\beta)(2\mu+1)$$

such that $\beta = \frac{2(\mu+1)}{4+3\mu-6\mu^2}$. Therefore, the following open problems are raised.

Q1: Is this estimate sharp for all $\alpha, \beta \in \mathbb{R}$ and $-1 \le \mu \le 1$, which satisfy

$$\alpha - (2\mu-3)\beta < 2, \quad (-3\mu-2)\alpha - (2\mu+1)\beta < 2(2\mu+1)$$

and

$$\lambda_0 = (\alpha+2\beta)\mu + 2(1-\alpha-\beta)(2\mu+1)$$

such that $\beta = \frac{2(\mu+1)}{4+3\mu-6\mu^2}$.

Q2: What values of α, β and μ provide the class $\mathcal{MF}^{\mu}_{\alpha,\beta}$ in connection with the nonlinear operator $\wp^{\mu}_{\alpha,\beta}(f)$, consisting of univalent functions?

(The only cases we know the affirmative answer for are $\alpha = 0, \mu = 1$ and $\beta < 2$.)

9. Conjecture

The filtrations constructed in Theorems 7 and 10 are strict by definition.

10. Conclusions

This research is avid to a systematic and comprehensive analysis of linearization models for one-parameter continuous semi-groups, functional equations, different classes of univalent functions and their applications to various problems of complex dynamics, in order to establish a connection between the Fekete–Szegö functional and the class of infinitesimal generators.

Author Contributions: Conceptualization, M.N. and S.Z.H.B.; methodology, M.N. and S.Z.H.B.; software, M.N. and S.Z.H.B.; validation, S.N.M.; formal analysis, S.N.M.; investigation, M.N. and S.Z.H.B.; resources, F.T.; data curation, F.T.; writing—original draft preparation, M.N.; writing—review and editing, S.N.M.; visualization, J.-S.R.; supervision, S.Z.H.B.; project administration, J.-S.R.; funding acquisition, J.-S.R. All authors have read and agreed to the published version of the manuscript.

Funding: 1. The research work of the fourth author is supported by the researchers Supporting Project Number (RSP2023R401), King Saud University, Riyadh, Saudi Arabia. 2. The research work of the third author is supported by the National Research Foundation of Korea (NRF) grant, funded by the Korean government (MSIT) (No. NRF-2022R1A2C2004874). 3. The research work of the third author is supported by the Korea Institute of Energy Technology Evaluation and Planning (KETEP) and the Ministry of Trade, Industry & Energy (MOTIE) of the Republic of Korea (No. 20214000000280). 4. The research work of the fifth author is supported by Project number (Ref No. 20-16231/NRPU/R&D/HEC/2021-2020), Higher Education Commission of Pakistan.

Data Availability Statement: No data is used in this study.

Conflicts of Interest: The authors declare no conflict of interest.

References

1. Keogh, F.R.; Merkes, E.P. A coefficient inequality for certain classes of analytic functions. *Proc Amer. Math. Soc.* **1969**, *20*, 8–12. [CrossRef]
2. Elin, M.; Jacobzon, F. Estimates on some functionals over non-linear resolvents. *arXiv* **2021**, arXiv:2105.09582. [CrossRef]
3. Bracci, F.; Contreras, M.D.; Díaz-Madrigal, S. *Continuos Semigroups of Holomorphic Self-Maps of the Unit Disc*; Springer: Berlin/Heidelberg, Germany, 2020.
4. Elin, M.; Reich, S.; Shoikhet, D. *Numerical Range of Holomorpic Mappings and Applications*; Birkhäuser: Cham, Switzerland, 2019.
5. Elin, M.; Shoikhet, D. Linearization models for complex dynamical systems. *Topics in Univalent Functions, Functions Equations and Semigroup Theory*; Birkhäuser: Basel, Switzerland, 2010.
6. Berkson, E.; Porta, H. Semigroups of analytic functions and composition operators. *Michigan Math. J.* **1978**, *25*, 101–115. [CrossRef]
7. Thomas, D.K.; Tuneski, N.; Vasudevarao, A. *Univalent Functions: A Primer*; De Gruyter Studies in Mathematics, 69; De Gruyter: Berlin, Germany, 2018.
8. Miller, S.S.; Mocanu, P.T. Univalent solutions of Briot—Bouquet differential equations. *J. Diff. Equations* **1985**, *56*, 297–309. [CrossRef]
9. Elin, M.; Jacobzon, F.; Tuneski, N. The Fekete–Szegö functional and filtration of generators. *Rend. Del Circ. Mat. Palermo Ser. 2* **2023**, *72*, 2811–2829. [CrossRef]
10. Jack, I.S. Functions starlike and convex of order α. *J. London Math. Soc. Ser. 2* **1971**, *3*, 469–474. [CrossRef]
11. Mocanu, P.T. Une propriété de convexité généralisée dans la théorie de la représentation conformé. *Mathematica* **1969**, *11*, 127–133.
12. Al-Amiri, H. Certain analogy of the α-convex functions. *Rev. Roumaine Math. Pures Appl. XXIII* **1978**, *10*, 1449–1454.
13. Fukui, S. On $\alpha-$convex functions of order β. *Internat. J. Math. Math. Sci.* **1997**, *20*, 769–772. [CrossRef]
14. Miller, S.S.; Mocanu, P.T.; Reade, M.O. All alpha-convex functions are starlike. *Rev. Roumaine Math. Pure Appl.* **1972**, *17*, 1395–1397.
15. Ravichandran, V.; Darus, V. On a class of α-convex functions. *J. Anal. Appl.* **2004**, *2*, 17–25.

fractal and fractional

MDPI

Article

Advances in Ostrowski-Mercer Like Inequalities within Fractal Space

Miguel Vivas-Cortez [1], Muhammad Uzair Awan [2,*], Usama Asif [2], Muhammad Zakria Javed [2] and Hüseyin Budak [3]

1 Escuela de Ciencias Fsicas y Matemáticas, Facultad de Ciencias Exactas y Naturales, Pontificia Universidad Católica del Ecuador, Av. 12 de Octubre 1076, Apartado, Quito 17-01-2184, Ecuador; mjvivas@puce.edu.ec
2 Department of Mathematics, Government College University, Faisalabad 38000, Pakistan
3 Department of Mathematics, Faculty of Science and Arts, Düzce University, Düzce 81620, Turkey
* Correspondence: awan.uzair@gmail.com

Abstract: The main idea of the current investigation is to explore some new aspects of Ostrowski's type integral inequalities implementing the generalized Jensen–Mercer inequality established for generalized s-convexity in fractal space. To proceed further with this task, we construct a new generalized integral equality for first-order local differentiable functions, which will serve as an auxiliary result to restore some new bounds for Ostrowski inequality. We establish our desired results by employing the equality, some renowned generalized integral inequalities like Hölder's, power mean, Yang-Hölder's, bounded characteristics of the functions and considering generalized s-convexity characteristics of functions. Also, in support of our main findings, we deliver specific applications to means, and numerical integration and graphical visualization are also presented here.

Keywords: convex; Jensen-Mercer; Ostrowski; fractal; inequalities; means

Citation: Vivas-Cortez, M.; Awan, M.U.; Asif, U.; Javed, M.Z.; Budak, H. Advances in Ostrowski-Mercer Like Inequalities within Fractal Space. *Fractal Fract.* **2023**, *7*, 689. https://doi.org/10.3390/fractalfract7090689

Academic Editor: Hari Mohan Srivastava

Received: 31 July 2023
Revised: 26 August 2023
Accepted: 30 August 2023
Published: 16 September 2023

1. Introduction

Fractals have been used in many different scientific disciplines since it first came into existence over a hundred years ago. But in the last four decades, its influence has increased many times in mathematics. Mandelbrot has published many books on this topic and introduced the notion of a fractal set, whose Hausdroff dimensions strictly increase the topological dimensions. After this major development, numerous studies have been done regarding this issue. In [1], Yang computed some $\varpi^{\dagger}$-level sets assuming that $\varpi^{\dagger}$ is the dimension of the fractal set.

The theory of convexity has its own very crucial character in the growth of inequalities, and several integral inequalities are restored by considering the notion of convex functions and its generalized forms. Recently, various kinds of novel and innovative convexity have been established. One of them is the generalized convexity defined over the fractal set. After this, many notable and fruitful extensions over fractal sets have been made essentially by making use of non-negative mapping h and parameter $s \in (0,1]$ and some strong convexities.

Fractional calculus, which deals with non-integer order derivatives and integrals, is one of the key calculus modifications devised recently for a better understanding and depiction of real-world issues. The fractional calculus over the fractal set, frequently referred to as the local fractal calculus, was first developed in 2012 by Yang [1]. The creation of photographs, small-angle scattering theory, the music industry, soil mechanics, etc., are all fields where fractals are beneficial. In non-differentiable problems pertaining to science and engineering nowadays, fractal calculus outperforms wholly and practically. For more details, see [2–4]. Inspired by the pre-mentioned facts, Mo et al. [5] introduced the concept of generalized convexity over $\mathbb{R}^{\varpi^{\dagger}}$ and have discussed some algebraic properties of this new class and developed the fractal version of well-known integral inequalities.

In 2017 Sarikaya and Budak et al. [6] formulated the Ostrowski-type integral inequalities by considering the class of generalized convexity and local fractional approach. In [7], the authors have explored the notion of generalized s-convexity and established some new integral inequalities. In [8], the authors explored the Simpson's like inequalities through a novel class of convexity named (s, p)-convex functions in the frame of local fractional calculus. Kilicman and Saleh [9] studied some new aspects of generalized convexity and developed some applications for integral inequalities. Chu et al. [10] introduced the conception of exponential convex functions over the fractal set and by implementing this notion developed some new unified bounds of integral inequalities. In 2020, Sanchez and Sanabria [11] reported the new class of strongly convex functions defined over $\mathbb{R}^{\varpi^\dagger}$ and discussed some algebraic properties. By using this notion, some strong fractal versions of fundamental inequalities of Jensen's type have been obtained. Luo et al. [12] have reported some weighted Hermite–Hadamard type inequalities associated with h-convexity defined over $\mathbb{R}^{\varpi^\dagger}$ and have discussed some special cases to enhance the study with previous results in the literature. In 2020, Sun et al. [13] focused on generalized harmonic convexity to prove some new estimates of trapezium-type inequalities with the help of local identities. Sun et al. [14] have examined the Hermite–Hadamard type inequalities involving the class of generalized harmonic convex mappings defined over the fractal set in association with local fractional calculus. In 2021, Weibing Sun [15] focused on Ostrowski-type inequalities implementing the generalized convex functions through fractal concepts. Razzak et al. [16] have introduced the notion of generalized F convex mapping to explore some new integral inequalities with the help of local fractal calculus. In [17], Kian and Moslehian derived the Jensen–Mercer inequality for operator convexity and some other related inequalities. After this series of work has been done, for further investigation see [18–22]. The first time, Butt and colleagues [23] examined the local fractional variants of Jensen–Mercer inequality and some other inequalities of trapezoidal type in association with the newly proved Jensen–Mercer inequality. In [24], authors investigated the well-known Jensen–Mercer inequality through generalized convexity defined by non-negative mapping h in the context of the fractal domain. In 2017, the authors of [25] studied the Jensen–Mercer inequality from the perspective of harmonic convexity over the fractal domain. In [26], Kalsoom and her colleagues studied Hermite–Hadamard–Fejer-type inequalities involving h-harmonically convex mappings. In [27], the authors developed new counterparts of Simpson's schemes involving generalized p convexity. Erden and Sarikaya [28] investigated the new error estimates for Bullen-type inequalities along with applications. In [29], Wenbing Sun implemented the s-preinvex mappings to acquire new local fractional analogs of Hermite–Hadamard-type inequalities and applications. Du et al. [30] explored certain integral inequalities based on m-convexity convexity over the fractal set and discussed their applications as well. In [31], Yu and his colleagues derived a new variant of improved power-mean inequality in the fractal domain and established new fractional mid-point inequalities and some interesting applications.

2. Preliminaries

Here, $\mathbb{N}, \mathbb{Z}, \mathbb{Q}$ and $\mathbb{R}$ donate the set of natural numbers, set of integers, set of rational numbers, and set of real numbers, respectively. Through the idea of Yang [1], we recall basic concepts and known results regarding local fractional calculus.

Let us start by the notion of $\varpi^\dagger$ type set of element sets: In the following sequel, Mo and Sui [5] introduced a new class of convex functions over the fractal domain, which is defined as

1. $\mathbb{Z}^{\varpi^\dagger} := \{\pm 0^{\varpi^\dagger}, \pm 1^{\varpi^\dagger}, \pm 2^{\varpi^\dagger}, ...\} =: \varpi^\dagger$ type set of irrational number.
2. $\mathbb{Q}^{\varpi^\dagger} := \{v^{\varpi^\dagger} = \left(\frac{p_1}{q_1}\right)^{\varpi^\dagger} : p_1, q_1 \in \mathbb{Z}, q_2 \neq 0\} =: \varpi^\dagger$ type set of irrational number.
3. $\mathbb{Q}'^{\varpi^\dagger} := \{v^{\varpi^\dagger} \neq \left(\frac{p_1}{q_1}\right)^{\varpi^\dagger} : p_1, q_1 \in \mathbb{Z}, q_2 \neq 0\} =: \varpi^\dagger$ type set of irrational number.
4. $\mathbb{R}^{\varpi^\dagger} := \mathbb{Q}^{\varpi^\dagger} \cup \mathbb{Q}'^{\varpi^\dagger} =: \varpi^\dagger$ type set of real number.

We also consider two binary operations, the addition '+' and multiplication '$*$' on the $\varpi^{\dagger}$-type set $\mathbb{R}^{\varpi^{\dagger}}$ of real numbers as follows.

$$c^{\varpi^{\dagger}} + d^{\varpi^{\dagger}} := (c+d)^{\varpi^{\dagger}} \qquad \& \qquad c^{\varpi^{\dagger}} * d^{\varpi^{\dagger}} = c^{\varpi^{\dagger}} d^{\varpi^{\dagger}} := (cd)^{\varpi^{\dagger}}.$$

and both $c^{\varpi^{\dagger}} + d^{\varpi^{\dagger}}, c^{\varpi^{\dagger}} d^{\varpi^{\dagger}} \in \mathbb{R}^{\varpi^{\dagger}}$.

- Further more one can observe that $(\mathbb{R}^{\varpi^{\dagger}}, +)$ forms commutative group. For any $c^{\varpi^{\dagger}}, d^{\varpi^{\dagger}}, e^{\varpi^{\dagger}} \in \mathbb{R}^{\varpi^{\dagger}}$.
  $c^{\varpi^{\dagger}} + d^{\varpi^{\dagger}} = d^{\varpi^{\dagger}} + c^{\varpi^{\dagger}}$.
  $(c^{\varpi^{\dagger}} + d^{\varpi^{\dagger}}) + e^{\varpi^{\dagger}} = c^{\varpi^{\dagger}} + (d^{\varpi^{\dagger}} + e^{\varpi^{\dagger}})$.
  $0^{\varpi^{\dagger}}$ is the additive identity of $\mathbb{R}^{\varpi^{\dagger}}$, $0^{\varpi^{\dagger}} + c^{\varpi^{\dagger}} = c^{\varpi^{\dagger}} + 0^{\varpi^{\dagger}}, \forall c^{\varpi^{\dagger}} \in \mathbb{R}^{\varpi^{\dagger}}$.
  For any $c^{\varpi^{\dagger}}$ then there exist $(-c)^{\varpi^{\dagger}} \in \mathbb{R}^{\varpi^{\dagger}}$ such that $c^{\varpi^{\dagger}} + (-c)^{\varpi^{\dagger}} = 0^{\varpi^{\dagger}}$.
- Also, $(\mathbb{R}^{\varpi^{\dagger}}, *)$ $\{0\}$ forms a commutative group. For any $c^{\varpi^{\dagger}}, d^{\varpi^{\dagger}}, e^{\varpi^{\dagger}} \in \mathbb{R}^{\varpi^{\dagger}}$.
  $c^{\varpi^{\dagger}} d^{\varpi^{\dagger}} = d^{\varpi^{\dagger}} c^{\varpi^{\dagger}}$
  $(c^{\varpi^{\dagger}} d^{\varpi^{\dagger}}) e^{\varpi^{\dagger}} = c^{\varpi^{\dagger}} (d^{\varpi^{\dagger}} e^{\varpi^{\dagger}})$
  $1^{\varpi^{\dagger}} \in \mathbb{R}^{\varpi^{\dagger}}$ then for each $c^{\varpi^{\dagger}} \in \mathbb{R}^{\varpi^{\dagger}}$ such that $1^{\varpi^{\dagger}} c^{\varpi^{\dagger}} = c^{\varpi^{\dagger}} 1^{\varpi^{\dagger}} = c^{\varpi^{\dagger}}$.
  For each $c^{\varpi^{\dagger}} \in \mathbb{R}^{\varpi^{\dagger}}$ $\{0\}$ then there exist $\left(\frac{1}{c}\right)^{\varpi^{\dagger}}$ such that $c^{\varpi^{\dagger}} \left(\frac{1}{c}\right)^{\varpi^{\dagger}} = \left(c\frac{1}{c}\right)^{\varpi^{\dagger}} = 1^{\varpi^{\dagger}}$.

Remark 1. • *$(\mathbb{R}^{\varpi^{\dagger}}, +, *)$ forms field.*

- *If the order $<$ relation is defined on $\mathbb{R}^{\varpi^{\dagger}}$ is defined as follows: $c^{\varpi^{\dagger}} < d^{\varpi^{\dagger}} \Leftrightarrow c < d$ in $\mathbb{R}$. Then, $(\mathbb{R}^{\varpi^{\dagger}}, +, *)$ is an ordered field.*

Now, we have local fractional continuity, which is described as

Definition 1. *A non-differentiable mapping $\Upsilon : \mathbb{R} \to \mathbb{R}^{\varpi^{\dagger}}$, $v \to \Upsilon(v)$ is named as local fractional continuous at v_0, if for any $\epsilon > 0$ then there exist $\delta > 0$ such that*

$$|\Upsilon(v) - \Upsilon(v_0)| < \epsilon^{\varpi^{\dagger}}, \qquad |v - v_0| < \delta.$$

If $\Upsilon(v)$ is local continuous at (w_1, w_2), then $\Upsilon(v) \in C_{\varpi^{\dagger}}(w_1, w_2)$.

Now, we have a look at local differentiability, which is given as

Definition 2. *The local fractional derivative of $\Upsilon(v)$ of order $\varpi^{\dagger}$ at $v = v_0$ is stated as*

$$\Upsilon^{\varpi^{\dagger}}(v) = {}_{v_0}D_v^{\varpi^{\dagger}} \Upsilon(v) = \left| \frac{d^{\varpi^{\dagger}} \Upsilon(v)}{(dv)^{\varpi^{\dagger}}} \right|_{v=v_0} = \lim_{v \to v_0} \frac{\Delta^{\varpi^{\dagger}}(\Upsilon(v) - \Upsilon(v_0))}{(v - v_0)^{\varpi^{\dagger}}}.$$

where $\Delta^{\varpi^{\dagger}}(\Upsilon(v) - \Upsilon(v_0)) = \Gamma(1 + \varpi^{\dagger})(\Upsilon(v) - \Upsilon(v_0))$.

Let $\Upsilon^{\varpi^{\dagger}}(v) = D_v^{\varpi^{\dagger}} \Upsilon(v)$. If there exists $\Upsilon^{(l+1)\varpi^{\dagger}}(v) = \overbrace{D_v^{\varpi^{\dagger}} \Upsilon(v).D_v^{\varpi^{\dagger}} \Upsilon(v) \ldots D_v^{\varpi^{\dagger}} \Upsilon(v)}^{(l+1) times}$ for any $v \in [w_1, w_2]$, then it is denoted by $\Upsilon \in D_{(l+1)\varpi^{\dagger}}$, where $k = 1, 2, 3, \ldots$.

Now, we describe the local integration of $\Upsilon(v) \in C_{\varpi^{\dagger}}(w_1, w_2)$.

Definition 3. *Let $\triangle = \{\mathfrak{x}_0, \mathfrak{x}_1, \mathfrak{x}_2, \ldots, \mathfrak{x}_n\}$ where $n \in \mathbb{N}$ is a partition of $[w_1, w_2]$ such that $\mathfrak{x}_0 < \mathfrak{x}_1 < \mathfrak{x}_2 < \cdots < \mathfrak{x}_n$. Then, the local fractional integral of Υ on $[w_1, w_2]$ is defined as*

$${}_{w_1}I_{w_2}^{\varpi^{\dagger}} \Upsilon(\mathfrak{x}) = \frac{1}{\Gamma(1 + \varpi^{\dagger})} \int_{w_1}^{b} f(\mathfrak{x})(d\mathfrak{x})^{\varpi^{\dagger}} = \frac{1}{\Gamma(1 + \varpi^{\dagger})} \lim_{\triangle \mathfrak{x}_i \to 0} \sum_{i=1}^{n} \Upsilon(\mathfrak{x}_i (\triangle \mathfrak{x})^{\varpi^{\dagger}},$$

where $\triangle \mathfrak{x}_i = \nu_i - \nu_{i-1}$ for $i = 1, 2, 3, \ldots, n$.

From the above expression, it is clear that ${}_{w_1}I_{w_2}^{\varpi^\dagger}\Upsilon(\mathfrak{x}) = 0$ *if* $w_1 = w_2$ *and* ${}_{w_1}I_{w_2}^{\varpi^\dagger}\Upsilon(\mathfrak{x}) = -{}_{w_2}I_{w_1}^{\varpi^\dagger}\Upsilon(\mathfrak{x})$ *when* $w_1 < w_2$. *For any* $\mathfrak{x} \in [w_1, w_2]$, *if there exist* ${}_{w_1}I_{w_2}^{\varpi^\dagger}\Upsilon(\mathfrak{x})$, *then it is denoted by* $\Upsilon(v) \in I_{\mathfrak{x}}^{\varpi^\dagger}[w_1, w_2]$.

Lemma 1. *The following equalities hold:*

1. *(Local fractional integration is anti-differentiation) If* $\Upsilon(\mathfrak{x}) = r^{\varpi^\dagger}(\mathfrak{x}) \in C_{\varpi^\dagger}[w_1, w_2]$, *then*

$$ {}_{w_1}I_{w_2}^{\varpi^\dagger} g(\mathfrak{x}) = r(w_2) - r(w_1). $$

2. *Local fractional derivative of* $\mathfrak{x}^{l\varpi^\dagger}$ *is*

$$ \frac{d^{\varpi^\dagger}\mathfrak{x}^{l\varpi^\dagger}}{(d\mathfrak{x})^{\varpi^\dagger}} = \frac{\Gamma(1 + l\varpi^\dagger)}{\Gamma(1 + (l-1)\varpi^\dagger)}\mathfrak{x}^{(l-1)\varpi^\dagger}. $$

3. *Local fractional integration of* $\mathfrak{x}^{l\varpi^\dagger}$ *is*

$$ \frac{1}{\Gamma(1+\varpi^\dagger)}\int_{w_1}^{w_2} \mathfrak{x}^{l\varpi^\dagger}(d\mathfrak{x})^{\varpi^\dagger} = \frac{\Gamma(1 + l\varpi^\dagger)}{\Gamma(1 + (l+1)\varpi^\dagger)}(w_2{}^{(l+1)\varpi^\dagger} - w_1{}^{(l+1)\varpi^\dagger}). $$

In 2014, Mo et al. [5] introduced the concept of generalized convexity over fractal set $\mathbb{R}^{\varpi^\dagger}$, which is stated as

Definition 4. *Any mapping* $\Upsilon : [w_1, w_2] \to \mathbb{R}^{\varpi^\dagger}$ *is said to be a generalized convexity on fractal set, if*

$$ \Upsilon(\nu w_1 + (1-\nu)w_2) \le \nu^{\varpi^\dagger} + (1-\nu)^{\varpi^\dagger}\Upsilon(w_2), \tag{1} $$

$\nu \in [w_1, w_2]$ *and* $0 < \varpi^\dagger \le 1$.

Also, Υ *is said to be a generalized concave* $\Leftrightarrow -\Upsilon$ *is a generalized convex function.*

If the inequality (2) holds strictly, then it is known as a strictly generalized convex function.

Now, we give the second local derivative test for generalized convexity proved by Mo et al. [5].

Theorem 1. *Let* $\Upsilon \in D_{2\varpi^\dagger}(w_1, w_2)$. *Then* Υ *is said to be a generalized convex (generalized concave) function, if and only if,*

$$ \Upsilon^{2\varpi^\dagger}(\mathfrak{x}) > 0 \quad (\Upsilon^{2\varpi^\dagger} < 0), \quad \mathfrak{x} \in (w_1, w_2). $$

In [7], Mo and Sui explored the notion generalized s-convexity mappings, which are stated as

Definition 5. *Any mapping* $\Upsilon : [w_1, w_2] \to \mathbb{R}^{\varpi^\dagger}$ *is said to be generalized* s*-convexity on a fractal set, if*

$$ \Upsilon(\nu w_1 + (1-\nu)w_2) \le \nu^{s\varpi^\dagger}\Upsilon w_1 + (1-\nu)^{s\varpi^\dagger}\Upsilon(w_2), \tag{2} $$

$\nu \in [0,1], \quad s \in (0,1]$ *and* $0 < \varpi^\dagger \le 1$.

Our first concerned inequality regarding generalized convex functions is generalized Jensen inequality, which is stated as

Theorem 2. *Let* $\Upsilon : [w_1, w_2] \to \mathbb{R}^{\varpi^\dagger}$ $(0 < \varpi^\dagger \leq 1)$ *be a generalized convex function. Then, for any* $\mathfrak{x}_i \in [w_1, w_2]$ *and* $\nu_i \in [0,1]$ *with* $\sum_{i=1}^{n} \nu_i = 1$*, then*

$$\Upsilon\left(\sum_{i=1}^{n} \nu_i \mathfrak{x}_i\right) \leq \sum_{i=1}^{n} \nu_i^{\varpi^\dagger} \Upsilon(\mathfrak{x}_i),$$

Now, we revisit another consequence of Jensen's inequality for two points, which is described as follows:

Theorem 3. *Let* $\Upsilon : [w_1, w_2] \to \mathbb{R}^{\varpi^\dagger}$ $(0 < \varpi^\dagger \leq 1)$ *be a generalized convex function, then*

$$\Upsilon\left(\frac{w_1 + w_2}{2}\right) \leq \frac{\Gamma(1+\varpi^\dagger)}{(w_2 - w_1)^{\varpi^\dagger}} \, {}_{w_1}I_{w_2}^{\varpi^\dagger} \Upsilon(\mathfrak{x}) \leq \frac{\Upsilon(w_1) + \Upsilon(w_2)}{2^{\varpi^\dagger}}, \tag{3}$$

where $0 < \varpi^\dagger \leq 1$*. For more details, see [5].*

Recently, in 2022, Xu and colleagues [24] established a new variant of Jensen–Mercer inequality involving h-convex functions over the fractal set, which is followed as

Theorem 4. *Let* $h : J \to \mathbb{R}$ *be non-negative supermultiplicative mapping,* $h \neq 0$*. Let* $\nu_1, \nu_2, \ldots, \nu_n$ *be a positive real numbers* $(n \geq 2)$ *such that* $W_n = \sum_{k=1}^{n} \nu_k$ *and* $\sum_{k=1}^{n} h\left(\frac{\nu_k}{W_n}\right)$*. If* $\Upsilon : I = [w_1, w_2] \to \mathbb{R}^{\varpi^\dagger}$ *is a generalized h-convex mapping, then for any positive finite sequence* $\{\mathfrak{x}_k\} \in I$*, then*

$$\Upsilon\left(w_1 + w_2 - \frac{1}{W_n} \sum_{k=1}^{n} \nu_k \mathfrak{x}_k\right) \leq \Upsilon(w_1) + \Upsilon(w_2) - \sum_{k=1}^{n} h^{\varpi^\dagger}\left(\frac{\nu_k}{W_n}\right) \Upsilon(\mathfrak{x}_k).$$

Remark 2 ([24])**.**
1. *If* $h^{\varpi^\dagger}(\nu) = \nu^{\varpi^\dagger}$*, then it reduces to a Jensen–Mercer inequality for generalized convex mappings, which is proved in [23].*
2. *If* $h^{\varpi^\dagger}(\nu) = \nu^{s\varpi^\dagger}$*, then it reduces to Jensen–Mercer inequality for generalized s-convex mappings.*

Motivated by the research work going on, we have organized the current study to investigate Ostrowski's type inequalities via generalized s-convexity in the second sense over fractal space. The novelty of our research is that we will propose some new upper bounds for the remainder in the well-known Ostrowski quadrature rule. We have distributed our study in several parts. Initially, we give a brief introduction of the current research and some essential facts, which are required for further proceedings. In the next part, we will propose new local fractional counterparts of Osrowski–Mercer inequality involving s-convexity of the functions along with Holder's type inequalities. Later, applications and numerical and graphical illustrations of our primary findings will be discussed in detail. We hope the problem's idea and technique will attract interested readers' attention.

3. Main Results

The current portion of the study is specified for the detailed investigation of Ostrowski's type inequalities over fractal settings. The substantial part of this study is to formulate a new identity involving local differentiable mappings.

Lemma 2. *Let* $\Upsilon : I = [w_1, w_2] \to \mathbb{R}^{\varpi^\dagger}$ $(0 < \varpi^\dagger \leq 1)$ *be function, such that* $\Upsilon \in D_{\varpi^\dagger}(I^\circ)$ *where* I° *is the interior of I and* $\Upsilon^{\varpi^\dagger} \in C_{\varpi^\dagger}(w_1, w_2)$*, where* $[\mathfrak{u}_1, \mathfrak{u}_2] \subseteq [w_1, w_2]$ *and* $\mathfrak{x} \in [\mathfrak{u}_1, \mathfrak{u}_2]$*, then*

$$(\mathfrak{x} - \mathfrak{u}_1)^{\varpi^\dagger} \Upsilon(w_1 + \mathfrak{x} - \mathfrak{u}_1) + (\mathfrak{u}_2 - \mathfrak{x})^{\varpi^\dagger} \Upsilon(w_2 + \mathfrak{x} - \mathfrak{u}_2) - \Gamma(1+\varpi^\dagger)\left[{}_{a}I_{w_1+\mathfrak{x}-\mathfrak{u}_1}^{\varpi^\dagger} \Upsilon(\mathfrak{u}) + {}_{(w_2+\mathfrak{x}-\mathfrak{u}_2)}I_{w_2}^{\varpi^\dagger} \Upsilon(\mathfrak{u})\right]$$

$$
\begin{aligned}
&= \frac{(\mathfrak{x}-\mathfrak{u}_1)^{2\varpi^\dagger}}{\Gamma(\varpi^\dagger+1)} \int_0^1 \nu^{\varpi^\dagger} \mathrm{Y}^{\varpi^\dagger}(w_1+\mathfrak{x}-(\nu\mathfrak{u}_1+(1-\nu)\mathfrak{x}))(dt)^{\varpi^\dagger} \\
&- \frac{(\mathfrak{u}_2-\mathfrak{x})^{2\varpi^\dagger}}{\Gamma(\varpi^\dagger+1)} \int_0^1 \nu^{\varpi^\dagger} \mathrm{Y}^{\varpi^\dagger}(w_2+\mathfrak{x}-(\nu\mathfrak{u}_2+(1-\nu)\mathfrak{x}))(dt)^{\varpi^\dagger}
\end{aligned} \tag{4}
$$

Proof. Consider the right hand side of (4), we have

$$
I = (\mathfrak{x}-\mathfrak{u}_1)^{2\varpi^\dagger} I_1 - (\mathfrak{u}_2-\mathfrak{x})^{2\varpi^\dagger} I_2, \tag{5}
$$

where,

$$
\begin{aligned}
I_1 &= \frac{1}{\Gamma(\varpi^\dagger+1)} \int_0^1 \nu^{\varpi^\dagger} \mathrm{Y}^{\varpi^\dagger}(w_1+\mathfrak{x}-(\nu\mathfrak{u}_1+(1-\nu)\mathfrak{x}))(dt)^{\varpi^\dagger} \\
&= \frac{1}{(\mathfrak{x}-\mathfrak{u}_1)^{\varpi^\dagger}} \left[\mathrm{Y}(w_1+\mathfrak{x}-\mathfrak{u}_1) - \frac{\Gamma(1+\varpi^\dagger)}{(\mathfrak{x}-\mathfrak{u}_1)^{\varpi^\dagger}\Gamma(1+\varpi^\dagger)} \int_{w_1}^{w_1+\mathfrak{x}-\mathfrak{u}_1} \mathrm{Y}(\mathfrak{u})(d\mathfrak{u})^{\varpi^\dagger} \right] \\
&= \frac{\mathrm{Y}(w_1+\mathfrak{x}-\mathfrak{u}_1)}{(\mathfrak{x}-\mathfrak{u}_1)^{\varpi^\dagger}} - \frac{\Gamma(1+\varpi^\dagger)}{(\mathfrak{x}-\mathfrak{u}_1)^{2\varpi^\dagger}} {}_{w_1}I^{\varpi^\dagger}_{w_1+\mathfrak{x}-\mathfrak{u}_1} \mathrm{Y}(\mathfrak{u}),
\end{aligned} \tag{6}
$$

similarly, we obtain

$$
\begin{aligned}
I_2 &= \frac{1}{\Gamma(\varpi^\dagger+1)} \int_0^1 \nu^{\varpi^\dagger} \mathrm{Y}^{\varpi^\dagger}(w_2+\mathfrak{x}-(\nu\mathfrak{u}_2+(1-\nu)\mathfrak{x}))(dt)^{\varpi^\dagger} \\
&= -\frac{\mathrm{Y}(w_2+\mathfrak{x}-\mathfrak{u}_2)}{(\mathfrak{u}_2-\mathfrak{x})^{\varpi^\dagger}} - \frac{\Gamma(1+\varpi^\dagger)}{(\mathfrak{u}_2-\mathfrak{x})^{2\varpi^\dagger}} {}_{(w_2+\mathfrak{x}-\mathfrak{u}_2)}I^{\varpi^\dagger}_{w_2} \mathrm{Y}(\mathfrak{u}),
\end{aligned} \tag{7}
$$

Substituting (6) and (7) in (5), we obtain (4). □

Remark 3. *If we set $\mathfrak{u}_1 = w_1$ and $\mathfrak{u}_2 = w_2$ in Lemma 2, then we obtain Lemma 3 of [15].*

Theorem 5. *Under the assumptions of Lemma 2, If $|\mathrm{Y}^{\varpi^\dagger}|$ be a generalized s-convex function in second sense, then*

$$
\begin{aligned}
&\left| (\mathfrak{x}-\mathfrak{u}_1)^{\varpi^\dagger}\mathrm{Y}(w_1+\mathfrak{x}-\mathfrak{u}_1) + (\mathfrak{u}_2-\mathfrak{x})^{\varpi^\dagger}\mathrm{Y}(w_2+\mathfrak{x}-\mathfrak{u}_2) - \Gamma(1+\varpi^\dagger)\left[{}_aI^{\varpi^\dagger}_{w_1+\mathfrak{x}-\mathfrak{u}_1}\mathrm{Y}(\mathfrak{u}) + {}_{(w_2+\mathfrak{x}-\mathfrak{u}_2)}I^{\varpi^\dagger}_{w_2}\mathrm{Y}(\mathfrak{u}) \right] \right| \\
&\le (\mathfrak{x}-\mathfrak{u}_1)^{2\varpi^\dagger} \left[\frac{\Gamma(1+\varpi^\dagger)}{\Gamma(1+2\varpi^\dagger)} |\mathrm{Y}^{\varpi^\dagger}(w_1)| + \left[\frac{\Gamma(1+\varpi^\dagger)}{\Gamma(1+2\varpi^\dagger)} - B_{\varpi^\dagger}(2,s+1) \right] |\mathrm{Y}^{\varpi^\dagger}(\mathfrak{x})| \right. \\
&\left. -\frac{\Gamma(1+(s+1)\varpi^\dagger)}{\Gamma(1+(s+2)\varpi^\dagger)} |\mathrm{Y}^{\varpi^\dagger}(\mathfrak{u}_1)| \right] + (\mathfrak{u}_2-\mathfrak{x})^{2\varpi^\dagger} \left[\frac{\Gamma(1+\varpi^\dagger)}{\Gamma(1+2\varpi^\dagger)} |\mathrm{Y}^{\varpi^\dagger}(w_2)| \right. \\
&\left. + \left[\frac{\Gamma(1+\varpi^\dagger)}{\Gamma(1+2\varpi^\dagger)} - B_{\varpi^\dagger}(2,s+1) \right] |\mathrm{Y}^{\varpi^\dagger}(\mathfrak{x})| - \frac{\Gamma(1+(s+1)\varpi^\dagger)}{\Gamma(1+(s+2)\varpi^\dagger)} |\mathrm{Y}^{\varpi^\dagger}(\mathfrak{u}_2)| \right],
\end{aligned} \tag{8}
$$

$B_{\varpi^\dagger}(.,.)$ is the well-known local beta function and is defined as

$$
B_{\varpi^\dagger}(m_1,m_2) = \frac{1}{\Gamma(1+\varpi^\dagger)} \int_0^1 (\nu)^{m_1\varpi^\dagger-1}(1-\nu)^{m_2\varpi^\dagger-1}(d\nu)^{\varpi^\dagger}.
$$

Proof. Applying the modulus property and Jensen–Mercer inequality for generalized s-convex function in equality Lemma 2, we have

$$
\begin{aligned}
&\left| (\mathfrak{x}-\mathfrak{u}_1)^{\varpi^\dagger}\mathrm{Y}(w_1+\mathfrak{x}-\mathfrak{u}_1) + (\mathfrak{u}_2-\mathfrak{x})^{\varpi^\dagger}\mathrm{Y}(w_2+\mathfrak{x}-\mathfrak{u}_2) - \Gamma(1+\varpi^\dagger)\left[{}_aI^{\varpi^\dagger}_{w_1+\mathfrak{x}-\mathfrak{u}_1}\mathrm{Y}(\mathfrak{u}) + {}_{(w_2+\mathfrak{x}-\mathfrak{u}_2)}I^{\varpi^\dagger}_{w_2}\mathrm{Y}(\mathfrak{u}) \right] \right| \\
&\le \frac{(\mathfrak{x}-\mathfrak{u}_1)^{2\varpi^\dagger}}{\Gamma(\varpi^\dagger+1)} \int_0^1 \left| \nu^{\varpi^\dagger}\mathrm{Y}^{\varpi^\dagger}(w_1+\mathfrak{x}-(\nu\mathfrak{u}_1+(1-\nu)\mathfrak{x})) \right| (dt)^{\varpi^\dagger}
\end{aligned}
$$

$$+\frac{(\mathfrak{u}_2-\mathfrak{x})^{2\varpi^{\dagger}}}{\Gamma(\varpi^{\dagger}+1)}\int_0^1\left|\nu^{\varpi^{\dagger}}\mathrm{Y}^{\varpi^{\dagger}}(w_2+\mathfrak{x}-(\nu\mathfrak{u}_2+(1-\nu)\mathfrak{x}))\right|(dt)^{\varpi^{\dagger}}$$
$$\leq\frac{(\mathfrak{x}-\mathfrak{u}_1)^{2\varpi^{\dagger}}}{\Gamma(\varpi^{\dagger}+1)}\int_0^1\nu^{\varpi^{\dagger}}\left[|\mathrm{Y}^{\varpi^{\dagger}}(w_1)|+|\mathrm{Y}^{\varpi^{\dagger}}(\mathfrak{x})|-\nu^{\varpi^{\dagger}s}|\mathrm{Y}^{\varpi^{\dagger}}(\mathfrak{u}_1)|-(1-\nu)^{\varpi^{\dagger}s}|\mathrm{Y}^{\varpi^{\dagger}}(\mathfrak{x})|\right](dt)^{\varpi^{\dagger}}$$
$$+\frac{(\mathfrak{u}_2-\mathfrak{x})^{2\varpi^{\dagger}}}{\Gamma(\varpi^{\dagger}+1)}\int_0^1\nu^{\varpi^{\dagger}}\left[|\mathrm{Y}^{\varpi^{\dagger}}(w_2)|+|\mathrm{Y}^{\varpi^{\dagger}}(\mathfrak{x})|-\nu^{\varpi^{\dagger}s}|\mathrm{Y}^{\varpi^{\dagger}}(\mathfrak{u}_2)|-(1-\nu)^{\varpi^{\dagger}s}|\mathrm{Y}^{\varpi^{\dagger}}(\mathfrak{x})|\right](dt)^{\varpi^{\dagger}}$$
$$\leq(\mathfrak{x}-\mathfrak{u}_1)^{2\varpi^{\dagger}}\left[\frac{\Gamma(1+\varpi^{\dagger})}{\Gamma(1+2\varpi^{\dagger})}|\mathrm{Y}^{\varpi^{\dagger}}(w_1)|+\left[\frac{\Gamma(1+\varpi^{\dagger})}{\Gamma(1+2\varpi^{\dagger})}-B_{\varpi^{\dagger}}(2,s+1)\right]|\mathrm{Y}^{\varpi^{\dagger}}(\mathfrak{x})|\right.$$
$$\left.-\frac{\Gamma(1+(s+1)\varpi^{\dagger})}{\Gamma(1+(s+2)\varpi^{\dagger})}|\mathrm{Y}^{\varpi^{\dagger}}(\mathfrak{u}_1)|\right]+(\mathfrak{u}_2-\mathfrak{x})^{2\varpi^{\dagger}}\left[\frac{\Gamma(1+\varpi^{\dagger})}{\Gamma(1+2\varpi^{\dagger})}|\mathrm{Y}^{\varpi^{\dagger}}(w_2)|\right.$$
$$\left.+\left[\frac{\Gamma(1+\varpi^{\dagger})}{\Gamma(1+2\varpi^{\dagger})}-B_{\varpi^{\dagger}}(2,s+1)\right]|\mathrm{Y}^{\varpi^{\dagger}}(\mathfrak{x})|-\frac{\Gamma(1+(s+1)\varpi^{\dagger})}{\Gamma(1+(s+2)\varpi^{\dagger})}|\mathrm{Y}^{\varpi^{\dagger}}(\mathfrak{u}_2)|\right],$$

which gives the inequality (8). □

Corollary 1. *If we take $s=1$ in (8), then*

$$\left|(\mathfrak{x}-\mathfrak{u}_1)^{\varpi^{\dagger}}\mathrm{Y}(w_1+\mathfrak{x}-\mathfrak{u}_1)+(\mathfrak{u}_2-\mathfrak{x})^{\varpi^{\dagger}}\mathrm{Y}(w_2+\mathfrak{x}-\mathfrak{u}_2)-\Gamma(1+\varpi^{\dagger})\left[{}_aI^{\varpi^{\dagger}}_{w_1+\mathfrak{x}-\mathfrak{u}_1}\mathrm{Y}(\mathfrak{u})+{}_{(w_2+\mathfrak{x}-\mathfrak{u}_2)}I^{\varpi^{\dagger}}_{w_2}\mathrm{Y}(\mathfrak{u})\right]\right|$$
$$\leq(\mathfrak{x}-\mathfrak{u}_1)^{2\varpi^{\dagger}}\left[\frac{\Gamma(1+\varpi^{\dagger})}{\Gamma(1+2\varpi^{\dagger})}|\mathrm{Y}^{\varpi^{\dagger}}(w_1)|+\left[\frac{\Gamma(1+\varpi^{\dagger})}{\Gamma(1+2\varpi^{\dagger})}-B_{\varpi^{\dagger}}(2,2)\right]|\mathrm{Y}^{\varpi^{\dagger}}(\mathfrak{x})|-\frac{\Gamma(1+2\varpi^{\dagger})}{\Gamma(1+3\varpi^{\dagger})}|\mathrm{Y}^{\varpi^{\dagger}}(\mathfrak{u}_1)|\right]$$
$$+(\mathfrak{u}_2-\mathfrak{x})^{2\varpi^{\dagger}}\left[\frac{\Gamma(1+\varpi^{\dagger})}{\Gamma(1+2\varpi^{\dagger})}|\mathrm{Y}^{\varpi^{\dagger}}(w_2)|+\left[\frac{\Gamma(1+\varpi^{\dagger})}{\Gamma(1+2\varpi^{\dagger})}-B_{\varpi^{\dagger}}(2,2)\right]|\mathrm{Y}^{\varpi^{\dagger}}(\mathfrak{x})|-\frac{\Gamma(1+2\varpi^{\dagger})}{\Gamma(1+3\varpi^{\dagger})}|\mathrm{Y}^{\varpi^{\dagger}}(\mathfrak{u}_2)|\right].$$

Corollary 2. *If we set $\mathfrak{u}_1=w_1$ and $\mathfrak{u}_2=w_2$ in (8), then we obtain*

$$\left|(\mathfrak{x}-\mathfrak{u}_1)^{\varpi^{\dagger}}\mathrm{Y}(w_1+\mathfrak{x}-\mathfrak{u}_1)+(\mathfrak{u}_2-\mathfrak{x})^{\varpi^{\dagger}}\mathrm{Y}(w_2+\mathfrak{x}-\mathfrak{u}_2)-\Gamma(1+\varpi^{\dagger})\left[{}_aI^{\varpi^{\dagger}}_{w_1+\mathfrak{x}-\mathfrak{u}_1}\mathrm{Y}(\mathfrak{u})+{}_{(w_2+\mathfrak{x}-\mathfrak{u}_2)}I^{\varpi^{\dagger}}_{w_2}\mathrm{Y}(\mathfrak{u})\right]\right|$$
$$\leq(\mathfrak{x}-\mathfrak{u}_1)^{2\varpi^{\dagger}}\left[\frac{\Gamma(1+\varpi^{\dagger})}{\Gamma(1+2\varpi^{\dagger})}|\mathrm{Y}^{\varpi^{\dagger}}(w_1)|+\left[\frac{\Gamma(1+\varpi^{\dagger})}{\Gamma(1+2\varpi^{\dagger})}-B_{\varpi^{\dagger}}(2,2)\right]|\mathrm{Y}^{\varpi^{\dagger}}(\mathfrak{x})|-\frac{\Gamma(1+2\varpi^{\dagger})}{\Gamma(1+3\varpi^{\dagger})}|\mathrm{Y}^{\varpi^{\dagger}}(\mathfrak{u}_1)|\right]$$
$$+(\mathfrak{u}_2-\mathfrak{x})^{2\varpi^{\dagger}}\left[\frac{\Gamma(1+\varpi^{\dagger})}{\Gamma(1+2\varpi^{\dagger})}|\mathrm{Y}^{\varpi^{\dagger}}(w_2)|+\left[\frac{\Gamma(1+\varpi^{\dagger})}{\Gamma(1+2\varpi^{\dagger})}-B_{\varpi^{\dagger}}(2,2)\right]|\mathrm{Y}^{\varpi^{\dagger}}(\mathfrak{x})|-\frac{\Gamma(1+2\varpi^{\dagger})}{\Gamma(1+3\varpi^{\dagger})}|\mathrm{Y}^{\varpi^{\dagger}}(\mathfrak{u}_2)|\right].$$

Corollary 3. *If we set $\mathfrak{u}_1=w_1$, $\mathfrak{u}_2=w_2$ and $\mathfrak{x}=\frac{w_1+w_2}{2}$ in (8), then we obtain*

$$\left|\frac{(w_2-w_1)^{\varpi^{\dagger}}\mathrm{Y}\left(\frac{w_1+w_2}{2}\right)}{\Gamma(1+\varpi^{\dagger})}-\frac{1}{\Gamma(1+\varpi^{\dagger})}\int_{w_1}^{b}f(\mathfrak{u})(d\mathfrak{u})^{\varpi^{\dagger}}\right|$$
$$\leq\frac{1}{\Gamma(1+\varpi^{\dagger})}\left(\frac{w_2-w_1}{2}\right)^{2\varpi^{\dagger}}\left[\left(\frac{\Gamma(1+\varpi^{\dagger})}{\Gamma(1+2\varpi^{\dagger})}-\frac{\Gamma(1+(s+1)\varpi^{\dagger})}{\Gamma(1+(s+2)\varpi^{\dagger})}\right)|\mathrm{Y}^{\varpi^{\dagger}}(w_1)|\right.$$
$$\left.+2^{\varpi^{\dagger}}\left[\frac{\Gamma(1+\varpi^{\dagger})}{\Gamma(1+2\varpi^{\dagger})}-B_{\varpi^{\dagger}}(2,s+1)\right]\left|\mathrm{Y}^{\varpi^{\dagger}}\left(\frac{w_1+w_2}{2}\right)\right|+\left(\frac{\Gamma(1+\varpi^{\dagger})}{\Gamma(1+2\varpi^{\dagger})}-\frac{\Gamma(1+(s+1)\varpi^{\dagger})}{\Gamma(1+(s+2)\varpi^{\dagger})}\right)|\mathrm{Y}^{\varpi^{\dagger}}(w_2)|\right].$$

Theorem 6. *Under the assumptions of Lemma 2, if $|\mathrm{Y}^{\varpi^{\dagger}}|^q$ be a generalized s-convex function in second sense, then*

$$\left|(\mathfrak{x}-\mathfrak{u}_1)^{\varpi^{\dagger}}\mathrm{Y}(w_1+\mathfrak{x}-\mathfrak{u}_1)+(\mathfrak{u}_2-\mathfrak{x})^{\varpi^{\dagger}}\mathrm{Y}(w_2+\mathfrak{x}-\mathfrak{u}_2)-\Gamma(1+\varpi^{\dagger})\left[{}_aI^{\varpi^{\dagger}}_{w_1+\mathfrak{x}-\mathfrak{u}_1}\mathrm{Y}(\mathfrak{u})+{}_{(w_2+\mathfrak{x}-\mathfrak{u}_2)}I^{\varpi^{\dagger}}_{w_2}\mathrm{Y}(\mathfrak{u})\right]\right|$$
$$\leq\left(\frac{\Gamma(1+\varpi^{\dagger}p)}{\Gamma(1+(p+1)\varpi^{\dagger})}\right)^{\frac{1}{p}}\left[(\mathfrak{x}-\mathfrak{u}_1)^{2\varpi^{\dagger}}\left(\frac{1}{\Gamma(\varpi^{\dagger}+1)}|\mathrm{Y}^{\varpi^{\dagger}}(w_1)|^q\right.\right.$$
$$\left.+\left(\frac{1}{\Gamma(\varpi^{\dagger}+1)}-\frac{\Gamma(1+\varpi^{\dagger}s)}{\Gamma(1+(s+1)\varpi^{\dagger})}\right)|\mathrm{Y}^{\varpi^{\dagger}}(\mathfrak{x})|^q-\frac{\Gamma(1+\varpi^{\dagger}s)}{\Gamma(1+(s+1)\varpi^{\dagger})}|\mathrm{Y}^{\varpi^{\dagger}}(\mathfrak{u}_1)|^q\right)^{\frac{1}{q}}$$

$$+(\mathfrak{u}_2-\mathfrak{x})^{2\varpi^\dagger}\left(\frac{1}{\Gamma(\varpi^\dagger+1)}|\Upsilon^{\varpi^\dagger}(w_2)|^q\right.$$
$$\left.\left.+\left(\frac{1}{\Gamma(\varpi^\dagger+1)}-\frac{\Gamma(1+\varpi^\dagger s)}{\Gamma(1+(s+1)\varpi^\dagger)}\right)|\Upsilon^{\varpi^\dagger}(\mathfrak{x})|^q-\frac{\Gamma(1+\varpi^\dagger s)}{\Gamma(1+(s+1)\varpi^\dagger)}|\Upsilon^{\varpi^\dagger}(\mathfrak{u}_2)|^q\right)^{\frac{1}{q}}\right], \tag{9}$$

where $p^{-1}+q^{-1}=1$.

Proof. Applying the modulus property, Hölder's inequality, and generalized convexity property of $|\Upsilon^{\varpi^\dagger}|^q$, then

$$\left|(\mathfrak{x}-\mathfrak{u}_1)^{\varpi^\dagger}\Upsilon(w_1+\mathfrak{x}-\mathfrak{u}_1)+(\mathfrak{u}_2-\mathfrak{x})^{\varpi^\dagger}\Upsilon(w_2+\mathfrak{x}-\mathfrak{u}_2)-\Gamma(1+\varpi^\dagger)\left[{}_aI^{\varpi^\dagger}_{w_1+\mathfrak{x}-\mathfrak{u}_1}\Upsilon(\mathfrak{u})+{}_{(w_2+\mathfrak{x}-\mathfrak{u}_2)}I^{\varpi^\dagger}_{w_2}\Upsilon(\mathfrak{u})\right]\right|$$
$$\leq\frac{(\mathfrak{x}-\mathfrak{u}_1)^{2\varpi^\dagger}}{\Gamma(\varpi^\dagger+1)}\int_0^1\left|\nu^{\varpi^\dagger}\Upsilon^{\varpi^\dagger}(w_1+\mathfrak{x}-(\nu\mathfrak{u}_1+(1-\nu)\mathfrak{x}))\right|(dt)^{\varpi^\dagger}$$
$$+\frac{(\mathfrak{u}_2-\mathfrak{x})^{2\varpi^\dagger}}{\Gamma(\varpi^\dagger+1)}\int_0^1\left|\nu^{\varpi^\dagger}\Upsilon^{\varpi^\dagger}(w_2+\mathfrak{x}-(\nu\mathfrak{u}_2+(1-\nu)\mathfrak{x}))\right|(dt)^{\varpi^\dagger}$$
$$\leq(\mathfrak{x}-\mathfrak{u}_1)^{2\varpi^\dagger}\left(\frac{1}{\Gamma(\varpi^\dagger+1)}\int_0^1\nu^{\varpi^\dagger p}(dt)^{\varpi^\dagger}\right)^{\frac{1}{p}}\left(\frac{1}{\Gamma(\varpi^\dagger+1)}\int_0^1\left|\Upsilon^{\varpi^\dagger}(w_1+\mathfrak{x}-(\nu\mathfrak{u}_1+(1-\nu)\mathfrak{x}))\right|(dt)^{\varpi^\dagger}\right)^{\frac{1}{q}}$$
$$+(\mathfrak{u}_2-\mathfrak{x})^{2\varpi^\dagger}\left(\frac{1}{\Gamma(\varpi^\dagger+1)}\int_0^1\nu^{\varpi^\dagger p}(dt)^{\varpi^\dagger}\right)^{\frac{1}{p}}\left(\frac{1}{\Gamma(\varpi^\dagger+1)}\int_0^1\left|\Upsilon^{\varpi^\dagger}(w_2+\mathfrak{x}-(\nu\mathfrak{u}_2+(1-\nu)\mathfrak{x}))\right|(dt)^{\varpi^\dagger}\right)^{\frac{1}{q}}$$
$$\leq(\mathfrak{x}-\mathfrak{u}_1)^{2\varpi^\dagger}\left(\frac{1}{\Gamma(\varpi^\dagger+1)}\int_0^1\nu^{\varpi^\dagger p}(dt)^{\varpi^\dagger}\right)^{\frac{1}{p}}$$
$$\times\left(\frac{1}{\Gamma(\varpi^\dagger+1)}\int_0^1\left[|\Upsilon^{\varpi^\dagger}(w_1)|^q+|\Upsilon^{\varpi^\dagger}(\mathfrak{x})|^q-\nu^{\varpi^\dagger s}|\Upsilon^{\varpi^\dagger}(\mathfrak{u}_1)|^q-(1-\nu)^{\varpi^\dagger s}|\Upsilon^{\varpi^\dagger}(\mathfrak{x})|^q\right](dt)^{\varpi^\dagger}\right)^{\frac{1}{q}}$$
$$+(\mathfrak{u}_2-\mathfrak{x})^{2\varpi^\dagger}\left(\frac{1}{\Gamma(\varpi^\dagger+1)}\int_0^1\nu^{\varpi^\dagger p}(dt)^{\varpi^\dagger}\right)^{\frac{1}{p}}$$
$$\times\left(\frac{1}{\Gamma(\varpi^\dagger+1)}\int_0^1\left[|\Upsilon^{\varpi^\dagger}(w_2)|^q+|\Upsilon^{\varpi^\dagger}(\mathfrak{x})|^q-\nu^{\varpi^\dagger s}|\Upsilon^{\varpi^\dagger}(\mathfrak{u}_2)|^q-(1-\nu)^{\varpi^\dagger s}|\Upsilon^{\varpi^\dagger}(\mathfrak{x})|^q\right](dt)^{\varpi^\dagger}\right)^{\frac{1}{q}}$$
$$\leq\left(\frac{\Gamma(1+\varpi^\dagger p)}{\Gamma(1+(p+1)\varpi^\dagger)}\right)^{\frac{1}{p}}\left[(\mathfrak{x}-\mathfrak{u}_1)^{2\varpi^\dagger}\left(\frac{1}{\Gamma(\varpi^\dagger+1)}|\Upsilon^{\varpi^\dagger}(w_1)|^q\right.\right.$$
$$\left.+\left(\frac{1}{\Gamma(\varpi^\dagger+1)}-\frac{\Gamma(1+\varpi^\dagger s)}{\Gamma(1+(s+1)\varpi^\dagger)}\right)|\Upsilon^{\varpi^\dagger}(\mathfrak{x})|^q-\frac{\Gamma(1+\varpi^\dagger s)}{\Gamma(1+(s+1)\varpi^\dagger)}|\Upsilon^{\varpi^\dagger}(\mathfrak{u}_1)|^q\right)^{\frac{1}{q}}$$
$$+(\mathfrak{u}_2-\mathfrak{x})^{2\varpi^\dagger}\left(\frac{1}{\Gamma(\varpi^\dagger+1)}|\Upsilon^{\varpi^\dagger}(w_2)|^q\right.$$
$$\left.\left.+\left(\frac{1}{\Gamma(\varpi^\dagger+1)}-\frac{\Gamma(1+\varpi^\dagger s)}{\Gamma(1+(s+1)\varpi^\dagger)}\right)|\Upsilon^{\varpi^\dagger}(\mathfrak{x})|^q-\frac{\Gamma(1+\varpi^\dagger s)}{\Gamma(1+(s+1)\varpi^\dagger)}|\Upsilon^{\varpi^\dagger}(\mathfrak{u}_2)|^q\right)^{\frac{1}{q}}\right],$$

which completes the proof. □

Corollary 4. *If we take* $s=1$ *in (9), then*

$$\left|(\mathfrak{x}-\mathfrak{u}_1)^{\varpi^\dagger}\Upsilon(w_1+\mathfrak{x}-\mathfrak{u}_1)+(\mathfrak{u}_2-\mathfrak{x})^{\varpi^\dagger}\Upsilon(w_2+\mathfrak{x}-\mathfrak{u}_2)-\Gamma(1+\varpi^\dagger)\left[{}_aI^{\varpi^\dagger}_{w_1+\mathfrak{x}-\mathfrak{u}_1}\Upsilon(\mathfrak{u})+{}_{(w_2+\mathfrak{x}-\mathfrak{u}_2)}I^{\varpi^\dagger}_{w_2}\Upsilon(\mathfrak{u})\right]\right|$$
$$\leq\left(\frac{\Gamma(1+\varpi^\dagger p)}{\Gamma(1+(p+1)\varpi^\dagger)}\right)^{\frac{1}{p}}\left[(\mathfrak{x}-\mathfrak{u}_1)^{2\varpi^\dagger}\left(\frac{1}{\Gamma(\varpi^\dagger+1)}|\Upsilon^{\varpi^\dagger}(w_1)|^q\right.\right.$$
$$\left.+\left(\frac{1}{\Gamma(\varpi^\dagger+1)}-\frac{\Gamma(1+\varpi^\dagger)}{\Gamma(1+2\varpi^\dagger)}\right)|\Upsilon^{\varpi^\dagger}(\mathfrak{x})|^q-\frac{\Gamma(1+\varpi^\dagger)}{\Gamma(1+2\varpi^\dagger)}|\Upsilon^{\varpi^\dagger}(\mathfrak{u}_1)|^q\right)^{\frac{1}{q}}$$

$$+(\mathfrak{u}_2-\mathfrak{x})^{2\varpi^{\dagger}}\left(\frac{1}{\Gamma(\varpi^{\dagger}+1)}|\Upsilon^{\varpi^{\dagger}}(w_2)|^q\right.$$
$$\left.\left.+\left(\frac{1}{\Gamma(\varpi^{\dagger}+1)}-\frac{\Gamma(1+\varpi^{\dagger})}{\Gamma(1+2\varpi^{\dagger})}\right)|\Upsilon^{\varpi^{\dagger}}(\mathfrak{x})|^q-\frac{\Gamma(1+\varpi^{\dagger})}{\Gamma(1+2\varpi^{\dagger})}|\Upsilon^{\varpi^{\dagger}}(\mathfrak{u}_2)|^q\right)^{\frac{1}{q}}\right],$$

Corollary 5. *If we set* $\mathfrak{u}_1=w_1,\mathfrak{u}_2=w_2$ *and* $\mathfrak{x}=\frac{w_1+w_2}{2}$ *in (9), then we obtain*

$$\left|\frac{(w_2-w_1)^{\varpi^{\dagger}}\Upsilon\left(\frac{w_1+w_2}{2}\right)}{\Gamma(1+\varpi^{\dagger})}-\frac{1}{\Gamma(1+\varpi^{\dagger})}\int_{w_1}^{b}f(\mathfrak{u})(d\mathfrak{u})^{\varpi^{\dagger}}\right|$$
$$\leq\frac{1}{\Gamma(1+\varpi^{\dagger})}\left(\frac{\Gamma(1+\varpi^{\dagger}p)}{\Gamma(1+(p+1)\varpi^{\dagger})}\right)^{\frac{1}{p}}$$
$$\times\left[\left(\frac{w_2-w_1}{2}\right)^{2\varpi^{\dagger}}\left(\left(\frac{1}{\Gamma(\varpi^{\dagger}+1)}-\frac{\Gamma(1+\varpi^{\dagger}s)}{\Gamma(1+(s+1)\varpi^{\dagger})}\right)|\Upsilon^{\varpi^{\dagger}}(w_1)|^q\right.\right.$$
$$\left.+\left(\frac{1}{\Gamma(\varpi^{\dagger}+1)}-\frac{\Gamma(1+\varpi^{\dagger}s)}{\Gamma(1+(s+1)\varpi^{\dagger})}\right)\left|\Upsilon^{\varpi^{\dagger}}\left(\frac{w_1+w_2}{2}\right)\right|^q\right)^{\frac{1}{q}}$$
$$+\left(\frac{w_2-w_1}{2}\right)^{2\varpi^{\dagger}}\left(\left(\frac{1}{\Gamma(\varpi^{\dagger}+1)}-\frac{\Gamma(1+\varpi^{\dagger}s)}{\Gamma(1+(s+1)\varpi^{\dagger})}\right)|\Upsilon^{\varpi^{\dagger}}(w_2)|^q\right.$$
$$\left.\left.+\left(\frac{1}{\Gamma(\varpi^{\dagger}+1)}-\frac{\Gamma(1+\varpi^{\dagger}s)}{\Gamma(1+(s+1)\varpi^{\dagger})}\right)\left|\Upsilon^{\varpi^{\dagger}}\left(\frac{w_1+w_2}{2}\right)\right|^q\right)^{\frac{1}{q}}\right].$$

Remark 4. *If we set* $\mathfrak{u}_1=w_1$ *and* $\mathfrak{u}_2=w_2$ *in inequality , then we obtain special case of inequality (3.16), as proved in [15].*

Theorem 7. *Under the assumptions of Lemma 2, if* $|\Upsilon^{\varpi^{\dagger}}|^q$ *be a generalized s-convex function in second sense, then*

$$\left|(\mathfrak{x}-\mathfrak{u}_1)^{\varpi^{\dagger}}\Upsilon(w_1+\mathfrak{x}-\mathfrak{u}_1)+(\mathfrak{u}_2-\mathfrak{x})^{\varpi^{\dagger}}\Upsilon(w_2+\mathfrak{x}-\mathfrak{u}_2)-\Gamma(1+\varpi^{\dagger})\left[{}_aI^{\varpi^{\dagger}}_{w_1+\mathfrak{x}-\mathfrak{u}_1}\Upsilon(\mathfrak{u})+{}_{(w_2+\mathfrak{x}-\mathfrak{u}_2)}I^{\varpi^{\dagger}}_{w_2}\Upsilon(\mathfrak{u})\right]\right|$$
$$\leq\left(\frac{\Gamma(1+\varpi^{\dagger})}{\Gamma(1+2\varpi^{\dagger})}\right)^{1-\frac{1}{q}}\left((\mathfrak{x}-\mathfrak{u}_1)^{2\varpi^{\dagger}}\left[\frac{\Gamma(1+\varpi^{\dagger})}{\Gamma(1+2\varpi^{\dagger})}|\Upsilon^{\varpi^{\dagger}}(w_1)|^q+\left[\frac{\Gamma(1+\varpi^{\dagger})}{\Gamma(1+2\varpi^{\dagger})}-B_{\varpi^{\dagger}}(2,s+1)\right]|\Upsilon^{\varpi^{\dagger}}(\mathfrak{x})|^q\right.\right.$$
$$\left.-\frac{\Gamma(1+(s+1)\varpi^{\dagger})}{\Gamma(1+(s+2)\varpi^{\dagger})}|\Upsilon^{\varpi^{\dagger}}(\mathfrak{u}_1)|^q\right]^{\frac{1}{q}}+(\mathfrak{u}_2-\mathfrak{x})^{2\varpi^{\dagger}}\left[\frac{\Gamma(1+\varpi^{\dagger})}{\Gamma(1+2\varpi^{\dagger})}|\Upsilon^{\varpi^{\dagger}}(w_2)|^q\right.$$
$$\left.\left.+\left[\frac{\Gamma(1+\varpi^{\dagger})}{\Gamma(1+2\varpi^{\dagger})}-B_{\varpi^{\dagger}}(2,s+1)\right]|\Upsilon^{\varpi^{\dagger}}(\mathfrak{x})|^q-\frac{\Gamma(1+(s+1)\varpi^{\dagger})}{\Gamma(1+(s+2)\varpi^{\dagger})}|\Upsilon^{\varpi^{\dagger}}(\mathfrak{u}_2)|^q\right]^{\frac{1}{q}}\right),\tag{10}$$

where $p^{-1}+q^{-1}=1$ *and* $B_{\varpi^{\dagger}}(w_1,w_2)=\frac{1}{\Gamma(1+\varpi^{\dagger})}\int_0^1\nu^{w_1\alpha}(1-\nu)^{w_2\alpha}$ *is a well known beta function over the fractal set.*

Proof. Applying the power mean inequality and generalized convexity property of the $|\Upsilon^{\varpi^{\dagger}}|^q$, then

$$\left|(\mathfrak{x}-\mathfrak{u}_1)^{\varpi^{\dagger}}\Upsilon(w_1+\mathfrak{x}-\mathfrak{u}_1)+(\mathfrak{u}_2-\mathfrak{x})^{\varpi^{\dagger}}\Upsilon(w_2+\mathfrak{x}-\mathfrak{u}_2)\right.$$
$$\left.-\Gamma(1+\varpi^{\dagger})\left[{}_aI^{\varpi^{\dagger}}_{w_1+w_2-\mathfrak{u}_1}\Upsilon(\mathfrak{u})+{}_{(w_2+\mathfrak{x}-\mathfrak{u})}I^{\varpi^{\dagger}}_{w_2}\Upsilon(\mathfrak{u})\right]\right|$$
$$\leq\frac{(\mathfrak{x}-\mathfrak{u}_1)^{2\varpi^{\dagger}}}{\Gamma(\varpi^{\dagger}+1)}\int_0^1\left|\nu^{\varpi^{\dagger}}\Upsilon^{\varpi^{\dagger}}(w_1+\mathfrak{x}-(\nu\mathfrak{u}_1+(1-\nu)\mathfrak{x}))\right|(dt)^{\varpi^{\dagger}}$$

$$+\frac{(\mathfrak{u}_2-\mathfrak{x})^{2\varpi^\dagger}}{\Gamma(\varpi^\dagger+1)}\int_0^1\left|\nu^{\varpi^\dagger}\Upsilon^{\varpi^\dagger}(w_2+\mathfrak{x}-(\nu\mathfrak{u}_2+(1-\nu)\mathfrak{x}))\right|(dt)^{\varpi^\dagger}$$

$$\leq(\mathfrak{x}-\mathfrak{u}_1)^{2\varpi^\dagger}\left(\frac{1}{\Gamma(\varpi^\dagger+1)}\int_0^1\nu^{\varpi^\dagger}(dt)^{\varpi^\dagger}\right)^{1-\frac{1}{q}}$$

$$\times\left(\frac{1}{\Gamma(\varpi^\dagger+1)}\int_0^1\left|\nu^{\varpi^\dagger}\Upsilon^{\varpi^\dagger}(w_1+\mathfrak{x}-(\nu\mathfrak{u}_1+(1-\nu)\mathfrak{x}))\right|(dt)^{\varpi^\dagger}\right)^{\frac{1}{q}}$$

$$+(\mathfrak{u}_2-\mathfrak{x})^{2\varpi^\dagger}\left(\frac{1}{\Gamma(\varpi^\dagger+1)}\int_0^1\nu^{\varpi^\dagger}(dt)^{\varpi^\dagger}\right)^{1-\frac{1}{q}}$$

$$\times\left(\frac{1}{\Gamma(\varpi^\dagger+1)}\int_0^1\left|\nu^{\varpi^\dagger}\Upsilon^{\varpi^\dagger}(w_2+\mathfrak{x}-(\nu\mathfrak{u}_2+(1-\nu)\mathfrak{x}))\right|(dt)^{\varpi^\dagger}\right)^{\frac{1}{q}}$$

$$\leq(\mathfrak{x}-\mathfrak{u}_1)^{2\varpi^\dagger}\left(\frac{1}{\Gamma(\varpi^\dagger+1)}\int_0^1\nu^{\varpi^\dagger}(dt)^{\varpi^\dagger}\right)^{1-\frac{1}{q}}$$

$$\times\left(\frac{1}{\Gamma(\varpi^\dagger+1)}\int_0^1\nu^{\varpi^\dagger}\left[|\Upsilon^{\varpi^\dagger}(w_1)|^q+|\Upsilon^{\varpi^\dagger}(\mathfrak{x})|^q-\nu^{\varpi^\dagger s}|\Upsilon^{\varpi^\dagger}(\mathfrak{u}_1)|^q-(1-\nu)^{\varpi^\dagger s}|\Upsilon^{\varpi^\dagger}(\mathfrak{x})|^q\right](dt)^{\varpi^\dagger}\right)^{\frac{1}{q}}$$

$$+(\mathfrak{u}_2-\mathfrak{x})^{2\varpi^\dagger}\left(\frac{1}{\Gamma(\varpi^\dagger+1)}\int_0^1\nu^{\varpi^\dagger}(dt)^{\varpi^\dagger}\right)^{1-\frac{1}{q}}$$

$$\times\left(\frac{1}{\Gamma(\varpi^\dagger+1)}\int_0^1\nu^{\varpi^\dagger}\left[|\Upsilon^{\varpi^\dagger}(w_2)|^q+|\Upsilon^{\varpi^\dagger}(\mathfrak{x})|^q-\nu^{\varpi^\dagger s}|\Upsilon^{\varpi^\dagger}(\mathfrak{u}_2)|^q-(1-\nu)^{\varpi^\dagger s}|\Upsilon^{\varpi^\dagger}(\mathfrak{x})|^q\right](dt)^{\varpi^\dagger}\right)^{\frac{1}{q}}$$

$$\leq\left(\frac{\Gamma(1+\varpi^\dagger)}{\Gamma(1+2\varpi^\dagger)}\right)^{1-\frac{1}{q}}\left((\mathfrak{x}-\mathfrak{u}_1)^{2\varpi^\dagger}\left[\frac{\Gamma(1+\varpi^\dagger)}{\Gamma(1+2\varpi^\dagger)}|\Upsilon^{\varpi^\dagger}(w_1)|^q+\left[\frac{\Gamma(1+\varpi^\dagger)}{\Gamma(1+2\varpi^\dagger)}-B_{\varpi^\dagger}(2,s+1)\right]|\Upsilon^{\varpi^\dagger}(\mathfrak{x})|^q\right.\right.$$

$$\left.-\frac{\Gamma(1+(s+1)\varpi^\dagger)}{\Gamma(1+(s+2)\varpi^\dagger)}|\Upsilon^{\varpi^\dagger}(\mathfrak{u}_1)|^q\right]^{\frac{1}{q}}+(\mathfrak{u}_2-\mathfrak{x})^{2\varpi^\dagger}\left[\frac{\Gamma(1+\varpi^\dagger)}{\Gamma(1+2\varpi^\dagger)}|\Upsilon^{\varpi^\dagger}(w_2)|^q\right.$$

$$\left.\left.+\left[\frac{\Gamma(1+\varpi^\dagger)}{\Gamma(1+2\varpi^\dagger)}-B_{\varpi^\dagger}(2,s+1)\right]|\Upsilon^{\varpi^\dagger}(\mathfrak{x})|^q-\frac{\Gamma(1+(s+1)\varpi^\dagger)}{\Gamma(1+(s+2)\varpi^\dagger)}|\Upsilon^{\varpi^\dagger}(\mathfrak{u}_2)|^q\right]^{\frac{1}{q}}\right),$$

which completes the proof. □

Corollary 6. *If we take $s=1$ in (10), then*

$$\left|(\mathfrak{x}-\mathfrak{u}_1)^{\varpi^\dagger}\Upsilon(w_1+\mathfrak{x}-\mathfrak{u}_1)+(\mathfrak{u}_2-\mathfrak{x})^{\varpi^\dagger}\Upsilon(w_2+\mathfrak{x}-\mathfrak{u}_2)-\Gamma(1+\varpi^\dagger)\left[{}_aI^{\varpi^\dagger}_{w_1+\mathfrak{x}-\mathfrak{u}_1}\Upsilon(\mathfrak{u})+{}_{(w_2+\mathfrak{x}-\mathfrak{u}_2)}I^{\varpi^\dagger}_{w_2}\Upsilon(\mathfrak{u})\right]\right|$$

$$\leq\left(\frac{\Gamma(1+\varpi^\dagger)}{\Gamma(1+2\varpi^\dagger)}\right)^{1-\frac{1}{q}}\left((\mathfrak{x}-\mathfrak{u}_1)^{2\varpi^\dagger}\left[\frac{\Gamma(1+\varpi^\dagger)}{\Gamma(1+2\varpi^\dagger)}|\Upsilon^{\varpi^\dagger}(w_1)|^q+\left[\frac{\Gamma(1+\varpi^\dagger)}{\Gamma(1+2\varpi^\dagger)}-B_{\varpi^\dagger}(2,2)\right]|\Upsilon^{\varpi^\dagger}(\mathfrak{x})|^q\right.\right.$$

$$\left.-\frac{\Gamma(1+2\varpi^\dagger)}{\Gamma(1+3\varpi^\dagger)}|\Upsilon^{\varpi^\dagger}(\mathfrak{u}_1)|^q\right]^{\frac{1}{q}}+(\mathfrak{u}_2-\mathfrak{x})^{2\varpi^\dagger}\left[\frac{\Gamma(1+\varpi^\dagger)}{\Gamma(1+2\varpi^\dagger)}|\Upsilon^{\varpi^\dagger}(w_2)|^q\right.$$

$$\left.\left.+\left[\frac{\Gamma(1+\varpi^\dagger)}{\Gamma(1+2\varpi^\dagger)}-B_{\varpi^\dagger}(2,2)\right]|\Upsilon^{\varpi^\dagger}(\mathfrak{x})|^q-\frac{\Gamma(1+2\varpi^\dagger)}{\Gamma(1+3\varpi^\dagger)}|\Upsilon^{\varpi^\dagger}(\mathfrak{u}_2)|^q\right]^{\frac{1}{q}}\right).$$

Corollary 7. *If we set $\mathfrak{u}_1=w_1,\mathfrak{u}_2=w_2$ and $\mathfrak{x}=\frac{w_1+w_2}{2}$ in (10), then we obtain*

$$\left|\frac{(w_2-w_1)^{\varpi^\dagger}\Upsilon\left(\frac{w_1+w_2}{2}\right)}{\Gamma(1+\varpi^\dagger)}-\frac{1}{\Gamma(1+\varpi^\dagger)}\int_{w_1}^b f(\mathfrak{u})(d\mathfrak{u})^{\varpi^\dagger}\right|$$

$$\leq\frac{1}{\Gamma(1+\varpi^\dagger)}\left(\frac{\Gamma(1+\varpi^\dagger)}{\Gamma(1+2\varpi^\dagger)}\right)^{1-\frac{1}{q}}\left(\left(\frac{w_2-w_1}{2}\right)^{2\varpi^\dagger}\left[\left(\frac{\Gamma(1+\varpi^\dagger)}{\Gamma(1+2\varpi^\dagger)}-\frac{\Gamma(1+(s+1)\varpi^\dagger)}{\Gamma(1+(s+2)\varpi^\dagger)}\right)|\Upsilon^{\varpi^\dagger}(w_1)|^q\right.\right.$$

$$+\left[\frac{\Gamma(1+\varpi^{\dagger})}{\Gamma(1+2\varpi^{\dagger})}-B_{\varpi^{\dagger}}(2,s+1)\right]\left|\Upsilon^{\varpi^{\dagger}}\left(\frac{w_1+w_2}{2}\right)\right|^{q}\Bigg]^{\frac{1}{q}}$$
$$+\left(\frac{w_2-w_1}{2}\right)^{2\varpi^{\dagger}}\Bigg[\left(\frac{\Gamma(1+\varpi^{\dagger})}{\Gamma(1+2\varpi^{\dagger})}-\frac{\Gamma(1+(s+1)\varpi^{\dagger})}{\Gamma(1+(s+2)\varpi^{\dagger})}\right)|\Upsilon^{\varpi^{\dagger}}(w_2)|^{q}$$
$$+\left[\frac{\Gamma(1+\varpi^{\dagger})}{\Gamma(1+2\varpi^{\dagger})}-B_{\varpi^{\dagger}}(2,s+1)\right]\left|\Upsilon^{\varpi^{\dagger}}\left(\frac{w_1+w_2}{2}\right)\right|^{q}\Bigg]^{\frac{1}{q}}\Bigg).$$

Theorem 8. *Assume that all the conditions of Lemma 2 are satisfied, if $|\Upsilon^{\varpi^{\dagger}}|^{q}$ is generalized s-convex on the interval $[w_1,w_2]$ for $p,q>0$ with $\frac{1}{p}+\frac{1}{q}=1$, then*

$$\left|(\mathfrak{r}-\mathfrak{u}_1)^{\varpi^{\dagger}}\Upsilon(w_1+\mathfrak{r}-\mathfrak{u}_1)+(\mathfrak{u}_2-\mathfrak{r})^{\varpi^{\dagger}}\Upsilon(w_2+\mathfrak{r}-\mathfrak{u}_2)-\Gamma(1+\varpi^{\dagger})\left[{}_{a}I^{\varpi^{\dagger}}_{w_1+w_2-\mathfrak{u}_1}\Upsilon(\mathfrak{u})+{}_{(w_2+\mathfrak{r}-\mathfrak{u})}I^{\varpi^{\dagger}}_{w_2}\Upsilon(\mathfrak{u})\right]\right|$$
$$\leq(\mathfrak{r}-\mathfrak{u}_1)^{2\varpi^{\dagger}}\Bigg\{(B_{\varpi^{\dagger}}(p+1,2))^{\frac{1}{p}}\Bigg(\frac{\Gamma(\varpi^{\dagger}+1)}{\Gamma(2\varpi^{\dagger}+1)}|\Upsilon^{\varpi^{\dagger}}(w_1)|^{q}$$
$$+\left[\frac{\Gamma(\varpi^{\dagger}+1)}{\Gamma(2\varpi^{\dagger}+1)}-B_{\varpi^{\dagger}}(s+1,2)\right]|\Upsilon^{\varpi^{\dagger}}(\mathfrak{r})|^{q}-\frac{\Gamma(1+(s+1)\varpi^{\dagger})}{\Gamma(1+(s+2)\varpi^{\dagger})}|\Upsilon^{\varpi^{\dagger}}(\mathfrak{u}_1)|^{q}\Bigg)^{\frac{1}{q}}$$
$$+\left(\frac{\Gamma(1+(p+1)\varpi^{\dagger})}{\Gamma(1+(p+2)\varpi^{\dagger})}\right)^{\frac{1}{p}}\Bigg(\frac{\Gamma(\varpi^{\dagger}+1)}{\Gamma(2\varpi^{\dagger}+1)}|\Upsilon^{\varpi^{\dagger}}(w_1)|^{q}$$
$$+\left[\frac{\Gamma(\varpi^{\dagger}+1)}{\Gamma(2\varpi^{\dagger}+1)}-B_{\varpi^{\dagger}}(2,s+1)\right]|\Upsilon^{\varpi^{\dagger}}(\mathfrak{r})|^{q}-\frac{\Gamma(1+(s+1)\varpi^{\dagger})}{\Gamma(1+(s+2)\varpi^{\dagger})}|\Upsilon^{\varpi^{\dagger}}(\mathfrak{u}_1)|^{q}\Bigg)^{\frac{1}{q}}\Bigg\}$$
$$+(\mathfrak{u}_2-\mathfrak{r})^{2\varpi^{\dagger}}\Bigg\{(B_{\varpi^{\dagger}}(p+1,2))^{\frac{1}{p}}\Bigg(\frac{\Gamma(\varpi^{\dagger}+1)}{\Gamma(2\varpi^{\dagger}+1)}|\Upsilon^{\varpi^{\dagger}}(w_2)|^{q}$$
$$+\left[\frac{\Gamma(\varpi^{\dagger}+1)}{\Gamma(2\varpi^{\dagger}+1)}-B_{\varpi^{\dagger}}(s+1,2)\right]|\Upsilon^{\varpi^{\dagger}}(\mathfrak{r})|^{q}-\frac{\Gamma(1+(s+1)\varpi^{\dagger})}{\Gamma(1+(s+2)\varpi^{\dagger})}|\Upsilon^{\varpi^{\dagger}}(\mathfrak{u}_2)|^{q}\Bigg)^{\frac{1}{q}}$$
$$+\left(\frac{\Gamma(1+(p+1)\varpi^{\dagger})}{\Gamma(1+(p+2)\varpi^{\dagger})}\right)^{\frac{1}{p}}\Bigg(\frac{\Gamma(\varpi^{\dagger}+1)}{\Gamma(2\varpi^{\dagger}+1)}|\Upsilon^{\varpi^{\dagger}}(w_2)|^{q}$$
$$+\left[\frac{\Gamma(\varpi^{\dagger}+1)}{\Gamma(2\varpi^{\dagger}+1)}-B_{\varpi^{\dagger}}(2,s+1)\right]|\Upsilon^{\varpi^{\dagger}}(\mathfrak{r})|^{q}-\frac{\Gamma(1+(s+1)\varpi^{\dagger})}{\Gamma(1+(s+2)\varpi^{\dagger})}|\Upsilon^{\varpi^{\dagger}}(\mathfrak{u}_2)|^{q}\Bigg)^{\frac{1}{q}}\Bigg\}.$$

Proof. Employing Lemma 2 and the Holder–Yang's inequality, we find that

$$\begin{aligned}
&\left|(\mathfrak{r}-\mathfrak{u}_1)^{\varpi^\dagger}\Upsilon(w_1+\mathfrak{r}-\mathfrak{u}_1)+(\mathfrak{u}_2-\mathfrak{r})^{\varpi^\dagger}\Upsilon(w_2+\mathfrak{r}-\mathfrak{u}_2)-\Gamma(1+\varpi^\dagger)\left[{}_aI^{\varpi^\dagger}_{w_1+\mathfrak{r}-\mathfrak{u}_1}\Upsilon(\mathfrak{u})+{}_{(w_2+\mathfrak{r}-\mathfrak{u}_2)}I^{\varpi^\dagger}_{w_2}\Upsilon(\mathfrak{u})\right]\right|\\
&\leq \frac{(\mathfrak{r}-\mathfrak{u}_1)^{2\varpi^\dagger}}{\Gamma(\varpi^\dagger+1)}\int_0^1\left|\nu^{\varpi^\dagger}\Upsilon^{\varpi^\dagger}(w_1+\mathfrak{r}-(\nu\mathfrak{u}_1+(1-\nu)\mathfrak{r}))\right|(dt)^{\varpi^\dagger}\\
&+\frac{(\mathfrak{u}_2-\mathfrak{r})^{2\varpi^\dagger}}{\Gamma(\varpi^\dagger+1)}\int_0^1\left|\nu^{\varpi^\dagger}\Upsilon^{\varpi^\dagger}(w_2+\mathfrak{r}-(\nu\mathfrak{u}_2+(1-\nu)\mathfrak{r}))\right|(dt)^{\varpi^\dagger}\\
&\leq (\mathfrak{r}-\mathfrak{u}_1)^{2\varpi^\dagger}\left\{\left(\frac{1}{\Gamma(1+\varpi^\dagger)}\int_0^1(1-\nu)^{\varpi^\dagger}\nu^{p\varpi^\dagger}(d(\nu))^{\varpi^\dagger}\right)^{\frac{1}{p}}\right.\\
&\times\left(\frac{1}{\Gamma(1+\varpi^\dagger)}\int_0^1(1-\nu)^{\varpi^\dagger}|\Upsilon^{\varpi^\dagger}(w_1+\mathfrak{r}-(\nu\mathfrak{u}_1+(1-\nu)\mathfrak{r}))|^q(d(\nu))^{\varpi^\dagger}\right)^{\frac{1}{q}}\\
&\left.+\left(\frac{1}{\Gamma(1+\varpi^\dagger)}\int_0^1\nu^{\varpi^\dagger}\nu^{p\varpi^\dagger}(d(\nu))^{\varpi^\dagger}\right)^{\frac{1}{p}}\left(\frac{1}{\Gamma(1+\varpi^\dagger)}\int_0^1\nu^{\varpi^\dagger}|\Upsilon^{\varpi^\dagger}(w_1+\mathfrak{r}-(\nu\mathfrak{u}_1+(1-\nu)\mathfrak{r}))|^q(d(\nu))^{\varpi^\dagger}\right)^{\frac{1}{q}}\right\}\\
&+(\mathfrak{u}_2-\mathfrak{r})^{2\varpi^\dagger}\left\{\left(\frac{1}{\Gamma(1+\varpi^\dagger)}\int_0^1(1-\nu)^{\varpi^\dagger}\nu^{p\varpi^\dagger}(d(\nu))^{\varpi^\dagger}\right)^{\frac{1}{p}}\right.\\
&\times\left(\frac{1}{\Gamma(1+\varpi^\dagger)}\int_0^1(1-\nu)^{\varpi^\dagger}|\Upsilon^{\varpi^\dagger}(w_2+\mathfrak{r}-(\nu\mathfrak{u}_2+(1-\nu)\mathfrak{r}))|^q(d(\nu))^{\varpi^\dagger}\right)^{\frac{1}{q}}\\
&\left.+\left(\frac{1}{\Gamma(1+\varpi^\dagger)}\int_0^1\nu^{\varpi^\dagger}\nu^{p\varpi^\dagger}(d(\nu))^{\varpi^\dagger}\right)^{\frac{1}{p}}\left(\frac{1}{\Gamma(1+\varpi^\dagger)}\int_0^1\nu^{\varpi^\dagger}|\Upsilon^{\varpi^\dagger}(w_2+\mathfrak{r}-(\nu\mathfrak{u}_2+(1-\nu)\mathfrak{r}))|^q(d(\nu))^{\varpi^\dagger}\right)^{\frac{1}{q}}\right\}.
\end{aligned}$$

Owing to the generalized s-convexity of the mapping $|\Upsilon^{\varpi^\dagger}|^q$, we find that

$$\begin{aligned}
&\left|(\mathfrak{r}-\mathfrak{u}_1)^{\varpi^\dagger}\Upsilon(w_1+\mathfrak{r}-\mathfrak{u}_1)+(\mathfrak{u}_2-\mathfrak{r})^{\varpi^\dagger}\Upsilon(w_2+\mathfrak{r}-\mathfrak{u}_2)-\Gamma(1+\varpi^\dagger)\left[{}_aI^{\varpi^\dagger}_{w_1+\mathfrak{r}-\mathfrak{u}_1}\Upsilon(\mathfrak{u})+{}_{(w_2+\mathfrak{r}-\mathfrak{u}_2)}I^{\varpi^\dagger}_{w_2}\Upsilon(\mathfrak{u})\right]\right|\\
&\leq (\mathfrak{r}-\mathfrak{u}_1)^{2\varpi^\dagger}\left\{\left(\frac{1}{\Gamma(1+\varpi^\dagger)}\int_0^1(1-\nu)^{\varpi^\dagger}\nu^{p\varpi^\dagger}(d(\nu))^{\varpi^\dagger}\right)^{\frac{1}{p}}\right.\\
&\times\left(\frac{1}{\Gamma(1+\varpi^\dagger)}\int_0^1(1-\nu)^{\varpi^\dagger}[|\Upsilon^{\varpi^\dagger}(w_1)|^q+|\Upsilon^{\varpi^\dagger}(\mathfrak{r})|^q-\nu^{s\varpi^\dagger}|\Upsilon^{\varpi^\dagger}(\mathfrak{u}_1)|^q-(1-\nu)^{s\varpi^\dagger}|\Upsilon^{\varpi^\dagger}(\mathfrak{r})|^q](d(\nu))^{\varpi^\dagger}\right)^{\frac{1}{q}}\\
&+\left(\frac{1}{\Gamma(1+\varpi^\dagger)}\int_0^1\nu^{\varpi^\dagger}\nu^{p\varpi^\dagger}(d(\nu))^{\varpi^\dagger}\right)^{\frac{1}{p}}\\
&\left.\times\left(\frac{1}{\Gamma(1+\varpi^\dagger)}\int_0^1\nu^{\varpi^\dagger}[|\Upsilon^{\varpi^\dagger}(w_1)|^q+|\Upsilon^{\varpi^\dagger}(\mathfrak{r})|^q-\nu^{s\varpi^\dagger}|\Upsilon^{\varpi^\dagger}(\mathfrak{u}_1)|^q-(1-\nu)^{s\varpi^\dagger}|\Upsilon^{\varpi^\dagger}(\mathfrak{r})|^q](d(\nu))^{\varpi^\dagger}\right)^{\frac{1}{q}}\right\}\\
&+(\mathfrak{u}_2-\mathfrak{r})^{2\varpi^\dagger}\left\{\left(\frac{1}{\Gamma(1+\varpi^\dagger)}\int_0^1(1-\nu)^{\varpi^\dagger}\nu^{p\varpi^\dagger}(d(\nu))^{\varpi^\dagger}\right)^{\frac{1}{p}}\right.\\
&\times\left(\frac{1}{\Gamma(1+\varpi^\dagger)}\int_0^1(1-\nu)^{\varpi^\dagger}[|\Upsilon^{\varpi^\dagger}(w_2)|^q+|\Upsilon^{\varpi^\dagger}(\mathfrak{r})|^q-\nu^{s\varpi^\dagger}|\Upsilon^{\varpi^\dagger}(\mathfrak{u}_2)|^q-(1-\nu)^{s\varpi^\dagger}|\Upsilon^{\varpi^\dagger}(\mathfrak{r})|^q](d(\nu))^{\varpi^\dagger}\right)^{\frac{1}{q}}\\
&+\left(\frac{1}{\Gamma(1+\varpi^\dagger)}\int_0^1\nu^{\varpi^\dagger}\nu^{p\varpi^\dagger}(d(\nu))^{\varpi^\dagger}\right)^{\frac{1}{p}}\\
&\left.\times\left(\frac{1}{\Gamma(1+\varpi^\dagger)}\int_0^1\nu^{\varpi^\dagger}[|\Upsilon^{\varpi^\dagger}(w_2)|^q+|\Upsilon^{\varpi^\dagger}(\mathfrak{r})|^q-\nu^{s\varpi^\dagger}|\Upsilon^{\varpi^\dagger}(\mathfrak{u}_2)|^q-(1-\nu)^{s\varpi^\dagger}|\Upsilon^{\varpi^\dagger}(\mathfrak{r})|^q](d(\nu))^{\varpi^\dagger}\right)^{\frac{1}{q}}\right\}\\
&\leq (\mathfrak{r}-\mathfrak{u}_1)^{2\varpi^\dagger}\left\{(B_{\varpi^\dagger}(p+1,2))^{\frac{1}{p}}\left(\frac{\Gamma(\varpi^\dagger+1)}{\Gamma(2\varpi^\dagger+1)}|\Upsilon^{\varpi^\dagger}(w_1)|^q\right.\right.
\end{aligned}$$

$$+\left[\frac{\Gamma(\varpi^{\dagger}+1)}{\Gamma(2\varpi^{\dagger}+1)}-B_{\varpi^{\dagger}}(s+1,2)\right]|Y^{\varpi^{\dagger}}(\mathfrak{x})|^{q}-\frac{\Gamma(1+(s+1)\varpi^{\dagger})}{\Gamma(1+(s+2)\varpi^{\dagger})}|Y^{\varpi^{\dagger}}(u_1)|^{q}\Bigg)^{\frac{1}{q}}$$
$$+\left(\frac{\Gamma(1+(p+1)\varpi^{\dagger})}{\Gamma(1+(p+2)\varpi^{\dagger})}\right)^{\frac{1}{p}}\left(\frac{\Gamma(\varpi^{\dagger}+1)}{\Gamma(2\varpi^{\dagger}+1)}|Y^{\varpi^{\dagger}}(w_1)|^{q}\right.$$
$$\left.+\left[\frac{\Gamma(\varpi^{\dagger}+1)}{\Gamma(2\varpi^{\dagger}+1)}-B_{\varpi^{\dagger}}(2,s+1)\right]|Y^{\varpi^{\dagger}}(\mathfrak{x})|^{q}-\frac{\Gamma(1+(s+1)\varpi^{\dagger})}{\Gamma(1+(s+2)\varpi^{\dagger})}|Y^{\varpi^{\dagger}}(u_1)|^{q}\right)^{\frac{1}{q}}\Bigg\}$$
$$+(u_2-\mathfrak{x})^{2\varpi^{\dagger}}\Bigg\{(B_{\varpi^{\dagger}}(p+1,2))^{\frac{1}{p}}\left(\frac{\Gamma(\varpi^{\dagger}+1)}{\Gamma(2\varpi^{\dagger}+1)}|Y^{\varpi^{\dagger}}(w_2)|^{q}\right.$$
$$\left.+\left[\frac{\Gamma(\varpi^{\dagger}+1)}{\Gamma(2\varpi^{\dagger}+1)}-B_{\varpi^{\dagger}}(s+1,2)\right]|Y^{\varpi^{\dagger}}(\mathfrak{x})|^{q}-\frac{\Gamma(1+(s+1)\varpi^{\dagger})}{\Gamma(1+(s+2)\varpi^{\dagger})}|Y^{\varpi^{\dagger}}(u_2)|^{q}\right)^{\frac{1}{q}}$$
$$+\left(\frac{\Gamma(1+(p+1)\varpi^{\dagger})}{\Gamma(1+(p+2)\varpi^{\dagger})}\right)^{\frac{1}{p}}\left(\frac{\Gamma(\varpi^{\dagger}+1)}{\Gamma(2\varpi^{\dagger}+1)}|Y^{\varpi^{\dagger}}(w_2)|^{q}\right.$$
$$\left.+\left[\frac{\Gamma(\varpi^{\dagger}+1)}{\Gamma(2\varpi^{\dagger}+1)}-B_{\varpi^{\dagger}}(2,s+1)\right]|Y^{\varpi^{\dagger}}(\mathfrak{x})|^{q}-\frac{\Gamma(1+(s+1)\varpi^{\dagger})}{\Gamma(1+(s+2)\varpi^{\dagger})}|Y^{\varpi^{\dagger}}(u_2)|^{q}\right)^{\frac{1}{q}}\Bigg\}.$$

In this way, we concluded our required result. □

Corollary 8. *If we take $s=1$ in Theorem 8, then we have the following inequality:*

$$\left|(\mathfrak{x}-u_1)^{\varpi^{\dagger}}Y(w_1+\mathfrak{x}-u_1)+(u_2-\mathfrak{x})^{\varpi^{\dagger}}Y(w_2+\mathfrak{x}-u_2)-\Gamma(1+\varpi^{\dagger})\left[{}_{a}I^{\varpi^{\dagger}}_{w_1+\mathfrak{x}-u_1}Y(u)+{}_{(w_2+\mathfrak{x}-u_2)}I^{\varpi^{\dagger}}_{w_2}Y(u)\right]\right|$$
$$\leq(\mathfrak{x}-u_1)^{2\varpi^{\dagger}}\Bigg\{(B_{\varpi^{\dagger}}(p+1,2))^{\frac{1}{p}}\left(\frac{\Gamma(\varpi^{\dagger}+1)}{\Gamma(2\varpi^{\dagger}+1)}|Y^{\varpi^{\dagger}}(w_1)|^{q}\right.$$
$$\left.+\left[\frac{\Gamma(\varpi^{\dagger}+1)}{\Gamma(2\varpi^{\dagger}+1)}-B_{\varpi^{\dagger}}(2,2)\right]|Y^{\varpi^{\dagger}}(\mathfrak{x})|^{q}-\frac{\Gamma(1+2\varpi^{\dagger})}{\Gamma(1+3\varpi^{\dagger})}|Y^{\varpi^{\dagger}}(u_1)|^{q}\right)^{\frac{1}{q}}$$
$$+\left(\frac{\Gamma(1+(p+1)\varpi^{\dagger})}{\Gamma(1+(p+2)\varpi^{\dagger})}\right)^{\frac{1}{p}}\left(\frac{\Gamma(\varpi^{\dagger}+1)}{\Gamma(2\varpi^{\dagger}+1)}|Y^{\varpi^{\dagger}}(w_1)|^{q}\right.$$
$$\left.+\left[\frac{\Gamma(\varpi^{\dagger}+1)}{\Gamma(2\varpi^{\dagger}+1)}-B_{\varpi^{\dagger}}(2,2)\right]|Y^{\varpi^{\dagger}}(\mathfrak{x})|^{q}-\frac{\Gamma(1+2\varpi^{\dagger})}{\Gamma(1+3\varpi^{\dagger})}|Y^{\varpi^{\dagger}}(u_1)|^{q}\right)^{\frac{1}{q}}\Bigg\}$$
$$+(u_2-\mathfrak{x})^{2\varpi^{\dagger}}\Bigg\{(B_{\varpi^{\dagger}}(p+1,2))^{\frac{1}{p}}\left(\frac{\Gamma(\varpi^{\dagger}+1)}{\Gamma(2\varpi^{\dagger}+1)}|Y^{\varpi^{\dagger}}(w_2)|^{q}\right.$$
$$\left.+\left[\frac{\Gamma(\varpi^{\dagger}+1)}{\Gamma(2\varpi^{\dagger}+1)}-B_{\varpi^{\dagger}}(2,2)\right]|Y^{\varpi^{\dagger}}(\mathfrak{x})|^{q}-\frac{\Gamma(1+2\varpi^{\dagger})}{\Gamma(1+3\varpi^{\dagger})}|Y^{\varpi^{\dagger}}(u_2)|^{q}\right)^{\frac{1}{q}}$$
$$+\left(\frac{\Gamma(1+(p+1)\varpi^{\dagger})}{\Gamma(1+(p+2)\varpi^{\dagger})}\right)^{\frac{1}{p}}\left(\frac{\Gamma(\varpi^{\dagger}+1)}{\Gamma(2\varpi^{\dagger}+1)}|Y^{\varpi^{\dagger}}(w_2)|^{q}\right.$$
$$\left.+\left[\frac{\Gamma(\varpi^{\dagger}+1)}{\Gamma(2\varpi^{\dagger}+1)}-B_{\varpi^{\dagger}}(2,2)\right]|Y^{\varpi^{\dagger}}(\mathfrak{x})|^{q}-\frac{\Gamma(1+2\varpi^{\dagger})}{\Gamma(1+3\varpi^{\dagger})}|Y^{\varpi^{\dagger}}(u_2)|^{q}\right)^{\frac{1}{q}}\Bigg\}.$$

Corollary 9. *If we set $u_1=w_1, u_2=w_2$ and $\mathfrak{x}=\frac{w_1+w_2}{2}$ in (8), then we obtain*

$$\left|\frac{(w_2-w_1)^{\varpi^{\dagger}}Y\left(\frac{w_1+w_2}{2}\right)}{\Gamma(1+\varpi^{\dagger})}-\frac{1}{\Gamma(1+\varpi^{\dagger})}\int_{w_1}^{b}f(u)(du)^{\varpi^{\dagger}}\right|$$
$$\leq\frac{1}{\Gamma(1+\varpi^{\dagger})}\left(\frac{w_2-w_1}{2}\right)^{2\varpi^{\dagger}}(B_{\varpi^{\dagger}}(p+1,2))^{\frac{1}{p}}\Bigg\{\left(\left(\frac{\Gamma(\varpi^{\dagger}+1)}{\Gamma(2\varpi^{\dagger}+1)}-\frac{\Gamma(1+(s+1)\varpi^{\dagger})}{\Gamma(1+(s+2)\varpi^{\dagger})}\right)|Y^{\varpi^{\dagger}}(w_1)|^{q}\right.$$

$$+\left[\frac{\Gamma(\varpi^{\dagger}+1)}{\Gamma(2\varpi^{\dagger}+1)}-B_{\varpi^{\dagger}}(s+1,2)\right]\left|Y^{\varpi^{\dagger}}\left(\frac{w_1+w_2}{2}\right)\right|^{q}\Bigg)^{\frac{1}{q}}$$
$$+\Bigg(\left(\frac{\Gamma(\varpi^{\dagger}+1)}{\Gamma(2\varpi^{\dagger}+1)}-\frac{\Gamma(1+(s+1)\varpi^{\dagger})}{\Gamma(1+(s+2)\varpi^{\dagger})}\right)|Y^{\varpi^{\dagger}}(w_2)|^{q}$$
$$+\left[\frac{\Gamma(\varpi^{\dagger}+1)}{\Gamma(2\varpi^{\dagger}+1)}-B_{\varpi^{\dagger}}(s+1,2)\right]\left|Y^{\varpi^{\dagger}}\left(\frac{w_1+w_2}{2}\right)\right|^{q}\Bigg)^{\frac{1}{q}}\Bigg\}$$
$$+\frac{1}{\Gamma(1+\varpi^{\dagger})}\left(\frac{w_2-w_1}{2}\right)^{2\varpi^{\dagger}}\left(\frac{\Gamma(1+(p+1)\varpi^{\dagger})}{\Gamma(1+(p+2)\varpi^{\dagger})}\right)^{\frac{1}{p}}$$
$$\times\Bigg\{\Bigg(\left(\frac{\Gamma(\varpi^{\dagger}+1)}{\Gamma(2\varpi^{\dagger}+1)}-\frac{\Gamma(1+(s+1)\varpi^{\dagger})}{\Gamma(1+(s+2)\varpi^{\dagger})}\right)|Y^{\varpi^{\dagger}}(w_1)|^{q}$$
$$+\left[\frac{\Gamma(\varpi^{\dagger}+1)}{\Gamma(2\varpi^{\dagger}+1)}-B_{\varpi^{\dagger}}(2,s+1)\right]\left|Y^{\varpi^{\dagger}}\left(\frac{w_1+w_2}{2}\right)\right|^{q}\Bigg)^{\frac{1}{q}}$$
$$+\Bigg(\left(\frac{\Gamma(\varpi^{\dagger}+1)}{\Gamma(2\varpi^{\dagger}+1)}-\frac{\Gamma(1+(s+1)\varpi^{\dagger})}{\Gamma(1+(s+2)\varpi^{\dagger})}\right)|Y^{\varpi^{\dagger}}(w_2)|^{q}$$
$$+\left[\frac{\Gamma(\varpi^{\dagger}+1)}{\Gamma(2\varpi^{\dagger}+1)}-B_{\varpi^{\dagger}}(2,s+1)\right]\left|Y^{\varpi^{\dagger}}\left(\frac{w_1+w_2}{2}\right)\right|^{q}\Bigg)^{\frac{1}{q}}\Bigg\}.$$

Theorem 9. *Assume that all the assumptions of Lemma 2 are satisfied, if $|Y^{\varpi^{\dagger}}|\leq M^{\varpi^{\dagger}}$, where $M^{\varpi^{\dagger}}\in\mathbb{R}^{\varpi^{\dagger}},\varpi^{\dagger}\in(0,1]$, then*

$$\left|(\mathfrak{x}-\mathfrak{u}_1)^{\varpi^{\dagger}}Y(w_1+\mathfrak{x}-\mathfrak{u}_1)+(\mathfrak{u}_2-\mathfrak{x})^{\varpi^{\dagger}}Y(w_2+\mathfrak{x}-\mathfrak{u}_2)-\Gamma(1+\varpi^{\dagger})\left[{}_{a}I^{\varpi^{\dagger}}_{w_1+\mathfrak{x}-\mathfrak{u}_1}Y(\mathfrak{u})+{}_{(w_2+\mathfrak{x}-\mathfrak{u}_2)}I^{\varpi^{\dagger}}_{w_2}Y(\mathfrak{u})\right]\right|$$
$$\leq\frac{M^{\varpi^{\dagger}}\Gamma(1+\varpi^{\dagger})}{\Gamma(1+2\varpi^{\dagger})}[(\mathfrak{x}-\mathfrak{u}_1)^{2\varpi^{\dagger}}+(\mathfrak{u}_2-\mathfrak{x})^{2\varpi^{\dagger}}] \quad (11)$$

Proof. By taking the absolute value in Lemma 2 and using $|Y^{\varpi^{\dagger}}|\leq M^{\varpi^{\dagger}},0<\varpi^{\dagger}\leq 1$, we have

$$\left|(\mathfrak{x}-\mathfrak{u}_1)^{\varpi^{\dagger}}Y(w_1+\mathfrak{x}-\mathfrak{u}_1)+(\mathfrak{u}_2-\mathfrak{x})^{\varpi^{\dagger}}Y(w_2+\mathfrak{x}-\mathfrak{u}_2)-\Gamma(1+\varpi^{\dagger})\left[{}_{a}I^{\varpi^{\dagger}}_{w_1+\mathfrak{x}-\mathfrak{u}_1}Y(\mathfrak{u})+{}_{(w_2+\mathfrak{x}-\mathfrak{u}_2)}I^{\varpi^{\dagger}}_{w_2}Y(\mathfrak{u})\right]\right|$$
$$\leq\frac{(\mathfrak{x}-\mathfrak{u}_1)^{2\varpi^{\dagger}}}{\Gamma(\varpi^{\dagger}+1)}\int_0^1\left|\nu^{\varpi^{\dagger}}Y^{\varpi^{\dagger}}(w_1+\mathfrak{x}-(\nu\mathfrak{u}_1+(1-\nu)\mathfrak{x}))\right|(dt)^{\varpi^{\dagger}}$$
$$+\frac{(\mathfrak{u}_2-\mathfrak{x})^{2\varpi^{\dagger}}}{\Gamma(\varpi^{\dagger}+1)}\int_0^1\left|\nu^{\varpi^{\dagger}}Y^{\varpi^{\dagger}}(w_2+\mathfrak{x}-(\nu\mathfrak{u}_2+(1-\nu)\mathfrak{x}))\right|(dt)^{\varpi^{\dagger}}$$
$$\leq\frac{M^{\varpi^{\dagger}}(\mathfrak{x}-\mathfrak{u}_1)^{2\varpi^{\dagger}}}{\Gamma(\varpi^{\dagger}+1)}\int_0^1\nu^{\varpi^{\dagger}}(dt)^{\varpi^{\dagger}}+\frac{M^{\varpi^{\dagger}}(\mathfrak{u}_2-\mathfrak{x})^{2\varpi^{\dagger}}}{\Gamma(\varpi^{\dagger}+1)}\int_0^1\nu^{\varpi^{\dagger}}(dt)^{\varpi^{\dagger}}$$
$$\leq\frac{M^{\varpi^{\dagger}}\Gamma(1+\varpi^{\dagger})}{\Gamma(1+2\varpi^{\dagger})}[(\mathfrak{x}-\mathfrak{u}_1)^{2\varpi^{\dagger}}+(\mathfrak{u}_2-\mathfrak{x})^{2\varpi^{\dagger}}],$$

which gives the inequality (11). □

Corollary 10. *If we set $\mathfrak{u}_1=w_1,\mathfrak{u}_2=w_2$ and $\mathfrak{x}=\frac{w_1+w_2}{2}$ in (11), then we obtain*

$$\left|\frac{(w_2-w_1)^{\varpi^{\dagger}}Y\left(\frac{w_1+w_2}{2}\right)}{\Gamma(1+\varpi^{\dagger})}-\frac{1}{\Gamma(1+\varpi^{\dagger})}\int_{w_1}^{b}f(\mathfrak{u})(d\mathfrak{u})^{\varpi^{\dagger}}\right|\leq\frac{2^{\varpi^{\dagger}}M^{\varpi^{\dagger}}}{\Gamma(1+2\varpi^{\dagger})}\left(\frac{w_2-w_1}{2}\right)^{2\varpi^{\dagger}}.$$

Theorem 10. *Under the assumption of Lemma 2, if $|\Upsilon^{\varpi^\dagger}|$ satisfies the generalized s-convexity defined on the interval $[w_1, w_2]$, and $\Upsilon^{\varpi^\dagger}$ is bounded, i.e., $||\Upsilon^{\varpi^\dagger}||_\infty = sup_{\nu \in [w_1,w_2]}|\Upsilon^{\varpi^\dagger}| < \infty$, then*

$$\begin{aligned}
&\left|(\mathfrak{x} - \mathfrak{u}_1)^{\varpi^\dagger}\Upsilon(w_1 + \mathfrak{x} - \mathfrak{u}_1) + (\mathfrak{u}_2 - \mathfrak{x})^{\varpi^\dagger}\Upsilon(w_2 + \mathfrak{x} - \mathfrak{u}_2) - \Gamma(1+\varpi^\dagger)\left[{}_aI^{\varpi^\dagger}_{w_1+\mathfrak{x}-\mathfrak{u}_1}\Upsilon(\mathfrak{u}) + {}_{(w_2+\mathfrak{x}-\mathfrak{u}_2)}I^{\varpi^\dagger}_{w_2}\Upsilon(\mathfrak{u})\right]\right| \\
&\leq \left[\frac{2^{\varpi^\dagger}\Gamma(\varpi^\dagger+1)}{\Gamma(2\varpi^\dagger+1)} - \frac{\Gamma(1+(s+1)\varpi^\dagger)}{\Gamma(1+(s+2)\varpi^\dagger)} - B_{\varpi^\dagger}(2, s+1)\right]||\Upsilon^{\varpi^\dagger}||_\infty[(\mathfrak{x}-\mathfrak{u}_1)^{2\varpi^\dagger} + (\mathfrak{u}_2-\mathfrak{x})^{2\varpi^\dagger}],
\end{aligned}$$

Proof. Considering the integral identity derived in Lemma 2 and taking advantage of the property of the modulus, we have

$$\begin{aligned}
&\left|(\mathfrak{x} - \mathfrak{u}_1)^{\varpi^\dagger}\Upsilon(w_1 + \mathfrak{x} - \mathfrak{u}_1) + (\mathfrak{u}_2 - \mathfrak{x})^{\varpi^\dagger}\Upsilon(w_2 + \mathfrak{x} - \mathfrak{u}_2) - \Gamma(1+\varpi^\dagger)\left[{}_aI^{\varpi^\dagger}_{w_1+\mathfrak{x}-\mathfrak{u}_1}\Upsilon(\mathfrak{u}) + {}_{(w_2+\mathfrak{x}-\mathfrak{u}_2)}I^{\varpi^\dagger}_{w_2}\Upsilon(\mathfrak{u})\right]\right| \\
&\leq \frac{(\mathfrak{x}-\mathfrak{u}_1)^{2\varpi^\dagger}}{\Gamma(\varpi^\dagger+1)}\int_0^1 \left|\nu^{\varpi^\dagger}\Upsilon^{\varpi^\dagger}(w_1 + \mathfrak{x} - (\nu\mathfrak{u}_1 + (1-\nu)\mathfrak{x}))\right|(dt)^{\varpi^\dagger} \\
&+ \frac{(\mathfrak{u}_2-\mathfrak{x})^{2\varpi^\dagger}}{\Gamma(\varpi^\dagger+1)}\int_0^1 \left|\nu^{\varpi^\dagger}\Upsilon^{\varpi^\dagger}(w_2 + \mathfrak{x} - (\nu\mathfrak{u}_2 + (1-\nu)\mathfrak{x}))\right|(dt)^{\varpi^\dagger}.
\end{aligned}$$

We employ the generalized s-convexity of the mapping $|\Upsilon^{\varpi^\dagger}|$ defined on $[w_1, w_2]$, then

$$\begin{aligned}
&\left|(\mathfrak{x} - \mathfrak{u}_1)^{\varpi^\dagger}\Upsilon(w_1 + \mathfrak{x} - \mathfrak{u}_1) + (\mathfrak{u}_2 - \mathfrak{x})^{\varpi^\dagger}\Upsilon(w_2 + \mathfrak{x} - \mathfrak{u}_2) - \Gamma(1+\varpi^\dagger)\left[{}_aI^{\varpi^\dagger}_{w_1+\mathfrak{x}-\mathfrak{u}_1}\Upsilon(\mathfrak{u}) + {}_{(w_2+\mathfrak{x}-\mathfrak{u}_2)}I^{\varpi^\dagger}_{w_2}\Upsilon(\mathfrak{u})\right]\right| \\
&\leq \frac{(\mathfrak{x}-\mathfrak{u}_1)^{2\varpi^\dagger}}{\Gamma(\varpi^\dagger+1)}\int_0^1 \nu^{\varpi^\dagger}\left[|\Upsilon^{\varpi^\dagger}(w_1)| + |\Upsilon^{\varpi^\dagger}(\mathfrak{x})| - \nu^{\varpi^\dagger s}|\Upsilon^{\varpi^\dagger}(\mathfrak{u}_1)| - (1-\nu)^{\varpi^\dagger s}|\Upsilon^{\varpi^\dagger}(\mathfrak{x})|\right](dt)^{\varpi^\dagger} \\
&+ \frac{(\mathfrak{u}_2-\mathfrak{x})^{2\varpi^\dagger}}{\Gamma(\varpi^\dagger+1)}\int_0^1 \nu^{\varpi^\dagger}\left[|\Upsilon^{\varpi^\dagger}(w_2)| + |\Upsilon^{\varpi^\dagger}(\mathfrak{x})| - \nu^{\varpi^\dagger s}|\Upsilon^{\varpi^\dagger}(\mathfrak{u}_2)| - (1-\nu)^{\varpi^\dagger s}|\Upsilon^{\varpi^\dagger}(\mathfrak{x})|\right](dt)^{\varpi^\dagger} \\
&\leq \left[\frac{2\Gamma(\varpi^\dagger+1)}{\Gamma(2\varpi^\dagger+1)} - \frac{\Gamma(1+(s+1)\varpi^\dagger)}{\Gamma(1+(s+2)\varpi^\dagger)} - B_{\varpi^\dagger}(2, s+1)\right]||\Upsilon^{\varpi^\dagger}||_\infty[(\mathfrak{x}-\mathfrak{u}_1)^{2\varpi^\dagger} + (\mathfrak{u}_2-\mathfrak{x})^{2\varpi^\dagger}],
\end{aligned}$$

which is the desired the result asserted in Theorem 10. □

Corollary 11. *If we take $s = 1$ in Theorem 10, then*

$$\begin{aligned}
&\left|(\mathfrak{x} - \mathfrak{u}_1)^{\varpi^\dagger}\Upsilon(w_1 + \mathfrak{x} - \mathfrak{u}_1) + (\mathfrak{u}_2 - \mathfrak{x})^{\varpi^\dagger}\Upsilon(w_2 + \mathfrak{x} - \mathfrak{u}_2) - \Gamma(1+\varpi^\dagger)\left[{}_aI^{\varpi^\dagger}_{w_1+\mathfrak{x}-\mathfrak{u}_1}\Upsilon(\mathfrak{u}) + {}_{(w_2+\mathfrak{x}-\mathfrak{u}_2)}I^{\varpi^\dagger}_{w_2}\Upsilon(\mathfrak{u})\right]\right| \\
&\leq \left[\frac{2\Gamma(\varpi^\dagger+1)}{\Gamma(2\varpi^\dagger+1)} - \frac{\Gamma(1+2\varpi^\dagger)}{\Gamma(1+3\varpi^\dagger)} - B_{\varpi^\dagger}(2, 2)\right]||\Upsilon^{\varpi^\dagger}||_\infty[(\mathfrak{x}-\mathfrak{u}_1)^{2\varpi^\dagger} + (\mathfrak{u}_2-\mathfrak{x})^{2\varpi^\dagger}].
\end{aligned}$$

4. Applications

In this section, we are going to present some applications of our main findings. First, we develop some relation between generalized means by considering some results obtained in the previous section. Further, we examine more applications to numerical integration.

4.1. Generalized Special Means

Here, we recapture the renowned generalized means between two numbers $w_1{}^{\varpi^\dagger}, w_2{}^{\varpi^\dagger} \in \mathbb{R}^{\varpi^\dagger}$.

1. The generalized arithmetic mean:

$$A_{\varpi^\dagger}(w_1, w_2) = \frac{w_1{}^{\varpi^\dagger} + w_2{}^{\varpi^\dagger}}{2^{\varpi^\dagger}} = \left(\frac{w_1 + w_2}{2}\right)^{\varpi^\dagger},$$

2. The generalized Weighted arithmetic mean:

$$_{w}A_{\varpi^{\dagger}}(w_1, w_2; m_1, m_2) = \frac{m_1^{\varpi^{\dagger}} {w_1}^{\varpi^{\dagger}} + m_2^{\varpi^{\dagger}} w_2^{\varpi^{\dagger}}}{(w_1 + w_2)^{\varpi^{\dagger}}}.$$

3. The generalized log-p-mean:

$$L_{\varpi^{\dagger},p}(w_1, w_2) = \left[\frac{\Gamma(1+p\varpi^{\dagger})}{\Gamma(1+(1+p)\varpi^{\dagger})} \frac{{w_2}^{(p+1)\varpi^{\dagger}} - {w_1}^{(p+1)\varpi^{\dagger}}}{(p+1)(w_2 - w_1)^{\varpi^{\dagger}}}\right]^{\frac{1}{p}}; \ p \in \mathbb{R} \setminus \{-1, 0\}.$$

Proposition 1. *All the assumptions of Theorem 5 are satisfied, then the following relation holds:*

$$\begin{aligned}
&\Big|(\mathfrak{u}_2 - \mathfrak{u}_1)^{\varpi^{\dagger}} \ _{\omega}A_{\varpi^{\dagger}}((\mathfrak{x} - \mathfrak{u}_1), (\mathfrak{u}_2 - \mathfrak{x}), (w_1 + \mathfrak{x} - \mathfrak{u}_1)^s, (w_2 + \mathfrak{x} - \mathfrak{u}_2)^s) \\
&\quad -\Gamma(1+\varpi^{\dagger})\Big[(\mathfrak{x} - \mathfrak{u}_1)L^s_{s,\varpi^{\dagger}}(w_1 + \mathfrak{x} - \mathfrak{u}_1, w_1) + (\mathfrak{u}_2 - \mathfrak{x})L^s_{s,\varpi^{\dagger}}(w_2, w_2 + \mathfrak{x} - \mathfrak{u}_2)\Big]\Big| \\
&\leq (\mathfrak{x} - \mathfrak{u}_1)^{2\varpi^{\dagger}}\Bigg[\frac{2^{\varpi^{\dagger}}\Gamma(1+\varpi^{\dagger})\Gamma(1+s\varpi^{\dagger})}{\Gamma(1+2\varpi^{\dagger})\Gamma(1+(s-1)\varpi^{\dagger})} A_{\varpi^{\dagger}}({w_1}^{s-1}, \mathfrak{x}^{s-1}) \\
&\quad - \frac{\Gamma(1+s\varpi^{\dagger})}{\Gamma(1+(s-1)\varpi^{\dagger})}\Bigg[B_{\varpi^{\dagger}}(2, s+1)\mathfrak{x}^{(s-1)\varpi^{\dagger}} + \frac{\Gamma(1+(s+1)\varpi^{\dagger})}{\Gamma(1+(s+2)\varpi^{\dagger})}\mathfrak{u}_1^{(s-1)\varpi^{\dagger}}\Bigg]\Bigg] \\
&\quad + (\mathfrak{u}_2 - \mathfrak{x})^{2\varpi^{\dagger}}\Bigg[\frac{2^{\varpi^{\dagger}}\Gamma(1+\varpi^{\dagger})\Gamma(1+s\varpi^{\dagger})}{\Gamma(1+2\varpi^{\dagger})\Gamma(1+(s-1)\varpi^{\dagger})} w_{1\varpi^{\dagger}}({w_2}^{s-1}, \mathfrak{x}^{s-1}) \\
&\quad - \frac{\Gamma(1+s\varpi^{\dagger})}{\Gamma(1+(s-1)\varpi^{\dagger})}\Bigg[B_{\varpi^{\dagger}}(2, s+1)\mathfrak{x}^{(s-1)\varpi^{\dagger}} + \frac{\Gamma(1+(s+1)\varpi^{\dagger})}{\Gamma(1+(s+2)\varpi^{\dagger})}\mathfrak{u}_2^{(s-1)\varpi^{\dagger}}\Bigg]\Bigg].
\end{aligned}$$

Proof. The assertion follows directly by substituting $\Upsilon(\mathfrak{u}) = \mathfrak{u}^{\varpi^{\dagger}s}$ with $0 < \varpi^{\dagger}, s \leq 1$ in inequality (8). □

Proposition 2. *All the assumptions of Theorem 6 are satisfied, then the following relation holds:*

$$\begin{aligned}
&\Big|(\mathfrak{u}_2 - \mathfrak{u}_1)^{\varpi^{\dagger}} \ _{\omega}A_{\varpi^{\dagger}}((\mathfrak{x} - \mathfrak{u}_1), (\mathfrak{u}_2 - \mathfrak{x}), (w_1 + \mathfrak{x} - \mathfrak{u}_1)^s, (w_2 + \mathfrak{x} - \mathfrak{u}_2)^s) \\
&\quad -\Gamma(1+\varpi^{\dagger})\Big[(\mathfrak{x} - \mathfrak{u}_1)L^s_{s,\varpi^{\dagger}}(w_1 + \mathfrak{x} - \mathfrak{u}_1, w_1) + (\mathfrak{u}_2 - \mathfrak{x})L^s_{s,\varpi^{\dagger}}(w_2, w_2 + \mathfrak{x} - \mathfrak{u}_2)\Big]\Big| \\
&\leq \left(\frac{\Gamma(1+\varpi^{\dagger}p)}{\Gamma(1+(p+1)\varpi^{\dagger})}\right)^{\frac{1}{p}}\Bigg[(\mathfrak{x} - \mathfrak{u}_1)^{2\varpi^{\dagger}}\Bigg(\frac{1}{\Gamma(\varpi^{\dagger}+1)}\left(\frac{\Gamma(1+s\varpi^{\dagger})}{\Gamma(1+(s-1)\varpi^{\dagger})}\right)^q A_{\varpi^{\dagger}}({w_1}^{(s-1)q}, \mathfrak{x}^{(s-1)q}) \\
&\quad - \frac{\Gamma(1+\varpi^{\dagger}s)}{\Gamma(1+(s+1)\varpi^{\dagger})}\left(\frac{\Gamma(1+s\varpi^{\dagger})}{\Gamma(1+(s-1)\varpi^{\dagger})}\right)^q A_{\varpi^{\dagger}}(\mathfrak{x}^{(s-1)q}, \mathfrak{u}_1^{(s-1)q})\Bigg)^{\frac{1}{q}} \\
&\quad + (\mathfrak{u}_2 - \mathfrak{x})^{2\varpi^{\dagger}}\Bigg(\frac{1}{\Gamma(\varpi^{\dagger}+1)}\left(\frac{\Gamma(1+s\varpi^{\dagger})}{\Gamma(1+(s-1)\varpi^{\dagger})}\right)^q A_{\varpi^{\dagger}}({w_2}^{(s-1)q}, \mathfrak{x}^{(s-1)q}) \\
&\quad - \frac{\Gamma(1+\varpi^{\dagger}s)}{\Gamma(1+(s+1)\varpi^{\dagger})}\left(\frac{\Gamma(1+s\varpi^{\dagger})}{\Gamma(1+(s-1)\varpi^{\dagger})}\right)^q A_{\varpi^{\dagger}}(\mathfrak{x}^{(s-1)q}, \mathfrak{u}_2^{(s-1)q})\Bigg)^{\frac{1}{q}}\Bigg].
\end{aligned}$$

Proof. The assertion follows directly by substituting $\Upsilon(\mathfrak{u}) = \mathfrak{u}^{\varpi^{\dagger}s}$ with $0 < \varpi^{\dagger}$, $s \leq 1$ in inequality (9). □

Proposition 3. *All the assumptions of Theorem 9 are satisfied, then the following relation holds:*

$$\Big|(\mathfrak{u}_2 - \mathfrak{u}_1)^{\varpi^{\dagger}} \ _{\omega}A_{\varpi^{\dagger}}((\mathfrak{x} - \mathfrak{u}_1), (\mathfrak{u}_2 - \mathfrak{x}), (w_1 + \mathfrak{x} - \mathfrak{u}_1)^s, (w_2 + \mathfrak{x} - \mathfrak{u}_2)^s)$$

$$-\Gamma(1+\varpi^{\dagger})\Big[(\mathfrak{x}-\mathfrak{u}_1)L^{s}_{s,\varpi^{\dagger}}(w_1+\mathfrak{x}-\mathfrak{u}_1,w_1)+(\mathfrak{u}_2-\mathfrak{x})L^{s}_{s,\varpi^{\dagger}}(w_2,w_2+\mathfrak{x}-\mathfrak{u}_2)\Big]\Big|$$
$$\leq M^{\varpi^{\dagger}}\left[\frac{2^{\varpi^{\dagger}}\Gamma(1+\varpi^{\dagger})}{\Gamma(1+2\varpi^{\dagger})}-\frac{\Gamma(1+(s+1)\varpi^{\dagger})}{\Gamma(1+(s+2)\varpi^{\dagger})}-B_{\varpi^{\dagger}}(2,s+1)\right]\left[(\mathfrak{x}-\mathfrak{u}_1)^{2\varpi^{\dagger}}+(\mathfrak{u}_2-\mathfrak{x})^{2\varpi^{\dagger}}\right].$$

Proof. The assertion follows directly by substituting $\Upsilon(\mathfrak{u})=\mathfrak{u}^{\varpi^{\dagger}s}$ with $0<\varpi^{\dagger},s\leq 1$ in Theorem 9. □

4.2. The Quadrature Formula

Here, we present some applications to generalized midpoint rules. If we divide the interval $[w_1,w_2]$ into J subintervals $\mathfrak{x}_i,\mathfrak{x}_{i+1}$ with $i=0,1,\ldots,J-1$, then one finds a partition $\mathcal{P}: w_1=\mathfrak{x}_0<\mathfrak{x}_1<\cdots<\mathfrak{x}_{j-1}<\mathfrak{x}_j=w_2$. Furthermore, we take into account the undermentioned quadrature formula

$$\begin{aligned}{}_{z}I^{\varpi^{\dagger}}_{w_2}\Upsilon(y)&=\frac{1}{\Gamma(1+\varpi^{\dagger})}\int_{w_1}^{w_2}\Upsilon(y)(d(y))^{\varpi^{\dagger}}\\&=T_s(\Upsilon,\gamma)+E_s(\Upsilon,\gamma),\end{aligned}$$

where

$$T_s(\Upsilon,\gamma)=(w_2-w_1)^{\varpi^{\dagger}}\Upsilon\left(\frac{w_1+w_2}{2}\right).$$

Proposition 4. *If all the assumptions of Theorem 8 are held, then*

$$\begin{aligned}|E_s(\gamma,\gamma)|\leqslant&\sum_{i=1}^{n}\frac{1}{\Gamma(1+\varpi^{\dagger})}\left(\frac{\mathfrak{x}_{i+1}-\mathfrak{x}_i}{2}\right)^{2\varpi^{\dagger}}(B_{\varpi^{\dagger}}(p+1,2))^{\frac{1}{p}}\\
&\times\left\{\left(\left(\frac{\Gamma(\varpi^{\dagger}+1)}{\Gamma(2\varpi^{\dagger}+1)}-\frac{\Gamma(1+(s+1)\varpi^{\dagger})}{\Gamma(1+(s+2)\varpi^{\dagger})}\right)\left|\gamma^{\varpi^{\dagger}}(\mathfrak{x}_i)\right|^{q}+\left[\frac{\Gamma(\varpi^{\dagger}+1)}{\Gamma(2\varpi^{\dagger}+1)}-B_{\varpi^{\dagger}}(s+1,2)\right]\left|\gamma^{\dagger}\left(\frac{\mathfrak{x}_i+\mathfrak{x}_{i+1}}{2}\right)\right|^{q}\right)^{\frac{1}{q}}\right.\\
&\left.+\left(\left(\frac{\Gamma(\varpi^{\dagger}+1)}{\Gamma(2\varpi^{\dagger}+1)}-\frac{\Gamma(1+(s+1)\varpi^{\dagger})}{\Gamma(1+(s+2)\varpi^{\dagger})}\right)\left|\gamma^{\varpi^{\dagger}}(\mathfrak{x}_{i+1})\right|^{q}+\left[\frac{\Gamma(\varpi^{\dagger}+1)}{\Gamma(2\varpi^{\dagger}+1)}-B_{\omega^{\dagger}}(s+1,2)\right]\left|\sigma^{\dagger}\left(\frac{\mathfrak{x}_i+\mathfrak{x}_{i+1}}{2}\right)\right|^{q}\right)^{\frac{1}{q}}\right\}\\
&+\sum_{i=1}^{n}\frac{1}{\Gamma(1+\varpi^{\dagger})}\left(\frac{\mathfrak{x}_{i+1}-\mathfrak{x}_i}{2}\right)^{2\varpi^{\dagger}}\left(\frac{\Gamma(1+(p+1)\varpi^{\dagger})}{\Gamma(1+(p+2)\varpi^{\dagger})}\right)^{\frac{1}{p}}\\
&\times\left\{\left(\left(\frac{\Gamma(\varpi^{\dagger}+1)}{\Gamma(2\varpi^{\dagger}+1)}-\frac{\Gamma(1+(s+1)\varpi^{\dagger})}{\Gamma(1+(s+2)\varpi^{\dagger})}\right)\left|\gamma^{\omega^{\dagger}}(\mathfrak{x}_i)\right|^{q}+\left[\frac{\Gamma(\varpi^{\dagger}+1)}{\Gamma(2\varpi^{\dagger}+1)}-B_{\omega^{\dagger}}(2,s+1)\right]\left|\gamma^{\dagger}\left(\frac{\mathfrak{x}_i+\mathfrak{x}_{i+1}}{2}\right)\right|^{q}\right)^{\frac{1}{q}}\right.\\
&\left.+\left(\left(\frac{\Gamma(\omega^{\dagger}+1)}{\Gamma(2\varpi^{\dagger}+1)}-\frac{\Gamma(1+(s+1)\varpi^{\dagger})}{\Gamma(1+(s+2)\varpi^{\dagger})}\right)\left|\gamma^{\omega^{\dagger}}(\tilde{r}_{i+1})\right|^{q}+\left[\frac{\Gamma(\omega^{\dagger}+1)}{\Gamma(2\omega^{\dagger}+1)}-B_{\omega^{\dagger}}(2,s+1)\right]\left|\gamma^{\dagger}\left(\frac{\tilde{p}_i+\mathfrak{p}_{i+1}}{2}\right)\right|^{q}\right)^{\frac{1}{q}}\right\}.\end{aligned}$$

Proof. The assertion follows directly by taking the sum from $n=0$ to $n-1$ over subinterval $[\mathfrak{x}_i,\mathfrak{x}_{i+1}]$ in Theorem 8. □

Proposition 5. *If all the assumptions of Theorem 10 are held, then*

$$E_s(\Upsilon,\gamma)|\leq\frac{2^{\varpi^{\dagger}}||\Upsilon^{\varpi^{\dagger}}||_{\infty}}{\Gamma(1+\varpi^{\dagger})}\left(\frac{\mathfrak{x}_{i+1}-\mathfrak{x}_i}{2}\right)^{2\varpi^{\dagger}}\left[\frac{2\Gamma(\varpi^{\dagger}+1)}{\Gamma(2\varpi^{\dagger}+1)}-\frac{\Gamma(1+(s+1)\varpi^{\dagger})}{\Gamma(1+(s+2)\varpi^{\dagger})}-B_{\varpi^{\dagger}}(2,s+1)\right].$$

Proof. The assertion follows directly by taking the sum from $n=0$ to $n-1$ over subinterval $[\mathfrak{x}_i,\mathfrak{x}_{i+1}]$ in Theorem 10. □

5. Examples

The following section is organized to increase the impact and visibility of main outcomes by establishing some numerical and graphical simulations.

Example 1. *If all the assumptions of Theorem 5 are satisfied, and we one consider the mapping* $\Upsilon(\mathfrak{u}) = \frac{\Gamma(1+2\varpi^{\dagger})}{\Gamma(1+3\varpi^{\dagger})}\left(\frac{\mathfrak{u}^3}{3}\right)^{\varpi^{\dagger}}$ *on* $\mathbb{R}^+$ *the generalized convex functions and also* $\left|\Upsilon^{\varpi^{\dagger}}(\mathfrak{u})\right| = \left(\frac{\mathfrak{u}^2}{3}\right)^{\varpi^{\dagger}}$ *is a generalized convex mapping. By specifying the values of* $w_1 = 0, \mathfrak{u}_1 = 1, \mathfrak{u}_2 = 3, w_2 = 4$, *s = 0.8, then*

$$\left|\frac{(\mathfrak{x}-1)^4}{9} + \frac{(3-\mathfrak{x})(1+\mathfrak{x})}{9} - \frac{(\mathfrak{x}-1)^4 + 4^4 - (1+\mathfrak{x})^4}{36}\right|$$
$$\leq (\mathfrak{x}-1)^2\left(\frac{13\mathfrak{x}^2}{138} - \frac{5}{42}\right) + (3-\mathfrak{x})^2\left(\frac{8}{3} + \frac{13\mathfrak{x}^2}{138} - \frac{15}{14}\right).$$

We regard $\mathfrak{x} \in [1,3]$ *as a variable to plot a graph between the left and right-hand side of inequality (8).*

Figure 1 depicts the comparative analysis between the left and right sides of Theorem 5. Here red and green colors reflect the left and right-hand sides respectively.

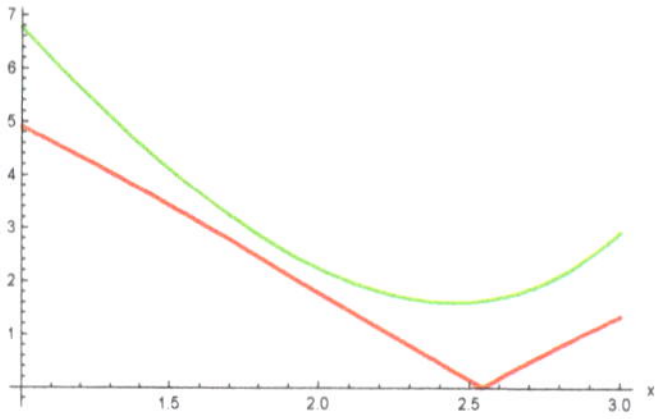

Figure 1. Comparative analysis between both sides of Theorem 5.

Example 2. *If all the assumptions of Theorem 6 are satisfied, and we one consider the mapping* $\Upsilon(\mathfrak{u}) = \frac{\Gamma(1+2\varpi^{\dagger})}{\Gamma(1+3\varpi^{\dagger})}\left(\frac{\mathfrak{u}^3}{3}\right)^{\varpi^{\dagger}}$ *on* $\mathbb{R}^+$ *the generalized convex functions and also* $\left|\Upsilon^{\varpi^{\dagger}}(\mathfrak{u})\right| = \left(\frac{\mathfrak{u}^2}{3}\right)^{\varpi^{\dagger}}$ *is a generalized convex mapping. By specifying the values of* $w_1 = 0, \mathfrak{u}_1 = 1, \mathfrak{u}_2 = 3, w_2 = 4$, *s = 1, then*

$$\left|\frac{(\mathfrak{x}-1)^4}{9} + \frac{(3-\mathfrak{x})(1+\mathfrak{x})}{9} - \frac{(\mathfrak{x}-1)^4 + 4^4 - (1+\mathfrak{x})^4}{36}\right|$$
$$\leq (\mathfrak{x}-1)^2\left(\frac{\mathfrak{x}^4-1}{54}\right)^{\frac{1}{2}} + (3-\mathfrak{x})^2\left(\frac{256}{27} + \frac{\mathfrak{x}^4}{54} - \frac{3}{2}\right)^{\frac{1}{2}}.$$

We regard $\mathfrak{x} \in [1,3]$ *as a variable to plot a graph between the left and right-hand side of inequality 9).*

Figure 2 depicts the comparative analysis between the left and right sides of Theorem 5. Here red and green colors reflect the left and right-hand sides respectively.

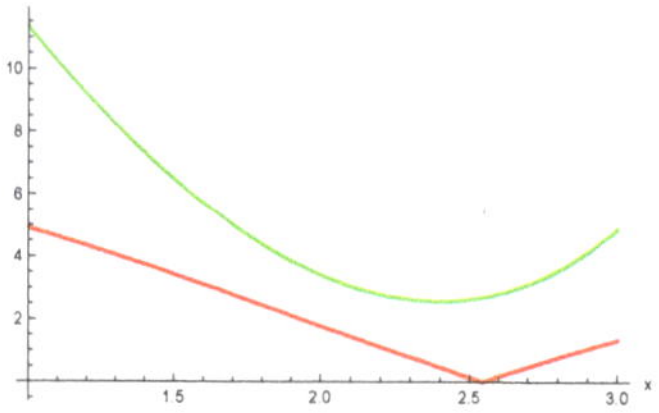

Figure 2. Comparative analysis between the left and right sides of Theorem 6.

Example 3. *If all the assumptions of Theorem 7 are satisfied, and we one consider the mapping* $Y(u) = \frac{\Gamma(1+2\varpi^{\dagger})}{\Gamma(1+3\varpi^{\dagger})}\left(\frac{u^3}{3}\right)^{\varpi^{\dagger}}$ *on* $\mathbb{R}^+$ *the generalized convex functions and also* $\left|Y^{\varpi^{\dagger}}(u)\right| = \left(\frac{u^2}{3}\right)^{\varpi^{\dagger}}$ *be a generalized convex mapping. By specifying the values of* $w_1 = 0, u_1 = 1, u_2 = 3, w_2 = 4$, *s = 1, then*

$$\left|\frac{(\mathfrak{r}-1)^4}{9} + \frac{(3-\mathfrak{r})(1+\mathfrak{r})}{9} - \frac{(\mathfrak{r}-1)^4 + 4^4 - (1+\mathfrak{r})^4}{36}\right|$$
$$\leq (\mathfrak{r}-1)^2\left(\frac{\mathfrak{r}^4-1}{54}\right)^{\frac{1}{2}} + (3-\mathfrak{r})^2\left(\frac{256}{36} + \frac{\mathfrak{r}^4}{54} - \frac{3}{2}\right)^{\frac{1}{2}}.$$

We regard $\mathfrak{r} \in [1,3]$ *as a variable to plot a graph between the left and right-hand side of inequality (10).*

Figure 3 depicts the comparative analysis between the left and right sides of Theorem 7. Here red and green colors reflect the left and right-hand sides respectively.

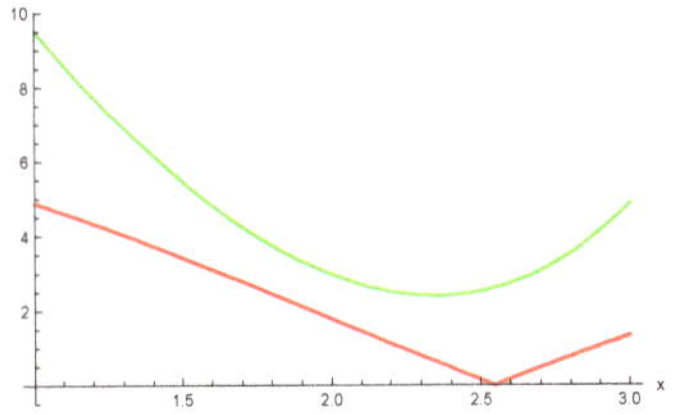

Figure 3. Comparative analysis between the left and right sides of Theorem 7.

Example 4. *If all the assumptions of Theorem 8 are satisfied, and we consider the mapping* $Y(u) = \frac{\Gamma(1+2\varpi^{\dagger})}{\Gamma(1+3\varpi^{\dagger})}\left(\frac{u^3}{3}\right)^{\varpi^{\dagger}}$ *on* $\mathbb{R}^+$ *the generalized convex functions and also* $\left|Y^{\varpi^{\dagger}}(u)\right| = \left(\frac{u^2}{3}\right)^{\varpi^{\dagger}}$ *is a generalized convex mapping. By specifying the values of* $w_1 = 0, u_1 = 1, u_2 = 3, w_2 = 4$, *s = 1, then*

$$\left|\frac{(\mathfrak{r}-1)^4}{9} + \frac{(3-\mathfrak{r})(1+\mathfrak{r})}{9} - \frac{(\mathfrak{r}-1)^4 + 4^4 - (1+\mathfrak{r})^4}{36}\right|$$
$$\leq 0.7886(\mathfrak{r}-1)^2\left(\frac{\mathfrak{r}^4-1}{27}\right)^{\frac{1}{2}} + 0.7886(3-\mathfrak{r})^2\left(\frac{126}{9} + \frac{\mathfrak{r}^4}{27} - 3\right)^{\frac{1}{2}}.$$

We regard $\mathfrak{r} \in [1,3]$ *as a variable to plot a graph between the left- and right-hand side of Theorem 8.*

Figure 4 depicts the comparative analysis between the left and right sides of Theorem 7. Here red and green colors reflect the left and right-hand sides respectively.

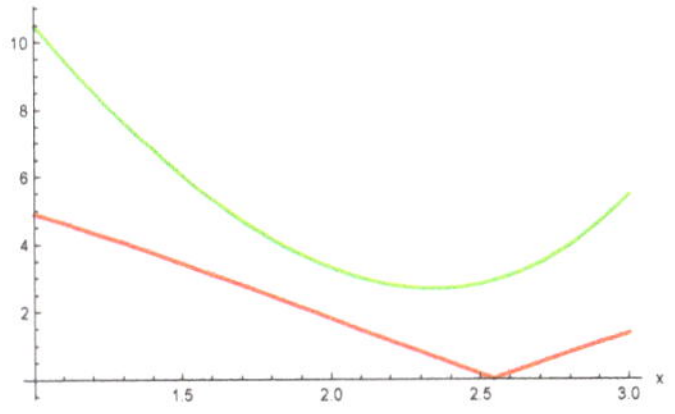

Figure 4. Comparative analysis between the left and right sides of Theorem 8.

Example 5. *If all the assumptions of Theorem 10 are satisfied, and we consider the mapping* $Y(u) = \frac{\Gamma(1+2\varpi^{\dagger})}{\Gamma(1+3\varpi^{\dagger})}\left(\frac{u^3}{3}\right)^{\varpi^{\dagger}}$ *on* $\mathbb{R}^+$ *the generalized convex functions and also* $\left|Y^{\varpi^{\dagger}}(u)\right| = \left(\frac{u^2}{3}\right)^{\varpi^{\dagger}}$

be a generalized convex mapping. By specifying the values of $w_1 = 0, \mathfrak{u}_1 = 1, \mathfrak{u}_2 = 3, w_2 = 4,$ *s = 1, then*

$$\left|\frac{(\mathfrak{x}-1)^4}{9} + \frac{(3-\mathfrak{x})(1+\mathfrak{x})}{9} - \frac{(\mathfrak{x}-1)^4 + 4^4 - (1+\mathfrak{x})^4}{36}\right|$$
$$\leq \frac{8}{3}\Big((\mathfrak{x}-1)^2 + (3-\mathfrak{x})^2\Big).$$

We regard $\mathfrak{x} \in [1,3]$ *as a variable to plot the graph between the left- and right-hand side of Theorem 10.*

Figure 5 depicts the comparative analysis between the left and right sides of Theorem 7. Here red and green colors reflect the left and right-hand sides respectively.

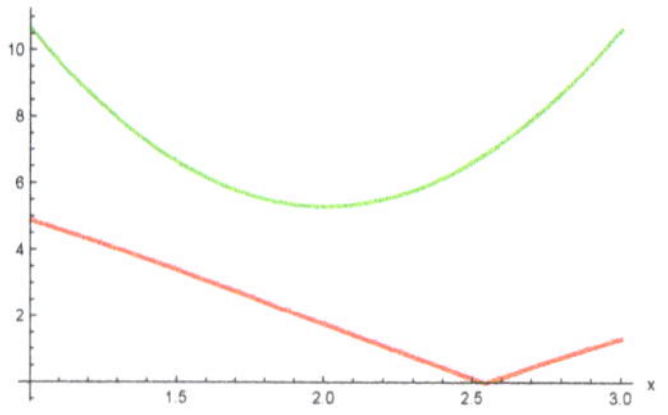

Figure 5. Comparative analysis between the left and right sides of Theorem 10.

6. Conclusions

Numerous techniques have been utilized to formulate the precise upper bounds of quadrature or cubature rules. In this regard, various well-known inequalities have been generalized and modified via different approaches like quantum calculus, fractional calculus, interval analysis, and fractal domains. The current study contains several integral inequalities of Ostrowski's type which have been explored here invoking the local differentiable functions and some classical concepts of inequalities as well. Furthermore, we have supported our primary findings with interesting applications and numerical examples with figures. In the future, we will conclude some new variants of other related inequalities through the implementation of majorization concepts and some generalized local fractional operators in association with generalized Mittag–Leffler functions. Also, this work can be explored by utilizing other classes of convexity. I hope this study will be a major development in the literature and bring curiosity to interested readers.

Author Contributions: Conceptualization, M.U.A., U.A. and H.B.; methodology, M.V.-C., M.U.A., U.A., M.Z.J. and H.B.; software, M.U.A., U.A. and M.Z.J.; validation, M.V.-C., M.U.A., U.A., M.Z.J. and H.B.; formal analysis, M.V.-C., M.U.A., U.A., M.Z.J. and H.B.; investigation, M.V.-C., M.U.A., U.A., M.Z.J. and H.B.; resources, M.V.-C., M.U.A., U.A., M.Z.J. and H.B.; writing—original draft preparation, U.A. and M.Z.J.; writing—review and editing, M.U.A.; visualization, M.V.-C., M.U.A., U.A., M.Z.J. and H.B.; supervision, M.U.A.; funding acquisition, M.V.-C. All authors have read and agreed to the published version of the manuscript.

Funding: This Study was supported via funding from Pontificia Universidad Católica del Ecuador project: RESULTADOS CUALITATIVOS DE ECUACIONES DIFERENCIALES FRACCIONARIAS LOCALES Y DESIGUALDADES INTEGRALES Cod: 070-UIO-2022.

Data Availability Statement: Not applicable.

Acknowledgments: The authors are thankful to the editor and the anonymous reviewers for their valuable comments and suggestions.

Conflicts of Interest: The authors declare no conflict of interest.

References

1. Yang, X.J. *Advanced Local Fractional Calculus and Its Applications*; World Science: New York, NY, USA, 2012.
2. Kolwankar, K.M.; Gangal, A.D. *Local fractional Calculus: A Calculus for Fractal Space-Time, in Fractals: Theory and Applications in Engineering*; Springer, London, UK, 1999; pp. 171–181.
3. Zhao, Y.; Cheng, D.F.; Yang, X.J. Approximation solutions for local fractional Schrodinger equation in the one-dimensional cantorian system. *Adv. Math.* **2013**, *2013*, 291386. [CrossRef]
4. Mandelbrot, B.B. *The Fractal Geometry of Nature*; Macmillan: New York, NY, USA, 1983.
5. Mo, H.; Sui, X. Generalized-convex functions on fractal sets. *Abstr. Appl. Anal.* **2014**, *2014*, 254737. [CrossRef]
6. Sarikaya, M.; Budak, H. Generalized Ostrowski-type inequalities for local fractional integrals. *Proc. Am. Math. Soc.* **2017**, *145*, 1527–1538. [CrossRef]
7. Mo, H.; Sui, X. Hermite-Hadamard-type inequalities for generalized s-convex functions on real linear fractal set $\mathbb{R}^{\varpi^{\dagger}}$, $(0 < \varpi^{\dagger} < 1)$. *Math. Sci.* **2017**, *11*, 241–246.
8. Zhou, Y.; Du, T. The Simpson-type integral inequalities involving twice local fractional differentiable generalized (s, p) convexity and their applications. *Fractals* **2023**, *31*, 1–32. [CrossRef]
9. Kilicman, A.; Saleh, W. Notions of generalized s-convex functions on fractal sets. *J. Inequalities Appl.* **2015**, *2015*, 312. [CrossRef]
10. Chu, Y.M.; Rashid, S.; Abdeljawad, T.; Khalid, A.; Kalsoom, H. On new generalized unified bounds via generalized exponentially harmonically s-convex functions on fractal sets. *Adv. Differ. Equ.* **2021**, *2021*, 218. [CrossRef]
11. Sanchez, R.V.; Sanabria, J.E. Strongly convexity on fractal sets and some inequalities. *Proyecciones* **2020**, *39*, 1–13. [CrossRef]
12. Luo, C.; Wang, H.; Du, T. Fejer-Hermite-Hadamard type inequalities involving generalized h-convexity on fractal sets and their applications. *Chaos Solitons Fractals* **2020**, *131*, 109547. [CrossRef]
13. Sun, W.; Liu, Q. Hadamard type local fractional integral inequalities for generalized harmonically convex functions and applications. *Math. Methods Appl. Sci.* **2020**, *43*, 5776–5787. [CrossRef]
14. Sun, W.; Xu, R. Some new Hermite-Hadamard type inequalities for generalized harmonically convex functions involving local fractional integrals. *AIMS Math.* **2021**, *6*, 10679–10695. [CrossRef]
15. Sun, W. Local fractional Ostrowski-type inequalities involving generalized h-convex functions and some applications for generalized moments. *Fractals* **2021**, *29*, 2150006. [CrossRef]
16. Razzaq, A.; Rasheed, T.; Shaokat, S. Generalized Hermite-Hadamard type inequalities for generalized F-convex function via local fractional integrals. *Chaos Solitons Fractals* **2023**, *168*, 113172. [CrossRef]
17. Kian, M.; Moslehian, M. Refinements of the operator Jensen-Mercer inequality. *Electron. J. Linear Algebra* **2013**, *26*, 742–753. [CrossRef]
18. Adil Khan, M.; Anwar, S.; Khalid, S.; Sayed, Z.M.M.M. Inequalities of the Type Hermite-Hadamard-Jensen-Mercer for Strong Convexity. *Math. Probl. Eng.* **2021**, *2021*, 5386488. [CrossRef]
19. Adil Khan, M.; Husain, Z.; Chu, Y.M. New estimates for Csiszar divergence and zipf-mandelbrot entropy via jensen-mercer's inequality. *Complexity* **2020**, *2020*, 8928691. [CrossRef]
20. Vivas-Cortez, M.; Ali, M.A.; Kashuri, A.; Budak, H. Generalizations of fractional Hermite-Hadamard-Mercer-like inequalities for convex functions. *AIMS Math.* **2021**, *6*, 9397–9421. [CrossRef]
21. Vivas-Cortez, M.; Awan, M.U.; Javed, M.Z.; Kashuri, A.; Noor, M.A.; Noor, K.I. Some new generalized k-fractional Hermite-Hadamard-Mercer type integral inequalities and their applications. *AIMS Math.* **2022**, *7*, 3203–3220. [CrossRef]
22. Al-Sa'di, S.U.; Bibi, M.; Muddassar, M. Some Hermite-Hadamard's type local fractional integral inequalities for generalized γ-preinvex function with applications. *Math. Methods Appl. Sci.* **2023**, *46*, 2941–2954. [CrossRef]
23. Butt, S.I.; Yousaf, S.; Ahmad, H.; Nofal, T.A. Jensen-Mercer inequality and related results in the fractal sense with applications. *Fractals* **2022**, *30*, 2240008. [CrossRef]
24. Xu, P.; Butt, S.I.; Yousaf, S.; Aslam, A.; Zia, T.J. Generalized Fractal Jensen-Mercer and Hermite-Mercer type inequalities via h-convex functions involving Mittag-Leffler kernel. *Alex. Eng. J.* **2022**, *61*, 4837–4846. [CrossRef]
25. Butt, S.I.; Agarwal, P.; Yousaf, S.; Guirao, J.L. Generalized fractal Jensen and Jensen-Mercer inequalities for harmonic convex function with applications. *J. Inequalities Appl.* **2022**, *2022*, 1.
26. Kalsoom, H.; Latif, M.A.; Khan, Z.A.; Vivas-Cortez, M. Some New Hermite-Hadamard-Fejer fractional type inequalities for h-convex and harmonically h-convex interval-valued Functions. *Mathematics* **2021**, *10*, 74. [CrossRef]
27. Abdeljawad, T.; Rashid, S.; Hammouch, Z.; Işcan, İ; Chu, Y.M. Some new Simpson-type inequalities for generalized p-convex function on fractal sets with applications. *Adv. Differ. Equ.* **2020**, *2020*, 496.
28. Erden, S.; Sarikaya, M.Z. Generalized Bullen-type inequalities for local fractional integrals and their applications. *RGMIA Res. Rep. Collect* **2015**, *18*, 81.
29. Sun, W. Hermite-Hadamard type local fractional integral inequalities for generalized s-preinvex functions and their generalization. *Fractals* **2021**, *29*, 2150098.

30. Du, T.; Wang, H.; Khan, M.A.; Zhang, Y. Certain integral inequalities considering generalized m-convexity on fractal sets and their applications. *Fractals* **2019**, *27*, 1950117. [CrossRef]
31. Yu, S.; Mohammed, P.O.; Xu, L.; Du, T. An improvement of the power-mean integral inequality in the frame of fractal space and certain related midpoint-type integral inequalities. *Fractals* **2022**, *30*, 2250085. [CrossRef]

fractal and fractional

MDPI

Article

On Bounds of k-Fractional Integral Operators with Mittag-Leffler Kernels for Several Types of Exponentially Convexities

Ghulam Farid [1], Hala Safdar Khan [1], Ferdous M. O. Tawfiq [2], Jong-Suk Ro [3,4,*] and Saira Zainab [5,*]

[1] Department of Mathematics, COMSATS University Islamabad, Attock Campus, Attock 43600, Pakistan; ghlmfarid@ciit-attock.edu.pk (G.F.); khanhala0698@gmail.com (H.S.K.)
[2] Department of Mathematics, College of Science, King Saud University, P.O. Box 22452, Riyadh 11495, Saudi Arabia; ftoufic@ksu.edu.sa
[3] School of Electrical and Electronics Engineering, Chung-Ang University, Dongjak-gu, Seoul 06974, Republic of Korea
[4] Department of Intelligent Energy and Industry, Chung-Ang University, Dongjak-gu, Seoul 06974, Republic of Korea
[5] School of Electrical Engineering and Computer Science (SEECS), National University of Sciences and Technology (NUST), Sector H-12, Islamabad 44000, Pakistan
* Correspondence: jongsukro@gmail.com (J.-S.R.); saira.zainab@seecs.edu.pk (S.Z.)

Abstract: This paper aims to study the bounds of k-integral operators with the Mittag-Leffler kernel in a unified form. To achieve these bounds, the definition of exponentially $(\alpha, h-m)-p$-convexity is utilized frequently. In addition, a fractional Hadamard type inequality which shows the upper and lower bounds of k-integral operators simultaneously is presented. The results are directly linked with the results of many published articles.

Keywords: convex function; exponentially $(\alpha, h-m)-p$-convex function; Mittag-Leffler function; generalized integral operators

MSC: 26A51; 26A33; 33E12

Citation: Farid, G.; Khan, H.S.; Tawfiq, F.M.O.; Ro, J.-S.; Zainab, S. On Bounds of k-Fractional Integral Operators with Mittag-Leffler Kernels for Several Types of Exponentially Convexities. *Fractal Fract.* **2023**, 7, 617. https://doi.org/10.3390/fractalfract7080617

Academic Editors: Ivanka Stamova, Eze Nwaeze and Seth Kermausuor

Received: 14 July 2023
Revised: 3 August 2023
Accepted: 8 August 2023
Published: 11 August 2023

1. Introduction

Special functions, including trigonometric, hyperbolic, exponential, gamma, beta, and many others, have fascinating and unique characteristics. They play very important role in the fields of mathematical analysis, complex analysis, geometric function theory, physics, and statistics. The well known Mittag-Leffler function introduced in [1] represents a vital contribution to the class of special functions. It is very frequently used in applied sciences in regard to the generalization and extension of classical concepts; for further details, readers are referred to [2–5].

The Mittag-Leffler function is frequently utilized in the formation of generalizations of fractional integral operators. Fractional integral operators lead to the theory of fractional calculus, fractional analysis, fractional differential equations, and fractional dynamic systems; see [6–8]. The aim of this paper is to estimate fractional integral operators containing a specific Mittag-Leffler function via various types of exponential convexities.

The Mittag-Leffler function is a generalization of exponential, trigonometric, and hyperbolic functions, and is defined with the help of the gamma function. Likewise, the beta function can be utilized to extend the Mittag-Leffler function. In the following, we provide the definitions of the gamma function, beta function, ϖ-beta function, and pochhammer symbol.

Definition 1 ([5]). *The gamma function for* $\Phi > 0$ *is defined by:*

$$\Gamma(\Phi) = \int_0^\infty e^{-w} w^{\Phi-1} dw. \tag{1}$$

Definition 2 ([5]). *The beta function is defined by:*

$$\beta(\Psi, \Phi) = \int_0^1 w^{\Psi-1}(1-w)^{\Phi-1} dw,$$

where $\Re(\Psi), \Re(\Phi) > 0$.

Definition 3 ([9]). *The definition of the* ϖ*-beta function is defined by:*

$$\beta_\varpi(\Psi, \Phi) = \int_0^1 w^{\Psi-1}(1-w)^{\Phi-1} e^{-\frac{\varpi}{w(1-w)}} dw,$$

where $\min\{\Re(\Psi), \Re(\Phi)\} > 0$ *and* $\Re R(\varpi) > 0$.

Definition 4 ([5]). *The pochhammer symbol for* $r \in \mathbb{C}$ *is defined by:*

$$(r)_{n\lambda} = \frac{\Gamma(r + n\lambda)}{\Gamma(r)}. \tag{2}$$

By introducing additional parameters, almost all special functions can be extended and generalized. For more detailed study, we refer readers to [9–11]. By using these extended special functions, fractional integrals have been extended to k-fractional integral operators. For instance, in [11], k-analogues of Riemann–Liouville fractional integrals were defined, while in [12] k-analogues of Liouville–Caputo fractional derivatives were defined. For more detailed study on further such extensions, see [13–15]. The $k-$analogue of the gamma function [10] is defined by:

$$\Gamma_k(\Phi) = \int_0^\infty w^{\Phi-1} e^{\frac{-w^k}{k}} dw, \tag{3}$$

where $z \in \mathbb{C}$ with $\Re(\Phi) > 0$ and $k > 0$.

Fractional integral operators ($\mathcal{IO}$s) are very frequently used when generalizing integral inequalities. Almost all classical integral inequalities have been published for different integral operators. Due to the importance of $\mathcal{IO}$s, many researchers have defined the several $\mathcal{IO}$s by adopting different approaches. By applying the Mittag-Leffler function (4), Zhang et al. [15] defined the following generalized k-$\mathcal{IO}$ which is directly linked with many well-known $\mathcal{IO}$s:

Definition 5. *Let* $\mathcal{Y}$ *be a positive and integrable function and let* $\mathcal{Z}$ *be a differentiable and strictly increasing function such that* $\mathcal{Y}, \mathcal{Z} : [\mu, \nu] \to \mathbb{R}$ *with* $0 < \mu < \nu$. *Additionally, let* $\varsigma, \varphi, \rho, \Psi, r$, $\eta \in \mathbb{C}$, $\varsigma, \epsilon, \Phi \geq 0$ *with* $k > 0$ *and* $0 < \lambda \leq \epsilon + \varsigma$. *Then, for* $\delta \in [\mu, \nu]$, *we have:*

$$\left({}^{k}_{\mathcal{Z}}\mathcal{D}^{\rho,\epsilon,\lambda,r}_{\varsigma,\eta,\varphi,\Psi,\mu^+}\mathcal{Y}\right)(\varpi;\Phi) = \int_\mu^\varpi (\mathcal{Z}(\varpi) - \mathcal{Z}(\delta))^{\frac{\eta}{k}-1} E^{\rho,\epsilon,\lambda,r}_{\varsigma,\eta,\varphi,k}\left(\Psi(\mathcal{Z}(\varpi) - \mathcal{Z}(\delta))^{\frac{\varsigma}{k}};\Phi\right)\mathcal{Y}(\delta)d(\mathcal{Z}(\delta)), \tag{4}$$

$$\left({}^{k}_{\mathcal{Z}}\mathcal{D}^{\rho,\epsilon,\lambda,r}_{\varsigma,\eta,\varphi,\Psi,\nu^-}\mathcal{Y}\right)(\varpi;\Phi) = \int_\varpi^\nu (\mathcal{Z}(\delta) - \mathcal{Z}(\varpi))^{\frac{\eta}{k}-1} E^{\rho,\epsilon,\lambda,r}_{\varsigma,\eta,\varphi,k}\left(\Psi(\mathcal{Z}(\delta) - \mathcal{Z}(\varpi))^{\frac{\varsigma}{k}};\Phi\right)\mathcal{Y}(\delta)d(\mathcal{Z}(\delta)) \tag{5}$$

which are called generalized k-$\mathcal{IO}$*s, where the Mittag-Leffler function is provided by:*

$$E^{\rho,\epsilon,\lambda,r}_{\varsigma,\eta,\varphi,k}(\delta;\Phi) = \sum_{n=0}^\infty \frac{\beta_p(\rho + n\lambda, r - \rho)}{\beta(\rho, r - \rho)} \frac{(r)_{n\lambda}}{k\Gamma_k(\varsigma n + \eta)} \frac{\delta^n}{(\varphi)_{n\epsilon}}. \tag{6}$$

Remark 1. *The $\mathcal{IO}$s (4) and (5) can reproduce several well-known $\mathcal{IO}$s which already exist in the literature. For example, for $k = 1$, the $\mathcal{IO}$s defined in [16] are obtained. For $k = 1$ and $\mathcal{Z}(\varpi) = \varpi$, the $\mathcal{IO}$s defined in [17] are obtained. For $k = 1$, $\mathcal{Z}(\varpi) = \varpi$ and $\Phi = 0$, the $\mathcal{IO}$s defined in [18] are obtained. For $k = 1$, $\mathcal{Z}(\varpi) = \varpi$ and $\epsilon = \Psi = 1$, the $\mathcal{IO}$s defined in [19] are obtained. For $k = 1$, $\mathcal{Z}(\varpi) = \varpi$, $\Phi = 0$, and $\epsilon = \Psi = 1$, the $\mathcal{IO}$s defined in [20] are obtained. For $k = 1$, $\mathcal{Z}(\varpi) = \varpi$, $\Phi = 0$, and $\lambda = \epsilon = \Psi = 1$, the $\mathcal{IO}$s defined in [21] are obtained. For $k = 1$, $\mathcal{Z}(\varpi) = \frac{\varpi^\eta}{\eta}$, $\eta > 0$, and $\Psi = \Phi = 0$, the $\mathcal{IO}$s defined in [22] are obtained. For $k = 1$, $\mathcal{Z}(\varpi) = ln\varpi$ and $\Psi = \Phi = 0$, the $\mathcal{IO}$s defined in [23] are obtained. For $\mathcal{Z}(\varpi) = \frac{\varpi^{\eta+1}}{\eta+1}$ and $\Psi = \Phi = 0$, the $\mathcal{IO}$s defined in [14] are obtained. For $k = 1$, $\mathcal{Z}(\varpi) = \frac{\varpi^{\eta+\zeta}}{\eta+\zeta}$ and $\Psi = \Phi = 0$, the $\mathcal{IO}$s defined in [24] are obtained. For $\mathcal{Z}(\varpi) = \frac{(\varpi-\mu)^\eta}{\eta}$, $\eta > 0$ in (4), and $\mathcal{Z}(\varpi) = -\frac{(\nu-\varpi)^\eta}{\eta}$, $\eta > 0$ in (5) with $\Psi = \Phi = 0$, the $\mathcal{IO}$s defined in [13] are obtained. For $\mathcal{Z}(\varpi) = \frac{(\varpi-\mu)^\eta}{\eta}$, $\eta > 0$ in (4), and $\mathcal{Z}(\varpi) = -\frac{(\nu-\varpi)^\eta}{\eta}$ $\eta > 0$ in (5) with $k = 1$ and $\Psi = \Phi = 0$, the $\mathcal{IO}$s defined in [25] are obtained. For $\Psi = \Phi = 0$, the $\mathcal{IO}$s defined in [26] are obtained. For $\Psi = \Phi = 0$ and $\mathcal{Z}(\varpi) = \varpi$, the $\mathcal{IO}$s defined in [11] are obtained. For $\Psi = \Phi = 0$, $\mathcal{Z}(\varpi) = \varpi$, and $k = 1$, the classical Riemann–Liouville $\mathcal{IO}$s are obtained.*

From k-$\mathcal{IO}$s (4) and (5), for constant function we can write:

$$\left({}^{k}_{\mathcal{Z}}\mathcal{D}^{\rho,\epsilon,\lambda,r}_{\varsigma,\eta,\varphi,\Psi,\mu^+}1\right)(\varpi;\Phi)=k(\mathcal{Z}(\varpi)-\mathcal{Z}(\mu))^{\frac{\eta}{k}}E^{\rho,\epsilon,\lambda,r}_{\varsigma,\eta+k,\varphi,k}\left(\Psi(\mathcal{Z}(\varpi)-\mathcal{Z}(\mu))^{\frac{\varsigma}{k}};\Phi\right):=\mathcal{F}_{\frac{\eta}{k},\mu^+}(\varpi;\Phi), \tag{7}$$

$$\left({}^{k}_{\mathcal{Z}}\mathcal{D}^{\rho,\epsilon,\lambda,r}_{\varsigma,\eta,\varphi,\Psi,\nu^-}1\right)(\varpi;\Phi)=k(\mathcal{Z}(\nu)-\mathcal{Z}(\varpi))^{\frac{\eta}{k}}E^{\rho,\epsilon,\lambda,r}_{\varsigma,\eta+k,\varphi,k}\left(\Psi(\mathcal{Z}(\nu)-\mathcal{Z}(\varpi))^{\frac{\varsigma}{k}};\Phi\right):=\mathcal{F}_{\frac{\eta}{k},\nu^-}(\varpi;\Phi). \tag{8}$$

Next, we provide the definition of newly defined functions, namely, exponentially $(\alpha, h-m)-p$-convex functions, as follows:

Definition 6 ([27]). *A function $\mathcal{Y} : (0,\nu] \to \mathbb{R}$ is said to be exponentially $(\alpha, h-m)-p$-convex functions if $\mathcal{Y}$ is positive and*

$$\mathcal{Y}\left((\delta\mu^p + (1-\delta)\nu^p)^{\frac{1}{p}}\right) \leq h(\delta^\alpha)\frac{\mathcal{Y}(\mu)}{e^{\omega\mu}} + mh(1-\delta^\alpha)\frac{\mathcal{Y}(\nu)}{e^{\omega\nu}} \tag{9}$$

is valid, while $J \subseteq \mathbb{R}$ is an interval involving $(0,1)$ and $h : J \to \mathbb{R}$ is a positive function with $(\delta\mu^p + (1-\delta)\nu^p)^{\frac{1}{p}} \in (0,\nu]$, $(\alpha, m) \in [0,1]^2$, $0 < \delta < 1$, and $\omega \in \mathbb{R}$.

Remark 2. *The function satisfying (9) produces various kinds of convex functions. For example, for $p = 1$, exponentially $(\alpha, h-m)$-convex functions are obtained. For $h(\delta) = \delta$, exponentially $(\alpha, m)-p$-convex functions are obtained. For $m = 1$, exponentially $(\alpha, h)-p$-convex functions are obtained. For $\alpha = 1$, exponentially $(h-m)-p$-convex functions are obtained. For $p = m = 1$, exponentially (α, h)-convex functions are obtained. For $\alpha = m = 1$, exponentially (h, p)-convex functions are obtained. For $p = \alpha = m = 1$, exponentially h-convex functions are obtained. For $h(\delta) = \delta$, and $p = 1$, exponentially (α, m)-convex functions are obtained. For $h(\delta) = \delta$ and $m = 1$, exponentially (α, p)-convex functions are obtained. For $h(\delta) = \delta$ and $\alpha = 1$, exponentially (m, p)-convex functions are obtained. For $h(\delta) = \delta$ and $p = m = 1$, exponentially α-convex functions are obtained. For $h(\delta) = \delta$ and $p = \alpha = 1$, exponentially m-convex functions are obtained. For $h(\delta) = \delta$ and $\alpha = m = 1$, exponentially p-convex functions are obtained. For $h(\delta) = \delta$ and $p = \alpha = m = 1$, exponentially convex functions are obtained.*

In recent years, many authors have derived the bounds of several $\mathcal{IO}$s for different kinds of convex functions. For example, Farid [28] established the bounds of Riemann–Liouville $\mathcal{IO}$s using convex functions. Mehmood and Farid [29] provided the bounds of generalized Riemann–Liouville k-$\mathcal{IO}$s via m-convex functions. Yu et al. [30] proved the bounds of generalized $\mathcal{IO}$s involving the Mittag-Leffler function in their kernels via strongly exponentially $(\alpha, h-m)$-convex functions. Inspired by these previous works, the aim of this paper is to derive the bounds of generalized k-$\mathcal{IO}$s for exponentially $(\alpha, h-m)-p$-convex functions.

In the upcoming section, we first derive the bounds of the k-$\mathcal{IO}$s provided in (4) and (5) for functions satisfying (9) and derive a modulus inequality for these operators. Further, an identity is proved to derive the Hadamard type inequality for k-$\mathcal{IO}$s via exponentially $(\alpha, h-m)-p$-convex functions. In particular cases, the presented results provide bounds of various $\mathcal{IO}$s.

2. Main Results

First, we provide the bounds of k-$\mathcal{IO}$s via exponentially $(\alpha, h-m)-p$-convex functions:

Theorem 1. *Let $\mathcal{Y}:[\mu,\nu]\longrightarrow\mathbb{R}$ be a positive, integrable, and exponentially $(\alpha,h-m)-p$-convex functions with $m\in(0,1]$. In addition, let $\mathcal{Z}$ be differentiable and strictly increasing with $\mathcal{Z}'\in L_1[\mu,\nu]$. Then, for $\eta,\zeta\geq k$ and $\omega\in\mathbb{R}$, we have:*

$$\begin{aligned}
&\left({}_{\mathcal{Z}}^{k}\mathcal{D}^{\rho,\epsilon,\lambda,r}_{\varsigma,\eta,\varphi,\Psi,\mu^+}\mathcal{Y}\circ\mathcal{U}\right)(\varpi;\Phi)+\left({}_{\mathcal{Z}}^{k}\mathcal{D}^{\rho,\epsilon,\lambda,r}_{\varsigma,\zeta,\varphi,\Psi,\nu^-}\mathcal{Y}\circ\mathcal{U}\right)(\varpi;\Phi) \quad (10)\\
&\leq(\varpi-\mu)\Big(\mathcal{Z}(\varpi)-\mathcal{Z}(\mu)\Big)^{\frac{\eta}{k}-1}E^{\rho,\epsilon,\lambda,r}_{\varsigma,\eta,\varphi,k}\left(\Psi(\mathcal{Z}(\varpi)-\mathcal{Z}(\mu))^{\frac{\varsigma}{k}};\Phi\right)\\
&\left[\frac{\mathcal{Y}((\mu)^{\frac{1}{p}})}{e^{\omega((\mu)^{\frac{1}{p}})}}\mathcal{T}^{\mu}_{\varpi}\Big(h,\mathcal{R}^{\alpha};\mathcal{Z}'\Big)+m\frac{\mathcal{Y}\Big((\frac{\varpi}{m})^{\frac{1}{p}}\Big)}{e^{\omega\left((\frac{\varpi}{m})^{\frac{1}{p}}\right)}}\mathcal{T}^{\mu}_{\varpi}\Big(h,1-\mathcal{R}^{\alpha};\mathcal{Z}'\Big)\right]\\
&+(\nu-\varpi)\Big(\mathcal{Z}(\nu)-\mathcal{Z}(\varpi)\Big)^{\frac{\zeta}{k}-1}E^{\rho,\epsilon,\lambda,r}_{\varsigma,\zeta,\varphi,k}\left(\Psi(\mathcal{Z}(\nu)-\mathcal{Z}(\varpi))^{\frac{\varsigma}{k}};\Phi\right)\\
&\left[\frac{\mathcal{Y}((\nu)^{\frac{1}{p}})}{e^{\omega((\nu)^{\frac{1}{p}})}}\mathcal{T}^{\nu}_{\varpi}\Big(h,\mathcal{R}^{\alpha};\mathcal{Z}'\Big)+m\frac{\mathcal{Y}\Big((\frac{\varpi}{m})^{\frac{1}{p}}\Big)}{e^{\omega\left((\frac{\varpi}{m})^{\frac{1}{p}}\right)}}\mathcal{T}^{\nu}_{\varpi}\Big(h,1-\mathcal{R}^{\alpha};\mathcal{Z}'\Big)\right],
\end{aligned}$$

where $\mathcal{U}(\delta)=\delta^{\frac{1}{p}}$, $\mathcal{T}^{\mu}_{\varpi}\Big(h,\mathcal{R}^{\alpha};\mathcal{Z}'\Big)=\int_0^1 h(\mathcal{R}^{\alpha})\mathcal{Z}'(\varpi-\mathcal{R}(\varpi-\mu))d\mathcal{R}$, $\mathcal{T}^{\mu}_{\varpi}\Big(h,1-\mathcal{R}^{\alpha};\mathcal{Z}'\Big)=\int_0^1 h(1-\mathcal{R}^{\alpha})\mathcal{Z}'(\varpi-\mathcal{R}(\varpi-\mu))d\mathcal{R}$.

Proof. Under the given assumptions, the following inequalities hold:

$$\begin{aligned}
&(\mathcal{Z}(\varpi)-\mathcal{Z}(\delta))^{\frac{\eta}{k}-1}E^{\rho,\epsilon,\lambda,r}_{\varsigma,\eta,\varphi,k}\left(\Psi(\mathcal{Z}(\varpi)-\mathcal{Z}(\delta))^{\frac{\varsigma}{k}};\Phi\right)\mathcal{Z}'(\delta) \quad (11)\\
&\leq(\mathcal{Z}(\varpi)-\mathcal{Z}(\mu))^{\frac{\eta}{k}-1}E^{\rho,\epsilon,\lambda,r}_{\varsigma,\eta,\varphi,k}\left(\Psi(\mathcal{Z}(\varpi)-\mathcal{Z}(\mu))^{\frac{\varsigma}{k}};\Phi\right)\mathcal{Z}'(\delta),\quad \mu<\delta<\varpi,
\end{aligned}$$

$$\begin{aligned}
&(\mathcal{Z}(\delta)-\mathcal{Z}(\varpi))^{\frac{\zeta}{k}-1}E^{\rho,\epsilon,\lambda,r}_{\varsigma,\zeta,\varphi,k}\left(\Psi(\mathcal{Z}(\delta)-\mathcal{Z}(\varpi))^{\frac{\varsigma}{k}};\Phi\right)\mathcal{Z}'(\delta) \quad (12)\\
&\leq(\mathcal{Z}(\nu)-\mathcal{Z}(\varpi))^{\frac{\zeta}{k}-1}E^{\rho,\epsilon,\lambda,r}_{\varsigma,\zeta,\varphi,k}\left(\Psi(\mathcal{Z}(\nu)-\mathcal{Z}(\varpi))^{\frac{\varsigma}{k}};\Phi\right)\mathcal{Z}'(\delta),\quad \varpi<\delta<\nu.
\end{aligned}$$

By utilizing the exponentially $(\alpha,h-m)-p$-convexity of $\mathcal{Y}$, we can obtain the following:

$$\mathcal{Y}((\delta)^{\frac{1}{p}})\leq h\left(\frac{\varpi-\delta}{\varpi-\mu}\right)^{\alpha}\frac{\mathcal{Y}((\mu)^{\frac{1}{p}})}{e^{\omega((\mu)^{\frac{1}{p}})}}+mh\left(1-\left(\frac{\varpi-\delta}{\varpi-\mu}\right)^{\alpha}\right)\frac{\mathcal{Y}\Big((\frac{\varpi}{m})^{\frac{1}{p}}\Big)}{e^{\omega\left((\frac{\varpi}{m})^{\frac{1}{p}}\right)}}, \quad (13)$$

$$\mathcal{Y}((\delta)^{\frac{1}{p}}) \leq h\left(\frac{\delta-\varpi}{\nu-\varpi}\right)^{\alpha}\frac{\mathcal{Y}((\nu)^{\frac{1}{p}})}{e^{\omega((\nu)^{\frac{1}{p}})}} + mh\left(1-\left(\frac{\delta-\varpi}{\nu-\varpi}\right)^{\alpha}\right)\frac{\mathcal{Y}\left((\frac{\varpi}{m})^{\frac{1}{p}}\right)}{e^{\omega\left((\frac{\varpi}{m})^{\frac{1}{p}}\right)}}. \tag{14}$$

From inequalities (11) and (13), the following inequality is valid:

$$\int_{\mu}^{\varpi}(\mathcal{Z}(\varpi)-\mathcal{Z}(\delta))^{\frac{\eta}{k}-1}E^{\rho,\epsilon,\lambda,r}_{\varsigma,\eta,\varphi,k}\left(\Psi(\mathcal{Z}(\varpi)-\mathcal{Z}(\delta))^{\frac{\varsigma}{k}};\Phi\right)\mathcal{Z}'(\delta)\mathcal{Y}((\delta)^{\frac{1}{p}})d\delta$$
$$\leq \left(\mathcal{Z}(\varpi)-\mathcal{Z}(\mu)\right)^{\frac{\eta}{k}-1}E^{\rho,\epsilon,\lambda,r}_{\varsigma,\eta,\varphi,k}\left(\Psi(\mathcal{Z}(\varpi)-\mathcal{Z}(\mu))^{\frac{\varsigma}{k}};\Phi\right)\left[\frac{\mathcal{Y}((\mu)^{\frac{1}{p}})}{e^{\omega((\mu)^{\frac{1}{p}})}}\right.$$
$$\left.\int_{\mu}^{\varpi}h\left(\frac{\varpi-\delta}{\varpi-\mu}\right)^{\alpha}\mathcal{Z}'(\delta)d\delta + \frac{m\mathcal{Y}\left((\frac{\varpi}{m})^{\frac{1}{p}}\right)}{e^{\omega\left((\frac{\varpi}{m})^{\frac{1}{p}}\right)}}\int_{\mu}^{\varpi}h\left(1-\left(\frac{\varpi-\delta}{\varpi-\mu}\right)^{\alpha}\right)\mathcal{Z}'(\delta)d\delta\right].$$

By utilizing the integral operator (4) on the left-hand side and making the substitution $\mathcal{R}=(\varpi-\delta)/(\varpi-\mu)$ on the right-hand side, we obtain:

$$\left({}^{k}_{\mathcal{Z}}\mathcal{D}^{\rho,\epsilon,\lambda,r}_{\varsigma,\eta,\varphi,\Psi,\mu^{+}}\mathcal{Y}\circ\mathcal{U}\right)(\varpi;\Phi) \leq (\varpi-\mu)\left(\mathcal{Z}(\varpi)-\mathcal{Z}(\mu)\right)^{\frac{\eta}{k}-1}$$
$$E^{\rho,\epsilon,\lambda,r}_{\varsigma,\eta,\varphi,k}\left(\Psi(\mathcal{Z}(\varpi)-\mathcal{Z}(\mu))^{\frac{\varsigma}{k}};\Phi\right)\left[\frac{\mathcal{Y}((\mu)^{\frac{1}{p}})}{e^{\omega((\mu)^{\frac{1}{p}})}}\int_{0}^{1}h(\mathcal{R}^{\alpha})\mathcal{Z}'(\varpi-\mathcal{R}(\varpi-\mu))d\mathcal{R}\right.$$
$$\left.+\frac{m\mathcal{Y}\left((\frac{\varpi}{m})^{\frac{1}{p}}\right)}{e^{\omega\left((\frac{\varpi}{m})^{\frac{1}{p}}\right)}}\int_{0}^{1}h(1-\mathcal{R}^{\alpha})\mathcal{Z}'(\varpi-\mathcal{R}(\varpi-\mu))d\mathcal{R}\right].$$

The above inequality can be written in the following form:

$$\left({}^{k}_{\mathcal{Z}}\mathcal{D}^{\rho,\epsilon,\lambda,r}_{\varsigma,\eta,\varphi,\Psi,\mu^{+}}\mathcal{Y}\circ\mathcal{U}\right)(\varpi;\Phi) \tag{15}$$
$$\leq (\varpi-\mu)\left(\mathcal{Z}(\varpi)-\mathcal{Z}(\mu)\right)^{\frac{\eta}{k}-1}E^{\rho,\epsilon,\lambda,r}_{\varsigma,\eta,\varphi,k}\left(\Psi(\mathcal{Z}(\varpi)-\mathcal{Z}(\mu))^{\frac{\varsigma}{k}};\Phi\right)$$
$$\left[\frac{\mathcal{Y}((\mu)^{\frac{1}{p}})}{e^{\omega((\mu)^{\frac{1}{p}})}}\mathcal{T}^{\mu}_{\varpi}\left(h,\mathcal{R}^{\alpha};\mathcal{Z}'\right)+\frac{m\mathcal{Y}\left((\frac{\varpi}{m})^{\frac{1}{p}}\right)}{e^{\omega\left((\frac{\varpi}{m})^{\frac{1}{p}}\right)}}\mathcal{T}^{\mu}_{\varpi}\left(h,1-\mathcal{R}^{\alpha};\mathcal{Z}'\right)\right].$$

On the other hand, by multiplying (12) and (14) and adopting the same approach as we did for (11) and (13), the following inequality can be obtained:

$$\left({}^{k}_{\mathcal{Z}}\mathcal{D}^{\rho,\epsilon,\lambda,r}_{\varsigma,\zeta,\varphi,\Psi,\nu^{-}}\mathcal{Y}\circ\mathcal{U}\right)(\varpi;\Phi) \leq (\nu-\varpi)\left(\mathcal{Z}(\nu)-\mathcal{Z}(\varpi)\right)^{\frac{\zeta}{k}-1}$$
$$E^{\rho,\epsilon,\lambda,r}_{\varsigma,\zeta,\varphi,k}\left(\Psi(\mathcal{Z}(\nu)-\mathcal{Z}(\varpi))^{\frac{\varsigma}{k}};\Phi\right)\left[\frac{\mathcal{Y}((\nu)^{\frac{1}{p}})}{e^{\omega((\nu)^{\frac{1}{p}})}}\int_{0}^{1}h(\mathcal{R}^{\alpha})\mathcal{Z}'(\varpi-\mathcal{R}(\varpi-\nu))d\mathcal{R}\right.$$
$$\left.+\frac{m\mathcal{Y}\left((\frac{\varpi}{m})^{\frac{1}{p}}\right)}{e^{\omega\left((\frac{\varpi}{m})^{\frac{1}{p}}\right)}}\int_{0}^{1}h(1-\mathcal{R}^{\alpha})\mathcal{Z}'(\varpi-\mathcal{R}(\varpi-\nu))d\mathcal{R}\right].$$

The above inequality takes the following form:

$$\begin{aligned}&\left({}_{\mathcal{Z}}^{k}\mathcal{D}^{\rho,\epsilon,\lambda,r}_{\varsigma,\zeta,\varphi,\Psi,\nu^-}\mathcal{Y}\circ\mathcal{U}\right)(\varpi;\Phi)\\&\leq(\nu-\varpi)\left(\mathcal{Z}(\nu)-\mathcal{Z}(\varpi)\right)^{\frac{\zeta}{k}-1}E^{\rho,\epsilon,\lambda,r}_{\varsigma,\zeta,\varphi,k}\left(\Psi(\mathcal{Z}(\nu)-\mathcal{Z}(\varpi))^{\frac{\zeta}{k}};\Phi\right)\\&\left[\frac{\mathcal{Y}((\nu)^{\frac{1}{p}})}{e^{\omega((\nu)^{\frac{1}{p}})}}\mathcal{T}^{\nu}_{\varpi}\left(h,\mathcal{R}^{\alpha};\mathcal{Z}'\right)+m\frac{\mathcal{Y}\left((\frac{\varpi}{m})^{\frac{1}{p}}\right)}{e^{\omega\left((\frac{\varpi}{m})^{\frac{1}{p}}\right)}}\mathcal{T}^{\nu}_{\varpi}\left(h,1-\mathcal{R}^{\alpha};\mathcal{Z}'\right)\right].\end{aligned}\tag{16}$$

By adding the inequalities (15) and (16), the inequality (10) is obtained. □

Corollary 1. *For $\eta=\zeta$ in (10), the following inequality is valid:*

$$\begin{aligned}&\left({}_{\mathcal{Z}}^{k}\mathcal{D}^{\rho,\epsilon,\lambda,r}_{\varsigma,\eta,\varphi,\Psi,\mu^+}\mathcal{Y}\circ\mathcal{U}\right)(\varpi;\Phi)+\left({}_{\mathcal{Z}}^{k}\mathcal{D}^{\rho,\epsilon,\lambda,r}_{\varsigma,\eta,\varphi,\Psi,\nu^-}\mathcal{Y}\circ\mathcal{U}\right)(\varpi;\Phi)\\&\leq(\varpi-\mu)\left(\mathcal{Z}(\varpi)-\mathcal{Z}(\mu)\right)^{\frac{\eta}{k}-1}E^{\rho,\epsilon,\lambda,r}_{\varsigma,\eta,\varphi,k}\left(\Psi(\mathcal{Z}(\varpi)-\mathcal{Z}(\mu))^{\frac{\eta}{k}};\Phi\right)\\&\left[\frac{\mathcal{Y}((\mu)^{\frac{1}{p}})}{e^{\omega((\mu)^{\frac{1}{p}})}}\mathcal{T}^{\mu}_{\varpi}\left(h,\mathcal{R}^{\alpha};\mathcal{Z}'\right)+\frac{m\mathcal{Y}\left((\frac{\varpi}{m})^{\frac{1}{p}}\right)}{e^{\omega\left((\frac{\varpi}{m})^{\frac{1}{p}}\right)}}\mathcal{T}^{\mu}_{\varpi}\left(h,1-\mathcal{R}^{\alpha};\mathcal{Z}'\right)\right]\\&+(\nu-\varpi)\left(\mathcal{Z}(\nu)-\mathcal{Z}(\varpi)\right)^{\frac{\eta}{k}-1}E^{\rho,\epsilon,\lambda,r}_{\varsigma,\eta,\varphi,k}\left(\Psi(\mathcal{Z}(\nu)-\mathcal{Z}(\varpi))^{\frac{\zeta}{k}};\Phi\right)\\&\left[\frac{\mathcal{Y}((\nu)^{\frac{1}{p}})}{e^{\omega((\nu)^{\frac{1}{p}})}}\mathcal{T}^{\nu}_{\varpi}\left(h,\mathcal{R}^{\alpha};\mathcal{Z}'\right)+\frac{m\mathcal{Y}\left((\frac{\varpi}{m})^{\frac{1}{p}}\right)}{e^{\omega\left((\frac{\varpi}{m})^{\frac{1}{p}}\right)}}\mathcal{T}^{\nu}_{\varpi}\left(h,1-\mathcal{R}^{\alpha};\mathcal{Z}'\right)\right].\end{aligned}\tag{17}$$

Remark 3. *From Theorem 1, a large number of new bounds for all kinds of $\mathcal{IO}$s (as identified in Remark 1) via all kinds of convex functions (as identified in Remark 2) can be obtained.*

In the following, we provide the modulus inequality for k-$\mathcal{IO}$s via exponentially $(\alpha,h-m)-p$-convex functions:

Theorem 2. *Let $\mathcal{Y}:[\mu,\nu]\longrightarrow\mathbb{R}$ be positive integrable and let $|\mathcal{Y}'|$ be an exponentially $(\alpha,h-m)-p$-convex function with $m\in(0,1]$. In addition, let $\mathcal{Z}$ be differentiable and strictly increasing with $\mathcal{Z}'\in L_1[\mu,\nu]$. Then, for $\eta,\zeta\geq k$ and $\omega\in\mathbb{R}$, we have:*

$$\begin{aligned}&\left|\left({}_{\mathcal{Z}}^{k}\mathcal{D}^{\rho,\epsilon,\lambda,r}_{\varsigma,\eta,\varphi,\Psi,\mu^+}(\mathcal{Z}*\mathcal{Y})\circ\mathcal{U}\right)(\varpi,w;\Phi)+\left({}_{\mathcal{Z}}^{k}\mathcal{D}^{\rho,\epsilon,\lambda,r}_{\varsigma,\zeta,\varphi,\Psi,\nu^-}(\mathcal{Z}*\mathcal{Y})\circ\mathcal{U}\right)(\varpi,w;\Phi)\right|\\&\leq(\varpi-\mu)\left(\mathcal{Z}(\varpi)-\mathcal{Z}(\mu)\right)^{\frac{\eta}{k}-1}E^{\rho,\epsilon,\lambda,r}_{\varsigma,\eta,\varphi,k}\left(\Psi(\mathcal{Z}(\varpi)-\mathcal{Z}(\mu))^{\frac{\varsigma}{k}};\Phi\right)\\&\left[\frac{|\mathcal{Y}'((\mu)^{\frac{1}{p}})|}{e^{\omega((\mu)^{\frac{1}{p}})}}\mathcal{T}^{\mu}_{\varpi}\left(h,\mathcal{R}^{\alpha};\mathcal{Z}'\right)+\frac{m\left|\mathcal{Y}'\left((\frac{\varpi}{m})^{\frac{1}{p}}\right)\right|}{e^{\omega\left((\frac{\varpi}{m})^{\frac{1}{p}}\right)}}\mathcal{T}^{\mu}_{\varpi}\left(h,1-\mathcal{R}^{\alpha};\mathcal{Z}'\right)\right]\\&+(\nu-\varpi)\left(\mathcal{Z}(\nu)-\mathcal{Z}(\varpi)\right)^{\frac{\zeta}{k}-1}E^{\rho,\epsilon,\lambda,r}_{\varsigma,\zeta,\varphi,k}\left(\Psi(\mathcal{Z}(\nu)-\mathcal{Z}(\varpi))^{\frac{\varsigma}{k}};\Phi\right)\\&\left[\frac{|\mathcal{Y}'((\nu)^{\frac{1}{p}})|}{e^{\omega((\nu)^{\frac{1}{p}})}}\mathcal{T}^{\nu}_{\varpi}\left(h,\mathcal{R}^{\alpha};\mathcal{Z}'\right)+\frac{m\left|\mathcal{Y}'\left((\frac{\varpi}{m})^{\frac{1}{p}}\right)\right|}{e^{\omega\left((\frac{\varpi}{m})^{\frac{1}{p}}\right)}}\mathcal{T}^{\nu}_{\varpi}\left(h,1-\mathcal{R}^{\alpha};\mathcal{Z}'\right)\right],\end{aligned}\tag{18}$$

where

$$\left({}_{\mathcal{Z}}^{k}\mathcal{D}^{\rho,\epsilon,\lambda,r}_{\varsigma,\eta,\varphi,\Psi,\mu^+}(\mathcal{Z}*\mathcal{Y})\circ\mathcal{U}\right)(\varpi,w;\Phi)$$
$$:=\int_{\mu}^{\varpi}(\mathcal{Z}(\varpi)-\mathcal{Z}(\delta))^{\frac{\eta}{k}-1}E^{\rho,\epsilon,\lambda,r}_{\varsigma,\eta,\varphi,k}\left(\Psi(\mathcal{Z}(\varpi)-\mathcal{Z}(\delta))^{\frac{\varsigma}{k}};\Phi\right)\mathcal{Z}'(\delta)\mathcal{Y}'((\delta)^{\frac{1}{p}})d\delta$$

and

$$\left({}_{\mathcal{Z}}^{k}\mathcal{D}^{\rho,\epsilon,\lambda,r}_{\varsigma,\zeta,\varphi,\Psi,\nu^-}(\mathcal{Z}*\mathcal{Y})\circ\mathcal{U}\right)(\varpi,w;\Phi)$$
$$:=\int_{\varpi}^{\nu}(\mathcal{Z}(\delta)-\mathcal{Z}(\varpi))^{\frac{\zeta}{k}-1}E^{\rho,\epsilon,\lambda,r}_{\varsigma,\zeta,\varphi,k}\left(\Psi(\mathcal{Z}(\delta)-\mathcal{Z}(\varpi))^{\frac{\varsigma}{k}};\Phi\right)\mathcal{Z}'(\delta)\mathcal{Y}'((\delta)^{\frac{1}{p}})d\delta.$$

Proof. By utilizing the strongly exponentially $(\alpha,h-m)-p$-convexity of $|\mathcal{Y}'|$, the following inequality holds:

$$|\mathcal{Y}'((\delta)^{\frac{1}{p}})|\leq h\left(\frac{\varpi-\delta}{\varpi-\mu}\right)^{\alpha}\frac{|\mathcal{Y}'((\mu)^{\frac{1}{p}})|}{e^{\omega((\mu)^{\frac{1}{p}})}}+mh\left(1-\left(\frac{\varpi-\delta}{\varpi-\mu}\right)^{\alpha}\right)\frac{|\mathcal{Y}'((\frac{\varpi}{m})^{\frac{1}{p}})|}{e^{\omega\left((\frac{\varpi}{m})^{\frac{1}{p}}\right)}}. \tag{19}$$

The above inequality can be written in the following form:

$$-\left(h\left(\frac{\varpi-\delta}{\varpi-\mu}\right)^{\alpha}\frac{|\mathcal{Y}'((\mu)^{\frac{1}{p}})|}{e^{\omega((\mu)^{\frac{1}{p}})}}+mh\left(1-\left(\frac{\varpi-\delta}{\varpi-\mu}\right)^{\alpha}\right)\frac{|\mathcal{Y}'((\frac{\varpi}{m})^{\frac{1}{p}})|}{e^{\omega\left((\frac{\varpi}{m})^{\frac{1}{p}}\right)}}\right) \tag{20}$$
$$\mathcal{Y}'((\delta)^{\frac{1}{p}})\leq\left(h\left(\frac{\varpi-\delta}{\varpi-\mu}\right)^{\alpha}\frac{|\mathcal{Y}'((\mu)^{\frac{1}{p}})|}{e^{\omega((\mu)^{\frac{1}{p}})}}+mh\left(1-\left(\frac{\varpi-\delta}{\varpi-\mu}\right)^{\alpha}\right)\frac{|\mathcal{Y}'((\frac{\varpi}{m})^{\frac{1}{p}})|}{e^{\omega\left((\frac{\varpi}{m})^{\frac{1}{p}}\right)}}\right).$$

Now, by multiplying the inequality (11) with the first inequality of (20) and integrating over $[\mu,\varpi]$, we obtain the following:

$$\int_{\mu}^{\varpi}(\mathcal{Z}(\varpi)-\mathcal{Z}(\delta))^{\frac{\eta}{k}-1}E^{\rho,\epsilon,\lambda,r}_{\varsigma,\eta,\varphi,k}\left(\Psi(\mathcal{Z}(\varpi)-\mathcal{Z}(\delta))^{\frac{\varsigma}{k}};\Phi\right)\mathcal{Z}'(\delta)\mathcal{Y}'((\delta)^{\frac{1}{p}})d\delta \tag{21}$$
$$\leq(\mathcal{Z}(\varpi)-\mathcal{Z}(\mu))^{\frac{\eta}{k}-1}E^{\rho,\epsilon,\lambda,r}_{\varsigma,\eta,\varphi,k}\left(\Psi(\mathcal{Z}(\varpi)-\mathcal{Z}(\mu))^{\frac{\varsigma}{k}};\Phi\right)\left(\frac{|\mathcal{Y}'((\mu)^{\frac{1}{p}})|}{e^{\omega((\mu)^{\frac{1}{p}})}}\int_{\mu}^{\varpi}h\left(\frac{\varpi-\delta}{\varpi-\mu}\right)^{\alpha}\right.$$
$$\left.\mathcal{Z}'(\delta)d\delta+\frac{m|\mathcal{Y}'((\frac{\varpi}{m})^{\frac{1}{p}})|}{e^{\omega\left((\frac{\varpi}{m})^{\frac{1}{p}}\right)}}\int_{\mu}^{\varpi}h\left(1-\left(\frac{\varpi-\delta}{\varpi-\mu}\right)^{\alpha}\right)\mathcal{Z}'(\delta)d\delta\right).$$

After simplifying the inequality (21), we have

$$\left({}_{\mathcal{Z}}^{k}\mathcal{D}^{\rho,\epsilon,\lambda,r}_{\varsigma,\eta,\varphi,\Psi,\mu^+}(\mathcal{Z}*\mathcal{Y})\circ\mathcal{U}\right)(\varpi,w;\Phi) \tag{22}$$
$$\leq(\varpi-\mu)\Big(\mathcal{Z}(\varpi)-\mathcal{Z}(\mu)\Big)^{\frac{\eta}{k}-1}E^{\rho,\epsilon,\lambda,r}_{\varsigma,\eta,\varphi,k}\left(\Psi(\mathcal{Z}(\varpi)-\mathcal{Z}(\mu))^{\frac{\varsigma}{k}};\Phi\right)$$
$$\left[\frac{|\mathcal{Y}'((\mu)^{\frac{1}{p}})|}{e^{\omega((\mu)^{\frac{1}{p}})}}\mathcal{T}^{\mu}_{\varpi}\left(h,\mathcal{R}^{\alpha};\mathcal{Z}'\right)+\frac{m|\mathcal{Y}'\left((\frac{\varpi}{m})^{\frac{1}{p}}\right)|}{e^{\omega\left((\frac{\varpi}{m})^{\frac{1}{p}}\right)}}\mathcal{T}^{\mu}_{\varpi}\left(h,1-\mathcal{R}^{\alpha};\mathcal{Z}'\right)\right].$$

By using the second inequality of (20) and following the same approach as we did for the first inequality, we can obtain the following:

$$\left({}^{k}_{\mathcal{Z}}\mathcal{D}^{\rho,\epsilon,\lambda,r}_{\varsigma,\eta,\varphi,\Psi,\mu^{+}}(\mathcal{Z}*\mathcal{Y})\circ\mathcal{U}\right)(\varpi,w;\Phi) \tag{23}$$
$$\geq -(\varpi-\mu)\Big(\mathcal{Z}(\varpi)-\mathcal{Z}(\mu)\Big)^{\frac{\eta}{k}-1}E^{\rho,\epsilon,\lambda,r}_{\varsigma,\eta,\varphi,k}\Big(\Psi(\mathcal{Z}(\varpi)-\mathcal{Z}(\mu))^{\frac{\varsigma}{k}};\Phi\Big)$$
$$\left[\frac{|\mathcal{Y}'((\mu)^{\frac{1}{p}})|}{e^{\omega((\mu)^{\frac{1}{p}})}}\mathcal{T}^{\mu}_{\varpi}\Big(h,\mathcal{R}^{\alpha};\mathcal{Z}'\Big)+\frac{m|\mathcal{Y}'\Big((\frac{\varpi}{m})^{\frac{1}{p}}\Big)|}{e^{\omega\left((\frac{\varpi}{m})^{\frac{1}{p}}\right)}}\mathcal{T}^{\mu}_{\varpi}\Big(h,1-\mathcal{R}^{\alpha};\mathcal{Z}'\Big)\right].$$

From inequalities (22) and (23), we have:

$$\left|\left({}^{k}_{\mathcal{Z}}\mathcal{D}^{\rho,\epsilon,\lambda,r}_{\varsigma,\eta,\varphi,\Psi,\mu^{+}}(\mathcal{Z}*\mathcal{Y})\circ\mathcal{U}\right)(\varpi,w;\Phi)\right| \tag{24}$$
$$\leq (\varpi-\mu)\Big(\mathcal{Z}(\varpi)-\mathcal{Z}(\mu)\Big)^{\frac{\eta}{k}-1}E^{\rho,\epsilon,\lambda,r}_{\varsigma,\eta,\varphi,k}\Big(\Psi(\mathcal{Z}(\varpi)-\mathcal{Z}(\mu))^{\frac{\varsigma}{k}};\Phi\Big)$$
$$\left[\frac{|\mathcal{Y}'((\mu)^{\frac{1}{p}})|}{e^{\omega((\mu)^{\frac{1}{p}})}}\mathcal{T}^{\mu}_{\varpi}\Big(h,\mathcal{R}^{\alpha};\mathcal{Z}'\Big)+\frac{m|\mathcal{Y}'\Big((\frac{\varpi}{m})^{\frac{1}{p}}\Big)|}{e^{\omega\left((\frac{\varpi}{m})^{\frac{1}{p}}\right)}}\mathcal{T}^{\mu}_{\varpi}\Big(h,1-\mathcal{R}^{\alpha};\mathcal{Z}'\Big)\right].$$

Again, by utilizing the strongly exponentially $(\alpha,h-m)-p$-convexity of $|\mathcal{Y}'|$, we have

$$|\mathcal{Y}'((\delta)^{\frac{1}{p}})|\leq h\left(\frac{\delta-\varpi}{\nu-\varpi}\right)^{\alpha}\frac{|\mathcal{Y}'((\nu)^{\frac{1}{p}})|}{e^{\omega((\nu)^{\frac{1}{p}})}}+mh\left(1-\left(\frac{\delta-\varpi}{\nu-\varpi}\right)^{\alpha}\right)\frac{|\mathcal{Y}'\Big((\frac{\varpi}{m})^{\frac{1}{p}}\Big)|}{e^{\omega\left((\frac{\varpi}{m})^{\frac{1}{p}}\right)}}. \tag{25}$$

By following the same approach as we did for (11) and (19), from (12) and (25) we can obtain:

$$\left|\left({}^{k}_{\mathcal{Z}}\mathcal{D}^{\rho,\epsilon,\lambda,r}_{\varsigma,\zeta,\varphi,\Psi,\nu^{-}}(\mathcal{Z}*\mathcal{Y})\circ\mathcal{U}\right)(\varpi,w;\Phi)\right| \tag{26}$$
$$\leq (\nu-\varpi)\Big(\mathcal{Z}(\nu)-\mathcal{Z}(\varpi)\Big)^{\frac{\zeta}{k}-1}E^{\rho,\epsilon,\lambda,r}_{\varsigma,\zeta,\varphi,k}\Big(\Psi(\mathcal{Z}(\nu)-\mathcal{Z}(\varpi))^{\frac{\varsigma}{k}};\Phi\Big)$$
$$\left[\frac{|\mathcal{Y}'((\nu)^{\frac{1}{p}})|}{e^{\omega((\nu)^{\frac{1}{p}})}}\mathcal{T}^{\nu}_{\varpi}\Big(h,\mathcal{R}^{\alpha};\mathcal{Z}'\Big)+\frac{m|\mathcal{Y}'\Big((\frac{\varpi}{m})^{\frac{1}{p}}\Big)|}{e^{\omega\left((\frac{\varpi}{m})^{\frac{1}{p}}\right)}}\mathcal{T}^{\nu}_{\varpi}\Big(h,1-\mathcal{R}^{\alpha};\mathcal{Z}'\Big)\right].$$

By adding the inequalities (24) and (26), the required inequality (18) is obtained. □

Corollary 2. *For $\eta=\zeta$ in (18), the following inequality is valid:*

$$\left|\left({}^{k}_{\mathcal{Z}}\mathcal{D}^{\rho,\epsilon,\lambda,r}_{\varsigma,\eta,\varphi,\Psi,\mu^{+}}(\mathcal{Z}*\mathcal{Y})\circ\mathcal{U}\right)(\varpi,w;\Phi)+\left({}^{k}_{\mathcal{Z}}\mathcal{D}^{\rho,\epsilon,\lambda,r}_{\varsigma,\eta,\varphi,\Psi,\nu^{-}}(\mathcal{Z}*\mathcal{Y})\circ\mathcal{U}\right)(\varpi,w;\Phi)\right| \tag{27}$$
$$\leq (\varpi-\mu)\Big(\mathcal{Z}(\varpi)-\mathcal{Z}(\mu)\Big)^{\frac{\eta}{k}-1}E^{\rho,\epsilon,\lambda,r}_{\varsigma,\eta,\varphi,k}\Big(\Psi(\mathcal{Z}(\varpi)-\mathcal{Z}(\mu))^{\frac{\varsigma}{k}};\Phi\Big)$$
$$\left[\frac{|\mathcal{Y}'((\mu)^{\frac{1}{p}})|}{e^{\omega((\mu)^{\frac{1}{p}})}}\mathcal{T}^{\mu}_{\varpi}\Big(h,\mathcal{R}^{\alpha};\mathcal{Z}'\Big)+\frac{m|\mathcal{Y}'\Big((\frac{\varpi}{m})^{\frac{1}{p}}\Big)|}{e^{\omega\left((\frac{\varpi}{m})^{\frac{1}{p}}\right)}}\mathcal{T}^{\mu}_{\varpi}\Big(h,1-\mathcal{R}^{\alpha};\mathcal{Z}'\Big)\right]$$
$$+(\nu-\varpi)\Big(\mathcal{Z}(\nu)-\mathcal{Z}(\varpi)\Big)^{\frac{\zeta}{k}-1}E^{\rho,\epsilon,\lambda,r}_{\varsigma,\eta,\varphi,k}\Big(\Psi(\mathcal{Z}(\nu)-\mathcal{Z}(\varpi))^{\frac{\varsigma}{k}};\Phi\Big)$$
$$\left[\frac{|\mathcal{Y}'((\nu)^{\frac{1}{p}})|}{e^{\omega((\nu)^{\frac{1}{p}})}}\mathcal{T}^{\nu}_{\varpi}\Big(h,\mathcal{R}^{\alpha};\mathcal{Z}'\Big)+\frac{m|\mathcal{Y}'\Big((\frac{\varpi}{m})^{\frac{1}{p}}\Big)|}{e^{\omega\left((\frac{\varpi}{m})^{\frac{1}{p}}\right)}}\mathcal{T}^{\nu}_{\varpi}\Big(h,1-\mathcal{R}^{\alpha};\mathcal{Z}'\Big)\right],$$

Remark 4. *From Theorem 2, the bounds for all $\mathcal{I}\mathcal{O}$s (provided in Remark 1) via all kinds of convex functions (provided in Remark 2) can be obtained.*

The following identity is useful to prove the Hadamard-type inequality:

Lemma 1. *Let* $\mathcal{Y} : [\mu, m\nu] \to \mathbb{R}$, $\mu < m\nu$, *be an exponentially* $(\alpha, h-m) - p$*-convex function. If the condition*

$$\frac{\mathcal{Y}((\varpi)^{\frac{1}{p}})}{e^{\omega((\varpi)^{\frac{1}{p}})}} = \frac{\mathcal{Y}\left(\frac{(\mu^p + m\nu^p - \varpi)^{\frac{1}{p}}}{m}\right)}{e^{\omega\left(\frac{(\mu^p + m\nu^p - \varpi)^{\frac{1}{p}}}{m}\right)}} \tag{28}$$

holds for $m \in (0,1]$, *then we have*

$$\mathcal{Y}\left(\left(\frac{\mu^p + m\nu^p}{2}\right)^{\frac{1}{p}}\right) \le \frac{\mathcal{Y}((\varpi)^{\frac{1}{p}})}{e^{\omega((\varpi)^{\frac{1}{p}})}}\left(h\left(\frac{1}{2^\alpha}\right) + mh\left(1 - \frac{1}{2^\alpha}\right)\right). \tag{29}$$

Proof. We use the following identity:

$$\left(\frac{\mu^p + m\nu^p}{2}\right)^{\frac{1}{p}} = \left[\frac{1}{2}\left(\left(\frac{\varpi - \mu^p}{m\nu^p - \mu^p} m\nu^p + \frac{m\nu^p - \varpi}{m\nu^p - \mu^p}\mu^p\right)^{\frac{1}{p}}\right)^p \right. \tag{30}$$

$$\left. + m\left(1 - \frac{1}{2}\right)\left(\left(\frac{\frac{\varpi - \mu^p}{m\nu^p - \mu^p}\mu^p + \frac{m\nu^p - \varpi}{m\nu^p - \mu^p} m\nu^p}{m}\right)^{\frac{1}{p}}\right)^p\right]^{\frac{1}{p}}.$$

By applying the exponentially $(\alpha, h-m) - p$-convexity of $\mathcal{Y}$, we obtain:

$$\mathcal{Y}\left(\left(\frac{\mu^p + m\nu^p}{2}\right)^{\frac{1}{p}}\right) \le h\left(\frac{1}{2^\alpha}\right)\frac{\mathcal{Y}\left(\left(\frac{\varpi - \mu^p}{m\nu^p - \mu^p} m\nu^p + \frac{m\nu^p - \varpi}{m\nu^p - \mu^p}\mu^p\right)^{\frac{1}{p}}\right)}{e^{\omega\left(\left(\frac{\varpi - \mu^p}{m\nu^p - \mu^p} m\nu^p + \frac{m\nu^p - \varpi}{m\nu^p - \mu^p}\mu^p\right)^{\frac{1}{p}}\right)}} \tag{31}$$

$$+ mh\left(1 - \frac{1}{2^\alpha}\right)\frac{\mathcal{Y}\left(\left(\frac{\frac{\varpi - \mu^p}{m\nu^p - \mu^p}\mu^p + \frac{m\nu^p - \varpi}{m\nu^p - \mu^p} m\nu^p}{m}\right)^{\frac{1}{p}}\right)}{e^{\omega\left(\left(\frac{\frac{\varpi - \mu^p}{m\nu^p - \mu^p}\mu^p + \frac{m\nu^p - \varpi}{m\nu^p - \mu^p} m\nu^p}{m}\right)^{\frac{1}{p}}\right)}}$$

$$= h\left(\frac{1}{2^\alpha}\right)\frac{\mathcal{Y}((\varpi)^{\frac{1}{p}})}{e^{\omega((\varpi)^{\frac{1}{p}})}} + mh\left(1 - \frac{1}{2^\alpha}\right)\frac{\mathcal{Y}\left(\frac{(\mu^p + m\nu^p - \varpi)^{\frac{1}{p}}}{m}\right)}{e^{\omega\left(\frac{(\mu^p + m\nu^p - \varpi)^{\frac{1}{p}}}{m}\right)}}.$$

By using the assumption provided in (28), the required inequality (29) is obtained. □

In the following, we provide the Hadamarad type inequality for k-$\mathcal{IO}$s via exponentially $(\alpha, h-m) - p$-convex functions:

Theorem 3. *With the same conditions on $\mathcal{Y}$, $\mathcal{Z}$, and h as in Theorem 1, and additionally if* (28) *is satisfied, then we have:*

$$\frac{\mathcal{Q}(\omega)}{\left(h\left(\frac{1}{2^{\alpha}}\right)+mh\left(1-\frac{1}{2^{\alpha}}\right)\right)}\left[\mathcal{Y}\left(\left(\frac{\mu^{p}+m\nu^{p}}{2}\right)^{\frac{1}{p}}\right)\left(\mathcal{F}_{\frac{\eta}{k},\mu^{+}}(\nu;\Phi)+\mathcal{F}_{\frac{\zeta}{k},\nu^{-}}(\mu;\Phi)\right)\right] \tag{32}$$
$$\leq\left({}^{k}_{\mathcal{Z}}\mathcal{D}^{\rho,\epsilon,\lambda,r}_{\varsigma,\eta,\varphi,\Psi,\mu^{+}}\mathcal{Y}\circ\mathcal{U}\right)(\nu;\Phi)+\left({}^{k}_{\mathcal{Z}}\mathcal{D}^{\rho,\epsilon,\lambda,r}_{\varsigma,\zeta,\varphi,\Psi,\nu^{-}}\mathcal{Y}\circ\mathcal{U}\right)(\mu;\Phi)$$
$$\leq(\nu-\mu)\Big((\mathcal{Z}(\nu)-\mathcal{Z}(\mu))^{\frac{\eta}{k}-1}E^{\rho,\epsilon,\lambda,r}_{\varsigma,\eta,\varphi,k}\left(\Psi(\mathcal{Z}(\nu)-\mathcal{Z}(\mu))^{\frac{\varsigma}{k}};\Phi\right)$$
$$+(\mathcal{Z}(\nu)-\mathcal{Z}(\mu))^{\frac{\zeta}{k}-1}E^{\rho,\epsilon,\lambda,r}_{\varsigma,\zeta,\varphi,k}\left(\Psi(\mathcal{Z}(\nu)-\mathcal{Z}(\mu))^{\frac{\varsigma}{k}};\Phi\right)\Big)$$
$$\left[\frac{\mathcal{Y}((\nu)^{\frac{1}{p}})}{e^{\omega((\nu)^{\frac{1}{p}})}}\mathcal{T}^{\mu}_{\nu}\left(h,\mathcal{R}^{\alpha};\mathcal{Z}'\right)+\frac{m\mathcal{Y}\left((\frac{\mu}{m})^{\frac{1}{p}}\right)}{e^{\omega(\frac{\mu}{m})^{\frac{1}{p}}}}\mathcal{T}^{\mu}_{\nu}\left(h,1-\mathcal{R}^{\alpha};\mathcal{Z}'\right)\right].$$

where $\mathcal{U}(\delta)=\delta^{\frac{1}{p}}$ *and* $\mathcal{Q}(\omega)=e^{\omega\mu}$ *for* $\omega\geq 0$; $\mathcal{Q}(\omega)=e^{\omega\nu}$ *for* $\omega<0$.

Proof. Under the given assumptions, the following inequalities hold:

$$(\mathcal{Z}(\varpi)-\mathcal{Z}(\mu))^{\frac{\zeta}{k}-1}E^{\rho,\epsilon,\lambda,r}_{\varsigma,\zeta,\varphi,k}\left(\Psi(\mathcal{Z}(\varpi)-\mathcal{Z}(\mu))^{\frac{\varsigma}{k}};\Phi\right)\mathcal{Z}'(\varpi) \tag{33}$$
$$\leq(\mathcal{Z}(\nu)-\mathcal{Z}(\mu))^{\frac{\zeta}{k}-1}E^{\rho,\epsilon,\lambda,r}_{\varsigma,\zeta,\varphi,k}\left(\Psi(\mathcal{Z}(\nu)-\mathcal{Z}(\mu))^{\frac{\varsigma}{k}};\Phi\right)\mathcal{Z}'(\varpi),\quad \varpi\in[\mu,\nu],$$

$$(\mathcal{Z}(\nu)-\mathcal{Z}(\varpi))^{\frac{\eta}{k}-1}E^{\rho,\epsilon,\lambda,r}_{\varsigma,\eta,\varphi,k}\left(\Psi(\mathcal{Z}(\nu)-\mathcal{Z}(\varpi))^{\frac{\varsigma}{k}};\Phi\right)\mathcal{Z}'(\varpi) \tag{34}$$
$$\leq(\mathcal{Z}(\nu)-\mathcal{Z}(\mu))^{\frac{\eta}{k}-1}E^{\rho,\epsilon,\lambda,r}_{\varsigma,\eta,\varphi,k}\left(\Psi(\mathcal{Z}(\nu)-\mathcal{Z}(\mu))^{\frac{\varsigma}{k}};\Phi\right)\mathcal{Z}'(\varpi)\quad \varpi\in[\mu,\nu].$$

By utilizing the strongly exponential $(\alpha,h-m)-p$-convexity of $\mathcal{Y}$, we obtain:

$$\mathcal{Y}((\varpi)^{\frac{1}{p}})\leq h\left(\frac{\varpi-\mu}{\nu-\mu}\right)^{\alpha}\frac{\mathcal{Y}((\nu)^{\frac{1}{p}})}{e^{\omega((\nu)^{\frac{1}{p}})}}+mh\left(1-\left(\frac{\varpi-\mu}{\nu-\mu}\right)^{\alpha}\right)\frac{\mathcal{Y}\left((\frac{\mu}{m})^{\frac{1}{p}}\right)}{e^{\omega(\frac{\mu}{m})^{\frac{1}{p}}}}. \tag{35}$$

From inequalities (33) and (35), the following inequality holds:

$$\int_{\mu}^{\nu}(\mathcal{Z}(\varpi)-\mathcal{Z}(\mu))^{\frac{\zeta}{k}-1}E^{\rho,\epsilon,\lambda,r}_{\varsigma,\zeta,\varphi,k}\left(\Psi(\mathcal{Z}(\varpi)-\mathcal{Z}(\mu))^{\frac{\varsigma}{k}};\Phi\right)\mathcal{Z}'(\varpi)\mathcal{Y}((\varpi)^{\frac{1}{p}})d\varpi$$
$$\leq(\mathcal{Z}(\nu)-\mathcal{Z}(\mu))^{\frac{\zeta}{k}-1}E^{\rho,\epsilon,\lambda,r}_{\varsigma,\zeta,\varphi,k}\left(\Psi(\mathcal{Z}(\nu)-\mathcal{Z}(\mu))^{\frac{\varsigma}{k}};\Phi\right)\left[\frac{\mathcal{Y}((\nu)^{\frac{1}{p}})}{e^{\omega((\nu)^{\frac{1}{p}})}}\right.$$
$$\left.\int_{\mu}^{\nu}h\left(\frac{\varpi-\mu}{\nu-\mu}\right)^{\alpha}\mathcal{Z}'(\varpi)d\varpi+\frac{m\mathcal{Y}\left((\frac{\mu}{m})^{\frac{1}{p}}\right)}{e^{\omega(\frac{\mu}{m})^{\frac{1}{p}}}}\int_{\mu}^{\nu}h\left(1-\left(\frac{\varpi-\mu}{\nu-\mu}\right)^{\alpha}\right)\mathcal{Z}'(\varpi)d\varpi\right].$$

By utilizing the integral operator (5) on the left-hand side and making the substitution $\mathcal{R} = (\varpi - \mu)/(\nu - \mu)$ on the right-hand side, we obtain the following:

$$\left({}_{\mathcal{Z}}^{k}\mathcal{D}^{\rho,\epsilon,\lambda,r}_{\varsigma,\zeta,\varphi,\Psi,\nu^-}\mathcal{Y}\circ\mathcal{U}\right)(\mu;\Phi) \le (\nu-\mu)(\mathcal{Z}(\nu)-\mathcal{Z}(\mu))^{\frac{\zeta}{k}-1} \tag{36}$$

$$E^{\rho,\epsilon,\lambda,r}_{\varsigma,\zeta,\varphi,k}\left(\Psi(\mathcal{Z}(\nu)-\mathcal{Z}(\mu))^{\frac{\varsigma}{k}};\Phi\right)\left[\frac{\mathcal{Y}((\nu)^{\frac{1}{p}})}{e^{\omega((\nu)^{\frac{1}{p}})}}\int_0^1 h(\mathcal{R}^{\alpha})\mathcal{Z}'(\mu+\mathcal{R}(\nu-\mu))d\mathcal{R}\right.$$

$$\left.+\frac{m\mathcal{Y}\left((\frac{\mu}{m})^{\frac{1}{p}}\right)}{e^{\omega(\frac{\mu}{m})^{\frac{1}{p}}}}\int_0^1 h(1-\mathcal{R}^{\alpha})\mathcal{Z}'(\mu+\mathcal{R}(\nu-\mu))d\mathcal{R}\right].$$

The above inequality takes the following form:

$$\begin{aligned}&\left({}_{\mathcal{Z}}^{k}\mathcal{D}^{\rho,\epsilon,\lambda,r}_{\varsigma,\zeta,\varphi,\Psi,\nu^-}\mathcal{Y}\circ\mathcal{U}\right)(\mu;\Phi)\\&\le(\nu-\mu)(\mathcal{Z}(\nu)-\mathcal{Z}(\mu))^{\frac{\zeta}{k}-1}E^{\rho,\epsilon,\lambda,r}_{\varsigma,\zeta,\varphi,k}\left(\Psi(\mathcal{Z}(\nu)-\mathcal{Z}(\mu))^{\frac{\varsigma}{k}};\Phi\right)\\&\left[\frac{\mathcal{Y}((\nu)^{\frac{1}{p}})}{e^{\omega((\nu)^{\frac{1}{p}})}}\mathcal{T}^{\mu}_{\nu}\left(h,\mathcal{R}^{\alpha};\mathcal{Z}'\right)+\frac{m\mathcal{Y}\left((\frac{\mu}{m})^{\frac{1}{p}}\right)}{e^{\omega(\frac{\mu}{m})^{\frac{1}{p}}}}\mathcal{T}^{\mu}_{\nu}\left(h,1-\mathcal{R}^{\alpha};\mathcal{Z}'\right)\right].\end{aligned}\tag{37}$$

Similarly, from inequalities (34) and (35), after simplification, the following inequality is obtained:

$$\begin{aligned}&\left({}_{\mathcal{Z}}^{k}\mathcal{D}^{\rho,\epsilon,\lambda,r}_{\varsigma,\eta,\varphi,\Psi,\mu^+}\mathcal{Y}\circ\mathcal{U}\right)(\nu;\Phi)\\&\le(\nu-\mu)(\mathcal{Z}(\nu)-\mathcal{Z}(\mu))^{\frac{\eta}{k}-1}E^{\rho,\epsilon,\lambda,r}_{\varsigma,\eta,\varphi,k}\left(\Psi(\mathcal{Z}(\nu)-\mathcal{Z}(\mu))^{\frac{\varsigma}{k}};\Phi\right)\\&\left[\frac{\mathcal{Y}((\nu)^{\frac{1}{p}})}{e^{\omega((\nu)^{\frac{1}{p}})}}\mathcal{T}^{\mu}_{\nu}\left(h,\mathcal{R}^{\alpha};\mathcal{Z}'\right)+\frac{m\mathcal{Y}\left((\frac{\mu}{m})^{\frac{1}{p}}\right)}{e^{\omega(\frac{\mu}{m})^{\frac{1}{p}}}}\mathcal{T}^{\mu}_{\nu}\left(h,1-\mathcal{R}^{\alpha};\mathcal{Z}'\right)\right].\end{aligned}\tag{38}$$

By adding the inequalities (37) and (38), we obtain:

$$\begin{aligned}&\left({}_{\mathcal{Z}}^{k}\mathcal{D}^{\rho,\epsilon,\lambda,r}_{\varsigma,\eta,\varphi,\Psi,\mu^+}\mathcal{Y}\circ\mathcal{U}\right)(\nu;\Phi)+\left({}_{\mathcal{Z}}^{k}\mathcal{D}^{\rho,\epsilon,\lambda,r}_{\varsigma,\zeta,\varphi,\Psi,\nu^-}\mathcal{Y}\circ\mathcal{U}\right)(\mu;\Phi)\\&\le(\nu-\mu)\left((\mathcal{Z}(\nu)-\mathcal{Z}(\mu))^{\frac{\eta}{k}-1}E^{\rho,\epsilon,\lambda,r}_{\varsigma,\eta,\varphi,k}\left(\Psi(\mathcal{Z}(\nu)-\mathcal{Z}(\mu))^{\frac{\varsigma}{k}};\Phi\right)\right.\\&\left.+(\mathcal{Z}(\nu)-\mathcal{Z}(\mu))^{\frac{\zeta}{k}-1}E^{\rho,\epsilon,\lambda,r}_{\varsigma,\zeta,\varphi,k}\left(\Psi(\mathcal{Z}(\nu)-\mathcal{Z}(\mu))^{\frac{\varsigma}{k}};\Phi\right)\right)\\&\left[\frac{\mathcal{Y}((\nu)^{\frac{1}{p}})}{e^{\omega((\nu)^{\frac{1}{p}})}}\mathcal{T}^{\mu}_{\nu}\left(h,\mathcal{R}^{\alpha};\mathcal{Z}'\right)+\frac{m\mathcal{Y}\left((\frac{\mu}{m})^{\frac{1}{p}}\right)}{e^{\omega(\frac{\mu}{m})^{\frac{1}{p}}}}\mathcal{T}^{\mu}_{\nu}\left(h,1-\mathcal{R}^{\alpha};\mathcal{Z}'\right)\right].\end{aligned}\tag{39}$$

Now, multiplying the inequality (29) with $(\mathcal{Z}(\varpi)-\mathcal{Z}(\mu))^{\frac{\zeta}{k}-1}E^{\rho,\epsilon,\lambda,r}_{\varsigma,\zeta,\varphi,k}\left(\Psi(\mathcal{Z}(\varpi)-\mathcal{Z}(\mu))^{\frac{\varsigma}{k}};\Phi\right)$ $\mathcal{Z}'(\varpi)$ and integrating over $[\mu,\nu]$, we have:

$$\mathcal{Y}\left(\left(\frac{\mu^p+m\nu^p}{2}\right)^{\frac{1}{p}}\right)\int_\mu^\nu(\mathcal{Z}(\varpi)-\mathcal{Z}(\mu))^{\frac{\zeta}{k}-1}E^{\rho,\epsilon,\lambda,r}_{\varsigma,\zeta,\varphi,k}\left(\Psi(\mathcal{Z}(\varpi)-\mathcal{Z}(\mu))^{\frac{\varsigma}{k}};\Phi\right)\mathcal{Z}'(\varpi)d\varpi \quad (40)$$
$$\leq\left(h\left(\frac{1}{2^\alpha}\right)+mh\left(1-\frac{1}{2^\alpha}\right)\right)\int_\mu^\nu(\mathcal{Z}(\varpi)-\mathcal{Z}(\mu))^{\frac{\zeta}{k}-1}E^{\rho,\epsilon,\lambda,r}_{\varsigma,\zeta,\varphi,k}\left(\Psi(\mathcal{Z}(\varpi)-\mathcal{Z}(\mu))^{\frac{\varsigma}{k}};\Phi\right)$$
$$\times\mathcal{Z}'(\varpi)\frac{\mathcal{Y}((\varpi)^{\frac{1}{p}})}{e^{\omega((\varpi)^{\frac{1}{p}})}}d\varpi.$$

By utilizing the integral operator from (5) and (8), we obtain:

$$\frac{\mathcal{Q}(\omega)}{\left(h\left(\frac{1}{2^\alpha}\right)+mh\left(1-\frac{1}{2^\alpha}\right)\right)}\left(\mathcal{Y}\left(\left(\frac{\mu^p+m\nu^p}{2}\right)^{\frac{1}{p}}\right)\mathcal{F}_{\frac{\zeta}{k},\nu^-}(\mu;\Phi)\right)\leq\left({}^k_{\mathcal{Z}}\mathcal{D}^{\rho,\epsilon,\lambda,r}_{\varsigma,\zeta,\varphi,\Psi,\nu^-}\mathcal{Y}\circ\mathcal{U}\right)(\mu;\Phi). \quad (41)$$

Similarly, by multiplying the inequality (29) with $(\mathcal{Z}(\nu)-\mathcal{Z}(\varpi))^{\frac{\eta}{k}-1}E^{\rho,\epsilon,\lambda,r}_{\varsigma,\eta,\varphi,k}\left(\Psi(\mathcal{Z}(\nu)-\mathcal{Z}(\varpi))^{\frac{\varsigma}{k}};\Phi\right)\mathcal{Z}'(\varpi)$ and integrating over $[\mu,\nu]$, then utilizing integral (4) and (7), we obtain:

$$\frac{\mathcal{Q}(\omega)}{\left(h\left(\frac{1}{2^\alpha}\right)+mh\left(1-\frac{1}{2^\alpha}\right)\right)}\left(\mathcal{Y}\left(\left(\frac{\mu^p+m\nu^p}{2}\right)^{\frac{1}{p}}\right)\mathcal{F}_{\frac{\eta}{k},\mu^+}(\nu;\Phi)\right)\leq\left({}^k_{\mathcal{Z}}\mathcal{D}^{\rho,\epsilon,\lambda,r}_{\varsigma,\eta,\varphi,\Psi,\mu^+}\mathcal{Y}\circ\mathcal{U}\right)(\nu;\Phi). \quad (42)$$

By adding the inequalities (41) and (42), we obtain:

$$\frac{\mathcal{Q}(\omega)}{\left(h\left(\frac{1}{2^\alpha}\right)+mh\left(1-\frac{1}{2^\alpha}\right)\right)}\left[\mathcal{Y}\left(\left(\frac{\mu^p+m\nu^p}{2}\right)^{\frac{1}{p}}\right)\left(\mathcal{F}_{\frac{\eta}{k},\mu^+}(\nu;\Phi)+\mathcal{F}_{\frac{\zeta}{k},\nu^-}(\mu;\Phi)\right)\right] \quad (43)$$
$$\leq\left({}^k_{\mathcal{Z}}\mathcal{D}^{\rho,\epsilon,\lambda,r}_{\varsigma,\eta,\varphi,\Psi,\mu^+}\mathcal{Y}\circ\mathcal{U}\right)(\nu;\Phi)+\left({}^k_{\mathcal{Z}}\mathcal{D}^{\rho,\epsilon,\lambda,r}_{\varsigma,\zeta,\varphi,\Psi,\nu^-}\mathcal{Y}\circ\mathcal{U}\right)(\mu;\Phi).$$

From inequalities (39) and (43), the required inequality (32) is obtained. □

Corollary 3. *For $\eta=\zeta$ in (32), the following inequality is valid:*

$$\frac{\mathcal{Q}(\omega)}{\left(h\left(\frac{1}{2^\alpha}\right)+mh\left(1-\frac{1}{2^\alpha}\right)\right)}\left[\mathcal{Y}\left(\left(\frac{\mu^p+m\nu^p}{2}\right)^{\frac{1}{p}}\right)\left(\mathcal{F}_{\frac{\eta}{k},\mu^+}(\nu;\Phi)+\mathcal{F}_{\frac{\eta}{k},\nu^-}(\mu;\Phi)\right)\right] \quad (44)$$
$$\leq\left({}^k_{\mathcal{Z}}\mathcal{D}^{\rho,\epsilon,\lambda,r}_{\varsigma,\eta,\varphi,\Psi,\mu^+}\mathcal{Y}\circ\mathcal{U}\right)(\nu;\Phi)+\left({}^k_{\mathcal{Z}}\mathcal{D}^{\rho,\epsilon,\lambda,r}_{\varsigma,\eta,\varphi,\Psi,\nu^-}\mathcal{Y}\circ\mathcal{U}\right)(\mu;\Phi)$$
$$\leq(\nu-\mu)(\mathcal{Z}(\nu)-\mathcal{Z}(\mu))^{\frac{\eta}{k}-1}E^{\rho,\epsilon,\lambda,r}_{\varsigma,\eta,\varphi,k}\left(\Psi(\mathcal{Z}(\nu)-\mathcal{Z}(\mu))^{\frac{\varsigma}{k}};\Phi\right)$$
$$\left[\frac{\mathcal{Y}((\nu)^{\frac{1}{p}})}{e^{\omega((\nu)^{\frac{1}{p}})}}\mathcal{T}^\mu_\nu\left(h,\mathcal{R}^\alpha;\mathcal{Z}'\right)+\frac{m\mathcal{Y}\left(\left(\frac{\mu}{m}\right)^{\frac{1}{p}}\right)}{e^{\omega(\frac{\mu}{m})^{\frac{1}{p}}}}\mathcal{T}^\mu_\nu\left(h,1-\mathcal{R}^\alpha;\mathcal{Z}'\right)\right].$$

Remark 5. *From Theorem 3, Hadamard-type inequalities for all kinds of $\mathcal{IO}$s (provided in Remark 1) for all kinds of convex functions (provided in Remark 2) can be obtained.*

3. Concluding Remarks

In this article, we have investigated the bounds of k-$\mathcal{IO}$s. These bounds were achieved by applying thedefinition of exponentially $(\alpha,h-m)-p$-convex functions. The presented results provide a large number of new bounds of several $\mathcal{IO}$s for various kinds of convexities using convenient substitutions. Further, an identity is established to prove the Hadamard-type inequality for k-$\mathcal{IO}$s via exponentially $(\alpha, h-m)-p$-convex functions.

Author Contributions: Conceptualization, G.F., H.S.K., F.M.O.T., J.-S.R. and S.Z.; investigation, H.S.K.; validation, G.F., H.S.K., F.M.O.T., J.-S.R. and S.Z.; formal analysis, S.Z.; writing—original draft, G.F. and H.S.K.; writing—review and editing, G.F., H.S.K., F.M.O.T., J.-S.R. and S.Z. All authors have read and agreed to the published version of the manuscript.

Funding: This research received no external funding.

Data Availability Statement: Not applicable.

Acknowledgments: The research work of the fourth author was supported by a National Research Foundation of Korea (NRF) grant funded by the Korean government (MSIT) (No. NRF-2022R1A2C2004874), the Korean Institute of Energy Technology Evaluation and Planning (KETEP), and the Ministry of Trade, Industry, and Energy (MOTIE) of the Republic of Korea (No. 20214000000280). The research work of the third author is supported by a grant under project number RSP2023R440 from King Saud University, Riyadh, Saudi Arabia.

Conflicts of Interest: The authors declare no conflict of interest.

References

1. Mittag-Leffler, G. Sur la nouvelle fonction $E(x)$. *C. R. Acad. Sci. Paris.* **1903**, *137*, 554–558.
2. Wiman, A. Uber den fundamentalsatz in der Teorie der Funktionen $E(x)$. *Acta Math.* **1905**, *29*, 191–201. [CrossRef]
3. Shukla, A.K.; Prajapati, J.C. On a generalization of Mittag-Leffler function and its properties. *J. Math. Anal. Appl.* **2007**, *336*, 797–811. [CrossRef]
4. Srivastava, H.M.; Kumar, A.; Das, S.; Mehrez, K. Geometric properties of a certain class of Mittag–Leffler-type functions. *Fractal Fract.* **2020**, *6*, 54. [CrossRef]
5. Rainville, E.D. *Special Functions*; Macmillan: New York, NY, USA, 1960.
6. Almoneef, A.A.; Barakat, M.A.; Hyder, A.-A. Analysis of the fractional HIV model under proportional Hadamard-Caputo operators. *Fractal Fract.* **2023**, *7*, 220. [CrossRef]
7. Saadeh, R.; Abdoon, M.A.; Qazza, A.; Berir, M. A numerical solution of generalized Caputo fractional initial value problems. *Fractal Fract.* **2023**, *7*, 332. [CrossRef]
8. Cheng, X.; Zheng, Y.; Zhang, X. Arbitrage in the Hermite binomial market. *Fractal Fract.* **2022**, *6*, 702. [CrossRef]
9. Chaudhry, M.A.; Qadir, A.; Rafique, M.; Zubair, S.M. Extension of Euler's beta function. *J. Comput. Appl. Math.* **1997**, *78*, 19–32. [CrossRef]
10. Diaz, R.; Pariguan, E. On hypergeometric functions and Pochhammer k-symbol. *Divulg. Matemticas* **2007**, *15*, 179–192.
11. Mubeen, S.; Habibullah, G.M. k-fractional integrals and applications. *Int. J. Contemp. Math. Sci.* **2012**, *7*, 89–94.
12. Farid, G.; Javed, A. On Hadamard and Fejer-Hadamard inequalities for Caputo k-fractional derivatives. *Int. J. Nonlinear Anal. Appl.* **2018**, *9*, 69–81.
13. Habib, S.; Mubeen, S.; Naeem, M.N. Chebyshev type integral inequalities for generalized k-fractional conformable integrals. *J. Inequal. Spec. Func.* **2018**, *9*, 53–65.
14. Sarikaya, M.Z.; Dahmani, M.; Kiris, M.E.; Ahmad, F. (k,s)-Riemann-Liouville fractional integral and applications. *Hacet. J. Math. Stat.* **2016**, *45*, 77–89. [CrossRef]
15. Zhang, Z.; Farid, G.; Mehmood, S.; Nonlaopon, K.; Yan, T. Generalized k-fractional integral operators associated with Pólya-Szegö and Chebyshev types inequalities. *Fractal Fract.* **2022**, *6*, 90. [CrossRef]
16. Mehmood, S.; Farid, G.; Khan, K.A.; Yussouf, M. New fractional Hadamard and Fejér-Hadamard inequalities associated with exponentially (h,m)-convex function. *Eng. Appl. Sci. Lett.* **2020**, *3*, 9–18. [CrossRef]
17. Andrić, M.; Farid, G.; Pečarić, J. A further extension of Mittag-Leffler function. *Fract. Calc. Appl. Anal.* **2018**, *21*, 1377–1395. [CrossRef]
18. Salim, T.O.; Faraj, A.W. A generalization of Mittag-Leffler function and integral operator associated with integral calculus. *J. Frac. Calc. Appl.* **2012**, *3*, 1–13.
19. Rahman, G.; Baleanu, D.; Qurashi, M.A.; Purohit, S.D.; Mubeen, S.; Arshad, M. The extended Mittag-Leffler function via fractional calculus. *J. Nonlinear Sci. Appl.* **2017**, *10*, 4244–4253. [CrossRef]
20. Srivastava, H.M.; Tomovski, Z. Fractional calculus with an integral operator containing generalized Mittag-Leffler function in the kernal. *Appl. Math. Comput.* **2009**, *211*, 198–210. [CrossRef]
21. Prabhakar, T.R. A singular integral equation with a generalized Mittag-Leffler function in the kernel. *Yokohama Math. J.* **1971**, *19*, 7–15.
22. Chen, H.; Katugampola, U.N. Hermite-Hadamard and Hermite-Hadamard-Fejér type inequalities for generalized fractional integrals. *J. Math. Anal. Appl.* **2017**, *446*, 1274–1291. [CrossRef]

23. Kilbas, A.A.; Srivastava, H.M. Trujillo, J.J. *Theory and Applications of Fractional Differential Equations*; North-Holland Mathematics Studies, 204; Elsevier: New York, NY, USA; London, UK, 2006.
24. Khan, T.U.; Khan, M.A. Generalized conformable fractional operators. *J. Comput. Appl. Math.* **2019**, *346*, 378–389. [CrossRef]
25. Jarad, F.; Ugurlu, E.; Abdeljawad, T.; Baleanu, D. On a new class of fractional operators. *Adv. Differ. Equ.* **2017**, *2017*, 247. [CrossRef]
26. Kwun, Y.C.; Farid, G.; Nazeer, W.; Ullah, S.; Kang, S.M. Generalized Riemann-Liouville *k*-fractional integrals associated with Ostrowski type inequalities and error bounds of Hadamard inequalities. *IEEE Access* **2018**, *6*, 64946–64953. [CrossRef]
27. Zhang, X.; Farid, G.; Yasmeen, H.; Nonlaopon, K. Some generalized formulas of Hadamard-type fractional integral inequalities. *J. Funct. Spaces.* **2022**, *2022*, 12. [CrossRef]
28. Farid, G. Some Riemann-Liouville fractional integral inequalities for convex functions. *J. Anal.* **2019**, *27*, 1095–1102. [CrossRef]
29. Mehmood, S.; Farid, G. *m*-Convex functions associated with bounds of *k*-fractional integrals. *Adv. Inequal. Appl.* **2020**, *2020*, 20.
30. Yu, T.; Farid, G.; Mahreen, K.;Jung, Chahn Y.; Shim, S.H. On generalized strongly convex functions and unified integral operators. *Math. Probl. Eng.* **2021**, *2021*, 6695781. [CrossRef]

fractal and fractional

MDPI

Article

Certain New Reverse Hölder- and Minkowski-Type Inequalities for Modified Unified Generalized Fractional Integral Operators with Extended Unified Mittag–Leffler Functions

Wengui Yang [1,2]

[1] Normal School, Sanmenxia Polytechnic, Sanmenxia 472000, China; yangwg8088@163.com

[2] Mathematics Teaching and Research Office, Sanmenxia College of Applied Engineering, Sanmenxia 472000, China

Abstract: In this article, we obtain certain novel reverse Hölder- and Minkowski-type inequalities for modified unified generalized fractional integral operators (FIOs) with extended unified Mittag–Leffler functions (MLFs). The predominant results of this article generalize and extend the existing fractional Hölder- and Minkowski-type integral inequalities in the literature. As applications, the reverse versions of weighted Radon-, Jensen- and power mean-type inequalities for modified unified generalized FIOs with extended unified MLFs are also investigated.

Keywords: Hölder's inequalities; Minkowski's inequalities; weighted Radon-type inequalities; Jensen-type inequalities; power mean-type inequalities; fractional integral operators

MSC: 26D10; 26A33

Citation: Yang, W. Certain New Reverse Hölder- and Minkowski-Type Inequalities for Modified Unified Generalized Fractional Integral Operators with Extended Unified Mittag–Leffler Functions. *Fractal Fract.* **2023**, *7*, 613. https://doi.org/10.3390/fractalfract7080613

Academic Editors: Ivanka Stamova, Eze Nwaeze and Seth Kermausuor

Received: 4 July 2023
Revised: 5 August 2023
Accepted: 8 August 2023
Published: 9 August 2023

1. Introduction

Let us begin with the following well-known Young inequality [1,2]:

$$\mathcal{A}^{1-\mathrm{v}}\mathcal{B}^{\mathrm{v}} \leqslant (1-\mathrm{v})\mathcal{A} + \mathrm{v}\mathcal{B} \quad \text{for } \forall \mathcal{A}, \mathcal{B} > 0 \text{ and } \mathrm{v} \in [0,1]. \tag{1}$$

The foregoing formula (1) is also sometimes known as v-weighted arithmetic-geometric mean inequality. For example, by employing the Kantorovich constant, Zuo et al. [3] showed the refined version of the above classical Young inequality. In the paper [4], Sababheh and Choi obtained some multiple refined versions of Young-type inequalities containing real numbers and matrix operators. By making use of Marichev-Saigo-Maeda fractional integral operators (FIOs), the author [5] obtained some new weighted Young-type Marichev-Saigo-Maeda FIO inequalities. In 2002, Tominaga [6] established the reverse inequality of Young with Specht's ratio as

$$(1-\mathrm{v})\mathcal{A} + \mathrm{v}\mathcal{B} \leqslant S(\mathcal{A}/\mathcal{B})\mathcal{A}^{1-\mathrm{v}}\mathcal{B}^{\mathrm{v}} \quad \text{for } \forall \mathcal{A}, \mathcal{B} > 0 \text{ and } \mathrm{v} \in [0,1], \tag{2}$$

where $S(h)$ stands for the Specht's ratio given by $S(h) = h^{1/(h-1)}/(e \log h^{1/(h-1)})$ for $h > 0$ and $h \neq 1$. For some characteristics of Specht's ratio, the reader can see the reference [6]. In the same paper [6], Tominaga showed the following converse difference inequality for the Young inequality

$$(1-\mathrm{v})\mathcal{A} + \mathrm{v}\mathcal{B} - \mathcal{A}^{1-\mathrm{v}}\mathcal{B}^{\mathrm{v}} \leqslant L(\mathcal{A}, \mathcal{B}) \log S(\mathcal{A}/\mathcal{B}) \quad \text{for } \forall \mathcal{A}, \mathcal{B} > 0 \text{ and } \mathrm{v} \in [0,1], \tag{3}$$

where $L(*, \star)$ represents the logarithmic mean defined by $L(x,y) = (y-x)/(\log y - \log x)$, $x \neq y$ and $L(x,x) \equiv x$ for two positive real constants x and y.

In 2012, Furuichi [7] presented the following refined Young inequalities associating v-weighted geometric mean with v-weighted arithmetic mean:

$$\mathcal{A}^{1-\mathrm{v}}\mathcal{B}^{\mathrm{v}} \leqslant S((\mathcal{A}/\mathcal{B})^{\mathrm{r}})\mathcal{A}^{1-\mathrm{v}}\mathcal{B}^{\mathrm{v}} \leqslant (1-\mathrm{v})\mathcal{A} + \mathrm{v}\mathcal{B} \text{ for } \forall \mathcal{A}, \mathcal{B} > 0, \tag{4}$$

where $\mathrm{v} \in [0,1]$, $\mathrm{r} = \min\{\mathrm{v}, 1-\mathrm{v}\}$.

For $1/\mathrm{p} + 1/\mathrm{q} = 1$ with $\mathrm{p} > 1$, $\mathrm{r} = \min\{1/\mathrm{p}, 1/\mathrm{q}\}$, the above inequalities (2), (3) and (4) can be represented as

$$\mathcal{A}^{\frac{1}{\mathrm{p}}}\mathcal{B}^{\frac{1}{\mathrm{q}}} \leqslant S\left(\left(\frac{\mathcal{A}}{\mathcal{B}}\right)^{\mathrm{r}}\right)\mathcal{A}^{\frac{1}{\mathrm{p}}}\mathcal{B}^{\frac{1}{\mathrm{q}}} \leqslant \frac{\mathcal{A}}{\mathrm{p}} + \frac{\mathcal{B}}{\mathrm{q}} \leqslant S\left(\frac{\mathcal{A}}{\mathcal{B}}\right)\mathcal{A}^{\frac{1}{\mathrm{p}}}\mathcal{B}^{\frac{1}{\mathrm{q}}} \text{ for } \forall \mathcal{A}, \mathcal{B} > 0,\ \mathrm{v} \in [0,1], \tag{5}$$

$$\frac{\mathcal{A}}{\mathrm{p}} + \frac{\mathcal{B}}{\mathrm{q}} - \mathcal{A}^{\frac{1}{\mathrm{p}}}\mathcal{B}^{\frac{1}{\mathrm{q}}} \leqslant L(\mathcal{A}, \mathcal{B}) \log S\left(\frac{\mathcal{A}}{\mathcal{B}}\right) \text{ for } \forall \mathcal{A}, \mathcal{B} > 0 \text{ and } \mathrm{v} \in [0,1]. \tag{6}$$

The famous classical Hölder's and Minkowski's inequalities declares that (see [1,2])

$$\sum_{i=1}^{n} \mathfrak{A}_i \mathfrak{B}_i \leqslant \left(\sum_{i=1}^{n} \mathfrak{A}_i^{\mathrm{p}}\right)^{\frac{1}{\mathrm{p}}} \left(\sum_{i=1}^{n} \mathfrak{B}_i^{\mathrm{q}}\right)^{\frac{1}{\mathrm{q}}}, \tag{7}$$

$$\left(\sum_{i=1}^{n} (\mathfrak{A}_i + \mathfrak{B}_i)^{\mathrm{p}}\right)^{\frac{1}{\mathrm{p}}} \leqslant \left(\sum_{i=1}^{n} \mathfrak{A}_i^{\mathrm{p}}\right)^{\frac{1}{\mathrm{p}}} + \left(\sum_{i=1}^{n} \mathfrak{B}_i^{\mathrm{q}}\right)^{\frac{1}{\mathrm{q}}}, \tag{8}$$

where $1/\mathrm{p} + 1/\mathrm{q} = 1$ with $\mathrm{p} > 1$, $\{\mathfrak{A}_i\}_{i=1}^{n}$ and $\{\mathfrak{B}_i\}_{i=1}^{n}$ are nonnegative real sequences.

The integral analogues of the preceding Hölder's inequality (7) and Minkowski's inequality (8) are given as

$$\int_a^b \mathfrak{F}(x)\mathfrak{G}(x)dx \leqslant \left(\int_a^b \mathfrak{F}^{\mathrm{p}}(x)dx\right)^{\frac{1}{\mathrm{p}}} \left(\int_a^b \mathfrak{G}^{\mathrm{q}}(x)dx\right)^{\frac{1}{\mathrm{q}}}, \tag{9}$$

$$\left(\int_a^b (\mathfrak{F}(x) + \mathfrak{G}(x))^{\mathrm{p}}dx\right)^{\frac{1}{\mathrm{p}}} \leqslant \left(\int_a^b \mathfrak{F}^{\mathrm{p}}(x)dx\right)^{\frac{1}{\mathrm{p}}} + \left(\int_a^b \mathfrak{G}^{\mathrm{q}}(x)dx\right)^{\frac{1}{\mathrm{q}}}, \tag{10}$$

where $1/\mathrm{p} + 1/\mathrm{q} = 1$ with $\mathrm{p} > 1$, $\mathfrak{F}$ and $\mathfrak{G}$ express two nonnegative continuous functions on $[a, b]$. The mentioned sum forms (7) and (8) and integral analogs (9) and (10) of Hölder's and Minkowski's inequalities have attracted the attention of a large number of scholars. For instance, Manjegani [8] presented some extensions of Hölder-type trace inequalities for operators. By employing the fractional quantum integrals, Yang [9] gave some fractional quantum Hölder- and Minkowski-type integral inequalities. Based on the local FIOs, Chen et al. [10] investigated the Hölder-type functional inequalities and the reverse version. Furthermore, Minkowski- and Dresher-type inequalities for local FIOs were also presented. By means of the generalized proportional FIOs, Rahman et al. [11] introduced reverse nonlocal fractional Minkowski-type inequalities and some related inequalities.

In 2016, using Specht's ratio, Zhao and Cheung [12] investigated a new reverse version of the foregoing Hölder's inequality. They proved that the following inequality held for $1/\mathrm{p} + 1/\mathrm{q} = 1$ with $\mathrm{p} > 1$,

$$\left(\int_a^b \mathfrak{F}^{\mathrm{p}}(x)dx\right)^{\frac{1}{\mathrm{p}}} \left(\int_a^b \mathfrak{G}^{\mathrm{q}}(x)dx\right)^{\frac{1}{\mathrm{q}}} \leqslant \int_a^b S\left(\frac{Y\mathfrak{F}^{\mathrm{p}}(x)}{X\mathfrak{G}^{\mathrm{q}}(x)}\right)\mathfrak{F}(x)\mathfrak{G}(x)dx, \tag{11}$$

where $\mathfrak{F}$ and $\mathfrak{G}$ demonstrate two continuous positive functions on $[a, b]$,

$$X = \int_a^b \mathfrak{F}^{\mathrm{p}}(x)dx \quad \text{and} \quad Y = \int_a^b \mathfrak{G}^{\mathrm{q}}(x)dx. \tag{12}$$

By substituting $\mathfrak{F}, g$ for $\mathfrak{F}^{\mathbb{p}}, g^{\mathbb{q}}$, respectively, the inequality (12) can be given as

$$\left(\int_a^b \mathfrak{F}(x)dx\right)^{\frac{1}{\mathbb{p}}}\left(\int_a^b \mathfrak{G}(x)dx\right)^{\frac{1}{\mathbb{q}}} \leqslant \int_a^b S\left(\frac{Y\mathfrak{F}(x)}{X\mathfrak{G}(x)}\right)\mathfrak{F}^{\frac{1}{\mathbb{p}}}(x)\mathfrak{G}^{\frac{1}{\mathbb{q}}}(x)dx, \tag{13}$$

where $1/\mathbb{p}+1/\mathbb{q}=1$ with $\mathbb{p}>1$, $\mathfrak{F}$ and $\mathfrak{G}$ stand for two continuous positive functions on $[a,b]$,

$$X = \int_a^b \mathfrak{F}(x)dx \quad \text{and} \quad Y = \int_a^b \mathfrak{G}(x)dx. \tag{14}$$

Based on Specht's ratio and the diamond-α integral on an arbitrary time scale, El-Deeb et al. [13] obtained some new reverse versions of Hölder-type inequalities on an arbitrary time scale, which can be seen as the extensions of the inequalities (11) and (13).

In 2020, Benaissa and Budak [14] improved the reverse version of the Hölder's inequality mentioned above. They showed that, for $\hbar, \ell > 0$, $1/\mathbb{p}+1/\mathbb{q}=1$ with $\mathbb{p}>1$,

$$\left(\int_a^b w(x)\mathfrak{F}^{\hbar}(x)dx\right)^{\frac{1}{\mathbb{p}}}\left(\int_a^b w(x)\mathfrak{G}^{\ell}(x)dx\right)^{\frac{1}{\mathbb{q}}} \leqslant \left(\frac{\mathbb{M}}{\mathbb{m}}\right)^{\frac{1}{\mathbb{p}\mathbb{q}}}\int_a^b w(x)\mathfrak{F}^{\frac{\hbar}{\mathbb{p}}}(x)\mathfrak{G}^{\frac{\ell}{\mathbb{q}}}(x)dx, \tag{15}$$

where $\mathfrak{F}$ and g stand for two continuous positive functions on $[a,b]$ satisfying $0<\mathbb{m}\leqslant \mathfrak{F}^{\hbar}(x)/\mathfrak{G}^{\ell}(x)\leqslant \mathbb{M}$ for all $x\in[a,b]$, and w is continuous positive weight function. When $w(x)=1$, Zhao and Cheung [12] presented the special case of the above reverse Hölder-type inequality (15). Agarwal et al. [15], Yin and Qi [16], and Zakarya et al. [17] considered the reverse Hölder-type inequalities for Δ-integral and diamond-α integral on an arbitrary time scales similar to the inequality (15), respectively. In 2022, using the diamond-α integral on an arbitrary time scale and introducing two parameters, Benaissa [18] obtained a generalized form of the anterior reverse Hölder's inequality.

In 2010, Set et al. [19] investigated the new reverse analog of a Minkowski-type inequality and the related result. They showed that, for $1\leqslant\mathbb{p}$, f and g are continuous positive functions on $[a,b]$ satisfying $0<\mathbb{m}\leqslant\mathfrak{F}(t)/\mathfrak{G}(t)\leqslant\mathbb{M}$ for all $t\in[a,b]$, then

$$\left(\int_a^b \mathfrak{F}^{\mathbb{p}}(x)dx\right)^{\frac{1}{\mathbb{p}}}+\left(\int_a^b \mathfrak{G}^{\mathbb{p}}(x)dx\right)^{\frac{1}{\mathbb{p}}} \leqslant \mathbb{c}_1\left(\int_a^b (\mathfrak{F}(x)+\mathfrak{G}(x))^{\mathbb{p}}dx\right)^{\frac{1}{\mathbb{p}}}, \tag{16}$$

$$\left(\int_a^b \mathfrak{F}^{\mathbb{p}}(x)dx\right)^{\frac{2}{\mathbb{p}}}+\left(\int_a^b \mathfrak{G}^{\mathbb{p}}(x)dx\right)^{\frac{2}{\mathbb{p}}} \geqslant \mathbb{c}_2\left(\int_a^b \mathfrak{F}^{\mathbb{p}}(x)dx\right)^{\frac{1}{\mathbb{p}}}\left(\int_a^b \mathfrak{G}^{\mathbb{p}}(x)dx\right)^{\frac{1}{\mathbb{p}}}, \tag{17}$$

where

$$\mathbb{c}_1 = \frac{\mathbb{M}(\mathbb{m}+1)+(\mathbb{M}+1)}{(\mathbb{m}+1)(\mathbb{M}+1)} \quad \text{and} \quad \mathbb{c}_2 = \frac{(\mathbb{m}+1)(\mathbb{M}+1)}{\mathbb{M}}-2. \tag{18}$$

Based on the Riemann–Liouville FIOs, Zoubir [20] considered the reverse Minkowski-type fractional integral inequalities similar to the inequalities (16) and (18). Later, Chinchane and Pachpatte [21] and Taf and Brahim [22], Chinchane and Pachpatte [23], Chinchane [24], Sousa and Oliveira [25], Rashid [26], and Aljaaidi et al. [27] investigated the reverse fractional Minkowski's inequalities for the Hadamard FIOs, Saigo FIOs, generalized k-FIOs, Katugampola FIOs, generalized $\mathcal{K}$-FIOs and proportional FIOs, respectively.

In this paper, inspired by the mentioned papers, we will consider certain new reverse Hölder- and Minkowski-type inequalities for modified unified generalized FIOs with extended unified Mittag–Leffler functions (MLFs). The principal results of this article generalize and extend the existing fractional Hölder- and Minkowski-type integral inequalities in the literature. As applications, the reverse analogues of weighted Radon-, Jensen- and power mean-type inequalities for modified unified generalized FIOs with extended unified MLFs are also given.

2. Preliminaries

In this section, we will first present the generalized Q function, which can be seen as the generalization of the canonical MLF.

Definition 1 ([28]). *Let $Q^{\lambda,\rho,\theta,k,n}_{\alpha,\beta,\gamma,\delta,\mu,\nu}(\cdot;\cdot,\cdot)$ be the generalized Q function defined by*

$$Q^{\lambda,\rho,\theta,k,n}_{\alpha,\beta,\gamma,\delta,\mu,\nu}(t;\underline{\mathscr{A}},\underline{\mathscr{B}}) = \sum_{l=0}^{\infty} \frac{\prod_{i=1}^{n} B(\mathscr{B}_i,l)(\lambda)_{\rho l}(\theta)_{kl}t^l}{\prod_{i=1}^{n} B(\mathscr{A}_i,l)(\gamma)_{\delta l}(\mu)_{\nu l}\Gamma(\alpha l+\beta)}, \tag{19}$$

where $k \in (0,1) \cup \mathbb{N}$, the generalized Pochhammer symbol $(\lambda)_{\rho l} = (\Gamma(\lambda+\rho l)/\Gamma(\lambda))$, $\Gamma(\cdot)$ and $B(\cdot,\cdot)$ denotes the well-known gamma function and beta function, respectively, $\underline{\mathscr{A}} = (\mathscr{A}_1,\mathscr{A}_2,\cdots,\mathscr{A}_n)$, $\underline{\mathscr{B}} = (\mathscr{B}_1,\mathscr{B}_2,\cdots,\mathscr{B}_n)$, $\alpha,\beta,\gamma,\delta,\mu,\nu,\lambda,\rho,\theta,\mathscr{A}_i,\mathscr{B}_i \in \mathbb{C}$, $\min\{\mathscr{R}(\alpha),\mathscr{R}(\beta),\mathscr{R}(\gamma),\mathscr{R}(\delta),\mathscr{R}(\lambda),\mathscr{R}(\theta),\mathscr{R}(\rho)\} > 0$, and $\mathscr{R}(\alpha)$ demonstrates the real part of complex number α.

Based on the generalized Q function above, Zhou et al. [29] presented the following generalized FIOs.

Definition 2 ([29]). *The generalized FIOs ${}_QI^{\omega,\lambda,\rho,\theta,k,n}_{u^+,\alpha,\beta,\gamma,\delta,\mu,\nu}\psi(x;\underline{\mathscr{A}},\underline{\mathscr{B}})$ and ${}_QI^{\omega,\lambda,\rho,\theta,k,n}_{v^-,\alpha,\beta,\gamma,\delta,\mu,\nu}\psi(x;\underline{\mathscr{A}},\underline{\mathscr{B}})$ with the generalized Q function (19) are introduced as*

$${}_QI^{\omega,\lambda,\rho,\theta,k,n}_{u^+,\alpha,\beta,\gamma,\delta,\mu,\nu}\psi(x;\underline{\mathscr{A}},\underline{\mathscr{B}}) = \int_u^x (x-s)^{\beta-1} Q^{\lambda,\rho,\theta,k,n}_{\alpha,\beta,\gamma,\delta,\mu,\nu}(\omega(x-s)^{\alpha};\underline{\mathscr{A}},\underline{\mathscr{B}})\psi(s)ds, \tag{20}$$

$${}_QI^{\omega,\lambda,\rho,\theta,k,n}_{v^-,\alpha,\beta,\gamma,\delta,\mu,\nu}\psi(x;\underline{\mathscr{A}},\underline{\mathscr{B}}) = \int_x^v (s-x)^{\beta-1} Q^{\lambda,\rho,\theta,k,n}_{\alpha,\beta,\gamma,\delta,\mu,\nu}(\omega(s-x)^{\alpha};\underline{\mathscr{A}},\underline{\mathscr{B}})\psi(s)ds. \tag{21}$$

In 2018, Andrić et al. [30] first introduced an extended generalized MLF as follows.

Definition 3 ([30]). *Assume that $\alpha,\beta,\gamma,\lambda,\theta \in \mathbb{C}$, $\min\{\mathscr{R}(\alpha),\mathscr{R}(\beta),\mathscr{R}(\gamma),\mathscr{R}(\lambda),\mathscr{R}(\theta)\} > 0$, $\mathscr{R}(\theta) > \mathscr{R}(\lambda)$ and $0 < k \leq r + \mathscr{R}(\alpha)$ for $p \geq 0$, $r > 0$. Then, define the extended generalized MLF $E^{\lambda,\theta,k,r}_{\alpha,\beta,\gamma}(t;p)$ by the following series*

$$E^{\lambda,\theta,k,r}_{\alpha,\beta,\gamma}(t;p) = \sum_{l=0}^{\infty} \frac{B_p(\gamma+lk,\theta-\lambda)}{B(\lambda,\theta-\lambda)} \frac{(\theta)_{lk}}{(\gamma)_{lr}} \frac{t^n}{\Gamma(\alpha l+\beta)}, \tag{22}$$

where, $\min\{\mathscr{R}(x),\mathscr{R}(y),\mathscr{R}(p)\} > 0$, $B_p(*,\star)$ denotes a generalization of the beta function by

$$B_p(x,y) = \int_0^1 s^{x-1}(1-s)^{y-1}e^{-\frac{p}{s(1-s)}}ds. \tag{23}$$

Second, Andrić et al. [30] gave the following extended generalized FIOs with the extended generalized MLF.

Definition 4 ([30]). *The extended generalized FIOs $\varepsilon^{\omega,\lambda,\theta,k,r}_{u^+,\alpha,\beta,\gamma}\psi(x;p)$ and $\varepsilon^{\omega,\lambda,\theta,k,r}_{v^-,\alpha,\beta,\gamma,\delta,\mu,\nu}\psi(x;p)$ with the above extended generalized MLF (22) are presented by the following forms*

$$\varepsilon^{\omega,\lambda,\theta,k,r}_{u^+,\alpha,\beta,\gamma}\psi(x;p) = \int_u^x (x-s)^{\beta-1} E^{\lambda,\theta,k,r}_{\alpha,\beta,\gamma}(\omega(x-s)^{\alpha};p)\psi(s)ds, \tag{24}$$

$$\varepsilon^{\omega,\lambda,\theta,k,r}_{v^-,\alpha,\beta,\gamma}\psi(x;p) = \int_x^v (s-x)^{\beta-1} E^{\lambda,\theta,k,r}_{\alpha,\beta,\gamma}(\omega(s-x)^{\alpha};p)\psi(s)ds. \tag{25}$$

By employing the extended generalized MLF above, Farid [31,32] introduced the following unified FIOs with regard to an increasing function.

Definition 5 ([31,32]). *Suppose that $\psi,\xi : [u,v] \to \mathbb{R}$, $0 < u < v$, are two continuous functions so that ψ is positive satisfying $\psi \in L_1[u,v]$, and ξ is strictly increasing and differentiable. Also let ϕ be a positive* *function so that ϕ/x be an increasing on $[u,+\infty)$ and $\omega,\alpha,\beta,\gamma,\lambda,\theta\in\mathbb{C}$, $\min\{\mathscr{R}(\alpha),\mathscr{R}(\beta),\mathscr{R}(\gamma),\mathscr{R}(\lambda),\mathscr{R}(\theta)\}>0$, $\mathscr{R}(\theta)>\mathscr{R}(\lambda)$ with $p\geq 0$, $r>0$ and $0<k\leq r+\mathscr{R}(\alpha)$. Then, for $x\in[u,v]$, the left and right-side unified FIOs $\left({}^{\phi}_{\xi}F^{\omega,\lambda,\theta,k,r}_{u^+,\alpha,\beta,\gamma}\psi\right)(x;p)$ and $\left({}^{\phi}_{\xi}F^{\omega,\lambda,\theta,k,r}_{v^-,\alpha,\beta,\gamma}\psi\right)(x;p)$ are introduced by*

$$\left({}^{\phi}_{\xi}F^{\omega,\lambda,\theta,k,r}_{u^+,\alpha,\beta,\gamma}\psi\right)(x;p)=\int_u^x\frac{\phi(\xi(x)-\xi(s))}{\xi(x)-\xi(s)}E^{\lambda,\theta,k,r}_{\alpha,\beta,\gamma}(\omega(\xi(x)-\xi(s))^{\alpha};p)\psi(s)d(\xi(s)),\tag{26}$$

$$\left({}^{\phi}_{\xi}F^{\omega,\lambda,\theta,k,r}_{v^-,\alpha,\beta,\gamma}\psi\right)(x;p)=\int_x^v\frac{\phi(\xi(s)-\xi(x))}{\xi(s)-\xi(x)}E^{\lambda,\theta,k,r}_{\alpha,\beta,\gamma}(\omega(\xi(s)-\xi(x))^{\alpha};p)\psi(s)d(\xi(s)).\tag{27}$$

In 2005, Raina gave the following definition of Mittag–Leffler-like function (MLLF).

Definition 6 ([33]). *Let $\mathcal{E}^{\sigma,k}_{\rho,\lambda}(x)$ and $\Gamma_k(\varrho)$ be the MLLF and k-gamma function introduced by*

$$\mathcal{E}^{\sigma,k}_{\rho,\lambda}(x)=\sum_{n=0}^{\infty}\frac{\sigma(n)x^n}{k\Gamma_k(\rho kn+\lambda)},\ \rho,\lambda>0,\ \text{and}\ \Gamma_k(\varrho)=\int_0^{\infty}\exp\left(-\frac{t^k}{k}\right)t^{\varrho-1}dt,\tag{28}$$

where $|x|<\mathcal{R}$, the coefficient $\sigma(n)$ is a bounded positive sequence for $n\in\mathbb{N}_0=\mathbb{N}\cup\{0\}$ and a positive constant $\mathcal{R}$. The k-gamma function satisfies the relations $\Gamma_k(\varrho+k)=\varrho\Gamma_k(\varrho)$, $\Gamma_k(\varrho)=k^{\varrho/k-1}\Gamma_k(\varrho/k)$, and $\Gamma(\varrho)=\lim_{k\to 1}\Gamma_k(\varrho)$.

In 2022, taking advantage of the MLLF, the author [34,35] introduced the following generalized FIOs.

Definition 7 ([34,35]). *Assume that ψ,ξ are two continuous functions from $[u,v]$ to $\mathbb{R}$ for $0<u<v$ so that $\psi\in L_1[u,v]$ is positive, and ξ is a strictly increasing and differentiable function. Also suppose that ϕ/x is an increasing function on $[u,+\infty)$ for a positive function ϕ and $\omega\in\mathbb{R}$, $\rho,\lambda,\mu>0$. Then for $x\in[u,v]$, the left and right-side generalized FIOs ${}^{\phi}_{\xi}\mathcal{F}^{\Omega,\omega,\sigma,k}_{u^+,\alpha,\rho,\lambda}\psi(x)$ and ${}^{\phi}_{\xi}\mathcal{F}^{\Omega,\omega,\sigma,k}_{v^-,\alpha,\rho,\lambda}\psi(x)$ with the MLLF (28) are given by*

$${}^{\phi}_{\xi}\mathcal{F}^{\Omega,\omega,\sigma,k}_{u^+,\alpha,\rho,\lambda}\psi(x)=\aleph^{-1}(x)\int_u^x\frac{\phi(\xi(x)-\xi(s))}{\xi(x)-\xi(s)}\aleph(s)\mathcal{E}^{\sigma,k}_{\rho,\lambda}(\omega(\xi(x)-\xi(s))^{\alpha})\psi(s)d(\xi(s)),\tag{29}$$

$${}^{\phi}_{\xi}\mathcal{F}^{\Omega,\omega,\sigma,k}_{v^-,\alpha,\rho,\lambda}\psi(x)=\aleph^{-1}(x)\int_x^v\frac{\phi(\xi(s)-\xi(x))}{\xi(s)-\xi(x)}\aleph(s)\mathcal{E}^{\sigma,k}_{\rho,\lambda}(\omega(\xi(s)-\xi(x))^{\alpha})\psi(s)d(\xi(s)),\tag{30}$$

where $\aleph(s)$ stands for a weighted function satisfying $\aleph(s)>0$ for all $s\in[u,v]$.

In 2021, Zhang et al. [36] introduced a new MLF unifying the generalized Q function (19) and extended MLF (22). Moreover, the following FIOs involving the unified MLF as its kernel were established as

Definition 8 ([36]). *Let $\underline{\mathscr{A}}=(\mathscr{A}_1,\mathscr{A}_2,\cdots,\mathscr{A}_n)$, $\underline{\mathscr{B}}=(\mathscr{B}_1,\mathscr{B}_2,\cdots,\mathscr{B}_n)$, $\underline{\mathscr{C}}=(\mathscr{C}_1,\mathscr{C}_2,\cdots,\mathscr{C}_n)$, where $\mathscr{A}_i,\mathscr{B}_i,\mathscr{C}_i$, $i=1,2,\ldots,n$, such that $\forall i$, $\mathscr{R}(\mathscr{A}_i),\mathscr{R}(\mathscr{B}_i),\mathscr{R}(\mathscr{C}_i)>0$. Furthermore, let $\alpha,\beta,\gamma,\delta,\mu,v,\rho,\theta,t\in\mathbb{C}$, $\min\{\mathscr{R}(\alpha),\mathscr{R}(\beta),\mathscr{R}(\gamma),\mathscr{R}(\delta),\mathscr{R}(\lambda),\mathscr{R}(\theta)\}>0$, $k\in(0,1)\cup\mathbb{N}$ with $p\geqslant 0$, and $k+\mathscr{R}(\rho)<\mathscr{R}(\delta+v+\alpha)$ with $\mathscr{I}(\rho)=\mathscr{I}(\delta+v+\alpha)$, $\mathscr{I}(\alpha)$ denotes the imaginary part of complex number α. Then, we present the unified MLF by*

$$M^{\lambda,\rho,\theta,k,n}_{\alpha,\beta,\gamma,\delta,\mu,v}(t;\underline{\mathscr{A}},\underline{\mathscr{B}},\underline{\mathscr{C}},p)=\sum_{l=0}^{\infty}\frac{\prod_{i=1}^{n}B_p(\mathscr{B}_i,\mathscr{A}_i)(\lambda)_{\rho l}(\theta)_{kl}t^l}{\prod_{i=1}^{n}B(\mathscr{C}_i,\mathscr{A}_i)(\gamma)_{\delta l}(\mu)_{vl}\Gamma(\alpha l+\beta)}.\tag{31}$$

Definition 9 ([36]). *The generalized FIOs $I^{\omega,\lambda,\rho,\theta,k,n}_{u^+,\alpha,\beta,\gamma,\mu,v}\psi(x;\underline{\mathscr{A}},\underline{\mathscr{B}},\underline{\mathscr{C}},p)$ and $I^{\omega,\lambda,\rho,\theta,k,n}_{v^-,\alpha,\beta,\gamma,\mu,v}\psi(x;\underline{\mathscr{A}},\underline{\mathscr{B}},\underline{\mathscr{C}},p)$ with the unified MLF (31) are obtained by*

$$I^{\omega,\lambda,\rho,\theta,k,n}_{u^+,\alpha,\beta,\gamma,\mu,\nu}\psi(x;\underline{\mathscr{A}},\underline{\mathscr{B}},\underline{\mathscr{C}},p) = \int_u^x (x-s)^{\beta-1} \cdot M^{\lambda,\rho,\theta,k,n}_{\alpha,\beta,\gamma,\delta,\mu,\nu}(\omega(x-s)^{\alpha};\underline{\mathscr{A}},\underline{\mathscr{B}},\underline{\mathscr{C}},p)\psi(s)ds, \quad (32)$$

$$I^{\omega,\lambda,\rho,\theta,k,n}_{v^-,\alpha,\beta,\gamma,\mu,\nu}\psi(x;\underline{\mathscr{A}},\underline{\mathscr{B}},\underline{\mathscr{C}},p) = \int_x^v (s-x)^{\beta-1} \cdot M^{\lambda,\rho,\theta,k,n}_{\alpha,\beta,\gamma,\delta,\mu,\nu}(\omega(s-x)^{\alpha};\underline{\mathscr{A}},\underline{\mathscr{B}},\underline{\mathscr{C}},p)\psi(s)ds. \quad (33)$$

In 2022, making use of the unified MLF above, Gao et al. [37] presented the unified generalized FIOs as follows.

Definition 10 ([37]). *Assume that ψ, ξ are two continuous functions from $[u,v]$ to $\mathbb{R}$ for $0 < u < v$ so that $\psi \in L_1[u,v]$ is positive, and ξ is a strictly increasing and differentiable function. Also suppose that ϕ/x is an increasing function on $[u,+\infty)$ for a positive function ϕ and $\omega \in \mathbb{R}$. Let $\underline{\mathscr{A}} = (\mathscr{A}_1,\mathscr{A}_2,\cdots,\mathscr{A}_n)$, $\underline{\mathscr{B}} = (\mathscr{B}_1,\mathscr{B}_2,\cdots,\mathscr{B}_n)$, $\underline{\mathscr{C}} = (\mathscr{C}_1,\mathscr{C}_2,\cdots,\mathscr{C}_n)$, where $\mathscr{A}_i,\mathscr{B}_i,\mathscr{C}_i$, $i = 1,2,\ldots,n$, such that $\forall i$, $\mathscr{R}(\mathscr{A}_i),\mathscr{R}(\mathscr{B}_i),\mathscr{R}(\mathscr{C}_i) > 0$. Furthermore, let $\omega,\alpha,\beta,\gamma,\delta,\mu,\nu,\rho,\theta$, $t \in \mathbb{C}$, $\min\{\mathscr{R}(\alpha),\mathscr{R}(\beta),\mathscr{R}(\gamma),\mathscr{R}(\delta),\mathscr{R}(\lambda),\mathscr{R}(\theta)\} > 0$, $k \in (0,1)\cup\mathbb{N}$ with $p \geqslant 0$, and $k+\mathscr{R}(\rho) < \mathscr{R}(\delta+\nu+\alpha)$ with $\mathscr{I}(\rho) = \mathscr{I}(\delta+\nu+\alpha)$. Then, for $x \in [u,v]$, the left and right-side unified generalized FIOs $({}^{\phi}_{\xi}\Omega^{\omega,\lambda,\rho,\theta,k,n}_{u^+,\alpha,\beta,\gamma,\mu,\nu}\psi)(x;p)$ and $({}^{\phi}_{\xi}\Omega^{\omega,\lambda,\rho,\theta,k,n}_{v^-,\alpha,\beta,\gamma,\mu,\nu}\psi)(x;p)$ with the unified MLF (31) are given by*

$$({}^{\phi}_{\xi}\Omega^{\omega,\lambda,\rho,\theta,k,n}_{u^+,\alpha,\beta,\gamma,\mu,\nu}\psi)(x;p) = \int_u^x \frac{\phi(\xi(x)-\xi(s))}{\xi(x)-\xi(s)} \cdot M^{\lambda,\rho,\theta,k,n}_{\alpha,\beta,\gamma,\delta,\mu,\nu}(\omega(\xi(x)-\xi(s))^{\alpha};p)\psi(s)d(\xi(s)), \quad (34)$$

$$({}^{\phi}_{\xi}\Omega^{\omega,\lambda,\rho,\theta,k,n}_{v^-,\alpha,\beta,\gamma,\mu,\nu}\psi)(x;p) = \int_x^v \frac{\phi(\xi(s)-\xi(x))}{\xi(s)-\xi(x)} \cdot M^{\lambda,\rho,\theta,k,n}_{\alpha,\beta,\gamma,\delta,\mu,\nu}(\omega(\xi(s)-\xi(x))^{\alpha};p)\psi(s)d(\xi(s)). \quad (35)$$

In 2022, by means of the modified extended beta function, Abubakar et al. [38] gave the following extended unified MLF, which can be seen as the extensions of gamma, beta, and hypergeometric MLFs.

Definition 11 ([38]). *Let $\underline{\mathscr{A}} = (\mathscr{A}_1,\mathscr{A}_2,\cdots,\mathscr{A}_n)$, $\underline{\mathscr{B}} = (\mathscr{B}_1,\mathscr{B}_2,\cdots,\mathscr{B}_n)$, $\underline{\mathscr{C}} = (\mathscr{C}_1,\mathscr{C}_2,\cdots,\mathscr{C}_n)$, where $\mathscr{A}_i,\mathscr{B}_i,\mathscr{C}_i$, $i = 1,2,\ldots,n$, such that $\forall i$, $\mathscr{R}(\mathscr{A}_i),\mathscr{R}(\mathscr{B}_i),\mathscr{R}(\mathscr{C}_i) > 0$. Furthermore, let $\alpha,\beta,\gamma,\delta,\mu,\nu,\rho,\theta,t \in \mathbb{C}$, $\min\{\mathscr{R}(\alpha),\mathscr{R}(\beta),\mathscr{R}(\gamma),\mathscr{R}(\delta),\mathscr{R}(\lambda),\mathscr{R}(\theta)\} > 0$, $k \in (0,1)\cup\mathbb{N}$ with $p \geqslant 0$, and $k+\mathscr{R}(\rho) < \mathscr{R}(\delta+\nu+\alpha)$ with $\mathscr{I}(\rho) = \mathscr{I}(\delta+\nu+\alpha)$. Then the extended unified MLF is presented by*

$${}^{\varrho_1,\varrho_2}_{\sigma_1,\sigma_2}M^{\lambda,\rho,\theta,k,n}_{\alpha,\beta,\gamma,\delta,\mu,\nu}(t;\underline{\mathscr{A}},\underline{\mathscr{B}},\underline{\mathscr{C}},\sigma) = \sum_{l=0}^{\infty} \frac{\prod_{i=1}^{n} B^{\varrho_1,\varrho_2}_{\sigma_1,\sigma_2}(\mathscr{B}_i,\mathscr{A}_i,\varsigma)(\lambda)_{\rho l}(\theta)_{kl}t^l}{\prod_{i=1}^{n} B(\mathscr{C}_i,\mathscr{A}_i)(\gamma)_{\delta l}(\mu)_{\nu l}\Gamma(\alpha l+\beta)}, \quad (36)$$

where $B^{\varrho_1,\varrho_2}_{\sigma_1,\sigma_2}(*,\cdot,\star)$ denotes the modified extended beta function defined by

$$B^{\varrho_1,\varrho_2}_{\sigma_1,\sigma_2}(\tau_1,\tau_2,\varsigma) = \int_0^1 s^{\tau_1-1}(1-s)^{\tau_2-1}\varsigma^{\left(-\frac{\sigma_1}{s^{\varrho_1}}-\frac{\sigma_2}{(1-s)^{\varrho_2}}\right)}ds, \quad (37)$$

for $\min\{\mathscr{R}(\tau_1),\mathscr{R}(\tau_2),\mathscr{R}(\sigma_1),\mathscr{R}(\sigma_2),\mathscr{R}(\varrho_1),\mathscr{R}(\varrho_2)\} > 0$, $\varsigma \in (0,\infty)\backslash\{1\}$.

Finally, the following definition of modified unified generalized FIOs will be introduced based on the extended unified MLF.

Definition 12. *Assume that ψ, ξ are two continuous functions from $[u,v]$ to $\mathbb{R}$ for $0 < u < v$ so that $\psi \in L_1[u,v]$ is positive, and ξ is a strictly increasing and differentiable function. Also suppose that ϕ/x is an increasing function on $[u,+\infty)$ for a positive function ϕ and $\omega \in \mathbb{R}$. Let $\underline{\mathscr{A}} = (\mathscr{A}_1, \mathscr{A}_2, \cdots, \mathscr{A}_n)$, $\underline{\mathscr{B}} = (\mathscr{B}_1, \mathscr{B}_2, \cdots, \mathscr{B}_n)$, $\underline{\mathscr{C}} = (\mathscr{C}_1, \mathscr{C}_2, \cdots, \mathscr{C}_n)$, where $\mathscr{A}_i, \mathscr{B}_i, \mathscr{C}_i$, $i = 1,2,n,\ldots$, such that $\forall i$, $\mathscr{R}(\mathscr{A}_i), \mathscr{R}(\mathscr{B}_i), \mathscr{R}(\mathscr{C}_i) > 0$. Furthermore, let $\omega, \alpha, \beta, \gamma, \delta, \mu, \nu, \rho, \theta$, $t \in \mathbb{C}$, $\min\{\mathscr{R}(\alpha), \mathscr{R}(\beta), \mathscr{R}(\gamma), \mathscr{R}(\delta), \mathscr{R}(\lambda), \mathscr{R}(\theta)\} > 0$, $k \in (0,1) \cup \mathbb{N}$ with $p \geqslant 0$, and $k + \mathscr{R}(\rho) < \mathscr{R}(\delta + \nu + \alpha)$ with $\mathscr{I}(\rho) = \mathscr{I}(\delta + \nu + \alpha)$. Then, for $x \in [u,v]$, the left and right-side modified unified generalized FIOs $({}^{\phi}_{\xi}\Theta^{M}_{u^+}\psi)(x;\sigma)$ and $({}^{\phi}_{\xi}\Theta^{M}_{v^-}\psi)(x;\sigma)$ with the extended unified MLF (36) are defined by*

$$\begin{aligned}({}^{\phi}_{\xi}\Theta^{M}_{u^+}\psi)(x;\sigma) =& ({}^{\phi,\varrho_1,\varrho_2}_{\xi,\sigma_1,\sigma_2}\Theta^{\omega,\lambda,\rho,\theta,k,n}_{u^+,\alpha,\beta,\gamma,\mu,\nu}\psi)(x;\sigma) \\ =& \aleph^{-1}(x)\int_u^x \aleph(t)\mathscr{M}_x^t({}^{\varrho_1,\varrho_2}_{\sigma_1,\sigma_2}M^{\lambda,\rho,\theta,k,n}_{\alpha,\beta,\gamma,\delta,\mu,\nu}, \xi, \phi)\psi(t)d(\xi(t)), \qquad (38)\\ ({}^{\phi}_{\xi}\Theta^{M}_{v^-}\psi)(x;\sigma) =& ({}^{\phi,\varrho_1,\varrho_2}_{\xi,\sigma_1,\sigma_2}\Theta^{\omega,\lambda,\rho,\theta,k,n}_{v^-,\alpha,\beta,\gamma,\mu,\nu}\psi)(x;\sigma) \\ =& \aleph^{-1}(x)\int_x^v \aleph(t)\mathscr{M}_t^x({}^{\varrho_1,\varrho_2}_{\sigma_1,\sigma_2}M^{\lambda,\rho,\theta,k,n}_{\alpha,\beta,\gamma,\delta,\mu,\nu}, \xi, \phi)\psi(t)d(\xi(t)), \qquad (39)\end{aligned}$$

where $\aleph(s)$ stands for a weighted function satisfying $\aleph(t) > 0$ for all $t \in [u,v]$ and the kernel function $\mathscr{M}_x^t({}^{\varrho_1,\varrho_2}_{\sigma_1,\sigma_2}M^{\lambda,\rho,\theta,k,n}_{\alpha,\beta,\gamma,\delta,\mu,\nu}, \xi, \phi)$ is given as

$$\begin{aligned}\mathscr{M}_x^t({}^{\varrho_1,\varrho_2}_{\sigma_1,\sigma_2}M^{\lambda,\rho,\theta,k,n}_{\alpha,\beta,\gamma,\delta,\mu,\nu}, \xi, \phi) =& \frac{\phi(\xi(x)-\xi(t))}{\xi(x)-\xi(t)} \\ &\cdot {}^{\varrho_1,\varrho_2}_{\sigma_1,\sigma_2}M^{\lambda,\rho,\theta,k,n}_{\alpha,\beta,\gamma,\delta,\mu,\nu}(\omega(\xi(x)-\xi(t))^{\alpha}; \underline{\mathscr{A}}, \underline{\mathscr{B}}, \underline{\mathscr{C}}, \sigma). \qquad (40)\end{aligned}$$

Remark 1. *The unified MLF (31) can be seen as the generalization of the generalized Q function (19) and extended MLF (22); however, the unified MLF (31) can be seen as the special case of the extended unified MLF (36). Therefore, the modified unified generalized FIOs (38) and (39) includes the FIOs (20) and (21), (24) and (25), the unified FIOs (26) and (27), the unified generalized FIOs (34) and (35). From ([34], Remarks 9 and 10) and ([35], Remarks 2.2 and 2.3), we point out that the raised previously unified FIOs (26) and (27) can produce a great number of existent FIOs according to distinct setting values of the relevant parameters and functions.*

For the sake of convenience, we always assume that all of the modified unified generalized FIOs exist throughout the article.

3. Reverse Hölder Type Inequalities

In this section, we will establish some new reverse Hölder-type inequalities for modified unified generalized FIOs.

Theorem 1. *Assume that f, g, w are three continuous positive functions on $[u,v]$. Let $1/\mathrm{p} + 1/\mathrm{q} = 1$ satisfying $\mathrm{p} > 1$. Then, for $x \in [u,v]$, we have the following FIO inequalities*

$$\begin{aligned}({}^{\phi}_{\xi}\Theta^{M}_{u^+}wfg)(x;\sigma) \leqslant& \left({}^{\phi}_{\xi}\Theta^{M}_{u^+}S\left(\left(\frac{\mathscr{G}_1 f^{\mathrm{p}}}{\mathscr{F}_1 g^{\mathrm{q}}}\right)^{\mathrm{r}}\right)wfg\right)(x;\sigma) \\ \leqslant& ({}^{\phi}_{\xi}\Theta^{M}_{u^+}wf^{\mathrm{p}})^{\frac{1}{\mathrm{p}}}(x;\sigma)({}^{\phi}_{\xi}\Theta^{M}_{u^+}wg^{\mathrm{q}})^{\frac{1}{\mathrm{q}}}(x;\sigma) \leqslant \left({}^{\phi}_{\xi}\Theta^{M}_{u^+}S\left(\frac{\mathscr{G}_1 f^{\mathrm{p}}}{\mathscr{F}_1 g^{\mathrm{q}}}\right)wfg\right)(x;\sigma), \qquad (41)\end{aligned}$$

$$\begin{aligned}({}^{\phi}_{\xi}\Theta^{M}_{u^+}wf^{\mathrm{p}})^{\frac{1}{\mathrm{p}}}(x;\sigma)({}^{\phi}_{\xi}\Theta^{M}_{u^+}wg^{\mathrm{q}})^{\frac{1}{\mathrm{q}}}(x;\sigma) - ({}^{\phi}_{\xi}\Theta^{M}_{u^+}wfg)(x;\sigma) \leqslant& ({}^{\phi}_{\xi}\Theta^{M}_{u^+}wf^{\mathrm{p}})^{\frac{1}{\mathrm{p}}}(x;\sigma) \\ \cdot ({}^{\phi}_{\xi}\Theta^{M}_{u^+}wg^{\mathrm{q}})^{\frac{1}{\mathrm{q}}}(x;\sigma)\left({}^{\phi}_{\xi}\Theta^{M}_{u^+}L\left(\frac{wf^{\mathrm{p}}}{\mathscr{F}_1}, \frac{wg^{\mathrm{q}}}{\mathscr{G}_1}\right)\log S\left(\frac{\mathscr{G}_1 f^{\mathrm{p}}}{\mathscr{F}_1 g^{\mathrm{q}}}\right)\right)&(x;\sigma), \qquad (42)\end{aligned}$$

where $\mathrm{r} = \min\{1/\mathrm{p}, 1/\mathrm{q}\}$, $\mathscr{F}_1 = ({}^{\phi}_{\xi}\Theta^{M}_{u+} w f^{\mathrm{p}})(x;\sigma)$, $\mathscr{G}_1 = ({}^{\phi}_{\xi}\Theta^{M}_{u+} w g^{\mathrm{q}})(x;\sigma)$, $L(*,\star)$ *and* $S(\cdot)$ *denote the logarithmic mean and Specht's ratio, respectively.*

Proof. Let $\mathcal{A} = w(t)f^{\mathrm{p}}(t)/\mathscr{F}_1$ and $\mathcal{B} = w(t)g^{\mathrm{q}}(t)/\mathscr{G}_1$ in (5), then

$$\frac{w(t)f(t)g(t)}{\mathscr{F}_1^{\frac{1}{\mathrm{p}}}\mathscr{G}_1^{\frac{1}{\mathrm{q}}}} \leqslant S\left(\left(\frac{\mathscr{G}_1 f^{\mathrm{p}}(t)}{\mathscr{F}_1 g^{\mathrm{q}}(t)}\right)^{\mathrm{r}}\right)\frac{w(t)f(t)g(t)}{\mathscr{F}_1^{\frac{1}{\mathrm{p}}}\mathscr{G}_1^{\frac{1}{\mathrm{q}}}} \leqslant \frac{w(t)f^{\mathrm{p}}(t)}{\mathrm{p}\mathscr{F}_1} + \frac{w(t)g^{\mathrm{q}}(t)}{\mathrm{q}\mathscr{G}_1} \leqslant S\left(\frac{\mathscr{G}_1 f^{\mathrm{p}}(t)}{\mathscr{F}_1 g^{\mathrm{q}}(t)}\right)\frac{w(t)f(t)g(t)}{\mathscr{F}_1^{\frac{1}{\mathrm{p}}}\mathscr{G}_1^{\frac{1}{\mathrm{q}}}}. \quad (43)$$

Multiplying simultaneously both sides of (43) by $\aleph^{-1}(x)\aleph(t)\mathscr{M}_x^t({}^{\varrho_1,\varrho_2}_{\sigma_1,\sigma_2}M^{\lambda,\rho,\theta,k,n}_{\alpha,\beta,\gamma,\delta,\mu,\nu}, \xi, \phi)\xi'(t)$ $w(t)$ and integrating the acquired inequality with regard to t from u to x, we claim based on the operator (38)

$$\frac{({}^{\phi}_{\xi}\Theta^{M}_{u+} wfg)(x;\sigma)}{\mathscr{F}_1^{\frac{1}{\mathrm{p}}}\mathscr{G}_1^{\frac{1}{\mathrm{q}}}} \leqslant \frac{\left({}^{\phi}_{\xi}\Theta^{M}_{u+} S\left(\left(\frac{\mathscr{G}_1 f^{\mathrm{p}}}{\mathscr{F}_1 g^{\mathrm{q}}}\right)^{\mathrm{r}}\right) wfg\right)(x;\sigma)}{\mathscr{F}_1^{\frac{1}{\mathrm{p}}}\mathscr{G}_1^{\frac{1}{\mathrm{q}}}} \leqslant \frac{({}^{\phi}_{\xi}\Theta^{M}_{u+} wf^{\mathrm{p}})(x;\sigma)}{\mathrm{p}\mathscr{F}_1} + \frac{({}^{\phi}_{\xi}\Theta^{M}_{u+} wg^{\mathrm{q}})(x;\sigma)}{\mathrm{q}\mathscr{G}_1} \leqslant \frac{\left({}^{\phi}_{\xi}\Theta^{M}_{u+} S\left(\frac{\mathscr{G}_1 f^{\mathrm{p}}}{\mathscr{F}_1 g^{\mathrm{q}}}\right) wfg\right)(x;\sigma)}{\mathscr{F}_1^{\frac{1}{\mathrm{p}}}\mathscr{G}_1^{\frac{1}{\mathrm{q}}}}. \quad (44)$$

According to the definitions of $\mathscr{F}_1$ and $\mathscr{G}_1$, the inequalities (44) can be rewritten as

$$\frac{({}^{\phi}_{\xi}\Theta^{M}_{u+} wfg)(x;\sigma)}{\mathscr{F}_1^{\frac{1}{\mathrm{p}}}\mathscr{G}_1^{\frac{1}{\mathrm{q}}}} \leqslant \frac{\left({}^{\phi}_{\xi}\Theta^{M}_{u+} S\left(\left(\frac{\mathscr{G}_1 f^{\mathrm{p}}}{\mathscr{F}_1 g^{\mathrm{q}}}\right)^{\mathrm{r}}\right) wfg\right)(x;\sigma)}{\mathscr{F}_1^{\frac{1}{\mathrm{p}}}\mathscr{G}_1^{\frac{1}{\mathrm{q}}}} \leqslant 1 \leqslant \frac{\left({}^{\phi}_{\xi}\Theta^{M}_{u+} S\left(\frac{\mathscr{G}_1 f^{\mathrm{p}}}{\mathscr{F}_1 g^{\mathrm{q}}}\right) wfg\right)(x;\sigma)}{\mathscr{F}_1^{\frac{1}{\mathrm{p}}}\mathscr{G}_1^{\frac{1}{\mathrm{q}}}}, \quad (45)$$

which are the desired inequalities (41). Let $\mathcal{A} = w(t)f^{\mathrm{p}}(t)/\mathscr{F}_1$ and $\mathcal{B} = w(t)g^{\mathrm{q}}(t)/\mathscr{G}_1$ in (6), then

$$\frac{w(t)f^{\mathrm{p}}(t)}{\mathrm{p}\mathscr{F}_1} + \frac{w(t)g^{\mathrm{q}}(t)}{\mathrm{q}\mathscr{G}_1} - \frac{w(t)f(t)g(t)}{\mathscr{F}_1^{\frac{1}{\mathrm{p}}}\mathscr{G}_1^{\frac{1}{\mathrm{q}}}} \leqslant L\left(\frac{w(t)f^{\mathrm{p}}(t)}{\mathscr{F}_1}, \frac{w(t)g^{\mathrm{q}}(t)}{\mathscr{G}_1}\right)\log S\left(\frac{\mathscr{G}_1 f^{\mathrm{p}}(t)}{\mathscr{F}_1 g^{\mathrm{q}}(t)}\right). \quad (46)$$

Multiplying simultaneously both sides of (46) by $\aleph^{-1}(x)\aleph(t)\mathscr{M}_x^t({}^{\varrho_1,\varrho_2}_{\sigma_1,\sigma_2}M^{\lambda,\rho,\theta,k,n}_{\alpha,\beta,\gamma,\delta,\mu,\nu}, \xi, \phi)\xi'(t)$ $w(t)$ and integrating the achieved inequality in regard to t from u to x, we gain based on the operator (38)

$$\frac{({}^{\phi}_{\xi}\Theta^{M}_{u+} wf^{\mathrm{p}})(x;\sigma)}{\mathrm{p}\mathscr{F}_1} + \frac{({}^{\phi}_{\xi}\Theta^{M}_{u+} wg^{\mathrm{q}})(x;\sigma)}{\mathrm{q}\mathscr{G}_1} - \frac{({}^{\phi}_{\xi}\Theta^{M}_{u+} wfg)(x;\sigma)}{\mathscr{F}_1^{\frac{1}{\mathrm{p}}}\mathscr{G}_1^{\frac{1}{\mathrm{q}}}} \leqslant \left({}^{\phi}_{\xi}\Theta^{M}_{u+} L\left(\frac{wf^{\mathrm{p}}}{\mathscr{F}_1}, \frac{wg^{\mathrm{q}}}{\mathscr{G}_1}\right)\log S\left(\frac{\mathscr{G}_1 f^{\mathrm{p}}}{\mathscr{F}_1 g^{\mathrm{q}}}\right)\right)(x;\sigma), \quad (47)$$

which are the anticipated inequalities (42). This completes the proof. □

Remark 2. *It follows from (41) that* $\left({}^{\phi}_{\xi}\Theta^{M}_{u^+}wfg\right)(x;\sigma) \leqslant \left({}^{\phi}_{\xi}\Theta^{M}_{u^+}wf^{\mathbb{p}}\right)^{\frac{1}{\mathbb{p}}}(x;\sigma)\left({}^{\phi}_{\xi}\Theta^{M}_{u^+}wg^{\mathbb{q}}\right)^{\frac{1}{\mathbb{q}}}(x;\sigma)$ *for* $1/\mathbb{p}+1/\mathbb{q}=1$ *with* $\mathbb{p}>1$, *which is Hölder-type inequalities for modified unified generalized FIOs. The reverse of the above inequality holds also when* $0<\mathbb{p}<1$ *and when* $\mathbb{p}<0$ *or* $\mathbb{q}<0$.

Theorem 2. *Suppose that* f,g,w *are three continuous positive functions on* $[u,v]$. *Let* $1/\mathbb{p}+1/\mathbb{q}=1$ *satisfying* $\mathbb{p}<0$ *(or* $\mathbb{q}<0$*). Then, for* $x\in[u,v]$, *we have the following FIO inequalities*

$$\begin{aligned}
&\left({}^{\phi}_{\xi}\Theta^{M}_{u^+}wf^{\mathbb{p}}\right)^{\frac{1}{\mathbb{p}}}(x;\sigma)\left({}^{\phi}_{\xi}\Theta^{M}_{u^+}wg^{\mathbb{q}}\right)^{\frac{1}{\mathbb{q}}}(x;\sigma)\\
&\leqslant \left({}^{\phi}_{\xi}\Theta^{M}_{u^+}wf^{\mathbb{p}}\right)^{\frac{1}{\mathbb{p}}}(x;\sigma)\left({}^{\phi}_{\xi}\Theta^{M}_{u^+}S\left(\left(\frac{\mathscr{G}_2f^{\mathbb{p}}}{\mathscr{F}_2fg}\right)^{\mathbb{r}}\right)wg^{\mathbb{q}}\right)^{\frac{1}{\mathbb{q}}}(x;\sigma)\leqslant\left({}^{\phi}_{\xi}\Theta^{M}_{u^+}wfg\right)^{\mathbb{q}}(x;\sigma)\\
&\leqslant \left({}^{\phi}_{\xi}\Theta^{M}_{u^+}wf^{\mathbb{p}}\right)^{\frac{1}{\mathbb{p}}}(x;\sigma)\left({}^{\phi}_{\xi}\Theta^{M}_{u^+}S\left(\frac{\mathscr{G}_2f^{\mathbb{p}}}{\mathscr{F}_2fg}\right)wg^{\mathbb{q}}\right)^{\frac{1}{\mathbb{q}}}(x;\sigma),
\end{aligned}\tag{48}$$

$$\begin{aligned}
&\left({}^{\phi}_{\xi}\Theta^{M}_{u^+}wfg\right)^{\mathbb{q}}(x;\sigma)-\left({}^{\phi}_{\xi}\Theta^{M}_{u^+}wf^{\mathbb{p}}\right)^{\frac{\mathbb{q}}{\mathbb{p}}}(x;\sigma)\left({}^{\phi}_{\xi}\Theta^{M}_{u^+}wg^{\mathbb{q}}\right)(x;\sigma)\\
&\leqslant\left({}^{\phi}_{\xi}\Theta^{M}_{u^+}wfg\right)^{\mathbb{q}}(x;\sigma)\left({}^{\phi}_{\xi}\Theta^{M}_{u^+}L\left(\frac{wf^{\mathbb{p}}}{\mathscr{F}_2},\frac{wfg}{\mathscr{G}_2}\right)\log S\left(\frac{\mathscr{G}_2f^{\mathbb{p}}}{\mathscr{F}_2fg}\right)\right)(x;\sigma),
\end{aligned}\tag{49}$$

where $\mathbb{r}=\min\{\mathbb{q},1-\mathbb{q}\}$ *(or* $\mathbb{r}=\min\{\mathbb{p},1-\mathbb{p}\}$*),* $\mathscr{F}_2=\left({}^{\phi}_{\xi}\Theta^{M}_{u^+}wf^{\mathbb{p}}\right)(x;\sigma)$, $\mathscr{G}_2=\left({}^{\phi}_{\xi}\Theta^{M}_{u^+}wfg\right)$ $(x;\sigma)$, $L(*,\star)$ *and* $S(\cdot)$ *denote the logarithmic mean and Specht's ratio, respectively.*

Proof. Suppose that $\mathbb{p}<0$ (if $\mathbb{q}<0$, the idea is really the same). Let $\mathbb{P}=-\mathbb{p}/\mathbb{q}$ and $\mathbb{Q}=1/\mathbb{q}$, then we obtain $1/\mathbb{P}+1/\mathbb{Q}=1$ satisfying $\mathbb{P}>1$ and $\mathbb{Q}>1$. Assume that F,G,w are three continuous positive functions on $[u,v]$ with $\mathbb{R}=\min\{1/\mathbb{P},1/\mathbb{Q}\}$. It follows from (41) and (42) that

$$\begin{aligned}
&\left({}^{\phi}_{\xi}\Theta^{M}_{u^+}wFG\right)(x;\sigma)\leqslant\left({}^{\phi}_{\xi}\Theta^{M}_{u^+}S\left(\left(\frac{\mathscr{G}_2F^{\mathbb{P}}}{\mathscr{F}_2G^{\mathbb{Q}}}\right)^{\mathbb{R}}\right)wFG\right)(x;\sigma)\\
&\leqslant\left({}^{\phi}_{\xi}\Theta^{M}_{u^+}wF^{\mathbb{P}}\right)^{\frac{1}{\mathbb{P}}}(x;\sigma)\left({}^{\phi}_{\xi}\Theta^{M}_{u^+}wG^{\mathbb{Q}}\right)^{\frac{1}{\mathbb{Q}}}(x;\sigma)\leqslant\left({}^{\phi}_{\xi}\Theta^{M}_{u^+}S\left(\frac{\mathscr{G}_2F^{\mathbb{P}}}{\mathscr{F}_2G^{\mathbb{Q}}}\right)wFG\right)(x;\sigma),
\end{aligned}\tag{50}$$

$$\begin{aligned}
&\left({}^{\phi}_{\xi}\Theta^{M}_{u^+}wF^{\mathbb{P}}\right)^{\frac{1}{\mathbb{P}}}(x;\sigma)\left({}^{\phi}_{\xi}\Theta^{M}_{u^+}wG^{\mathbb{Q}}\right)^{\frac{1}{\mathbb{Q}}}(x;\sigma)-\left({}^{\phi}_{\xi}\Theta^{M}_{u^+}wFG\right)(x;\sigma)\leqslant\left({}^{\phi}_{\xi}\Theta^{M}_{u^+}wF^{\mathbb{P}}\right)^{\frac{1}{\mathbb{P}}}(x;\sigma)\\
&\cdot\left({}^{\phi}_{\xi}\Theta^{M}_{u^+}wG^{\mathbb{Q}}\right)^{\frac{1}{\mathbb{Q}}}(x;\sigma)\left({}^{\phi}_{\xi}\Theta^{M}_{u^+}L\left(\frac{wF^{\mathbb{P}}}{\mathscr{F}_2},\frac{wG^{\mathbb{Q}}}{\mathscr{G}_2}\right)\log S\left(\frac{\mathscr{G}_2F^{\mathbb{P}}}{\mathscr{F}_2G^{\mathbb{Q}}}\right)\right)(x;\sigma),
\end{aligned}\tag{51}$$

where $\mathscr{F}_2=\left({}^{\phi}_{\xi}\Theta^{M}_{u^+}wF^{\mathbb{p}}\right)(x;\sigma)$ and $\mathscr{G}_2=\left({}^{\phi}_{\xi}\Theta^{M}_{u^+}wG^{\mathbb{q}}\right)(x;\sigma)$.

Letting $F=f^{-\mathbb{q}}$ and $G=f^{\mathbb{q}}g^{\mathbb{q}}$ in the inequalities (50) and (51), we obtain

$$\begin{aligned}
&\left({}^{\phi}_{\xi}\Theta^{M}_{u^+}wg^{\mathbb{q}}\right)(x;\sigma)\leqslant\left({}^{\phi}_{\xi}\Theta^{M}_{u^+}S\left(\left(\frac{\mathscr{G}_2f^{\mathbb{p}}}{\mathscr{F}_2fg}\right)^{\mathbb{r}}\right)wg^{\mathbb{q}}\right)(x;\sigma)\\
&\leqslant\left({}^{\phi}_{\xi}\Theta^{M}_{u^+}wf^{\mathbb{p}}\right)^{\frac{-\mathbb{q}}{\mathbb{p}}}(x;\sigma)\left({}^{\phi}_{\xi}\Theta^{M}_{u^+}wfg\right)^{\mathbb{q}}(x;\sigma)\leqslant\left({}^{\phi}_{\xi}\Theta^{M}_{u^+}S\left(\frac{\mathscr{G}_2f^{\mathbb{p}}}{\mathscr{F}_2fg}\right)wg^{\mathbb{q}}\right)(x;\sigma),
\end{aligned}\tag{52}$$

$$\begin{aligned}
&\left({}^{\phi}_{\xi}\Theta^{M}_{u^+}wf^{\mathbb{p}}\right)^{\frac{-\mathbb{q}}{\mathbb{p}}}(x;\sigma)\left({}^{\phi}_{\xi}\Theta^{M}_{u^+}wfg\right)^{\mathbb{q}}(x;\sigma)-\left({}^{\phi}_{\xi}\Theta^{M}_{u^+}wg^{\mathbb{q}}\right)(x;\sigma)\leqslant\left({}^{\phi}_{\xi}\Theta^{M}_{u^+}wf^{\mathbb{p}}\right)^{\frac{-\mathbb{q}}{\mathbb{p}}}(x;\sigma)\\
&\cdot\left({}^{\phi}_{\xi}\Theta^{M}_{u^+}wfg\right)^{\mathbb{q}}(x;\sigma)\left({}^{\phi}_{\xi}\Theta^{M}_{u^+}L\left(\frac{wf^{\mathbb{p}}}{\mathscr{F}_2},\frac{wfg}{\mathscr{G}_2}\right)\log S\left(\frac{\mathscr{G}_2f^{\mathbb{p}}}{\mathscr{F}_2fg}\right)\right)(x;\sigma).
\end{aligned}\tag{53}$$

Multiplying simultaneously both sides of (52) and (53) by $\left({}^{\phi}_{\xi}\Theta^{M}_{u^+}wf^{\mathbb{p}}\right)^{\frac{\mathbb{q}}{\mathbb{p}}}(x;\sigma)$, we obtain

$$\left({}_{\xi}^{\phi}\Theta_{u^+}^{M} wf^{\mathrm{p}}\right)^{\frac{\mathrm{q}}{\mathrm{p}}}(x;\sigma)\left({}_{\xi}^{\phi}\Theta_{u^+}^{M} wg^{\mathrm{q}}\right)(x;\sigma)$$
$$\leqslant \left({}_{\xi}^{\phi}\Theta_{u^+}^{M} wf^{\mathrm{p}}\right)^{\frac{\mathrm{q}}{\mathrm{p}}}(x;\sigma)\left({}_{\xi}^{\phi}\Theta_{u^+}^{M} S\left(\left(\frac{\mathscr{G}_2 f^{\mathrm{p}}}{\mathscr{F}_2 fg}\right)^{\mathrm{r}}\right) wg^{\mathrm{q}}\right)(x;\sigma) \leqslant \left({}_{\xi}^{\phi}\Theta_{u^+}^{M} wfg\right)^{\mathrm{q}}(x;\sigma)$$
$$\leqslant \left({}_{\xi}^{\phi}\Theta_{u^+}^{M} wf^{\mathrm{p}}\right)^{\frac{\mathrm{q}}{\mathrm{p}}}(x;\sigma)\left({}_{\xi}^{\phi}\Theta_{u^+}^{M} S\left(\frac{\mathscr{G}_2 f^{\mathrm{p}}}{\mathscr{F}_2 fg}\right) wg^{\mathrm{q}}\right)(x;\sigma), \quad (54)$$

$$\left({}_{\xi}^{\phi}\Theta_{u^+}^{M} wfg\right)^{\mathrm{q}}(x;\sigma) - \left({}_{\xi}^{\phi}\Theta_{u^+}^{M} wf^{\mathrm{p}}\right)^{\frac{\mathrm{q}}{\mathrm{p}}}(x;\sigma)\left({}_{\xi}^{\phi}\Theta_{u^+}^{M} wg^{\mathrm{q}}\right)(x;\sigma)$$
$$\leqslant \left({}_{\xi}^{\phi}\Theta_{u^+}^{M} wfg\right)^{\mathrm{q}}(x;\sigma)\left({}_{\xi}^{\phi}\Theta_{u^+}^{M} L\left(\frac{wf^{\mathrm{p}}}{\mathscr{F}_2}, \frac{wfg}{\mathscr{G}_2}\right)\log S\left(\frac{\mathscr{G}_2 f^{\mathrm{p}}}{\mathscr{F}_2 fg}\right)\right)(x;\sigma). \quad (55)$$

which are the desired inequalities (48) and (49). This completes the proof. □

By substituting f, g for $f^{\mathrm{p}}, g^{\mathrm{q}}$ in (41) and (48), respectively, we derive the following corollary.

Corollary 1. (a) *Under the assumptions of Theorem 1, inequalities* (41) *can be rewritten as*

$$\left({}_{\xi}^{\phi}\Theta_{u^+}^{M} wf^{\frac{1}{\mathrm{p}}}g^{\frac{1}{\mathrm{q}}}\right)(x;\sigma) \leqslant \left({}_{\xi}^{\phi}\Theta_{u^+}^{M} S\left(\left(\frac{\mathscr{G}_1^* f}{\mathscr{F}_1^* g}\right)^{\mathrm{r}}\right) wf^{\frac{1}{\mathrm{p}}}g^{\frac{1}{\mathrm{q}}}\right)(x;\sigma)$$
$$\leqslant \left({}_{\xi}^{\phi}\Theta_{u^+}^{M} wf\right)^{\frac{1}{\mathrm{p}}}(x;\sigma)\left({}_{\xi}^{\phi}\Theta_{u^+}^{M} wg\right)^{\frac{1}{\mathrm{q}}}(x;\sigma) \leqslant \left({}_{\xi}^{\phi}\Theta_{u^+}^{M} S\left(\frac{\mathscr{G}_1^* f}{\mathscr{F}_1^* g}\right) wf^{\frac{1}{\mathrm{p}}}g^{\frac{1}{\mathrm{q}}}\right)(x;\sigma). \quad (56)$$

where $\mathscr{F}_1^* = \left({}_{\xi}^{\phi}\Theta_{u^+}^{M} wf\right)(x;\sigma)$ *and* $\mathscr{G}_1^* = \left({}_{\xi}^{\phi}\Theta_{u^+}^{M} wg\right)(x;\sigma)$.

(b) *Under the conditions of Theorem 2, inequalities* (48) *can be rewritten as*

$$\left({}_{\xi}^{\phi}\Theta_{u^+}^{M} wf\right)^{\frac{1}{\mathrm{p}}}(x;\sigma)\left({}_{\xi}^{\phi}\Theta_{u^+}^{M} wg\right)^{\frac{1}{\mathrm{q}}}(x;\sigma)$$
$$\leqslant \left({}_{\xi}^{\phi}\Theta_{u^+}^{M} wf\right)^{\frac{1}{\mathrm{p}}}(x;\sigma)\left({}_{\xi}^{\phi}\Theta_{u^+}^{M} S\left(\left(\frac{\mathscr{G}_2^* f}{\mathscr{F}_2^* f^{\frac{1}{\mathrm{p}}}g^{\frac{1}{\mathrm{q}}}}\right)^{\mathrm{r}}\right) wg\right)^{\frac{1}{\mathrm{q}}}(x;\sigma) \leqslant \left({}_{\xi}^{\phi}\Theta_{u^+}^{M} wf^{\frac{1}{\mathrm{p}}}g^{\frac{1}{\mathrm{q}}}\right)^{\mathrm{q}}(x;\sigma)$$
$$\leqslant \left({}_{\xi}^{\phi}\Theta_{u^+}^{M} wf\right)^{\frac{1}{\mathrm{p}}}(x;\sigma)\left({}_{\xi}^{\phi}\Theta_{u^+}^{M} S\left(\frac{\mathscr{G}_2^* f}{\mathscr{F}_2^* f^{\frac{1}{\mathrm{p}}}g^{\frac{1}{\mathrm{q}}}}\right) hg^{\mathrm{q}}\right)^{\frac{1}{\mathrm{q}}}(x;\sigma), \quad (57)$$

where $\mathscr{F}_2^* = \left({}_{\xi}^{\phi}\Theta_{u^+}^{M} wf\right)(x;\sigma)$ *and* $\mathscr{G}_2^* = \left({}_{\xi}^{\phi}\Theta_{u^+}^{M} wf^{\frac{1}{\mathrm{p}}}g^{\frac{1}{\mathrm{q}}}\right)(x;\sigma)$.

Theorem 3. *Let* $1/\mathrm{p} + 1/\mathrm{q} = 1$ *with* $\mathrm{p} > 1$. *Assume that* f, g, w *are three continuous positive functions on* $[u, v]$ *satisfying* $0 < \mathrm{m} \leqslant f^{\mathrm{p}}(t)/g^{\mathrm{q}}(t) \leqslant \mathrm{M}$ *for all* $t \in [u, v]$. *Then, for* $x \in [u, v]$, *we have the following fractional integral inequalities*

$$\left(\frac{\mathrm{m}}{\mathrm{M}}\right)^{\frac{1}{\mathrm{pq}}}\left({}_{\xi}^{\phi}\Theta_{u^+}^{M} wfg\right)(x;\sigma) \leqslant \left({}_{\xi}^{\phi}\Theta_{u^+}^{M} S\left(\frac{\mathscr{G}_1 f^{\mathrm{p}}}{\mathscr{F}_1 g^{\mathrm{q}}}\right) wfg\right)(x;\sigma), \quad (58)$$

where $S(\cdot)$ *denotes the Specht's ratio,* $\mathscr{F}_1 = \left({}_{\xi}^{\phi}\Theta_{u^+}^{M} hf^{\mathrm{p}}\right)(x;\sigma)$ *and* $\mathscr{G}_1 = \left({}_{\xi}^{\phi}\Theta_{u^+}^{M} hg^{\mathrm{q}}\right)(x;\sigma)$.

Proof. It follows from (41) that

$$\left({}_{\xi}^{\phi}\Theta_{u^+}^{M} wf^{\mathrm{p}}\right)^{\frac{1}{\mathrm{p}}}(x;\sigma)\left({}_{\xi}^{\phi}\Theta_{u^+}^{M} wg^{\mathrm{q}}\right)^{\frac{1}{\mathrm{q}}}(x;\sigma) \leqslant \left({}_{\xi}^{\phi}\Theta_{u^+}^{M} S\left(\frac{\mathscr{G}_1 f^{\mathrm{p}}}{\mathscr{F}_1 g^{\mathrm{q}}}\right) wfg\right)(x;\sigma). \quad (59)$$

Since $0 < \mathrm{m} \leqslant f^{\mathrm{p}}(t)/g^{\mathrm{q}}(t) \leqslant \mathbb{M}$, then we observe

$$\mathbb{M}^{-1/\mathrm{p}} f(t) \leqslant g^{\mathrm{q}/\mathrm{p}}(t) \text{ and } \mathrm{m}^{1/\mathrm{q}} g(t) \leqslant f^{\mathrm{p}/\mathrm{q}}(t). \tag{60}$$

Multiplying the above inequality (60) by $g(t)$ and $f(t)$, respectively, then we obtain

$$\mathbb{M}^{-1/\mathrm{p}} f(t)g(t) \leqslant g^{\mathrm{q}/\mathrm{p}+1}(t) = g^{\mathrm{q}}(t) \text{ and } \mathrm{m}^{1/\mathrm{q}} f(t)g(t) \leqslant f^{\mathrm{p}/\mathrm{q}+1}(t) = f^{\mathrm{p}}(t). \tag{61}$$

Multiplying simultaneously the inequalities (61) by $\aleph^{-1}(x)\aleph(t)\mathscr{M}_x^t({}_{\sigma_1,\sigma_2}^{\varrho_1,\varrho_2}M_{\alpha,\beta,\gamma,\delta,\mu,\nu}^{\lambda,\rho,\theta,k,n}, \xi, \phi)$ $\xi'(t)w(t)$ and integrating the acquired inequalities with regard to t from u to x, we claim based on the operator (38)

$$\begin{aligned} \frac{1}{\mathbb{M}^{\frac{1}{\mathrm{p}}}} ({}_{\xi}^{\phi}\Theta_{u^+}^{M} wfg)(x;\sigma) &\leqslant ({}_{\xi}^{\phi}\Theta_{u^+}^{M} wg^{\mathrm{q}})(x;\sigma), \\ \mathrm{m}^{\frac{1}{\mathrm{q}}} ({}_{\xi}^{\phi}\Theta_{u^+}^{M} wfg)(x;\sigma) &\leqslant ({}_{\xi}^{\phi}\Theta_{u^+}^{M} wf^{\mathrm{p}})(x;\sigma). \end{aligned} \tag{62}$$

Combining (59) and (62) yields the following inequality

$$\left(\frac{\mathrm{m}}{\mathbb{M}}\right)^{\frac{1}{\mathrm{pq}}} ({}_{\xi}^{\phi}\Theta_{u^+}^{M} wfg)(x;\sigma) \leqslant \left({}_{\xi}^{\phi}\Theta_{u^+}^{M} S\left(\frac{\mathscr{G}_1 f^{\mathrm{p}}}{\mathscr{F}_1 g^{\mathrm{q}}}\right) wfg\right)(x;\sigma), \tag{63}$$

which is the desired inequality (58). This completes the proof. □

Theorem 4. *Let $1/\mathrm{p} + 1/\mathrm{q} = 1$ with $\mathrm{p} > 1$. Suppose that f, g, w are three continuous positive functions on $[u,v]$ satisfying $0 < \mathrm{m} \leqslant f(t)/g(t) \leqslant \mathbb{M}$ for all $t \in [u,v]$. Then, for $x \in [u,v]$, we have the following FIO inequalities*

$$\left(\frac{\mathrm{m}}{\mathbb{M}}\right)^{\frac{1}{\mathrm{pq}}} \left({}_{\xi}^{\phi}\Theta_{u^+}^{M} wf^{\frac{1}{\mathrm{p}}} g^{\frac{1}{\mathrm{q}}}\right)(x;\sigma) \leqslant \left({}_{\xi}^{\phi}\Theta_{u^+}^{M} S\left(\frac{\mathscr{G}_1^* f}{\mathscr{F}_1^* g}\right) wf^{\frac{1}{\mathrm{p}}} g^{\frac{1}{\mathrm{q}}}\right)(x;\sigma), \tag{64}$$

$$\frac{\mathrm{m}^{\frac{1}{\mathrm{p}^2}}}{\mathbb{M}^{\frac{1}{\mathrm{q}^2}}} \left({}_{\xi}^{\phi}\Theta_{u^+}^{M} wf^{\frac{1}{\mathrm{q}}} g^{\frac{1}{\mathrm{p}}}\right)(x;\sigma) \leqslant \left({}_{\xi}^{\phi}\Theta_{u^+}^{M} S\left(\frac{\mathscr{G}_1^* f}{\mathscr{F}_1^* g}\right) wf^{\frac{1}{\mathrm{p}}} g^{\frac{1}{\mathrm{q}}}\right)(x;\sigma), \tag{65}$$

where $S(\cdot)$ denotes the Specht's ratio, $\mathscr{F}_1^* = ({}_{\xi}^{\phi}\Theta_{u^+}^{M} wf)(x;\sigma)$ and $\mathscr{G}_1^* = ({}_{\xi}^{\phi}\Theta_{u^+}^{M} wg)(x;\sigma)$.

Proof. It follows from (56) that

$$({}_{\xi}^{\phi}\Theta_{u^+}^{M} wf)^{\frac{1}{\mathrm{p}}}(x;\sigma)({}_{\xi}^{\phi}\Theta_{u^+}^{M} wg)^{\frac{1}{\mathrm{q}}}(x;\sigma) \leqslant \left({}_{\xi}^{\phi}\Theta_{u^+}^{M} S\left(\frac{\mathscr{G}_1 f}{\mathscr{F}_1 g}\right) wf^{\frac{1}{\mathrm{p}}} g^{\frac{1}{\mathrm{q}}}\right)(x;\sigma). \tag{66}$$

Since $0 < \mathrm{m} \leqslant f(t)/g(t) \leqslant \mathbb{M}$, then we observe

$$\frac{1}{\mathbb{M}^{\frac{1}{\mathrm{p}}}} f^{\frac{1}{\mathrm{p}}}(t) g^{\frac{1}{\mathrm{q}}}(t) \leqslant g^{\frac{1}{\mathrm{p}}+\frac{1}{\mathrm{q}}}(t) = g(t) \text{ and } \mathrm{m}^{\frac{1}{\mathrm{q}}} f^{\frac{1}{\mathrm{p}}}(t) g^{\frac{1}{\mathrm{q}}}(t) \leqslant f^{\frac{1}{\mathrm{p}}+\frac{1}{\mathrm{q}}}(t) = f(t), \tag{67}$$

$$\frac{1}{\mathbb{M}^{\frac{1}{\mathrm{q}}}} f^{\frac{1}{\mathrm{q}}}(t) g^{\frac{1}{\mathrm{p}}}(t) \leqslant g^{\frac{1}{\mathrm{p}}+\frac{1}{\mathrm{q}}}(t) = g(t) \text{ and } \mathrm{m}^{\frac{1}{\mathrm{p}}} f^{\frac{1}{\mathrm{q}}}(t) g^{\frac{1}{\mathrm{p}}}(t) \leqslant f^{\frac{1}{\mathrm{p}}+\frac{1}{\mathrm{q}}}(t) = f(t). \tag{68}$$

Multiplying simultaneously the inequalities (67) and (68) by $\aleph^{-1}(x)\aleph(t)\mathscr{M}_x^t({}_{\sigma_1,\sigma_2}^{\varrho_1,\varrho_2}M_{\alpha,\beta,\gamma,\delta,\mu,\nu}^{\lambda,\rho,\theta,k,n},$ $\xi, \phi)\xi'(t)w(t)$ and integrating the acquired inequalities in regard to t from u to x, we gain based on the operator (38)

$$\begin{aligned} \frac{1}{\mathbb{M}^{\frac{1}{\mathrm{p}}}} ({}_{\xi}^{\phi}\Theta_{u^+}^{M} wf^{\frac{1}{\mathrm{p}}} g^{\frac{1}{\mathrm{q}}})(x;\sigma) &\leqslant ({}_{\xi}^{\phi}\Theta_{u^+}^{M} wg)(x;\sigma), \\ \mathrm{m}^{\frac{1}{\mathrm{q}}} ({}_{\xi}^{\phi}\Theta_{u^+}^{M} wf^{\frac{1}{\mathrm{p}}} g^{\frac{1}{\mathrm{q}}})(x;\sigma) &\leqslant ({}_{\xi}^{\phi}\Theta_{u^+}^{M} wf)(x;\sigma), \end{aligned} \tag{69}$$

$$\frac{1}{\mathbb{M}^{\frac{1}{q}}}\left({}_{\xi}^{\phi}\Theta_{u^+}^{M} w f^{\frac{1}{q}} g^{\frac{1}{p}}\right)(x;\sigma) \leqslant \left({}_{\xi}^{\phi}\Theta_{u^+}^{M} w g\right)(x;\sigma),$$
$$\mathbb{m}^{\frac{1}{p}}\left({}_{\xi}^{\phi}\Theta_{u^+}^{M} w f^{\frac{1}{q}} g^{\frac{1}{p}}\right)(x;\sigma) \leqslant \left({}_{\xi}^{\phi}\Theta_{u^+}^{M} w f\right)(x;\sigma), \tag{70}$$

Combining (66), (69) and (70) yields the following inequalities

$$\left(\frac{\mathbb{m}}{\mathbb{M}}\right)^{\frac{1}{pq}}\left({}_{\xi}^{\phi}\Theta_{u^+}^{M} w f^{\frac{1}{p}} g^{\frac{1}{q}}\right)(x;\sigma) \leqslant \left({}_{\xi}^{\phi}\Theta_{u^+}^{M} S\left(\frac{\mathcal{G}_1^* f}{\mathcal{F}_1^* g}\right) w f^{\frac{1}{p}} g^{\frac{1}{q}}\right)(x;\sigma), \tag{71}$$

$$\frac{\mathbb{m}^{\frac{1}{p^2}}}{\mathbb{M}^{\frac{1}{q^2}}}\left({}_{\xi}^{\phi}\Theta_{u^+}^{M} w f^{\frac{1}{q}} g^{\frac{1}{p}}\right)(x;\sigma) \leqslant \left({}_{\xi}^{\phi}\Theta_{u^+}^{M} S\left(\frac{\mathcal{G}_1^* f}{\mathcal{F}_1^* g}\right) w f^{\frac{1}{p}} g^{\frac{1}{q}}\right)(x;\sigma), \tag{72}$$

which are the expected inequalities (64) and (65). This completes the proof. □

Theorem 5. *Let $\hbar, \ell > 0$, $1/\mathbb{p} + 1/\mathbb{q} = 1$ with $\mathbb{p} > 1$. Assume that f, g, w are three continuous positive functions on $[u, v]$ satisfying $0 < \mathbb{m} \leqslant f^{\hbar}(t)/g^{\ell}(t) \leqslant \mathbb{M}$ for all $t \in [u, v]$. Then, for $x \in [u, v]$, we achieve the following FIO inequalities*

$$\begin{aligned}&\left({}_{\xi}^{\phi}\Theta_{u^+}^{M} w f^{\frac{\hbar}{p}} g^{\frac{\ell}{q}}\right)(x;\sigma) \leqslant \left({}_{\xi}^{\phi}\Theta_{u^+}^{M} w f^{\hbar}\right)^{\frac{1}{p}}(x;\sigma)\left({}_{\xi}^{\phi}\Theta_{u^+}^{M} w g^{\ell}\right)^{\frac{1}{q}}(x;\sigma)\\ &\leqslant \left(\frac{\mathbb{M}}{\mathbb{m}}\right)^{\frac{1}{pq}}\left({}_{\xi}^{\phi}\Theta_{u^+}^{M} w f^{\frac{\hbar}{p}} g^{\frac{\ell}{q}}\right)(x;\sigma) \leqslant \left(\frac{\mathbb{M}}{\mathbb{m}}\right)^{\frac{1}{pq}}\left({}_{\xi}^{\phi}\Theta_{u^+}^{M} w f^{\hbar}\right)^{\frac{1}{p}}(x;\sigma)\left({}_{\xi}^{\phi}\Theta_{u^+}^{M} w g^{\ell}\right)^{\frac{1}{q}}(x;\sigma),\end{aligned} \tag{73}$$

$$\begin{aligned}&\left({}_{\xi}^{\phi}\Theta_{u^+}^{M} w f^{\frac{\hbar}{p}} g^{\frac{\ell}{q}}\right)(x;\sigma) \leqslant \left({}_{\xi}^{\phi}\Theta_{u^+}^{M} w f^{\hbar}\right)^{\frac{1}{p}}(x;\sigma)\left({}_{\xi}^{\phi}\Theta_{u^+}^{M} w g^{\ell}\right)^{\frac{1}{q}}(x;\sigma)\\ &\leqslant \frac{\mathbb{M}^{\frac{1}{p^2}}}{\mathbb{m}^{\frac{1}{q^2}}}\left({}_{\xi}^{\phi}\Theta_{u^+}^{M} w f^{\frac{\hbar}{q}} g^{\frac{\ell}{p}}\right)(x;\sigma) \leqslant \frac{\mathbb{M}^{\frac{1}{p^2}}}{\mathbb{m}^{\frac{1}{q^2}}}\left({}_{\xi}^{\phi}\Theta_{u^+}^{M} w f^{\hbar}\right)^{\frac{1}{q}}(x;\sigma)\left({}_{\xi}^{\phi}\Theta_{u^+}^{M} w g^{\ell}\right)^{\frac{1}{p}}(x;\sigma),\end{aligned} \tag{74}$$

$$\begin{aligned}\left({}_{\xi}^{\phi}\Theta_{u^+}^{M} w f^{\frac{\hbar}{p}}\right)^{p}(x;\sigma)\left({}_{\xi}^{\phi}\Theta_{u^+}^{M} w g^{\frac{\ell}{q}}\right)^{q}(x;\sigma) &\leqslant \frac{\mathbb{M}}{\mathbb{m}}\left({}_{\xi}^{\phi}\Theta_{u^+}^{M} w (f^{\hbar} g^{\ell})^{\frac{1}{2p}}\right)^{p}(x;\sigma)\\ &\cdot \left({}_{\xi}^{\phi}\Theta_{u^+}^{M} w (f^{\hbar} g^{\ell})^{\frac{1}{2q}}\right)^{q}(x;\sigma).\end{aligned} \tag{75}$$

Proof. It follows from Remark 2 that

$$\left({}_{\xi}^{\phi}\Theta_{u^+}^{M} w f^{\frac{\hbar}{p}} g^{\frac{\ell}{q}}\right)(x;\sigma) \leqslant \left({}_{\xi}^{\phi}\Theta_{u^+}^{M} w f^{\hbar}\right)^{\frac{1}{p}}(x;\sigma)\left({}_{\xi}^{\phi}\Theta_{u^+}^{M} w g^{\ell}\right)^{\frac{1}{q}}(x;\sigma). \tag{76}$$

Since $0 < \mathbb{m} \leqslant f^{\hbar}(t)/g^{\ell}(t) \leqslant \mathbb{M}$, then we observe

$$f^{\hbar}(t) = f^{\frac{\hbar}{p}+\frac{\hbar}{q}}(t) = \mathbb{M}^{\frac{1}{q}} f^{\frac{\hbar}{p}}(t) g^{\frac{\ell}{q}}(t), \quad g^{\ell}(t) = g^{\frac{\ell}{p}+\frac{\ell}{q}}(t) \leqslant \mathbb{m}^{-\frac{1}{p}} f^{\frac{\hbar}{p}}(t) g^{\frac{\ell}{q}}(t), \tag{77}$$

$$f^{\hbar}(t) = f^{\frac{\hbar}{p}+\frac{\hbar}{q}}(t) = \mathbb{M}^{\frac{1}{p}} f^{\frac{\hbar}{q}}(t) g^{\frac{\ell}{p}}(t), \quad g^{\ell}(t) = g^{\frac{\ell}{p}+\frac{\ell}{q}}(t) \leqslant \mathbb{m}^{-\frac{1}{q}} f^{\frac{\hbar}{q}}(t) g^{\frac{\ell}{p}}(t). \tag{78}$$

Substituting (77) and (78) into (76) and using the Hölder-type inequalities, we obtain the desired inequalities (73) and (74). Also since $0 < \mathbb{m} \leqslant f^{\hbar}(t)/g^{\ell}(t) \leqslant \mathbb{M}$, then we have the following inequalities

$$\mathbb{m} + 1 \leqslant \frac{f^{\hbar}(t) + g^{\ell}(t)}{g^{\ell}(t)} \leqslant \mathbb{M} + 1, \quad \frac{\mathbb{M}+1}{\mathbb{M}} \leqslant \frac{f^{\hbar}(t) + g^{\ell}(t)}{f^{\hbar}(t)} \leqslant \frac{\mathbb{m}+1}{\mathbb{m}}. \tag{79}$$

That is,

$$f^{\hbar}(t) \leqslant \frac{\mathbb{M}}{\mathbb{M}+1}\left(f^{\hbar}(t) + g^{\ell}(t)\right), \quad g^{\ell}(t) \leqslant \frac{1}{\mathbb{m}+1}\left(f^{\hbar}(t) + g^{\ell}(t)\right), \tag{80}$$

$$(f^{\hbar}(t)+g^{\ell}(t))^2 \leqslant \frac{(\mathrm{m}+1)(\mathbb{M}+1)}{\mathrm{m}} f^{\hbar}(t)g^{\ell}(t)$$

$$\Rightarrow f^{\hbar}(t)+g^{\ell}(t) \leqslant \left(\frac{(\mathrm{m}+1)(\mathbb{M}+1)}{\mathrm{m}}\right)^{\frac{1}{2}} (f^{\hbar}(t)g^{\ell}(t))^{\frac{1}{2}}. \quad (81)$$

It follows from (80) and (81) that based on the operator (38)

$$\begin{aligned}
&\left({}^{\phi}_{\xi}\Theta^{M}_{u^+} w f^{\frac{\hbar}{\mathrm{p}}}\right)^{\mathrm{p}}(x;\sigma)\left({}^{\phi}_{\xi}\Theta^{M}_{u^+} w g^{\frac{\ell}{\mathrm{q}}}\right)^{\mathrm{q}}(x;\sigma) \\
&\leqslant \frac{\mathbb{M}}{\mathbb{M}+1}\left({}^{\phi}_{\xi}\Theta^{M}_{u^+} w (f^{\hbar}+g^{\ell})^{\frac{1}{\mathrm{p}}}\right)^{\mathrm{p}}(x;\sigma)\frac{1}{\mathrm{m}+1}\left({}^{\phi}_{\xi}\Theta^{M}_{u^+} w (f^{\hbar}+g^{\ell})^{\frac{1}{\mathrm{q}}}\right)^{\mathrm{q}}(x;\sigma) \\
&\leqslant \frac{\mathbb{M}}{\mathrm{m}}\left({}^{\phi}_{\xi}\Theta^{M}_{u^+} w (f^{\hbar}g^{\ell})^{\frac{1}{2\mathrm{p}}}\right)^{\mathrm{p}}(x;\sigma)\left({}^{\phi}_{\xi}\Theta^{M}_{u^+} w (f^{\hbar}g^{\ell})^{\frac{1}{2\mathrm{q}}}\right)^{\mathrm{q}}(x;\sigma), \quad (82)
\end{aligned}$$

which implies the desired inequality (75). The proof of Theorem 5 is completed. □

When $\hbar=\ell=1$, from Theorem 5, we have following corollary.

Corollary 2. *For $1/\mathrm{p}+1/\mathrm{q}=1$ with $\mathrm{p}>1$. Suppose that f,g,w are three continuous positive functions on $[u,v]$ satisfying $0<\mathrm{m}\leqslant f(t)/g(t)\leqslant \mathbb{M}$ for all $t\in[u,v]$. Then, for $x\in[u,v]$, we have the following FIO inequalities*

$$\begin{aligned}
\left({}^{\phi}_{\xi}\Theta^{M}_{u^+} w f\right)^{\frac{1}{\mathrm{p}}}(x;\sigma)\left({}^{\phi}_{\xi}\Theta^{M}_{u^+} w g\right)^{\frac{1}{\mathrm{q}}}(x;\sigma) &\leqslant \left(\frac{\mathbb{M}}{\mathrm{m}}\right)^{\frac{1}{\mathrm{pq}}}\left({}^{\phi}_{\xi}\Theta^{M}_{u^+} w f^{\frac{1}{\mathrm{p}}} g^{\frac{1}{\mathrm{q}}}\right)(x;\sigma) \\
&\leqslant \left(\frac{\mathbb{M}}{\mathrm{m}}\right)^{\frac{1}{\mathrm{pq}}}\left({}^{\phi}_{\xi}\Theta^{M}_{u^+} w f\right)^{\frac{1}{\mathrm{p}}}(x;\sigma)\left({}^{\phi}_{\xi}\Theta^{M}_{u^+} w g\right)^{\frac{1}{\mathrm{q}}}(x;\sigma), \quad (83)
\end{aligned}$$

$$\begin{aligned}
\left({}^{\phi}_{\xi}\Theta^{M}_{u^+} w f\right)^{\frac{1}{\mathrm{p}}}(x;\sigma)\left({}^{\phi}_{\xi}\Theta^{M}_{u^+} w g\right)^{\frac{1}{\mathrm{q}}}(x;\sigma) &\leqslant \frac{\mathbb{M}^{\frac{1}{\mathrm{p}^2}}}{\mathrm{m}^{\frac{1}{\mathrm{q}^2}}}\left({}^{\phi}_{\xi}\Theta^{M}_{u^+} w f^{\frac{1}{\mathrm{q}}} g^{\frac{1}{\mathrm{p}}}\right)(x;\sigma) \\
&\leqslant \frac{\mathbb{M}^{\frac{1}{\mathrm{p}^2}}}{\mathrm{m}^{\frac{1}{\mathrm{q}^2}}}\left({}^{\phi}_{\xi}\Theta^{M}_{u^+} w f\right)^{\frac{1}{\mathrm{q}}}(x;\sigma)\left({}^{\phi}_{\xi}\Theta^{M}_{u^+} w g\right)^{\frac{1}{\mathrm{p}}}(x;\sigma), \quad (84)
\end{aligned}$$

$$\begin{aligned}
\left({}^{\phi}_{\xi}\Theta^{M}_{u^+} w f^{\frac{1}{\mathrm{p}}}\right)^{\mathrm{p}}(x;\sigma)\left({}^{\phi}_{\xi}\Theta^{M}_{u^+} w g^{\frac{1}{\mathrm{q}}}\right)^{\mathrm{q}}(x;\sigma) &\leqslant \frac{\mathbb{M}}{\mathrm{m}}\left({}^{\phi}_{\xi}\Theta^{M}_{u^+} w (fg)^{\frac{1}{2\mathrm{p}}}\right)^{\mathrm{p}}(x;\sigma) \\
&\quad\cdot\left({}^{\phi}_{\xi}\Theta^{M}_{u^+} w (fg)^{\frac{1}{2\mathrm{q}}}\right)^{\mathrm{q}}(x;\sigma). \quad (85)
\end{aligned}$$

When $\hbar=\mathrm{p}$ and $\ell=\mathrm{q}$, from Theorem 5, we gain following corollary.

Corollary 3. *For $1/\mathrm{p}+1/\mathrm{q}=1$ with $\mathrm{p}>1$. Suppose that f,g,w are three continuous positive functions on $[u,v]$ satisfying $0<\mathrm{m}\leqslant f^{\mathrm{p}}(t)/g^{\mathrm{q}}(t)\leqslant \mathbb{M}$ for all $t\in[u,v]$. Then, for $x\in[u,v]$, we have the following FIO inequalities*

$$\begin{aligned}
\left({}^{\phi}_{\xi}\Theta^{M}_{u^+} w f^{\mathrm{p}}\right)^{\frac{1}{\mathrm{p}}}(x;\sigma)\left({}^{\phi}_{\xi}\Theta^{M}_{u^+} w g^{\mathrm{q}}\right)^{\frac{1}{\mathrm{q}}}(x;\sigma) &\leqslant \left(\frac{\mathbb{M}}{\mathrm{m}}\right)^{\frac{1}{\mathrm{pq}}}\left({}^{\phi}_{\xi}\Theta^{M}_{u^+} w f g\right)(x;\sigma) \\
&\leqslant \left(\frac{\mathbb{M}}{\mathrm{m}}\right)^{\frac{1}{\mathrm{pq}}}\left({}^{\phi}_{\xi}\Theta^{M}_{u^+} w f^{\mathrm{p}}\right)^{\frac{1}{\mathrm{p}}}(x;\sigma)\left({}^{\phi}_{\xi}\Theta^{M}_{u^+} w g^{\mathrm{q}}\right)^{\frac{1}{\mathrm{q}}}(x;\sigma), \quad (86)
\end{aligned}$$

$$\begin{aligned}
\left({}^{\phi}_{\xi}\Theta^{M}_{u^+} w f^{\mathrm{p}}\right)^{\frac{1}{\mathrm{p}}}(x;\sigma)\left({}^{\phi}_{\xi}\Theta^{M}_{u^+} w g^{\mathrm{q}}\right)^{\frac{1}{\mathrm{q}}}(x;\sigma) &\leqslant \frac{\mathbb{M}^{\frac{1}{\mathrm{p}^2}}}{\mathrm{m}^{\frac{1}{\mathrm{q}^2}}}\left({}^{\phi}_{\xi}\Theta^{M}_{u^+} w f g\right)(x;\sigma) \\
&\leqslant \frac{\mathbb{M}^{\frac{1}{\mathrm{p}^2}}}{\mathrm{m}^{\frac{1}{\mathrm{q}^2}}}\left({}^{\phi}_{\xi}\Theta^{M}_{u^+} w f^{\mathrm{p}}\right)^{\frac{1}{\mathrm{q}}}(x;\sigma)\left({}^{\phi}_{\xi}\Theta^{M}_{u^+} w g^{\mathrm{q}}\right)^{\frac{1}{\mathrm{p}}}(x;\sigma), \quad (87)
\end{aligned}$$

$$\left({}_{\xi}^{\phi}\Theta_{u^+}^{M} wf\right)^{\mathbb{p}}(x;\sigma)\left({}_{\xi}^{\phi}\Theta_{u^+}^{M} wg\right)^{\mathbb{q}}(x;\sigma) \leqslant \frac{\mathbb{M}}{\mathbb{m}}\left({}_{\xi}^{\phi}\Theta_{u^+}^{M} w(f^{\mathbb{p}}g^{\mathbb{q}})^{\frac{1}{2\mathbb{p}}}\right)^{\mathbb{p}}(x;\sigma) \cdot \left({}_{\xi}^{\phi}\Theta_{u^+}^{M} w(f^{\mathbb{p}}g^{\mathbb{q}})^{\frac{1}{2\mathbb{q}}}\right)^{\mathbb{q}}(x;\sigma). \quad (88)$$

Theorem 6. *For $\kappa, \vartheta, \mathbb{p}, \mathbb{q}, \mathbb{p}', \mathbb{q}' > 0$. Suppose that f, g, w are three continuous positive functions on $[u, v]$ satisfying $0 < \kappa < \mathbb{m} \leqslant \vartheta f(t)/g(t) \leqslant \mathbb{M}$ for all $t \in [u, v]$. Then, for $x \in [u, v]$, we have the following FIO inequality*

$$\left({}_{\xi}^{\phi}\Theta_{u^+}^{M} wf^{\mathbb{p}}\right)^{\frac{1}{\mathbb{p}}}(x;\sigma)\left({}_{\xi}^{\phi}\Theta_{u^+}^{M} wg^{\mathbb{q}}\right)^{\frac{1}{\mathbb{q}}}(x;\sigma) \leqslant \frac{\mathbb{M}}{\mathbb{m}}\left(\frac{\vartheta}{\mathbb{m}}\right)^{\frac{2\mathbb{p}'}{\mathbb{p}'+\mathbb{q}'}}(\mathbb{m}+\kappa)^{\frac{\mathbb{p}'-\mathbb{q}'}{\mathbb{p}'+\mathbb{q}'}}(\mathbb{M}+\kappa)^{\frac{\mathbb{q}'-\mathbb{p}'}{\mathbb{p}'+\mathbb{q}'}} \cdot \left({}_{\xi}^{\phi}\Theta_{u^+}^{M} w(f^{\mathbb{p}'}g^{\mathbb{q}'})^{\frac{\mathbb{p}}{\mathbb{p}'+\mathbb{q}'}}\right)^{\frac{1}{\mathbb{p}}}(x;\sigma)\left({}_{\xi}^{\phi}\Theta_{u^+}^{M} w(f^{\mathbb{p}'}g^{\mathbb{q}'})^{\frac{\mathbb{q}}{\mathbb{p}'+\mathbb{q}'}}\right)^{\frac{1}{\mathbb{q}}}(x;\sigma). \quad (89)$$

Proof. Since $0 < \kappa < \mathbb{m} \leqslant \vartheta f(t)/g(t) \leqslant \mathbb{M}$ for all $t \in [a, b]$, we have

$$\mathbb{m}+\kappa \leqslant \frac{\vartheta f(t)+\kappa g(t)}{g(t)} \leqslant \mathbb{M}+\kappa, \quad \frac{\mathbb{M}+\kappa}{\mathbb{M}} \leqslant \frac{\vartheta f(t)+\kappa g(t)}{\vartheta f(t)} \leqslant \frac{\mathbb{m}+\kappa}{\mathbb{m}}. \quad (90)$$

From the left inequalities of (90), we can obtain

$$\vartheta\left(\frac{\mathbb{M}+\kappa}{\mathbb{M}}\right)\left({}_{\xi}^{\phi}\Theta_{u^+}^{M} wf^{\mathbb{p}}\right)^{\frac{1}{\mathbb{p}}}(x;\sigma) \leqslant \left({}_{\xi}^{\phi}\Theta_{u^+}^{M} w(\vartheta f+\kappa g)^{\mathbb{p}}\right)^{\frac{1}{\mathbb{p}}}(x;\sigma), \quad (91)$$

$$(\mathbb{m}+\kappa)\left({}_{\xi}^{\phi}\Theta_{u^+}^{M} wg^{\mathbb{q}}\right)^{\frac{1}{\mathbb{q}}}(x;\sigma) \leqslant \left({}_{\xi}^{\phi}\Theta_{u^+}^{M} w(\vartheta f+\kappa g)^{\mathbb{q}}\right)^{\frac{1}{\mathbb{q}}}(x;\sigma). \quad (92)$$

Multiplying these inequalities (91) and (92), we obtain

$$\frac{\vartheta}{\mathbb{M}}(\mathbb{m}+\kappa)(\mathbb{M}+\kappa)\left({}_{\xi}^{\phi}\Theta_{u^+}^{M} wf^{\mathbb{p}}\right)^{\frac{1}{\mathbb{p}}}(x;\sigma)\left({}_{\xi}^{\phi}\Theta_{u^+}^{M} wg^{\mathbb{q}}\right)^{\frac{1}{\mathbb{q}}}(x;\sigma) \leqslant \left({}_{\xi}^{\phi}\Theta_{u^+}^{M} w(\vartheta f+\kappa g)^{\mathbb{p}}\right)^{\frac{1}{\mathbb{p}}}(x;\sigma)\left({}_{\xi}^{\phi}\Theta_{u^+}^{M} w(\vartheta f+\kappa g)^{\mathbb{q}}\right)^{\frac{1}{\mathbb{q}}}(x;\sigma). \quad (93)$$

On the other hand, from the right inequalities of (90), we have

$$(\vartheta f(t)+\kappa g(t))^{\mathbb{p}'} \leqslant \left(\frac{\vartheta}{\mathbb{m}}(\mathbb{m}+\kappa)\right)^{\mathbb{p}'} f^{\mathbb{p}'}(t), \quad (\vartheta f(t)+\kappa g(t))^{\mathbb{q}'} \leqslant (\mathbb{M}+\kappa)^{\mathbb{q}'} g^{\mathbb{q}'}(t). \quad (94)$$

By multiplying the inequalities (94) and raising the resulting inequality to power $1/(\mathbb{p}'+\mathbb{q}')$, we achieve

$$\vartheta f(t)+\kappa g(t) \leqslant \left(\frac{\vartheta}{\mathbb{m}}(\mathbb{m}+\kappa)\right)^{\frac{\mathbb{p}'}{\mathbb{p}'+\mathbb{q}'}}(\mathbb{M}+\kappa)^{\frac{\mathbb{q}'}{\mathbb{p}'+\mathbb{q}'}}\left(f^{\mathbb{p}'}(t)g^{\mathbb{q}'}(t)\right)^{\frac{1}{\mathbb{p}'+\mathbb{q}'}}. \quad (95)$$

Based on the operator (38) and inequality (95), we derive

$$\left({}_{\xi}^{\phi}\Theta_{u^+}^{M} w(\vartheta f+\kappa g)^{\mathbb{p}}\right)^{\frac{1}{\mathbb{p}}}(x;\sigma) \leqslant \left(\frac{\vartheta}{\mathbb{m}}(\mathbb{m}+\kappa)\right)^{\frac{\mathbb{p}'}{\mathbb{p}'+\mathbb{q}'}}(\mathbb{M}+\kappa)^{\frac{\mathbb{q}'}{\mathbb{p}'+\mathbb{q}'}} \cdot \left({}_{\xi}^{\phi}\Theta_{u^+}^{M} w(f^{\mathbb{p}'}g^{\mathbb{q}'})^{\frac{\mathbb{p}}{\mathbb{p}'+\mathbb{q}'}}\right)^{\frac{1}{\mathbb{p}}}(x;\sigma), \quad (96)$$

$$\left({}_{\xi}^{\phi}\Theta_{u^+}^{M} w(\vartheta f+\kappa g)^{\mathbb{q}}\right)^{\frac{1}{\mathbb{q}}}(x;\sigma) \leqslant \left(\frac{\vartheta}{\mathbb{m}}(\mathbb{m}+\kappa)\right)^{\frac{\mathbb{p}'}{\mathbb{p}'+\mathbb{q}'}}(\mathbb{M}+\kappa)^{\frac{\mathbb{q}'}{\mathbb{p}'+\mathbb{q}'}} \cdot \left({}_{\xi}^{\phi}\Theta_{u^+}^{M} w(f^{\mathbb{p}'}g^{\mathbb{q}'})^{\frac{\mathbb{q}}{\mathbb{p}'+\mathbb{q}'}}\right)^{\frac{1}{\mathbb{q}}}(x;\sigma). \quad (97)$$

Multiplying these inequalities (96) and (97), we obtain

$$\left({}^{\phi}_{\xi}\Theta^{M}_{u^+}w(\vartheta f+\kappa g)^{\mathrm{p}}\right)^{\frac{1}{\mathrm{p}}}(x;\sigma)\left({}^{\phi}_{\xi}\Theta^{M}_{u^+}w(\vartheta f+\kappa g)^{\mathrm{p}}\right)^{\frac{1}{\mathrm{p}}}(x;\sigma)\leqslant\left(\frac{\vartheta}{\mathrm{m}}(\mathrm{m}+\kappa)\right)^{\frac{2\mathrm{p}'}{\mathrm{p}'+\mathrm{q}'}}$$

$$\cdot(\mathbb{M}+\kappa)^{\frac{2\mathrm{q}'}{\mathrm{p}'+\mathrm{q}'}}\left({}^{\phi}_{\xi}\Theta^{M}_{u^+}w(f^{\mathrm{p}'}g^{\mathrm{q}'})^{\frac{\mathrm{p}}{\mathrm{p}'+\mathrm{q}'}}\right)^{\frac{1}{\mathrm{p}}}(x;\sigma)\left({}^{\phi}_{\xi}\Theta^{M}_{u^+}w(f^{\mathrm{p}'}g^{\mathrm{q}'})^{\frac{\mathrm{q}}{\mathrm{p}'+\mathrm{q}'}}\right)^{\frac{1}{\mathrm{q}}}(x;\sigma), \quad (98)$$

which implies the anticipated inequality (89). The proof of Theorem 6 is completed. □

Theorem 7. *For $\hbar,\ell>0$, $1/\mathrm{p}+1/\mathrm{q}=1/\mathrm{p}'+1/\mathrm{q}'=1$ with $\mathrm{p}\geqslant\mathrm{p}'>1$. Let f,g and w be three continuous positive functions on $[u,v]$ satisfying $0<\mathrm{m}\leqslant f^{\hbar}(t)/g^{\ell}(t)\leqslant\mathbb{M}$ for any $t\in[u,v]$. Then, for $x\in[u,v]$, we have the following FIO inequality*

$$\left({}^{\phi}_{\xi}\Theta^{M}_{u^+}wf^{\frac{\mathrm{p}'\hbar}{\mathrm{p}}}\right)^{\frac{1}{\mathrm{p}'}}(x;\sigma)\left({}^{\phi}_{\xi}\Theta^{M}_{u^+}wg^{\frac{\mathrm{q}\ell}{\mathrm{q}'}}\right)^{\frac{1}{\mathrm{q}}}(x;\sigma)\leqslant\frac{\mathbb{M}^{\frac{1}{\mathrm{pq}}}}{\mathrm{m}^{\frac{1}{\mathrm{p}'\mathrm{q}'}}}\left({}^{\phi}_{\xi}\Theta^{M}_{u^+}w\right)^{\frac{2}{\mathrm{p}'}-\frac{2}{\mathrm{p}}}(x;\sigma)$$

$$\cdot\left({}^{\phi}_{\xi}\Theta^{M}_{u^+}wf^{\frac{\hbar}{\mathrm{p}}}g^{\frac{\ell}{\mathrm{q}}}\right)^{\frac{1}{\mathrm{p}}}(x;\sigma)\left({}^{\phi}_{\xi}\Theta^{M}_{u^+}wf^{\frac{\hbar}{\mathrm{p}'}}g^{\frac{\ell}{\mathrm{q}'}}\right)^{\frac{1}{\mathrm{q}'}}(x;\sigma), \quad (99)$$

$$\left({}^{\phi}_{\xi}\Theta^{M}_{u^+}wf^{\frac{\mathrm{p}'\hbar}{\mathrm{p}}}\right)^{\frac{1}{\mathrm{p}'}}(x;\sigma)\left({}^{\phi}_{\xi}\Theta^{M}_{u^+}wg^{\frac{\mathrm{q}\ell}{\mathrm{q}'}}\right)^{\frac{1}{\mathrm{q}}}(x;\sigma)\leqslant\frac{\mathbb{M}^{\frac{1}{\mathrm{p}^2}}}{\mathrm{m}^{\frac{1}{\mathrm{q}'^2}}}\left({}^{\phi}_{\xi}\Theta^{M}_{u^+}w\right)^{\frac{2}{\mathrm{p}'}-\frac{2}{\mathrm{p}}}(x;\sigma)$$

$$\cdot\left({}^{\phi}_{\xi}\Theta^{M}_{u^+}wf^{\frac{\hbar}{\mathrm{q}}}g^{\frac{\ell}{\mathrm{p}}}\right)^{\frac{1}{\mathrm{p}}}(x;\sigma)\left({}^{\phi}_{\xi}\Theta^{M}_{u^+}wf^{\frac{\hbar}{\mathrm{q}'}}g^{\frac{\ell}{\mathrm{p}'}}\right)^{\frac{1}{\mathrm{q}'}}(x;\sigma). \quad (100)$$

Proof. Since $1/\mathrm{p}+1/\mathrm{q}=1/\mathrm{p}'+1/\mathrm{q}'=1$ with $\mathrm{p}\geqslant\mathrm{p}'>1$, then $\mathrm{q}'\geqslant\mathrm{q}>1, 0<\mathrm{p}'/\mathrm{p}\leqslant1$ and $0<\mathrm{q}/\mathrm{q}'\leqslant1$. Form Remark 2, we have

$$\left({}^{\phi}_{\xi}\Theta^{M}_{u^+}wf^{\mathrm{p}}\right)(x;\sigma)=\left({}^{\phi}_{\xi}\Theta^{M}_{u^+}(w^{\frac{\mathrm{p}'-\mathrm{p}}{\mathrm{p}'}})(w^{\frac{\mathrm{p}}{\mathrm{p}'}}f^{\mathrm{p}})\right)(x;\sigma)$$

$$\geqslant\left({}^{\phi}_{\xi}\Theta^{M}_{u^+}w\right)^{\frac{\mathrm{p}'-\mathrm{p}}{\mathrm{p}'}}(x;\sigma)\left({}^{\phi}_{\xi}\Theta^{M}_{u^+}wf^{\mathrm{p}'}\right)^{\frac{\mathrm{p}}{\mathrm{p}'}}(x;\sigma), \quad (101)$$

$$\left({}^{\phi}_{\xi}\Theta^{M}_{u^+}wf^{\mathrm{q}'}\right)(x;\sigma)=\left({}^{\phi}_{\xi}\Theta^{M}_{u^+}(w^{\frac{\mathrm{q}-\mathrm{q}'}{\mathrm{q}}})(w^{\frac{\mathrm{q}'}{\mathrm{q}}}f^{\mathrm{q}'})\right)(x;\sigma)$$

$$\geqslant\left({}^{\phi}_{\xi}\Theta^{M}_{u^+}w\right)^{\frac{\mathrm{q}-\mathrm{q}'}{\mathrm{q}}}(x;\sigma)\left({}^{\phi}_{\xi}\Theta^{M}_{u^+}wf^{\mathrm{q}}\right)^{\frac{\mathrm{q}'}{\mathrm{q}}}(x;\sigma). \quad (102)$$

It follows from the hypothesis $0<\mathrm{m}\leqslant f^{\hbar}(t)/g^{\ell}(t)\leqslant\mathbb{M}$ that

$$f^{\hbar}(t)\leqslant\mathbb{M}g^{\ell}(t)\Rightarrow f^{\frac{\hbar}{\mathrm{q}}}(t)\leqslant\mathbb{M}^{\frac{1}{\mathrm{q}}}g^{\frac{\ell}{\mathrm{q}}}(t)\Rightarrow f^{\hbar}(t)\leqslant\mathbb{M}^{\frac{1}{\mathrm{q}}}f^{\frac{\hbar}{\mathrm{p}}}(t)g^{\frac{\ell}{\mathrm{q}}}(t). \quad (103)$$

Multiplying simultaneously the inequalities (103) by $\aleph^{-1}(x)\aleph(t)\mathscr{M}_x^t({}^{\varrho_1,\varrho_2}_{\sigma_1,\sigma_2}M^{\lambda,\rho,\theta,k,n}_{\alpha,\beta,\gamma,\delta,\mu,\nu},\xi,\phi)$ $\xi'(t)w(t)$ and integrating the acquired inequalities with regard to t from u to x, we obtain, based on the operator (38)

$$\left({}^{\phi}_{\xi}\Theta^{M}_{u^+}wf^{\hbar}\right)^{\frac{1}{\mathrm{p}}}(x;\sigma)\leqslant\mathbb{M}^{\frac{1}{\mathrm{pq}}}\left({}^{\phi}_{\xi}\Theta^{M}_{u^+}wf^{\frac{\hbar}{\mathrm{p}}}g^{\frac{\ell}{\mathrm{q}}}\right)^{\frac{1}{\mathrm{p}}}(x;\sigma). \quad (104)$$

Replacing f with $f^{\frac{\hbar}{\mathrm{p}}}$ in (101), we deduce

$$\left({}^{\phi}_{\xi}\Theta^{M}_{u^+}wf^{\hbar}\right)(x;\sigma)\geqslant\left({}^{\phi}_{\xi}\Theta^{M}_{u^+}w\right)^{\frac{\mathrm{p}'-\mathrm{p}}{\mathrm{p}'}}(x;\sigma)\left({}^{\phi}_{\xi}\Theta^{M}_{u^+}wf^{\frac{\mathrm{p}'\hbar}{\mathrm{p}}}\right)^{\frac{\mathrm{p}}{\mathrm{p}'}}(x;\sigma), \quad (105)$$

that is,

$$\left({}^{\phi}_{\xi}\Theta^{M}_{u^+}wf^{\frac{\mathrm{p}'\hbar}{\mathrm{p}}}\right)^{\frac{1}{\mathrm{p}'}}(x;\sigma)\leqslant\left({}^{\phi}_{\xi}\Theta^{M}_{u^+}w\right)^{\frac{\mathrm{p}-\mathrm{p}'}{\mathrm{pp}'}}(x;\sigma)\left({}^{\phi}_{\xi}\Theta^{M}_{u^+}wf^{\hbar}\right)^{\frac{1}{\mathrm{p}}}(x;\sigma). \quad (106)$$

Combining (104) and (106) yields

$$\left({}^{\phi}_{\xi}\Theta^{M}_{u^+} w f^{\frac{\mathbb{p}'\hbar}{\mathbb{p}}}\right)^{\frac{1}{\mathbb{p}'}}(x;\sigma) \leqslant \mathbb{M}^{\frac{1}{\mathbb{p}\mathbb{q}}}\left({}^{\phi}_{\xi}\Theta^{M}_{u^+} w\right)^{\frac{\mathbb{p}-\mathbb{p}'}{\mathbb{p}\mathbb{p}'}}(x;\sigma)\left({}^{\phi}_{\xi}\Theta^{M}_{u^+} w f^{\frac{\hbar}{\mathbb{p}}} g^{\frac{\ell}{\mathbb{q}}}\right)^{\frac{1}{\mathbb{p}}}(x;\sigma). \tag{107}$$

On the other hand, from the hypothesis $0 < \mathbb{m} \leqslant f^{\hbar}(t)/g^{\ell}(t) \leqslant \mathbb{M}$, we achieve

$$g^{\ell}(t) \leqslant \frac{1}{\mathbb{m}} f^{\hbar}(t) \Rightarrow g^{\frac{\ell}{\mathbb{p}'}}(t) \leqslant \frac{1}{\mathbb{m}^{\frac{1}{\mathbb{p}'}}} f^{\frac{\hbar}{\mathbb{p}'}}(t) \Rightarrow g^{\ell}(t) \leqslant \frac{1}{\mathbb{m}^{\frac{1}{\mathbb{p}'}}} f^{\frac{\hbar}{\mathbb{p}'}}(t) g^{\frac{\ell}{\mathbb{q}'}}(t). \tag{108}$$

Multiplying simultaneously the inequalities (108) by $\aleph^{-1}(x)\aleph(t)\mathscr{M}^{t}_{x}\left({}^{\varrho_1,\varrho_2}_{\sigma_1,\sigma_2}M^{\lambda,\rho,\theta,k,n}_{\alpha,\beta,\gamma,\delta,\mu,\nu}, \xi, \phi\right)$ $\xi'(t)w(t)$ and integrating the obtained inequalities in regard to t from u to x, we achieve based on the operator (38)

$$\left({}^{\phi}_{\xi}\Theta^{M}_{u^+} w g^{\ell}\right)^{\frac{1}{\mathbb{q}'}}(x;\sigma) \leqslant \frac{1}{\mathbb{m}^{\frac{1}{\mathbb{p}'\mathbb{q}'}}}\left({}^{\phi}_{\xi}\Theta^{M}_{u^+} w f^{\frac{\hbar}{\mathbb{p}'}} g^{\frac{\ell}{\mathbb{q}'}}\right)^{\frac{1}{\mathbb{q}'}}(x;\sigma). \tag{109}$$

Replacing f with $g^{\frac{\ell}{\mathbb{q}'}}$ in (102), we deduce

$$\left({}^{\phi}_{\xi}\Theta^{M}_{u^+} w g^{\ell}\right)(x;\sigma) \geqslant \left({}^{\phi}_{\xi}\Theta^{M}_{u^+} w\right)^{\frac{\mathbb{q}-\mathbb{q}'}{\mathbb{q}}}(x;\sigma)\left({}^{\phi}_{\xi}\Theta^{M}_{u^+} w g^{\frac{\mathbb{q}\ell}{\mathbb{q}'}}\right)^{\frac{\mathbb{q}'}{\mathbb{q}}}(x;\sigma), \tag{110}$$

that is,

$$\left({}^{\phi}_{\xi}\Theta^{M}_{u^+} w g^{\frac{\mathbb{q}\ell}{\mathbb{q}'}}\right)^{\frac{1}{\mathbb{q}}}(x;\sigma) \leqslant \left({}^{\phi}_{\xi}\Theta^{M}_{u^+} w\right)^{\frac{\mathbb{q}'-\mathbb{q}}{\mathbb{q}\mathbb{q}'}}(x;\sigma)\left({}^{\phi}_{\xi}\Theta^{M}_{u^+} w g^{\ell}\right)^{\frac{1}{\mathbb{q}'}}(x;\sigma). \tag{111}$$

Combining (108) and (110) yields

$$\left({}^{\phi}_{\xi}\Theta^{M}_{u^+} w g^{\frac{\mathbb{q}\ell}{\mathbb{q}'}}\right)^{\frac{1}{\mathbb{q}}}(x;\sigma) \leqslant \frac{1}{\mathbb{m}^{\frac{1}{\mathbb{p}'\mathbb{q}'}}}\left({}^{\phi}_{\xi}\Theta^{M}_{u^+} w\right)^{\frac{\mathbb{q}'-\mathbb{q}}{\mathbb{q}\mathbb{q}'}}(x;\sigma)\left({}^{\phi}_{\xi}\Theta^{M}_{u^+} w f^{\frac{\hbar}{\mathbb{p}'}} g^{\frac{\ell}{\mathbb{q}'}}\right)^{\frac{1}{\mathbb{q}'}}(x;\sigma). \tag{112}$$

By multiplying the inequalities (107) and (111), then we achieve the desired inequality (99). Similar to the proof of inequality (99), we also deduce inequality (100). The proof of Theorem 7 is completed. □

Remark 3. *If* $\mathbb{p} = \mathbb{p}'$, *it is easy to see that the inequalities* (99) *and* (100) *reduce to the second inequalities of* (73) *and* (74), *respectively.*

4. Reverse Minkowski Type Inequalities

In this section, we will consider some reverse Minkowski-type inequalities for modified unified generalized FIOs with extended unified MLFs.

Theorem 8. *Suppose that* f, g, w *are three continuous positive functions on* $[u, v]$ *satisfying* $0 < \mathbb{m} \leqslant f(t)/g(t) \leqslant \mathbb{M}$ *for any* $t \in [u, v]$ *and* $\mathbb{p} \geqslant 1$. *Then, for* $x \in [u, v]$, *the following FIO inequalities hold*

$$\begin{aligned}\left({}^{\phi}_{\xi}\Theta^{M}_{u^+} w (f+g)^{\mathbb{p}}\right)^{\frac{1}{\mathbb{p}}}(x;\sigma) &\leqslant \left({}^{\phi}_{\xi}\Theta^{M}_{u^+} w f^{\mathbb{p}}\right)^{\frac{1}{\mathbb{p}}}(x;\sigma) + \left({}^{\phi}_{\xi}\Theta^{M}_{u^+} w g^{\mathbb{p}}\right)^{\frac{1}{\mathbb{p}}}(x;\sigma) \\ &\leqslant \mathbb{c}_1 \left({}^{\phi}_{\xi}\Theta^{M}_{u^+} w (f+g)^{\mathbb{p}}\right)^{\frac{1}{\mathbb{p}}}(x;\sigma),\end{aligned} \tag{113}$$

where $\mathbb{c}_1$ *is defined in* (18).

Proof. When $\mathbb{p} = 1$, the first inequality of (113) becomes an equation. When $\mathbb{p} > 1$, by taking advantage of the Hölder's inequality in Remark 2, we can obtain for $1/\mathbb{p} + 1/\mathbb{q} = 1$

$$\left({}_{\xi}^{\phi}\Theta_{u^+}^{M} w(f+g)^{\mathbb{p}}\right)(x;\sigma) = \left({}_{\xi}^{\phi}\Theta_{u^+}^{M} w(f+g)(f+g)^{\mathbb{p}-1}\right)(x;\sigma)$$
$$= \left({}_{\xi}^{\phi}\Theta_{u^+}^{M} wf(f+g)^{\mathbb{p}-1}\right)(x;\sigma) + \left({}_{\xi}^{\phi}\Theta_{u^+}^{M} wg(f+g)^{\mathbb{p}-1}\right)(x;\sigma)$$
$$\leqslant \left(\left({}_{\xi}^{\phi}\Theta_{u^+}^{M} wf^{\mathbb{p}}\right)^{\frac{1}{\mathbb{p}}}(x;\sigma) + \left({}_{\xi}^{\phi}\Theta_{u^+}^{M} wg^{\mathbb{p}}\right)^{\frac{1}{\mathbb{p}}}(x;\sigma)\right)\left({}_{\xi}^{\phi}\Theta_{u^+}^{M} w(f+g)^{\mathbb{q}(\mathbb{p}-1)}\right)^{\frac{1}{\mathbb{q}}}(x;\sigma). \quad (114)$$

Since $1/\mathbb{p} + 1/\mathbb{q} = 1$, then $\mathbb{q}(\mathbb{p}-1) = \mathbb{p}$. Multiplying the inequality (114) by $\left({}_{\xi}^{\phi}\Theta_{u^+}^{M} w(f+g)^{\mathbb{p}}\right)^{-1/\mathbb{q}}(x;\sigma)$, we can acquire the first inequality of (113).

Since $0 < \mathbb{m} \leqslant f(t)/g(t) \leqslant \mathbb{M}$, then we can observe

$$(\mathbb{M}+1)f(t) \leqslant \mathbb{M}(f(t)+g(t)) \Rightarrow (\mathbb{M}+1)^{\mathbb{p}} f^{\mathbb{p}}(t) \leqslant \mathbb{M}^{\mathbb{p}}(f(t)+g(t))^{\mathbb{p}}. \quad (115)$$

Multiplying simultaneously the inequality (115) by $\aleph^{-1}(x)\aleph(t)\mathscr{M}_x^t({}_{\sigma_1,\sigma_2}^{\varrho_1,\varrho_2}M_{\alpha,\beta,\gamma,\delta,\mu,\nu}^{\lambda,\rho,\theta,k,n}, \xi, \phi)$ $\xi'(t)w(t)$ and integrating the acquired inequality in regard to t from u to x, we gain based on the operator (38)

$$\left({}_{\xi}^{\phi}\Theta_{u^+}^{M} wf^{\mathbb{p}}\right)^{\frac{1}{\mathbb{p}}}(x;\sigma) \leqslant \frac{\mathbb{M}}{\mathbb{M}+1}\left({}_{\xi}^{\phi}\Theta_{u^+}^{M} w(f+g)^{\mathbb{p}}\right)^{\frac{1}{\mathbb{p}}}(x;\sigma). \quad (116)$$

Also since $0 < \mathbb{m} \leqslant f(t)/g(t) \leqslant \mathbb{M}$, then we can write

$$(\mathbb{m}+1)g(t) \leqslant f(t)+g(t) \Rightarrow (\mathbb{m}+1)^{\mathbb{p}} g^{\mathbb{p}}(t) \leqslant (f(t)+g(t))^{\mathbb{p}}. \quad (117)$$

Multiplying simultaneously the inequality (117) by $\aleph^{-1}(x)\aleph(t)\mathscr{M}_x^t({}_{\sigma_1,\sigma_2}^{\varrho_1,\varrho_2}M_{\alpha,\beta,\gamma,\delta,\mu,\nu}^{\lambda,\rho,\theta,k,n}, \xi, \phi)$ $\xi'(t)w(t)$ and integrating the obtained inequality with regard to t from u to x, we acquire based on the operator (38)

$$\left({}_{\xi}^{\phi}\Theta_{u^+}^{M} wg^{\mathbb{p}}\right)^{\frac{1}{\mathbb{p}}}(x;\sigma) \leqslant \frac{1}{\mathbb{m}+1}\left({}_{\xi}^{\phi}\Theta_{u^+}^{M} w(f+g)^{\mathbb{p}}\right)^{\frac{1}{\mathbb{p}}}(x;\sigma). \quad (118)$$

Adding (116) and (118) yields the second inequality of (113). This completes the proof. □

Theorem 9. *Assume that f, g, w are three continuous positive functions on $[u,v]$ satisfying $0 < \mathbb{m} \leqslant f(t)/g(t) \leqslant \mathbb{M}$ for all $t \in [u,v]$ and $\mathbb{p} \geqslant 1$. Then, for $x \in [u,v]$, we have the following fractional integral inequality*

$$\left({}_{\xi}^{\phi}\Theta_{u^+}^{M} wf^{\mathbb{p}}\right)^{\frac{2}{\mathbb{p}}}(x;\sigma) + \left({}_{\xi}^{\phi}\Theta_{u^+}^{M} wg^{\mathbb{p}}\right)^{\frac{2}{\mathbb{p}}}(x;\sigma)$$
$$\geqslant \mathbb{c}_2\left({}_{\xi}^{\phi}\Theta_{u^+}^{M} wf^{\mathbb{p}}\right)^{\frac{1}{\mathbb{p}}}(x;\sigma)\left({}_{\xi}^{\phi}\Theta_{u^+}^{M} wg^{\mathbb{p}}\right)^{\frac{1}{\mathbb{p}}}(x;\sigma), \quad (119)$$

where $\mathbb{c}_2$ is defined in (18).

Proof. Combining (116) and (118) yields the following inequality

$$\left({}_{\xi}^{\phi}\Theta_{u^+}^{M} wf^{\mathbb{p}}\right)^{\frac{1}{\mathbb{p}}}(x;\sigma)\left({}_{\xi}^{\phi}\Theta_{u^+}^{M} wg^{\mathbb{p}}\right)^{\frac{1}{\mathbb{p}}}(x;\sigma) \leqslant \frac{\mathbb{M}\left({}_{\xi}^{\phi}\Theta_{u^+}^{M} w(f+g)^{\mathbb{p}}\right)^{\frac{2}{\mathbb{p}}}(x;\sigma)}{(\mathbb{m}+1)(\mathbb{M}+1)}. \quad (120)$$

Applying Minkowski's inequality to the right side of (120), we have

$$\frac{\mathbb{M}\left({}_{\xi}^{\phi}\Theta_{u^+}^{M} w(f+g)^{\mathbb{p}}\right)^{\frac{2}{\mathbb{p}}}(x;\sigma)}{(\mathbb{m}+1)(\mathbb{M}+1)} \leqslant \left(\left({}_{\xi}^{\phi}\Theta_{u^+}^{M} wf^{\mathbb{p}}\right)^{\frac{1}{\mathbb{p}}}(x;\sigma) + \left({}_{\xi}^{\phi}\Theta_{u^+}^{M} wg^{\mathbb{p}}\right)^{\frac{1}{\mathbb{p}}}(x;\sigma)\right)^2. \quad (121)$$

According to the inequalities (120) and (121), we have the desired inequality (119). This completes the proof. □

Theorem 10. *Let* $1/\mathbb{p}+1/\mathbb{q}=1$ *with* $\mathbb{p}>1$. *Let* f, g *and* w *be three continuous positive functions on* $[u,v]$ *satisfying* $0<\mathbb{m}\leqslant f(t)/g(t)\leqslant \mathbb{M}$ *for all* $t\in[u,v]$. *Then, for* $x\in[u,v]$, *we have the following fractional integral inequality*

$$\big({}_{\xi}^{\phi}\Theta_{u^+}^{M} wfg\big)(x;\sigma) \leqslant \mathbb{c}_3\big({}_{\xi}^{\phi}\Theta_{u^+}^{M} w(f^{\mathbb{p}}+g^{\mathbb{p}})\big)(x;\sigma)+\mathbb{c}_4\big({}_{\xi}^{\phi}\Theta_{u^+}^{M} w(f^{\mathbb{q}}+g^{\mathbb{q}})\big)(x;\sigma), \tag{122}$$

where $\mathbb{c}_3=2^{\mathbb{p}-1}\mathbb{M}^{\mathbb{p}}/(\mathbb{p}(\mathbb{M}+1)^{\mathbb{p}})$ *and* $\mathbb{c}_4=2^{\mathbb{q}-1}/(\mathbb{q}(\mathbb{m}+1)^{\mathbb{q}})$.

Proof. Similar to (116) and (118), we can easily obtain

$$\big({}_{\xi}^{\phi}\Theta_{u^+}^{M} wf^{\mathbb{p}}\big)(x;\sigma) \leqslant \frac{\mathbb{M}^{\mathbb{p}}}{(\mathbb{M}+1)^{\mathbb{p}}}\big({}_{\xi}^{\phi}\Theta_{u^+}^{M} w(f+g)^{\mathbb{p}}\big)(x;\sigma), \tag{123}$$

$$\big({}_{\xi}^{\phi}\Theta_{u^+}^{M} wg^{\mathbb{q}}\big)(x;\sigma) \leqslant \frac{1}{(\mathbb{m}+1)^{\mathbb{q}}}\big({}_{\xi}^{\phi}\Theta_{u^+}^{M} w(f+g)^{\mathbb{q}}\big)(x;\sigma). \tag{124}$$

It follows from Young inequality $\mathcal{A}^{1/\mathbb{p}}\mathcal{B}^{1/\mathbb{q}}\leqslant \mathcal{A}/\mathbb{p}+\mathcal{B}/\mathbb{q}$ with $\mathcal{A}=f^{\mathbb{p}}(t)$ and $\mathcal{B}=g^{\mathbb{q}}(t)$ that we have the following FIO inequality

$$\big({}_{\xi}^{\phi}\Theta_{u^+}^{M} wfg\big)(x;\sigma) \leqslant \frac{1}{\mathbb{p}}\big({}_{\xi}^{\phi}\Theta_{u^+}^{M} wf^{\mathbb{p}}\big)(x;\sigma)+\frac{1}{\mathbb{q}}\big({}_{\xi}^{\phi}\Theta_{u^+}^{M} wg^{\mathbb{q}}\big)(x;\sigma). \tag{125}$$

Substituting (123) and (124) into (125) yields

$$\begin{aligned}\big({}_{\xi}^{\phi}\Theta_{u^+}^{M} wfg\big)(x;\sigma) \leqslant{}& \frac{\mathbb{M}^{\mathbb{p}}}{\mathbb{p}(\mathbb{M}+1)^{\mathbb{p}}}\big({}_{\xi}^{\phi}\Theta_{u^+}^{M} w(f+g)^{\mathbb{p}}\big)(x;\sigma)\\ &+\frac{1}{\mathbb{q}(\mathbb{m}+1)^{\mathbb{q}}}\big({}_{\xi}^{\phi}\Theta_{u^+}^{M} w(f+g)^{\mathbb{q}}\big)(x;\sigma).\end{aligned} \tag{126}$$

Applying the inequality $(\mathcal{A}+\mathcal{B})^{\mathbb{j}}\leqslant 2^{\mathbb{j}-1}(\mathcal{A}^{\mathbb{j}}+\mathcal{B}^{\mathbb{j}})$, $\mathbb{j}>1$, $\mathcal{A},\mathcal{B}$, to the right part of (126), we have the following inequalities

$$\big({}_{\xi}^{\phi}\Theta_{u^+}^{M} w(f+g)^{\mathbb{p}}\big)(x;\sigma) \leqslant 2^{\mathbb{p}-1}\big({}_{\xi}^{\phi}\Theta_{u^+}^{M} w(f^{\mathbb{p}}+g^{\mathbb{p}})\big)(x;\sigma), \tag{127}$$

$$\big({}_{\xi}^{\phi}\Theta_{u^+}^{M} w(f+g)^{\mathbb{q}}\big)(x;\sigma) \leqslant 2^{\mathbb{q}-1}\big({}_{\xi}^{\phi}\Theta_{u^+}^{M} w(f^{\mathbb{q}}+g^{\mathbb{q}})\big)(x;\sigma). \tag{128}$$

Substituting (127) and (128) into (126) yields the desired inequality (122). This completes the proof. □

Theorem 11. *Suppose that* f, g, w *are three continuous positive functions on* $[u,v]$ *satisfying* $0<\mathbb{m}_1\leqslant f(t)\leqslant \mathbb{M}_1$ *and* $0<\mathbb{m}_2\leqslant g(t)\leqslant \mathbb{M}_2$ *for all* $t\in[u,v]$ *and* $\mathbb{p}\geqslant 1$. *Then, for* $x\in[u,v]$, *the following FIO inequalities hold*

$$\big({}_{\xi}^{\phi}\Theta_{u^+}^{M} wf^{\mathbb{p}}\big)^{\frac{1}{\mathbb{p}}}(x;\sigma)+\big({}_{\xi}^{\phi}\Theta_{u^+}^{M} wg^{\mathbb{p}}\big)^{\frac{1}{\mathbb{p}}}(x;\sigma) \leqslant \mathbb{c}_5\big({}_{\xi}^{\phi}\Theta_{u^+}^{M} w(f+g)^{\mathbb{p}}\big)^{\frac{1}{\mathbb{p}}}(x;\sigma), \tag{129}$$

where $\mathbb{c}_5=\big(\mathbb{M}_1(\mathbb{m}_1+\mathbb{M}_2)+\mathbb{M}_2(\mathbb{m}_2+\mathbb{M}_1)\big)/\big((\mathbb{m}_1+\mathbb{M}_2)(\mathbb{m}_2+\mathbb{M}_1)\big)$.

Proof. It follows from the hypothesis $0<\mathbb{m}_2\leqslant g(t)\leqslant \mathbb{M}_2$ that

$$\frac{1}{\mathbb{M}_2}\leqslant\frac{1}{g(t)}\leqslant\frac{1}{\mathbb{m}_2}. \tag{130}$$

Carrying the product between (130) and $0 < \mathbb{m}_1 \leqslant f(t) \leqslant \mathbb{M}_1$, we can observe

$$\frac{\mathbb{m}_1}{\mathbb{M}_2} \leqslant \frac{f(t)}{g(t)} \leqslant \frac{\mathbb{M}_1}{\mathbb{m}_2}. \tag{131}$$

According to the second inequality of (113), we can gain the desired inequality (129). The proof of Theorem 11 is completed. □

Theorem 12. *Assume that f, g, w are three continuous positive functions on $[u, v]$ satisfying $0 < \mathbb{m} \leqslant f(t)/g(t) \leqslant \mathbb{M}$ for all $t \in [u, v]$. Then, for $x \in [u, v]$, the following FIO inequalities hold*

$$\frac{1}{\mathbb{M}}\left({}_{\xi}^{\phi}\Theta_{u^+}^{M} wfg\right)(x;\sigma) \leqslant \frac{1}{(\mathbb{m}+1)(\mathbb{M}+1)}\left({}_{\xi}^{\phi}\Theta_{u^+}^{M} w(f+g)^2\right)(x;\sigma) \leqslant \frac{1}{\mathbb{m}}\left({}_{\xi}^{\phi}\Theta_{u^+}^{M} wfg\right)(x;\sigma). \tag{132}$$

Proof. Since $0 < \mathbb{m} \leqslant f(t)/g(t) \leqslant \mathbb{M}$, we have

$$(\mathbb{m}+1)g(t) \leqslant f(t) + g(t) \leqslant (\mathbb{M}+1)g(t). \tag{133}$$

It follows from $0 < \mathbb{m} \leqslant f(t)/g(t) \leqslant \mathbb{M}$ that $(1/\mathbb{M}) \leqslant g(t)/f(t) \leqslant (1/\mathbb{m})$, which implies

$$\left(\frac{\mathbb{M}+1}{\mathbb{M}}\right)f(t) \leqslant f(t) + g(t) \leqslant \left(\frac{\mathbb{m}+1}{\mathbb{m}}\right)f(t). \tag{134}$$

Realizing the product between (133) and (134) yields

$$\frac{1}{\mathbb{M}}f(t)g(t) \leqslant \frac{1}{(\mathbb{m}+1)(\mathbb{M}+1)}(f(t)+g(t))^2 \leqslant \frac{1}{\mathbb{m}}f(t)g(t). \tag{135}$$

Multiplying simultaneously the inequality (135) by $\aleph^{-1}(x)\aleph(t)\mathscr{M}_x^t({}^{\varrho_1,\varrho_2}_{\sigma_1,\sigma_2}M^{\lambda,\rho,\theta,k,n}_{\alpha,\beta,\gamma,\delta,\mu,\nu}, \xi, \phi)$ $\xi'(t)w(t)$ and integrating the obtained inequality in regard to t from u to x, we deduce based on the operator (38)

$$\frac{1}{\mathbb{M}}\left({}_{\xi}^{\phi}\Theta_{u^+}^{M} wfg\right)(x;\sigma) \leqslant \frac{1}{(\mathbb{m}+1)(\mathbb{M}+1)}\left({}_{\xi}^{\phi}\Theta_{u^+}^{M} w(f+g)^2\right)(x;\sigma) \leqslant \frac{1}{\mathbb{m}}\left({}_{\xi}^{\phi}\Theta_{u^+}^{M} wfg\right)(x;\sigma), \tag{136}$$

which is the desired inequality (132). This completes the proof. □

Theorem 13. *Suppose that f, g, w are three continuous positive functions on $[u, v]$ satisfying $0 < \kappa < \mathbb{m} \leqslant f(t)/g(t) \leqslant \mathbb{M}$ for all $t \in [u, v]$ and $\mathbb{p} \geqslant 1$. Then, for $x \in [u, v]$, we obtain*

$$\frac{\mathbb{M}+1}{\mathbb{M}-\kappa}\left({}_{\xi}^{\phi}\Theta_{u^+}^{M} w(f-\kappa g)^{\mathbb{p}}\right)^{\frac{1}{\mathbb{p}}}(x;\sigma) \leqslant \left({}_{\xi}^{\phi}\Theta_{u^+}^{M} wf^{\mathbb{p}}\right)^{\frac{1}{\mathbb{p}}}(x;\sigma) + \left({}_{\xi}^{\phi}\Theta_{u^+}^{M} wg^{\mathbb{p}}\right)^{\frac{1}{\mathbb{p}}}(x;\sigma) \leqslant \frac{\mathbb{m}+1}{\mathbb{m}-\kappa}\left({}_{\xi}^{\phi}\Theta_{u^+}^{M} w(f-\kappa g)^{\mathbb{p}}\right)^{\frac{1}{\mathbb{p}}}(x;\sigma). \tag{137}$$

Proof. Taking $0 < \kappa < \mathbb{m} \leqslant f(t)/g(t) \leqslant \mathbb{M}$, we have

$$\mathbb{m} - \kappa \leqslant \frac{f(t) - \kappa g(t)}{g(t)} \leqslant \mathbb{M} - \kappa \Rightarrow \frac{1}{\mathbb{M}-\kappa} \leqslant \frac{g(t)}{f(t) - \kappa g(t)} \leqslant \frac{1}{\mathbb{m}-\kappa}, \tag{138}$$

which demonstrates

$$\left(\frac{1}{\mathbb{M}-\kappa}\right)^{\mathbb{p}}(f(t)-\kappa g(t))^{\mathbb{p}} \leqslant g^{\mathbb{p}}(t) \leqslant \left(\frac{1}{\mathbb{m}-\kappa}\right)^{\mathbb{p}}(f(t)-\kappa g(t))^{\mathbb{p}}. \tag{139}$$

Multiplying simultaneously the inequality (139) by $\aleph^{-1}(x)\aleph(t)\mathscr{M}_x^t({}^{\varrho_1,\varrho_2}_{\sigma_1,\sigma_2}M^{\lambda,\rho,\theta,k,n}_{\alpha,\beta,\gamma,\delta,\mu,\nu},\xi,\phi)$ $\xi'(t)w(t)$ and integrating the resulting inequality with regard to t from u to x, we achieve based on the operator (38)

$$\frac{1}{\mathbb{M}-\kappa}\left({}^{\phi}_{\xi}\Theta^{M}_{u^+}w(f-\kappa g)^{\mathbb{p}}\right)^{\frac{1}{\mathbb{p}}}(x;\sigma)\leqslant\left({}^{\phi}_{\xi}\Theta^{M}_{u^+}wg^{\mathbb{p}}\right)^{\frac{1}{\mathbb{p}}}(x;\sigma)$$
$$\leqslant\frac{1}{\mathbb{m}-\kappa}\left({}^{\phi}_{\xi}\Theta^{M}_{u^+}w(f-\kappa g)^{\mathbb{p}}\right)^{\frac{1}{\mathbb{p}}}(x;\sigma). \quad (140)$$

It follows also from $0<\kappa<\mathbb{m}\leqslant f(t)/g(t)\leqslant\mathbb{M}$ that

$$\frac{1}{\mathbb{M}}\leqslant\frac{g(t)}{f(t)}\leqslant\frac{1}{\mathbb{m}}\Rightarrow\frac{\mathbb{m}-\kappa}{\mathbb{m}}\leqslant\frac{f(t)-\kappa g(t)}{f(t)}\leqslant\frac{\mathbb{M}-\kappa}{\mathbb{M}}, \quad (141)$$

which implies

$$\left(\frac{\mathbb{M}}{\mathbb{M}-\kappa}\right)^{\mathbb{p}}(f(t)-\kappa g(t))^{\mathbb{p}}\leqslant f^{\mathbb{p}}(t)\leqslant\left(\frac{\mathbb{m}}{\mathbb{m}-\kappa}\right)^{\mathbb{p}}(f(t)-\kappa g(t))^{\mathbb{p}}. \quad (142)$$

Multiplying simultaneously the inequality (142) by $\aleph^{-1}(x)\aleph(t)\mathscr{M}_x^t({}^{\varrho_1,\varrho_2}_{\sigma_1,\sigma_2}M^{\lambda,\rho,\theta,k,n}_{\alpha,\beta,\gamma,\delta,\mu,\nu},\xi,\phi)$ $\xi'(t)w(t)$ and integrating the obtained result with regard to t from u to x, we gain based on the operator (38)

$$\frac{\mathbb{M}}{\mathbb{M}-\kappa}\left({}^{\phi}_{\xi}\Theta^{M}_{u^+}w(f-\kappa g)^{\mathbb{p}}\right)^{\frac{1}{\mathbb{p}}}(x;\sigma)\leqslant\left({}^{\phi}_{\xi}\Theta^{M}_{u^+}wf^{\mathbb{p}}\right)^{\frac{1}{\mathbb{p}}}(x;\sigma)$$
$$\leqslant\frac{\mathbb{m}}{\mathbb{m}-\kappa}\left({}^{\phi}_{\xi}\Theta^{M}_{u^+}w(f-\kappa g)^{\mathbb{p}}\right)^{\frac{1}{\mathbb{p}}}(x;\sigma). \quad (143)$$

Adding (140) and (143) yields the desired inequality (137). This completes the proof. □

Theorem 14. *Let f,g and w be three continuous positive functions on $[u,v]$ satisfying $0<\mathbb{m}\leqslant f(t)/g(t)\leqslant\mathbb{M}$ for all $t\in[u,v]$ and $\mathbb{p}\geqslant 1$. Then, for $x\in[u,v]$, we have the following inequality*

$$\left({}^{\phi}_{\xi}\Theta^{M}_{u^+}wf^{\mathbb{p}}\right)^{\frac{1}{\mathbb{p}}}(x;\sigma)+\left({}^{\phi}_{\xi}\Theta^{M}_{u^+}wg^{\mathbb{p}}\right)^{\frac{1}{\mathbb{p}}}(x;\sigma)\leqslant 2\left({}^{\phi}_{\xi}\Theta^{M}_{u^+}wh^{\mathbb{p}}(f,g)\right)^{\frac{1}{\mathbb{p}}}(x;\sigma), \quad (144)$$

where $h(f(t),g(t))=\max\{(\mathbb{M}/\mathbb{m}+1)f(t)-\mathbb{M}g(t),((\mathbb{m}+\mathbb{M})g(t)-f(t))/\mathbb{m}\}$.

Proof. Since $0<\mathbb{m}\leqslant f(t)/g(t)\leqslant\mathbb{M}$, we have

$$0\leqslant\mathbb{m}\leqslant\mathbb{m}+\mathbb{M}-\frac{f(t)}{g(t)}\leqslant\mathbb{M}. \quad (145)$$

It follows from (145) that

$$g(t)\leqslant\frac{(\mathbb{m}+\mathbb{M})g(t)-f(t)}{\mathbb{m}}\leqslant h(f(t),g(t)). \quad (146)$$

Multiplying simultaneously the inequality (146) by $\aleph^{-1}(x)\aleph(t)\mathscr{M}_x^t({}^{\varrho_1,\varrho_2}_{\sigma_1,\sigma_2}M^{\lambda,\rho,\theta,k,n}_{\alpha,\beta,\gamma,\delta,\mu,\nu},\xi,\phi)$ $\xi'(t)w(t)$ and integrating the obtained result in regard to t from u to x, we achieve based on the operator (38)

$$\left({}^{\phi}_{\xi}\Theta^{M}_{u^+}wg^{\mathbb{p}}\right)^{\frac{1}{\mathbb{p}}}(x;\sigma)\leqslant\left({}^{\phi}_{\xi}\Theta^{M}_{u^+}wh^{\mathbb{p}}(f,g)\right)^{\frac{1}{\mathbb{p}}}(x;\sigma). \quad (147)$$

Also since $0 < \mathbb{m} \leqslant f(t)/g(t) \leqslant \mathbb{M}$, then $(1/\mathbb{M}) \leqslant g(t)/f(t) \leqslant (1/\mathbb{m})$, which implies

$$\frac{1}{\mathbb{M}} \leqslant \frac{1}{\mathbb{M}} + \frac{1}{\mathbb{m}} - \frac{g(t)}{f(t)} \leqslant \frac{1}{\mathbb{m}}. \tag{148}$$

It follows from (148) that

$$f(t) \leqslant \left(\frac{\mathbb{M}}{\mathbb{m}} + 1\right) f(t) - \mathbb{M} g(t) \leqslant h(f(t), g(t)). \tag{149}$$

Multiplying simultaneously the inequality (149) by $\aleph^{-1}(x)\aleph(t)\mathscr{M}_x^t({}_{\sigma_1,\sigma_2}^{\varrho_1,\varrho_2}M_{\alpha,\beta,\gamma,\delta,\mu,\nu}^{\lambda,\rho,\theta,k,n}, \xi, \phi)$ $\xi'(t)w(t)$ and integrating the resulting inequality in regard to t from u to x, we achieve based on the operator (38)

$$\left({}_{\xi}^{\phi}\Theta_{u^+}^{M} w f^{\mathbb{p}}\right)^{\frac{1}{\mathbb{p}}}(x;\sigma) \leqslant \left({}_{\xi}^{\phi}\Theta_{u^+}^{M} w h^{\mathbb{p}}(f,g)\right)^{\frac{1}{\mathbb{p}}}(x;\sigma). \tag{150}$$

Adding (147) and (150) yields the desired inequality (144). The proof of Theorem 14 is completed. □

Theorem 15. *Assume that f, g, w are three continuous positive functions on $[u, v]$ satisfying $0 < \mathbb{m} \leqslant f(t)/g(t) + g(t)/f(t) \leqslant \mathbb{M}$ for all $t \in [u, v]$ and $\mathbb{p} \geqslant 1$. Then, for $x \in [u, v]$, we have*

$$\mathbb{m}\left({}_{\xi}^{\phi}\Theta_{u^+}^{M} w f^{\mathbb{p}} g^{\mathbb{p}}\right)^{\frac{1}{\mathbb{p}}}(x;\sigma) \leqslant \left({}_{\xi}^{\phi}\Theta_{u^+}^{M} w (f^2+g^2)^{\mathbb{p}}\right)^{\frac{1}{\mathbb{p}}}(x;\sigma) \leqslant \mathbb{M}\left({}_{\xi}^{\phi}\Theta_{u^+}^{M} w f^{\mathbb{p}} g^{\mathbb{p}}\right)^{\frac{1}{\mathbb{p}}}(x;\sigma), \tag{151}$$

$$\begin{aligned}\frac{1}{\mathbb{M}}\left({}_{\xi}^{\phi}\Theta_{u^+}^{M} w (f^2+g^2)^{\mathbb{p}}\right)^{\frac{1}{\mathbb{p}}}(x;\sigma) &\leqslant \left({}_{\xi}^{\phi}\Theta_{u^+}^{M} w f^{\mathbb{p}} g^{\mathbb{p}}\right)^{\frac{1}{\mathbb{p}}}(x;\sigma) \\ &\leqslant \frac{1}{\mathbb{m}}\left({}_{\xi}^{\phi}\Theta_{u^+}^{M} w (f^2+g^2)^{\mathbb{p}}\right)^{\frac{1}{\mathbb{p}}}(x;\sigma).\end{aligned} \tag{152}$$

Proof. Since $0 < \mathbb{m} \leqslant f(t)/g(t) + g(t)/f(t) \leqslant \mathbb{M}$, we have

$$\mathbb{m} \leqslant \frac{f^2(t)+g^2(t)}{f(t)g(t)} \leqslant \mathbb{M} \Rightarrow \mathbb{m} f^{\mathbb{p}}(t) g^{\mathbb{p}}(t) \leqslant (f^2(t)+g^2(t))^{\mathbb{p}} \leqslant \mathbb{M} f^{\mathbb{p}}(t) g^{\mathbb{p}}(t). \tag{153}$$

$$\begin{aligned}\frac{1}{\mathbb{M}} \leqslant \frac{f(t)g(t)}{f^2(t)+g^2(t)} \leqslant \frac{1}{\mathbb{m}} \Rightarrow \frac{1}{\mathbb{M}}(f^2(t)+g^2(t))^{\mathbb{p}} &\leqslant f^{\mathbb{p}}(t) g^{\mathbb{p}}(t) \\ &\leqslant \frac{1}{\mathbb{m}}(f^2(t)+g^2(t))^{\mathbb{p}}.\end{aligned} \tag{154}$$

Multiplying simultaneously the inequalities (153) and (154) by $\mathscr{M}_x^t({}_{\sigma_1,\sigma_2}^{\varrho_1,\varrho_2}M_{\alpha,\beta,\gamma,\delta,\mu,\nu}^{\lambda,\rho,\theta,k,n}, \xi, \phi)$ $\aleph^{-1}(x)\aleph(t)\xi'(t)w(t)$ and integrating the obtained results with regard to t from u to x, we gain based on the operator (38)

$$\mathbb{m}\left({}_{\xi}^{\phi}\Theta_{u^+}^{M} w f^{\mathbb{p}} g^{\mathbb{p}}\right)^{\frac{1}{\mathbb{p}}}(x;\sigma) \leqslant \left({}_{\xi}^{\phi}\Theta_{u^+}^{M} w (f^2+g^2)^{\mathbb{p}}\right)^{\frac{1}{\mathbb{p}}}(x;\sigma) \leqslant \mathbb{M}\left({}_{\xi}^{\phi}\Theta_{u^+}^{M} w f^{\mathbb{p}} g^{\mathbb{p}}\right)^{\frac{1}{\mathbb{p}}}(x;\sigma), \tag{155}$$

$$\begin{aligned}\frac{1}{\mathbb{M}}\left({}_{\xi}^{\phi}\Theta_{u^+}^{M} w (f^2+g^2)^{\mathbb{p}}\right)^{\frac{1}{\mathbb{p}}}(x;\sigma) &\leqslant \left({}_{\xi}^{\phi}\Theta_{u^+}^{M} w f^{\mathbb{p}} g^{\mathbb{p}}\right)^{\frac{1}{\mathbb{p}}}(x;\sigma) \\ &\leqslant \frac{1}{\mathbb{m}}\left({}_{\xi}^{\phi}\Theta_{u^+}^{M} w (f^2+g^2)^{\mathbb{p}}\right)^{\frac{1}{\mathbb{p}}}(x;\sigma),\end{aligned} \tag{156}$$

which are the anticipated inequalities (151) and (152). This completes the proof. □

Remark 4. *By using the different settings of the parameters and functions in* (38)*, Theorems 8 and 9 can reduce to the reverse Minkowski-type Riemann–Liouville FIO inequalities [20], the reverse Minkowski-type Hadamard FIO inequalities [20,21], the reverse Minkowski-type generalized k-*

FIO inequalities [24], the reverse Minkowski-type Katugampola FIO inequalities [25], the reverse weighted Minkowski-type inequalities for generalized FIOs with the Wright function [39] and the reverse weighted Minkowski-type inequalities for weighted FIOs with a monotonically increasing function [40], respectively.

5. Some Applications

In this section, by utilizing the reverse Hölder- and Minkowski-type inequalities obtained in the front, we will present some other inequalities for modified unified generalized FIOs with extended unified MLFs.

Theorem 16 (Jensen's inequality). *Let f and w be three continuous positive functions on $[u,v]$ and $0<\ell<\hbar$. Then, for $x\in[u,v]$, we have FIO inequalities*

$$\frac{\left({}_{\xi}^{\phi}\Theta_{u^+}^{M}wf^{\ell}\right)^{\frac{1}{\ell}}(x;\sigma)}{\left({}_{\xi}^{\phi}\Theta_{u^+}^{M}w\right)^{\frac{1}{\ell}}(x;\sigma)}\leqslant\frac{\left({}_{\xi}^{\phi}\Theta_{u^+}^{M}wf^{\hbar}\right)^{\frac{1}{\hbar}}(x;\sigma)}{\left({}_{\xi}^{\phi}\Theta_{u^+}^{M}w\right)^{\frac{1}{\hbar}}(x;\sigma)}\leqslant\frac{\left({}_{\xi}^{\phi}\Theta_{u^+}^{M}S\left(\frac{\mathscr{G}_3f^{\hbar}}{\mathscr{F}_3}\right)wf^{\ell}\right)^{\frac{1}{\ell}}(x;\sigma)}{\left({}_{\xi}^{\phi}\Theta_{u^+}^{M}w\right)^{\frac{1}{\ell}}(x;\sigma)},\tag{157}$$

where $S(\cdot)$ denotes the Specht's ratio, $\mathscr{F}_3=\left({}_{\xi}^{\phi}\Theta_{u^+}^{M}wf^{\hbar}\right)(x;\sigma)$ and $\mathscr{G}_3=\left({}_{\xi}^{\phi}\Theta_{u^+}^{M}w\right)(x;\sigma)$.

Proof. Since $0<\ell<\hbar$, then $\mathbb{p}=\hbar/\ell>1$ and $\mathbb{q}=\hbar/(\hbar-\ell)>1$. By employing the Hölder's inequality in Remark 2, we have

$$\begin{aligned}\left({}_{\xi}^{\phi}\Theta_{u^+}^{M}wf^{\ell}\right)^{\frac{1}{\ell}}(x;\sigma)&=\left({}_{\xi}^{\phi}\Theta_{u^+}^{M}(w^{\ell/\hbar}f^{\ell})w^{1-\ell/\hbar}\right)^{\frac{1}{\ell}}(x;\sigma)\\&\leqslant\left(\left({}_{\xi}^{\phi}\Theta_{u^+}^{M}(w^{\ell/\hbar}f^{\ell})^{\hbar/\ell}\right)^{\frac{\ell}{\hbar}}(x;\sigma)\left({}_{\xi}^{\phi}\Theta_{u^+}^{M}(w^{1-\ell/\hbar})^{\hbar/(\hbar-\ell)}\right)^{\frac{\hbar-\ell}{\hbar}}(x;\sigma)\right)^{\frac{1}{\ell}}\\&=\left({}_{\xi}^{\phi}\Theta_{u^+}^{M}wf^{\hbar}\right)^{\frac{1}{\hbar}}(x;\sigma)\left({}_{\xi}^{\phi}\Theta_{u^+}^{M}w\right)^{\frac{1}{\ell}-\frac{1}{\hbar}}(x;\sigma),\end{aligned}\tag{158}$$

which implies the left inequality of (157). From the hypotheses, we obtain

$$\begin{aligned}&\left({}_{\xi}^{\phi}\Theta_{u^+}^{M}S\left(\frac{\mathscr{G}_3f^{\hbar}}{\mathscr{F}_3}\right)wf^{\ell}\right)^{\frac{1}{\ell}}(x;\sigma)\\&\quad=\left({}_{\xi}^{\phi}\Theta_{u^+}^{M}S\left(\frac{\mathscr{G}_3(w^{\ell/\hbar}f^{\ell})^{\hbar/\ell}}{\mathscr{F}_3(w^{1-\ell/\hbar})^{\hbar/(\hbar-\ell)}}\right)(w^{\ell/\hbar}f^{\ell})w^{1-\ell/\hbar}\right)^{\frac{1}{\ell}}(x;\sigma).\end{aligned}\tag{159}$$

By employing the third inequality of (41) to the right-hand part of (159), we observe

$$\begin{aligned}&\left({}_{\xi}^{\phi}\Theta_{u^+}^{M}S\left(\frac{\mathscr{G}_3(w^{\ell/\hbar}f^{\ell})^{\hbar/\ell}}{\mathscr{F}_3(w^{1-\ell/\hbar})^{\hbar/(\hbar-\ell)}}\right)(w^{\ell/\hbar}f^{\ell})w^{1-\ell/\hbar}\right)^{\frac{1}{\ell}}(x;\sigma)\\&\quad\geqslant\left(\left({}_{\xi}^{\phi}\Theta_{u^+}^{M}(w^{\ell/\hbar}f^{\ell})^{\hbar/\ell}\right)^{\frac{\ell}{\hbar}}(x;\sigma)\left({}_{\xi}^{\phi}\Theta_{u^+}^{M}(w^{1-\ell/\hbar})^{\hbar/(\hbar-\ell)}\right)^{\frac{\hbar-\ell}{\hbar}}(x;\sigma)\right)^{\frac{1}{\ell}}\\&\quad=\left({}_{\xi}^{\phi}\Theta_{u^+}^{M}wf^{\hbar}\right)^{\frac{1}{\hbar}}(x;\sigma)\left({}_{\xi}^{\phi}\Theta_{u^+}^{M}w\right)^{\frac{1}{\ell}-\frac{1}{\hbar}}(x;\sigma),\end{aligned}\tag{160}$$

which implies the right-hand desired inequality (157). The proof of Theorem 16 is completed. □

Theorem 17 (Weighted power mean inequality). *Assume that f, w are two continuous positive functions on $[u,v]$ and $0<\ell$. Then, for $x\in[u,v]$, we have FIO inequalities*

$$\frac{\left({}^{\phi}_{\xi}\Theta^{M}_{u^+}wf^{\ell}\right)^{\frac{1}{\ell}}(x;\sigma)}{\left({}^{\phi}_{\xi}\Theta^{M}_{u^+}w\right)^{\frac{1}{\ell}}(x;\sigma)} \leqslant \frac{\left({}^{\phi}_{\xi}\Theta^{M}_{u^+}wf^{2\ell}\right)^{\frac{1}{2\ell}}(x;\sigma)}{\left({}^{\phi}_{\xi}\Theta^{M}_{u^+}w\right)^{\frac{1}{2\ell}}(x;\sigma)} \leqslant \frac{\left({}^{\phi}_{\xi}\Theta^{M}_{u^+}S\left(\frac{\mathscr{F}_3^*}{\mathscr{G}_3 f^{2\ell}}\right)wf^{\ell}\right)^{\frac{1}{\ell}}(x;\sigma)}{\left({}^{\phi}_{\xi}\Theta^{M}_{u^+}w\right)^{\frac{1}{\ell}}(x;\sigma)}, \tag{161}$$

where $S(\cdot)$ denotes the Specht's ratio, $\mathscr{F}_3^*=\left({}^{\phi}_{\xi}\Theta^{M}_{u^+}wf^{2\ell}\right)(x;\sigma)$ and $\mathscr{G}_3=\left({}^{\phi}_{\xi}\Theta^{M}_{u^+}w\right)(x;\sigma)$.

Proof. From the left-hand inequality of (157) with $\hbar=2\ell$, we know the left-hand inequality of (161) holds. From the hypotheses, we obtain

$$\left({}^{\phi}_{\xi}\Theta^{M}_{u^+}S\left(\frac{\mathscr{F}_3^*}{\mathscr{G}_3 f^{2\ell}}\right)wf^{\ell}\right)^{\frac{1}{\ell}}(x;\sigma)=\left({}^{\phi}_{\xi}\Theta^{M}_{u^+}S\left(\frac{\mathscr{F}_3^* w}{\mathscr{G}_3 wf^{2\ell}}\right)(w^{1/2}f^{\ell})w^{1/2}\right)^{\frac{1}{\ell}}(x;\sigma). \tag{162}$$

By applying the third inequality of (41) with $\mathbb{p}=\mathbb{q}=1/2$ to the right-hand part of (162), we can acquire

$$\begin{aligned}&\left({}^{\phi}_{\xi}\Theta^{M}_{u^+}S\left(\frac{\mathscr{F}_3^* w}{\mathscr{G}_3 wf^{2\ell}}\right)(w^{1/2}f^{\ell})w^{1/2}\right)^{\frac{1}{\ell}}(x;\sigma)\\ &\qquad\geqslant\left(\left({}^{\phi}_{\xi}\Theta^{M}_{u^+}wf^{2\ell}\right)^{\frac{1}{2}}(x;\sigma)\left({}^{\phi}_{\xi}\Theta^{M}_{u^+}w\right)^{\frac{1}{2}}(x;\sigma)\right)^{\frac{1}{\ell}}\\ &\qquad=\left({}^{\phi}_{\xi}\Theta^{M}_{u^+}wf^{2\ell}\right)^{\frac{1}{2\ell}}(x;\sigma)\left({}^{\phi}_{\xi}\Theta^{M}_{u^+}w\right)^{\frac{1}{\ell}-\frac{1}{2\ell}}(x;\sigma),\end{aligned} \tag{163}$$

which implies the right-hand anticipated inequality (161). The proof of Theorem 17 is completed. □

Theorem 18 (Radon's inequality). *Suppose that f,g,w be three continuous positive functions on $[u,v]$ and $0<\ell$, $1\leqslant\hbar$. Then, for $x\in[u,v]$, we have FIO inequalities*

$$\begin{aligned}\frac{\left({}^{\phi}_{\xi}\Theta^{M}_{u^+}wfg^{\hbar-1}\right)^{\ell+\hbar}(x;\sigma)}{\left({}^{\phi}_{\xi}\Theta^{M}_{u^+}wg^{\hbar}\right)^{\ell+\hbar-1}(x;\sigma)}&\leqslant\left({}^{\phi}_{\xi}\Theta^{M}_{u^+}w\left(\frac{f^{\ell+\hbar}}{g^{\ell}}\right)\right)(x;\sigma)\\ &\leqslant\frac{\left({}^{\phi}_{\xi}\Theta^{M}_{u^+}S\left(\frac{\mathscr{G}_4 f^{\ell+\hbar}}{\mathscr{F}_4 g^{\ell+\hbar}}\right)wf^{\hbar}\right)^{\frac{\ell+\hbar}{\hbar}}(x;\sigma)}{\left({}^{\phi}_{\xi}\Theta^{M}_{u^+}wg^{\hbar}\right)^{\frac{\ell}{\hbar}}(x;\sigma)},\end{aligned} \tag{164}$$

where $S(\cdot)$ denotes the Specht's ratio, $\mathscr{F}_4=\left({}^{\phi}_{\xi}\Theta^{M}_{u^+}wf^{\frac{\ell+\hbar}{\hbar}}/g^{\ell}\right)(x;\sigma)$ and $\mathscr{G}_4=\left({}^{\phi}_{\xi}\Theta^{M}_{u^+}wg^{\hbar}\right)(x;\sigma)$.

Proof. For the convex $\Lambda(t)=t^{\ell+\hbar}$ on $[0,+\infty)$, then we have following inequality

$$\Lambda\left(\frac{\left({}^{\phi}_{\xi}\Theta^{M}_{u^+}w\Upsilon\right)(x;\sigma)}{\left({}^{\phi}_{\xi}\Theta^{M}_{u^+}w\right)(x;\sigma)}\right)\leqslant\frac{\left({}^{\phi}_{\xi}\Theta^{M}_{u^+}\Lambda(w\Upsilon)\right)(x;\sigma)}{\left({}^{\phi}_{\xi}\Theta^{M}_{u^+}w\right)(x;\sigma)}\quad\text{for positive function }\Upsilon. \tag{165}$$

By applying the above inequality (165) with $w=wg$ and $\Upsilon=f/g$, we can obtain

$$\begin{aligned}&\left({}^{\phi}_{\xi}\Theta^{M}_{u^+}w\left(\frac{f^{\ell+\hbar}}{g^{\ell}}\right)\right)(x;\sigma)=\left({}^{\phi}_{\xi}\Theta^{M}_{u^+}wg^{\hbar}\left(\frac{f}{g}\right)^{\ell+\hbar}\right)(x;\sigma)\\ &\quad\geqslant\left({}^{\phi}_{\xi}\Theta^{M}_{u^+}wg^{\hbar}\right)(x;\sigma)\left(\frac{\left({}^{\phi}_{\xi}\Theta^{M}_{u^+}wfg^{\hbar-1}\right)(x;\sigma)}{\left({}^{\phi}_{\xi}\Theta^{M}_{u^+}wg^{\hbar}\right)(x;\sigma)}\right)^{\ell+\hbar}=\frac{\left({}^{\phi}_{\xi}\Theta^{M}_{u^+}wfg^{\hbar-1}\right)^{\ell+\hbar}(x;\sigma)}{\left({}^{\phi}_{\xi}\Theta^{M}_{u^+}wg^{\hbar}\right)^{\ell+\hbar-1}(x;\sigma)},\end{aligned} \tag{166}$$

which is the left-hand desired inequality (164). For $\mathbb{p} = (\ell + \hbar)/\hbar$ and $\mathbb{q} = (\ell + \hbar)/\ell$, by replacing $f(t)$ and $g(t)$ by $\mathscr{U}(t)$ and $\mathscr{V}(t)$ in (41), respectively, we have

$$\big({}^{\phi}_{\xi}\Theta^{M}_{u^+} w\mathscr{U}^{\frac{\ell+\hbar}{\hbar}}\big)^{\frac{\hbar}{\ell+\hbar}}(x;\sigma)\big({}^{\phi}_{\xi}\Theta^{M}_{u^+} w\mathscr{V}^{\frac{\ell+\hbar}{\ell}}\big)^{\frac{\ell}{\ell+1}}(x;\sigma) \leqslant \left({}^{\phi}_{\xi}\Theta^{M}_{u^+} S\Big(\frac{\widehat{\mathscr{G}_1}\mathscr{U}^{\frac{\ell+\hbar}{\hbar}}}{\widehat{\mathscr{F}_1}\mathscr{V}^{\frac{\ell+\hbar}{\ell}}}\Big) w\mathscr{U}\mathscr{V}\right)(x;\sigma), \quad (167)$$

where $\widehat{\mathscr{F}_1} = \big({}^{\phi}_{\xi}\Theta^{M}_{u^+} w\mathscr{U}^{\frac{\ell+\hbar}{\hbar}}\big)(x;\sigma)$ and $\widehat{\mathscr{G}_1} = \big({}^{\phi}_{\xi}\Theta^{M}_{u^+} w\mathscr{V}^{\frac{\ell+\hbar}{\ell}}\big)(x;\sigma)$.

Letting $\mathscr{U} = (\mathscr{X}/\mathscr{Y})^{\hbar/(\ell+\hbar)}$ and $\mathscr{V} = \mathscr{X}^{\ell/(\ell+\hbar)}\mathscr{Y}^{\hbar/(\ell+\hbar)}$ in (167) yields

$$\Big({}^{\phi}_{\xi}\Theta^{M}_{u^+} w\Big(\frac{\mathscr{X}}{\mathscr{Y}}\Big)\Big)^{\frac{\hbar}{\ell+\hbar}}(x;\sigma)\Big({}^{\phi}_{\xi}\Theta^{M}_{u^+} w\big(\mathscr{X}\mathscr{Y}^{\frac{\hbar}{\ell}}\big)\Big)^{\frac{\ell}{\ell+\hbar}}(x;\sigma) \leqslant \left({}^{\phi}_{\xi}\Theta^{M}_{u^+} S\Big(\frac{\overline{\mathscr{G}}_1}{\overline{\mathscr{F}}_1\mathscr{Y}^{\frac{\ell+\hbar}{\ell}}}\Big) w\mathscr{X}\right)(x;\sigma), \quad (168)$$

where $\overline{\mathscr{F}}_1 = \big({}^{\phi}_{\xi}\Theta^{M}_{u^+} w\mathscr{X}/\mathscr{Y}\big)(x;\sigma)$ and $\overline{\mathscr{G}}_1 = \big({}^{\phi}_{\xi}\Theta^{M}_{u^+} w\mathscr{X}\mathscr{Y}^{\frac{\hbar}{\ell}}\big)(x;\sigma)$.

Replacing $\mathscr{X}$ and $\mathscr{Y}$ by $f^{\hbar}(t)$ and $(g(t)/f(t))^{\ell}$, we can observe

$$\Big({}^{\phi}_{\xi}\Theta^{M}_{u^+} w\Big(\frac{f^{\ell+\hbar}}{g^{\ell}}\Big)\Big)^{\frac{\hbar}{\ell+\hbar}}(x;\sigma)\Big({}^{\phi}_{\xi}\Theta^{M}_{u^+} wg^{\hbar}\Big)^{\frac{\ell}{\ell+\hbar}}(x;\sigma) \leqslant \Big({}^{\phi}_{\xi}\Theta^{M}_{u^+} S\Big(\frac{\mathscr{G}_4 f^{\ell+\hbar}}{\mathscr{F}_4 g^{\ell+\hbar}}\Big) wf^{\hbar}\Big)(x;\sigma), \quad (169)$$

where $\mathscr{F}_4 = \big({}^{\phi}_{\xi}\Theta^{M}_{u^+} wf^{\frac{\ell+\hbar}{\hbar}}/g^{\ell}\big)(x;\sigma)$ and $\mathscr{G}_4 = \big({}^{\phi}_{\xi}\Theta^{M}_{u^+} wg^{\hbar}\big)(x;\sigma)$. The foregoing inequality (169) can yield the right-hand inequality of (164). This completes the proof. □

Theorem 19. *For $0 < \ell$ and $1 \leqslant \hbar$, assume that f, g, w are three continuous positive functions satisfying $0 < \mathbb{m} \leqslant (f(t)/g(t))^{\ell+\hbar} \leqslant \mathbb{M}$, $t \in [u,v]$. Then, for $x \in [u,v]$, we have*

$$\Big({}^{\phi}_{\xi}\Theta^{M}_{u^+} w\Big(\frac{f^{\ell+\hbar}}{g^{\ell}}\Big)\Big)^{\hbar}(x;\sigma) \leqslant \Big(\frac{\mathbb{M}}{\mathbb{m}}\Big)^{\frac{\ell\hbar}{\ell+\hbar}} \frac{\big({}^{\phi}_{\xi}\Theta^{M}_{u^+} wf^{\hbar}\big)^{\ell+\hbar}(x;\sigma)}{\big({}^{\phi}_{\xi}\Theta^{M}_{u^+} wg^{\hbar}\big)^{\ell}(x;\sigma)}. \quad (170)$$

Proof. For $\mathbb{p} = (\ell + \hbar)/\hbar$ and $\mathbb{q} = (\ell + \hbar)/\ell$, making $f = \mathscr{U}$ and $g = \mathscr{V}$ in the left-hand inequality of (86) yields with $\mathbb{m} \leqslant \mathscr{U}^{\mathbb{p}}/\mathscr{V}^{\mathbb{q}} \leqslant \mathbb{M}$

$$\big({}^{\phi}_{\xi}\Theta^{M}_{u^+} w\mathscr{U}^{\frac{\ell+\hbar}{\hbar}}\big)^{\frac{\hbar}{\ell+\hbar}}(x;\sigma)\big({}^{\phi}_{\xi}\Theta^{M}_{u^+} w\mathscr{V}^{\frac{\ell+\hbar}{\ell}}\big)^{\frac{\ell}{\ell+\hbar}}(x;\sigma) \leqslant \Big(\frac{\mathbb{M}}{\mathbb{m}}\Big)^{\frac{\ell\hbar}{(\ell+\hbar)^2}}\big({}^{\phi}_{\xi}\Theta^{M}_{u^+} w\mathscr{U}\mathscr{V}\big)(x;\sigma). \quad (171)$$

Let $\mathscr{U} = f^{\hbar}/g^{\ell\hbar/(\ell+\hbar)}$ and $\mathscr{V} = g^{\ell\hbar/(\ell+\hbar)}$, from the condition $0 < \mathbb{m} \leqslant (f(t)/g(t))^{\ell+\hbar} \leqslant \mathbb{M}$, then $\mathbb{m} \leqslant \mathscr{U}^{\mathbb{p}}/\mathscr{V}^{\mathbb{q}} \leqslant \mathbb{M}$. Using the inequality (171), we obtain

$$\Big({}^{\phi}_{\xi}\Theta^{M}_{u^+} w\Big(\frac{f^{\ell+\hbar}}{g^{\ell}}\Big)\Big)^{\frac{\hbar}{\ell+\hbar}}(x;\sigma)\big({}^{\phi}_{\xi}\Theta^{M}_{u^+} wg^{\hbar}\big)^{\frac{\ell}{\ell+\hbar}}(x;\sigma) \leqslant \Big(\frac{\mathbb{M}}{\mathbb{m}}\Big)^{\frac{\ell\hbar}{(\ell+\hbar)^2}}\big({}^{\phi}_{\xi}\Theta^{M}_{u^+} wf^{\hbar}\big)(x;\sigma), \quad (172)$$

which is the right-hand anticipated inequality (170) by traightforward calculation. This completes the proof. □

Theorem 20. *Suppose that f, g, w are three continuous positive functions on $[u,v]$ satisfying $0 < \mathbb{m} \leqslant f(t)/g(t) \leqslant \mathbb{M}$ for all $t \in [u,v]$ and $\mathbb{p} \geqslant 1$. Then, for $x \in [u,v]$, the following FIO inequality holds*

$$\left({}_{\xi}^{\phi}\Theta_{u^+}^{M} w f^{\mathbb{P}}\right)(x;\sigma) + \left({}_{\xi}^{\phi}\Theta_{u^+}^{M} w g^{\mathbb{P}}\right)(x;\sigma) \leqslant \mathbb{c}_6 \left({}_{\xi}^{\phi}\Theta_{u^+}^{M} w (f+g)^{\mathbb{P}}\right)(x;\sigma) + \mathbb{c}_7 \left({}_{\xi}^{\phi}\Theta_{u^+}^{M} w (f-g)^{\mathbb{P}}\right)(x;\sigma), \quad (173)$$

where $\mathbb{c}_6 = ((\mathbb{M}+1)^{\mathbb{P}} + \mathbb{M}^{\mathbb{P}}(\mathbb{m}+1)^{\mathbb{P}})/(2(\mathbb{m}+1)^{\mathbb{P}}(\mathbb{M}+1)^{\mathbb{P}})$ *and* $\mathbb{c}_7 = (1+\mathbb{m}^{\mathbb{P}})/(2(\mathbb{m}-1)^{\mathbb{P}})$.

Proof. It follows from (116) and (118) with $\kappa = 1$ that

$$\left({}_{\xi}^{\phi}\Theta_{u^+}^{M} w f^{\mathbb{P}}\right)(x;\sigma) + \left({}_{\xi}^{\phi}\Theta_{u^+}^{M} w g^{\mathbb{P}}\right)(x;\sigma) \leqslant \left(\left(\frac{1}{\mathbb{m}+1}\right)^{\mathbb{P}} + \left(\frac{\mathbb{M}}{\mathbb{M}+1}\right)^{\mathbb{P}}\right) \cdot \left({}_{\xi}^{\phi}\Theta_{u^+}^{M} w (f+g)^{\mathbb{P}}\right)(x;\sigma). \quad (174)$$

On the other hand, from (140) and (143), we have

$$\left({}_{\xi}^{\phi}\Theta_{u^+}^{M} w g^{\mathbb{P}}\right)(x;\sigma) + \left({}_{\xi}^{\phi}\Theta_{u^+}^{M} w f^{\mathbb{P}}\right)(x;\sigma) \leqslant \left(\left(\frac{1}{\mathbb{m}-1}\right)^{\mathbb{P}} + \left(\frac{\mathbb{m}}{\mathbb{m}-1}\right)^{\mathbb{P}}\right) \cdot \left({}_{\xi}^{\phi}\Theta_{u^+}^{M} w (f-g)^{\mathbb{P}}\right)(x;\sigma). \quad (175)$$

Adding (174) and (175) yields the expected inequality (173). This finishes the proof. □

6. Conclusions

In this paper, we have investigated certain novel reverse Hölder- and Minkowski-type inequalities for modified unified generalized FIOs with extended unified MLFs. A large amount of the existing fractional Hölder- and Minkowski-type integral inequalities in the literature can be seen as the special cases of the main results of this paper. As applications, the reverse analogs of weighted Radon-, Jensen- and power mean-type inequalities for modified unified generalized FIOs with extended unified MLFs have been also presented. Following the main results of this article, we will investigate some Grüss-, Pólya-Szegö-, Beckenbach-, Bellman-type inequalities and related results for modified unified generalized FIOs with extended unified MLFs in future research.

Funding: This research was funded by the High-level Talent Fund Project of Sanmenxia Polytechnic under Grant No. SZYGCCRC-2021-009 and the Key Scientific Research Programmes of Higher Education of Henan Province under Grant No. 21B110005.

Institutional Review Board Statement: Not applicable.

Informed Consent Statement: Not applicable.

Data Availability Statement: Data sharing is not applicable to this paper as no datasets were generated or analyzed during the current study.

Acknowledgments: The author would like to express my gratitude to the editor and the anonymous reviewers for their ponderable comments and suggestions.

Conflicts of Interest: The author declares no conflict of interest.

References

1. Hardy, G.H.; Littlewood, J.E.; Pólya, G. *Inequalities*; Cambridge University Press: Cambridge, UK, 1952.
2. Mitrinović, D.S.; Pečarić, J.; Fink, A.M. *Classical and New Inequalities in Analysis*; Kluwer Academic Publishers Group: Dordrecht, The Netherlands, 1993.
3. Zuo, H.; Shi, G.; Fujii, M. Refined Young inequality with Kantorovich constant. *J. Math. Inequal* **2011**, *5*, 551–556. [CrossRef]
4. Sababheh, M.; Choi, D. A complete refinement of Young's inequality. *J. Math. Anal. Appl.* **2016**, *440*, 379–393. [CrossRef]
5. Yang, W. Certain weighted young and Pólya-Szegö-type inequalities involving Marichev-Saigo-Maeda fractional integral operators with applications. *Filomat* **2022**, *36*, 5161–5178. [CrossRef]

6. Tominaga, M. Specht's ratio in the Young inequality. *Sci. Math. Japon.* **2002**, *55*, 583–588.
7. Furuichi, S. Refined Young inequalities with Specht's ratio. *J. Egypt. Math. Soc.* **2012**, *20*, 46–49. [CrossRef]
8. Manjegani, S.M. Hölder and Young inequalities for the trace of operators. *Positivity* **2007**, *11*, 239–250. [CrossRef]
9. Yang, W. Some new fractional quantum integral inequalities. *Appl. Math. Lett.* **2012**, *25*, 963–969. [CrossRef]
10. Chen, G.; Liang, J.; Srivastava, H.M.; Lv, C. Local fractional integral Hölder-type inequalities and some related results. *Fractal Fract.* **2022**, *6*, 195. [CrossRef]
11. Rahman, G.; Khan, A.; Abdeljawad, T.; Nisar, K.S. The Minkowski inequalities via generalized proportional fractional integral operators. *Adv. Differ. Equ.* **2019**, *2019*, 287. [CrossRef]
12. Zhao, C.J.; Cheung, W.S. Hölder's reverse inequality and its applications. *Publ. Inst. Math.* **2016**, *99*, 211–216. [CrossRef]
13. El-Deeb, A.A.; Elsennary, H.A.; Cheung, W.S. Some reverse Hölder inequalities with Specht's ratio on time scales. *J. Nonlinear Sci. Appl.* **2018**, *11*, 444–455. [CrossRef]
14. Benaissa, B.; Budak, H. More on reverse of Hölder's integral inequality. *Korean J. Math.* **2020**, *28*, 9–15.
15. Agarwal, R.P.; O'Regan, D.; Saker, S.H. *Hardy Type Inequalities on Time Scales*; Springer International Publishing: Cham, Switzerland, 2016.
16. Yin, L.; Qi, F. Some integral inequalities on time scales. *Results Math.* **2013**, *64*, 371–381. [CrossRef]
17. Zakarya, M.; Abdelhamid, H.A.; Alnemer, G.; Rezk, H.M. More on Hölder's inequality and it's reverse via the diamond-alpha integral. *Symmetry* **2020**, *12*, 1716. [CrossRef]
18. Benaissa, B. A generalization of reverse Hölder's inequality via the diamond-α integral on time scales. *Hacet J. Math. Stat.* **2022**, *51*, 383–389. [CrossRef]
19. Set, E.; Özdemir, M.; Dragomir, S. On the Hermite-Hadamard inequality and other integral inequalities involving two functions. *J. Inequal. Appl.* **2010**, *2010*, 148102. [CrossRef]
20. Dahmani, Z. On Minkowski and Hermite-Hadamard integral inequalities via fractional integration. *Ann. Funct. Anal.* **2010**, *1*, 51–58. [CrossRef]
21. Chinchane, V.L.; Pachpatte, D.B. New fractional inequalities via Hadamard fractional integral. *Int. J. Funct. Anal. Oper. Theory Appl.* **2013**, *5*, 165–176.
22. Taf, S.; Brahim, K. Some new results using Hadamard fractional integral. *Int. J. Nonlinear Anal. Appl.* **2015**, *7*, 103–109.
23. Chinchane, V.L.; Pachpatte, D.B. New fractional inequalities involving Saigo fractional integral operator. *Math. Sci. Lett.* **2014**, *3*, 133–139. [CrossRef]
24. Chinchane, V.L. New approach to Minkowski's fractional inequalities using generalized k-fractional integral operator. *J. Indian Math. Soc.* **2018**, *85*, 32–41. [CrossRef]
25. Sousa, J.V.C.; Oliveira, E.C. The Minkowski's inequality by means of a generalized fractional integral. *AIMS Math.* **2018**, *3*, 131–147. [CrossRef]
26. Rashid, S.; Hammouch, Z.; Kalsoom, H.; Ashraf, R.; Chu, Y.M. New investigation on the generalized $\mathcal{K}$-fractional integral operators. *Front. Phys.* **2020**, *8*, 25. [CrossRef]
27. Aljaaidi, T.A.; Pachpatte, D.B.; Shatanawi, W.; Abdo, M.S.; Abodayeh, K. Generalized proportional fractional integral functional bounds in Minkowski's inequalities. *Adv. Differ. Equ.* **2021**, *2021*, 419. [CrossRef]
28. Bhatnagar, D.; Pandey, R.M. A study of some integral transforms on Q function. *South East Asian J. Math. Math. Sci.* **2020**, *16*, 99–110.
29. Zhou, S.S.; Farid, G.; Ahmad, A. Fractional versions of Minkowski-type fractional integral inequalities via unified Mittag–Leffler function. *Adv. Contin. Discret. Model.* **2022**, *2022*, 9. [CrossRef]
30. Andrić, M.; Farid, G.; Pečarić, J. A further extension of Mittag–Leffler function. *Fract. Calc. Appl. Anal.* **2018**, *21*, 1377–1395. [CrossRef]
31. Farid, G. A unified integral operator and further its consequences. *Open J. Math. Anal.* **2020**, *4*, 1–7. [CrossRef]
32. Farid, G. Study of inequalities for unified integral operators of generalized convex functions. *Open J. Math. Sci.* **2021**, *5*, 80–93. [CrossRef]
33. Raina, R.K. On generalized Wright's hypergeometric functions and fractional calculus operators. *East Asian Math. J.* **2005**, *21*, 191–203.
34. Yang, W. Certain new Chebyshev and Grüss-type inequalities for unified fractional integral operators via an extended generalized Mittag–Leffler function. *Fractal Fract.* **2022**, *6*, 182. [CrossRef]
35. Yang, W. Certain new weighted young- and Pólya-Szegö-type inequalities for unified fractional integral operators via an extended generalized Mittag–Leffler function with applications. *Fractals* **2022**, *30*, 2250106. [CrossRef]
36. Zhang, Y.; Farid, G.; Salleh, Z.; Ahmad, A. On a unified Mittag–Leffler function and associated fractional integral operator. *Math. Probl. Eng.* **2021**, *2021*, 6043769. [CrossRef]
37. Gao, T.;Farid, G.; Ahmad, A.; Luangboon, W.; Nonlaopon, K. Fractional Minkowski-type integral inequalities via the unified generalized fractional integral operator. *J. Funct. Spaces* **2022**, *2022*, 2890981. [CrossRef]
38. Abubakar, U.M.; Kabara, S.; Hassan, A.A.; Idris, A. Extended unified Mittag–Leffler function and its properties. *ResearchGate* **2022**. Available online: https://www.researchgate.net/publication/357713705 (accessed on 5 August 2023).

39. Liko, R.; Mohammed, P.O.; Kashuri, A.; Hamed, Y.S. Reverse Minkowski Inequalities Pertaining to New Weighted Generalized Fractional Integral Operators. *Fractal Fract.* **2022**, *6*, 131. [CrossRef]
40. Yildiz, Ç.; Gürbüz, M. The Minkowski type inequalities for weighted fractional operators. *Commun. Fac. Sci. Univ. Ank. Ser. A1 Math. Stat.* **2022**, *71*, 884–897. [CrossRef]

fractal and fractional

MDPI

Article

Certain Novel Fractional Integral Inequalities via Fuzzy Interval Valued Functions

Miguel Vivas-Cortez [1], Rana Safdar Ali [2], Humira Saif [2], Mdi Begum Jeelani [3], Gauhar Rahman [4,*] and Yasser Elmasry [5]

1 Escuela de Ciencias Físicas y Matemáticas, Facultad de Ciencias Exactas y Naturales, Pontificia Universidad Católica del Ecuador, Av. 12 de Octubre 1076, Apartado, Quito 17-01-2184, Ecuador; mjvivas@puce.edu.ec
2 Department of Mathematics, University of Lahore, Lahore 54000, Pakistan; safdar.ali@math.uol.edu.pk (R.S.A.); pmat07213019@student.uol.edu.pk (H.S.)
3 Department of Mathematics and Statistics, College of Science, Imam Mohammad Ibn Saud Islamic University, Riyadh 13314, Saudi Arabia; mbshaikh@imamu.edu.sa
4 Department of Mathematics and Statistics, Hazara University, Mansehra 21300, Pakistan
5 Department of Mathematics, Faculty of Science, King Khalid University, P.O. Box 9004, Abha 61466, Saudi Arabia; sadek@kku.edu.sa
* Correspondence: drgauhar.rahman@hu.edu.pk

Abstract: Fuzzy-interval valued functions (FIVFs) are the generalization of interval valued and real valued functions, which have a great contribution to resolve the problems arising in the theory of interval analysis. In this article, we elaborate the convexities and pre-invexities in aspects of FIVFs and investigate the existence of fuzzy fractional integral operators (FFIOs) having a generalized Bessel–Maitland function as their kernel. Using the class of convexities and pre-invexities FIVFs, we prove some Hermite–Hadamard (H-H) and trapezoid-type inequalities by the implementation of FFIOs. Additionally, we obtain other well known inequalities having significant behavior in the field of fuzzy interval analysis.

Keywords: convex (FIV) function; fuzzy fractional integral operator; pre-invex FIV function; Hermite–Hadamard (H-H)-type inequality; trapezoid-type inequality; extended generalized Bessel–Maitland function

MSC: 26D10; 26D15; 26D10; 26D53; 05A30

Citation: Vivas-Cortez, M.; Ali, R.S.; Saif, H.; Jeelani, M.B.; Rahman, G.; Elmasry, Y. Certain Novel Fractional Integral Inequalities via Fuzzy Interval Valued Functions. *Fractal Fract.* **2023**, *7*, 580. https://doi.org/10.3390/fractalfract7080580

Academic Editor: Palle Jorgensen

Received: 9 June 2023
Revised: 4 July 2023
Accepted: 6 July 2023
Published: 28 July 2023

1. Introduction

The theory of convexity is a dynamic, addictive, and significant area of study that has made major contributions to other fields of research, such as mathematical analysis, optimization problems, control theories, economics, finance, and game theory. By the theory of convexity, researchers have created unified numerical structures that can be used to resolve the wide range of problems, which have arisen in pure and applied mathematics. Convexity has been through significant advancements, generalizations, and extensions in a few decades. The study of fractional analysis has increased the demand of fractional operators in different areas of mathematics. To fulfil this requirement, many researchers have worked to develop the fractional operators by utilizing the non-singular special functions as their kernel and obtained modified versions of inequalities. Generalized fractional operators are one of the techniques used to improve the fractional inequalities for different convexities and pre-invexities, which have significant applications in the field of analysis.

Fractional calculus is the generalization of classical calculus, which plays an important role in pure, applied, and computation fields of mathematics. The research work in the field of fractional analysis has made a great contribution in various directions, such as signal-image processing, biology, physics, control operator theory, computer structure optimizations, and fluid dynamics [1–3]. During the last few decades, most of the scientists have worked to obtain the generalized versions of well-known inequalities and discussed a huge number of applications in the fields of analysis and discrete optimization. Many authors have worked extensively [4–12] and discussed the refinements and extensions in different areas of mathematics. The advanced analysis of inequalities is possible for the development of fractional operators by means of their kernel in multi-dimension functions, which play an ideal role to create new horizons to study the behavior of inequalities in multi-discipline branches of mathematics.

There are many significant applications of fuzzy set theory, which deals with the problems incorporating ambiguous, vague, and imprecise information, and makes decisions for individual or group collaboration. This initiative developed the idea of interval analysis [13] by Moore Ramon in 1966. Many scientists are attracted towards this field because of to its decision-making evaluation. The investigation on interval analysis proved to be beneficial in global optimization and constraint solution algorithms for decision makers and in the last few decades, it has become very popular among experts. It has provided effective and valid results, minimized the errors, and improved the accuracy. Due to this motivation, several researchers started their research in inequalities to get the desired results.

Zhao et al. [14] were the first who introduced the interval-valued-function (IVF). Many mathematicians introduced a strong relation between inequalities and IVFs by the implementation of different integral operators [15–19]. Many scholars have elaborated the applications of fuzzy differential equations and fuzzy interval analysis, which deal with many mathematical or computer modules [20–24]. In different research articles, many people illustrated several inequalities, such as Hermite–Hadamard inequality, Jensen inequality, Mercer inequality, Schur inequality, and trapezoid-type inequalities with the help of a fuzzy interval valued function [25,26].

Motivation

Convexity and generalized convexity are important concepts in optimization under the fuzzy domain, which provide fuzzy variational inequalities as a result of characterizing the optimality condition of convexity. Variational inequality and fuzzy set theory have generated strong techniques, which resolved many mathematical problems related to minimization theory and interval analysis. Fuzzy mappings are also termed as fuzzy-IVFs. There are many fractional integrals that contain fuzzy-IVFs for lower and upper cases. The behavior of well known inequalities can be checked by the successful implementation of such kinds of fractional integrals. These investigations demonstrate that this strategy is important from both a theoretical and a practical standpoint to transform the actual integral inequalities to the fuzzy integral inequalities.

2. Preliminaries

In this section, we will discuss the basic definitions and results, which help to understand the concepts of our new results.

Definition 1. *[27] Let $k \in \mathbb{R}$ be convex set, then the convex function for $\digamma : K \to \mathbb{R}$ is defined as follows:*

$$\digamma\left[\sigma u + (1-\sigma)v\right] \leq \sigma\digamma(u) + (1-\sigma)\digamma(v). \tag{1}$$

for $\sigma \in [0,1], \forall\ \eth, v \in K$.

The concave function for $\digamma$ is to have the reversed inequality, defined in Equation (1).

Definition 2. *The Hermite–Hadamard type inequality [28–31] is as follows:*

$$\digamma\left(\frac{\jmath+\aleph}{2}\right) \leq \frac{1}{\aleph-\jmath}\int_{\jmath}^{\aleph}\digamma(z)dz \leq \frac{\digamma(\jmath)+\digamma(\aleph)}{2}. \tag{2}$$

where $F : K \to R$ is the convex function, and $[\jmath, \aleph] \in K \subseteq \mathbb{R}, \jmath < \aleph, \jmath, \aleph \in R$.

The modified form of fractional H-H inequality for the convex function is as follows:

$$F\left(\frac{\jmath+\aleph}{2}\right) \leq \frac{1}{2\varsigma(v,\eth)^{\nu'+1}}\left[\mathcal{I}^{\eth^+}_{v,v'}(\Omega, F) + \mathcal{I}^{v^-}_{\eth,v'}(\Omega, F)\right] \leq \frac{F(\jmath)+F(\aleph)}{2} \tag{3}$$

Definition 3. *[25] Let $F : [\eth, v] \subset \mathbb{R} \to \Omega_c^+$ (a space of all positive closed and bounded intervals of $\mathbb{R}$) is a convex IVF given by $F(\alpha) = [F(\alpha)_*, F(\alpha)^*]$ for all $\alpha \in [\eth, v]$ where $F(\alpha)_*$ is convex function and $F(\alpha)^*$ is concave function. If F is Riemann integrable function, then:*

$$F\left(\frac{\alpha+\Lambda}{2}\right) \supseteq (IR)\frac{1}{\Lambda-\alpha}\int_\alpha^\Lambda F(z)dz \supseteq \frac{F(\alpha)+F(\Lambda)}{2} \tag{4}$$

The Hermite–Hadamard inequality for inclusion relation is as follows:

$$F\left(\frac{\alpha+\Lambda}{2}\right) \supseteq \frac{1}{2\varsigma(v,\eth)^{\nu'+1}}\left[\mathcal{I}^{\eth^+}_{v,v'}(\Omega, F) + \mathcal{I}^{v^-}_{\eth,v'}(\Omega, F)\right] \supseteq \frac{F(\alpha)+F(\Lambda)}{2} \tag{5}$$

Proposition 1. *[16] If $F, \daleth \in \mathbb{F}_0$, then for $\mathbb{F}_0$, relation " $\preccurlyeq$ " is defined as:*

$$F \preccurlyeq \daleth \text{ if and only if } [F]^\imath \leq_I [\daleth]^\imath \text{ for all } \imath \in [0,1], \tag{6}$$

the relation given above is also called partial order relation.

For $F, \daleth \in \mathbb{F}_0$, their scalar and vector properties are defined for $\imath \in [0,1]$, as follows:

$$\begin{aligned}(F \tilde{+} \daleth)^\imath &= (F)^\imath + (\daleth)^\imath \\ (F \tilde{+} \daleth)^\imath &= F + (\daleth)^\imath \\ (\wp . F)^\imath &= \wp.(F)^\imath \\ (F \tilde{\times} \daleth)^\imath &= (F)^\imath \times (\daleth)^\imath\end{aligned}$$

The Hukuhara difference of F and $\daleth$, for $\beth \in \mathbb{F}_0$ and $F = \daleth \tilde{+} \beth$, then $\beth$ is the Hukuhara difference of F and $\daleth$, which is defined as follows:

$$\begin{aligned}(\beth)^*(\imath) = (F \tilde{-} \daleth)^*(\imath) = F^*(\imath) - \daleth^*(\imath), \\ (\beth)_*(\imath) = (F \tilde{-} \daleth)_*(\imath) = F_*(\imath) - \daleth_*(\imath)\end{aligned}$$

Definition 4. *[11] Let P partition be the partition on the closed interval $[\eth, v]$ as the form:*

$$P = \eth = \jmath_1 < \jmath_2 < \jmath_3 < \jmath_4 < \jmath_5 < \ldots.\jmath_k = v.$$

The subintervals containing point P have a maximum length, which is called the mesh of a partition and defined as follows:

$$mesh(P) = max(\jmath_j - \jmath_{j-1} : j = 1,2,3...k) \tag{7}$$

Let $P(\sigma, [\eth, v])$ be the set of all $p \in P(\sigma, [\eth, v])$ and $mesh(p) < \sigma$. By taking arbitrary point $\daleth_j$ on each subinterval $[\jmath_{j-1}, \jmath_j]$, where $1 \leq j \leq k$, such that:

$$S(F, p, \sigma) = \sum_{j=1}^{k} F(\daleth_j)(\jmath_j - \jmath_{j-1}),$$

where $F : [\eth, v] \to \mathbb{R}_I$ is the real valued function and $S(F, p, \sigma)$ is called the Riemann sum of F corresponding to $p \in P(\sigma, [\eth, v])$.

Definition 5. *[32] A function $\digamma : [\eth, v] \to \mathbb{R}_I$ is called the Reimann integrable (IR-integrable) on the closed interval $[\eth, v]$ if there exists $B \in \mathbb{R}_I$ and for each ϵ and $\sigma > 0$, such that:*

$$d(S(\digamma, P, \sigma), B) < \epsilon.$$

for every Riemann sum of $\digamma$ corresponding to the partition $P \in p(\sigma, [\eth, v])$, and arbitrary choice of $\daleth_j \in [\jmath_{j-1}, \jmath_j]$ for $1 \leq j \leq k$; then, we have B be the IR-integral of $\digamma$ on $[\eth, v]$, which is denoted by $B = (IR)\int_{\eth}^{v} \digamma(t)dt$.

Theorem 1. *[33] The real interval valued function $\digamma : [\eth, v] \subseteq \mathbb{R} \to \mathbb{R}_I$ and $\digamma(\jmath) = [\digamma_*, \digamma^*]$; then, $\digamma$ is the integrable function on $[\eth, v]$ if and only if $\digamma_*$ and $\digamma^*$ are both integrable functions over $[\eth, v]$, if:*

$$(IR)\int_{\eth}^{v} \digamma(\jmath)dx = \left[(R)\int_{\eth}^{v} \digamma_*(\jmath), (R)\int_{\eth}^{v} \digamma^*(\jmath)dx\right]. \tag{8}$$

The representation of integrable function real valued functions and generalized integrable interval valued functions are $R_{[c,d]}, IR_{[\eth,v]}$, respectively.

Definition 6. *[34] If for each $\imath \in [0,1]$ and let $\digamma : k \subseteq R \to \mathbb{F}_0$ be fuzzy IVF, the $\imath$-levels define on IVF $\digamma : k \subseteq R \to \Omega_c$ are given by $\digamma_\imath(\jmath) = [\digamma_*(\jmath, \imath), \digamma^*(\jmath, \imath)], \forall \jmath \in \Omega$. Both the real-valued functions $\digamma_*(\jmath, \imath), \digamma^*(\jmath, \imath) : \Omega \to \mathbb{R}$, called the upper and lower functions of $\digamma$.*

Remark 1. *Let $\digamma : k \subseteq R \to \mathbb{F}_0$ be the FIV function, and for each $\imath \in [0,1]$, then $\digamma(\jmath)$ is called the continuous function at $\jmath \in \Omega$, and both the left and right real valued functions $\digamma_*(\jmath, \imath), \digamma^*(\jmath, \imath)$ are continuous at $\jmath \in K$.*

Definition 7. *[11] Let all closed and bounded intervals Ω_C of $\mathbb{R}$ and $\tau \in \Omega_C$, described as follows:*

$$\tau = [\tau_*, \tau^*] = \{\alpha \in \mathbb{R} | \tau_* \preccurlyeq \alpha \preccurlyeq \tau^*\}, (\tau_*, \tau^* \in \mathbb{R}).$$

- If $\tau_* = \tau^*$, then we say that τ is degenerate.
- If $\tau_* \geq 0$, then $[\tau_*, \tau^*]$ is said to be a positive interval. All positive intervals are denoted by Ω_C^+ and defined as:

$$\Omega_C^+ = \{[\tau_*, \tau^*] : [\tau_*, \tau^*] \in \Omega_C \quad and \quad \tau_* \geq 0\}.$$

Definition 8. *[11] Let $\sigma \in \mathbb{R}$ and $\sigma\tau$ be defined as:*

$$\sigma\tau = [\sigma\tau_*, \sigma\tau^*] \ if \ \sigma > 0, \ [\sigma\tau^*, \sigma\tau_*] \ if \ \sigma \preccurlyeq 0. \tag{9}$$

Algebraic Minkowski properties are defined for $\tau, \varsigma \in \Omega_C$ as follows:

$$[\varsigma_*, \varsigma^*] - [\tau_*, \tau^*] = [\varsigma_* - \tau_*, \varsigma^* - \tau^*]$$
$$, [\varsigma_*, \varsigma^*] + [\tau_*, \tau^*] = [\varsigma_* + \tau_*, \varsigma^* + \tau^*]$$

The inclusion " $\subseteq$ " property is defined as:

$$\varsigma \subseteq \tau, \ then \ [\varsigma_*, \varsigma^*] \subseteq [\tau_*, \tau^*] \ implies \ that \ \varsigma_* \preccurlyeq \tau_*, \varsigma^* \preccurlyeq \tau^*.$$

Remark 2. *[35] The relation " $\preccurlyeq_1$ " is defined on Ω_C as follows:*

$$[\sigma_*, \sigma^*] \preccurlyeq_1 [\tau_*, \tau^*] \text{ if and only if } \sigma_* \preccurlyeq \tau_*, \sigma^* \preccurlyeq \tau^*$$

for all $[\sigma_*, \sigma^*], [\tau_*, \tau^*] \in \Omega_C$, is an order relation. We have $[\sigma_*, \sigma^*], [\tau_*, \tau^*] \in \Omega_C$, then $[\sigma_*, \sigma^*] \preccurlyeq_1 [\tau_*, \tau^*]$ if and only if $\sigma_* \preccurlyeq \tau_*$ or $\sigma^* \preccurlyeq \tau^*, \sigma < \tau$.

Definition 9. *[11] For $\eth, v \in K$, $\lambda \in [0,1]$, if $F : K \times K \to \mathbb{R}$ is the bi-function, then the invex set $K \subseteq \mathbb{R}$ is defined as follows:*

$$v + \lambda F(\eth, v) \in K.$$

Definition 10. *[11] Let K be an invex set with respect to ς and $F : K \to \mathbb{R}$ is the pre-invex function, defined for $\jmath, \aleph \in K$ as follows:*

$$F(\aleph + \lambda\varsigma(\jmath, \aleph)) \leq \lambda F(\jmath) + (1-\lambda)F(\aleph), \tag{10}$$

where $\lambda \in [0,1]$.

Definition 11. *[22] If $F : K \to \mathbb{R}$, then the convex fuzzy interval valued function is defined as follows:*

$$F\left[\sigma\eth + (1-\sigma)v\right] \preccurlyeq \sigma F(\eth)\tilde{+}(1-\sigma)F(v). \tag{11}$$

for $\sigma \in [0,1]$, $\forall \eth, v \in K$, and then we call F concave if inequality (11) is reversed.

Remark 3. *If $F_*(\jmath, \imath) = F^*(\jmath, \imath)$ and $\imath = 1$, then we obtain the inequality (1).*

Definition 12. *[23] The pre-invex FIV function $F : K \to \mathbb{R}$ is defined for $\jmath, \aleph \in K$ and $\lambda \in [0,1]$ as follows:*

$$F(\aleph + \lambda\varsigma(\jmath, \aleph)) \preccurlyeq \lambda F(\jmath)\tilde{+}(1-\lambda)F(\aleph), \tag{12}$$

where K is an open invex set with respect to ς if we reversed the inequality (12), then named as pre-incave FIV functions.

Definition 13. *[36] The gamma function is defined in an integral form as follows:*

$$\Gamma(\sigma) = \int_0^\infty z^{\sigma-1}e^{-z}dz,$$

for $\Re(t) > 0$.

Definition 14. *[36] The Pochammer's symbol is defined as follows:*

$$(\wp)_\sigma = \left\{ \begin{array}{ll} 1, & \text{for } \sigma = 0, \wp \neq 0 \\ \wp(\wp+1)\cdots(\wp+\sigma-1), & \text{for } \sigma \geq 1, \end{array} \right\}$$

For $\sigma \in \mathbb{N}$ and $\wp \in \mathbb{C}$:

$$\begin{aligned} (\wp)_n &= \frac{\Gamma(\wp+n)}{\Gamma(\wp)} \\ (\wp)_{kn} &= \frac{\Gamma(\wp+kn)}{\Gamma(\wp)} \end{aligned}$$

where Γ is the gamma function.

Definition 15. *[37] The beta function for $\Re(m) > 0$ and $\Re(n) > 0$ is defined as follows:*

$$\begin{aligned}\Lambda(g,h) &= \int_0^1 \sigma^{g-1}(1-\sigma)^{h-1}d\sigma \\ &= \frac{\Gamma(g)\Gamma(h)}{\Gamma(g+h)}.\end{aligned}$$

Definition 16. *[38] The extended version of beta functions is defined for $\Re(g) > 0$, $\Re(h) > 0$, $\Re(p) > 0$ as follows:*

$$\Lambda_p(g,h) = \int_0^1 z^{g-1}(1-z)^{h-1}exp(\frac{-p}{z(1-z)})dz.$$

If we replace $p = 1$, then the extended beta function is going to replace the classical beta function.

Definition 17. *[39,40] The generalized Bessel–Maitland (eight-parameter) function is defined as follows:*

$$J_{\xi,\hbar,m,\sigma}^{\beth,\Theta,\sigma,\vartheta}(\aleph) = \sum_{p=0}^{\infty} \frac{(\Theta)_{\hbar p}(\vartheta)_{\sigma p}(-\aleph)^p}{\wp(\xi p + \beth + 1)(\sigma)_{mp}}, \tag{13}$$

where $\digamma, \beth, \sigma, \digamma, \vartheta \in \mathbb{C}$, $\Re(\digamma) > 0$, $\Re(\digamma) > 0$, $\Re(\nu) \geq -1$, $\Re(\sigma) > 0$, $\Re(\vartheta) > 0$; $m, \hbar, \sigma \geq 0$ and $\hbar > \Re(\digamma) + \sigma, m$.

Definition 18. *[40] The extended version of the Bessel–Maitland function is defined for $\Xi, \gimel, \nu, \wp, \rho, c \in \mathbb{C}$, $\Re(\Xi) > 0$, $\Re(\nu) \geq -1$, $\Re(\gimel) > 0$, $\Re(\rho) > 0$, $\Re(\wp) > 0$; $\hbar, \sigma, m \geq 0$ and $\hbar, m > \Re(\Xi) + \sigma$ as follows:*

$$J_{v,\gimel,\rho,\wp}^{\Xi,\hbar,m,\sigma,c}(\Omega; p) = \sum_{n=0}^{\infty} \frac{\Lambda_p(\gimel + \hbar n, c - \gimel)(c)_{\hbar n}(\wp)_{\sigma n}}{\Lambda(\gimel, c - \gimel)\wp(\Xi n + v + 1)(\rho)_{mn}}(-\Omega)^n. \tag{14}$$

Definition 19. *Let $\digamma : K \subseteq \mathbb{R} \to \mathbb{R}$ be the positive real valued function, then the Godunova–Levin FIV function is defined as follows:*

$$\digamma(\sigma\eth + (1-\sigma)v) \preccurlyeq \frac{\digamma(\eth)}{\sigma} \tilde{+} \frac{\digamma(v)}{1-\sigma},$$

where $\eth, v \in K$, $\sigma \in (0,1)$

Definition 20. *Let $h : (0,1) \to \mathbb{R}$ and $\digamma : K \to \mathbb{R}$ be the non-negative real valued function, the h-Godunova–Levin FIV function is defined for $\sigma \in (0,1)$, $\eth, v \in K$ as follows:*

$$\digamma(\sigma\eth + (1-\sigma)v) \preccurlyeq \frac{\digamma(\eth)}{h(\sigma)} \tilde{+} \frac{\digamma(v)}{h(1-\sigma)}.$$

Definition 21. *A real valued function $\digamma : K \to \mathbb{R}$ is said to be h-Godunova–Levin pre-invex FIV function with respect to ς if for all $\eth, v \in K$, $\Phi \in (0,1)$ as follows:*

$$\digamma(\eth + \Phi\varsigma(v,\eth)) \preccurlyeq \frac{\digamma(\eth)}{h(1-\Phi)} \tilde{+} \frac{\digamma(v)}{h(\Phi)}$$

holds.

Definition 22. *[40] The generalized fractional integral operators having an extended version of the Bessel–Maitland function as their kernel are defined for* $\Xi, \nu, \daleth, \rho, \wp, c \in \mathbb{C}$, $\Re(\Xi) > 0$, $\Re(\nu) \geq -1$, $\Re(\rho) > 0$, $\Re(\daleth) > 0$, $\Re(\wp) > 0$; $\hbar, \sigma, m \geq 0$ *and* $\hbar, m > \Re(\Xi) + \sigma$ *as follows:*

$$\left(\mathfrak{T}^{\Xi,\hbar,m,\sigma,c}_{v,\daleth,\rho,\wp;p^+} f\right)(\jmath, r) = \int_p^{\jmath} (\jmath - t)^v \mathrm{J}^{\Xi,\hbar,m,\sigma,c}_{v,\daleth,\rho,\wp}(\Omega(\jmath - t)^{\Xi}; r) f(\eth) d\eth, (\jmath > p)$$

and

$$\left(\mathfrak{T}^{\Xi,\hbar,m,\sigma,c}_{v,\daleth,\rho,\wp;q^-} f\right)(\jmath, r) = \int_{\jmath}^{q} (t - \jmath)^v \mathrm{J}^{\Xi,\hbar,m,\sigma,c}_{v,\daleth,\rho,\wp}(\Omega(t - \jmath)^{\Xi}; r) f(\eth) d\eth, (\jmath < q).$$

Remark 4. *The generalized fractional operators are represented in short notations [41] as follows:*

$$(\mathcal{I}^{\eth^+}_{v,v'})(\Omega, F) = (\mathfrak{T}^{\Xi,\hbar,m,\sigma,c}_{v',\daleth,\rho,\wp;\eth^+} F)(v, p)$$
$$(\mathcal{I}^{v^-}_{\eth,v'})(\Omega, F) = (\mathfrak{T}^{\Xi,\hbar,m,\sigma,c}_{v',\daleth,\rho,\wp;v^-} F)(\eth, p).$$

and

$$\int_v^u (v - x)^{v'} \mathcal{J}^{\Xi,\hbar,m,\sigma,c}_{v',\daleth,\rho,\imath}(\Omega(\frac{v - x}{\varsigma(v, \eth)})^{\Xi}; p) dx = (\mathfrak{I}^{v^-}_{\eth,v'})(\Omega', 1)$$

3. Hermite–Hadamard (H-H) Integral Inequalities via Convex FIVF

Here, we define the left- and right-sided generalized fuzzy fractional integral operators, discuss the existence of H-H type inequality for the h-Godnova–Levin convex FIVF, and deduce some corollaries from our main results.

Definition 23. *The left- and right-sided generalized fuzzy fractional integral operators based on the left and right end point function for* $\Xi, \nu, \daleth, \rho, \wp, c \in \mathbb{C}$, $\Re(\Xi) > 0$, $\Re(\nu) \geq -1$, $\Re(\daleth) > 0$, $\Re(\rho) > 0$, $\Re(\wp) > 0$; $\hbar, m, \sigma \geq 0$ *and* $m, \hbar > \Re(\Xi) + \sigma$ *are defined as follows:*

$$\left[\left(\mathfrak{T}^{\Xi,\hbar,m,\sigma,c}_{v,\daleth,\rho,\wp;p^+} f\right)(\jmath, r)\right]^{\imath} = \int_p^{\jmath} (\jmath - t)^v \mathrm{J}^{\Xi,\hbar,m,\sigma,c}_{v,\daleth,\rho,\wp}(\Omega(\jmath - t)^{\Xi}; r) f_{\imath}(\eth) d\eth$$

$$= \int_p^{\jmath} (\jmath - t)^v \mathrm{J}^{\Xi,\hbar,m,\sigma,c}_{v,\daleth,\rho,\wp}(\Omega(\jmath - t)^{\Xi}; r) [f_*(\eth, \imath), f^*(\eth, \imath)] d\eth, (\jmath > p)$$

where

$$\left(\mathfrak{T}^{\Xi,\hbar,m,\sigma,c}_{v,\daleth,\rho,\wp;p^+} f_*\right)((\jmath, r), \imath) = \int_p^{\jmath} (\jmath - t)^v \mathrm{J}^{\Xi,\hbar,m,\sigma,c}_{v,\daleth,\rho,\wp}(\Omega(\jmath - t)^{\Xi}; r) f_*(\eth, \imath) d\eth, (\jmath > p)$$

$$\left(\mathfrak{T}^{\Xi,m,\hbar,\sigma,c}_{v,\daleth,\rho,\wp;p^+} f^*\right)((\jmath, r), \imath) = \int_p^{\jmath} (\jmath - t)^v \mathrm{J}^{\Xi,m,\hbar,\sigma,c}_{v,\daleth,\rho,\wp}(\Omega(\jmath - t)^{\Xi}; r) f^*(\eth, \imath) d\eth, (\jmath > p)$$

On the same pattern, we can easily define the right-sided generalized fractional integral operator based on left and right end point functions.

Remark 5. *The generalized fuzzy fractional integral operators are represented in short notations as follows:*

$$\int_u^v (x - u)^{v'} \mathcal{J}^{\Xi,\hbar,m,\sigma,c}_{v',\daleth,\rho,\imath}(\Omega(\frac{x - u}{\varsigma(v, \eth)})^{\Xi}; p) F_*(x, \imath) dx = (\mathfrak{I}^{\eth^+}_{v,v'})(\Omega'; F_*)$$
$$\int_v^u (v - x)^{v'} \mathcal{J}^{\Xi,\hbar,m,\sigma,c}_{v',\daleth,\rho,\imath}(\Omega(\frac{v - x}{\varsigma(v, \eth)})^{\Xi}; p) F_*(x, \imath) dx = (\mathfrak{I}^{v^-}_{\eth,v'})(\Omega'; F_*) \quad (15)$$

Theorem 2. *Let $h : (0,1) \to \mathbb{R}$ be a positive function, $h(\sigma) \neq 0$ and h-Godunova Levin convex fuzzy interval valued function $\digamma : [\eth, v] \to \mathbb{R}$ with $\digamma \in L_1[\eth, v]$ and $0 < \eth < v$, then with the generalized fractional integral described in* (22)*, we have;*

$$\frac{h(\frac{1}{2})}{2}\digamma\left(\frac{\eth+v}{2}\right)(\beth^{v^-}_{\eth,v'})(\Omega',1) \preccurlyeq \frac{1}{2}\Big[\left(\beth^{v^-}_{\eth,v'}\right)(\Omega',\digamma)\tilde{+}\left(\beth^{\eth^+}_{v,v'}\right)(\Omega',\digamma)\Big]$$
$$\preccurlyeq \frac{\digamma(\eth)\tilde{+}\digamma(v)}{2}\int_0^1\Big[\frac{1}{h(\sigma)}+\frac{1}{h(1-\sigma)}\Big]\sigma^{v'}\mathcal{J}^{\Xi,\hbar,m,\sigma,c}_{v',\beth,\rho,\imath}(\Omega\sigma^{\Xi};p)d\sigma, \tag{16}$$

where $\Omega' = \frac{\Omega}{\varsigma(v,\eth)^{\Xi}}$

Proof. Consider $\digamma$ to be the h-Godunova–Levin convex function for $\jmath, \aleph \in [\eth, v]$, we have:

$$\digamma(\hbar\jmath + (1-\hbar)\aleph) \leq \frac{\digamma(\jmath)}{h(\hbar)} + \frac{\digamma(\aleph)}{h(1-\hbar)}$$

Replacing the values $\jmath = \sigma\eth + (1-\sigma)v, \aleph = (1-\sigma)\eth + \sigma v$ and $\hbar = \frac{1}{2}$, we have:

$$\digamma(\frac{\eth+v}{2}) \leq \frac{1}{h(\frac{1}{2})}[\digamma(\sigma\eth+(1-\sigma)v)+\digamma((1-\sigma)\eth+\sigma v)]$$
$$h(\frac{1}{2})\digamma(\frac{\eth+v}{2}) \leq \digamma(\sigma\eth+(1-\sigma)v)+\digamma((1-\sigma)\eth+\sigma v)$$

If we take for every $\imath \in [0,1]$, then we have:

$$\digamma(\frac{\eth+v}{2},\imath) \leq \frac{1}{h(\frac{1}{2})}[\digamma_*(\sigma\eth+(1-\sigma)v,\imath)+\digamma_*((1-\sigma)\eth+\sigma v),\imath] \tag{17}$$

Multiplying by $\sigma^{v'}\mathcal{J}^{\Xi,\hbar,m,\sigma,c}_{v',\beth,\rho,\imath}(\Omega\sigma^{\Xi};p)$ in Equation (17) and then integrating with respect to σ over the interval $[0,1]$, we have:

$$h(\frac{1}{2})\digamma_*(\frac{\eth+v}{2},\imath)\int_0^1\sigma^{v'}\mathcal{J}^{\Xi,\hbar,m,\sigma,c}_{v',\beth,\rho,\imath}(\Omega\sigma^{\Xi};p)d\sigma \leq \int_0^1\sigma^{v'}\mathcal{J}^{\Xi,\hbar,m,\sigma,c}_{v',\beth,\rho,\imath}(\Omega\sigma^{\Xi};p)\digamma_*(\sigma\eth+(1-\sigma)v,\imath)d\sigma$$
$$+\int_0^1\sigma^{v'}\mathcal{J}^{\Xi,\hbar,m,\sigma,c}_{v',\beth,\rho,\imath}(\Omega\sigma^{\Xi};p)\digamma_*((1-\sigma)\eth+\sigma v,\imath)d\sigma$$

$$h(\frac{1}{2})\digamma_*(\frac{\eth+v}{2},\imath)\sum_{n=0}^{\infty}\frac{\Lambda_p(\beth+\hbar n,c-\beth)(c)_{\hbar n}(\imath)_{\sigma n}}{\Lambda(\beth,c-\beth)\imath(\Xi n+v'+1)(\rho)_{mn}}(-\Omega)^n\int_0^1\sigma^{v'+\Xi n}d\sigma$$
$$\leq \sum_{n=0}^{\infty}\frac{\Lambda_p(\beth+\hbar n,c-\beth)(c)_{\hbar n}(\imath)_{\sigma n}}{\Lambda(\beth,c-\beth)\imath(\Xi n+v'+1)(\rho)_{mn}}(-\Omega)^n\Big[\int_0^1\sigma^{v'+\Xi n}\digamma_*(\sigma\eth+(1-\sigma)v,\imath)d\sigma$$
$$+\int_0^1\sigma^{v'+\Xi n}\digamma_*((1-\sigma)\eth+\sigma v,\imath)d\sigma\Big]. \tag{18}$$

After simplification of the integral inequality (18) by using (15), we obtain:

$$\frac{h(\frac{1}{2})}{2}\digamma_*(\frac{\eth+v}{2},\imath)(\beth^{v^-}_{\eth,v'})(\Omega',1) \leq \frac{1}{2}\Big[(\beth^{\eth^+}_{v,v'})(\Omega';\digamma_*)+(\beth^{v^-}_{\eth,v'})(\Omega';\digamma_*)\Big]. \tag{19}$$

Now, again consider the h-Godunova–Levin convex on $\digamma$:

$$\digamma(\sigma\eth+(1-\sigma)v) \leq \frac{\digamma(\eth)}{h(\sigma)}+\frac{\digamma(v)}{h(1-\sigma)} \tag{20}$$

Re-writing Equation (20), we have:

$$F((1-\sigma)\eth+\sigma v) \leq \frac{F(\eth)}{h(1-\sigma)} + \frac{F(v)}{h(\sigma)}. \tag{21}$$

Adding Equations (20) and (21) gives the following inequality:

$$F(\sigma\eth+(1-\sigma)v) + F((1-\sigma)\eth+\sigma v) \leq (F(\eth)+F(v))\left[\frac{1}{h(\sigma)} + \frac{1}{h(1-\sigma)}\right].$$

If we take for every $\imath \in [0,1]$, then we are given the following inequality:

$$F_*(\sigma\eth+(1-\sigma)v,\imath) + F_*((1-\sigma)\eth+\sigma v,\imath) \leq (F_*(\eth,\imath)+F_*(v,\imath))\left[\frac{1}{h(\sigma)} + \frac{1}{h(1-\sigma)}\right] \tag{22}$$

Multiplying by $\sigma^{v'} \mathcal{J}_{v',\daleth,\rho,\imath}^{\Xi,\hbar,m,\sigma,c}(\omega\sigma^{\Xi};p)$ in Equation (22), then integrating with respect to σ over the interval $[0,1]$, we get:

$$\begin{aligned}\int_0^1 \sigma^{v'} \mathcal{J}_{v',\daleth,\rho,\imath}^{\Xi,\hbar,m,\sigma,c}(\Omega\sigma^{\Xi};p)F_*(\sigma\eth+(1-\sigma)v,\imath)d\sigma + \int_0^1 \sigma^{v'} \mathcal{J}_{v',\daleth,\rho,\imath}^{\Xi,\hbar,m,\sigma,c}(\Omega\sigma^{\Xi};p)F_*((1-\sigma)\eth+\sigma v,\imath)d\sigma \\ \leq (F_*(\eth,\imath)+F_*(v,\imath))\int_0^1 \left[\frac{1}{h(\sigma)} + \frac{1}{h(1-\sigma)}\right]\sigma^{v'} \mathcal{J}_{v',\daleth,\rho,\imath}^{\Xi,\hbar,m,\sigma,c}(\Omega\sigma^{\Xi};p)d\sigma.\end{aligned} \tag{23}$$

After simplification of the inequality (23), we have:

$$\frac{1}{2}\left[(\mathfrak{I}_{v,v'}^{\eth^+})(\Omega';F_*) + (\mathfrak{I}_{\eth,v'}^{v^-})(\Omega';F_*)\right] \leq \frac{F_*(\eth,\imath)+F_*(v,\imath)}{2}\int_0^1 \left[\frac{1}{h(\sigma)} + \frac{1}{h(1-\sigma)}\right]\sigma^{v'} \mathcal{J}_{v',\daleth,\rho,\imath}^{\Xi,\hbar,m,\sigma,c}(\Omega\sigma^{\Xi};p)d\sigma. \tag{24}$$

Combining (19) and (24), we get inequality.

$$\begin{aligned}\frac{h(\frac{1}{2})}{2}F_*\left(\frac{\eth+v}{2},\imath\right)(\mathfrak{I}_{\eth,v'}^{v^-})(\Omega',1) &\leq \frac{1}{2}\left[(\mathfrak{I}_{v,v'}^{\eth^+})(\Omega';F_*) + (\mathfrak{I}_{\eth,v'}^{v^-})(\Omega';F_*)\right] \\ &\leq \frac{F_*(\eth,\imath)+F_*(v,\imath)}{2}\int_0^1 \left[\frac{1}{h(\sigma)} + \frac{1}{h(1-\sigma)}\right]\sigma^{v'} \mathcal{J}_{v',\daleth,\rho,\imath}^{\Xi,\hbar,m,\sigma,c}(\Omega\sigma^{\Xi};p)d\sigma.\end{aligned} \tag{25}$$

Similarly for F^*:

$$\begin{aligned}\frac{h(\frac{1}{2})}{2}F^*\left(\frac{\eth+v}{2},\imath\right)(\mathfrak{I}_{\eth,v'}^{v^-})(\Omega',1) &\leq \frac{1}{2}\left[(\mathfrak{I}_{v,v'}^{\eth^+})(\Omega';F^*) + (\mathfrak{I}_{\eth,v'}^{v^-})(\Omega';F^*)\right] \\ &\leq \frac{F^*(\eth,\imath)+F^*(v,\imath)}{2}\int_0^1 \left[\frac{1}{h(\sigma)} + \frac{1}{h(1-\sigma)}\right]\sigma^{v'} \mathcal{J}_{v',\daleth,\rho,\imath}^{\Xi,\hbar,m,\sigma,c}(\Omega\sigma^{\Xi};p)d\sigma.\end{aligned} \tag{26}$$

From Equations (25) and (26):

$$\begin{aligned}&\frac{h(\frac{1}{2})}{2}\left[F^*\left(\frac{\eth+v}{2},\imath\right),F_*\left(\frac{\eth+v}{2},\imath\right)\right](\mathfrak{I}_{\eth,v'}^{v^-})(\Omega',1) \\ &\leq_I \left[(\mathfrak{I}_{v,v'}^{\eth^+})(\Omega';F_*) + (\mathfrak{I}_{\eth,v'}^{v^-})(\Omega';F_*)\right],\left[(\mathfrak{I}_{v,v'}^{\eth^+})(\Omega';F^*) + (\mathfrak{I}_{\eth,v'}^{v^-})(\Omega';F^*)\right] \\ &\leq_I \left[\{F^*(\eth,\imath)+F^*(v,\imath)\},\{F_*(\eth,\imath)+F_*(v,\imath)\}\right]\int_0^1 \left[\frac{1}{h(\sigma)} + \frac{1}{h(1-\sigma)}\right]\sigma^{v'} \mathcal{J}_{v',\daleth,\rho,\imath}^{\Xi,\hbar,m,\sigma,c}(\Omega\sigma^{\Xi};p)d\sigma.\end{aligned}$$

After simplification:

$$\frac{h(\frac{1}{2})}{2}\mathcal{F}\left(\frac{\eth+v}{2}\right)(\mathfrak{I}^{v-}_{\eth,v'})(\Omega',1) \preccurlyeq \frac{1}{2}\Big[\left(\mathfrak{I}^{v-}_{\eth,v'}\right)(\Omega',\mathcal{F})\tilde{+}\left(\mathfrak{I}^{\eth+}_{v,v'}\right)(\Omega',\mathcal{F})\Big] \preccurlyeq \frac{\mathcal{F}(\eth)\tilde{+}\mathcal{F}(v)}{2}$$
$$\int_0^1 [\frac{1}{h(\sigma)}+\frac{1}{h(1-\sigma)}]\sigma^{v'}\mathcal{J}^{\Xi,\hbar,m,\sigma,c}_{v',\beth,\rho,\iota}(\Omega\sigma^{\Xi};p)d\sigma,$$

□

Corollary 1. *We obtain H-H-type inequality for the p-type FIV function if we substitute $h(\sigma)=1$ in Theorem 2:*

$$\frac{1}{2}\mathcal{F}\left(\frac{\eth+v}{2}\right)(\mathcal{I}^{v-}_{\eth,v'})(\Omega',1) \preccurlyeq \frac{1}{2}\Big[\left(\mathcal{I}^{v-}_{\eth,v'}\right)(\Omega',\mathcal{F})\tilde{+}\left(\mathcal{I}^{\eth+}_{v,v'}\right)(\Omega',\mathcal{F})\Big]$$
$$\preccurlyeq (\mathcal{F}(\eth)\tilde{+}\mathcal{F}(v))(\mathcal{I}^{\eth+}_{v,v'})(\Omega',1)$$

Corollary 2. *We obtained H-H-type inequality for the s-Godunova–Levin FIV function after replacing $h(\sigma)=\sigma^s$ in Theorem 2.*

$$\frac{(\frac{1}{2})^s}{2}\mathcal{F}\left(\frac{\eth+v}{2}\right)(\mathcal{I}^{v-}_{\eth,v'})(\Omega','1) \preccurlyeq \frac{1}{2}\Big[\left(\mathcal{I}^{v-}_{\eth,v'}\right)(\Omega',\mathcal{F})\tilde{+}\left(\mathcal{I}^{\eth+}_{v,v'}\right)(\Omega',\mathcal{F})\Big] \preccurlyeq \frac{\mathcal{F}(\eth)\tilde{+}\mathcal{F}(v)}{2}$$
$$\int_0^1 [\frac{1}{\sigma^s}+\frac{1}{(1-\sigma)^s}]\sigma^{v'}\mathcal{J}^{\Xi,\hbar,m,\sigma,c}_{v',\beth,\rho,\wp}(\Omega\sigma^{\Xi};p)d\sigma.$$

Corollary 3. *Putting the value $h(\sigma)=\frac{1}{\sigma}$ in Theorem 2, we obtain Hermite–Hadamard-type inequality for the FIV convex function.*

$$\mathcal{F}\left(\frac{\eth+v}{2}\right)(\mathcal{I}^{v-}_{\eth,v'})(\Omega',1) \preccurlyeq \frac{1}{2}\Big[\left(\mathcal{I}^{v-}_{\eth,v'}\right)(\Omega',\mathcal{F})\tilde{+}\left(\mathcal{I}^{\eth+}_{v,v'}\right)(\Omega',\mathcal{F})\Big]$$
$$\preccurlyeq \frac{\mathcal{F}(\eth)\tilde{+}\mathcal{F}(v)}{2}(\mathcal{I}^{\eth+}_{v,v'})(\Omega',1)$$

Corollary 4. *If we take $h(\sigma)=\sigma$ in Theorem 2, we obtain Hermite–Hadamard-type inequality for the Godunova–Levin FIV function.*

$$\frac{1}{4}\mathcal{F}\left(\frac{\eth+v}{2}\right)(\mathcal{I}^{v-}_{\eth,v'})(\Omega',1) \preccurlyeq \frac{1}{2}\Big[\left(\mathcal{I}^{v-}_{\eth,v'}\right)(\Omega',\mathcal{F})\tilde{+}\left(\mathcal{I}^{\eth+}_{v,v'}\right)(\Omega',\mathcal{F})\Big] \preccurlyeq \frac{\mathcal{F}(\eth)\tilde{+}\mathcal{F}(v)}{2}$$
$$\int_0^1 [\frac{\sigma^{v'-1}}{1-\sigma}]\mathcal{J}^{\Xi,\hbar,m,\sigma,c}_{v',\beth,\rho,\wp}(\Omega\sigma^{\Xi};p)d\sigma.$$

Corollary 5. *If we choose $h(\sigma)=\frac{1}{\sigma^s}$ in Theorem 2, we obtain Hermite–Hadamard-type inequality for the s-convex FIV function.*

$$2^{s-1}\mathcal{F}\left(\frac{\eth+v}{2}\right)(\mathcal{I}^{v-}_{\eth,v'})(\Omega',1) \preccurlyeq \frac{1}{2}\Big[\left(\mathcal{I}^{v-}_{\eth,v'}\right)(\Omega',\mathcal{F})\tilde{+}\left(\mathcal{I}^{\eth+}_{v,v'}\right)(\Omega',\mathcal{F})\Big]$$
$$\preccurlyeq \frac{\mathcal{F}(\eth)\tilde{+}\mathcal{F}(v)}{2}\int_0^1 [\sigma^s+(1-\sigma)^s]\sigma^{v'}\mathcal{J}^{\Xi,\hbar,m,\sigma,c}_{v',\beth,\rho,\wp}(\Omega\sigma^{\Xi};p)d\sigma.$$

4. Applications of Trapezoid Type Inequalities via Pre-Invex Fuzzy Interval Valued Function (FIV)

In this section, we discuss the important result in the form of lemma, which are used to develop our main results related to the trapezoid-type inequalities by the implementation of generalized fractional operators for the h-Godunova–Levin pre-invex fuzzy interval valued function.

Lemma 1. *Let J be an open invex set with respect to $\varsigma : J \times J \to \mathbb{R}$, $\varsigma(v,\eth) > 0$ for $\eth, v \in J$, $F \in L_1[\eth, \eth + \varsigma(v,\eth)]$ be a differentiable function and $F : J = [\eth, \eth + \varsigma(v,\eth)] \to \mathbb{R}$ with $\eth, v \in \mathbb{R}$, then the following result holds:*

$$\frac{F(\eth)\tilde{+}F(\eth+\varsigma(v,\eth))}{2}\mathcal{J}^{\Xi,\hbar,m,\sigma,c}_{v',\beth,\rho,\wp}(\Omega;p) - \frac{1}{2\varsigma(v,\eth)^{v'}}\Big[(\mathcal{I}^{\eth^+}_{\eth+\varsigma(v,\eth),v'-1})(\Omega';F)\tilde{+} (\mathcal{I}^{(\eth+\beth_1(v,\eth))^-}_{\eth,v'-1})(\Omega';F)\Big] = \frac{\varsigma(v,\eth)}{2}J \tag{27}$$

where $\Omega' = \frac{\Omega}{\varsigma(v,\eth)^{\Xi}}$ *and* $J = \int_0^1 \sigma^{v'}\mathcal{J}^{\Xi,\hbar,m,\sigma,c}_{v',\beth,\rho,\wp}(\Omega(\sigma)^{\Xi};p)F'(\eth+\sigma\varsigma(v,\eth))d\sigma + \int_0^1 -(1-\sigma)^{v'} \mathcal{J}^{\Xi,\hbar,m,\sigma,c}_{v',\beth,\rho,\wp}(\Omega(1-\sigma)^{\Xi};p)F'(\eth+\sigma\varsigma(v,\eth))d\sigma,$

Proof. Consider the integral:

$$J = \int_0^1 \sigma^{v'}\mathcal{J}^{\Xi,\hbar,m,\sigma,c}_{v',\beth,\rho,\wp}(\Omega(\sigma)^{\Xi};p)F'(\eth+\sigma\varsigma(v,\eth))d\sigma + \int_0^1 -(1-\sigma)^{v'} \mathcal{J}^{\Xi,\hbar,m,\sigma,c}_{v',\beth,\rho,\wp}(\Omega(1-\sigma)^{\Xi};p)F'(\eth+\sigma\varsigma(v,\eth))d\sigma.$$

Therefore, by taking the value of $\imath \in [0,1]$, we have:

$$J = \int_0^1 \sigma^{v'}\mathcal{J}^{\Xi,\hbar,m,\sigma,c}_{v',\beth,\rho,\wp}(\Omega(\sigma)^{\Xi};p)F'_*(\eth+\sigma\varsigma(v,\eth),\imath)d\sigma + \int_0^1 -(1-\sigma)^{v'} \mathcal{J}^{\Xi,\hbar,m,\sigma,c}_{v',\beth,\rho,\wp}(\Omega(1-\sigma)^{\Xi};p)F'_*(\eth+\sigma\varsigma(v,\eth),\imath)d\sigma. \tag{28}$$

Now, we take the integrals:

$$J_1 = \int_0^1 \sigma^{v'}\mathcal{J}^{\Xi,\hbar,m,\sigma,c}_{v',\beth,\rho,\wp}(\Omega(\sigma)^{\Xi};p)F'_*(\eth+\sigma\varsigma(v,\eth),\imath)d\sigma$$
$$J_1 = \sum_{n=0}^{\infty}\frac{\Lambda_p(\beth+\hbar n, c-\beth)(c)_{\hbar n}(\wp)_{\sigma n}}{\Lambda(\beth, c-\beth)\wp(\Xi n+v'+1)(\rho)_{mn}}(-\Omega)^n\int_0^1 \sigma^{v'+\Xi n}F'_*(\eth+\sigma\varsigma(v,\eth),\imath)d\sigma.$$
$$J_2 = \int_0^1 -(1-\sigma)^{v'}\mathcal{J}^{\Xi,\hbar,m,\sigma,c}_{v',\beth,\rho,\wp}(\Omega(1-\sigma)^{\Xi};p)F'_*(\eth+\sigma\varsigma(v,\eth),\imath)d\sigma.$$

$$J_2 = \sum_{n=0}^{\infty}\frac{\Lambda_p(\beth+\hbar n, c-\beth)(c)_{\hbar n}(\wp)_{\sigma n}}{\Lambda(\beth, c-\beth)\wp(\Xi n+v'+1)(\rho)_{mn}}(-\Omega)^n\int_0^1 -(1-\sigma)^{v'+\Xi n}F'_*(\eth+\sigma\varsigma(v,\eth),\imath)d\sigma.$$

For solving the integral J_1:

$$J_1 = \sum_{n=0}^{\infty}\frac{\Lambda_p(\beth+\hbar n, c-\beth)(c)_{\hbar n}(\wp)_{\sigma n}}{\Lambda(\beth, c-\beth)\wp(\Xi n+v'+1)(\rho)_{mn}}(-\Omega)^n\Big[\sigma^{v'+\Xi n}\frac{F_*(\eth+\sigma\varsigma(v,\eth),\imath)}{\varsigma(v,\eth)}\Big|_0^1 - \frac{v'+\Xi n}{\varsigma(v,\eth)}\int_0^1 \sigma^{v'+\Xi n-1}F_*(\eth+\sigma\varsigma(v,\eth),\imath)d\sigma\Big]$$
$$J_1 = \sum_{n=0}^{\infty}\frac{\Lambda_p(\beth+\hbar n, c-\beth)(c)_{\hbar n}(\wp)_{\sigma n}}{\Lambda(\beth, c-\beth)\wp(\Xi n+v'+1)(\rho)_{mn}}(-\Omega)^n\Big[\frac{F_*(\eth+\varsigma(v,\eth),\imath)}{\varsigma(v,\eth)} - \frac{v'+\Xi n}{\varsigma(v,\eth)}\int_0^1 \sigma^{v'+\Xi n-1}F(\eth+\sigma\varsigma(v,\eth))d\sigma\Big]$$
$$J_1 = \frac{F_*(\eth+\varsigma(v,\eth),\imath)}{\varsigma(v,\eth)}\mathcal{J}^{\Xi,\hbar,m,\sigma,c}_{v',\beth,\rho,\wp}(\Omega;p) - \frac{1}{(\varsigma(v,\eth))^{v'+1}}(\mathcal{I}^{(\eth+\varsigma(v,\eth),\imath)^-}_{\eth,v'-1})(\Omega';F_*)$$

By applying the same procedure for lower FIVF of the integral J_2, we have:

$$J_2 = \frac{F_*(\eth, \imath)}{\varsigma(v,\eth)} \mathcal{J}^{\Xi,\hbar,m,\sigma,c}_{v',\beth,\rho,\wp}(\Omega; p) - \frac{1}{(\varsigma(v,\eth))^{v'+1}} (\mathcal{I}^{\eth^+}_{(\eth+\varsigma(v,\eth),\imath),v'-1})(\Omega', F_*) \tag{29}$$

Substituting the values of J_1 and J_2 in (28), we have:

$$J = \frac{F_*(\eth,\imath) + F_*(\eth+\varsigma(v,\eth),\imath)}{\varsigma(v,\eth)} \mathcal{J}^{\Xi,\hbar,m,\sigma,c}_{v',\beth,\rho,\wp}(\Omega; p) - \frac{1}{(\varsigma(v,\eth))^{v'+1}} \Big[(\mathcal{I}^{(\eth+\varsigma(v,\eth),\imath)^-}_{\eth,v'-1})(\Omega', F_*) + (\mathcal{I}^{(\eth,\imath)^+}_{\eth+\varsigma(v,\eth),v'-1})(\Omega', F_*)\Big]. \tag{30}$$

Similarly, solving the expression of J for upper FIVF F^*, we obtain:

$$J = \frac{F^*(\eth,\imath) + F^*(\eth+\varsigma(v,\eth),\imath)}{\varsigma(v,\eth)} \mathcal{J}^{\Xi,\hbar,m,\sigma,c}_{v',\beth,\rho,\wp}(\Omega; p) - \frac{1}{(\varsigma(v,\eth))^{v'+1}} \times \Big[(\mathcal{I}^{(\eth+\varsigma(v,\eth),\imath)^-}_{\eth,v'-1})(\Omega', F^*) + (\mathcal{I}^{(\eth,\imath)^+}_{\eth+\varsigma(v,\eth),v'-1})(\Omega', F^*)\Big]. \tag{31}$$

By combining (30) and (31), we get:

$$J = \frac{F^*(\eth,\imath), F_*(\eth,\imath) + F^*(\eth+\varsigma(v,\eth),\imath), F_*(\eth+\varsigma(v,\eth),\imath)}{\varsigma(v,\eth)} \mathcal{J}^{\Xi,\hbar,m,\sigma,c}_{v',\beth,\rho,\wp}(\Omega; p) - \frac{1}{(\varsigma(v,\eth))^{v'+1}} \times$$
$$\Big[(\mathcal{I}^{(\eth+\varsigma(v,\eth),\imath)^-}_{\eth,v'-1})(\Omega', F^*) + (\mathcal{I}^{(\eth,\imath)^+}_{\eth+\varsigma(v,\eth),v'-1})(\Omega', F^*), (\mathcal{I}^{(\eth+\varsigma(v,\eth),\imath)^-}_{\eth,v'-1})(\omega', F^*) + (\mathcal{I}^{(\eth,\imath)^+}_{\eth+\varsigma(v,\eth),v'-1})(\Omega', F^*)\Big].$$
$$J = \frac{F(\eth)\tilde{+}F(\eth+\varsigma(v,\eth))}{\varsigma(v,\eth)} \mathcal{J}^{\Xi,\hbar,m,\sigma,c}_{v',\beth,\rho,\wp}(\Omega; p) - \frac{1}{(\varsigma(v,\eth))^{v'+1}} \Big[(\mathcal{I}^{(\eth+\varsigma(v,\eth))^-}_{\eth,v'-1})(\Omega', F) \tilde{+}(\mathcal{I}^{\eth^+}_{(\eth+\varsigma(v,\eth)),v'-1})(\Omega', F)\Big]. \tag{32}$$

Multiplying by $\frac{\varsigma(v,\eth)}{2}$, we get the required result. □

Theorem 3. *Let $J \in \mathbb{R}$ be a differentiable function on J with a function $F : J = [\eth, \eth+\varsigma(v,\eth)] \to (0,\infty)$ for the generalized the fractional integral defined in (22) with the restricted extended generalized Bessel–Maitland function to a real valued function and suppose that $|F'|$ is a h-Godunova–Levin pre-invex FIV function on J, then we have:*

$$\Big|\frac{F(\eth)\tilde{+}F(\eth+\varsigma(v,\eth))}{2} \mathcal{J}^{\Xi,\hbar,m,\sigma,c}_{v',\beth,\rho,\wp}(\Omega; p) - \frac{1}{2\varsigma(v,\eth)^{v'}} \Big[(\mathcal{I}^{\eth^+}_{\eth+\varsigma(v,\eth),v'-1})(\Omega', F)\tilde{+} (\mathcal{I}^{(\eth+\varsigma(v,\eth))^-}_{\eth,v'-1})(\Omega', F)\Big]\Big|$$
$$\preccurlyeq \frac{\varsigma(v,\eth)}{2}(|F'(\eth)|\tilde{+}|F'(v)|)\int_0^1 \sum_{n=0}^{\infty}\Big|\frac{\Lambda_p(\beth+\hbar n, c-\beth)(c)_{\hbar n}(\wp)_{\sigma n}}{\Lambda(\beth, c-\beth)\wp(\Xi n+v'+1)(\rho)_{mn}}(-\Omega)^n\Big| \Big|\frac{\sigma^{v'+\Xi n} - (1-\sigma)^{v'+\Xi n}}{h(\sigma)}\Big| d\sigma.$$

Proof. By considering previous lemma and taking mod on both sides:

$$\Big|\frac{F(\eth)\tilde{+}F(\eth+\varsigma(v,\eth))}{2} \mathcal{J}^{\Xi,\hbar,m,\sigma,c}_{v',\beth,\rho,\wp}(\Omega; p) - \frac{1}{2\varsigma(v,\eth)^{v'}} \Big[(\mathcal{I}^{\eth^+}_{\eth+\varsigma(v,\eth),v'-1})(\Omega', F)\tilde{+} (\mathcal{I}^{(\eth+\varsigma(v,\eth))^-}_{\eth,v'-1})(\Omega', F)\Big]\Big| = \Big|\frac{\varsigma(v,\eth)}{2} J\Big|$$

by taking the value $\imath \in [0,1]$, we have:

$$= \left| \frac{\varsigma(v, \eth)}{2} J \right|$$

$$\leq \frac{\varsigma(v,\eth)}{2} \sum_{n=0}^{\infty} \left| \frac{\Lambda_p(\beth + \hbar n, c - \beth)(c)_{\hbar n}(\wp)_{\sigma n}}{\Lambda(\beth, c - \beth)\wp(\Xi n + v' + 1)(\rho)_{mn}} (-\Omega)^n \right| \int_0^1 |\sigma^{v'+\Xi n} - (1-\sigma)^{v'+\Xi n}|$$
$$|F'_*(\eth + \sigma\varsigma(v,\eth), \imath)| d\sigma$$
$$\leq \frac{\varsigma(v,\eth)}{2} \sum_{n=0}^{\infty} \left| \frac{\Lambda_p(\beth + \hbar n, c - \beth)(c)_{\hbar n}(\wp)_{\sigma n}}{\Lambda(\beth, c - \beth)\wp(\Xi n + v' + 1)(\rho)_{mn}} (-\Omega)^n \right| \int_0^1 |\sigma^{v'+\Xi n} - (1-\sigma)^{v'+\Xi n}|$$
$$\left| \frac{F'_*](\eth)}{h(\sigma)} + \frac{F'_*(v)}{h(1-\sigma)} \right| d\sigma.$$

$$\leq \frac{\varsigma(v,\eth)}{2} \sum_{n=0}^{\infty} \left| \frac{\Lambda_p(\beth + \hbar n, c - \beth)(c)_{\hbar n}(\wp)_{\sigma n}}{\Lambda(\beth, c - \beth)\wp(\Xi n + v' + 1)(\rho)_{mn}} (-\Omega)^n \right|$$
$$\left[|F'_*(\eth)| \int_0^1 |\sigma^{v'+\Xi n} - (1-\sigma)^{v'+\Xi n}| \left| \frac{1}{h(\sigma)} \right| d\sigma + |F'_*(v)| \int_0^1 |\sigma^{v'+\Xi n} - (1-\sigma)^{v'+\Xi n}| \left| \frac{1}{h(1-\sigma)} \right| d\sigma \right]$$
$$= \frac{\varsigma(v,\eth)}{2} (|F'_*(\eth,\imath)| + |F'_*(v,\imath)|) \int_0^1 \sum_{n=0}^{\infty} \left| \frac{\Lambda_p(\beth + \hbar n, c - \beth)(c)_{\hbar n}(\wp)_{\sigma n}}{\Lambda(\beth, c - \beth)\wp(\Xi n + v' + 1)(\rho)_{mn}} (-\Omega)^n \right|$$
$$\left| \frac{\sigma^{v'+\Xi n} - (1-\sigma)^{v'+\Xi n}}{h(\sigma)} \right| d\sigma. \tag{33}$$

Similarly, if we solve for upper FIV function F^*, we have:

$$\leq \frac{\varsigma(v,\eth)}{2} (|F'^*(\eth,\imath)| + |F'^*(v,\imath)|) \int_0^1 \sum_{n=0}^{\infty} \left| \frac{\Lambda_p(\beth + \hbar n, c - \beth)(c)_{\hbar n}(\wp)_{\sigma n}}{\Lambda(\beth, c - \beth)\wp(\Xi n + v' + 1)(\rho)_{mn}} (-\Omega)^n \right| \times$$
$$\left| \frac{\sigma^{v'+\Xi n} - (1-\sigma)^{v'+\Xi n}}{h(\sigma)} \right| d\sigma. \tag{34}$$

By combining Equations (33) and (34), we have the required result:

$$\leq \frac{\varsigma(v,\eth)}{2} (|F'_*(\eth,\imath)| + |F'_*(v,\imath)|, |F'^*(\eth,\imath)| + |F'^*(v,\imath)|)$$
$$\int_0^1 \sum_{n=0}^{\infty} \left| \frac{\Lambda_p(\beth + \hbar n, c - \beth)(c)_{\hbar n}(\wp)_{\sigma n}}{\Lambda(\beth, c - \beth)\wp(\Xi n + v' + 1)(\rho)_{mn}} (-\Omega)^n \right| \left| \frac{\sigma^{v'+\Xi n} - (1-\sigma)^{v'+\Xi n}}{h(\sigma)} \right| d\sigma.$$
$$\preccurlyeq \frac{\varsigma(v,\eth)}{2} (|F'(\eth)| \tilde{+} |F'(v)|) \int_0^1 \sum_{n=0}^{\infty} \left| \frac{\Lambda_p(\beth + \hbar n, c - \beth)(c)_{\hbar n}(\wp)_{\sigma n}}{\Lambda(\beth, c - \beth)\wp(\Xi n + v' + 1)(\rho)_{mn}} (-\Omega)^n \right|$$
$$\left| \frac{\sigma^{v'+\Xi n} - (1-\sigma)^{v'+\Xi n}}{h(\sigma)} \right| d\sigma.$$

□

Corollary 6. *Taking $\varsigma(v,\eth) = v - \eth$ in Theorem 3, we obtain the following inequality:*

$$\left|\frac{F(\eth)\tilde{+}F(v)}{2}\mathcal{J}^{\Xi,\hbar,m,\sigma,c}_{v',\beth,\rho,\wp}(\Omega;p) - \frac{1}{2(v-\eth)^{v'}}\left[(\mathcal{I}^{\eth^+}_{v,v'-1})(\Omega',F)\tilde{+}(\mathcal{I}^{v^-}_{\eth,v'-1})(\Omega',F)\right]\right|$$
$$\preccurlyeq \frac{v-\eth}{2}(|F'(\eth)|\tilde{+}|F'(v)|)\int_0^1\sum_{n=0}^{\infty}\left|\frac{\Lambda_p(\beth+\hbar n, c-\beth)(c)_{\hbar n}(\wp)_{\sigma n}}{\Lambda(\beth,c-\beth)\wp(\Xi n+v'+1)(\rho)_{mn}}(-\Omega)^n\right|$$
$$\left|\frac{\sigma^{v'+\Xi n}-(1-\sigma)^{v'+\Xi n}}{h(\sigma)}\right|d\sigma.$$

Theorem 4. *Let $F : J = [\eth, \eth+\varsigma(v,\eth)] \to (0,\infty)$ be a differentiable function on $J \in \mathbb{R}$, and suppose that $|F'|^q$ is a h-Godunova–Levin pre-invex FIV function on J with $p > 1$ and $q = (p)(p-1)^{-1}$, then for the generalized fractional integral defined in (22) with the restricted extended generalized Bessel–Maitland function to a real valued function, we have:*

$$\left|\frac{F(\eth)\tilde{+}F(\eth+\varsigma(v,\eth))}{2}\mathcal{J}^{\Xi,\hbar,m,\sigma,c}_{v',\beth,\rho,\wp}(\Omega;p) - \frac{1}{2\varsigma(v,\eth)^{v'}}\left[(\mathcal{I}^{\eth^+}_{\eth+\varsigma(v,\eth),v'-1})(\Omega',F)\tilde{+}(\mathcal{I}^{(\eth+\varsigma(v,\eth))^-}_{\eth,v'-1})(\Omega',F)\right]\right|$$
$$\preccurlyeq \frac{\varsigma(v,\eth)}{2}(|F'(\eth)|^q\tilde{+}|F'(v)|^q)^{\frac{1}{q}}$$
$$\left(\int_0^1\left|\sigma^{v'}\mathcal{J}^{\Xi,\hbar,m,\sigma,c}_{v',\beth,\rho,\wp}(\Omega\sigma^{\Xi};p)-(1-\sigma)^{v'}\mathcal{J}^{\Xi,\hbar,m,\sigma,c}_{v',\beth,\rho,\wp}(\Omega(1-\sigma)^{\Xi};p)\right|^p d\sigma\right)^{\frac{1}{p}}\left(\int_0^1\frac{1}{h(\sigma)}d\sigma\right)^{\frac{1}{q}}.$$

Proof. By using Lemma 1, we have:

$$\left|\frac{F(\eth)\tilde{+}F(\eth+\varsigma(v,\eth))}{2}\mathcal{J}^{\Xi,\hbar,m,\sigma,c}_{v',\beth,\rho,\wp}(\Omega;p) - \frac{1}{2\varsigma(v,\eth)^{v'}}\left[(\mathcal{I}^{\eth^+}_{\eth+\varsigma(v,\eth),v'-1})(\Omega',F)\tilde{+}(\mathcal{I}^{(\eth+\varsigma(v,\eth))^-}_{\eth,v'-1})(\Omega',F)\right]\right|$$
$$= \left|\frac{\varsigma(v,\eth)}{2}J\right|$$

by taking the value $\iota \in [0,1]$, we have:

$$= \left|\frac{\varsigma(v,\eth)}{2}J\right|$$

$$\leq \frac{\varsigma(v,\eth)}{2}\int_0^1\left|\sigma^{v'}\mathcal{J}^{\Xi,\hbar,m,\sigma,c}_{v',\beth,\rho,\wp}(\Omega\sigma^{\Xi};p)-(1-\sigma)^{v'}\mathcal{J}^{\Xi,\hbar,m,\sigma,c}_{v',\beth,\rho,\wp}(\Omega(1-\sigma)^{\Xi};p)\right|\left|F'_*(\eth+\sigma\varsigma(v,\eth),\iota)\right|d\sigma$$

Using Hölder's integral inequality, we have:

$$\leq \frac{\varsigma(v,\eth)}{2}\left(\int_0^1\left|\sigma^{v'}\mathcal{J}^{\Xi,\hbar,m,\sigma,c}_{v',\beth,\rho,\wp}(\Omega\sigma^{\Xi};p)-(1-\sigma)^{v'}\mathcal{J}^{\Xi,\hbar,m,\sigma,c}_{v',\beth,\rho,\wp}(\Omega(1-\sigma)^{\Xi};p)\right|^p d\sigma\right)^{\frac{1}{p}}\times$$
$$\left(\int_0^1|F'_*(\eth+\sigma\varsigma(v,\eth),\iota)|^q d\sigma\right)^{\frac{1}{q}} \tag{35}$$

where $p^{-1}+q^{-1}=1$.

Considering the h-Godunova–Levin pre-invex FIV function $|F'_*|^q$, we have:

$$\int_0^1|F'_*(\eth+\sigma\varsigma(v,\eth))|^q d\sigma \leq \int_0^1\left(\frac{|F'(\eth)|^q}{h(\sigma)}+\frac{|F'(v)|^q}{h(1-\sigma)}\right)d\sigma$$
$$\leq (|F'_*(\eth,\iota)|^q+|F'_*(v,\iota)|^q)\int_0^1\frac{1}{h(\sigma)}d\sigma. \tag{36}$$

By using Equation (36) in Equation (35), we obtain:

$$\leq \frac{\varsigma(v,\eth)}{2}\left(|F'_*(\eth,\imath)|^q + |F'_*(v,\imath)|^q\right)^{\frac{1}{q}}$$

$$\left(\int_0^1 \left|\sigma^{v'} \mathcal{J}^{\Xi,\hbar,m,\sigma,c}_{v',\beth,\rho,\wp}(\Omega\sigma^{\Xi};p) - (1-\sigma)^{v'} \mathcal{J}^{\Xi,\hbar,m,\sigma,c}_{v',\beth,\rho,\wp}(\Omega(1-\sigma)^{\Xi};p)\right|^p d\sigma\right)^{\frac{1}{p}} \left(\int_0^1 \frac{1}{h(\sigma)} d\sigma\right)^{\frac{1}{q}}. \quad (37)$$

Similarly, if we solve for upper FIV function for $|F'^*|^q$, we are given the following inequality:

$$\leq \frac{\varsigma(v,\eth)}{2}\left(|F'^*(\eth,\imath)|^q + |F'^*(v,\imath)|^q\right)^{\frac{1}{q}}$$

$$\left(\int_0^1 \left|\sigma^{v'} \mathcal{J}^{\Xi,\hbar,m,\sigma,c}_{v',\beth,\rho,\wp}(\Omega\sigma^{\Xi};p) - (1-\sigma)^{v'} \mathcal{J}^{\Xi,\hbar,m,\sigma,c}_{v',\beth,\rho,\wp}(\Omega(1-\sigma)^{\Xi};p)\right|^p d\sigma\right)^{\frac{1}{p}} \left(\int_0^1 \frac{1}{h(\sigma)} d\sigma\right)^{\frac{1}{q}}. \quad (38)$$

By combining Equations (37) and (38), we have:

$$\leq_I \frac{\varsigma(v,\eth)}{2}\left(|F'_*(\eth,\imath)|^q + |F'_*(v,\imath)|^q, |F'^*(\eth,\imath)|^q + |F'^*(v,\imath)|^q\right)^{\frac{1}{q}}$$

$$\left(\int_0^1 \left|\sigma^{v'} \mathcal{J}^{\Xi,\hbar,m,\sigma,c}_{v',\beth,\rho,\wp}(\Omega\sigma^{\Xi};p) - (1-\sigma)^{v'} \mathcal{J}^{\Xi,\hbar,m,\sigma,c}_{v',\beth,\rho,\wp}(\Omega(1-\sigma)^{\Xi};p)\right|^p d\sigma\right)^{\frac{1}{p}} \left(\int_0^1 \frac{1}{h(\sigma)} d\sigma\right)^{\frac{1}{q}}. \quad (39)$$

After replacing the value $|F'_*(\eth,\imath)|^q + |F'_*(v,\imath)|^q, |F'^*(\eth,\imath)|^q + |F'^*(v,\imath)|^q \preccurlyeq |F'(\eth)|^q \tilde{+} |F'(v)|^q$, we have the required result. □

Theorem 5. *With the assumptions of Theorem 4, we get the inequality related to Hermite–Hadamard inequality as follows:*

$$\left|\frac{F(\eth)\tilde{+}F(\eth+\varsigma(v,\eth))}{2}\mathcal{J}^{\Xi,\hbar,m,\sigma,c}_{v',\beth,\rho,\wp}(\Omega;p) - \frac{1}{2\varsigma(v,\eth)^{v'}}\left[(\mathcal{I}^{\eth^+}_{\eth+\varsigma(v,\eth),v'-1})(\Omega',F)\tilde{+}(\mathcal{I}^{(\eth+\varsigma(v,\eth))^-}_{\eth,v'-1})(\Omega',F)\right]\right|$$

$$\preccurlyeq \frac{\varsigma(v,\eth)}{2^{\frac{1}{q}}}\left(|F'(\eth)|^q\tilde{+}|F'(v)|^q\right)^{\frac{1}{q}}\left[\mathcal{J}^{\Xi,\hbar,m,\sigma,c}_{v'+1,\beth,\rho,\wp}(\Omega;p) - \left(\frac{1}{2}\right)^{v'}\mathcal{J}^{\Xi,\hbar,m,\sigma,c}_{v'+1,\beth,\rho,\wp}\left(\Omega\left(\frac{1}{2}\right)^{\Xi};p\right)\right]^{1-\frac{1}{q}}$$

$$\left[\int_0^1 \frac{\left|\sigma^{v'} \mathcal{J}^{\Xi,\hbar,m,\sigma,c}_{v',\beth,\rho,\wp}(\Omega\sigma^{\Xi};p) - (1-\sigma)^{v'} \mathcal{J}^{\Xi,\hbar,m,\sigma,c}_{v',\beth,\rho,\wp}(\Omega(1-\sigma)^{\Xi};p)\right|}{h(\sigma)} d\sigma\right]^{\frac{1}{q}},$$

where $v', \Xi \in \mathbb{R}^+$.

Proof. Considering Lemma 1, we have:

$$\left|\frac{F(\eth)\tilde{+}F(\eth+\varsigma(v,\eth))}{2}\mathcal{J}^{\Xi,\hbar,m,\sigma,c}_{v',\beth,\rho,\wp}(\Omega;p) - \frac{1}{2\varsigma(v,\eth)^{v'}}\left[(\mathcal{I}^{\eth^+}_{\eth+\varsigma(v,\eth),v'-1})(\Omega',F)\tilde{+}(\mathcal{I}^{(\eth+\varsigma(v,\eth))^-}_{\eth,v'-1})(\Omega',F)\right]\right| = \left|\frac{\varsigma(v,\eth)}{2}J\right|$$

by taking the value $\imath \in [0,1]$, we have:

$$= \left|\frac{\varsigma(v,\eth)}{2}J\right|$$

$$\leq \frac{\varsigma(v,\eth)}{2}\int_0^1 \left|\sigma^{v'} \mathcal{J}^{\Xi,\hbar,m,\sigma,c}_{v',\beth,\rho,\wp}(\Omega\sigma^{\Xi};p) - (1-\sigma)^{v'} \mathcal{J}^{\Xi,\hbar,m,\sigma,c}_{v',\beth,\rho,\wp}(\Omega(1-\sigma)^{\Xi};p)\right|\left|F'_*(\eth+\sigma\varsigma(v,\eth),\imath)\right| d\sigma.$$

By applying the power mean inequality, we get:

$$\left|\frac{F(\eth)+F(\eth+\varsigma(v,\eth))}{2}\mathcal{J}^{\Xi,\hbar,m,\sigma,c}_{v',\beth,\rho,\wp}(\Omega;p)-\frac{1}{2\varsigma(v,\eth)^{v'}}\left[\left(\mathcal{I}^{\eth^{+}}_{\eth+\varsigma(v,\eth),v'-1}\right)(\Omega',F)+\left(\mathcal{I}^{(\eth+\varsigma(v,\eth))^{-}}_{\eth,v'-1}\right)(\Omega',F)\right]\right|$$
$$\leq\frac{\varsigma(v,\eth)}{2}\left(\int_0^1\left|\sigma^{v'}\mathcal{J}^{\Xi,\hbar,m,\sigma,c}_{v',\beth,\rho,\wp}(\Omega\sigma^{\Xi};p)-(1-\sigma)^{v'}\mathcal{J}^{\Xi,\hbar,m,\sigma,c}_{v',\beth,\rho,\wp}(\Omega(1-\sigma)^{\Xi};p)\right|d\sigma\right)^{1-\frac{1}{q}}\times$$
$$\left(\int_0^1\left|\sigma^{v'}\mathcal{J}^{\Xi,\hbar,m,\sigma,c}_{v',\beth,\rho,\wp}(\Omega\sigma^{\Xi};p)-(1-\sigma)^{v'}\mathcal{J}^{\Xi,\hbar,m,\sigma,c}_{v',\beth,\rho,\wp}(\Omega(1-\sigma)^{\Xi};p)\right|\left|F'_*(\eth+\sigma\varsigma(v,\eth),\imath)\right|^q d\sigma\right)^{\frac{1}{q}}. \quad (40)$$

Let

$$I=\int_0^1\left|\sigma^{v'}\mathcal{J}^{\Xi,\hbar,m,\sigma,c}_{v',\beth,\rho,\wp}(\Omega\sigma^{\Xi};p)-(1-\sigma)^{v'}\mathcal{J}^{\Xi,\hbar,m,\sigma,c}_{v',\beth,\rho,\wp}(\Omega(1-\sigma)^{\Xi};p)\right|\left|F'_*(\eth+\sigma\varsigma(v,\eth),\imath)\right|^q d\sigma$$

By applying the definition of the h-Godunova–Levin pre-invex function FIV function on $\left|F'_*(\eth+\sigma\varsigma(v,\eth),\imath)\right|^q$, we have:

$$\leq\int_0^1\frac{\left|\sigma^{v'}\mathcal{J}^{\Xi,\hbar,m,\sigma,c}_{v',\beth,\rho,\wp}(\Omega\sigma^{\Xi};p)-(1-\sigma)^{v'}\mathcal{J}^{\Xi,\hbar,m,\sigma,c}_{v',\beth,\rho,\wp}(\Omega(1-\sigma)^{\Xi};p)\right|}{h(\sigma)}|F'_*(\eth,\imath)|^q$$
$$+\frac{\left|\sigma^{v'}\mathcal{J}^{\Xi,\hbar,m,\sigma,c}_{v',\beth,\rho,\wp}(\Omega\sigma^{\Xi};p)-(1-\sigma)^{v'}\mathcal{J}^{\Xi,\hbar,m,\sigma,c}_{v',\beth,\rho,\wp}(\Omega(1-\sigma)^{\Xi};p)\right|}{h(1-\sigma)}|F'_*(v,\imath)|^q\Big)d\sigma$$
$$=\left(|F'_*(\eth,\imath)|^q+|F'_*(v,\imath)|^q\right)$$
$$\int_0^1\frac{|\sigma^{v'}\mathcal{J}^{\Xi,\hbar,m,\sigma,c}_{v',\beth,\rho,\wp}(\Omega\sigma^{\Xi};p)-(1-\sigma)^{v'}\mathcal{J}^{\Xi,\hbar,m,\sigma,c}_{v',\beth,\rho,\wp}(\Omega(1-\sigma)^{\Xi};p)|}{h(\sigma)}. \quad (41)$$

Similarly, we solve for the upper FIV function $|F'^*|^q$:

$$I\leq\int_0^1\frac{\left|\sigma^{v'}\mathcal{J}^{\Xi,\hbar,m,\sigma,c}_{v',\beth,\rho,\wp}(\Omega\sigma^{\Xi};p)-(1-\sigma)^{v'}\mathcal{J}^{\Xi,\hbar,m,\sigma,c}_{v',\beth,\rho,\wp}(\Omega(1-\sigma)^{\Xi};p)\right|}{h(\sigma)}|F'^*(\eth,\imath)|^q$$
$$+\frac{\left|\sigma^{v'}\mathcal{J}^{\Xi,\hbar,m,\sigma,c}_{v',\beth,\rho,\wp}(\Omega\sigma^{\Xi};p)-(1-\sigma)^{v'}\mathcal{J}^{\Xi,\hbar,m,\sigma,c}_{v',\beth,\rho,\wp}(\Omega(1-\sigma)^{\Xi};p)\right|}{h(1-\sigma)}|F'^*(v,\imath)|^q\Big)d\sigma$$
$$=\left(|F'^*(\eth,\imath)|^q+|F'^*(v,\imath)|^q\right)\int_0^1\frac{|\sigma^{v'}\mathcal{J}^{\Xi,\hbar,m,\sigma,c}_{v',\beth,\rho,\wp}(\Omega\sigma^{\Xi};p)-(1-\sigma)^{v'}\mathcal{J}^{\Xi,\hbar,m,\sigma,c}_{v',\beth,\rho,\wp}(\Omega(1-\sigma)^{\Xi};p)|}{h(\sigma)}. \quad (42)$$

Combining the upper and lower value of FIV function for I, we have:

$$I\leq_I\left(|F'_*(\eth,\imath)|^q+|F'_*(v,\imath)|^q,|F'^*(\eth,\imath)|^q+|F'^*(v,\imath)|^q\right)$$
$$\int_0^1\frac{|\sigma^{v'}\mathcal{J}^{\Xi,\hbar,m,\sigma,c}_{v',\beth,\rho,\wp}(\Omega\sigma^{\Xi};p)-(1-\sigma)^{v'}\mathcal{J}^{\Xi,\hbar,m,\sigma,c}_{v',\beth,\rho,\wp}(\Omega(1-\sigma)^{\Xi};p)|}{h(\sigma)}.$$
$$\preccurlyeq\left(|F'(\eth)|^q\tilde{+}|F'(v)|^q\right)\int_0^1\frac{|\sigma^{v'}\mathcal{J}^{\Xi,\hbar,m,\sigma,c}_{v',\beth,\rho,\wp}(\Omega\sigma^{\Xi};p)-(1-\sigma)^{v'}\mathcal{J}^{\Xi,\hbar,m,\sigma,c}_{v',\beth,\rho,\wp}(\Omega(1-\sigma)^{\Xi};p)|}{h(\sigma)}. \quad (43)$$

Now, consider the integral:

$$\int_0^1 \left|\sigma^{v'} \mathcal{J}^{\Xi,\hbar,m,\sigma,c}_{v',\beth,\rho,\wp}(\Omega\sigma^{\Xi};p) - (1-\sigma)^{v'} \mathcal{J}^{\Xi,\hbar,m,\sigma,c}_{v',\beth,\rho,\wp}(\Omega(1-\sigma)^{\Xi};p)\right|$$
$$= \sum_{n=0}^{\infty} \left|\frac{\Lambda_p(\beth+\hbar n, c-\beth)(c)_{\hbar n}(\wp)_{\sigma n}}{\Lambda(\beth, c-\beth)\wp(\Xi n + v' + 1)(\rho)_{mn}}(-\Omega)^n\right| \int_0^1 \left|\sigma^{v'+\Xi n} - (1-\sigma)^{v'+\Xi n}\right| d\sigma$$
$$= \sum_{n=0}^{\infty} \left|\frac{\Lambda_p(\beth+\hbar n, c-\beth)(c)_{\hbar n}(\wp)_{\sigma n}}{\Lambda(\beth, c-\beth)\wp(\Xi n + v' + 1)(\rho)_{mn}}(-\Omega)^n\right| \left[\int_0^{\frac{1}{2}} \left((1-\sigma)^{v'+\Xi n} - \sigma^{v'+\Xi n}\right) d\sigma + \int_{\frac{1}{2}}^1 \left(\sigma^{v'+\Xi n} - (1-\sigma)^{v'+\Xi n}\right)\right]$$
$$= 2\left[\mathcal{J}^{\Xi,\hbar,m,\sigma,c}_{v'+1,\beth,\rho,\wp}(\Omega;p) - \left(\frac{1}{2}\right)^{v'} \mathcal{J}^{\Xi,\hbar,m,\sigma,c}_{v'+1,\beth,\rho,\wp}\left(\Omega\left(\frac{1}{2}\right)^{\Xi};p\right)\right]. \tag{44}$$

Putting the values (43) and (44) in (40), we have the required result. □

5. Conclusions

In research work, we investigated the existence of inequalities such as Hermite–Hadamard-type inequalities and trapezoid-type inequalities for *h*-Godunova–Levin convex and pre-invex fuzzy interval valued functions by the implementation of FFIPs. The obtained inequalities are the generalizations and extensions by means of fuzzy interval valued functions. A lot of work could be conducted in the field of analysis by improving the convex and non-convex functions in FIVFs. In future work, we will attempt to investigate this idea for generalized convex fuzzy-IVFs and various applications in fuzzy-interval nonlinear programming. The new area of research in convex analysis and optimization theory can be found by applying this idea.

Author Contributions: Conceptualization, M.V.-C., R.S.A., H.S., M.B.J., G.R. and Y.E.; methodology, M.V.-C., R.S.A., H.S., M.B.J., G.R. and Y.E.; software, M.V.-C., R.S.A. and H.S.; validation, M.B.J., G.R. and Y.E.; formal analysis, M.V.-C., R.S.A., H.S., M.B.J., G.R. and Y.E.; investigation, M.V.-C., R.S.A., H.S., M.B.J., G.R. and Y.E.; resources, M.V.-C. and M.B.J.; data curation, M.V.-C., R.S.A., H.S., M.B.J., G.R. and Y.E.; writing—original draft preparation, M.V.-C., R.S.A., H.S., M.B.J., G.R. and Y.E.; writing—review and editing, M.V.-C., R.S.A., H.S., M.B.J., G.R. and Y.E.; visualization, M.V.-C., R.S.A., H.S., M.B.J., G.R. and Y.E.; supervision, M.V.-C., G.R. and Y.E.; project administration, Y.E.; funding acquisition, M.V.-C. All authors have read and agreed to the published version of the manuscript.

Funding: This research received no external funding.

Data Availability Statement: Not Applicable.

Acknowledgments: The authors extend their appreciation to the Deanship of Scientific Research at King Khalid University for funding this work through the Large Groups under grant number (RGP.2/120/44).

Conflicts of Interest: The authors declare no conflict of interest.

References

1. Abdeljawad, T.; Baleanu, D. Monotonicity results for fractional difference operators with discrete exponential kernels. *Adv. Differ. Equations* **2017**, *2017*, 1–9. [CrossRef]
2. Agarwal, R.; Purohit, D.S. A mathematical fractional model with nonsingular kernel for thrombin receptor activation in calcium signalling. *Math. Methods Appl. Sci.* **2019**, *42*, 7160–7171. [CrossRef]
3. Agarwal, R.; Yadav, M.P.; Baleanu, D.; Purohit, S. Existence and Uniqueness of Miscible Flow Equation through Porous Media with a Non Singular Fractional Derivative. *AIMS Math.* **2020**, *5*, 1062–1073. [CrossRef]
4. Khan, M.A.; Begum, S.; Khurshid, Y.; Chu, M.Y. Ostrowski type inequalities involving conformable fractional integrals. *J. Inequalities Appl.* **2018**, *2018*, 1–14.
5. Khan, M.A.; Chu, M.Y.; Kashuri, A.; Liko, R.; Ali, G. Conformable fractional integrals versions of Hermite-Hadamard inequalities and their generalizations. *J. Funct. Spaces* **2018**, *2018*, 6928130.

6. Mohammed, O.P.; Abdeljawad, T. Integral inequalities for a fractional operator of a function with respect to another function with nonsingular kernel. *Adv. Differ. Equ.* **2020**, *2020*, 1–19. [CrossRef]
7. Mohammed, O.P.; Aydi, H.; Kashuri, A.; Hamed, S.Y.; Abualnaja, M.K. Midpoint inequalities in fractional calculus defined using positive weighted symmetry function kernels. *Symmetry* **2021**, *13*, 550. [CrossRef]
8. Fejér, L. Uber die fourierreihen, II. *Math. Naturwiss. Anz. Ungar. Akad. Wiss* **1906**, *24*, 369–390.
9. Mehmood, S.; Zafar, F.; Asmin, N. New Hermite-Hadamard-Fejér type inequalities for (η_1, η_2)-convex functions via fractional calculus. *Sci. Asia* **2020**, *46*, 102–108. [CrossRef]
10. Aslani, S.M.; Delavar, M.R.; Vaezpour, S.M. Inequalities of Fejér Type Related to Generalized Convex Functions. *Int. J. Anal. Appl.* **2018**, *6*, 38–49.
11. Delavar, M.R.; Aslani, S.M.; Sen, M.D.L. Hermite-Hadamard-Fejér inequality related to generalized convex functions via fractional integrals. *J. Math.* **2018**, *2018*, 5864091.
12. Gordji, M.E.; Delavar, M.R.; Sen, M.D.L. On Φ-convex functions. *J. Math. Inequal.* **2016**, *10*, 173–183. [CrossRef]
13. Moore, E.R.; Kearfott, R.B.; Michael, J.C. *Introduction to Interval Analysis;* Society for Industrial and Applied Mathematics: Philadelphia, PA, USA, 2009.
14. Zhao, D.; An, T.; Ye, G.; Liu, W. New Jensen and Hermite-Hadamard type inequalities for h-convex interval-valued functions. *J. Inequalities Appl.* **2018**, *2018*, 302. [CrossRef]
15. Costa, T. Jensen's inequality type integral for fuzzy-interval-valued functions. *Fuzzy Sets Syst.* **2017**, *327*, 31–47. [CrossRef]
16. Costa, T.M.; Romn-Flores, H. Some integral inequalities for fuzzy-interval-valued functions. *Inf. Sci.* **2017**, *420*, 110–125. [CrossRef]
17. Romn-Flores, H.; Chalco-Cano, Y.; Lodwick, W. Some integral inequalities for interval-valued functions. *Comput. Appl. Math.* **2018**, *37*, 1306–1318. [CrossRef]
18. Romn-Flores, H.; Chalco-Cano, Y.; Silva, G.N. A note on Gronwall type inequality for interval-valued functions. In Proceedings of the 2013 Joint IFSA World Congress and NAFIPS Annual Meeting (IFSA/NAFIPS), Edmonton, AB, Canada, 24–28 June 2013; pp. 1455–1458.
19. Chalco-Cano, Y.; Flores-Franulic, A.; Romn-Flores, H. Ostrowski type inequalities for interval-valued functions using generalized Hukuhara derivative. *Comput. Appl. Math.* **2012**, *31*, 457–472.
20. Agarwal, P.A.; Baleanu, D.; Nieto, J.J.; Torres, F.D.; Zhou, Y. A survey on fuzzy fractional differential and optimal control nonlocal evolution equations. *J. Comput. Appl. Math.* **2018**, *339*, 3–29. [CrossRef]
21. Diamond, P.; Kloeden, P. Metric spaces of fuzzy sets. *Fuzzy Sets Syst.* **1990**, *35*, 241–249. [CrossRef]
22. Nanda, S.; Kar, K. Convex fuzzy mappings. *Fuzzy Sets Syst.* **1992**, *48*, 129–132. [CrossRef]
23. Noor, M.A. Fuzzy preinvex functions. *Fuzzy Sets Syst.* **1994**, *64*, 95–104. [CrossRef]
24. Bede, B.; Gal, S.G. Generalizations of the differentiability of fuzzy-number-valued functions with applications to fuzzy differential equations. *Fuzzy Sets Syst.* **2005**, *151*, 581–599. [CrossRef]
25. Khan, M.B.; Mohammed, P.O.; Noor, M.A.; Hamed, Y.S. New Hermite-Hadamard inequalities in fuzzy-interval fractional calculus and related inequalities. *Symmetry* **2021**, *13*, 673. [CrossRef]
26. Khan, B.M.; Noor, M.A.; Shah, N.A.; Abualnaja, K.M.; Botmart, T. Some New Versions of Hermite-Hadamard Integral Inequalities in Fuzzy Fractional Calculus for Generalized Pre-Invex Functions via Fuzzy-Interval-Valued Settings. *Fractal Fract.* **2022**, *6*, 83. [CrossRef]
27. Toader, G.H. Some generalizations of the convexity. In *Proceedings of the Colloquium on Approximation and Optimization;* Universitatea Cluj-Napoca: Cluj Napoca, Romania, 1984; pp. 329–338.
28. Peajcariaac, J.E.; Tong, Y.L. *Convex Functions, Partial Orderings, and Statistical Applications;* Academic Press: Cambridge, MA, USA, 1992.
29. Qiang, X.; Farid, G.; Yussouf, M.; Khan, K.A.; Rahman, A.U. New generalized fractional versions of Hadamard and Fejér inequalities for harmonically convex functions. *J. Inequalities Appl.* **2020**, *2020*, 1–13. [CrossRef]
30. Iscan, I.; Wu, S. Hermite-Hadamard type inequalities for harmonically convex functions via fractional integrals. *Appl. Math. Comput.* **2014**, *238*, 237–244.
31. Ion, D.A. Some estimates on the Hermite-Hadamard inequality through quasi-convex functions. *Ann. Univ. Craiova-Math. Comput. Sci. Ser.* **2007**, *34*, 82–87.
32. Stefanini, L.; Bede, B. Generalized Hukuhara differentiability of interval-valued functions and interval differential equations. *Nonlinear Anal. Theory Methods Appl.* **2009**, *71*, 1311–1328. [CrossRef]
33. Moore, R.E. *Interval Analysis;* Prentice Hall: Englewood Cliffs, NJ, USA, 1966.
34. Kaleva, O. Fuzzy Differential Equations. *Fuzzy Sets Syst.* **1987**, *24*, 301–317. [CrossRef]
35. Khan, M.B.; Noor, M.A.; Al-Shomrani, M.M.; Abdullah, L. Some novel inequalities for LR-h-convex interval-valued functions by means of pseudo-order relation. *Math. Methods Appl. Sci.* **2022**, *45*, 1310–1340. [CrossRef]
36. Rainville, E.D. *Special Functions;* Chelsea Publ. Co.: Bronx, NY, USA, 1971.
37. Petojevic, A. A note about the Pochhammer symbol. *Math. Moravica* **2008**, **12**, 37–42. [CrossRef]
38. Mubeen, S.; Ali, S.R.S.; Nayab, I.; Rahman, G.; Abdeljawad, T.; Nisar, K.S. Integral transforms of an extended generalized multi-index Bessel function. *AIMS Math.* **2020**, *5*, 7531–7547. [CrossRef]
39. Ali, R.S.; Mubeen, S.; Nayab,I.; Araci,S.; Rahman,G.; Nisar, K.S. Some Fractional Operators with the Generalized Bessel-Maitland Fuction *Discret. Dyn. Nat. Soc.* **2020**, *2020*, 1378457. [CrossRef]

40. Ali, S.; Mubeen, S.; Ali, R.S.; Rahman, G.; Morsy, A.; Nisar, K.S.; Purohit, S.D.; Zakarya, M. Dynamical significance of generalized fractional integral inequalities via convexity. *AIMS Math.* **2021**, *6*, 9705–9730. [CrossRef]
41. Ali, R.S.; Mubeen, S.; Ali, S.; Rahman, G.; Younis, J.; Ali, A. Generalized Hermite–Hadamard-Type Integral Inequalities for-Godunova–Levin Functions. *J. Funct. Spaces* **2022**, *2022*, 9113745. [CrossRef]

fractal and fractional

Article

Exploration of Hermite–Hadamard-Type Integral Inequalities for Twice Differentiable h-Convex Functions

Miguel Vivas-Cortez [1], Muhammad Samraiz [2,*], Muhammad Tanveer Ghaffar [2], Saima Naheed [2], Gauhar Rahman [3] and Yasser Elmasry [4]

1 Escuela de Ciencias Físicas y Matemáticas, Facultad de Ciencias Exactas y Naturales, Pontificia Universidad Católica del Ecuador, Av. 12 de Octubre 1076, Apartado, Quito 17-01-2184, Ecuador; mjvivas@puce.edu.ec
2 Department of Mathematics, University of Sargodha, Sargodha 40100, Pakistan; tanvirmalik364@gmail.com (M.T.G.); saima.naheed@uos.edu.pk or saimasamraiz@gmail.com (S.N.)
3 Department of Mathematics and Statistics, Hazara University Mansehra, Mansehra 21300, Pakistan; gauhar55uom@gmail.com or drgauhar.rahman@hu.edu.pk
4 Department of Mathematics, Faculty of Science, King Khalid University, P.O. Box 9004, Abha 61466, Saudi Arabia; sadek@kku.edu.sa
* Correspondence: muhammad.samraiz@uos.edu.pk or msamraizuos@gmail.com

Abstract: The significance of fractional calculus cannot be underestimated, as it plays a crucial role in the theory of inequalities. In this paper, we study a new class of mean-type inequalities by incorporating Riemann-type fractional integrals. By doing so, we discover a novel set of such inequalities and analyze them using different mathematical identities. This particular class of inequalities is introduced by employing a generalized convexity concept. To validate our work, we create visual graphs and a table of values using specific functions to represent the inequalities. This approach allows us to demonstrate the validity of our findings and further solidify our conclusions. Moreover, we find that some previously published results emerge as special consequences of our main findings. This research serves as a catalyst for future investigations, encouraging researchers to explore more comprehensive outcomes by using generalized fractional operators and expanding the concept of convexity.

Keywords: Hermite–Hadamard-type inequalities; generalized Riemann-type integrals; h-convex function; Hölder's inequality

MSC: 26A33; 26D15

Citation: Vivas-Cortez, M.; Samraiz, M.; Ghaffar, M.T.; Naheed, S.; Rahman, G.; Elmasry, Y. Exploration of Hermite–Hadamard-Type Integral Inequalities for Twice Differentiable h-Convex Functions. *Fractal Fract.* **2023**, *7*, 532. https://doi.org/10.3390/fractalfract7070532

Academic Editor: Agnieszka B. Malinowska

Received: 23 May 2023
Revised: 18 June 2023
Accepted: 20 June 2023
Published: 7 July 2023

1. Introduction and Preliminaries

Fractional calculus deals with arbitrary order integrals and derivatives that are employed in several applications. In recent years, the area related to fractional differential and integral equations has received much attention from numerous mathematicians and specialists [1]. The derivatives of fractional order represent physical models of multiple phenomena in many fields, including engineering [2,3], mathematical physics [4], fractional calculus [5] and bio-engineering [6]. The idea of convexity has been modernized, extended and expanded in several ways [7,8]. Convexity has a significant impact on our daily lives because of its numerous applications in commerce [9], industry [10], medicine [11] and the arts [12]. Geometrically convex functions in n-dimensions and s-dimensions have been derived. Some classes of convex functions, such as geometrically convex and s-convex, were investigated by Yang and Hudzik et al. in [13,14], respectively. Functional analysis, optimization and control theory all depend on convexity in significant ways [15]. Due to the activities of its definition, convexity has a strong character in the area of inequalities. The idea of convexity has played a significant and astonishing role in integral inequalities that are equally important for both fields of pure and applied mathematics [16,17].

It is obvious that without inequalities, mathematical techniques are meaningless. The mathematician presented extensions, refinements and modifications of classical inequalities such as Hermite–Hadamard inequalities [18,19], Ostrowski inequalities [20], Olsen inequalities [21], Gagliardo–Nirenberg inequalities [22] and Hardy-type inequalities [23].

The classical Hermite–Hadamard inequality was first introduced in 1893 [24]. Peter Korus [25,26] successfully updated a class of Hermite–Hadamard inequalities by incorporating the class of generalized convex derivatives. Some other authors studied the Fejer–Hadamard inequalities for convex functions in [27–32]. This inequality basically provides the bounds of the average value of a convex function. Moreover, it provides error boundaries of specific means relations and numerous numerical quadrature rules of integration such as rectangular, trapezoidal and Simpson [33,34]. For further studies, we refer the reader to articles [35,36] and book [37]. In the proposed work, we first establish some identities involving fractional integrals of the Riemann-type. Such identities will then be used to investigate Hermite–Hadamard-type integral inequalities for twice differentiable h-convex functions. The Hölders inequality will be utilized to create this class. The gamma function is defined in [38] by the following.

Definition 1. *The Euler gamma function defined for* $Re(y) > 0$, *as*

$$\Gamma(y) = \int_0^\infty \xi^{y-1} e^{-\xi} d\xi.$$

In [39], Mubeen et al. defined the following definition of the k-gamma function.

Definition 2. *The k-gamma functions defined for* $Re(y) > 0$, *as*

$$\Gamma_k(y) = \lim_{m\to\infty} \frac{m! k^m (mk)^{\frac{y}{k}-1}}{(y)_{m,k}},$$

where $(y)_{m,k}$ *is the Pochhammer k-symbols for* $k > 0$ *and factorial function. The integral form is given by*

$$\Gamma_k(y) = \int_0^\infty \xi^{y-1} \exp^{(-\frac{\xi^k}{k})} d\xi.$$

Clearly, $\Gamma(y) = \lim_{k\to 1} \Gamma_k(y)$, *and the relation between classical gamma and k-gamma is* $\Gamma_k(y) = k^{\frac{y}{k}-1}\Gamma(\frac{y}{k})$. *Additionally,* $\Gamma_k(y+k) = y\Gamma_k(y)$.

The following expression represents the complete beta function as defined in reference [40].

Definition 3. *The complete beta function is defined as*

$$\beta(\imath_1, \imath_2) = \int_0^1 \xi^{\imath_1 - 1}(1-\xi)^{\imath_2 - 1} d\xi,$$

where $Re(\imath_1) > 0, Re(\imath_2) > 0$.

The incomplete beta function [41] and relation between beta and gamma functions are given in the following.

Definition 4. *The incomplete beta function is defined as*

$$\beta_y(\imath_1, \imath_2) = \int_0^y \xi^{\imath_1 - 1}(1-\xi)^{\imath_2 - 1} d\xi,$$

where $y \in [0,1]$ *and* $\imath_1 > 0, \imath_2 > 0$. *The notable relation between the beta and gamma function is stated as*

$$\beta(\imath_1, \imath_2) = \beta(\imath_2, \imath_1) = \frac{\Gamma(\imath_1)(\imath_2)}{\Gamma(\imath_1 + \imath_2)}.$$

The definition of the h-convex function presented in [42] is defined as follows.

Definition 5. *Let* $h : \Omega \to \Re$ *be a positive increasing function. A function* $\bar{\bar{\wedge}} : \aleph \to \Re$ *is h-convex, if* $\bar{\bar{\wedge}}$ *is nonnegative on* $\aleph$, $\xi \in (0,1)$, *and for all* $\imath_1, \imath_2 \in \aleph$, *we have*

$$\bar{\bar{\wedge}}(\xi\imath_1 + (1-\xi)\imath_2) \leq h(\xi)\,\bar{\bar{\wedge}}(\imath_1) + h(1-\xi)\,\bar{\bar{\wedge}}(\imath_2). \tag{1}$$

This definition generalizes the following convexities.

(i) *If we set* $h(\xi) = l$ *in (1), then we obtain the convex function*

$$\bar{\bar{\wedge}}(\xi\imath_1 + (1-\xi)\imath_2) \leq \xi\,\bar{\bar{\wedge}}(\imath_1) + (1-\xi)\,\bar{\bar{\wedge}}(\imath_2).$$

(ii) *If we set* $h(\xi) = l^s$ *in (1), then we obtain the s-convex function in the second sense*

$$\bar{\bar{\wedge}}(\xi\imath_1 + (1-\xi)\imath_2) \leq \xi^s\,\bar{\bar{\wedge}}(\imath_1) + (1-\xi)^s\,\bar{\bar{\wedge}}(\imath_2).$$

(iii) *If we set* $h(\xi) = \frac{1}{\xi}$ *in (1), then we obtain the Godunova Levin functions.*

$$\bar{\bar{\wedge}}(\xi\imath_1 + (1-\xi)\imath_2) \leq \frac{\bar{\bar{\wedge}}(\imath_1)}{\xi} + \frac{\bar{\bar{\wedge}}(\imath_2)}{1-\xi}.$$

Definition 6 ([43]). *Let* $\bar{\bar{\wedge}} \in L[\imath_1, \imath_2]$, *then the Riemann–Liouville fractional integrals of the order* ζ *are defined by*

$$(\mathcal{F}^{\zeta}_{\imath_1^+}\bar{\bar{\wedge}})(y) = \frac{1}{\Gamma(\zeta)}\int_{\imath_1}^{y}(y-\xi)^{\zeta-1}\,\bar{\bar{\wedge}}(\xi)d\xi, \quad (0 \leq \imath_1 < y),$$

and

$$(\mathcal{F}^{\zeta}_{\imath_2^-}\bar{\bar{\wedge}})(y) = \frac{1}{\Gamma(\zeta)}\int_{y}^{\imath_2}(\xi-y)^{\zeta-1}\,\bar{\bar{\wedge}}(\xi)d\xi, \quad (0 \leq y < \imath_2),$$

are known as the left- and right-sided Riemann–Liouville fractional integrals with $\Gamma(.)$ *as the gamma function.*

Definition 7 ([39]). *Let* $\bar{\bar{\wedge}} \in L[\imath_1, \imath_2]$, *then the fractional integrals of order* ζ *defined by*

$$(\mathcal{F}^{\zeta}_{\imath_1^+,k}\bar{\bar{\wedge}})(y) = \frac{1}{k\Gamma_k(\zeta)}\int_{\imath_1}^{y}(y-\xi)^{\frac{\zeta}{k}-1}\,\bar{\bar{\wedge}}(\xi)d\xi, \quad (0 \leq \imath_1 < y),$$

and

$$(\mathcal{F}^{\zeta}_{\imath_2^-,k}\bar{\bar{\wedge}})(y) = \frac{1}{k\Gamma_k(\zeta)}\int_{y}^{\imath_2}(\xi-y)^{\frac{\zeta}{k}-1}\,\bar{\bar{\wedge}}(\xi)d\xi, \quad (0 \leq y < \imath_2),$$

are known as the left- and right-sided k-Riemann–Liouville fractional integrals with a k-gamma function.

To establish the main results, we need to recall the following lemmas presented in [44,45], respectively.

Lemma 1. *For all $\xi \in [0,1]$, we have*

$$(1-\xi)^q \leq 2^{1-q} - \xi^q \quad for\, q \in [0,1],$$
$$(1-\xi)^q \leq 2^{1-q} - \xi^q \quad for\, q \in [1,\infty).$$

Lemma 2. *Let $\overline{\overline{\wedge}} : [\imath_1, \imath_2] \to \Re$ be a function such that $\overline{\overline{\wedge}}''$ exists on $(\imath_1, \imath_2)$ with $\imath_1 < \imath_2$ if $\overline{\overline{\wedge}}'' \in L[\imath_1, \imath_2]$; then, the equation for k-fractional integrals is as follows:*

$$\frac{\overline{\overline{\wedge}}(\imath_1) + \overline{\overline{\wedge}}(\imath_2)}{2} - \frac{\Gamma_k(\zeta + k)}{2(\imath_2 - \imath_1)^{\frac{\zeta}{k}}} \left[\mathcal{F}^{\zeta}_{\imath_1^+, k} \overline{\overline{\wedge}}(\imath_2) + \mathcal{F}^{\zeta}_{\imath_2^-, k} \overline{\overline{\wedge}}(\imath_1) \right]$$
$$= \frac{(\imath_2 - \imath_1)^2}{2} \int_0^1 \frac{1 - (1-\xi)^{\frac{\zeta}{k}+1} - \xi^{\frac{\zeta}{k}+1}}{\frac{\zeta}{k}+1} \overline{\overline{\wedge}}''(\xi \imath_1 + (1-\xi)\imath_2) d\xi. \tag{2}$$

The motivation behind this work is to explore and analyze a new set of inequalities that involve mean-type concepts by employing more general convexity and fractional integrals. The Höder's inequality is used to establish these results that have applications in diverse areas, including mathematics, statistics, engineering and computer science, where it serves as a valuable tool for analyzing and solving a wide range of problems. Through visual representations and validation of our findings, we seek to contribute to the existing body of knowledge and inspire further research in this area, potentially leading to advancements in mathematical theory and applications.

2. Main Results

In this section, we first present some important identities using a generalized fractional operator of the Riemann-type. Secondly, we explore Hermite–Hadamard inequalities by first establishing some identities.

Lemma 3. *Let $\overline{\overline{\wedge}} : [\imath_1, \imath_2] \to \Re$ be a function such that $\overline{\overline{\wedge}}''$ exists on $(\imath_1, \imath_2)$ with $\imath_1 < \imath_2$ if $\overline{\overline{\wedge}}'' \in L[\imath_1, \imath_2]$; then, we have the identity*

$$\frac{\Gamma_k(\zeta + k)}{(\imath_2 - \imath_1)^{\frac{\zeta}{k}}} \left[\mathcal{F}^{\zeta}_{\imath_1^+, k} \overline{\overline{\wedge}}(\imath_2) + \mathcal{F}^{\zeta}_{\imath_2^-, k} \overline{\overline{\wedge}}(\imath_1) \right] - \overline{\overline{\wedge}}\left(\frac{\imath_1 + \imath_2}{2}\right)$$
$$= (\imath_2 - \imath_1)^2 \int_0^1 p(\xi) \overline{\overline{\wedge}}''(\xi \imath_1 + (1-\xi)\imath_2) d\xi,$$

where

$$p(\xi) = \begin{cases} \xi - \frac{1-(1-\xi)^{\frac{\zeta}{k}+1} - \xi^{\frac{\zeta}{k}+1}}{\frac{\zeta}{k}+1}, & \xi \in [0, \frac{1}{2}), \\ 1 - \xi - \frac{1-(1-\xi)^{\frac{\zeta}{k}+1} - \xi^{\frac{\zeta}{k}+1}}{\frac{\zeta}{k}+1}, & \xi \in [\frac{1}{2}, 1). \end{cases} \tag{3}$$

Proof. Consider

$$\begin{aligned}
&\int_0^1 p(\xi) \overline{\overline{\wedge}}''(\xi \imath_1 + (1-\xi)\imath_2) d\xi \\
&= \int_0^{\frac{1}{2}} \left[\xi - \frac{1-(1-\xi)^{\frac{\zeta}{k}+1} - \xi^{\frac{\zeta}{k}+1}}{\frac{\zeta}{k}+1} \right] \overline{\overline{\wedge}}''(\xi \imath_1 + (1-\xi)\imath_2) d\xi \\
&+ \int_{\frac{1}{2}}^1 \left[1 - \xi - \frac{1-(1-\xi)^{\frac{\zeta}{k}+1} - \xi^{\frac{\zeta}{k}+1}}{\frac{\zeta}{k}+1} \right] \overline{\overline{\wedge}}''(\xi \imath_1 + (1-\xi)\imath_2) d\xi \\
&= \int_0^{\frac{1}{2}} \xi \overline{\overline{\wedge}}''(\xi \imath_1 + (1-\xi)\imath_2) d\xi + \int_{\frac{1}{2}}^1 (1-\xi) \overline{\overline{\wedge}}''(\xi \imath_1 + (1-\xi)\imath_2) d\xi \\
&- \int_0^1 \frac{1-(1-\xi)^{\frac{\zeta}{k}+1} - \xi^{\frac{\zeta}{k}+1}}{\frac{\zeta}{k}+1} \overline{\overline{\wedge}}''(\xi \imath_1 + (1-\xi)\imath_2) d\xi.
\end{aligned} \tag{4}$$

Integrating by parts, we obtain

$$\int_0^{\frac{1}{2}} \xi \,\bar{\bar{\curlywedge}}''\,(\xi\imath_1+(1-\xi)\imath_2)d\xi$$
$$=\frac{1}{2(\imath_1-\imath_2)}\bar{\bar{\curlywedge}}'\left(\frac{\imath_1+\imath_2}{2}\right)-\frac{1}{(\imath_1-\imath_2)^2}\left[\bar{\bar{\curlywedge}}\left(\frac{\imath_1+\imath_2}{2}\right)-\bar{\bar{\curlywedge}}(\imath_2)\right]d\xi, \tag{5}$$

and

$$\int_{\frac{1}{2}}^1 (1-\xi)\,\bar{\bar{\curlywedge}}''\,(\xi\imath_1+(1-\xi)\imath_2)d\xi$$
$$=\frac{-1}{2(\imath_1-\imath_2)}\bar{\bar{\curlywedge}}'\left(\frac{\imath_1+\imath_2}{2}\right)+\frac{1}{(\imath_1-\imath_2)^2}\left[\bar{\bar{\curlywedge}}(\imath_1)-\bar{\bar{\curlywedge}}(\frac{\imath_1+\imath_2}{2})\right]. \tag{6}$$

Substituting (5) and (6) in (4), we obtain

$$\int_0^1 p(\xi)\,\bar{\bar{\curlywedge}}''\,(\xi\imath_1+(1-\xi)\imath_2)d\xi$$
$$=\frac{\bar{\bar{\curlywedge}}(\imath_1)+\bar{\bar{\curlywedge}}(\imath_2)}{(\imath_1-\imath_2)^2}-\frac{2}{(\imath_1-\imath_2)^2}\bar{\bar{\curlywedge}}\left(\frac{\imath_1+\imath_2}{2}\right) \tag{7}$$
$$-\int_0^1\frac{1-(1-\xi)^{\frac{\zeta}{k}+1}-\xi^{\frac{\zeta}{k}+1}}{\frac{\zeta}{k}+1}\bar{\bar{\curlywedge}}''\,(\xi\imath_1+(1-\xi)\imath_2)d\xi.$$

Multiplying $\frac{(\imath_2-\imath_1)^2}{2}$ with (7) on both sides, we can write

$$\frac{(\imath_2-\imath_1)^2}{2}\int_0^1 p(\xi)\,\bar{\bar{\curlywedge}}''\,(\xi\imath_1+(1-\xi)\imath_2)d\xi$$
$$=\frac{\bar{\bar{\curlywedge}}(\imath_1)+\bar{\bar{\curlywedge}}(\imath_2)}{2}-\bar{\bar{\curlywedge}}\left(\frac{\imath_1+\imath_2}{2}\right) \tag{8}$$
$$-\frac{(\imath_2-\imath_1)^2}{2}\int_0^1\frac{1-(1-\xi)^{\frac{\zeta}{k}+1}-\xi^{\frac{\zeta}{k}+1}}{\frac{\zeta}{k}+1}\bar{\bar{\curlywedge}}''\,(\xi\imath_1+(1-\xi)\imath_2)d\xi.$$

Substituting Lemma 2 into (8), we obtain the required result.
Hence, the proof is complete. □

Lemma 4. *Let $\bar{\bar{\curlywedge}}:[\imath_1,\imath_2]\to\Re$ be a function such that $\bar{\bar{\curlywedge}}''$ exists on $(\imath_1,\imath_2)$ with $\imath_1<\imath_2$ if $\bar{\bar{\curlywedge}}''\in L[\imath_1,\imath_2]$, $\curlywedge>0$; then, the identity*

$$\frac{\bar{\bar{\curlywedge}}(\imath_1)+\bar{\bar{\curlywedge}}(\imath_2)}{(\curlywedge+1)}+\frac{2}{\curlywedge+1}\bar{\bar{\curlywedge}}\left(\frac{\imath_1+\imath_2}{2}\right)-\frac{\Gamma_k(\zeta+k)}{\curlywedge(\imath_2-\imath_1)^{\frac{\zeta}{k}}}\left[\mathcal{F}^{\zeta}_{\imath_1^+,k}\bar{\bar{\curlywedge}}(\imath_2)+\mathcal{F}^{\zeta}_{\imath_2^-,k}\bar{\bar{\curlywedge}}(\imath_1)\right]$$
$$=(\imath_2-\imath_1)^2\int_0^1 m(l)\,\bar{\bar{\curlywedge}}''\,(\xi\imath_1+(1-\xi)\imath_2)d\xi,$$

holds with

$$m(\xi)=\begin{cases}\frac{1-(1-\xi)^{\frac{\zeta}{k}+1}-\xi^{\frac{\zeta}{k}+1}}{\curlywedge(\frac{\zeta}{k}+1)}-\frac{\xi}{\curlywedge+1}, & \xi\in[0,\frac{1}{2}),\\ \frac{1-(1-\xi)^{\frac{\zeta}{k}+1}-\xi^{\frac{\zeta}{k}+1}}{\curlywedge(\frac{\zeta}{k}+1)}-\frac{1-\xi}{\curlywedge+1}, & \xi\in[\frac{1}{2},1).\end{cases} \tag{9}$$

Proof. Multiplying $\frac{1}{\curlywedge(\curlywedge+1)}$ with Lemma 2, then

$$\frac{\doublebarwedge(\iota_1)+\doublebarwedge(\iota_2)}{\leftthreetimes(\leftthreetimes+1)}-\frac{\Gamma_k(\zeta+k)}{\leftthreetimes(\leftthreetimes+1)(\iota_2-\iota_1)^{\frac{\zeta}{k}}}\left[\mathcal{F}^{\zeta}_{\iota_1^+,k}\doublebarwedge(\iota_2)+\mathcal{F}^{\zeta}_{\iota_2^-,k}\doublebarwedge(\iota_1)\right]$$
$$=\frac{(\iota_2-\iota_1)^2}{\leftthreetimes(\leftthreetimes+1)}\int_0^1\frac{1-(1-\xi)^{\frac{\zeta}{k}+1}-\xi^{\frac{\zeta}{k}+1}}{\frac{\zeta}{k}+1}\doublebarwedge''(\xi\iota_1+(1-\xi)\iota_2)d\xi. \tag{10}$$

Multiplying $\frac{-1}{\leftthreetimes+1}$ with Lemma 3, then

$$\frac{2}{\leftthreetimes+1}\doublebarwedge\left(\frac{\iota_1+\iota_2}{2}\right)-\frac{\Gamma_k(\zeta+k)}{(\leftthreetimes+1)(\iota_2-\iota_1)^{\frac{\zeta}{k}}}\left[\mathcal{F}^{\zeta}_{\iota_1^+,k}\doublebarwedge(\iota_2)+\mathcal{F}^{\zeta}_{\iota_2^-,k}\doublebarwedge(\iota_1)\right]$$
$$=-\frac{(\iota_2-\iota_1)^2}{\leftthreetimes+1}\int_0^1 p(\xi)\doublebarwedge''(\xi\iota_1+(1-\xi)\iota_2)d\xi. \tag{11}$$

Hence, (10) and (11) yield

$$\frac{\doublebarwedge(\iota_1)+\doublebarwedge(\iota_2)}{\leftthreetimes(\leftthreetimes+1)}+\frac{2}{\leftthreetimes+1}\doublebarwedge\left(\frac{\iota_1+\iota_2}{2}\right)-\frac{\Gamma_k(\zeta+k)}{\leftthreetimes(\iota_2-\iota_1)^{\frac{\zeta}{k}}}\left[\mathcal{F}^{\zeta}_{\iota_1^+,k}\doublebarwedge(\iota_2)+\mathcal{F}^{\zeta}_{\iota_2^-,k}\doublebarwedge(\iota_1)\right]$$
$$=\frac{(\iota_2-\iota_1)^2}{\leftthreetimes(\leftthreetimes+1)}\int_0^1\frac{1-(1-\xi)^{\frac{\zeta}{k}+1}-\xi^{\frac{\zeta}{k}+1}}{\frac{\zeta}{k}+1}\doublebarwedge''(\xi\iota_1+(1-\xi)\iota_2)d\xi$$
$$-\frac{(\iota_2-\iota_1)^2}{\leftthreetimes+1}\int_0^1 p(\xi)\doublebarwedge''(\xi\iota_1+(1-\xi)\iota_2)d\xi$$
$$=(\iota_2-\iota_1)^2\int_0^1 m(\xi)\doublebarwedge''(\xi\iota_1+(1-\xi)\iota_2)d\xi,$$

where $m(\xi)$ is defined by (9). The required proof is complete. □

By using Lemma 2 and Lemma 1, we obtain the following results.

Theorem 1. *Let $\doublebarwedge:[\iota_1,\iota_2]\to\Re$ be a function such that $|\doublebarwedge''|$ exists and is measurable. Let $|\doublebarwedge''|$ be a monotonic positive function and h-convex on $[\iota_1,\iota_2]$; then, for some fixed $\zeta\in(0,\infty)$, $0\le\iota_1<\iota_2$ the inequality*

$$\left|\frac{\doublebarwedge(\iota_1)+\doublebarwedge(\iota_2)}{2}-\frac{\Gamma_k(\zeta+k)}{2(\iota_2-\iota_1)^{\frac{\zeta}{k}}}\left[\mathcal{F}^{\zeta}_{\iota_1^+,k}\doublebarwedge(\iota_2)+\mathcal{F}^{\zeta}_{\iota_2^-,k}\doublebarwedge(\iota_1)\right]\right|$$
$$\le M\frac{k(\iota_2-\iota_1)^2}{2(\zeta+k)}\left(\left|\doublebarwedge''(\iota_1)\right|+\left|\doublebarwedge''(\iota_2)\right|\right)\left(\frac{\zeta}{\zeta+2k}\right) \tag{12}$$

holds, where h is bounded by M.

Proof. By using Lemma 2, we have

$$\left|\frac{\doublebarwedge(\iota_1)+\doublebarwedge(\iota_2)}{2}-\frac{\Gamma_k(\zeta+k)}{2(\iota_2-\iota_1)^{\frac{\zeta}{k}}}\left[\mathcal{F}^{\zeta}_{\iota_1^+,k}\doublebarwedge(\iota_2)+\mathcal{F}^{\zeta}_{\iota_2^-,k}\doublebarwedge(\iota_1)\right]\right|$$
$$\le\frac{(\iota_2-\iota_1)^2}{2}\int_0^1\left|\frac{1-(1-\xi)^{\frac{\zeta}{k}+1}-\xi^{\frac{\zeta}{k}+1}}{\frac{\zeta}{k}+1}\right|\left|\doublebarwedge''(\xi\iota_1+(1-\xi)\iota_2)\right|d\xi.$$

By using the h-convexity of $|\doublebarwedge''|$, we can write

$$\leq \frac{(\imath_2-\imath_1)^2}{2}\int_0^1\left|\frac{1-(1-\xi)^{\frac{\zeta}{k}+1}-\xi^{\frac{\zeta}{k}+1}}{\frac{\zeta}{k}+1}\right|\left(h(\xi)\left|\overline{\overline{\wedge}}''(\imath_1)\right|+h(1-\xi)\left|\overline{\overline{\wedge}}''(\imath_2)\right|\right)d\xi$$

$$\leq \frac{(\imath_2-\imath_1)^2}{2}\int_0^1\left|\frac{1-(1-\xi)^{\frac{\zeta}{k}+1}-\xi^{\frac{\zeta}{k}+1}}{\frac{\zeta}{k}+1}\right|\left(M\left|\overline{\overline{\wedge}}''(\imath_1)\right|+M\left|\overline{\overline{\wedge}}''(\imath_2)\right|\right)d\xi$$

$$\leq M\frac{k(\imath_2-\imath_1)^2}{2(\zeta+k)}\left(\left|\overline{\overline{\wedge}}''(\imath_1)\right|+\left|\overline{\overline{\wedge}}''(\imath_2)\right|\right)\left(\frac{\zeta}{\zeta+2k}\right).$$

The required proof is complete. □

Example 1. *The inequality presented in Theorem 1 can be verified by sketching the graph of (29). For this purpose, we substitute $\overline{\overline{\wedge}}(\xi)=e^{\xi}$ and obtain the following*

$$\mathcal{F}^{\zeta}_{\imath_1^+,k}e^{\imath_2}=\frac{1}{k\Gamma_k(\zeta)}\int_{\imath_1}^{\imath_2}(\imath_2-\xi)^{\frac{\zeta}{k}-1}e^{\xi}d\xi, \tag{13}$$

and

$$\mathcal{F}^{\zeta}_{\imath_2^-,k}e^{\imath_1}=\frac{1}{k\Gamma_k(\zeta)}\int_{\imath_1}^{\imath_2}(\xi-\imath_1)^{\frac{\zeta}{k}-1}e^{\xi}d\xi. \tag{14}$$

By utilizing the expressions (13) and (14) in (29), we obtain

$$\begin{aligned}&\frac{e^{\imath_1}+e^{\imath_2}}{2}-\frac{Mk(\imath_2-\imath_1)^2}{2(\zeta+k)}(|e^{\imath_1}|+|e^{\imath_2}|)\left(\frac{\zeta}{\zeta+2k}\right)\\&\leq\frac{\Gamma_k(\zeta+k)}{2k\Gamma_k(\zeta)(\imath_2-\imath_1)^{\frac{\zeta}{k}}}\int_{\imath_1}^{\imath_2}[(\imath_2-\xi)^{\frac{\zeta}{k}-1}+(\xi-\imath_1)^{\frac{\zeta}{k}-1}]e^{\xi}d\xi\\&\leq\frac{e^{\imath_1}+e^{\imath_2}}{2}+\frac{Mk(\imath_2-\imath_1)^2}{2(\zeta+k)}(|e^{\imath_1}|+|e^{\imath_2}|)\left(\frac{\zeta}{\zeta+2k}\right).\end{aligned} \tag{15}$$

Corresponding to the choice of the parameters $M=1$, $\imath_1=0$, $\imath_2=1$, $k=1$, with $1\leq\zeta\leq4$, the graph of the double inequality (15) is as below.

$$p_0(\zeta)=1.8591\left(1-\frac{1}{\zeta+1}\right)+\frac{3.7183}{(\zeta+1)(\zeta+2)}.$$

$$p_1(\zeta)=\frac{\zeta}{2}\int_0^1\left[(1-\xi)^{\zeta-1}+\xi^{\zeta-1}\right]e^{\xi}d\xi.$$

$$p_2(\zeta)=1.8591\left(1+\frac{1}{\zeta+1}\right)-\frac{3.7183}{(\zeta+1)(\zeta+2)}.$$

The numerical values in Table 1 corresponds to Figure 1.

Table 1. The comparison results in Example 1 between the double inequality are presented in the following table.

Functions	1	1.5	2	2.5	3	3.5	4
$p_0(\zeta)$	1.54927	1.54041	1.54926	1.56401	1.58024	1.5962	1.61122
$p_1(\zeta)$	1.71828	1.71428	1.71828	1.72494	1.73227	1.73947	1.74625
$p_2(\zeta)$	2.16893	2.17779	2.16894	2.15419	2.13796	2.122	2.10698

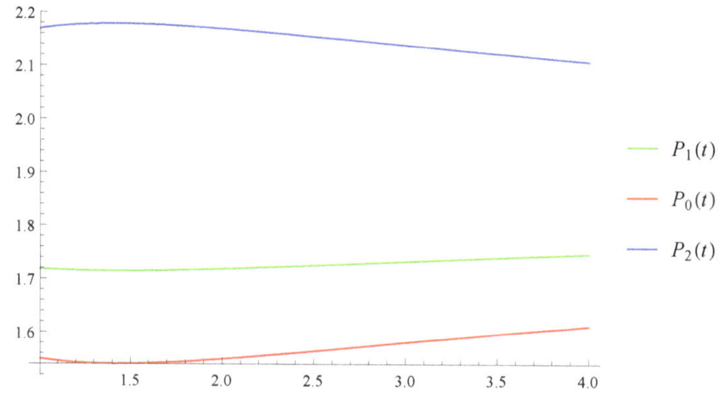

Figure 1. The graph of Theorem 1 for the choice of order $1 \le \zeta \le 4$ is presented in Figure 1.

Remark 1. *By substituting $h(\xi) = \xi$ and $k = 1$ in Theorem 1, we arrive at ([46] Theorem 3.1) with a choice $s = 1$, i.e.,*

$$\left|\frac{\bar{\bar{\wedge}}(\imath_1)+\bar{\bar{\wedge}}(\imath_2)}{2} - \frac{\Gamma(\zeta+1)}{2(\imath_2-\imath_1)^{\zeta}}\left[\mathcal{F}^{\zeta}_{\imath_1^+}\bar{\bar{\wedge}}(\imath_2)+\mathcal{F}^{\zeta}_{\imath_2^-}\bar{\bar{\wedge}}(\imath_1)\right]\right| \le \frac{(\imath_2-\imath_1)^2}{2(\zeta+1)}\left(\left|\bar{\bar{\wedge}}''(\imath_1)\right|+\left|\bar{\bar{\wedge}}''(\imath_2)\right|\right)\left(\frac{1}{2}-\frac{1}{\zeta+3}\right).$$

Remark 2. *By substituting $h(\xi) = \xi^s$ and $k = 1$ in Theorem 1, we obtain ([46] Theorem 3.1), i.e.,*

$$\left|\frac{\bar{\bar{\wedge}}(\imath_1)+\bar{\bar{\wedge}}(\imath_2)}{2} - \frac{\Gamma(\zeta+1)}{2(\imath_2-\imath_1)^{\zeta}}\left[\mathcal{F}^{\zeta}_{\imath_1^+}\bar{\bar{\wedge}}(\imath_2)+\mathcal{F}^{\zeta}_{\imath_2^-}\bar{\bar{\wedge}}(\imath_1)\right]\right| \le \frac{(\imath_2-\imath_1)^2}{2(\zeta+1)}\left(\left|\bar{\bar{\wedge}}''(\imath_1)\right|+\left|\bar{\bar{\wedge}}''(\imath_2)\right|\right)\left(\frac{1}{s+1}-\frac{1}{\zeta+s+2}\right).$$

Theorem 2. *Let the $\bar{\bar{\wedge}} : [\imath_1, \imath_2] \to \Re$ be a function such that the $\bar{\bar{\wedge}}''$ exists. Let $0 < \omega_2 < \infty$, $\left|\bar{\bar{\wedge}}''\right|^{\omega_2} \in L[\imath_1, \imath_2]$ be an h-convex monotonic positive function on $[\imath_1, \imath_2]$, $0 \le \imath_1 < \imath_2$. Then, the inequality*

$$\left|\frac{\bar{\bar{\wedge}}(\imath_1)+\bar{\bar{\wedge}}(\imath_2)}{2} - \frac{\Gamma_k(\zeta+k)}{2(\imath_2-\imath_1)^{\frac{\zeta}{k}}}\left[\mathcal{F}^{\zeta}_{\imath_1^+,k}\bar{\bar{\wedge}}(\imath_2)+\mathcal{F}^{\zeta}_{\imath_2^-,k}\bar{\bar{\wedge}}(\imath_1)\right]\right| \le M\frac{(\imath_2-\imath_1)^2\max\left(1-2^{1-\frac{\zeta}{k}}, 2^{1-\frac{\zeta}{k}}-1\right)}{2(\frac{\zeta}{k}+1)}\left(\left|\bar{\bar{\wedge}}''(\imath_1)\right|^{\omega_2}+\left|\bar{\bar{\wedge}}''(\imath_2)\right|^{\omega_2}\right)^{\frac{1}{\omega_2}} \quad (16)$$

holds with $|h(x)| \le M$ and $\frac{1}{\omega_1}+\frac{1}{\omega_2} = 1$.

Proof. The proof of this result is divided into two cases.

Case (i): Let $\zeta \in (0,1)$. By using Lemmas 1 and 2 and applying Hölder's inequality,

$$\begin{aligned}
&\left|\frac{\overline{\overline{\wedge}}(\imath_1)+\overline{\overline{\wedge}}(\imath_2)}{2}-\frac{\Gamma_k(\zeta+k)}{2(\imath_2-\imath_1)^{\frac{\zeta}{k}}}\left[\mathcal{F}^{\zeta}_{\imath_1^+,k}\overline{\overline{\wedge}}(\imath_2)+\mathcal{F}^{\zeta}_{\imath_2^-,k}\overline{\overline{\wedge}}(\imath_1)\right]\right| \\
&\leq \frac{(\imath_2-\imath_1)^2}{2}\int_0^1\left|\frac{1-(1-\xi)^{\frac{\zeta}{k}+1}-\xi^{\frac{\zeta}{k}+1}}{\frac{\zeta}{k}+1}\right|\left|\overline{\overline{\wedge}}''(\xi\imath_1+(1-\xi)\imath_2)\right|d\xi \\
&\leq \frac{(\imath_2-\imath_1)^2}{2(\frac{\zeta}{k}+1)}\left(\int_0^1\left|1-(1-\xi)^{\frac{\zeta}{k}}-\xi^{\frac{\zeta}{k}}\right|^{\omega_1}dl\right)^{\frac{1}{\omega_1}}\left(\int_0^1\left|\overline{\overline{\wedge}}''(\xi\imath_1+(1-\xi)\imath_2)\right|^{\omega_2}d\xi\right)^{\frac{1}{\omega_2}} \\
&\leq \frac{(\imath_2-\imath_1)^2}{2(\frac{\zeta}{k}+1)}\left(\int_0^1\left|(1-\xi)^{\frac{\zeta}{k}}+\xi^{\frac{\zeta}{k}}-1\right|^{\omega_1}d\xi\right)^{\frac{1}{\omega_1}}\left(\int_0^1\left|\overline{\overline{\wedge}}''(\xi\imath_1+(1-\xi)\imath_2)\right|^{\omega_2}d\xi\right)^{\frac{1}{\omega_2}} \\
&\leq \frac{(\imath_2-\imath_1)^2}{2(\frac{\zeta}{k}+1)}\left(\int_0^1\left(2^{1-\frac{\zeta}{k}}-1\right)^{\omega_1}d\xi\right)^{\frac{1}{\omega_1}}\left(\int_0^1\left|\overline{\overline{\wedge}}''(\xi\imath_1+(1-\xi)\imath_2)\right|^{\omega_2}d\xi\right)^{\frac{1}{\omega_2}} \\
&\leq \frac{(\imath_2-\imath_1)^2}{2(\frac{\zeta}{k}+1)}\left(2^{1-\frac{\zeta}{k}}-1\right)\left(\int_0^1\left|\overline{\overline{\wedge}}''(\xi\imath_1+(1-\xi)\imath_2)\right|^{\omega_2}d\xi\right)^{\frac{1}{\omega_2}}.
\end{aligned}$$

By using the h-convexity of $|\overline{\overline{\wedge}}''|^{\omega_2}$,

$$\begin{aligned}
&\leq \frac{(\imath_2-\imath_1)^2}{2(\frac{\zeta}{k}+1)}\left(2^{1-\frac{\zeta}{k}}-1\right)\left(\int_0^1\left(h(\xi)\left|\overline{\overline{\wedge}}''(\imath_1)\right|^{\omega_2}+h(1-\xi)\left|\overline{\overline{\wedge}}''(\imath_2)\right|^{\omega_2}\right)d\xi\right)^{\frac{1}{\omega_2}} \\
&\leq \frac{(\imath_2-\imath_1)^2}{2(\frac{\zeta}{k}+1)}\left(2^{1-\frac{\zeta}{k}}-1\right)\left(\int_0^1\left(M\left|\overline{\overline{\wedge}}''(\imath_1)\right|^{\omega_2}+M\left|\overline{\overline{\wedge}}''(\imath_2)\right|^{\omega_2}\right)d\xi\right)^{\frac{1}{\omega_2}} \\
&\leq M\frac{(\imath_2-\imath_1)^2}{2(\frac{\zeta}{k}+1)}\left(2^{1-\frac{\zeta}{k}}-1\right)\left(\left|\overline{\overline{\wedge}}''(\imath_1)\right|^{\omega_2}+\left|\overline{\overline{\wedge}}''(\imath_2)\right|^{\omega_2}\right)^{\frac{1}{\omega_2}}.
\end{aligned}$$

Case (ii): Let $\zeta\in[1,\infty)$. By using Lemmas 1 and 2 and applying Hölder's inequality,

$$\begin{aligned}
&\left|\frac{\overline{\overline{\wedge}}(\imath_1)+\overline{\overline{\wedge}}(\imath_2)}{2}-\frac{\Gamma_k(\zeta+k)}{2(\imath_2-\imath_1)^{\frac{\zeta}{k}}}\left[\mathcal{F}^{\zeta}_{\imath_1^+,k}\overline{\overline{\wedge}}(\imath_2)+\mathcal{F}^{\zeta}_{\imath_2^-,k}\overline{\overline{\wedge}}(\imath_1)\right]\right| \\
&\leq \frac{(\imath_2-\imath_1)^2}{2}\int_0^1\left|\frac{1-(1-\xi)^{\frac{\zeta}{k}+1}-\xi^{\frac{\zeta}{k}+1}}{\frac{\zeta}{k}+1}\right|\left|\overline{\overline{\wedge}}''(\xi\imath_1+(1-\xi)\imath_2)\right|d\xi \\
&\leq \frac{(\imath_2-\imath_1)^2}{2(\frac{\zeta}{k}+1)}\left(\int_0^1\left|1-(1-\xi)^{\frac{\zeta}{k}}-\xi^{\frac{\zeta}{k}}\right|^{\omega_1}d\xi\right)^{\frac{1}{\omega_1}}\left(\int_0^1\left|\overline{\overline{\wedge}}''(\xi\imath_1+(1-\xi)\imath_2)\right|^{\omega_2}d\xi\right)^{\frac{1}{\omega_2}} \\
&\leq \frac{(\imath_2-\imath_1)^2}{2(\frac{\zeta}{k}+1)}\left(\int_0^1\left(1-2^{1-\frac{\zeta}{k}}\right)^{\omega_1}d\xi\right)^{\frac{1}{\omega_1}}\left(\int_0^1\left|\overline{\overline{\wedge}}''(\xi\imath_1+(1-\xi)\imath_2)\right|^{\omega_2}d\xi\right)^{\frac{1}{\omega_2}} \\
&\leq \frac{(\imath_2-\imath_1)^2}{2(\frac{\zeta}{k}+1)}\left(1-2^{1-\frac{\zeta}{k}}\right)\left(\int_0^1\left|\overline{\overline{\wedge}}''(\xi\imath_1+(1-\xi)\imath_2)\right|^{\omega_2}d\xi\right)^{\frac{1}{\omega_2}}.
\end{aligned}$$

By using the h-convexity of $|\overline{\overline{\wedge}}''|^{\omega_2}$, we obtain

$$\leq \frac{(\imath_2-\imath_1)^2}{2(\frac{\zeta}{k}+1)}\left(1-2^{1-\frac{\zeta}{k}}\right)\left(\int_0^1\left(h(\xi)\left|\overline{\overline{\wedge}}''(\imath_1)\right|^{\omega_2}+h(1-\xi)\left|\overline{\overline{\wedge}}''(\imath_2)\right|^{\omega_2}\right)d\xi\right)^{\frac{1}{\omega_2}}$$
$$\leq \frac{(\imath_2-\imath_1)^2}{2(\frac{\zeta}{k}+1)}\left(1-2^{1-\frac{\zeta}{k}}\right)\left(\int_0^1\left(M\left|\overline{\overline{\wedge}}''(\imath_1)\right|^{\omega_2}+M\left|\overline{\overline{\wedge}}''(\imath_2)\right|^{\omega_2}\right)d\xi\right)^{\frac{1}{\omega_2}}$$
$$\leq M\frac{(\imath_2-\imath_1)^2}{2(\frac{\zeta}{k}+1)}\left(1-2^{1-\frac{\zeta}{k}}\right)\left(\left|\overline{\overline{\wedge}}''(\imath_1)\right|^{\omega_2}+\left|\overline{\overline{\wedge}}''(\imath_2)\right|^{\omega_2}\right)^{\frac{1}{\omega_2}}.$$

Hence, the proof is complete. □

Example 2. *The inequality presented in Theorem 2 can be verified by sketching the graph of (31). For this purpose, we substitute $\overline{\overline{\wedge}}(\xi)=\xi^2$ and obtain the following relations*

$$\mathcal{F}^{\zeta}_{\imath_1^+,k}\imath_2^2=\frac{1}{k\Gamma_k(\zeta)}\int_{\imath_1}^{\imath_2}(\imath_2-\xi)^{\frac{\zeta}{k}-1}\xi^2 d\xi, \tag{17}$$

and

$$\mathcal{F}^{\zeta}_{\imath_2^-,k}\imath_1^2=\frac{1}{k\Gamma_k(\zeta)}\int_{\imath_1}^{\imath_2}(\xi-\imath_1)^{\frac{\zeta}{k}-1}\xi^2 d\xi. \tag{18}$$

By utilizing (17) and (18) in (31), we obtain

$$\begin{aligned}&\frac{\imath_1^2+\imath_2^2}{2}-\frac{M(\imath_2-\imath_1)^2\max(1-2^{1-\frac{\zeta}{k}},2^{1-\frac{\zeta}{k}}-1)}{2(\frac{\zeta}{k}+1)}\left(|2|^{\omega_2+1}\right)^{\frac{1}{\omega_2}}\\ \leq\;&\frac{\Gamma_k(\zeta+k)}{2k\Gamma_k(\zeta)(\imath_2-\imath_1)^{\frac{\zeta}{k}}}\int_{\imath_1}^{\imath_2}[(\imath_2-\xi)^{\frac{\zeta}{k}-1}+(\xi-\imath_1)^{\frac{\zeta}{k}-1}]\xi^2 d\xi\\ \leq\;&\frac{\imath_1^2+\imath_2^2}{2}+\frac{M(\imath_2-\imath_1)^2\max(1-2^{1-\frac{\zeta}{k}},2^{1-\frac{\zeta}{k}}-1)}{2(\frac{\zeta}{k}+1)}\left(|2|^{\omega_2+1}\right)^{\frac{1}{\omega_2}}.\end{aligned} \tag{19}$$

Corresponding to the choice of the parameters $M=1$, $\imath_1=0$, $\imath_2=1$, $\omega_1=2$, $\omega_2=2$, $k=1$, with $0\leq\zeta\leq 2$, the graph of the double inequality (19) is as below.

$$p_0(\zeta)=\frac{1}{2}-\frac{\sqrt{2}}{\zeta+1}.$$
$$p_1(\zeta)=\frac{\zeta}{2}\int_0^1[(1-\xi)^{\zeta-1}+\xi^{\zeta-1}]\xi^2 d\xi.$$
$$p_2(\zeta)=\frac{1}{2}+\frac{\sqrt{2}}{\zeta+1}.$$

The numerical values in Table 2 corresponds to Figure 2.

Table 2. The comparison results in Example 2 between the double inequality are presented in the following table.

Functions	0	0.4	0.8	1.2	1.6	2
$p_0(\zeta)$	−0.914214	−0.510153	−0.285674	−0.142824	−0.0439283	0.0285955
$p_1(\zeta)$	0	0.380952	0.34127	0.329545	0.32906	0.333333
$p_2(\zeta)$	1.91421	1.51015	1.28567	1.14282	1.04393	0.971405

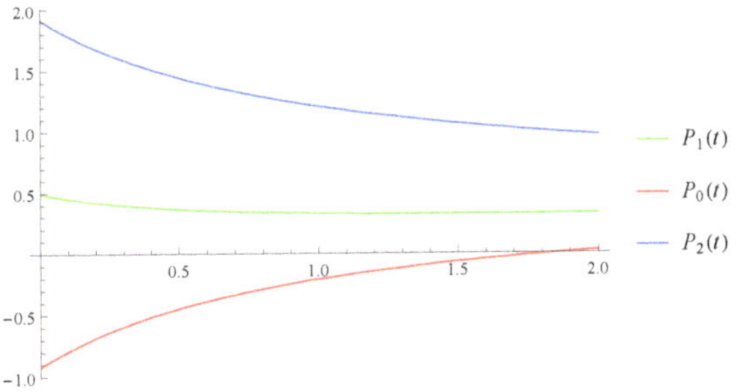

Figure 2. The graph of Theorem 2 for the choice of order $0 \leq \zeta \leq 2$ is presented in Figure 2.

Remark 3. *By substituting $h(\xi) = \xi$ and $k = 1$ in Theorem 2, we obtain ([46] Theorem 3.2) with the choice $s = 1$, i.e.,*

$$\left| \frac{\overline{\overline{\wedge}}(\imath_1) + \overline{\overline{\wedge}}(\imath_2)}{2} - \frac{\Gamma(\zeta+1)}{2(\imath_2 - \imath_1)^{\zeta}} \left[\mathcal{F}^{\zeta}_{\imath_1^+} \overline{\overline{\wedge}}(\imath_2) + \mathcal{F}^{\zeta}_{\imath_2^-} \overline{\overline{\wedge}}(\imath_1) \right] \right|$$
$$\leq \frac{(\imath_2 - \imath_1)^2 \max(1 - 2^{1-\zeta}, 2^{1-\zeta} - 1)}{2(\zeta+1)} \left(\frac{\left|\overline{\overline{\wedge}}''(\imath_1)\right|^{\omega_2} + \left|\overline{\overline{\wedge}}''(\imath_2)\right|^{\omega_2}}{2} \right)^{\frac{1}{\omega_2}},$$

where $\frac{1}{\omega_1} + \frac{1}{\omega_2} = 1$.

Remark 4. *By substituting $h(\xi) = \xi^s$ and $k = 1$ in Theorem 2, we obtain ([46] Theorem 3.2), i.e.,*

$$\left| \frac{\overline{\overline{\wedge}}(\imath_1) + \overline{\overline{\wedge}}(\imath_2)}{2} - \frac{\Gamma(\zeta+1)}{2(\imath_2 - \imath_1)^{\zeta}} \left[\mathcal{F}^{\zeta}_{\imath_1^+} \overline{\overline{\wedge}}(\imath_2) + \mathcal{F}^{\zeta}_{\imath_2^-} \overline{\overline{\wedge}}(\imath_1) \right] \right|$$
$$\leq \frac{(\imath_2 - \imath_1)^2 \max(1 - 2^{1-\zeta}, 2^{1-\zeta} - 1)}{2(\zeta+1)} \left(\frac{\left|\overline{\overline{\wedge}}''(\imath_1)\right|^{\omega_2} + \left|\overline{\overline{\wedge}}''(\imath_2)\right|^{\omega_2}}{s+1} \right)^{\frac{1}{\omega_2}},$$

where $\frac{1}{\omega_1} + \frac{1}{\omega_2} = 1$.

In the next two results, we used Lemma 3.

Theorem 3. *Let the $\overline{\overline{\wedge}} : [\imath_1, \imath_2] \to \Re$ be a differentiable mapping $|\overline{\overline{\wedge}}''|$, is measurable, and $|\overline{\overline{\wedge}}''|$ is a monotonic positive function and h-convex on $[\imath_1, \imath_2]$, $0 \leq \imath_1 < \imath_2$; then, we have the result*

$$\left| \frac{\Gamma_k(\zeta+k)}{2(\imath_2 - \imath_1)^{\frac{\zeta}{k}}} \left[\mathcal{F}^{\zeta}_{\imath_1^+,k} \overline{\overline{\wedge}}(\imath_2) + \mathcal{F}^{\zeta}_{\imath_2^-,k} \overline{\overline{\wedge}}(\imath_1) \right] - \overline{\overline{\wedge}}\left(\frac{\imath_1 + \imath_2}{2}\right) \right|$$
$$\leq M \frac{(\imath_2 - \imath_1)^2}{2} \left(\left|\overline{\overline{\wedge}}''(\imath_1)\right| + \left|\overline{\overline{\wedge}}''(\imath_2)\right| \right) \left(\frac{1}{4} - \frac{1}{\frac{\zeta}{k}+1} + \frac{2}{(\frac{\zeta}{k}+1)(\frac{\zeta}{k}+2)} \right), \quad (20)$$

where $|h(x)| \leq M$ *and* $\zeta \in (0, \infty)$.

Proof. By using Lemma 3, we can write

$$\left| \frac{\Gamma_k(\zeta+k)}{2(\imath_2 - \imath_1)^{\frac{\zeta}{k}}} \left[\mathcal{F}^{\zeta}_{\imath_1^+,k} \overline{\overline{\wedge}}(\imath_2) + \mathcal{F}^{\zeta}_{\imath_2^-,k} \overline{\overline{\wedge}}(\imath_1) \right] - \overline{\overline{\wedge}}\left(\frac{\imath_1 + \imath_2}{2}\right) \right|$$
$$\leq \frac{(\imath_2 - \imath_1)^2}{2} \int_0^1 |p(\xi)| \left|\overline{\overline{\wedge}}''(\xi\imath_1 + (1-\xi)\imath_2)\right| d\xi.$$

By using the h-convexity of $|\overline{\overline{\wedge}}''|$, we have

$$\begin{aligned}
&\leq \frac{(\imath_2-\imath_1)^2}{2}\int_0^1\left(|p(\xi)|\left(h(\xi)\left|\overline{\overline{\wedge}}''(\imath_1)\right|+h(1-\xi)\left|\overline{\overline{\wedge}}''(\imath_2)\right|\right)\right)d\xi \\
&\leq \frac{(\imath_2-\imath_1)^2}{2}\int_0^1|p(\xi)|\left(M\left|\overline{\overline{\wedge}}''(\imath_1)\right|+M\left|\overline{\overline{\wedge}}''(\imath_2)\right|\right)d\xi \\
&\leq M\frac{(\imath_2-\imath_1)^2}{2}\int_0^1\left(|p(\xi)|\left(\left|\overline{\overline{\wedge}}''(\imath_1)\right|+\left|\overline{\overline{\wedge}}''(\imath_2)\right|\right)\right)d\xi \\
&\leq M\frac{(\imath_2-\imath_1)^2}{2}\left(\left|\overline{\overline{\wedge}}''(\imath_1)\right|+\left|\overline{\overline{\wedge}}''(\imath_2)\right|\right)\int_0^1|p(\xi)|d\xi \\
&\leq M\frac{(\imath_2-\imath_1)^2}{2}\left(\left|\overline{\overline{\wedge}}''(\imath_1)\right|+\left|\overline{\overline{\wedge}}''(\imath_2)\right|\right)\left(\int_0^{\frac{1}{2}}\left|\xi-\frac{1-(1-\xi)^{\frac{\zeta}{k}+1}-\xi^{\frac{\zeta}{k}+1}}{\frac{\zeta}{k}+1}\right|d\xi\right. \\
&\left.+\int_{\frac{1}{2}}^1\left|1-\xi-\frac{1-(1-\xi)^{\frac{\zeta}{k}+1}-\xi^{\frac{\zeta}{k}+1}}{\frac{\zeta}{k}+1}\right|d\xi\right) \\
&\leq M\frac{(\imath_2-\imath_1)^2}{2(\frac{\zeta}{k}+1)}\left(\left|\overline{\overline{\wedge}}''(\imath_1)\right|+\left|\overline{\overline{\wedge}}''(\imath_2)\right|\right)\left(\int_0^{\frac{1}{2}}\left|\xi\frac{\zeta}{k}+\xi-1+(1-\xi)^{\frac{\zeta}{k}+1}\right.\right. \\
&\left.\left.+\xi^{\frac{\zeta}{k}+1}\right|d\xi+\int_{\frac{1}{2}}^1\left|\frac{\zeta}{k}+1-\xi\frac{\zeta}{k}-1-\xi+(1-\xi)^{\frac{\zeta}{k}+1}+\xi^{\frac{\zeta}{k}+1}\right|d\xi\right) \\
&\leq M\frac{(\imath_2-\imath_1)^2}{2}\left(\left|\overline{\overline{\wedge}}''(\imath_1)\right|+\left|\overline{\overline{\wedge}}''(\imath_2)\right|\right)\left(\frac{1}{4}-\frac{1}{\frac{\zeta}{k}+1}+\frac{2}{(\frac{\zeta}{k}+1)(\frac{\zeta}{k}+2)}\right).
\end{aligned}$$

Hence, the desired result is proved. □

Example 3. *The inequality presented in Theorem 3 can be verified by sketching the graph of (20). For this purpose, by utilizing the expressions (13) and (14) in (20), we obtain*

$$\begin{aligned}
&e^{\left(\frac{\imath_1+\imath_2}{2}\right)}-\frac{M(\imath_2-\imath_1)^2}{2}(|e^{\imath_1}|+|e^{\imath_2}|)\left(\frac{1}{4}-\frac{1}{\frac{\zeta}{k}+1}+\frac{2}{(\frac{\zeta}{k}+1)(\frac{\zeta}{k}+2)}\right) \\
&\leq \frac{\Gamma_k(\zeta+k)}{2k\Gamma_k(\zeta)(\imath_2-\imath_1)^{\frac{\zeta}{k}}}\int_{\imath_1}^{\imath_2}\left[(\imath_2-\xi)^{\frac{\zeta}{k}-1}+(\xi-\imath_1)^{\frac{\zeta}{k}-1}\right]e^{\xi}d\xi \qquad (21)\\
&\leq e^{\left(\frac{\imath_1+\imath_2}{2}\right)}+\frac{M(\imath_2-\imath_1)^2}{2}(|e^{\imath_1}|+|e^{\imath_2}|)\left(\frac{1}{4}-\frac{1}{\frac{\zeta}{k}+1}+\frac{2}{(\frac{\zeta}{k}+1)(\frac{\zeta}{k}+2)}\right).
\end{aligned}$$

Corresponding to the choice of the parameters $M=1$, $\imath_1=0$, $\imath_2=1$, $k=1$, with $1\leq\zeta\leq4$, the graph of the double inequality (21) is as below.

$$\begin{aligned}
p_0(\zeta)&=1.6487-1.8591\left(\frac{1}{4}-\frac{1}{\zeta+1}+\frac{2}{(\zeta+1)(\zeta+2)}\right). \\
p_1(\zeta)&=\frac{\zeta}{2}\int_0^1\left[(1-\xi)^{\zeta-1}+\xi^{\zeta-1}\right]e^{\xi}d\xi. \\
p_2(\zeta)&=1.6487+1.8591\left(\frac{1}{4}-\frac{1}{\zeta+1}+\frac{2}{(\zeta+1)(\zeta+2)}\right).
\end{aligned}$$

The numerical values in Table 3 corresponds to Figure 3.

Table 3. The comparison results in Example 3 between the double inequality are presented in the following table.

Functions	1	1.5	2	2.5	3	3.5	4
$p_0(\zeta)$	1.49378	1.50263	1.49378	1.47902	1.46279	1.44683	1.43181
$p_1(\zeta)$	1.71828	1.71428	1.71828	1.72494	1.73227	1.73947	1.74625
$p_2(\zeta)$	1.80363	1.79477	1.80363	1.81838	1.83461	1.85057	1.8656

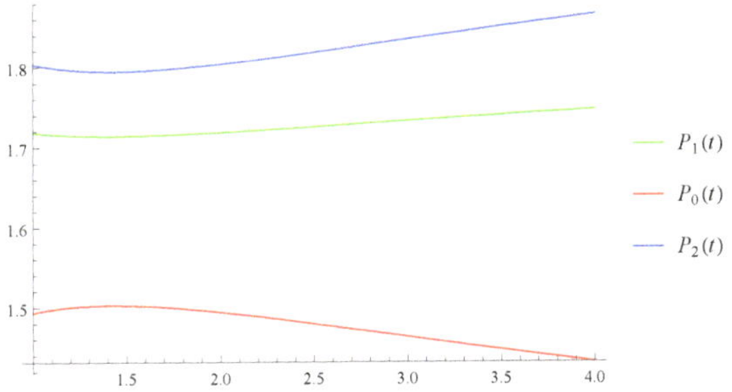

Figure 3. The graph of Theorem 3 for the choice of order $1 \leq \zeta \leq 4$ is presented in Figure 3.

Remark 5. *By substituting $h(\xi) = \xi$ and $k = 1$ in Theorem 3, we obtain ([46] Theorem 4.1) with the choice $s = 1$.*

$$\begin{aligned}
&\left|\frac{\Gamma(\zeta+1)}{2(\iota_2-\iota_1)^\zeta}\left[\mathcal{F}^\zeta_{\iota_1^+}\overline{\overline{\wedge}}(\iota_2)+\mathcal{F}^\zeta_{\iota_2^-}\overline{\overline{\wedge}}(\iota_1)\right]-\overline{\overline{\wedge}}\left(\frac{\iota_1+\iota_2}{2}\right)\right| \\
&\leq \frac{(\iota_2-\iota_1)^2\left|\overline{\overline{\wedge}}''(\iota_1)\right|}{2(\zeta+1)}\left[\frac{1}{\zeta+3}-\frac{\zeta+1}{8}+2\beta(2,\zeta+2)\right] \\
&+\frac{(\iota_2-\iota_1)^2\left|\overline{\overline{\wedge}}''(\iota_2)\right|}{2(\zeta+1)}\left[\frac{1}{\zeta+3}-\frac{\zeta-5}{8}+2\beta(\zeta+2,2)\right].
\end{aligned}$$

Remark 6. *By substituting $h(\zeta) = \xi^s$ and $k = 1$ in Theorem 3, we obtain ([46] Theorem 4.1).*

$$\begin{aligned}
&\left|\frac{\Gamma(\zeta+1)}{2(\iota_2-\iota_1)^\zeta}\left[\mathcal{F}^\zeta_{\iota_1^+}\overline{\overline{\wedge}}(\iota_2)+\mathcal{F}^\zeta_{\iota_2^-}\overline{\overline{\wedge}}(\iota_1)\right]-\overline{\overline{\wedge}}\left(\frac{\iota_1+\iota_2}{2}\right)\right| \\
&\leq \frac{(\iota_2-\iota_1)^2\left|\overline{\overline{\wedge}}''(\iota_1)\right|}{2(\zeta+1)}\left[\frac{\zeta-\zeta 2^{-s-1}-2^{-s-1}}{1+s}-\frac{\zeta+1}{2+s}\right. \\
&\left.+2\beta(\zeta+2,s+1)+\frac{1}{\zeta+s+2}\right] \\
&+\frac{(\iota_2-\iota_1)^2\left|\overline{\overline{\wedge}}''(\iota_2)\right|}{2(\zeta+1)}\left[\frac{\zeta 2^{-s-1}-2^{-s-1}-1}{1+s}-\frac{1}{\zeta+s+2}+2\beta(\zeta+2,s+1)\right].
\end{aligned}$$

Theorem 4. *Consider a function $\overline{\overline{\wedge}}$ defined on the interval $[\iota_1, \iota_2]$ such that its second derivative, denoted by $\overline{\overline{\wedge}}''$, exists on this interval. Assume that the function $\left|\overline{\overline{\wedge}}''\right|^{\omega_2}$ belongs to the class of integrable functions $L[\iota_1, \iota_2]$ and is both h-convex and a positive monotonic function. Additionally, suppose that $0 \leq \iota_1 < \iota_2$. Then, the inequality*

$$\left|\frac{\Gamma_k(\zeta+k)}{2(\iota_2-\iota_1)^{\frac{\zeta}{k}}}\left[\mathcal{F}^{\zeta}_{\iota_1^+,k}\bar{\bar{\wedge}}(\iota_2)+\mathcal{F}^{\zeta}_{\iota_2^-,k}\bar{\bar{\wedge}}(\iota_1)\right]-\bar{\bar{\wedge}}\left(\frac{\iota_1+\iota_2}{2}\right)\right|$$
$$\leq M\frac{(\iota_2-\iota_1)^2}{2(\frac{\zeta}{k}+1)}\left(\left|\bar{\bar{\wedge}}''(\iota_1)\right|^{\omega_2}+\left|\bar{\bar{\wedge}}''(\iota_2)\right|^{\omega_2}\right)^{\frac{1}{\omega_2}} \tag{22}$$
$$\times\left(\frac{\left(\frac{\zeta}{k}+1\right)2^{-\omega_1-1}-\left(\frac{\zeta}{k}\right)^{\omega_1+1}+\left(\frac{\zeta}{k}+0.5\right)^{\omega_1+1}}{\omega_1+1}\right)^{\frac{1}{\omega_1}}$$

holds, where $|h(x)|\leq M$ *and* $\frac{1}{\omega_1}+\frac{1}{\omega_2}=1$.

Proof. By using Hölder's inequality and Lemma 3, we have

$$\left|\frac{\Gamma_k(\zeta+k)}{2(\iota_2-\iota_1)^{\frac{\zeta}{k}}}\left[\mathcal{F}^{\zeta}_{\iota_1^+,k}\bar{\bar{\wedge}}(\iota_2)+\mathcal{F}^{\zeta}_{\iota_2^-,k}\bar{\bar{\wedge}}(\iota_1)\right]-\bar{\bar{\wedge}}\left(\frac{\iota_1+\iota_2}{2}\right)\right|$$
$$\leq\frac{(\iota_2-\iota_1)^2}{2}\int_0^1\left(|p(\xi)|\left|\bar{\bar{\wedge}}''(\xi\iota_1+(1-\xi)\iota_2)\right|\right)d\xi$$
$$\leq\frac{(\iota_2-\iota_1)^2}{2}\left(\int_0^1|p(\xi)|^{\omega_1}d\xi\right)^{\frac{1}{\omega_1}}\left(\int_0^1\left|\bar{\bar{\wedge}}''(\xi\iota_1+(1-\xi)\iota_2)\right|^{\omega_2}d\xi\right)^{\frac{1}{\omega_2}}.$$

By using the h-convexity of $|\bar{\bar{\wedge}}''|^{\omega_2}$, we obtain

$$\leq\frac{(\iota_2-\iota_1)^2}{2}\left(\int_0^1|p(\xi)|^{\omega_1}d\xi\right)^{\frac{1}{\omega_1}}$$
$$\times\left(\int_0^1\left(h(\xi)\left|\bar{\bar{\wedge}}''(\iota_1)\right|^{\omega_2}+h(1-\xi)\left|\bar{\bar{\wedge}}''(\iota_2)\right|^{\omega_2}\right)d\xi\right)^{\frac{1}{\omega_2}}$$
$$\leq\frac{(\iota_2-\iota_1)^2}{2}\left(\int_0^1|p(\xi)|^{\omega_1}d\xi\right)^{\frac{1}{\omega_1}}\left(\int_0^1\left(M\left|\bar{\bar{\wedge}}''(\iota_1)\right|^{\omega_2}+M\left|\bar{\bar{\wedge}}''(\iota_2)\right|^{\omega_2}\right)d\xi\right)^{\frac{1}{\omega_2}}$$
$$\leq M\frac{(\iota_2-\iota_1)^2}{2}\left(\left|\bar{\bar{\wedge}}''(\iota_1)\right|^{\omega_2}+\left|\bar{\bar{\wedge}}''(\iota_2)\right|^{\omega_2}\right)^{\frac{1}{\omega_2}}\left(\int_0^1|p(\xi)|^{\omega_1}d\xi\right)^{\frac{1}{\omega_1}}$$
$$\leq M\frac{(\iota_2-\iota_1)^2}{2}\left(\left|\bar{\bar{\wedge}}''(\iota_1)\right|^{\omega_2}+\left|\bar{\bar{\wedge}}''(\iota_2)\right|^{\omega_2}\right)^{\frac{1}{\omega_2}}$$
$$\times\left(\int_0^{\frac{1}{2}}\left|\xi-\frac{1-(1-\xi)^{\frac{\zeta}{k}+1}-\xi^{\frac{\zeta}{k}+1}}{\frac{\zeta}{k}+1}\right|^{\omega_1}d\xi\right.$$
$$\left.+\int_{\frac{1}{2}}^1\left|1-\xi-\frac{1-(1-\xi)^{\frac{\zeta}{k}+1}-\xi^{\frac{\zeta}{k}+1}}{\frac{\zeta}{k}+1}\right|^{\omega_1}d\xi\right)^{\frac{1}{\omega_1}}$$
$$\leq M\frac{(\iota_2-\iota_1)^2}{2(\frac{\zeta}{k}+1)}\left(\left|\bar{\bar{\wedge}}''(\iota_1)\right|^{\omega_2}+\left|\bar{\bar{\wedge}}''(\iota_2)\right|^{\omega_2}\right)^{\frac{1}{\omega_2}}$$

$$\times\left(\int_0^{\frac{1}{2}}\left|\xi\frac{\zeta}{k}+\xi-1+(1-\xi)^{\frac{\zeta}{k}+1}+\xi^{\frac{\zeta}{k}+1}\right|^{\omega_1}d\xi\right.$$

$$\left.+\int_{\frac{1}{2}}^{1}\left|\frac{\zeta}{k}+1-\xi\frac{\zeta}{k}-1-\xi+(1-\xi)^{\frac{\zeta}{k}+1}+\xi^{\frac{\zeta}{k}+1}\right|^{\omega_1}d\xi\right)^{\frac{1}{\omega_1}}$$

$$\leq M\frac{(\imath_2-\imath_1)^2}{2((\frac{\zeta}{k}+1))}\left(\left|\overline{\overline{\wedge}}''(\imath_1)\right|^{\omega_2}+\left|\overline{\overline{\wedge}}''(\imath_2)\right|^{\omega_2}\right)^{\frac{1}{\omega_2}}$$

$$\times\left(\int_0^{\frac{1}{2}}\left|(\frac{\zeta}{k}+1)\xi\right|^{\omega_1}d\xi+\int_{\frac{1}{2}}^{1}\left|\frac{\zeta}{k}-\xi+1\right|^{\omega_1}d\xi\right)^{\frac{1}{\omega_1}}$$

$$\leq M\frac{(\imath_2-\imath_1)^2}{2(\frac{\zeta}{k}+1)}\left(\left|\overline{\overline{\wedge}}''(\imath_1)\right|^{\omega_2}+\left|\overline{\overline{\wedge}}''(\imath_2)\right|^{\omega_2}\right)^{\frac{1}{\omega_2}}$$

$$\times\left(\int_0^{\frac{1}{2}}\left(\frac{\zeta}{k}+1\right)\xi^{\omega_1}d\xi+\int_{\frac{1}{2}}^{1}\left(\frac{\zeta}{k}-\xi+1\right)^{\omega_1}d\xi\right)^{\frac{1}{\omega_1}}$$

$$\leq M\frac{(\imath_2-\imath_1)^2}{2(\frac{\zeta}{k}+1)}\left(\left|\overline{\overline{\wedge}}''(\imath_1)\right|^{\omega_2}+\left|\overline{\overline{\wedge}}''(\imath_2)\right|^{\omega_2}\right)^{\frac{1}{\omega_2}}$$

$$\times\left(\frac{(\frac{\zeta}{k}+1)2^{-\omega_1-1}-(\frac{\zeta}{k})^{\omega_1+1}+(\frac{\zeta}{k}+0.5)^{\omega_1+1}}{\omega_1+1}\right)^{\frac{1}{\omega_1}}.$$

This completes the result. □

Remark 7. *By substituting $h(\xi)=\xi$ and $k=1$ in Theorem 4, we obtain ([46] Theorem 4.2) with the choice $s=1$.*

$$\frac{\Gamma(\zeta+1)}{2(\imath_2-\imath_1)^{\zeta}}\left[\mathcal{F}^{\zeta}_{\imath_1^+}\overline{\overline{\wedge}}(\imath_2)+\mathcal{F}^{\zeta}_{\imath_2^-}\overline{\overline{\wedge}}(\imath_1)\right]-\overline{\overline{\wedge}}\left(\frac{\imath_1+\imath_2}{2}\right)$$

$$\leq\frac{(\imath_2-\imath_1)^2}{2(\zeta+1)}\left(\frac{\left|\overline{\overline{\wedge}}''(\imath_1)\right|^{\omega_2}+\left|\overline{\overline{\wedge}}''(\imath_2)\right|^{\omega_2}}{2}\right)^{\frac{1}{\omega_2}}$$

$$\times\left(\frac{(\zeta+1)2^{-\omega_1-1}+(\zeta+0.5)^{\omega_1+1}-\zeta^{\omega_1+1}}{\omega_1+1}\right)^{\frac{1}{\omega_1}},$$

where $\frac{1}{\omega_1}+\frac{1}{\omega_2}=1$.

Remark 8. *By substituting $h(\xi)=\xi^s$ and $k=1$ in Theorem 4, we obtain ([46] Theorem 4.2).*

$$\frac{\Gamma(\zeta+1)}{2(\imath_2-\imath_1)^{\zeta}}\left[\mathcal{F}^{\zeta}_{\imath_1^+}\overline{\overline{\wedge}}(\imath_2)+\mathcal{F}^{\zeta}_{\imath_2^-}\overline{\overline{\wedge}}(\imath_1)\right]-\overline{\overline{\wedge}}\left(\frac{\imath_1+\imath_2}{2}\right)$$

$$\leq\frac{(\imath_2-\imath_1)^2}{2(\zeta+1)}\left(\frac{\left|\overline{\overline{\wedge}}''(\imath_1)\right|^{\omega_2}+\left|\overline{\overline{\wedge}}''(\imath_2)\right|^{\omega_2}}{s+1}\right)^{\frac{1}{\omega_2}}$$

$$\times\left(\frac{(\zeta+1)2^{-\omega_1-1}+(\zeta+0.5)^{\omega_1+1}-\zeta^{\omega_1+1}}{\omega_1+1}\right)^{\frac{1}{\omega_1}},$$

where $\frac{1}{\omega_1}+\frac{1}{\omega_2}=1$.

By using Lemma 4, we obtain the next two results.

Theorem 5. *Suppose we have a function $\overline{\overline{\wedge}}$ defined on the interval $[\imath_1, \imath_2]$ such that the absolute value of its second derivative, denoted by $|\overline{\overline{\wedge}}''|$, exists. If $|\overline{\overline{\wedge}}''|$ is both monotonic and positive and it is also h-convex on the interval $[\imath_1, \imath_2]$, where $0 \leq \imath_1 < \imath_2$, then the following inequality holds:*

$$\begin{aligned}
&\left|\frac{\overline{\overline{\wedge}}(\imath_1)+\overline{\overline{\wedge}}(\imath_2)}{\wedge(\wedge+1)}+\frac{2}{\wedge+1}\overline{\overline{\wedge}}\left(\frac{\imath_1+\imath_2}{2}\right)-\frac{\Gamma_k(\zeta+k)}{\wedge(\imath_2-\imath_1)^{\frac{\zeta}{k}}}\left[\mathcal{F}^{\zeta}_{\imath_1^+,k}\overline{\overline{\wedge}}(\imath_2)+\mathcal{F}^{\zeta}_{\imath_2^-,k}\overline{\overline{\wedge}}(\imath_1)\right]\right|\\
&\leq M\frac{(\imath_2-\imath_1)^2}{\wedge(\wedge+1)(\frac{\zeta}{k}+1)}\left(\left|\overline{\overline{\wedge}}''(\imath_1)\right|+\left|\overline{\overline{\wedge}}''(\imath_2)\right|\right)\\
&\times\max\left[\frac{\wedge+1}{2}-\frac{\wedge(\frac{\zeta}{k}+1)}{8}-\frac{\wedge+1}{\frac{\zeta}{k}+2},\frac{-\wedge-1}{2}+\frac{\wedge(\frac{\zeta}{k}+1)}{8}+\frac{\wedge+1}{\frac{\zeta}{k}+2}\right]\\
&+M\frac{(\imath_2-\imath_1)^2}{\wedge(\wedge+1)(\frac{\zeta}{k}+1)}\left(\left|\overline{\overline{\wedge}}''(\imath_1)\right|+\left|\overline{\overline{\wedge}}''(\imath_2)\right|\right)\\
&\times\max\left[\frac{\wedge+1}{2}-\frac{\wedge(\frac{\zeta}{k}+1)}{8}-\frac{\wedge+1}{\frac{\zeta}{k}+2},\frac{-\wedge-1}{2}+\frac{\wedge(\frac{\zeta}{k}+1)}{8}+\frac{\wedge+1}{\frac{\zeta}{k}+2}\right],
\end{aligned} \tag{23}$$

where $|h(x)| \leq M$.

Proof. By using Lemma 4, we can write

$$\begin{aligned}
&\left|\frac{\overline{\overline{\wedge}}(\imath_1)+\overline{\overline{\wedge}}(\imath_2)}{\wedge(\wedge+1)}+\frac{2}{\wedge+1}\overline{\overline{\wedge}}\left(\frac{\imath_1+\imath_2}{2}\right)-\frac{\Gamma_k(\zeta+k)}{\wedge(\imath_2-\imath_1)^{\frac{\zeta}{k}}}\left[\mathcal{F}^{\zeta}_{\imath_1^+,k}\overline{\overline{\wedge}}(\imath_2)+\mathcal{F}^{\zeta}_{\imath_2^-,k}\overline{\overline{\wedge}}(\imath_1)\right]\right|\\
&\leq(\imath_2-\imath_1)^2\int_0^1\left(|m(\xi)|\left|\overline{\overline{\wedge}}''(\xi\imath_1+(1-\xi)\imath_2)\right|\right)d\xi.
\end{aligned}$$

By using the h-convexity of $|\overline{\overline{\wedge}}''|$, we can write

$$\begin{aligned}
&\leq(\imath_2-\imath_1)^2\int_0^1|m(\xi)|\left(h(\xi)\left|\overline{\overline{\wedge}}''(\imath_1)\right|+h(1-\xi)\left|\overline{\overline{\wedge}}''(\imath_2)\right|\right)d\xi\\
&\leq(\imath_2-\imath_1)^2\int_0^1|m(\xi)|\left(M\left|\overline{\overline{\wedge}}''(\imath_1)\right|+M\left|\overline{\overline{\wedge}}''(\imath_2)\right|\right)d\xi\\
&\leq M(\imath_2-\imath_1)^2\left(\left|\overline{\overline{\wedge}}''(\imath_1)\right|+\left|\overline{\overline{\wedge}}''(\imath_2)\right|\right)\int_0^1|m(\xi)|d\xi\\
&\leq M(\imath_2-\imath_1)^2\left(\left|\overline{\overline{\wedge}}''(\imath_1)\right|+\left|\overline{\overline{\wedge}}''(\imath_2)\right|\right)\\
&\times\left(\int_0^{\frac{1}{2}}\left|\frac{1-(1-\xi)^{\frac{\zeta}{k}+1}-\xi^{\frac{\zeta}{k}+1}}{\wedge(\frac{\zeta}{k}+1)}-\frac{\xi}{\wedge+1}\right|d\xi\right.\\
&\left.+\int_{\frac{1}{2}}^1\left|\frac{1-(1-\xi)^{\frac{\zeta}{k}+1}-\xi^{\frac{\zeta}{k}+1}}{\wedge(\frac{\zeta}{k}+1)}-\frac{1-\xi}{\wedge+1}\right|d\xi\right)\\
&\leq M\frac{(\imath_2-\imath_1)^2}{\wedge(\wedge+1)(\frac{\zeta}{k}+1)}\left(\left|\overline{\overline{\wedge}}''(\imath_1)\right|+\left|\overline{\overline{\wedge}}''(\imath_2)\right|\right)\\
&\times\left(\int_0^{\frac{1}{2}}\left|\wedge+1-(\wedge+1)((1-\xi)^{\frac{\zeta}{k}+1}+\xi^{\frac{\zeta}{k}+1})-\wedge(\frac{\zeta}{k}+1)\xi\right|d\xi\right.\\
&\left.+\int_{\frac{1}{2}}^1\left|\wedge+1-(\wedge+1)((1-\xi)^{\frac{\zeta}{k}+1}+\xi^{\frac{\zeta}{k}+1})-\wedge(\frac{\zeta}{k}+1)(1-\xi)\right|d\xi\right).
\end{aligned} \tag{24}$$

However,

$$\begin{aligned}
&\int_0^{\frac{1}{2}}\left[\wedge+1-(\wedge+1)((1-\xi)^{\frac{\zeta}{k}+1}+\xi^{\frac{\zeta}{k}+1})-\wedge(\frac{\zeta}{k}+1)\xi\right]d\xi\\
&\leq\frac{\wedge+1}{2}-\frac{\wedge(\frac{\zeta}{k}+1)}{8}-\frac{\wedge+1}{\frac{\zeta}{k}+2},
\end{aligned}$$

and

$$\int_0^{\frac{1}{2}} \left[-\lambda - 1 + (\lambda+1)((1-\xi)^{\frac{\zeta}{k}+1} + \xi^{\frac{\zeta}{k}+1}) + \lambda(\frac{\zeta}{k}+1)\xi \right] d\xi$$
$$\leq \frac{-\lambda-1}{2} + \frac{\lambda(\frac{\zeta}{k}+1)}{8} + \frac{\lambda+1}{\frac{\zeta}{k}+2}.$$

Additionally,

$$\int_{\frac{1}{2}}^1 \left[\lambda + 1 - (\lambda+1)((1-\xi)^{\frac{\zeta}{k}+1} + \xi^{\frac{\zeta}{k}+1}) - \lambda(\frac{\zeta}{k}+1)(1-\xi) \right] d\xi$$
$$\leq \frac{\lambda+1}{2} - \frac{\lambda(\frac{\zeta}{k}+1)}{8} - \frac{\lambda+1}{\frac{\zeta}{k}+2},$$

and

$$\int_{\frac{1}{2}}^1 \left[-\lambda - 1 + (\lambda+1)((1-\xi)^{\frac{\zeta}{k}+1} + \xi^{\frac{\zeta}{k}+1}) + \lambda(\frac{\zeta}{k}+1)(1-\xi) \right] d\xi$$
$$\leq \frac{-\lambda-1}{2} + \frac{\lambda(\frac{\zeta}{k}+1)}{8} + \frac{\lambda+1}{\frac{\zeta}{k}+2}.$$

Substituting these values of integrals in (24), we obtain the required result. □

Example 4. *The inequality presented in Theorem 5 can be verified by sketching the graph of (23). For this purpose, by utilizing (17) and (18) in (23), we obtain*

$$\begin{aligned}
&\frac{\iota_1^2+\iota_2^2}{\lambda(\lambda+1)} + \frac{2}{\lambda+1}\left(\frac{\iota_1+\iota_2}{2}\right)^2 - M\frac{4(\iota_2-\iota_1)^2}{\lambda(\lambda+1)(\frac{\zeta}{k}+1)} \\
&\times \max\left[\frac{\lambda+1}{2} - \frac{\lambda(\frac{\zeta}{k}+1)}{8} - \frac{\lambda+1}{\frac{\zeta}{k}+2}, \frac{-\lambda-1}{2} + \frac{\lambda(\frac{\zeta}{k}+1)}{8} + \frac{\lambda+1}{\frac{\zeta}{k}+2}\right] \\
-&M\frac{4(\iota_2-\iota_1)^2}{\lambda(\lambda+1)(\frac{\zeta}{k}+1)} \\
&\times \max\left[\frac{\lambda+1}{2} - \frac{\lambda(\frac{\zeta}{k}+1)}{8} - \frac{\lambda+1}{\frac{\zeta}{k}+2}, \frac{-\lambda-1}{2} + \frac{\lambda(\frac{\zeta}{k}+1)}{8} + \frac{\lambda+1}{\frac{\zeta}{k}+2}\right] \\
&\leq \frac{\Gamma_k(\zeta+k)}{k\lambda\Gamma_k(\zeta)(\iota_2-\iota_1)^{\frac{\zeta}{k}}} \int_{\iota_1}^{\iota_2} \left[(\iota_2-\xi)^{\frac{\zeta}{k}-1} + (\xi-\iota_1)^{\frac{\zeta}{k}-1}\right] e^{\xi} d\xi \\
&\leq \frac{\iota_1^2+\iota_2^2}{\lambda(\lambda+1)} + \frac{2}{\lambda+1}\left(\frac{\iota_1+\iota_2}{2}\right)^2 + M\frac{4(\iota_2-\iota_1)^2}{\lambda(\lambda+1)(\frac{\zeta}{k}+1)} \\
&\times \max\left[\frac{\lambda+1}{2} - \frac{\lambda(\frac{\zeta}{k}+1)}{8} - \frac{\lambda+1}{\frac{\zeta}{k}+2}, \frac{-\lambda-1}{2} + \frac{\lambda(\frac{\zeta}{k}+1)}{8} + \frac{\lambda+1}{\frac{\zeta}{k}+2}\right] \\
+&M\frac{4(\iota_2-\iota_1)^2}{\lambda(\lambda+1)(\frac{\zeta}{k}+1)} \\
&\times \max\left[\frac{\lambda+1}{2} - \frac{\lambda(\frac{\zeta}{k}+1)}{8} - \frac{\lambda+1}{\frac{\zeta}{k}+2}, \frac{-\lambda-1}{2} + \frac{\lambda(\frac{\zeta}{k}+1)}{8} + \frac{\lambda+1}{\frac{\zeta}{k}+2}\right].
\end{aligned} \tag{25}$$

Corresponding to the choice of the parameters $M = 1$, $\iota_1 = 0$, $\iota_2 = 1$, $\lambda = 1$, $k = 1$, with $0 \leq \zeta \leq 2$, the graph of the double inequality (25) is as below.

$$p_0(\zeta) = \frac{3}{4} - \frac{1}{\zeta+1}.$$
$$p_1(\zeta) = \zeta \int_0^1 [(1-\xi)^{\zeta-1} + \xi^{\zeta-1}]\xi^2 d\xi.$$
$$p_2(\zeta) = \frac{3}{4} + \frac{1}{\zeta+1}.$$

The numerical values in Table 4 corresponds to Figure 4.

Table 4. The comparison results in Example 4 between the double inequality are presented in the following table.

Functions	0	0.4	0.8	1.2	1.6	2
$p_0(\zeta)$	−0.25	0.357143	0.194444	0.295455	0.365385	0.416667
$p_1(\zeta)$	0	0.761905	0.68254	0.659091	0.65812	0.666667
$p_2(\zeta)$	1.75	1.46429	1.30556	1.20455	1.13462	1.083333

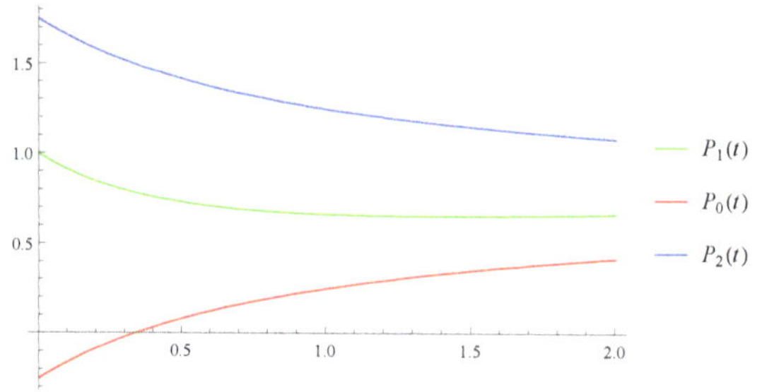

Figure 4. The graph of Theorem 5 for the choice of order $0 \le \zeta \le 2$ is presented in Figure 4.

Remark 9. *By substituting $h(\xi) = \xi$ and $k = 1$ in Theorem 5, we obtain ([46] Theorem 5.1) with the choice $s = 1$.*

$$\left| \frac{\bar{\bar{\wedge}}(\imath_1) + \bar{\bar{\wedge}}(\imath_2)}{\lambda(\lambda+1)} + \frac{2}{\lambda+1} \bar{\bar{\wedge}} \left(\frac{\imath_1 + \imath_2}{2} \right) - \frac{\Gamma(\zeta+1)}{\lambda(\imath_2 - \imath_1)^{\zeta}} \left[\mathcal{F}^{\zeta}_{\imath_1^+} \bar{\bar{\wedge}}(\imath_2) + \mathcal{F}^{\zeta}_{\imath_2^-} \bar{\bar{\wedge}}(\imath_1) \right] \right|$$
$$\le \frac{(\imath_2 - \imath_1)^2}{\lambda(\lambda+1)(\zeta+1)} \max\left(\left[\lambda + 1 - (\lambda+1)2^{-\zeta} \right] \left[\frac{\left|\bar{\bar{\wedge}}''(\imath_1)\right| + 3\left|\bar{\bar{\wedge}}''(\imath_2)\right|}{8} \right] \right.$$
$$\left. - \lambda(\zeta+1) \left[\frac{\left|\bar{\bar{\wedge}}''(\imath_1)\right| + 57\left|\bar{\bar{\wedge}}''(\imath_2)\right|}{24} \right], \lambda(\zeta+1) \left[\frac{\left|\bar{\bar{\wedge}}''(\imath_1)\right| + 57\left|\bar{\bar{\wedge}}''(\imath_2)\right|}{24} \right] \right)$$
$$+ \frac{(\imath_2 - \imath_1)^2}{\lambda(\lambda+1)(\zeta+1)} \max\left(\left[1 - \lambda\zeta - (\lambda+1)2^{-\zeta} \right] \left[\frac{3\left|\bar{\bar{\wedge}}''(\imath_1)\right| - \left|\bar{\bar{\wedge}}''(\imath_2)\right|}{8} \right] \right.$$
$$\left. + \lambda(\zeta+1) \left[\frac{7\left|\bar{\bar{\wedge}}''(\imath_1)\right| + 57\left|\bar{\bar{\wedge}}''(\imath_2)\right|}{24} \right], \lambda(\zeta+1) \left[\frac{\left|\bar{\bar{\wedge}}''(\imath_1)\right| + 27\left|\bar{\bar{\wedge}}''(\imath_2)\right|}{12} \right] \right).$$

Remark 10. *By substituting $h(\xi) = \xi^s$ and $k = 1$ in Theorem 5, we obtain ([46] Theorem 5.1).*

$$\left| \frac{\bar{\bar{\wedge}}(\imath_1) + \bar{\bar{\wedge}}(\imath_2)}{\lambda(\lambda+1)} + \frac{2}{\lambda+1} \bar{\bar{\wedge}} \left(\frac{\imath_1 + \imath_2}{2} \right) - \frac{\Gamma(\zeta+1)}{\lambda(\imath_2 - \imath_1)^{\zeta}} \left[\mathcal{F}^{\zeta}_{\imath_1^+} \bar{\bar{\wedge}}(\imath_2) + \mathcal{F}^{\zeta}_{\imath_2^-} \bar{\bar{\wedge}}(\imath_1) \right] \right|$$

$$\leq \frac{(\iota_2-\iota_1)^2}{\leftthreetimes(\leftthreetimes+1)(\zeta+1)}\max\left(\left[\frac{2^{-s-1}\left|\bar{\bar{\wedge}}''(\iota_1)\right|+(1-2^{-s-1})\left|\bar{\bar{\wedge}}''(\iota_2)\right|}{s+1}\right]\right.$$

$$\times\left[\leftthreetimes+1-(\leftthreetimes+1)2^{-\zeta}\right]-\leftthreetimes(\zeta+1)\left[\frac{2^{-s-2}\left|\bar{\bar{\wedge}}''(\iota_1)\right|}{s+2}+\beta_{0.5}(2,s+1)\left|\bar{\bar{\wedge}}''(\iota_2)\right|\right]$$

$$,\leftthreetimes(\zeta+1)\left[\frac{2^{-s-2}\left|\bar{\bar{\wedge}}''(\iota_1)\right|}{s+2}+\beta_{0.5}(2,s+1)\left|\bar{\bar{\wedge}}''(\iota_2)\right|\right]\Bigg)$$

$$+\frac{(\iota_2-\iota_1)^2}{\leftthreetimes(\leftthreetimes+1)(\zeta+1)}\max\left(\left[\frac{(1-2^{-s-1})\left|\bar{\bar{\wedge}}''(\iota_1)\right|-2^{-s-1}\left|\bar{\bar{\wedge}}''(\iota_2)\right|}{s+1}\right]\right.$$

$$\times\left[\leftthreetimes+1-(\leftthreetimes+1)2^{-\zeta}-\leftthreetimes(\zeta+1)\right]+\leftthreetimes(\zeta+1)\left[\frac{(1-2^{-s-2})\left|\bar{\bar{\wedge}}''(\iota_1)\right|}{s+2}\right.$$

$$\left.+\beta_{0.5}(s+1,2)\left|\bar{\bar{\wedge}}''(\iota_2)\right|\right],$$

$$\leftthreetimes(\zeta+1)\left[\frac{(1-2^{-s-1})\left|\bar{\bar{\wedge}}''(\iota_1)\right|-2^{-s-1}\left|\bar{\bar{\wedge}}''(\iota_2)\right|}{s+1}-\frac{(1-2^{-s-2})\left|\bar{\bar{\wedge}}''(\iota_1)\right|}{s+2}\right.$$

$$\left.\left.-\beta_{0.5}(s+1,2)\left|\bar{\bar{\wedge}}''(\iota_2)\right|\right]\right).$$

Theorem 6. *Let the* $\bar{\bar{\wedge}}:[\iota_1,\iota_2]\rightarrow\Re$ *be a function such that* $|\bar{\bar{\wedge}}''|$ *exists on* $[\iota_1,\iota_2]$. *Let* $0<\omega_2<\infty$, $|\bar{\bar{\wedge}}''|^q\in L[\iota_1,\iota_2]$ *be an h-convex, monotonic positive function where* $0\leq\iota_1<\iota_2$. *Then, the following inequality*

$$\left|\frac{\bar{\bar{\wedge}}(\iota_1)+\bar{\bar{\wedge}}(\iota_2)}{\leftthreetimes(\leftthreetimes+1)}+\frac{2}{\leftthreetimes+1}\bar{\bar{\wedge}}\left(\frac{\iota_1+\iota_2}{2}\right)-\frac{\Gamma_k(\zeta+k)}{\leftthreetimes(\iota_2-\iota_1)^{\frac{\zeta}{k}}}\left[\mathcal{F}^{\zeta}_{\iota_1^+,k}\bar{\bar{\wedge}}(\iota_2)+\mathcal{F}^{\zeta}_{\iota_2^-,k}\bar{\bar{\wedge}}(\iota_1)\right]\right|$$
$$\leq\frac{M(\iota_2-\iota_1)^2}{[\leftthreetimes(\leftthreetimes+1)(\frac{\zeta}{k}+1)]^{1+\omega_1^{-1}}}\left(\left|\bar{\bar{\wedge}}''(\iota_1)\right|^{\omega_2}+\left|\bar{\bar{\wedge}}''(\iota_2)\right|^{\omega_2}\right)^{\frac{1}{\omega_2}}$$
$$\times\left(\max\left[\left[\leftthreetimes+1-(\leftthreetimes+1)2^{-\frac{\zeta}{k}}\right]^{\omega_1+1}-\left[1+0.5\leftthreetimes(1-\frac{\zeta}{k})-(1+\leftthreetimes)2^{-\frac{\zeta}{k}}\right]^{\omega_1+1},\right.\right. \tag{26}$$
$$\left.\left[\leftthreetimes(\frac{\zeta}{k}+1)\right]^{\omega_1+1}2^{-\omega_1-1}\right]+\max\left[\left[\leftthreetimes+1-(\leftthreetimes+1)2^{-\frac{\zeta}{k}}\right]^{\omega_1+1}\right.$$
$$\left.\left.-\left[1+0.5\leftthreetimes(1-\frac{\zeta}{k})-(\leftthreetimes+1)2^{-\frac{\zeta}{k}}\right]^{\omega_1+1},\left[0.5\leftthreetimes(\frac{\zeta}{k}+1)\right]^{\omega_1+1}\right]\right)^{\frac{1}{\omega_1}}$$

holds, where $|h(x)|\leq M$ *and* $\frac{1}{\omega_1}+\frac{1}{\omega_2}=1$.

Proof. By using the Hölder's inequality and Lemma 4, we can write

$$\left|\frac{\bar{\bar{\wedge}}(\iota_1)+\bar{\bar{\wedge}}(\iota_2)}{\leftthreetimes(\leftthreetimes+1)}+\frac{2}{\leftthreetimes+1}\bar{\bar{\wedge}}\left(\frac{\iota_1+\iota_2}{2}\right)-\frac{\Gamma_k(\zeta+k)}{\leftthreetimes(\iota_2-\iota_1)^{\frac{\zeta}{k}}}\left[\mathcal{F}^{\zeta}_{\iota_1^+,k}\bar{\bar{\wedge}}(\iota_2)+\mathcal{F}^{\zeta}_{\iota_2^-,k}\bar{\bar{\wedge}}(\iota_1)\right]\right|$$
$$\leq(\iota_2-\iota_1)^2\int_0^1\left(|m(\xi)|\left|\bar{\bar{\wedge}}''(\xi\iota_1+(1-\xi)\iota_2)\right|\right)d\xi$$
$$\leq(\iota_2-\iota_1)^2\left(\int_0^1|m(\xi)|^{\omega_1}d\xi\right)^{\frac{1}{\omega_1}}\left(\int_0^1\left|\bar{\bar{\wedge}}''(\xi\iota_1+(1-\xi)\iota_2)\right|^{\omega_2}d\xi\right)^{\frac{1}{\omega_2}}.$$

By using the h-convexity of $|\overline{\overline{\wedge}}''|^{\omega_2}$, we can write

$$
\begin{aligned}
&\leq (\iota_2-\iota_1)^2\left(\int_0^1 |m(\xi)|^{\omega_1} d\xi\right)^{\frac{1}{\omega_1}} \\
&\times\left(\int_0^1 \left(h(\xi)\left|\overline{\overline{\wedge}}''(\iota_1)\right|^{\omega_2}+h(1-\xi)\left|\overline{\overline{\wedge}}''(\iota_2)\right|^{\omega_2}\right)d\xi\right)^{\frac{1}{\omega_2}} \\
&\leq (\iota_2-\iota_1)^2\left(\int_0^1 |m(\xi)|^{\omega_1} d\xi\right)^{\frac{1}{\omega_1}}\left(\int_0^1\left(M\left|\overline{\overline{\wedge}}''(\iota_1)\right|^{\omega_2}+M\left|\overline{\overline{\wedge}}''(\iota_2)\right|^{\omega_2}\right)d\xi\right)^{\frac{1}{\omega_2}} \\
&\leq M(\iota_2-\iota_1)^2\left(\left|\overline{\overline{\wedge}}''(\iota_1)\right|^{\omega_2}+\left|\overline{\overline{\wedge}}''(\iota_2)\right|^{\omega_2}\right)^{\frac{1}{\omega_2}}\left(\int_0^1 |m(\xi)|^{\omega_1} d\xi\right)^{\frac{1}{\omega_1}} \\
&\leq M(\iota_2-\iota_1)^2\left(\left|\overline{\overline{\wedge}}''(\iota_1)\right|^{\omega_2}+\left|\overline{\overline{\wedge}}''(\iota_2)\right|^{\omega_2}\right)^{\frac{1}{\omega_2}} \\
&\times\left(\int_0^{\frac{1}{2}}\left|\frac{1-(1-\xi)^{\frac{\zeta}{k}+1}-\xi^{\frac{\zeta}{k}+1}}{\wedge(\frac{\zeta}{k}+1)}-\frac{\xi}{\wedge+1}\right|^{\omega_1} d\xi\right. \qquad (27) \\
&\left.+\int_{\frac{1}{2}}^1\left|\frac{1-(1-\xi)^{\frac{\zeta}{k}+1}-\xi^{\frac{\zeta}{k}+1}}{\wedge(\frac{\zeta}{k}+1)}-\frac{1-\xi}{\wedge+1}\right|^{\omega_1} d\xi\right)^{\frac{1}{\omega_1}} \\
&\leq M\frac{(\iota_2-\iota_1)^2}{\wedge(\wedge+1)(\frac{\zeta}{k}+1)}\left(\left|\overline{\overline{\wedge}}''(\iota_1)\right|^{\omega_2}+\left|\overline{\overline{\wedge}}''(\iota_2)\right|^{\omega_2}\right)^{\frac{1}{\omega_2}} \\
&\times\left(\int_0^{\frac{1}{2}}\left|\wedge+1-(\wedge+1)((1-\xi)^{\frac{\zeta}{k}+1}+\xi^{\frac{\zeta}{k}+1})-\wedge(\frac{\zeta}{k}+1)\xi\right|^{\omega_1} d\xi\right. \\
&\left.+\int_{\frac{1}{2}}^1\left|\wedge+1-(\wedge+1)((1-\xi)^{\frac{\zeta}{k}+1}+\xi^{\frac{\zeta}{k}+1})-\wedge(\frac{\zeta}{k}+1)(1-\xi)\right|^{\omega_1} d\xi\right)^{\frac{1}{\omega_1}}.
\end{aligned}
$$

However,

$$
\begin{aligned}
&\int_0^{\frac{1}{2}}\left[\wedge+1-(\wedge+1)((1-\xi)^{\frac{\zeta}{k}+1}+\xi^{\frac{\zeta}{k}+1})-\wedge(\frac{\zeta}{k}+1)\xi\right]^{\omega_1} d\xi \\
&\leq\frac{\left[\wedge+1-(\wedge+1)2^{-\frac{\zeta}{k}}\right]^{\omega_1+1}-\left[1+0.5\wedge(1-\frac{\zeta}{k})-(1+\wedge)2^{-\frac{\zeta}{k}}\right]^{\omega_1+1}}{\wedge(\omega_1+1)(\frac{\zeta}{k}+1)},
\end{aligned}
$$

and

$$
\begin{aligned}
&\int_0^{\frac{1}{2}}\left[-\wedge-1+(\wedge+1)((1-\xi)^{\frac{\zeta}{k}+1}+\xi^{\frac{\zeta}{k}+1})+\wedge(\frac{\zeta}{k}+1)\xi\right]^{\omega_1} d\xi \\
&\leq\frac{\left[\wedge(\frac{\zeta}{k}+1)\right]^{\omega_1+1}2^{-\omega_1-1}}{\wedge(\omega_1+1)(\frac{\zeta}{k}+1)}.
\end{aligned}
$$

Additionally

$$
\begin{aligned}
&\int_{\frac{1}{2}}^1\left[\wedge+1-(\wedge+1)((1-\xi)^{\frac{\zeta}{k}+1}+\xi^{\frac{\zeta}{k}+1})-\wedge(\frac{\zeta}{k}+1)(1-\xi)\right]^{\omega_1} d\xi \\
&\leq\frac{\left[\wedge+1-(\wedge+1)2^{-\frac{\zeta}{k}}\right]^{\omega_1+1}-\left[1+0.5\wedge(1-\frac{\zeta}{k})-(\wedge+1)2^{-\frac{\zeta}{k}}\right]^{\omega_1+1}}{\wedge(\omega_1+1)(\frac{\zeta}{k}+1)},
\end{aligned}
$$

and

$$\int_{\frac{1}{2}}^{1}\left[-\lambda-1+(\lambda+1)((1-\xi)^{\frac{\zeta}{k}+1}+\xi^{\frac{\zeta}{k}+1})+\lambda(\frac{\zeta}{k}+1)(1-\xi)\right]^{\omega_1}d\xi$$
$$\leq\frac{\left[0.5\lambda(\frac{\zeta}{k}+1)\right]^{\omega_1+1}}{\lambda(\omega_1+1)(\frac{\zeta}{k}+1)}.$$

Substituting the values of integrals in (27), we obtain the required result. The proof is complete. □

Example 5. *The inequality presented in Theorem 6 can be verified by sketching the graph of (26). For this purpose, by utilizing these expressions (13) and (14) in (23), we obtain*

$$\begin{aligned}
&\frac{e^{\iota_1}+e^{\iota_2}}{\lambda(\lambda+1)}+\frac{2}{\lambda+1}e^{(\frac{\iota_1+\iota_2}{2})}-\frac{(\iota_2-\iota_1)^2}{[\lambda(\lambda+1)(\frac{\zeta}{k}+1)]^{1+\omega_1^{-1}}}\left(|e^{\iota_1}|^{\omega_2}+|e^{\iota_2}|^{\omega_2}\right)^{\frac{1}{\omega_2}}\\
&\times\Bigg(\max\Bigg[\left[\lambda+1-(\lambda+1)2^{-\frac{\zeta}{k}}\right]^{\omega_1+1}-\left[1+0.5\lambda(1-\frac{\zeta}{k})-(1+\lambda)2^{-\frac{\zeta}{k}}\right]^{\omega_1+1},\\
&\left[\lambda(\frac{\zeta}{k}+1)\right]^{\omega_1+1}2^{-\omega_1-1}\Bigg]+\max\Bigg[\left[\lambda+1-(\lambda+1)2^{-\frac{\zeta}{k}}\right]^{\omega_1+1}\\
&-\left[1+0.5\lambda(1-\frac{\zeta}{k})-(\lambda+1)2^{-\frac{\zeta}{k}}\right]^{\omega_1+1},\left[0.5\lambda(\frac{\zeta}{k}+1)\right]^{\omega_1+1}\Bigg]\Bigg)^{\frac{1}{\omega_1}}\\
&\leq\frac{\Gamma_k(\zeta+k)}{k\lambda\Gamma_k(\zeta)(\iota_2-\iota_1)^{\frac{\zeta}{k}}}\int_{\iota_1}^{\iota_2}\left[(\iota_2-\xi)^{\frac{\zeta}{k}-1}+(\xi-\iota_1)^{\frac{\zeta}{k}-1}\right]e^{\xi}d\xi \qquad (28)\\
&\leq\frac{e^{\iota_1}+e^{\iota_2}}{\lambda(\lambda+1)}+\frac{2}{\lambda+1}e^{(\frac{\iota_1+\iota_2}{2})}+\frac{(\iota_2-\iota_1)^2}{[\lambda(\lambda+1)(\frac{\zeta}{k}+1)]^{1+\omega_1^{-1}}}\left(|e^{\iota_1}|^{\omega_2}+|e^{\iota_2}|^{\omega_2}\right)^{\frac{1}{\omega_2}}\\
&\times\Bigg(\max\Bigg[\left[\lambda+1-(\lambda+1)2^{-\frac{\zeta}{k}}\right]^{\omega_1+1}-\left[1+0.5\lambda(1-\frac{\zeta}{k})-(1+\lambda)2^{-\frac{\zeta}{k}}\right]^{\omega_1+1},\\
&\left[\lambda(\frac{\zeta}{k}+1)\right]^{\omega_1+1}2^{-\omega_1-1}\Bigg]+\max\Bigg[\left[\lambda+1-(\lambda+1)2^{-\frac{\zeta}{k}}\right]^{\omega_1+1}\\
&-\left[1+0.5\lambda(1-\frac{\zeta}{k})-(\lambda+1)2^{-\frac{\zeta}{k}}\right]^{\omega_1+1},\left[0.5\lambda(\frac{\zeta}{k}+1)\right]^{\omega_1+1}\Bigg]\Bigg)^{\frac{1}{\omega_1}}.
\end{aligned}$$

Corresponding to the choice of the parameters $M=1$, $\iota_1=0$, $\iota_2=1$, $\lambda=1$, $\omega_1=2$, $\omega_2=2$, $k=1$, with $1\leq\zeta\leq 4$, the graph of the double inequality (28) is as below.

$$p_0(\zeta)=3.5078-\frac{2.0240}{(\zeta+1)^{\frac{3}{2}}}.$$
$$p_1(\zeta)=\zeta\int_0^1\left[(1-\xi)^{\zeta-1}+\xi^{\zeta-1}\right]e^{\xi}d\xi.$$
$$p_2(\zeta)=3.5078+\frac{2.0240}{(\zeta+1)^{\frac{3}{2}}}.$$

The numerical values in Table 5 corresponds to Figure 5.

Table 5. The comparison results in Example 5 between the double inequality are presented in the following table.

Functions	1	1.5	2	2.5	3	3.5	4
$p_0(\zeta)$	2.79221	2.99576	3.11828	3.19869	3.2548	3.29577	3.32677
$p_1(\zeta)$	3.43656	3.42856	3.43656	3.44989	3.46454	3.47895	3.49251
$p_2(\zeta)$	4.22339	4.01984	3.89732	3.81691	3.7608	3.71983	3.68883

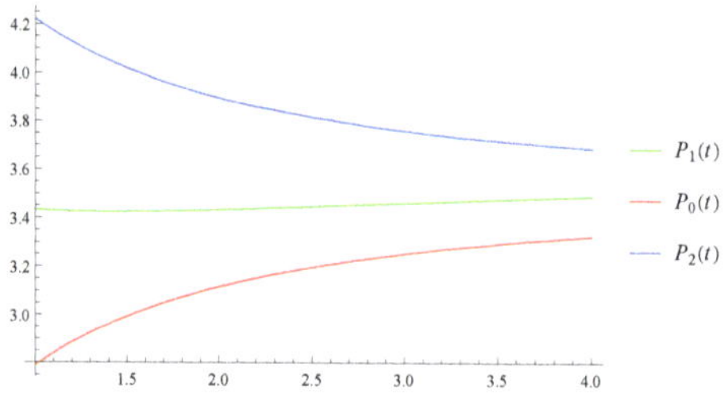

Figure 5. The graph of Theorem 6 for the choice of order $1 \leq \zeta \leq 4$ is presented in Figure 5.

Remark 11. *By substituting $h(\xi) = \xi$ and $k = 1$ in Theorem 6, we obtain ([46] Theorem 5.2) with the choice $s = 1$.*

$$\left|\frac{\bar{\bar{\wedge}}(\iota_1)+\bar{\bar{\wedge}}(\iota_2)}{\lambda(\lambda+1)}+\frac{2}{\lambda+1}\bar{\bar{\wedge}}\left(\frac{\iota_1+\iota_2}{2}\right)-\frac{\Gamma(\zeta+1)}{\lambda(\iota_2-\iota_1)^{\zeta}}\left[\mathcal{F}^{\zeta}_{\iota_1^+}\bar{\bar{\wedge}}(\iota_2)+\mathcal{F}^{\zeta}_{\iota_2^-}\bar{\bar{\wedge}}(\iota_1)\right]\right|$$
$$\leq \frac{(\iota_2-\iota_1)^2}{[\lambda(\lambda+1)(\zeta+1)]^{1+\omega_1^{-1}}}\left(\frac{\left|\bar{\bar{\wedge}}''(\iota_1)\right|^{\omega_2}+\left|\bar{\bar{\wedge}}''(\iota_1)\right|^{\omega_2}}{2}\right)^{\frac{1}{\omega_2}}$$
$$\times\Big(\max\Big([\lambda+1-(\lambda+1)2^{-\zeta}]^{\omega_1+1}+[1+0.5\lambda(1-\zeta)-(1+\lambda)2^{-\zeta}]^{\omega_1+1},$$
$$[\lambda(\zeta+1)]^{\omega_1+1}2^{-\omega_1-1}\Big)$$
$$+\max\Big([\lambda+1-(\lambda+1)2^{-\zeta}]^{\omega_1+1}-[1+0.5\lambda(1-\zeta)+(1+\lambda)2^{-\zeta}]^{\omega_1+1},$$
$$[0.5\lambda(\zeta+1)]^{\omega_1+1}\Big)\Big)^{\frac{1}{\omega_1}},$$

where $\frac{1}{\omega_1}+\frac{1}{\omega_2}=1$.

Remark 12. *By substituting $h(\xi) = \xi^s$ and $k = 1$ in Theorem 6, we obtain ([46] Theorem 5.2).*

$$\left|\frac{\bar{\bar{\wedge}}(\iota_1)+\bar{\bar{\wedge}}(\iota_2)}{\lambda(\lambda+1)}+\frac{2}{\lambda+1}\bar{\bar{\wedge}}\left(\frac{\iota_1+\iota_2}{2}\right)-\frac{\Gamma(\zeta+1)}{\lambda(\iota_2-\iota_1)^{\zeta}}\left[\mathcal{F}^{\zeta}_{\iota_1^+}\bar{\bar{\wedge}}(\iota_2)+\mathcal{F}^{\zeta}_{\iota_2^-}\bar{\bar{\wedge}}(\iota_1)\right]\right|$$
$$\leq \frac{(\iota_2-\iota_1)^2}{[\lambda(\lambda+1)(\zeta+1)]^{1+\omega_1^{-1}}}\left(\frac{\left|\bar{\bar{\wedge}}''(\iota_1)\right|^{\omega_2}+\left|\bar{\bar{\wedge}}''(\iota_1)\right|^{\omega_2}}{s+1}\right)^{\frac{1}{\omega_2}}$$
$$\times\Big[\max\Big([\lambda+1-(\lambda+1)2^{-\zeta}]^{\omega_1+1}+[1+0.5\lambda(1-\zeta)-(1+\lambda)2^{-\zeta}]^{\omega_1+1},$$
$$[\lambda(\zeta+1)]^{\omega_1+1}2^{-\omega_1-1}\Big)$$
$$+\max\Big([\lambda+1-(\lambda+1)2^{-\zeta}]^{\omega_1+1}-[1+0.5\lambda(1-\zeta)+(1+\lambda)2^{-\zeta}]^{\omega_1+1},$$
$$[0.5\lambda(\zeta+1)]^{\omega_1+1}\Big)\Big]^{\frac{1}{\omega_1}},$$

where $\frac{1}{\omega_1} + \frac{1}{\omega_2} = 1$.

3. Some Applications to the Main Results in Terms of Means

In mathematics, the means we employ hold profound significance in various domains such as problem-solving, statistical analysis, optimization problems and mathematical proofs. This section contains applications of thhe main results in terms of means. The representation of the means are given as follows:

(i) The arithmetic mean:
$A = A(\imath_1, \imath_2) = \frac{\imath_1+\imath_2}{2}, \imath_1, \imath_2 \in \mathbb{R}^+$

(ii) The logarithmic mean:
$L(\imath_1, \imath_2) = \frac{\imath_2-\imath_1}{\ln \imath_2 - \ln \imath_1}, \imath_1 \neq \imath_2\ \imath_1, \imath_2 \in \mathbb{R}^+$

Proposition 1. *Let* $\imath_1, \imath_2 \in \mathbb{R}^+$, $\imath_1 < \imath_2$; *then, we have the following inequalities.*

$$|A(e^{\imath_1}, e^{\imath_2}) - L(e^{\imath_1}, e^{\imath_2})| \leq \frac{(\imath_2 - \imath_1)^2 (e^{\imath_1} + e^{\imath_2})}{12}. \tag{29}$$

Proof. Using Theorem (1) and making some simplification, we can write this as

$$\left| \frac{\overline{\overline{\wedge}}(\imath_1) + \overline{\overline{\wedge}}(\imath_2)}{2} - \frac{k}{2(\imath_2 - \imath_1)^{\frac{\zeta}{k}}} \int_{\imath_1}^{\imath_2} [(y-\xi)^{\frac{\zeta}{k}-1} + (\xi - y)^{\frac{\zeta}{k}-1}] \overline{\overline{\wedge}}(\xi) d\xi \right|$$
$$\leq M \frac{k(\imath_2 - \imath_1)^2}{2(\zeta + k)} \left(\left| \overline{\overline{\wedge}}''(\imath_1) \right| + \left| \overline{\overline{\wedge}}''(\imath_2) \right| \right) \left(\frac{\zeta}{\zeta + 2k} \right). \tag{30}$$

By substituting $\overline{\overline{\wedge}}(\xi) = e^{\xi}$, $k = 1$, $\zeta = 1$ and $M = 1$ in (30), we can write this as

$$\left| \frac{e^{\imath_1} + e^{\imath_2}}{2} - \frac{1}{(\imath_2 - \imath_1)} \int_{\imath_1}^{\imath_2} e^{\xi} d\xi \right| \leq \frac{(\imath_2 - \imath_1)^2 (e^{\imath_1} + e^{\imath_2})}{12}$$
$$\left| \frac{e^{\imath_1} + e^{\imath_2}}{2} - \frac{(e^{\imath_2} - e^{\imath_1})}{(\imath_2 - \imath_1)} \right| \leq \frac{(\imath_2 - \imath_1)^2 (e^{\imath_1} + e^{\imath_2})}{12}.$$

This proved relation (29). □

Proposition 2. *Let* $\imath_1, \imath_2 \in \mathbb{R}^+$, $\imath_1 < \imath_2$; *then, we have the following inequalities.*

$$\left| A(e^{\imath_1}, e^{\imath_2}) + e^{A(e^{\imath_1}, e^{\imath_2})} - 2L(e^{\imath_1}, e^{\imath_2}) \right| \leq \frac{(\imath_2 - \imath_1)^2 (e^{\imath_1} + e^{\imath_2})}{24}. \tag{31}$$

Proof. Using Theorem (5) and making some simplification, we can write this as

$$\left| \frac{\overline{\overline{\wedge}}(\imath_1) + \overline{\overline{\wedge}}(\imath_2)}{\lambda(\lambda+1)} + \frac{2}{\lambda+1} \overline{\overline{\wedge}}\left(\frac{\imath_1 + \imath_2}{2} \right) - \frac{k}{\lambda(\imath_2 - \imath_1)^{\frac{\zeta}{k}}} \int_{\imath_1}^{\imath_2} [(y-\xi)^{\frac{\zeta}{k}-1} + (\xi - y)^{\frac{\zeta}{k}-1}] \overline{\overline{\wedge}}(\xi) d\xi \right|$$
$$\leq M \frac{(\imath_2 - \imath_1)^2}{\lambda(\lambda+1)(\frac{\zeta}{k}+1)} \left(\left| \overline{\overline{\wedge}}''(\imath_1) \right| + \left| \overline{\overline{\wedge}}''(\imath_2) \right| \right)$$
$$\times \max \left[\frac{\lambda+1}{2} - \frac{\lambda(\frac{\zeta}{k}+1)}{8} - \frac{\lambda+1}{\frac{\zeta}{k}+2}, \frac{-\lambda-1}{2} + \frac{\lambda(\frac{\zeta}{k}+1)}{8} + \frac{\lambda+1}{\frac{\zeta}{k}+2} \right] \tag{32}$$
$$+ M \frac{(\imath_2 - \imath_1)^2}{\lambda(\lambda+1)(\frac{\zeta}{k}+1)} \left(\left| \overline{\overline{\wedge}}''(\imath_1) \right| + \left| \overline{\overline{\wedge}}''(\imath_2) \right| \right)$$
$$\times \max \left[\frac{\lambda+1}{2} - \frac{\lambda(\frac{\zeta}{k}+1)}{8} - \frac{\lambda+1}{\frac{\zeta}{k}+2}, \frac{-\lambda-1}{2} + \frac{\lambda(\frac{\zeta}{k}+1)}{8} + \frac{\lambda+1}{\frac{\zeta}{k}+2} \right].$$

By substituting $\overline{\overline{\curlywedge}}(\xi) = e^{\xi}, k = 1, \zeta = 1, \curlywedge = 1$ and $M = 1$ in (32), we can write

$$\left|\frac{e^{\imath_1} + e^{\imath_2}}{2} + e^{\left(\frac{\imath_1+\imath_2}{2}\right)} - \frac{2}{(\imath_2 - \imath_1)} \int_{\imath_1}^{\imath_2} e^{\xi} d\xi \right| \leq \frac{(\imath_2 - \imath_1)^2 (e^{\imath_1} + e^{\imath_2})}{24}$$
$$\left|\frac{e^{\imath_1} + e^{\imath_2}}{2} + e^{\left(\frac{\imath_1+\imath_2}{2}\right)} - \frac{2(e^{\imath_2} - e^{\imath_1})}{(\imath_2 - \imath_1)} \right| \leq \frac{(\imath_2 - \imath_1)^2 (e^{\imath_1} + e^{\imath_2})}{24}.$$

This completes the proof of (31). □

4. Concluding Remarks

Convexity, a concept that originated from Archimedes around 250 B.C., is a simple and intuitive notion with far-reaching implications in various aspects of our daily lives, including industry, business, medicine and art. Its application is particularly prominent in the field of inequalities, which holds significant importance in optimization theory. In our recent research, we focused on exploring the Hermite–Hadamard integral inequality by employing h-convex functions and a Riemann-type fractional integral. By leveraging Hölder's inequality, we introduced novel findings that have broad implications for inequality theory. These results were derived based on a newly established identity, allowing us to extend previously published findings and broaden the scope of our investigation. To establish the validity of our obtained results, we represented the double inequalities using graphical representations and tables of values. This comprehensive approach provides concrete evidence supporting our conclusions and further solidifies the significance of our research. Our research serves as a catalyst for future investigations, encouraging researchers to explore more comprehensive outcomes by incorporating generalized fractional operators and expanding the scope of convexities. By embracing these broader perspectives, we anticipate the discovery of more general results that can advance the theory of inequalities and enrich the field of fractional calculus.

Author Contributions: Conceptualization, M.S., Y.E. and M.T.G.; methodology, S.N. and G.R.; software, M.S. Y.E. and M.T.G.; validation, M.T.G. and G.R.; formal analysis, M.S. and S.N.; investigation, M.T.G., M.S., S.N. and M.V.-C.; data duration, G.R., M.T.G. and S.N.; writing—original draft preparation, M.S. and M.T.G.; writing—review and editing, M.S., M.T.G. and S.N.; visualization, M.T.G.; supervision, Y.E., G.R. and M.S.; project administration, Y.E. and M.S., funding acquisition, M.V.-C. All authors have read and agreed to the published version of the manuscript.

Funding: This research received no external funding.

Data Availability Statement: Not applicable.

Acknowledgments: The authors extend their appreciation to the Deanship of Scientific Research at King Khalid University for funding this work through the Large Groups under grant number (RGP.2/120/44).

Conflicts of Interest: The authors declare that they have no competing interest.

References

1. Kilbas, A.A.; Srivastava, H.M.; Trujillo, J.J. *Theory and Applications of Fractional Differential Equations*; Elsevier: Amsterdam, The Netherlands, 2006.
2. Loverro, A. *Fractional Calculus: History, Definitions and Applications for the Engineer*; Rapport Technique; Univeristy of Notre Dame, Department of Aerospace and Mechanical Engineering: Notre Dame, IN, USA, 2004; pp. 1–28.
3. Samraiz, M.; Umer, M.; Abduljawad, T.; Naheed, S.; Rahman, G.; Shah, K. On Riemann-type weighted fractional operator and solution to cauchy problems. *Comput. Model. Eng. Sci.* **2023**, *136*, 901–919. [CrossRef]
4. Singh, J.; Anastassiou, G.A.; Baleanu, D.; Kumar, D. On weighted fractional operators with applications to mathematical models arising in physics. In *Advances in Mathematical Modelling, Applied Analysis and Computation*; Lecture Notes in Networks and Systems; Springer: Cham, Switzerland, 2023; Volume 666.
5. Ray, S.S.; Atangana, A.; Noutchie, S.C.; Kurulay, M.; Bildik, N.; Kilicman, A. Fractional calculus and its applications in applied mathematics and other sciences. *Math. Probl. Eng.* **2014**, *2014*, 849395. [CrossRef]
6. Magin, R. Fractional calculus in bioengineering, Part 1. *Crit. Rev. Biomed. Eng.* **2004**, *32*, 104.

7. Beckenbach, E.F. Convex functions. *Bull. Am. Math. Soc.* **1948**, *54*, 439–460. [CrossRef]
8. Avriel, M. *r*-Convex functions. *Math. Program.* **1972**, *2*, 309–323. [CrossRef]
9. Niculescu, C.P.; Persson, L.E. *Convex Functions and Their Applications: A Contemporary Approach*; CMC Books in Mathematics: New York, NY, USA, 2004.
10. Ramli, A.A.; Watada, J.; Pedrycz, W. A combination of genetic algorithm-based fuzzy C-means with a convex hull-based regression for real-time fuzzy switching regression analysis: Application to industrial intelligent data analysis. *IEEJ Trans. Electr. Electron. Eng.* **2014**, *9*, 71–82. [CrossRef]
11. Xu, J.; Noo, F. Convex optimization algorithms in medical image reconstruction in the age of AI. *Phys. Med. Biol.* **2022**, *67*, 07TR01. [CrossRef]
12. Rockafellar, R.T. *Convex Analysis*; Princeton University Press: Princeton, NJ, USA, 1970.
13. Yang, D.H. About inequality of geometrically convex function, Hebei university learned journal. *Natur. Sci. Ed.* **2002**, *22*, 325–328.
14. Hudzik, H.; Maligranda, L. Some remarks on *s*-convex functions. *Aequationes Math.* **1994**, *48*, 100–111. [CrossRef]
15. Bertsimas, D.; Brown, D.B.; Caramanis, C. Theory and applications of robust optimization. *SIAM Rev.* **2011**, *53*, 464–501. [CrossRef]
16. Artacho, F.J.A.; Borwein, J.M.; Marquez, V.M.; Yao, L. Applications of convex analysis within mathematics. *Math. Program.* **2014**, *148*, 49–88. [CrossRef]
17. Bullen, P.S. *Handbook of Means and Their Inequalities*; Springer Science and Business Media: Berlin/Heidelberg, Germany, 2003.
18. Dragomir, S.S. *Operator Inequalities of Ostrowski and Trapezoidal Type*; Springer: New York, NY, USA, 2011.
19. Mitrinovic, D.S.; Pecaric, J.E.; Fink, A.M. *Classical and New Inequalities in Analysis*; Springer Science and Business Media: Berlin/Heidelberg, Germany, 1993.
20. Gavrea, B.; Gavrea, I. On some Ostrowski type inequalities. *Gen. Math.* **2010**, *18*, 33–44.
21. Gunawan, H. Fractional integrals and generalized Olsen inequalities. *Kyungpook Math. J.* **2009**, *49*, 31–39. [CrossRef]
22. Sawano, Y.; Wadade, H. On the Gagliardo-Nirenberg type inequality in the critical Sobolev-Morrey space. *J. Fourier Anal. Appl.* **2013**, *19*, 20–47. [CrossRef]
23. Ciatti, P.; Cowling, M.G.; Ricci, F. Hardy and uncertainty inequalities on stratified Lie groups. *Adv. Math.* **2015**, *277*, 365–387. [CrossRef]
24. Hadamard, J. Etude sur les proprietes des fonctions entieres et en particulier dune fonction consideree par Riemann. *J. Math. Pures Appl.* **1893**, *9*, 171–216.
25. Korus, P. Some Hermite-Hadamard type inequalities for functions of generalized convex derivative. *Acta Math. Hungar.* **2021**, *165*, 463–473. [CrossRef]
26. Vivas-Cortez, M.; Ali, M.A.; Kashuri, A.; Budak, H. Generalizations of fractional Hermite-Hadamard-Mercer like inequalities for convex functions. *AIMS Math.* **2021**, *6*, 9397–9421. [CrossRef]
27. Baleanu, D.; Samraiz, M.; Perveen, Z.; Iqbal, S.; Nisar, K.S.; Rahman, G. Hermite-Hadamard-Fejer type inequalities via fractional integral of a function concerning another function. *AIMS Math.* **2021**, *6*, 4280–4295. [CrossRef]
28. Farid, G.; Yussouf, M.; Nonlaopon, K. Fejer-Hadamard type inequalities for $(\alpha,h\text{-}m)$-p-convex functions via extended generalized fractional integrals. *Fractal Fract.* **2021**, *5*, 253. [CrossRef]
29. Kang, S.M.; Farid, G.; Nazeer, W.; Tariq, B. Hadamard and Fejer-Hadamard inequalities for extended generalized fractional integrals involving special functions. *J. Inequal. Appl.* **2018**, *2018*, 119. [CrossRef] [PubMed]
30. Vivas-Cortez, M.; Hernández, H.; Jorge, E. On some new generalized Hermite Hadamard Fejér-inequalities for product of two operator convex functions. *Appl. Math. Inf. Sci.* **2017**, *11*, 983–992. [CrossRef]
31. Vivas-Cortez, M.; Ali, M.A.; Budak, H.; Kalsoom, H.; Agarwal, P. Some new Hermite–Hadamard and related inequalities for convex functions via (p, q)-integral. *Entropy* **2021**, *23*, 828. [CrossRef] [PubMed]
32. Kalsoom, H.; Latif, M.A.; Khan, Z.A.;Vivas-Cortez, M. Some New Hermite-Hadamard-Fejér fractional type inequalities for h-convex and harmonically h-Convex interval-valued Functions. *Mathematics* **2021**, *10*, 74. [CrossRef]
33. Kwun, Y.C.; Farid, G.; Nazeer, W.; Ullah, S.; Kang, S.M. Generalized riemann-liouville *k*-fractional integrals associated with Ostrowski type inequalities and error bounds of hadamard inequalities. *IEEE Access* **2018**, *6*, 64946–64953. [CrossRef]
34. Budak, H.; Hezenci, F.; Kara, H. On generalized Ostrowski, Simpson and Trapezoidal type inequalities for co-ordinated convex functions via generalized fractional integrals. *Adv. Differ. Equ.* **2021**, *2021*, 312. [CrossRef]
35. Khan, M.A.; Chu, Y.; Khan, T.U.; Khan, J. Some new inequalities of Hermite-Hadamard type for *s*-convex functions with applications. *Open Math.* **2017**, *15*, 1414–1430. [CrossRef]
36. Rashid, S.; Kalsoom, H.; Hammouch, Z.; Ashraf, R.; Baleanu, D.; Chu, Y.M. New multi-parametrized estimates having pth-order differentiability in fractional calculus for predominating *h*-convex functions in Hilbert space. *Symmetry* **2020**, *12*, 222. [CrossRef]
37. Mitrinović, D.S. *Analytic Inequalities*; Springer: Berlin, Germany, 1970.
38. Davis, P.J. Leonhard euler's integral: A historical profile of the gamma function: In memoriam: Milton abramowitz. *Am. Math. Mon.* **1959**, *66*, 849–869.
39. Mubeen, S.; Habibullah, G.M. *k*-Fractional integrals and application. *Int. J. Contemp. Math. Sci.* **2012**, *7*, 89–94.
40. Chaudhry, M.A.; Qadir, A.; Rafique, M.; Zubair, S.M. Extension of Euler's beta function. *J. Comput. Appl. Math.* **1997**, *78*, 19–32.
41. DiDonato, A.R.; Jarnagin, M.P. The efficient calculation of the incomplete beta-function ratio for half-integer values of the parameters *a*, *b*. *Math. Comp.* **1967**, *21*, 652–662. [CrossRef]

42. Varosanec, S. On h-convexity. *J. Math. Anal. Appl.* **2007**, *326*, 303–311.
43. Mubeen, S.H.; Iqbal, S.; Iqbal, Z. On Ostrowski type inequalities for generalized k-fractional integrals. *J. Inequal. Spec. Funct.* **2017**, *8*, 107–118.
44. Deng, J.; Wang, J. Fractional Hermite-Hadamard inequalities for (a,m)-logarithmically convex functions. *J. Inequal. Appl.* **2013**, *2013*, 364.
45. Hussain, R.; Ali, A.; Gulshan, G.; Latif, A.; Rauf, K. Hermite-Hadamard type inequalities for k-Riemann-Liouville fractional integrals via two kinds of convexity. *Austral. J. Math. Anal. Appl.* **2016**, *13*, 1–12.
46. Liao, Y.; Deng, J.; Wang, J. Riemann-Liouville fractional Hermite-Hadamard inequalities. Part II: For twice differentiable geometric-arithmetically s-convex functions. *J. Inequal. Appl.* **2013**, *2013*, 517.

fractal and fractional

Article

On Further Inequalities for Convex Functions via Generalized Weighted-Type Fractional Operators

Çetin Yıldız [1,*], Gauhar Rahman [2] and Luminiţa-Ioana Cotîrlă [3,*]

[1] Department of Mathematics, K.K. Education Faculty, Atatürk University, Erzurum 25320, Turkey
[2] Department of Mathematics and Statistic, Hazara University, Mansehra 21300, Pakistan; drgauhar.rahman@hu.edu.pk
[3] Department of Mathematics, Technical University of Cluj-Napoca, 400020 Cluj-Napoca, Romania
* Correspondence: cetin@atauni.edu.tr (Ç.Y.); luminita.cotirla@math.utcluj.ro (L.-I.C.)

Abstract: Several inequalities for convex functions are derived in this paper using the monotonicity properties of functions and a generalized weighted-type fractional integral operator, which allows the integration of a function κ with respect to another function in fractional order. Additionally, it is clear that the results were generalizations of the previously presented findings. In addition, different types of inequalities are obtained using the basic features of mathematical analysis. Finally, we believe that the methodology used in this work will inspire additional research in this field.

Keywords: convex functions; generalized weighted-type fractional operators; Minkowski inequality; young inequality

MSC: 26A15; 26A51; 26D10

Citation: Yıldız, Ç.; Rahman, G.; Cotîrlă, L.-I. On Further Inequalities for Convex Functions via Generalized Weighted-Type Fractional Operators. *Fractal Fract.* **2023**, 7, 513. https://doi.org/10.3390/fractalfract7070513

Academic Editors: Seth Kermausuor and Eze Nwaeze

Received: 9 May 2023
Revised: 20 June 2023
Accepted: 22 June 2023
Published: 28 June 2023

1. Introduction

With the extensive content and daily addition of new fractional operators, particularly in recent years, fractional calculus plays a significant role in the subject of inequality theory. Some algebraic features, such as the semigroup property, are present in some of these fractional operators but not in others. In addition, while some of them do not, some of them occasionally have a singularity difficulty. Therefore, the application areas of the operators can differ. The generalizations of fractional integrals have been provided by scholars continuously using various methods. For us, providing a generalization of inequalities that includes all consequences that have so far been demonstrated for various fractional integrals is always interesting and inspiring.

Convex analysis has become one of the important application areas of fractional analysis (see [1–9]). In addition, several mathematicians have studied certain inequalities for convex functions using different types of integral operators (for example, the R-L fractional integral operator, the conformable fractional integral operator, tempered fractional integral operators, generalized proportional integral operators, and generalized proportional Hadamard integral operators). These studies have helped to develop different aspects of operator analysis [10–16]. Different from other mapping classes, convex functions have several applications in the areas of optimization theory, probability theory, statistics, mathematics, and applied sciences. Furthermore, its geometric formulation is very important. It is also one of the cornerstones of the theory of inequality and has developed into the main motivating reason behind one variety of inequalities. Convex functions may be used in many fields of mathematical analysis and statistics, but the one in which they have been most successfully used is inequality theory [17–22].

First, we recall the elementary notation in convex analysis:

Definition 1. *A set $F \subset \mathbb{R}$ is said to be convex if*

$$\varphi\theta + (1-\varphi)\gamma \in F$$

for each $\theta, \gamma \in F$ and $\varphi \in [0,1]$.

Definition 2. *The mapping $\kappa_1 : F \rightarrow \mathbb{R}$, is said to be convex if the following inequality holds:*

$$\kappa_1(\varphi\theta + (1-\varphi)\gamma) \leq \varphi\kappa_1(\theta) + (1-\varphi)\kappa_1(\gamma)$$

for all $\theta, \gamma \in F$, and $\varphi \in [0,1]$. We say that κ_1 is concave if $(-\kappa_1)$ is convex.

The properties and definitions of the convex functions have recently ascribed a significant role to its theory and practice in the field of fractional integral operators.

The following inequality was established in [23] by Ngo et al.:

$$\int_0^1 g_1^{\zeta+1}(\rho)d\rho \geq \int_0^1 \rho^{\zeta} g_1^{\zeta}(\rho)d\rho$$

and

$$\int_0^1 g_1^{\zeta+1}(\rho)d\rho \geq \int_0^1 \rho g_1^{\zeta}(\rho)d\rho,$$

where $\zeta > 0$ and $g_1 > 0$ and the continuous function on $[0,1]$ is such that

$$\int_{\varkappa}^1 g_1(\rho)d\rho \geq \int_{\varkappa}^1 \rho d\rho, \quad \varkappa \in [0,1].$$

Then, Liu et al. established the following inequalities in [24]:

$$\int_\theta^\gamma g_1^{\zeta+\vartheta}(\rho)d\rho \geq \int_\theta^\gamma (\rho-\theta)^{\zeta} g_1^{\vartheta}(\rho)d\rho,$$

where $\zeta > 0$, $\vartheta > 0$, and $g_1 > 0$ and the continuous function on $[\theta, \gamma]$ is such that

$$\int_\theta^\gamma g_1^{\xi}(\rho)d\rho \geq \int_0^1 (\rho-\theta)^{\xi}d\rho, \quad \xi = \min(1,\vartheta), \ \rho \in [0,1].$$

The following two theorems were obtained by Liu in [25]:

Theorem 1. *Let κ_1 and κ_2 be continuous and positive functions with $\kappa_1 \leq \kappa_2$ on $[\theta, \gamma]$ such that κ_1 is increasing and $\frac{\kappa_1}{\kappa_2}$ ($\kappa_2 \neq 0$) is decreasing. If ξ is a convex function, then the inequality*

$$\frac{\int_\theta^\gamma \kappa_1(\varpi)d\varpi}{\int_\theta^\gamma \kappa_2(\varpi)d\varpi} \geq \frac{\int_\theta^\gamma \xi(\kappa_1(\varpi))d\varpi}{\int_\theta^\gamma \xi(\kappa_2(\varpi))d\varpi}.$$

holds where $\xi(0) = 0$.

Theorem 2. *Let κ_1, κ_2, and κ_3 be continuous and positive functions with $\kappa_1 \leq \kappa_2$ on $[\theta, \gamma]$ such that κ_1 and κ_3 are increasing and $\frac{\kappa_1}{\kappa_2}$ ($\kappa_2 \neq 0$) is decreasing. If ξ is a convex function, then the inequality*

$$\frac{\int_\theta^\gamma \kappa_1(\varpi)d\varpi}{\int_\theta^\gamma \kappa_2(\varpi)d\varpi} \geq \frac{\int_\theta^\gamma \xi(\kappa_1(\varpi))\kappa_3(\varpi)d\varpi}{\int_\theta^\gamma \xi(\kappa_2(\varpi))\kappa_3(\varpi)d\varpi}$$

holds where $\xi(0) = 0$.

For functions in $L_p[\theta, \gamma]$, defined as follows, several novel conclusions were obtained:

Definition 3. *For $p \in [1, \infty)$, if the function κ holds*

$$\left(\int_{\theta}^{\gamma} |\kappa(\tau)|^p d\varpi \right)^{\frac{1}{p}} < \infty,$$

then it is said to be in $L_p[\theta, \gamma]$.

The well-known Minkowski inequality has been presented as follows in the mathematical literature (see [26]):

Theorem 3. *$\int_{\theta}^{\gamma} \kappa^p(\varpi) d\varpi$ and $\int_{\theta}^{\gamma} \hbar^p(\varpi) d\varpi$ are positive finite reals for $p \geq 1$. Then, the inequality*

$$\left(\int_{\theta}^{\gamma} (\kappa(\varpi) + \hbar(\varpi))^p d\varpi \right)^{\frac{1}{p}} \leq \left(\int_{\theta}^{\gamma} \kappa^p(\varpi) d\varpi \right)^{\frac{1}{p}} + \left(\int_{\theta}^{\gamma} \hbar^p(\varpi) d\varpi \right)^{\frac{1}{p}}$$

holds.

L. Bougoffa in [27] derives the reverse Minkowski inequality for Riemann–Liouville fractional integrals, which is explained as follows:

Theorem 4. *Let $\kappa, \hbar \in L_p[\theta, \gamma]$ and $\kappa, \hbar > 0$, with $1 \leq p < \infty$, $0 < \int_{\theta}^{\gamma} \kappa^p(\varpi) d\varpi < \infty$ and $0 < \int_{\theta}^{\gamma} \hbar^p(\varpi) d\varpi < \infty$. If $0 \leq \eta \leq \frac{\kappa(\varpi)}{\hbar(\varpi)} \leq \aleph$ for $\eta, \aleph \in \mathbb{R}^+$ and every $\varpi \in [\theta, \gamma]$, then the inequality*

$$\left(\int_{\theta}^{\gamma} \kappa^p(\varpi) d\varpi \right)^{\frac{1}{p}} + \left(\int_{\theta}^{\gamma} \hbar^p(\varpi) d\varpi \right)^{\frac{1}{p}} \leq c \left(\int_{\theta}^{\gamma} (\kappa(\varpi) + \hbar(\varpi))^p d\varpi \right)^{\frac{1}{p}}$$

holds where $c = \frac{\aleph(\eta+1) + (\aleph+1)}{(\eta+1)(\aleph+1)}$.

Z. Dahmani provided the reverse Minkowski and Hadamard inequalities utilizing the Riemann–Liouville fractional integral in [28]. Set et al. presented some inequalities of reverse Minkowski and Hermite–Hadamard involving two functions using the classical Riemann integral in [29]. Chinchane and Pachpatte established the reverse Minkowski inequality via the Saigo fractional integral operator in [30]. Vanterler et al. studied the reverse Minkowski inequalities and some other related inequalities by means of the Katugampola fractional integral operator in [31]. The reverse Minkowski inequality and other fractional inequalities in [32] were established by Rahman et al. using the generalized proportional fractional integral operators. By taking general kernels into account in [33], Iqbal et al. were able to achieve novel conclusions for Minkowski and associated inequalities. There are many studies on the reverse Minkowski inequality in the literature. The "Young's inequality" theorem is as follows (see [34]):

Theorem 5. *Let $[0, k]$ be an interval with $k > 0$, and h be an increasing, continuous function on $[0, k]$. If $\gamma \in [0, \hbar(k)]$, $\theta \in [0, k]$, $\hbar(0) = 0$ and $\hbar^{-1}$ stands for the inverse function of h, then*

$$\int_0^{\theta} \hbar(\varpi) d\varpi + \int_0^{\gamma} \hbar^{-1}(\varpi) d\varpi \geq \theta\gamma. \tag{1}$$

Different forms of Young's inequality are defined as follows:

$$\frac{1}{r}\theta^r + \frac{1}{s}\gamma^s \geq \theta\gamma, \quad \theta, \gamma \geq 0, \ r \geq 1 \text{ and } \frac{1}{r} + \frac{1}{s} = 1.$$

In other words, this inequality illustrates the relationship between the geometric and arithmetic means.

2. Preliminaries

The application of fractional integral operators is another method for obtaining extensions of the traditional integral inequalities that are known from the literature. By using different versions of fractional integrals, many extensions, generalizations, and variations of inequalities, such as those of Hermite–Hadamard, Simpson, Ostrowski, Minkowski, Chebyshev, and Grüss, have been obtained.

Now, some fractional integral operators used to obtain integral inequalities will be given. First of them is the Riemann–Liouville fractional integral operator (see [35]), which is widely used in fractional calculus.

Definition 4. *Let $\kappa \in L_1[\theta, \gamma]$. $J^{\ell}_{\theta+}\kappa$ and $J^{\ell}_{\gamma-}\kappa$ (Riemann–Liouville fractional integral operators) of order $\ell > 0$ with $\theta \geq 0$ are defined by*

$$J^{\ell}_{\theta+}\kappa(\varkappa) = \frac{1}{\Gamma(\ell)}\int_{\theta}^{\varkappa}(\varkappa - \varpi)^{\ell-1}\kappa(\varpi)d\varpi, \quad \varkappa > \theta$$

and

$$J^{\ell}_{\gamma-}\kappa(\varkappa) = \frac{1}{\Gamma(\ell)}\int_{\varkappa}^{\gamma}(\varpi - \varkappa)^{\ell-1}\kappa(\varpi)d\varpi, \quad \varkappa < \gamma,$$

respectively, where $\Gamma(\ell) = \int_0^{\infty} e^{-u}u^{\ell-1}du$. Here, $J^{0}_{\theta+}\kappa(\varkappa) = J^{0}_{\gamma-}\kappa(\varkappa) = \kappa(\varkappa)$. The fractional integral becomes the classical integral when $\ell = 1$.

Definition 5 ([36]). *Suppose that the function $\Psi : [0, \infty) \to [0, \infty)$ satisfies the conditions given below:*

$$\int_0^1 \frac{\Psi(\varpi)}{\varpi}d\varpi < \infty, \tag{2}$$

$$\frac{1}{\rho} \leq \frac{\Psi(\hbar_1)}{\Psi(\hbar_2)} \leq \rho, \frac{1}{2} \leq \frac{\hbar_1}{\hbar_2} \leq 2, \tag{3}$$

$$\frac{\Psi(\hbar_2)}{\hbar_2^2} \leq \varphi\frac{\Psi(\hbar_1)}{\hbar_1^2}, \hbar_1 \leq \hbar_2, \tag{4}$$

$$\left|\frac{\Psi(\hbar_2)}{\hbar_2^2} - \frac{\Psi(\hbar_1)}{\hbar_1^2}\right| \leq \zeta|\hbar_2 - \hbar_1|\frac{\Psi(\hbar_2)}{\hbar_2^2}, \frac{1}{2} \leq \frac{\hbar_1}{\hbar_2} \leq 2, \tag{5}$$

where $\rho, \varphi, \zeta > 0$ are independent of $\hbar_1, \hbar_2 > 0$. If $\Psi(\hbar_2)\hbar_2^{\alpha}$ is increasing for some $\alpha > 0$ and $\frac{\Psi(\hbar_2)}{\hbar_2^{\mu}}$ is decreasing for some $\mu > 0$, then Ψ satisfies (2)–(5).

It became important to obtain more general versions of the new results when fractional integral operators were utilized more frequently. As a result, weighted integral operators started to be introduced. While generalized versions of the findings in the literature may also be obtained, novel results are also produced with these operators. The following list includes one of the most useful weighted integral operators lately presented:

Definition 6 ([37]). *The generalized weighted-type fractional integral operators, on both the right and left side, are respectively defined by:*

$$\begin{aligned}\left({}^{\wp}_{\omega}\Im^{\Psi}_{\theta+}\kappa\right)(\varkappa) &= \omega^{-1}(\varkappa)\int_{\theta}^{\varkappa}\frac{\Psi(\wp(\varkappa) - \wp(\varpi))}{\wp(\varkappa) - \wp(\varpi)}\omega(\varpi)\wp'(\varpi)\kappa(\varpi)d\varpi, \ \theta < \varkappa \\ \left({}^{\wp}_{\omega}\Im^{\Psi}_{\gamma-}\kappa\right)(\varkappa) &= \omega^{-1}(\varkappa)\int_{\varkappa}^{\gamma}\frac{\Psi(\wp(\varpi) - \wp(x))}{\wp(\varpi) - \wp(x)}\omega(\varpi)\wp'(\varpi)\kappa(\varpi)d\varpi, \ \gamma > \varkappa\end{aligned} \tag{6}$$

where $\omega^{-1}(\varkappa) = \frac{1}{\omega(\varkappa)}, \omega(\varkappa) \neq 0$.

These important special cases of the generalized weighted-type fractional integral operators are mentioned below:

Remark 1. *In Definition 6:*

- *If we consider* $\Psi(\wp(\varkappa)) = \wp(\varkappa)$, *we obtain*

$$\begin{aligned}\left({}_{\omega}^{\wp}\Im_{\theta+}\kappa\right)(\varkappa) &= \omega^{-1}(\varkappa)\int_{\theta}^{\varkappa}\omega(\varpi)\wp'(\varpi)\kappa(\varpi)d\varpi,\ \theta<\varkappa\\ \left({}_{\omega}^{\wp}\Im_{\gamma-}\kappa\right)(\varkappa) &= \omega^{-1}(\varkappa)\int_{\varkappa}^{\gamma}\omega(\varpi)\wp'(\varpi)\kappa(\varpi)d\varpi,\ \gamma>\varkappa.\end{aligned}$$

- *If we consider* $\wp(\varkappa) = \varkappa$, *then*

$$\begin{aligned}\left({}_{\omega}^{\wp}\Im_{\theta+}\kappa\right)(\varkappa) &= \omega^{-1}(\varkappa)\int_{\theta}^{\varkappa}\frac{\Psi(\varkappa-\varpi)}{\varkappa-\varpi}\omega(\varpi)\kappa(\varpi)d\varpi,\ \theta<\varkappa\\ \left({}_{\omega}^{\wp}\Im_{\gamma-}\kappa\right)(\varkappa) &= \omega^{-1}(\varkappa)\int_{\varkappa}^{\gamma}\frac{\Psi(\varpi-\varkappa)}{\varpi-\varkappa}\omega(\varpi)\kappa(\varpi)d\varpi,\ \gamma>\varkappa.\end{aligned}$$

  In addition, if we take $\omega(\varkappa) = 1$,, *we obtain the generalized fractional operators in [38].*

- *If we consider* $\Psi(\wp(\varkappa)) = \frac{\wp^{\ell}(\varkappa)}{\Gamma(k)}$, *then we obtain*

$$\begin{aligned}\left({}_{\omega}^{\wp}\Im_{\theta+}^{\ell}\kappa\right)(\varkappa) &= \frac{\omega^{-1}(\varkappa)}{\Gamma(\ell)}\int_{\theta}^{\varkappa}[\wp(\varkappa)-\wp(\varpi)]^{\ell-1}\omega(\varpi)\wp'(\varpi)\kappa(\varpi)d\varpi,\ \theta<\varkappa\\ \left({}_{\omega}^{\wp}\Im_{\gamma-}^{\ell}\kappa\right)(\varkappa) &= \frac{\omega^{-1}(\varkappa)}{\Gamma(\ell)}\int_{\varkappa}^{\gamma}[\wp(\varpi)-\wp(\varkappa)]^{\ell-1}\omega(\varpi)\wp'(\varpi)\kappa(\varpi)d\varpi,\ \gamma>\varkappa\end{aligned}$$

  where $\ell\in\mathbb{C}$ *with* $\Re(\ell)>0$ *[39].*

- *If we consider* $\wp(\varkappa) = \varkappa$ *and* $\Psi(\wp(\varkappa)) = \frac{\varkappa^{\ell}}{\Gamma(\ell)}$, *then*

$$\begin{aligned}\left({}_{\omega}\Im_{\theta+}^{\ell}\kappa\right)(\varkappa) &= \frac{\omega^{-1}(\varkappa)}{\Gamma(\ell)}\int_{\theta}^{\varkappa}[\varkappa-\varpi]^{\ell-1}\omega(\varpi)\kappa(\varpi)d\varpi,\ \theta<\varkappa\\ \left({}_{\omega}^{\wp}\Im_{\gamma-}^{\ell}\kappa\right)(\varkappa) &= \frac{\omega^{-1}(\varkappa)}{\Gamma(\ell)}\int_{\varkappa}^{\gamma}[\varpi-\varkappa]^{\ell-1}\omega(\varpi)\kappa(\varpi)d\varpi,\ \gamma>\varkappa.\end{aligned}$$

  In addition to the above identities, if we choose $\omega(\varkappa) = 1$, *we obtain classical Riemann–Liouville fractional integral operators.*

- *If we consider* $\wp(\varkappa) = \ln\varkappa$ *and* $\Psi(\wp(\varkappa)) = \frac{(\ln\varkappa)^{\ell}}{\Gamma(\ell)}$, *then the operators reduce to the weighted Hadamard fractional integrals as follows:*

$$\begin{aligned}\left({}_{\omega}\Im_{\theta+}^{\ell}\kappa\right)(\varkappa) &= \frac{\omega^{-1}(\varkappa)}{\Gamma(\ell)}\int_{\theta}^{\varkappa}[\ln\varkappa-\ln\varpi]^{\ell-1}\omega(\varpi)\kappa(\varpi)\frac{d\varpi}{\varpi},\ \theta<x\\ \left({}_{\omega}\Im_{\gamma-}^{\ell}\kappa\right)(\varkappa) &= \frac{\omega^{-1}(\varkappa)}{\Gamma(\ell)}\int_{\varkappa}^{\gamma}[\ln\varpi-\ln\varkappa]^{\ell-1}\omega(\varpi)\kappa(\varpi)\frac{d\varpi}{\varpi},\ \gamma>x.\end{aligned}$$

- *If we consider* $\wp(\varkappa) = \varkappa^{\tau}$ *and* $\Psi(\wp(\varkappa)) = \frac{\varkappa^{\tau}}{\tau}$, *then the operators reduce to the weighted Katugampola fractional integrals as follows:*

$$\begin{aligned}\left({}_{\omega}\Im_{\theta+}^{\ell}\kappa\right)(\varkappa) &= \frac{\omega^{-1}(\varkappa)}{\Gamma(\ell)}\int_{\theta}^{\varkappa}\left[\frac{\varkappa^{\tau}-\varpi^{\tau}}{\tau}\right]^{\ell-1}\omega(\varpi)\kappa(\varpi)\frac{d\varpi}{\varpi^{1-\tau}},\ \theta<\varkappa\\ \left({}_{\omega}\Im_{\gamma-}^{\ell}\kappa\right)(\varkappa) &= \frac{\omega^{-1}(\varkappa)}{\Gamma(\ell)}\int_{\varkappa}^{\gamma}\left[\frac{\varpi^{\tau}-\varkappa^{\tau}}{\tau}\right]^{\ell-1}\omega(\varpi)\kappa(\varpi)\frac{d\varpi}{\varpi^{1-\tau}},\ \gamma>\varkappa.\end{aligned}$$

- *In addition, to obtain the different version of the fractional integral operator that is defined in [9,37], one can choose $\omega(\varkappa) = 1$ in (6).*

This article discussed several important inequalities (such as Hadamard, Grüss, Chebyshev, Fejer, and Minkowski types) via the generalized weighted-type fractional integral operators (6) with increasing, decreasing, positive, continuous, and convex functions. The existing inequalities associated with increasing, decreasing, positive, continuous, and convex functions are also restored by applying specific conditions as given in the remarks. By applying certain conditions on $\wp$ and Ψ described in the literature, several other varieties of fractional integral inequalities can be established.

The main purpose of this article is to generalize some classical integral inequalities using the generalized weighted-type fractional integral operators. In addition, we used the basic features of mathematical analysis to achieve our main results.

The article is arranged as follows: We recall some of the notations, definitions, results, and introductory facts that were used in Sections 1 and 2 and are utilized throughout the remaining chapters of this work. In Section 3, we introduce some inequalities for convex functions utilizing the generalized weighted-type fractional integral operators. In Section 4, we give results of the reverse Minkowski inequality, which is the first of our main results. Finally, in Section 5, we present some other related results involving constant generalized weighted-type fractional integral operators.

3. New Inequalities Involving Generalized Weighted-Type Fractional Operators

This section introduces some inequalities for convex functions using the generalized weighted-type fractional integral operators.

Theorem 6. *Let κ_1 and κ_2 be two positive continuous functions on $[\theta,\gamma]$ and $\kappa_1 \le \kappa_2$ on $[\theta,\gamma]$. If $\frac{\kappa_1}{\kappa_2}$ is decreasing and κ_1 is increasing on $[\theta,\gamma]$, then for a convex function ξ with $\xi(0)=0$, the generalized weighted-type fractional integral operator given by (6) satisfies the following inequality:*

$$\frac{\left({}^{\wp}_{\omega}\Im^{\Psi}_{\theta+}\kappa_1\right)(\varkappa)}{\left({}^{\wp}_{\omega}\Im^{\Psi}_{\theta+}\kappa_2\right)(\varkappa)} \ge \frac{\left({}^{\wp}_{\omega}\Im^{\Psi}_{\theta+}\xi\circ\kappa_1\right)(\varkappa)}{\left({}^{\wp}_{\omega}\Im^{\Psi}_{\theta+}\xi\circ\kappa_2\right)(\varkappa)}, \tag{7}$$

where $\varkappa > \theta > 0$.

Proof. $\frac{\xi(\varkappa)}{\varkappa}$ is increasing since ξ is defined as convex function satisfying $\xi(0)=0$. Moreover, the function $\frac{\xi(\kappa_1(\varkappa))}{\kappa_1(\varkappa)}$ is also increasing as κ_1 is increasing. Clearly, the function $\frac{\kappa_1(\varkappa)}{\kappa_2(\varkappa)}$ is decreasing. Thus, for all $[\theta,\varkappa]$, $\theta < \varkappa \le \gamma$, it can be written

$$\left(\frac{\xi(\kappa_1(\varpi))}{\kappa_1(\varpi)} - \frac{\xi(\kappa_1(\varphi))}{\kappa_1(\varphi)}\right)\left(\frac{\kappa_1(\varphi)}{\kappa_2(\varphi)} - \frac{\kappa_1(\varpi)}{\kappa_2(\varpi)}\right) \ge 0.$$

It follows that

$$\begin{aligned}&\frac{\xi(\kappa_1(\varpi))}{\kappa_1(\varpi)}\frac{\kappa_1(\varphi)}{\kappa_2(\varphi)} + \frac{\xi(\kappa_1(\varphi))}{\kappa_1(\varphi)}\frac{\kappa_1(\varpi)}{\kappa_2(\varpi)}\\ &- \frac{\xi(\kappa_1(\varphi))}{\kappa_1(\varphi)}\frac{\kappa_1(\varphi)}{\kappa_2(\varphi)} - \frac{\xi(\kappa_1(\varpi))}{\kappa_1(\varpi)}\frac{\kappa_1(\varpi)}{\kappa_2(\varpi)} \ge 0.\end{aligned} \tag{8}$$

Multiplying (8) by $\kappa_2(\varpi)\kappa_2(\varphi)$, we have

$$\begin{aligned}&\frac{\xi(\kappa_1(\varpi))}{\kappa_1(\varpi)}\kappa_1(\varphi)\kappa_2(\varpi) + \frac{\xi(\kappa_1(\varphi))}{\kappa_1(\varphi)}\kappa_1(\varpi)\kappa_2(\varphi)\\ &- \frac{\xi(\kappa_1(\varphi))}{\kappa_1(\varphi)}\kappa_1(\varphi)\kappa_2(\varpi) - \frac{\xi(\kappa_1(\varpi))}{\kappa_1(\varpi)}\kappa_1(\varpi)\kappa_2(\varphi) \ge 0.\end{aligned} \tag{9}$$

Now, multiplying both sides of (9) by $\omega^{-1}(\varkappa)\frac{\Psi(\wp(\varkappa)-\wp(\varpi))}{\wp(\varkappa)-\wp(\varpi)}\omega(\varpi)\wp'(\varpi)$ and then integrating with regard to the variable ϖ from θ to $\varkappa$, we obtain

$$\begin{aligned}&\omega^{-1}(\varkappa)\int_{\theta}^{\varkappa}\frac{\Psi(\wp(\varkappa)-\wp(\varpi))}{\wp(\varkappa)-\wp(\varpi)}\frac{\xi(\kappa_1(\varpi))}{\kappa_1(\varpi)}\omega(\varpi)\wp'(\varpi)\kappa_1(\varphi)\kappa_2(\varpi)d\varpi\\&+\omega^{-1}(\varkappa)\int_{\theta}^{\varkappa}\frac{\Psi(\wp(\varkappa)-\wp(\varpi))}{\wp(\varkappa)-\wp(\varpi)}\frac{\xi(\kappa_1(\varphi))}{\kappa_1(\varphi)}\omega(\varpi)\wp'(\varpi)\kappa_1(\varpi)\kappa_2(\varphi)d\varpi\\&-\omega^{-1}(\varkappa)\int_{\theta}^{\varkappa}\frac{\Psi(\wp(\varkappa)-\wp(\varpi))}{\wp(\varkappa)-\wp(\varpi)}\frac{\xi(\kappa_1(\varphi))}{\kappa_1(\varphi)}\omega(\varpi)\wp'(\varpi)\kappa_1(\varphi)\kappa_2(\varpi)d\varpi\\&-\omega^{-1}(\varkappa)\int_{\theta}^{\varkappa}\frac{\Psi(\wp(\varkappa)-\wp(\varpi))}{\wp(\varkappa)-\wp(\varpi)}\frac{\xi(\kappa_1(\varpi))}{\kappa_1(\varpi)}\omega(\varpi)\wp'(\varpi)\kappa_1(\varpi)\kappa_2(\varphi)d\varpi\geq 0.\end{aligned}$$

Then, it follows that

$$\begin{aligned}&\kappa_1(\varphi)\left({}^{\wp}_{\omega}\Im^{\Psi}_{\theta+}\frac{\xi\circ\kappa_1}{\kappa_1}\kappa_2\right)(\varkappa)+\frac{\xi(\kappa_1(\varphi))}{\kappa_1(\varphi)}\kappa_2(\varphi)\left({}^{\wp}_{\omega}\Im^{\Psi}_{\theta+}\kappa_1\right)(\varkappa)\\&-\frac{\xi(\kappa_1(\varphi))}{\kappa_1(\varphi)}\kappa_1(\varphi)\left({}^{\wp}_{\omega}\Im^{\Psi}_{\theta+}\kappa_2\right)(\varkappa)-\kappa_2(\varphi)\left({}^{\wp}_{\omega}\Im^{\Psi}_{\theta+}\frac{\xi\circ\kappa_1}{\kappa_1}\kappa_1\right)(\varkappa)\geq 0.\end{aligned}\quad(10)$$

Again, by multiplying both sides of (10) by $\omega^{-1}(\varkappa)\frac{\Psi(\wp(\varkappa)-\wp(\varphi))}{\wp(\varkappa)-\wp(\varphi)}\omega(\varphi)\wp'(\varphi)$ and then integrating from θ to $\varkappa$ with regard to φ, we have

$$\begin{aligned}&\left({}^{\wp}_{\omega}\Im^{\Psi}_{\theta+}\kappa_1\right)(\varkappa)\left({}^{\wp}_{\omega}\Im^{\Psi}_{\theta+}\frac{\xi\circ\kappa_1}{\kappa_1}\kappa_2\right)(\varkappa)+\left({}^{\wp}_{\omega}\Im^{\Psi}_{\theta+}\frac{\xi\circ\kappa_1}{\kappa_1}\kappa_2\right)(\varkappa)\left({}^{\wp}_{\omega}\Im^{\Psi}_{\theta+}\kappa_1\right)(\varkappa)\\&\geq\left({}^{\wp}_{\omega}\Im^{\Psi}_{\theta+}\xi\circ\kappa_1\right)(\varkappa)\left({}^{\wp}_{\omega}\Im^{\Psi}_{\theta+}\kappa_2\right)(\varkappa)+\left({}^{\wp}_{\omega}\Im^{\Psi}_{\theta+}\kappa_2\right)(\varkappa)\left({}^{\wp}_{\omega}\Im^{\Psi}_{\theta+}\xi\circ\kappa_1\right)(\varkappa).\end{aligned}\quad(11)$$

It follows that

$$\frac{\left({}^{\wp}_{\omega}\Im^{\Psi}_{\theta+}\kappa_1\right)(\varkappa)}{\left({}^{\wp}_{\omega}\Im^{\Psi}_{\theta+}\kappa_2\right)(\varkappa)}\geq\frac{\left({}^{\wp}_{\omega}\Im^{\Psi}_{\theta+}\xi\circ\kappa_1\right)(\varkappa)}{\left({}^{\wp}_{\omega}\Im^{\Psi}_{\theta+}\frac{\xi\circ\kappa_1}{\kappa_1}\kappa_2\right)(\varkappa)}.\quad(12)$$

Now, since $\frac{\xi(\varkappa)}{\varkappa}$ is an increasing function and $\kappa_1\leq\kappa_2$ on $[\theta,\gamma]$, we obtain

$$\frac{\xi(\kappa_1(\varpi))}{\kappa_1(\varpi)}\leq\frac{\xi(\kappa_2(\varpi))}{\kappa_2(\varpi)}\quad(13)$$

for $[\theta,\varkappa]$.

Multiplying both sides of (13) by $\omega^{-1}(\varkappa)\frac{\Psi(\wp(\varkappa)-\wp(\varpi))}{\wp(\varkappa)-\wp(\varpi)}\omega(\varpi)\wp'(\varpi)\kappa_2(\varpi)$ and then integrating with regard to the variable ϖ from θ to $\varkappa$, we have

$$\begin{aligned}&\omega^{-1}(\varkappa)\int_{\theta}^{\varkappa}\frac{\Psi(\wp(\varkappa)-\wp(\varpi))}{\wp(\varkappa)-\wp(\varpi)}\frac{\xi(\kappa_1(\varpi))}{\kappa_1(\varpi)}\omega(\varpi)\wp'(\varpi)\kappa_2(\varpi)d\varpi\\\leq\;&\omega^{-1}(\varkappa)\int_{\theta}^{\varkappa}\frac{\Psi(\wp(\varkappa)-\wp(\varpi))}{\wp(\varkappa)-\wp(\varpi)}\frac{\xi(\kappa_2(\varpi))}{\kappa_2(\varpi)}\omega(\varpi)\wp'(\varpi)\kappa_2(\varpi)d\varpi,\end{aligned}$$

which yields

$$\left({}^{\wp}_{\omega}\Im^{\Psi}_{\theta+}\frac{\xi\circ\kappa_1}{\kappa_1}\kappa_2\right)(\varkappa)\leq\left({}^{\wp}_{\omega}\Im^{\Psi}_{\theta+}\xi\circ\kappa_2\right)(\varkappa).\quad(14)$$

Hence, from (12) and (14), we have (7). □

Remark 2. *If we take* $\omega(\varkappa)=\varkappa$, $\wp(\varkappa)=\varkappa$, $\varkappa=\gamma$, *and* $\Psi(\wp(\varkappa))=\wp(\varkappa)$ *in Theorem 6, we obtain Theorem 1.*

Theorem 7. *Let κ_1, κ_2, and κ_3 be positive continuous functions and $\kappa_1 \leq \kappa_2$ on $[\theta, \gamma]$. If $\frac{\kappa_1}{\kappa_2}$ is decreasing and κ_1 and κ_3 are increasing on $[\theta, \gamma]$, then, for a convex function ξ with $\xi(0) = 0$, the weighted fractional operator shows the following inequality (6):*

$$\frac{\left({}^{\wp}_{\omega}\Im^{\Psi}_{\theta+}\kappa_1\right)(\varkappa)}{\left({}^{\wp}_{\omega}\Im^{\Psi}_{\theta+}\kappa_2\right)(\varkappa)} \geq \frac{\left({}^{\wp}_{\omega}\Im^{\Psi}_{\theta+}(\xi \circ \kappa_1)\kappa_3\right)(\varkappa)}{\left({}^{\wp}_{\omega}\Im^{\Psi}_{\theta+}(\xi \circ \kappa_2)\kappa_3\right)(\varkappa)},$$

where $\varkappa > \theta > 0$.

Proof. Since $\kappa_1 \leq \kappa_2$ on $[\theta, \gamma]$ and $\frac{\xi(\varkappa)}{\varkappa}$ is increasing for $\varpi, \varphi \in [\theta, \varkappa], \theta < \varkappa \leq \gamma$, we obtain

$$\frac{\xi(\kappa_1(\varpi))}{\kappa_1(\varpi)} \leq \frac{\xi(\kappa_2(\varpi))}{\kappa_2(\varpi)}. \tag{15}$$

Multiplying both sides of (15) by $\omega^{-1}(\varkappa)\frac{\Psi(\wp(\varkappa)-\wp(\varpi))}{\wp(\varkappa)-\wp(\varpi)}\omega(\varpi)\wp'(\varpi)\kappa_2(\varpi)\kappa_3(\varpi)$ and then integrating with regard to the variable ϖ from θ to $\varkappa$, we have

$$\begin{aligned}
&\omega^{-1}(\varkappa)\int_{\theta}^{\varkappa}\frac{\Psi(\wp(\varkappa)-\wp(\varpi))}{\wp(\varkappa)-\wp(\varpi)}\frac{\xi(\kappa_1(\varpi))}{\kappa_1(\varpi)}\omega(\varpi)\wp'(\varpi)\kappa_2(\varpi)\kappa_3(\varpi)d\varpi \\
\leq\ &\omega^{-1}(\varkappa)\int_{\theta}^{\varkappa}\frac{\Psi(\wp(\varkappa)-\wp(\varpi))}{\wp(\varkappa)-\wp(\varpi)}\frac{\xi(\kappa_2(\varpi))}{\kappa_2(\varpi)}\omega(\varpi)\wp'(\varpi)\kappa_2(\varpi)\kappa_3(\varpi)d\varpi
\end{aligned}$$

which, by virtue of (6), can be written as

$$\left({}^{\wp}_{\omega}\Im^{\Psi}_{\theta+}\frac{\xi \circ \kappa_1}{\kappa_1}\kappa_2\kappa_3\right)(\varkappa) \leq \left({}^{\wp}_{\omega}\Im^{\Psi}_{\theta+}(\xi \circ \kappa_2)\kappa_3\right)(\varkappa). \tag{16}$$

Moreover, $\frac{\xi(\varpi)}{\varpi}$ is increasing, since $\xi(0) = 0$ and the function ξ is convex. Since κ_1 is increasing, so is $\frac{\xi(\kappa_1(\varpi))}{\kappa_1(\varpi)}$. Obviously, the function $\frac{\kappa_1(\varpi)}{\kappa_2(\varpi)}$ is decreasing for $\varpi, \varphi \in [\theta, \varkappa]$, $\theta < \varkappa \leq \gamma$.Thus,

$$\left(\frac{\xi(\kappa_1(\varpi))}{\kappa_1(\varpi)}\kappa_3(\varpi) - \frac{\xi(\kappa_1(\varphi))}{\kappa_1(\varphi)}\kappa_3(\varphi)\right)(\kappa_1(\varphi)\kappa_2(\varpi) - \kappa_1(\varpi)\kappa_2(\varphi)) \geq 0.$$

It becomes

$$\begin{aligned}
&\frac{\xi(\kappa_1(\varpi))\kappa_3(\varpi)}{\kappa_1(\varpi)}\kappa_1(\varphi)\kappa_2(\varpi) + \frac{\xi(\kappa_1(\varphi))\kappa_3(\varphi)}{\kappa_1(\varphi)}\kappa_1(\varpi)\kappa_2(\varphi) \\
&- \frac{\xi(\kappa_1(\varphi))\kappa_3(\varphi)}{\kappa_1(\varphi)}\kappa_1(\varphi)\kappa_2(\varpi) - \frac{\xi(\kappa_1(\varpi))\kappa_3(\varpi)}{\kappa_1(\varpi)}\kappa_1(\varpi)\kappa_2(\varphi) \geq 0.
\end{aligned} \tag{17}$$

Multiplying both sides of (17) by $\omega^{-1}(\varkappa)\frac{\Psi(\wp(\varkappa)-\wp(\varpi))}{\wp(\varkappa)-\wp(\varpi)}\omega(\varpi)\wp'(\varpi)$ and then integrating with regard to the variable ϖ from θ to $\varkappa$, we obtain

$$\begin{aligned}
&\omega^{-1}(\varkappa)\int_{\theta}^{\varkappa}\frac{\Psi(\wp(\varkappa)-\wp(\varpi))}{\wp(\varkappa)-\wp(\varpi)}\frac{\xi(\kappa_1(\varpi))\kappa_3(\varpi)}{\kappa_1(\varpi)}\omega(\varpi)\wp'(\varpi)\kappa_1(\varphi)\kappa_2(\varpi)d\varpi \\
&+\omega^{-1}(\varkappa)\int_{\theta}^{\varkappa}\frac{\Psi(\wp(\varkappa)-\wp(\varpi))}{\wp(\varkappa)-\wp(\varpi)}\frac{\xi(\kappa_1(\varphi))\kappa_3(\varphi)}{\kappa_1(\varphi)}\omega(\varpi)\wp'(\varpi)\kappa_1(\varpi)\kappa_2(\varphi)d\varpi \\
&-\omega^{-1}(\varkappa)\int_{\theta}^{\varkappa}\frac{\Psi(\wp(\varkappa)-\wp(\varpi))}{\wp(\varkappa)-\wp(\varpi)}\frac{\xi(\kappa_1(\varphi))\kappa_3(\varphi)}{\kappa_1(\varphi)}\omega(\varpi)\wp'(\varpi)\kappa_1(\varphi)\kappa_2(\varpi)d\varpi \\
&-\omega^{-1}(\varkappa)\int_{\theta}^{\varkappa}\frac{\Psi(\wp(\varkappa)-\wp(\varpi))}{\wp(\varkappa)-\wp(\varpi)}\frac{\xi(\kappa_1(\varpi))\kappa_3(\varpi)}{\kappa_1(\varpi)}\omega(\varpi)\wp'(\varpi)\kappa_1(\varpi)\kappa_2(\varphi)d\varpi \geq 0.
\end{aligned}$$

This follows that

$$\kappa_1(\varphi)\left({}^{\wp}_{\omega}\Im^{\Psi}_{\theta+}\frac{\xi\circ\kappa_1}{\kappa_1}\kappa_2\kappa_3\right)(\varkappa)+\frac{\xi(\kappa_1(\varphi))\kappa_3(\varphi)}{\kappa_1(\varphi)}\kappa_2(\varphi)\left({}^{\wp}_{\omega}\Im^{\Psi}_{\theta+}\kappa_1\right)(\varkappa)$$

$$-\frac{\xi(\kappa_1(\varphi))\kappa_3(\varphi)}{\kappa_1(\varphi)}\kappa_1(\varphi)\left({}^{\wp}_{\omega}\Im^{\Psi}_{\theta+}\kappa_2\right)(\varkappa)-\kappa_2(\varphi)\left({}^{\wp}_{\omega}\Im^{\Psi}_{\theta+}(\xi\circ\kappa_1)\kappa_3\right)(\varkappa)\geq 0. \quad (18)$$

Again, multiplying both sides of (18) by $\omega^{-1}(\varkappa)\frac{\Psi(\wp(\varkappa)-\wp(\varphi))}{\wp(\varkappa)-\wp(\varphi)}\omega(\varphi)\wp'(\varphi)$ and then integrating with regard to the variable φ from θ to $\varkappa$, we have

$$\begin{aligned}&\left({}^{\wp}_{\omega}\Im^{\Psi}_{\theta+}\kappa_1\right)(\varkappa)\left({}^{\wp}_{\omega}\Im^{\Psi}_{\theta+}\frac{\xi\circ\kappa_1}{\kappa_1}\kappa_2\kappa_3\right)(\varkappa)+\left({}^{\wp}_{\omega}\Im^{\Psi}_{\theta+}\frac{\xi\circ\kappa_1}{\kappa_1}\kappa_2\kappa_3\right)(\varkappa)\left({}^{\wp}_{\omega}\Im^{\Psi}_{\theta+}\kappa_1\right)(\varkappa)\\ \geq\ &\left({}^{\wp}_{\omega}\Im^{\Psi}_{\theta+}\kappa_2\right)(\varkappa)\left({}^{\wp}_{\omega}\Im^{\Psi}_{\theta+}(\xi\circ\kappa_1)\kappa_3\right)(\varkappa)+\left({}^{\wp}_{\omega}\Im^{\Psi}_{\theta+}\kappa_2\right)(\varkappa)\left({}^{\wp}_{\omega}\Im^{\Psi}_{\theta+}(\xi\circ\kappa_1)\kappa_3\right)(\varkappa).\end{aligned}$$

Therefore, we can write

$$\frac{\left({}^{\wp}_{\omega}\Im^{\Psi}_{\theta+}\kappa_1\right)(\varkappa)}{\left({}^{\wp}_{\omega}\Im^{\Psi}_{\theta+}\kappa_2\right)(\varkappa)}\geq\frac{\left({}^{\wp}_{\omega}\Im^{\Psi}_{\theta+}(\xi\circ\kappa_1)\kappa_3\right)(\varkappa)}{\left({}^{\wp}_{\omega}\Im^{\Psi}_{\theta+}\frac{\xi\circ\kappa_1}{\kappa_1}\kappa_2\kappa_3\right)(\varkappa)}. \quad (19)$$

Hence, from (16) and (19), we obtain the required result. □

Remark 3. *If we take $\omega(\varkappa)=\varkappa$, $\wp(\varkappa)=\varkappa$, $\varkappa=\gamma$, and $\Psi(\wp(\varkappa))=\wp(\varkappa)$ in Theorem 7, we obtain Theorem 2.*

4. Reverse Minkowski Inequalities for Generalized Weighted-Type Fractional Integral Operators

In this section, the results of the reverse Minkowski inequality using the generalized weighted-type fractional integral operators are given.

Theorem 8. *Let $\kappa,\hbar\in L[\theta,\varkappa]$ be two positive functions on $[0,\infty)$, such that $\left({}^{\wp}_{\omega}\Im^{\Psi}_{\theta+}\kappa^p\right)(\varkappa)$ and $\left({}^{\wp}_{\omega}\Im^{\Psi}_{\theta+}\hbar^p\right)(\varkappa)$ are finite reals for $\varkappa>\theta>0$, $p\geq 1$. If $0\leq\eta\leq\frac{\kappa(\varpi)}{\hbar(\varpi)}\leq\aleph$ holds for $\eta,\aleph\in\mathbb{R}^+$ and $\varpi\in[\theta,\varkappa]$, then*

$$\left({}^{\wp}_{\omega}\Im^{\Psi}_{\theta+}\kappa^p\right)^{\frac{1}{p}}(\varkappa)+\left({}^{\wp}_{\omega}\Im^{\Psi}_{\theta+}\hbar^p\right)^{\frac{1}{p}}(\varkappa)\leq c_1\left({}^{\wp}_{\omega}\Im^{\Psi}_{\theta+}(\kappa+\hbar)^p\right)^{\frac{1}{p}}(\varkappa), \quad (20)$$

with $c_1=\frac{\aleph(\eta+1)+(N+1)}{(\eta+1)(\aleph+1)}$.

Proof. Assuming the given condition $\frac{\kappa(\varpi)}{\hbar(\varpi)}\leq\aleph$, $\varpi\in[\theta,\varkappa]$, it can be written as

$$\kappa(\varpi)\leq\aleph(\kappa(\varpi)+\hbar(\varpi))-\aleph\kappa(\varpi)$$

which implies that

$$(\aleph+1)^p\kappa^p(\varpi)\leq\aleph^p(\kappa(\varpi)+\hbar(\varpi))^p. \quad (21)$$

Multiplying both sides of (21) by $\omega^{-1}(\varkappa)\frac{\Psi(\wp(\varkappa)-\wp(\varpi))}{\wp(\varkappa)-\wp(\varpi)}\omega(\varpi)\wp'(\varpi)$ and then integrating with respect to ϖ from θ to $\varkappa$, we have

$$\begin{aligned}&(\aleph+1)^p\omega^{-1}(\varkappa)\int_{\theta}^{\varkappa}\frac{\Psi(\wp(\varkappa)-\wp(\varpi))}{\wp(\varkappa)-\wp(\varpi)}\omega(\varpi)\wp'(\varpi)\kappa^p(\varpi)d\varpi\\ \leq\ &\aleph^p\omega^{-1}(\varkappa)\int_{\theta}^{\varkappa}\frac{\Psi(\wp(\varkappa)-\wp(\varpi))}{\wp(\varkappa)-\wp(\varpi)}\omega(\varpi)\wp'(\varpi)(\kappa+\hbar)^p(\varpi)d\varpi.\end{aligned}$$

Consequently, we can write

$$\left({}^{\wp}_{\omega}\Im^{\Psi}_{\theta+}\kappa^{p}\right)^{\frac{1}{p}}(\varkappa) \leq \frac{\aleph}{\aleph+1}\left({}^{\wp}_{\omega}\Im^{\Psi}_{\theta+}(\kappa+\hbar)^{p}\right)^{\frac{1}{p}}(\varkappa). \tag{22}$$

Nevertheless, as $\eta\hbar(\varpi) \leq \kappa(\varpi)$, it follows

$$\left(1+\frac{1}{\eta}\right)^{p}\hbar^{p}(\varpi) \leq \left(\frac{1}{\eta}\right)^{p}(\kappa(\varpi)+\hbar(\varpi))^{p}. \tag{23}$$

Now, multiplying both sides of (23) by $\omega^{-1}(\varkappa)\frac{\Psi(\wp(\varkappa)-\wp(\varpi))}{\wp(\varkappa)-\wp(\varpi)}\omega(\varpi)\wp'(\varpi)$ and then integrating with respect to ϖ from θ to $\varkappa$, we obtain

$$\left({}^{\wp}_{\omega}\Im^{\Psi}_{\theta+}\hbar^{p}\right)^{\frac{1}{p}}(\varkappa) \leq \frac{1}{\eta+1}\left({}^{\wp}_{\omega}\Im^{\Psi}_{\theta+}(\kappa+\hbar)^{p}\right)^{\frac{1}{p}}(\varkappa). \tag{24}$$

From (22) and (24), the required result follows. □

Remark 4. *If we choose $\omega(\varkappa) = \varkappa$, $\wp(\varkappa) = \varkappa$, $\varkappa = \gamma$, and $\Psi(\wp(\varkappa)) = \wp(\varkappa)$ in Theorem 8, we obtain Theorem 4.*

With the help of generalized weighted-type fractional operators, inequality (20) is a variant of the reverse Minkowski inequality.

Theorem 9. *Let $\kappa, \hbar \in L[\theta, \varkappa]$ be two positive functions on $[0, \infty)$, such that $({}^{\wp}_{\omega}\Im^{\Psi}_{\theta+}\kappa^{p})(\varkappa)$ and $({}^{\wp}_{\omega}\Im^{\Psi}_{\theta+}\hbar^{p})(\varkappa)$ are finite reals for $\varkappa > \theta > 0$, $p \geq 1$. If $0 \leq \eta \leq \frac{\kappa(\varpi)}{\hbar(\varpi)} \leq \aleph$ holds for $\eta, \aleph \in \mathbb{R}^{+}$ and $\varpi \in [\theta, \varkappa]$, then*

$$\left({}^{\wp}_{\omega}\Im^{\Psi}_{\theta+}\kappa^{p}\right)^{\frac{2}{p}}(\varkappa) + \left({}^{\wp}_{\omega}\Im^{\Psi}_{\theta+}\hbar^{p}\right)^{\frac{2}{p}}(\varkappa) \geq c_2\left({}^{\wp}_{\omega}\Im^{\Psi}_{\theta+}\kappa^{p}\right)^{\frac{1}{p}}(\varkappa)\left({}^{\wp}_{\omega}\Im^{\Psi}_{\theta+}\hbar^{p}\right)^{\frac{1}{p}}(\varkappa),$$

with $c_2 = \frac{(\aleph+1)(\eta+1)}{\aleph} - 2$.

Proof. Multiplying inequality (22) by inequality (24), we have

$$\frac{(\aleph+1)(\eta+1)}{\aleph}\left({}^{\wp}_{\omega}\Im^{\Psi}_{\theta+}\kappa^{p}\right)^{\frac{1}{p}}(\varkappa)\left({}^{\wp}_{\omega}\Im^{\Psi}_{\theta+}\hbar^{p}\right)^{\frac{1}{p}}(\varkappa) \leq \left({}^{\wp}_{\omega}\Im^{\Psi}_{\theta+}(\kappa+\hbar)^{p}\right)^{\frac{2}{p}}(\varkappa). \tag{25}$$

On the right side of (25), using the Minkowski inequality, we obtain

$$\begin{aligned}&\frac{(\aleph+1)(\eta+1)}{\aleph}\left({}^{\wp}_{\omega}\Im^{\Psi}_{\theta+}\kappa^{p}\right)^{\frac{1}{p}}(\varkappa)\left({}^{\wp}_{\omega}\Im^{\Psi}_{\theta+}\hbar^{p}\right)^{\frac{1}{p}}(\varkappa)\\ \leq\ &\left[\left({}^{\wp}_{\omega}\Im^{\Psi}_{\theta+}\kappa^{p}\right)^{\frac{1}{p}}(\varkappa) + \left({}^{\wp}_{\omega}\Im^{\Psi}_{\theta+}\hbar^{p}\right)^{\frac{1}{p}}(\varkappa)\right]^{2}.\end{aligned}$$

Then, we have

$$\begin{aligned}&\left({}^{\wp}_{\omega}\Im^{\Psi}_{\theta+}\kappa^{p}\right)^{\frac{2}{p}}(\varkappa) + \left({}^{\wp}_{\omega}\Im^{\Psi}_{\theta+}\hbar^{p}\right)^{\frac{2}{p}}(\varkappa)\\ \geq\ &\left[\frac{(\aleph+1)(\eta+1)}{\aleph} - 2\right]\left({}^{\wp}_{\omega}\Im^{\Psi}_{\theta+}\kappa^{p}\right)^{\frac{1}{p}}(\varkappa)\left({}^{\wp}_{\omega}\Im^{\Psi}_{\theta+}\hbar^{p}\right)^{\frac{1}{p}}(x)\end{aligned}$$

which is the desired result. □

5. Other Related Inequalities via Generalized Weighted-Type Fractional Operators

Finally, the generalized weighted-type fractional operators are used in this section to derive a number of related inequalities.

Theorem 10. *Let $\kappa, \hbar \in L[\theta, \varkappa]$ and $\kappa, \hbar > 0$ on $[0, \infty)$, such that $\left({}^{\wp}_{\omega}\Im^{\Psi}_{\theta+}\kappa^{p}\right)(\varkappa)$ and $\left({}^{\wp}_{\omega}\Im^{\Psi}_{\theta+}\hbar^{p}\right)(\varkappa)$ are finite reals for $\varkappa > \theta > 0$, $p, q \geq 1$ and $\frac{1}{p} + \frac{1}{q} = 1$. If $0 \leq \eta \leq \frac{\kappa(\varpi)}{\hbar(\varpi)} \leq \aleph$ holds for $\eta, \aleph \in \mathbb{R}^{+}$ and $\varpi \in [\theta, \varkappa]$, then the inequality shown below holds for generalized weighted-type fractional operators:*

$$\left({}^{\wp}_{\omega}\Im^{\Psi}_{\theta+}\kappa\right)^{\frac{1}{p}}(\varkappa)\left({}^{\wp}_{\omega}\Im^{\Psi}_{\theta+}\hbar\right)^{\frac{1}{q}}(\tau) \leq \left(\frac{\aleph}{\eta}\right)^{\frac{1}{qp}}\left({}^{\wp}_{\omega}\Im^{\Psi}_{\theta+}\kappa^{\frac{1}{p}}.\hbar^{\frac{1}{q}}\right)(\varkappa).$$

Proof. Applying the specified condition $\frac{\kappa(\varpi)}{\hbar(\varpi)} \leq \aleph, \varpi \in [\theta, \varkappa]$, it can be written

$$\begin{aligned} \kappa(\varpi) &\leq \aleph\hbar(\varpi) \\ \aleph^{-\frac{1}{q}}\kappa^{\frac{1}{q}}(\varpi) &\leq \hbar^{\frac{1}{q}}(\varpi). \end{aligned} \tag{26}$$

Multiplying both sides of (26) by $\kappa^{\frac{1}{p}}(\varpi)$, we can rewrite it as

$$\aleph^{-\frac{1}{q}}\kappa(\varpi) \leq \kappa^{\frac{1}{p}}(\varpi)\hbar^{\frac{1}{q}}(\varpi) \tag{27}$$

where $\frac{1}{p} + \frac{1}{q} = 1$.

Multiplying both sides of (27) by $\omega^{-1}(\varkappa)\frac{\Psi(\wp(\varkappa)-\wp(\varpi))}{\wp(\varkappa)-\wp(\varpi)}\omega(\varpi)\wp'(\varpi)$ and then integrating, we obtain

$$\begin{aligned} &\aleph^{-\frac{1}{q}}\omega^{-1}(\varkappa)\int_{\theta}^{\varkappa}\frac{\Psi(\wp(\varkappa)-\wp(\varpi))}{\wp(\varkappa)-\wp(\varpi)}\omega(\varpi)\wp'(\varpi)\kappa(\varpi)d\varpi \\ \leq\ &\omega^{-1}(\varkappa)\int_{\theta}^{\varkappa}\frac{\Psi(\wp(\varkappa)-\wp(\varpi))}{\wp(\varkappa)-\wp(\varpi)}\omega(\varpi)\wp'(\varpi)\kappa^{\frac{1}{p}}(\varpi)\hbar^{\frac{1}{q}}(\varpi)d\varpi. \end{aligned}$$

From generalized weighted-type fractional operators, we then have

$$\aleph^{-\frac{1}{pq}}\left({}^{\wp}_{\omega}\Im^{\Psi}_{\theta+}\kappa\right)^{\frac{1}{p}}(\varkappa) < \left({}^{\wp}_{\omega}\Im^{\Psi}_{\theta+}\kappa^{\frac{1}{p}}.\hbar^{\frac{1}{q}}\right)^{\frac{1}{p}}(\varkappa). \tag{28}$$

On the other hand, as $\eta \leq \frac{\kappa(\varpi)}{\hbar(\varpi)}$, it follows that

$$\eta^{\frac{1}{p}}\hbar^{\frac{1}{p}}(\varpi) \leq \kappa^{\frac{1}{p}}(\varpi). \tag{29}$$

Multiplying both sides of (29) by $\hbar^{\frac{1}{q}}(\varpi)$ and using the relation $\frac{1}{p} + \frac{1}{q} = 1$, we obtain

$$\eta^{\frac{1}{p}}\hbar(\varpi) \leq \kappa^{\frac{1}{p}}(\varpi)\hbar^{\frac{1}{q}}(\varpi). \tag{30}$$

Multiplying both sides of (30) by $\omega^{-1}(\varkappa)\frac{\Psi(\wp(\varkappa)-\wp(\varpi))}{\wp(\varkappa)-\wp(\varpi)}\omega(\varpi)\wp'(\varpi)$ and then integrating, we have

$$\eta^{\frac{1}{pq}}\left({}^{\wp}_{\omega}\Im^{\Psi}_{\theta+}\hbar\right)^{\frac{1}{q}}(\varkappa) \leq \left({}^{\wp}_{\omega}\Im^{\Psi}_{\theta+}\kappa^{\frac{1}{p}}.\hbar^{\frac{1}{q}}\right)^{\frac{1}{q}}(\varkappa). \tag{31}$$

Conducting the product between (28) and (31), we have

$$\left({}^{\wp}_{\omega}\Im^{\Psi}_{\theta+}\kappa\right)^{\frac{1}{p}}(\varkappa)\left({}^{\wp}_{\omega}\Im^{\Psi}_{\theta+}\hbar\right)^{\frac{1}{q}}(\varkappa) \leq \left(\frac{\aleph}{\eta}\right)^{\frac{1}{qp}}\left({}^{\wp}_{\omega}\Im^{\Psi}_{\theta+}\kappa^{\frac{1}{p}}\hbar^{\frac{1}{q}}\right)(\varkappa).$$

where $\frac{1}{p}+\frac{1}{q}=1$. Thus, the proof is completed. □

Theorem 11. *For $p,q \geq 1$ and $\frac{1}{p}+\frac{1}{q}=1$. Let $\kappa,\hbar \in L[\theta,\varkappa]$ and $\kappa,\hbar > 0$ on $[0,\infty)$, such that $\left({}^{\wp}_{\omega}\Im^{\Psi}_{\theta+}\kappa^{p}\right)(\varkappa)$ and $\left({}^{\wp}_{\omega}\Im^{\Psi}_{\theta+}\hbar^{p}\right)(\varkappa)$ are finite reals for $\varkappa > \theta > 0$. If $0 \leq \eta \leq \frac{\kappa(\varpi)}{\hbar(\varpi)} \leq \aleph$ for $\eta,\aleph \in \mathbb{R}^{+}$ and for all $\varpi \in [\theta,\varkappa]$, then*

$$\left({}^{\wp}_{\omega}\Im^{\Psi}_{\theta+}\kappa\hbar\right)(\varkappa) \leq c_3\left({}^{\wp}_{\omega}\Im^{\Psi}_{\theta+}(\kappa^{p}+\hbar^{p})\right)(\varkappa) + c_4\left({}^{\wp}_{\omega}\Im^{\Psi}_{\theta+}(\kappa^{q}+\hbar^{q})\right)(\varkappa)$$

with $c_3 = \frac{2^{p-1}\aleph^{p}}{p(\aleph+1)^{p}}$ and $c_4 = \frac{2^{q-1}}{q(\eta+1)^{q}}$.

Proof. The following inequality is obtained using the following hypothesis:

$$(\aleph+1)^{p}\kappa^{p}(\varpi) \leq \aleph^{p}(\kappa+\hbar)^{p}(\varpi). \tag{32}$$

Multiplying both sides of (32) by $\omega^{-1}(\varkappa)\frac{\Psi(\wp(\varkappa)-\wp(\varpi))}{\wp(\varkappa)-\wp(\varpi)}\omega(\varpi)\wp'(\varpi)$ and then integrating, we have

$$\left({}^{\wp}_{\omega}\Im^{\Psi}_{\theta+}\kappa^{p}\right)(\varkappa) \leq \frac{\aleph^{p}}{(\aleph+1)^{p}}\left({}^{\wp}_{\omega}\Im^{\Psi}_{\theta+}(\kappa+\hbar)^{p}\right)(\varkappa). \tag{33}$$

For $\varpi \in [\theta,\varkappa]$, since $0 \leq \eta \leq \frac{\kappa(\varpi)}{\hbar(\varpi)}$ holds, we obtain

$$(\eta+1)^{q}\hbar^{q}(\varpi) \leq (\kappa+\hbar)^{q}(\varpi). \tag{34}$$

Similarly, multiplying both sides of (34) by $\omega^{-1}(\varkappa)\frac{\Psi(\wp(\varkappa)-\wp(\varpi))}{\wp(\varkappa)-\wp(\varpi)}\omega(\varpi)\wp'(\varpi)$ and then integrating, we can write

$$\left({}^{\wp}_{\omega}\Im^{\Psi}_{\theta+}\hbar^{q}\right)(\varkappa) \leq \frac{1}{(\eta+1)^{q}}\left({}^{\wp}_{\omega}\Im^{\Psi}_{\theta+}(\kappa+\hbar)^{q}\right)(\varkappa). \tag{35}$$

Using Young's inequality, we have

$$\kappa(\varpi)\hbar(\varpi) \leq \frac{1}{p}\kappa^{p}(\varpi) + \frac{1}{q}\hbar^{q}(\varpi), \tag{36}$$

again multiplying both sides of (36) by $\omega^{-1}(\varkappa)\frac{\Psi(\wp(\varkappa)-\wp(\varpi))}{\wp(\varkappa)-\wp(\varpi)}\omega(\varpi)\wp'(\varpi)$ and then integrating, we obtain

$$\left({}^{\wp}_{\omega}\Im^{\Psi}_{\theta+}\kappa\hbar\right)(\varkappa) \leq \frac{1}{p}\left({}^{\wp}_{\omega}\Im^{\Psi}_{\theta+}\kappa^{p}\right)(\varkappa) + \frac{1}{q}\left({}^{\wp}_{\omega}\Im^{\Psi}_{\theta+}\hbar^{q}\right)(\varkappa). \tag{37}$$

Using (33) and (35) in (37), we obtain

$$\begin{aligned}\left({}^{\wp}_{\omega}\Im^{\Psi}_{\theta+}\kappa\hbar\right)(\varkappa) \leq\ & \frac{\aleph^{p}}{p(\aleph+1)^{p}}\left({}^{\wp}_{\omega}\Im^{\Psi}_{\theta+}(\kappa+\hbar)^{p}\right)(\varkappa) \\ & + \frac{1}{q(\eta+1)^{q}}\left({}^{\wp}_{\omega}\Im^{\Psi}_{\theta+}(\kappa+\hbar)^{q}\right)(\varkappa).\end{aligned} \tag{38}$$

Utilizing the identity $(\varsigma+\rho)^{r} \leq 2^{r-1}(\varsigma^{r}+\rho^{r})$, $r>1$, $\varsigma,\rho>0$ in (38), we obtain

$$\begin{aligned}\left({}^{\wp}_{\omega}\Im^{\Psi}_{\theta+}\kappa\hbar\right)(\varkappa) \leq\ & \frac{2^{p-1}\aleph^{p}}{p(\aleph+1)^{p}}\left({}^{\wp}_{\omega}\Im^{\Psi}_{\theta+}(\kappa^{p}+\hbar^{p})\right)(\varkappa) \\ & + \frac{2^{q-1}}{q(\eta+1)^{q}}\left({}^{\wp}_{\omega}\Im^{\Psi}_{\theta+}(\kappa^{q}+\hbar^{q})\right)(\varkappa).\end{aligned}$$

This is the required result. □

Theorem 12. *Let $\kappa, \hbar \in L[\theta, \varkappa]$ and $\kappa, \hbar > 0$ on $[0, \infty)$, such that $\left({}^{\wp}_{\omega}\Im^{\Psi}_{\theta+}\kappa^p\right)(\varkappa)$ and $\left({}^{\wp}_{\omega}\Im^{\Psi}_{\theta+}\hbar^p\right)(\varkappa)$ are finite reals for $\varkappa > \theta > 0$. If $0 < c < \eta \leq \frac{\kappa(\varpi)}{\hbar(\varpi)} \leq \aleph$ for $\eta, \aleph \in \mathbb{R}^+$ and for all $\varpi \in [\theta, \varkappa]$, then the following inequalities hold:*

$$\begin{aligned} \frac{\aleph+1}{\aleph-c}\left({}^{\wp}_{\omega}\Im^{\Psi}_{\theta+}(\kappa-c\hbar)^p\right)^{\frac{1}{p}}(\varkappa) &\leq \left({}^{\wp}_{\omega}\Im^{\Psi}_{\theta+}\kappa^p\right)^{\frac{1}{p}}(\varkappa)+\left({}^{\wp}_{\omega}\Im^{\Psi}_{\theta+}\hbar^p\right)^{\frac{1}{p}}(\varkappa) \\ &\leq \frac{\eta+1}{\eta-c}\left({}^{\wp}_{\omega}\Im^{\Psi}_{\theta+}(\kappa-c\hbar)^p\right)^{\frac{1}{p}}(\varkappa) \end{aligned}$$

for $p \geq 1$.

Proof. By using the hypothesis $0 < c < \eta \leq \aleph$, we obtain

$$\eta c \leq \aleph c \quad \Longrightarrow \quad \eta c + \eta \leq \eta c + \aleph \leq \aleph c + \aleph \quad \Longrightarrow \quad (\aleph+1)(\eta-c) \leq (\eta+1)(\aleph-c).$$

The conclusion is that

$$\frac{\aleph+1}{\aleph-c} \leq \frac{\eta+1}{\eta-c}.$$

In addition,

$$\eta \leq \frac{\kappa(\varpi)}{\hbar(\varpi)} \leq \aleph \quad \Longrightarrow \quad \eta - c \leq \frac{\kappa(\varpi)-c\hbar(\varpi)}{\hbar(\varpi)} \leq \aleph - c$$

$$\Longrightarrow \frac{(\kappa(\varpi)-c\hbar(\varpi))^p}{(\aleph-c)^p} \leq \hbar^p(\varpi) \leq \frac{(\kappa(\varpi)-c\hbar(\varpi))^p}{(\eta-c)^p}. \tag{39}$$

Multiplying both sides of (39) by $\omega^{-1}(\varkappa)\frac{\Psi(\wp(\varkappa)-\wp(\varpi))}{\wp(\varkappa)-\wp(\varpi)}\omega(\varpi)\wp'(\varpi)$ and then integrating, we obtain

$$\begin{aligned} &\frac{\omega^{-1}(\varkappa)}{(\aleph-c)^p}\int_{\theta}^{\varkappa}\frac{\Psi(\wp(\varkappa)-\wp(\varpi))}{\wp(\varkappa)-\wp(\varpi)}\omega(\varpi)\wp'(\varpi)(\kappa(\varpi)-c\hbar(\varpi))^p d\varpi \\ \leq\ &\omega^{-1}(\varkappa)\int_{\theta}^{\varkappa}\frac{\Psi(\wp(\varkappa)-\wp(\varpi))}{\wp(\varkappa)-\wp(\varpi)}\omega(\varpi)\wp'(\varpi)\hbar^p(\varpi)d\varpi \\ \leq\ &\frac{\omega^{-1}(\varkappa)}{(\eta-c)^p}\int_{\theta}^{\varkappa}\frac{\Psi(\wp(\varkappa)-\wp(\varpi))}{\wp(\varkappa)-\wp(\varpi)}\omega(\varpi)\wp'(\varpi)(\kappa(\varpi)-c\hbar(\varpi))^p d\varpi \end{aligned}$$

Then, we can write

$$\begin{aligned} \frac{1}{\aleph-c}\left({}^{\wp}_{\omega}\Im^{\Psi}_{\theta+}(\kappa-c\hbar)^p\right)^{\frac{1}{p}}(\varkappa) &\leq \left({}^{\wp}_{\omega}\Im^{\Psi}_{\theta+}\hbar^p\right)^{\frac{1}{p}}(\varkappa) \\ &\leq \frac{1}{\eta-c}\left({}^{\wp}_{\omega}\Im^{\Psi}_{\theta+}(\kappa-c\hbar)^p\right)^{\frac{1}{p}}(\varkappa). \end{aligned} \tag{40}$$

Again, we have

$$\frac{1}{\aleph} \leq \frac{\hbar(\varpi)}{\kappa(\varpi)} \leq \frac{1}{\eta} \Longrightarrow \frac{\eta-c}{\eta c} \leq \frac{\kappa(\varpi)-c\hbar(\varpi)}{c\kappa(\varpi)} \leq \frac{\aleph-c}{c\aleph}$$

which implies

$$\left(\frac{\aleph}{\aleph-c}\right)^p(\kappa(\varpi)-c\hbar(\varpi))^p \leq \kappa^p(\varpi) \leq \left(\frac{\eta}{\eta-c}\right)^p(\kappa(\varpi)-c\hbar(\varpi))^p. \tag{41}$$

By using the same procedures with (41), we obtain

$$\begin{aligned}\frac{\aleph}{\aleph - c}\left({}^{\wp}_{\omega}\Im^{\Psi}_{\theta+}(\kappa - c\hbar)^p\right)^{\frac{1}{p}}(\varkappa) &\leq \left({}^{\wp}_{\omega}\Im^{\Psi}_{\theta+}\kappa^p\right)^{\frac{1}{p}}(\varkappa) \\ &\leq \frac{\eta}{\eta - c}\left({}^{\wp}_{\omega}\Im^{\Psi}_{\theta+}(\kappa - c\hbar)^p\right)^{\frac{1}{p}}(\varkappa).\end{aligned} \tag{42}$$

Adding (40) and (42), the required result is obtained. □

Theorem 13. *Let $\kappa, \hbar \in L[\theta, \varkappa]$ and $\kappa, \hbar > 0$ on $[0, \infty)$, such that $\left({}^{\wp}_{\omega}\Im^{\Psi}_{\theta+}\kappa^p\right)(\varkappa)$ and $\left({}^{\wp}_{\omega}\Im^{\Psi}_{\theta+}\hbar^p\right)(\varkappa)$ are finite reals for $\varkappa > \theta > 0$. If $0 \leq a \leq \kappa(\varpi) \leq A$ and $0 \leq b \leq \hbar(\varpi) \leq B$, $\varpi \in [\theta, \varkappa]$, then*

$$\left({}^{\wp}_{\omega}\Im^{\Psi}_{\theta+}\kappa^p\right)^{\frac{1}{p}}(\varkappa) + \left({}^{\wp}_{\omega}\Im^{\Psi}_{\theta+}\hbar^p\right)^{\frac{1}{p}}(\varkappa) \leq c_5\left({}^{\wp}_{\omega}\Im^{\Psi}_{\theta+}(\kappa + \hbar)^p\right)^{\frac{1}{p}}(\varkappa) \tag{43}$$

with $c_5 = \frac{A(a+B)+B(b+A)}{(a+B)(b+A)}$ and $p \geq 1$.

Proof. As a result of the conditions, it follows that

$$\frac{1}{B} \leq \frac{1}{\hbar(\varpi)} \leq \frac{1}{b}. \tag{44}$$

Considering the product of (44) and $0 \leq a \leq \kappa(\varpi) \leq A$, we obtain

$$\frac{a}{B} \leq \frac{\kappa(\varpi)}{\hbar(\varpi)} \leq \frac{A}{b}. \tag{45}$$

From (45), we obtain

$$\hbar^p(\varpi) \leq \left(\frac{B}{a + B}\right)^p (\kappa(\varpi) + \hbar(\varpi))^p \tag{46}$$

and

$$\kappa^p(\varpi) \leq \left(\frac{A}{b + A}\right)^p (\kappa(\varpi) + \hbar(\varpi))^p. \tag{47}$$

Multiplying both sides of (46) and (47) by $\omega^{-1}(\varkappa)\frac{\Psi(\wp(\varkappa)-\wp(\varpi))}{\wp(\varkappa)-\wp(\varpi)}\omega(\varpi)\wp'(\varpi)$ and then integrating, we obtain

$$\left({}^{\wp}_{\omega}\Im^{\Psi}_{\theta+}\hbar^p\right)^{\frac{1}{p}}(\varkappa) \leq \frac{B}{a + B}\left({}^{\wp}_{\omega}\Im^{\Psi}_{\theta+}(\kappa + \hbar)^p\right)^{\frac{1}{p}}(\varkappa) \tag{48}$$

and

$$\left({}^{\wp}_{\omega}\Im^{\Psi}_{\theta+}\kappa^p\right)^{\frac{1}{p}}(\varkappa) \leq \frac{A}{b + A}\left({}^{\wp}_{\omega}\Im^{\Psi}_{\theta+}(\kappa + \hbar)^p\right)^{\frac{1}{p}}(\varkappa), \tag{49}$$

respectively. Adding (48) and (49) completes the proof of (43). □

Theorem 14. *Let $\kappa, \hbar \in L[\theta, \varkappa]$ and $\kappa, \hbar > 0$ on $[0, \infty)$, such that $\left({}^{\wp}_{\omega}\Im^{\Psi}_{\theta+}\kappa^p\right)(\varkappa)$ and $\left({}^{\wp}_{\omega}\Im^{\Psi}_{\theta+}\hbar^p\right)(\varkappa)$ are finite reals for $\varkappa > \theta > 0$. If $0 \leq \eta \leq \frac{\kappa(\varpi)}{\hbar(\varpi)} \leq \aleph$ for $\eta, \aleph \in \mathbb{R}^+$ and for all $\varpi \in [\theta, \varkappa]$, then we have*

$$\frac{1}{\aleph}\left({}^{\wp}_{\omega}\Im^{\Psi}_{\theta+}\kappa\hbar\right)(\varkappa) \leq \frac{1}{(\eta + 1)(\aleph + 1)}\left({}^{\wp}_{\omega}\Im^{\Psi}_{\theta+}(\kappa + \hbar)^2\right)(\varkappa) \leq \frac{1}{\eta}\left({}^{\wp}_{\omega}\Im^{\Psi}_{\theta+}\kappa\hbar\right)(\varkappa).$$

Proof. Using $0 \leq \eta \leq \frac{\kappa(\varpi)}{\hbar(\varpi)} \leq \aleph$, we have

$$\hbar(\varpi)(\eta + 1) \leq \hbar(\varpi) + \kappa(\varpi) \leq \hbar(\varpi)(\aleph + 1). \tag{50}$$

In addition, it follows that $\frac{1}{\aleph} \leq \frac{\hbar(\varpi)}{\kappa(\varpi)} \leq \frac{1}{\eta}$, which yields

$$\kappa(\varpi)\left(\frac{\aleph+1}{\aleph}\right) \leq \hbar(\varpi) + \kappa(\varpi) \leq \kappa(\varpi)\left(\frac{\eta+1}{\eta}\right). \tag{51}$$

Evaluating the product between (50) and (51), we obtain

$$\frac{\kappa(\varpi)\hbar(\varpi)}{\aleph} \leq \frac{(\hbar(\varpi)+\kappa(\varpi))^2}{(\eta+1)(\aleph+1)} \leq \frac{\kappa(\varpi)\hbar(\varpi)}{\eta}. \tag{52}$$

Multiplying both sides of (52) by $\omega^{-1}(\varkappa)\frac{\Psi(\wp(\varkappa)-\wp(\varpi))}{\wp(\varkappa)-\wp(\varpi)}\omega(\varpi)\wp'(\varpi)$ and then integrating, we have

$$\begin{aligned} & \frac{\omega^{-1}(\varkappa)}{\aleph}\int_\theta^\varkappa \frac{\Psi(\wp(\varkappa)-\wp(\varpi))}{\wp(\varkappa)-\wp(\varpi)}\omega(\varpi)\wp'(\varpi)\kappa(\varpi)\hbar(\varpi)d\varpi \\ \leq \; & \frac{\omega^{-1}(\varkappa)}{(\eta+1)(\aleph+1)}\int_\theta^\varkappa \frac{\Psi(\wp(\varkappa)-\wp(\varpi))}{\wp(\varkappa)-\wp(\varpi)}\omega(\varpi)\wp'(\varpi)(\hbar(\varpi)+\kappa(\varpi))^2 d\varpi \\ \leq \; & \frac{\omega^{-1}(\varkappa)}{\eta}\int_\theta^\varkappa \frac{\Psi(\wp(\varkappa)-\wp(\varpi))}{\wp(\varkappa)-\wp(\varpi)}\omega(\varpi)\wp'(\varpi)\kappa(\varpi)\hbar(\varpi)d\varpi. \end{aligned}$$

Hence,

$$\frac{1}{\aleph}({}_\omega^\wp\Im_{\theta+}^\Psi \kappa\hbar)(\varkappa) \leq \frac{1}{(\eta+1)(\aleph+1)}\left({}_\omega^\wp\Im_{\theta+}^\Psi(\kappa+\hbar)^2\right)(\varkappa) \leq \frac{1}{\eta}({}_\omega^\wp\Im_{\theta+}^\Psi \kappa\hbar)(\varkappa).$$

This completes the proof. □

Theorem 15. *Let $\kappa, \hbar \in L[\theta, \varkappa]$ and $\kappa, \hbar > 0$ on $[0,\infty)$, such that $({}_\omega^\wp\Im_{\theta+}^\Psi \kappa^p)(\varkappa)$ and $({}_\omega^\wp\Im_{\theta+}^\Psi \hbar^p)(\varkappa)$ are finite reals for $\varkappa > \theta > 0$. If $0 < \eta \leq \frac{\kappa(\varpi)}{\hbar(\varpi)} \leq \aleph$ holds for $\eta, \aleph \in \mathbb{R}^+$ and for all $\varpi \in [\theta, \varkappa]$, then*

$$({}_\omega^\wp\Im_{\theta+}^\Psi \kappa^p)^{\frac{1}{p}}(\varkappa) + ({}_\omega^\wp\Im_{\theta+}^\Psi \hbar^p)^{\frac{1}{p}}(\varkappa) \leq 2\left({}_\omega^\wp\Im_{\theta+}^\Psi \mathcal{F}^p(\kappa,\hbar)\right)^{\frac{1}{p}}(\varkappa) \tag{53}$$

holds. $\mathcal{F}(\kappa(\varpi),\hbar(\varpi)) = \max\left\{\aleph\left[\left(\frac{\aleph}{\eta}+1\right)\kappa(\varpi) - \aleph\hbar(\varpi)\right], \frac{(\aleph+\eta)\hbar(\varpi)-\kappa(\varpi)}{\eta}\right\}$.

Proof. From the hypothesis $0 < \eta \leq \frac{\kappa(\varpi)}{\hbar(\varpi)} \leq \aleph$, we obtain

$$0 < \eta \leq \aleph + \eta - \frac{\kappa(\varpi)}{\hbar(\varpi)} \tag{54}$$

and

$$\aleph + \eta - \frac{\kappa(\varpi)}{\hbar(\varpi)} \leq \aleph. \tag{55}$$

Hence, using (54) and (55), we obtain

$$\hbar(\varpi) < \frac{(\aleph+\eta)\hbar(\varpi)-\kappa(\varpi)}{\eta} \leq \mathcal{F}(\kappa(\varpi),\hbar(\varpi)), \tag{56}$$

where $\mathcal{F}(\kappa(\varpi),\hbar(\varpi)) = \max\left\{\aleph\left[\left(\frac{\aleph}{\eta}+1\right)\kappa(\varpi) - \aleph\hbar(\varpi)\right], \frac{(\aleph+\eta)\hbar(\varpi)-\kappa(\varpi)}{\eta}\right\}$.

Using the hypothesis, it follows that $0 < \frac{1}{\aleph} \leq \frac{\hbar(\varpi)}{\kappa(\varpi)} \leq \frac{1}{\eta}$. In this way, we have

$$\frac{1}{\aleph} \leq \frac{1}{\aleph} + \frac{1}{\eta} - \frac{\hbar(\varpi)}{\kappa(\varpi)} \tag{57}$$

and

$$\frac{1}{\aleph}+\frac{1}{\eta}-\frac{\hbar(\varpi)}{\kappa(\varpi)}\leq\frac{1}{\eta}. \tag{58}$$

From (57) and (58), we obtain

$$\frac{1}{\aleph}\leq\frac{\left(\frac{1}{\aleph}+\frac{1}{\eta}\right)\kappa(\varpi)-\hbar(\varpi)}{\kappa(\varpi)}\leq\frac{1}{\eta},$$

which can be rewritten as

$$\begin{aligned}\kappa(\varpi) &\leq \aleph\left(\frac{1}{\aleph}+\frac{1}{\eta}\right)\kappa(\varpi)-\aleph\hbar(\varpi)\\ &= \left(\frac{\aleph}{\eta}+1\right)\kappa(\varpi)-\aleph\hbar(\varpi)\\ &\leq \aleph\left[\left(\frac{\aleph}{\eta}+1\right)\kappa(\varpi)-\aleph\hbar(\varpi)\right]\\ &\leq \mathcal{F}(\kappa(\varpi),\hbar(\varpi)). \end{aligned}\tag{59}$$

We can write from (56) and (59)

$$\kappa^p(\varpi) \leq \mathcal{F}^p(\kappa(\varpi),\hbar(\varpi)) \tag{60}$$

$$\hbar^p(\varpi) \leq \mathcal{F}^p(\kappa(\varpi),\hbar(\varpi)). \tag{61}$$

Multiplying both sides of (60) by $\omega^{-1}(\varkappa)\frac{\Psi(\wp(\varkappa)-\wp(\varpi))}{\wp(\varkappa)-\wp(\varpi)}\omega(\varpi)\wp'(\varpi)$ and then integrating, we have

$$\begin{aligned}&\omega^{-1}(\varkappa)\int_\theta^\varkappa\frac{\Psi(\wp(\varkappa)-\wp(\varpi))}{\wp(\varkappa)-\wp(\varpi)}\omega(\varpi)\wp'(\varpi)\kappa^p(\varpi)d\varpi\\ \leq\ &\omega^{-1}(\varkappa)\int_\theta^\varkappa\frac{\Psi(\wp(\varkappa)-\wp(\varpi))}{\wp(\varkappa)-\wp(\varpi)}\omega(\varpi)\wp'(\varpi)\mathcal{F}^p(\kappa(\varpi),\hbar(\varpi))d\varpi.\end{aligned}$$

Accordingly, it can be written as

$$\left({}^{\wp}_{\omega}\Im^{\Psi}_{\theta+}\kappa^p\right)^{\frac{1}{p}}(\varkappa)\leq\left({}^{\wp}_{\omega}\Im^{\Psi}_{\theta+}\mathcal{F}^p(\kappa,\hbar)\right)^{\frac{1}{p}}(\varkappa). \tag{62}$$

Using the same procedure as above, for (61), we have

$$\left({}^{\wp}_{\omega}\Im^{\Psi}_{\theta+}\hbar^p\right)^{\frac{1}{p}}(\varkappa)\leq\left({}^{\wp}_{\omega}\Im^{\Psi}_{\theta+}\mathcal{F}^p(\kappa,\hbar)\right)^{\frac{1}{p}}(\varkappa). \tag{63}$$

The required result (53) follows from (62) and (63). □

6. Conclusions

Mathematical inequalities are of significant importance in the study of mathematics and related fields. Future research on integral inequalities will now be encouraged by these recommendations to examine how integral inequalities can be extended using fractional calculus operators. In this study, first of all, we presented several definitions of fractional integral operators, and then we showed some inequalities utilizing the monotonicity properties of functions for the generalized weighted-type fractional operators. The acquired results reflect an expansion of certain previously published results. Different types of inequalities were also obtained using this operator. We would like to emphasize, in particular, that these operators can be used to obtain new types of integral inequalities and results.

Author Contributions: Conceptualization, Ç.Y., G.R. and L.-I.C.; methodology, Ç.Y., G.R. and L.-I.C.; validation, Ç.Y., G.R. and L.-I.C.; formal analysis, Ç.Y., G.R. and L.-I.C.; investigation, Ç.Y., G.R. and L.-I.C.; resources: Ç.Y.; writing—original draft preparation, Ç.Y.; writing—review and editing, Ç.Y.; visualization, Ç.Y., G.R. and L.-I.C.; supervision: Ç.Y.; project administration, Ç.Y.; funding acquisition: L.-I.C. All authors have read and agreed to the published version of the manuscript.

Funding: This research received no external funding.

Data Availability Statement: Not applicable.

Conflicts of Interest: The authors declare no conflict of interest.

References

1. Botmart, T.; Sahoo, S.K.; Kodamasingh, B.; Amer, M.; Latif, F.J.; Kashuri, A. Certain midpoint-type Fejér and Hermite-Hadamard inclusions involving fractional integrals with an exponential function in kernel. *AIMS Math.* **2023**, *8*, 5616–5638. [CrossRef]
2. Yildiz, Ç.; Cotîrlă, L.I. Examining the Hermite–Hadamard Inequalities for $k-$Fractional Operators Using the Green Function. *Fractal Fract.* **2023**, *7*, 161. [CrossRef]
3. Khan, T.U.; Khan, M.A. Generalized conformable fractional operators. *J. Comput. Appl. Math.* **2019**, *346*, 378–389. [CrossRef]
4. Hyder, A.-A.; Budak, H.; Barakat, M.A. New Versions of Midpoint Inequalities Based on Extended Riemann–Liouville Fractional Integrals. *Fractal Fract.* **2023**, *7*, 442. [CrossRef]
5. Osler, T.J. The fractional derivative of a composite function. *SIAM J. Math. Anal.* **1970**, *1*, 288–293. [CrossRef]
6. Almeira, R. A Caputo fractional derivative of a function with respect to another function. *Commun. Nonlinear Sci. Numer. Simul.* **2017**, *44*, 460–481. [CrossRef]
7. Sarikaya, M.Z.; Budak, H. Generalized Ostrowski type inequalities for local fractional integrals. *Proc. Am. Math. Soc.* **2017**, *145*, 1527–1538. [CrossRef]
8. Rahman, G.; Samraiz, M.; Naheed, S.; Kashuri, A.; Nonlaopon, K. New classes of unified fractional integral inequalities. *AIMS Math.* **2022**, *7*, 15563–15583. [CrossRef]
9. Rahman, G.; Aldosary, S.F.; Samraiz, M.; Nisar, K.S. Some double generalized weighted fractional integral inequalities associated with monotone Chebyshev functionals. *Fractal Fract.* **2021**, *5*, 275. [CrossRef]
10. Dahmani, Z. A note on some new fractional results involving convex functions. *Acta Math. Univ. Comen.* **2012**, *LXXXI*, 241–246.
11. Rahman, G.; Nisar, K.S.; Abdeljawad, T.; Ullah, S. Certain Fractional Proportional Integral Inequalities via Convex Functions. *Mathematics* **2020**, *8*, 222. [CrossRef]
12. Çelik, B.; Gürbüz, M.; Özdemir, M.E.; Set, E. On integral inequalities related to the weighted and the extended Chebyshev functionals involving different fractional operators. *J. Inequal. Appl.* **2020**, 246. [CrossRef]
13. Qi, H.; Nazeer, W.; Abbas, F.; Liao, W. Some inequalities of Hermite-Hadamard type for $MT-h-$convex functions via classical and generalized fractional integrals. *J. Funct. Spaces* **2022** , *9*, 766–777. [CrossRef]
14. Rahman, G.; Nisar, K.S.; Abdeljawad, T. Tempered Fractional Integral Inequalities for Convex Functions. *Mathematics* **2020**, *8*, 500. [CrossRef]
15. Set, E.; Butt, S.I.; Akdemir, A.O.; Karaoğlan, A.; Abdeljawad, T. New integral inequalities for differentiable convex functions via Atangana-Baleanu fractional integral operators. *Chaos Solitons Fractals* **2021**, *143*, 110554. [CrossRef]
16. Rahman, G.; Abdeljawad, T.; Jarad, F.; Khan, A.; Nisar, K.S. Certain inequalities via generalized proportional Hadamard fractional integral operators. *Adv. Differ. Equ.* **2019**, *2019*, 454. [CrossRef]
17. Gürbüz, M.; Yıldız, Ç. Some new inequalities for convex functions via Riemann-Liouville fractional integrals. *Appl. Math. Nonlinear Sci.* **2021**, *6*, 537–544. [CrossRef]
18. Dragomir, S.S. Inequalities for double integrals of Schur convex functions on symmetric and convex domains. *Mat. Vesn.* **2021**, *73*, 63–74.
19. Sarıkaya, M.Z.; Budak, H.; Erden, S. On new inequalities of Simpson's type for generalized convex functions. *Korean J. Math.* **2019**, *27*, 279–295.
20. Khan, M.A.; Saeed, T.; Nwaeze, E.R. A New advanced class of convex functions with related results. *Axioms* **2023**, *12*, 195. [CrossRef]
21. Wu, Y.; Yin, H.P.; Guo, B.N. Generalizations of Hermite-Hadamard type integral inequalities for convex functions. *Axioms* **2021**, *10*, 136. [CrossRef]
22. Gürbüz, M.; Özdemir, M.E. On some inequalities for product of different kinds of convex functions. *Turk. J. Sci.* **2020**, *5*, 23–27.
23. Ngo, Q.A.; Thang, D.D.; Dat, T.T.; Tuan, D.A. Notes on an integral inequality. *J. Inequal. Pure Appl. Math.* **2006**, *7*, 120.
24. Liu, W.J.; Cheng, G.S.; Li, C.C. Further development of an open problem concerning an integral inequality. *J. Inequal. Pure Appl. Math.* **2008**, *9*, 14.
25. Liu, W.J.; Ngŏ, Q.A.; Huy, V.N. Several interesting integral inequalities. *J. Math. Inequal.* **2009**, *3*, 201–212. [CrossRef]
26. Hardy, G.H.; Littewood, J.E.; Pòlya, G. *Minkowski's Inequality and Minkowski's Inequality for Integrals, 2.11, 5.7, and 6.13 in Inequalities*, 2nd ed.; Cambridge University Press: Cambridge, UK, 1988; pp. 123, 3032, 146150.
27. Bougoffa, L. On Minkowski and Hardy integral inequalities. *J. Inequal. Pure Appl. Math.* **2006**, *7*, 60.

28. Dahmani, Z. On Minkowski and Hermite-Hadamard integral inequalities via fractional integration. *Ann. Funct. Anal.* **2010**, *1*, 51–58. [CrossRef]
29. Set, E.; Özdemir, M.E.; Dragomir, S.S. On the HermiteHadamard inequality and other integral inequalities involving two functions. *J. Inequal. Appl.* **2010**, 148102. [CrossRef]
30. Chinchane, V.L.; Pachpatte, D.B. New fractional inequalities involving Saigo fractional integral operator. *Math. Sci. Lett.* **2014**, *3*, 133–139. [CrossRef]
31. da Vanterler, J.; Sousa, C.; de Oliveira Capelas, E. The Minkowski's inequality by means of a generalized fractional integral. *AIMS Math.* **2018**, *3*, 131–142. [CrossRef]
32. Rahman, G.; Khan, A.; Abdeljawad, T.; Nisar, K.S. The Minkowski inequalities via generalized pro-portional fractional integral operators. *Adv. Differ. Equ.* **2019**, *2019*, 287. [CrossRef]
33. Iqbal, S.; Samraiz, M.; Khan, M.A.; Rahman, G.; Nonlaopon, K. New Minkowski and related inequalities via general kernels and measures. *J. Inequal. Appl.* **2023**, *1*, 1–23. [CrossRef]
34. Mitrinović, D.S.; Pečarić, J.E.; Fink, A.M. *Classical and New Inequalities in Analysis*; Kluwer Academic Publishers: London, UK, 1993; p. 55.
35. Kilbas, A.A. Hadamard-type fractional calculus. *J.Korean Math. Soc.* **2001**, *38*, 1191–1204.
36. Sarikaya, M.Z.; Yildirim, H. On generalization of the Riesz potential. *Indian J. Math. Math. Sci.* **2007**, *3*, 231–235.
37. Rahman, G.; Hussain, A.; Ali, A.; Nisar, K.S.; Mohamed, R.N. More General Weighted-Type Fractional Integral Inequalities via Chebyshev Functionals. *Fractal Fract.* **2021**, *5*, 232. [CrossRef]
38. Sarikaya, M.Z.; Ertugral, F. On the generalized Hermite-Hadamard inequalities. *Ann. Univ. Craiova-Math. Com. Sci. Ser.* **2020**, *47*, 193–213.
39. Jarad, F.; Abdeljawad, T.; Shah, K. On the weighted fractional operators of a function with respect to another function. *Fractals* **2020**, *28*, 12. [CrossRef]

fractal and fractional

Article

Several Quantum Hermite–Hadamard-Type Integral Inequalities for Convex Functions

Loredana Ciurdariu [1,*] and Eugenia Grecu [2]

1 Department of Mathematics, Politehnica University of Timisoara, 300006 Timisoara, Romania
2 Department of Management, Politehnica University of Timisoara, 300006 Timisoara, Romania; eugenia.grecu@upt.ro
* Correspondence: loredana.ciurdariu@upt.ro

Abstract: The aim of this study was to present several improved quantum Hermite–Hadamard-type integral inequalities for convex functions using a parameter. Thus, a new quantum identity is proven to be used as the main tool in the proof of our results. Consequently, in some special cases several new quantum estimations for q-midpoints and q-trapezoidal-type inequalities are derived with an example. The results obtained could be applied in the optimization of several economic geology problems.

Keywords: quantum calculus; convex functions; Hermite–Hadamard-type inequalities

Citation: Ciurdariu, L.; Grecu, E. Several Quantum Hermite–Hadamard-Type Integral Inequalities for Convex Functions. *Fractal Fract.* **2023**, *7*, 463. https://doi.org/10.3390/fractalfract7060463

Academic Editors: Seth Kermausuor and Eze Nwaeze

Received: 4 May 2023
Revised: 1 June 2023
Accepted: 5 June 2023
Published: 7 June 2023

1. Introduction

The field of mathematical inequalities and applications has seen great advancements in the last three decades. This has a significant impact on areas such as physics, earth sciences, engineering [1], statistics [2], economics [3] and approximation theory [4], information theory [5] and numerical analysis [6,7]. "Mathematical inequalities have streamlined the concept of classical convexity" [8]. It is known that "the scientific observations and calculations rely on convex functions and their relationship to mathematical inequalities" [8]. Integral inequalities represent a fundamental way to establish qualitative or quantitative mathematical results. The strong correlation between different convexities and symmetric functions, as well as between convex functions and integral inequalities, open a broad framework for studying a large category of complex problems.

Convexity is a natural concept for solving many problems in mathematics with numerous uses in industry, business and medicine. Various types of convexities have been investigated, such as, h-convexity defined by Varosanec [9], exponentially convex functions introduced by Bernstein [10] with covariance analysis applications, r-convex functions studied by Avriel [11], convex functions on coordinates introduced by Dragomir [12], h-convexity on coordinates introduced by Alomari et al. [13], exponentially h-convexity defined by Rashid et al. [14], and exponential h-convex functions [15] on coordinates given by W. Iqbal et al. On the other hand, Pal and Wong provided a base for exponential convex functions in the fields of information theory [16] and optimization theory. An important generalization of convexity was given in 1981 [17], by the introduction of invexity, due to its importance in optimization. Studies on convex and pre-invex functions have potential applications [18] in maximizing the likelihood [19] from multiple linear regressions [20] involving Gauss–Laplace distributions.

Quantum calculus has various applications in the interdisciplinary field of quantum information theory. This field contains many subfields, such as computer science, information theory [21], philosophy, and cryptography. Quantum calculus (i.e., q-calculus) is known as the study of calculus without limitations. This topic has become a reliable instrument in many areas of physics [22] and mathematics in recent years. The quantum integral inequalities are more useful and interesting than their classical equivalents. Jackson studied the quantum difference operator [23]. The first use of quantum calculus and the difference equations [23] was in physics and chemistry problems. Siegel investigated string theory [24] involving quantum calculus. Recently, new applications have been established in various branches of physics and mathematics. In [25], in 1969, Agarwal studied q-fractional derivatives for the first time. q-calculus concepts [26] on finite intervals was used to find quantum analogues of known mathematical definitions and results. New quantum analogues [27] of the Ostrowski inequalities [28], using first-order quantum differentiable convex mappings, were presented by Noor et al. Several bounds for the left-hand side (LHS) of quantum H–H inequalities [29] were established. New quantum analogues of the classical Simpson's inequality were presented [30] for pre-invex functions. These new q-analogues of the (s, m) that generalized (s, m) pre-invex functions were given in [31] by Deng et al. The mathematical field [32] of time scale calculus contains quantum calculus as a subfield. "In studying quantum calculus, we are concerned with a specific time scale, called the q-time scale, defined as: $T = q^{\mathbb{N}_0} = \{q^t : t \in \mathbb{N}_0\}$", see [32].

Many inequalities, especially the Hermite–Hadamard (H–H)-type inequalities, contain a kind of symmetry, an important characteristic as symmetry commonly has a central role [21] in finding the correct way to solve dynamic inequalities. This famous inequality [12] has had many improvements and extensions [13] during recent decades [33], see, for example, [34], and nowadays, for quantum and post-quantum calculus, fractional calculus and fuzzy environment. Recently new generalizations and refinements of H–H-type integral inequalities for quantum [29,31] and post-quantum calculus [35,36] have been obtained, e.g., [37,38] and the references cited therein.

Motivated by [36], we aimed to obtain new parametrized q-H–H-type inequalities for third-order q-differentiable functions using a new quantum identity, concerning the third-order q-left and right derivatives. These results are different from the results of [39] and are similar to the results of [36]. Our work represents the case when the functions accept the third q-derivative instead of the first q-derivative, see [36], and the left term of these inequalities contains two integrals defined as two new intervals, $[a, \lambda b + (1 - \lambda)a]$ and $[\lambda a + (1 - \lambda)b, b]$, different from intervals $[a, x]$ and $[x, b]$ which appear in [39] and [35]. The values of the parameter λ change these intervals in a different way, which is advantageous. Furthermore, here new terms appear in the left term of these inequalities with different coefficients of the third q-derivatives in the right term.

The paper is structured as four sections as follows. Section 2 provides a brief summary of the fundamental definitions and properties regarding quantum calculus and the H–H integral inequality. In Section 3, we state and prove our main results in Lemma 1, Theorems 4–6. In these theorems and consequent new q-midpoints, trapezoidal and q-H–H-type integral inequalities are established for three times differentiable convex functions. Many consequences are formulated with a given example. Figure and several calculus in Example 1 were performed using the Matlab R2023a software version. Applications to special cases of real numbers are presented in Section 3 using the newly generated results. In Section 4, a discussion and conclusions are drawn.

2. Preliminary on q-Calculus and Inequalities

The classical H–H inequality says that "if $\theta : [a, b] \to \mathbb{R}$ is a convex function, then the following inequality holds:

$$\theta\left(\frac{a+b}{2}\right) \le \frac{1}{b-a}\int_a^b \theta(x)dx \le \frac{\theta(a)+\theta(b)}{2}. \tag{1}$$

When θ is a concave function, then the previous inequality holds but in the opposite direction", see [40].

We assume that $0 < q < 1$. Let $[a, b]$ be a real interval, where $a < b$. We assume that $[n]_q = \frac{1-q^n}{1-q} = 1 + q + \ldots + q^{n-2} + q^{n-1}$, $n \in \mathbb{N}$.

Now we present some important definitions, remarks and lemmas of the q-calculus which will be used throughout this paper.

Definition 1 ([36]). *The right or q^b-derivative of $\theta : [a,b] \to \mathbb{R}$ at $x \in [a,b]$ is expressed as:*

$$^{b}D_q\theta(x) = \frac{\theta(qx + (1-q)b) - \theta(x)}{(1-q)(b-x)}, \quad x \neq b.$$

Definition 2 ([36,41]). *The left or q_a-derivative of $\theta : [a,b] \to \mathbb{R}$ at $x \in [a,b]$ is expressed as:*

$$_{a}D_q\theta(x) = \frac{\theta(x) - \theta(qx + (1-q)a)}{(1-q)(x-a)}, \quad x \neq a.$$

Definition 3 ([36]). *The right or q^b-integral of $\theta : [a,b] \to \mathbb{R}$ at $x \in [a,b]$ is defined as:*

$$\int_x^b \theta(t)^b d_q t = (1-q)(b-x)\sum_{n=0}^{\infty} q^n\theta(q^n x + (1-q^n)b) = (b-a)\int_0^1 \theta(tb + (1-t)x)^1 d_q t.$$

Definition 4 ([36]). *The left or q_a-integral of $\theta : [a,b] \to \mathbb{R}$ at $x \in [a,b]$ is defined as:*

$$\int_a^x \theta(t)_a d_q t = (1-q)(x-a)\sum_{n=0}^{\infty} q^n\theta(q^n x + (1-q^n)a) = (b-a)\int_0^1 \theta(tx + (1-t)a) d_q t.$$

Definition 5 ([36]). *We have the equality for q_a-integrals, defined as*

$$\int_a^b (x-a)^{\alpha}\,{}_a d_q x = \frac{(b-a)^{\alpha+1}}{[\alpha+1]_q},$$

for $\alpha \in \mathbb{R} - \{-1\}$.

The fundamental properties of these derivatives and integrals can be found in [41,42]. Recently, new refinements and generalizations of q-H–H integral inequalities for q-differentiable functions were given in [36].

Theorem 1 ([36]). *"We assume that the conditions of Lemma 2 ([36]) hold. If $|_aD_q\theta|$ and $|^bD_q\theta|$ are convex on $[a,b]$, then the following inequality holds:*

$$\Big|\frac{1}{2\lambda(b-a)}\left(\int_a^{\lambda b+(1-\lambda)a} \theta(t)_a d_q t + \int_{\lambda a+(1-\lambda)b}^{b} \theta(t)^b d_q t\right) - \frac{\theta(\lambda b + (1-\lambda)a) + \theta(\lambda a + (1-\lambda)b)}{2}\Big|$$

$$\leq \frac{\lambda q(b-a)}{2[2]_q[3]_q}[([3]_q - \lambda[2]_q)[|^bD_q\theta(b)| + |_aD_q\theta(a)|] + \lambda[2]_q[|^bD_q\theta(a)| + |_aD_q\theta(b)|]]."$$

Theorem 2 ([36]). *"We assume that the conditions of Lemma 2 ([36]) hold. If $|_aD_q\theta|^s$ and $|^bD_q\theta|^s$, $s > 1$ are convex, then the following inequality holds:*

$$\Big|\frac{1}{2\lambda(b-a)}\left(\int_a^{\lambda b+(1-\lambda)a} \theta(t)_a d_q t + \int_{\lambda a+(1-\lambda)b}^{b} \theta(t)^b d_q t\right) - \frac{\theta(\lambda b + (1-\lambda)a) + \theta(\lambda a + (1-\lambda)b)}{2}\Big|$$

$$\leq \frac{\lambda q(b-a)}{2}\left(\frac{1}{[r+1]_q}\right)^{\frac{1}{r}}\Big[\left(\frac{[2]_q - \lambda}{[2]_q}|^bD_q\theta(b)|^s + \frac{\lambda}{[2]_q}|^bD_q\theta(a)|^s\right)^{\frac{1}{s}}$$

$$+\left(\frac{[2]_q - \lambda}{[2]_q}|_aD_q\theta(a)|^s + \frac{\lambda}{[2]_q}|_aD_q\theta(b)|^s\right)^{\frac{1}{s}}\Big],$$

where $s^{-1} + r^{-1} = 1$."

Theorem 3 ([36]). *"We assume that the conditions of Lemma 2 ([36]) hold. If* $|{}_aD_q\theta|^s$ *and* $|{}^bD_q\theta|^s$*,* $s \geq 1$ *are convex, then the following inequality holds:*

$$
\begin{aligned}
&\left|\frac{1}{2\lambda(b-a)}\left(\int_a^{\lambda b+(1-\lambda)a}\theta(t)_a d_q t+\int_{\lambda a+(1-\lambda)b}^{b}\theta(t)^b d_q t\right)-\frac{\theta(\lambda b+(1-\lambda)a)+\theta(\lambda a+(1-\lambda)b)}{2}\right| \\
&\leq \frac{\lambda q(b-a)}{2[2]_q}\left[\left(\frac{([3]_q-\lambda[2]_q)|{}^bD_q\theta(b)|^s+\lambda[2]_q|{}^bD_q\theta(a)|^s}{[3]_q}\right)^{\frac{1}{s}}\right. \\
&\left.+\left(\frac{([3]_q-\lambda[2]_q)|{}_aD_q\theta(a)|^s+\lambda[2]_q|{}_aD_q\theta(b)|^s}{[3]_q}\right)^{\frac{1}{s}}\right]."
\end{aligned}
$$

3. Results

A new quantum identity is given below as the main tool in the proof of our results. New estimates of parametrized q-H–H-type integral inequalities for three time quantum differentiable functions are presented below starting from the results from [36]. In addition, new consequent terms and applications, including an example, are given to illustrate the investigated results.

Lemma 1. *Let* $\theta : [a,b] \to \mathbb{R}$ *be a third-order q-differentiable function with* ${}_aD_q^3\theta$ *and* ${}^bD_q^3\theta$ *continuous and q-integrable functions on* $[a,b]$*, respectively. Thus, the following equality holds,*

$$
{}_a^bP_q(\lambda)=\frac{\lambda^3(b-a)^3}{2}\int_0^1 q^6t^3[{}^bD_q^3\theta((1-\lambda t)b+\lambda ta)-{}_aD_q^3\theta((1-\lambda t)a+\lambda tb)]d_qt, \tag{2}
$$

where

$$
\begin{aligned}
{}_a^bP_q(\lambda) &= \frac{[2]_q[3]_q}{2\lambda(b-a)}\left[\int_{\lambda a+(1-\lambda)b}^{b}\theta(t)^b d_qt+\int_a^{\lambda b+(1-\lambda a)}\theta(t)_a d_qt\right] \\
&- \frac{1-q[2]_q[3]_q(1-q)}{2(1-q)^2}[\theta(\lambda a+(1-\lambda)b)+\theta(\lambda b+(1-\lambda)a)] \\
&- \frac{q(1-q[3]_q)}{2(1-q)^2}[\theta(q\lambda a+(1-q\lambda)b)+\theta(q\lambda b+(1-q\lambda)a)] \\
&- \frac{q^2}{2(1-q)^2}[\theta(q^2\lambda a+(1-q^2\lambda)b)+\theta(q^2\lambda b+(1-q^2\lambda)a)].
\end{aligned}
$$

Proof. Using Definition 1, Definition 3 and calculus, we obtain

$$
\begin{aligned}
I_1 &= \int_0^1 t^{3b}D_q^3\theta((1-\lambda t)b+\lambda ta)d_qt \\
&= \int_0^1 \frac{1}{q^3(1-q)^3\lambda^3(b-a)^3}[\theta(q^3\lambda ta+b(1-q^3\lambda t))-[3]_q\theta(q^2\lambda ta+b(1-q^2\lambda t) \\
&+ q[3]_q\theta(q\lambda ta+b(1-q\lambda t))-q^3\theta(\lambda ta+(1-\lambda t)b)]d_qt \\
&= \frac{1}{(b-a)^3\lambda^3q^3(1-q)^2}\left[\sum_{n=0}^{\infty}q^n\theta(q^{n+3}\lambda a+b(1-q^{n+3}\lambda))\right. \\
&- [3]_q\sum_{n=0}^{\infty}q^n\theta(q^{n+2}\lambda a+b(1-q^{n+2}\lambda)) \\
&+ \left.q[3]_q\sum_{n=0}^{\infty}q^n\theta(q^{n+1}\lambda a+b(1-q^{n+1}\lambda))-q^3\sum_{n=0}^{\infty}q^n\theta(q^n\lambda a+b(1-q^n\lambda))\right] \\
&= \frac{1-q}{(b-a)^3\lambda^3q^3(1-q)^3}\left[\frac{1}{q^3}\sum_{n=3}^{\infty}q^n\theta(q^n\lambda a+b(1-q^n\lambda))-\frac{[3]_q}{q^2}\sum_{n=2}^{\infty}q^n\theta(q^n\lambda a+b(1-q^n\lambda))\right.
\end{aligned}
$$

$$
\begin{aligned}
&+ \quad [3]_q \sum_{n=1}^{\infty} q^n\theta(q^n\lambda a+b(1-q^n\lambda)) - q^3\sum_{n=0}^{\infty} q^n\theta(q^n\lambda a+b(1-q^n\lambda))] \\
&= \quad \frac{1-q}{(b-a)^3\lambda^3q^3(1-q)^3}\{\frac{1}{q^3}[\sum_{n=0}^{\infty} q^n\theta(q^n\lambda a+b(1-q^n\lambda)) - \theta(\lambda a+b(1-\lambda)) \\
&- \quad q\theta(q\lambda a+b(1-q\lambda)) - q^2\theta(q^2\lambda a+b(1-q^2\lambda))] \\
&- \quad \frac{[3]_q}{q^2}[\sum_{n=0}^{\infty} q^n\theta(q^n\lambda a+b(1-q^n\lambda)) - \theta(\lambda a+b(1-\lambda)) - q\theta(q\lambda a+b(1-q\lambda))] \\
&+ \quad [3]_q[\sum_{n=0}^{\infty} q^n\theta(q^n\lambda a+b(1-q^n\lambda)) - \theta(\lambda a+b(1-\lambda))] - q^3\sum_{n=0}^{\infty} q^n\theta(q^n\lambda a+b(1-q^n\lambda))]\} \\
&= \quad \frac{1}{(b-a)^4\lambda^4q^3(1-q)^3}\left(\frac{1}{q^3}-\frac{[3]_q}{q^2}+[3]_q-q^3\right)\int_{\lambda a+b(1-\lambda)}^{b} \theta(t)\,{}^{b}d_qt \\
&- \quad \frac{1}{(b-a)^3\lambda^3q^3(1-q)^2}\left(\frac{1}{q^3}-\frac{[3]_q}{q^2}+[3]_q\right)\theta(\lambda a+b(1-\lambda)) \\
&- \quad \frac{1}{(b-a)^3\lambda^3q^5(1-q)^2}(1-q[3]_q)\theta(q\lambda a+b(1-q\lambda)) \\
&- \quad \frac{1}{(b-a)^3\lambda^3q^4(1-q)^2}\theta(q^2\lambda a+b(1-q^2\lambda)).
\end{aligned}
$$

In the same way, from Definition 2, Definition 4 and calculus, we obtain

$$
\begin{aligned}
I_2 \quad &= \quad \int_0^1 t^3\,{}_aD_q^3\theta((1-\lambda t)a+\lambda tb)d_qt \\
&= \quad \int_0^1 \frac{1}{q^3(1-q)^3\lambda^3(b-a)^3}[-\theta(q^3\lambda tb+a(1-q^3\lambda t)) + [3]_q\theta(q^2\lambda tb+a(1-q^2\lambda t) \\
&- \quad q[3]_q\theta(q\lambda tb+a(1-q\lambda t)) + q^3\theta(\lambda tb+(1-\lambda t)a)]d_qt \\
&= \quad \frac{1}{(b-a)^3\lambda^3q^3(1-q)^2}[-\sum_{n=0}^{\infty} q^n\theta(q^{n+3}\lambda b+a(1-q^{n+3}\lambda)) \\
&+ \quad [3]_q\sum_{n=0}^{\infty} q^n\theta(q^{n+2}\lambda b+a(1-q^{n+2}\lambda)) \\
&- \quad q[3]_q\sum_{n=0}^{\infty} q^n\theta(q^{n+1}\lambda b+a(1-q^{n+1}\lambda)) + q^3\sum_{n=0}^{\infty} q^n\theta(q^n\lambda b+a(1-q^n\lambda))] \\
&= \quad \frac{1-q}{(b-a)^3\lambda^3q^3(1-q)^3}[-\frac{1}{q^3}\sum_{n=3}^{\infty} q^n\theta(q^n\lambda b+a(1-q^n\lambda)) \\
&+ \quad \frac{[3]_q}{q^2}\sum_{n=2}^{\infty} q^n\theta(q^n\lambda b+a(1-q^n\lambda)) - [3]_q\sum_{n=1}^{\infty} q^n\theta(q^n\lambda b+a(1-q^n\lambda)) \\
&+ \quad q^3\sum_{n=0}^{\infty} q^n\theta(q^n\lambda b+a(1-q^n\lambda))] \\
&= \quad \frac{1-q}{(b-a)^3\lambda^3q^3(1-q)^3}\{-\frac{1}{q^3}[\sum_{n=0}^{\infty} q^n\theta(q^n\lambda b+a(1-q^n\lambda)) - \theta(\lambda b+a(1-\lambda)) \\
&-q \quad \theta(q\lambda b+a(1-q\lambda)) - q^2\theta(q^2\lambda b+a(1-q^2\lambda))] + \frac{[3]_q}{q^2}[\sum_{n=0}^{\infty} q^n\theta(q^n\lambda b+a(1-q^n\lambda)) \\
&- \quad \theta(\lambda b+a(1-\lambda)) - q\theta(q\lambda b+a(1-q\lambda))]
\end{aligned}
$$

$$
\begin{aligned}
&- \quad [3]_q[\sum_{n=0}^{\infty} q^n\theta(q^n\lambda b + a(1-q^n\lambda)) - \theta(\lambda b + a(1-\lambda))] + q^3\sum_{n=0}^{\infty} q^n\theta(q^n\lambda b + a(1-q^n\lambda))]\} \\
&= \quad \frac{1}{(b-a)^4\lambda^4 q^3(1-q)^3}\left(-\frac{1}{q^3} + \frac{[3]_q}{q^2} - [3]_q + q^3\right)\int_a^{\lambda b + a(1-\lambda)} \theta(t)_a d_q t \\
&+ \quad \frac{1}{(b-a)^3\lambda^3 q^3(1-q)^2}\left(\frac{1}{q^3} - \frac{[3]_q}{q^2} + [3]_q\right)\theta(\lambda b + a(1-\lambda)) \\
&+ \quad \frac{1}{(b-a)^3\lambda^3 q^5(1-q)^2}(1-q[3]_q)\theta(q\lambda b + a(1-q\lambda)) \\
&+ \quad \frac{1}{(b-a)^3\lambda^3 q^4(1-q)^2}\theta(q^2\lambda b + a(1-q^2\lambda)).
\end{aligned}
$$

By subtracting I_2 from I_1 and multiplying the result by $\frac{\lambda^3 q^6(b-a)^3}{2}$, it follows that

$$
\begin{aligned}
\frac{\lambda^3 q^6(b-a)^3}{2}(I_1 - I_2) &= \frac{[2]_q[3]_q}{2\lambda(b-a)}[\int_{\lambda a+(1-\lambda)b}^{b} \theta(t)^b d_q t + \int_a^{\lambda b+(1-\lambda)a} \theta(t)_a d_q t] \\
&- \frac{1-q[2]_q[3]_q(1-q)}{2(1-q)^2}[\theta(\lambda a + b(1-\lambda)) + \theta(\lambda b + a(1-\lambda))] \\
&- \frac{q(1-q[3]_q)}{2(1-q)^2}[\theta(q\lambda a + b(1-q\lambda)) + \theta(q\lambda b + a(1-q\lambda))] \\
&- \frac{q^2}{2(1-q)^2}[\theta(q^2\lambda a + b(1-q^2\lambda)) + \theta(q^2\lambda b + a(1-q^2\lambda))],
\end{aligned}
$$

and thus, the proof is complete. □

Theorem 4. *We assume that the hypotheses of Lemma 1 are satisfied. If* $|_aD_q^3\theta|$ *and* $|^bD_q^3\theta|$ *are convex on* $[a,b]$ *then the following inequality holds:*

$$
\begin{aligned}
|_a^b P_q(\lambda)| &= |\frac{[2]_q[3]_q}{2\lambda(b-a)}[\int_{\lambda a+(1-\lambda)b}^{b} \theta(t)^b d_q t + \int_a^{\lambda b+(1-\lambda a)} \theta(t)_a d_q t] \\
&- \frac{1-q[2]_q[3]_q(1-q)}{2(1-q)^2}[\theta(\lambda a + (1-\lambda)b) + \theta(\lambda b + (1-\lambda)a)] \\
&- \frac{q(1-q[3]_q)}{2(1-q)^2}[\theta(q\lambda a + (1-q\lambda)b) + \theta(q\lambda b + (1-q\lambda)a)] \\
&- \frac{q^2}{2(1-q)^2}[\theta(q^2\lambda a + (1-q^2\lambda)b) + \theta(q^2\lambda b + (1-q^2\lambda)a)]| \\
&\leq \frac{\lambda^3 q^6(b-a)^3}{2[4]_q[5]_q}\{([5]_q - \lambda[4]_q)[|^bD_q^3\theta(b)| + |_aD_q^3\theta(a)|] \\
&\quad +\lambda[4]_q[|^bD_q^3\theta(a)| + |_aD_q^3\theta(b)|]\}. \qquad (3)
\end{aligned}
$$

Proof. By using Lemma 1, we obtain

$$\begin{aligned}
|{}_a^bP_q(\lambda)| &= |\frac{[2]_q[3]_q}{2\lambda(b-a)}[\int_{\lambda a+(1-\lambda)b}^{b}\theta(t)^b d_qt + \int_a^{\lambda b+(1-\lambda a)}\theta(t)_a d_qt] \\
&- \frac{1-q[2]_q[3]_q(1-q)}{2(1-q)^2}[\theta(\lambda a+(1-\lambda)b)+\theta(\lambda b+(1-\lambda)a)] \\
&- \frac{q(1-q[3]_q)}{2(1-q)^2}[\theta(q\lambda a+(1-q\lambda)b)+\theta(q\lambda b+(1-q\lambda)a)] \\
&- \frac{q^2}{2(1-q)^2}[\theta(q^2\lambda a+(1-q^2\lambda)b)+\theta(q^2\lambda b+(1-q^2\lambda)a)]| \\
&\leq \frac{\lambda^3q^6(b-a)^3}{2}\{\int_0^1 t^3|{}^bD_q^3\theta((1-\lambda t)b+\lambda ta)|d_qt \\
&+ \int_0^1 t^3|{}_aD_q^3\theta((1-\lambda t)a+\lambda tb)|d_qt\}
\end{aligned}$$

and then with the help of convexity of $|{}_aD_q^3\theta|$ and $|{}^bD_q^3\theta|$, we have

$$\begin{aligned}
|{}_a^bP_q(\lambda)| &\leq \frac{\lambda^3q^6(b-a)^3}{2}\{\int_0^1 t^3[(1-\lambda t)|{}^bD_q^3\theta(b)|+\lambda t|{}^bD_q^3\theta(a)|]d_qt \\
&+ \int_0^1 t^3[(1-\lambda t)|{}_aD_q^3\theta(a)|+\lambda t|{}_aD_q^3\theta(b)|]d_qt\} \\
&= \frac{\lambda^3q^6(b-a)^3}{2}\{[|{}^bD_q^3\theta(b)|+|{}_aD_q^3\theta(a)|]\int_0^1 t^3(1-\lambda t)d_qt \\
&+ [|{}^bD_q^3\theta(a)|+|{}_aD_q^3\theta(b)|]\int_0^1 t^4\lambda d_qt\} \\
&= \frac{\lambda^3q^6(b-a)^3}{2}\{(\frac{1}{[4]_q}-\frac{\lambda}{[5]_q})[|{}^bD_q^3\theta(b)|+|{}_aD_q^3\theta(a)|] \\
&+ \frac{\lambda}{[5]_q}[|{}^bD_q^3\theta(a)|+|{}_aD_q^3\theta(b)|]\}.
\end{aligned}$$

Using calculus we obtain the desired inequality. □

Remark 1. *If we take $\lambda = 1$ in Theorem 4, the following trapezoid-type inequality is obtained:*

$$\begin{aligned}
|{}_a^bP_q(1)| &= |\frac{[2]_q[3]_q}{2(b-a)}[\int_a^b\theta(t)^b d_qt+\int_a^b\theta(t)_a d_qt] - \frac{1-q[2]_q[3]_q(1-q)}{2(1-q)^2}[\theta(a)+\theta(b)] \\
&- \frac{q(1-q[3]_q)}{2(1-q)^2}[\theta(qa+(1-q)b)+\theta(qb+(1-q)a)] \\
&- \frac{q^2}{2(1-q)^2}[\theta(q^2a+(1-q^2)b)+\theta(q^2b+(1-q^2)a)]| \\
&\leq \frac{q^6(b-a)^3}{2[4]_q[5]_q}\{([5]_q-[4]_q)[|{}^bD_q^3\theta(b)|+|{}_aD_q^3\theta(a)|]+[4]_q[|{}^bD_q^3\theta(a)|+|{}_aD_q^3\theta(b)|]\}.
\end{aligned}$$

Remark 2. *If we assign $\lambda = \frac{1}{2}$ in Theorem 4, then the following midpoint-type inequality is obtained:*

$$
\begin{aligned}
|{}_a^bP_q(\frac{1}{2})| &= |\frac{[2]_q[3]_q}{(b-a)}[\int_{\frac{a+b}{2}}^{b} \theta(t)^b d_qt + \int_a^{\frac{a+b}{2}} \theta(t)_a d_qt] - \frac{1-q[2]_q[3]_q(1-q)}{2(1-q)^2}\theta(\frac{a+b}{2}) \\
&- \frac{q(1-q[3]_q)}{2(1-q)^2}[\theta(\frac{q}{2}a + (1-\frac{q}{2})b) + \theta(\frac{q}{2}b + (1-\frac{q}{2})a)] \\
&- \frac{q^2}{2(1-q)^2}[\theta(\frac{q^2}{2}a + (1-\frac{q^2}{2})b) + \theta(\frac{q^2}{2}b + (1-\frac{q^2}{2})a)]| \\
&\leq \frac{q^6(b-a)^3}{32[4]_q[5]_q}\{(2[5]_q - [4]_q)[|{}^bD_q^3\theta(b)| + |{}_aD_q^3\theta(a)|] + [4]_q[|{}^bD_q^3\theta(a)| + |{}_aD_q^3\theta(b)|]\}.
\end{aligned}
$$

Remark 3. *If we assign $\lambda = \frac{1}{[2]_q}$ in Theorem 4, then the following inequality is obtained:*

$$
\begin{aligned}
|{}_a^bP_q(\frac{1}{[2]_q})| &= |\frac{[2]_q^2[3]_q}{2(b-a)}[\int_{\frac{a+qb}{[2]_q}}^{b} \theta(t)^b d_qt + \int_a^{\frac{qa+b}{[2]_q}} \theta(t)_a d_qt] - \frac{1-q[2]_q[3]_q(1-q)}{2(1-q)^2}[\theta(\frac{a+qb}{[2]_q}) \\
&+ \theta(\frac{qa+b}{[2]_q})] - \frac{q(1-q[3]_q)}{2(1-q)^2}[\theta(\frac{qa+b}{[2]_q}) + \theta(\frac{qb+a}{[2]_q})] \\
&- \frac{q^2}{2(1-q)^2}[\theta(\frac{q^2a + b([2]_q - q^2)}{[2]_q}) + \theta(\frac{q^2b + a([2]_q - q^2)}{[2]_q})]| \\
&\leq \frac{q^6(b-a)^3}{2[2]_q^4[4]_q[5]_q}\{([2]_q[5]_q - [4]_q)[|{}^bD_q^3\theta(b)| + |{}_aD_q^3\theta(a)|] \\
&+ [4]_q[|{}^bD_q^3\theta(a)| + |{}_aD_q^3\theta(b)|]\}.
\end{aligned}
$$

Theorem 5. *We assume that the conditions from Lemma 1 hold. If $|{}_aD_q^3\theta|^s$ and $|{}^bD_q^3\theta|^s$ are convex functions when $s > 1$ then the following inequality holds:*

$$
\begin{aligned}
|{}_a^bP_q(\lambda)| &\leq \frac{\lambda^3q^6(b-a)^3}{2}\left(\frac{1}{[3r+1]_q}\right)^{\frac{1}{r}}\{[\frac{[2]_q-\lambda}{[2]_q}|{}^bD_q^3\theta(b)|^s + \frac{\lambda}{[2]_q}|{}^bD_q^3\theta(a)|^s]^{\frac{1}{s}} \\
&+ [\frac{[2]_q-\lambda}{[2]_q}|{}_aD_q^3\theta(a)|^s + \frac{\lambda}{[2]_q}|{}_aD_q^3\theta(b)|^s]^{\frac{1}{s}}\},
\end{aligned}
$$

where $\frac{1}{s} + \frac{1}{r} = 1$.

Proof. This time, the parameters will be applied to Holder's inequality after being used before the modulus properties in Theorem 4, obtaining:

$$
\begin{aligned}
|{}_a^bP_q(\lambda)| &\leq \frac{\lambda^3q^6(b-a)^3}{2}\{\int_0^1 t^3|{}^bD_q^3\theta((1-\lambda t)b + \lambda ta)|d_qt \\
&+ \int_0^1 t^3|{}_aD_q^3\theta((1-\lambda t)a + \lambda tb)|d_qt\} \\
&\leq \frac{\lambda^3q^6(b-a)^3}{2}[\left(\int_0^1 t^{3r}d_qt\right)^{\frac{1}{r}}\left(\int_0^1 |{}^bD_q^3\theta((1-\lambda t)b + \lambda ta)|^s d_qt\right)^{\frac{1}{s}} \\
&+ \left(\int_0^1 t^{3r}d_qt\right)^{\frac{1}{r}}\left(\int_0^1 |{}_aD_q^3\theta((1-\lambda t)a + \lambda tb)|^s d_qt\right)^{\frac{1}{s}}].
\end{aligned}
$$

Now we use the convex functions $|{}_aD_q^3\theta|^s$ and $|{}^bD_q^3\theta|^s$ to obtain

$$
\begin{aligned}
|{}_a^bP_q(\lambda)| &\le \frac{\lambda^3 q^6 (b-a)^3}{2}\left(\frac{1}{[3r+1]_q}\right)^{\frac{1}{r}}[\left(\int_0^1 (1-\lambda t)|{}^bD_q^3\theta(b)|^s d_qt + \int_0^1 \lambda t|{}^bD_q^3\theta(a)|^s d_qt\right)^{\frac{1}{s}} \\
&+ \left(\int_0^1 (1-\lambda t)|{}_aD_q^3\theta(a)|^s d_qt + \int_0^1 \lambda t|{}_aD_q^3\theta(b)|^s d_qt\right)^{\frac{1}{s}}] \\
&= \frac{\lambda^3 q^6 (b-a)^3}{2}\left(\frac{1}{[3r+1]_q}\right)^{\frac{1}{r}}\{[\frac{[2]_q-\lambda}{[2]_q}|{}^bD_q^3\theta(b)|^s + \frac{\lambda}{[2]_q}|{}^bD_q^3\theta(a)|^s]^{\frac{1}{s}} \\
&+ [\frac{[2]_q-\lambda}{[2]_q}|{}_aD_q^3\theta(a)|^s + \frac{\lambda}{[2]_q}|{}_aD_q^3\theta(b)|^s]^{\frac{1}{s}}\},
\end{aligned}
$$

which completes the proof. □

Remark 4. *If we assign $\lambda = 1$ in Theorem 5, then the following trapezoid-type inequality is obtained:*

$$
\begin{aligned}
|{}_a^bP_q(1)| &= |\frac{[2]_q[3]_q}{2(b-a)}[\int_a^b \theta(t)\,{}^bd_qt + \int_a^b \theta(t)\,{}_ad_qt] - \frac{1-q[2]_q[3]_q(1-q)}{2(1-q)^2}[\theta(a)+\theta(b)] \\
&- \frac{q(1-q[3]_q)}{2(1-q)^2}[\theta(qa+(1-q)b)+\theta(qb+(1-q)a)] \\
&- \frac{q^2}{2(1-q)^2}[\theta(q^2a+(1-q^2)b)+\theta(q^2b+(1-q^2)a)]| \\
&\le \frac{q^6(b-a)^3}{2}\left(\frac{1}{[3r+1]_q}\right)^{\frac{1}{r}}\{[\frac{[2]_q-1}{[2]_q}|{}^bD_q^3\theta(b)|^s + \frac{1}{[2]_q}|{}^bD_q^3\theta(a)|^s]^{\frac{1}{s}} \\
&+ [\frac{[2]_q-1}{[2]_q}|{}_aD_q^3\theta(a)|^s + \frac{1}{[2]_q}|{}_aD_q^3\theta(b)|^s]^{\frac{1}{s}}\}.
\end{aligned}
$$

Remark 5. *If we assign $\lambda = \frac{1}{2}$ in Theorem 5, then the following midpoint-type inequality is obtained:*

$$
\begin{aligned}
|{}_a^bP_q(\tfrac{1}{2})| &= |\frac{[2]_q[3]_q}{(b-a)}[\int_{\frac{a+b}{2}}^b \theta(t)\,{}^bd_qt + \int_a^{\frac{a+b}{2}} \theta(t)\,{}_ad_qt] - \frac{1-q[2]_q[3]_q(1-q)}{2(1-q)^2}\theta(\frac{a+b}{2}) \\
&- \frac{q(1-q[3]_q)}{2(1-q)^2}[\theta(\frac{q}{2}a+(1-\frac{q}{2})b)+\theta(\frac{q}{2}b+(1-\frac{q}{2})a)] \\
&- \frac{q^2}{2(1-q)^2}[\theta(\frac{q^2}{2}a+(1-\frac{q^2}{2})b)+\theta(\frac{q^2}{2}b+(1-\frac{q^2}{2})a)]| \\
&\le \frac{q^6(b-a)^3}{16}\left(\frac{1}{[2]_q}\right)^{\frac{1}{s}}\left(\frac{1}{[3r+1]_q}\right)^{\frac{1}{r}}\{[(2[2]_q-1)|{}^bD_q^3\theta(b)|^s + |{}^bD_q^3\theta(a)|^s]^{\frac{1}{s}} \\
&+ [(2[2]_q-1)||{}_aD_q^3\theta(a)|^s + |{}_aD_q^3\theta(b)|^s]^{\frac{1}{s}}\}.
\end{aligned}
$$

Theorem 6. *We assume that the conditions from Lemma 1 hold. If $|{}_aD_q^3\theta|^s$ and $|{}^bD_q^3\theta|^s$ are convex functions for $s \ge 1$, then the following inequality holds:*

$$
\begin{aligned}
|{}_a^bP_q(\lambda)| &\le \frac{\lambda^3 q^6 (b-a)^3}{2[4]_q[5]_q^{\frac{1}{s}}} \\
&\times \{[([5]_q-\lambda[4]_q)|{}^bD_q^3\theta(b)|^s + \lambda[4]_q|{}^bD_q^3\theta(a)|^s]^{\frac{1}{s}} \\
&+ [([5]_q-\lambda[4]_q)|{}_aD_q^3\theta(a)|^s + \lambda[4]_q|{}_aD_q^3\theta(b)|^s]^{\frac{1}{s}}\}.
\end{aligned}
$$

Proof. By applying the properties of modulus and the power mean inequality we obtain,

$$|{}_a^bP_q(\lambda)| \leq \frac{\lambda^3 q^6 (b-a)^3}{2}\{\left(\int_0^1 t^3 d_q t\right)^{1-\frac{1}{s}}\left(\int_0^1 t^3 |{}^bD_q^3\theta((1-\lambda t)b+\lambda ta)|^s d_q t\right)^{\frac{1}{s}}$$

$$+\left(\int_0^1 t^3 d_q t\right)^{1-\frac{1}{s}}\left(\int_0^1 t^3 |{}_aD_q^3\theta((1-\lambda t)a+\lambda tb)|^s d_q t\right)^{\frac{1}{s}}\}.$$

By using the convexity of the functions $|{}_aD_q^3\theta|^s$ and $|{}^bD_q^3\theta|^s$ we have,

$$\begin{aligned}
|{}_a^bP_q(\lambda)| \leq & \frac{\lambda^3 q^6 (b-a)^3}{2}\frac{1}{[4]_q^{1-\frac{1}{s}}}\{\left(\int_0^1 (t^3(1-\lambda t))|{}^bD_q^3\theta(b)|^s + \lambda t^4 |{}^bD_q^3\theta(a)|^s) d_q t\right)^{\frac{1}{s}} \\
+ & \left(\int_0^1 (t^3(1-\lambda t))|{}_aD_q^3\theta(a)|^s + \lambda t^4 |{}_aD_q^3\theta(b)|^s) d_q t\right)^{\frac{1}{s}}\} \\
= & \frac{\lambda^3 q^6 (b-a)^3}{2}\frac{1}{[4]_q^{1-\frac{1}{s}}}\{[(\frac{1}{[4]_q}-\frac{\lambda}{[5]_q})|{}^bD_q^3\theta(b)|^s + \frac{\lambda}{[5]_q}|{}^bD_q^3\theta(a)|^s]^{\frac{1}{s}} \\
+ & [(\frac{1}{[4]_q}-\frac{\lambda}{[5]_q})|{}_aD_q^3\theta(a)|^s + \frac{\lambda}{[5]_q}|{}_aD_q^3\theta(b)|^s)]^{\frac{1}{s}}\} \\
= & \frac{\lambda^3 q^6 (b-a)^3}{2[4]_q[5]_q^{\frac{1}{s}}}\{[([5]_q-\lambda[4]_q)|{}^bD_q^3\theta(b)|^s + \lambda[4]_q|{}^bD_q^3\theta(a)|^s]^{\frac{1}{s}} \\
+ & [([5]_q-\lambda[4]_q)|{}_aD_q^3\theta(a)|^s + \lambda[4]_q|{}_aD_q^3\theta(b)|^s)]^{\frac{1}{s}}\}.
\end{aligned}$$

Therefore, the proof is complete. □

Remark 6. *If we take $\lambda = 1$ in Theorem 6, then the following trapezoid-type inequality is obtained:*

$$\begin{aligned}
|{}_a^bP_q(1)| = & |\frac{[2]_q[3]_q}{2(b-a)}[\int_a^b \theta(t)^b d_q t + \int_a^b \theta(t)_a d_q t] - \frac{1-q[2]_q[3]_q(1-q)}{2(1-q)^2}[\theta(a)+\theta(b)] \\
- & \frac{q(1-q[3]_q)}{2(1-q)^2}[\theta(qa+(1-q)b)+\theta(qb+(1-q)a)] \\
- & \frac{q^2}{2(1-q)^2}[\theta(q^2a+(1-q^2)b)+\theta(q^2b+(1-q^2)a)]| \\
\leq & \frac{q^6(b-a)^3}{2[4]_q[5]_q^{\frac{1}{s}}}\{[([5]_q-[4]_q)|{}^bD_q^3\theta(b)|^s + [4]_q|{}^bD_q^3\theta(a)|^s]^{\frac{1}{s}} \\
+ & [([5]_q-[4]_q)|{}_aD_q^3\theta(a)|^s + [4]_q|{}_aD_q^3\theta(b)|^s]^{\frac{1}{s}}\}.
\end{aligned}$$

Remark 7. *If we take $\lambda = \frac{1}{2}$ in Theorem 6, then the following midpoint-type inequality holds:*

$$\begin{aligned}
|{}_a^bP_q(\frac{1}{2})| = & |\frac{[2]_q[3]_q}{(b-a)}[\int_{\frac{a+b}{2}}^b \theta(t)^b d_q t + \int_a^{\frac{a+b}{2}} \theta(t)_a d_q t] - \frac{1-q[2]_q[3]_q(1-q)}{2(1-q)^2}\theta(\frac{a+b}{2}) \\
- & \frac{q(1-q[3]_q)}{2(1-q)^2}[\theta(\frac{q}{2}a+(1-\frac{q}{2})b)+\theta(\frac{q}{2}b+(1-\frac{q}{2})a)] \\
- & \frac{q^2}{2(1-q)^2}[\theta(\frac{q^2}{2}a+(1-\frac{q^2}{2})b)+\theta(\frac{q^2}{2}b+(1-\frac{q^2}{2})a)]| \\
\leq & \frac{q^6(b-a)^3}{16[2]_q^{\frac{1}{s}}[4]_q[5]_q^{\frac{1}{s}}}\{[(2[5]_q-[4]_q)|{}^bD_q^3\theta(b)|^s + [4]_q|{}^bD_q^3\theta(a)|^s]^{\frac{1}{s}} \\
+ & [(2[5]_q-[4]_q)|{}_aD_q^3\theta(a)|^s + [4]_q|{}_aD_q^3\theta(b)|^s]^{\frac{1}{s}}\}.
\end{aligned}$$

Example 1. *Let us consider the convex function $\theta : [0,1] \to \mathbb{R}$ defined by $\theta(x) = x^5$ and $\lambda = 1$, which satisfies the conditions of Theorem 4. Using calculus, under these assumptions, we obtain for the left-hand side of inequality (3), the expression,*

$$|\frac{[2]_q[3]_q}{2}[\int_0^1 \theta(t)^1 d_q t + \int_0^1 \theta(t)_0 d_q t] - \frac{1 - q[2]_q[3]_q(1-q)}{2(1-q)^2}[\theta(0) + \theta(1)]$$

$$\begin{aligned}
&- \frac{q(1-q[3]_q)}{2(1-q)^2}[\theta(1-q) + \theta(q)] - \frac{q^2}{2(1-q)^2}[\theta(1-q^2) + \theta(q^2)]| \\
&= |\frac{[2]_q[3]_q}{2}[\int_0^1 t^{51} d_q t + \int_0^1 t^5{}_0 d_q t] - \frac{1 - q[2]_q[3]_q(1-q)}{2(1-q)^2} \\
&- \frac{q(1-q[3]_q)}{2(1-q)^2}[(1-q)^5 + q^5] - \frac{q^2}{2(1-q)^2}[(1-q^2)^5 + q^{10}]| \\
&= |\frac{[2]_q[3]_q}{2}(1-q)[\sum_0^\infty q^n(1-q^n)^5 + \sum_0^\infty q^{6n}] - \frac{1 - q[2]_q[3]_q(1-q)}{2(1-q)^2} \\
&- \frac{q(1-q[3]_q)}{2(1-q)^2}[(1-q)^5 + q^5] - \frac{q^2}{2(1-q)^2}[(1-q^2)^5 + q^{10}]| \\
&= |\frac{[2]_q[3]_q}{2}[1 - \frac{5}{[2]_q} + \frac{10}{[3]_q} - \frac{10}{[4]_q} + \frac{5}{[5]_q}] - \frac{1 - q[2]_q[3]_q(1-q)}{2(1-q)^2} \\
&- \frac{q(1-q[3]_q)}{2(1-q)^2}[(1-q)^5 + q^5] - \frac{q^2}{2(1-q)^2}[(1-q^2)^5 + q^{10}]|.
\end{aligned}$$

Then, using calculus, the right-hand side of inequality (3) becomes:

$$\frac{q^6}{2[4]_q[5]_q}\{([5]_q - [4]_q)[|^1D_q^3\theta(1)| + |_0D_q^3\theta(0)|] + [4]_q[|^1D_q^3\theta(0)| + |_0D_q^3\theta(1)|]\}.$$

Thus, in this case inequality (3) becomes,

$$\begin{aligned}
&|\frac{[2]_q[3]_q}{2}[1 - \frac{5}{[2]_q} + \frac{10}{[3]_q} - \frac{10}{[4]_q} + \frac{5}{[5]_q}] - \frac{1 - q[2]_q[3]_q(1-q)}{2(1-q)^2} \\
&- \frac{q(1-q[3]_q)}{2(1-q)^2}[(1-q)^5 + q^5] - \frac{q^2}{2(1-q)^2}[(1-q^2)^5 + q^{10}]| \\
&\le \frac{q^6}{2[4]_q[5]_q}\{([5]_q - [4]_q)[|^1D_q^3\theta(1)| + |_0D_q^3\theta(0)|] + [4]_q[|^1D_q^3\theta(0)| + |_0D_q^3\theta(1)|]\}. \quad (4)
\end{aligned}$$

On the other hand we have, ${}_0D_q^3\theta(x) = [5]_q[4]_q[3]_q x^2$,; therefore, ${}_0D_q^3\theta(0) = 0$ and ${}_0D_q^3\theta(1) = [5]_q[4]_q[3]_q$. Using this in our case gives,

$${}^1D_q^3\theta(x) = \frac{(q^3x + 1 - q^3)^5 - [3]_q(q^2x + 1 - q^2)^5 + q[3]_q(qx + 1 - q)^5 - q^3x^5}{q^3(1-q)^3(1-x)^3}$$

finding that ${}^1D_q^3\theta(0) = q^9 + 3q^8 + 6q^7 + 4q^6 - 4q^5 - 14q^4 - 11q^3 + q^2 + 8q + 6$ and ${}^1D_q^3\theta(1) = 10(q^3 + 2q^2 + 2q + 1)$.

One can see the validity of inequality (4) in Figure 1, where the red line represents the left term of inequality (4) and the right term is represented by the blue line in the figure.

The results could be used to optimise economic geology analyses; for example, in the study of metal ore resources, fossil fuels, and other materials of commercial value.

Here the Matlab R2023a software version was utilized to create Figure 1 and perform partial calculus operations of last two derivatives.

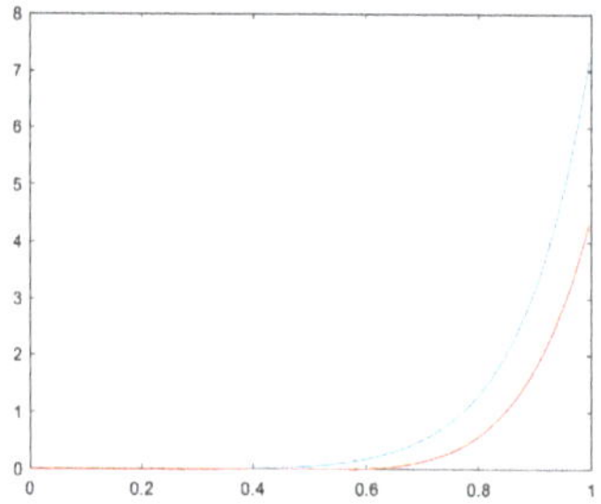

Figure 1. An example for inequality (3) from Theorem 4.

Remark 8. *If we consider the same convex function $\theta : [0,1] \to \mathbb{R}$ defined by $\theta(x) = x^5$ and $\lambda = \frac{1}{2}$, or $\lambda = \frac{1}{[2]_q}$ the analogue inequalities and figures can be analysed as in Example 1.*

Some important applications to the special means of real numbers can be found in [38], where the definitions of the arithmetic mean, harmonic mean and geometric mean are discussed. Similar inequalities can be obtained in our case and we formulate these results for the arithmetic mean.

Remark 9. *If we assume $|_aD_q^3\theta| \leq M$ and $|^bD_q^3\theta| \leq M$ in Remark 1, we obtain*

$$\begin{aligned}
&|\frac{[2]_q[3]_q}{2(b-a)}[\int_a^b \theta(t)^b d_qt + \int_a^b \theta(t)_a d_qt] - \frac{1-q[2]_q[3]_q(1-q)}{2(1-q)^2}[\theta(a)+\theta(b)] \\
&-\frac{q(1-q[3]_q)}{2(1-q)^2}[\theta(qa+(1-q)b)+\theta(qb+(1-q)a)] \\
&-\frac{q^2}{2(1-q)^2}[\theta(q^2a+(1-q^2)b)+\theta(q^2b+(1-q^2)a)]| \leq \frac{Mq^6(b-a)^3}{[4]_q}.
\end{aligned}$$

Proposition 1. *For $a, b \in \mathbb{R}$, $a < b$ we have,*

$$\begin{aligned}
&|\frac{[2]_q[3]_q}{b-a}\mathcal{A}(\theta_1,\theta_2) - \frac{1-q[2]_q[3]_q(1-q)}{(1-q)^2}\mathcal{A}(a^5,b^5) \\
&-\frac{q(1-q[3]_q)}{(1-q)^2}\mathcal{A}((qa+(1-q)b)^5,(qb+(1-q)a)^5) \\
&-\frac{q^2}{(1-q)^2}\mathcal{A}((q^2a+(1-q^2)b)^5,(q^2b+(1-q^2)a)^5)| \leq \frac{Mq^6(b-a)^3}{[4]_q},
\end{aligned}$$

where

$$\theta_1 = (1-q)(b-a)\sum_{n=0}^{\infty} q^n(q^na+(1-q^n)b)^5$$

and

$$\theta_2 = (1-q)(b-a)\sum_{n=0}^{\infty} q^n(q^nb+(1-q^n)a)^5.$$

Proof. The inequality from Remark 9 used for the function $\theta(x) = x^5$ leads to the desired result. □

Remark 10. *If we assume* $|{}_aD_q^3\theta| \leq M$ *and* $|{}^bD_q^3\theta| \leq M$ *in Remark 2, we obtain*

$$\begin{aligned}&|\frac{[2]_q[3]_q}{(b-a)}[\int_{\frac{a+b}{2}}^{b}\theta(t)^b d_q t+\int_a^{\frac{a+b}{2}}\theta(t)_a d_q t]-\frac{1-q[2]_q[3]_q(1-q)}{2(1-q)^2}\theta(\frac{a+b}{2})\\&-\frac{q(1-q[3]_q)}{2(1-q)^2}[\theta(\frac{q}{2}a+(1-\frac{q}{2})b)+\theta(\frac{q}{2}b+(1-\frac{q}{2})a)]\\&-\frac{q^2}{2(1-q)^2}[\theta(\frac{q^2}{2}a+(1-\frac{q^2}{2})b)+\theta(\frac{q^2}{2}b+(1-\frac{q^2}{2})a)]|\leq\frac{Mq^6(b-a)^3}{8[4]_q}.\end{aligned}$$

Proposition 2. *For* $a, b \in \mathbb{R}$, $a < b$ *we have,*

$$\begin{aligned}&|\frac{2[2]_q[3]_q}{b-a}\mathcal{A}(\theta_1',\theta_2')-\frac{1-q[2]_q[3]_q(1-q)}{(1-q)^2}\mathcal{A}^5(a,b)\\&-\frac{q(1-q[3]_q)}{(1-q)^2}\mathcal{A}((\frac{q}{2}a+(1-\frac{q}{2})b)^5,(\frac{q}{2}b+(1-\frac{q}{2})a)^5)\\&-\frac{q^2}{(1-q)^2}\mathcal{A}((\frac{q^2}{2}a+(1-\frac{q^2}{2})b)^5,(\frac{q^2}{2}b+(1-\frac{q^2}{2})a)^5)|\leq\frac{Mq^6(b-a)^3}{8[4]_q},\end{aligned}$$

where

$$\theta_1'=\frac{(1-q)(b-a)}{2}\sum_{n=0}^{\infty}q^n(q^n\mathcal{A}(a,b)+(1-q^n)b)^5$$

and

$$\theta_2'=\frac{(1-q)(b-a)}{2}\sum_{n=0}^{\infty}q^n(q^n\mathcal{A}(a,b)+(1-q^n)a)^5.$$

Proof. The inequality from Remark 10 used for the function $\theta(x) = x^5$ leads to the desired result. □

Proposition 3. *For* $a, b \in \mathbb{R}$, $a < b$ *we have,*

$$\begin{aligned}&|\frac{[2]_q[3]_q}{2(b-a)}\mathcal{A}(\theta_1,\theta_2)-\frac{1-q[2]_q[3]_q(1-q)}{(1-q)^2}\mathcal{A}(a^5,b^5)\\&-\frac{q(1-q[3]_q)}{(1-q)^2}\mathcal{A}((qa+(1-q)b)^5,(qb+(1-q)a)^5)\\&-\frac{q^2}{(1-q)^2}\mathcal{A}((q^2a+(1-q^2)b)^5,(q^2b+(1-q^2)a)^5)|\leq\frac{Mq^6(b-a)^3}{[3r+1]_q^{\frac{1}{r}}},\end{aligned}$$

where

$$\theta_1=(1-q)(b-a)\sum_{n=0}^{\infty}q^n(q^na+(1-q^n)b)^5$$

and

$$\theta_2=(1-q)(b-a)\sum_{n=0}^{\infty}q^n(q^nb+(1-q^n)a)^5.$$

Proof. The inequality from Remark 4 used for the function $\theta(x) = x^5$ leads to the desired result. □

Proposition 4. *For $a, b \in \mathbb{R}$, $a < b$ we have,*

$$\begin{aligned}
&|\frac{2[2]_q[3]_q}{b-a}\mathcal{A}(\theta_1', \theta_2') - \frac{1 - q[2]_q[3]_q(1-q)}{(1-q)^2}\mathcal{A}^5(a,b) \\
&- \frac{q(1-q[3]_q)}{(1-q)^2}\mathcal{A}((\frac{q}{2}a + (1-\frac{q}{2})b)^5, (\frac{q}{2}b + (1-\frac{q}{2})a)^5) \\
&- \frac{q^2}{(1-q)^2}\mathcal{A}((\frac{q^2}{2}a + (1-\frac{q^2}{2})b)^5, (\frac{q^2}{2}b + (1-\frac{q^2}{2})a)^5)| \leq \frac{Mq^6(b-a)^3 2^{\frac{1}{s}}}{8[3r+1]_q^{\frac{1}{r}}},
\end{aligned}$$

where

$$\theta_1' = \frac{(1-q)(b-a)}{2}\sum_{n=0}^{\infty} q^n (q^n \mathcal{A}(a,b) + (1-q^n)b)^5$$

and

$$\theta_2' = \frac{(1-q)(b-a)}{2}\sum_{n=0}^{\infty} q^n (q^n \mathcal{A}(a,b) + (1-q^n)a)^5.$$

Proof. The inequality from Remark 5 for function $\theta(x) = x^5$ leads to the desired result. □

Analogue inequalities can be obtained if the function $\theta(x) = x^5$ is chosen in Remarks 6 and 7.

4. Discussion and Conclusions

In this paper, several new parametrized q-H–H-type integral inequalities were given for functions whose third left and right q-derivatives are convex. Some basic inequalities, such as quantum Holder's inequality and power mean inequality, were used to obtain new bounds and an auxiliary quantum lemma was utilized in the demonstrations. Some consequences and an example were presented to illustrate the generated results. Using Matlab, Figure 1 confirms the results obtained in Section 3. Some interesting applications to special means have been presented. Many consequences arise in certain special cases of the parameter and an interesting problem to study may be to use these methods to prove q-fractional inequalities and similar inequalities for different kinds of convexities. The present study could be used to better guide the exploration of mineral resources. In our opinion this research could be very useful in structural geology, stratigraphic optimization, economic exploitation of mineral deposits, and building materials such as stones or gypsum.

We are confident that the ideas and techniques investigated here will inspire further studies on functional analysis and statistics.

Author Contributions: Conceptualization, L.C. and E.G.; methodology, L.C.; software, L.C.; validation, L.C. and E.G.; formal analysis, L.C.; investigation, L.C. and E.G.; resources, L.C. and E.G.; data curation, L.C.; writing—original draft preparation, L.C.; writing—review and editing, L.C. and E.G.; visualization, L.C. and E.G.; supervision, L.C. and E.G.; project administration, L.C. and E.G.; funding acquisition, L.C. and E.G. All authors have read and agreed to the version of the manuscript.

Funding: This research received no external funding.

Data Availability Statement: This study did not report any data.

Conflicts of Interest: The authors declare no conflict of interest.

References

1. Cloud, M.J.; Drachman, B.C.; Lebedev, L.P. *Inequalities with Applications to Engineering*; Springer: London, UK, 2014.
2. Liao, J.G.; Berg, A. Sharpening Jensen's inequality. *Am. Stat.* **2019**, *73*, 278–281.
3. Khan, M.A.; Anwar, S.; Khalid, S.; Sayed, Z.M.M.M. Inequalities of the type Hermite-Hadamard-Jensen-Mercer for strong convexity. *Math. Probl. Eng.* **2021**, *2021*, 5386488.
4. Fridli, S.; Schipp, F. Strong approximation via Sidon type inequalities. *J. Approx. Theory* **1998**, *94*, 263–284. [CrossRef]

5. Milovanovic, G.V.; Rassias, M.T. *Analytic Number Theory, Approximation Theory and Special Functions*; Springer: Berlin/Heidelberg, Germany, 2014; p. 891.
6. Dragomir, S.S. Inequalities with applications in numerical analysis. *AIP Conf. Proc.* **2007**, *936*, 681.
7. Dragomir, S.S.; Rassias, M.T. *Ostrowski Type Inequalities and Applications in Numerical Integration*; Springer: Berlin/Heidelberg, Germany, 2013; p. 504.
8. Kalsoom, H.; Vivas-Cortez, M. q_1q_2-Ostrowski-type integral inequalities involving property of generalized higher-order strongly n-polynomial preinvexity. *Symmetry* **2022**, *14*, 717. [CrossRef]
9. Varosanec, S. On h-convexity. *J. Math. Anal. Appl.* **2007**, *326*, 303–311. [CrossRef]
10. Bernstein, S.N. Sur les fonctions absolument monotones. *Acta Math.* **1929**, *52*, 1–66. [CrossRef]
11. Avriel, M. r-Convex functions. *Math. Program.* **1972**, *2*, 309–323. [CrossRef]
12. Dragomir, S.S. On Hadamard's inequality for convex functions on the co-ordinates in a rectangle from the plane. *Taiwan J. Math.* **2001**, *5*, 775–788.
13. Alomari, M.; Latif, M.A. On Hadamard-type inequalities for h-convex functions on the co-ordinates. *Int. J. Math. Anal.* **2009**, *3*, 1645–1656.
14. Rashid, S.; Noor, M.A.; Noor, K.I. Some new estimates for exponentially (h,m)-convex functions via extended generalized fractional integral operators. *Korean J. Math.* **2019**, *27*, 843–860.
15. Iqbal, W.; Rehman, A.U.; Farid, G.; Rathour, L.; Sharma, M.K.; Mishra, N. Further on Petrovic's types inequalities. *J. Appl. Math. Inform.* **2022**, *40*, 1021–1034.
16. Pal, S.; Wong, T.K. Exponentially concave functions and a new information geometry. *Ann. Probab.* **2018**, *46*, 1070–1113. [CrossRef]
17. Hanson, M.A. On sufficiency of the Kuhn-Tucker conditions. *J. Math. Anal. Appl.* **1981**, *80*, 545–550. [CrossRef]
18. Kilbas, A.A.; Srivastava, H.M.; Trujillo, J.J. *Theory and Applications of Fractional Differential Equations; North-Holland Mathematical Studies*; Elsevier (North-Holland) Science Publishers: Amsterdam, The Netherlands; London, UK; New York, NY, USA, 2006; Volume 204.
19. Srivastava, H.M.; Karlsson, P.W. *Gaussian Hypergeometric Series*; Halsted Press (Ellis Horwood Limited, Chichester): Chichester, UK; John Wiley and Sons: New York, NY, USA; Chichester, UK; Brisbane, Australia; Toronto, ON, Canada, 1985.
20. Barnett, N.S.; Dragomir, S.S. Some elementary inequalities for the expectation and variance of a random variable whose pdf is defined on a finite interval. *RGMIA Res. Rep. Coll.* **1999**, *2*, 1–7.
21. El-Deeb, A.A.; Awrejcewicz, J. Ostrowski-trapezoidal-Gruss-type on (q,ω)-Hahn difference operator. *Symmetry* **2022**, *14*, 1776. [CrossRef]
22. Dasgupta, A.; Fajardo-Montenegro, J. Aspects of Quantum Gravity Phenomenology and Astrophysics. *Universe* **2023**, *9*, 128. [CrossRef]
23. Jackson, F.H. On q-difference equations. *Am. J. Math.* **1910**, *32*, 305–314. [CrossRef]
24. Siegel, W. *Introduction to String Field Theory. Advanced Series in Mathematical Physics*; World Scientific: Teaneck, NJ, USA, 1998; Volume 8.
25. Agarwal, R. A propos d'une note de m. pierre humbert. *Comptes Rendus De L'Academie Des Sci.* **1953**, *236*, 2031–2032.
26. Tariboon, J.; Ntouyas, S.K. Quantum calculus on finite intervals and aplications to impulsive difference equations. *Adv. Differ. Equ.* **2013**, *2013*, 282. [CrossRef]
27. Noor, M.; Noor, K.; Awan, M. Quantum Ostrowski inequalities for q-differentiable convex functions. *J. Math. Inequal.* **2016**, *10*, 1013–1018. [CrossRef]
28. Sahoo, S.K.; Kashuri, A.; Aljuaid, M.; Mishra, S.; Sen, M. On Ostrowski-Mercer's type fractional inequalities for convex functions and applications. *Fractal Fract.* **2023**, *7*, 215. [CrossRef]
29. Alp, N.; Sarikaya, M.Z.; Kunt, M.; Iscan, I. q_2-Hermite-Hadamard inequalities and quantum estimates for midpoint type inequalities via convex and quasi-convex functions. *J. King Saud Univ. Sci.* **2018**, *30*, 193–203. [CrossRef]
30. Deng, Y.; Awan, M.U.; Wu, S. Quantum Integral Inequalities of Simpson-Type for Strongly Preinvex Functions. *Mathematics* **2019**, *7*, 751. [CrossRef]
31. Deng, Y.; Kalsoom, H.; Wu, S. Some new quantum Hermite-Hadamard-Type Estimates Within a Class of Generalized (s,m)-Preinvex Functions. *Symmetry* **2019**, *10*, 1283. [CrossRef]
32. Kara, H.; Budak, H.; Alp, N.; Kalsoom, H.; Sarikaya, M.Z. On new generalized quantum integrals and related Hermite-Hadamard inequalities. *J. Inequalities Appl.* **2021**, *2021*, 180. [CrossRef]
33. Khan, A.; Chu, Y.M.; Khan, T.U.; Khan, J. Some new inequalities of Hermite-Hadamard type for s-convex functions with applications. *Open Math.* **2017**, *15*, 1414–1430. [CrossRef]
34. Latif, M.A.; Dragomir, S. New inequalities of Hermite-Hadamard type for n-times differentiable convex and concave functions with applications. *Filomat* **2016**, *30*, 2609–2621. [CrossRef]
35. Luangboon, W.; Nonlaopon, K.; Tariboon, J.; Ntouyas, S.K.; Budak, H. Post-Quantum Ostrowski type integral inequalities for twice (p,q)-differentiable functions. *J. Math. Ineq.* **2022**, *16*, 1129–1144. [CrossRef]
36. Alp, N.; Budak, H.; Sarikaya, M.Z.; Ali, M.A. On new refinements and generalizations of q-Hermite-Hadamard inequalities for convex functions. *Rocky Mountain J. Math.* **2023**. Available online: https://projecteuclid.org/journals/rmjm/rocky-mountain-journal-of-mathematics/DownloadAcceptedPapers/220708-Budak.pdf (accessed on 4 June 2023).

37. Jhanthanam, S.; Tariboon, J.; Ntouyas, S.K.; Nonlaopon, K. On q-Hermite-Hadamard inequalities for differentiable convex functions. *Mathematics* **2019**, *7*, 632. [CrossRef]
38. Zhao, D.; Ali, M.A.; Luangboon, W.; Budak, H.; Nonlaopon, K. Some Generalizations of Different Types of Quantum Integral Inequalities for Differentiable Convex Functions with Applications. *Fractal Fract.* **2022**, *6*, 129. [CrossRef]
39. Ciurdariu, L.; Grecu, E. Post-quantum integral inequalities for three-times (p,q)-differential functions. *Symmetry* **2023**, *246*, 15.
40. Hadamard, J. Etude sur les proprietes des fonctions entieres en particulier d'une fonction consideree par Riemann. *J. Math. Pures. Appl.* **1893**, *58*, 171–215.
41. Tariboon, J.; Ntouyas, S.K. Quantum integral inequalities on finite intervals. *J. Inequal. Appl.* **2014**, *13*, 121. [CrossRef]
42. Ernst, T. *A Comprehensive Treatment of q-Calculus*; Springer: Basel, Switerland, 2012.

fractal and fractional

MDPI

Article

Some Novel Inequalities for LR-(k,h-m)-p Convex Interval Valued Functions by Means of Pseudo Order Relation

Vuk Stojiljković [1,*,†], Rajagopalan Ramaswamy [2,†], Ola A. Ashour Abdelnaby [2,†] and Stojan Radenović [3]

1 Faculty of Science, University of Novi Sad, Trg Dositeja Obradovića 3, 21000 Novi Sad, Serbia
2 Department of Mathematics, College of Science and Humanities, Prince Sattam bin Abdulaziz Univeristy, Al-Kharj 16278, Saudi Arabia
3 Faculty of Mechanical Engineering, University of Belgrade, Kraljice Marije 16, 11120 Beograd, Serbia
* Correspondence: vuk.stojiljkovic999@gmail.com; Tel.: +381-640123911
† These authors contributed equally to this work.

Abstract: In this paper, a new type of convexity is defined, namely, the left–right-(k,h-m)-p IVM (set-valued function) convexity. Utilizing the definition of this new convexity, we prove the Hadamard inequalities for noninteger Katugampola integrals. These inequalities generalize the noninteger Hadamard inequalities for a convex IVM, (p,h)-convex IVM, p-convex IVM, h-convex, s-convex in the second sense and many other related well-known classes of functions implicitly. An apt number of numerical examples are provided as supplements to the derived results.

Keywords: convex set-valued functions; left–right-(k,h-m)-p-convex set-valued functions; Katugampola noninteger integral operators; Hermite–Hadamard inequality

MSC: 26D10; 26A33

Citation: Stojiljković, V.; Ramaswamy, R.; Abdelnaby, O.A.A. Radenović, S. Some Novel Inequalities for LR-(k,h-m)-p Convex Interval Valued Functions by Means of Pseudo Order Relation. *Fractal Fract.* **2022**, 6, 726. https://doi.org/10.3390/fractalfract6120726

Academic Editors: Ivanka Stamova, Eze Nwaeze and Seth Kermausuor

Received: 28 October 2022
Accepted: 6 December 2022
Published: 9 December 2022

1. Introduction

From the time when Gauss, Cauchy, Chebyshev, to mention the most important, gave a theoretical background on the approximative methods, the big theory of inequalities started to develop. At the end of the 19th century and the beginning of the 20th century, a large number of inequalities were proven, and some of them became the classics we know today, while the rest of them remained isolated results. The first book to connect all the inequalities and make them formally as the field we know today is the book Inequalities, written by Hardy et al. [1]. The book Inequalities was the first of its kind to be dedicated solely to inequalities and therefore was an instrumental book to the field. This paper concerns itself with convex inequalities, the ones using the notion of convexity introduced by Jensen. Since Jensen discovered the first convex inequality [2], various inequalities have been discovered as a consequence of Jensen's inequality [3]. A variety of applications of convex inequalities exist in, for example, the fields of numerical analysis, physics and optimization problems. The following books can be referred to for more information [4–12].

Hadamard [13] gave the following:

Let $\mathfrak{L} : \mathbb{I} \to \mathbb{R}$ be a convex function on $\mathbb{I}$ in $\mathbb{R}$ and $\omega_1, \omega_2 \in \mathbb{I}$ such that $\omega_1 < \omega_2$, then

$$\mathfrak{L}\left(\frac{\omega_1 + \omega_2}{2}\right) \leqslant \frac{1}{\omega_2 - \omega_1} \int_{\omega_1}^{\omega_2} \mathfrak{L}(t)dt \leqslant \frac{\mathfrak{L}(\omega_1) + \mathfrak{L}(\omega_2)}{2}.$$

Various generalizations have been reported over the years [14–16]. The Hermite–Hadamard inequality has been obtained using many different convex generalizations of the Jensen's inequality, see [17–19]. We apply the set-valued function setting (IVM) in tandem with convexity properties along with noninteger integral operators.

In 1695, l'Hopital sent a letter to Leibniz. In his message, an important question about the order of the derivative emerged: What might be a derivative of order $\frac{1}{2}$? That letter sparked the interest of many upcoming mathematicians to investigate further into the matter of noninteger derivatives. Then, in 1822, Fourier suggested an integral representation in order to define the derivative, and his version can be considered as the first definition of the derivative of an arbitrary positive order. Abel in 1826 solved an integral equation associated with a tautochrone problem, which was the first application of FC (noninteger calculus). After Abel, many mathematicians proceeded to work in the field such as Riemann, Grünwald and Letnikov, Hadamard, Weyl and many more. In the late half of the 20th century, Caputo formulated a definition, more restrictive than the Riemann–Liouville one but more appropriate to discuss problems involving noninteger differential equations with initial conditions. Noninteger calculus was found to be useful in physics as well; for example, Whatcraft and Meerschaert (2008) described a noninteger conservation of mass, acoustic wave equations for complex media and many others. Different types of noninteger integrals and derivatives have been defined throughout the years; we refer the interested reader to the following books [20,21] for more information on the matter. Generalizations and the usage of the noninteger calculus in the field of inequalities is also widespread, see [22–28] for more information.

One of the highly influential papers in the last year was the paper written by Khan et al. [29], which brought the notion of fuzzy convex inequalities and as such is worth to mention. The notion itself is a broad field which can be investigated further on. See the cited paper for more information thereon.

The motivation behind this paper is to introduce a new class of IVM, namely left–right-(k,h-m)-p-convex inequalities. The defined IVM inequality generalizes previously defined IVM convex inequalities. Namely, it contains in itself a previously defined p,h-convex IVM. For more information about noninteger calculus, see the following [20,21,30,31].

2. Preliminaries

We require the following definitions and monograph in the sequel:

The following notion of IVM is used, which contains sets in itself .

$$\mathbb{K}_c = \{[\mathfrak{S}_*, \mathfrak{S}^*] : \mathfrak{S}_*, \mathfrak{S}^* \in \mathbb{R} \; and \; \mathfrak{S}_* \leqslant \mathfrak{S}^*\}.$$

The range $[\mathfrak{S}_*, \mathfrak{S}^*]$ is a positive range if $\mathfrak{S}_* \geqslant 0$ and is given as follows

$$\mathbb{K}_c^+ = \{[\mathfrak{S}_*, \mathfrak{S}^*] : \mathfrak{S}_*, \mathfrak{S}^* \in \mathbb{R} \; and \; \mathfrak{S}_* \geqslant 0\}.$$

The elementary operations for $[\mathfrak{T}_*, \mathfrak{T}^*], [\mathfrak{S}_*, \mathfrak{S}^*] \in K_c$ and $\omega_6 \in \mathbb{R}$ are defined as follows:

$$[\mathfrak{T}_*, \mathfrak{T}^*] + [\mathfrak{S}_*, \mathfrak{S}^*] = [\mathfrak{T}_* + \mathfrak{S}_*, \mathfrak{T}^* + \mathfrak{S}^*],$$

$$[\mathfrak{T}_*, \mathfrak{T}^*] \cdot [\mathfrak{S}_*, \mathfrak{S}^*] = [\min\{\mathfrak{T}_*\mathfrak{S}_*, \mathfrak{T}^*\mathfrak{S}_*, \mathfrak{T}_*\mathfrak{S}^*, \mathfrak{T}^*\mathfrak{S}^*\}, \max\{\mathfrak{T}_*, \mathfrak{S}_*, \mathfrak{T}^*\mathfrak{S}_*, \mathfrak{T}_*\mathfrak{S}^*, \mathfrak{T}^*\mathfrak{S}^*\}]$$

and

$$\omega_6 \cdot [\mathfrak{T}_*, \mathfrak{T}^*] = \begin{cases} [\omega_6\mathfrak{T}_*, \omega_6\mathfrak{T}^*], (\omega_6 > 0), \\ \{0\}, (\omega_6 = 0), \\ [\omega_6\mathfrak{T}^*, \omega_6\mathfrak{T}_*], (\omega_6 < 0) \end{cases},$$

respectively, and the difference is given by

$$\mathfrak{T} - \mathfrak{S} = [\mathfrak{T}_*, \mathfrak{T}^*] - [\mathfrak{S}_*, \mathfrak{S}^*] = [\mathfrak{T}_* - \mathfrak{S}^*, \mathfrak{T}^* - \mathfrak{S}_*].$$

The mathematical notion $\mathfrak{S} \supseteq \mathfrak{T}$ gives us

$$\mathfrak{S} \supseteq \mathfrak{T} \; if \; and \; only \; if [\mathfrak{S}_*, \mathfrak{S}^*] \supseteq [\mathfrak{T}_*, \mathfrak{T}^*] \; if \; and \; only \; if [\mathfrak{T}_* \geqslant \mathfrak{S}_*, \mathfrak{S}^* \geqslant \mathfrak{T}^*]$$

Remark 1 ([32]). *The relation "$\leqslant_p$" defined on K_c by*

$$[\mathfrak{T}_*, \mathfrak{T}^*] \leqslant_p [\mathfrak{S}_*, \mathfrak{S}^*]$$

$\iff \mathfrak{T}_* \leqslant \mathfrak{S}_*, \mathfrak{T}^* \leqslant \mathfrak{S}^*$ *for all* $[\mathfrak{T}_*, \mathfrak{T}^*], [\mathfrak{S}_*, \mathfrak{S}^*] \in \mathbb{R}$ *is a pseudo-order relation; for more details, see [32].*

The integral given by Moore [32] is introduced as:

Theorem 1 ([32]). *Given* $\mathfrak{L} : [\rho_1, \rho_2] \subset \mathbb{R} \to K_c$ *a set-valued function such that*

$$\mathfrak{L}(\psi_5) = [\mathfrak{L}_*(\psi_5), \mathfrak{L}^*(\psi_5)].$$

Then, $\mathfrak{L}$ *is Riemann integrable over* $[\rho_1, \rho_2] \iff \mathfrak{L}_*$ *and* $\mathfrak{L}^*$ *are both Riemann integrable over* $[\rho_1, \rho_2]$.

$$(IR)\int_{\rho_1}^{\rho_2} \mathfrak{L}(\psi_5)d\psi_5 = \left[(R)\int_{\rho_1}^{\rho_2} \mathfrak{L}_*(\psi_5)d\psi_5, (R)\int_{\rho_1}^{\rho_2} \mathfrak{L}^*(\psi_5)d\psi_5\right]$$

Definition 1 ([33]). *For the set* $Y^\star$ *in* $\mathbb{R}$*, a function* $\mathfrak{F} : Y^\star \to \mathbb{R}$ *is convex on* $Y^\star$ *if*

$$\mathfrak{F}(\omega_6\psi_5 + (1-\omega_6)\psi_6) \leqslant \omega_6\mathfrak{F}(\psi_5) + (1-\omega_6)f(\psi_6)$$

for all $\psi_5, \psi_6 \in Y^\star$ *and* $\omega_6 \in [0,1]$ *holds and is a concave function if the inequality is of the opposite sign.*

Khan et al. [34] proposed the following:

Definition 2. *The set-valued function* $\mathscr{L} : \mathscr{W}^\star \to K_c^+$ *is left–right-convex set-valued on a convex set* $\mathscr{W}^\star$ *in all cases*$\rho_1, \rho_2 \in \mathscr{W}^\star$ *and* $\omega_6 \in [0,1]$*, we have*

$$\mathscr{L}(\omega_6\rho_1 + (1-\omega_6)\rho_2) \leqslant_p \omega_6\mathscr{L}(\rho_1) + (1-\omega_6)\mathscr{L}(\rho_2).$$

If the inequality is of the opposite sign, then $\mathscr{L}$ *is left–right-concave on* $\mathscr{W}^\star$*. Moreover,* $\mathscr{L}$ *is affine on* $\mathscr{W}^\star \iff$ *it is both left–right-convex and left–right-concave on* $\mathscr{W}^\star$*.*

Now, we introduce the concept of the Katugampola noninteger integral operator for a set-valued function.

Definition 3. *Let* $q \geqslant 1$, $c \in \mathbb{R}$ *and* $\chi_c^q(u,v)$ *be the set of all complex-valued Lebesgue integrable set-valued functions* Q *on* $[\psi_5, \psi_6]$ *for which the norm* $||Q||\chi_c^q$ *is introduced by*

$$||Q||\chi_c^q = \left(\int_u^v |n^c Q(n)|^q \frac{dn}{n}\right)^{\frac{1}{q}} < +\infty$$

for $1 \leqslant q < +\infty$ *and*

$$||Q||\chi_c^{+\infty} = ess \sup_{u \leqslant n \leqslant v} n^c |Q(n)|.$$

Katugampola [35] presented a new noninteger integral to generalize the Riemann–Liouville and Hadamard noninteger integrals under certain conditions.

Let $p, \xi_\star > 0$ *and* $\mathfrak{F} \in L[\psi_5, \psi_6]$ *be the collection of all complex-valued Lebesgue integrable IVMs on* $[\psi_5, \psi_6]$*. Then, the set of left and right Katugampola noninteger integrals of* $\mathfrak{F} \in L[\psi_5, \psi_6]$ *with order* $\xi_\star > 0$ *are introduced by*

$$J_{\psi_5^+}^{p,\xi_\star}\mathfrak{F}(x) = \frac{p^{1-\xi_\star}}{\Gamma(\xi_\star)}\int_{\psi_5}^{x}(x^p - \mu^p)^{\xi_\star - 1}\mu^{p-1}\mathfrak{F}(\mu)d\mu \quad (x > \psi_5),$$

$$J_{\psi_6^-}^{p,\xi_\star}\mathfrak{F}(x) = \frac{p^{1-\xi_\star}}{\Gamma(\xi_\star)}\int_{x}^{\psi_6}(\mu^p - x^p)^{\xi_\star - 1}\mu^{p-1}\mathfrak{F}(\mu)d\mu \quad (x < \psi_6)$$

where $\Gamma(\xi_\star) = \int_0^{+\infty} e^{-x}x^{\xi_\star - 1}dx$ *is the Euler gamma function [36]*

Zhang and Wang [37] established the concept of p-convex functions given below.

Definition 4. *Let $p \in \mathbb{R}$ with $p \neq 0$. Then, the set $\Upsilon^\star$ is p-convex if*

$$[\rho x^p + (1-\rho)y^p]^{\frac{1}{p}} \in \Upsilon^\star$$

for all $x, y \in \Upsilon^\star, \rho \in [0,1]$, where $p = 2n+1$ and $n \in \mathcal{N}$ or p is an odd number.

Definition 5. *Let $\mathbb{I}$ be a p-convex set. A function $\mathfrak{F} : \mathbb{I} \to \mathbb{R}$ is a p-convex function or belongs to the class PC(I), if*

$$\mathfrak{F}\left((\rho x^p + (1-\rho)y^p)^{\frac{1}{p}}\right) \leqslant \rho\mathfrak{F}(x) + (1-\rho)f(y)$$

for all $x, y \in [\psi_5, \psi_6]$, $\rho \in [0,1]$. If the inequality is of the opposite sign, then $\mathfrak{F}$ is called a p-concave function.

The following definition is utilized by Khan et al. to produce generalizations of the HH inequality [38–40].

Definition 6. *The IVM $\mathfrak{L} : [\psi_5, \psi_6] \to K_c^+$ is a left–right-p-convex IVM in all cases $\tau_2, \tau_3 \in [\psi_5, \psi_6]$ and $\rho \in [0,1]$ and we have*

$$\mathfrak{L}\left([\rho\tau_2^p + (1-\rho)\tau_3^p]^{\frac{1}{p}}\right) \leqslant_p \rho\mathfrak{L}(\tau_2) + (1-\rho)\mathfrak{L}(\tau_3).$$

If the inequality is of the opposite sign, then $\mathfrak{L}$ is left–right-p-concave on $[\psi_5, \psi_6]$. The set of all left–right-p-convex (left–right-p-concave) IVMs is denoted by

$$Left - RightSX([\psi_5, \psi_6], K_c^+, p) \quad (Left - RightSV([\psi_5, \psi_6], K_c^+, p)).$$

Definition 7. *Let $J \subset \mathbb{R}$ be a set having in itself $(0,1)$ and let $\tau : J \to \mathbb{R}$ be a positive function, including zero. Let $\mathbb{I} \subset (0, +\infty)$ be a set and $p \in \mathbb{R} - 0$. A function $\mathscr{L} : \mathbb{I} \to \mathbb{R}$ is $(k, h\text{-}m)$-p convex, if*

$$\mathscr{L}\left([x^p\xi_\star + m(1-\xi_\star)y^p]^{\frac{1}{p}}\right) \leqslant \tau(\xi_\star^k)\mathscr{L}(x) + m\tau(1-\xi_\star^k)\mathscr{L}(y)$$

holds provided $[x^p\xi_\star + m(1-\xi_\star)y^p]^{\frac{1}{p}} \in \mathbb{I}$ for all $\xi_\star \in [0,1]$ and $(k,m) \in [0,1]$. If the inequality is of the opposite sign, then $\mathscr{L}$ is said to be $(k, h\text{-}m)$-p-concave. The set of all $(k, h\text{-}m)$-p-convex (concave) functions is denoted by

$$KHMPX(\mathbb{I}, p)\,,\; KHMPV(\mathbb{I}, p),$$

respectively. The set of all $(k, h\text{-}m)$-p-convex (concave) functions defined on closed, positive and bounded sets of $\mathbb{R}$ is given, respectively, by

$$KHMPX([\psi_5, \psi_6], K_c^+, p), \;\; KHMPV([\psi_5, \psi_6], K_c^+, p).$$

The motivation behind defining the $(k, h\text{-}m)$-p-convex IVM is the definition given by [41] above.

Now we define a new type, namely a $(k, h\text{-}m)$-p-*convex* I-V-F.

Definition 8. *Let $J \subset \mathbb{R}$ be a set containing $(0,1)$ and let $\tau : J \to \mathbb{R}$ be a positive function including zero. Let $\mathbb{I}$ be a positive subset of $\mathbb{R}$ and $p \in \mathbb{R} - 0$. The IVM $\mathscr{F} : [\psi_5, \psi_6] \to K_c^+$ is a left–right-$(k, h\text{-}m)$-p-convex IVM if*

$$\mathscr{F}\left([u^p\xi_\star + m(1-\xi_\star)v^p]^{\frac{1}{p}}\right) \leqslant_p \tau(\xi_\star^k)\mathscr{F}(u) + m\tau(1-\xi_\star^k)\mathscr{F}(v)$$

holds, provided $[u^p\xi_\star + m(1-\xi_\star)v^p]^{\frac{1}{p}} \in \mathbb{I}$ *for all* $\xi_\star \in [0,1]$ *and* $(k,m) \in [0,1]$. *If the inequality is of the opposite sign, then* $\mathscr{F}$ *is a left–right-*$(k, h\text{-}m)$*-p-concave IVM. The set of all left–right-*$(k, h\text{-}m)$*-p-convex (left–right-*$(k, h\text{-}m)$*-p-concave) IVMs is denoted by*

$$Left-RightSKHMPX([\psi_5,\psi_6],K_c^+,p) \quad (Left-RightSKHMPV([\psi_5,\psi_6],K_c^+,p)).$$

$\mathscr{F}$ *is left–right-(k,h-m)-p-affine* $\iff$ *it is both left–right-(k,h-m)-p-convex and left–right(k,h-m)-p-concave.*

The set of all left–right-(k,h-m)-p-affine IVMs is denoted by $Left\text{-}RightSKHMPA$ $([\psi_5,\psi_6],K_c^+,p))$.

Remark 2.

- *Setting* $k,m=1$, *we get the p,h-convex IVM introduced by Khan et al. [42] given by*

$$\mathscr{F}\left([x^p\xi_\star + (1-\xi_\star)y^p]^{\frac{1}{p}}\right) \leqslant_p q(\xi_\star)\mathscr{F}(x) + q(1-\xi_\star)\mathscr{F}(y).$$

- *Setting* $k,m=1, q(t)=t$, *we get a p-convex IVM.*
- *Setting* $p,m=1, q(t)=t, k=1$ *we get a convex IVM, namely we obtain*

$$\mathscr{F}(\omega_6\rho_1 + (1-\omega_6)\rho_2) \leqslant_p \omega_6\mathscr{F}(\rho_1) + (1-\omega_6)\mathscr{F}(\rho_2).$$

In the following, we obtain new HH type inequalities and as a consequence of the said generalization in the IVM sense, we obtain the results reported in the recent literature.

3. Main Results

Theorem 2. *Let* $J \subset \mathbb{R}$ *be a set containing* $(0,1)$ *and let* $\tau : J \to \mathbb{R}$ *be a positive function including zero. Let* $\mathbb{I} \subset (0,+\infty)$ *be a set,* $p \in \mathbb{R}-0$ *and* $\mathscr{F} : [\psi_5,\psi_6] \to K_c^+$ *be an IVM introduced by* $\mathscr{F}(x) = [\mathscr{F}_*,\mathscr{F}^*]$, *for all* $x \in [\psi_5,\psi_6]$. *Then,* $\mathscr{F} \in Left-RightSKHMPX([\psi_5,\psi_6],K_c^+,p)$ $\iff$, $\mathscr{F}_*,\mathscr{F}^* \in KHMPX([\psi_5,\psi_6],K_c^+,p)$.

Proof. Assume that $\mathscr{F}_*,\mathscr{F}^* \in KHMPX([\psi_5,\psi_6],K_c^+,p)$. Then, for all $x,y \in [\psi_5,\psi_6]$, $\xi_\star \in [0,1]$ and $(k,m) \in [0,1]$, we have

$$\mathscr{F}_*\left([x^p\xi_\star + m(1-\xi_\star)y^p]^{\frac{1}{p}}\right) \leqslant \tau(\xi_\star^k)\mathscr{F}_*(x) + m\tau(1-\xi_\star^k)\mathscr{F}_*(y),$$

and

$$\mathscr{F}^*\left([x^p\xi_\star + m(1-\xi_\star)y^p]^{\frac{1}{p}}\right) \leqslant \tau(\xi_\star^k)\mathscr{F}^*(x) + m\tau(1-\xi_\star^k)\mathscr{F}^*(y).$$

From the inequality defined in Definition 8 and the order relation $\leqslant_p$, we have

$$\left[\mathscr{F}_*\left([x^p\xi_\star + m(1-\xi_\star)y^p]^{\frac{1}{p}}\right), \mathscr{F}^*\left([x^p\xi_\star + m(1-\xi_\star)y^p]^{\frac{1}{p}}\right)\right]$$

$$\leqslant_p \left[\tau(\xi_\star^k)\mathscr{F}_*(x) + m\tau(1-\xi_\star^k)\mathscr{F}_*(y), \tau(\xi_\star^k)\mathscr{F}^*(x) + m\tau(1-\xi_\star^k)\mathscr{F}^*(y)\right],$$

$$= \tau(\xi_\star^k)[\mathscr{F}_*(x),\mathscr{F}^*(x)] + m\tau(1-\xi_\star^k)[\mathscr{F}_*(y),\mathscr{F}^*(y)],$$

that is

$$\mathscr{F}\left([x^p\xi_\star + m(1-\xi_\star)y^p]^{\frac{1}{p}}\right) \leqslant_p \tau(\xi_\star^k)\mathscr{F}(x) + m\tau(1-\xi_\star^k)\mathscr{F}(y), \text{ for all } x,y \in [\psi_5,\psi_6], \xi_\star \in [0,1].$$

Hence, $\mathscr{F} \in Left\text{-}RightSKHMPX([\psi_5,\psi_6],K_c^+,p)$.

Conversely, let $\mathscr{F} \in Left\text{-}RightSKHMPX([\psi_5, \psi_6], K_c^+, p)$. Then, for all $x, y \in [\psi_5, \psi_6]$, $\xi_\star \in [0,1]$ and $(k, m) \in [0,1]$, we have

$$\mathscr{F}\left([x^p\xi_\star + m(1-\xi_\star)y^p]^{\frac{1}{p}}\right) \leqslant_p \tau(\xi_\star^k)\mathscr{F}(x) + m\tau(1-\xi_\star^k)\mathscr{F}(y),$$

that is

$$\left[\mathscr{F}_*\left([x^p\xi_\star + m(1-\xi_\star)y^p]^{\frac{1}{p}}\right), \mathscr{F}^*\left([x^p\xi_\star + m(1-\xi_\star)y^p]^{\frac{1}{p}}\right)\right] \leqslant_p$$
$$\tau(\xi_\star^k)[\mathscr{F}_*(x), \mathscr{F}^*(y)] + m\tau(1-\xi_\star^k)[\mathscr{F}_*(y), \mathscr{F}^*(y)]$$
$$= \left[\tau(\xi_\star^k)\mathscr{F}_*(x) + m\tau(1-\xi_\star^k)\mathscr{F}_*(y), \tau(\xi_\star^k)\mathscr{F}^*(x) + m\tau(1-\xi_\star^k)\mathscr{F}^*(y)\right].$$

Hence, we have

$$\mathscr{F}_*\left([x^p\xi_\star + m(1-\xi_\star)y^p]^{\frac{1}{p}}\right) \leqslant_p \tau(\xi_\star^k)\mathscr{F}_*(x) + m\tau(1-\xi_\star^k)\mathscr{F}_*(y),$$

and

$$\mathscr{F}^*\left([x^p\xi_\star + m(1-\xi_\star)y^p]^{\frac{1}{p}}\right) \leqslant_p \tau(\xi_\star^k)\mathscr{F}^*(x) + m\tau(1-\xi_\star^k)\mathscr{F}^*(y).$$

□

Remark 3. *If $\mathscr{F}_* = \mathscr{F}^*$ then the left–right-(k,h-m)-p-convex function becomes a $(k, h\text{-}m)$-p-convex function.*

If $k, m = 1$, then the left–right-(k,h-m)-p IVM becomes a left–right-(p,h)-convex IVM [42].

If $\mathscr{F}_* = \mathscr{F}^*, m, p, k = 1$, $h(\xi_\star) = \xi_\star^s$ and $s \in (0,1]$, then the left–right-(k,h-m)-p-convex IVM becomes an s-convex function in the second sense, see [43].

If $m = 1, k = 1$ and $h(\xi_\star) = \xi_\star$ we get a p-convex IVM.

If $\mathscr{F}_* = \mathscr{F}^*$ with $m = 1, p = 1, \xi_\star = 1$, then the left–right-(k,h-m)-p-convex IVM reduces to an h-convex function, see [44].

If $\mathscr{F}_* = \mathscr{F}^*$ with $h(\xi_\star) = 1$ and $m = 1, p = 1$, then the left–right-(k,h-m)-p-convex IVM reduces to the a p-convex function, see [45].

If $\mathscr{F}_* = \mathscr{F}^*$ with $k, p, m = 1$ and $h(\xi_\star) = \xi_\star$, then left–right-(k,h-m)-p-convex IVM reduces to the classical convex function.

Theorem 3. *Let $\mathscr{F} : [a,b] \to \mathbb{K}_c^+$ be an IVM that is left–right-$(k, h\text{-}m)$-p-convex. Then, the inequality holds in one of the cases:*

1. $a > 0, b > a, 0 < m < \frac{a}{b}$
2. $a > 0, b < a, 0 < m \leqslant 1$

$$\mathscr{F}\left([\frac{a^p + m^p b^p}{2}]^{\frac{1}{p}}\right) \leqslant_p \frac{\Gamma(\beta+1)p^\beta}{(a^p - m^p b^p)^\beta}\left(\chi_{a^-}^{p,\beta}\mathscr{F}(mb)\tau\left(\frac{1}{2^k}\right) + m^{p\beta+p}\tau\left(1-\frac{1}{2^k}\right)\chi_{b^+}^{p,\beta}\mathscr{F}\left(\frac{a}{m}\right)\right)$$
$$\leqslant_p \beta p \cdot \left(\tau\left(\frac{1}{2^k}\right)\mathscr{F}(a) + m^p\tau\left(1-\frac{1}{2^k}\right)\mathscr{F}(b)\right)\int_0^1 t^{\beta p-1}\tau(t^{\xi_\star p})dt$$
$$+\beta p \cdot \left(\tau\left(\frac{1}{2^k}\right)m^p\mathscr{F}(b) + \tau\left(1-\frac{1}{2^k}\right)\mathscr{F}(a)\right)\int_0^1 t^{\beta p-1}\tau(1-t^{\xi_\star p})dt.$$

Proof. From the statement of a left–right-(k,h-m)-p-convex IVM, we have

$$\mathscr{F}\left([x^p\xi_\star + m(1-\xi_\star)y^p]^{\frac{1}{p}}\right) \leqslant_p \tau(\xi_\star^k)\mathscr{F}(x) + m\tau(1-\xi_\star^k)\mathscr{F}(y).$$

Setting $\xi_\star = \frac{1}{2}, m \to m^p$, we obtain

$$\mathscr{F}\left([\frac{x^p + m^p y^p}{2}]^{\frac{1}{p}}\right) \leqslant_p \tau\left(\frac{1}{2^k}\right)\mathscr{F}(x) + m^p\tau\left(1 - \frac{1}{2^k}\right)\mathscr{F}(y).$$

Setting $x^p = m^p(1-t^p)b^p + t^p a^p, y^p = (1-t^p)\frac{a^p}{m^p} + b^p t^p$, we obtain

$$\mathscr{F}\left([\frac{a^p + m^p b^p}{2}]^{\frac{1}{p}}\right)$$

$$\leqslant_p \tau\left(\frac{1}{2^k}\right)\mathscr{F}\left(\left[m^p(1-t^p)b^p + t^p a^p\right]^{\frac{1}{p}}\right) + m^p\tau\left(1 - \frac{1}{2^k}\right)\mathscr{F}\left(\left[(1-t^p)\frac{a^p}{m^p} + b^p t^p\right]^{\frac{1}{p}}\right).$$

It follows from the statement of the IVM

$$\mathscr{F}_*\left([\frac{a^p + m^p b^p}{2}]^{\frac{1}{p}}\right)$$

$$\leqslant \tau\left(\frac{1}{2^k}\right)\mathscr{F}_*\left(\left[m^p(1-t^p)b^p + t^p a^p\right]^{\frac{1}{p}}\right) + m^p\tau\left(1 - \frac{1}{2^k}\right)\mathscr{F}_*\left(\left[(1-t^p)\frac{a^p}{m^p} + b^p t^p\right]^{\frac{1}{p}}\right),$$

and

$$\mathscr{F}^*\left([\frac{a^p + m^p b^p}{2}]^{\frac{1}{p}}\right)$$

$$\leqslant \tau\left(\frac{1}{2^k}\right)\mathscr{F}^*\left(\left[m^p(1-t^p)b^p + t^p a^p\right]^{\frac{1}{p}}\right) + m^p\tau\left(1 - \frac{1}{2^k}\right)\mathscr{F}^*\left(\left[(1-t^p)\frac{a^p}{m^p} + b^p t^p\right]^{\frac{1}{p}}\right).$$

Multiplying the inequalities with $t^{\beta p-1}$ and integrating with respect to the variable used, we get

$$\frac{\mathscr{F}_*\left([\frac{a^p + m^p b^p}{2}]^{\frac{1}{p}}\right)}{\beta p} \leqslant$$

$$\int_0^1 t^{\beta p-1}\tau\left(\frac{1}{2^k}\right)\mathscr{F}_*\left(\left[m^p(1-t^p)b^p + t^p a^p\right]^{\frac{1}{p}}\right)dt$$

$$+ \int_0^1 t^{\beta p-1} m^p\tau\left(1 - \frac{1}{2^k}\right)\mathscr{F}_*\left(\left[(1-t^p)\frac{a^p}{m^p} + b^p t^p\right]^{\frac{1}{p}}\right)dt,$$

and

$$\frac{\mathscr{F}^*\left([\frac{a^p + m^p b^p}{2}]^{\frac{1}{p}}\right)}{\beta p} \leqslant$$

$$\int_0^1 t^{\beta p-1}\tau\left(\frac{1}{2^k}\right)\mathscr{F}^*\left(\left[m^p(1-t^p)b^p + t^p a^p\right]^{\frac{1}{p}}\right)dt$$

$$+ \int_0^1 t^{\beta p-1} m^p\tau\left(1 - \frac{1}{2^k}\right)\mathscr{F}^*\left(\left[(1-t^p)\frac{a^p}{m^p} + b^p t^p\right]^{\frac{1}{p}}\right)dt.$$

Focusing towards the right and setting $(1-t^p)m^p b^p + t^p a^p = k^p$ in the first integral and $(1-t^p)\frac{a^p}{m^p} + b^p t^p = k^p$ in the second integral, we obtain

$$= \frac{\tau\left(\frac{1}{2^k}\right)}{(a^p - m^p b^p)^\beta}\int_{mb}^{a} \mathscr{F}_*(k)(k^p - m^p b^p)^{\beta-1} k^{p-1} dk$$

$$+ \frac{\tau\left(1 - \frac{1}{2^k}\right)m^{p+p\beta}}{(a^p - b^p m^p)^\beta}\int_b^{\frac{a}{m}} \mathscr{F}_*(k)\left(\frac{a^p}{m^p} - k^p\right)^{\beta-1} k^{p-1} dk,$$

and

$$= \frac{\tau\left(\frac{1}{2^k}\right)}{(a^p - m^p b^p)^\beta} \int_{mb}^{a} \mathscr{F}^*(k)(k^p - m^p b^p)^{\beta-1} k^{p-1} dk$$

$$+ \frac{\tau\left(1-\frac{1}{2^k}\right) m^{p+p\beta}}{(a^p - b^p m^p)^\beta} \int_{b}^{\frac{a}{m}} \mathscr{F}^*(k) \left(\frac{a^p}{m^p} - k^p\right)^{\beta-1} k^{p-1} dk.$$

What we get when we recognize it in terms of a Katugampola integral is

$$= \frac{\Gamma(\beta)p^{\beta-1}}{(a^p - m^p b^p)^\beta} \left(\chi_{a^-}^{p,\beta} \mathscr{F}_*(mb) \tau\left(\frac{1}{2^k}\right) + m^{p\beta+p} \tau\left(1-\frac{1}{2^k}\right) \chi_{b^+}^{p,\beta} \mathscr{F}_*\left(\frac{a}{m}\right) \right),$$

and

$$= \frac{\Gamma(\beta)p^{\beta-1}}{(a^p - m^p b^p)^\beta} \left(\chi_{a^-}^{p,\beta} \mathscr{F}^*(mb) \tau\left(\frac{1}{2^k}\right) + m^{p\beta+p} \tau\left(1-\frac{1}{2^k}\right) \chi_{b^+}^{p,\beta} \mathscr{F}^*\left(\frac{a}{m}\right) \right),$$

which together yields

$$\left[\mathscr{F}_*\left([\frac{a^p + m^p b^p}{2}]^{\frac{1}{p}} \right), \mathscr{F}^*\left([\frac{a^p + m^p b^p}{2}]^{\frac{1}{p}} \right) \right] \leqslant_p$$

$$\left(\frac{\Gamma(\beta)p^{\beta-1}}{(a^p - m^p b^p)^\beta} \left(\chi_{a^-}^{p,\beta} \mathscr{F}_*(mb) \tau\left(\frac{1}{2^k}\right) + m^{p\beta+p} \tau\left(1-\frac{1}{2^k}\right) \chi_{b^+}^{p,\beta} \mathscr{F}_*\left(\frac{a}{m}\right), \right) \right.$$

$$\left. \frac{\Gamma(\beta)p^{\beta-1}}{(a^p - m^p b^p)^\beta} \left(\chi_{a^-}^{p,\beta} \mathscr{F}^*(mb) \tau\left(\frac{1}{2^k}\right) + m^{p\beta+p} \tau\left(1-\frac{1}{2^k}\right) \chi_{b^+}^{p,\beta} \mathscr{F}^*\left(\frac{a}{m}\right) \right) \right),$$

from which we get the original left part of the inequality.

Now to obtain the upper inequality, we use the left–right-(k,h-m)-p-convexity and apply the IVM property to the following expression

$$\tau\left(\frac{1}{2^k}\right) \mathscr{F}\left(\left[m^p(1-t^p)b^p + t^p a^p \right]^{\frac{1}{p}} \right)$$

$$+ m^p \tau\left(1-\frac{1}{2^k}\right) \mathscr{F}\left(\left[(1-t^p)\frac{a^p}{m^p} + b^p t^p \right]^{\frac{1}{p}} \right)$$

and multiply it with $t^{\beta p-1}$, while integrating the expression; hence, we obtain

$$\frac{\Gamma(\beta)p^{\beta-1}}{(a^p - m^p b^p)^\beta} \left(\chi_{a^-}^{p,\beta} \mathscr{F}^*(mb) \tau\left(\frac{1}{2^k}\right) + m^{p\beta+p} \tau\left(1-\frac{1}{2^k}\right) \chi_{b^+}^{p,\beta} \mathscr{F}^*\left(\frac{a}{m}\right) \right) \leqslant$$

$$\left(\tau\left(\frac{1}{2^k}\right) \mathscr{F}^*(a) + m^p \tau\left(1-\frac{1}{2^k}\right) \mathscr{F}^*(b) \right) \int_0^1 t^{\beta p-1} \tau(t^{\xi_* p}) dt$$

$$+ \left(\tau\left(\frac{1}{2^k}\right) m^p \mathscr{F}^*(b) + \tau\left(1-\frac{1}{2^k}\right) \mathscr{F}^*(a) \right) \int_0^1 t^{\beta p-1} h\left(1 - t^{\xi_* p}\right) dt,$$

and

$$\frac{\Gamma(\beta)p^{\beta-1}}{(a^p - m^p b^p)^\beta} \left(\chi_{a^-}^{p,\beta} \mathscr{F}_*(mb) \tau\left(\frac{1}{2^k}\right) + m^{p\beta+p} \tau\left(1-\frac{1}{2^k}\right) \chi_{b^+}^{p,\beta} \mathscr{F}_*\left(\frac{a}{m}\right) \right) \leqslant$$

$$\left(\tau\left(\frac{1}{2^k}\right) \mathscr{F}_*(a) + m^p \tau\left(1-\frac{1}{2^k}\right) \mathscr{F}_*(b) \right) \int_0^1 t^{\beta p-1} \tau(t^{\xi_* p}) dt$$

$$+ \left(\tau\left(\frac{1}{2^k}\right) m^p \mathscr{F}_*(b) + \tau\left(1-\frac{1}{2^k}\right) \mathscr{F}_*(a) \right) \int_0^1 t^{\beta p-1} h\left(1 - t^{\xi_* p}\right) dt,$$

From which we get the original right-hand side inequality. Connecting the left- and right-hand side inequalities, we obtain the original inequality

$$\mathscr{F}\left([\frac{a^p+m^pb^p}{2}]^{\frac{1}{p}}\right) \leqslant_p \frac{\Gamma(\beta+1)p^\beta}{(a^p-m^pb^p)^\beta}\left(\chi^{p,\beta}_{a^-}\mathscr{F}(mb)\tau\left(\frac{1}{2^k}\right)+m^{p\beta+p}\tau\left(1-\frac{1}{2^k}\right)\chi^{p,\beta}_{b^+}\mathscr{F}\left(\frac{a}{m}\right)\right)$$

$$\leqslant_p \beta p\cdot\left(\tau\left(\frac{1}{2^k}\right)\mathscr{F}(a)+m^p\tau\left(1-\frac{1}{2^k}\right)\mathscr{F}(b)\right)\int_0^1 t^{\beta p-1}\tau(t^{\xi_\star p})dt$$

$$+\beta p\cdot\left(\tau\left(\frac{1}{2^k}\right)m^p\mathscr{F}(b)+\tau\left(1-\frac{1}{2^k}\right)\mathscr{F}(a)\right)\int_0^1 t^{\beta p-1}\tau(1-t^{\xi_\star p})dt.$$

□

Setting $p=3, k=\frac{1}{2}$ in the theorem, we obtain a new inequality of the left–right-(k,h-m)-p-convex type.

Corollary 1.

$$\mathscr{F}\left([\frac{a^3+m^3b^3}{2}]^{\frac{1}{3}}\right) \leqslant_p \frac{\Gamma(\beta+1)3^\beta}{(a^3-m^3b^3)^\beta}\left(\chi^{3,\beta}_{a^-}\mathscr{F}(mb)h\left(\frac{1}{2^{\frac{1}{2}}}\right)+m^{3\beta+3}h\left(1-\frac{1}{2^{\frac{1}{2}}}\right)\chi^{3,\beta}_{b^+}\mathscr{F}\left(\frac{a}{m}\right)\right)$$

$$\leqslant_p 3\beta\cdot\left(h\left(\frac{1}{2^{\frac{1}{2}}}\right)\mathscr{F}(a)+m^3h\left(1-\frac{1}{2^{\frac{1}{2}}}\right)\mathscr{F}(b)\right)\int_0^1 t^{\beta 3-1}h(t^{3\xi_\star})dt$$

$$+3\beta\cdot\left(h\left(\frac{1}{2^{\frac{1}{2}}}\right)m^3\mathscr{F}(b)+h\left(1-\frac{1}{2^{\frac{1}{2}}}\right)\mathscr{F}(a)\right)\int_0^1 t^{3\beta-1}h(1-t^{3\xi_\star})dt.$$

Theorem 4. *If the conditions are the same as in Theorem 3, then, the inequality holds in the following case with* $a\geqslant 0, b>a, \frac{a}{b}<m\leqslant 1$

$$\mathscr{F}\left([\frac{a^p+m^pb^p}{2}]^{\frac{1}{p}}\right) \leqslant_p \tau\left(\frac{1}{2^k}\right)\frac{\Gamma(\beta+1)2^\beta}{p^{-\beta}(m^pb^p-a^p)^\beta}\chi^{\beta,p}_{\left(\left(\frac{a^p}{2m^p}+\frac{b^p}{2}\right)^{\frac{1}{p}}\right)^-}\mathscr{F}\left(\frac{a}{m}\right)$$

$$+\tau\left(\frac{2^k-1}{2^k}\right)\frac{m^{p\beta+p}2^\beta\Gamma(\beta+1)}{p^{-\beta}(m^pb^p-a^p)^\beta}\chi^{\beta,p}_{\left(\left(\frac{a^p}{2}+\frac{b^pm^p}{2}\right)^{\frac{1}{p}}\right)^+}\mathscr{F}(mb)$$

$$\leqslant_p \beta p\left(\tau\left(\frac{1}{2^k}\right)\mathscr{F}(a)+m^p\tau\left(\frac{2^k-1}{2^k}\right)\mathscr{F}(b)\right)\int_0^1 h\left(\left(\frac{t^p}{2}\right)^{\xi_\star}\right)t^{\beta p-1}dt$$

$$+\beta p\left(\tau\left(\frac{1}{2^k}\right)m^p\mathscr{F}(b)+\tau\left(\frac{2^k-1}{2^k}\right)\mathscr{F}(a)\right)\int_0^1 h\left(1-\left(\frac{t^p}{2}\right)^{\xi_\star}\right)t^{\beta p-1}dt.$$

Proof. From the statement of the left–right-(k,h-m)-p-convex IVM, we have

$$\mathscr{F}\left([x^p\xi_\star+m(1-\xi_\star)y^p]^{\frac{1}{p}}\right) \leqslant_p \tau(\xi_\star^k)\mathscr{F}(x)+m\tau(1-\xi_\star^k)\mathscr{F}(y).$$

Setting $\xi_\star=\frac{1}{2}, m\to m^p$, we obtain

$$\mathscr{F}\left([\frac{x^p+m^py^p}{2}]^{\frac{1}{p}}\right) \leqslant_p \tau\left(\frac{1}{2^k}\right)\mathscr{F}(x)+m^p\tau\left(1-\frac{1}{2^k}\right)\mathscr{F}(y).$$

Setting $x^p=\frac{(at)^p}{2}+\frac{m^p(2-t^p)}{2}b^p, y^p=\frac{(bt)^p}{2}+\frac{(2-t^p)}{2}(\frac{a}{m})^p$ in the inequality, we get the following

$$\mathscr{F}\left([\frac{a^p+m^pb^p}{2}]^{\frac{1}{p}}\right) \leqslant_p \tau\left(\frac{1}{2^k}\right)\mathscr{F}\left([\frac{(at)^p}{2}+\frac{m^p(2-t^p)}{2}b^p]^{\frac{1}{p}}\right)$$

$$+m^p\tau\left(1-\frac{1}{2^k}\right)\mathscr{F}\left([\frac{(bt)^p}{2}+\frac{(2-t^p)}{2}\left(\frac{a}{m}\right)^p]^{\frac{1}{p}}\right).$$

It follows from the statement of the IVM that

$$\mathscr{F}_*\left([\frac{a^p+m^pb^p}{2}]^{\frac{1}{p}}\right)\leqslant\tau\left(\frac{1}{2^k}\right)\mathscr{F}_*\left([\frac{(at)^p}{2}+\frac{m^p(2-t^p)}{2}b^p]^{\frac{1}{p}}\right)$$

$$+m^p\tau\left(1-\frac{1}{2^k}\right)\mathscr{F}_*\left([\frac{(bt)^p}{2}+\frac{(2-t^p)}{2}\left(\frac{a}{m}\right)^p]^{\frac{1}{p}}\right),$$

and

$$\mathscr{F}^*\left([\frac{a^p+m^pb^p}{2}]^{\frac{1}{p}}\right)\leqslant\tau\left(\frac{1}{2^k}\right)\mathscr{F}^*\left([\frac{(at)^p}{2}+\frac{m^p(2-t^p)}{2}b^p]^{\frac{1}{p}}\right)$$

$$+m^p\tau\left(1-\frac{1}{2^k}\right)\mathscr{F}^*\left([\frac{(bt)^p}{2}+\frac{(2-t^p)}{2}\left(\frac{a}{m}\right)^p]^{\frac{1}{p}}\right).$$

Multiplying the inequalities with $t^{\beta p-1}$ and integrating with respect to the variable used, we get

$$\frac{\mathscr{F}_*\left([\frac{a^p+m^pb^p}{2}]^{\frac{1}{p}}\right)}{\beta p}\leqslant\int_0^1 t^{p\beta-1}\tau\left(\frac{1}{2^k}\right)\mathscr{F}_*\left([\frac{(at)^p}{2}+\frac{m^p(2-t^p)}{2}b^p]^{\frac{1}{p}}\right)dt$$

$$+\int_0^1 t^{\beta p-1}m^p\tau\left(1-\frac{1}{2^k}\right)\mathscr{F}_*\left([\frac{(bt)^p}{2}+\frac{(2-t^p)}{2}\left(\frac{a}{m}\right)^p]^{\frac{1}{p}}\right)dt,$$

and

$$\frac{\mathscr{F}^*\left([\frac{a^p+m^pb^p}{2}]^{\frac{1}{p}}\right)}{p\beta}\leqslant\int_0^1 t^{\beta p-1}\tau\left(\frac{1}{2^k}\right)\mathscr{F}^*\left([\frac{(at)^p}{2}+\frac{m^p(2-t^p)}{2}b^p]^{\frac{1}{p}}\right)dt$$

$$+\int_0^1 t^{\beta p-1}m^p\tau\left(1-\frac{1}{2^k}\right)\mathscr{F}^*\left([\frac{(bt)^p}{2}+\frac{(2-t^p)}{2}\left(\frac{a}{m}\right)^p]^{\frac{1}{p}}\right)dt.$$

Focusing on the lower end point function $\mathscr{F}_*$ and introducing the following substitution to the first integral $k^p=\frac{a^pt^p}{2}+\frac{m^p(2-t^p)}{2}b^p$ while nothing that $mb\geqslant a$, we get

$$\int_0^1 t^{p\beta-1}\tau\left(\frac{1}{2^k}\right)\mathscr{F}_*\left([\frac{(at)^p}{2}+\frac{m^p(2-t^p)}{2}b^p]^{\frac{1}{p}}\right)dt$$

$$=\frac{2^\beta}{(m^pb^p-a^p)^\beta}\int_{(\frac{a^p+b^pm^p}{2})^{\frac{1}{p}}}^{bm}\mathscr{F}_*(k)(m^pb^p-k^p)^{\beta-1}k^{p-1}dk$$

$$=\frac{2^\beta\Gamma(\beta)p^{\beta-1}}{(m^pb^p-a^p)^\beta}\chi^{p,\beta}_{((\frac{a^p+m^pb^p}{2})^{\frac{1}{p}})+}\mathscr{F}_*(bm).$$

Introducing a substitution to the second integral, namely, $k^p=\frac{(bt)^p}{2}+\frac{(2-t^p)}{2}\left(\frac{a}{m}\right)^p$, we get in a similar manner

$$\int_0^1 t^{\beta p-1}m^p\tau\left(1-\frac{1}{2^k}\right)\mathscr{F}_*\left([\frac{(bt)^p}{2}+\frac{(2-t^p)}{2}\left(\frac{a}{m}\right)^p]^{\frac{1}{p}}\right)dt$$

$$=\int_{\frac{a}{m}}^{\left(\frac{b^p}{2}+\frac{a^p}{2m^p}\right)^{\frac{1}{p}}}\mathscr{F}_*(k)\left(k^p-\frac{a^p}{m^p}\right)^{\beta-1}k^{p-1}dk\cdot\frac{1}{(\frac{b^p}{2}-\frac{a^p}{2m^p})^\beta}$$

$$=\frac{m^{p\beta}\Gamma(\beta)2^\beta}{p^{1-\beta}(m^pb^p-a^p)^\beta}\chi^{\beta,p}_{\left((\frac{a^p}{2m^p}+\frac{b^p}{2})^{\frac{1}{p}}\right)^-}\mathscr{F}_*\left(\frac{a}{m}\right).$$

We obtain similar equalities with the upper end function, namely,

$$\int_0^1 t^{p\beta-1}\tau\left(\frac{1}{2^k}\right)\mathscr{F}^*\left([\frac{(at)^p}{2}+\frac{m^p(2-t^p)}{2}b^p]^{\frac{1}{p}}\right)dt$$

$$=\frac{2^\beta}{(m^pb^p-a^p)^\beta}\int_{(\frac{a^p+b^pm^p}{2})^{\frac{1}{p}}}^{bm}\mathscr{F}^*(k)(m^pb^p-k^p)^{\beta-1}k^{p-1}dk$$

$$=\frac{2^\beta\Gamma(\beta)p^{\beta-1}}{(m^pb^p-a^p)^\beta}\chi^{p,\beta}_{((\frac{a^p+m^pb^p}{2})^{\frac{1}{p}})+}\mathscr{F}^*(bm).$$

$$\int_0^1 t^{\beta p-1}m^p\tau\left(1-\frac{1}{2^k}\right)\mathscr{F}^*\left([\frac{(bt)^p}{2}+\frac{(2-t^p)}{2}\left(\frac{a}{m}\right)^p]^{\frac{1}{p}}\right)dt$$

$$=\int_{\frac{a}{m}}^{\left(\frac{b^p}{2}+\frac{a^p}{2m^p}\right)^{\frac{1}{p}}}\mathscr{F}^*(k)\left(k^p-\frac{a^p}{m^p}\right)^{\beta-1}k^{p-1}dk\cdot\frac{1}{(\frac{b^p}{2}-\frac{a^p}{2m^p})^\theta}$$

$$=\frac{m^{p\beta}\Gamma(\beta)2^\beta}{p^{1-\beta}(m^pb^p-a^p)^\beta}\chi^{\beta,p}_{\left(\left(\frac{a^p}{2m^p}+\frac{b^p}{2}\right)^{\frac{1}{p}}\right)^-}\mathscr{F}^*\left(\frac{a}{m}\right).$$

Hence, we obtain

$$\left(\frac{\mathscr{F}_*\left([\frac{a^p+m^pb^p}{2}]^{\frac{1}{p}}\right)}{\beta p},\frac{\mathscr{F}^*\left([\frac{a^p+m^pb^p}{2}]^{\frac{1}{p}}\right)}{\beta p}\right)\leqslant$$

$$\left(\tau\left(\frac{1}{2^k}\right)\frac{p^{\beta-1}\Gamma(\beta)2^\beta}{p^{-\beta+1}(m^pb^p-a^p)^\beta}\chi^{\beta,p}_{\left(\left(\frac{a^p}{2m^p}+\frac{b^p}{2}\right)^{\frac{1}{p}}\right)^-}\mathscr{F}_*\left(\frac{a}{m}\right)\right.$$

$$+\tau\left(\frac{2^k-1}{2^k}\right)\frac{m^{p\beta+p}2^\beta\Gamma(\beta)}{p^{-\beta+1}(m^pb^p-a^p)^\beta}\chi^{\beta,p}_{\left(\left(\frac{a^p}{2}+\frac{b^pm^p}{2}\right)^{\frac{1}{p}}\right)^+}\mathscr{F}_*(mb),$$

$$\tau\left(\frac{1}{2^k}\right)\frac{p^{\beta-1}\Gamma(\beta)2^\beta}{p^{-\beta+1}(m^pb^p-a^p)^\beta}\chi^{\beta,p}_{\left(\left(\frac{a^p}{2m^p}+\frac{b^p}{2}\right)^{\frac{1}{p}}\right)^-}\mathscr{F}^*\left(\frac{a}{m}\right)$$

$$\left.+\tau\left(\frac{2^k-1}{2^k}\right)\frac{m^{p\beta+p}2^\beta\Gamma(\beta)}{p^{-\beta+1}(m^pb^p-a^p)^\beta}\chi^{\beta,p}_{\left(\left(\frac{a^p}{2}+\frac{b^pm^p}{2}\right)^{\frac{1}{p}}\right)^+}\mathscr{F}^*(mb)\right)$$

and the left inequality follows.

Using the definition of the left–right-(k,h-m)-p-convex function towards the right

$$\tau\left(\frac{1}{2^k}\right)\mathscr{F}\left([\frac{(at)^p}{2}+\frac{m^p(2-t^p)}{2}b^p]^{\frac{1}{p}}\right)$$

$$+m^p\tau\left(1-\frac{1}{2^k}\right)\mathscr{F}\left([\frac{(bt)^p}{2}+\frac{(2-t^p)}{2}\left(\frac{a}{m}\right)^p]^{\frac{1}{p}}\right),$$

while using the definition of the IVM property, multiplying with $t^{p\beta-1}$ and integrating with respect to the variable used, we obtain

$$\tau\left(\frac{1}{2^k}\right)\frac{\Gamma(\beta)2^\beta}{p^{-\beta+1}(m^pb^p-a^p)^\beta}\chi^{\beta,p}_{\left(\left(\frac{a^p}{2m^p}+\frac{b^p}{2}\right)^{\frac{1}{p}}\right)^-}\mathscr{F}\left(\frac{a}{m}\right)$$

$$+\tau\left(\frac{2^k-1}{2^k}\right)\frac{2^{\beta}m^{p\beta+p}\Gamma(\beta)}{p^{-\beta+1}(m^pb^p-a^p)^{\beta}}\chi^{\beta,p}_{\left(\left(\frac{a^p}{2}+\frac{b^pm^p}{2}\right)^{\frac{1}{p}}\right)^+}\mathscr{F}(mb)$$

$$\leqslant\left(\tau\left(\frac{1}{2^k}\right)\mathscr{F}(a)+m^p\tau\left(\frac{2^k-1}{2^k}\right)\mathscr{F}(b)\right)\int_0^1 h\left(\left(\frac{t^p}{2}\right)^{\xi_\star}\right)t^{\beta p-1}dt$$

$$+\left(\tau\left(\frac{1}{2^k}\right)m^p\mathscr{F}(b)+\tau\left(\frac{2^k-1}{2^k}\right)\mathscr{F}(a)\right)\int_0^1 h\left(1-\left(\frac{t^p}{2}\right)^{\xi_\star}\right)t^{\beta p-1}dt.$$

Now, connecting the left- and right-hand sides, we obtain the original inequality. □

Setting $p=3, k=\frac{1}{2}$, we get a new IVM noninteger inequality.

Corollary 2.

$$\mathscr{F}\left([\frac{a^3+m^3b^3}{2}]^{\frac{1}{3}}\right)\leqslant_p h\left(\frac{1}{2^{\frac{1}{2}}}\right)\frac{\Gamma(\beta+1)2^{\beta}}{3^{-\beta}(m^3b^3-a^3)^{\beta}}\chi^{\beta,3}_{\left(\left(\frac{a^3}{2m^3}+\frac{b^3}{2}\right)^{\frac{1}{3}}\right)^-}\mathscr{F}\left(\frac{a}{m}\right)$$

$$+h\left(\frac{2^{\frac{1}{2}}-1}{2^{\frac{1}{2}}}\right)\frac{m^{3\beta+3}2^{\beta}\Gamma(\beta+1)}{3^{-\beta}(m^3b^3-a^3)^{\beta}}\chi^{\beta,3}_{\left(\left(\frac{a^3}{2}+\frac{b^3m^3}{2}\right)^{\frac{1}{3}}\right)^+}\mathscr{F}(mb)$$

$$\leqslant_p 3\beta\left(h\left(\frac{1}{2^{\frac{1}{2}}}\right)\mathscr{F}(a)+m^3h\left(\frac{2^{\frac{1}{2}}-1}{2^{\frac{1}{2}}}\right)\mathscr{F}(b)\right)\int_0^1 h\left(\left(\frac{t^3}{2}\right)^{\xi_\star}\right)t^{3\beta-1}dt$$

$$+3\beta\left(h\left(\frac{1}{2^{\frac{1}{2}}}\right)m^3\mathscr{F}(b)+h\left(\frac{2^{\frac{1}{2}}-1}{2^{\frac{1}{2}}}\right)\mathscr{F}(a)\right)\int_0^1 h\left(1-\left(\frac{t^3}{2}\right)^{\xi_\star}\right)t^{3\beta-1}dt.$$

Corollary 3. *Setting $\mathscr{F}_*=\mathscr{F}^*, h(t)=t, m, k, \xi_\star=1$, we get a classical noninteger p-convex inequality, namely,*

$$\mathscr{F}\left([\frac{a^p+m^pb^p}{2}]^{\frac{1}{p}}\right)\leqslant\frac{\Gamma(\beta+1)2^{\beta}}{2p^{-\beta}(b^p-a^p)^{\beta}}\chi^{\beta,p}_{\left(\left(\frac{a^p}{2}+\frac{b^p}{2}\right)^{\frac{1}{p}}\right)^-}\mathscr{F}(a)$$

$$+\frac{2^{\beta-1}\Gamma(\beta+1)}{p^{-\beta}(b^p-a^p)^{\beta}}\chi^{\beta,p}_{\left(\left(\frac{a^p}{2}+\frac{b^pm^p}{2}\right)^{\frac{1}{p}}\right)^+}\mathscr{F}(b)$$

$$\leqslant\beta p\left(\frac{1}{2}\mathscr{F}(a)+\frac{1}{2}\mathscr{F}(b)\right)\int_0^1\left(\frac{t^p}{2}\right)t^{\beta p-1}dt$$

$$+\beta p\left(\frac{1}{2}\mathscr{F}(b)+\frac{1}{2}\mathscr{F}(a)\right)\int_0^1\left(1-\left(\frac{t^p}{2}\right)\right)t^{\beta p-1}dt.$$

Example 1. *Setting $k=1, h(t)=t, m=1$, we recover a left–right-p-convex IVM, which is also a left–right-(k,h-m)-p-convex IVM.*

Using a similar construction as in the paper [23] and setting $p=1, \beta=\frac{1}{3}, k, \xi_\star=1$:

$$\mathscr{F}\left([\frac{a^p+m^pb^p}{2}]^{\frac{1}{p}}\right)\leqslant_p\tau\left(\frac{1}{2^k}\right)\frac{\Gamma(\beta+1)2^{\beta}}{p^{-\beta}(m^pb^p-a^p)^{\beta}}\chi^{\beta,p}_{\left(\left(\frac{a^p}{2m^p}+\frac{b^p}{2}\right)^{\frac{1}{p}}\right)^-}\mathscr{F}\left(\frac{a}{m}\right)$$

$$+\tau\left(\frac{2^k-1}{2^k}\right)\frac{m^{p\beta+p}2^{\beta}\Gamma(\beta+1)}{p^{-\beta}(m^pb^p-a^p)^{\beta}}\chi^{\beta,p}_{\left(\left(\frac{a^p}{2}+\frac{b^pm^p}{2}\right)^{\frac{1}{p}}\right)^+}\mathscr{F}(mb)$$

$$\leqslant_p \beta p\left(\tau\left(\frac{1}{2^k}\right)\mathscr{F}(a)+m^p\tau\left(\frac{2^k-1}{2^k}\right)\mathscr{F}(b)\right)\int_0^1 h\left(\left(\frac{t^p}{2}\right)^{\xi_\star}\right)t^{\beta p-1}dt$$

$$+\beta p\left(\tau\left(\frac{1}{2^k}\right)m^p\mathscr{F}(b)+\tau\left(\frac{2^k-1}{2^k}\right)\mathscr{F}(a)\right)\int_0^1 h\left(1-\left(\frac{t^p}{2}\right)^{\xi_\star}\right)t^{\beta p-1}dt.$$

$$\mathscr{F}_*\left([\frac{a^p+m^pb^p}{2}]^{\frac{1}{p}}\right)=\frac{1}{2},$$

$$\tau\left(\frac{1}{2^k}\right)\frac{\Gamma(\beta+1)2^{\beta}}{p^{-\beta}(m^pb^p-a^p)^{\beta}}\chi^{\beta,p}_{\left(\left(\frac{a^p}{2m^p}+\frac{b^p}{2}\right)^{\frac{1}{p}}\right)^-}\mathscr{F}_*\left(\frac{a}{m}\right)$$

$$+\tau\left(\frac{2^k-1}{2^k}\right)\frac{m^{p\beta+p}2^{\beta}\Gamma(\beta+1)}{p^{-\beta}(m^pb^p-a^p)^{\beta}}\chi^{\beta,p}_{\left(\left(\frac{a^p}{2}+\frac{b^pm^p}{2}\right)^{\frac{1}{p}}\right)^+}\mathscr{F}_*(mb)=\frac{1}{2},$$

$$\beta p\left(\tau\left(\frac{1}{2^k}\right)\mathscr{F}_*(a)+m^p\tau\left(\frac{2^k-1}{2^k}\right)\mathscr{F}_*(b)\right)\int_0^1 h\left(\left(\frac{t^p}{2}\right)^{\xi_\star}\right)t^{\beta p-1}dt$$

$$+\beta p\left(\tau\left(\frac{1}{2^k}\right)m^p\mathscr{F}_*(b)+\tau\left(\frac{2^k-1}{2^k}\right)\mathscr{F}_*(a)\right)\int_0^1 h\left(1-\left(\frac{t^p}{2}\right)^{\xi_\star}\right)t^{\beta p-1}dt=\frac{1}{2}.$$

Therefore, we get

$$\frac{1}{2}\leqslant\frac{1}{2}\leqslant\frac{1}{2}.$$

Now evaluating the top point function, we achieve

$$\mathscr{F}\left([\frac{a^p+m^pb^p}{2}]^{\frac{1}{p}}\right)=1.648,$$

$$\tau\left(\frac{1}{2^k}\right)\frac{\Gamma(\beta+1)2^{\beta}}{p^{-\beta}(m^pb^p-a^p)^{\beta}}\chi^{\beta,p}_{\left(\left(\frac{a^p}{2m^p}+\frac{b^p}{2}\right)^{\frac{1}{p}}\right)^-}\mathscr{F}\left(\frac{a}{m}\right)$$

$$+\tau\left(\frac{2^k-1}{2^k}\right)\frac{m^{p\beta+p}2^{\beta}\Gamma(\beta+1)}{p^{-\beta}(m^pb^p-a^p)^{\beta}}\chi^{\beta,p}_{\left(\left(\frac{a^p}{2}+\frac{b^pm^p}{2}\right)^{\frac{1}{p}}\right)^+}\mathscr{F}(mb)=1.712,$$

$$\beta p\left(\tau\left(\frac{1}{2^k}\right)\mathscr{F}(a)+m^p\tau\left(\frac{2^k-1}{2^k}\right)\mathscr{F}(b)\right)\int_0^1 h\left(\left(\frac{t^p}{2}\right)^{\xi_\star}\right)t^{\beta p-1}dt$$

$$+\beta p\left(\tau\left(\frac{1}{2^k}\right)m^p\mathscr{F}(b)+\tau\left(\frac{2^k-1}{2^k}\right)\mathscr{F}(a)\right)\int_0^1 h\left(1-\left(\frac{t^p}{2}\right)^{\xi_\star}\right)t^{\beta p-1}dt=1.859.$$

Hence, we achieve

$$[\frac{1}{2},1.648]\leqslant_p[\frac{1}{2},1.712]\leqslant_p[\frac{1}{2},1.859],$$

which verifies our result.

Theorem 5. *Using the same conditions as in Theorem 3 and $a \geqslant 0, b > a, \frac{a}{b} < m \leqslant 1$ results in the following inequality:*

$$\mathscr{F}\left([\frac{a^p + m^p b^p}{2}]^{\frac{1}{p}}\right) \leqslant_p$$

$$\frac{\tau\left(\frac{1}{2^{\xi_\star}}\right)2^\theta p^\theta \Gamma(\theta+1)}{(b^p m^p - a^p)^\theta} \chi^{\theta,p}_{\left(\left(\frac{q}{2}(a^p - m^p b^p) + \frac{a^p}{2} + \frac{b^p m^p}{2}\right)^{\frac{1}{p}}\right)^+} \mathscr{F}\left(\left(\frac{q}{2}(a^p - b^p m^p) + m^p b^p\right)^{\frac{1}{p}}\right)$$

$$+\frac{\tau\left(1-\frac{1}{2^{\xi_\star}}\right)m^{p+\theta p}2^\theta p^\theta \Gamma(\theta+1)}{(b^p m^p - a^p)^\theta} \chi^{p,\theta}_{\left(\left(\frac{q}{2}(b^p - \frac{a^p}{m^p}) + \frac{a^p}{2m^p} + \frac{b^p}{2}\right)^{\frac{1}{p}}\right)^-} \mathscr{F}\left(\left(\frac{q}{2}(b^p - \frac{a^p}{m^p}) + \frac{a^p}{m^p}\right)^{\frac{1}{p}}\right)$$

$$\leqslant_p \left(\left(\tau\left(\frac{1}{2^{\xi_\star}}\right)\mathscr{F}(a) + \tau\left(1-\frac{1}{2^{\xi_\star}}\right)m^p \mathscr{F}(b)\right)\int_0^1 h\left(\left(\frac{q+t^p}{2}\right)^k\right)t^{\theta p-1}dt\right)\theta p$$

$$+\left(\left(\tau\left(\frac{1}{2^{\xi_\star}}\right)\mathscr{F}(b)m^p + \tau\left(1-\frac{1}{2^{\xi_\star}}\right)\mathscr{F}(a)\right)\int_0^1 h\left(1-\left(\frac{q+t^p}{2}\right)^k\right)t^{\theta p-1}dt\right)\theta p.$$

Proof. Since $\mathscr{F}$ is left–right-(k ,h-m)-p-convex, we have the following inequality

$$\mathscr{F}\left((tx^p + m(1-t)y^p)^{\frac{1}{p}}\right) \leqslant_p h(t^{\xi_\star}).\mathscr{F}(x) + mh(1-t^{\xi_\star}).\mathscr{F}(y).$$

Setting $t = \frac{1}{2}, m \to m^p$ and $x^p = \frac{q+t^p}{2}a^p + \left(1-\frac{q+t^p}{2}\right)b^p m^p, y^p = \frac{q+t^p}{2}b^p + \left(1-\frac{q+t^p}{2}\right)\frac{a^p}{m^p}$ in the inequality, we achieve

$$\mathscr{F}\left([\frac{a^p + m^p b^p}{2}]^{\frac{1}{p}}\right) \leqslant_p \tau\left(\frac{1}{2^{\xi_\star}}\right)\mathscr{F}\left((\frac{q+t^p}{2}a^p + \left(1-\frac{q+t^p}{2}\right)b^p m^p)^{\frac{1}{p}}\right)$$

$$+\tau\left(1-\frac{1}{2^{\xi_\star}}\right)m^p \mathscr{F}\left((\frac{q+t^p}{2}b^p + \left(1-\frac{q+t^p}{2}\right)\frac{a^p}{m^p})^{\frac{1}{p}}\right).$$

It follows from the statement of the IVM that

$$\mathscr{F}_*\left([\frac{a^p + m^p b^p}{2}]^{\frac{1}{p}}\right) \leqslant \tau\left(\frac{1}{2^{\xi_\star}}\right)\mathscr{F}_*\left((\frac{q+t^p}{2}a^p + \left(1-\frac{q+t^p}{2}\right)b^p m^p)^{\frac{1}{p}}\right)$$

$$+\tau\left(1-\frac{1}{2^{\xi_\star}}\right)m^p \mathscr{F}_*\left((\frac{q+t^p}{2}b^p + \left(1-\frac{q+t^p}{2}\right)\frac{a^p}{m^p})^{\frac{1}{p}}\right),$$

and

$$\mathscr{F}^*\left([\frac{a^p + m^p b^p}{2}]^{\frac{1}{p}}\right) \leqslant \tau\left(\frac{1}{2^{\xi_\star}}\right)\mathscr{F}^*\left((\frac{q+t^p}{2}a^p + \left(1-\frac{q+t^p}{2}\right)b^p m^p)^{\frac{1}{p}}\right)$$

$$+\tau\left(1-\frac{1}{2^{\xi_\star}}\right)m^p \mathscr{F}^*\left((\frac{q+t^p}{2}b^p + \left(1-\frac{q+t^p}{2}\right)\frac{a^p}{m^p})^{\frac{1}{p}}\right).$$

Multiplying the inequalities with $t^{\theta p-1}$ and integrating with respect to the variable used, we get

$$\frac{\mathscr{F}_*\left([\frac{a^p + m^p b^p}{2}]^{\frac{1}{p}}\right)}{\theta p} \leqslant \int_0^1 t^{p\theta-1}\tau\left(\frac{1}{2^{\xi_\star}}\right)\mathscr{F}_*\left((\frac{q+t^p}{2}a^p + \left(1-\frac{q+t^p}{2}\right)b^p m^p)^{\frac{1}{p}}\right)dt$$

$$+\int_0^1 t^{p\theta-1}\tau\left(1-\frac{1}{2^{\xi_\star}}\right)m^p \mathscr{F}_*\left((\frac{q+t^p}{2}b^p + \left(1-\frac{q+t^p}{2}\right)\frac{a^p}{m^p})^{\frac{1}{p}}\right)dt,$$

and

$$\frac{\mathscr{F}^*\left(\left[\frac{a^p+m^pb^p}{2}\right]^{\frac{1}{p}}\right)}{\theta p} \leqslant \int_0^1 t^{p\theta-1}\tau\left(\frac{1}{2\xi_\star}\right)\mathscr{F}^*\left(\left(\frac{q+t^p}{2}a^p+\left(1-\frac{q+t^p}{2}\right)b^pm^p\right)^{\frac{1}{p}}\right)dt$$
$$+\int_0^1 t^{p\theta-1}\tau\left(1-\frac{1}{2\xi_\star}\right)m^p\mathscr{F}^*\left(\left(\frac{q+t^p}{2}b^p+\left(1-\frac{q+t^p}{2}\right)\frac{a^p}{m^p}\right)^{\frac{1}{p}}\right)dt.$$

Introducing the substitution $z^p = \frac{q+t^p}{2}a^p + (1-\frac{q+t^p}{2})b^pm^p$ in the first integral and $z^p = \frac{q+t^p}{2}b^p + (1-\frac{q+t^p}{2})a^pm^p$ in the second integral, we get for the first and second integrals, respectively,

$$\int_0^1 t^{p\beta-1}\tau\left(\frac{1}{2\xi_\star}\right)\mathscr{F}_*\left(\left(\frac{q+t^p}{2}a^p+\left(1-\frac{q+t^p}{2}\right)b^pm^p\right)^{\frac{1}{p}}\right)dt =$$

$$\int_{\left(\frac{q}{2}(a^p-b^pm^p)+\frac{a^p}{2}+\frac{m^pb^p}{2}\right)^{\frac{1}{p}}}^{\left(\frac{q}{2}(a^p-m^pb^p)+b^pm^p\right)^{\frac{1}{p}}} \mathscr{F}_*(z)(b^pm^p+\frac{q}{2}(a^p-b^pm^p)-z^p)^{\frac{\theta}{k}-1}z^{p-1}dz\cdot\frac{2^\theta}{(b^pm^p-a^p)^\theta}$$
$$=\frac{\tau\left(\frac{1}{2\xi_\star}\right)2^\theta\Gamma(\theta)}{p^{1-\theta}(b^pm^p-a^p)^\theta}\chi^{\theta,p}_{\left(\left(\frac{q}{2}(a^p-m^pb^p)+\frac{a^p}{2}+\frac{b^pm^p}{2}\right)^{\frac{1}{p}}\right)^+}\mathscr{F}_*\left(\left(\frac{q}{2}(a^p-b^pm^p)+m^pb^p\right)^{\frac{1}{p}}\right),$$

and

$$\int_0^1 t^{p\beta-1}\tau\left(1-\frac{1}{2\xi_\star}\right)m^p\mathscr{F}_*\left(\left(\frac{q+t^p}{2}b^p+\left(1-\frac{q+t^p}{2}\right)\frac{a^p}{m^p}\right)^{\frac{1}{p}}\right)dt$$
$$=\int_{\left(\frac{q}{2}\left(b^p-\frac{a^p}{m^p}\right)+\frac{a^p}{m^p}\right)^{\frac{1}{p}}}^{\left(\frac{q}{2}\left(b^p-\frac{a^p}{m^p}\right)+\frac{a^p}{2m^p}+\frac{b^p}{2}\right)^{\frac{1}{p}}}\mathscr{F}_*(z)\left(z^p-\frac{q}{2}(b^p-\frac{a^p}{m^p})-\frac{a^p}{m^p}\right)^{\frac{\theta}{k}}\cdot\frac{2^\theta m^{\theta p}}{(m^pb^p-a^p)^\theta}$$
$$=\frac{2^\theta m^{p\theta}\Gamma(\theta)}{p^{1-\theta}(b^pm^p-a^p)^\theta}\chi^{\theta,p}_{\left(\left(\frac{q}{2}(b^p-\frac{a^p}{m^p})+\frac{a^p}{2m^p}+\frac{b^p}{2}\right)^{\frac{1}{p}}\right)^+}\mathscr{F}_*\left(\left(\frac{q}{2}(b^p-\frac{a^p}{m^p})+\frac{a^p}{m^p}\right)^{\frac{1}{p}}\right).$$

Using a similar technique leads us to the equalities for the upper end point functions,

$$\int_0^1 t^{p\beta-1}\tau\left(\frac{1}{2\xi_\star}\right)\mathscr{F}^*\left(\left(\frac{q+t^p}{2}a^p+\left(1-\frac{q+t^p}{2}\right)b^pm^p\right)^{\frac{1}{p}}\right)dt$$

$$=\int_{\left(\frac{q}{2}(a^p-b^pm^p)+\frac{a^p}{2}+\frac{m^pb^p}{2}\right)^{\frac{1}{p}}}^{\left(\frac{q}{2}(a^p-m^pb^p)+b^pm^p\right)^{\frac{1}{p}}} \mathscr{F}^*(z)(b^pm^p+\frac{q}{2}(a^p-b^pm^p)-z^p)^{\frac{\theta}{k}-1}z^{p-1}dz\cdot\frac{2^\theta}{(b^pm^p-a^p)^\theta}$$
$$=\frac{\tau\left(\frac{1}{2\xi_\star}\right)2^\theta\Gamma(\theta)}{p^{1-\theta}(b^pm^p-a^p)^\theta}\chi^{\theta,p}_{\left(\left(\frac{q}{2}(a^p-m^pb^p)+\frac{a^p}{2}+\frac{b^pm^p}{2}\right)^{\frac{1}{p}}\right)^+}\mathscr{F}^*\left(\left(\frac{q}{2}(a^p-b^pm^p)+m^pb^p\right)^{\frac{1}{p}}\right),$$

and

$$\int_0^1 t^{p\beta-1}\tau\left(1-\frac{1}{2\xi_\star}\right)m^p\mathscr{F}^*\left(\left(\frac{q+t^p}{2}b^p+\left(1-\frac{q+t^p}{2}\right)\frac{a^p}{m^p}\right)^{\frac{1}{p}}\right)dt$$
$$=\int_{\left(\frac{q}{2}\left(b^p-\frac{a^p}{m^p}\right)+\frac{a^p}{m^p}\right)^{\frac{1}{p}}}^{\left(\frac{q}{2}\left(b^p-\frac{a^p}{m^p}\right)+\frac{a^p}{2m^p}+\frac{b^p}{2}\right)^{\frac{1}{p}}}\mathscr{F}^*(z)\left(z^p-\frac{q}{2}(b^p-\frac{a^p}{m^p})-\frac{a^p}{m^p}\right)^{\frac{\theta}{k}}\cdot\frac{2^\theta m^{\theta p}}{(m^pb^p-a^p)^\theta}$$
$$=\frac{2^\theta m^{p\theta}\Gamma(\theta)}{p^{1-\theta}(b^pm^p-a^p)^\theta}\chi^{\theta,p}_{\left(\left(\frac{q}{2}(b^p-\frac{a^p}{m^p})+\frac{a^p}{2m^p}+\frac{b^p}{2}\right)^{\frac{1}{p}}\right)^+}\mathscr{F}^*\left(\left(\frac{q}{2}(b^p-\frac{a^p}{m^p})+\frac{a^p}{m^p}\right)^{\frac{1}{p}}\right).$$

Hence, we achieve

$$\left(\frac{\mathscr{F}_*\left([\frac{a^p+m^pb^p}{2}]^{\frac{1}{p}}\right)}{\theta p}, \frac{\mathscr{F}^*\left([\frac{a^p+m^pb^p}{2}]^{\frac{1}{p}}\right)}{\theta p}\right)$$

$$\leqslant_p \left(\frac{\tau\left(\frac{1}{2\xi_\star}\right)2^\theta p^{\theta-1}\Gamma(\theta)}{(b^pm^p-a^p)^\theta}\chi^{\theta,p}_{\left(\left(\frac{q}{2}(a^p-m^pb^p)+\frac{a^p}{2}+\frac{b^pm^p}{2}\right)^{\frac{1}{p}}\right)^+}\mathscr{F}_*\left(\left(\frac{q}{2}(a^p-b^pm^p)+m^pb^p\right)^{\frac{1}{p}}\right)\right.$$

$$+\frac{\tau\left(1-\frac{1}{2\xi_\star}\right)m^{p+\theta p}2^\theta p^{\theta-1}\Gamma(\theta)}{(b^pm^p-a^p)^\theta}\chi^{p,\theta}_{\left(\left(\frac{q}{2}(b^p-\frac{a^p}{m^p})+\frac{a^p}{2m^p}+\frac{b^p}{2}\right)^{\frac{1}{p}}\right)^-}\mathscr{F}_*\left(\left(\frac{q}{2}(b^p-\frac{a^p}{m^p})+\frac{a^p}{m^p}\right)^{\frac{1}{p}}\right),$$

$$\frac{\tau\left(\frac{1}{2\xi_\star}\right)2^\theta p^{\theta-1}\Gamma(\theta)}{(b^pm^p-a^p)^\theta}\chi^{\theta,p}_{\left(\left(\frac{q}{2}(a^p-m^pb^p)+\frac{a^p}{2}+\frac{b^pm^p}{2}\right)^{\frac{1}{p}}\right)^+}\mathscr{F}^*\left(\left(\frac{q}{2}(a^p-b^pm^p)+m^pb^p\right)^{\frac{1}{p}}\right)$$

$$\left.+\frac{\tau\left(1-\frac{1}{2\xi_\star}\right)m^{p+\theta p}2^\theta p^{\theta-1}\Gamma(\theta)}{(b^pm^p-a^p)^\theta}\chi^{p,\theta}_{\left(\left(\frac{q}{2}(b^p-\frac{a^p}{m^p})+\frac{a^p}{2m^p}+\frac{b^p}{2}\right)^{\frac{1}{p}}\right)^-}\mathscr{F}^*\left(\left(\frac{q}{2}(b^p-\frac{a^p}{m^p})+\frac{a^p}{m^p}\right)^{\frac{1}{p}}\right)\right),$$

from which we achieve the left inequality.

Now, we obtain the right side. Using the definition of the left–right-(k,h-m)-p-convex function towards the right, we achieve

$$\tau\left(\frac{1}{2\xi_\star}\right)\mathscr{F}\left(\left(\frac{q+t^p}{2}a^p+\left(1-\frac{q+t^p}{2}\right)b^pm^p\right)^{\frac{1}{p}}\right)$$

$$+\tau\left(1-\frac{1}{2\xi_\star}\right)m^p\mathscr{F}\left(\left(\frac{q+t^p}{2}b^p+\left(1-\frac{q+t^p}{2}\right)\frac{a^p}{m^p}\right)^{\frac{1}{p}}\right)\leqslant_p$$

$$\left(\left(\tau\left(\frac{1}{2\xi_\star}\right)\mathscr{F}(a)+\tau\left(1-\frac{1}{2\xi_\star}\right)m^p\mathscr{F}(b)\right)h\left(\left(\frac{q+t^p}{2}\right)^k\right)t^{\theta p-1}\right)$$

$$+\left(\left(\tau\left(\frac{1}{2\xi_\star}\right)\mathscr{F}(b)m^p+\tau\left(1-\frac{1}{2\xi_\star}\right)\mathscr{F}(a)\right)h\left(1-\left(\frac{q+t^p}{2}\right)^k\right)t^{\theta p-1}\right).$$

Multiplying the inequality with $t^{\theta p-1}$ and integrating the expression, then using the IVM property, we obtain the right-hand side. Now, taking the product with the constant from the left part, we achieve the original inequality

$$\mathscr{F}\left([\frac{a^p+m^pb^p}{2}]^{\frac{1}{p}}\right)\leqslant_p$$

$$\frac{\tau\left(\frac{1}{2\xi_\star}\right)2^\theta p^\theta\Gamma(\theta+1)}{(b^pm^p-a^p)^\theta}\chi^{\theta,p}_{\left(\left(\frac{q}{2}(a^p-m^pb^p)+\frac{a^p}{2}+\frac{b^pm^p}{2}\right)^{\frac{1}{p}}\right)^+}\mathscr{F}\left(\left(\frac{q}{2}(a^p-b^pm^p)+m^pb^p\right)^{\frac{1}{p}}\right)$$

$$+\frac{\tau\left(1-\frac{1}{2\xi_\star}\right)m^{p+\theta p}2^\theta p^\theta\Gamma(\theta+1)}{(b^pm^p-a^p)^\theta}\chi^{p,\theta}_{\left(\left(\frac{q}{2}(b^p-\frac{a^p}{m^p})+\frac{a^p}{2m^p}+\frac{b^p}{2}\right)^{\frac{1}{p}}\right)^-}\mathscr{F}\left(\left(\frac{q}{2}(b^p-\frac{a^p}{m^p})+\frac{a^p}{m^p}\right)^{\frac{1}{p}}\right)$$

$$\leqslant_p\left(\left(\tau\left(\frac{1}{2\xi_\star}\right)\mathscr{F}(a)+\tau\left(1-\frac{1}{2\xi_\star}\right)m^p\mathscr{F}(b)\right)\int_0^1h\left(\left(\frac{q+t^p}{2}\right)^k\right)t^{\theta p-1}dt\right)\theta p$$

$$+\left(\left(\tau\left(\frac{1}{2\xi_\star}\right)\mathscr{F}(b)m^p+\tau\left(1-\frac{1}{2\xi_\star}\right)\mathscr{F}(a)\right)\int_0^1h\left(1-\left(\frac{q+t^p}{2}\right)^k\right)t^{\theta p-1}dt\right)\theta p.$$

□

Corollary 4. *Setting $p = 3, \xi_\star = 3$, we achieve a new noninteger HH type inequality*

$$\mathscr{F}\left([\frac{a^3 + m^3b^3}{2}]^{\frac{1}{3}}\right) \leqslant_p$$

$$\frac{h\left(\frac{1}{2^3}\right)2^\theta 3^\theta \Gamma(\theta+1)}{(b^3m^3 - a^3)^\theta} \chi^{\theta,3}_{\left(\left(\frac{q}{2}(a^2 - m^3b^3) + \frac{a^3}{2} + \frac{b^3m^3}{2}\right)^{\frac{1}{3}}\right)^+} \mathscr{F}\left(\left(\frac{q}{2}(a^3 - b^3m^3) + m^3b^3\right)^{\frac{1}{3}}\right)$$

$$+\frac{h\left(1 - \frac{1}{2^3}\right)m^{3+3\theta}2^\theta 3^\theta \Gamma(\theta+1)}{(b^3m^3 - a^3)^\theta} \chi^{3,\theta}_{\left(\left(\frac{q}{2}(b^3 - \frac{a^3}{m^3}) + \frac{a^3}{2m^3} + \frac{b^3}{2}\right)^{\frac{1}{3}}\right)^-} \mathscr{F}\left(\left(\frac{q}{2}(b^3 - \frac{a^3}{m^3}) + \frac{a^3}{m^3}\right)^{\frac{1}{3}}\right)$$

$$\leqslant_p \left(\left(h\left(\frac{1}{2^3}\right)\mathscr{F}(a) + h\left(1 - \frac{1}{2^3}\right)m^3\mathscr{F}(b)\right) \int_0^1 h\left(\left(\frac{q+t^3}{2}\right)^3\right) t^{3\theta-1}dt\right)3\theta$$

$$+\left(\left(h\left(\frac{1}{2^3}\right)\mathscr{F}(b)m^3 + h\left(1 - \frac{1}{2^3}\right)\mathscr{F}(a)\right) \int_0^1 h\left(1 - \left(\frac{q+t^3}{2}\right)^3\right) t^{3\theta-1}dt\right)3\theta.$$

4. Conclusions

We introduced a novel type of IVM, namely the left–right-(k,h-m)-p-convex function, which generalized the previously defined p,h-convex IVM given by Khan et al. As a consequence of the generalization, many new inequalities followed. We achieved new variations of the Hermite–Hadamard inequality in combination with noninteger operators which generalized the previous HH type results. Because of the IVM environment, by letting the upper and lower bound be the same, we recovered previous results from the (k,h-m)-p-convexity to the classical convexity.

Author Contributions: Conceptualization, V.S. and S.R.; methodology, V.S., S.R., R.R. and O.A.A.A.; formal analysis, V.S., S.R. and O.A.A.A.; writing–original draft preparation, V.S. and S.R.; supervision, R.R., O.A.A.A. and S.R. All authors have read and agreed to the published version of the manuscript.

Funding: This research received no external funding.

Data Availability Statement: Not applicable.

Acknowledgments: The research is supported by the Deanship of Scientific Research, Prince Sattam bin Abdulaziz University, Alkharj. The authors convey their sincere thanks to the anonymous reviewers for their valuable comments, which helped bring the manuscript to its present form.

Conflicts of Interest: The authors declare no conflict of interest.

References

1. Hardy, G.H.; Littlewood, J.E.; Pólya, G. *Inequalities*; Cambridge University Press: Cambridge, UK, 1952; 324p.
2. Siricharuanun, P.; Erden, S.; Ali, M.A.; Budak, H.; Chasreechai, S.; Sitthiwirattham, T. Some New Simpson's and Newton's Formulas Type Inequalities for Convex Functions in Quantum Calculus. *Mathematics* **2021**, *9*, 1992. [CrossRef]
3. You, X.; Ali, M.A.; Budak, H.; Reunsumrit, J.; Sitthiwirattham, T. Hermite–Hadamard–Mercer-Type Inequalities for Harmonically Convex Mappings. *Mathematics* **2021**, *9*, 2556. [CrossRef]
4. Sarikaya, M.Z.; Yildirim, H. On Hermite–Hadamard type inequalities for Riemann-Liouville fractional integrals. *Miskolc Math. Notes* **2016**, *17*, 1049–1059. [CrossRef]
5. Chen, H.; Katugampola, U.N. Hermite–Hadamard and Hermite–Hadamard-Fejr type inequalities for generalized fractional integrals. *J. Math. Anal. Appl.* **2017**, *446*, 1274–1291. [CrossRef]
6. Han, J.; Mohammed, P.O.; Zeng, H. Generalized fractional integral inequalities of Hermite–Hadamard-type for a convex function. *Open Math.* **2020**, *18*, 794–806. [CrossRef]
7. Awan, M.U.; Talib, S.; Chu, Y.M.; Noor, M.A.; Noor, K.I. Some new refinements of Hermite–Hadamard-type inequalities involving-Riemann-Liouville fractional integrals and applications. *Math. Probl. Eng.* **2020**, 2020, 3051920. [CrossRef]
8. Aljaaidi, T.A.; Pachpatte, D.B. The Minkowski's inequalities via f-Riemann-Liouville fractional integral operators. *Rendiconti del Circolo Matematico di Palermo Series 2* **2021**, *70*, 893–906. [CrossRef]

9. Mohammed, P.O.; Aydi, H.; Kashuri, A.; Hamed, Y.S.; Abualnaja, K.M. Midpoint inequalities in fractional calculus defined using positive weighted symmetry function kernels. *Symmetry* **2021**, *13*, 550. [CrossRef]
10. Mohammed, P.O.; Abdeljawad, T.; Jarad, F.; Chu, Y.M. Existence and uniqueness of uncertain fractional backward difference equations of Riemann-Liouville type. *Math. Probl. Eng.* **2020**, *2020*, 6598682. [CrossRef]
11. Mitrinović, D.S. *Analytic Inequalities*; Springer: Berlin/Heidelberg, Germany, 1970.
12. Pečarić, J.; Proschan, F.; Tong, Y. *Convex Functions, Partial Orderings, and Statistical Applications*; Academic Press, Inc.: Cambridge, MA, USA, 1992.
13. Hadamard, J. Étude sur les propriétés des fonctions entières en particulier d'une fonction considéréé par Riemann. *J. Math. Pures Appl.* **1893**, *58*, 171–215.
14. Cristescu, G. Hadamard type inequalities for convolution of h-convex functions. *Ann. Tiberiu Popoviciu Semin. Funct. Equ. Approx. Convexity* **2010**, *8*, 3–11.
15. Dragomir, S.S. An inequality improving the first Hermite-Hadamard inequality for convex functions defined on linear spaces and applications for semi-inner products. *J. Inequal. Pure Appl. Math.* **2002**, *3*, 31.
16. Dragomir, S.S.; Fitzpatrick, S. The Hadamard inequalities for sconvex functions in the second sense. *Demonstr. Math.* **1999**, *32*, 687–696.
17. El Farissi, A. Simple proof and refeinment of Hermite-Hadamard inequality. *J. Math. Ineq.* **2010**, *4*, 365–369. [CrossRef]
18. Kikianty, E.; Dragomir, S.S. Hermite-Hadamard's inequality and the p-HH-norm on the Cartesian product of two copies of a normed space. *Math. Inequal. Appl.* **2010**. [CrossRef]
19. Mitrinović, D.S.; Lacković, I.B. Hermite and convexity. *Aequ. Math.* **1985**, *28*, 229–232. [CrossRef]
20. Hermann, R. *Fractional Calculus an Introduction for Physicists*; World Scientific Publishing Co. Pte. Ltd.: Singapore, 2011; p. 596224.
21. Oldham, K.B.; Spanier, J. *The Fractional Calculus Theory and Applications of Differentation and Integration to Arbitrary Order*; Academic Press, Inc.: London, UK, 1974.
22. Stojiljković, V.; Ramaswamy, R.; Alshammari, F.; Ashour, O.A.; Alghazwani, M.L.H.; Radenović, S. Hermite–Hadamard Type Inequalities Involving (k-p) Fractional Operator for Various Types of Convex Functions. *Fractal Fract.* **2022**, *6*, 376. [CrossRef]
23. Stojiljković, V.; Ramaswamy, R.; Ashour Abdelnaby, O.A.; Radenović, S. Riemann-Liouville Fractional Inclusions for Convex Functions Using Interval Valued Setting. *Mathematics* **2022**, *10*, 3491. [CrossRef]
24. Afzal, W.; Abbas, M.; Macías-Díaz, J.E.; Treanţă, S. Some H-Godunova–Levin Function Inequalities Using Center Radius (Cr) Order Relation. *Fractal Fract.* **2022**, *6*, 518. [CrossRef]
25. Afzal, W.; Alb Lupaş, A.; Shabbir, K. Hermite–Hadamard and Jensen-Type Inequalities for Harmonical (h1, h2)-Godunova–Levin Interval-Valued Functions. *Mathematics* **2022**, *10*, 2970. [CrossRef]
26. Afzal, W.; Shabbir, K.; Treanţă, S.; Nonlaopon, K. Jensen and Hermite-Hadamard type inclusions for harmonical h-Godunova-Levin functions. *AIMS Math.* **2023**, *8*, 3303–3321. [CrossRef]
27. Khan, M.B.; Noor, M.A.; Noor, K.I.; Ab Ghani, A.T.; Abdullah, L. Extended Perturbed Mixed Variational-Like Inequalities for Fuzzy Mappings. *J. Math.* **2021**, *2021*, 6652930. [CrossRef]
28. Khan, M.B.; Noor, M.A.; Noor, K.I.; Chu, Y.-M. New Hermite-Hadamard Type Inequalities for (h1, h2)-Convex Fuzzy-IntervalValued Functions. *Adv. Differ. Equ.* **2021**, *2021*, 6–20. [CrossRef]
29. Khan, M.B.; Mohammed, P.O.; Noor, M.A.; Hamed, Y.S. New Hermite–Hadamard Inequalities in Fuzzy-Interval Fractional Calculus and Related Inequalities. *Symmetry* **2021**, *13*, 673. [CrossRef]
30. Yang, X.J. *General Fractional Derivatives Theory, Methods and Applications*; Taylor and Francis Group: London, UK, 2019.
31. Budak, H.; Tunç, T.; Sarikaya, M.Z. Fractional Hermite–Hadamard type inequalities for interval-valued functions. *Proc. Am. Math. Soc.* **2019**, *148*, 705–718. [CrossRef]
32. Moore, R.E. *Interval Analysis*; Prentice Hall: Englewood Cliffs, NJ, USA, 1966.
33. Jensen, J.L.W.V. Sur les fonctions convexes et les inégalités entre les valeurs moyennes. *Acta Math.* **1906**, *30*, 175–193. [CrossRef]
34. Khan, M.B.; Cătas, A.; Saeed, T. Generalized Fractional Integral Inequalities for p-Convex Fuzzy Interval-Valued Mappings. *Fractal Fract.* **2022**, *6*, 324. [CrossRef]
35. Katugampola, U.N. A new approach to generalized fractional derivatives. *Bull. Math. Anal. Appl.* **2014**, *6*, 1–15.
36. Abramowitz, M.; Stegun, I.A. *Handbook of Mathematical Functions: With Formulas, Graphs, and Mathematical Tables*; MR1225604; Dover Publications: New York, NY, USA, 1992.
37. Fang, Z.; Shi, R. On the (p,h)-convex function and some integral inequalities. *J. Inequalities Appl.* **2014**, *2014*, 45. [CrossRef]
38. Khan, M.B.; Mohammed, P.O.; Noor, M.A.; Baleanu, D.; Guirao, J.L.G. Some New Fractional Estimates of Inequalities for LR-p-Convex Interval-Valued Functions by Means of Pseudo Order Relation. *Axioms* **2021**, *10*, 175. 10.3390/axioms10030175. [CrossRef]
39. Zhang, D.; Guo, C.; Chen, D.; Wang, G. Jensen's inequalities for set-valued and fuzzy set-valued functions. *Fuzzy Sets Syst.* **2020**, *404*, 178–204. [CrossRef]
40. Costa, T.M. Jensen's inequality type integral for fuzzy-interval-valued functions. *Fuzzy Sets Syst.* **2017**, *327*, 31–47. [CrossRef]
41. Jia, W.; Yussouf, M.; Farid, G.; Khan, K.A. Hadamard and Fejér–Hadamard inequalities for (α, h–m)– p–convex functions via Riemann–Liouville fractional integrals. *Math. Probl. Eng.* **2021**, *2021*, 9945114. [CrossRef]
42. Khan, M.B.; Noor, M.A.; Noor, K.I. Some Novel Inequalities for LR-(p,h)-Convex Interval Valued Functions by Means of Pseudo Order Relation. *Math. Methods Appl. Sci.* **2021**, *45*, 1310–1340. [CrossRef]

43. Özdemir, M.E.; Yıldız, Ç.; Akdemir, A.O.; Set, E. On some inequalities for s-convex functions and applications. *J. Inequalities Appl.* **2013**, *2013*, 333. [CrossRef]
44. Varošanec, S. On h-convexity. *J. Math. Anal. Appl.* **2007**, *326*, 303–311. [CrossRef]
45. Noor, M.A.; Awan, M.U.; Noor, K.I.; Postolache, M. Some Integral Inequalities for p-Convex Functions. *Filomat* **2016**, *30*, 2435–2444. [CrossRef]

MDPI AG
Grosspeteranlage 5
4052 Basel
Switzerland
Tel.: +41 61 683 77 34

Fractal and Fractional Editorial Office
E-mail: fractalfract@mdpi.com
www.mdpi.com/journal/fractalfract

www.ingramcontent.com/pod-product-compliance
Lightning Source LLC
LaVergne TN
LVHW070210100526
838202LV00015B/2025